AUSTRALIAN DICTIONARY

OF BIOGRAPHY

General Editor

DOUGLAS PIKE

AUSTRALIAN
DICTIONARY
OF BIOGRAPHY

VOLUME 4 : 1851-1890

D-J

Section Editors

BEDE NAIRN
GEOFFREY SERLE
RUSSEL WARD

MELBOURNE UNIVERSITY PRESS

First published 1972
Reprinted 1979, 1990
Printed in Australia by
Brown Prior Anderson Pty Ltd, Burwood, Victoria, for
Melbourne University Press, Carlton, Victoria 3053
U.S.A. and Canada: International Specialized Book Services, Inc.,
5602 N.E. Hassalo Street, Portland, Oregon 97213–3640
United Kingdom, Ireland and Europe: Europa Publications Limited,
18 Bedford Square, London WC1B 3JN

National Library of Australia Cataloguing-in-Publication entry

Australian dictionary of biography. Volume 4. 1851–1890, D–J.

Bibliography
ISBN 0 522 84034 5

1. Australia — Biography. 2. Australia — History — 1981–1890.
I. Nairn, Noel Bede, joint ed. II. Serle, Alan Geoffrey, joint ed.
III. Ward, Russel Braddock, 1914–, joint ed.
920′.094

PREFACE

This volume of the *Australian Dictionary of Biography* is the second of four for the 1851-1890 section. The first volume of this section and the two for 1788-1850 have already been published; six have been planned for the third section 1891-1939. This chronological division was designed to simplify production, for over six thousand articles are likely to be included. A general index volume will be prepared when the three sections are completed.

The placing of each individual's name in the appropriate section has been generally determined by when he did his most important work (*floruit*). For articles that overlap the chronological division, preference has usually been given to the earlier period, although most of the important Federationists will appear in the third section.

The selection of names for inclusion in the *Dictionary* has been the result of much consultation and co-operation. After quotas were estimated, Working Parties in each State prepared provisional lists, which were widely circulated and carefully amended. Many of the names were obviously significant and worthy of inclusion. Others, less notable, were chosen simply as samples of the Australian experience. Some had to be omitted through lack of material, and thereby joined the great anonymous mass whose members richly deserve a more honoured place; however, many thousands of these names are accumulating in a 'Biographical Register' at the *Dictionary* headquarters in the Australian National University.

Most authors were nominated by the Working Parties, and the burden of writing has been shared almost equally by university historians and by members of Historical and Genealogical Societies and other specialists. Most of the unsigned entries were prepared in the *Dictionary* office.

The *Dictionary* is an all-Australian, Commonwealth-wide project based on consultation and co-operation. The Australian National University has borne the cost of the headquarters staff, of much research and of some special contingencies, while other Australian Universities have supported the project in various ways. Its policies have been determined by the National Committee of representatives from the Departments of History in each Australian University. At Canberra the Editorial Board has kept in touch with all these representatives and, through them, with the Working Parties, librarians, archivists and other local experts, as well as overseas correspondents and research assistants in each Australian capital. With such varied support the *Australian Dictionary of Biography* can truly be called a national project.

Canberra
May 1972   D.P.

ACKNOWLEDGMENTS

Special thanks are due to Professor J. A. La Nauze for his helpful guidance as Chairman of the Editorial Board and to Professor G. Sawer for acting in his absence. Those who helped in planning the shape of the work have been acknowledged in earlier volumes.

For this volume the *Dictionary* is grateful for many privileges extended by the Australian Universities, especially the Australian National University.

For assistance overseas thanks are due to Mrs Judy Egerton and Peter Saunders, Liaison Officer of the National Library of Australia in London; Dr T. I. Rae, National Library of Scotland; N. C. Buck, St John's College, Cambridge; Kenneth Emsley, Durham; Professor Alan R. Tippett, Fuller Theology Seminary, California; the officials of the Public Record Office, Somerset House and the County Records Offices, and the host of clergy, archivists and others who have answered calls for help.

The *Dictionary* deeply regrets the death of such notable contributors to this volume as K. G. Allars, Colonel P. Dale, V. W. E. Goodin, A. Gross, C. Lack, N. S. Lynravn, Dr C. F. Macdonald, Dr B. R. Marshall, Mrs I. Mead and especially Dr C. H. Currey.

Within Australia the *Dictionary* is greatly indebted to countless librarians and archivists in Canberra and each State, to the secretaries of many Historical and Genealogical Societies, to the Registrars-General of Births, Marriages and Deaths, and of Probates, whose generous co-operation has solved many problems. Warm thanks for the free gift of their time and talents are due to all contributors and all members of the National Committee, Editorial Board and the Working Parties. For particular advice the *Dictionary* owes much to Professor J. J. Auchmuty, Dr A. Barnard, Dr D. Barwick, John Bennett, Dr J. Cumpston, G. A. Fairbairn, Professor B. Gandevia, Dr N. Gunson, Mrs E. Harcus, Dr R. M. Hartwell, Miss Mary Lazarus, Richard Lord, D. McCorquodale, J. McCristal o.f.m., Miss A. M. Mitchell, Miss P. M. Quinn (archivist, Bank of New South Wales), Mrs V. Parsons, E. R. Pretyman, Miss Ann Pugh (librarian, Institution of Engineers), Dr F. B. Smith, Frank Strahan, G. M. Tobin, Mrs R. N. Wardle, Miss Carole Woods and many others. Grateful acknowledgment is also due to the Director and staff of Melbourne University Press; to the editorial staff: N. B. Nairn from September 1965, H. J. Gibbney from July 1965, Nan Phillips from 1967, Martha Campbell and Sally O'Neill from September 1967 and Suzanne Edgar from March 1969; to the painstaking assistance of Audrey Ferguson and Ruth Frappell in Sydney, Noelene Hall in Brisbane, Jessie Serle and Kathleen Thomson in Melbourne, Marjorie Findlay and E. Zalums in Adelaide, Wendy Birman in Perth, Mary Nicholls in Tasmania and Margery Walton in New Zealand; to the secretarial staff, especially Dorothy Smith.

COMMITTEES

COMMITTEES

AUTHORS

ABBOTT, G. J.:
Dibbs, T.; Gordon, S.
ALLARS, K. G.*:
Innes, J.
ANDREWS, B. G.:
Farrell; Hopkins, L.
ANTILL, J. M.:
Hickson.
AUBREY, Keith H.:
Greenway.
AUSTIN, C. G.:
Dalrymple.
AUSTIN, K. A.:
Devine.

BANKS, Maxwell R.:
Gould.
BARNARD, Alan:
Elder, D.; Goldsbrough.
BARNES, John:
Furphy; James, J. S.
BARRETT, Bernard:
FitzGibbon.
BARRON, Eleanor E.:
Gowlland.
BARROW, Elizabeth:
Dobson, F.
BARTLETT, Geoffrey:
Francis; Grant; Jones, C.
BATTYE, O. K.:
Harper.
BEEVER, E. A.:
Elliott; James, C.
BEEVER, Margot:
Gillies; Harker; Heales; Jenner.
BELL, Harold F.:
Gilfillan; Joseph.
BELL, Jacqueline:
Douglas, A. D.; Fraser, S., auctioneer.
BENNETT, J. M.:
Darley, F.; Hargrave.
BERGMAN, George F. J.:
Davis; Hoffnung; Hyam.
BIRMAN, Wendy:
Dempster; Henderson, E.; Hensman;
Hooley; Horrocks; Humble, G.
BLAESS, F. J. H.*:
Eggers.
BLAINEY, Ann:
Horne, R.
BLAINEY, Geoffrey:
Johns, P.
BLAKE, L. J.:
Derry; Hagenauer.
BODI, Leslie:
Gerstaecker.
BOLGER, Peter:
Dunne, W.; Facy.
* deceased.

BOLTON, G. C.:
Daintree; Fitzgerald, T. H.; Gregory, A.;
Hamilton, John, politician; Hann.
BRADSHAW, F. Maxwell:
Hetherington.
BRAMSTED, E. K.:
Garran.
BRERETON, Roslyn:
Fulton.
BROWNFOOT, Janice N.:
Dugdale.
BURKE, Iris:
Freeman.
BURKE, Keast:
Degotardi; Freeman; Holtermann.
BURNS, P. L.:
Douglas, W.
BURNS WOODS, Janice:
Evans, G.; Ireland.
BUXTON, Gordon:
Freeling; Gormly.

CABLE, K. J.:
Druitt; Ellis; Garnsey; Gordon, A.;
Gunther; Hose; Howard.
CAHILL, A. E.:
Jennings, P.
CALDWELL, Margaret:
Graham, J., physician; Henning.
CAMPBELL, A. W.:
Graves, J. W.
CANE, Alan V.:
Everett.
CANNON, Michael:
Fink.
CARTER, M.:
Drury, E.; Fraser, S., auctioneer; Haly;
Harding.
CAVANOUGH, Maurice:
Hales, T.
CHAMBERS, Don:
Henderson, W.
CHISHOLM, A. H.:
Elsey; Helms.
CLARK, Manning:
Hope, R.
CLARK, S. B.:
Fowler, F.
CLAUGHTON, S. G.:
Hurst.
CLOSE, Cecily:
Foy.
CORRIS, Peter:
Dawson, J.
CRANFIELD, Louis R.:
Esmond.
CRAWFORD, G. H.:
Dodds.

CROOK, D. P.:
Finch-Hatton.
CROWLEY, F. K.:
Darling, C.; Fraser, M.
CURREY, C. H.*:
Denison.
CURTIS, Winifred M.:
Hooker.

DALE, P.*:
Gore, J.
DALEY, Louise T.:
Dangar, W.; Dawson, R.; Irving, C.
DE GARIS, B. K.:
Heaton.
DENHOLM, David:
Finch-Hatton.
DENHOLM, Zita:
Edkins.
DE PURY, G. G.:
De Pury.
DERHAM, David:
Derham.
DICKEY, Brian:
Fitzpatrick, M.; Fosbery; Halloran.
DOCKER, E.:
Docker.
DOLLERY, E. M.:
Dobson, W.; Giblin.
DOUGAN, Alan:
Fullerton; Geikie; Grimm; Johnstone, T.
DOW, Gwyneth M.:
Higinbotham, G.
DOW, Hume:
Dow.
DOWLING, A. R.:
Dowling, J.
DOWLING, Austin:
Gaunt.
DOXFORD, C. F.:
Graves, J. A.
DRAPER, Sandra:
Donaldson, S.
DRISCOLL, W. P.:
Fallon.
DUCKER, Sophie C.:
Harvey.
DUFFY, C. J.:
Gibbons.
DUNKERLEY, J. S.:
Farr.
DURACK, Mary:
Durack.
DWYER, D. J.:
Fitzgerald, N.

EARNSHAW, John:
Hayes, W.
EDGELOE, V. A.:
Fergusson.
ELFORD, Ken:
Hely.
ELLIS, Ian:
Hungerford.

ELLIS, W. F.:
Holyman.
ELSE-MITCHELL, R.:
Gregory, D.
EUNSON, Warwick:
Davitt.
EVANS, Wilson P.:
Fullarton.

FAIRFAX, J. O.:
Fairfax.
FENDLEY, G. C.:
Irving, M.
FERGUSON, Audrey:
Dalgleish.
FINDLAY, Marjorie:
Daly; Gilbert, Joseph.
FINNIS, H. J.:
Evans, M.
FISCHER, G. L.:
Hussey.
FITZGERALD, R. T.:
Hall, G.
FITZHARDINGE-SETON, Peter C.:
Fitzhardinge.
FORBES, John R.:
Isaacs.
FORSTER, Harley W.:
Ferres.
FORSYTH, J. H.:
Goodchap.
FREELAND, J. M.:
Hunt, J.
FREEMAN, R. D.:
Davies, J. M.
FRENCH, E. L.:
Harris, R.
FRENCH, M.:
Dunn.

GARDEN, Donald S.:
Fairbairn; Franklyn; Frencham; Gordon, G.; Gresham.
GARRETT, John:
Jones, P.
GASCOIGNE, S. C. B.:
Ellery.
GEEVES, Philip:
Gannon; Holt, T.
GIBBNEY, H. J.:
D'Albertis; Dowie; Edinburgh; Erskine; Favenc; Fleming, J.; Forbes, H.; Gibson; Goldie; Heath; Hemmant; Henderson, J.; Hernsheim; Hunter, G.; Ingham; Ivory; James, H.
GIBSON, M.:
Fleming, V.
GILBERT, L. A.:
De Vis; Dietrich; FitzGerald, R. D.
GILL, J. C. H.:
Gill, J.
GINNIVAN, Paul E.:
Donaghy.

GOLLAN, Robin:
  Fletcher, J.; Gregson.
GOODIN, V. W. E.*:
  Farnell.
GOODMAN, Rupert:
  Ewart.
GOSSE, Fayette:
  Elder, W.; Gosse.
GRANT, James:
  Goodman.
GRAVELL, Margaret:
  Godfrey.
GRAY, Nancy:
  Fisher, T.; Hall, T.
GREEN, F. C.:
  Davies, John, convict; *Dodery; Douglas, A.; Fenton.*
GREEN, Louis:
  Giles.
GREEN, R. M.:
  Green, R.
GRIFFIN, James:
  Fisher, J. C.
GRIFFITH, R. G. De B.:
  Holroyd, E.
GRIGSBY, J. R. J.:
  Duffy, J.; Goold, J.
GROSS, Alan*:
  Dallachy; Guilfoyle.
GUNSON, Niel:
  Gainford; Gill, W.; Gosman; Halley; Haydon; Hitchcock.
GUNTHORPE, S. G.:
  Dowse.

HADGRAFT, Cecil:
  Foott; Forbes, W.
HARDY, Patsy:
  Degraves.
HARPER, Harry:
  Hutchinson.
HARTWELL, R. M.:
  Dalgety.
HASSELL, C. W.:
  Hassell.
HAWKER, G. N.:
  Jacob.
HENNING, G. R.:
  Huddart.
HENRY, Margaret:
  Foott.
HENRY, Marian R.:
  Fox.
HENWOOD, John:
  Fincham.
HESELTINE, H. P.:
  Holdsworth.
HICKS, Neville:
  Derrington.
HILL, A. C.:
  Goode.
HILL, A. J.:
  Edwards.

HILL, Dorothy:
  Jack.
HINCE, Kenneth:
  Elsasser.
HOBAN, Ruth:
  Forster, W. M.
HOLT, H. T. E.:
  Deffell; Holroyd, A.; Josephson.
HOLT, L. V.:
  De Boos.
HONE, J. Ann:
  Danks; Dennis; Dowling, T.; Fanning, E.; Fetherstonhaugh; Fisken; Flower; Greene; Guthrie; Hamilton, T.; Highett; Hopkins, J.
HORTON, W. M.:
  Foley.
HOUGH, G. J.:
  Jones, J.
HOWE, Renate:
  Eggleston; Fraser, A.
HUXLEY, Molly:
  Duffield; Duncan, J.

IRVING, T. H.:
  Holden.

JOHNSON, Robert A.:
  Everard; Halfey.
JOHNSTON, W. Ross:
  Garrick.
JONES, Dorothy:
  Eden; Johnstone, R.
JOYCE, R. B.:
  Douglas, J.

KEATING, John D.:
  Duncan, G.
KEESING, Nancy:
  Hardy, J.
KELLY, David St Leger:
  Gwynne; Hubbe.
KENNEDY, Richard:
  Embling.
KENT, H. S. K.:
  Darling, J.
KIERS, Dorothy:
  Harrison, J.
KINGSTON, Beverley:
  Dutton; Hodgson, C.
KIRK, Pauline M.:
  Hume.
KIRSOP, Wallace:
  Gotch.
KNIGHT, Kenneth W.:
  Houston.
KNOX, B. A.:
  Herbert; Hotham.
KRAMER, Leonie:
  Gordon, A. L.

LACK, Clem*:
  Dalrymple; Harris, J. and G.; Henry, E.; Jardine.

LAMB, P. N. :
Eagar.
LA NAUZE, J. A. :
Hearn; Jevons.
LANGMORE, Diane L. :
Humffray.
LANSBURY, Coral :
Dickens.
LEA-SCARLETT, E. J. :
Day; Delany; Fitzpatrick, C.; Gale;
Greville.
LEGGE, J. S. :
Grice.
LINANE, T. J. :
Dunne, P.; Fitzpatrick, J.
LOANE, M. L. :
Hodgson, W.
LOVE, J. H. :
Finlayson.
LYNRAVN, N. S.* :
Forster, A.
LYONS, Mark :
Goold, S.

MACANALLY, P. M. :
Donaghy.
McCALLUM, Austin :
Glenny.
McCARTHY, Susan :
Hopwood.
MACDONALD, Colin* :
FitzGerald, T. N.
McDONALD, D. I. :
Hunter, H.
McGUIRE, F. M. :
Heyne.
McKAY, P. T. :
Douglas, A.
McLAREN, Ian F. :
Dwight; Ham.
McLAUGHLIN, John Kennedy :
Dickinson.
MACLAURIN, E. C. B. :
Fitzgerald, R.
McMARTIN, Arthur :
Henry, L.
MACNAB, Ken :
Dymock.
MAHER, J. T. :
Drury, A.
MAIN, J. M. :
Fisher, C.
MALONE, Betty :
Foster, J.; Haines.
MANSFIELD, Bruce E. :
Dibbs, G.
MARKS, E. N. :
Diggles.
MARSHALL, B. R.* :
Handfield.
MARTIN, A. W. :
Hay.
MEAD, Isabella J.* :
Dowling, R.; Du Croz.

MEDCALF, M. :
Johnston, J.
MERRIFIELD, S. :
Don; Douglass.
MILLAR, T. B. :
Disney.
MITCHELL, Ann M. :
Dalgarno.
MITCHELL, Bruce :
Fraser, A. C.; Hargraves.
MOREY, G. C. :
Hoskins.
MORLEY, J. A. :
Dowling, C.
MORRIS, Christopher :
Giffen.
MORRIS, David :
Greenwood.
MORRISON, A. A. :
Deuchar; Douglas, A. D.; Drury, E.;
Edmondstone; Eliott; Finney; Forbes, F.;
Gordon, P.; Gore, St G.; Graham, C.;
Griffin; Haly; Harding; Hill, C.; Hope, L.;
Jordan.
MORRISSEY, Sylvia :
Ievers.

NAIRN, Bede :
Dalley; Davies, John, ironmonger; Dixon,
F.; Driver; Forster, W.; Garrard; Garvan;
George; Higgins.
NEESON, I. J. :
Hayter.
NICHOLLS, Mary :
Horne, T.
NICKS, Beverley A. :
Davenport.
NOYE, R. J. :
Duryea; Foelsche.
NUNN, H. W. :
Hodgkinson, C.

O'DONNELL, Dan :
Hannell.
O'KEEFFE, Mary :
Donaldson, J.
O'KELLY, G. J. :
Dalton, Joseph.
OLDHAM, Ray :
Jewell.
O'NEILL, K. M. :
Fauchery.
O'NEILL, Sally :
Dilke; Gunson; Hardy, T.; Hart, J.; Henty;
Hughes, J.
O'SULLIVAN, David M. :
Gillbee.

PALMER, Imelda :
Frayne.
PARNABY, Joy E. :
Duffy, C.
PARSONS, George :
Ferguson, M.; Humble, W.

PATENALL, Dianne:
  Faithfull; Falkiner.
PENZIG, Edgar F.:
  Gardiner; Gilbert, John; Hall, B.
PEREZ, E.:
  Griver.
PERRIGNON, W. B.:
  Faucett.
PERRY, Warren:
  Downes.
PHILLIPS, Nan:
  Greenup.
PHILLIPS, Walter:
  Jefferis.
PLAYFORD, Phillip E.:
  Hardman.
POORTEN, Helen M. VAN DER:
  Darrell; Jennings, E.
POWELL, Owen:
  Hobbs.
POYNTER, J. R.:
  Felton; Grimwade.
PRETYMAN, E. R.:
  Gill, H.; Hamilton, John, parliamentarian.
PRICE, G. A.:
  Garrett.
PROEVE, H. F. W.:
  Heidenreich.
PRYOR, Oswald:
  Hancock.

RADI, Heather:
  Haynes.
RADIC, Maureen Thérèse:
  Herz; Horsley.
RATHBONE, R. W.:
  Darvall; Flood.
RAYNER, K.:
  Glennie.
REDMOND, Elizabeth M.:
  Fraser, S., contractor.
REFSHAUGE, Richard:
  Hamilton, R.
REIGER, Kerreen M.:
  Davies, D.
REYNOLDS, John:
  Davies, Joseph; Fitzgerald, G.; Harrap;
  Hart, W.
RICHARDSON, G. D.:
  Dixson, H.
RICKARD, John:
  Dampier; Hopkins, F.
RIMMER, Gordon:
  Du Cane.
ROBERTS, Kim:
  Hunt, C.
ROBERTSON, J. R.:
  Davies, M.; Hamilton, E.
ROBIN, A. DE Q.:
  Hale.
RUNDLE, J. H.:
  Eade.
RUSSELL, K. F.:
  Eades; Halford.

RUTLEDGE, Martha:
  Dalley; Dalton, James; Dangar, T.;
  Dowling, V.; Ewan; Forsyth, A.; Fosbery;
  Foster, W.; Frazer; Garland; Gordon, S.;
  Harris, J.; Hill, G. & R.; Hurley, John,
  innkeeper; Hurley, John, speculator;
  Inglis; Jaques; Jeanneret; Johnson, R.;
  Joubert.
RYAN, J. S.:
  Dexter; Donnithorne.

SACK, P. G.:
  Finsch.
SACLIER, M. J.:
  Elyard; Grubb.
SAUNDERS, G. E.:
  Hartley.
SCAMMELL, A. F.:
  Faulding.
SCARFE, Janet:
  Green, S.
SELLECK, R. J. W.:
  Gladman.
SENYARD, J. E.:
  Glass.
SERLE, Geoffrey:
  Gaunson.
SHANAHAN, Mary:
  Forrest.
SHARMAN, R. C.:
  Drysdale.
SHOESMITH, Dennis:
  Hayes, C.; Holt, J.; Jefferson.
SIMPSON, K.:
  Hunt, T.
SMART, D. B.:
  Fletcher, J. H.
SMITH, F. B.:
  Hodgson, R.
STANNER, W. E. H.:
  Fison; Howitt, A.
STAPLES, A. C.:
  Hayward.
STOODLEY, June:
  Fryar; Hodgkinson, W.
STRAHAN, Frank:
  Dennys; Graham, J., merchant.
SULLIVAN, C. M.:
  Innes, F.
SWAN, K. J.:
  Desailly; Forsyth, G.; Horsfall; Jones, A.

TAMBLYN, M.:
  Johns, J.
TARNAY, S. M.:
  Goethe; Herlitz.
TAYLOR, A. W.:
  Headlam.
TAYLOR, Herbert R.:
  Gore, T.
TEALE, Ruth:
  Darley, B.; Davies, W.; Dean; De Lissa;
  Fanning, W.; Freehill; Froude; Gardener;
  Goodlet; Hall, H.; Halliday; Hammond;

Hixson; Hordern; Houlding; Humphery; Ironside.

THOMPSON, John R.:
Hogan.

THORPE, Osmund:
Geoghegan.

TIPPING, Marjorie J.:
Guerard.

TREGENZA, John:
Hardy, A.

TURNER, Ian:
Harrison, H.

TURNER, I. S.:
Gurney.

TURNER, J. W.:
Farthing.

TURNEY, Cliff:
Huffer; Johnson, E.

VAN DISSEL, Dirk:
Gardner; Hughes, W.

WALKER, Mary Howitt:
Howitt, W.

WALKER, R. B.:
Davidson; Fletcher, W.; Gilmore.

WALKLEY, Gavin:
Garlick.

WALSH, G. P.:
De Mestre; Deniehy; Dickson; Ebsworth; Egan; Farmer; Fowler, R.; Hill, J.; Hudson; Jasprizza.

WARD, John M.:
Flanagan; Goodenough.

WATERSON, D. B.:
De Satgé; Gregory, A.; Groom; Hodgson, A.

WETTENHALL, R. L.:
Falconer; Higinbotham, T.; Hull.

WILLIS, R. W. G.:
Greeves.

WILSON, H. Margaret:
Hall, W.

WINKS, Robin W.:
Jervois.

WOODS, Carole:
Fellows; Ford; Fry; Gray, M.; Griffith; Gurner; Haddon; Harriman; Haverfield; Johnston, J. S.

YAXLEY, M. L.:
Gould.

ZALUMS, E.:
James, J. C.

ZUBANS, Ruth:
Folingsby.

REFERENCES

The following works of reference have been widely used but have not been listed in the sources at the foot of the articles:

D. Blair, *Cyclopaedia of Australasia* (Melbourne, 1881)

B. Burke, *A Genealogical and Heraldic History of the Colonial Gentry* (London, 1891)

J. A. Ferguson, *Bibliography of Australia*, 1-7 (Sydney, 1941-69)

H. M. Green, *A History of Australian Literature*, 1-2 (Sydney, 1961)

J. H. Heaton, *Australian Dictionary of Dates and Men of the Time* (London, 1879)

F. Johns, *An Australian Biographical Dictionary* (Melbourne, 1934)

P. Mennell, *The Dictionary of Australasian Biography* (London, 1892)

E. M. Miller, *Australian Literature . . . to 1935*, 1-2 (Melbourne, 1940) extended to 1950, by F. T. Macartney (Sydney, 1956)

W. Moore, *The Story of Australian Art*, 1-2 (Sydney, 1934)

P. C. Mowle, *A Genealogical History of Pioneer Families in Australia* (Sydney, 1939)

P. Serle, *Dictionary of Australian Biography*, 1-2 (Sydney, 1949)

Australian Encyclopaedia, 1-2 (Sydney, 1925)

Australian Encyclopaedia, 1-10 (Sydney, 1958)

Dictionary of National Biography (London, 1885-1971)

D

DAINTREE, RICHARD (1832-1878), geologist and photographer, was born on 13 December 1832 at Hemingford Abbots, Huntingdonshire, England, son of Richard Daintree, farmer, and his wife Elizabeth. He matriculated at Christ's College, Cambridge, in 1851, but left after a year because of ill health and in 1852 joined the gold rush to Victoria. Unsuccessful as a prospector, he accepted appointment in February 1854 as assistant geologist to his friend, Alfred Selwyn [q.v.], in the Victorian Geological Survey, and served with it until 1856. On a visit to England to study assaying and metallurgy at the Royal School of Mines Laboratory, he became interested in photography, and on his return to Melbourne in 1857 may have collaborated with Antoine Fauchery [q.v.] in a volume of photographic studies modestly entitled *Australia*. When he rejoined the Geological Survey as a field surveyor in January 1859, he pioneered the use of photography in field-work. In the next five years his routine duties included mapping and search for coal seams, and his growing dissatisfaction with this life was not assuaged by controversy with Professor Frederick McCoy [q.v.] in defence of the palaeontological theories of W. B. Clarke [q.v.] for whom Daintree developed an almost filial regard.

In 1864 Daintree left the Geological Survey to become a resident partner with William Hann [q.v.] in pastoral properties in the new Burdekin country of North Queensland. There Daintree was able to indulge his taste for both photography and prospecting. His discoveries in 1865-67 included several indications of gold, a copper deposit on the Einasleigh and the first systematic examination of the Bowen River (Collinsville) coal seams. When the pastoral boom collapsed Daintree used his knowledge to open up goldfields at Cape River in 1867, Gilbert in 1869 and Etheridge in 1869-70; they played an important part in tiding North Queensland over the depression, although only the Etheridge proved permanent and was soon overshadowed by other finds. But for Daintree's pioneering work in attracting prospectors to North Queensland, the gold resources of this area would probably not have been developed so early.

Daintree advocated a government geological survey in Queensland, and when it began in 1868 he was geologist in charge of the northern division until 1870. In that year he made some of his finest photographic studies. At the 1871 Exhibition of Art and Industry in London, Daintree's collection of photographs and geological specimens formed the mainstay of Queensland's contribution, and he was sent to England as commissioner in charge of this display, although much of it was lost when the ship carrying Daintree and his family was wrecked. In London he soon established himself as an enthusiastic and effective propagandist for Queensland and, on the unexpected resignation of Archibald Archer [q.v.] as Queensland's agent-general, was appointed to the vacancy early in 1872. With great energy he stimulated assisted immigration to Queensland, travelled widely to lecture on the colony's resources and produced attractive handbooks illustrated by his own photographs. From 1874, however, his administration was increasingly criticized by the premier, Arthur Macalister [q.v.], who was disturbed by the quality of some of the new migrants and by growing evidence of inefficiency in the agent-general's staff. Eventually in the winter of 1875-76 Macalister went to London; his personal investigation revealed that Daintree, although thoroughly honest and hard-working, had trusted the routine business of his office to clerks who used their expertise as a cover for various malpractices. The offenders were dismissed and Daintree, whose health had deteriorated, resigned in 1876. Daintree wintered twice in south France, hoping to recover enough strength to devote himself to the study of petrology. He continued to attend scientific meetings but succumbed to tuberculosis and other ailments at Beckenham, Kent, on 20 June 1878, soon after his appointment as C.M.G. In Melbourne on 1 December 1857 he had married Lettice Agnes, daughter of Henry Foot, a surveyor of Brighton; she survived him with two sons and six daughters.

Daintree's importance as a pioneer geologist lies more in his work as a prospector than in the controversies in which he was involved. His photographs, taken under difficult conditions by the cumbersome wet-plate process, are superb specimens of the art and present a vivid picture of early settlement in Queensland. His enthusiasm, skill and capacity for friendship distinguished him in his profession, although these qualities were not enough to make him a success in the agent-general's office or to avoid the tragedy of his last years.

G. C. Bolton, *Richard Daintree, a photographic memoir* (Brisb, 1965); A. Mozley, 'Richard Daintree; first government geologist of Northern Queensland', *Qld Heritage*, 1 (1965) no 2; A. M. Healy, 'Ophir to Bulolo: the history of the gold search in New Guinea', *Hist Studies*, no 45, Oct 1965; W. B. Clarke papers (ML); Maryvale papers, held by Edgar Clarke, Maryvale station, Charters Towers, Qld.

G. C. BOLTON

D'ALBERTIS, LUIGI MARIA (1841-1901), explorer, was born on 21 November 1841 at Voltri, Italy, into an old Florentine family. He abandoned his education for the Piedmontese army in deference to his father's support of the temporal power of the Pope and spent several years hunting in the Alps and Apennines; at 18 he joined Garibaldi's army. Trained by the French savant, Abbé Armand David, and inspired to devote his life to science, he joined Odoardo Beccari in November 1876 on an expedition to western New Guinea. He reached the peak of Mount Arfak Geb but was compelled by fever to retreat and arrived in Sydney on 1 February 1873 in the corvette *Vettor Pisani* to recuperate. An account of the journey was published in the *Melbourne Review*, 1876. D'Albertis left for Europe via America with a fine collection of specimens on 20 December 1873.

In April 1874 D'Albertis left Italy with one companion and set up a base on Yule Island. To gain ascendancy over the natives he publicly kissed the women and, with a shell full of burning methylated spirits, ostentatiously threatened to set the ocean alight. His homesick companion left, most of his native employees deserted and on 8 November he sailed for Somerset by the mission steamer *Ellengowan*. He then joined Rev. Samuel Macfarlane and H. M. Chester [q.v.] in a trip of 150 miles up the Fly River after which he returned to Italy.

Determined to conquer the Fly, D'Albertis returned to Sydney in February 1876. In the borrowed government launch *Neva*, he left Somerset with Lawrence Hargrave, engineer and scientist, the 17-year-old Clarence Wilcox, a crew of South Sea Islanders, Negroes and Chinese, a sheep and a dog. They entered the Fly on 23 May under both Italian and New South Wales flags and steamed upstream for forty-five days; they stopped at times for collecting but low water forced their retreat on 7 July. D'Albertis inhibited native hostility by firing rockets loaded with dynamite; his unscrupulous ethnological collecting was often criticized by later travellers. He claimed to have reached about 5°30′S., but Sir William MacGregor later doubted that he had passed 6°11′S. They

emerged from the Fly on 17 July but did not reach Somerset till 21 November.

D'Albertis left Somerset again on 3 May 1877 with Preston, an English engineer, five Chinese and three Islanders. The voyage was disastrous. One Chinese died after a beating from D'Albertis. The rest of the crew deserted and by November D'Albertis was left with Preston and one Islander to bring the *Neva* into Somerset on 4 January 1878. The deserters accused D'Albertis of murder but he successfuly prosecuted them and after bitter correspondence with Chester left for Sydney in the warship *Cristoforo Colombo*. He arrived in England on 1 July 1878 and after giving papers to the Royal Geographical Society, the Anthropological Institute and the Royal Colonial Institute he returned to Italy where in 1880 he published the Italian edition of his two-volume *New Guinea: What I did and what I saw*. He then judged his life's work complete and retired to hunt from a Papuan-style lodge in the Pontine Marshes. An unrepentant chain smoker, he died of mouth cancer on 2 September 1901.

Though D'Albertis's latin temperament and theatrical behaviour were not popular in Australia, Sir Hubert Murray described him as 'a great explorer and a most gifted man' but added, 'I should not like to have been the first white man to follow in his footsteps. The natives would have expected too much'.

S. Macfarlane, *Among the cannibals of New Guinea* (Lond, 1888); British New Guinea, *Annual report 1890-91*; A. Wichmann, *Nova Guinea*, 2 (Leiden, 1910); J. H. P. Murray, *Papua or British New Guinea* (Lond, 1912); D. Bartolini (ed), *Enciclopedia Italiana di scienze, lettere ed arti*, 12 (Rome, 1949); G. Souter, *New Guinea; the last unknown* (Syd, 1963); V&P (LA NSW), 1876-77, 5, 887; *Town and Country J*, 4 May 1878; H. M. Laracy, 'Italians on the Pacific frontier', paper to Istituto Italiana di Cultura seminar, Melb 1968; Hargrave papers (NL); Souter papers (NL); Col Sec in-letters 1876/268, 1878/2614 (QA).

H. J. GIBBNEY

DALE, ROBERT WILLIAM (1829-1895), Congregational minister, was born on 1 December 1829 at Newington Butts, London, son of Robert Dale, hat trimmer, and his wife Elizabeth, née Young. At 15 he became an assistant schoolmaster, joined the Congregational Church in Andover and began to preach and contribute to religious magazines. He entered Spring College, Birmingham, to study theology in 1847 and went to the University of London (B.A., 1850; M.A., 1853), winning the gold medal in philosophy. He then became assistant to John Angell James at the Carr's Lane Chapel, Birmingham, was elected pastor there after James died in 1859, and retained the office for thirty-six years. With his powerful ministry and enthusiasm for missions and church extension, he was outstanding as a promoter of education in Birmingham and in 1886 shared in the creation of the Free Church Mansfield College at Oxford. He was a prolific and influential writer, always emphasizing the practical issues of his doctrines rather than expounding theology as a polemic. He disliked divinity titles and by 1869 had discarded the use of 'reverend' but, although he never used the D.D. awarded to him at Yale in 1877, he yielded when the University of Glasgow gave him an honorary doctorate of laws in 1883. A month after his last sermon at Carr's Lane, he died on 13 March 1895. He was survived by his wife Elizabeth, née Dowling, whom he had married on 21 February 1855, and by two daughters and a son, Alfred William Winterslow, sometime vice-chancellor of the University of Liverpool.

Dale had rejected an invitation to a leading pastorate in Melbourne in 1862, but in 1887 he went with his wife and daughter to Hobart and for fifteen weeks toured Victoria, South Australia and New South Wales. Everywhere they met 'hospitality that surpassed all expectations', not only from the Congregational Unions which had invited him but also from all other denominations. He was also cheered by the passionate affection for Britain which, he believed, made Australians ultra-sensitive to criticisms in the English press. His *Impressions of Australia* (London, 1889), reprinted from the *Contemporary Review*, was one of the most acute surveys of that time. From observation, he recorded and tried to explain the differences of 'national character' in the three colonies. From wide-ranging interviews and study of parliamentary reports and the *Victorian Year Book* he expounded the resources, education, politics, religion and morals that justify Australia's 'buoyant faith in the future'. During his visit the frenzy over Broken Hill in the stock exchanges and the preparation of Sydney's centenary made him over-sanguine on some subjects, yet his wisdom and tolerant insight must have leavened the quality of British migrants who flocked to Australia after the depression of the 1890s.

DALGARNO, ISABELLA (1805-1878), temperance advocate, was born in the parish of Plains, Aberdeen, Scotland, daughter of James Gossip, crofter, and his wife Isabella, née Robertson. In 1830 she married Joseph (1807?-1895), son of Samuel Dalgarno, a shoemaker of Aberdeen, whose family had seafaring connexions.

Mrs Dalgarno was attracted to the temperance cause in Liverpool about 1840. When she returned to Aberdeen she was persuaded to speak at public meetings, her friends 'having represented that the novelty of such an exhibition would attract a numerous audience'. Mrs Dalgarno did not lack courage. She was later lectured from the bench by a Melbourne magistrate for her presumption at speaking before men in public. In 1841 she was presented with a silver medal, the first of many, this one a token of esteem for her services as president to the Aberdeen Female Teetotal Society. Soon afterwards she went to sea with her husband, who by then was rated a master of merchant vessels.

In the 1840s and early 1850s Captain Dalgarno made regular trips to the Australian colonies, first in the *Arab* and later in the *Lochnagar* (*Loch-Na-Gar*); he usually finished at Melbourne but also called at Adelaide and sometimes at Launceston. Whenever in port Mrs Dalgarno would contact local temperance agencies; she sparked the Melbourne Total Abstinence Society, established in 1842, into such new life that popular myth believed her to be responsible for its foundation.

Mrs Dalgarno's first recorded public appearances in Melbourne were in 1843, but her impact was really felt next year when the evident power of her oratory, delivered with broad Scots accent and heavy humour, drew large crowds to her meetings. The press admired her intentions but deplored the trenchant abuse which she and her colleagues heaped upon publicans and drinkers. The publicans led by Phillip Anderson of the Commercial Inn took revenge by wrecking one temperance meeting in a violent free-for-all on 20 May 1844. Mrs Dalgarno's sincerity was doubted because the *Arab* was known to carry large stocks of grog. In self-defence she and her husband countered that they had no control over the *Arab*'s cargo : 'the people at home did not care what they sent out so that they could get a handsome profit...They would drown [the colonies] with strong drink, and smother them with broken bottles'. Captain Dalgarno had also been accused of alcoholism, but as he testified to the success of enforcing teetotalism on his crews in 1844 and with his wife was always prominent and respected in Melbourne temperance circles, there seems little evidence for the suggestion. No doubt there was real sting to the taunts of 'where's your breeches?'. Perhaps the controversy helped, but it was noted that Melbourne suffered less from the prevailing evils of intemperance when Mrs Dalgarno was at her peak in the 1840s.

In 1852 the Dalgarnos settled permanently in Williamstown, Victoria, where Joseph had acquired property; he was a town councillor in 1866-69; he established a general store in Douglas Parade which later dealt mainly in drapery and operated under his name until 1928. In Williamstown the couple concentrated on local temperance effort. Joseph, though a well-known raconteur of sailing experiences, rarely gave temperance speeches; but Mrs Dalgarno continued to address meetings in and around Melbourne almost until her death. They were both attached to the United Free Methodist Church and associated with other denominations. The marriage was childless. Isabella died on 18 June 1878. Joseph married a widow, Hannah Simmons, in 1882; he died on 7 April 1895. Isabella and Joseph were buried together in the old Williamstown cemetery.

Garryowen (E. Finn), *The chronicles of early Melbourne*, 2 (Melb, 1888), p 531; M. M. Love, 'Woman's work', *Temperance in Australia*, memorial volume of the International Temperance Convention, 1888 (Melb, 1889); *Port Phillip Patriot*, 9 Mar, 4 May 1843, 23, 27 May, 25 July 1844, 13 Nov 1845, 2 Jan 1846; *Port Phillip Gazette*, 18, 22, 25 May, 1 June 1844; *Port Phillip Herald*, 24, 31 May 1844; *Williamstown Advertiser*, 13 Apr 1895; *Williamstown Chronicle*, 13 Apr 1895; information from W. P. Evans, historian to City of Williamstown, and Mrs Dorothy Ford, Northcote, Vic.

ANN M. MITCHELL

DALGETY, FREDERICK GONNERMAN (1817-1894), merchant and financier, was born on 3 December 1817 in Canada, son of Alexander Dalgety, army officer, and his wife Elizabeth, née Doidge. He arrived at Sydney on 2 June 1834 in the *Dryade* and became a clerk in T. C. Breillat [q.v.] & Co. In December 1842 he moved to Melbourne as manager of a new firm which he rapidly made his own and by 1848 was an independent and well-to-do merchant, concentrating on 'the settlers' trade', providing merchandise for the squatters and buying their produce. He visited England in 1849 to strengthen his facilities for credit and the disposal of colonial produce and returned to Victoria in 1851. In the gold rush Dalgety continued with general business, enlarged his pastoral trade, sold merchandise to the diggers and bought much gold from them; in 1851-55 he made about £150,000 from his gold speculations alone. In 1854 he moved to London to establish the headquarters of a metropolitan-colonial enterprise dealing mainly with the Victorian pastoral industry. He took with him as London partner F. A. Du Croz [q.v.], and left C. Ibbotson as a colonial manager-partner in Geelong; he

returned to Victoria in 1857 to establish James Blackwood [q.v.] as another manager-partner in Melbourne. These four men between them were mainly responsible for the expansion and success of the Dalgety business; until 1884 only one other partner, E. T. Doxat, was added to the London firm. Dalgety lived in England after 1859, making one last trip to Australia and New Zealand in 1881. By 1884 Dalgety had firms in London, Melbourne, Geelong, Launceston, Dunedin (opened in 1859), Christchurch (1860) and Sydney (1878), with ten partners and a combined capital of £900,000, of which Dalgety held £300,000 and his original partners £350,000. In 1884 the firms were incorporated into a joint-stock company, Dalgety & Co., in which Dalgety continued in active management as largest shareholder and chairman of directors until his death.

On 12 December 1855 Dalgety married Blanche Trosse Allen; she died on 11 April 1883. He held various civic offices in Hampshire and was high sheriff in 1877; he was also by purchase lord of the manors and patron of the livings of East Tytherley and Lockerley. In 1868-73 he had built Lockerley Hall, a mansion and estate worth £238,000. He died there on 20 March 1894, survived by five daughters and five sons, none of whom went into the business. He left at least seven stations in New Zealand valued at £160,000 and personalty at more than £479,900. Except for an abortive Kimberley speculation, his private property in Australia had been sold profitably in the 1880s.

Dalgety's importance to Australia was his role in the development of large-scale facilities for financing and organizing the production and marketing of rural produce. He was one of the first merchants to see clearly the potentiality and needs of the squatters, and to exploit the mercantile and financial resources of Britain for the growing requirements of the Australian economy. Since Britain provided both market and capital Dalgety realized, earlier than most, the greater strength of a business with its London headquarters closely co-operating with colonial branches. Except for the important gold interlude, wool was the core of Dalgety's business and it grew with the pastoral industry; by 1880 his firms were consigning over 70,000 bales a year, about 90 per cent of the firms' colonial exports, and about 7 per cent of the total Australasian clip exported. Beginning as a merchant for the squatters, he gradually widened his activities to provide wool-growers with such necessary services as finance, transport, storage, insurance, technical advice and wool sales. With the rapid growth of the pastoral industry after 1860 when technical change and the consolidation of freeholds demanded large capital outlays, Dalgety was increasingly involved in finance; his firms contributed about 10 per cent of the inflow of British long-term capital into the industry by pastoral finance companies from 1866 until 1884 when his private partnerships were forced into incorporation by the increasing demand for capital and the competition of joint-stock companies and banks. However, in the next three years Dalgety branches were opened in Queensland and Western Australia, and the properties and assets of the company increased by 50 per cent. Dalgety & Co. continued to grow after its founder died and in 1962 merged with the New Zealand Loan and Mercantile Agency Co. Ltd; with assets of £44 million in 1963 it was the largest pastoral combine operating in the antipodes.

Dalgety had no interests outside his business, family and estates; his only pastime was shooting. He never dabbled in politics although, as the largest Australian woolimporter in London, he was the natural focus of Australian pastoral and London wool interests, and chairman of the Colonial Wool Merchants' Association. The upbringing of his children was gentlemanly, not commercial; he married his eldest daughter into the aristocracy with a dowry of £20,000.

P. L. Brown (ed), *Clyde Company papers*, 2-6 (Lond, 1952-68); Dalgety papers (Lockerley Hall, Hampshire); Dalgety & Co. Ltd Archives (Leadenhall St, Lond); Dalgety & Co. Ltd records, Aust branches (ANU Archives).

R. M. HARTWELL

DALGLEISH, DANIEL CAMERON (1827-1870), engineer and politician, was born at Alloa, Scotland, son of Adam Dalgleish, an excise supervisor. On leaving school he was apprenticed to an engineering firm in Edinburgh and later worked in London. He became a member of the Amalgamated Society of Engineers which was formed in January 1851. Next January Manchester and London employers combined to lock out their engineers when the A.S.E.'s threat to ban systematic overtime was carried out. The dispute ended in defeat for the union, and the employers refused to reinstate any engineers who did not sign a document renouncing membership or support of any trade union. Dalgleish was among the small number who refused to sign and who decided to migrate. A group of Christian Socialists, who had assisted the men by subscriptions and letters in the lockout, supported the migration project, and one of them, Augustus Vansittart, advanced

about £1000 to pay the passages of twenty-seven engineers and their families in the *Frances Walker*, sailing for Sydney. The loan was later repaid in full.

The first overseas branch of the A.S.E. (now the Amalgamated Engineering Union) in Australia was formed at sea by these men on 8 October 1852 and Dalgleish was on the first committee. In Sydney he found work in his trade and later set up his own engineering shop. In November 1860 Dalgleish advertised in the *Empire* that he would contest West Sydney in the Legislative Assembly election as a representative of Labor. On the hustings he claimed to favour free selection, an elective Upper House, universal and purely secular education, no state aid to religion, courts of conciliation in industrial matters and payment of members of parliament. He denied that he was either a protectionist or a free trader.

Dalgleish won West Sydney in December and held the seat until parliament dissolved in 1864. He was conscientious in attendance, served on select committees and was prolific with petitions; he took a special interest in bills dealing with relations between employers and employees, and technical engineering problems. As a speaker he was long winded and dwelt on detail; to David Buchanan [q.v.] he was 'a most imperturbable and unalloyed nuisance in the House. A man who will speak upwards of thirty times in one night'. Some time after his election Dalgleish was presented with a purse of 165 sovereigns. 'Called as you were from the ranks of labor to represent your own class in the people's House of Parliament', the accompanying testimonial stated, 'and being chosen in this Electorate for making the experiment of the representative of Labour from its own ranks . . . We have felt it our bounden duty to assist you to our utmost to carry out this experiment to a successful issue'.

In the 1864-65 elections Dalgleish described himself as an independent free trader but he was criticized for his support of various tariff measures. He successively lost West Sydney, Goldfields South and the Glebe, where his campaign led to his charging Thomas Holt [q.v.] with electoral impersonation and to a Supreme Court action in which he was discredited; Holt declined to collect the £500 damages and costs he won. In February 1866 Dalgleish was appointed engineer-surveyor to the Steam Navigation Board, and inspector in October. On 18 February 1870 he died in Sydney Infirmary from head injuries received a week earlier when he was thrown from a horse. He left a widow, Emma, and several children. He was buried with Masonic honours. Members of the iron trades joined the funeral procession and his friend Rev. J. D. Lang [q.v.] delivered the funeral oration.

C. E. Raven, *Christian socialism, 1848-1854* (Lond, 1920); Australian Engineering Union, *Souvenir, 25th anniversary* (Syd, 1946); J. B. Jefferys, *The story of the engineers, 1800-1945* (Lond, 1946); *Town and Country J*, 26 Feb 1870; MS cat under D. C. Dalgleish (ML); CO 201/542.
                                    AUDREY FERGUSON

DALLACHY, JOHN (1808?-1871), botanist and curator, was born in Morayshire, Scotland, son of John Dallachy, soldier, and his wife, née Lumsdaine. He became a gardener at Haddo House, seat of the earl of Aberdeen, who was interested in raising Australian plants from seed. Through the influence of Sir William Hooker, Dallachy spent some years on the staff of Kew Gardens; he returned later to Haddo House as head gardener. With an introduction from the earl of Aberdeen, Dallachy went to Ceylon in 1847 to manage a coffee plantation but next year moved to Melbourne where he was first employed as gardener to J. B. Were [q.v.] at Brighton. On 12 March 1849 Dallachy was appointed overseer of the Melbourne Botanic Gardens, established three years earlier. He was promoted superintendent in 1852 but in August 1857 his friend Ferdinand Mueller [q.v.] was appointed director of the gardens while Dallachy assumed the title of curator with his salary reduced from £400 to £300.

Dallachy's term in charge of the gardens was not marked by any lasting landscape development. His chief interest lay in collecting botanical specimens, many of them valuable for interchange with gardens in Britain and elsewhere. He made several expeditions: to the Baw Baws where he is reputed to have found the headwaters of the River Yarra; to Mount Macedon in August 1849; Mount Disappointment in January 1850; and the Pentland Hills in August 1850. In 1853 he joined Mueller in an expedition to the Ovens valley and Mount Buffalo. In 1858 he collected drought-resistant species along the River Murray near Wentworth and the Darling River as far north as Mount Murchison near Wilcannia. In 1860 he investigated the Wimmera River and Lake Hindmarsh. Next year he resigned as curator and set up a nursery at Prahran. When that venture failed he went to north Queensland where he continued to collect for the Victorian herbarium. In 1864 at Mueller's request he joined a party led by G. E. Dalrymple [q.v.] to form a settlement at Rockingham Bay. The luxuriant flora fascinated him and he settled in the district with his family. A

Presbyterian, he had married Ann Matheson in Scotland about 1839. He died on 4 June 1871 at Vale of Herbert, Herbert River, Cardwell, survived by three sons and two of his three daughters. He is best remembered as a botanist and meticulous collector of native species. J. H. Maiden in 1908 claimed Dallachy as perhaps the best Australian botanical collector 'to whom justice has not been done'.

P. C. Morrison (ed), *Melbourne's garden* (Melb, 1946); D. Jones, *Cardwell Shire story* (Brisb, 1961); J. H. Maiden, 'Records of Victorian botanists', *Vic Naturalist*, 25 (1908-09); C. Daley, 'Baron Sir Ferdinand Von Mueller', *VHM*, 10 (1924-25); information from Roy Botanic Gardens & National Herbarium, Melb.
                                        ALAN GROSS

DALLEY, WILLIAM BEDE (1831-1888), 'patriot, scholar and statesman', was born in George Street, Sydney, on 5 July 1831, son of John Dalley, store-keeper, and Catherine Spillane, who were both convicts. Educated at St Mary's seminary where he formed a lifelong friendship with Archbishop Polding [q.v.] he left in 1845 intending to work in Hordern's [q.v.] drapery shop, but Polding persuaded him to resume his studies at the Sydney College. After working as a clerk in Thomas Burdekin's office, in 1853 he was articled to Frederick Wright Unwin and on 5 July 1856 was admitted to the Bar. He spent the first £20 he earned on a dinner that cost £25. Virtually unknown in the early 1850s, his stirring street-corner speeches on the Constitution bill had thrust him into prominence while his natural geniality and generosity endeared him to most colonists. In 1856 at a banquet for C. G. Duffy [q.v.] he stamped his reputation as an orator by replying in place of Daniel Deniehy [q.v.] to the toast 'Our Native Country'. In December Dalley was nominated by Henry Parkes [q.v.] for the seat of Sydney, and won after stressing the rights of the native-born to an active political career.

In parliament he supported the liberal policies of Charles Cowper and John Robertson [qq.v.], and introduced six public bills, including one to amend the licensing laws and one to abolish the death penalty for rape, but only his amendment, abolishing the religious test in the Affiliated Colleges Partial Endowment Act, was passed in 1858. He also introduced six private bills, three of which were carried. To help Cowper in the 1858 elections he sacrificed his own chances for Sydney, but won Cumberland Boroughs. From November 1858 to February 1859 he was solicitor-general under Cowper. In 1859 he won Windsor, but in February 1860 re-

signed his seat to visit England, Ireland and
Europe. At a farewell banquet he paid tribute to his political opponents, and Rev. J.
D. Lang [q.v.] hoped that he would return
'better prepared to fight the great fight for
the liberties of the people of this country'.
After his return Dalley was nominated to
the Legislative Council on 10 May 1861 but
was not sworn in. The same year Dalley
was appointed an immigration commissioner
with Parkes and returned to London. They
toured Great Britain and published several
pamphlets but it was 'a matter of controversy in the colony whether they actually
sent out one solitary emigrant or not'. In
1862-64 Dalley represented Carcoar in the
assembly.

Short and thickset, with a jovial and often
glowing countenance, Dalley set trends in
colonial dress: colourful cravats and button-
holes reflected his unique flair and style. He
saluted friends and acquaintances alike as
'Old boy' and found it virtually impossible
to resist any appeal to his generosity. In
1860 he was guyed as 'little tiptop' in
Deniehy's sparkling The Attorney-General
of New Barataria, but quickly recovered his
poise. He helped Deniehy in many ways
and cherished his friendship along with that
of other colonial connoisseurs, including
Professor Badham, Sir Alfred Stephen,
Henry Kendall and N. D. Stenhouse [qq.v.].
By the mid-1860s he was renowned as the
most scintillating conversationalist and
after-dinner speaker in the colony.

Over many years Dalley made editorial
and other contributions to the Freeman's
Journal; in 1865 he was its editor and part
proprietor and improved both its tone and
appearance. The next year G. B. Barton
[q.v.] wrote that 'Fortunately, or unfortunately Dalley has withdrawn from political
life, the asperities of which are foreign to his
nature; and could we be certain that Literature would gain what has been lost to Politics, we should have infinite reason to re-
joice'. He supported financially the Sydney
Punch and wrote consistently for it, including a masterly series of satirical political biographies. He wrote many articles, reviews
and letters for the Sydney Morning Herald;
in 1881 the Bulletin considered that his
Herald review of Lord Beaconsfield's Endym-
ion 'should alone entitle him to rank
amongst the most subtle and refined critics
of the age'. His patronage of the arts extended to many young and struggling painters
and writers.

At the Bar Dalley's eloquence and in-
stinctive grace charmed juries, winning him
many victories, particularly on the criminal
side. In two notable cases, however, he did
not succeed. One was his defence in 1864 of
the bushranger Frank Gardiner [q.v.],

whom he had probably known as a boy, the
other in 1868 of H. J. O'Farrell [q.v.] for
the shooting of the duke of Edinburgh. He
commanded some of the highest fees taken
in criminal matters, his affluence being augmented in 1871 by a substantial legacy from
his father. Financial independence and demand for his services encouraged him to
accept only important cases. Dalley could
hold his place with any barrister, not only in
advocacy but in legal argument, and at his
peak he was briefed in many fields of the
law. He became a Q.C. in 1877.

But Dalley found in politics the best
medium for his versatile talents. If by 1865
he had tired of electoral campaigning he
still revelled in the excitement of parliament
and the political power it provided to complement his social prestige and legal eminence. In 1870-73 he was a member of the
Legislative Council. On 20 May 1872 he
excoriated Parkes for his 'entire, absolute
and unqualified falsehoods' designed to
arouse 'bitter sectarian animosities' after the
attempted assassination of the duke of
Edinburgh; with Edward Butler [q.v.] in
mind, he deplored Parkes's 'dishonest and
scandalous alliance' with the Roman
Catholics, and derided his financial delin-
quencies: 'If Parkes lives long enough he
will rule over a nation, not of admirers and
friends, but of — creditors'. He also berated
the other members of Parkes's cabinet and
his reference to G. A. Lloyd [q.v.], 'I fancy
silence is an eulogium—and a courtesy',
revealed the latent snobbery that sometimes laced his luminous wit.

On 15 June 1872 at St John's Church of
England, Darlinghurst, he married Eleanor
Jane, daughter of William Long, merchant.
The union brought him great happiness and
strengthened his friendship with Sir James
Martin [q.v.], whose wife was Isabella
Long, though it strained temporarily Dalley's relations with his Church. But he had
always been an essentially loyal and devoted
Catholic, although disdainful at times of the
confusion of many clerics about divine and
worldly affairs and their failure to adapt
charitably to the Australian environment:
his nativism led him to seek a Roman Catholic Church that was Australian rather than
Irish in sentiment, a goal accentuated by his
Benedictine training and some misgivings
about the zeal of many Irishmen; but he was
outnumbered, and despite his religious liberalism and social enlightenment became in
effect a prize exhibit of the Irish. He remained as tolerant of the gaucheries of many of
his co-religionists as of the philistinism of
many of his fellow colonists. In 1879 when
opposing publicly Parkes's education bill,
he stressed that 'We will not give [our
opponents] the luxury of supposing that

they have been able . . . "to freeze the genial current of the soul"'.

In 1872 Dalley strongly supported a petition to the governor to exercise the prerogative of mercy and set Gardiner free. The bushranger's release in 1874 led to the fall of Parkes's government, and on 9 February 1875 Dalley became attorney-general under Robertson and returned to the council. Although the *Illustrated Sydney News* thought that to 'crush the leader of that Opposition seems to be Mr. Dalley's special mission—his sole reason for returning to political life', in his two and a half years in the cabinet he revealed his capacity for concentrated hard work; his legal opinions filled five volumes. In 1876 Dalley declined a Supreme Court judgeship and persuaded Sir William Manning [q.v.] to accept it. He served as attorney-general in Robertson's short-lived ministry in 1877.

In April 1880 Dalley retired from the Legislative Council. He told Stephen that 'The severance of my connection with it was a painful effort, but it was one I felt it absolutely necessary to make in the interests of my family and of my own repose'. Parkes wrote a 'sympathetic letter' and Dalley replied, 'I too, like yourself, have a keen and consoling remembrance of times when you and I enjoyed other relations than those in which circumstance and conviction have more recently placed us towards each other. I shall not willingly let the recollection to be tarnished and shall I trust always think of you, however we may be fated to differ from each other, as one whose friendship it was my privilege to possess when I was accumulating the first honours of my life'. By this time Dalley was active in a wide range of public affairs. He was a member of the committee of the Australian Club, vice-president and honorary counsel for the Society for the Prevention of Cruelty to Animals, a trustee of the Public Library, and fellow of St John's College. He was a steward of the Australian Jockey Club, a member of the Royal Sydney Yacht Squadron and a member of the Southern Cross Masonic Lodge. He was also a magistrate of the City of Sydney and a fellow of the Senate of the University of Sydney.

Leaving six young children, his wife died of typhoid fever on 17 January 1881. Grief-stricken, Dalley withdrew from public life, sold his house, Clairveaux, at Rose Bay and lived at Sutton Forest, devoting himself to his children. When he returned to Sydney he built a 'castle', Marinella, at Manly. On 10 August he was briefed by prominent Chinese to protest against the stringency of the Chinese restriction bill. He was permitted to speak from the floor of the council and argued that the measure was against the spirit of English legislation and 'at direct variance with the liberal spirit of the age'. The council modified the most objectionable clauses.

Yielding to his political instinct and his sense of duty and affection for Sir Alexander Stuart [q.v.], Dalley returned to public life on 5 January 1883 as attorney-general. The *Goulburn Herald* contrasted Dalley's intellect with his indolence and thought him likely to prove more 'ornamental than useful'. But the next three years were to be his most active. Not only was he required to give legal opinions on many complicated issues such as the legality of summoning parliament to legalize the running of steam tramways, and three appeals to the Privy Council, he was also responsible for government legislation in the Legislative Council. The complicated Criminal Law Amendment Act, first drafted by Stephen and introduced by Edward Butler in 1873, was finally carried by Dalley in 1883. He failed in his attempts to simplify bankruptcy proceedings and to restrict the power of the judges in contempt of court cases, but carried the Prisoners' Labour Sentences Act. He amended the Matrimonial Causes Act by altering court procedure : he had also aimed to extend the grounds of divorce to desertion after five years and for injury or attempted murder, or for administering poison, but dropped the relevant clauses when he saw that opposition to them would delay the urgently needed procedural reforms.

Dalley was a leading New South Wales member of the Intercolonial Convention held in Sydney in December 1883. His native-born bias stressed the imperial authority of England as the mother country and the local primacy of New South Wales as the mother colony and led him, with his fastidious urbanity, to look askance at James Service's [q.v.] crude annexation plans and to reflect his colony's lack of interest in a Federal Council; but he helped the convention to reach reasonable compromises, and later explained his government's sensible policy in a gruelling series of banquets from Grafton to Albury.

The long parliamentary session of 9 October 1883 to 1 November 1884 concentrated on the land bill amendment and was a serious physical strain on the ministry. The tumultuous late night sittings broke the health of Stuart, and Dalley became acting colonial secretary as well as attorney-general from 7 October 1884 to 11 May 1885. He adroitly averted a collision between the two Houses over the land bill, and on 12 February 1885 electrified Australia by offering Britain a New South Wales contingent to help in the Sudan campaign.

Dalley was a discerning imperialist able to judge nicely the often incongruous pressures of colonial and empire needs. In early 1885, at a critical period of the federation movement, he assessed majority opinion exactly and strengthened both Australian nationalism and the imperial connexion. His object in offering the troops for the Sudan was 'to testify to the readiness of the Australian colonies to give instant and practical help to the Empire . . . conceiving that such a course cannot be without a beneficial effect upon those who may, in dealing adversely with the Imperial interest, fail to recognize the esteem, the sympathy, and the adherence of the Colonies'. A significant minority, led by Henry Parkes, did not reduce Dalley's enthusiastic public support. The soldiers left on 3 March and parliament overwhelmingly approved in April. But the exertions weakened his health further and the *Sydney Morning Herald* tried to postpone his retirement by remarking that 'During the last three years he has been more indefatigable and more brilliant than ever . . . it will be much to be regretted if he cannot be persuaded to sacrifice his inclination for repose'. The ministry resigned on 6 October and Dalley declined a commission to form a new cabinet. In 1888 he told R. Burdett Smith [q.v.] that he had 'only tasted suffering and the grossest misrepresentation' over the Sudan contingent and that 'I now scarcely ever open my mouth about a subject in which I thought I should have shared in the glory of our country in its achievements'.

In 1886 Dalley was twice honoured; a bust of him by Simonetti [q.v.] was placed in the Legislative Council and he became Australia's first privy councillor. The same year, saddened by Martin's death, he declined the vacant chief justiceship, but prevailed upon Frederick Darley [q.v.] to accept it.

Always opposed to the death penalty, on 20 January 1887 Dalley joined Parkes, Bishop Barry [q.v.] and Cardinal Moran in a deputation to the governor for clemency in the Mount Rennie rape case. Seriously ill that year, Dalley's public appearances were limited to those connected with Church affairs. His last great political effort was to modify the Chinese restriction bill of 1888. Despite failing strength Dalley still enjoyed the pleasures of life. On 24 June 1888 he wrote to Stephen 'I have a decent cook, a few bottles of dear old Martin's best wine—and I could send any day . . . a pair of charming gentle horses well driven to bring you out to lunch'. At the centennial celebrations, he represented the laity and offered an address to the seven governors at St Mary's Cathedral; he also spoke at the opening of St Vincent's Hospital's new wing

and the installation of Dr O'Brien as rector of St John's College. He died on 28 October 1888 at his house, Annerly, Darling Point, from cardiac disease, renal disease and uraemia, and was survived by three sons and two daughters. Buried in Waverley cemetery, he was mourned throughout the continent as a great Australian patriot. Many leading newspapers carried eulogistic editorials as well as long obituaries. Sir John Robertson quickly organized public meetings and a subscription to erect in Hyde Park a statue of Dalley, where it stands today looking down Macquarie Street to the Law Courts and Parliament House. There is a stained-glass window and commemorative plaque in St Mary's Cathedral, Sydney, and a plaque in St Paul's Cathedral, London. He made for himself a unique position in society, in literature, and in the law and was described by the *Argus* as 'one of the pioneer statesmen of the new world'. Sir Alfred Stephen perceived him as 'the loveable William Bede Dalley, himself a lover of romance, and in whose company no man could feel dull'.

G. B. Barton, *Literature in New South Wales* (Syd, 1866); J. A. Froude, *Oceana, or England and her colonies* (Lond, 1886); W. Blacket, *May it please your honour* (Syd, 1927); A. B. Piddington, *Worshipful masters* (Syd, 1929); B. R. Penny, 'The age of empire: an Australian episode', *Hist Studies*, no 41, Nov 1963; *Empire* (Syd), 24 Feb 1860; *Illustrated Sydney News*, 10 Mar 1875; *SMH*, 11 Aug 1881; *Freeman's J* (Syd), 14 Oct 1882, 3, 7, 10 Nov, 15, 22 Dec 1888; *Bulletin*, 26 Feb 1881, 28 Nov 1891; *Goulburn Herald*, 9 Jan 1883; *Sydney Mail*, 27 Jan 1883; *The Times*, 5 Nov 1888; *Catholic Weekly* (Syd), 9 Jan 1958; letters to Lord Angus Loftus (ML); Parkes letters (ML); MS cat under W. B. Dalley (ML); uncat MS, W. M. Manning, Sir Alfred Stephen, R. Town & Co, W. Windeyer (ML); CO 201/598-611. BEDE NAIRN
MARTHA RUTLEDGE

DALRYMPLE, GEORGE AUGUSTUS FREDERICK ELPHINSTONE (1826-1876), explorer, public servant and politician, was born on 6 May 1826, the tenth son of Lieut-Colonel Robert Dalrymple Horn Elphinstone of Aberdeenshire, Scotland, and his wife Graeme, née Hepburn. He was the younger brother of E. G. B. E. Dalrymple [q.v.]. He left Scotland in the 1840s and became a coffee planter in Ceylon. He arrived in Australia between 1856 and 1858 and went to the Darling Downs where he was unable to take up land as he had intended. The unoccupied north attracted him and in February 1859 he published in Brisbane *Proposals for the Establishment of a New Pastoral Settlement in North Australia*. His proposed syndicate soon attracted subscribers and he organized an expedition to explore the Burdekin River watershed (Kennedy district). His party, including Ernest Henry and P. F. Sellheim [qq.v.], set out from near Rockhampton in August and reached the site of Bowen.

The Queensland government countermanded the decision to open the new district for settlement in January 1860 and the syndicate's plans to tender for runs were forestalled. In compensation Dalrymple was made commissioner for crown lands in the Kennedy district. In August he went with Lieutenant J. W. Smith in the *Spitfire* to explore the coast and examine Port Denison as a port of access for the Kennedy. As officer in charge of the proposed settlement of Bowen, Dalrymple then planned the expedition to establish the township and led the overland section. After he arrived Bowen was proclaimed on 11 April 1861. He was soon beset by official duties in a frontier town and by problems of administering the new Land Act, but neglected his mounting clerical tasks for more adventurous field-work. When Dalrymple went south on sick·leave he fell out with his superior, A. C. Gregory [q.v.]. In 1862 when several land commissioners, including Dalrymple, were to be replaced by professional surveyors, he resigned rather than accept alternative posts offered him in Bowen.

Early next year with W. J. Scott [q.v.], his brother Arthur and R. G. W. Herbert [q.v.] as 'sleeping partner', Dalrymple formed Scott Bros Dalrymple & Co., took up the Valley of Lagoons run on the Upper Burdekin River, and became its manager. He brought in his large collection of books and pictures but was often absent from the station. At Rockhampton he was drawn into a minor scandal involving a friend's wife; while vindicating his own and his friend's honour Dalrymple assaulted the police magistrate, John Jardine, and was fined £500. In 1864 Dalrymple and Arthur Scott established Cardwell on Rockingham Bay as a port for inland stations north of Bowen. The expedition, initiated by the company but with official backing, included J. Morrill and J. Dallachy [qq.v.]. Dalrymple led a small party inland to the Valley of Lagoons and returned, hacking out a dray route to the coast.

Dalrymple sold his interests in the company to go into politics. In March 1865 he was elected the first member for Kennedy in the Legislative Assembly. He was colonial secretary in Herbert's ministry from July to August 1866 but held no other office, although as a supporter of the Northern Separation League and its president in 1866

he was favoured as premier for the proposed new colony. He did not contest Kennedy in 1867 but went to Britain to recover his health. He returned to Queensland in 1869 and with A. J. Bogle took up Oxford Downs on the Upper Burdekin. The venture failed, as did his imported traction engine which proved impracticable on northern roads. Insolvent, he was lucky to get a government post as assistant gold commissioner on the Gilbert diggings in October 1871. Next year he had charge of the diggings and was also sent to find a route for a telegraph over the Sea View Range near Cardwell. In September 1873 he led an official exploration of the coast north of Cardwell. They reached the Endeavour River in October, just before Cooktown sprang up as the port for the Palmer goldfields. They returned to Cardwell in December and Dalrymple, sick with fever, went to Brisbane. He hoped to explore the coast north of Cooktown but in 1874 was given charge of the government settlement at Somerset on Cape York. He sailed for Somerset in May but soon after he arrived was incapacitated by fever and a stroke. He was taken south by mail steamer and granted leave in September. After a summer in Scotland he went to St Leonards, Sussex, where he died, unmarried, on 22 January 1876.

Dalrymple had been elected a fellow of the Royal Geographical Society in November 1867. He was a successful explorer, a dashing leader, restless, impatient of official parsimony and red tape. Through his policy of vigilance and restraint he seldom had trouble with the Aboriginals on his expeditions. Dalrymple's appreciation of natural beauty is amply expressed in his exploration reports. Many features of northern Queensland commemorate his name and many more were named by him.

G. C. Bolton, *A thousand miles away* (Brisb, 1963); J. Farnfield, *Frontiersman* (Melb, 1968); G. C. Bolton, 'The Valley of Lagoons: a study in exile', *Business Archives and History*, 4 (1964) no 2; CO 201/508/461; information supplied by Mrs Penelope E. Lovell, New York, USA.
                                                    C. G. AUSTIN
                                                    CLEM LACK

DALTON, JAMES (1834-1919), merchant and pastoralist, was born in Duntryleague, Limerick, Ireland, son of James Dalton, innkeeper, and his first wife Eleanor, née Ryan. Because of the famine he went to New South Wales with his father in the late 1840s. In 1849 James senior opened a bark and slab store in Orange. In 1853 James junior set up as a store-keeper in Orange, where he married Margaret Mary Collins in 1858. In that year his brother Thomas joined him and the firm became known as Dalton Bros. James helped displaced miners and in 1857 promised to build a mill if they grew wheat; his flour-mill was built in 1861. The firm's business expanded until it became the largest wholesale distributor west of the Blue Mountains. They had great success producing roasted and ground coffee on a large scale and later built large wool stores in Orange, where in 1865 they built an impressive retail store in Summer Street. By 1871 they had acquired three stations in the Lachlan district.

Dalton Bros continued to flourish in the 1870s and in 1876 James built Duntryleague, a mansion set in magnificent grounds, reputedly for £50,000. Aware that the coming of the railway, for which James had turned the first sod in 1874, would mean the end of wholesale distributors in the west Dalton Bros established an importing agency in Sydney, managed by Thomas, and in 1878 built Dalton House, Pitt Street. They built stores in lower Fort Street and had a wharf and bond and free warehouses at Millers Point. In 1878 James bought Ammerdown, near Orange, and later, Kangaroobie.

James Dalton provided funds and leadership for the Irish nationalist movement in New South Wales. In 1882 his presiding over an Irish Land League meeting was questioned in the Legislative Assembly. He was closely associated with the visit of the Irish nationalists, John [q.v.] and William Redmond, to the colony in 1883. As president of the local branch of the Irish National League, Dalton with two other magistrates signed an address of welcome to Redmond, which praised their 'resolute resistance to the oppressive proceedings of a foreign senate'. The address provoked a public outcry and a demand for the removal of the 'seditious' justices. The premier, Alexander Stuart [q.v.], requested explanations from the three magistrates, but found them unacceptable. Dalton claimed that he had done nothing incompatible with his 'oath of fealty as a magistrate'. Asked to resign, he refused and was dismissed on 28 April. The bond between the Daltons and Redmonds was cemented when on 4 September John Redmond married Dalton's half-sister Johanna; later William Redmond married Dalton's daughter Eleanor. In 1883-84 Dalton was in Britain and America.

Dalton was an active townsman, a member of such local bodies as the local council and mayor of Orange in 1869. In 1885 he built the Australian Hall because the Redmonds had been obliged to lecture in a shop. In the early 1890s he dissolved the partnership with Thomas, sold his Sydney interests and formed two family companies, Dalton Bros in Orange and Dalton Estates Ltd covering his pastoral holdings, to which he had added Belowra in the 1880s, Gobala, Nevertire, in 1898 and the Lookout at Mullion.

The Dalton family was one of the colony's richest and most influential Catholic families. Thomas, a papal knight, became mayor of Orange in 1877, represented Orange in the assembly in 1882-91 and was a member of the Legislative Council in 1892-1901. He died in Sydney on 26 June 1901. His daughter Blanche married Sir Mark Sheldon. James's second son, James Joseph, became the first native-born Australian member of the House of Commons when he was elected for West Donegal in 1890 in the Parnell interest. Despite exceptional enterprise and business ability James was kindly, unassuming and ever ready to help an Irishman in distress. He was a friend of Cardinal Moran and Bishop Dunne and a benefactor of St Mary's Cathedral. He received a papal knighthood in 1877. He died aged 85 on 17 March 1919 at Duntryleague, Orange. Predeceased by his wife, he was survived by four sons and four daughters. His estate was worth £73,000.

H. N. Maitland (ed), *New South Wales, 1920-1923* (Syd, 1923); J. Jervis et al, *Orange 1860-1960*, O. and A. Ziegler eds (Orange, 1960); PD (LA NSW), 1883, 848, 1545-65; SMH, 9 Mar, 18 Apr 1883; *Freeman's J* (Syd), 21 Apr, 12 May 1883, 19 Mar 1919; *Dubbo Dispatch*, 18 Mar 1919; G. M. Tobin, The sea-divided Gael: a study of the Irish home rule movement in Victoria and New South Wales, 1880-1916 (M.A. thesis, ANU, 1970); Mahon papers (NL); printed cat under Dalton (ML); CO 201/598.

MARTHA RUTLEDGE

DALTON, JOSEPH (1817-1905), Jesuit priest, was born on 2 December 1817 at Waterford, Ireland. He was educated at the Jesuit colleges of Clongowes and Tullabeg and entered the Society of Jesus in December 1836. For the next thirty years he studied and worked in Jesuit Houses in Ireland, and became rector of St Stanislaus College, Tullabeg.

Austrian Jesuits had begun a mission to the German settlers near Clare, South Australia, in 1848 but were diffident to extend their work to Victoria where Dr Goold [q.v.] was eager to found an Irish Jesuit Mission. The Jesuit priests, William Kelly [q.v.] and Joseph Lentaigne, reached Melbourne in September 1865. Dalton was appointed superior of the mission and arrived in April 1866. The first of his many tasks was to revive St Patrick's College, which had opened at East Melbourne in

1854 with a government grant but closed after eight years through maladministration. Dalton appointed Kelly to its staff and by 1880 'Old Patricians' could boast many graduates at the University of Melbourne, and two of its three doctorates in law. At St Patrick's Dalton was also persuaded by Goold to train candidates for the diocesan priesthood, but he resisted Goold's pressure for a more ambitious college until he had sufficient resources. On land bought at Kew in 1871 he built Xavier College which opened in 1878 and cost £40,000.

Dalton was also entrusted by Goold with the parochial care of a very large area centred on Richmond where some of the colony's most eminent laymen lived. With W. W. Wardell [q.v.] and a magnificent site, Dalton worked towards the grandiose St Ignatius Church, capable of seating almost his entire 4000 parishioners. In his district he built other chapels, schools and churches, including the Church of the Immaculate Conception, Hawthorn. He gave many retreats, lectured often on secular education, and engaged in controversy which led once to litigation. He went with Goold to reorganize the diocese of Auckland in 1869 and after Archbishop Polding [q.v.] died, the Irish Jesuit Mission was invited to Sydney in 1878. As superior there Dalton took charge within eight months of the North Sydney district, founded St Kilda House, the forerunner of St Aloysius College, Milson's Point, and was its first rector. He also bought 118 acres at Riverview where, as rector, he opened St Ignatius College. There he lived after his retirement in 1883 and died on 5 January 1905.

Dalton founded two great public schools and made more than a dozen foundations, of which only one at Dunedin proved abortive; they involved debts of at least £120,000 which were mostly paid by 1883. He published nothing and his inner life is not revealed in his diary (1866-88). Those who knew him well attested that he was first and foremost a holy priest, and he was widely revered in Richmond and Riverview. His energy and vision were striking, and his work established the Irish Jesuits in the eastern colonies.

J. Ryan, *The Society of Jesus in Australia* (priv print, 1911); papers and St Patrick's College records (Jesuit Provincial Archives, Hawthorn, Vic).   G. J. O'KELLY

DALY, SIR DOMINICK (1798-1868), governor, was born on 11 August 1798 at Ardfry, Ireland, the third son of Dominick Daly of Benmore, County Galway, and his wife Joanna Harriet, daughter of Joseph Blake of Ardfry, sister of Lord Wallscourt and widow of Richard Burke of Glinsk. He was educated at Oscott College, Birmingham, and at 24 went to Lower Canada as secretary to the lieut-governor, Sir Francis Burton. As secretary to the Executive Council created by Lord Durham he won mention in Appendix C of the famous report and appointment as secretary to the United Province Council in 1841-48. The last survivor of Colonial Office 'bureaucracy' in Canada, he was nicknamed 'the perpetual secretary' but respected for his firm, if detached, belief in democratic processes, and popular for his conviviality. After responsible government he joined the Executive Council and later became commissioner of woods and forests. He was lieut-governor of Tobago in 1851-54 and of Prince Edward Island in 1854-59. He was knighted in 1856.

Daly was appointed governor of South Australia in October 1861. With his wife and two daughters he arrived in February 1862 at Melbourne where he visited Governor Barkly and met leading politicians. He reached Adelaide on 4 March, the day his predecessor, Sir Richard MacDonnell, was farewelled. That Daly ignored the lack of an official welcome because of his early arrival was indicative of a disposition which was also able to dispel the early prejudice against him as a Roman Catholic. South Australians came to know him as a kindly ageing gentleman, accessible, devoted to duty and a peacemaker noted for his cheerful impartiality. His first duty of sending condolences to the Queen on the death of the Prince Consort was melancholy but it was followed by the happier report of the return of J. M. Stuart's [q.v.] expedition which led to annexation of the Northern Territory to South Australia in 1863. Unfortunately pastoral expansion was halted by drought in 1864 but the boom in copper mining revived the economy and led to an extension of railways and agricultural settlement. Political crises were therefore frequent and the administration changed nine times in 1862-68. More serious was the controversy which led to the removal of Judge Boothby [q.v.] from the Supreme Court bench in 1867. Daly loyally supported each premier in turn, zealously advocating more production and immigration as the surest roads to prosperity, and more than any other governor he recommended leading colonists for royal honours. A month before the duke of Edinburgh's visit in October 1867 Daly asked for an extension of his term, chiefly because of his wife's paralysis, but his own health was rapidly declining and he died in office on 19 February 1868. Despite searing heat, people lined the streets for the state funeral and he was buried in the Catholic section of West Terrace cemetery.

On 20 May 1826 he had married Caroline Maria, daughter of Ralph Gore of Barrowmount, County Kilkenny; she died at Glenelg on 16 July 1872, aged 71, survived by three sons and two ·daughters.

W. S. Kelly, *Rural development in South Australia* (Adel, 1962); *Register* (Adel), 20-28 Feb 1868; *Illustrated Adel Post*, 25 Mar 1868; Governor's confidential dispatches (SAA); CO 13/111-25.   MARJORIE FINDLAY

DAMPIER, ALFRED (1848?-1908), actor-manager, was born at Horsham, Sussex, England, son of John Dampier, builder, and his wife Mary, née Daly. He was educated at Charterhouse School and began work in a barrister's office, but an interest in amateur theatricals diverted him to a stage career. His main experience in England was in the Manchester company headed by Henry Irving. In 1866 Irving moved on to London and fame, and in the following years Dampier graduated to the rank of leading man.

In 1873 Dampier was invited to Melbourne by H. R. Harwood, representative of a theatrical syndicate which included G. S. Coppin [q.v.]. He made his colonial début at the Royal Theatre, playing Mephistopheles in his own adaptation of Goethe's *Faust*. He formed his own company and in 1877, as Hamlet, made his first appearance in Sydney. For the next thirty years Dampier and his company were a notable part of the Austra.ian theatrical scene. Although he retained a reputation as a Shakespearian actor, Dampier found himself committed by necessity to the popular medium of melodrama, and he used, according to the tastes of the time, an increasing amount of spectacular scenic effects. Many of his plays were either his own adaptations or those of friends and colleagues; in 1876-82, for example, he staged five plays by F. R. C. Hopkins [q.v.], all derived from European works despite their local authorship.

Dampier's distinction for promoting a native Australian drama seems to date from his successful production in 1886 of *For the Term of His Natural Life*, which was followed by *Robbery Under Arms* in 1890 and *The Miner's Right* in 1891; all three were adapted for the stage by Dampier himself. Although advertised as plays of literary importance, Dampier took great liberties with the originals, particularly in providing happy endings. It is clear that these plays were of no great quality, but many applauded the Australian spirit of the productions. He also produced several of his own melodramas, amongst them *Marvellous Melbourne* (1889, co-author T. Somers), *This Great City* (1891), and *To The West* (1896, co-author K. Mackay). While relying on traditional devices of the form, these melodramas used a range of stock Australian characters and revealed an aggressive, nascent nationalism. *Marvellous Melbourne*, timed for the 1888-89 exhibition, was a particular success; it concluded, appropriately, with the heroine's horse winning the Melbourne Cup off stage.

Contemporary reviews suggest that as an actor Dampier was sound rather than brilliant. He was generally praised for his elocutionary powers, presence and sense of restraint. His company toured Australia and New Zealand, but was particularly associated with the Alexandra Theatre in Melbourne and the Royal Standard in Sydney. He visited the United States in 1878 and made several trips to England; there he produced Hopkins's *All For Gold* in 1881 and *Robbery Under Arms* in 1894, but neither appears to have been successful. In the depression of 1893 he became insolvent but soon recovered.

At Birmingham in 1869 Dampier had married Katherine Alice, daughter of T. H. Russell, R.A. Katherine had been a pianist, but in Australia she and her children appeared regularly with her husband's company. Dampier died of a cerebral haemorrhage on 23 May 1908 at his home in Paddington, Sydney, and was buried in the Anglican section of Waverley cemetery. He was survived by his wife, who died aged 66 in the United States on 8 March 1915, and by one son and two daughters.

P. McGuire et al, *The Australian theatre* (Melb, 1948); G. L. C. Rees, *Towards an Australian drama* (Syd, 1953); H. Porter, *Stars of Australian stage and screen* (Adel, 1965); *Shakespearean Q*, Jan 1924; *Daily Telegraph* (Syd), 7 June 1906; *SMH*, 25 May 1908; MS cat under A. Dampier (ML).   JOHN RICKARD

DANGAR, THOMAS GORDON GIBBONS (1829-1890), pastoralist and politician, was born on 27 November 1829 in Sydney, son of Matthew John Gibbons, cooper, and his wife Charlotte Selina, née Hutchinson. In 1832 at Maitland his widowed mother married Thomas Dangar; the family moved to Scone where she died in 1838 and Dangar brought up the boy as his own son and gave him his name. At Scone Dangar was postmaster and later store-keeper. In December 1840 the store was held up by bushrangers led by Edward Davis [q.v.] and young Thomas gave evidence at the trial in Sydney. He was

educated in Paterson and Singleton and later
at the Sydney College. A long illness prevented him reading for the Bar.

In 1847 Dangar went to New England.
He helped to form a station beyond the
Condamine and then pioneered the Lower
Barwon and Warrego districts. About 1850
he made his headquarters at Bullerawa on
the Namoi River. By 1854 he was in partnership with William Dangar on the Liverpool
Plains and later leased other runs there and
in the Warrego district. He twice petitioned
parliament for redress and inquiry into his
disputes with the Lands Department.

In 1855 Dangar became a magistrate. In
January 1865 he was elected to the Legislative Assembly for the Gwydir; his election
was declared void in May because he held a
government mail contract but he was immediately re-elected. He represented the
Gwydir until at his insistence division of
the electorate was incorporated in the
Electoral Act of 1880; apart from the twelfth
parliament he then represented the Namoi
till his death. Unobtrusive but hard working, Dangar was a very successful 'roads and
bridges' politician. He helped to procure the
extension of the inland telegraph to the
Queensland border. In 1873 he corresponded with Henry Parkes [q.v.] over the
appointment of additional magistrates at
Wee Waa. Although he attended parliament
irregularly, he introduced seven public bills
and one private, most of them on parochial
matters or livestock. According to the Bulletin he was 'a kindly old man who said
little but got a culvert put agin the door of
every constituent'. About 1858 in letters to
the press, Dangar had advocated locks on
the Darling; the suggestion was then
ridiculed but steamers later reached as far
as Walgett.

'Tom' Dangar reputedly housed and provided for twenty-five old convicts, 'who had
finished their useful life'. He left a collection
of pictures, maps and books, and for his own
use devised a peculiar book-plate depicting
the combined arms of the only Gibbons
family in Burke's Peerage and those of
Charles Gordon, eleventh marquess of
Huntly. Dangar died of diabetes on 4 July
1890 at his home in Cavendish Street,
Petersham, and was buried in the family
vault at St Luke's Church of England,
Scone. He was survived by his wife
Catherine Annabella, née Mackenzie, whom
he had married at Wangan, near Pilliga. He
left her £2800 in trust for his son, Thomas
Eclipse Vivian.

E. M. Dangar, The Dangars from St Neot,
Cornwall (Syd, 1966); V&P (LA NSW), 1862,
4, 1075, 1869, 2, 161, 1873-74, 3, 1889; SMH, 25
Feb 1851, 6, 20 May 1876, 21 Nov 1888, 5 July
1890; Town and Country J, 19 Mar 1887, 12
July 1890; Newcastle Morning Herald, 7 Feb
1912; information from A. J. Gray, Scone.

                                        MARTHA RUTLEDGE

DANGAR, WILLIAM JOHN (1829-
1890), pastoralist, HENRY CARY (1830-
1917), barrister, politician and sportsman,
FREDERICK HOLKHAM (1831-1921), merchant and financier, ALBERT AUGUSTUS
(1840-1913), pastoralist, and FRANCIS
RICHARD (1845-1873), landowner, were
sons of Henry Dangar [q.v.] and his wife
Grace, née Sibley. William John was born
on 16 March 1829 at St Neot, Cornwall,
England, and as an infant went to Sydney
with his parents. They lived at Port
Stephens until 1833 and then moved to
Neotsfield, Hunter River. In 1846 on his
return from school in Sydney he was con-
fronted with his father's overriding
ambition to make him a squatter. Although
unco-operative and independent, he was sent
to work on his father's stations under
A. H. Palmer [q.v.]. While his parents were
abroad in 1852-55 he managed Neotsfield
under the guidance of his uncle William
who wrote regretfully 'he wont confide in
anyone'. On his father's return he left home
and on 14 February 1856 married Marian,
daughter of John Phelps of Paterson. After
his father died he inherited Neotsfield, and
in 1874 withdrew from Dangar Brothers.
He died without issue on 3 August 1890,
leaving an estate valued at £214,900.

Henry Cary was born on 4 June 1830 at
Port Stephens and educated at Sydney College. In 1846 on the advice of his uncle
Richard he sailed for England in the Persian.
In 1849 he entered Trinity College, Cambridge (B.A., 1853; M.A., 1857). After touring the Continent with his parents he was
admitted to the Middle Temple and to the
Bar in 1854. Back in Australia he was a
stabilizing influence in the troubled family
affairs although unwilling to practise law.
In 1861 by his father's will he inherited the
family properties at St Neot, Cornwall, but
they had all been sold except one cottage. As
compensation his mother gave him Grantham, the family home at Potts Point,
Sydney. On 19 September 1865 he married
Lucy, daughter of Commander John Lamb,
R.N. A silent partner in Dangar Brothers,
Dangar Gilchrist & Co. and other enterprises, he represented West Sydney in the
Legislative Assembly in 1874-77 and East
Sydney in 1880-82. Although conservative
he supported the revision of the land laws.
When appointed to the Legislative Council
in 1883 he was known as 'a regular attender
and serious debater' who worked for colonial
expansion, but was attacked by the Bulletin

as a 'Tory' on the immigration issue. He inherited Neotsfield from William John in 1890. A member of the Australian Jockey Club for forty-two years his racing colours were well known as was his generosity in sending the New South Wales Rifle Team to compete in Philadelphia. He donated the cloisters of St Paul's College in the University of Sydney and was a founder and trustee of the Union Club, a director of the Royal Prince Alfred Hospital and a councillor of the New South Wales Academy of Art. He died at Potts Point on 25 April 1917, survived by four sons and four daughters.

The third brother, Frederick Holkham, was born on 23 October 1831 at Port Stephens. In 1846 his parents smiled at his love of the sea and his voyage to Calcutta in .the *Royal Saxon*; his willingness to examine progressive ideas was encouraged by his uncle Richard, and he became the family financial adviser. At 17 he was exporting kauri gum from New Zealand to London. In 1855 with an advance of £2000 from his father he joined Rundle [q.v.], Dangar & Co., general merchants of Sydney and London. In 1858 he married his sister-in-law Elizabeth Phelps. With a wedding present of £15,000 from his father he bought in 1859 a partnership in Dangar, Gilchrist & Co., established on 1 December 1858 by his uncle Richard and James Gilchrist, merchant of Armidale and Glen Innes. From his father he inherited properties at Muswellbrook and Maitland, and Holkham station at Aberdeen which had been sold, but he was compensated by cancellation of the £2000 debt. In 1868 he inherited the Australian estate of his uncle William and bought a half share in the *Hawkesbury*, 1100 tons. Later, with George Dibbs [q.v.], he bought the *Gladstone*, an iron screw barque, to carry wool to the London sales. In 1889 the *Neotsfield* was built to his specifications and designed for the comfort of the crew. He also supported the training ships, *Medway* and *Port Jackson*, operated by Devitt & Moore. In 1870 Gilchrist retired from the firm and was replaced by C. T. Gedye. In 1879 Frederick Dangar also retired and after disposing of his colonial interests made his home at Ealing, London. He died there on 26 March 1921, predeceased by his wife and survived by two sons and one daughter; his estate was sworn at £76,000. He was well known for his generosity and his ready friendship with people in all walks of life. In New South Wales he had been president of the National Shipwreck Relief Society and the Cricket Association, and director of the Commercial Banking Co. of Sydney, the Australian General Assurance Co., the Sydney Infirm-

ary and Dispensary and the Shale & Oil Co. Ltd. He was also a member of the Royal Colonial Institute for forty years.

The fourth son, Albert Augustus, was born on 8 June 1840 at Neotsfield. A delicate child, he attended school at Newcastle; at 12 he went with his parents to England and studied at the Truro Grammar School, Cornwall, and in Germany. After three years at sea in the service of Duncan Dunbar he returned to New South Wales to work under A. H. Palmer in the management of his father's properties. In 1863-97 he was general manager of the pastoral holdings of Dangar Brothers. From his father he inherited 'properties at Newcastle and within 5 miles thereof', valued at £3000 in 1852 but worth £108,181 in 1906. He married Mary Phoebe, daughter of Edwin Rouse, at Windsor on 11 September 1866. In that year he also bought Baroona station near Singleton. Although called a 'Perigrinating Plutocrat' in 1903 he was highly respected at Singleton, where he donated a cottage hospital in 1906 and generous funds to rebuilding the Church of All Saints in 1911. He was a founder and president of the Pastoralists' Union, a principal in the Cobar Copper Syndicate and first donor to the Dreadnought Fund. His major hobby was the breeding of pure stock. He died at Baroona on 5 April 1913, survived by four sons and four daughters; his probate was sworn at over £300,000.

The youngest son, Francis Richard, was born on 14 February 1845 at Neotsfield and educated at The King's School, Parramatta. By his father's will and codicil he received a life interest entailed to his descendants in 'leasehold properties in the Gostwyck group without stock and equipment', and the squattage of Yarrowyck. After his mother died in 1869 he leased the stations to Dangar Brothers in which he held a fifth interest for £480 and went to England. He died unmarried in London on 12 October 1873, leaving an estate worth £51,000.

A. D. Fraser (ed), *This century of ours* (Syd, 1938); E. M. Dangar, *The Dangars from St Neot, Cornwall* (Syd, 1966); E. C. Rowland, 'The life and times of Henry Dangar', *JRAHS*, 39 (1953); *SMH*, 4 Dec 1880, 4 Mar 1882, 27 May 1885, 26, 27 Apr 1917, 30 Mar 1921; *Bulletin*, 6 June 1885; *Truth* (Syd), 11 Oct 1903; Dangar papers (Univ New England Archives).

LOUISE T. DALEY

DANKS, JOHN (1828-1902), businessman, was born in January 1828 at Wednesbury, Staffordshire, England, son of John Danks, a wrought iron and gas tube manufacturer, and his wife Hannah, née Hickman. At 8 he was apprenticed to his father but finished his training with another firm and then joined his brothers, Samuel and Thomas, in starting an iron and tube works in Wednesbury. In 1857 the brothers and their families arrived in the *Shaftesbury* at Melbourne. After several unsuccessful ventures the brothers became hardware manufacturers, dealing 'in nearly everything suitable for plumbers, engineers, gasfitters and water supply'; one of their first jobs was the manufacture of pipe connexions for the Yan Yean water supply.

In 1860 Thomas retired and the firm continued as J. & S. Danks until 1871 when Samuel retired. The next twenty years brought rapid expansion: branch shops were established in Sydney and in Christchurch, New Zealand; John's son, Aaron, became a partner and in 1885 started a brassfoundry in England; Danks won prizes at the Philadelphia, Sydney and Melbourne International Exhibitions. The number of his employees grew from 35 to 150 and his contemporaries attributed his success to his being 'just the man for the time', one 'whose business was continually enlarged by the demands of a growing city'. Danks believed more in his own ability and in the beneficial effects of the tariff which he had forcefully advocated when the question was vital to manufacturers. In September 1874 he had helped to form the Manufacturers' Association and next year called the meeting from which the Protection League developed; Danks became president of the Emerald Hill (South Melbourne) branch.

The first serious check to Danks's success was the depression of the 1890s; by the end of 1892 the sheet lead mill was idle and 1894 brought a £1503 deficit. Danks was severely shocked but his son could soon write, 'my father has quite pulled himself together again and looks as well as ever'. Indeed, in that year manufacturing was started in Sydney, to the annoyance of their Melbourne rival, John McIlwraith [q.v.], with whom, however, they reached an agreement. In 1896 Danks won the contract for the City of Melbourne sewerage and two years later it was still making up for the decline in ordinary business. By 1900 he had 200 employees and a capital of £300,000.

Danks was a member of the Emerald Hill Council in 1871-80 and as mayor in 1874-76 was painstaking in his efforts for the ratepayers. In 1877 he unsuccessfully contested the Emerald Hill seat in the Legislative Assembly. He was a founder and director of the Australian and European Bank and a commissioner at the 1888 Paris Exhibition. Deeply religious, he was active in the Methodist Church and a Sunday schoolteacher for thirty years. He gave £3000 to the Cecil Street Wesleyan Church, support-

ed many charities and hospitals, and towards the end of his life marked each birthday by giving away £100.

A charming man of slight build, Danks was little changed by success. In his few years of semi-retirement he was happiest at his turning lathe, explaining 'I was always a mechanic and all my people before me were mechanics . . . [there are] few better mechanics here than myself'. He loved his garden and enjoyed music, being able to 'knock out a tune on almost any instrument'. He filled his house with paintings (he gave £100 to the Wednesbury Art Gallery) and his fine library included many books on art, science and metal-work. He continued to own land in Staffordshire but had no wish to return there because 'an Australian can never get used to the English climate'. He died after a short illness at his home, Vermont, Merton Crescent, South Melbourne, on 28 February 1902; he was survived by his wife Ann, née Turner, and by one daughter and one son of their eight children.

H. M. Humphreys (ed), *Men of the time in Australia: Victorian series*, 1st ed (Melb, 1878); A. Sutherland et al, *Victoria and its metropolis*, 2 (Melb, 1888); J. Smith (ed), *Cyclopedia of Victoria*, 1 (Melb, 1903); *A'sian Trade Review*, 15 Feb 1882; *Table Talk*, 26 Sept 1901; *Age*, 1 Mar 1902; Danks papers (ANU Archives).

J. ANN HONE

DAPLYN, ALFRED JAMES (1844-1926), artist, was born in London. He studied at the Slade School in London, the National Academy in New York, under Leon Gérome at L'Ecole Nationale des Beaux Arts in Paris and in Rome. He also studied under Carolus-Duran and Corot, and sought inspiration at artist colonies in Pont-Aven and Barbizon in France; some of his work was exhibited at the Old Salon, London. He migrated to Melbourne in 1881 and next year exhibited his 'Showery Weather' and 'The Boat-Builder' at the Victorian Academy of Arts; according to the *Argus*, 25 March 1882, he 'painted in the low tones after the French method, and in the style of the "impressionists"', possibly the first use of the word in an Australian context. Certainly his *plein air* painting gave effects of light and atmosphere not possible in a studio, and his works were broader than those of Piguenit, Chevalier and even Buvelot [qq.v.] whose methods were becoming rather old-fashioned.

Daplyn moved to Sydney in 1884, became secretary of the New South Wales Art Society and its instructor in painting in 1885-92. Among the artists he influenced were C. E. Conder [q.v.], Sydney Long and perhaps most of all, Julian Ashton, with whom he often painted on the Hawkesbury River. One of the many paintings exhibited by Daplyn was 'The moon is up and yet 'tis not night'; it was bought by the trustees of the National Gallery of New South Wales in 1900 and sold in 1946. About 1892 he visited at Vailima his old friend, Robert Louis Stevenson, whom he had met in his student days in France, and painted for nearly a year in Samoa. He then returned to Sydney and set up as an art expert, giving lessons and making illustrations. In 1902 he published *Landscape Painting from Nature in Australia*, a manual for the student in oil and water colours. In 1913 a substantial legacy took him to Paris and London; after World War I he made a sketching tour in Belgium. By 1920 he was back in Sydney; in 1924 he returned to England. Aged 82 he died at Chelsea on 19 July 1926. He left his 'paintings, pictures and books' to the artist William Lister Lister.

J. R. Ashton, *Now came still evening on* (Syd, 1941); Bernard Smith, *Australian painting 1788-1960* (Melb, 1962); A. McCulloch, *Encyclopedia of Australian art* (Lond, 1968); *Argus*, 25 Mar 1882; *Bulletin*, 5 Aug 1926; *Australasian*, 7 Aug 1926; MS cat under Daplyn (ML).

DARLEY, BENJAMIN (1811-1864), captain and merchant, was born in February 1811 in Dublin, son of Benjamin Darley, master mariner, and his wife Mary Catherine, née Deey. He went to sea and by 21 had his own command in the West Indian trade. He arrived at Sydney in February 1840 as captain of the *Eweretta*, 356 tons, owned by Ellice & Co. of London. By 1847 he had made seven voyages with merchandise from London and wool from Sydney. After 1844, under contract to Robert Towns [q.v.], he made his return voyages through the Fiji and Samoan islands for sandalwood. On 6 February 1847 at Trinity Church, Sydney, Darley married Katharine, daughter of D'Arcy Wentworth [q.v.] and Ann Lawes. With his bride he sailed in the *Eweretta*, arrived in London in July, sold his share in the ship and returned to Sydney on 26 December. In the next four years he ran a sheep station at Wellington Valley, but in the gold rush sold the station. With Towns as partner he bought the patent slip at Balmain, later moving it to Darling Harbour. They also acquired several ships in the eastern trade, including the *Phoenix*, *Onyx* and *Vernon*. About 1860 Darley's affairs seem to have floundered, and in May Towns wrote that Darley 'will never lose and I question if he will ever *gain* by adventure'.

Darley helped to found the Sydney Exchange in 1852 and was a director for life. In 1854 he joined the Sydney Chamber of Commerce, was auditor in 1856, director in 1857 and committee member for life. After 1857 he was a director of the Australian Gaslight Co. and the Waratah Coal Co. Towns and Darley were also agents for the Derwent and Tamar Fire, Life and Marine Insurance Co. In June 1854 he became a non-official member of the Steam Navigation Board, and of the Pilot Board from July 1857 until March 1862 when he was dismissed with H. T. Fox and Charles Smith [qq.v.]. He was also rear-commodore of the Sydney Yacht Club. He died on 22 June 1864, leaving an estate of £16,000, and was buried in St Jude's cemetery, Randwick. He was survived by a son and four daughters. In November 1867 his widow married William Thomas Bassett, stock and station agent, and after long effort disposed profitably of estates inherited from her father. She died in London on 14 November 1898; her probate was valued at £73,000, mostly derived from her father's estate.

G. Forbes, *History of Sydney* (Syd, 1926); D. Shineberg, *They came for sandalwood* (Melb, 1967); Sel Cttee on the Pilot Board Evidence, *V&P* (LA NSW), 1862, 2, 1086; W. J. Lyons, 'Prominent business figures of Sydney in the 1850's', *Business Archives and History*, May 1957; R. Towns papers (ML); Wentworth papers (ML); Darley papers (NL).

RUTH TEALE

DARLEY, SIR FREDERICK MATTHEW (1830-1910), chief justice and lieut-governor, was born on 18 September 1830 in Ireland, the first child of Henry Darley of Wingfield, Bray, County Wicklow, and his wife Maria Louisa, née West. The family came from Arles (d'Arlé) at the Conquest, settling in the English Midlands; some migrated to Ireland in the seventeenth century and won repute in Dublin as builders and architects. Frederick's grandfather introduced legal leanings and Henry Darley was described by Lord St Leonards as 'not only the best officer in the Court of Chancery in Ireland, but the best officer he had ever come across'. Frederick's parents, 'eminent for piety and learning', saw to his education before he entered Dungannon College, County Tyrone, where his uncle, Rev. John Darley (later Anglican bishop of Kilmore), was headmaster. Well grounded in classics, Frederick entered Trinity College, Dublin (B.A., 1851). Called to the Bar at the King's Inns on 18 January 1853, he went to London where he read in the chambers of Richard Holmes Coote. He was admitted to the English Bar before returning to practise on the Munster Circuit. In 1858 one of the judges commended his industry and expressed pleasure at having 'so nice a fellow, and so educated and good a lawyer practising before me'.

At Hunsdon, Hertfordshire, on 13 December 1860 Darley married Lucy Forest, daughter of Captain Sylvester John Browne and sister of the novelist 'Rolf Boldrewood' (T. A. Browne [q.v.]). The Australian interests of Captain Browne and of Benjamin Darley [q.v.], strengthened by recommendation of the colonial Bar by Chief Justice Sir Alfred Stephen [q.v.] in a chance meeting, probably decided Darley to migrate. Farewelled by his Munster colleagues with a dinner and a gift of silver, he sailed with his wife in the *Swiftsure* from Plymouth in January 1862. On 2 June he was admitted to the New South Wales Bar. He found his first eleven years the 'most trying' of his life. He lost many early cases but clients trusted his devotion and he won a varied practice, distinguished by his command of procedure. Diligence brought its return. He was in the Bar's front rank on taking silk in 1878: 'I have been very hard worked this month. In Court all day and every day often with a case going on in each Court. I sometimes get tired of the perpetual grind, however it means money. I fancy I will earn £700 this month, one of the busiest in the year—next month I will not earn more than £300 perhaps'.

Darley's zeal attracted James Martin [q.v.] who in 1868 nominated him to the Legislative Council. His career there was likened to that of a model legislator or of a 'standing counsel of Parliament'. He gave much time to matters of legislative policy and draftsmanship, most notably in equity, company law, matrimonial causes and bankruptcy. His criticisms of the English Judicature Acts did much to influence their rejection in New South Wales. His range in debate was diverse but, beyond supporting free trade, he was uninterested in politics and remained independent even on becoming vice-president of the Executive Council in the Parkes [q.v.] ministry in 1881; he said that he never changed his seat whatever government was in office. Of his several journeys abroad, one was as representative commissioner to the Bordeaux Wine Exhibition in 1882. At home he largely restricted his public interests to the council and represented it on the Senate of the University of Sydney. He also served on the committee of the Australian Club and was active in a few charitable institutions.

On Martin's death in 1886 W. B. Dalley [q.v.] was invited to become chief justice but declined. Darley was offered the vacancy; regretting his 'ungracious act', he shrank from the loss of income it would cause. Julian Salomons [q.v.] took the proffered commission but resigned before being sworn in. Darley then agreed in the public interest to make the financial sacrifice and was sworn in as chief justice on 7 December. Unlike his predecessors he brought no aura of statesmanship or political involvement to that bench; his sole concern was the due administration of the law. Distinguished in appearance, courteously dignified, adept at judicial management and robust in constitution, he adorned his high office. He was a sound, pragmatic jurist, delivering many clear, concise decisions for the Full Bench, and taking more than his share of sittings alone or with a jury. He had no pretensions of legal brilliance and some of his judgments seem insipid, particularly when compared to those of the foundation Justices of the High Court. Yet he could rise to juridical heights. His clashes with the government in the cases of 1888 under the Chinese Influx Restriction Acts produced his most masterly decisions: his censures of crown lands legislation were vigorous: his command of legal principle was often apparent (e.g., *Walker v. Solomon*, 1890; *In re Wilson*, 1891; *In re McIntosh*, 1894; *Australian Joint Stock Bank v. Bailey*, 1897). He had a liberal approach when interpreting beneficial statutes, at times infusing reform into his construction of the law. More often he was over-cautious, and inept in using precedent. He eschewed trespassing on statutory policy; parliamentary criticism of him in 1904 for excessive comment on the Industrial Arbitration Act was partisan and unfair. Apart from that incident, he enjoyed uniform public confidence. A humanitarian, he advocated improvement in prison methods and reduction of court delays, especially in country criminal trials. He emphatically resisted attempted encroachments by the executive on judicial independence. His public manner, always serious, conservative and ceremonious, and his detachment may have misled those who have belittled his ability as a judge.

Late in 1901 Darley's health failed. Surgery so enfeebled him that lobbying for the chief justiceship began. When he took leave in England in 1902 the press reported that his judicial career had ended, but medical attention in Edinburgh achieved such restoration that Darley accepted membership of the English royal commission on the South African war. He was well qualified, having acted as a royal commissioner on colonial defence in 1881 and being thoroughly informed in military matters, as evidenced in his parliamentary speeches. His forensic competence aided the commission and its work stimulated his recovery. He resumed his seat on the bench when he returned to Sydney in 1903.

Darley became lieut-governor in 1891. Administrative skill, urbanity, fervour for protocol, and noble deportment all fitted him for the role which he filled to the satisfaction of local society and of the Colonial Office. Ironically his longest term from 1 November 1900 to 27 May 1902 thrust upon him a major part in the trappings of Federation. His anxiety for the mother State's supremacy contributed to the 'Hopetoun blunder'; although his official speeches reflected public feeling without personal conviction, his private assessment in 1902 was that 'Australian Federation is so far a pronounced failure'.

Darley lived at Quambi, Albert Street, Woollahra, and 'rusticated' at Lilianfels, Katoomba. His work was recognized by many honours. He was knighted in 1887 and appointed K.C.M.G. in 1897 and G.C.M.G. in 1901; he became a privy councillor in 1905. His old university conferred on him an honorary LL.D. in 1903. In 1909 on his retirement from the bench he returned to Britain and the Royal Colonial Institute elected him resident fellow. He had sought no recognition and never aspired to any public office. Characteristically he wished to be remembered only as 'an old Irish gentleman'. He died in London on 4 January 1910 and was buried in the family vault at Dublin; memorial services were held in England, Ireland and in Sydney. Lady Darley had been a great helpmate to him. Her interests extended beyond the domestic distaff: 'Mother is inclined to go in for all sorts of things and generally do a great deal too much', wrote Darley to his son in 1896. She was a member of numerous charitable and benevolent organizations, and an accomplished hostess. A lady of great culture, she had, according to her brother, a contralto voice 'worthy of scientific cultivation', while her letters matched his concinnity. Sometimes she would write to politicians on contentious issues, of which she could speak more freely than her husband and, 'as a woman and mother', more emotively. She died in England in 1913, survived by two sons and four of her six daughters.

Of several extant portraits, that by Longstaff in the Supreme Court House, Sydney, is noteworthy.

'Men of eminence in New South Wales. Sir Frederick Matthew Darley', *Syd Q Mag*, Sept 1887; Attorney-General's and Justice Department papers (NSWA); Darley papers (NL); F. M. and C. W. Darley papers (ML); Griffith papers (Dixson Lib, Syd); J. See papers (ML); Way papers (SAA); family letters and information from R. C. Lewis-Crosby, Dublin, and D. Darley, Epping, NSW.   J. M. BENNETT

DARLING, Sir CHARLES HENRY (1809-1870), military officer and governor, was born on 19 February 1809 at Annapolis Royal, Nova Scotia, the eldest son of Major-General Henry Charles Darling, sometime lieut-governor of Tobago, and his wife Isabella, the eldest daughter of Charles Cameron, sometime governor of the Bahamas. With a recommendation from Sandhurst, Charles joined the 57th Regiment as an ensign in 1826 and next year went with his regiment to New South Wales. He served as assistant private secretary and after 1830 as military secretary to his uncle, Governor Darling. In 1831 he returned to Sandhurst. In 1833-39 he served as military secretary to Sir Lionel Smith in the West Indies and in 1839-41 was captain of an unattached company. He then retired from the army and settled in Jamaica. At Barbados in 1835 he had married the eldest daughter of Alan Dalzell; she died in 1837 and in 1839 he married the eldest daughter of Joshua Bushill Nurse; she had one daughter and died in 1848.

Recommended by Lord Elgin, Darling was appointed agent-general for immigration and adjutant-general of militia in Jamaica in 1843 and became a member of the Legislative Council. He served as secretary to two governors, Major-General Sackville Berkeley and Sir Charles Grey, and in 1847 was appointed lieut-governor of St Lucia. In 1851 he married Elizabeth Isabella Caroline, the only daughter of Christopher Salter of Buckinghamshire; they had four sons. In that year he was transferred to Cape Colony as lieut-governor, and from May to December 1854 acted as administrator when parliamentary government was being established. His appointment as governor of Newfoundland in May 1855 was made permanent in February 1857. While in office he helped to inaugurate parliamentary government. He then served as governor of Jamaica, Honduras and the Bay Islands until 1863. He was appointed K.C.B. in 1862.

In September 1863, Darling took up duty as governor of Victoria. The governorship was one of the best paid and most highly prized in the empire, and Victoria appeared fortunate to have a governor with long experience of colonial administration and first-hand knowledge of parliamentary government. But the Colonial Office soon had misgivings about the wisdom of Darling's appointment. In his first year he became involved in the Australia-wide controversy over the continuance of convict transportation to Western Australia, and was privately censured by the secretary of state for the colonies, Edward Cardwell, for allowing his cabinet ministers too free a rein in their official dealings with the other Australian colonial governments. He was also rebuked for being a public, and thereby a partisan, supporter of the anti-transportation policy, but the matter was settled when the British government decided to end transportation within three years. The significance of this conflict lay partly in the close personal affinity which Darling had quickly established with his cabinet ministers, and partly in his eagerness to establish *rapport* with progressive colonial opinion. He soon became so personally involved in local political crises that he was unable to maintain the role expected of all colonial governors, that they should act as independent arbiters between contending factions in parliament and between social divisions in the community. He allowed his vice-regal authority to be used by the progressives as a bludgeon on the conservatives, and for this he was abruptly removed from office.

In the early 1860s Victoria was plagued by three controversial issues: reform of the crown land laws; proposals to change the customs tariff; and the parliamentary power of the pastoralists and free traders who dominated the Legislative Council. The council was elected on a property- and rurally-weighted franchise, whilst the Legislative Assembly was elected by manhood suffrage and represented the urban and working classes. Both Houses of the parliament had the power to accept or reject any new legislation. The McCulloch [q.v.] government, elected with a large majority in the assembly in November 1864, began to change the law in the three fields and provoked constitutional struggles with the council that brought chaos to the parliamentary system and involved the public and the press in controversy on an unprecedented scale. These important disputes between the progressive post-gold majority in the assembly and the conservative pre-gold majority in the council drew attention to the difficulty of grafting British parliamentary institutions on to a novel colonial society at a time when the British government, convinced of the virtues of free trade, was reluctant to make the colony completely independent especially in matters of manufacturing, trade and commerce. The disputes also made great demands on the governor's prudence and tact.

The council thwarted its own reform early in 1865 but the land issue was solved for the time being by Grant's [q.v.] Act of March 1865. However, the McCulloch government's attempt to introduce the first major protective tariff in Australia led to the main crisis. The assembly tacked the tariff bill to the annual appropriation bill, but the government had miscalculated the strength of feeling in the council where the bill was thrown out in July. With Darling's approval, the government continued to collect the new protective customs duties, relying on a resolution of the assembly. But the funds from the Customs House were inadequate to meet day-to-day administrative expenses, especially the need to pay the civil servants. The government then negotiated a series of short-term loans with the London Chartered Bank, whose sole local director was the premier. The bank then sued the Crown for the return of the money; by a series of court actions the government confessed judgment and the bank was repaid by vouchers drawn on consolidated revenue. The procedure incensed the council, the other private banks, the *Argus* and a large section of the commercial community. After a Supreme Court decision the government ceased to collect the new duties and seemed likely to be able to resist the council indefinitely. The assembly decided not to pass any appropriation bill until the council had passed the tariff. Darling tried in vain to arrange a conference between the two Houses, but in November the assembly sent up a separate tariff bill which the council promptly rejected. Thereupon Darling agreed to the government's request to dissolve parliament, and at the assembly elections in January 1866, the McCulloch government was returned with a two-thirds majority; the council, being indissoluble, retained its political complexion. After further disputes, another rejection of the tariff bill and the resignation and reinstatement of the McCulloch government, a conference was arranged in April and the tariff bill was eventually passed by both Houses of parliament.

Meanwhile in December 1865 twenty-two former cabinet ministers, who had served as members of the Executive Council, petitioned the Queen complaining of the financial and constitutional irregularities which Darling had permitted. When transmitting the petition Darling commented adversely on both the petition and the character of the petitioners and stated that it would be impossible for him to accept any of them in the future as cabinet ministers because he believed that they were conspiring to remove him. But Cardwell had already decided that Darling's actions had made him unfit for office; he was recalled to London and his successor appointed. Popular indignation over Darling's 'recall' was widespread. Petitions, public meetings and torchlight processions preceded the departure of 'the people's Governor', whom many believed had become a martyr in the cause of progress; others hinted that he was being sacrificed as part of a deal between the Colonial Office in London on the one hand, and the Legislative Council, the free traders and the pastoralists of Melbourne on the other. The assembly then resolved to make a grant of £20,000 to Lady Darling because the governor was not allowed to receive a direct gift. More constitutional crises ensued and Darling put his case to his superiors for the redress of his wrongs, on the ground that he had properly accepted the advice of his responsible advisers. But the response he received in the English press and in the British parliament was unsympathetic. Eventually the secretary of state informed Darling and the Legislative Assembly that Darling could not accept the grant. As a result Darling resigned from the colonial service in April 1867, and the Victorian government then included the grant in the annual estimates. The council rejected the appropriation bill. The McCulloch government resigned but was returned to office. A further appropriation bill was rejected by the council and the constitutional struggle now appeared interminable. A fresh assembly election merely reinforced the progressives in their determination to press the issue, especially as no alternative government was possible. Finally in May 1868 Darling was allowed to withdraw his resignation and in July was granted a retrospective pension. Broken in spirit and fortune he died on 25 January 1870 at Cheltenham, England. At his death a separate bill was passed by both Houses of the Victorian parliament, at the instigation of the McCulloch government, which granted a pension to Darling's widow and a sum for the education of her children.

As a vice-regal representative, a constitutional head of state and an officer of the British government Darling had been a failure. He had been neither prudent nor cautious and had allowed his partisan sympathy to undermine the functioning of the parliament and the rule of law. He had become a mouthpiece of McCulloch and his ministers, especially of the attorney-general, George Higinbotham [q.v.]. Doubtless the Colonial Office was justified in recalling him but perhaps the judgment of history ought to allow him to continue as a martyr in the democratic cause. Perhaps the odd feature of the Victorian imbroglio of 1864-68 was that Darling should have become 'the people's Governor', for neither his training, experience nor temperament fitted him to be a political Samson in the cause of democracy. Yet he was honestly convinced that the pre-gold Victorian Establishment was deliberately impeding development of the colony, and he never seemed to realize that a governor had the right to reach such a conclusion, but not to act upon it.

D. P. Clarke, 'The Colonial Office and the constitutional crises in Victoria, 1865-68', *Hist Studies*, no 18, May 1952; F. K. Crowley, Aspects of the constitutional conflicts . . . Victorian legislature, 1864-1868 (M.A. thesis, Univ Melb, 1947).   F. K. CROWLEY

DARLING, JOHN (1831-1905), merchant and grain exporter, was born on 23 February 1831 in Edinburgh, into a family originally from Duns in Berwickshire. Admitted to a George Heriot free school in Edinburgh, John left at 11 after his father died. He was apprenticed to an Edinburgh typefounder and remained with the firm until October 1854. Seeing little prospect of advancement, he decided to follow friends to South Australia. Early in 1855 he arrived at Adelaide in the *Achilles* with his wife Isabella, née Ferguson, and two sons. After brief employment in a general store and two years in a bakery, Darling tried to set up as a contractor; at a well-chosen site on the Glen Osmond Road he also built a small general store which his wife managed. The contracting failed and he joined the Adelaide firm of Giles & Smith, grain and flour merchants. Darling became its manager but after five years transferred to R. G. Bowen's wheat and grain store in Waymouth Street.

In 1867 Darling took over Bowen's business and noted that in his first six weeks he cleared as much as he had earned in three years as an employee. In 1872 he took his twenty-year-old son, John, into partnership and changed the firm's name to John Darling & Son. With branches in South Australia's wheat belt the firm acquired interests in many agricultural properties and flour mills, bought grain from growers and exported extensively to eastern Australia. When Victoria became self-supporting in grain Darling turned to the international market. He travelled overseas in 1871 and was soon shipping cargoes to many European ports. In the 1880s he lived for some years in Melbourne where he founded another main office and, after a second visit to America and Europe, became known as the 'Grain King', the biggest shipper of wheat from Australia. By 1890 the firm also had immense interests in flour-milling and shipping together with a large London office managed by his son Charles. Darling could justly claim: 'I carried grain and flour on my back for 12 years. I have since then carried grain and flour on my brain for over 35 years'.

Consistent with the ethics of many self-made men, Darling conscientiously served his stint in the South Australian parliament. In the assembly he represented West Adelaide in 1870-71 and again in 1876-78 after a break for health and business reasons. He represented Yatala in 1878-81 and Stanley in 1885-87; he served in the Downer government as commissioner of Public Works in 1885 for four months only, resigning because of press criticism. In 1888-97 Darling represented North District in the Legislative Council. Throughout his political career Darling described himself as 'a moderate Protectionist'. Although he seldom spoke his words carried weight and his unrivalled knowledge of agriculture and trade proved valuable to many select committees and royal commissions.

Darling was a generous supporter of many philanthropies, and as an active member of the Independent and Baptist Churches helped their missions, worked as a lay preacher and served on committees. Proud of his Scottish origin he was a member of the Adelaide Caledonian Society and its chief in 1892-94. Through his son Joseph, he became interested in cricket and helped to found the Adelaide Oval. Darling died in Adelaide on 10 April 1905, leaving an estate worth £67,500, most of it to be invested in a trust fund for his wife and children, and the remainder to charities and favoured employees.

His eldest son JOHN DARLING junior was born on 24 January 1852 in Edinburgh. He took over the management of his father's firm in 1897 and continued to extend its business, becoming known as the 'Wheat King' of Australia. As an active member of the Chamber of Commerce, the Shipowners Association, the South Australian Employers Union and the Australian Employers Federation, he foresaw the clash with trade unionism, especially on the waterfront, and fought with undiminished zeal for freedom of contract long after the strikes ended. In 1892 he became a director of Broken Hill Pty Co. Ltd and was chairman of directors in 1907-14.

Like his father, Darling served in the South Australian parliament, representing East Torrens in 1896-1902 and Torrens in 1902-05. He was also a generous supporter of the Baptist Church and many philanthropic movements. He died in Melbourne on 27 March 1914 and was buried in Adelaide, survived by his wife Jessie, daughter of the merchant, Alexander Dowie, and by four sons and five daughters. His estate, valued at £1,694,500 was reduced by a third in death duties, and the remainder, apart from special legacies, was placed in a trust fund for his family.

J. J. Pascoe, History of Adelaide and vicinity (Adel, 1901); T. Gill, History and topography of Glen Osmond (Adel, 1905); H. E. Hughes, Our first hundred years: the Baptist Church in South Australia (Adel, 1937); Observer (Adel), 30 May 1903, 15 Apr 1905; Argus, 30 Mar 1914; Advertiser (Adel), 7 May 1968; information from the family and the Baptist Church in SA.
                                    H. S. K. KENT

DARRELL, FANNY; see CATHCART

DARRELL, GEORGE FREDERICK PRICE (1851?-1921), dramatist and theatrical manager, was born in England probably the son of G. F. P. Darrell and his wife Jane, née Cartere. In 1865 he went to the New Zealand goldfields, but soon joined Simonsen's New Zealand touring opera company. In 1869 he was in Melbourne and Sydney as leading juvenile actor to Walter Montgomery [q.v.].

In September 1869 Darrell left Sydney for Auckland as a member of Mrs Robert Heir's [Fanny Cathcart, q.v.] company, with a tour to California intended, but they did not leave New Zealand. On 20 January 1870 at St George's Church, Shortlands, Kent, he married Fanny Heir. He returned to Australia as her stage manager. She was 36 at the time, and some years past her best. There were no children of this otherwise successful union.

The Darrells toured extensively through New Zealand, to Brisbane, Adelaide, and western New South Wales. In 1873-74 they visited the United States where Darrell laid the basis for his future career as a commercial playwright and leading manager. By 1877 he formed 'Darrell's Dramatic Company for the Production of Australian Plays', and presented his Transported for Life and next year Back from the Grave in spectacular productions at Melbourne and Sydney.

Not all of his later plays were so acclaimed; The Forlorn Hope, playing in Melbourne when Mrs Darrell died in January 1880, was rejected by critics for its 'tendency to claptrap and . . . sentimentality'. The New Zealand Mail considered that he owed all of his success as an actor and author to his wife. On 12 January 1880 the Australian Natives' Association gave him a complimentary benefit in Melbourne for his services to 'Patriotic Drama', and thereafter he called himself a 'Native Australian Dramatist'.

In April 1883 Darrell produced his best known piece, The Sunny South, at Melbourne, with Essie Jenyns [q.v.] in the starring role. He was to perform in this play himself over 1500 times. At London on 27 October 1884, he opened with it at the Grand Theatre, Islington, and received acclaim never before given to a colonial dramatist; but the season was interrupted when he was injured by a bowie knife. Success went to his head, and he adopted a notoriously arrogant and 'Dandyish' public style. A fellow-playwright reported that Darrell considered *The Sunny South* worthy of comparison only with *Hamlet*. In September 1898 it was again produced in London, and made another record for an Australian playwright; in 1914 it was made into a film in Australia.

He continued to turn out numerous pieces on Australian themes, and spent much of his time in England. In 1887 a lengthy illness prevented him from acting or writing, and in May he complained in the London *Era* that English playwrights were plagiarizing his 'original dramas'. In fact Darrell's highly episodic plays were themselves derivative of contemporary European dramas, and relied for their novelty on spectacular scenic tableaux and such exotic colonial stereotypes as 'The Wool King'. Australian critics remained lukewarm to Darrell's works, but popular support allowed him to continue producing them and other sensational dramas. On 23 August 1887 a complimentary benefit at Melbourne, organized by his confrères, realized more than £400. George Coppin [q.v.] presented him with an illuminated address for his services to the native drama.

Darrell remained a prominent manager until the turn of the century, when he faded into relative obscurity as a writer of short stories. In 1916 he published *The Belle of the Bush* (Sydney) and made a final stage appearance reading militaristic poems for the Shakespeare Anzac Day performance at Sydney's Adelphi Theatre. On 6 May 1886 in New Zealand he had married Christine (Cissie) Peachey, a young actress in one of his companies. Their son Rupert became a prominent pantomime actor in Australia and United States.

Ill health, financial difficulties, and the departure of Rupert for the United States seemed to have made Darrell increasingly despondent. On 27 January 1921 he disappeared from his lodgings in Darlinghurst, Sydney, leaving a suicide note to the effect that he was 'going on a long voyage'. Next day his body was washed up on Dee Why beach. His funeral on 31 January was organized and paid for by J. C. Williamson [q.v.] Ltd; he was buried in the Anglican section of Rookwood cemetery.

G. L. C. Rees, *Towards an Australian drama* (Syd, 1953); G. L. Dann, 'Australian drama from *Sunny South* to *Fire on the Snow*', *Qld Writing*, 1954; *Illustrated Aust News*, Jan 1880; *New Zealand Mail*, 28 May 1881.

HELEN M. VAN DER POORTEN

DARVALL, SIR JOHN BAYLEY (1809-1883), barrister and politician, was born on 19 November 1809 at Felixkirk, Yorkshire, England, the second son of Major Edward Darvall and his wife Emily, née Johnson, an heiress with whom he had eloped in 1805. John was educated at Eton and Trinity College, Cambridge (B.A., 1833; M.A., 1837). On 15 June 1833 he was admitted to the Middle Temple. He became articled to his uncle, Sir John Bayley, and was later marshal to Lord Bayley. In 1838 he was called to the Bar. On 27 September 1837 at Tewkesbury, Gloucestershire, he had married Elizabeth Flora, daughter of Colonel John Shapland. In August 1839 they arrived at Sydney in the *Abberton*. His parents, two brothers and three sisters arrived in the *Alfred* in January 1840, accompanied by friends with Indian connexions. Darvall became 'intimately connected with the monied and pastoral interests of the colony', and was appointed a director of the Sydney Banking Co. and the Australian Banking Co. He was also involved with other companies which collapsed in the slump of the early 1840s. In 1842 he joined an association formed to petition for permission to introduce Indian coolies in place of convict labour. On 16 September 1839 he had been admitted to the colonial Bar and soon had a flourishing practice. In December 1846 his opposing counsel in a Supreme Court case was Richard Windeyer [q.v.], who charged him with unfair conduct and called him a liar. Darvall promptly struck his opponent and was committed to gaol for fourteen days for 'contempt and outrage', while Windeyer received twenty days.

In July 1844 Darvall was nominated to the Legislative Council, where he loyally supported the government until he resigned in 1848, unable to reconcile his conscience with nomineeism. Later that year he was returned for Bathurst by one vote; in 1850-56 he represented Cumberland. In public speeches he seemed indifferent to what others thought of his words and actions, and often appeared eager to provoke opposition; one speech led George Macleay [q.v.] to comment, 'Is not Darvall an extraordinary fellow! perpetually out-Darvalling himself'. In 1850 he had become a foundation fellow of the Senate of the University of Sydney, in 1851 declined a judgeship in Victoria and in 1853 was appointed a Queen's Counsel. He was also a founding director of the Australian Joint Stock Bank, a member of the Sydney Chamber of Commerce, a trustee of the Australian Club and served on many charitable and public committees.

With his aristocratic connexions and intellectual pride Darvall was detached in colonial politics and never a strong party

man. He aligned himself with Charles
Cowper, J. D. Lang and Henry Parkes
[qq.v.], and the popular opposition to
Wentworth's [q.v.] Constitution bill. In
1853 he attacked the proposal for a nominated upper house and ridiculed Wentworth's 'Botany Bay aristocracy' and the
putting of legislative power 'into the hands
of people yet unborn, and of merit yet un-
tried'. He also wanted a redistribution of
electorates and in 1854 moved resolutions in
the council condemning the Constitution
and praying for the intervention of the
imperial government, maintaining that the
constituents wanted 'a representative legislature and a just distribution of the elective
franchise'; he also condemned the two-thirds
majority clause required for constitutional
amendments. The resolutions were rejected
by 24 votes to 10 but later the hereditary
clauses were withdrawn, the nominee
appointments limited to five years and the
two-thirds clause nullified by the imperial
parliament.

In April 1856 Darvall was elected for the
North Riding of Cumberland to the first
Legislative Assembly and in June took
office as solicitor-general in the first ministry
under Stuart Donaldson [q.v.]. Condemned
by the liberals for deserting their cause, Darvall claimed that an attack by the *Empire*
'transgressed the limits of party warfare by
misrepresenting my political opinions . . . I
took office to assist in carrying out those
ideas at the earliest convenient period'. This
letter alarmed W. M. Manning [q.v.] who
warned James Macarthur [q.v.]: 'I am
afraid that electioneering interests are leading both Donaldson & Darvall to break faith
with me—and I think with you. We must
be on our guard'. The ministry was reconciled but the assembly proved obstructive;
urged by Darvall, Donaldson resigned on
25 August. Darvall was solicitor-general in
H. W. Parker's [q.v.] ministry from October
1856 to May 1857, and then attorney-general until September. Darvall resigned in
November but was elected for the Hawkesbury on 25 June 1859. Disturbed by the land
question and the apparent results of manhood suffrage, he joined the conservative
Constitutional Association. For opposition
to free selection before survey he was received with hostility in the 1860 election and,
taunted with inattention to 'roads and
bridges', retired from the contest in disgust.

Alarmed at the democratic pressure which
led Governor Young to 'swamp' the Legislative Council, Darvall was more than ever
convinced that the Upper House should be
elective. Pledged to its reform, he was nominated to the council in June 1861. In the
debate on the Legislative Council bill in
December he created a sensation with his

bitter remarks on rampant democracy which
would 'if unchecked, bring the fine colony
to ruin', but he still demanded that the
council should be representative, refrain
from amending money bills and yield to the
assembly in any clash of opinion. He also
advocated G. K. Holden's [q.v.] plan to introduce the Hare system of proportional representation for the council. Throughout
1862 Darvall sat on the select committee on
the Legislative Council bill but did not
attend any debates in the next session. In
June 1863 he resigned to contest a by-election for East Maitland. Although he had
opposed the separation of Moreton Bay and
the restrictive anti-Chinese legislation which
he considered 'cruel, unkind and disgraceful', and had equivocated over the abolition
of state aid to religion, he called himself a
'liberal' and, supported by the *Maitland
Mercury*, was returned in June. In August
he became attorney-general under Cowper.
For this about-turn he was severely criticized
and his ministerial re-election was fiercely
contested by Parkes. Darvall maintained
that 'The colony must have an Attorney
General, and the Government had chosen
him'. He believed that 'their policy was
one which he could conscientiously uphold'.
He wrote to Parkes: 'before you lend yourself to the very unusual course of opposing
a reelection on taking Office I beg you to
consider that you are the last man from
whom I could expect such exhibitions of personal ill will'. When Darvall won the hard-
fought contest by fifty-nine votes Parkes
declared that his opponent and friends had
solicited votes 'with the electoral roll in the
right hand and the grog bottle in the left'.

Cowper's government fell in October. In
November 1864 Darvall was returned for
West Sydney and next February became
attorney-general under Cowper. In May he
outlined proposed reforms in the administration of justice but in June 1865 he resigned. A week later the *Sydney Morning
Herald* was regretting his departure for England. He was praised for his 'inimitable
charm' and 'perfect control of temper', but
William Walker [q.v.] commented that he
was 'too fond of ease and elegance, with his
comfortable circumstances, to be a successful
or persevering politician in a democratic
country like this'. Yet to Governor Young
he was 'the most accomplished speaker in
New South Wales'. Certainly he was a commanding figure in the courts and legislature.

In England Darvall practised at the Bar
and enjoyed 'a little of that cultured ease
that the colony failed to afford'. In 1866 he
became a director of the Bank of Australasia
and was appointed C.M.G. in 1869 and
K.C.M.G. in 1877. Almost blind in his last
years, he was visited by Parkes, who des-

cribed him as always a 'gallant-hearted man'. He died on 28 December 1883 at his home in London, survived by four sons and two of his three daughters. He left an estate of £60,000 in England and £20,000 in New South Wales.

R. J. Flanagan, *The history of New South Wales* (Lond, 1862); G. B. Barton (ed), *The poets and prose writers of New South Wales* (Syd, 1866); W. Walker, *Miscellanies*, 1st ed (Windsor, 1884) p 93; H. Parkes, *Fifty years in the making of Australian history* (Lond, 1892); *SMH*, 24 July 1844, 23 Dec 1846, 2 Aug 1850, 23 Aug 1853, 18 Oct 1854, 17 June 1856, 1 Jan 1884; *Empire* (Syd), 7 Feb 1855, 12 Apr, 10, 11, 12 June 1856, 13 Dec 1861, 15, 22 May, 22 June 1865; *Maitland Mercury*, 18, 30 June, 6, 8, 13 Aug 1863; *Old Times*, June-July 1903; P. Loveday, Parliamentary government in New South Wales, 1856-1870 (Ph.D. thesis, Univ Syd, 1962); Cowper letters (ML); Darvall papers (ML); S. A. Donaldson ministry letters (ML); Kater papers (NL); CO 201/518, 531, 533-34, 542, 584; information from Dr A. R. Darvall, Carlingford, NSW.   R. W. RATHBONE

DAVENPORT, SIR SAMUEL (1818-1906), landowner and parliamentarian, was born on 5 March 1818 at Shirburn, Oxfordshire, England, the fourth son of George Davenport, banker, and his wife Jane Devereux, née Davies. His father, descendant of an old Cheshire family, became an agent of the South Australian Co. and a director of the South Australian Banking Co.; in 1839 with two partners he paid £4416 for a special survey of 4000 acres and a town reserve and sent his son Francis to South Australia to select the site. Francis arrived at Adelaide in February 1840 and applied for the land near Port Lincoln; in June he cancelled that claim and selected the survey on the upper branches of the River Angas. There the new township was named Macclesfield, but before surveys were completed he visited England.

Samuel and his brother Robert arrived at Adelaide in February 1843. With Samuel was his wife Margaret Fraser, only daughter of William Lennox Cleland, barrister, of Calcutta; they had married on 1 June 1842. The brothers soon moved to Macclesfield where they managed the survey after Francis died on 8 April 1843. Samuel and his wife lived in a stone cottage on sixty acres at the township of Macclesfield while Robert bought near-by Watergate. With an annual allowance from his father, Samuel was able to 'gain colonial experience . . . without . . . being crowded with fears for a year or two of the extent of success'. His first ventures were mainly in mixed farming and he experimented with almonds and vines

which had first interested him while in the south of France as a youth. He later bought a run at Rivoli Bay where he ran some 6000 sheep, but disease killed half of them in full wool. In 1860 he bought Talowie near Port Augusta and turned to horses and cattle; his success upheld his contention that large-stock holdings were the chief source of profits in South Australia. From 1849 he lived mostly at his home in Beaumont where he later gave land for a common. At Macclesfield Davenport was genuinely concerned with the welfare of his tenants and made his rental terms attractive to prospective settlers in the area. From the outset he maintained the traditional values of the liberal squire; for instance, in December 1843 he wrote of the Christmas fare which he and Robert as proprietors had provided for their tenants at Macclesfield; one of the first cricket matches in the colony was included in the festivities. Without the leisure and comforts of many English country gentlemen, Davenport continued his interest in reading and he ordered many publications from England both for his private and a community library. He was also interested in geology and mineralogy and in technological developments.

In 1846-48 Davenport was a nominee in the Legislative Council where he opposed state aid to religion. He contested Hindmarsh without success in a by-election in 1854 but in 1855 was nominated to the part-elective Legislative Council. He was elected to the first Legislative Council under responsible government in 1857 and with J. H. Fisher [q.v.] administered the oath of allegiance to the councillors on 22 April. He served as commissioner of public works from March to August in the Finniss [q.v.] ministry and in September under Torrens [q.v.]. In May 1861 he was asked by Governor MacDonnell to form a ministry but failed; in 1866 he resigned from the council.

Davenport was an ardent promoter of agriculture and new industries in South Australia. In 1864-72 he published several pamphlets, three of them dealing with the cultivation of olives and manufacture of olive oil, silk and tobacco in the colony. For his great interest in these subjects he was elected president of the Royal Agricultural and Horticultural Society and later of the South Australian branch of the Royal Geographical Society of Australasia. He was also a trustee of the Savings Bank, a director of several companies and for twenty years president of the Chamber of Manufactures. In 1849-52 he served as a city commissioner. In 1860 as a trustee of the Poonindie institution he gave evidence to the select committee on Aboriginals. In 1851 he represented the colony as executive commissioner at the Great Exhibition in London, and at exhibitions in Philadelphia in 1876, Sydney in 1879 and Melbourne in 1880, at the Colonial and Indian Exhibition in 1886 and the International Exhibition at Melbourne in 1888.

He was knighted in 1884 and in 1886 appointed K.C.M.G. and given an honorary doctorate by the University of Cambridge. A patrician figure, he died at Beaumont on 3 September 1906. His wife had pre-deceased him on 6 February 1902; they had no children. He left an estate worth £6400 mainly to his nephew. Obituarists praised his 'honourable record both in public and private life' and both Houses of parliament adjourned for his funeral.

B. S. Baldwin (ed), Letters of Samuel Davenport . . . 1842-1849, *South Australiana*, Mar, Sept 1967, Sept 1968; B. A. Cocker, Special surveys and the Wakefield theory (B.A. Hons. thesis, Univ Adel, 1967); V. T. Sumfield, Memorial notices of Sir Samuel Davenport (SAA); Davenport letters (SAA).

                          BEVERLEY A. NICKS

DAVIDSON, JOHN (1834-1881), Presbyterian minister and scholar, was born in Kinghorn, Fife, Scotland, son of John Davidson, dominie of Burntisland. He attended the Universities of St Andrews in 1851-55 and Edinburgh in 1855-56 but took no degree. He studied divinity in 1856-58 and 1860-61, became a licentiate of the Free Church Presbytery of Kinross and in 1864 was ordained minister of Langholm, Dumfriesshire. In 1869 he was called to Adelaide and arrived with his wife and children in the *Carnaquheen* in June 1870. At Chalmers Church, North Terrace, he was soon 'instrumental in raising his congregation to a high state of prosperity'.

In 1872 W. W. Hughes [q.v.] offered £20,000 to Union College, an institution for the education of Presbyterian, Congregational and Baptist ministers. Davidson and others on the college council suggested that the endowment be devoted to founding a university. Hughes agreed and the University Act was passed in 1874. Despite criticism in parliament that he was not a graduate or 'of any great culture' Davidson was appointed the first Hughes professor of English literature and mental and moral philosophy. With Rev. Henry Reed [q.v.] he began to conduct classes, although formal academic work did not begin at the university until March 1876. Davidson resigned from Chalmers Church in 1877 but continued to preach on most Sundays at various churches. He was also in constant demand outside the university as a popular lecturer.

He held his chair until he died from a liver complaint at Glenelg on 22 July 1881, aged 47. He was survived by his wife Harriet, daughter of Hugh Miller, author and geologist, and his wife Lydia, née Falconer. They had met on the Continent and were married in 1860; she had great refinement, was a novelist and poet, and regularly contributed to local journals, but after visiting Scotland in 1877 became a confirmed invalid and died aged 44 on 21 December 1883, survived by four children.

Davidson was one of the many supporters of William Robertson Smith (1846-1894), whose entries on biblical subjects in the ninth edition of the *Encyclopaedia Britannica* (1877) alarmed Presbyterian leaders and cost him his chair at the Free Church College, Aberdeen. Davidson's theological views were also too advanced for some of his congregation, but his expositions were always sincere and scrupulously fair. His purity of style and close reasoning were attractive even to students who had little taste for the subtleties of metaphysics and his manliness won him widespread respect and friendship.

Chalmers Church jubilee and annual reports, 1851-1901 (Adel, 1901); PD (SA), 1874, 2063a; *Presbyterian Mag* (SA), Aug 1881; *Register* (Adel), 4, 23, 25 July 1881, 22 Dec 1883; biographical index (SAA).

                          R. B. WALKER

DAVIES, DAVID MORTIMER (1840?-1894), politician, was born in Blaina, Monmouthshire, England, son of Thomas Davies, miner, and his wife Annie, née Lewis. He was educated for the church at Brecon Independent College, Monmouthshire, but doubts about his religious calling led him to forsake the ministry for farming and mining. He arrived in Adelaide in 1866 and served the Welsh congregation at Wallaroo. Next year he moved to Victoria and settled at Ross Creek in the Buninyong district. There he ministered to the Welsh Congregationalists in the mining communities around Sebastopol, Smythesdale and Scarsdale. When his liberal views became unacceptable to his deacons, he resigned and was elected a member of the Legislative Assembly for Grenville in 1877. His election was challenged on the ground that he was a minister of religion, but the objection failed and he represented Grenville until 1894. A strong liberal and protectionist, he acted as whip in the Berry [q.v.] government and sat on many royal commissions. As a staunch member of the earlier National Liberal League and a persistent advocate of Liberal policies, he resented Alfred Deakin's coalition with the Conservatives under Gillies [q.v.] in 1886. In letters to Deakin he emphasized his long and costly loyalty and pressed his claim for recompense as minister of mines. When Deakin rejected this plea, Davies relented and accepted appointment as minister without portfolio in October 1887. In June 1889 he became commissioner of public works and vice-president of the Board of Land and Works in the coalition government and was minister of mines from June to November 1890.

Davies was also prominent in local government. He served on the Buninyong Borough Council for many years, was elected mayor three times and was a justice of the peace for the Southern Bailiwick. Well known especially in the Ballarat district as an amateur astronomer, he delivered the inaugural lecture at the opening of the Ballarat observatory. His many other interests ranged from entomology to mineralogical and geological collections, the spectrum, telephone and phonograph. In the Welsh community he was particularly prominent; he emphasized the contribution of the Welsh to British greatness rather than narrow Welsh patriotism. After 1890 poor health reduced his public activities and in 1893 he suffered such severe loss in the bank crisis that he had to part with his beloved home at Buninyong. After protracted illness he died aged 54 in Errard Street South. Ballarat, on 18 June 1894 and was buried in the Ballarat old cemetery with many Buninyong councillors as pall-bearers. The Legislative Assembly adjourned for the day as a mark of respect to a member who, without taking a leading role in debates, had given long and faithful service in the House. He was survived by his wife Sarah, née Phillips, and by five sons and one daughter.

A. Sutherland et al, Victoria and its metropolis, 2 (Melb, 1888); J. Hughes, Australia revisited (Lond, 1891); Age, 19-21 June 1894; Argus, 19 June 1894; Ballarat Courier, 19, 20 June 1894; S. M. Ingham, Some aspects of Victorian liberalism (M.A. thesis, Univ Melb, 1950); Deakin letters, 1540/6866-71 (NL).

KERREEN M. REIGER

DAVIES, JOHN (1813-1872), convict, hotel-keeper, journalist and newspaper proprietor, was born in London, son of Michael John Davies and his wife Hannah, née Benjamin. On 15 July 1830 at Maidstone his father, managing clerk in a London attorney's office, was tried for obtaining goods by false pretences and sentenced to transportation for seven years; in December he arrived at Sydney in the Florentia with his wife, two sons and three daughters. He was assigned to the Australian Agricultural Co. at Port Stephens, moved to Port Macquarie in 1834 and, after his discharge, became a publican in Sydney. About 1871 he started the weekly, Australian, at Windsor, where he died on 27 December 1873.

John Davies was convicted of fraud at the Middlesex Court on 6 December 1830 and sentenced to transportation for seven years. In August 1831 he arrived at Hobart Town in the Argyle, aged 18, single, a clerk and a Jew. On the voyage he had been employed as a barber for his fellow prisoners. According to his gaol report, he was 'a bad character, audacious and impudent'. He was sent to government service in New South Wales and by 1834 he had joined his father at Port Macquarie. He was discharged in October 1837, worked in various jobs and then moved to Melbourne where he joined the Hebrew Congregation, set up as a pastry-cook and in October 1840 opened the Imperial Hotel; it passed to his creditors within seven months. With great self-confidence he became a reporter for the Port Phillip Gazette by February 1842 and in May was appointed chief constable at Portland. By October he was back in Melbourne writing aggressively for the Gazette and attempting to organize support for Judge Willis [q.v.]. As an amateur actor he played the part of a ghoulish comedian in a performance at the Pavilion, Melbourne's wooden theatre. Though never popular he was bustling and energetic, and when engaged on any undertaking his impudence and persistence brought success. In 1845 he organized the opening performance at a new theatre as a benefit to himself. Soon afterwards he married Elizabeth Hills and left for New South Wales, where in Sydney he worked as a government clerk, and in 1847 at Wellington became chief constable. On a visit to Melbourne in 1848 he made a vicious attack in Fawkner's [q.v.] Port Phillip Patriot on the wife of William Kerr [q.v.]. Fawkner made a public apology but Davies was charged with criminal libel; found guilty, he pleaded for a mitigated sentence and was fined £15.

In 1850 Davies left New South Wales and took his wife and two sons to Van Diemen's Land, where he acquired a hotel at Brighton. In 1852 he took over the Waterloo Hotel in Hobart and in partnership with George Auber Jones [q.v.] published the Hobarton Guardian. It was incorporated on 5 July 1854 with the first issue of the Hobarton Mercury. With Davies as sole proprietor it became a daily in 1858 and by 1860 had absorbed four other papers, the Colonial Times, Tasmanian Daily News, Daily Courier and Hobart Town Courier. In 1859 and 1864 he published Tasmanian almanacs.

In October 1871 two of his sons, John George and Charles Ellis, took over the *Mercury*, then Hobart's only newspaper. In 1854 Davies had also become part-proprietor of the Theatre Royal, Hobart, and under his guidance it was extensively reconstructed.

In Tasmania Davies became notorious for settling disputes by physical violence. In 1852 he was in hospital recovering from injuries received in a brawl, for which he demanded compensation from A. T. C. Yates, editor of the *Daily News*. In 1855 he was defendant in a Supreme Court action by Washington McMinn, solicitor, who claimed £1000 damages from an assault by Davies; the verdict was for the plaintiff with damages assessed at £5. In 1860 he was sentenced to one month's imprisonment for an assault on Samuel Prout Hill [q.v.]. In that year he had another fracas with Yates in a public street, and soon afterwards Davies charged J. C. Hall of the *Hobart Town Advertiser* with assault.

In 1861 Davies was elected to the House of Assembly as a member for Hobart, but because of a petition claiming that he was ineligible for election since he had printing contracts with the government he resigned and in 1862 was elected member for Devon, a northern electorate. He was defeated in September 1871 but won the Franklin seat. After a heart attack he died at his home, Windemere, Macquarie Street, Hobart, on 11 June 1872 and was buried with Anglican rites.

L. M. Goldman, *The Jews in Victoria in the nineteenth century* (Melb, 1954); M. Roe, *A history of the Theatre Royal, Hobart, from 1834* (Hob, 1965); M. Weidenhofer (ed), *Garryowen's Melbourne . . . 1835-1852* (Melb, 1967); *Port Phillip Gazette*, 17 Oct 1840, 5 May 1841, 11 May, 11 Sept, 15 Oct 1842; correspondence file under John Davies (TA).   F. C. GREEN

DAVIES, JOHN (1839-1896), ironmonger and politician, was born on 2 March 1839 at Sydney, son of John Davies, engineer, and his wife Honorah, née Roberts. Baptized a Roman Catholic, he had little education and at 9 worked as a messenger in an ironworks. Astute and frugal he matured as a teetotaller and non-smoker, became a blacksmith and in 1864 set up as an ironmonger in York Street. His Catholicism eroded, he joined the Loyal Orange Lodge, and on 3 April 1861 at Sydney he married Elizabeth Eaton according to Presbyterian rites. He emerged from obscurity to be president of the Protestant Friendly Society in 1864 and to rally Protestant support for James Martin's [q.v.] 1863-65 ministry and for the Martin-Parkes [q.v.] 1866-68 ministry; he was useful in the campaign for the Public Schools Act of 1866.

In 1868 H. J. O'Farrell's [q.v.] attempt to assassinate the duke of Edinburgh exacerbated the sectarian strand of colonial politics and improved conditions for the ascent of Davies. In July he became president of the Protestant Political Association, newly formed to secure the return of Protestants to parliament and the city council, and provoked the first of many public censures when W. J. Macleay [q.v.] claimed that 'Mr. Davies is simply a political loafer . . . No language could be too strong to expose the character of the people . . . whose pretended Protestantism is simply a political cry'. But Davies found sustenance in such attacks and in the 1870s from his widening base of leadership of multifarious political, temperance and wowser fraternities he became a significant political organizer. In 1874 he was elected to the city council, where he stayed until 1882, and to represent East Sydney in parliament, where, rebuffed by Parkes's earlier links with E. Butler [q.v.], he became J. Robertson's [q.v.] ingratiating 'whipper-in'. W. B. Dalley [q.v.], friend and associate of Robertson, subtly disturbed Davies's zealotry; they joined Robertson's 1877 ministry, Davies as postmaster-general. Davies was whip for the Parkes-Robertson 1878-83 coalition and in 1880-81 exhilarated his temperance supporters by helping to pass restrictive licensing laws. In 1880 he had lost his seat in East Sydney, but won South Sydney, where the breweries were.

In 1875 Davies had become a magistrate and in 1879 as acting British commissioner at Sydney for the Melbourne International Exhibition was appointed C.M.G. In 1882 he was a commissioner for the Amsterdam Exhibition. In 1881-82 he was an effective chairman of the royal commission on friendly societies. His enemies increased : in 1879 he was assaulted on one of his frequent harbour picnics; on 14 February 1880 the infant *Bulletin*, gaily unaware of its own brand of dissimulation, lampooned him as a chameleon who 'used the Orange institution . . . at the same time that he retained the support of the other sect by exposing to their gaze . . . an Agnus Dei upon his breast, and getting for some poor Irish labourers billets under the Corporation'; to the *Bulletin* he remained 'oleaginous John'. His 1882 appointment to the licensing bench aroused George Reid and the 'liquor interest' to ask how a teetotaller could cope with the duties. Slanders and libels enveloped him. In March 1883 he won a verdict of 40s. against the alderman, J. D. Young, and in June a more significant farthing, with costs, against John Harris [q.v.], mayor of Sydney.

In 1882 Davies lost South Sydney but in 1885 was at the head of the poll, allegedly with the aid of an 'underground bit of machinery, which is painted green, and fires up on alcohol'. In 1886 he was a member of the royal commission on intoxicating drink. He could not adjust his style to the 'fiscal elections' of 1887, lost his seat and was appointed to the Legislative Council by Parkes. He also helped to organize the laying of the foundation stone of the Queen's statue at the top of King Street, and in 1888 with others he proposed a statue in Dalley's memory. In 1887 he became a commissioner of the Adelaide Jubilee and Melbourne Centennial Exhibitions and was appointed chairman of the Casual Labour Board, entrusted with the expenditure of £250,000. Davies worked long hours on the board but in 1889 an inquiry found that he had apparently embezzled £112. Although counsel reported that Davies had 'sailed very close to the wind' and no criminal charge could be laid against him, he was charged and acquitted; later, after a convulsive debate, he was voted £1102 for his services.

By this time, according to the *Newcastle Morning Herald*, Davies was 'a positive blight on the public life of New South Wales'. Anathema to Catholics, publicans, the fastidious middle-class, journalists and cartoonists, he had raised himself from poverty and obscurity to notoriety and comparative affluence, inspiring envy and arousing feelings of guilt in his detractors. He had provided a necessary, if often tawdry, leadership to a significant part of the population; his political manipulations reflected the peculiarities of colonial politics. His wide philanthropy, including the relief of destitute children, was not just the façade that his actions often suggested. He was not impervious to the Christianity he patronized. He died on 23 May 1896, survived by his wife, one son and five daughters, and was buried in the Anglican section of Waverley cemetery. His estate was valued at £6296.

Illustrated Sydney News, 29 Nov 1879; *Bulletin*, 14 Feb 1880; *Freeman's J* (Syd), 29 July 1882; *Daily Telegraph* (Syd), 25 May 1896; Parkes letters (ML).   BEDE NAIRN

DAVIES, SIR JOHN MARK (1840-1919), solicitor, politician and speculator, GEORGE SCHOEN (1841-1910), banker, company manager and accountant, JOSEPH BARTLETT (1843-1924), accountant, banker and speculator, and SIR MATTHEW HENRY (1850-1912), solicitor, speculator, politician and philanthropist, were sons of Ebenezer Davies and his wife Ruth, née Bartlett. Their father was born on 17 July 1808 at Tetfield, Gloucestershire, England, the sixth child of John Davies, Congregational minister, and his wife Dorothy Anna Maria, née Schoen. He had little education and, because his parents could not support him, left home at an early age. He was employed in general trading in London and later acquired a straw hat manufactory at Halstead, Essex. After inheriting an annuity of about £500 from a Welsh uncle he migrated with his family in the *Travencore* and landed in November 1849 at Geelong. He became a tannery and property owner and a director of the Geelong and Melbourne Railway Co. His wife died in 1853 at Geelong and in 1857 he married Jane Vines. He was a tireless worker in the interests of Geelong. He was also deeply religious, though something of a tyrant to his family, convinced that his duty to his children was only to educate them. He died at Armadale on 15 May 1886, survived by most of the six sons and six daughters of his first marriage and four sons and one daughter of the second.

His eldest son, John Mark, was born on 8 February 1840 at Halstead. He was educated in Geelong, articled at 18 and admitted to the Supreme Court as a solicitor and proctor in December 1863. He went into practice in Melbourne with J. M. Campbell as his partner. Like his brothers he had attended the Bible-class of James Balfour [q.v.] and was a regular worshipper in the Presbyterian Church. In 1865 he married Emily Frances Scales; they had six sons and five daughters. He won profit and repute in the legal profession, and bought twenty-five acres at Malvern where he started to build the large mansion which later became Malvern Grammar School. In the land boom of the 1880s he speculated in bank and mortgage company shares and in 1886 formed the General Land and Savings Co. Ltd. He represented South Yarra Province in the Legislative Council in 1889-95, and in James Munro's [q.v.] cabinet was minister of justice from November 1890 to February 1892 and for two months in 1891 acting chief secretary and minister of health. He was largely responsible for the Voluntary Liquidation Act, 1891, which became significant in the depression.

The second son, George Schoen, was born on 26 October 1841 at Halstead. After education at Geelong Grammar School he joined the Geelong branch of the London Chartered Bank of Australia. He married Sarah Ann Staples; they had one son. After his wife died he moved to Melbourne in 1867, joined the Australian Deposit and Mortgage Bank Ltd and married Jessie

Agnes MacMurtrie. Conscientious and competent, he became manager of the bank in 1883. He resigned in February 1889 to manage the Gascoigne group of companies for his brother Matthew Henry.

The third son, Joseph Bartlett, was born on 30 September 1843 at Halstead. He was educated at Geelong Grammar School and became an accountant. He tended to be led by his brother Matthew Henry and in 1882 was appointed managing director of his Freehold Investment and Banking Co. Ltd, which was primarily engaged in land subdivision.

The most notorious son was Matthew Henry. He was born on 1 February 1850 at Geelong. He went to the Grammar School and Geelong College and matriculated at the University of Melbourne in 1869. After some freelance journalism he was articled to his brother John Mark in February 1870. On 23 March 1875 he married Elizabeth Locke, eldest daughter of Dr Peter Mercer, Presbyterian minister. In April he was admitted a solicitor of the Supreme Court and set up his own practice. He was honorary secretary to the council of the Law Institute of Victoria for five years, became a justice of the peace and served as mayor of Prahran in 1881-82. After failing to win the East Bourke Boroughs seat he represented St Kilda in the Legislative Assembly in 1883-88 and Toorak in 1889-92. In 1886 he was a minister without portfolio in the Gillies [q.v.] government and visited London for the Indian and Colonial Exhibition. He sat on several committees of inquiry and as chairman of the royal commission on banking laws recommended the removal of restrictions for lending money on the security of freehold property. In October 1887 by a majority of one he was elected Speaker; he adorned the office by his impartiality and skill in conducting business smartly without limiting discussion. When knighted in 1890 he was already well known for his gifts to the Imperial Institute, public charities and the Young Men's Christian Association, and for founding the Cheltenham Convalescent Home. He was also well known for the splendour of his Toorak mansion and his lavish entertainment. His boundless energy combined with personal charm to make him an irrepressible advocate for the 'great city of Melbourne' which he and his fellow speculators hoped to build.

Much of his early legal work was connected with the property dealings of one of the greatest 'land boomers', C. H. James [q.v.]. By 1877 Davies had himself begun speculating in land. He formed his first company in 1882 and by 1887 had organized a network of about forty companies; their respectability owed much to the sponsorship of James Balfour. Davies was also active on the board of the *Daily Telegraph*. The great crisis in his affairs was in 1892. His Mercantile Bank declared an 8 per cent dividend in February but suspended payment in March. He resigned from parliament in April and left for England in the *City of Chicago* which was wrecked on the Irish coast on 2 July. With 200 other passengers Davies scaled the cliff on a 300-foot rope ladder and lost all his luggage. He reached London too late for a meeting of depositors who resolved to apply for voluntary liquidation of the bank. At a meeting in October he made a long statement but was severely criticized by angry shareholders. He returned to Melbourne to find most of his other companies in difficulty. In January 1893 he was committed for trial for conspiracy to defraud by means of a false balance sheet. The trial was delayed until May but before it ended the attorney-general, Sir Bryan O'Loghlen [q.v.], decided to withdraw the charges. Davies was stricken with severe nervous prostration and ordered a complete change of scene; he sailed with his wife in the *Salier*. Meanwhile the solicitor-general, Isaac Isaacs, had issued new writs. A telegram to Adelaide arrived too late for Davies's arrest. He was arrested in Colombo by a Victorian detective who had followed on a later ship, although Davies said he would return voluntarily. After several trials failed to unravel the transactions of his companies, he was acquitted but had to file his schedule in bankruptcy in 1894. His reputed assets of £650,000 in 1890 were gone yet he was soon discharged on the ground that his liabilities of £280,000 were caused by the depression. All his companies disappeared, with losses to the public of over £4 million. Davies returned to his legal practice. He failed to win the Melbourne seat in parliament but later became deputy-grand master of Freemasons and president of the Philharmonic Society. His health deteriorated but did not affect his handsome and unruffled appearance. He died at Mentone on 26 November 1912, survived by his second wife Margaret, née Boyle, and by two sons and four daughters.

Joseph Bartlett, who had borrowed large sums to prop up his company before it was liquidated in February 1892, went bankrupt in April 1894 for £594,000, the highest personal debt of the family, and paid a ¼d in the £. His valuable art collection and fine furniture were sold and after his discharge he worked as an accountant until his death on 28 October 1924 at a private hospital in Malvern. By his wife Mary Forrest, née Gardner, he had two sons and seven daughters.

George Schoen also lost heavily on shares

in his brother's companies, but he remained solvent by selling his assets and practising as an accountant. A staunch Presbyterian, he was a church elder and for ten years member of the assembly. He was highly respected, but unlike Matthew Henry was quiet and unassuming. He died on 1 February 1910 at his home in Malvern, survived by his wife and four sons.

John Mark struggled in vain in 1892 to reconstruct Matthew Henry's Mercantile Bank but his own company failed in 1893 and paid only 2s. in the £. He had to sell most of his land and other assets; despite heavy losses on his speculations, he remained solvent, although his debts were not finally wiped off until 1906. Meanwhile in 1895 he represented Victoria at the sixth session of the Federal Council, and in the September elections lost his seat for South Yarra. He represented Melbourne in the Legislative Council in 1899-1919. He was solicitor-general in Allan McLean's ministry in 1899-1900, and again in 1902-03 under W. H. Irvine, who also appointed him minister of public instruction for seven months in 1903 and attorney-general in 1903-04. In Bent's [q.v.] ministry he was attorney-general and solicitor-general in 1904-09. He acted as premier and treasurer in Bent's absence in 1907 and next year went to London as chairman of the Victorian commission to the Empire Exhibition. While in office he led the government party in the council and out of office was unofficial leader. On 6 July 1910 he was nominated president of the council by Balfour and elected unanimously. A competent parliamentarian, he was a tower of strength in cabinet and debate. After his resignation in June 1919 because of a stroke, members of both Houses waxed lyrical in praise. Without ostentation he supported many charities and served on many committees such as that of the Austin Hospital. In January 1918 he was appointed K.C.M.G. He died at his home in Malvern on 12 September 1919 and was given a state funeral. He was survived by his wife and by three sons and five daughters of their thirteen children.

Victorian Reports, 1893-94; E. H. Sugden and F. W. Eggleston, *George Swinburne a biography* (Syd, 1931); M. Cannon, *The land boomers* (Melb, 1966); PD (Vic), 1912, 1919; *Messenger* (Presbyterian, Vic & Tas), 18 Mar 1910; *A'sian Insurance and Banking Record*, 16 (1892); *Australasian*, 2 June 1888, 9 July, 20 Aug, 10 Dec 1892, 7 Jan, 8 July, 19 Aug 1893; *Argus*, 2 Jan 1890, 3 Feb 1910, 13 Sept 1919, 29 Oct 1924; *Town and Country J*, 19 Nov 1892.

R. D. FREEMAN

DAVIES, JOSEPH (1839-1922), mine manager, was born in Hobart Town, the second son of James Davies, shipsmith. At 12 he went to Ballarat and the goldfields at Bendigo and Castlemaine. In 1854 he returned to Tasmania where he received his first instruction in geology from John Nicholas Clemons. In 1858 he went to Victoria and gained experience of quartz mining in South Gippsland, where by 1872 he became manager of the Ophir mine and was recognized as an expert in mineralogy and chemistry.

Davies returned to Tasmania in 1877 and worked on the Lefroy goldfield until June when the Dally brothers discovered a reef at Brandy Creek on the western side of the River Tamar near the townsite of Beaconsfield. On 12 August Davies was appointed manager of the Dally brothers' mine. In October William Hart and William Grubb [qq.v.] of Launceston bought the mine and formed the Tasmania Gold Mining and Quartz Crushing Co., with Davies as manager. By November 1878 the mine was paying dividends and a uniform average yield was maintained for the next twenty-five years, 'an indication of the richness of the mine and his capable management'. Although the 'Tasmania' was continually flooded Davies later acquired other small mines on the same lode. Operations extended and the mining force was greatly increased until the mine was the largest employer of mine labour in Tasmania, and among the largest steadily producing reef gold mines in Australia. Davies made a fine collection of rocks and mineral types from the field and prepared detailed geological maps of the area which attracted the attention of professional geologists. As an acknowledged expert in reef mining under excessively wet conditions, he was often called to advise mainland mining companies with similar problems. In 1886 he published *History of the Tasmanian Gold Mining and Quartz Crushing Company*. He was elected a fellow of the Royal Society of Tasmania and became a corresponding member of the Geological Society of London.

Davies did not confine his activities to management and professional studies, but became an active leader in the new community. He was a justice of the peace, a master in the Masonic fraternity, chairman of the Local Schools' Board of Advice, a Methodist local preacher and a vigorous advocate of temperance. According to a visiting clergyman, 'The excellent character of the Company's miners is well-known and much of their sobriety and steadiness was no doubt due to the example of Davies'. His six hundred employees were carefully selected, and a court conviction or habitual drunkenness usually debarred a man from employment. Bad language was also discouraged. In one crisis he had to stand down a hundred men, but he believed in equal sacrifice and voluntarily cut his own pay from £8 to £6 10s. a week. He retired in 1902 and received a bonus of £1000. In his long service the Tasmania had yielded some eighteen tons of gold and dividends of over £750,000.

Davies became general manager of the Queen Margaret gold mine opened in 1896 at Bulong, east of Coolgardie, Western Australia, and returned in 1909 to his home, the Grove, at George Town. He died there on 16 September 1922, survived by his wife Elizabeth, née Trevaskis, whom he had married at Ballarat in 1872, and by their three sons and four daughters.

Cyclopedia of Tasmania, 2 (Hob, 1900); J. Kerrison, Beaconsfield gold (Beaconsfield, 1963); Examiner (Launceston), 18 Sept 1922.

JOHN REYNOLDS

DAVIES, MAURICE COLEMAN (1835-1913), timber merchant, building contractor and pastoralist, was born in London, son of John Davies and his wife Catherine, née Hart (1795-1889). At 5 he went to Van Diemen's Land with his parents, who took up pastoral pursuits. After some eleven years he went to Victoria and worked on the Blackwood diggings. He then engaged in a mercantile and shipping business in Melbourne and later in Adelaide, where in 1867 he opened as a general commission agent and merchant in Gilbert Place. When he moved to Grenfell Street in 1877, he was dividing his time between South and Western Australia. As a member of Baillie, Davies & Wishart in South Australia he carried out several government contracts. One of them, for the second section of the Melbourne-Adelaide railway, introduced Davies to Western Australian hardwoods, and on Christmas eve 1875 in Perth he applied for a lease of 1920 acres of forest in the Bunbury district. In 1876 he set up a steam sawmill in the Collie Ranges, about twenty miles from Bunbury. The Collie mills operated successfully for eight years. Private visitors and government officials were favourably impressed with the efficiency of his station and, although Davies disputed with local authorities over the upkeep of roads used by his horse and bullock teams, an official investigation left no doubt that Davies's operations greatly benefited the district. For several years until 1878 he was also a shareholder in the Jarrahdale and Rockingham Timber Co.

Jarrah (Eucalyptus marginata) was milled at Collie, and in 1883 Davies owned a tuart (Eucalyptus gomphocephala) mill on the Capel River. But the timber whose name is almost synonymous with his own is karri (Eucalyptus diversicolor). He claimed, probably correctly, that karri was unknown to the world's timber users before he began milling it. By 1877 he was interested in the timber between Cape Hamelin and Augusta in the extreme south-west. He took up a licence to cover the area and began cutting in 1879 in what became the Karridale estate; there in the 1880s and 1890s he built several large mills, townships, roads, railways and jetties, and installed a telephone system, library and sports ground. He shipped timber from Hamelin Bay on the west coast, and Flinders Bay on the south coast. Under Davies a close-knit, self-sufficient patriarchal society developed on the estate. Much use was made of the truck system and money was almost unknown; the account of each employee was credited with wages and interest and debited with expenses such as rent and purchases at the company store. Davies recruited his labour from afar and at least once tried to indenture Chinese workers. His venture prospered and in 1890 Karridale was the colony's biggest single timber-exporting station, accounting for over one-third of total shipments. In 1897, when large amounts of English capital were being invested in the Western Australian timber industry, his interests were bought by the M. C. Davies Karri and Jarrah Co., incorporated in London with a capital of £250,000; Davies was its first managing director. The company operated the Karridale mills until in 1902 it was absorbed, with seven other major timber companies, into Millars' Karri and Jarrah Co. Ltd. Thereafter he had no active role in sawmilling.

Davies had become involved in the goldmining industry and was a shareholder in the West Australian Shipping Association, formed about 1884, but his most important investments were in the pastoral industry. In 1881 he helped to form the Kimberley Pastoral Co. and was its managing director until 1913. The company took up the Liveringa station on the Fitzroy River. Davies also had a share in the station of the Luluigui Pastoral Co. Ltd, downstream from Liveringa. In 1884 he bought Balmaningarra in the Kimberleys and his family controlled Napier Downs. He also had large holdings in the Kojonup and Katanning areas, under the name of the Palmirup Grazing Co. In his last decade his pastoral interests overshadowed those in the timber industry. Described as a retired pastoralist, he died at his home, Peradeniya, St George's Terrace, Perth, on 10 May 1913. He held large shares in several companies not connected with rural industry, and his land investments in

Perth alone were valued at £8000. He also had property at various towns and suburbs in Western Australia, at Adelaide and at Colombo, Ceylon. His probate was sworn at nearly £38,000.

In Adelaide on 24 March 1858 he had married Sarah Salom (b. 26 September 1838). He was survived by six sons and two daughters of their twelve children. The sons became prominent in the timber industry: despite the family wealth each began his career as a labourer; two were Australian directors of the M. C. Davies Karri and Jarrah Co. and in 1902 five held high positions in the firm. One, Walter David 'Karri' (b. 14 June 1867), achieved prominence at the time of the Jameson raid as a member of the Uitlanders' Reform Committee; he later fought in the Boer war.

M. C. Davies was one of the handful of men whose career bridged the pioneering phase of Western Australian timber industry, the boom of the 1890s and the consolidation of the early twentieth century. His financial rewards were a measure of his skill as a timberman; none before him had worked Western Australia's forests so successfully and on such a scale. His greatest contribution to the colony's development was probably his promotion of karri. His efforts to bring it to the notice of buyers included showing it at the Indian and Colonial Exhibition in London in 1886 and at Melbourne in 1888 where he won a trophy. He and his sons travelled widely in their attempts to open new markets for karri. At times his business practices were criticized; his company was detected selling karri as jarrah for marine works, and several controversies arose over the alleged leniency of the government's terms when granting him timber licences. But he rose high in the social scale of the colony. His burial in the Jewish section of Karrakatta cemetery was attended by representatives of many leading families.

Herald (Fremantle), 1 Nov 1879, 19 Nov 1881, 6 Jan 1883; West Australian, 11 Feb, 22 July 1881, 25 Jan 1886, 12, 13 May 1913; B. F. Hamling, Maurice Coleman Davies of Karridale and Liveringa, essay, 1961, Claremont Teachers' College (WAA); CSO records (Battye Lib, Perth).   J. R. ROBERTSON

DAVIES, WILLIAM (1824-1890), storekeeper and parliamentarian, was born in Manchester, England, son of Thomas Davies and his wife Ann Maria. From the merchant marine he went into commerce and about 1849 arrived in New South Wales. At Goulburn he became book-keeper in the Australian Stores but soon left for Melbourne where he was shipping reporter for the Argus. In 1852 he joined the Araluen gold rush; on 11 May at Surry Hills he married Maria Cooper, governess to the children of Rev. William Schofield [q.v.]. He returned to Goulburn and by 1856 was managing the Australian Stores. In 1860 he went into partnership with Maurice Alexander [q.v.] and others, and soon had stores throughout the southern districts. In 1877 Alexander sold out, leaving Davies as sole proprietor. At Goulburn in May 1880 Davies opened large new premises in Auburn Street, where he employed seventy hands. He was also a director of the Australian Copper Mining Co., and in 1879 first chairman of the Goulburn Gas Co. In the 1880s he floated the Berrima Coal Mining and Railway Co. and in 1885 the Goulburn Foundry and Engineering Co. Ltd.

Davies was a member of the Goulburn Municipal Council in 1859-87, was responsible for the revival of local government after it lapsed in 1863-68 and served eight times as mayor. Although an excellent speaker his reserved manner, his Wesleyan ties and opposition to horse-racing and other sports brought him into conflict with other aldermen. He helped to form the Goulburn volunteer fire brigade in 1876 and was elected a trustee for the insurance companies. He was also a local magistrate and a trustee of the Mechanics' Institute.

For many years Davies was a steward of the Goulburn Wesleyan circuit. He was prominent in the Home Mission Society from its foundation in 1859 and in the local branch of the British and Foreign Bible Society. For over thirty-two years he was superintendent of the main Wesleyan Sunday school and after 1874 a delegate to the New South Wales Wesleyan Conference. In the 1860s he was a trustee and shareholder of the Methodist denominational school, and strongly advocated conversion of the Methodist and Presbyterian schools into a public school. When Parkes [q.v.] opened the public school in the Methodist building in 1868 Davies was chairman of the board. In October 1881 he opened the public school in South Goulburn. His eldest son was the first pupil enrolled at Newington House. In May 1878 Davies helped to lay the foundation stone of Newington College at Stanmore and became a life member of its council.

In 1877-80 Davies represented Argyle in the Legislative Assembly. He supported the Parkes ministry and in 1889-90 was a councillor of the Free Trade and Liberal Association of New South Wales. In 1887 Davies had to assign his estate. His bankruptcy was caused by his debt of £11,000 to the Oriental Bank as chairman of the Berrima Coal Mining Co. and by the costs of buying out his partners and the outlay on his store and large new home, Carrawarra. He sold the store and in May retired to Sydney as manager of the Sydney and Provincial Building Society. He lived at Redfern, was superintendent of the Newtown Methodist Sunday school and continued to be active in Wesleyan affairs. He died aged 66 on 14 August 1890, survived by his widow, two sons and two daughters. His estate was valued at £2627 and heavy life insurance met his creditors.

G. Wilson, *Goulburn and the southern highlands* (Syd, 1916); R. T. Wyatt, *The history of Goulburn, N.S.W.* (Goulburn, 1941); *Goulburn Herald*, 28 Feb, 18 Mar, 4 Nov 1863, 9 Feb, 22, 25 Mar 1876, 15 May 1880, 16 Aug 1890; *Goulburn Evening Penny Post*, 16, 19 Aug 1890; *SMH*, 16 Aug 1890; Council of Education in-letters (NSWA).   RUTH TEALE

DAVIS, ALEXANDER BARNARD (1828-1913), Jewish minister, was born on 15 August 1828 in London. Orphaned at 12, he was educated by Rev. H. A. Henry of St Albans and then, whilst teaching himself Hebrew, at Holland House, Hammersmith, by Rev. H. M. Meyers of Ramsgate. He became a master of Westminster Jews' Free School in 1848; in 1852, recommended by the chief rabbi of England, Dr Adler, he accepted the ministry of the Portsmouth Synagogue. In June 1853 he married Blanche Annie (1832-1892), daughter of Bartolomew Harris, stationer of Hatton Garden, London. In 1854 he became minister at Kingston, Jamaica, where his progressive views united members of the Portuguese and German Jewish communities. He returned to England in 1861 and accepted the ministry of the York Street Synagogue, Sydney. He arrived with his family on 17 August 1862. He was installed on 14 September at the reconsecration of the renovated synagogue and soon aroused the drooping congregation.

Davis soon realized the inadequacy of religious education in the Jewish community. In 1863 he founded the Jewish Sabbath school and was its president until 1882. He later established the Society for the Diffusion of Religious Knowledge in unison with the London association; it was equipped with a lending library and a children's savings bank. In 1868 he joined the committee of the Sydney Hebrew Orthodox Denominational School and in 1873 was its president; in 1882 he was president of the Sydney Jewish Board of Education. In 1869 he published *Jewish Rites explained . . . and Prayers for children* (Sydney, 1869); its third edition was printed in 1902. He also produced two pamphlets: *Questions upon the principles and duties of the Jewish Religion* (Sydney, 1866) and *De-votions for children and Jewish families*, and in 1895-96 wrote many articles for the *Australasian Hebrew*. He was the first to admit girls to religious classes and to conduct confirmation services for girls in the synagogue. He is also said to have initiated the first mixed choir in any synagogue of the British empire. In 1872 he founded the local branch of the Anglo-Jewish Association and was its first president. He greatly assisted in breaching the gulf between the York Street and the dissenting Macquarie Street Synagogues, and in uniting the Sydney Jewish community after the building of the Great Synagogue in Elizabeth Street. He consecrated it on 4 March 1878 and became its first minister. In 1883 while on leave in England he collected funds for a home for the aged poor, the Sir Moses Montefiore Jewish Home, which was opened in 1889 in Dowling Street, Sydney, and later transferred to Hunter's Hill. In 1903 he retired and was appointed emeritus minister. He died on 16 December 1913 and was buried in the Jewish section of the Rookwood cemetery. He left an estate worth £8000. His wife had died on 6 June 1892, survived by three daughters and six of her nine sons. The eldest, Ernest Lawton, was a leading Sydney stockbroker and sometime chairman of the Sydney Stock Exchange; the two youngest sons, Oscar and William, were medical practitioners.

Davis never claimed the title of 'Rabbi', although it was freely accorded to him. He was strong and sincere and an excellent preacher. An incident in 1871 showed the wide public esteem earned by Davis: he was accused by his maid of indecent assault, and acquitted; the case was notable for Edward Butler's [q.v.] defence and David Buchanan's [q.v.] prosecution and Davis's complete vindication received warm approval from all sections of the community. He supported Palestine welfare appeals but not the nascent Zionist movement in 1901. Imbued with Anglo-Jewish traditions, he misjudged the importance of Jewish migration to Australia as a means of survival, and had misgivings in the 1890s when Russian Jews, fleeing from pogroms, began to migrate to Australia. His name will always be associated with dignified services, religious education and unification of the Sydney Jewish community.

D. J. Benjamin, 'Essays in the history of Jewish education in New South Wales', *Aust Jewish Hist Soc, J*, 4 (1954-58); *Hebrew Standard of A'sia*, Dec 1913; *SMH*, 14, 17, 19, Oct 1871.   GEORGE F. J. BERGMAN

DAVITT, ARTHUR (1808-1860), educationist, was born in Drogheda, Ireland, son of James Davitt and his wife Mary. According to his own account, he became 'an excellent classical scholar' in Ireland and for the next twenty years was 'A Professor of Modern Languages in Paris, at Sens and other colleges on the continent'; in 1842 he 'underwent a general examination at the Sorbonne . . . and received his degree with the highest distinction'. A footnote adds that a prerequisite of this examination was a bachelor's degree. In 1845 in Jersey he married Marie Antoinette Hélène Léontine Heseltine (1820-1879) of Dublin; they had no children. In 1847 he was appointed inspector of schools for the Athy district under the commissioners of National Education, Ireland. In 1851-54 his wife taught drawing in the Irish National Board's Model School for Girls in Marlborough Street, Dublin.

They arrived at Melbourne on 31 July 1854 to take up a joint appointment with the National Board of Education, Davitt as principal of the Model and Normal Schools and his wife as superintendent of the female pupils and trainees. The Model Schools for boys, girls and infants were opened on 18 September. In 1859 a financial recession led to the closure of the training institution and the dismissal of the Davitts. Davitt died on 24 January 1860 at the National Hotel, Moorabool Street, Geelong. Mrs Davitt taught at various Victorian schools for the next fifteen years. She died at Fitzroy on 6 January 1879.

In his pamphlet, *Origin and Progress of the National System of Education: its real principles, and special adaptability to the circumstances of a mixed community* (Melbourne, 1856), Davitt answered charges against the National system and its suitability for Victorian needs. In 1855 he had been criticized on pedagogical grounds for his unwillingness to temper the Irish system to the viable social structure. His caution was to be expected in a community split by the rivalries of the National and Denominational systems, and there is ample evidence that he liberalized and enriched the studies of his pupils and students. The Training College opened in May 1855, with twelve students and in 1856 the first residents were admitted. When Davitt left 169 teachers had been trained, 130 of them deemed worthy of classification for National schools' appointments. The system of classification devised by Davitt and Inspector Orlebar had significant similarities to the complex one still operating in Victorian schools. Davitt also initiated the system of paid monitors in 1854 and pupil teachers in 1857. Despite his heavy responsibility he established industrial classes for adults and in 1857 some of his trainees were able to

attend lectures at the University of Melbourne.

Unfortunately the Davitts were involved in frequent quarrels with their staff and much correspondence passed between the board and the principal whose worsening health sapped the composure he might have displayed. Mrs Davitt's 'overbearing self-esteem' apparently increased her husband's difficulties. The commissioners several times rebuked Davitt for a 'deficiency on your part which is not consistent with harmonious working'. His dismissal may have arisen from such deficiencies rather than from reduction of the education grant for 1859. Yet he often exhibited a tolerance and understanding more commendable than those of his associates. Many of the differences were trivial and today would never reach the central authorities, but at that time the officers of the National Board occupied rooms in the Model School. Davitt's founding and development of the Model Schools and Training College became significant in 1870; adequate teacher training was then urgently needed and the authorities revived his establishment.

J. A. Allan, *The old Model School . . . 1852-1904* (Melb, 1934); E. Sweetman, *History of the Melbourne Teachers' College and its predecessors* (Melb, 1939); National Board of Education, letters and papers 1854-59 (VA).

WARWICK EUNSON

DAWSON, JAMES (1806-1900), pastoralist and friend of the Aboriginals, was born on 5 July 1806 at Bonnytoun, West Lothian, Scotland, the youngest son of Adam Dawson and his wife Frances, née McKell. Business reversals in London and the ill health of his wife Joan Anderson, née Park, niece of the African explorer Mungo Park, caused Dawson to migrate with her to Port Phillip. They arrived in May 1840 and Dawson bought a small property on the Yarra above Anderson's Creek. Prosperity and an expanding dairy herd caused him to move in 1844 to the Western District where he took up a cattle-run near Port Fairy. Dawson lost ground in the depression of the 1840s and, although he attempted to survive by using a boiling-down plant, he was declared bankrupt in 1845. However, he continued on the land, profited in the gold rushes and sold his station in 1866 and leased land near Camperdown where he lived for the rest of his life as a farmer, amateur taxidermist and protector, friend and student of the Aboriginals. His only child, Isabella, helped him in his studies. A Presbyterian, he died at Camperdown on 19 April 1900.

Dawson is remembered as an amateur

ethnographer (his *Australian Aborigines. The Languages and Customs of several tribes of Aborigines in the Western District of Victoria, Australia* was published in Melbourne in 1881) and for his sympathetic interest in the Aboriginals. He was appointed a protector of Aborigines and gave evidence to the 1877 royal commission on their condition, severely criticizing the assumptions upon which current native policy was based and its results. He considered that the Aboriginals were entitled to government support without obligation, and that it was unfair to restrict their movements and to press unpalatable employment and religion upon them.

In the 1880s Dawson collected money from the settlers around Camperdown for a monument to the last local Aboriginals; it stands in the Camperdown cemetery. An acquaintance later recalled that, when some settlers refused to contribute, Dawson rushed to Melbourne with an account he had written of the early ill treatment of the Aboriginals. He demanded that the *Argus* editor, F. W. Haddon [q.v.], publish this attack on the settlers but was refused: 'Dawson however insisted and, when Haddon ordered him out of the room, old Jimmy Dawson went for him with his umbrella'.

Dawson was well known locally as an irascible teller-of-tales about the maltreatment of the Aboriginals, and his book clearly reflects his sympathy for them. On some subjects, particularly on the nature of authority within the Aboriginal community, the book is unreliable, as E. M. Curr [q.v.] was the first to show. Dawson got much of his information from the detribalized Aboriginals at the Framlingham reserve. In his desire to put them in a good light, he often pleaded their case to unsympathetic officials. He dedicated his book to this 'ill-used and interesting people', and his reputation as their sincere friend is secure.

R. Boldrewood (T. A. Browne), *Old Melbourne memories*, 1st ed (Melb, 1884); H. Nisbet, *A colonial tramp*, 2nd ed (Lond, 1896); A. Henderson (ed), *Early pioneer families of Victoria and Riverina* (Melb, 1936); *Portland Gazette*, 9 Dec 1845; Boyer to Stephens, MS cat under Dawson (ML).   PETER CORRIS

DAWSON, ROBERT BARRINGTON (1815-1891), studmaster, civil servant and pastoralist, was born at Great Bentley, Essex, England, the eldest son of Robert Dawson [q.v.] and his first wife Anne, née Taylor. His formal education at Uxbridge School ended in 1830 when he went to Madeira to work for a Portuguese wine merchant. He arrived at Sydney in 1835 and gained ex-perience on stations in the Hunter, Castlereagh and Liverpool Plains districts. In 1840 he returned to England with a commission to buy and import sixteen thoroughbred mares and stallions of much-needed bloodlines. At Belford, Hunter River, in 1841 he established a stud whence he later exported 'walers' for the Indian army and imported high-caste Arab sires, a breed on which he was a recognized authority. In 1844 he entertained Leichhardt [q.v.] on his way to Port Essington, and the Dawson River was named after him in gratitude for his financial assistance. Ruined by drought in 1848-49 and the failure of his Indian partner, Dawson sailed for California in February 1850 with A. A. Leycester and John Maister. They found no payable gold but maintained themselves by shooting game and growing vegetables for the San Francisco market. Dawson returned in 1851 and collected firewood for sale to Sydney householders, but a bushfire consumed his stacks. A trip to the Nundle gold-diggings was equally unfortunate.

In 1857 Dawson was appointed road superintendent for the Bathurst-Hartley district, and in Sydney married the widow Jessie Terry. He resigned from the department of roads in 1867 to become commissioner of crown lands for the Clarence, Richmond and Tweed including parts of New England, the Gwydir and Liverpool Plains. In this enormous district he had to ride long distances, and inspect all types of country in order to administer appraisal courts, but he held the appointment until commissionerships were abolished in 1881 and was compensated for his compulsory retirement. He then managed his property, Bentley, between Casino and Lismore where his ingenious and cultivated mind led him to build a homestead of wattle and daub with a bark roof to suit the climate. Aged 75 he died there on 19 January 1891 and was buried with Anglican rites at Casino. His wife and their two sons, Arthur David and Robert Leycester, inherited his estate worth over £8400.

Slight of figure, friendly of temperament and an accomplished horseman Dawson may have benefited in his youth from the natural sympathy accorded to his father's son by the squatters, but he later proved himself an able administrator and a competent and democratic grazier.

R. L. Dawson, 'Leaves from a crown lands commissioner's letters. Richmond River district', Richmond River Hist Soc, J, 1 (1937); R. L. Dawson, 'Casino and the building of Bentley', Richmond River Hist Soc, J, 2 (1938); *Maitland Mercury*, 18 Mar 1843; Clarence and Richmond River districts, papers 1868-71 (held by Mrs. C. A. Richardson).   LOUISE T. DALEY

DAY, GEORGE (1826-1906), entrepreneur and parliamentarian, was born on 29 October 1826 in the Hawkesbury River district, New South Wales, son of John Day, a farmer at Cornwallis, and his wife Sarah, née Connolly. At 14, after schooling at Windsor and Richmond, he joined his brother James, manager of a station in the Monaro; later they moved to Omeo, Victoria. In 1852 George went to the Bendigo goldfields and after six successful months opened a store on the new Livingstone Creek goldfield at Omeo, and then helped to manage four Gippsland stations. In May 1856 with his brother he leased Tabletop station near Albury for their cattle and for wheat-growing after a small crop returned a bumper harvest. When the Tabletop lease expired in 1859 they bought Quat Quatta station on the Murray River for £15,000. A few years later the brothers paid a much larger sum for Yarra Yarra station on Billabong Creek where they ran six thousand cattle.

About 1860 Day moved to Albury and was appointed a justice of the peace. In 1861 he rented the Fanny Ceres flour-mill and later bought it. Goldfield demand sent profits up to 300 per cent on the milling and he brought wheat by steamboat from as far as South Australia. At the mill he was book-keeper, wheat-buyer and sometimes engine attendant. In local affairs he served as alderman of the Albury Municipal Council in 1868-78, and as mayor in 1869, 1870 and 1873; he was also president of the local racing club and for many years president of the District Hospital Board.

In 1874-89 Day represented the Hume and Albury electorates in the New South Wales Legislative Assembly, where he enjoyed repute as a supporter of free selection. He was an active legislator, bringing down five public and twelve private bills, of which thirteen were passed, including several affecting public utilities in Albury and Broken Hill. Several times he declined ministerial office. Narrowly defeated in 1889 he was nominated to the Legislative Council and held the seat until he died on 13 July 1906. His last years had been spent at Lewisham, Sydney, where he was a staunch supporter of the Roman Catholic Church; for his benefactions to the hospital of the Little Company of Mary, he was appointed a knight commander of St Gregory by Pope Leo XIII. He left an estate worth more than £26,500. In 1849 Day had married Eliza, daughter of John Williams, of Grosse's Plain, Monaro; she died without issue in 1905.

Day's active contribution to parliamentary life gave him distinction among his contemporaries. Equally, as a tycoon he appealed to the nineteenth-century respect for the self-made man, a role he embodied in his own life, though his achievements were mostly local and sectional.

Albury Daily News, 13 July 1906; *Freeman's J* (Syd), 21 July 1906.   E. J. LEA-SCARLETT

DEAN, HORACE (1814-1887), physician, journalist and store-keeper, was born on 10 November 1814 in Chicago, United States of America, probably son of Horace Williams who had migrated from London with his mother, née Dean. He claimed an education in medicine but the diplomas he later exhibited have not been acknowledged by Dartmouth College, New Hampshire, or the St Louis School of Medicine, Missouri. In 1846 he was a surgeon and cavalry captain in the Mexican war. In a duel next year he killed an officer and fled to England where he spent some months in a lunatic asylum. As Horace Dean on 25 April 1849 at Hastings he married Jane Ann Mitchell, and in November arrived at Adelaide as surgeon in the *Augusta*.

With a forged medical diploma, Dean set up a practice in Angaston; in October 1850 he was naturalized and admitted to the roll of qualified medical practitioners. He became a justice of the peace in March 1851, and acted in 1852 as an honorary special magistrate. As second stipendiary magistrate of the northern districts early in 1853, he fell out with George Fife Angas [q.v.], who claimed that Dean had reported to the governor 'that all in Angaston hated the landlord and were afraid of him'. Angas then wrote to friends in America who challenged Dean's identity and qualifications. Before Sir Richard MacDonnell in September 1855 Dean allowed himself to be passed off as Colonel Thomas Haskell; in reply to the governor's letter Jefferson Davis, the United States secretary of war, showed conclusively that this claim was false. Meanwhile the 'persecution' by Angas continued; Dean had to resign as magistrate in November 1855 and was struck off the medical roll in 1857. Convinced that it was 'necessary to remit these questions to the decision of the people', he stood for Barossa in the first Legislative Assembly elections. On the hustings Dean professed contempt for all 'would-be aristocrats' who attempted 'to monopolize the fat of the land', and urged electors to 'overwhelm the Upper House in its own ruins' if Angas attempted to 'control the representatives of the people'. Dean was elected in March 1857 but disqualified in May by the Court of Disputed Returns. He was re-elected in June but again disqualified. He then proposed to start an 'altogether democratic' paper, but could not find the capital.

Dean went to Melbourne, then Sydney where he wrote for the *Empire* and in 1858 settled as a store-keeper at Tinonee on the Manning River. He practised medicine although he never registered in New South Wales. He encouraged attempts to grow sugar-cane, cotton and tobacco and to mine for gold, copper and limestone. In April 1865 he started the *Manning River News*. Still an artful demagogue, he was elected in December 1869 for the Hastings but was disqualified because he was in government pay as a postmaster. In July 1870 he was returned by what he called 'the unanimous will of an outraged people' but was again disqualified under naturalization conditions. Still hopeful of re-election, he proposed in 1872 to start a Sydney daily; when Parkes [q.v.] refused to be his political editor, his enthusiasm waned. After a short stay in Uralla, in 1875 Dean bought a store in Grafton and entered local politics. He became mayor in 1878 but was removed within six months for 'gross mismanagement'. His intention to stand again for parliament aroused opposition and he retired to write an autobiography, but a flood carried away his papers and ruined his store. He died on 8 May 1887, survived by four sons and four daughters; his wife predeceased him by seven weeks. His estate was valued at £7236.

Grafton and district . . . Fifty years of progress 1859-1909 (Syd, 1909); F. A. Fitzpatrick, *Peeps into the past* (Parramattta, 1914); *Government Gazette* (SA), 3 Oct.1850, 19 Feb 1852, 27 Jan 1853; *Register* (Adel), 10 Nov 1849, 2 Jan-18 July 1857; *SMH*, 6-24 Dec 1869, 7 May, 23 June, 8 July, 24 Sept 1870; *Empire* (Syd), 24 Sept 1870; *Clarence & Richmond Examiner*, 16 Feb, 17 Aug-14 Sept 1878, 10 May 1887; Parkes letters (ML); D. McFarlane newspaper cuttings (ML); information from George Clinch, Petersham, NSW.   RUTH TEALE

DE BOOS, CHARLES EDWARD AUGUSTUS (1819-1900), journalist and police magistrate, was born on 24 May 1819 in London, son of Henry Charles de Boos and reputedly grandson of a French count. After education at Addiscombe, Surrey, he went to Spain as a volunteer in the Carlist war. He went to Sydney in 1839 and took up land on the Hunter River. Unsuccessful on the land, he became a journalist first on the *Monitor*, then the *Sydney Gazette*. In 1851 he went to Melbourne and was commissioned by the *Argus* to report on the Victorian goldfields. He spent five months at Ballarat, Forest Creek and Bendigo, and in 1853 went to the Ovens on a similar mission. In 1854 he became a shorthand writer in the Victorian Legislative Council. In 1856 de Boos returned to Sydney and

joined the *Sydney Morning Herald*. In the first parliamentary recess he visited the New South Wales goldfields and as the *Herald's* special correspondent later reported on all the newly-discovered fields. The knowledge he acquired of mining, its laws and the needs of miners was later to benefit him. In 1862 he created the countryman, 'Mr John Smith', who described the doings of parliament and the politicians in a primitive form of 'Strine'. 'John Smith' was resurrected in the *Sydney Mail* and *Herald* during the duke of Edinburgh's visit in 1868, and again in 1870 after a tense election. *The Congewoi Correspondence*, 'letters of Mr. John Smith edited by Mr. Chas De Boos', was published in 1874. The most enduring work of de Boos was as the *Herald's* parliamentary reporter. After a century his weekly column, 'The Collective Wisdom of New South Wales' in 1867-73, still brings to life a host of politicians and well-known figures, for his quick ear caught many exchanges omitted in the official reports. In 1867 de Boos published, first as a serial, *Fifty Years Ago: An Australian Tale* and dedicated it to John Fairfax [q.v]. A revised edition appeared in 1906 as *Settler and Savage*. In 1871 his 'Random Notes by a Wandering Reporter' recorded his impressions of New South Wales.

De Boos's evidence before the 1870 royal commission on the goldfields led to his appointment in January 1875 as mining warden of the Southern Tumut and Adelong mining districts, and in May as a magistrate. In December 1879 he became warden for the Lachlan and in August 1880 for the Hunter and Macleay mining districts; he was also appointed police magistrate and coroner at Copeland. In 1881-82 at Temora de Boos was accused of partiality, insobriety and improper language. Three times in the Legislative Assembly in 1882 William Forster [q.v.] asked questions about his conduct and was told by the minister of justice that he had been reprimanded, although some of the complaints had not been substantiated. De Boos ceased to be a mining warden in July 1883 but remained police magistrate at Copeland until he retired on 15 June 1889. An obituarist claimed that he had more than justified his appointment as a mining warden and in 1881 had been presented with a gold medal 'as a mark of esteem' by Chinese miners in the Braidwood district. In retirement de Boos published several short stories. He was a prominent Freemason and a member of the New Brunswick Grand Lodge. He died on 30 October 1900 of senile decay at his daughter's home, Congewoi, Ryde. He was predeceased by his wife Sarah, née Stone, whom he had married in 1848, two sons and three daughters, and survived by one son and three daughters. He was buried in the Anglican section of Rookwood cemetery.

V&P (LA NSW), 1871-72, 2, 369, 1872-73, 2, 966, 1880-81, 1, 315, 1882, 1, 84, 111, 122, 1883-84, 4, 486; *Sydney Mail*, 1856-73; SMH, 1856-73, 31 Oct 1900; MS and printed cat under de Boos (ML).   L. V. HOLT

DE CASTELLA; *see* CASTELLA

DEFFELL, GEORGE HIBBERT (1819-1895), judge, was born on 30 May 1819 in London, the third son of John Henry Deffell, merchant, and his wife Elizabeth, née Mackenzie. He was educated at Harrow in 1832-37 and played in its cricket eleven. He graduated at Trinity College, Cambridge (B.A., 1842; M.A., 1845). He was admitted to the Inner Temple in 1839 and called to the Bar on 20 November 1846. On 10 July 1850 in London he married the 17-year-old Julia Gross of Ipswich, Suffolk: their only child, John Thomas, was born on 6 June 1851.

He arrived in Sydney on 6 January 1856 with his wife and child in the *La Hogue* and was admitted to the Bar of the New South Wales Supreme Court on 4 February. In directing Deffell's admission, Sir Alfred Stephen [q.v.] quoted a letter from Lord Campbell, a close friend of Deffell and his family, who believed that 'from his legal proficiency, honourable character, and agreeable manners, [Deffell] will be a valuable acquisition to the Sydney bar'.

In July he unsuccessfully applied for the chair of constitutional law or modern history at the University of Sydney, and on 25 August was appointed a commissioner for reporting upon claims to grants of land. In December he unsuccessfully applied to be appointed crown prosecutor in the Moreton Bay District, but on 1 April 1857 was appointed master in Equity of the Supreme Court of New South Wales. In June 1865 he was persuaded to accept the appointment of chief commissioner of insolvent estates and, as an economy measure, to continue to carry on the mastership temporarily until the administration of the Equity Court was amended. He became chief commissioner on 30 June and prepared a draft amendment bill but the government delayed dealing with it and he soon found that he could not perform both offices. He then tried to resign as master, persisted in his attempts and finally had to support them with the opinions of the judges that it was impossible for him to continue 'without a denial of justice pro tanto to suitors and to creditors and insol-

vents'. Only then was he relieved of his position as master in May 1866.

In the last half of 1887 the unprecedented course was taken by the government of passing three separate Acts to enable Deffell to perform different functions in the Supreme Court. Two of these Acts were required because an insufficient number of Supreme Court judges were available to constitute a full court of three to hear a number of appeals then pending and great hardship was being suffered by some litigants. An Act was quickly passed appointing Deffell to assist in disposing of sixteen of these appeals and he was sworn in as a temporary judge for that limited purpose on 15 August 1887. After only six appeals had been dealt with, another judge became unavailable through illness. No further appeals could be heard and, while Deffell could find nothing to do, the government had to appoint a barrister to hold a circuit court. Another Act was then rushed through parliament to give him further powers of a puisne judge until 28 December 1887, by which time the new bankruptcy bill was expected to be in force.

Deffell was largely instrumental in bringing about the much needed reforms in bankruptcy law because he considered the forty-six-year-old Act which he had had to administer a scandal and disgrace to the jurisprudence of the country. He was acknowledged as a most experienced administrator of the bankruptcy law, as well as a painstaking and capable equity man, and his accomplishments were lauded in parliament when the bankruptcy bill was debated. In consequence a third Act, the Bankruptcy Act of 1887, provided for his appointment as the first judge in bankruptcy and a judge of the Supreme Court; he was sworn in on 3 January 1888.

Ill health compelled Deffell to retire on 9 November 1889. He had lived for many years at Bayfield, Hunter's Hill, on the river front where his stone jetty was renowned for blackbream fishing. Two days after he retired, he and his wife left in the *Arcadia* for England, followed by a launch chartered by many legal friends whose cheers farewelled him at the Heads. The hope had been expressed that, when his health was restored, he might return to serve the colony with his wealth of experience and legal knowledge, but he remained in England and died at Tunbridge Wells on 21 September 1895.

Government-Gazette (NSW), 26 Aug 1856, 3 Apr 1857, 30 June 1865; S. A. Donaldson letters (ML); Macarthur papers (ML); documents formerly held by F. H. Deffell (ML).

                                        H. T. E. HOLT

DEGOTARDI, JOHN (1823-1882), printer and photographer, was born on 26 September 1823 at Laibach (Ljubljana), Yugoslavia, son of John Degotardi, a printer of Graz, Austria. As a young man he travelled in Germany, Switzerland, France and Denmark. In 1848 he became a compositor with the firm of J. Wertheim in London. There in 1852 he married Nina Frankel, whom he had met in Germany. Next year they arrived at Sydney in the *Panthea*. He worked briefly for the *Sydney Morning Herald* and then set up in business as an engraver and printer in premises at 20 York Street where he produced the first series of a monthly magazine, *The Spirit of the Age*, in 1855-56. By 1859 he had moved to Robin Hood Lane, off George Street. Among his best known productions were two sheet music editions of Henry Kendall's [q.v.] first separately-published song, *Silent Tears* (1859). Unfortunately several errors appeared in the words; the poet's letter of correction was printed in the *Empire*, but the words were engraved on copper and could not be changed.

Degotardi was always deeply interested in photography, but its appeal was quickened by the introduction of the wet-plate process and the invention of photolithography by J. W. Osborne [q.v.] of Melbourne in August 1859. Some of his experiments in photolithography are preserved by the family, one being a copy of a letter from Captain Cook to Joseph Banks [qq.v.]. In 1861 he printed privately a twenty-four page pamphlet, *The Art of Printing in its various branches*, the first publication on this topic to be issued in Australia; it is attractive typographically and includes examples of various methods of printing. On 26 September 1862 he advertised a perspective by photolithography of government buildings.

In the association of photography with printing, Degotardi was far ahead of his time; that he did not proceed to the etching of plates from photographic negatives, the next stage in photo-reproduction, was perhaps because of his failing health. He turned instead to landscape photography, for which there was a growing popular demand from a public tiring of steel engravings and chromolitho prints. His high standards won him awards at four exhibitions: Victoria in 1866, Sydney Intercolonial in 1870, London 'All Fine Arts' in 1873 and Sydney International in 1879. His last years were marred by his wife's death in 1872 and soon afterwards by a slight stroke. He died at St Vincent's Hospital, Sydney, on 16 December 1882, and was buried in the Catholic section of Rookwood cemetery. He was survived by three sons and one daughter of his eight children. Four generations of his descendants adopted photography as a profession.

Degotardi was the first Australian to realize the possibilities promised by the association of photography with printing. His pamphlet on printing contains a long and sincere panegyric on photography ending 'Photography will be handed down to posterity as the truest and most lasting monument to the combined powers of man, art and nature'.   KEAST BURKE

DEGRAVES, WILLIAM (1821-1883), flour-miller, merchant and station-owner, was born in England, the second son of Peter Degraves [q.v.] and his wife Sophia, née McIntosh. He began work in his father's flour-mill and shipyard at Hobart Town. In 1849 he went to Melbourne and with his brother Charles as partner sought a site for a steam flour-mill. For £2000 they bought an acre with a frontage to Flinders Lane and Degraves Street. Their mill, built in 1851, was said to have cost £10,000. William also became a director of the Hobson's Bay Railway Co. As an importer and buyer of gold and wool, he was soon a leading merchant. His three-storied Free and Bonded Stores, one of the earliest in Melbourne, was built in 1865 at the corner of Flinders and Russell Streets, on an acre that cost him £8000. His home was at 182 Collins Street and he owned several other houses.

The main business of William Degraves & Co. was in Melbourne but branches spread to other centres and included flour-mills at Sandhurst, Malmsbury and Kyneton, and warehouses in the main railway towns; one at Echuca was served by a branch line much to the annoyance of local merchants who resented the special treatment of influential persons. Degraves was a director of the Union Bank of Australia. As a station-owner and land speculator he held at various times the runs of Woorooma and Westmeath in the Riverina, Coliban Park and Campaspe Mills estate near Kyneton, North and South Woodlands in the east Wimmera, Silesian Downs at Mount Carmel, a property at Elphinstone, and pastoral leases in South Australia. In the 1860s he was acclaimed one of the leading sheep and cattle breeders in Australia, with studs of imported Rambouillet rams and Shorthorn bulls. He was honourably mentioned for wool exhibits at the Paris Exhibition of 1867 and the first president of the National Agricultural Society of Victoria, formed in 1871.

Degraves represented South Province in the Legislative Council from 18 September 1860 until 24 May 1874. He was a member of the committee appointed 16 March 1865 to confer with a Legislative Assembly committee on the deadlock between the Houses over a proposed amendment to the Land Act of 1862. He was also a member of the royal commission on the Public Works Department in January 1873 but was unable to give the necessary attendance to join in the report. He was a reactionary and a staunch opponent of parliamentary reform, outspoken in his distrust of the 'levelling-system' and seeing in universal suffrage the cause of all mismanagement of public affairs. An immigration scheme he advocated was based on free land grants rather than free passages, a system which he believed would attract 'a higher class of citizen' who would also bring their servants with them. He also supported all projects for railway extension and irrigation by locking rivers.

Degraves saw himself as a squatter rather than as a businessman and bitterly criticized the administration of the Lands Department for failing to protect the rights of pastoralists against selectors and land jobbers. His concern seems to have been well founded : at one time reputed the Rothschild of Australia, Degraves retired to Tasmania about 1875 much reduced in wealth. He died in Hobart on 20 March 1883, a few days after returning from a visit to England. He left an estate worth £19,200 to his wife Robina, daughter of Major James Fraser; they were married in 1850. His brother Charles died in 1874.

R. V. Billis and A. S. Kenyon, *Pastures new* (Melb, 1930); H. M. Eastman, *Memoirs of a sheepman* (Deniliquin, 1953); R. B. Ronald, *The Riverina: people and properties* (Melb, 1960); Sel cttee on private wharf claims, Evidence, V&P (LA Vic), 1864, 1 (D16); E. A. Mackay, 'The first flour mills of Port Phillip', VHM, 16 (1937) no 4; *Illustrated Melb Post*, 25 May 1865; *Mercury*, 21 Mar 1883.

PATSY HARDY

DELANY, JOHN ALBERT (1852-1907), musician, was born on 6 July 1852 at Ratcliff, London, son of John Daniel Delany, journalist, and his wife Marie, née Walters. He went with his parents to New South Wales in infancy and had his first musical tuition at Newcastle where his father established a newspaper. Educated in Sydney by the Benedictine monks at Lyndhurst College, he began to study music with William John Cordner [q.v.], organist of St Mary's Cathedral, and joined the orchestra of the Victoria Theatre as a violinist.

In 1872 Delany was appointed choirmaster at the cathedral and organist in 1874 but resigned in 1877 to join the Lyster [q.v.] Opera Company in Melbourne as chorus-master. After some years with itinerant musical companies he returned to Sydney to take up a special appointment in September 1882 as musical director of the three-day celebrations marking the opening of the northern end of St Mary's Cathedral, in honour of which he composed his 'Triduum March'. After further travel he was appointed conductor at the Bijou Theatre, Melbourne, in 1884; next year he returned to Sydney to become conductor of the Liedertafel, a post which he retained until 1897; both Dame Nellie Melba and Ada Crossley made their Sydney débuts under his direction. In 1886 he was appointed musical director at St Mary's Cathedral where frequent changes in choirmasters had produced incongruities in choral standards. Delany set out to correct them by reintroducing plainsong and unaccompanied polyphony after years of neglect. His wide operatic training also qualified him to present polished performances of the concert Masses then popular. In 1894 Delany became a foundation member of the Sydney College of Music, a private conservatorium of which he later became chairman of the Board of Examiners. In 1895 on the death of N. G. Barnett [q.v.] he added the post of organist to his other duties at the cathedral. On the inauguration of the Commonwealth in 1901 he conducted the massed choirs in Centennial Park and was one of the conductors at the State concert attended by the duke of York. His greatest achievement was the presentation of the Australian *première* of Sir Edward Elgar's oratorio 'The Dream of Gerontius' in Sydney Town Hall on 21 December 1903, to mark the golden jubilee of the ordination of Patrick Francis Moran, archbishop of Sydney, who presented him with a papal decoration. Delany died at Paddington on 11 May 1907 and was buried in Waverley cemetery beneath a monument engraved with a theme from one of his Masses. His wife Jane Ann, née Sharp, whom he married in Sydney in 1872, had died in 1887 and he was survived by their two daughters, one of whom, Louisa Lilian Tridua, was named in honour of the Triduum of 1882 during which she was born.

Delany was a composer of considerable output, producing two Masses, many motets and a cantata, 'Captain Cook', to words by P. E. Quinn. Little of his work was published, although his 'Song of the Commonwealth', composed for the swearing-in 'of Lord Hopetoun as governor-general in 1901, was reissued in 1951 as a Catholic contribution to the Commonwealth golden jubilee. He was successful as a teacher and his best-known pupil, Harry Barton Dawkins, succeeded him as organist of St Mary's Cathedral. Delany's most important contribution to Australian music was as a conductor. The *première* of 'The Dream of Gerontius' showed both his skill and boldness in attempting so elaborate a work demanding unusually large orchestral and choral resources when its few performances in England had met with hostile criticism. His musical tastes were broad and even before the musical reforms of Pius X in 1903 he had advocated a re-evaluation of plain-song which he thought a superior form of church music to renaissance polyphony. He had great personal charm and was a witty and engaging conversationalist.

E. J. Lea-Scarlett, 'The music of St Mary's Cathedral, Sydney', Organ Soc, Syd, *J*, 2 (1964), 3 (1965); *Freeman's J* (Syd), 16 May 1907.

E. J. LEA-SCARLETT

DE LISSA, ALFRED (1838-1913), solicitor, was born in London, son of Solomon Aaron de Lissa and his wife Rosetta, née Solomon. After study at University College, London, he arrived in Sydney in 1854 with his family. His father set up as a cabinet maker and upholsterer but in October 1856 was declared bankrupt. Soon afterwards he began as an optician and in July 1861 was again insolvent. Alfred was articled to Want & Johnson [qq.v.] and was admitted a solicitor on 31 March 1866. Till 1878 he was a partner of David Lawrence Levy; he then practised alone and won repute in trademark cases. As one of the oldest practising solicitors in Sydney, he retired in 1912. He was a founder and first secretary of the Incorporated Law Institute of New South Wales.

De Lissa specialized in company law: he was a publicist with an elaborate and sometimes florid style. His first work, *Bankruptcy and Insolvency Law* (Sydney, 1881), advocated a legal limit of liability to prevent a trader from incurring debts of more than four times his capital, and a reform in the administration of insolvent estates by placing them under a 'bureau of insolvency', not the law courts. More substantial was his *Companies' Work and Mining Law in New South Wales and Victoria* (Sydney, 1894), in which he tabulated procedures for joint-stock companies. He also published *The Codification of Mercantile Law* (Sydney, 1897), a lecture to the conference of Australasian Chambers of Commerce, and *The Bill of Lading Question and Marine Insurance Policies*, read to the Institute of Bankers in August 1901.

On the eve of sailing for England in 1887 de Lissa had tried to interest Parkes [q.v.] in a finance company to introduce English capital 'for all kinds of industrial enterprise'.

In the financial crisis he assumed that the trend toward socialism was due to insufficient government intervention. On this theory he published several pamphlets in Sydney. His lecture, *Protection and Federation*, to the Granville School of Arts was chaired by Edmund Barton. His *Law of the Incomes* (1890), proposed a more equitable distribution between the incomes of workers and capitalists, a theme later developed in *Production, Distribution and Quesnay's Tableau Economique* (Sydney, 1896). In *The Labour Problem* (1891) he advocated a government bureau of industry to issue licences for restricting competition and limiting capital and employment in private industries. In January 1892 his lecture, 'The Organization of Industry', to the Hobart meeting of the Australasian Association for the Advancement of Science enlarged upon this system, hoping that in Australia at least, 'labour and capital may join hand in hand in the proud work of Anglo-Saxon progress'. In *Credit, Currency, and a National Bank* (1891), he showed that Australian banks were not overcommitted, and did not need a national bank. He lectured to the Institute of Bankers against *Bi-Metallism: or The Silver Question* (1892) and in *An Empire League: [by] Hoc Vincet Omnia* (1905) envisaged a British customs union with preferential tariff.

At Melbourne in 1873 de Lissa married Elizabeth, née Hart. A practising Jew, he had long been auditor of the Great Synagogue. He died on 25 February 1913 in Sydney, his debts greatly exceeding his assets. He was survived by his wife and two daughters; his son Horace, admitted a barrister on 14 November 1901, had died in 1912 in a riding accident.

C. D. W. Goodwin, *Economic enquiry in Australia* (Durham, N.C., 1966); *Hebrew Standard of A'sia*, 28 Feb 1913; *SMH*, 26 Feb 1913; *Telegraph* (Syd), 26 Feb 1913; Parkes letters (ML); Bankruptcy papers under de Lissa (NSWA).

RUTH TEALE

DE MESTRE, ETIENNE LIVINGSTONE (1832-1916), studmaster and turf identity, was born on 9 April 1832 at Sydney, the third son of Prosper de Mestre [q.v.], merchant, and his wife Mary Ann, née Black. He was an excellent horseman and at 15 he won a main event at the Bathurst races on his own horse Sweetheart. His father had taken up land at Terara near the mouth of the Shoalhaven River, where in the 1850s Etienne established a horse stud, stable and racetrack. He soon proved himself a successful trainer and South Coast and Monaro squatters were eager to add their most promising horses to his 'string'.

In 1859 he trained Veno, the winner of the first intercolonial Champion Challenge race in Melbourne. In 1861 and 1862 de Mestre won the first two Melbourne Cups with his horse Archer. In 1863 de Mestre again planned to run Archer despite his weight of 11 stone 4 pounds, but the Victoria Racing Club scratched him because de Mestre's telegraphed acceptance arrived late. De Mestre said he would never race again in Victoria, and other owners scratched their horses in sympathy. However, in 1867 with Tim Whiffler de Mestre won again, but by 1876 his rival 'Honest' John Tait [q.v.] had four wins to de Mestre's three. In that year ill-fortune prevented him from squaring the score when the *City of Melbourne*, carrying his entry Robin Hood from Sydney to Melbourne, ran into a heavy gale and nine horses including de Mestre's champion perished. Next year he won with Chester, owned by James White [q.v.], and his win in 1878 with Calamia gave him a record. De Mestre also won most of the other classic turf events in New South Wales and Victoria at least once.

He was closely associated with the brothers C. B. [q.v.] and H. Fisher and acquired some good stock at the dispersal of the Maribyrnong stud in 1877. But many of his best mares died during their first winter at Terara and his stud's progeny proved disappointing. Drought ruined his pastoral investments in Queensland. He ran into financial difficulties and his health failed.

Well again, he tried to recoup his losses by coupling two of his horses, Navigator and Gudarz, for the 1882 Victorian Derby and Melbourne Cup in the biggest single bet ever laid in the colonies to that time. Navigator won but Gudarz ran third, and though de Mestre was the largest winner over the whole meeting he was ruined. Some minor wins at the Shoalhaven Club averted final disaster for a few months, but in 1883 Terara was auctioned and the all-black livery of the Terara stable disappeared from the colonial racing world.

Gifts and loans from his numerous friends together with the proceeds of a special race meeting, held at Randwick to mark his retirement from the turf, enabled him to take up a small farm, Garryowen, at Moss Vale, where he died on 22 October 1916. He was buried in the Church of England cemetery at Bong Bong.

At St Matthias's Church, Paddington, on 27 December 1873 he had married Clara Eliza, daughter of George Rowe [q.v.] and sister of George W. S. Rowe, secretary of the Rosehill Racing Club; they had five sons and five daughters. The eldest son Etienne George (b. 1874) became a horse-trainer in England; the third son Hurtle Edwin (b. 1881) went to the Boer war and later took up the management of a leading stud in South Africa; the fourth son Edward McKenzie (b. 1887) settled at Binalong in New South Wales; the youngest son Leroy Leveson Laurent Joseph (Roy de Maistre, 1894-1968) achieved much success as an artist.

N. J. de Mestre, 'An account of the de Mestre family in Australia', *Descent*, 3 (1967-68), nos 3, 4; *SMH*, 13 Sept 1876, 8 Nov 1882, 23 Oct 1916, 29 Oct 1960; *Daily Telegraph* (Syd), 23 Oct 1916; *Daily Mirror* (Syd), 25 June 1960.

G. P. WALSH

DEMPSTER, JAMES McLEAN (1810-1890), mariner and grazier, was born in June 1810 in Scotland, on his father's estate, Muresk. At 14 he ran away to sea and gained his master's ticket ten years later. In 1829 he was engaged by Captain Charles Pratt to skipper his *Eagle*, in which the Pratt family migrated to the Swan River settlement, arriving in January 1830. A few years later, despite parental opposition, Dempster married Pratt's daughter, Anne Ellen; they had seven children.

A colourful character with a liking for adventure, Dempster had a varied career. Soon after he arrived at Fremantle he bought the schooner *Mary Ann*, 120 tons, in which he traded between Australia and Mauritius and then tried pearling on the north-west coast. After his marriage Dempster took up land on Rottnest Island where he grew hay and bred horses with some success and probably supervised the construction of some of the first buildings. He received much publicity in September 1838 when he took a whaleboat and Aboriginal crew to rescue the complement of the *Lancier* wrecked on Straggler Reefs. He was duly rewarded by the government of Mauritius despite the accidental loss of a chest with 5000 sovereigns. From Rottnest he moved to the Beverley district, where he established the property Addington. He had some trouble with Aboriginals and was reputed to have shot Turkey Cock, a notorious fellow who was chasing him with spear poised.

Dempster managed Buckland, his father-in-law's 8000-acre estate near Northam, but soon fell out with Pratt, returned to the sea and took sheep and the bloodhorse, Sonnambulist, to Mauritius. The venture was unsuccessful and Dempster went to Rottnest as superintendent of the penal settlement in April 1850. He became reconciled with Pratt and on 2 April 1853 returned to Buckland, where he died in May 1890. His wife had died on 6 August 1880 and on 31 December he married Hester Frances Shaw.

Two sons of Dempster's first marriage,

CHARLES EDWARD (b. Fremantle, 19 December 1839) and ANDREW (b. 2 February 1843), achieved distinction for their explorations, pioneering and community work. Their first expedition, thirty miles east of Roe's [q.v.] 1836 expedition, resulted in a grant from the government for further exploration. In 1861 with C. Harper [q.v.] and D. Clarkson the brothers pushed east, through rough scrub and salt-lake country to the Georgina Range. For their report on gold-bearing country near Yilgarn they received a reward of £500. In 1863 with government and private sponsorship the Dempster brothers chartered the *Emelia* and explored the south coast to Israelite Bay. Leaving the main party to return by sea, Charles and Andrew went by land to Esperance and thence to Perth, thus opening up a stock route. In August the Dempster brothers leased 304,000 acres at Esperance and stocked it with sheep, cattle and horses. With great ability and sound bushcraft the brothers took their stock overland with very slight loss. Charles farmed at Esperance until 1866 when he went to manage Buckland, which he later inherited. On 17 March 1867 he married Mary Margaret, daughter of Patrick Taylor, farmer of Albany, and his wife Mary Yates, née Bussell. He severed his connexion with Buckland in 1877 and went into business as a miller and storekeeper at Toodyay until he moved to Springfield, near Northam, in 1886.

He was nominated to the Legislative Council by Governor Weld, and represented Toodyay in 1873-74 and Eastern Province in 1894-1907. According to the press, he was a politician who 'never aspired to high places, yet as a man, his rugged individuality has won him a host of friends and admirers'. He was a justice of the peace, member of the Northam Roads Board and Agricultural Society, and a keen sportsman with an active interest in the turf, owning several notable race-horses. He died at Sydney on 22 July 1907 and was buried at Northam.

Andrew continued his pioneering activities at Esperance. He employed many ticket-of-leave men as shepherds and as builders of his beautiful limestone house, designed by his brother James and built for his bride Mary Emily Marsden whom Andrew married on 28 August 1867; she was a step-daughter of Rev. Charles Clay and a descendant of Samuel Marsden [q.v.]. Although farming had been reasonably profitable in the initial stages the sheep were soon affected with coast disease because the soil lacked cobalt. Dempster sought new pastures, first in the Dundas Hills, and in 1866 he established a property in the Fraser Range. He also acquired the cutter *Gypsy*, 20 tons, in which he took his wool to Ade-laide, fetched stores from Fremantle, carried sheep to the islands round Esperance and hunted seals, their skins selling for 30s. each. In 1875 he moved to Toodyay, but returned to Esperance in 1878 with a contract to build the police station. His interest in Esperance waned after his wife died on 12 October 1888, and near Northam he acquired a property which he named Muresk. He represented Eastern Province in the Legislative Council in 1903-04. He married a widow, Sarah Roe, née Clarkson, on 21 January 1891 and died on 6 March 1909.

The Avon Valley (Northam, 1905); PD (WA), 1907, 31, 355; *Perth Gazette*, 20 July 1860; *Northam Advertiser*, 24 July 1907; *Western Mail* (Perth), 27 July 1907; *West Australian*, 8 Aug 1907; *Muresk Mag*, Sept 1928; Dempster family papers (Battye Lib, Perth).

WENDY BIRMAN

DENIEHY, DANIEL HENRY (1828-1865), orator, man of letters, lawyer and politician, was born in Sydney on 18 August 1828, the only son of Henry Deniehy (d. 1850), produce merchant, and his wife Mary, née MacCarthy (d. 1883); he was baptized on 28 August in St Mary's Church. His father received a seven-year sentence at Cork for vagrancy in 1819 and arrived in the ship *Hadlow* in August 1820; his mother, also with a seven-year sentence, arrived in the ship *Almorah* in August 1824.

Deniehy was a precocious child and his parents recognized and cultivated his unusual talents. At several schools he studied French, Italian, classics and English literature and his teachers and tutors admired his quick and retentive memory. W. B. Dalley [q.v.] was a boyhood friend, and the artist Adelaide Ironside [q.v.] an early associate.

At 14 he went to England with his parents and read for a time with a university tutor; he visited many of the major art centres on the Continent and spent 'a swallow's season' in Ireland, where he met and was deeply impressed by leaders of the Young Ireland Party. He returned to Sydney in the immigrant ship *Elizabeth* on 29 April 1844, continued his schooling and was articled to the solicitor N. D. Stenhouse [q.v.]. In 1844 he published a novelette 'Love at First Sight' in the *Colonial Literary Journal;* he wrote criticism for the *People's Advocate,* and in 1847 some youthful verse in *Heads of the People.* Deniehy's association with Stenhouse gave him access to a fine library and he began forming his own famous library, later reputed to weigh over four tons. He was admitted as a solicitor on 3 May 1851. He did well at the law but gradually his love of literature prevailed and he became involved in radical politics. In 1851-53 he gave a number of lectures on poetry and French literature to the Sydney Mechanics' School of Arts.

In 1850 Deniehy fervently supported Rev. J. D. Lang's [q.v.] Australian League and worked with the liberal Constitution committee. Known as 'the boy orator', on 15 August 1853 he publicly derided W. C. Wentworth's [q.v.] proposed colonial nobility as 'a bunyip aristocracy', and soon ridiculed the scheme into oblivion. In 1854 he went to Goulburn to benefit his health and legal practice. A temporary estrangement from Henry Parkes [q.v.] was followed in December 1854 by a letter in which he indicated his misgivings about entering politics: 'My education, in the deep sense of the world, is not yet complete—I have not yet built myself into what I conceive to be the requisite spiritual and mental proportions—I have not yet learnt, thought, and observed enough'. Letters to Parkes in 1855 show an increasing political interest but no urgency to enter politics. However, after a stirring nomination speech that repeated his inner doubts, he won Argyle and as 'an extreme liberal' represented it from 13 February 1857 to 11 April 1859.

He made many excellent parliamentary speeches, particularly those on the land bill (1857), the electoral reform and the Chinese immigration bills (1858). In 1858 he returned to Sydney and was in great demand as an occasional speaker. His fame spread to Victoria and in September he spoke in Melbourne on the land bill and argued that 'the first great aim of statesmanship in a new country should be to people the soil,—in a word, to create a great community'. In the second Cowper [q.v.] ministry Deniehy opposed the appointment of L. H. Bayley [q.v.] as attorney-general, and immortalized the whole incident in a pungent satire entitled How I Became Attorney-General of New Barataria (Sydney, 1860); first published in the Southern Cross, which Deniehy founded in 1859 and edited, it is his longest written piece and his monument as a political satirist.

Deniehy still devoted much time to literature. In November 1857 he lectured approvingly on the poetry of his friend Charles Harpur [q.v.]. He also recognized the quality of William Forster's [q.v.] poetry. He wrote on a variety of topics for the Freeman's Journal, Southern Cross and other journals; in 1859-60 he composed a number of excellent obituary notices on eminent men of letters including his exemplar, Thomas De Quincey.

Deniehy's principles and independence brought him into conflict with his Church, first in January 1859 over his opposition to extra state aid and next month over Abbot Gregory's [q.v.] nomination of a Protestant to the Catholic orphanage at Parramatta. Deniehy addressed a protest meeting which found Gregory's act 'repugnant to the simplest Catholic interests' and passed a vote of no confidence in the Church administration. A committee of seven including Deniehy forwarded the resolutions to Archbishop Polding [q.v.] who demanded that the seven recant under pain of excommunication. They submitted except Deniehy, but all appealed to Rome.

In Deniehy's last term in parliament, representing East Macquarie from May to November 1860, he became extremely disillusioned with the moral tone of politics and politicians. Refusing to compromise his principles, he alienated even his best friends, and took to drink. His notable political work was on the land question, in particular some of the key clauses of the Robertson [q.v.] Land Act.

In 1862 Deniehy and his family went to Melbourne and he edited the Victorian. Rehabilitated for a time he wrote well, but after the death of his only surviving son he relapsed. The paper closed in April 1864 and he returned to Sydney to resume his legal practice. Henry Kendall [q.v.] noticed in him 'some flashes of the old light' even though most of his mental and physical strength had gone. 'It is bad at this time of day, this beginning the world over again; but it must be done now or never' he wrote to his wife in October. In a last desperate effort to restore himself he went to Bathurst, where, wavering between deep despair and flashes of optimism, he sank into complete alcoholism.

On 22 October 1865 in a Bathurst street Deniehy fell and struck his head. He died in hospital from 'loss of blood and fits induced by habits of intemperance'. Two days later a handful of mourners accompanied his body to the old Catholic cemetery. Peter White, the clerk of petty sessions, incurred the displeasure of the Church for reading the burial service.

Deniehy, slender of limb and delicately made, stood about 5 ft. 2 ins.; his face was freckled and his ample brow was overlaid by a shock of flaxen hair. His manners and speech were correct and his laugh bright and clear. His verse is generally facile and undistinguished, but his speeches are excellent examples of Irish oratory. His literary criticism, though highly praised by David Blair, G. B. Barton, Frank Fowler [qq.v.] and Sir Edward Bulwer Lytton, is somewhat marred by reckless superlatives and copious allusions. As a critic he believed that 'Criticism should be gentle' because 'all life, literature, politics are but processes of approximation'.

He ranged sensitively over the whole field of modern letters, from Stendahl to Emerson, from Heine to Mrs Jamieson with, as Walter Murdoch says, 'his bright intelligence and swift appreciation'.

He saw the colonial *milieu* as 'darkened by the nature and occasion of its first settlement and by the black history of its first decades' where 'Art had done nothing, but Nature everything'. He inexorably isolated himself from this environment and was finally defeated by it. Colonial society was harsh and generally unaccommodating to a man of his temperament, insight and sensitivity; and his life ended in mortification, personal tragedy and failure.

Deniehy left very little evidence by which to judge his undoubted political and literary talents and great human qualities. Any assessment of his importance must also consider his contemporaries' opinions, which are compelling even allowing for the Victorian weakness for 'young, blighted genius'. Many praised Deniehy's unassuming manner, warm-hearted and generous disposition, as well as his learning, wit and vivacity. Dalley, Barton and Stenhouse regarded him as one of the most gifted men that the colony had produced. To R. H. Horne [q.v.] Deniehy was the 'brightest spirit' of all young Australians. In 1883 Dalley recalled him as 'the most gifted Irish-Australian of our history' and said he might easily have occupied 'the highest place among the most gifted and honoured of modern Irishmen'. In September 1888 Daniel O'Connor [q.v.] and a group of admirers had Deniehy's remains removed from Bathurst and interred in Waverley cemetery by the Franciscan fathers. Over his grave a tall monument was erected 'as an admiring tribute to the graceful genius of one of Australia's most gifted and patriotic sons', with the verse,

The Vehement Voice Of The South,
Is Loud Where The Journalist Lies;
But Calm Hath Encompassed His Mouth,
And Sweet Is The Peace In His Eyes.

On 24 February 1852 at Sydney, Deniehy had married Adelaide Elizabeth, only daughter of John Casimir Hoalls, gentleman, and his wife Mary Elizabeth, née English. They had two sons and five daughters. He was survived by his wife and three daughters. On 7 July 1877 Deniehy's widow married John McGarvie Smith; there were no children. She died at Woollahra on 31 December 1908, aged 78, and was buried in the Church of England section of Waverley cemetery.

A statue of Deniehy by James White is on the Lands Department building in Sydney.

G. B. Barton, *Literature in New South Wales* (Syd, 1866); G. B. Barton (ed), *The poets and prose writers of New South Wales* (Syd, 1866); E. A. Martin, *The life and speeches of Daniel Henry Deniehy* (Melb, 1884); J. Normington-Rawling, *Charles Harpur, an Australian* (Syd, 1962); P. Loveday and A. W. Martin, *Parliament factions and parties* (Melb, 1966); B. T. Dowd, 'Daniel Henry Deniehy', *JRAHS*, 33 (1947); *Austral Light*, Apr 1894; *SMH*, 16 Aug 1853, 19 Feb 1857, 5, 13 Jan, 9, 28 Feb, 4 Mar 1859, 27 Oct 1865; *Freeman's J* (Syd), 19 Mar 1859, 28 Oct 1865, 13 May 1883; *Bathurst Times*, 25 Oct 1865; *Aust J*, Oct 1869; *Bulletin*, 15 Apr 1882, 1-29 Sept, 6 Oct 1888; *Town and Country J*, 17 Mar 1888; Parkes letters (ML).

G. P. WALSH

DENISON, SIR WILLIAM THOMAS (1804-1871), governor-general, was born on 3 May 1804 in London, son of John Denison and his second wife Charlotte, née Estwick. Like his brothers Evelyn (Viscount Ossington) and Edward (bishop of Salisbury) he went to Eton; he later entered the Royal Military College, graduating in 1826 as a lieutenant in the Royal Engineers. He worked on the Rideau Canal in Canada and won the prized Telford silver medal for an essay on timbers. He returned to England in 1832 and was the first editor of *Papers on subjects connected with the duties of the Corps of Royal Engineers.* He also instructed engineer cadets at Chatham where he set up an observatory, and later as an Admiralty officer he supervised the building and repair of dockyards and other works at Portsmouth, Woolwich and Bermuda. In November 1838 he married Caroline, daughter of Sir Phipps Hornby.

In April 1846 Gladstone dismissed Sir John Eardley-Wilmot from Van Diemen's Land and appointed Denison as lieutgovernor. Earl Grey, who succeeded Gladstone, endorsed Denison's appointment and had him knighted. After five months in the Colonial Office Denison sailed from Spithead and reached Hobart Town on 25 January 1847. He came with preconceived notions about punishment. To him its purpose was to deter : convicts were evil-doers and talk of their reform was 'maudlin sentimentality'. Since he believed that 'idleness . . . is at the root of ninety crimes out of a hundred', he wanted imprisonment to be accompanied by enforced labour, the prisoners to be encouraged by the prospect of tangible rewards with provision for their separate confinement when not at work or meals or during their instruction. His conviction was that 'to everyman the full penalty which the law allots to his offence should be meted out'.

In the colony he found various systems of punishment had been attempted. He was also to find in Grey a superior who had studied the subject more than he had. Denison had to implement a system that he thought defective but, set in his opinions, he modified wherever he could. When he arrived some 29,000 of the colony's population were under sentence. Their number had increased sharply after transportation to New South Wales had been discontinued in 1840 and the Colonial Office realized that the flow must be temporarily arrested. In May 1846 Gladstone had suspended the transportation of males to Van Diemen's Land for two years. Grey endorsed this decision and on 5 February 1847 wrote to Denison: 'it is not the intention that transportation should be resumed at the expiration of the two years'. By mischance, 'under the present system' had been omitted after 'transportation', but Denison took the dispatch to mean what it said; he also read it to his Legislative Council and told Grey that it was desirable to carry out fully the intention expressed. When he realized that Grey had meant no more than a change in the system when transportation was resumed, he felt bound to implement the Crown's policy. Thus he became the head of those in the colony who advocated continuance.

Denison had already antagonized some local leaders by his maladroit handling of a situation inherited from Eardley-Wilmot. By 1844 the annual cost of the island's police and gaols had risen to £36,737. In 1846 the British Treasury agreed to pay two-thirds of it but meanwhile the six unofficial nominees in the Legislative Council had become so incensed by the cost that they had resigned in October 1845, thus depriving Eardley-Wilmot of a quorum in the council. He had promptly replaced them by six other nominees all validly seated pending decision by the Colonial Office on the fate of the so-called Patriotic Six. The Colonial Office decided that the Patriotic Six had a case; Denison was advised to select the six most suitable of the twelve councillors but was given no formal instruments to appoint them lawfully. Probably Grey expected Denison to submit his selections to London so that the appointments could be approved and the others disallowed. After fruitless negotiations Denison declared the seats vacant and filled them with the Patriotic Six; on 20 July 1847 they were sworn in despite the doubts of the chief justice, Sir John Pedder [q.v.]. The dislodged men appealed to Grey who ordered the disallowance of their appointments and the approval of those made by Denison. He was also instructed to enact a statute giving retrospective validity to all the Acts 'of the present Councillors'. But no such measure was carried, for doubts had so shaken Deni-

son's confidence that on 30 July he had adjourned the council pending advice from London. He had acted impetuously, highhandedly and illegally but Grey chided him only for his 'errors of judgment'.

In 1846 the Legislative Council had enacted 'the Dog Act' (10 Vic. no 5), but its validity was successfully challenged in the Supreme Court in November 1847. Denison was disquieted when told that this decision adversely affected fifteen other revenue-providing local statutes and exposed about twenty more to legal challenge. All these could have been amended at once had the Legislative Council been able to function, but Denison decided to suspend his two judges and appoint 'others in their places'. The puisne judge, Algernon Montagu [q.v.], had already exposed himself to criticism and was dismissed on 30 December, but Pedder defended himself successfully before the Executive Council. At a public meeting on 15 January 1848 'the arbitrary and unconstitutional proceedings of the Lieutenant-Governor and his Executive Council' were vehemently condemned, and a petition was submitted to him for transmission to the Queen. 'The papers here', wrote Lady Denison, 'have never ceased predicting our recall', but Grey was content with a stern rebuke: he ascribed Denison's conduct to 'mistakes of judgment in a crisis of very unusual embarrassment' and avowed confidence in his ability.

The arrival of male convicts from May 1848 brought Denison more harassment not only from the Irish 'State prisoners' but also from the opponents of renewed transportation. Such colonial leaders as Richard Dry, Thomas Gregson and Michael Fenton [qq.v.], although prepared to return to the Legislative Council, were convinced that the burden on the colonial Treasury was intolerable. When Denison submitted the budget they rejected it but he decided to authorize government payments pending advice from London. Grey's advice would have disconcerted any man less self-assured than Denison: 'You are distinctly to understand that the course you have followed must not again be adopted should a similar case arise. You have taken upon yourself to contravene the fundamental law that renders the consent of the Legislature to the Estimates absolutely necessary'. An Indemnity Act was indispensable but since the Legislative Council was unlikely to pass it Grey decided to replace the dissentients by new members willing to approve the estimates. He gave the necessary instructions but enjoined Denison to avoid their use. Sir William was lucky. Three dissentients resigned and he replaced them with men on whom he could rely. The estimates were passed, but Denison's avowal that he had determined his course without consulting his legal advisers confirmed doubt of his knowledge of constitutional processes.

These shortcomings were offset by his zeal as an administrator. With competent help from such officers as James Bicheno, Peter Fraser, Adam Turnbull and Dr Hampton [qq.v.], Denison put the surveys on a sound footing, encouraged the use of local resources and introduced better methods of agriculture. As a skilled engineer he was specially interested in building docks, harbours and bridges, draining swamps, digging canals and extending irrigation. He had inherited a depleted Treasury and £92,000 of debts. His main sources of public revenue were from land and customs duties. While convicts might lawfully be transported, Van Diemen's Land was excepted from the Waste Lands Acts imposed on other Australian colonies, but the appropriation of land revenue remained in the Crown acting through the lieut-governor and his Executive Council. Denison used this power to strengthen the land fund by selling and leasing crown land, thus acquiring the means to open new country, test coal discoveries and liquidate the colony's debt. He had less freedom with customs duties but he believed in free trade and his changes in the tariff schedules were deemed by the Colonial Office to be 'judicious'.

One of Denison's abiding interests was education. He found that 6060 of the 9767 children in the colony between 4 and 14 were receiving no schooling. To meet this urgent need he introduced a bill in the council providing for an annual tax of 5s. on each free adult and dividing the colony into school districts, each controlled by a committee elected annually by those who paid the tax. His bill was rejected by the council. With characteristic pertinacity he reintroduced it twice but in vain. In 1853 he had to agree to a bill which threw the cost of schools on the colonial Treasury and provided for the control of education by a board whose secretary was the inspector-general, Thomas Arnold [q.v.]. The most acrimonious part of the debate on schooling was religious instruction. Sectarianism was rife and kept at high pitch by the Anglican Bishop Nixon, and the Presbyterian leader Lillie [qq.v.]. As a staunch Anglican, Denison frowned on such rivalries and favoured the scripture lessons of the Irish National system. The Church Act of 1837 (1 Vic. no 16) provided stipends for clergy of the Churches of England, Scotland and Rome, their entitlement dependent on the governor's approval of their appointment. Since each Anglican priest had to be licensed by the bishop, the head of the state and the

head of the church clashed, but the secular arm prevailed.

Constitution-making was a preoccupation of Earl Grey but, despite his clarity and understanding of the subject, he sought local opinion from the colonial governors. Denison did not fail him. On 15 August 1848 he recommended that, when the constitution of Van Diemen's Land was revised, it should provide for a bicameral legislature. Denison's report to Grey also included a derogatory appraisal of local society. His dispatch was confidential but it was laid on the table of the House of Commons and thus reached the colonial press. He was already unpopular for his advocacy of transportation and his overbearing methods, and this diatribe fanned the flames of local dissatisfaction. Grey, although partial to the bicameral system, decided to retain the unicameral system and the Constitution Act of 1850 (13 & 14 Vic. c. 59) empowered the establishment of a Legislative Council of twenty-four members, one-third appointed by the Crown and two-thirds elected.

Denison duly drafted a bill for the election of sixteen representatives, distributing them in a manner calculated 'to neutralize the radical tendencies of the towns'. In April 1851 he remarked, 'I do not despair of getting a Council in which the Government will have . . . a very strong minority despite all the storm getting up about transportation'. He belittled the leaders of the Anti-Transportation League which was formed at Launceston in January 1849 and by 1851 had developed into the Australasian League for the Abolition of Transportation. Underestimating its strength, he declared that were the question abstract he would be the first to pronounce against it, but he shared with Grey the view that cessation would injure the island's economy.

In the elections each of the sixteeen constituencies returned an anti-transportationist. Nomination to the other eight seats was left to Denison, subject to confirmation by the Colonial Office. They included Peter Fraser as acting colonial secretary, Adam Turnbull, Valentine Fleming and Francis Smith [qq.v.]. Grey and Denison attached great importance to the choice of the permanent colonial secretary. The former appointed H. S. Chapman [q.v.], who took office on 5 April 1852 when the relations between Sir William and the elected councillors were deteriorating. To Denison the gold rush to Victoria increased the colony's dependence on convict labour. The elected councillors, bent on implementing their constituents' mandate, planned to offset the exodus by subsidized immigration. On 14 September a motion requesting the Queen to revoke the Order in Council, in which

Van Diemen's Land and Norfolk Island were listed as places to which the empire's felons might be sent, was carried in the council by 16 votes to 4. For supporting the motion Turnbull and Chapman were both deprived of office. Denison commented in such terms on the motion that the council passed a motion of no confidence in him, and resolved that a copy be sent to London for publication in *The Times* and *Daily News*. Yet Denison was not without supporters. He was in the sixth year, the normal term of a governor, and the pouch which conveyed the no confidence motion also held a petition with 2220 signatures to extend his term.

Victorian gold relaxed the contention between governor and governed in the island. Sir John Pakington wrote to Denison on 14 December: 'Transportation would be disarmed of its terrors . . . if offenders should long continue to be sent to the Island in the immediate neighbourhood of the gold colonies of Australia'. Before this dispatch was sent the *St Vincent* had sailed from London, the last convict transport to eastern Australia. Denison did not cavil at this decision. He thought it unwise but it had been made by superior authority and he conceived it his duty to address himself loyally to the new situation. Thereafter his administration evoked general approbation.

One of his first actions was to ask the Colonial Office to give Van Diemen's Land equality with the mainland colonies in drafting its constitution. This request was granted and a new document was prepared by a committee elected by the Legislative Council on 25 April 1854. As passed on 31 October the Act (18 Vic. no 17) provided for a bicameral legislature: the Upper House was to have fifteen elected members and the House of Assembly thirty. Denison had kept in touch with the committee; he told it of the objections in London to the corresponding bill from New South Wales, with the result that Van Diemen's Land, although last of the four Australian colonies to draft its new Constitution, was first to win royal assent.

The end of transportation brought the island under the Waste Lands Act of 1842 and its regulations, a consequence that Denison and his legal advisers had overlooked. When it was pointed out by the Colonial Office, all the conflicting local regulations were suspended, but financial consequences were more serious. The Treasury commissioners in London decided to cease their annual contribution of £24,000 to the maintenance of the police and gaols; after hard bargaining Denison won agreement on a progressive reduction from 1 April 1854. More imperative was the sharp increase in the cost of living and in government salaries and wages. Governor and council agreed that the economic consequences of the gold mania could be offset only by increasing the colony's work force. Their immigration schemes did not please the Land and Emigration Commission in London and had to be revised, but a later plan which promised a steady stream of free people was accepted. Denison's resolute support of it helped to close the breach that had divided him from the council. This healing process was accelerated by his opposition to the Victorian Act to prevent the influx of 'Vandemonian' convicts with tickets-of-leave or conditional pardons. Denison secured some redress but the Victorian Legislative Council retained the substance of its defensive measure. Despite this lack of co-operation he sent troops to Melbourne when the *émeute* at Eureka led Sir Charles Hotham to invoke his aid.

The one questionable official act in Denison's last year in Hobart was his appointment of Valentine Fleming as chief justice when Pedder resigned in August 1854. The Colonial Office had preferred Thomas Horne [q.v.] but yielded when Denison emphasized 'the zeal, energy and courage with which Mr. Fleming had supported the Government'. One of Sir William's last official actions was to commend a petition from the Legislative Council that the island's name be changed to Tasmania. The request was granted and took effect on 1 January 1856. On 13 September 1854 Denison had acknowledged the dispatch appointing him governor of New South Wales. On 9 December he received two commissions, each dated 20 September, one as governor of New South Wales, the other as 'Governor-General in and over all our Colonies of New South Wales, Van Diemen's Land, Victoria, South Australia and Western Australia'. He sailed with his family for Sydney on 13 January 1855 after cordial farewells.

In his first year as governor-general, the Crimean war turned Denison's attention to the defence of Sydney against sea-borne attack. He strengthened the batteries at Dawes Point, hastened the building of a fort on Pinchgut (Fort Denison), installed other harbour batteries and provided for their manning by trained gunners. He then examined the Surveyor-General's Department and concluded that it required drastic overhaul. The death of Sir Thomas Mitchell [q.v.] relieved him of 'a great difficulty', and Colonel Barney [q.v.] was appointed surveyor-general. Public works were scrutinized and three commissioners appointed. In June the commissioner for railway construction sought Denison's advice on the vital issue of railway gauge. In July 1852 the directors of the Sydney Railway Co. had decided on a gauge of 5′ 3″ but in 1853 changed it to 4′ 8½″ which was used on the Sydney-Parramatta line opened by Denison in September 1855. Meanwhile the 5′ 3″ gauge had been adopted in South Australia and Victoria. The governor-general, unlike the Colonial Office, ignored the problems that would arise when lines differing in gauge reached the several borders.

As in Tasmania, Denison continued his interest in education. His visit to the two Orphan Schools at Parramatta led to a report from William Wilkins [q.v.] and two other inspectors 'to correct the minor evils of management' and plan for betterment. The Benevolent Society also attracted official attention but its honorary secretary, George Allen [q.v.], resisted intervention. In March Denison wrote to his mother : 'I have been hard at work for the last few days scheming out a plan of education'. His plan, presented to the Executive and Legislative Councils, was the same scheme for local school rates that he had tried to establish in Tasmania and had the same fate. He was able, however, to encourage the development of the infant University of Sydney and the Sydney Grammar School.

Denison presided on 14 May at the opening of the Sydney branch of the Royal Mint. Later he pressed the Colonial Office to give the new coinage the title of 'Coin of the Realm'. This was done in 1863 and by 1868 the Australian sovereign was legal tender throughout the Queen's dominions. Denison also enjoyed the mental stimulus of E. W. Ward and W. S. Jevons [qq.v.], officers of the Mint, and the two naturalists, Elsey and Mueller [qq.v.], who in 1856 went with A. C. Gregory's [q.v.] North Australian Expedition from the Victoria River to Brisbane. On their return Denison reported to London : 'Of this great continent, more than three-fourths is an absolute, howling wilderness', an astonishing deduction from the explorers' careful statements.

On 24 November 1855 Denison proclaimed the Constitution Act (17 Vic. no 41). With responsible government impending he was again sworn in as governor-general on 19 December under his new commission. His Executive Council ceased to function, although its members continued as heads of government departments and public business went on as usual. In need of advice, the governor-general constituted a provisional Executive Council of four 'gentlemen unconnected with party politics on whose impartiality and intelligence [he] could safely rely'. He soon found them inadequate and on 21 February 1856 gazetted Deas Thomson, Campbell Riddell and later Francis Merewether [qq.v.] as members of the provisional council. In accepting ap-

pointment Thomson stipulated that the council should do nothing 'which was not absolutely necessary . . . until the formal appointment of a responsible ministry', but much remained to be done before the Constitution became effective. The new parliament was to consist of an elected Legislative Assembly and a nominated Legislative Council. The first business, therefore, was the election of the new Legislative Assembly.

Since Denison declined to nominate the members of the Legislative Council until he had the advice of an Executive Council supported by a majority in the Legislative Assembly, he had to abide by the result of this election held between 11 March and 19 April. Thirty-four 'Conservatives' and twenty-four 'Liberals' were returned and Denison commissioned S. A. Donaldson [q.v.] to form a ministry. On 29 April Donaldson and his colleagues were sworn in as members of the Executive Council but the new ministers did not immediately take over their public departments. Had they done so, they would have become entitled to salaries with offices of profit under the Crown and obliged to resign and seek re-election. But no writs for such elections could be issued until the Legislative Council was created.

This complicated problem was happily solved when the existing departmental heads agreed to carry on until the Legislative Council was constituted, the parliament had met, the position of the ministry confirmed and provision made for the holding of elections for the vacated seats. Meanwhile the Executive Council, with Denison and his 'ministers without portfolios or salaries', prepared to nominate the members of the Legislative Council. On 29 April the names of suitable persons were listed, great care being taken to give representation to the various parties, creeds, classes and interests in the community. By the new Constitution their number was to be not less than twenty-one, but thirty-three took their seats when the Legislative Council was opened on 23 May. Soon afterwards Thomson and his colleagues were released and on 6 June Donaldson and his colleagues took the prescribed oaths of office and received their commissions. They were re-elected to the assembly and the establishment of responsible government in New South Wales was complete.

Throughout this transition Denison had been the leader. 'An unwilling instrument', he did not favour the change, but it had been so ordained and he implemented it with even temper, clarity of mind and expression, and a complete mastery of ways and means. Yet his insistence that the Executive Council 'should be recognized as the Governing Body' and that responsible government as it existed in England had not been established in New South Wales, brought some sharp exchanges between him and some of his ministers. His doubts were later strengthened by evidence of little 'instinct of party'. In private letters and sometimes in dispatches, Denison was harsh on his ministers: 'I have now been working responsible government for three years and a half . . . I have had five sets of Ministers besides numerous individual changes; not one single measure of social improvement has passed, and the only Acts of importance that have stood the ordeal are those of very questionable advantage'.

In 1857 he had written : 'The work of the Government is taken out of my hands, and placed in those of responsible Ministers as they are termed, so that I have less to think of in that way than I used to have; but I manage to make work for myself'. The Aboriginals posed one of many important problems in Tasmania. He had moved their remnants from Flinders Island to Oyster Bay and done what he could for their comfort. In New South Wales he was made pessimistic by reports on 'the native question'. In September 1858 he wrote to the Colonial Office: 'The physical peculiarities of the race, their want of stamina to resist the slightest access of disease, seem to render their gradual extinction a matter almost of necessity when coupled with the unproductiveness of the females'. Bulwer Lytton replied : 'I can only press upon the local Government the consideration that it is our duty, on Christian no less than on political grounds, not to relax our efforts in despair'. This dispatch reached Denison while he was engrossed with the establishment of Queensland, where the Aboriginals were more numerous and militant and their relations with the whites most inflamed. For those who remained in New South Wales he was quick to redress abuses that came to his notice but he never seemed to detect their spiritual malaise.

Denison doubted the wisdom of separating Queensland from New South Wales; the original decision of the Colonial Office placed the Clarence and New England districts in Queensland but Denison was able to have the boundary line changed to its present position. When the colony was established in 1859, he was given 'the very important duty of inaugurating [it] by appointing the Legislative Council and summoning the first Legislative Assembly'. With help from Sir George Bowen, Captain Wickham [q.v.] and officials conversant with the Moreton Bay district, he discharged those duties and the first parliament of Queensland opened on 22 May 1860.

Denison was invariably addressed as governor-general. Apart from his lapse on uniform railway gauge, he took an active and informed interest in many matters of intercolonial concern. According to Professor J. M. Ward, 'although he himself doubted whether a Governor-General were needed in the colonies, he succeeded, before the commencement of responsible government, in making significant use of the "titular preeminence" which had been conferred upon him . . . The most conspicuous of his successes was his contribution to the agreement of the colonies and Britain for the maintenance of steam postal services between Australia and the United Kingdom. He also eased the wrangling over tariffs that had followed the opening of the River Murray, and was active in bringing about a measure of intercolonial agreement concerning ocean lighthouses'.

The introduction of responsible government in New South Wales coincided with Denison's appointment as governor of Norfolk Island. His association with the island had begun while he was in Hobart. From August 1846 to January 1853 the administration of this penal station had reflected the capacity of the civil commandant, John Price [q.v.], to inspire dread. Denison upheld Price's régime but in 1852, alerted by the condemnatory report of Bishop Willson [q.v.], he decided that the penal station ought to be abandoned. His recommendation was approved in London where the Colonial Office suggested that the island was 'fit for the reception of a small body of settlers now existing at Pitcairn Island'. Denison was authorized to control their removal and resettlement. The *Morayshire* was chartered and the whole community of 194 landed on Norfolk Island on 8 June 1856. Unfortunately Denison's initial instructions directed that, apart from certain public reserves, the island was to be vested in the Pitcairners. This was not intended by the imperial authorities and the position was speedily clarified by the Colonial Office. When Denison visited the island in 1857 each family was given fifty acres in fee simple on the clear understanding that the title to all land not thus granted remained in the Crown. But the mischief was done. G. H. Nobbs [q.v.] and other islanders insisted that 'it was not with this understanding we left Pitcairn'. Their claim was untenable in law and in reason but it remained a persisting grievance. As governor of Norfolk Island Denison described himself as a colonial Solon. He welcomed the free hand given him in what he described as 'a singular little autocracy'. He gave their chief magistrate a code of rules, supplied their immediate wants and took a benign interest in their welfare.

When the native ruler and the missionaries in Tonga sought his help against French intrusion, Denison was unmoved but he supported the establishment of coaling stations on the projected steam postal route between Panama and Sydney, and for strategic reasons favoured the annexation of New Caledonia. By contrast his attitude to the maintenance of British rule in New Zealand was firm and sustained. He admired the Maoris but actively supported Governor Gore Browne. In April 1860, when hostilities began over the 'Waitara Purchase', he was quick to supply military assistance and to recommend his own ideas for fighting the Maori. Similarly on the outbreak of the Indian mutiny, he successfully advised the dispatch of the 77th Regiment to Calcutta. He also proposed that they should be strengthened by the local company of artillery but, after endorsing the suggestion, the Legislative Assembly refused to authorize the expenditure. Denison gave the assembly what he described as a 'sharp answer'; it was regarded as an affront to the House and was countered with a stiff rejoinder.

The last few weeks of his governor-generalship were clouded by an acute difference with his cabinet on the control of the great seal of the colony. The matter in issue, which related to a grant by the Crown of certain realty in Sydney that had escheated to Her Majesty in 1845, had been in debate between the law officers of the Crown in London and Sydney for years. It was brought to a head when on 8 September 1860 the secretary of state enjoined Denison to have the relevant deed, as approved by the law officer of the Treasury, perfected without further delay and delivered to the appropriate trustees. This action required the impressment upon the relevant deed of the great seal that was in the custody of the colonial secretary who was the prime minister, Charles Cowper [q.v.]. The ministry was opposed to the deed of grant as presented and argued that, by a convention of the Constitution, the control of the great seal of the colony was vested in it. 'My Commission', replied Denison, 'gives me authority to keep and use the Great Seal of the Colony and I am answerable to the Queen for the use I so make of it'. In obedience to his specific instructions from the Colonial Office, on 21 January 1861 he requested the delivery of the seal so that he might complete the deed.

As he had booked his passage to sail on 22 January 1861 for his new appointment as governor of the presidency of Madras, time came to his rescue. Cowper surrendered the seal and his ministry's resignation with it. Sir William promptly impressed the deed and returned the seal to the colonial secretary together with an intimation that he declined to accept the resignation. The government acquiesced but promptly requested a direction from the Queen that the great seal of the colony should not be used in future except on the advice of the colonial ministry.

Denison and his family arrived in Madras in February. They found the heat oppressive and several of the younger children were sent to relations in England. He made his country home at Guindy Park, about five miles from Government House, his main residence, but his refuge was at Ootacamund in the mountains about 7500 feet above sea level. There, among his other interests, he took an active part in the development of a Chinchora (quinine) plantation which became a boon to the natives.

Although the governor-general stood between him and the India Office, Denison was entitled as governor of Madras to communicate directly with the secretary of state for India. He continued his tireless correspondence with his superiors, often questioning the wisdom of their policy but always doing his best to implement it if his suggestions did not prevail. He remained zealous and efficient as an administrator, encouraging agriculture, extending irrigation and canals, promoting public health and advocating railways. He opened a school at Guindy for the children of his servants but never attempted to master the language and his comments upon the Hindus as a people were far from complimentary. While acting viceroy of India for six weeks in 1863 he altered policy by sending decisive reinforcements to an expeditionary force engaged with a troublesome tribe in Peshawar.

Denison's term in Madras ended in March 1866 and he returned to England by way of the Suez Canal which he examined and reported upon as an engineer. In 1868 he was appointed chairman of the inquiry into pollution of rivers in Britain. He gave many public lectures, some of which were published, and his eminently readable *Varieties of Vice-Regal Life* appeared in two volumes in 1870. He died at East Sheen, Surrey, on 19 January 1871. Lady Denison survived him until 1899. Of their thirteen children two had died in New South Wales.

In private life Denison was deeply devoted to his wife and children, his parents and his brothers. His first outdoor hobby in Hobart was his garden and in Sydney he had an aviary. His favourite pastimes were riding, fishing and shooting. As an ardent and informed conchologist he collected eight thousand species of Australian shells. He also had an interest in geology. In his big library he kept abreast of current literature and natural history. As a skilled engineer he turned readily to practical subjects and breathed fresh life into the scientific societies in Hobart and Sydney. But he remained unversed in philosophy and other humane disciplines that might have conditioned his severe judgments, quick temper and sense of personal superiority. An Anglican by faith, he was also a fervent fundamentalist to whom Darwinism was anathema. At a time when the spirit of Socrates was animating the discussions of accepted teaching and practices, Denison's limited vision and rigid mind made him insensitive to 'winds of change'.

J. West, *The history of Tasmania*, 1-2 (Launceston, 1852); G. O. Trevelyan, *The life and letters of Lord Macaulay*, 2 (Lond, 1876); W. A. Townsley, *The struggle for self-government in Tasmania 1842-1856* (Hob, 1951); J. M. Ward, *Earl Grey and the Australian colonies, 1846-1857* (Melb, 1958); R. J. Moore, *Sir Charles Wood's Indian policy, 1853-66* (Manchester, 1966); VDL Executive Council minutes 1846-55 (TA); NSW Executive Council minutes, vols 16-25 (NSWA); Mrs J. S. Barker, diaries 1855-56 (ML); Lady Eleanor Stephen diary (ML); Cowper letters, vol 1 (ML); MS cat under Sir William Thomas Denison (ML); East India Co. papers and accounts, vols 71 etc (ML); Denison papers 1837-62 (microfilm Oxford, ML, NL); GO dispatches (ML); CO 201/483-526, 202, 280/191-322.   C. H. CURREY

DENNIS, ALEXANDER (1811-1892), pastoralist, was born on 29 September 1811 at Trembath, in Penzance, Cornwall, England, son of Richard Dennis, farmer, and his wife Elizabeth, née Vinicombe. His grandfather, Alexander Dennis, a farmer and miller, was the author of *Journal of a Tour through great part of England and Scotland in the year 1810* (Penzance, 1816). His aunt Thomasin, self-taught in the classics, mathematics, chemistry and modern literature, was governess in the household of Josiah Wedgwood junior.

Alexander was thoroughly trained in farm work. In December 1837 he married Emma Williams, sister of E. P. Tregurtha [q.v.]. Finally heeding his brother-in-law's reports, Dennis sailed in the *John Bull* with his wife and daughter, his brothers John and William and four servants; they arrived at Port Phillip in January 1840. Alexander settled his family at George Town, Van Diemen's Land, while he bought stock and implements, which he took to Geelong in April. He joined his brothers, who had each contributed £1000 to the venture, and they drove 600 sheep into the Western District in search of land. They decided to buy the 5000-acre Keerangee-Balloort run near Birregurra from the Matson brothers. Alex-

ander brought his wife, daughter and new-born baby from George Town to the station in September. In 1842 the Dennis brothers took up Poliah station, north-west of Lake Corangamite. Financial difficulties prevented further expansion until 1848 when they bought Robertson's [q.v.] station on the Richardson River. The discovery of gold and the increased demand for meat allowed further development and in August 1853 they bought Carr's Plains adjoining Robertson's station which together included 70,000 acres.

The Birregurra run was Alexander's main interest. In 1848 he changed its name to Tarndwarncoort and employed a qualified mason and master carpenter to build a stone house to his own design; a bluestone wing was added in the late 1870s. He was an ardent horticulturalist and established a fine garden at Tarndwarncoort. His elder son, Richard, specialized in fruit-growing and raised American bronze turkeys; in 1880 he began breeding Polwarth sheep, first known as Dennis Comebacks. In 1867 Alexander bought Eeyeuk near Terang and leased it to his sons, for his brothers had returned to Cornwall. The Carr's Plain property was managed by his son-in-law, H. H. Wettenhall [q.v.], who later bought it.

Dennis took a great interest in community affairs. He was appointed a magistrate on 15 August 1849 and sat on the local bench in Colac where his decisions were painstaking and just. He became one of the first members of the District Roads Board in 1859, served on the Shire Council in 1868-73 and was its president in 1869-70. In Colac he was a member and president of the hospital committee and in 1859 helped to found the Agricultural Society of which he was a member for over thirty years. From his arrival in the district, when the Buntingdale reserve was proclaimed on part of his land, he was concerned with the plight of the Aboriginals. After the Buntingdale mission was abandoned in 1848 Tarndwarncoort became a meeting place for the Colac tribe. In 1867-79 Dennis was honorary correspondent to the Board for the Protection of the Aborigines.

Dennis sent his sons to Scotch College, Melbourne, and his grandsons attended Geelong College. In the district he was a 'veritable pillar' of the Wesleyan Church; at various times he was lay preacher, trustee, circuit steward, society steward and conference representative. In 1848 with others, he financed the building in Colac of a small wooden church which was long used by all denominations. Methodist services were held at Dennis's homestead until the late 1850s when the first Wesleyan church in the district was built on land he donated. He and his brothers had a chapel built at Carr's Plains; it was used for fifty years and served as a hall and school for the district. In 1883 Dennis gave £1000 for the building of the manse at Colac. He also helped to establish the Colac branch of the British and Foreign Bible Society. He died at Tarndwarncoort on 12 April 1892, survived by his wife, two sons and six daughters. His sons, sons-in-law and grandsons continued to maintain the properties and the traditional family links with Cornwall.

A. Henderson (ed), *Early pioneer families of Victoria and Riverina* (Melb, 1936); A. W. Dennis, *Six generations* (priv print, 1963); *Colac Reformer*, 14 Apr 1892.

J. ANN HONE

DENNYS, CHARLES JOHN (1818-1898), wool-broker and stock and station agent, was born in October 1818 in England, son of Nicholas Belfield Dennys, wine merchant of London, and his wife Eliza, née Lascelles. Part of his education was in Germany. In 1842 he migrated to Melbourne but soon moved to Geelong and farmed land on 'model' principles by the Barwon and Moorabool Rivers. In 1847 he bought the Barwon Melting Establishment, a tallow-rendering works near the Geelong breakwater. By 1850 a leather warehouse was added. He was helped by his cousin, Thomas Allen Lascelles junior, a business association which developed into Dennys Lascelles Ltd, one of the great Victorian wool-broking houses. Shortage of labour in the gold rushes led to the closing of the melting works in 1852 and in July Dennys formed a general agency business with his brother-in-law Edward Walton and cousin Lascelles under the name C. J. Dennys & Co. This partnership dissolved in March 1853 and Dennys left for England.

On his return Dennys decided to begin local wool auctions in Geelong. The usual practice for merchants had been to advance money to growers for their wool and to ship it for sale in London. Dennys's first sale, 160 bales from Gorinn station near Ararat, was in November 1857. Others had held earlier sales in Geelong, but they lacked the large premises offered by Dennys at his Western Wool Warehouse, an iron building on Victoria Terrace. In September 1858 Dennys advertised his intention to establish a 'Local Wool Mart', and claimed to have the support of the leading local merchant firms. He also invoked the traditional rivalry between Geelong and Melbourne by stating that one of his aims was to avoid the cost of shipping wool to Melbourne and that 'The auction sales held here last season have proved that this town is not beyond the pale of Melbourne buyers, Melbourne speculators, and Melbourne brokers'. He offered 849 bales at his sale on 9 November 1858 and sold 662.

In 1861 Dennys built new tallow works at Brown's Marsh, but wool remained his major interest. In 1864 his nephew Martin Lascelles Dennys came into partnership and the name C. J. Dennys & Co. was restored. The business prospered: in the 1867-68 selling season they catalogued 10,500 bales and Edward Harewood Lascelles [q.v.] became a partner. To provide larger premises they bought an old coal yard in Moorabool Street, Geelong, in December 1870. An imposing bluestone wool-store and offices were built and opened on 1 August 1872 with a third-floor banquet followed by a wool sale. Despite the company's success much of the wool had not been sold because high reserve prices were imposed by growers who, while overseas news came by sea mail, dreamt of the possibility of higher prices in London. For example, only 3600 bales of the 10,500 catalogued were sold in 1867-68. A big change came in 1872 when the opening of the telegraphic link with Britain brought the latest reports on London prices. In that year, too, Geelong had three woollen mills and a fourth was opened in 1874, and American buyers, attracted to his wool sales, popularized the term 'Geelong Wools' for the Western District clip. In the 1877-78 season the company sold 21,000 bales. Its name had been changed to Dennys Lascelles & Co. in 1875, and after M. L. Dennys withdrew in 1877 David Strachan became a partner. In September 1881 the prominent grazier, Sidney Austin, of Barwon Park, Winchelsea, joined the company and its name became Dennys, Lascelles, Austin & Co. Marcel Conran was admitted as a partner in 1889, together with George Young of Young Brothers, Horsham, whose firm became a subsidiary. Dennys remained the leading influence in the company until 1898 when 41,000 bales were sold.

Dennys had few notable activities outside his business career. He attended the first meeting of the District Council of Grant, held privately on 21 September 1843, and was appointed secretary at its first open meeting on 19 October. In July 1857 he was elected to the first South Barwon Municipal Council. In 1871 he unsuccessfully contested one of the two Legislative Assembly seats for Geelong East. He was a steward at the first Geelong horse-races in July 1843 and at the first Geelong regatta on 20 March 1844. In the early 1840s he served on the committee of the Geelong & Portland Bay Immigration Society. His early association with Germany led to his influencing many German migrants to the Geelong district. An Anglican, he had married his cousin Martha Elizabeth, daughter of Thomas Allen Lascelles senior [q.v.], in December 1855. Aged 80 he died on 4 February 1898 at his home, Claremont, Newtown Hill, survived by his daughters Laura, Emmeline and Ethel, wife of E. H. Lascelles. His estate was probated at only £3734. It is not known what money he had settled earlier on his family but his company's resources were severely strained in 1896 by expensive, if visionary, loans to struggling farmers on subdivisions in the Victorian Mallee.

Dennys was known for his kindliness and generosity. His career showed strong talent, imagination and resolution. A successful businessman, he exploited the opportunities offered by the rich Victorian Western District, for the benefit of Geelong as well as himself, and he was an influential pioneer of the process whereby domestic sales of Australian wool surpassed London sales by the mid-1890s.

HRA (1), 24, 26; W. R. Brownhill, *The history of Geelong and Corio Bay* (Melb, 1955); P. L. Brown, 'Historical summary', *Dennys, Lascelles Limited annual wool report and centenary review*, Aug 1957; P. L. Brown, *Clyde Company papers*, 4-5 (Lond, 1959, 1963); Dennys Lascelles Ltd papers (Univ Melb Archives).   FRANK STRAHAN

DENOVAN, WILLIAM DIXON CAMPBELL (1829-1906), miner, reformer, politician and public servant, was born on 20 December 1829 in Edinburgh, son of Francis Garden Denovan, shipbroker and sometime consul at Copenhagen, and his wife Margaret. He was educated at Inverarity, Forfarshire (Angus), and Dundee. At 18 he started his own school, hoping thereby to study at the University of Edinburgh and enter the Presbyterian ministry, but ill health made him abandon the project.

Denovan migrated in the *Mobile* to Melbourne in 1852 and in February 1853 went to Bendigo where his mother joined him. He became a miner and as a radical republican was soon prominent in the anti-licence movement, serving on its deputations, speaking at mass meetings which he helped to organize and drafting petitions for abolition of the licence tax. He also advocated the forcible ejection of Chinese miners but later canvassed for removal of their oppressive residence licence tax. By 1854 his zeal for reform had won him prominence as a goldfields leader and election as a diggers' representative at the Gold Fields Commission. His evidence explained the spread of poverty as individual miners were replaced by monopolistic companies, emphasized the diggers' right to representation in the Legislative Council and the need to unlock the land for smallholders. In 1855 he was elected to the first local mining court at Bendigo but soon moved to Ballarat where he was associated with the *Times* and *Star* and in 1856 began his own weekly, the *Nation and Advertiser*; it was short lived and he returned to Bendigo. He became a gold buyer for the Bank of Victoria but was burnt out in 1857. He then helped to found the Land League and became its honorary secretary, as usual following mining pursuits in his spare time.

After much persuasion Denovan accepted nomination in 1861 for Sandhurst in the Victorian Legislative Assembly. He headed the poll and the mining community paid his election expenses and provided an annual honorarium. In the assembly he generally supported the Heales [q.v.] ministry, and helped to secure grants for discoverers of gold and for surveying the Coliban channel to supply Bendigo and Castlemaine with water, but complained that parliament was no place for a poor man jealous of his independence and resigned in 1862. For about two years he edited the *Bendigo Evening News* and became a sharebroker in 1867 and a founder of the local stock exchange. In the next decade he won and lost a small fortune in mining speculation. He was given a purse of 307 sovereigns at his election to the City Council in 1877 and served with distinction as town clerk in 1877-92.

For years Denovan was honorary secretary of the Bendigo Liberal Association and remained a radical. In every crisis he was a willing public speaker, writing his speeches but delivering them oracularly without notes. He anticipated Henry George [q.v.] as an advocate of single tax with the State as sole landlord. By 1862 he had won renown as a spiritualist and in 1871 he formed the Bendigo Energetic Circle of free thinkers. His 700-page *Evidences of Spiritualism: Lectures, Addresses, and Record of the Spiritual Phenomena, culled from the Writings of Eminent Authors, Mediums, Magazines, and Newspapers connected with the Great Spiritual Movement of My Time; With Copious Memoranda of My Own Investigations and Experiences as to the Truth of These Things* (Melbourne, 1882) was probably then the best summary of the beliefs of Australian spiritualists. He contributed to many newspapers and as 'Dixon Campbell' wrote 'The Heir of Crayford Abbey', published in the *Australian Journal*, February 1887. He was also a prominent Freemason. After his mother died in 1888 he visited Britain. In retirement he continued his interests in mining and spiritualism until he died at Bendigo, aged 76 and unmarried, on 13 July 1906.

Demonax (D. Cameron), *The mysteries and miseries of Scripopolis* (Melb, 1872); H. M. Humphreys (ed), *Men of the time in Australia: Victorian series*, 1st ed (Melb, 1878); W. B. Kimberly, *Bendigo and vicinity* (Melb, 1895); G. Mackay, *Annals of Bendigo*, 1892-1909 (Bendigo, 1916); G. Serle, *The golden age* (Melb, 1963); V&P (LA Vic), 1854-55, 2 (A76), 1862-63, 3(10); *Age*, 11 June 1875; *Harbinger of Light*, 1 Oct 1904.

DE PURY, FREDERIC GUILLAUME (1831-1890), wine-grower, was born on 15 December 1831 at Neuchâtel, Switzerland, the eldest son of Edouard Charles Alexandre de Pury and his second wife, Julie de Sandoz-Travers. His father was a member of the Grand Council of Neuchâtel, and the family bore the hereditary title of baron, given them by Frederick II of Prussia. In 1851 Guillaume went to England to study English and agriculture and on 6 May 1852 he sailed for Victoria. There he first tended cattle at Yering, a property in the Yarra valley owned by Paul de Castella [q.v.]. In 1855 with C. H. de Castella he bought Dalry, a former out-station of Yering.

Guillaume was joined at Dalry by his brother Samuel (1836-1922) who had just arrived from Switzerland. In 1857 Samuel arranged to plant a hundred acres of vines on Yering but lost money after two years and relinquished the contract to Joseph Deschamps. In 1860 he bought a part of Yering near Lilydale and named it Cooring Yering. There he planted a vineyard of ten acres and built a house and wine cellar. In Switzerland six years later he became engaged; he returned to Victoria in 1867 but after his marriage in Switzerland next year to Louise Augusta Albana de Coulon he remained in Europe. Cooring Yering was sold in 1870. Samuel had taken a keen interest in the development of the Yarra valley area. He was a magistrate and in 1862 first president of the Upper Yarra District Roads Board and a member of it until he left the country.

Guillaume sold Dalry in 1858 and rented land on near-by Killara to graze sheep and breed horses. He visited Switzerland in 1861 while his brother looked after his interests at Killara. In 1863 with George Langdon he bought from Paul de Castella's creditors 900 acres of Yering which he called Yeringberg, and began a vineyard there. He bought out Langdon in 1869. Yeringberg was later enlarged to 1160 acres with some 60 acres under vines and the remaining area for grazing. By the mid-1880s de Pury had built cellars capable of storing over 30,000 gallons of wine and was making over 20,000 gallons

a year, much of it exported to England. The three vineyards of Yeringberg, St Hubert's and Yering were pioneer developments of the wine industry in the Lillydale district. However, profits declined and by 1921 when the vines of Yeringberg were uprooted wine production in the area had almost ceased. The dry table wines of the district were famous for lightness and quality. Wines made by Guillaume and later by his elder son George won gold medals in London, Bordeaux, Paris, Brussels and San Francisco, as well as many prizes in Australia.

Guillaume was a leader of the Swiss community of Lilydale. In 1875-90 he was consul for the Swiss Confederation in Melbourne. He became a justice of the peace in 1862 and was a member of the Upper Yarra District Roads Board for twenty-one years. When Lillydale was proclaimed a shire in 1872 he was one of its first councillors and .president for nine years. He and his wife gave substantial support towards building the Church of England at Lilydale. Guillaume took an interest in the Aboriginals of the Yarra tribe; he was a friend and adviser of Barak [q.v.] who often visited Yeringberg, and in 1881 served on a government inquiry into the condition of the Aboriginal station at Coranderrk.

On 2 February 1869 at St James's Cathedral, Melbourne, Guillaume married Adelaide Augusta, the eldest daughter of Charles Ibbotson of Geelong; they had two sons, George Alphonse (1870-1956) and Montague Edouard Victor (1873-1961). In 1883 the family visited Switzerland and returned to Victoria next year, leaving George to study in Neuchâtel. Guillaume was appointed a commissioner of the 1888 International Exhibition in Melbourne. Although his health was deteriorating he made two more trips to Switzerland and on the second died suddenly at Lausanne on 11 November 1890.

H. de Castella, *John Bull's vineyard. Australian sketches* (Melb, 1886); A. Sutherland et al, *Victoria and its metropolis*, 2 (Melb, 1888); A. Deschamps, *Back to Lilydale Re-Union* (Lilydale, 1931); F. de Castella, 'Early Victorian wine-growing', VHM, 19 (1941-42); L. J. Peel, 'Viticulture at Geelong and Lillydale', VHM, 36 (1965), no 4; *Age* (Melb), 14 Nov 1890; *Lilydale Express*, 2 May 1891; private papers (held by author).

G. G. DE PURY

DERHAM, FREDERICK THOMAS (1844-1922), businessman and politician, was born on 8 January 1844 at Bristol, England, the third of ten children of Thomas Plumley Derham, a Somerset auctioneer, and his wife Sarah Ann, née Watts. The family arrived in Melbourne in 1856. His father died in 1867 and his surviving elder brother in 1869; at 25 Frederick found himself the senior member of the family in Australia. He had married Ada Anderson on 13 January 1864 and had two sons before his elder brother died. Apparently undaunted by his responsibilities, he embarked on an active and successful career in business and politics. He was good looking and early showed more than usual ability. After completing his schooling he gained some commercial experience with Callender Caldwell & Co. of King Street, Melbourne. He then established his own business as a mercantile broker and agent, and developed a thriving export business, particularly in wheat. His wife died on 9 October 1874 leaving him with three sons and one daughter.

In the early 1850s Thomas Swallow [q.v.] had started a biscuit business and in 1854 established at Sandridge the first machine-equipped biscuit factory in Melbourne. In partnership with Thomas Harris Ariell from 1856, Swallow developed the firm into a large business which made biscuits not only for local but also for overseas markets. In 1877 Ariell died and Derham became Swallow's partner. On 13 April 1878 he married his partner's daughter, Frances Dodd; in the next nine years they had three daughters and two sons.

Swallow and Derham developed fruit canneries and preserving works in country centres, and established sugar plantations, crushing mills and treacle and golden syrup refineries in Queensland; their largest intercolonial venture was the development near Cairns of the Hambledon Mill, now part of the Colonial Sugar Refining Co. Ltd. In 1888 Swallow & Ariell was reformed as a limited liability company, with Swallow and Derham as joint managing directors. In 1890 Swallow died and the company was directed and managed by Derham until he suffered a serious illness in 1920. He died on 12 March 1922 at Kew and his eldest son, Frederick John, took his place as managing director.

Derham's political activities appear to have begun about the time of his partnership with Swallow. He was an outstandingly good public speaker and he became a member of the Sandridge Municipal Council and later mayor. In 1883 he was elected to the Legislative Assembly for Sandridge (Port Melbourne) and, described as 'a slight aesthetic looking gentleman, with a mild manner', he retained his seat until 1892. As postmaster-general in the Gillies [q.v.]-Deakin ministry in 1886-1890, he introduced the penny post into Victoria and also parcel post and country telephone services. In 1889, when he heard of the pneumatic tube method which had been introduced in Berlin for distributing letters and telegrams, he put in such a tube between the G.P.O.

and the new Stock Exchange building in Melbourne.

In politics he was conservative. He opposed whenever he could all measures which he saw as socialist in tendency. He was the founder and first president of the Victorian Employers' Union which he saw as a body necessarily called into being in answer to the 'ceaseless activities of the Labor Party' and to check 'rampant socialist legislation'. He opposed the legislation which established the Victorian Wages Board system and he thought that compulsory arbitration was a mistaken aim. He would have opposed the 'one man one vote' legislation had it been politically possible for him to do so. He was president of the Chamber of Manufactures from 1897 to 1903 and of the Victorian Mill-owners' Association. His last public political venture was as a candidate for the November 1903 Senate elections as an 'anti-socialist'. He was, none the less, a close friend of Alfred Deakin and they corresponded and worked together in politics without friction. He was himself a good, careful and successful employer who maintained high standards with respect to working conditions in his factories. Like that of so many contemporaries his fortune, which must have been considerable in the 1880s, was virtually destroyed in the great depression of the early 1890s. In 1892 he entered into a composition with his creditors and at that time, it has been reported, his liabilities exceeded his assets by an amount in the vicinity of £500,000.

In addition to business and politics Derham was also active in other affairs of a public and charitable nature. He was the first chairman of the Kindergarten Union and president of the Burnley Free Kindergarten. He was an active member of the Church of England and did much to support Holy Trinity Church, Port Melbourne, and Holy Trinity Church, Kew. He was a lover of good music and as an avid reader collected a large private library on a wide variety of subjects.

Frederick John Derham managed the company his father had done so much to develop until he died in 1932. His half-brother, Charles Alfred Melbourne Derham, M.C., managed the company until his death in 1959. The management then fell to Frederick Thomas's grandson, another Frederick Thomas Derham, until Swallow & Ariell Ltd was finally merged with a larger nation-wide organization.

H. M. Franklyn, A glance at Australia in 1880 (Melb, 1881); A. Sutherland et al, Victoria and its metropolis, 2 (Melb, 1888); J. Smith (ed), Cyclopedia of Victoria, 3 (Melb, 1905); J. W. Collinson, Early days of Cairns (Brisb, 1939); J. W. Collinson, More about Cairns: the second decade (Brisb, 1942); Weekly Times (Melb),

1895; *Table Talk*, 1899, 1901; *Scientific Australian*, 1900; *Table Talk Annual*, 1904; Swallow & Ariell Ltd records (Univ Melb Archives); family papers and records.

DAVID DERHAM

DERRINGTON, EDWIN HENRY (1830-1899), journalist and publicist, was born on 1 July 1830 at Birmingham, England, the first son and fourth child of Edwin Derrington, a Dissenting minister, and his wife Susannah, née Buggins. He became a compositor but was a reporter in Birmingham by 28 September 1852 when he married Elizabeth (b. 1831), daughter of William Shread. Their son was born in June 1853 but within ten months she and the child had died. Soon afterwards Derrington migrated to Australia. According to an obituary, he landed in Melbourne, but he was working for the *South Australian Register* by 1 September 1855 when he married Elizabeth Rosa Ekers at St Andrew's Church, Walkerville; of their nine children, eight survived childhood.

Derrington worked for the *Register* until he was appointed telegraph stationmaster at Mount Gambier on 1 January 1859. In September 1866 he became a partner in Blackwell, Derrington & Co., wholesale and retail store-keepers. When the partnership dissolved in 1869 he was owner-editor of the *Mount Gambier Standard* until 1872 when he moved to Moonta. There he founded and ran the *Yorke's Peninsula Advertiser and Miners' News* for eleven years. In 1878 he acquired the *Port Adelaide News* and was its owner-editor until 1883 and publisher until January 1885. He bought the *Adelaide Punch* in April 1882 but sold it in January 1884. His press speculations probably ended for financial reasons: in 1882 the colony had forty-seven newspapers for less than 300,000 people.

Attention to parochial problems was a necessity for editors but Derrington also pursued a vigorous liberal line on wider questions. He preferred property tax to the tariff as a source of revenue; he supported payment of parliamentarians, opposed selection of land before survey and sought universal education as a corollary to universal suffrage. He believed that female suffrage and a permanent executive would raise the quality of political life. In the conflict between Darwinian science and religion he saw the merits of the former; he also advocated more teaching hospitals to improve the standard of medicine, argued against the abolition of capital punishment, supported the exclusion of Chinese labour, and ridiculed the defence of Adelaide against Russian naval attack as 'A Lunatic Scare'. At Moonta he supported the miners who struck in 1874 when the mine directors attempted to reduce wages, and attributed the men's victory to orderly conduct and 'the power of moral suasion'.

Derrington's advocacy of local developments such as improved transport, proper drainage of the south-east and the establishment of a beet sugar industry must have pleased the residents of Mount Gambier. He represented them in the House of Assembly in 1872-73 and was commissioner of crown lands under Henry Ayers [q.v.] in 1872. He was not a skilful politician and his selection for the ministry 'after one afternoon of parliamentary experience' was a matter of expediency: the Ayers government wanted to shelve a proposed railway in the south-east and Derrington supported Mount Gambier commercial interests who wanted the line to be routed through their own area. In his undistinguished parliamentary career he began to quarrel with Ebenezer Ward [q.v.] who, he publicly asserted, was 'ignoring nearly all the qualities that make up private and public worth' and drowning his natural gifts 'in unnatural sensuousness, idleness, and unprincipledness'. Ward sued for damages of £2000. The chief justice, Samuel Way, seemed to think the defendant guilty but the six-day trial ended without agreement by the jury. A 'Derrington Defence Fund' was raised in excess of his legal costs.

In 1883 Derrington failed to win the Gumeracha seat. In succession he became the paid secretary of the Temperance Alliance, secretary of the Chamber of Manufactures and for two years a travelling lecturer for the Australian Mutual Provident Society. He was also active in the Bible Society, the Social Purity League and in Bible Christian, Primitive and Wesleyan Methodist affairs. He debated, sang, played the violin and painted with modest ability. The 'moral' tone of his utterances and his indifferent success in business suggest that he followed the Protestant ethic rather than the spirit of capitalism. When he died on 14 October 1899 the obituaries were sincere, for his energy and enthusiasm had helped his colony's cause.

SA Law Reports, 1880; *Libel case: Ward v. Derrington* (Adel, nd); *Port Adelaide News*, 14 Feb 1880; *Register* (Adel), 16 Oct 1899; family papers held by Mrs E. A. Hicks, Cumberland Park, SA.

NEVILLE HICKS

DERRY, JOHN DICKSON (1840-1913), surveyor and engineer, was born at Plymouth of an old Devonshire family. In 1859 he became a probationary engineer in the Public Works Department of the Indian government; he was best known and commended by the government for his part in building the Sirhind Canal in the Punjab, begun in 1878. He retired on a pension in 1880 and went to Victoria. There he was attracted by the surveys of George Gordon and A. Black [qq.v.] and their plans for water supply to the northern plains. Derry's initiative led to the formation of the Wimmera United Waterworks Trust on 6 October 1882. As its engineer he constructed several weirs and pumping stations and was mainly responsible for the Natimuk Channel.

In 1885 Derry went to California with Alfred Deakin, then chairman of the royal commission on water supply, to investigate irrigation methods; he wrote the second progress report for the commission. Back in the Wimmera in May 1885 Derry, with Samuel Carter [q.v.], recommended the building of the Wartook dam on the Mackenzie River in the Grampians. In July he resigned from the Wimmera waterworks and next month took up the Wimmera Shire's contract to build the dam; the first public irrigation storage in Australia, it was completed on 17 August 1886 and improved in 1887-88 at a total cost of £4635 3s. 8d. The dam was extended by Derry with Stuart Murray [q.v.] in 1889 at a further cost of £19,665. Derry acted as consultant for the Wimmera United Waterworks Trust and in February 1886 made a government survey of the Wimmera River sources. Later that year with G. J. Burke, Derry issued the irrigation report which laid the basis for the present channel system from the Wimmera to the Mallee region. After the 1886 Water Conservation Act, the Wimmera Shire set up its own trust for which Derry worked until September 1888 when it was absorbed into the new Western Wimmera Irrigation and Water Supply Trust. Employed on a commission basis as designing engineer from April 1889, Derry prepared an irrigation scheme for 200,000 acres north and south of the Wimmera River.

At Victoria's first Irrigation Conference in Melbourne in 1890 Derry spoke of his preparatory work for the 500-acre irrigation colony at Burnlea, and next year a company was formed to take it over from him. In several public projects he was associated with James Brake of the Horsham Borough Council, water commissioner and later politician, with whom he held an irrigation property at Nurrabiel. Derry was also active in plans for water supplies for Horsham, Pimpinio and Natimuk; he had an interest in Broken Hill's water problems and in 1892 gave gratuitous service to the Tucker village settlers at Wonwondah East near Horsham. Despite the trust's objections Derry proceeded with water surveys in connexion with the Co-operative Irrigation & Mercan-

tile Society's colony at Quantong near Horsham. His work outside the sphere of the trust and his failure to take up appointment in April 1891 as the trust's salaried resident engineer led to his dismissal in October. He was awarded £4713 in his claims against the trust but sued for more and received £650 under arbitration. Derry lived in Stawell, Murtoa, Horsham and finally St Kilda; he returned to England in 1894. He died suddenly of pneumonia on 12 March 1913 at Barnes, London, survived by his wife Edith, née Handley, their four daughters and one son who was in the Chinese consular service.

In 1865 Derry had become an associate member of the Institution of Civil Engineers in London and was elected a member in 1878; he wrote several papers on irrigation. Polished and formal in manner, he was an engineer of 'much ability and originality'. His memorial is the Wartook dam. Highly sensitive to criticism, he was frustrated by the attitude of some settlers and officials to his elaborate plans and practical achievements. He worked strenuously to develop the water resources of the Wimmera, but much of what he projected was scaled down when several irrigation colonies ran into difficulties and near-bankrupt trusts faced investigation by the royal commission on water supply in 1896.

G. Gordon and A. Black, Supply of water to the northern plains (Melb, 1882); Horsham Irrigation Colonizing Coy. Ltd. (Melb, 1890); R. F. McNab, The early settlement and water supply of the Wimmera and Mallee (Melb, 1944); State Rivers and Water Supply Com, Water resources of Victoria (Melb, 1962); A. S. Kenyon, 'Stuart Murray and irrigation in Victoria', VHM, 10 (1925) no 7; Aqua (Melb), May 1962, Feb, Nov 1963, Apr 1964; Horsham Times, May 1882, 8 Oct 1886, 3 Feb 1888, 18 Apr, 23, 29 May 1890; Wimmera Star, 20 June 1890, 22 May 1891; Inst of Civil Engineers (Lond), Records; Wimmera United Waterworks Trust, Minutes 1886-89; Shire of Wimmera Waterworks Trust, Minutes; Western Wimmera Irrigation and Water Supply, Minutes 1889-93.

L. J. BLAKE

DESAILLY, FRANCIS WILLIAM WISDOM (1816?-1889) and GEORGE PETER (1823?-1876), pastoralists, were the sons of Francis Desailly (d. 1864), physician, and his wife Ann, née Pigott. Francis junior was born in England and on 13 March 1821 arrived with his parents in Van Diemen's Land, where George was born at Brighton. With their father the brothers moved to the mainland in 1839 in the Britannia which was wrecked in Port Phillip Bay; George established a station at Arthur's Seat on the

Mornington Peninsula with the sheep rescued and later moved to Gippsland, where Francis joined him. In 1849 they visited California but by 1850 had taken up Coree station of 119,000 acres in the Riverina and Gunningrah in the Monaro. In 1858 angry squatters marched upstream and cut their large dam on Billabong Creek. George repaired it and built a log fortress on the summit. He threatened to shoot 'anyone who might attempt to open the dam'. It was again cut in 1860. Next year the Desaillys bought Bundure on Yanko Creek and in 1863 advertised its merino rams for sale. In the early 1860s they acquired either separately or in partnership many other runs, including Pomingalarna, near Wagga. By 1865 they held forty stations amounting to 1,118,000 acres. Both brothers were justices of the peace and active supporters of the Riverine Association, which aimed at separation from New South Wales. In 1863 they contributed £500 to its funds and George was for a time its president.

About 1864 the Desaillys sold Coree and Bundure for a reputed £80,000 and moved further west where they established the Mossgiel and Booligal stations on the Lachlan. They employed 300 men to fence, dig tanks and sink wells, and imported the first centrifugal pump and steam engine in the Riverina. By 1865 their Willanthry cut took water eleven miles from the Lachlan to their backblocks. George's dam was again breached by raiders chanting,

So now my dear Desailly
You've put up your dam in vain
If you put up another
Why we'll have to come again.

Despite the alleged £130,000 they had spent on water conservation and other improvements, the Desaillys were beaten by drought and in 1869 the mortgagees foreclosed. As they left the station it began to rain and their vehicles bogged. After a short and unsuccessful venture as stock and station agents in Melbourne, they bought Trida station, next to Mossgiel, with the assistance of their brother-in-law, W. A. Brodribb [q.v.]. By the mid-1870s they had prospered enough to retire to Melbourne 'on modest competences'.

George, who had been ailing for some time, died on 19 September 1876 at Brighton, Victoria, leaving five sons and four daughters. He had married Emma Jane Kennedy about 1856. He left her half his income and about £11,000 in trust. Francis died at his home in St Kilda on 2 August 1889 survived by his second wife Maria Jane, née Welsh, and at least three sons and three daughters who were all minors. His first wife, née Spottiswoode, had borne him a son.

HRA (3), 6, 26-27; J. Gormly, *Exploration and settlement in Australia* (Syd, 1921); R. B. Ronald, *The Riverina: people and properties* (Melb, 1960); A. Barnard, *The simple fleece* (Melb, 1962); A. McKay (ed), *Journals of the land commissioners for Van Diemen's Land, 1826-28* (Hob, 1962); *Riverine Herald*, 12 Aug 1863; *Wagga Wagga Advertiser*, 30 June 1869, 27 Sept. 1876; *Australasian*, 10, 17 Aug, 1889.

K. J. SWAN

DE SALIS, LEOPOLD FABIUS DIETEGAN FANE (1816-1898), pastoralist and politician, was born on 26 April 1816 in Florence, Italy, the second son of Jerome Fane, fourth Count de Salis, and his third wife Henrietta, née Foster. Educated at Eton, he studied sheep farming near Jedburgh, Scotland. He reached Sydney on 18 November 1840 in the *Royal George*. With a partner he acquired Darbalara on the Murrumbidgee, where they built a public house and charged excessive prices at the station store. De Salis wrote that 'Thro' very despair I determined to settle and content myself', and in 1844 he married Charlotte, daughter of George Macdonald. Next year the partners took up Junee station and by 1854 had added two other runs. In 1855 he sold out, planning to go to England; instead he bought Cuppacumbalong where he made improvements and planted Lombardy poplars along the river at Tharwa. He also introduced irrigation, pioneered the use of dams and made a lifelong study of meteorology.

A magistrate since 1844, de Salis was active on the bench : in 1866 he asked the colonial secretary for a detective to inquire into the shooting of cattle by a fellow magistrate. In December 1864 he was elected to the Legislative Assembly for Queanbeyan. A loyal supporter, he told his friend, Henry Parkes [q.v.], in November 1868 that it was 'in our best interests to educate the Catholics'; he also recommended the introduction of an income tax, to which labourers should contribute 'as an insurance against misfortune or improvidence'. His knowledge of local land conditions enabled de Salis to see both sides of the squatter-selector disputes : known as 'the selectors' friend', he opposed large estates but wanted more certain tenure for the squatter. Later he recognized that 'the chief burden of our Government is the inheritance from a Crown Colony of universal municipal responsibility'. In 1869 he was defeated by William Forster [q.v.], but in the 1872 election engineered his son's victory over 'the borough-mongering influences of the Rutledges . . . & the *personal* exertion of the priest'. De Salis urged Parkes to join Edward Butler [q.v.] and woo the Irish.

In July 1874 de Salis was appointed to the Legislative Council, pledged to its reconstruction on an elective basis. Reluctant to invest in Parkes's coal mine at Jervis Bay, he 'cheerfully' promised £100 a year to assist Parkes to continue as leader of the Opposition. An active member, de Salis introduced three unsuccessful bills. Characteristically he opposed the dispatch of the Sudan contingent, but as a devout Anglican was implacably against Sir Alfred Stephen's [q.v.] divorce reform bills. Cultured, independent and with much common sense, de Salis was a moderating influence in parliament, but increasingly left the management of his stations to his sons. In the Upper Murrumbidgee area he acquired Naas and Coolamon. In the 1870s de Salis Bros took up extensive land in Queensland, where their principal station was Strathmore, near Bowen, but lost all their holdings to the Union Bank by 1895. In 1893 de Salis had visited England to transfer entailed estates to his younger brother. On his return he lived with his daughter Nina, wife of William Farrer, at Lambrigg, Tharwa. With debts of over £100,000 he became insolvent in 1898; his benevolence and hospitality had contributed to his reverses. He died at Lambrigg on 20 November and was buried in the family cemetery at Cuppacumbalong, survived by three sons and his only daughter.

E. J. Lea-Scarlett, *Queanbeyan: district and people* (Queanbeyan, 1968); PD (LC NSW), 1880-98; A. W. Martin, 'Electoral contests in Yass and Queanbeyan in the 'seventies and 'eighties', JRAHS, 43 (1957); W. A. F. de Salis, 'Some family history', Canberra and District Hist Soc, *Papers*, 1960; *Queanbeyan Observer*, 22 Nov 1898; Parkes letters (ML); MS cat (ML); de Salis insolvency file (NSWA).

DE SATGE, OSCAR JOHN (1836-1906), pastoralist, was born on 20 November 1836 in England, the second son of Ernest Valentine, first vicomte de Satgé de St Jean, and his wife Caroline, daughter of Sherrington Sparkes, later high sheriff of Brecon. His father had been 'created' vicomte by the duchesse de Berry in 1830 on her appointment as regent for 'Henri V' but was exiled for involvement in a royalist revolt. The family, of Catalan origin, had long held seigneurial rights to the Château Thoren, Pyrenées Orientales, while the marriage of de Satgé's grandfather, Cosme (1769-1849), 12th baron de Thoren and préfect of Ariège, to Franciose Fausta Ballalud de St Jean, allied it to a connexion of antiquity and significance. De Satgé's brothers, Ernest Valentine Léon, later 2nd vicomte, and Henri Antoine, both married daughters of Edwin Tooth [q.v.].

De Satgé was educated at Rugby in 1849-52. He arrived in the *Essex* at Melbourne in May 1853. An introduction to La Trobe won him a clerkship in the Goldfields' Commission. He later served at Bendigo and as a parliamentary clerk but decided in December 1854 to seek pastoral experience. He joined his brother at stations on the Darling Downs, and drove cattle to Ipswich and a thousand miles to Victoria. In 1856-57 he worked on St George Gore's [q.v.] Yandilla property and in 1858 on Llangollen station near Cassilis. In 1861 he invested in a group of Peak Downs runs; his elder sister Ernestine, and his partner, Gordon Sandeman [q.v.] were married in 1862. In 1863 de Satgé sold most of his leases but retained Wolfgang Downs in partnership with James Milson [q.v.], with whom in 1872 he bought Coreena station, near Aramac. The partners disposed of Wolfgang in 1875 for over £100,000. After a visit to Europe and India in 1876-78 de Satgé returned to develop Coreena; he sold it in 1881 for £70,000 and devoted the proceeds to the acquisition, with Milson and other partners, of Carandotta, a three-million-acre lease on the Georgina River, and Augustus Downs on the Leichhardt River. Continuing his successful central Queensland policies de Satgé promoted a vigorous scheme of heavy stocking with extensive well-sinking and fencing. Capital was poured into the venture but, although the black soils were fertile and the seasons after 1881 generally agreeable, a disastrous drought in 1892 revealed the shaky foundations of the whole enterprise. Over 90,000 sheep and 10,000 cattle died and the Bank of New South Wales took over. De Satgé had retired to England in 1882 and at Madehurst, Sussex, on 3 August married Beatrice Elizabeth Fletcher; they had one son and two daughters. Apart from visits to Australia in 1883, 1888 and 1893 to inspect his properties, he lived at Elysee, Shorncliffe Road, Folkestone. He died there on 26 September 1906, leaving an estate worth £443.

In the Queensland Legislative Assembly de Satgé had represented Clermont in 1869-70 and 1870-72, Normanby in 1873-77 and Mitchell in 1881-82. First elected as a squatters' delegate to pass the 1869 pastoral leases bill, his superior social position, his comprehensive knowledge of the problems of the central and western Queensland squatters and his successful role as a Clermont 'roads and bridges' politician made him an effective pastoral leader. 'These', as he later nostalgically asserted, were 'the good old days when squatting constituencies returned representatives interested in the pursuit instead of Radicals ready to wage war against capital'. In February 1881 he attained momentary colonial fame by his determined opposition to McIlwraith's [q.v.] land-grant railway proposals and his later political victory in the crucial Mitchell constituency through which the line was to run. He was never prominent in the debates or in issues outside his pastoral province although his membership of the Queensland Pastoralists' Protection League in the 1860s and active involvement in metropolitan affairs earned him a perhaps undeserved reputation as an armchair manipulator and a powerful influence on pastoral land policies.

De Satgé's valuable and racy reminiscences, *Pages from the Journal of a Queensland Squatter* (London, 1901), reveal him as an able and shrewd pastoralist with much practical and financial skill. To his 'pure merino' contemporaries he was remarkably kind, intelligent and public spirited. A great club man, moving naturally by lineage, family connexions, occupation and wealth in the highest colonial social circles, he was a friend and confidant of governors. Politically inflexible and often imperceptive, distrustful of the colonial politicians and often resented by egalitarians, de Satgé with his distinguished appearance, courtly charm and perfect manners, was both an ornament and an example to the 'pure merinos' whose aspirations were so fully embodied in his person.

Etat présent de la noblesse française, 1st ed (Paris, 1866); *Pastoral Review*, 15 Dec 1906; *Folkestone, Hythe, Sandgate and Cheriton Herald*, 29 Sept 1906; *Brisbane Courier*, 28 Nov 1906; records held by the de Satgé family.

D. B. WATERSON

DEUCHAR, JOHN (1822-1872), pioneer and stock breeder, was born at Aberdeen, Scotland, son of John Deuchar, farmer, and his wife Margaret, née Rattary. He migrated to New South Wales in 1840, gained pastoral experience in the Hunter River district, and about 1842 drove sheep from Maitland to the Darling Downs for the Aberdeen Co., later the North British Australian Co. From 1844 he was cattle overseer for Patrick Leslie [q.v.] at Goomburra. After two years, with support from Walter Grey of Ipswich, he bought Canal Creek well stocked with Talgai merinos. In 1848 Deuchar sold Canal Creek, and succeeded Fred Bracker [q.v.] as manager of Rosenthal for the Aberdeen Co.; he also became travelling superintendent of the company's properties. On Rosenthal Deuchar had the first two thoroughbred merino rams on the Darling Downs, Camden Billy, already there when he took over the property, and German Billy, which he brought with him from Canal Creek. A fine

merino stud was developed from a blend of Negretti and Rambouillet strains.

Deuchar also began breeding cattle, especially Shorthorns, and brought to Rosenthal, Lord Raglan, the first imported Shorthorn bull to reach the Downs, and well-bred cattle from the Australian Agricultural Co.'s properties farther south. A lover of good horseflesh and specially dependent on it for his inspections, he also developed a racing stud. His stallion, Grey Arab, bought from one of the Aberdeen Co.'s properties, sired many fine horses, some of which Deuchar rode successfully at race meetings both on the flat and over the fences. He also introduced Omar Pasha, one of the first Clydesdale stallions on the Downs. In 1855 he went into partnership with Charles H. Marshall on Glengallan, also near Warwick, where he continued his work in stock breeding. His overseer, William Anderson, had been at school with him and had come to the colony on the same ship. Deuchar insisted on building up his own teams of employees; on taking over both Rosenthal and Glengallan he had dispersed the families on the properties and replaced them with other employees already known to him. Most of those displaced moved to Warwick and many became well-known pioneers of that town.

On 4 May 1857 at Paddington, Sydney, Deuchar married Eliza Charlotte, sixteen-year-old sister of Dr Lee of Warwick. In 1858-60 with his wife and infant daughter he visited Scotland. On his return he continued his developmental work at Glengallan and in 1867 built at a cost of £12,000 an impressive two-storied homestead with white stone quarried on the property. Although still standing (1968) the house is no longer in use. In 1870 he dissolved partnership with Marshall and retired to Mile End in Warwick, where he died aged 50 on 11 September 1872, survived by his wife, two daughters and six sons.

T. Hall, *The early history of Warwick district* (Toowoomba, 1923); D. Gunn, *Links with the past* (Brisb, 1937); *Brisbane Courier*, 16 Sept 1872; Leslie letters (Oxley Lib, Brisb).

A. A. MORRISON

DEVINE, EDWARD 'Cabbage Tree Ned' (1833?-1908), coach driver, was born probably on 10 August 1833 at Brighton, Van Diemen's Land, son of Thomas Devine, a free migrant who became a farmer at Cove Hill, near Brighton. Edward went to Victoria as a youth, and in 1854 was driving coaches on the Geelong-Ballarat Road. After Cobb & Co. acquired this route, Devine soon became one of their best-known drivers. For a time he drove the 'Leviathan' coach, the largest to appear in Australia, and by 1862 he was earning the very high wage of £17 a week. In that year he was assigned to drive H. H. Stephenson's cricketers, the first All-England team to visit Australia, on their tour of Victoria. His spectacular handling of a new coach with twelve magnificent light greys won him widespread fame. Something of a showman, he drove the cricketers right on to the oval at a match in Geelong. When the tour ended, the Englishmen presented him with a purse of 300 sovereigns at a complimentary dinner. In 1863 Devine went to New Zealand, where for fifteen years he drove for Cobb & Co., first on the South Road out of Dunedin, and later on the North Road from Dunedin to Palmerston and Oamaru. He retired from coaching in New Zealand in 1878, reputedly warning his suc-.cessor to 'mind the peat bog, and give my love to the tussocks'.

Devine acquired his nickname of 'Cabbage Tree Ned' by wearing a hat made from the fibrous leaves of the cabbage palm. A photograph taken in New Zealand shows that he was of medium build with a strong, broad face, square chin, straight nose and deep-set eyes. His generosity, free-spending habits and fund of tall stories enhanced his popularity; but he had weaknesses. A casual attitude to such details as way bills, a quick temper and a passion for practical jokes, some rather unfair, probably made him seem more human against the background of his unequalled skill as a whip, his shrewd judgment of horses and his calmness in emergencies. Stories about his achievements were legion. Once he drove a team of twenty-two with four postilions. Another time he was descending Fyansford Hill near Geelong when his horses bolted; Devine kept lashing them into greater speed to prevent the coach from over-running the wheelers until they could be safely pulled up on the opposite hill.

Devine's activities after 1878 are obscure and difficult to authenticate. He has been credited with a little more coach driving, spells of work as a barman and farm labourer, travelling with a stallion, running a livery stable in Melbourne and drifting to the Murchison goldfields in Western Australia. Certainly at Ballarat he gave an exhibition drive with an eight-horse team harnessed to a Cobb & Co. coach, and on 12 July 1904 was admitted to the Ballarat Benevolent Asylum. As driver of the institution's wagonette, he became a familiar figure on the city's streets. He died aged 71 and unmarried on 18 December 1908. Years later he was found to have been buried in an obscure corner of the Ballarat new cemetery. Admirers in Australia and New Zealand supported the appeal of a Memorial Committee to raise funds for his remains to be moved to a more prominent location with a fitting monument. On 7 February 1937 the new tomb with a distinctive headstone was unveiled by Frank Smiley, president of the Cobb & Co.'s Old Coach Drivers' Association.

E. M. Lovell-Smith, *Old coaching days in Otago and Southland* (Christchurch, 1931); K. A. Austin, *The lights of Cobb and Co.* (Adel, 1967); *Argus*, 19 Dec 1908; *Ballarat Star*, 19 Dec 1908; MS cat under Edward Devine, J. K. Moir collection, Lovell-Smith papers (LaT L).   K. A. AUSTIN

DE VIS, CHARLES WALTER (1829-1915), clergyman, zoologist and museum director, was born on 9 May 1829 at Birmingham, England, son of James Devis and Mary, née Chambers. The family was related to portrait painters of the same name. From Edward VI Grammar School, Birmingham, Charles went to Magdalene College, Cambridge (B.A., 1851; M.A., 1884). He was made deacon in 1851 and in 1853 was appointed rector of St John's, Brecon, Wales, but a keen interest in natural history led him to become curator of the Queen's Park Museum, Rochdale, Manchester. There he wrote his earliest scientific papers and joined the Anthropological Society.

De Vis left England in June 1870 for Queensland. He settled first at Black Gin Creek, near Rockhampton, and then at Clermont. After a visit to England he became librarian of the Rockhampton School of Arts. In 1880-81, under the pseudonym of 'Thickthorn', he contributed articles on geology and ornithology to the *Queenslander*. Their quality induced the trustees of the Queensland Museum in January 1882 to offer him the post of curator. He began work in February and in 1901 became director, holding office until he retired in 1905. He then filled the post of consulting specialist to the museum until 1912.

De Vis was an indefatigable writer and worker for natural science, especially in the fields of palaeontology and systematic vertebrate zoology. As A. G. Hamilton put it, de Vis 'tried to do for the Queensland fauna, what Mr. Bailey [q.v.] did for the flora, but under more unmanageable and difficult conditions'. Despite a small staff and limited budget, de Vis added much to the extent of the collections, their classification and display. He also built up a fine reference library and supervised the moving of the museum from the Public Library to the Exhibition Building, Bowen Park. The *Annals of the Queensland Museum* were commenced and attention was paid to the ethnological and biological products of New Guinea, whence his friend, Sir William MacGregor, sent great quantities of material.

Articles on birds, fish, reptiles, batrachians and marsupials, and accounts of his palae-ontological explorations poured from his pen. In the half century after 1865, he published some 130 papers in various journals including the Zoologist, the Journal of Anatomy and Physiology, Memoirs of the Anthropological Society of London, the Proceedings of the Linnean Society of New South Wales and those of the Royal Society of Queensland, the Annals of the Queensland Museum and the Annual Reports of the Administrator of H.M. Government in New Guinea. He had associations with the British and Australian Ornithologists Unions, the Australasian Association for the Advancement of Science, the Royal Geographical Society of Australasia and exhibitions held in London in 1886 and Melbourne in 1888. He was working to the end on a comparative vocabulary of Aboriginal languages. His first wife died in 1897; at Wellington, New Zealand, on 9 September 1898 he married a widow, Katherine Elizabeth Luckle, née Coulson. He died on 30 April 1915 and was buried in the Church of England section of the Toowong cemetery.

H. M. Whittell, The literature of Australian birds (Perth, 1954); A. G. Hamilton, 'Presidential address', Linnean Soc NSW, Procs, 41 (1916); T. H. Johnston, 'Presidential address', Roy Soc Qld, Procs, 28 (1916); G. Whitley, 'Some founders of Australian fish science', Aust Mus Mag, 9 (1948); G. Mack, 'The Queensland Museum, 1855-1955', Memoirs Qld Museum, 13 (1956) pt 2; Brisbane Courier, 3 May 1915; Daily Mail (Brisb), 3 May 1915.

L. A. GILBERT

DEXTER, CAROLINE (1819-1884), feminist, was born on 6 January 1819 in Nottingham, England, daughter of Richard Harper, watchmaker and jeweller, and his wife Mary, née Simson. She was educated privately in England and in Paris became well versed in French culture and friendly with the female novelist, 'George Sand' (1804-1876). At Nottingham in 1843 she married the painter, William Dexter, of Melbourne, Derbyshire. Despite success with the Royal Academy he decided to migrate; in the Bank of England he arrived at Sydney in October 1852. He taught drawing at Lyndhurst College, the Glebe, but soon went to Bendigo where he designed the diggers' banner and spoke at a protest meeting in August 1853. He was in Sydney in January 1855 when Caroline arrived in the

Marie Gabrielle. On the voyage she wrote 'The Emigrant', lines containing what little of nostalgia she allowed to creep into her writings.

In Sydney the Dexters opened a 'Gallery of Arts and School of Design', where Caroline proposed to teach 'elocution, composition and literature, grammar, writing and conversation'. This venture soon collapsed and in 1856 they moved to Gippsland where for a time they seemed happier and more productive: William did much painting, including 'Wood Ducks' and 'Dead Birds' (both in the National Gallery of Victoria), while Caroline began to write. Her Ladies Almanack: The Southern Cross or Australian Album and New Years Gift (Melbourne, 1857) correctly claimed to be 'The First Ladies' Almanack Published in the Colonies'.

The novelty of this work rather than its uneven quality probably discouraged subscriptions. With sketches, probably by her husband, of a native camp, an opossum by moonlight, a beautiful lubra and a bush hut, she produced remarkable vignettes of Australian life. Although the style suffers in quotation, her spirited writing is distinguished by its intensity towards the natives, exulting in the clear air, moonlight, colours of the wild flowers and shapes of majestic trees. Her interlarded maxims on how to manage a husband suggest a droll humour or increasing revolt against domestic fetters. Soon afterwards the Dexters separated. William returned to Sydney where he died in Redfern on 4 February 1860 aged 42.

Caroline moved to Melbourne still independent, dynamic and unconventional, startling society by opening an Institute of Hygiene and promulgating such novelties as divided skirts and abolition of corsets. Through her eager and practical interest in social reform and English feminist movements she met Harriet Clisby [q.v.], with whom she edited the first all-women publication, the Interpreter (1861); it ran to two issues. Caroline's contributions included an attack on an English manufacturing town, an appeal to colonists to forget their past and to remember England only for the passion of social reformers, the white man's betrayal of the 'noble savage', and a sketch of the remittance man useless either to Australia or to England.

In 1861 Caroline married William Lynch (b. Ireland 1839), a former pupil at Lyndhurst. Later he wrote: 'It was my wife's mind that attracted me, and from her I learned all that I know of art'. He became a prosperous solicitor and in 1880-81 was mayor of Brighton. With his wealth Caroline became a patron of local writers and artists, holding her salon at Bombala, her fashionable home in Brighton. She also helped her husband to assemble an extraordinary art collection, which included Richard Parkes Bonington's 'Low Tide at Boulogne', now in the National Gallery of Victoria. After she died on 19 August 1884, Lynch married Charlotte Mary Ochiltree; he died in Melbourne on 27 May 1901.

Caroline deserves to be remembered as a champion of women's rights and a friend to the Aboriginals. Though little of her writing remains, she contributed richly to the cultural life of Melbourne by her wit, love of local colour and zest for arts and letters.

H. Wilson, 'The Dexter mystery', Art in Australia, no 8, 1921; D. Wilcox and W. Moore, 'The wife of the artist—Caroline Dexter', Art in Australia, no 36, Feb 1931; Argus, 19 Aug 1853, 28 May 1901; Caroline Lynch to J. R. Sheridan 1871 (ML).   J. S. RYAN

DIBBS, SIR GEORGE RICHARD (1834-1904), politician, was born on 12 October 1834 in Sydney, the third son of Captain John Dibbs (b. 1790) and his wife Sophia Elizabeth (1809-1891). His father arrived in 1820 at Sydney and in 1822-27 was master of ships serving the Pacific stations of the London Missionary Society; when married at Scots Church on 16 December 1828 he was captain of the Lady Blackwood; in 1834 he disappeared. His resolute wife reared George and his brothers Thomas Allwright [q.v.] and John Campbell.

George's education was practical and commercial; he attended St Philip's Church of England School and at about 11, probably through his mother's influence with J. D. Lang [q.v.], entered the Australian College. His lifelong admiration for Lang, the 'pureminded patriot', did not check the family's drift from Presbyterianism into the Church of England, to which the mother was devoutly attached. In 1848 Dibbs became a junior clerk in William Brown & Co., wine merchants. At about 20 he joined his brother in J. C. Dibbs & Co., commission agents. The association was temporarily broken when George married Anne Maria (b. Staffordshire, 1835) at St Stephen's, Camperdown, on 18 March 1857 and joined her father, Ralph Mayer Robey [q.v.], first in his shipping agency and then in a sugarrefining and distilling business. It was sold in 1859 to the Colonial Sugar Co. and Dibbs returned to J. C. Dibbs & Co., as manager of the Newcastle branch and later the Sydney office.

Features of Dibbs's career indicated an impatience to live more adventurously than in an office. In 1855 he had sailed with

A. C. Gregory [q.v.] to the Victoria River, and then visited Singapore and perhaps India. A more revealing adventure began in 1865 when J. C. Dibbs & Co. decided to open a branch at Valparaiso under his charge. He sailed in September with his wife, son and three daughters in the Mary and Edith with coal for Chile; she was to return with Chilean wheat to Sydney where scarcity promised good prices. Although Chile was at war with Spain and the coast blockaded Dibbs got into Valparaiso, on one account by displaying the Union Jack and facing down 'the beggars', on another by abandoning his cargo and taking in a launch at night. He lived at Valparaiso as a corn factor until the failure of the Agra Bank brought down his branch and the company in 1866. The brothers worked hard to repay their creditors; in 1875 they were cleared by the Bankruptcy Court and able to extend into importing and shipowning, projects which had taken Dibbs to Britain in 1869.

By the early 1870s Dibbs was tolerably well known in Sydney's mercantile life. He was appointed to the Marine Services Board in 1872 and in 1873 challenged the Chamber of Commerce and the collector of customs with a pamphlet on Wharfage Accommodation . . . in the Port of Sydney. In 1874 he responded for the shipping interest at the merchants' annual dinner and in December was returned for West Sydney to the Legislative Assembly as a supporter of local business and city interests. His election was also a victory for the Public Schools League, newly formed to advocate 'national, compulsory, secular and free' education. He adhered to this cause less from sectarian rancour than from devotion to the principle: the 'absolute duty of the state to educate every child in it'. This led him to oppose the Parkes [q.v.] ministry which was then unwilling to disturb the balance created by the Education Act of 1866.

In June 1875 Dibbs fulfilled his electoral promise by proposing a bill to withdraw support from denominational schools but was defeated by 21 votes to 7; Robertson [q.v.], who had replaced Parkes as premier, promised to bring in a bill without any decisive change in policy and Parkes opposed the Public Schools League and any bill that would arouse denominational opinion. While the league waited hopefully for Robertson's bill Dibbs retained loose association with the ministry, but at a great public meeting in March 1876 he denounced Robertson's promised bill as a sham and betrayal. He then joined the group around Parkes, a connexion important in appreciating the relations between the two men. In division after division Dibbs voted with Parkes and after Parkes became premier in

March 1877 assured him of support. In the October elections this political friendship was at its height. Before the elections Dibbs had won repute as an enemy of labour by supporting the government's policy of assisted immigration, a question that brought an upsurge of working-class political activity. His meetings in West Sydney were plunged into 'uproar indescribable'. Even Dibbs quailed before the challenge, suspecting that working-class political action was a rising of 'brute force' against intelligence. Like Parkes he lost his seat.

One sequel to the campaign was the seamen's strike against the Australian Steam Navigation Co. It began in November 1878 when the company, pressed by competitors, extended its use of Chinese labour from Pacific island routes to the Australian coast, a decision which Dibbs as chairman of directors may not have approved. Attitudes soon hardened, partly because the strike became caught up in a wider agitation against Chinese immigration, partly because Dibbs, once the strike began, gave the directors and shareholders a pugnacious leadership. Although the company accepted a compromise in January 1879, it had been stubbornly opposed by the unions and a section of the press, while Parkes had accused it of provocation. As the company's lightning conductor, Dibbs seemed to have wrecked his political career but relief came from an unexpected quarter. His temperament, active but not cool, courageous but not disciplined, was litigious. While fighting the company's battles he was also gathering evidence for the divorce proceedings of his brother John whose wife had committed adultery with her solicitor, John Shepherd. Shepherd brought an action for slander and obtained a verdict for £2000 with costs. When Dibbs refused to pay, a writ of *ca. sa.* was issued and Shepherd, eager for the arrest, haunted the sheriff's office. At 11 p.m. on 7 May 1880 Dibbs was at last apprehended; he calmly undressed and challenged the bailiff to move his large bulk. What Shepherd's vindictiveness and his own *savoir-faire* began, was completed by patience and a good press during his year in gaol. In this 'cheery, pleasant retreat where one can do martyrdom for principle's sake with every comfort', he entertained his friends and restored his health by the manual labours that he loved, especially on the lathe supplied by Parkes. The new *Bulletin* became his champion: 'He holds the respect and esteem of the vast majority of the community, of all who admire steadfastness of character and the maintenance of principle against all consequences'. His imprisonment prepared the way for his return to parliament.

Dibbs also made overtures to political enemies. In October 1882 he read to the Trades and Labor Council a paper advocating as an alternative to strikes a court of conciliation on the French model, with wise adjudicators representative of both capital and labour putting faith not in legal machinery but in 'the unwritten law of a common interest ratified by mutual consent'. Exonerated by the former secretary of the Seamen's Union from responsibility for the strike, Dibbs stood for St Leonards in the December elections. He joined the Opposition under Alexander Stuart [q.v.] in condemning the refusal of the Parkes-Robertson coalition to reform the land laws and in favouring more orderly settlement and greater security for all occupiers of land, whether squatters or selectors, than was possible under the existing system. He was returned and, to the surprise of the press, was appointed colonial treasurer, although he claimed to have neither solicited nor bargained for office.

When Dibbs made his first financial statement in February 1883, the crucial decision had been firmly taken to suspend land sales. In a sanguine mood he proposed no new taxation, no tariff changes and no cut-back in public works. Later he recognized the decision to deprive the government of land revenue without alternative taxation as 'the gravest political blunder of my life; it was a cabinet decision but the odium was to be his. He saw clearly what had to be done. In his budget of January 1884 he proposed to create new revenue by a property tax to raise £1 million and, at the other end of the scale, increased duties on tea and tobacco. The press was well disposed and the ministry was not shaken by the clamours of the property-owners or by the threat of censure in the assembly, but the government's followers declined to support the property tax and Dibbs failed in this first attempt at fiscal reform which was long to preoccupy the colony's politics. However, in the faith that the country's future depended on a bold and comprehensive railway system he won the support of parliament for an unprecedented loan of over £14 million. His courage was admired, but he lacked the prudence to warn him that a revulsion of political feeling would leave him with an ineradicable reputation for extravagance.

Dibbs was taken by surprise when W. B. Dalley [q.v.], the acting premier, offered colonial troops for service in the Sudan in February 1885. At first he was cautious, but Dalley's boldness was congenial to him and to the Stuart administration, 'younger men', as B. R. Wise put it, 'of Australian birth, for whom the word "unconstitutional" possessed no terror'. He threw himself into the preparations and quickly pushed through the necessary legislation when parliament met in March.

The Sudan aroused patriotic fervour but did not reduce the government's difficulties: Stuart's illness; a long dispute with the Bank of New South Wales from which Dibbs withdrew the government's account; and the complexities of floating a large loan in London. In October Stuart retired and, when Dalley refused the call, Dibbs began to form his first ministry. According to the *Daily Telegraph* he had an impetuous temperament and imperious manner, British stubbornness, a rich manhood and a robust if undisciplined intellect. Anxious to be king-maker, the *Telegraph* was looking for a new combination of 'the young and vigorous and progressive'; the paper preferred Edmund Barton but Dibbs offered to be its leader. He reassembled the remnants of Stuart's ministry and added some younger men although failure to enlist Barton as attorney-general left his ministry weak.

In the elections of 1885 Parkes stood against Dibbs at St Leonards, attacked him mercilessly and won; Dibbs found refuge in the Murrumbidgee electorate. Throughout the colony the government polled rather badly yet Dibbs decided to meet parliament. In the new assembly he narrowly survived a censure vote but his ministry was destroyed by the revelation of a deficit of more than £1 million, the outcome of land policy, drought and failure to enforce new taxation.

In February 1886 Patrick Jennings [q.v.] became premier with Dibbs as his colonial secretary. The government's solution for the financial crisis included direct taxation and *ad valorem* duties on which public attention concentrated. The ministry was said to be 'sneaking in protection' and the *Sydney Morning Herald*, hitherto sympathetic, turned sharply against Dibbs. Although he called himself every inch a free trader and denied that *ad valorem* duties of 5 per cent were protective, he organized protectionist support and carried the measure in turbulent, all night sittings. Other measures were rejected by the Legislative Council and early in 1887 the ministry was dissolved.

The February elections decimated Dibbs's following and left the assembly divided. His only way out of political isolation was to join the Opposition to Parkes's free trade government. Opinion echoed Dibbs, who often quoted scripture, in referring to the road to Damascus when he publicly announced his adherence to protection in July. The change had been predicted in the Murrumbidgee election and was sincere, although he was always impatient with ideologies and remained suspect to the more doctrinaire protectionists. He gave experienced leadership to the large but unsteady protectionist party. Although he was not a social reformer, the 'inherent Toryism' often ascribed to him was hardly consistent with his support of law reform, divorce extension, one man one vote, courts of conciliation and even 'municipal socialism'. His relations with Parkes deteriorated in the crisis over Chinese immigration in May 1888. Dibbs's restless probing of the government's actions provoked Parkes to attack his 'genius for destruction, for degradation and for confusion' and to refer to his year's imprisonment, evidence to Dibbs of the tyrannous disposition of the 'mean, despicable, dastardly man'. When the Parkes ministry fell in February 1889, Dibbs formed a minority administration of sound men likely to reconcile different elements among the protectionists; his ministry was characterized above all as 'the country ministry'. He obtained a dissolution and campaigned on the tariff for solving the revenue problem and providing employment by protection against foreign competition. The protectionists swept the country electorates. Dibbs provocatively filled a number of Legislative Council seats, but when the assembly met he was defeated by 68 votes to 64 and Parkes returned to office.

Dibbs had never looked generously on other Australian colonies and his coolness to Parkes's revival of the federal question in 1889 was no surprise. Concluding that Dibbs would not wish to attend the Federal Convention of 1891 Parkes nominated J. P. Garvan [q.v.] but the outcry forced a ballot in which Dibbs was elected. Alfred Deakin called him 'the Ishmaelite of the Convention', isolated from the New South Wales delegation and opposed to everything brought forward by Parkes. Dibbs asserted Sydney's right to be federal capital and argued for a strong senate, but saw that colonial union was certain and that the most direct way of bringing it about was 'a federation of everything in common', based initially on a customs union.

In October 1891 Dibbs replaced Parkes with whom he had become partly reconciled during their illnesses in 1890. Again Dibbs chose the less doctrinaire of his party for his new ministry: 'the proselytes', said G. H. Reid, 'have crowded out all the apostles'. Barton could not lightly join Dibbs, a severe critic of his strong federalism, but accepted office as attorney-general in return for Dibbs's undertaking to allow him a free hand in federal matters and not to hinder open discussion of the convention bill in the assembly. Dibbs appears to have respected these obligations and the ministry was generally judged to be strong and intelligent. He began with characteristic bravura; the *Herald* called it 'a dangerous sense of exaltation'. He publicly renounced autocracy and rejoiced in colleagues with opinions of their own. Never a deep reader, he was largely indifferent to political ideas but he had clear notions of what constituted good government, above all, the equitable protection of all sections of the community. His immediate problem was to secure his own position. Despite his impulsiveness he shrewdly saw that Labor disunity on the fiscal question was the weak point in the political situation. With as little debate as possible he hastened through a customs duty bill. It gave an earnest to his party, though its protective effect was limited; it was lucrative, though the need for revenue did not then seem desperate; its immediate advantage was political, for it attached a group of Labor protectionists to the government and secured a majority. Dibbs saw the bill's weakness as a protectionist programme, but argued for proceeding by stages towards a fully protective tariff and a complete system of direct taxation. The government moved on with bills for electoral reform and conciliation and arbitration: the former, despite Legislative Council resistance, gave the colony one man one vote in 1893, but the latter provided no compulsion and its effect was small.

Dibbs visited London in 1892 hoping to improve his health and to convince critics that the Australian colonies were not extravagant or over-solicitous of their working classes. To English audiences he insisted on the purity and economy of administration in New South Wales, the security of its lands and public works, and the responsibility of its trades unions. He had promised Barton to speak 'in quiet style and with moderation' and on the tour he was never a prey to his temper. Although he made little progress in his financial business, his ease and tact won good opinions for himself and sympathy for the colony. Yet his steps in other areas threw his ministerial colleagues into alarm. His plans to persuade the French government to cease convict transportation to New Caledonia were thought to include recognition of a French protectorate in the New Hebrides; he cabled back, 'total misapprehension', and abandoned his visit to Paris. Provocatively he accepted a knighthood, finally on the insistence of the Queen and from her hands, but against the advice of Barton who thought refusal would be a politically inspiring gesture. To Dibbs his reception in England was 'like a dream' but he was not carried away by vanity. He was accused of succumbing to the aristocratic embrace and of apostasy to his republicanism, but it was 'only skin deep' and reflected the common colonial belief in eventual independence; in London he was careful to avoid identification with the Imperial Federation League.

Dibbs returned in September to a fulsome public welcome but a censure vote by the Opposition under Reid. On the same day the ministry ordered the arrest of strike leaders at Broken Hill for conspiracy. Reid and his supporters joined the government in rejecting a Labor amendment censuring its actions at Broken Hill, and four Labor protectionists helped Dibbs to survive Reid's censure. Assertions that he sided with the Broken Hill employers cannot be proved. On the contrary he urged them to hold out the olive branch and to use the new machinery for arbitration. He was hard on disorder but without vindictiveness, and towards Labor he was neither hostile nor obsequious. Though he preferred self help he had founded the Labor Bureau in February 1892 to bring together the unemployed and employers, but he refused to fix wages and condemned demonstrations by the unemployed.

By the beginning of 1893 the colony was moving into a great financial crisis. As usual Dibbs was too sanguine as catastrophe approached but bold and decisive when it struck. In 1892 the government resisted demands for retrenchment but next January it had to reduce its estimates and attempt to pass a new income tax bill. By April the estimates were still not adopted and Dibbs had to threaten with a dissolution those of his own party who wanted retrenchment. The Legislative Council threw out the income tax bill, but attention now had to be concentrated on the collapse of the banking system.

In that kind of emergency Dibbs came into his own. When panic threatened the Savings Bank of New South Wales he appeared at its doors and wrote in his own hand a proclamation guaranteeing its deposits. Continuing runs on the banks required more systematic action. Dibbs had foreseen such a catastrophe ten years earlier and had worked out a solution. A cabinet committee produced a simple measure making bank notes a first charge on the issuers' assets. Its purpose, said Dibbs, was not 'to assist the banks of this colony, because with private business and banking this Parliament has nothing whatever to do' but to 'save some thousands of our fellow-citizens from severe loss and misery'. The bill was accepted by large majorities in both Houses in May and he told Acting-Governor Darley [q.v.] that its mere passage would 'prove effective for the restoration of confidence'. The banks, however, 'unnerved by the swift march of destruction', lacked the will or the public spirit to take advantage of it and most of them closed their doors and prepared for reconstruction. T. A. Coghlan later claimed that without his 'bold, well conceived, and successful' action the crisis would have been worse than it was. 'For six weeks', wrote Dibbs himself, 'I never left my office to go home—but once—the storm is over—the ship saved'.

Success did not improve the government's position and in December it was defeated. Dibbs shrugged this off as a vote of no consequence and prorogued parliament because the new rolls and electorates required by the 1893 electoral reforms were not yet fixed. Dibbs ironically called this manoeuvre 'Cromwellian' and was accused of dictatorship. In early 1894 his opponents' indignation turned to hysteria: he was compared with Strafford, Alva and the Czar. With less abandon the government was attacked by the more radical or doctrinaire protectionists for his treachery in refusing to bring in a properly protective tariff. His defence was that amid his difficulties (worse, said the *Bulletin*, than had fallen to the lot of any cabinet in the colony's history) he could not face that long uphill struggle.

In 1894 the government passed its estimates and prepared the new electoral machinery. After long disdain of the federal question Dibbs suddenly appealed directly to the Victorian premier to begin a unification of New South Wales and Victoria into which the smaller colonies would eventually be drawn, but the idea fell flat. In the elections of mid-1894 the government was on the defensive while the Opposition promised social reform and solution of the fiscal problem by free trade and direct taxation. The protectionists, whose country support made them cautious about a land tax, were reduced in numbers but the existence of three parties, none with an absolute majority, permitted Dibbs's familiar manoeuvre of waiting to meet the new parliament. He even repeated the attempt to make appointments to the Legislative Council but the governor, Sir Robert Duff, refused the request and forced his resignation. As leader of the Opposition to Reid's ministry in 1894-95 Dibbs espoused a conservatism which has misleadingly coloured his whole career. He rejected payment of members and opposed measures he had long supported. A loose alliance with Parkes was prepared by intermediaries. In the circumstances the move was not so unholy as contemporaries pretended but it failed miserably. In the 1895 elections Reid presented Dibbs and Parkes as reactionary and unprincipled and both were defeated. Dibbs sympathized with Parkes on his handling by Reid and 'his revolutionary mob followers', claiming that such a defeat was more honourable than victory.

Dibbs was appointed managing trustee of the Savings Bank of New South Wales. Des-

pite occasional speculation about his return to lead the protectionist party and his own opposition to the form of Federation, he remained in political retirement until his death from heart disease at Passy, Hunter's Hill, on 5 August 1904. His wife, nine daughters and two sons survived him. He was buried at St Thomas's cemetery, North Sydney.

A portrait by Percy Spence, presented as a testimonial in 1893, is in the Public Library of New South Wales.

H. Parkes, *Fifty years in the making of Australian history* (Lond, 1892); B. R. Wise, *The making of the Australian Commonwealth, 1889-1900* (Lond, 1913); T. A. Coghlan, *Labour and industry in Australia*, 3-4 (Lond, 1918); B. E. Mansfield, *Australian democrat . . . the career of Edward William O'Sullivan, 1846-1910* (Syd, 1965); P. Loveday and A. W. Martin, *Parliament factions and parties* (Melb, 1966); A. R. Crane, 'The New South Wales Public Schools League 1874-1879', E. L. French (ed), *Melbourne studies in education 1964* (Melb, 1965); PD (NSW), 1883-95; N. B. Nairn, 'The political mastery of Sir Henry Parkes', *JRAHS*, 53 (1967); B. Dickey, 'The Broken Hill strike, 1892', *Labour Hist*, no 11, Nov 1966; N. J. Hubbard, Some aspects of the social and political career of George Dibbs in N.S.W. (M.A. thesis, Univ Syd, 1968); Col Sec papers, special bundles 1885-93 (NSWA); Barton papers and uncat MS (ML); Parkes letters (ML).

BRUCE E. MANSFIELD

DIBBS, SIR THOMAS ALLWRIGHT (1832-1923), banker, was born on 31 October 1832 in Sydney, the second son of John Dibbs, master mariner, and his wife Sophia Elizabeth, née Allwright. He attended the Australian College and at 14 began work in the Commercial Banking Co. of Sydney. He became its accountant in 1857, inspector in 1860, manager in March 1867 and general manager in 1882. At his retirement in 1915 he was voted a pension of £2000 and made an honorary director. He was also a substantial shareholder of the bank, having begun to buy shares in the early 1850s; he thereafter accumulated more by purchase.

The bank's annual report for 1923 recognized that 'the Bank, as it stands today is a monument to [Dibbs's] ability and faithful service'. Under his prudent management the bank progressed and was extolled for its success, particularly for its high annual dividends in 1867-92. In 1893 when several Sydney banks foundered, it weathered the crisis by closing its doors in May to permit reconstruction. This action, instituted on Dibbs's insistence, was justified but much criticized as completely unnecessary because the bank was then considered solvent. Its reopening in June in a healthy condition was later

credited to Dibbs's ability to do 'the right
thing at the right time', and increased his
repute for skilful management, clear judgment, quick perception, decisive action and
genuine concern for the welfare of the
bank's employees.

In his last thirty years with the Commercial Bank Dibbs became a doyen in the Australian banking community; his opinions on
banking and finance were much respected
and his advice was often sought by the New
South Wales government. His brother
George [q.v.] who was premier in 1891-94
may not have been as dependent on his advice as has sometimes been claimed, because
Thomas was in England in 1892 and because
the brothers were temporarily estranged.
Dibbs published a useful booklet, Interest
Tables, in 1877 and was also responsible for
shaping some important banking practices
in Sydney, particularly the form of the daily
settlement and the exchange system set up
in 1888. He also had a long association with
the Bankers' Institute of New South Wales
and was its president in 1901.

His family connexions, his standing in
financial circles and his wide interests won
Dibbs prominence in New South Wales. He
was appointed to the Civil Service Inquiry
Board in 1887 and was president of the committee of inquiry into public accounts in
1900. A keen yachtsman, he was a commodore of the Royal Sydney Yacht Squadron.
He was active in diocesan affairs of the
Church of England and his philanthropic
interests included the Sydney Naval Home
and the Queen Victoria Home for Consumptives; in June 1915 he gave his home, Gray-
thwaite, to the Commonwealth government
as a convalescent hospital for wounded soldiers. Equipped and furnished from the proceeds of a public appeal it was opened in
1916 under the control of the Red Cross
Society. Dibbs was knighted in 1917. He
died in Sydney on 18 March 1923, survived
by his wife Tryphena, née Gaden, whom he
had married at Sydney in 1857, and by six
daughters. His estate was sworn for probate
at more than £133,000.

A portrait is at the head office of the
Commercial Banking Co. of Sydney.

SMH, 15 June 1915, 19, 20 Mar 1923; Dibbs
family papers (ML).

G. J. ABBOTT

DICKENS, CHARLES (1812-1870), novelist, was born on 7 February 1812 in Portsmouth, England, son of John Dickens, a
clerk in the Navy Pay Office, and his wife
Elizabeth, née Barrow. Dickens received in-
termittent schooling and indifferent care
from his parents who were once obliged to
take up residence in Marshalsea prison for
debt. First apprenticed to the law, he began
writing unpaid pieces for popular journals.
Sketches by 'Boz', Dickens's pseudonym,
were published in two volumes in 1836 and
The Posthumous Papers of the Pickwick
Club in 1837. Sam Weller and Mr Pickwick
created a world-wide furore and Dickens's
imitators were legion. Pickwick parties were
held as far apart as Canada and Kangaroo
Island, whilst the first pirated edition of
Pickwick Papers was printed by Henry
Dowling [q.v.] of Tasmania in 1838.

Fame was assured for Dickens with the
publication of Oliver Twist in 1838 and
Nicholas Nickleby in 1839. As novelist,
journalist, public speaker and social critic,
his popularity was universal and the world
of his novels changed contemporary attitudes. At first aware of Australia only as a
place of penal servitude, Dickens in Pickwick Papers has the convict, John Edmunds,
transported and sent up country as a shepherd. The infamous Mr Squeers in Nicholas
Nickleby is similarly sent to the colony. Always fascinated by crime, Dickens acquired
knowledge of Norfolk Island from his friend
Alexander Maconochie [q.v.]. He never forgot Australia's prison origins and in his last
completed novel, Our Mutual Friend (1865),
Jenny Wren threatens her delinquent
father with transportation. Similarly in
David Copperfield, Mr Littimer and Uriah
Heep are dispatched to Australia to complete their sentences.

In 1849 Dickens was writing David Copperfield and faced with the problem of a satisfactory disposition of Micawber and his family. He had already met Samuel Sidney [q.v.],
who was advocating Australia as a home for
working class emigrants, and Mrs Caroline
Chisholm [q.v.] through a common friend,
Sidney Herbert. The last chapters of David
Copperfield embodied material from Sidney's
Australian Hand-Book (1848) and Wilkins
Micawber duly became the best known emigrant to Port Middlebay (Melbourne) where
he attained affluence and the office of magis-
trate. Micawber was accompanied by little
Em'ly, Peggotty, Martha Endell and Mrs
Gummidge. The downtrodden schoolmaster,
Mr Mell, founded an academy for boys at
Port Middlebay and his fiddling and oratory
delighted colonial society.

Household Words, Dickens's journal, began publication in 1850 and the first article
was an approving exposition of Mrs Chisholm's Family Colonization Loan Society.
Later articles and stories in that year were
written by Samuel Sidney. The discovery of
gold lent feasibility to Micawber's success
and mitigated the country's reputation as a
gaol. In Great Expectations (1861) Dickens
created Magwitch, the convict who amassed

wealth in New South Wales and so produced an English gentleman.

Dickens had contemplated a lecture tour of Australia in 1862 and intended to write a travel book, 'The Uncommercial Traveller Upside Down', but the tour was abandoned. In Australia, as in England, his novels were adapted as stage plays; with *Our Emily, Old Curiosity Shop* and *Cricket on the Hearth* as perennial favourites. The articles from *Household Words* and *All the Year Round* were widely published in the Australian press and helped to impose Dickens's own view of Australia on Australian life and society.

Dickens died on 9 June 1870. Of his surviving sons, Alfred D'Orsay Tennyson (b. 1845), had migrated to Australia in 1865. He bought a partnership in a stock and station agency in Hamilton, Victoria, but after his wife died left in 1882 to join the Melbourne branch of his brother's agency. After a lecture tour he died in the United States in 1912. The youngest son, Edward Bulwer Lytton (b. 1852), went to Australia in 1869 and settled at Wilcannia where he became manager of Momba station; in 1880 he married Constance Desailly. He opened a stock and station agency; was elected to the local council and bought a share in Yanda station near Bourke. He lost heavily from bad seasons and in 1886 he became a civil servant. He represented Wilcannia in the New South Wales Legislative Assembly in 1889-94. He died on 23 January 1902 at Moree and was buried by a Wesleyan minister.

C. Lansbury, 'Charles Dickens and his Australia', *JRAHS*, 52 (1966), and for bibliog.

CORAL LANSBURY

DICKINSON, SIR JOHN NODES (1806-1882), judge, was born at Grenada in the West Indies, son of Nodes Dickinson, F.R.C.S., a British army staff surgeon. He was educated at Fulham College and Caius College, Cambridge (B.A., 1829; M.A., 1832), and for the next eight years practised as a certificated special pleader. In 1840 he was called to the Bar at the Inner Temple, and at the Common Law Bar had, according to Judge J. S. Dowling [q.v.], 'the reputation of being a good sound lawyer and of being skilled in mercantile law'.

In 1844 a judgeship of the Supreme Court of New South Wales fell vacant on the appointment of W. W. Burton [q.v.] as a judge at Madras. Dickinson was considered for the vacancy but, being then a barrister of less than five years' standing, doubts arose as to his eligibility under the Act 4 Geo. IV, c. 96. The problem was referred to the English Crown law officers, who on 13 March advised that the statutory provisions related only to qualification as chief justice, not as puisne judge, of the colony. Dickinson was accordingly appointed judge, but to avoid all doubt as to the validity of his appointment he was furnished with two commissions differently worded. He was advised by Lord Stanley to present whichever of them was considered more appropriate after private discussion with the governor, the colonial law officers and the other judges of the Supreme Court. In June Dickinson sailed for Sydney in the *Garland Grove* with his wife Helen, daughter of Captain Henry Jauncey, R.N., of Dartmouth, Devon, whom he had married earlier that year. They arrived in Sydney on 13 October and he was sworn in next day, the last judge of the New South Wales Supreme Court appointed in England.

Dickinson's activities in the colony were not limited to his judicial duties. He took a keen interest in public affairs, constitutional development and law reform. On 16 September 1848 he was appointed to a royal commission to inquire into the constitution and practice of the courts of the colony. He had some novel ideas, which, however, were not adopted, particularly that the Supreme Court's jurisdictions should be made separate courts in distinct buildings, a separate Bar being associated with each.

In 1852, amidst increasing demands for responsible government in New South Wales, Dickinson published *A Letter to the Honorable the Speaker of the Legislative Council, on the formation of a Second Chamber in the Legislature of New South Wales*. Its interesting proposals included the creation of a local hereditary baronetage, that honour to be conferred on every fit and proper person having certain landed property qualifications in the colony, until seventy-five baronets had been so appointed. Thereafter a further twenty-five should be nominated without reference to property qualifications, and from the total there should be elected, either by themselves for a single parliamentary term or by popular vote for three parliamentary terms, thirty of their number, to form the Legislative Council. Nothing came of Dickinson's suggestion, although Wentworth [q.v.] later proposed a hereditary colonial aristocracy. On 13 May 1856 Dickinson was appointed to the first Legislative Council under responsible government, but, conscious of antipathy to judges taking part in politics, he resigned on 29 March 1858.

As a judge of the Supreme Court Dickinson carried out his duties ably and conscientiously, sometimes under difficulties; he once complained that 'the necessity of having to consider one day a point of Common Law, another day a point of Insolvency, and another day an Equity suit has been to me a source of the utmost distraction'. Yet he was highly competent, and his demeanour and impartiality were universally respected and admired. Dowling, who described him as 'an upright, conscientious, learned Judge', recalled that Dickinson exercised great control over his court and was 'exceedingly courteous' to the Bar. Dickinson never became a figure of controversy, and was the more acceptable in presiding at the hearing of several contentious cases of outstanding public interest. One was the great banking case of 1845, *Bank of Australasia* v. *Breillat* [q.v.] in which he presided at the first trial and was later a member of the Full Bench which presided over the trial at bar. Another was the celebrated Newtown ejectment case (*Doe dem. Devine* v. *Wilson and others*), where Dickinson presided over a special jury of twelve at a hearing lasting thirty days. His summing-up occupied three days. The *Sydney Morning Herald*, 23 September 1857, described Dickinson's conduct throughout the trial as 'a triumph of judicial discretion'.

From 15 February 1860 to 17 February 1861 Dickinson, as senior puisne judge, was acting chief justice of New South Wales during the absence of Sir Alfred Stephen [q.v.]. In this position and in recognition of his services to the colony .Dickinson was knighted in 1860. Dickinson and his family then lived at 239 Victoria Street, in the fashionable district of Darlinghurst but, according to Dowling, Dickinson was 'most unostentatious in his habits, and did not go much into society'. When Stephen returned Dickinson retired from the court and returned to England on a pension of £1050. He lived quietly, first at Bath and then in London, with his wife and their daughter Helen Mary. Still interested in law reform, Dickinson in 1861 published in London *A Letter to the Lord Chancellor on Law Consolidation*, wherein he recommended a codification of the law, along Continental lines, with a digest and an institute. In retirement he regularly corresponded with Sir Alfred Stephen. Dickinson died on 16 March 1882 while on a visit to Rome. He was survived by his wife and daughter, who were the executrices of his will, proved in London on 16 May 1882 at over £21,000.

His portrait, as acting chief justice, is in the President's Court, Supreme Court House, Sydney.

HRA (1), 23-26; V&P (LC NSW), 1856-58; SMH, 14, 15, 22 Oct 1844; *The Times*, 21 Mar 1882; *Old Times*, June, July 1903; Stephen papers (ML).   JOHN KENNEDY MCLAUGHLIN

DICKSON, JAMES (1813-1863), merchant and politician, was the son of Peter Dickson, farmer, of Seawick Park, Kirkcudbright, Scotland, and his wife Elizabeth, née Houston. Described as a tailor, he arrived in Australia as a bounty immigrant in the *Duchess of Northumberland* on 22 April 1838. He went to Maitland where he and his brother David established a general store that grew into a large and successful business. In the 1850s he leased over a quarter of a million acres in the New England, Warrego and Leichhardt districts, including Yarrow and Mihi Creeks, Oban, Pepperton and Cartland; he also held Glen Innis (25,000 acres) and Mole River (60,000 acres) with William Dumaresq [q.v.].

In 1857 Dickson won Northumberland Boroughs in the Legislative Assembly. He favoured free trade, electoral reform, municipal institutions and local taxation, the extension of railways, a national system of education and district courts with extended civil and criminal jurisdiction. He also supported 'extended religious liberty' but opposed further state aid because it was 'erroneous in principle and unjust in practice'. Before his success at the 1858 general election, he said that he was a supporter of the Cowper [q.v.] ministry and was against the undue influence exercised by the squatters in the first parliament. He also opposed an impost on Chinese, saying he would 'never consent to a tax on the human race'. He represented the seat until 11 April 1859. From 15 September until his death he represented East Maitland.

In 1852 Dickson was one of the founders of the Hunter River New Steam Navigation Co. After his election to parliament he moved to Sydney where he carried on business with Alexander Dickson and Robert Strachan as Dickson and Co., merchants, 15 Macquarie Place. In April 1858 he was elected with J. B. Watt [q.v.] to a committee to examine the possibility of establishing a Presbyterian college within the University of Sydney. He was an active member of the Presbyterian Church, both at Maitland and Newtown.

He died at his residence, Holmwood, Newtown, on 28 April 1863, and was buried in the Presbyterian cemetery at East Maitland: about 1905 his remains were transferred to Waverley cemetery. His estate was sworn for probate at £100,000.

At Maitland on 18 March 1842, he had married Agnes Graham, daughter of Robert Strachan of Gelston Lodge, Kirkcudbright, and sister of Mrs David Dickson; they had four sons and four daughters. The eldest daughter Jessie (b. 1843) married Lieutenant (later Major-General) John Soame Richardson [q.v.]. Dickson's wife, who was born in Dumfries, Scotland, died at Sydney on 25 October 1913, aged 91.

J. Cameron, *Centenary history of the Presbyterian Church in New South Wales* (Syd, 1905); *V&P (LA NSW)*, 1859-60, 3, 652-3, 691, 708; *Hunter River Gazette*, 19 Mar 1842; *SMH*, 26 Sept, 31 Oct, 5, 11 Nov 1857, 27 Jan, 6 Apr 1858, 29 Apr 1863; *Maitland Mercury*, 2 May 1863.   G. P. WALSH

DIETRICH, AMALIE (1821-1891), naturalist, was born at Siebenlehn, Saxony, daughter of Gottlieb Nelle(m), leatherworker, and his wife Cordel(ia). She was educated at the village school. Her passionate interest in natural history stemmed from a chance meeting with Wilhelm August Salomo Dietrich whom she married about 1846. He was ten years her senior and son of a lawyer whose family was long associated with botany; though trained as a chemist he preferred collecting natural history specimens for sale to apothecaries, institutions and students. The couple rented a house in Siebenlehn where they were joined by Amalie's parents who ran the household while Dietrich took Amalie on long collecting trips. In March 1848 their daughter Charitas Concordia Sophie was born. When Cordel Nelle died in 1852 the household deteriorated for Amalie was ill equipped to cope with domestic tasks. The Dietrichs parted but were reconciled in November 1853 and resumed their expeditions. Alone on a trip to Holland Amalie's health broke down. She finally left her husband, took her daughter to Hamburg and hawked her prepared collections. In 1862 she was introduced to the merchant, J. C. Godeffroy, who was persuaded by well-known scientists to send her to Australia to collect for his private museum.

Amalie sailed in *La Rochelle* and by August 1863 was in Brisbane. She took a house on the river and began collecting industriously. Her letters to Charitas told of much new material: the Brisbane River 'yielded . . . rich spoils'; Gladstone was not so bounteous; at Rockhampton she found that the heat, though 'unbearable' had produced 'such a wealth of vegetation that literally everything towers high above my head'. At the Fitzroy River she dissected crocodiles twenty-two feet long; she suffered fever, lost her house by fire and was rescued by Aboriginals from a water-lily swamp. In 1866 she went to Mackay, thence to Lake Elphinstone and by August 1869 was collecting around Bowen. She went with two assistants to the Holborne Islands, returned to Bowen and then continued to Brisbane and Sydney. At Melbourne in 1871 she met Ferdinand Mueller [q.v.]. By February 1872 she was at Tonga, and on 4 March 1873, accompanied by two pet eagles, she returned to Hamburg.

Amalie Dietrich was enchanted by the natural history resources of Australia and collected plants, insects, corals, shells, mammals, fish, birds and Aboriginal remains. 'What freedom I enjoy here as a collector', she wrote. 'No one circumscribes my zeal . . . I speedily forget the discomforts of heat and mosquitoes in the unbounded feeling of joy that animates me when, at every step, I light upon treasures that no one has secured before me'.

For thirteen years Amalie worked in Godeffroy's museum. When his collections became the property of the City of Hamburg, she was given a post in the Botanical Museum. On a visit to her daughter at Rendsburg she contracted pneumonia, died on 9 March 1891 and was buried in Rendsburg cemetery. She was fearless and single-minded in the cause of the natural science she so eagerly learned from her difficult and selfish husband. Completely unconcerned about personal comfort and appearance, she must have seemed unusually eccentric. Within a limited scientific circle she was highly respected as an ardent collector and accurate observer, and was honoured by the names of several plant and animal species (e.g. *Acacia dietrichiana, Bonamia dietrichiana, Nortonia amaliae* and *Odynerus dietrichianus*). Bentham [q.v.] referred to her specimens in his *Flora Australiensis*. She was elected a fellow of the Entomological Society of Stettin, and her fifty Australian wood specimens earned a gold medal at a horticultural exhibition. Some of her plant specimens went to Mueller and are in the National Herbarium, Melbourne.

C. Bischoff, *The hard road. The life story of Amalie Dietrich*, tr by A. L. Geddie (Lond, 1931); J. H. Maiden, 'Records of Australian botanists. First supplement', *Report 13th Meeting, A'sian Assn Advancement of Science* (Syd, 1912); G. Mulac-Teichmann, 'A tribute to the naturalist, Amalie Dietrich', *Vic Naturalist*, 81 (1964).   L. A. GILBERT

DIGGLES, SILVESTER (1817-1880), naturalist, artist and musician, was born on 24 January 1817, the eldest son of Edward Holt Diggles, ironmonger of Liverpool, England, and his wife Elizabeth, née Silvester. In May 1839 he married Eliza, daughter of John Bradley, tutor of Liverpool; they had two daughters and a son. With them he arrived at Sydney in November 1853, and moved to Brisbane in November 1854. There he taught drawing and music and also practised as a tuner and repairer of musical instruments. His wife died in August 1857 and in January 1858 he married Albina, daughter of John and Sarah Birkett of Barnby in the Willows, Nottinghamshire; they had two sons. Genial, friendly and an enthusiastic supporter of community activities, Diggles became a well-known and beloved citizen. He was a founder of the Brisbane Choral Society in 1859 and the Brisbane Philharmonic Society in 1861 and accompanist at church services and concerts. When the musicians of the city gave him a grand benefit concert in 1877, he was termed 'the father of music in Brisbane'. Sincerely religious, he had joined the New Jerusalem Church in 1846 and acted as its leader in Brisbane for some years; he also was a Mason.

Diggles helped to found the colony's first scientific institution, the Queensland Philosophical Society, on 1 March 1859 and published several papers in its *Transactions*; he also worked hard for the infant Queensland Museum which the society commenced in 1862. His special interests were ornithology and entomology, through which he had a wide circle of friends and correspondents. His outstanding publication was *The Ornithology of Australia* of which twenty-one parts were issued in 1865-70. Each part contains six lithographed hand-coloured plates, imperial quarto size, with accompanying descriptive notes. Between 1863 and 1875 he completed 325 plates illustrating about 600 birds, and the text but had no funds to publish more. His original plates and manuscript are in the Mitchell Library, Sydney. Diggles's major contribution to the knowledge of Australian fauna, however, was through the extensive collections of insects, particularly butterflies, moths and beetles, which he sent to overseas entomologists for description. In 1875 his health began to fail, due partly to worry over the *Ornithology*. He died at Kangaroo Point, Brisbane, on 21 March 1880, survived by two daughters of his first marriage and two sons of the second.

E. N. Marks, 'Silvester Diggles—a Queensland naturalist one hundred years ago', *Qld Naturalist*, 17 (July 1963), and for bibliog; E. N. Marks, 'Notes on Diggles "Ornithology of Australia"', *Qld Naturalist*, 17 (June 1965).

E. N. MARKS

DILKE, SIR CHARLES WENTWORTH (1843-1911), politician and author, was born on 4 September 1843 in London, son of Sir Charles Wentworth Dilke and his wife Mary, née Chatfield. He was educated privately and at Trinity Hall, Cambridge (LL.B., 1866; LL.M., 1869). He was called to the Bar at the Middle Temple in April 1866 but never practised. He planned to enter politics but first made a world tour, which he hoped would yield material for his work on radicalism and his interest in ideal commonwealths. He left England in June 1866 for America, then went to New Zealand and arrived at Sydney on 1 January 1867. After a brief visit to Queensland, he returned to Sydney via Newcastle, and in February went to Melbourne. Despite soaring summer temperatures he considered Victoria the 'most attractive as well as the most energetic' of the colonies, and visited Ballarat, Sandhurst, Echuca and Geelong. He liked Tasmania but saw it as the 'Ireland of the South', blighted by its convict past. In Melbourne again for the end of the Intercolonial Exhibition, he went on to Adelaide and Kapunda, and then to Western Australia. After his return to England his *Greater Britain: a record of travel in English-speaking countries during 1866 and 1867* (London, 1868) was published; it ran to eight editions and its short title became a catch phrase in imperialist debate. In 1869 he succeeded to the baronetcy and proprietorship of the *Athenaeum* and *Notes and Queries*.

Dilke represented Chelsea in the House of Commons in 1868-86. Earlier he had expressed republican views, which he later modified; in parliament he was leader of the radicals in Gladstone's government in 1880, under-secretary to the Foreign Office in 1880-82 and served in cabinet as president of the Local Government Board in 1882-85. Many saw him as a future premier but his career was cut short when he was cited as co-respondent in the spectacular divorce suit, *Crawford* v. *Crawford and Dilke* in 1885-86. Although he strongly protested his innocence, public opinion was against him; he lost his seat in parliament in July 1886 and turned to writing. His works referring to Australia include *The British Army* (1888), *Problems of Greater Britain* (1890), *Imperial Defence* (1892) written in collaboration with Spenser Wilkinson, and *The British Empire* (1899). In 1875 he had contributed to *Cobden Club Essays. Local government and taxation* edited by J. W. Probyn.

Dilke visited China and Japan in 1875, Greece and Constantinople in 1887-88 and India in 1888-89. In 1892-1911 he represented the Forest of Dean in parliament where he often spoke on foreign and imperial affairs. He had married Katherine Mary Eliza, née Sheil, in 1872; she died in 1874. On 3 October 1885 he married Emilia Francis Pattison, née Strong, who died in 1904. Dilke died in London on 26 January 1911, survived by a son of his first marriage.

Greater Britain established Dilke's reputation as an expert on colonial questions. The

Australasian, 28 January 1911, praised the 'grasp the radical statesman had upon empire politics'. His assessments of colonial democracy showed some weaknesses, but his interest in the Australian colonies persisted: in 1884 he urged Gladstone to annex New Guinea, taking what he said was 'the Australian view'. He corresponded with Alfred Deakin who described him as 'more ambitious than most of his' rivals, more industrious, more teachable and more versatile . . . one of the most trustworthy and intellectual of radicals . . . knowledge was his forte and omniscience his foible'. In speeches Dilke often referred to Australian experiments in labour and social legislation. As an exponent of imperial defence, he advocated a strong navy, a general staff at the War Office to operate on an imperial as well as a national level, and a regular army of high quality. Occasional articles by him appeared in the Australian press and in the 1890s he invested in Western Australian mining and newspapers.

S. L. Gwynn and G. M. Tuckwell, *The life of the Rt. Hon. Sir Charles W. Dilke* (Lond, 1917); R. Jenkins, *Sir Charles Dilke. A Victorian tragedy* (Lond, 1958); A. Deakin, *The federal story*, J. A. La Nauze ed (Melb, 1963); Mahon papers 937/3, 4 (NL).

SALLY O'NEILL

DISNEY, THOMAS ROBERT (1842-1915), soldier, was born on 16 October 1842, probably the son of James William King Disney and his wife Anna Maria, née Oliver, of Ireland. After joining the British army as a cadet on 1 January 1861, he was commissioned in the Royal Artillery on 18 December. He served in India in 1862-68, 1870-76, 1880-82 and 1893-95. He was present at the fall of Magdala, Abyssinia, in April 1868 and awarded the campaign medal. He was promoted captain in April 1875 and served as an adjutant in the Royal Horse Artillery from July 1877 to September 1880. He was made a temporary major in December 1881, becoming substantive next year.

In 1883 Disney was invited to command the reconstituted Victorian Military Forces, with the local rank of colonel. He assumed the rank on 1 September, was appointed on 1 December and remained commandant until 28 September 1888 when he left for England. His relations with the Victorian government were marred by a number of disputes, chiefly over the respective military responsibilities of the governor, the minister of defence and the commandant. In 1863 the secretary of state for the colonies had defined the military position of the governor as that of commander-in-chief of the local forces un-

til these were called out for actual service, when the command passed to the general or military officer of the district. Under the Victorian Discipline Act, 1870, the commandant was responsible to the governor-in-council. Disney claimed that he was responsible to the governor as his commander-in-chief; he made his inspection reports to him and listed him in the Volunteer Force as commander-in-chief. The attorney-general declined to give the minister of defence an opinion on the legal issue except at the request of the governor. In March 1885 Major-General M. F. Downes [q.v.], who had been commandant of the South Australian Forces, was appointed secretary of the Victorian Defence Department. Deference to Downes as senior officer and persuasion exerted by the minister of defence, Lieut-Colonel F. T. Sargood [q.v.], on the governor induced Disney to accede to the constitutional requirements.

Under Disney the permanent artillery force which had existed since 1871 was expanded and a permanent engineer section was created. Trained instructors were also provided for the militia forces, which were increased from 2789 in 1883 to 4451 in 1885 but reduced to 2852 by April 1888. A wider range of corps was introduced, including military commissariat and transport. A volunteer regiment of mounted rifles was raised in 1885 and the fixed defences were modernized. Disney must be given some credit for the improvement of the colony's defences, but his relations with the government remained prickly and he appeared to take only slight interest in the welfare of the forces he commanded.

On his return to the British army Disney held the rank of colonel from June 1896 until he retired in October 1899. He died at Dover on 2 March 1915, leaving a widow, Anne Eliza, and two sons, James William King and Thomas Brabazon.

W. H. Askwith (ed), *Kane's List of officers of the Royal Regiment of Artillery . . . to 1899, with notes on officers' services*, 4th ed (Lond, 1900); V&P (LA Vic), 1862-63, 4 (82); Victorian Defence Department file 85/1903 (CAO, Melb).

T. B. MILLAR

DIXON, FRANCIS BURDETT (1832-1884), trade unionist, was born near Leeds, Yorkshire, England, son of Joseph Dixon, stonemason, and his wife Susannah, née Bland. He served his apprenticeship as a stonemason and on 16 October 1854 in Preston, Lancashire, he married Elizabeth Chadwick, a weaver. In 1859 they migrated to Victoria with their two children and in 1864 moved to Sydney.

Both in Victoria and New South Wales

Dixon had occasional difficulty in getting work at his trade and had to go to the country as a labourer. He joined the Operative Stonemasons' Society and in 1866 became secretary of its central committee, but soon resigned 'in consequence of having to accept a job of piecework' which caused some members 'to take umbrage'. Dixon remained on the committee; in 1869 he was chairman and next year secretary again. In 1870 he set up his own business but within two months was back at his trade. Dixon was then the most prominent leader of his union and well known in Sydney's industrial circles. In 1871 he prosecuted the treasurer of the Sydney branch for embezzlement but the law prevented any criminal action: it was held that the man was a partner and the money was as much his as any other member's.

In 1869-71 Dixon was secretary and the most enterprising member of the Eight Hour System Extension League. He assessed the limitations of the league's objectives and on 13 October 1870 said that he 'very much wished to see a better organization in the form of a Trades Council'. The New South Wales Trades and Labor Council was founded in May 1871. Dixon served as delegate in 1872-82 and was several times president and secretary. From this wider platform he quickly became the spearhead of the labour movement in the 1870s. He fought particularly for the eight-hour day and after failing on a council deputation to persuade John Sutherland [q.v.], minister for public works, that railway workers should have it, Dixon perceived that direct political pressure should complement labour's industrial action. On 22 October 1873 he moved 'That this council take into consideration the advisability of bringing before [its affiliated] societies the propriety of direct labour representation in the Legislature'. The motion was passed unanimously but before it could be translated into action the council became embroiled in the 1873-74 iron trades strike; Dixon was its chief leader, reminding T. S. Mort [q.v.] that 'large establishments are erected and carried on' by employees, and helping to end the strike in February by his tenacious negotiating.

Dixon, with help from Angus Cameron and Jacob Garrard [qq.v.], renewed his political plan and the council agreed in June that it was 'expedient and highly desirable that Labor should be directly represented in Parliament'. Dixon expressed his views in a council circular that aimed to explain and rally support for the proposal: he stressed that manhood suffrage gave workers the opportunity to get their own kind into parliament to reshape and initiate legislation. Although the argument envisaged the general good, it was based on a class concept with political and economic implications running counter to colonial society; the *Maitland Mercury*, 22 October 1874, retorted that 'relations between capital and labour [cannot] be directly affected by any legislation—they are regulated by the law of supply and demand'. Dixon was the chief organizer of Cameron's election for West Sydney in December and his payment by the council until April 1876.

The failure of the political scheme persuaded the council to consolidate its independence as the chief industrial institution in New South Wales. Dixon guided and shaped the process more than any other unionist. Industrial action overlapped political in the agitation against assisted immigration and the entry of Chinese, but in a series of public meetings in 1877-78 Dixon was able to win wide community support without loss of labour's identity. He became a protectionist, and as his radicalism matured he saw the Chinese problem as a result of the 'over-competition' of capitalism and declared that the working class 'would not allow themselves to be degraded into a state of serfdom by competition amongst employers'. He organized maximum support for the Seamen's Union in the 1878-79 shipping strike but detached the council from its wider political background. He chaired the first Intercolonial Trade Union Congress in 1879 and exhorted members to show 'during the debates the gentlemanly feeling which I have seen characterise the . . . meetings of the Trades'.

Dixon had political ambitions himself, but failed at East Sydney in 1877 after revealing that he wanted 'to see the smoke of the factory chimneys here, to hear the roar of the puddlers' furnace and to see us working up the iron so plentiful in the land'. He declined to run again in 1880, but became president of the council for the last time in December 1882, alerted by E. W. O'Sullivan's tendency to weaken the council's independence, especially his attempt to get it to endorse George Dibbs's [q.v.] potentially disruptive arbitration scheme. By 1883 Dixon was suffering from the lung disease from which he died on 7 April 1884. His family was destitute and the Trades and Labor Council raised the money to bury him and one of his daughters who died on 10 April from a similar illness. The council also collected money for his wife and six surviving children, and for the monument erected over Dixon's grave in the Anglican section of Rookwood cemetery. At the unveiling on 20 September Daniel O'Connor [q.v.], in a long panegyric, told a large congregation that if Dixon had not suffered 'from the lack of means . . . [he] would have taken one of the highest positions in the country and held it with dignity and justice'. In 1971 the council renovated his grave.

Dixon was probably the most significant Australian trade unionist of the nineteenth century. From his home in Surry Hills he walked to and from no fewer than three meetings nearly every week in 1872-82, and his humane style invariably evoked a generous response from workers and employers, irrespective of the exigencies of any industrial problem. His leadership gave form and purpose to the Trades and Labor Council and helped it to become one of the most important institutions in New South Wales. His notion of labour's separate identity enabled it to repulse take-over attempts by other groups and complemented his vision of its need for direct political action which, although premature in 1874, provided the tradition and precedent for P. J. Brennan's [q.v.] successful moves to found the parliamentary Labor Party in 1889-91.

N. B. Nairn, 'The role of the Trades and Labour Council in New South Wales 1871-1891', *Historical Studies; selected articles*, 2nd s (Melb, 1967); *Sydney Mail*, 12 Apr 1884; *Evening News* (Syd), 22 Sept 1884; Operative Stonemasons' Soc (NSW), Central cttee minutes 1865-83 (ANU Archives); Eight Hours System Extension League minutes 1869-71 (ML); Trades and Labor Council minutes 1871-83 (ML).   BEDE NAIRN

DIXSON, HUGH (1810-1880), tobacco manufacturer, was born on 5 June 1810 in Edinburgh, the second son of Hugh Dixson, baker, and his wife Mary, née Scott. He was educated at Edinburgh High School, served an apprenticeship with a tobacconist and at 19 began his own business as a manufacturer and retailer of tobacco. On 11 April 1837 he married Helen, daughter of Robert Craig, a shawl manufacturer of Edinburgh. Deterred by high excise duties in Scotland and reputedly encouraged by John Dunmore Lang [q.v.] and by a relation who returned from Australia in 1838 Dixson decided to migrate. He arrived in Sydney with his wife and child in the *Glenswilly* on 29 October 1839. Immediately he opened a tobacco shop in George Street and sent home for 400 gross of pipes. This venture founded one of the largest enterprises of its kind in Australia, the Dixson Tobacco Co. Ltd.

Dixson invested in land, sugar and shipping, but without success. In 1860 he opened a store at Twofold Bay hoping to profit from the gold diggers at Kiandra, but the diggings declined and the store with them. He re-established his business in Sydney in 1862 and in the next fifteen years became the leading tobacco manufacturer in the colony,

gradually expanding his activities into larger premises, first in York Street and in 1875 in Castlereagh Street. He took a leading part in having the tariff on imported leaf reduced and he tried to foster the local tobacco-growing industry. His name appears on various public petitions, for example, in support of better provision for education and a better water supply, but mostly he devoted himself to his business, to improving the manufacture of tobacco and to varying his products to suit changing demands. He was a prominent Baptist and was respected as a good employer and for his honesty and industry. He brought a number of his relations to Sydney and helped to establish them there.

Dixson died in Sydney on 3 November 1880, and his wife on 5 February 1894. Of their ten children, five died in infancy. The eldest surviving son, (Sir) Hugh, and the second son, Robert, were taken into partnership with their father in 1864 when the firm became Dixson & Sons. Hugh became head of the firm on his father's death while Robert, father of Sir Hugh (Dixson) Denison and member of the South Australian House of Assembly in 1881-84, was the head of the Adelaide branch of the business. Two other sons, Craig and Thomas, became prominent medical practitioners. His daughter Isabella married Rev. F. Hibberd, a leading Baptist minister.

Biographical file (Dixson Lib, Syd).

G. D. RICHARDSON

DOBSON, FRANK STANLEY (1835-1895), lawyer and politician, was born on 20 April 1835 in Hobart Town, the second son of John Dobson, a solicitor from Durham, who migrated to Van Diemen's Land in 1833, and his wife Mary Ann, née Atkinson; he was a brother of Sir William and half-brother of Alfred [qq.v.] and Henry. His childhood was spent mainly at his uncle's house in the Tasmanian midlands and at Hutchins School. When Governor Denison was transferred to New South Wales Dobson went with him as tutor to his sons. He travelled with the family to England, and in 1856 entered St John's College, Cambridge (B.A., 1861; LL.B., 1860; LL.M., 1864; LL.D., 1870). He was admitted to the Middle Temple and called to the Bar in 1860. He returned to Australia and settled in Melbourne, was called to the Bar in 1861 and started a practice in Common Law. He became an examiner in French and German at the University of Melbourne and in 1863 was appointed lecturer in law. When his appointment was announced, one newspaper objected that 'being a good flute player is not a qualification for a law lectureship', but his close connexion with the university was retained for thirty-two years. He also became a Queen's Counsel in 1887.

Dobson's great interest was in the law of procedure, the law of wrongs and the law of obligations. For several years he was a certifying barrister to the Victorian Friendly Societies but in 1869 resigned. He was elected to the Legislative Council for the Southern Province in December 1870. When the Reform Act of 1880 enlarged the council, he represented the South Eastern Province and held the seat until 1895. He was several times offered a portfolio but refused until 1881 when Sir Bryan O'Loghlen [q.v.] persuaded him to take office as solicitor-general. In 1883-95 Dobson was chairman of committees, where his knowledge of constitutional law and parliamentary procedure was very useful. His activities were wide ranging. He was a member from 1880 of the royal commission on the promotion of technological and industrial instruction, a trustee of the Melbourne Public Library and National Gallery and in 1884 president of the Field Naturalists Club of Victoria. He became a fellow of the Linnean Society and an enthusiastic member of the Victorian Acclimatisation Society. For some years he represented Belvoir in the Church of England Assembly. He died at his home in South Yarra on 1 June 1895.

Dobson was married three times: first, at Christ Church, Hawthorn, on 27 June 1863 to Adelaide Whitehurst, who died on 24 August 1865; second, on 6 June 1871 to Edith Mary Carter, who died on 6 April 1874; third, at St David's Cathedral, Hobart. on 15 April 1879 to Henrietta Louisa Sharland, who survived him. His only children were a daughter who died in infancy and a son, Frank Temple, who graduated from Melbourne and Cambridge and became a solicitor in Melbourne.

H. M. Humphreys (ed), Men of the time in Australia: Victorian series, 1st ed (Melb, 1878); A. Sutherland et al, Victoria and its metropolis, 2 (Melb, 1881); J. L. Forde, Story of the Bar of Victoria (Melb, 1913); PD (LC Vic), 1871-95; Argus, 3 June 1895.

ELIZABETH BARROW

DOBSON, SIR WILLIAM LAMBERT (1833-1898), judge, was born on 24 April 1833 at Carr Hill, Gateshead, Durham, England, the elder son of John Dobson (1800-1865), solicitor, and his first wife Mary Ann, née Atkinson (1811-1837). With his parents he arrived at Hobart Town in the Mary on 18 January 1834. He attended Christ College

and in 1848 entered the Hutchins School where he became head boy. He then served as clerk in the Police Magistrate's Office and in 1853 left for England. He was admitted to the Middle Temple and after winning the first certificate, the highest honour awarded by the Council of Legal Education, was called to the Bar on 6 June 1856. He returned to Hobart, was admitted to practise as a barrister on 22 January 1857, appointed commissioner of the Caveat Board for the issue of crown grants, and later became crown solicitor and clerk of the peace. On 17 March 1859 at Launceston he married Fanny Louisa, daughter of Rev. W. H. Browne [q.v.]; they had two sons and four daughters.

Dobson represented Hobart in the House of Assembly in 1861-62 and Campbell Town in 1864-70. He was attorney-general in the administration of Weston [q.v.] from February to August 1861 and of T. D. Chapman [q.v.] until January 1863. He led the Opposition in the assembly from June 1864 to November 1866 when he became attorney-general and was virtually premier in Dry's [q.v.] ministry. When Dry died in August 1869 James Wilson [q.v.] became premier. Dobson continued as attorney-general until February 1870 when he was appointed a puisne judge in the Supreme Court. He had been as vigorous in opposition as he was strenuous in purpose while in office, and was responsible for many important measures including the Act abolishing imprisonment for debt (1867) and the Public Schools Act (1868) which gave Tasmania the first compulsory education in Australia.

He was appointed chief justice in February 1886 after acting in that office for a year while Sir Francis Smith [q.v.] was on leave. Dobson acted as deputy-governor in 1884, 1886-87 and 1892-93. Among other positions he was first chancellor of the University of Tasmania, president of the Tasmanian Council of Education and vice-president of the Royal Society of Tasmania. He was a member of the Linnean Society of London, a trustee of the Tasmanian Museum and Art Gallery and president of the cricket and football associations in southern Tasmania. He was also a consistent and pious churchman in the Anglican faith. On a visit to London in 1886 he was knighted by Queen Victoria and was appointed K.C.M.G. in 1897.

As a youth Dobson suffered from asthma and was nervous beyond measure. He mastered the latter affliction by sheer determination and outgrew the former. As chairman of the central committee of the Bush Fires Relief Fund he visited the burnt-out districts of southern Tasmania but contracted a fever and died on 17 March 1898 at Hobart. He was survived by his wife who died in her hundredth year in 1935. Of their sons, Frank Lambert (1861-1887) became a barrister of the Middle Temple and practised in Sydney, and William Percy (1864-1956) was a Queensland farmer.

Dobson's half-brother, ALFRED, was born on 18 August 1848 at Hobart Town, the fourth son of John Dobson and his second wife Kate, née Willis (1819-1868). He was educated at the Hutchins School. After a year in a bank, he served his articles and then went to London, entered the Inner Temple where he won a prize for conveyancing and first honours, and was called to the Bar on 26 January 1875. He returned to Hobart, was admitted to the colonial Bar and joined the family firm. In the House of Assembly he represented Glenorchy in 1877-87. He was attorney-general in the Fysh administration from August 1877 to March 1878 and leader of the Opposition in 1883-84. A careful politician and gentlemanly opponent, he was elected Speaker in July 1885, the first native-born in the colony of Tasmania to hold such office. In May 1877 he resigned and in June was appointed solicitor-general. An exceptionally able lawyer, he took part in many prominent legal cases. His other interests included membership of the Council of Education and of the Board of Legal Examiners. He was a director of the Colonial Mutual Life Association and served as advocate for the Anglican Diocese of Tasmania. In April 1901 Dobson was appointed agent-general for Tasmania in London where he sometimes acted on behalf of Victoria. With great energy he promoted Tasmania's interests, particularly its apple shipments, and represented the State at exhibitions and such official functions as the coronation. He was appointed C.M.G. in 1904 and a K.C. In 1907 he was offered the third judgeship on the Tasmanian bench, but declined. While returning from France to England on 5 December 1908 he fell from the Channel steamer and was drowned. At Bolden, Durham, on 17 December 1891 he had married Alice Ramsay, daughter of Bishop Sandford [q.v.]; she died on 7 December 1897, leaving a son. On 4 December 1907 in London Dobson married Mary Alice Walker who survived him.

Cyclopedia of Tasmania, 1 (Hob, 1900); F. C. Green (ed), A century of responsible government 1856-1956 (Hob, 1956); The Hutchins School Mag, no 102, Dec 1959; Mercury, 6 Feb 1870, 22 July 1878, 18 Mar 1898, 8 Dec 1908.   E. M. DOLLERY

DOCKER, JOSEPH (1802-1884), surgeon, landowner and politician, was born in London, the second son of Robert Docker, merchant, and his wife, née Perry. At 13 he left school and was apprenticed to Dr Thomas Docker of Dover, whose daughter Agnes he married in 1830. He joined the East India Co. as a surgeon, but resigned and went to Sydney in 1834 with his wife and son. He took up 10,000 acres on Dartbrook in the Upper Hunter district, naming the estate Thornthwaite. His wife died in childbirth in 1835 and Docker went to Britain where in 1839 at Edinburgh he married Matilda Brougham. He returned to Sydney with his wife, two female cousins, a farmer and several artisans.

At Thornthwaite for thirty years he worked as a grazier and cultivator and practised his profession. He became a justice of the peace in 1842 and later chairman of the bench of magistrates at Scone. After responsible government he contested the Phillip, Brisbane and Bligh seat in the Legislative Assembly; he was defeated by a neighbour, John Robertson [q.v.], but in May 1856 was appointed to the Legislative Council for five years. In 1861 when Robertson's free selection before survey bill reached the council Docker was a leading critic in the majority which opposed the measure. The government attempted to 'swamp' the council at its last sitting but the president and most members marched out leaving no quorum. When the first life appointments to the new Legislative Council were listed Docker's name was omitted and the land bill was passed in his absence. In 1863 he was appointed to the council by James Martin [q.v.], in whose second ministry he became postmaster-general in January 1866 and colonial secretary in September 1868. As representative of the government he successfully piloted Parkes's [q.v.] public schools bill through the Legislative Council against strong opposition. From December 1870 to May 1872 he was postmaster-general in the Martin-Robertson coalition. In February 1875 when he became minister of justice and public instruction the Miners' Advocate described him as 'the weak point in the [Robertson] ministry's armour ... given to old fogeyism and a desire to retard rather than advance good legislation'. However, he held office until the government was defeated in February 1877 and was then chairman of committees in the council until 1884.

Among his achievements Docker composed many songs, some of them published in England, painted in oils and watercolours, and was his own architect of Thornthwaite where he did much of the cabinet work and carved the family coat of arms on the façade of the stone steps at his front entrance. He was also an early enthusiast for photography and made most of his chemicals and apparatus. A friend once described him as the most accomplished gentleman in the colony. Docker died at his home in Sydney on 9 December 1884, aged 82. He was survived by a son of his first marriage and one daughter and six sons of the second, of whom Ernest, the eldest, became a District Court judge.

Miners' Advocate (Newcastle), 13 Feb 1875; *Town and Country J*, 27 Mar 1875, 13 Dec 1884; *Sydney Mail*, 27 Dec 1884; G. Lissant, Notes on the Docker family of Westmorland (ML). E. DOCKER

DODDS, SIR JOHN STOKELL (1848-1914), parliamentarian and judge, was born at Durham, England, son of William Dodds and his wife Annie, née Shute; his grandfather was vicar of Kirkleatham, Yorkshire. With his parents, a brother and a sister he arrived at Hobart Town in the *Union* on 24 September 1853. His father soon died and he was brought up by his mother to whose example and teaching he ascribed all his successes in life. He was educated at Hobart and was first employed there in shops. In 1867 he married Emma Augusta, daughter of Rev. James Norman and widow of G. H. Gatehouse; fifteen years his senior, she had three children by her first marriage. He was articled to William Pitt, solicitor, and admitted a legal practitioner of the Supreme Court of Tasmania in February 1872. Able and energetic, he built up a very large practice as a barrister and solicitor.

In 1878-87 Dodds represented East Hobart in the House of Assembly. Within a month of his first election, he became attorney-general in Crowther's [q.v.] ministry. In 1879 the government was defeated and, after negotiations led by W. R. Giblin [q.v.] and Dodds, the opposing parties agreed to form a coalition with Giblin as premier. Soon afterwards Dodds was asked to become treasurer but he was not willing and remained attorney-general. In 1881 Giblin prevailed on him to become treasurer and postmaster-general, and Giblin became attorney-general. In August 1884 Giblin resigned and Adye Douglas [q.v.] became premier. Dodds was attorney-general in the new government. He was also elected leader of the House of Assembly and remained so until 1887. When Douglas resigned in March 1886 he claimed the right to nominate the new premier to the governor. Dodds objected that this was unconstitutional, and particularly so because Douglas had accepted appointment as agent-general in London and was to be virtually a civil servant. However, the governor sent for Douglas's nominee, Agnew [q.v.], who undertook to form a government. On principle Dodds refused to serve in it and Agnew withdrew. The governor then sent for Dodds who formed a ministry with Agnew as premier. In 1885 Dodds had proposed to obtain royal assent by cable to enable rolls to be prepared for an election. He was much criticized in Tasmania but the Crown law officers approved his action.

While Dodds was treasurer and postmaster-general the subsidy paid by Tasmania towards the telegraph cable in Bass Strait was reduced by £1000 a year and the postal rate payable to Victoria was reduced by the same amount, postal, telegraph and cable charges were cut, a Post Office Savings Bank was established, telephone services began and 'pillar' street letter-boxes were installed. To inspect proposed public works he once went on foot from Mount Bischoff to the West Coast. While he was attorney-general bills were introduced to deal with settled estates (forerunner of the Settled Lands Act), to prevent the sale of obscene books etc., to regulate the sale of tobacco, to establish the office of agent-general, to regulate the sale of poisons and to provide retiring allowances for judges, registration of stock and crop mortgages and the inspection and regulation of fisheries; he was also active in introducing a new Education Act. In 1879 he protested strongly in the assembly against the practice of the Legislative Council of amending supply bills. In 1885 after suggesting for years in parliament that bribery and other corrupt practices took place at elections, he introduced an electoral amendments bill. Braddon alleged that if Dodds had any honesty and self respect he should be the first to introduce clauses to prevent such practices and that it had been shouted from the house tops that he had paid for his seat. Dodds promptly challenged the allegation and Braddon withdrew it.

Dodds attended several conferences and conventions in other colonies. In 1886 Douglas and he represented Tasmania at the first session of the Federal Council of Australasia in Hobart. His speeches were painstakingly prepared and he was appointed a member of a select committee to prepare standing rules and orders for the council, and a member of the standing and finance committees. He opposed the abolition of the office of governor and any severing of links with Britain. He supported a bill to enable the service of legal process in other colonies, and with Griffith and Berry [q.v.] formed a select committee to consider it. He spoke against the Federal Council evidence bill, the Australasian corporation bill and some of the provisions of the Australasian judgments bill, but Griffith prevailed and they were passed. He was also opposed by Griffith when he emphasized that Thursday Island was strategically less important for defence than King George Sound.

The government decided that Tasmania should be represented at the Colonial Conference in London in 1887 by Douglas as agent-general and Dodds as attorney-general. Despite protests in parliament he left for the conference, but he had already signed an undated acceptance of the position of puisne judge and an application for leave, and was duly appointed to the bench on 15 February. On 20 October 1898 he became chief justice. In the printed Tasmanian *Law Reports*, which commenced in 1897, Dodds is by far the least reported of the Tasmanian judges sitting alone; in the Full Court his impact was more important, but far greater contributions to Tasmanian law seem to have been made by other judges. He was appointed C.M.G. in 1889, knight in 1900 and K.C.M.G. in 1901. In 1914 he notified the government that he would retire in August, but he died at his home, Stoke, New Town, on 23 June 1914. He was predeceased by his wife and survived by two of their four sons.

According to his contemporaries, Dodds was able and quick, with a capacity to reduce the issues and avoid the determination of superfluous facts. As chief justice he administered the government from 14 August 1900 to 8 November 1901, and entertained at Government House the duke and duchess of York during their visit to open the first Federal parliament. He was appointed lieut-governor on 3 August 1903 and held this office until he died. He acted as governor from 16 April to 28 October 1904, from 21 May to 29 September 1909 and from 10 March until 4 June 1913. In the Boer war he raised by public subscription enough money to equip and send out a contingent of mounted infantry. With a deep interest in education, art, literature, music and sport, he served on the Council of the University of Tasmania and was chancellor in 1907-14; he was also patron or president of a host of societies in southern Tasmania. Lady Dodds was of retiring disposition and did not enjoy her necessary participation in public life.

Cyclopedia of Tasmania, 1 (Hob, 1900); Argus, 24 June 1914; Mercury, 25 June 1914; CSD papers (TA); Premier's Department papers (TA).   G. H. CRAWFORD

DODERY, WILLIAM (1819-1912), hotel proprietor, pastoralist and politician, was born in August 1819 at Clonmel, Tipperary, Ireland, son of George Dodery and his wife Grace (1797-1860). George Dodery had served in the ranks of the 1st Regiment at Waterloo and was stationed in Ireland with the 57th Regiment. In 1825 he went as a guard to Sydney with his wife and son in the transport Asia. Unlike Sudds, Thompson and other privates in the 57th he obtained his discharge by purchase in August 1827 and bought five £100 shares in the Bank of New South Wales. In 1831 he took his family to Launceston and next year petitioned Lieut-Governor Arthur for assistance after losing some £3000 'honestly acquired . . . by rigid frugality, a spirit of enterprise and persevering industry . . . in a maritime speculation'. Unsuccessful, he later returned to Sydney and bought the Racecourse Inn on the Parramatta Road; he died there on 6 June 1857 aged 63.

William attended school in Sydney and Launceston and then entered a merchant's office in Launceston. He visited Britain with his parents in 1835 and returned to his work in Launceston. On 15 March 1842 he married Mary, daughter of William Webb of Avoca. They soon went to Longford where in 1846 he became the proprietor of the new Blenheim Hotel. He also established a coach line between Longford and Launceston. In 1858 he sold the hotel and coach line and bought land in the Longford-Cressy district. In England with his wife in 1860 he bought horses and sheep for breeding and later won many prizes at agricultural shows for his Lincoln sheep. He also became well known as a race-horse breeder and owner and was a prominent amateur rider. Dodery was a member of local agricultural, horticultural and sporting societies and a liberal supporter of local charities. In 1870 he built his home, Lauraville, at Longford.

Dodery represented Norfolk Plains in the House of Assembly in 1861-70 and was a prominent advocate of the Launceston-Deloraine railway. In 1877 he was elected for Westmorland to the Legislative Council; on his retirement in 1907 he proudly claimed that he had to contest only one election in his parliamentary career. His presidency of the Legislative Council in 1904-07 prompted the Sydney Bulletin to refer to the Tasmanian council as 'the House of Dodery'. For over twenty years Dodery was a member of the Longford Municipal Council and its warden for eight years. He was a member of the Longford Road Trust, a territorial magistrate and a justice of the peace for Queensland. He died at Lauraville on 26 January 1912. His wife also died in that year aged 91. Of their eight children, the elder son, William, died in 1908 aged 60, and the younger, George, died in 1920.

V&P (HA Tas), 1862 (130), 1865 (64, 76), 1880 (114), 1884 (132); *Examiner* (Launceston), 28 Jan 1912; CSO 1/606/13833 (TA).

F. C. GREEN

DON, CHARLES JARDINE (1820-1866), stonemason and politician, was born on 12 June 1820 at Cupar-Angus, Forfarshire (Angus), Scotland, son of William Don and his wife Jeanette, née Rattery. His father, a stonemason, was an elder of the Relief Church, a branch of the United Presbyterians, but broke with them and joined the Church of Scotland. Don was educated at the village school and at 12 worked as a learner handloom weaver for ½d. a yard. At 17 he was apprenticed to his father and joined a mutual improvement society in which he learnt public speaking and, much to the disquiet of his teachers, developed his taste for radical writers, notably Tom Paine, John Cartwright and William Cobbett. As a journeyman he toured the main towns of Scotland speaking constantly. In 1842 he took part in the Chartist agitation and gained notoriety as a street orator particularly at the Market Cross, Edinburgh. In 1846 in Edinburgh he married Mary Louden, a Catholic, and in 1847-52 he lived in Glasgow, prominent in debating societies and as a student of Adam Smith. In 1853, attracted by the goldfields, he decided to migrate and arrived in Melbourne in the *Asia* with his wife and the younger of his two daughters.

Don went to the Ballarat diggings and returned to Melbourne to find his wife had died. At St Francis's Catholic Church, Melbourne, in 1855 he married Ellen Curtin. Meanwhile he had joined the Stonemasons' Union, becoming chairman in 1858, and was prominent as a leader of the movement for the eight-hour day; in 1857 he became secretary of the United Trades Association and in 1858 vice-president of the Victorian Eight Hours Labor League. After the Eureka stockade in 1854 and responsible government in 1856, Don had gravitated to politics, agitating on land and fiscal policy as well as industrial conditions. As 'the leading advocate of the working classes' he spoke almost nightly with M. W. Gray [q.v.] at the Eastern Market. The democratic pressure they and others wielded soon became a potent political influence. Don failed to win the Melbourne seat but in July 1857 became a delegate to a convention in protest against the conservative land bill of the Haines [q.v.] ministry; the convention held sixteen meetings, petitioned the Legislative Assembly and helped to defeat the bill in the Legislative Council. Don's activism continued with torchlight processions and revolutionary music and placards. In 1859

he won Collingwood and claimed to be the first of his class represented in 'any legislature within the British Empire'. Don was a vigorous member, speaking often and moving for an eight-hour clause in government contracts and for other progressive proposals. To E. Whitty, a leading English journalist, he had 'a cultured face . . . and dresses away from his class', and seemed 'a cross between a poet and a pirate'; Byron and his corsair', who unleashed 'the fury and frenzy of Feargus O'Connorism, of the most exaggerated kind'.

Don was not a successful politician; his working-class ardour went against the grain of colonial politics, even though he contributed to the mildly radical tone that the Victorian assembly acquired. His inability to adapt to the give and take of a parliamentarian was aggravated by his need to earn a living. At one stage he worked on Parliament House by day as a mason and in it by night as a member. His health began to fail and he began to drink heavily. An admirer of C. G. Duffy [q.v.], he offended his supporters by approving of Duffy's land bill in 1861; although Don finally voted against it he gradually lost electoral support and was unseated in 1864. He had failed as a hotel-keeper in Fitzroy in 1862, and his worsening health forced him into premature retirement in which his severe financial difficulties were barely relieved by his friends. At Collingwood on 27 September 1866 he died of pulmonary consumption, survived by a daughter of his first marriage and a son. He was buried in the Presbyterian section of the Melbourne cemetery.

R. Hamilton, *The combat and the victory* (Melb, 1866); S. Merrifield, 'Charles Jardine Don', *Recorder* (Labour Hist, Melb), Aug 1966; *Australasian*, 29 Sept 1866; *Illustrated Melb Post*, Oct 1866.   S. MERRIFIELD

DONAGHY, JOHN (1842-1894), businessman and politician, was born probably on 11 May 1842 at Liverpool, England, son of Michael Donaghy, rope-maker, and his wife Mary, née McManus. He arrived at Corio Bay, Geelong, with his parents about 1852. In 1854 his father established a rope-making industry in a shed near the Barwon River, at Marnock Vale, Geelong. After a short time on the Ballarat goldfields John joined his father in the business which was later known as Fairview Ropeworks. In 1864 a second site was bought at Geelong West for larger works and new machinery was imported from England and America. Later ropeworks were built at Port Adelaide and at Dunedin, New Zealand, and depots were established in Melbourne and Sydney.

About 1878 John and his younger brother Michael went into partnership with their father. After Michael senior died in 1883 John managed the business. It flourished; under John the first flat mining ropes in Australia were made, up-to-date machinery was used and the range of products broadened.

John Donaghy was a justice of the peace. He had long supported the movement for separate councils for Geelong and Geelong West. He became a councillor and was mayor of Geelong West in 1879-80 and 1885-86. He founded the first Geelong West Post and Telegraph Office in 1868. Later he chaired the meeting to form an Electric Tramway and Lighting Co. He helped to establish the first free library in the town, was vice-president of the Gordon Memorial Technical College and served on the hospital committee. At various times he was a member and president of the St Patrick's Society, president of the Geelong Yorick Club and vice-president of the Mechanics' Institute. He also supported the Fire Brigade, assisted at the opening of the mineral springs at Drysdale and presented Geelong West with its town clock. He was an active parishioner of St Mary's Catholic Church.

Donaghy represented Geelong in the Legislative Assembly in 1886-88. A zealous advocate for improvements in his electorate, he also supported the first grant of land to the Chaffey brothers and an extra tariff of 5 per cent to protect native industries. He died at Geelong West on 9 October 1894, survived by his wife Norah, née Darcy, whom he married in 1867, and by their three sons and two daughters. In 1968 the firm, M. Donaghy & Sons Pty Ltd, merged with another long-established rope and haulage company, James Miller Holdings Ltd.

T. W. H. Leavitt (ed), *Australian representative men* (Melb, 1887); J. F. Hogan, *The Irish in Australia* (Melb, 1888); A. Sutherland et al, *Victoria and its metropolis*, 2 (Melb, 1888); E. A. Vidler (ed), *The book of Geelong: its people, places, industries and amusements* (Geelong, 1897); M. Donaghy & Sons, Pty Ltd, *One hundred years of rope making, 1852-1952* (Geelong, 1952); W. R. Brownhill, *The history of Geelong and Corio Bay* (Melb, 1955); R. H. Holden, *The story of the Fairview Ropeworks* (Geelong, nd); *PD* (Vic), 1886.

P. M. MacAnally
Paul E. Ginnivan

DONALDSON, JOHN (1841-1896), pastoralist and politician, was born on 15 June 1841 at Purdeet, Mount Rouse, Victoria, son of Alexander Donaldson, pastoralist, and his wife Bridget, née McElroy. After his father's death he began to follow pastoral pursuits in a small way, and in time became the active partner in Moody, Donaldson, Inglis & Co. In 1876 he went to New South Wales to manage Pangee station and in 1881 moved to Queensland to manage another station, Mount Margaret, acquired by the company. In 1883 Donaldson was elected to the Legislative Assembly for the Warrego. His experience in other colonies led him to take an active interest in the debates on the 1884 land bill. Although a member of the Opposition he represented the government in a conference between the two Houses to settle their differences over the bill. In 1885 he became manager of the Union Mortgage and Agency Co. and the next year warned parliament against the 'wild cat' mining companies being floated in London.

When the Warrego electorate was divided in 1887 Donaldson retained part of his old seat as member for the Bulloo. He served under Thomas McIlwraith [q.v.] as postmaster-general and secretary of public instruction from 13 June 1888 and continued in those offices when B. D. Morehead [q.v.] became premier. On 19 November 1889 he was appointed colonial treasurer and on 24 July 1890 presented his budget. He showed that the colony's deficit had increased in the previous year from £484,000 to £969,000, which he proposed to meet by a property tax of 1d. in the £ on 'all property above the value of £500' and by an increase in duties on spirits. When his land and income tax bill was carried by only two votes, the government resigned on 12 August. Unable to support the Griffith-McIlwraith coalition, Donaldson became leader of the Opposition on 16 September but resigned his seat in August 1891. In March he had been one of the Queensland delegates to the National Australasian Convention at Sydney where he unsuccessfully urged that control of all the railways be given to the federal government. He was president of the Queensland branch of the Australian Natives' Association.

By 1891 Donaldson had become a local director of the Commercial Bank of Australia, a director of the Queensland Deposit Bank and Building Society, a member of the Brisbane Chamber of Commerce and president of the Agricultural and Industrial Association of Queensland. Proud of his descent, he was vice-president of the various Scottish societies and was associated with many different sporting organizations. His interest in the pastoral industry continued; he was a founder and later vice-president of the Queensland Stock Breeders and Graziers Association and a trustee of the United Pastoralists Association. Anxious about increasing labour disturbances and unable to resist the pressure of his friends, Donaldson consented to return to politics. After two defeats he was elected for the Logan in 1896 but resigned rather than let a petition against his return go to the Elections Tribunal. He was re-elected with an increased majority, but rarely appeared in the House. Always straightforward, Donaldson was popular and became known as 'honest John'. He died from kidney disease on 25 July 1896 at his Brisbane home, Knowsley, Coorparoo, and was buried in the Presbyterian section of Toowong cemetery. He was predeceased by his first wife Margaret, née Walker, whom he had married in Victoria in 1869, and her only daughter, but was survived by his second wife Gertrude Evelyn, née Willis, two sons by his first marriage and a son and two daughters by his second. In parliament John 'Plumper' Hoolan paid tribute to Donaldson: 'Although not of the same politics as myself, I learned to respect him long before I met him on the floor of the House, for his very generous and magnanimous dealings in certain commercial enterprises'.

Official report of the National Australasian Convention debates (Syd, 1891); C. A. Bernays, *Queensland politics during sixty years* (Brisb, 1919); PD (LA Qld), 1883-96; A. A. Morrison, 'Some lesser members of parliament in Queensland', JRQHS, 6 (1960-61); *Brisbane Courier*, 5 July 1896; *Age*, 27 July 1896; *Pastoral Review*, 15 Aug 1896.   MARY O'KEEFFE

DONALDSON, SIR STUART ALEXANDER (1812-1867), premier, merchant and pastoralist, was born on 16 December 1812, the third son of Stuart Alexander Donaldson and his wife, Betsy, née Cundall, of Snab Green, Lancashire, England. His father's London firm, Donaldson, Wilkinson & Co. (in 1838 Donaldson, Lambert & Co.) had colonial interests; in 1828 Donaldson senior wrote *Observations on the Cultivation of Tobacco in the Australian Colonies* and in that year and 1837 helped petitioners from Sydney.

At 15, after private tuition, Donaldson junior entered his father's firm. He progressed rapidly and was encouraged to travel. His notes of a trip from Hamburg to Berlin in 1830 show a bright turn of humour and acute observation. His qualities were soon recognized by his father's Sydney associates, Alexander Riley and Richard Jones [qq.v.], who asked him to send Stuart to the colony to stimulate the business of the London firm. Instead Donaldson went in 1831 to Mexico and later described his experiences vividly in *Mexico thirty years ago, as described in a series of private letters, by a youth* (London, 1866). He returned to England in May 1834 and when Richard Jones

renewed his offer Donaldson accepted, left England in the *Emma Eugenia* and arrived at Sydney on 5 May 1835.

Donaldson soon won a place in commercial life and the 'exclusive' circle at the Macarthurs' Vineyard and Camden estates. He did well at Richard Jones & Co., became a partner in 1837 and manager when Jones retired next year. In 1839 he was appointed agent for Lloyds of London. With success came his social *coup* when he took a leading part in founding the Australian Club in 1838; he served as treasurer, trustee, committeeman and in 1857-67 vice-president. In 1856 he was a founding member of the Union Club. Donaldson senior reflected these triumphs when he wrote 'I am not surprised at the gratification you appear to feel by the confidence reposed in you by the elite of your society'.

Donaldson also exploited the new outlets of pastoral expansion. In 1839 he sent James Graham [q.v.] as his agent to Melbourne, bought town and suburban land there and became a trustee of the Port Phillip Association. Early in 1840 he went to the New England district and took up the runs of Tenterfield and Clifton. With some 250,000 acres and 34,000 sheep, he saw himself as a 'sheep and cattle proprietor on a scale Suffolk people dont accustom themselves to think'. In 1841 he formed a business partnership with William Dawes and went to England. Donaldson was severely affected by the depression of the early 1840s and on his return in 1844 he found his business had been mismanaged and Richard Jones insolvent. The adversities of the London firm in the colony and New Zealand made Donaldson's financial position more precarious, but by 1851 he could boast that he had liquidated his debts and realized more than £30,000; his new interests included a tweed factory near Newcastle, shareholdings in many colonial companies and a trusteeship of the New South Wales Savings Bank. The gold rush brought him great wealth. In February 1853 he went to England and on 21 February 1854 married Amelia, daughter of Frederick Cowper of Carleton Hall, Cumberland. Donaldson returned to Sydney and in 1855 became consul-general for Sardinia.

In 1838 Donaldson became a magistrate but claimed that 'a politician I mean never to be'. He declined to stand for Port Phillip in 1845 and said he preferred moderate leaders in public affairs. However, his links with the Australian Club, Wentworth and Robert Lowe [qq.v.] and his improving finances drew him into politics. In February 1848 he won a by-election for Durham, and was returned by that electorate in July 1848, July 1849 and September 1851. He resigned in 1853 and was elected for Sydney Hamlets in February 1855. One contemporary described him as 'an animated and impetuous speaker', and others as 'bumptious' and full of 'self-esteem'; to close acquaintances he was a 'rattling, prattling, jovial companion' whose opinions always commanded attention. Charles Cowper [q.v.] thought him 'useless to the liberals'.

Donaldson soon won repute in the Legislative Council by his speeches on finance and the running of government departments. At the hustings in 1851 he had angered Sir Thomas Mitchell [q.v.] who demanded a public apology; it was published promptly in the press but Mitchell thought it insolent and challenged Donaldson to a duel. Both men were poor marksmen and after the affray remained unreconciled. With good humour Governor FitzRoy overlooked the offence, and Donaldson continued to advocate economy in the government. In December 1851 he moved that the council refrain from voting money in excess of the schedules prescribed by the Australian Colonies' Government Act of 1850, until their items were submitted for scrutiny. Triumphant, he then moved that the council reject the estimates and petition for the abolition of the schedules. Although supported by most elected members, his motion was narrowly defeated. He supported Wentworth's opposition to Earl Grey's Constitution proposals in 1848 and 1850. He was a member of both Grievances Committees and supported the 1851 Electoral Act. Donaldson was in England when Wentworth's Constitution bill was debated, but unlike Wentworth he adhered to an Upper House elected on a restricted franchise. He favoured a reduced price for crown land, and local control of land revenue. Among other legislative interests he had voted in 1848 in favour of the introduction of 'exiles' but, because Grey failed to send free immigrants as promised, he became an opponent of transportation and in 1850 denounced it as 'incompatible with the introduction of free institutions'. He also advocated steam communication with Britain, the introduction of cotton and tobacco growing and free trade. To encourage Caroline Chisholm [q.v.] he successfully moved the allocation of £10,000 for her Family Colonization Loan Society in 1852.

In the first elections under responsible government Donaldson was returned for Sydney Hamlets to the Legislative Assembly. The formation of the first ministry proved difficult. Deas Thomson [q.v.] failed, and James Macarthur [q.v.], doubting his own ability to win support in the assembly, recommended Donaldson to the governor. Hitherto he had worked with so many factions that one Sydney paper was at a loss to discover his political principles. Donaldson

preferred to call himself a liberal conservative who believed that 'a spicy opposition is always of service in a Colony, both to Governors and Governed'. On 22 January 1856 Governor Denison called on Donaldson to form a ministry. He wrote to his brother John that he hoped 'to reconcile the contending interests, to repress the selfishness of faction, to amalgamate the views of widely differing men and then to originate and carry out a colonial policy which will bear the test of examination . . . and all this in a colony perpetually changing in its social state and advancement politically'. Attempting to unite all the most talented politicians in the most acceptable combinations, he chose Thomas Holt, W. M. Manning, J. B. Darvall and G. R. Nichols [qq.v.]; the ministry was sworn in on 6 June. Only Manning had administrative experience, but James Macarthur attended cabinet meetings, nominally as a minister without portfolio. However, the arrangements proved untenable. Donaldson's relations were strained with Deas Thomson whose centralized administration, Donaldson believed, hampered the running of his department. He was also disheartened by the opposition of Martin, Murray, Parkes [qq.v.] and Cowper : 'we found the Assembly so intractable and we could not go on from night to night with majorities of two and three'. In July he learnt that his brother James had died, a tragedy that 'left a blank in me that never can be filled'. After defeat on a vote impugning the propriety of appointing judges to the Upper House, the ministry resigned on 25 August.

The measures proposed by the ministry were well suited to the colony's need and the resignation, particularly over a minor question, was condemned as hasty and imprudent. The only fundamental ministerial difference had been on the question of the Upper House, where Donaldson and Darvall favoured the elective principle. The ministry had agreed on the general questions of electoral representation, land, commercial and fiscal policy and law reform. Donaldson's reply to critics was, 'my colleagues and myself are all too independent of office to cling to it'.

The Cowper ministry that followed held office for five weeks. At the October elections Donaldson was defeated in the Sydney Hamlets but elected unopposed for the South Riding of Cumberland. As treasurer in the Parker [q.v.] ministry until 7 September 1857, Donaldson played a part in rearranging government administration into four main departments each represented in parliament by a minister, and in making the office of auditor-general a permanent and non-political office. In 1857 he was appointed a commissioner for railways and was elected for Cumberland in January 1858. In 1851-61 he was a member of the Senate of the University of Sydney. He had supported its foundation and his brother John helped to select the academic staff. Donaldson returned to England in June 1859, leaving his two brothers-in-law to manage his pastoral holdings.

With Sir Charles Nicholson, Sir William Burton, George Macleay [qq.v.] and Wentworth, Donaldson was active in the General Association for the Australian Colonies, formed in London in 1855. He was its chairman in 1860 and, when accused in 1863 of planning a penal settlement at Port Essington, he vigorously denied the charge in his *Copies of Letters to Sir Daniel Cooper* [q.v.]. He was knighted in 1860 and visited the colony on private business in 1861 and 1864. In April 1860 he unsuccessfully contested the seats of Dartmouth and later of Barnstaple in the House of Commons. Plagued by ill health he withdrew from public affairs and on 11 January 1867 died at Carleton Hall, Cumberland, survived by his wife. Their eldest son, Stuart, was master of Magdalene College, Cambridge, in 1904-15 and vice-chancellor in 1912-13; the second, Sir Hay Frederick, was educated at Eton and Trinity College, Cambridge, won repute as an engineer and in 1916 was drowned with Kitchener in the *Hampshire*; the third, St Clair George, became bishop of Brisbane and later of Salisbury; the youngest, Seton John Laing, was accidentally drowned while at Eton. The only daughter, Mary Ethel, married Rev. Algernon Lawley in 1896.

HRA (1), 21, 23, 24, 26; C. T. Dimont and F. de Witt Batty, *St. Clair Donaldson* (Lond, 1939); V&P (LC NSW), 1848-56; V&P (LA NSW), 1856-59; *Empire* (Syd), 7 Mar 1856; *SMH*, 23 Mar 1867; John and Stuart Alexander Donaldson papers (ML); Macarthur papers, v 27-8, 34 (ML); Riley papers (ML).

SANDRA DRAPER

DONNITHORNE, ELIZA EMILY (1826?-1886), recluse and eccentric, was born at Cape of Good Hope, youngest daughter of James Donnithorne and his wife Sarah Elizabeth, née Bampton. Her father, descendant of an old Cornish family, joined the East India Co. as a writer in 1792 and became master of the Mint and then judge and senior merchant in Mysore. About 1836 he retired to Sydney where he joined many public movements and won renown for his 'unbounded hospitality'. He invested in real estate and twice visited Melbourne to buy land. He settled at Cambridge Hall, 36 King Street, Newtown, where he died on 25 May 1852. Predeceased by his wife, whom he had married in 1807, and by two daughters in 1832, he was survived by two sons who had joined the British army and later settled in England, and by Eliza who inherited most of his estate.

Eliza was to have married in 1856. On the morning of the wedding 'the bride and her maid were already dressed for the ceremony; the wedding-breakfast was laid in the long dining-room, a very fine apartment. The wedding guests assembled—the stage was set, but the chief actor did not turn up to keep his appointment'. From that time her 'habits became eccentric'. She never again left the house, finding solace in books and opening the door only to the clergyman, physician and solicitor. The wedding breakfast remained undisturbed on the dining table and 'gradually mouldered away until nothing was left but dust and decay'. Eliza died in the house on 20 May 1886 and was buried in the same grave as her father at Camperdown cemetery where a headstone was later placed in his memory. Eliza's estate, including land and houses in Sydney, Melbourne and Britain, was valued at £12,000. The chief beneficiary was her housekeeper, Sarah Ann Bailey. She left her father's organ to her brother and her jewellery and books to his children, £200 each to the diocese of Sydney and the British and Foreign Bible Society, £50 to the Society for Prevention of Cruelty to Animals and 'an annuity of £5 for each of my six animals and £5 for all my birds'.

In Australian tradition Eliza's tragic story was used by Charles Dickens [q.v.] as the original for Miss Havisham in chapter 22 of his *Great Expectations* (1861). The identification of the Sydney personality and the Dickensian character is circumstantial but the chronology presents no inconsistencies and impossibilities. His *Household Words* contained many anecdotes about Australia in 1850-59 and the characters of Abel Magwitch and villainous Compeyson in *Great Expectations* indicate some knowledge of life in New South Wales. On the other hand Sydney people, after reading the novel, may have created the tradition by identifying Eliza with Miss Havisham.

J. R. Tyrrell, *Old books, old friends, old Sydney* (Syd, 1952); J. S. Ryan, 'A possible Australian source for Miss Havisham', *Aust Literary Studies*, Dec 1963.   J. S. RYAN

DORSEY, WILLIAM McTAGGART (1813-1878), medical practitioner, was born probably at Haunchwood House, Nuneaton, Warwickshire, England, son of Alexander Dorsey and his wife Elizabeth, née Donald.

He appears to have followed his brilliant brother, Alexander James Donald (1812-1894) to the University of Glasgow and to have acquired some knowledge of medicine. In 1837 at Glasgow he married Margaret Douglas.

In 1839 Dorsey bought land orders from the New Zealand Co. and sailed with his wife and two infants in the *Bengal Merchant*. They arrived at Port Nicholson (Wellington) in February 1840, were landed on the beach in torrential rain and had to find lodgings as best they could in the 'woods'. These troubles, capped by survey delays and threats of native attack, soon induced Dorsey to cut his losses. He took his family to Sydney where he was certified by the Medical Board on 12 October and practised at Bathurst until late in 1842 when he moved to the Moreton Bay District. In 1843 he bought one of the first town allotments at Limestone (Ipswich) for £12 10s., built a house, took up Stonehenge, a pastoral lease of 30,000 acres on the Darling Downs and stocked it with sheep. His practice in Ipswich was small but expanded as rapidly as the town. When J. D. Lang [q.v.] visited it in December 1845 he found 'a few presbyterians in the place and other protestants not unwilling to attend divine service'. In 1846 Dorsey was appointed a justice of the peace and by 1850 had chaired meetings to plan the building of Baptist and Anglican churches and a National school; he was also active in squatters' meetings to establish a local bank and to petition for the resumption of transportation to the Moreton Bay District. A hater of humbug and pointless delays, Dorsey held positive opinions; his blunt expression of them often roused antagonism. Once while treating an injured rider in a race-course booth he was disturbed by a drunk and promptly ordered his arrest. Court proceedings followed with Dorsey defending himself at a cost of £100, for which he sought reimbursement by the government because he had acted 'in the proper discharge of his Public Duty'; he won his claim after three years of angry letters.

In addition to his medical practice Dorsey pursued his squatting interests; in 1853-55 he bought many small freeholds in the Moreton Bay area and took large leases in the Leichhardt district. With two partners he acquired Grantham, a pastoral lease of 30,000 acres near Ipswich, in 1856 and then went to Scotland for further studies at the Universities of Glasgow (M.D., 1857) and Edinburgh (M.R.C.S., 1874). He returned to Queensland to find his runs mismanaged. He disposed of Grantham but became insolvent in 1862. He applied for leases in the Port Curtis area but was forestalled and in 1865 was appointed government medical officer

to serve the Ipswich immigration depot and the Police and Railway Departments at a salary of £70. In endless letters to the colonial secretary he appealed for adequate consulting rooms and for an allowance to supply medicine to his charges. In reply he was ordered to send vouchers for each item to the Treasury; by 1871 his salary had been reduced in stages to £50. After five years Dorsey ended the futile correspondence and concentrated on his private practice. Aged 64 he died of heart disease on 16 May 1878. His burial at Ipswich cemetery was largely attended and a contingent of the local volunteer artillery provided a band and fired three volleys over his grave. He was survived by his wife, three sons and three daughters, one of whom married J. P. Bell [q.v.].

A. E. Mulgan, *The city of the Strait* (Wellington, 1939); A. D. Gilchrist (ed), *John Dunmore Lang*, 2 (Melb, 1951); V&P (LC NSW), 1854, 1855, 2, 369; *Government Gazette* (NSW), 1841, 1844, 1846, 1862; *SMH*, 23, 31 Jan 1850; *Brisbane Courier*, 18, 22 May 1878; *Town and Country J*, 7 June 1878; Dorsey papers (QA).

DOUGLAS, SIR ADYE (1815-1906), lawyer and politician, was born on 31 May 1815 at Thorpe-next-Norwich, England, son of Captain Henry Osborne Douglas and his wife Eleanor, née Crabtree; his grandfather was Admiral Billy Douglas. Educated at schools in Hampshire and Normandy, he served articles with a legal firm in Southampton. He decided to migrate to Van Diemen's Land, sailed from London in the *Louisa Campbell* and arrived at Launceston in January 1839. He was admitted to practise in the Supreme Court in February but soon went to Port Phillip, where he ran sheep with his brother Henry near Mount Macedon. Late in 1842 he returned to Launceston where he founded a legal firm which still operates. Over the years he had several partners; the last, George Thomas Collins (1840-1927), had been articled by him. Douglas built up a flourishing local practice and acted for many important clients in Victoria. Deeply interested in the colony's welfare he realized that no progress was possible while convicts were sent to Tasmania. He became one of the founders of the Anti-Transportation League. He was elected one of the first aldermen in the Launceston Municipal Council, established in 1852 and held office until 1884, serving as mayor in 1865-66 and 1880-82.

Douglas was defeated at the elections for the first part-elective Legislative Council in 1851 but won a Launceston seat in 1855. He was prominent in the council's action against J. S. Hampton [q.v.], moving his arrest and the appeal to the Privy Council in defence of the Speaker, Michael Fenton [q.v.]. Under the new Constitution in 1856 he represented Launceston in the first House of Assembly where he succeeded in introducing a bill to provide a water supply for Launceston but failed to win support for a preliminary survey of the Hobart-Launceston railway. In 1857 he resigned and travelled in America, France and England. He became even more impressed by the need for railways. On his return he began to advocate the Launceston-Deloraine railway and in 1865 carried the bill for it against strong opposition; the first sod was turned by the duke of Edinburgh in 1868.

In the House of Assembly Douglas represented Westbury in 1862-70, Norfolk Plains in 1870-71 and Fingal in 1872-84. He then became premier and chief secretary and was elected for South Esk to the Legislative Council, where in 1885 he carried a bill for the appointment of an agent-general in London. He had represented Tasmania at the Sydney convention from which the Federal Council of Australasia was evolved. In 1886 at its first session in Hobart, Douglas predicted a 'United States of Australasia . . . independent of the little island in the Northern Hemisphere'. Called to order, he reminded members of the toasts of forty years ago to the 'Australian Republic'. In March he resigned as premier after appointing himself the first Tasmanian agent-general in London. He attended the Colonial Conference in 1887 but was recalled because his negotiations with the Tasmanian Main Line Railway Co. had failed. He represented Launceston in the Legislative Council in 1890-1904 and was its president in 1894-1904. As an active delegate to the federal conventions in 1891 and 1897-98 he won praise for his physical endurance; to (Sir) Isaac Isaacs, 'he looked like a Hebrew prophet with his long locks and long beard, speaking with kindly wisdom to his people'. Douglas was knighted in 1902, ranked by the governor as 'the first among living Tasmanians'. He died at his home, Ryehope, Hobart, on 10 April 1906 and was buried at Cornelian Bay cemetery.

Douglas had three sons and a daughter in the 1840s. On 10 July 1858 in London as a widower he married a widow Martha Matilda Collins, née Rolls. At Launceston on 18 January 1873 he married Charlotte Richards, by whom he had a daughter Eleanor before she died aged 22 on 23 July 1876. On 6 October 1877 in Adelaide he married Charlotte's sister Ida; they had four sons and four daughters.

W. A. Townsley, *The struggle for self-government in Tasmania 1842-1856* (Hob, 1951); F. C. Green (ed), *A century of respon-* *sible government 1856-1956* (Hob, 1956); *Mercury*, 1 Feb 1886; *Examiner* (Launceston), 11 Apr 1906; Van Diemen's Land Co, letters, 280 (TA); CSO 24/137, 208 (TA).   P. T. McKay
                                                  F. C. Green

DOUGLAS, ALEXANDER DOUGLAS (1843-1914), inspector of police and explorer, was born at St Helier, Channel Islands, son of Alexander Douglas Douglas, army officer, and his wife Ann, née Rouse. He joined the navy in 1857 as a cadet and served in the Tientsin campaign and the Taiping rebellion. His experiences gave him a taste for wandering and adventure. In 1865 he left the navy and migrated to Rockhampton, Queensland. For a time he satisfied his wanderlust by working as a teamster and drover. Attracted by police work he became an officer in the Queensland Native Police in 1872, and soon won promotion to sub-inspector in charge of the area from Cooktown to the Palmer River goldfield. In 1874 he was ordered to blaze a new trail from the goldfields to Cooktown, a task which suited his taste. His success secured him a second commission to find a practicable route to the new Normanby field, and in 1876 to yet another new goldfield, the Hodgkinson. For these achievements he ranks with the important explorers of the north.

In 1879 Douglas moved to a new station, Jundah, in the west, but next year was sent back to the north, this time to Biboohra on the Atherton Tableland. His services were much in demand and he was brought to Brisbane in 1881 to take charge of white police, but in 1882 he was sent to Herberton in the north. Once again exploratory duties called him : with four troopers, two old gold diggers and five Chinese, he blazed yet another trail, this time from Herberton to Mourilyan. On this trip the party was without rations and in continuous rain for twenty days, living mainly on roots, but the leadership of Douglas brought them through. He established a new native police camp at Mourilyan, and the government allocated to him a small steamship *Vigilant* to assist his patrols of the coast. At the end of 1884 he was given charge of the Townsville district, but from May to September 1885, during the Russian scare, because of his naval experience he was appointed commander of H.M.S. *Otter* in the Queensland navy. His next move was to Roma but in 1886 he was sent north to Georgetown in charge of the Gulf district. There he took charge of the largest gold escort, 26,000 oz., ever recorded in Queensland. In 1888 he moved his headquarters to Normanton where he remained until 1891. In 1893 he returned to Roma but in May 1898 became senior inspector of the Northern district, stationed at Townsville. In 1900 he was transferred to Brisbane and on 1 July succeeded John Stuart as chief inspector of the Queensland Police. He acted as commissioner four times and in 1902 went to Roma to investigate the Kenniff [q.v.] case. In 1905 Douglas was superannuated and returned to England where he died on 5 February 1914 in a private hospital near Portsmouth.

On 19 April 1884 at Charters Towers as a widower he had married Lucy, who at 3 had come to Australia in 1858 with her father Abraham Street, of Alva, Stirlingshire. They had no children. She died on 13 May 1905.

J. W. Collinson, *Early days of Cairns* (Brisb, 1939); H. A. Borland, *From wilderness to wealth . . . history of the district of Cairns* (Cairns, 1940); H. A. Borland, *Roadway of many memories, 1876-1951: Cairns district jubilee souvenir* (Brisb, 1951); Qld Police Department, *A centenary history of the Queensland Police Force 1864-1963* (Brisb, 1964); H. Holthouse, *River of gold* (Syd, 1967); R. A. Johnstone, 'Memoirs', *Queenslander*, 2 May 1903-11 Mar 1905.   A. A. MORRISON
                                      JACQUELINE BELL

DOUGLAS, JOHN (1828-1904), politician and administrator, was born on 6 March 1828 in London, the seventh son of Henry Alexander Douglas and his wife Elizabeth Dalzell, daughter of the earl of Carnwarth. His grandfather was Sir William Douglas of Kelhead and his uncle the famous marquess of Queensberry. When his parents died in 1837, his aunts took him to their home near Lockerbie, Dumfriesshire. He was educated at the Edinburgh Academy, Rugby in 1843-47 and the University of Durham (B.A., 1850). Entries from December 1848 to September 1850 in a diary suggest a not unusual youth: he worried about examinations, attended church regularly and with much conviction, and was closely attached to his family particularly his brothers Hugh and Edward and his sister Eliza. With a passion for walking he spent some time after graduation in the Lakes District and the Cheviots. In contemplation of entering the Church of England, he may have tutored in 1850 at Abbotsley, Huntingdonshire. He dabbled in geology, read Lyall's text and looked for 'specimens of epidote and chlorite'.

His interest in minerals possibly contributed to his decision to migrate with Edward to Australia. Certainly he had earlier expressed interest in the Californian gold rush. He had also been crossed in love. With

£2000 for acquiring land, the brothers sailed for Sydney as cabin passengers in the *Malacca* and arrived in August 1851. Next March John was appointed sub-commissioner of the southern goldfields at a salary of £200. He was stationed at Major's Creek near Araluen but resigned in September and in November took control of the police at Tuena goldfield. His salary was £300 in 1853 but on 21 June he resigned to join Edward on the land, possibly with Thomas Hood Hood who in 1852-53 held a depasturing licence for the 16,000-acre run Boree near Wellington. In 1854 with Hood they went to the Darling Downs and bought, reputedly for £50,000, the 64,000-acre station Talgai which in 1853 ran 20,900 sheep. Hood was nominated in 1855 to the New South Wales Legislative Council for the pastoral districts of Clarence and Darling Downs and held the seat until 1861. The Douglas brothers found other congenial acquaintances among the squatters, many of them newly arrived from Scotland. Nehemiah Bartley [q.v.] described John as a 'young, tall, well-made, slim swell . . . in his velvet coat, Bedford cords and boots', and he raced at local meetings. He also helped to establish the *Darling Downs Gazette* in 1858 and soon decided to enter politics 'as a kind of relaxation'.

Douglas represented the Darling Downs in the New South Wales Legislative Assembly from July to October 1859; 'As a liberal in heart as well as in principle' he generally supported the premier, Charles Cowper [q.v.], and claimed that 'his interests were identified' with those of the Downs. He also spoke on such matters as expenditure on roads and bridges in his electorate in comparison with receipts from land sales, and voted against Queensland inheriting on separation part of the public debt of New South Wales. In December 1860 he re-entered politics, holding the second seat for Camden until he resigned on 17 July 1861. He denied standing as 'Mr Cowper's nominee' and told Sir William Macarthur [q.v.] of his hopes to live near Sydney and to reconcile political opponents. The *Sydney Morning Herald* classified him as an obvious ministerialist and his nomination speech supported Cowper's associate, Robertson [q.v.], who was advocating free selection before survey. Meanwhile Douglas, besides holding Talgai until 1862, may have had an interest in another Hood property, Langton Downs near Clermont; on 13 July 1860 he bought in the Port Curtis district six pastoral runs, Tivoli, Borenia, Dundee, Montrose, Panuco and Tooloombah, sometimes collectively known as Tooloombah. When Douglas mortgaged them in 1860 to Gilchrist, Watt & Co. to raise £5000, they ran 1991 cattle. He had probably over-stocked and the evidence suggests that the Douglas brothers had not made the profits they expected from squatting. In 1861 Edward returned to Scotland; in Sydney John married Mary Ann Howe, the widowed daughter of Rev. William West Simpson.

Douglas moved to Brisbane in 1863 and was elected for Port Curtis to the Queensland Legislative Assembly where he remained independent of the Herbert [q.v.] ministry. When Macalister [q.v.] became premier in 1866 Douglas accepted office as a minister without portfolio from 1 to 28 February and postmaster-general from 1 March to 20 July and leader of the government in the Legislative Council. In 1867 he was elected for the Eastern Downs. He was treasurer from 19 December 1866 to 21 May 1867 and then secretary for public works until 15 August. He clashed, however, with Macalister and later opposed the squatter ministry of Mackenzie [q.v.]. As an ardent advocate of the pro-agriculturist provisions in the land bill of 1867, he strongly attacked squatters for their practice of dummying on the Darling Downs, and was appointed chairman of a select committee. Although the majority found his allegations unproven, Douglas refused to accept this verdict. Despite his attitudes he was returned for the Eastern Downs in 1868 and when the liberal Lilley [q.v.] became premier Douglas held office as postmaster-general from 12 December to 13 November 1869 and moved into the Legislative Council as leader of the government on the understanding that he would be appointed Queensland's emigration agent and agent-general in England at £1000 a year. In these posts from 15 September 1869 to 29 December 1870 he vigorously advocated migration to Queensland, tried vainly to promote a cable from Java to Queensland, made useful contacts with the Colonial Office but resigned after disagreements with the Palmer [q.v.] ministry. Later criticism of his work, doubts about his appointment and an alleged overcharge of £1320 which had 'lapsed in consequence of insolvency' led him to petition parliament. With Griffith's support a select committee of inquiry was appointed; its report on 30 July 1872 mainly exonerated Douglas. Meanwhile he had become insolvent on his own petition on 23 February 1872, owing £6767 15s. 9d. to Gilchrist, Watt & Co. for moneys advanced in 1860 and 1869.

After his return from England Douglas was easily defeated for East Moreton in November 1871, narrowly lost the Brisbane seat in November 1873 and was just beaten for Darling Downs in March 1875 in a campaign marked by sectarian bitterness.

On 23 April he was returned for Maryborough and in the Thorn [q.v.] ministry as secretary for public lands from 5 June 1876 to 8 March 1877 introduced two minor bills which became the Crown Lands Alienation Act and the Settled Districts Pastoral Leases Act. He was also vice-president of the Executive Council. He replaced Thorn as premier in 1877, combining this position with lands from 8 March to 7 November and with the colonial secretary-ship from 7 November 1877 to 21 January 1879. As leader of the Liberals against the Nationalists Douglas could do little while his party was losing popular support. He had alienated some voters by his desire to use land sale revenue to extend railways as far as the Gulf of Carpentaria. He found more support for his anti-Chinese legislation, keeping many of these unwanted migrants out of Queensland by quarantine regulations while his bill awaited royal assent. Always obstinate Douglas was found guilty of 'a very extraordinary breach of privilege' in 1880. He sent to the *Brisbane Courier* information given to a select committee despite standing orders which forbade publication before evidence was reported to parliament. Douglas had acted because he disliked 'any secret Legislative Committee, except when very weighty public considerations and the cause of morality demands secrecy', and he refused to apologize even after the assembly had voted that he was guilty of contempt. His parliamentary career was ended, though in 1883 he contested Brisbane without success.

During his political career and later he was a regular leader writer for the *Courier* and other colonial papers, winning praise from the journalist, Spencer Browne, for expounding in a 'bright and scholarly' way a variety of political, literary, scientific and educational issues. He had sat on the royal commission which in 1875 recommended the introduction of free, compulsory and secular education. He was a trustee of Brisbane Grammar School in 1874-77, the foundation president of the Spring Hill Mechanics' Institute in May 1864, and president of the influential North Brisbane School of Arts in 1872-85. His support of knowledge for its own sake and as a source of social and moral benefit was combined with more utilitarian arguments for technical education. 'The mechanic', he said, 'will certainly be no worse a mechanic, and he will undoubtedly be an infinitely better man and a more useful citizen if he knows something of the laws which govern the universe, and which surround him with the most inexhaustible beneficence'. He joined the Johnsonian Club founded in 1878 and was its president in 1880. His scientific and literary ideas were compatible with his religion; always a sincere Anglican, he was warden of All Saints and a member of the Diocesan Church Society in Brisbane. He was also a Freemason and district grand master. In 1877 he was appointed C.M.G.

In 1884 Douglas visited England where on 30 April he applied to the Colonial Office for appointment to the imperial service. Bramston [q.v.] thought his age was against him, but Herbert minuted that as 'a man of ability and high character' he should be considered. On 16 May he was assured that his name would be 'borne in mind' though 'few appointments' seemed suitable. Back in Queensland he resumed his journalism and sought through Griffith 'some form of administration'. In April 1885 he was offered the post of government resident and police magistrate at Thursday Island. In July he visited most of the islands of Torres Strait in his charge, and accompanied Captain Everill's expedition for the Geographical Society of Australasia up the Fly River in New Guinea. After Sir Peter Scratchley [q.v.] died in December 1885 Douglas was appointed special commissioner of the protectorate of British New Guinea; he remained in charge until its annexation in September 1888. As a commissioner with few defined powers Douglas realized that he could not achieve much, and hoped in 1887 that 'something [would soon be] settled—the present position is an absurd one'. His general lines of policy followed those of Scratchley and the spirit of J. E. Erskine's [q.v.] proclamation : to protect the Papuans yet to develop the island for Europeans. His long crusade for financial support from the Australian colonies was fruitless, since few Australian politicians had any interest in New Guinea despite the furore over the 1883 'annexation'. His 1887 diary shows that he spent the first three and last two months in Australia, often travelling to Sydney and Melbourne to interview politicians. He found time to walk with his sons in the Blue Mountains and near the family homes at Tenterfield and Sandgate, and in Thursday Island and New Guinea he patrolled regularly. Douglas was not chosen for the permanent appointment partly because the Colonial Office thought his wife 'unpresentable', but mainly because other candidates were preferred. In 1888 he returned to Thursday Island where, apart from a visit to Britain in 1902, he remained in charge until his death on 23 July 1904. He was survived by his second wife Sarah, née Hickey, whom he had married with Catholic rites in 1877, and by their four sons of whom the two eldest, despite his reservations, had completed their education at a Benedictine school in Scotland.

As a politician Douglas exemplified the independent local liberal member, uneasy in any party structure. He was not forceful enough to be a factional leader for long; in 1871 he was described as 'the d——est ass in the House', and others thought him vacillating. To William Coote [q.v.] in 1877, although Douglas was 'not an orator, not epigrammatic, not really argumentative nor imaginative . . . he has in fact a combination of talents each of which approaches to average excellence, and just falls short of the summit . . . a pleasant gentlemanly person of moderate acquirements'. Bernays [q.v.] claimed that he was more successful as a clever political wire-puller behind the scenes than on the floor of the House, but he was outmanoeuvred by Griffith. More clearly he was a leader in Brisbane's intellectual, literary and religious circles. As a conscientious administrator he had a sincere interest in his indigenous charges and the economic development of the islands. He wrote copious analyses of the problems of the area, particularly in his annual reports where he always supported transfer of some islands to New Guinea's control. In 1895 he warned that 'it looks as if these Japs, most indefatigable, persevering little fellows will before long possess themselves of the fishery' and he compared the position with that faced when in the Queensland government he sought to stem 'the first great Chinese invasion of Queensland'. In 1897 he sought 'to encourage the exercise of authority through Headmen . . . in all the Islands of any importance', who control 'their countrymen, partly in virtue of hereditary descent, and partly because they exercise a certain personal ascendancy'. He was also concerned in wider national problems. An ardent supporter of White Australia, he believed 'we must, through the length and breadth of Australia, be commandingly European', and he constantly advocated Federation, lecturing in its support as early as 1875 at Toowoomba and writing such articles as 'An Australian Nation' for the *Melbourne Review* in 1880; his *Past and Present of Thursday Island and Torres Straits* (Brisbane, 1900) ended with a plea for a 'yes' vote for the 'triumphant consummation of our Australian Constitutional Commonwealth'. His long rule at Thursday Island had been plagued by domestic and financial worries but he found compensation in his achievements, his intense religious beliefs and the progress of his sons. Port Douglas, in northern Queensland, was named while he was premier and a memorial chapel was built in the cathedral on Thursday Island.

R. Goodman, *Secondary education in Queensland* (Canberra, 1968); PD (Qld), 1863-

80; Annual reports for British New Guinea and Thursday Island, V&P (LA Qld), 1863-1904; W. Coote, 'The Hon. John Douglas', *Week*, 19 May 1877; SMH, 1859-61; *Brisbane Courier*, 25 July 1904; *Thursday Island Pilot*, 30 July 1904; J. X. Jobson, Sir Arthur Hunter Palmer (B.A. Hons thesis, Univ Qld, 1961); J. T. Cleary, The North Brisbane School of Arts (B.A. Hons thesis, Univ Qld, 1967); Eve Douglas, The Hon. John Douglas, 1828-1904 (ML); CSO, Land, Shipping, Treasury and Gold Commissioners, Records 1851-54 (NSWA); land, mortgage and insolvency records 1859-1904 (QA); GO dispatches 1859-1904 (QA); Palmer papers (Oxley Lib, Brisb); MS cat under John Douglas (ML); CO 234/44-45, 422/1-4.

R. B. JOYCE

DOUGLAS, WILLIAM BLOOMFIELD (1822-1906), naval officer and public servant, was born on 25 September 1822 in Aberystwyth, Wales, son of Richard William Clode Douglas and his wife Mary, née Johnson. His uncle, Rev. Francis Charles Johnson, married Emma, a sister of Sir James Brooke, first rajah of Sarawak. In January 1842 he entered the navy and became a captain's steward on H.M.S. *Wolverene* before resigning in September at Hong Kong. He then won distinction fighting pirates with Brooke in Sarawak in 1843-44. He also claimed to have served in a steam frigate in the Indian Navy. On 25 April 1848 at Embleton, Northumberland, he married Ellen, daughter of Christopher Atkinson, yeoman. At that time he was stationed at near-by Alnmouth, a coastguard station. To provide for his growing family he returned to the sea in September 1852.

In 1854 in command of the General Screw Steam Shipping Co.'s *Bosphorus*, a coastal mail vessel, Douglas successfully applied in Adelaide for the post of naval officer and harbourmaster. He assumed duty in December and in July 1858 became collector of customs as well. He also served as master of Trinity House and chairman of the Harbor Trust until these authorities and the post of naval officer were replaced in 1860 by a Marine Board with Douglas as its first president. He contributed as a commissioner or witness to official inquiries into South Australian lighthouses in 1855, harbours in 1855 and 1865 and defences in 1858, and surveyed Kangaroo Island and the Backstairs Passage in 1858, the Murray River mouth in 1859 and the west coast in 1867. He also served at various times on the Immigration Board, and as inspector of distilleries and stipendary magistrate.

In March 1870 Douglas was appointed government resident for the Northern Territory. Inspired perhaps by Brooke's example, he hoped to find fame and fortune on this new frontier. He governed like a white rajah but lacked the competence to introduce a suitable administration. He squandered money, ignored instructions and quarrelled with subordinates. He failed to control the gold rush which he encouraged and probably delayed the introduction of the 1872 mining regulations in order to protect his own investment. By early 1873 his ambitions were shattered and he had to be warned about his drinking. With a characteristic burst of energy he tried to put his administration in order but in June Thomas Reynolds [q.v.], the commissioner of crown lands, visited Palmerston (Darwin) and Douglas had to resign.

Douglas returned to Adelaide financially ruined. In April 1874 the government sent him to Singapore, on a mission he had proposed in 1871, to recruit Chinese miners for the Northern Territory. Almost 200 came to Australia in the first group but Douglas stayed in Singapore where in October he became acting police magistrate and in May 1875 second police magistrate. As British control extended in the Malay States he became acting assistant resident of Selangor in November and acting resident in April 1876. Selangor flourished in spite of Douglas's shortcomings. His incompetence was soon discovered and his work had to be closely supervised by the governor at Singapore. He spoke little Malay and his violent temper led to quarrels with important Malays and Chinese. In 1879 an inquiry found the treasury and land offices hopelessly disorganized and he was criticized for failing to extend his control to the mining districts in the interior. In response he moved to Kuala Lumpur and attempted to remedy the deficiencies in his administration, but in 1882 his son-in-law, Dominick Daniel Daly, whom he had appointed superintendent of public works, was dismissed for land jobbery; other irregularities were discovered and Douglas had to resign.

With a sick wife, a mentally retarded daughter and a son at school, Douglas was given a retirement allowance and a passage to England; instead he joined Daly who now had a job with the British North Borneo Co. His wife died in 1887 and he returned to England. His next move was to Canada where in 1893 he was employed by the tidal service of the Department of Marine and Fisheries. In 1895 he sat on an inquiry into pilotage dues in St John and in April 1897, giving his age as 65, became an examiner in the Department of Marine and Fisheries. On 31 January 1899 Douglas married Annie Maude, daughter of Ronald McDonald, collector of customs, Sydney, Nova Scotia. In 1900-03 he was a departmental inspector at Halifax and served again as an examiner before he died on 5 March 1906. The Halifax newspapers gave the 'Captain' favourable obituaries.

By his first wife Douglas had eight children; of his three sons, the eldest died young and the others served in Malaya and Sarawak. In Darwin his eldest daughter Harriet married D. D. Daly, a nephew of Governor Dominick Daly. She recorded her experiences in the Northern Territory in *Digging, Squatting, and Pioneering Life . . .* (London, 1887) and for years wrote a column from London for the *Sydney Morning Herald.*

H. Keppel, *The expedition to Borneo of H.M.S. Dido . . .* (Lond, 1845); E. Sadka, *The protected Malay states, 1874-1895* (Kuala Lumpur, 1968); PP (SA), 1855-56 (158), 1858 (88), 1870-71 (25, 148, 160); G. N. Hawker, The development of the South Australian civil service 1836-1916 (Ph.D. thesis, ANU, 1967); CO 273/74-119; CSO and NT letters (SAA); information from Mrs A. Noble, London, and Jack Cross, Adelaide.   P. L. BURNS

DOUGLASS, BENJAMIN (1830-1904), trade unionist, was born on 21 March 1830 at Greenwich, Kent, England, son of John Douglass, a Quaker and Chartist. As an apprentice plumber he married Mary Stacy at Wokingham, Berkshire. In January 1855, described as a bricklayer, he arrived at Portland in the *Shand*; next month he went to Melbourne where he at once became involved in trade union and radical activity, particularly the agitation for the eight-hour day, in which he was prominent for thirty years. In 1856 he became the first president of the Operative Plasterers' Society and a member of the first eight-hour committee which successfully gained the concession for some building trades workers on 21 March. Douglass was convinced of the need for continued union organization and in 1857 was one of the prime movers in the United Trades Association, which became the Trades Hall and Literary Institute Committee. He also saw the need for unskilled workers to belong to the union movement and helped to form an Organization of Labourers and in 1859, with C. J. Don [q.v.], the short-lived Political and Social Labour League.

By 1860 Douglass was one of the outstanding trade union leaders of Victoria. He had helped to clarify conditions in industries where subcontracting applied. In the 1860s his industrial work led him into political action to seek protection for local industries. In 1865 he was chairman of the Central Protection Committee and of Graham Berry's [q.v.] election committee, and in 1870 his prominence was recognized in his election as president of the Victorian Industries Protection League. In 1871 he was defeated at Collingwood in the general election. In 1872 he became secretary of the Australian Democratic Association in support of the Duffy [q.v.] ministry. He moved to Warrnambool where in 1874 he became secretary of a coal-mining company, helped to establish the Artisans' School of Design and became an employer and a member of the borough council.

Returning to Melbourne, Douglass became a clerk of works in the public service in 1881 and later an inspector; in 1884 he supervised the building of the law courts. In 1882 he had become a council member of the Working Men's College and was its vice-president until 1885. He was president of the Trades Hall Council in 1884-86 and chaired the 1884 Intercolonial Trades Union Congress. His increasing conservatism was reflected in his leadership of the trustees of the Trades Hall in the bitter struggle for control with affiliated unions in 1884-87. By the late 1890s he was opposed to strike action, although he had been prominent in the 1890 maritime strike and had encouraged George Higinbotham [q.v.] to donate to strike funds. Douglass was one of the two mourners who accompanied the family when Higinbotham was buried in 1892. Douglass remained active in community affairs until his death on 4 February 1904. He was buried in the Melbourne general cemetery, survived by five of his eight children.

For more than fifty years Douglass played a significant role in Victorian industrial history. His responsible co-operation with employers indicated the effects of protection in the colony and conditioned his drift away from the radical phase of his early career. On his death N. Levi [q.v.] of the Chamber of Manufactures commented that 'the men who were mixed up with the eight hours movement in the early days were different to what they are now'.

The history of capital and labour (Syd, 1888); *Argus,* 6 Feb 1905; Eight hour souvenir, *Co-operator,* 7 Oct 1912.   S. MERRIFIELD

DOW, JOHN LAMONT (1837-1923), politician and journalist, was born on 8 December 1837 at Kilmarnock, Ayrshire, Scotland, son of David Hill Dow (1818-1884), weaver, and his wife Agnes, née Lamont. In 1848 the family migrated to the Geelong district, where his father became a station overseer and Barrabool shire councillor. John was brought up to farming and stock-raising near Geelong; he claimed to have shorn in one season 'a daily average of 98 big wethers, not bare-bellied ewes'. In 1862 he joined a group sponsored by a pastoral company to explore Gulf of Carpentaria country, was among the founders of Burketown and became an early pastoralist on the Herbert River tableland. Ill from gulf-fever, he returned to Victoria in 1868 and worked on the land and as a miner until he joined the *Age* in 1873. He soon became agricultural editor of the *Leader*, a post he held until 1886 and again in 1892-1915.

On 15 September 1876 Dow addressed Ballarat's National Reform League on 'Our Land Acts and a Land Tax', using a giant map showing the vast areas held by squatters partly through dummies; he was later accused of 'Barnumising himself' into parliament. Adopting the 1860 'Unlock the Lands' slogan, he advocated a leasing system and was the first to propose taxes on land graduated by amount and quality alone, irrespective of improvements. The lecture was printed and widely distributed. In six months Dow addressed twenty-two country centres, helping to bring the selector vote behind Berry [q.v.] in the defeat of McCulloch [q.v.] in 1877. Elected for the new Kara Kara seat, Dow moved the address-in-reply on 26 June, pressing his radical liberal views. He held Kara Kara until 1893, often by walkover, nursing his electorate by helping selectors to peg out claims.

A 'Berryite' backbencher for nine years, he actively advocated land legislation, establishment of agricultural colleges, Syme's [q.v.] protectionism and temperance legislation. As a Wesleyan, he was a founding vice-president of the Victorian Alliance in 1881. In 1883 the *Australasian* sent his brother, Thomas Kirkland, to America and the *Leader* sent John; their articles on agricultural developments, later published as Thomas's *A Tour in America* and John's *The Australian in America*, were important in popularizing irrigation in Victoria. The *Age* deputed John to accompany Alfred Deakin, chairman of the royal commission on water supply and irrigation, which Dow later joined, on his 1885 mission to America; one result was the founding of Mildura.

In the 1886-90 Gillies [q.v.]-Deakin coalition government Dow was minister of lands, agriculture and mines, but soon relinquished the mines portfolio because of claims that it and agriculture were antagonistic. As lands minister he tripled forest reserves, reserved Wilson's Promontory as a national park and founded the Forests Department; more importantly his extensions of Tucker's [q.v.] 1884 Land Act expanded wheat and pastoral development in the Mallee. Dow's most significant effect on Victoria, however, was as minister for agriculture: in 1888 he sponsored large government bonuses to encourage agricultural, dairying, fruit and wine development. The bonus scheme led to the establishment of co-operative butter factories with an export worth £1 million by 1895 and made dairying a major Victorian industry. His political opponent Thomas Bent [q.v.] once said, 'Whenever I visit a dairying district, I raise my hat to the cow and to J. L. Dow'.

Dow's ministerial career was interrupted in May 1890 when he and the other directors of the Premier Permanent Building Society, of whom he had been one, were charged with fraud. In Dow's case, however, the charge was merely 'of a technical nature' and he was the only director not committed for trial. He rejoined the cabinet soon before it fell and was re-elected unopposed. Nevertheless, Dow had been involved in speculation, especially in Maitland coal through Felix Kabat, and forfeited his seat in 1893 when declared bankrupt. He admitted that he had speculated in mining 'all his life', and told the Insolvency Court, 'The next man that comes to you with a good thing, hit him with a club'.

His last parliamentary speech on 18 January 1893 helped to bring down the Shiels-Berry government that day; as 'an old, indurated and thick-skinned politician', he attacked his former leader, Berry, for compromising his liberal principles by joining Shiels. Dow re-entered politics only to contest the first Senate election in 1901 as 'a Syme candidate' and was narrowly defeated. In the *Leader* he had campaigned against bank foreclosures on farmers in 1895 and continued to write prolifically on land, stock-breeding, conservation and irrigation until his retirement in 1915. He died in Melbourne on 16 July 1923.

Dow saw his whole career in both politics and journalism as one lived in the farmers' interest: all his public work was dominated by the view that a balanced development of Victoria demanded rapid expansion of agriculture between the growing metropolis and the squatters' runs. His contributions to land legislation, dairying, irrigation and conservation justify this view. His belief from 1879 that 'without the mutual give-and-take of a reasonable compromise practical legislation is impossible' made him a skilled parliamentarian as well as Victoria's leading agricultural journalist for forty years. It was his misfortune, and possibly Victoria's, that his compulsive and careless mining speculations put him out of politics when his experience, political *nous* and abundant energy were combining to best effect. Naive in business—'honest, but takes it for granted that all others are honest too', said J. L. Purves [q.v.] who prosecuted him—yet shrewd in political controversy and something of a showman, his humour and rough-and-ready repartee made him a formidable but good-tempered opponent. Despite ill health from his Queensland pioneering and a game leg, he had a genial temperament; Deakin called him 'the best raconteur he had heard'.

In 1869 Dow married Marion Jane, daughter of William A. Orr of Toorak; they had three sons and five daughters. The eldest, David McKenzie (1870-1953), was official secretary for Australia in America in 1924-31 and acting commissioner-general in 1931-38.

His brother, Thomas Kirkland, agricultural journalist, was born on 4 July 1848 at Glasgow; after teaching in a State school near Ballarat in 1870-77 he joined the *Leader* but worked for the *Australasian* in 1881-90. He served on the first Council of Agricultural Education in 1884-90, was principal of Longerenong Agricultural College in 1890-96 and went overseas for the *Age* in 1898. He married Margaret Campbell, née Keith; they had two sons and three daughters. Thomas died at Tresco on 2 March 1918.

J. A. Alexander, *The life of George Chaffey* (Melb, 1928); M. Cannon, *The land boomers* (Melb, 1966); PD (Vic), 26 June, 4 Sept 1877, 25 June 1885, 7 Aug 1889, 18 Jan 1893; *Age*, 16 Sept 1876, 12, 20 Aug 1890, 13, 20 Apr 1893, 17 July 1923; *Vic Review*, 1 Dec 1879; S. M. Ingham, Some aspects of Victorian liberalism 1880-1900 (M.A. thesis, Univ Melb, 1950); J. E. Parnaby, The economic and political development of Victoria, 1877-1881 (Ph.D. thesis, Univ Melb, 1951); A. M. Mitchell, Temperance and the liquor question in later 19th century Victoria (M.A. thesis, Univ Melb, 1966); recollections of the late D. M. Cheesman, Barkly, Vic, and the late D. M. Dow.

HUME DOW

DOWIE, JOHN ALEXANDER (1847-1907), faith healer, was born on 25 May 1847 in Edinburgh, son of John Dowie, breechesmaker, and his wife Ann Macfarlan. His childhood was marked by poverty, sickness and precocious piety; in 1860 the family migrated to Adelaide where he was employed by an uncle and then in a wholesale grocery firm where he became junior partner. At 20 he forsook business to study for the Congregational ministry in Adelaide and Scotland and on 21 May 1872 was ordained to the pastorate of Alma and Hamley Bridge in South Australia.

His resignation nine months later was due, he said, to ill health; others said that he had quarrelled with his congregation. He was called in September 1873 to Manly, New South Wales, and in February 1875 to Newtown. In 1876 he visited Adelaide and

married his cousin Jane on 26 May. Although eloquent, Dowie was now markedly eccentric and in February 1878 he announced his resignation, holding up a glass of wine in the pulpit and crying, 'these be thy gods, O Israel'. He then conducted a mission in theatres and halls while his abusive tracts and sermons were ridiculed by the irreverent Sydney press.

In 1880 a confidence man borrowed money from Dowie by promising to donate £21,000 for a church. Dowie publicized the proposed gift widely and left for Adelaide to wait his benefactor's return from Europe but was disappointed to learn of his death. Five years later he recognized the 'deceased' in Melbourne and prosecuted him. In Adelaide Dowie became involved with the Salvation Army and won publicity by his legal action against the commissioner of police for obstructing the Army's work.

In November 1881 at Melbourne Dowie joined battle with Thomas Walker, a leading Spiritualist, and published a pamphlet on their controversy. He intended to return to Sydney but in May 1882 was invited to the Sackville Street Tabernacle, Collingwood. His authoritarian rule soon bred revolt; his story of it was recorded in *Sin in The Camp*. On 15 February 1883 he led a breakaway group to form a new tabernacle in Johnston Street, Fitzroy. In disputes over ownership the opposition barricaded themselves in the tabernacle; Dowie led his followers against them and was charged with organizing unauthorized processions. He insisted that he must obey the law of God rather than of man but then declared that if the court wanted its pound of flesh, he had fourteen stone to offer. He was gaoled for a month and fined for a second offence; when his sentence expired he refused to pay the fine and was gaoled again for seven days. Many liberals supported him and he was soon released. Dowie had already turned to faith healing and after a mission to New Zealand he left for the United States in June 1888. After two years in San Francisco he went to Chicago where by 1895 he was so notorious that a hundred charges were laid against him, although none succeeded.

On 22 February 1896 Dowie became general overseer of the Christian Catholic Church and in 1900 established Zion City, forty miles from Chicago. 'The new Elijah' owned all property there and leaseholders were prohibited from smoking, drinking, eating pork and establishing theatres, dance halls, doctors' surgeries and secret lodges. After trying in vain to convert New York in 1903 he launched a mission to the world in 1904. His visit to Dublin is mentioned in James Joyce's *Ulysses* but in Australia every appearance was marked by near riots stimulated partly by his blue, white, yellow and purple surplice and partly by the overbearing conduct of his train of Zion City guards. His increasingly luxurious way of life began to scandalize some of his supporters. He visited Mexico to set up a plantation and after a stroke on 24 September 1905 went to Jamaica. In his absence he was deposed on 20 April 1906 by Wilbur G. Voliva, his chief lieutenant. The ensuing litigation dragged on until he died at Zion City on 9 March 1907.

Dowie's success sprang mainly from his Biblical knowledge, personality and talent for showmanship. Whether he was mentally unbalanced or a cunning charlatan remains an open question. According to one commentator, 'there was a force in him whose tremors were felt at the ends of the earth. He had a wonderful faculty of persuasion . . . If he didn't impose on himself, he imposed himself on others. The instinct of accumulation was active and enterprising in him: he might have been a great financier and capitalist. He had a singularly copious repertoire of abusive epithets and his self opinionativeness combined with his inordinate pugnacity made him a reckless and somewhat dangerous antagonist'.

E. S. Kiek, *An apostle in Australia* (Lond, 1927); *Bulletin*, 10 Apr 1880, 25 June, 2, 30 July, 6 Aug 1881, 22 July, 2 Dec 1882; *Argus*, 5 May-26 June 1885, 9 Jan 1886; *Table Talk*, 27 Feb 1902; *Australasian*, 20 Feb 1904; J. H. Watson scrapbook, v 1 (ML); F. W. Cox diaries (Congregational Union Archives, Parkin College, Adel).   H. J. GIBBNEY

DOWLING, CHRISTOPHER VINCENT (1789-1873), Catholic priest, was born on 24 September 1789 in Dublin, and went at an early age to the famous Dominican College of Corpo-Santo in Lisbon, Portugal. There he joined the Dominican order, returned to Dublin in 1814 and was ordained by Archbishop Daniel Murray. During his eleven years in Dublin he was guardian of the Dominican Charity School in 1821 and subprior of the Dublin priory. In 1825, because of ill health, he was sent to France where he became pastor of Salignac in the Bordeaux diocese. Next year he was elected prior of the Dublin priory but did not return to Ireland to take up the office. In 1829 Dr Bramston, the Catholic vicar apostolic of London, appointed him to Newport in the Isle of Wight. After ten months he went to London and was ministering there, when at a request of the Colonial Office Bramston nominated him to go to New South Wales to replace the only official Catholic chaplain, Daniel Power, who had died in March 1830.

Dowling arrived at Sydney on 17 September 1831 in the *Mary Ann*, accompanied by his sister, Mary Theresa; on 8 May 1832 she married David Chambers, a solicitor. Dowling was referred to as an eloquent preacher, an able linguist, speaking French and Portuguese fluently, a good classical scholar and a frequent contributor to the press.

In Sydney he lived at Charlotte Place because John Joseph Therry [q.v.], who had been dismissed from the official chaplaincy by Governor Darling, refused to vacate the Chapel House at Hyde Park. Dowling secured government funds for the education of Catholic children and gained widespread support. But a bitter encounter between Dowling and Therry, in the course of which Dowling was assaulted, robbed and frequently insulted, continued until John McEncroe [q.v.] arrived in August 1832. Appointed chaplain for the Hawkesbury by Governor Bourke, Dowling went to Windsor. There he established a school and won the friendship of John Macarthur [q.v.] who gave the ground and some money for a Catholic chapel at Camden. Dowling performed the first Catholic marriage ceremony and baptism at Windsor on 1 January 1835. In September Bishop Polding [q.v.] appointed him to Maitland.

In August 1836 Dowling became the only resident priest north of Sydney. His parish covered the whole Hunter River district and extended north indefinitely. He met with mixed official receptions, the commandant at Harper's Hill in Maitland being particularly obstructive, but he maintained good relations with officials in Sydney and when the King died in 1837 signed appropriate letters to Queen Adelaide and Queen Victoria. On 27 February 1838 he attended the Government House levee after Governor Gipps was sworn in.

Ill health made his duties in the huge Maitland area most difficult and in March 1838 Polding informed Gipps that, as Dowling wished to have a 'less arduous situation', he hoped that the priest would take up the Catholic chaplaincy on Norfolk Island. However, in September Dowling moved to Newcastle as its first resident priest. He lived in a cottage on the Sandhills but for seven years said Mass and ran a school in Croasdill's Long Room above four dwellings in Newcomen Street. Catholic soldiers rented and furnished it for him. When it had to be vacated in 1845, the services took place in his house which had been the first hospital in Newcastle and was close to the old gaol. He regularly attended executions to console the condemned. His Newcastle parish extended from Lake Macquarie to Myall Lakes and included Raymond Terrace and Clarence Town. Owning no means of transport he either travelled by boat or walked. Later he lost the use of his legs and was carried by parishioners to call on sick or dying Catholics. In 1849 he began saying Mass in a government store-room in Watt Street, Newcastle. In 1852 the first Catholic Church of St Mary was built, a temporary structure, in Church Street; it was the only church Dowling built in an era of church builders.

His health continued to fail and despite assistant priests Dowling finally gave up his active ministry in 1863 and retired to his Sandhills cottage. Visited and revered by Catholics and others, he became a living legend in the district. When he died on 14 December 1873 men of all persuasions joined in mourning him. Crowds attended the lying-in-state in St Mary's. All ships in Newcastle Harbour flew their flags at half-mast and many shops closed when, at his own request, he was buried in St Joseph's Churchyard, East Maitland. He was one of the first ten Catholic priests, the fourth official Catholic chaplain and the first member of a religious order, to minister in Australia.

P. F. Moran, History of the Catholic Church in Australasia (Syd, 1895); E. M. O'Brien, Life and Letters of Archpriest John Joseph Therry, 1-2 (Syd, 1922); M. A. O'Hanlon, Dominican pioneers in New South Wales (Syd, 1949); H. Campbell, The diocese of Maitland 1866-1966 (Maitland, 1966); J. J. McGovern, 'John Bede Polding', pt 2, A'sian Catholic Record, 11 (1934) no 4; J. O'Brien (P. J. Hartigan), 'In diebus illis', A'sian Catholic Record, 20-21 (1943-44); Sydney Gazette, 20 Sept 1831; Australian, 23 Sept 1831, 17 Feb, 20 Apr 1832; Freeman's J (Syd), 20 Dec 1873, 3 Jan 1874; Catholic Weekly (Syd), 28 Aug 1952.

J. A. MORLEY

DOWLING, JAMES SHEEN (1819-1902), judge, was born on 2 December 1819 in London, the younger son of Sir James Dowling [q.v.] and his wife Maria, née Sheen. He arrived with his parents in the Hooghly in February 1828 at Sydney where his father took up an appointment as puisne judge of the Supreme Court. He was educated under J. D. Lang, Joseph Docker and William Cape [qq.v.] and transferred to the Sydney College when it opened in 1835. Cape formed a high opinion of his abilities and it was decided that he should study law in England. He became seriously ill in 1836 and was advised to take a long sea voyage to restore his health. Francis Forbes [q.v.] was then leaving for England and Dowling accompanied him. He arrived in London later that year and entered King's College (LL.B., 1841). He was admitted to the Middle Temple and called to the Bar in November

1843. He practised at the English Bar, gaining experience in pleading and conveyancing, and reported for his uncle Alfred Septimus Dowling for the weekly Legal Observer and Solicitor's Journal.

Dowling's projected return to New South Wales was hastened by news of his father's death. He took passage, again in the Hooghly, and arrived at Sydney in September 1845. Next month he was admitted to the colonial Bar, and immediately went into practice. He must have established a good reputation, for a year later he was appointed attorney-general for the proposed new colony, 'North Australia'. But the promotion was short lived; after three months at Port Curtis the project was abandoned. Sorely disappointed, as he had entertained hopes of further promotion there, he resumed his Sydney practice. In 1851 he was appointed police magistrate of Sydney and performed his duties creditably, particularly during the golden years. He was appointed crown prosecutor for the colony in 1857 but next year the office was abolished by the District Courts Act. Dowling was the junior of the first three judges to be appointed under this Act at a salary of £1000. He took the western district based at Bathurst, where he went to live in 1859. He returned to Sydney in 1861 after his appointment, at the same time as Alfred Cheeke [q.v.], as a judge of the metropolitan and coast districts, and chairman of Quarter Sessions in the Cumberland and coast districts. He became the senior District Court judge in 1865 on Cheeke's elevation to the Supreme Court bench.

Towards the end of 1888 Dowling's health began to fail and in February 1889 he resigned. He was persuaded, however, to remain and take leave to recover. He visited England, but on his return realized that he could not continue; his resignation in July was accepted and he received a pension of £750. Thereafter he lived quietly in Sydney where he recorded his reminiscences, now in the Mitchell Library. Apart from his own experiences, the volume includes descriptions of Sydney in his schooldays and sketches of contemporary legal figures. Though he claimed no literary merit for the work, it is a fund of information and a worthy contribution to the written history of New South Wales. Mild and kindly, his public activities were largely confined to his profession. Throughout his thirty years on the District Court bench, he dispensed justice with good sense and compassion, and his decisions were seldom, if ever, reversed. He was a noted wit and his court was reputed the most popular in the colony. Though he acted many times as a Supreme Court judge, he was interested neither in politics nor in accepting a 'political judgeship', and it was probably for this reason that he was never promoted to the superior court.

In 1849 at Sydney Dowling married Katherine Marion, third daughter of James Laidley [q.v.]; she predeceased him. He died at his home, Brougham, Woollahra, on 4 May 1902, survived by five sons and two daughters. The eldest son, James Arthur, was a solicitor and for twelve years president of the Board of Trustees, Public Library of New South Wales.

A portrait by Tom Roberts is held by M. R. L. Dowling of Sydney.

'Men of eminence in New South Wales. His Honor Judge Dowling', *Syd Q Mag*, Sept 1886; Dowling papers (ML). A. R. DOWLING

DOWLING, ROBERT HAWKER (1827-1886), artist, was born in England, the youngest son of Rev. Henry Dowling [q.v] and his wife Elizabeth, née Darke. At 7 he went to Van Diemen's Land with his parents in the *Janet*. As a youth he was deeply impressed by the tragedy of the Tasmanian Aboriginals. He was educated at Launceston and became a saddler. He showed an early ability for drawing and took lessons from Thomas Bock and Frederick Strange [qq.v.]. In August 1850, encouraged by his father, he changed his trade sign 'saddler' to 'portrait painter'. In 1851 he advertised in Wood's *Almanack* as a 'portrait and miniature painter, Charles Street, Launceston. Miniatures on ivory from one guinea upwards'. The press also reported on several portraits from his easel. In 1857, 'full of energy, pluck, resolution', he sailed in the *Pharamond* for England and entered Leigh's Academy, London. His 'Breakfasting out', a steel engraving of a London coffee stall scene, was exhibited at the Royal Academy in 1859 and his 'Tasmania Aborigines, Scene in the Bay of Fires' in 1860. Primarily a portrait, genre and history painter, he exhibited sixteen works at the Royal Academy in 1859-82; many were then lent to the Australian colonies, including 'A Sheikh and his Son entering Cairo on their return from a Pilgrimage to Mecca', later acquired by the National Gallery of Victoria. As 'an Australian artist of great promise', he was admitted to many art societies and had favourable press notices; Earl Spencer became his patron. In 1860 Dowling presented the city of Launceston with his 'Group of Natives of Tasmania', one of four historical group-portraits of Victorian and Tasmanian Aboriginals based on Bock's work. In reply Launceston subscribed 250 guineas for portraits of the Queen and Prince Consort which Dowling chose to paint from two Winter-

halter portraits of 1859. His copies arrived at Launceston in February 1863.

In 1885 Dowling returned to Australia. In Launceston he painted a portrait of the late Sir Richard Dry [q.v.] and in Melbourne a portrait of Governor Sir Henry Loch. He returned to England in the *Tigrisia* in April 1886 and died in London on 8 July. On 14 August 1849 he had married Arabella Dean; they had one daughter, Marion Beckford. Examples of his work are held by the National Gallery, university and Law Courts in Melbourne, by the Warrnambool Art Gallery and by the Queen Victoria Museum and Art Gallery, Launceston. A self-portrait is in Launceston.

H. Button, *Flotsam and jetsam* (Launceston, 1909); *Art J* (Lond), 1860, pp 169, 351, 379; *Examiner* (Launceston), 5, 19 Mar 1851, 25 Aug, 20, 23 Oct 1860, 19 Feb 1863, 16 Feb, 20 Oct 1864, 15, 17 July 1886; *Atlas* (Lond), 25 Aug 1860; *Cornwall Chronicle*, 20 Oct 1860, 29 June 1877; *Daily Telegraph* (Launceston), 23 Feb, 26 Mar 1885; *Tasmanian* (Launceston), 24 Apr 1886. ISABELLA J. MEAD

DOWLING, THOMAS (1820-1914), pastoralist, was born on 6 December 1820 at Colchester, Essex, England, son of Rev. Henry Dowling [q.v.], and his wife Elizabeth, née Darke. He went with his brother to Van Diemen's Land in 1838, was educated in Hobart Town and became a farmer. On 18 August 1842 he married Maria Jane Ware. In 1849 he crossed to Port Phillip, spent some time with his brother-in-law, Jeremiah George Ware, at Koort-Koort-Nong station and then either owned or rented a dairy at Lake Coragulac. In 1853 he bought Jellalabad station, 16,000 acres near Darlington, and with this area Dowling remained associated until his death. He built up a fine merino flock using rams from J. L. Currie's [q.v.] Larra stud and from the Bellevue and Parramore studs in Tasmania. Jellalabad merinos became widely known for the fine texture of their wool.

Dowling was appointed a magistrate for the Southern Bailiwick in 1854 and held the first police court at Timboon (Camperdown). He took his duties seriously and attended the police court every fortnight though this entailed a forty-mile ride over bush tracks. He was a member and chairman of the Road Board and in 1864 was elected to the Mortlake Shire Council of which he was president for twenty years and a member for fifty years. Dowling strove successfully for the establishment of schools in Darlington and Camperdown and was a trustee of the Darlington recreation reserve and the Darlington cemetery. He was treasurer of the Municipal Association of Victoria for over twenty years. In 1886-1904 he represented Nelson Province in the Legislative Council, where he advocated the surplus wealth tax as a means of removing all other forms of taxation.

Dowling remained active until his death on 8 July 1914. In Mortlake and Darlington he was the 'grand old man of the district and the last of the original squatters'. The removal of his strong grip on local affairs after his reign of fifty years must have seemed like the passing of an era. His wife had died in 1908 and he married Eliza Jane. She survived him with seven of the eleven children of his first marriage and many grandchildren.

J. Smith (ed), *Cyclopedia of Victoria*, 1 (Melb, 1903); *Leader* (Melb), 3 July 1880; *Terang Express*, 10 July 1914; *Colac Reformer*, 11 July 1914; *Mortlake Dispatch*, 11 July 1914.

J. ANN HONE

DOWLING, VINCENT JAMES (1835-1903), explorer and pastoralist, was born on 11 January 1835 at Flinton, South Head Road, near Sydney, the eldest son of James Willoughby Dowling and his wife Lillias, née Dickson. His father was a nephew and associate of Sir James Dowling [q.v.]. Vincent was educated by Rev. J. Wilkinson at Meads, Ashfield, until 1849 and then at Clapham, near London. He returned to New South Wales in 1851 and, after experience at Pomeroy, near Goulburn, held a New England run for about three years. He then bought mobs of sheep and cattle from the Richmond and Clarence Rivers and overlanded them to Victorian markets. His last trip in the 1858 drought was 'sufficient to sicken' him of overland work.

Early in 1859 Dowling drove 1200 Hereford heifers to establish a station on the Darling, which became known as Fort Bourke. When yards and living quarters had been erected, he started a garden. In 1860 he became a justice of the peace for New South Wales and in 1862 for Queensland. He sat on the bench at Bourke, Mudgee, Bathurst and Sofala. He soon found the Darling 'too civilized' and began exploring to the north and west; with an Aboriginal guide he traced the Paroo and Bulloo to their sources. He founded Caiwarroo and Eulo stations on the Paroo in 1861 and others on the Warrego and Cuttaburra Rivers, and Yantabulla and Birrawarra in New South Wales. About 1863 he went into partnership with G. H. Cox [q.v.]; by 1867 they had leased over 1300 square miles in the Warrego district of Queensland. Dowling was the active manager. In 1863 he had been saved by his 'long

American hat' from an Aboriginal spear in his head and in 1865 his brother John was murdered by natives. To such dangers were added arduous labour and intense loneliness, relieved only by books and the writing of bad poetry. 'God knows how it is all to end', he wrote in December 1865, 'but if this weather continues much longer, we must all go to the wall together'.

On 4 May 1866 at St Peter's Church of England, Cook's River, Dowling married Frances Emily, the fifth daughter of T. C. Breillat [q.v.]; he had courted her for eight years. Their first child was born in 1867 and Fanny went with Dowling to Thargomindah on the Bulloo; she was the first white woman in the area and he the farthest-out magistrate. He built up a fine herd of Herefords which he thought withstood drought better than Shorthorns. When Thargomindah was auctioned in 1874 it had a frontage of eighty miles on the Bulloo and nearly 1000 square miles of grassed mulga ridges and salt-bush plains. By 1875 Cox & Dowling had sold out in Queensland. In August 1876 Dowling left Sydney to tour the East, America and England where, despite ill health, he followed such famous hounds as those of the Pytchley Hunt.

He returned to Sydney in July 1877, bought Lue, Rylstone, from Dr J. C. Cox [q.v.], and settled down as a stud breeder. By 1884 Dowling had fenced Lue's 23,000 acres and subdivided it into about forty paddocks. With 1500 acres of lucerne and much prairie grass he raised the carrying capacity to 21,000 sheep and about 500 cattle. By 1891 he had 33,771 sheep on Lue and Slapdash. The Lue merino stud was famed for its wool which won many prizes. Dowling bought several rams from E. K. Cox [q.v.] at Rawdon and the 'champion ram' at the 1879 International Exhibition in Sydney. He continued to breed Herefords mainly with stock from Cressy, Tasmania. Bulls bred at Lue were later sent to his Queensland stations. He also bred carriage horses and Clydesdales.

In 1880 for £9500 he bought Gummin Gummin in the Warrumbungles where he ran sheep and cattle and bred 'walers' for the Indian Army. He later acquired Walla Walla, near Gilgandra, but never lost faith in Queensland. In the 1880s Cox & Dowling bought Connemara, north of Cooper's Creek, and were joined by S. A. Stephen [q.v.]; by 1896 the station had 25,000 cattle on 3000 square miles. The partners also acquired Pillicawarrina on the Macquarie River. On 19 September 1890, during the maritime strike, Dowling was one of six men who drove their wool to the Sydney wharves under police escort; the resulting turmoil led to the reading of the Riot Act. Dowling's last decade was clouded by anxiety over his muddled finances; before the 1902 drought ended large sums had to be borrowed to keep Connemara going, and selections on Pillicawarrina led to many complicated court cases.

Known as 'V.J.D.' Dowling loved all forms of sport: in his exploring days he hunted kangaroos and other game; a lover of horses, he was keen on racing and rode in steeplechases in Sydney. He owned racehorses and his four-in-hand was famous in Mudgee. He became vice-president of the Australian Jockey Club, the Royal Agricultural Society of New South Wales and the Stockowners Association, was a councillor of the Tax Payers Union and a member of the Bathurst Anglican Synod. He was not only widely read but had 'wonderful vitality' and great humour. He died from heart disease on 5 November 1903 at Neotsfield, Singleton, the home of his son-in-law, R. H. Dangar, and was buried in the Anglican cemetery at Mudgee. He was survived by his wife, two of his four sons and three daughters, to whom he left over £47,000.

C. McIvor, *The history and development of sheep farming* . . . (Syd, 1893); *Sydney Mail*, 24 Nov 1884; *Australasian*, 4 July 1885; *SMH*, 6 Nov 1903; *Pastoral Review*, 17 Nov 1903; G. H. Cox cash book and letters to George Stewart (held by Mrs R. R. B. Hickson, Mosman, NSW); V. J. Dowling diaries and letters (ML); S. A. and C. C. Stephen letter-books (held by A. E. Stephen, Sydney).

MARTHA RUTLEDGE

DOWNES, MAJOR FRANCIS (1834-1923), army officer, was born on 10 February 1834 at Dedham, Essex, England, the younger son of William Downes and his wife Ann, née Davey. He was educated at the Dedham Grammar School and entered the Royal Military Academy, Woolwich, in February 1848. He was appointed to the Royal Artillery as a second lieutenant in December 1852 and became lieutenant in February 1854 while on duty in Canada. He served in the Crimean war in 1854-56, became a captain in November 1859 and major in July 1872 when he was an instructor at the School of Gunnery in England. In 1877 he returned to regimental duties as a battery commander but soon accepted appointment as commandant of the military forces of South Australia for five years. In October Downes was promoted lieut-colonel and arrived in Adelaide. He set about his duties with energy and efficiency, and soon achieved some success in executing the government's military policy. In 1879 he offered to take 300 South Australian militia to serve in the Zulu war.

In February 1881 the New South Wales government appointed Downes a member of a royal commission to report on all aspects of the organization and administration of its military forces. In that year he became a local and temporary colonel in the British Army and a year later was placed on halfpay. Later he elected to be placed on the retired list because he believed that if he resumed duty in the British Army his prospects of promotion would be poor; he also wished to accept the South Australian government's invitation to stay longer because, he said, 'I was much interested in my work and felt there was much more to be done before a new hand took the wheel'. He was placed on the retired list of the British Army in October 1884 with the honorary rank of major-general. He resigned his command in South Australia in March 1885 and in April became the first permanent head of the Victorian Department of Defence. Although he had intended to live in New Zealand, he was persuaded by Lieut-Colonel Frederick Sargood [q.v.] to accept this civil appointment. In May he was appointed C.M.G. However, Downes was not happy as a civil servant because he was not accustomed to the continuous stream of paper work: 'it did not suit my out-of-doors nature'. To the regret of the Gillies [q.v.] ministry he resigned in March 1888. He returned to South Australia where in April he was reappointed commandant. The success of his earlier command enabled him to win the support of the government and the public. He made local arrangements for General Edwards's [q.v.] inspection of the colony's military forces in August 1889 and in 1890-91 served on an intercolonial committee of military commandants who inspected areas suitable for fixed defences at King George Sound, in Tasmania, at Thursday Island and Port Darwin and submitted its reports to the Australian governments through the Victorian minister for defence.

Downes had a riding accident on duty in November 1891 and resigned his command on 23 March 1893. With his family he left Adelaide for Victoria where he lived in Geelong and later in Brighton. Soon after the outbreak of the South African war in October 1899 he was invited by the premier Sir George Turner to succeed Major-General Sir Charles Holled Smith as military commandant in Victoria. Downes's appointment in November was temporary pending federation of the Australian colonies, but he organized and equipped five contingents for active service in South Africa. On 1 March 1901 the ministerial control of the six State military forces passed to the new Federal government. On 29 January 1902 Major-General Sir Edward Hutton, the first commander of the federal military forces, arrived in Melbourne and assumed command. In March 1902 Downes relinquished his Victorian command and was placed on the retired list of the Australian Military Forces with the rank of major-general. This time he had put away his sword for ever. He continued to live in Melbourne in retirement, devoting much time to charitable work, until he died on 15 October 1923 at his daughter's home in Middle Brighton. He was buried with military honours in the Church of England portion of the Brighton cemetery. His wife Helen Maria, née Chamberlin, whom he had married at Catton, Norwich, on 9 June 1858, had died on 21 January 1903 aged 62. They had one daughter and four sons, of whom Rupert (1885-1945) became major-general and director-general of medical services of the Australian Military Forces.

Because of his integrity, professional competence and moderation in the exercise of his powers Downes was a good example to the officers and men he commanded and a valued and trusted servant of the Australian governments he served. His official life was not free of conflicts and disappointments, but despite his toughening and tempering in the furnace of experience he remained a kindly and charitable man.

Government Gazette (SA), 1877-85, 1888-93; Government Gazette (Vic), 1885-88, 1899-1901; Government Gazette (Cwlth), 1901-02; correspondence . . ; on employment of Major-General M. F. Downes, PP (HC), 1890 (129); W. Perry, 'Major General M. F. Downes', VHM, 41 (1970); Argus, 1877-1902, 16 Oct 1923; autobiographical notes held by Mrs R. M. Downes, East Melbourne, Vic (copy SAA).

WARREN PERRY

DOWSE, THOMAS (1809-1885), merchant and town clerk, was born at Hackney, London, son of William Dowse and his wife Catherine, née Barron. An errand boy at 15, he was accused of theft, tried at Middlesex on 16 September 1824, convicted and sentenced to life imprisonment. He was sent to New South Wales in the Florentia which arrived in January 1828. At St John's, Parramatta, on 19 November 1832 he married Ann Kelly; of their seven children, Thomas George and William survived infancy.

In 1836 Dowse was granted a ticket-of-leave and a conditional pardon in 1839. Though not a prominent colonist, he had much knowledge of Sydney's commerce and shipping. When the Moreton Bay District was opened for free settlement he decided to go there to see what opportunity awaited 'a man with a wife and young family to push his fortunes'. He had no capital, but he was in good health and not afraid of hard work.

On 9 July 1842 in the Falcon he landed at night; cold, hungry and weary he thought Brisbane 'the abode of damn'd Spirits, so unmistakably miserable did all the surroundings appear', but he soon found friends from Sydney who made him welcome. Noticing the need of a ferry across the river, he bought a skiff which by 1843 had earned three times its value. By 1846 he was established as an auctioneer and commission agent, and also had the agency for the Sydney Morning Herald. At his premises in Queen Street he sold almost anything from shirts, frock coats, cutlery, looking-glasses and books to livestock. His auction mart also became a centre for discussion of social reform, for perhaps no one then had a greater horror of the degrading convict system or worked harder to end it.

In 1849 Dowse bought land near the Old Queen's Wharf, North Quay, but the subcollector of customs, W. A. Duncan [q.v.], did not recommend it as a sufferance wharf as he had hoped. On behalf of his friends, Coley, Harris and others who were also adversely affected, Dowse pursued the question officially in 1850 but Duncan's decision was maintained. Control by distant officials added to the agitation for separation of Moreton Bay from New South Wales, and Dowse played a leading part in the movement which raised great hostility between the squatters who controlled politics, and the free settlers in Brisbane. On 8 January 1851 two simultaneous meetings were held, one by the squatters to advocate separation and exiles, and another at Dowse's auction mart for 'petitioning the Queen to grant separation and to protest against the introduction of exiles'. Dowse's meeting was the larger and included many of Dr Lang's [q.v] immigrants. Eventually, through the combined efforts of Lang, James Swan, Dowse and others, separation was granted in 1859.

An incident at what is now Shorncliffe nearly cost Dowse and his two sons their lives in 1853. While preparing to build a cottage there, the party was attacked by Aboriginals. Dowse received a severe head wound and a son was speared in the leg but they managed to escape. A widower at 47, in Brisbane in 1856 he married Sarah Ann Fairfax; they had three sons and two daughters. Because of his work for separation and contributions to the press under the pseudonym of Old Tom, he was appointed with Walter Hill, director of the Botanic Gardens, to arrange the Queensland exhibit at the London Exhibition in 1862. In this task they were successful and received a public testimonial in 1864. When the first town clerk of Brisbane, W. M. Boyce, retired, Dowse was elected in January 1862. Although his friend, T. P. Pugh [q.v.], was in parliament frequent disagreements between the government and Brisbane City Council delayed important public works. Dowse retired from office in 1869 but continued in business until he died aged 75 at his home, Hillside, Milton, on 9 November 1885.

Custom's Dept, Moreton Bay correspondence, V&P (LC NSW), 1851, 2; *Moreton Bay Courier*, 17 May 1864, 24, 31 July 1869; *Queenslander*, 7 Aug 1909; Recollections of old times, NSW and Qld 1827-78 (Oxley Lib, Brisb).   S. G. GUNTHORPE

DOYNE, WILLIAM THOMAS (1823-1877), civil engineer, was born in Ireland, son of Rev. Thomas Doyne and his wife Sophia, née Armstrong. At 16 he studied engineering at the University of Durham for a year and was then articled to Edward Dixon, resident engineer of the London and South Western Railway. After experience in Hamburg and Ireland he worked on the London and North Western under Robert Stephenson in 1846. In 1847-51 he was managing engineer of the Rugby-Leamington line where, among other tasks, he built a wrought-iron lattice bridge. He was elected an associate of the Institution of Civil Engineers in 1849 and in 1851 with W. B. Blood submitted a paper on 'An investigation of the Strains upon the Diagonals of Lattice Beams, with the resulting Formulae', which won a prize and he became a full member of the institution. He was then working in Wales and in 1854 went to the Crimean war. He returned to England in 1856 and next year became chief engineer of a projected railway in Ceylon. After two years he moved to New Zealand where he helped to survey the tramway from Nelson to the copper mine at Dun Mountain. He then examined railways in New South Wales and Victoria.

In February 1861 Doyne was invited to plan the survey and construction of the Launceston-Deloraine railway, the first in Tasmania. Examined by a parliamentary committee, he reported with enthusiasm on the increased production, trade, communal happiness and savings from the 'extraordinary facilities afforded by the line of country' he had chosen. He spent six months supervising the surveyors of the railway. Later that year at the request of the West Tamar Road Trust, Doyne designed an elegant bridge to cross the South Esk at Launceston. Known as King's Bridge, a wrought-iron arch spanning 190 feet, its parts were made in Manchester and shipped from London in 1863. It was officially opened on 4 February 1864 and cost £12,000.

In 1862 Doyne calculated the cost of the Launceston-Deloraine railway at £317,000. Seven years later the directors found that it would exceed his estimate by £100,000. Press comments were unrestrained; Doyne sued for libel but did not recover a verdict for damages. A select committee of inquiry censured him. In 1870 the railway commissioners complained that he was absent from Tasmania while the railway was being built, leaving control to his partners and staff. Meanwhile Doyne had set himself up in general practice in Melbourne and his advice was sought by the governments of Queensland and Western Australia. In 1871 he was a member of a board appointed to inquire into the alleged silting-up of Hobson's Bay.

Doyne had married Helen Cox, probably at London in 1853. He died at St Kilda on 29 September 1877 aged 54, survived by a son and two daughters. Well read and a good conversationalist, he was described in the records of the Institution of Civil Engineers in London as a clever and painstaking engineer, a good mathematician, geologist and analytical chemist.

V&P (HAT), 1863 (70); R. M. Garvie, 'W. T. Doyne, bridge builder, and King's Bridge', PTHRA, 14 (1967).

DRAKE-BROCKMAN; *see* BROCKMAN

DRIVER, RICHARD (1829-1880), solicitor and politician, was born on 16 September 1829 at Cabramatta, New South Wales, son of Richard Driver, hotel-keeper, and his wife Elizabeth, née Powell, both of whom were born in New South Wales. He was articled to G. R. Nichols and J. Williams [qq.v.] and admitted as a solicitor in 1856. In 1859 he became solicitor to the Corporation of Sydney and began what soon grew into an extensive practice in the police courts. His fervour for reform of court procedures led to the important Holt, Dalgleish [qq.v.] case in 1865. Influenced by W. C. Wentworth's [q.v.] patriotism, Driver determined on a political career based on the rights of the native-born. At the 1858 general elections he failed in three seats and his views provoked the *Southern Cross*, 5 November 1859, to ask whether he sought to represent the 'cricketing clubs or the cabbage-tree mob?' Claiming that 'the natives of this country had never had a fair share of representation, either in the government . . . or in . . . patronage', he ran for East Sydney in 1859 on an *avant-garde* policy featuring the abolition of the Legislative Council and the need for a national bank. Failure did not reduce his radicalism, but when he won West Macquarie next year he was prepared to accept those 'who had adopted Australia as their Country'.

In 1860-80 Driver emerged as one of the chief law reformers in parliament and probably the most effective improver concerned with the development of Sydney. He also sought changes in the police force. He introduced about fifty bills, notably the criminal evidence amendment (1865) and the Sydney Common improvement (1866). An independent liberal in the 1860s, who in 1869 tried to remove two 'obnoxious clauses' from the Treason Felony Act, he was a circumspect supporter of Henry Parkes [q.v.] in the 1870s and, after declining the mines portfolio in Parkes's 1872-74 ministry, became minister for lands in his 1877 government. Driver was chairman of committees in 1872-76 and in 1878. His skill at and love for cricket sharpened his interest in the preservation of the Sydney Common (Moore Park) and while minister he provided £700 for improvements to the Sydney Cricket Ground; he also vested the ground in trustees and became one himself, representing the New South Wales Cricket Association.

In 1868 Driver became foundation president of the Australian Patriotic Association. Through his appreciation and encouragement of sport his intense nationalism widened beyond its Sydney confines; in 1860-80 he was a chief organizer of the visits of English cricket teams and of intercolonial matches, aware of their significance in the growth of an Australian identity. He drew up the first regulations of Tattersall's Club and was chairman in the 1860s and in 1875-80; a councillor of the Agricultural Society and a member of the Royal Sydney Yacht Club he was active in the administration of rowing, sailing and horse-racing. Before he died on 7 July 1880 he had become one of the most popular men in Sydney. Survived by his wife Elizabeth Margaret, née Marlow, whom he had married on 7 February 1871, he was buried with Masonic honours in the Anglican section of the Waverley cemetery. Driver Avenue, on the west side of the Sydney Cricket Ground, is named after him.

SMH, 8 July 1880; Town and Country J, 10 July 1880; Parkes letters (ML); CO 201/542.
BEDE NAIRN

DRUITT, THOMAS (1817-1891), Anglican clergyman and schoolmaster, was born on 21 October 1817 at Wimborne Minster, Dorset, England, the third son of Robert Druitt (1784-1822), surgeon, and his wife Jane, daughter of Rev. James Mavo, headmaster of Wimborne Grammar School and later proprietor of the Cheam School. The Druitt and Mayo families had produced men of some professional distinction; Thomas's eldest brother, Robert (1814-1883), became a notable medical man and author of The Surgeon's Vade Mecum, which ran to twelve editions in 1839-87. Thomas was educated at Wimborne Grammar School and proved a good classical scholar; his father's early death probably hindered his chances of a university education. After some teaching experience, he went to Portugal to follow a commercial career and married in Lisbon on 14 August 1845 Helena Hediveges Clementina, daughter of William Purvis, a Scottish merchant and a descendant of the Portuguese navigator, Cabral. In 1847 they returned to England and in November sailed for Sydney.

Druitt was appointed second master of St James's Grammar School in June 1848, and his wife taught French and Portuguese. Druitt fulfilled an old ambition on 3 June 1849 when he was made deacon by Bishop Broughton [q.v.] of Sydney; he was ordained priest by Broughton, in the presence of Bishop Selwyn of New Zealand, on 22 September 1850. He assisted at the services of St James's Church and took charge at St Bartholomew's, Pyrmont. He also acted as a chaplain at Victoria Barracks and served as honorary secretary of the Destitute Children's Asylum and on the committee of the Sydney Female Refuge. He was interested in music and became secretary of the Sydney Choral Society. Energetic and capable, Druitt was determined from the time of his arrival to play a full part in the life of Sydney.

Druitt succeeded Rev. Thomas Wall Bodenham as headmaster at St James's and maintained a prosperous school, lodging many boarders at his home in Elizabeth Street. In 1854 he transferred temporarily to Parramatta as acting headmaster of The King's School. The arrangement whereby he took charge while his wife was matron was not defined clearly and the arrival of the new headmaster, Rev. F. Armitage [q.v.], in 1855 led to misunderstanding. Druitt returned to his church and school and to charitable work in Sydney. The imminent opening of the Sydney Grammar School, with some government support, boded ill for St James's. Druitt's relations with the new bishop, Frederic Barker [q.v.], became strained over The King's School controversy; he resigned from St James's and his other appointments at the end of 1856 and 'undertook the spiritual charge of the widely extended district of Cooma'.

In the Monaro district Druitt began his major work for the Church of England in the colony. He reported in 1866 that his parish covered '10,000 square miles, inhabited by a sparse population, little educated and very unwilling to follow the teaching of a clergyman, and so situated that no assistance can be rendered to me, for during the ten years I have been here only three times has other voice than mine been heard from my pulpit'. In addition to Cooma, extensive out-stations and coastal areas had to be visited. Christ Church at Cooma, consecrated in 1850, was too remote to allow for a full range of services and Druitt held the evening service in the court-house until St Paul's Church was built. It was richly furnished and finally consecrated in 1872. He also built a new parsonage and school hall. His long incumbency was mostly a success and in his last years the work of the church in the Monaro was well organized.

A clergyman of strong opinions and emphatic actions, Druitt did not hesitate to remonstrate with the colonial secretary (who returned one letter as 'discreditable to yourself and disrespectful to the Government'), the Society for the Propagation of the Gospel (whose accredited missionary he was) or the bishops of Sydney and Goulburn if their support for his work seemed inadequate. At the Sydney Church Conference in 1858 he opposed strongly Bishop Barker's policy of securing legislation for a diocesan synod; he was always a forceful speaker at the Goulburn and provincial synods. But Druitt rose steadily in the ranks of the church. He became a canon of St Saviour's Cathedral, Goulburn, in 1877 and archdeacon of the South Coast in 1884. Druitt left Cooma in 1890 and after brief charge of Murrumburrah retired to Sydney. He died at Petersham on 30 December 1891, survived by his wife, five sons and four married daughters. A memorial window is in St Paul's, Cooma. In 1936 the ruined Christ Church was restored as a memorial to Broughton, Rev. Edward Gifford Pryce, a pioneer of Anglican work in the Monaro, and Druitt.

C. H. Mayo, A genealogical account of the Mayo and Elton families, 2nd ed (Lond, 1908); S. M. Johnstone, The history of The King's School, Parramatta (Syd, 1932); R. T. Wyatt, The history of the diocese of Goulburn (Syd, 1937); K. J. Cable, A short story of historic St James', Sydney, 2nd ed (Syd, 1964); Church Sentinel, Nov-Dec 1858; SMH, 20 Dec 1856; C. V. Nathan, The singing surgeon, the life of Dr Charles Nathan (held by author); SPG in-letters, D.29 (SPG Archives, Westminster); Col Sec, Clerical letters, vols 10, 11 (NSWA); information from C. V. Nathan, Vaucluse, NSW.

K. J. CABLE

DRURY, ALBERT VICTOR (1837-1907), public servant, was born on 28 August 1837 at Brussels, son of William Drury (1791-

1878) and his wife Anne, née Nicholas. His father entered Trinity College, Oxford (M.A., 1814), became a master at Harrow and was chaplain to the King of the Belgians in 1829-65 and to the English congregation in Brussels in 1829-78. Albert was educated in Brussels and reared in an atmosphere of close familiarity with people in high places. In 1855-61 he was a clerk in the War Office, London, and in 1862 went to Queensland to join his elder brother, Edward Robert [q.v.].

Albert began work in the Colonial Secretary's Office and in January 1867 was the fourth to be appointed clerk of the Executive Council of Queensland, a post he held for a record term of over thirty-seven years. He was a prominent figure in government circles and enjoyed the friendship of governors, premiers and many ministers of the Crown, and moved with them in the highest stratum of colonial society. The lonely bachelor, Governor Cairns, thought so highly of him that after his return to England he sent £300, insisting that Drury should visit him there. By virtue of his experience, ability and tact he became the confidant of those he served from the fourth ministry in 1866-67 to the twenty-second in 1903-04. The Imperial Service Order was conferred on him in 1903. Drury was something of an unofficial historian and kept many scrapbooks of newspaper cuttings, photographs, invitations, menus and other memorabilia relating to royalty and its representatives, governments and politicians. This collection, now in the Oxley Memorial Library, is a valuable source of reference to government activities and personalities. Drury retired in 1904 and died at his home in Brisbane on 6 September 1907, survived by his wife Mary, née Pring, whom he had married in 1864, and by four of their six children.

C. A. Bernays, Queensland politics during sixty years (Brisb, 1919); Justice Dept, Individual returns etc, JUS/103, 36/3882 (QA); Drury papers (Oxley Lib, Brisb).

J. T. MAHER

DRURY, EDWARD ROBERT (1832-1896), banker and soldier, was born in Brussels, the elder brother of Albert Victor Drury [q.v.]. He arrived at Melbourne in 1852, became a clerk in the Bank of Australasia in 1853 and was appointed manager of the Brisbane branch in 1860. Ten years later he was recalled to Sandhurst (Bendigo) but in May 1872 became general manager of the new Queensland National Bank in Brisbane, an institution which dominated the finances of Queensland until almost the end of the century. Drury followed a vigorous lending policy to assist the rapidly developing primary industries. A complete autocrat, he made advances without consulting his directors or recognizing any limits, sometimes even concealing accounts from the board. Yet the bank had a meteoric rise. As early as 1880 it had over thirty branches and held more than 40 per cent of the total deposits and advances in Queensland. A notable depositor was James Tyson [q.v.] who with £125,000 placed the first deposit in the Sydney branch. In 1881 construction of a new bank in Brisbane was begun; so magnificent were its stained glass and polished cedar that it became known as Drury's temple.

Drury's position was strengthened by his friendship with the new rising political stars, Thomas McIlwraith and Arthur Palmer [qq.v.], and by his brother, Albert Victor, clerk of the Executive Council. In 1879 the premier, McIlwraith, and Drury signed an agreement whereby the Queensland National Bank would for three years transact all government business. Although this monopoly continued until the 1890s it tended to disrupt normal business. Drury maintained his vigorous policy, lending often on name and position alone without collateral, notably to McIlwraith (£328,000) and himself (£67,000). But the strain grew too great, especially after the quarrel in 1891 between the Queensland government and the Bank of England, and on 15 May 1893 the Queensland National had to suspend payment. Drury still retained control and tried to reconstruct the bank but it remained shaky. In 1894-95 he was president of the Australian Association of Bankers. After his death on 3 February 1896 some sensational journals declared that Drury had not died but was living abroad, and that his coffin contained only stones; no proof was ever brought forward. In 1870 he had married Barbara Jane Grahame of New South Wales; they had four sons and four daughters.

Drury had always been interested in military pomp and in 1854 he joined the New South Wales Volunteer Rifles. He retained this interest in Queensland and strongly supported Governor Bowen's attempt to establish a colonial defence force. Bowen's plans failed and in 1866 Drury resigned from the forces, but in 1876 was gazetted major in the artillery, rising later to lieut-colonel and then colonel; several times he acted as commander of the Queensland Defence Forces and was deputed in 1885 to give evidence before the imperial royal commission on colonial defence. Contemporary evidence suggests that he thoroughly enjoyed appearing in full uniform. He was appointed C.M.G. in 1885. He never forgot his experiences in Belgium, became its consul in Queensland and was created a chevalier of the Belgian Order of Leopold.

R. Connolly, *John Drysdale and the Burdekin* (Syd, 1964); J. D. Bailey, *A hundred years of pastoral banking* (Oxford, 1966); *Queenslander*, 8 Feb 1896; *Town and Country J*, 15 Feb 1896.
        A. A. MORRISON
        M. CARTER

DRYSDALE, WILLIAM (1838-1902), businessman, **GEORGE RUSSELL** (1854?-1909), pastoralist and planter, and **JOHN** (1847-1928), engineer and planter, were born in Scotland, sons of John Drysdale of Kilrie, town clerk of Kirkcaldy, Fife, and his wife Mary, née Carstairs. The brothers were educated at Merchiston Castle School, Edinburgh. William entered a lawyer's office but soon left to replace his father as deputy-sheriff of Lanarkshire and for some years farmed the family estate at Kilrie. In 1868 he married Georgina Begbie; they had three sons and one daughter. John graduated as a civil engineer from the University of Edinburgh; he supervised the building of a railway in Devonshire and later another for the King of Siam. George arrived in Victoria in 1875. He joined his uncle George Russell [q.v.] who made him manager of South Thononga station on the Lachlan River. Another brother, Alexander Leslie, migrated to Victoria in 1877 and with George managed South Thononga until it was sold in 1883 for £175,000.

William arrived in Melbourne in 1883 as resident director of the New Zealand and Australian Land Co. He had gained a large holding in it after the failure of the City of Glasgow Bank in 1878 when he was appointed a director of the company formed to liquidate the bank's assets and of the reconstructed N.Z. & A.L. Co. which owed the bank some £2,200,000. In Australia William soon extended the Drysdale family interests. With his brother George and E. M. Young [q.v.] in 1883 he bought Bynya station in the Riverina and in May negotiated the purchase of Pioneer, a freehold sugar plantation on the Burdekin River, Queensland. A partnership was formed including William, George, Alexander and Arthur Drysdale, Young and John Bell, while shares were held in trust for members of the Russell and Tullis families; the venture was partly financed by the Australian Mortgage Land and Finance Co.

William visited Pioneer in August and then left for England. Appointed inspector for the A.M.L. & F. Co. in 1884, he returned to Melbourne in the *Khedive* in March 1885 with his wife and children. Young, now general manager of the A.M.L. & F. Co. in London, had hoped to strengthen it by the addition of the Drysdale interests, but William could not agree with the Melbourne manager, and Young soon decided that William's popularity in the card-rooms of Melbourne's leading clubs militated against proper management. His appointment was not renewed and he returned to Scotland in 1889. In 1891 he went to Melbourne as superintendent of the Union Mortgage and Agency Co.; four years later he left to join its London board. In 1898 he returned to Melbourne where he joined the board of the Union Mortgage and its affiliated company, the Australian Estates and Mortgage Co. Through his influence the Kalamia, Airdmillan and Seaforth sugar properties were bought by Australian Estates from the Australian and New Zealand Mortgage Co. Ltd. He died on 17 December 1902 at Prahran.

George, as the resident managing partner at Pioneer, supervised the building of the mill and began to irrigate the plantation; the mill's first sugar was crushed on 5 August 1884. He remained on the property until 1891 when he became pastoral inspector for the A.M.L. & F. Co. In 1902 he went to England where he lived at Walton-on-Thames, Surrey. He died on 5 August 1909 at Dunfermline. He was survived by his wife Mary, George Russell's daughter, whom he had married on 22 March 1888; they had two sons and a daughter; the artist, Sir George Russell Drysdale, is a grandson.

John arrived in Queensland in 1886 and, although not a member of the company, decided to join George in managing Pioneer. Despite the plantation's precarious finances he introduced many innovations. He extended the irrigation system, developing his own method of multiple spear pumping. He persuaded the company to adopt several machine inventions patented by Pioneer's consulting engineer, Henry Braby. To transport cane from the fields to the mill he built tramways which were later linked with the railway to Townsville. In 1895 he lit the mill with electricity and began to sell most of the production as raw sugar to the Colonial Sugar Refining Co. By 1899 he was virtually in sole control of Pioneer. In 1910 he bought 1280 acres on the Burdekin River, a shrewd buy which enabled him to bargain for government concessions to build a mill for the subdivided Inkerman sugar estates. He completed the mill in 1913. On 25 September 1914 Pioneer Sugar Mills Ltd took over the Pioneer and Inkerman mills, with John as a director. Drysdale Brothers retained ownership of the surrounding tenant farms and unsold freehold land.

Purposeful and able, blunt in speech and reticent in his own and the company's affairs, John ran his mills with a certain ruthless paternalism. To ensure an increasing supply of cane he bound farmers to him by long-term agreements and high payments. To obstruct attempts to build a rival co-operative mill in the district, he gave generous and often unfettered credit to farmers who supplied him regularly. By 1920 his direct assistance to local farmers totalled some £108,000; by 1927 over £300,000 was owed to him, though it limited the company's annual dividend to 5 per cent. Intolerant of government interference in the sugar milling business, he opposed trade union action, arbitration courts and price regulations and at first even suspected the Australian Sugar Producers' Association. At 57 he had married Georgina Selina Rose in England. She was living there when he died on 12 May 1928 at the Scottish Private Hospital, Paddington, Sydney. His remains were interred in Glasgow. He left an estate worth £81,700. A memorial is at Ayr, Queensland.

M. J. Fox (ed), The history of Queensland, 3 (Brisb, 1923); R. Connolly, John Drysdale and the Burdekin (Syd, 1964); J. D. Bailey, A hundred years of pastoral banking (Oxford, 1966); V&P (LA Qld), 1889, 4, 242; Roy com into the sugar industry of Australia, PP (Cwlth), 1912, 3, 1035; G. R. Drysdale, Will file 45/1911 (QA).   R. C. SHARMAN

DU CANE, SIR CHARLES (1825-1889), governor, was born on 5 December 1825 at Ryde, Isle of Wight, England, the eldest son of Charles Du Cane (1789-1850), naval commander, of Braxted Park, Witham, Essex, and his wife Frances, née Prideaux-Brune. He was educated at Charterhouse and Exeter College, Oxford (B.A., 1847; M.A., 1864). His election in 1852 to the House of Commons as Conservative member for Maldon was declared void on grounds of bribery by his agents. He represented North Essex in 1857-68 and was a civil lord of the Admiralty in 1866-68. In the House he supported the extension of the franchise to the intelligent portion of the working classes, but opposed the malt tax and the use of local rates to finance compulsory education. In June 1863 he married Georgiana Susan Copley, daughter of Baron Lyndhurst.

Du Cane was appointed governor of Tasmania, sailed with his wife and two children by way of Melbourne and Launceston, and was sworn in on 15 January 1869 at Hobart Town. He was the first occupant of the new Government House on the Domain. Settled ministries were then beginning to give stability in public administration after a long depression, although Du Cane later maintained that Tasmania's stagnation was due more to the shortcomings of her politicians and people than to the cessation of transportation and imperial expenditure. In Du Cane's term the arrangement was made whereby in the event of death, incapacity or absence of the governor, his office should be filled by the chief justice acting as administrator. Du Cane was faced with a minor constitutional crisis when the premier, J. M. Wilson [q.v.], was defeated over an income tax proposal and no other politician was willing to form a government, but Wilson withdrew his resignation and a general election followed. Generally Du Cane was able to keep aloof from sect and party. An Act was passed in 1872 to reduce the salary of future governors to £3500 and another in 1873 provided for the furnishing and maintenance of Government House out of the colony's consolidated revenue.

Sincerely interested in the progress of the colony, Du Cane went to many country agricultural shows and societies; he visited mines, laid foundation stones, opened the Launceston-Deloraine railway and travelled on the mainline railway before it was finished. He lectured everywhere, dazzling audiences with his dignity and classical erudition. His speeches were published widely in the mainland press and he drew large crowds on his travels to other Australasian colonies. He was a keen cricketer. In his term Tasmania was joined by telegraph to Victoria in 1869 and to England in 1872, tin mines were discovered at Mount Bischoff and imperial garrisons were withdrawn. Each occasion gave him opportunity to advocate closer harmony between colony and mother country, more development of internal communication, extension of public education and, above all, freedom of commerce to overcome 'the suicidal folly' of protective barriers between the colonies.

In November 1874 Du Cane left Hobart after a heavy round of farewells; even Truganini [q.v.] went to his last levee. He was appointed K.C.M.G. next year. In 1878 he became chairman of the Board of Customs at a salary of £2000, and a member of the royal commission on Factory Acts. He continued to promote emigration and one of his lectures, *Tasmania—Past and Present*, delivered at Colchester Town Hall in January 1877, was published. He also published his English translation of Homer's *Odyssey* in 1880. In Essex he was a justice of the peace and deputy lieutenant of the county. He died at Braxted Park on 25 February 1889, survived by his wife, who died on 11 June 1924, and by two sons and three daughters. Both sons made their careers in the services; one specialized in the design of high speed craft, including Bluebird II.

J. Fenton, A *history of Tasmania* (Hob, 1884); *Australasian*, 19 Dec 1868, 28 Nov 1874, 29 May 1875; *Examiner* (Launceston), 14 Jan 1869; *The Times*, 26 Feb, 6 Mar 1889; *Mercury*, 28 Feb 1889; CSD 7/30/349, 7/34/484 (TA); GO 27/1 (TA).　　　　　　GORDON RIMMER

DU CROZ, FREDERICK AUGUSTUS (1821-1897), merchant, was born in London, the eldest of three sons of John Du Croz, a dealer in glass and china who became a director of the Van Diemen's Land Co. and died at Merton, Surrey, on 13 March 1873. After training by his father Frederick sailed in the *Emu* and in March 1840 arrived at Launceston where he had been invited to manage Willis Keogh & Co. The firm was taken over by William Jackson with whom Du Croz soon became a partner. They bought land and wool, acted as import and export agents for many pastoral estates and became shipowners. At St John's Church on 20 December 1845 Du Croz married Margaret, daughter of Archibald McDowall, of Logan, Bothwell; they made their home at Fairplace (Pen-y-Bryn), off Elphin Road, Launceston.

In 1846 Jackson left to establish the head office of the firm in London and in November Gervase Bedford Du Croz arrived to join his brother in Launceston. Frederick was appointed agent for Lloyds in 1846 and became chairman of the Launceston Chamber of Commerce and a director of the Derwent and Tamar Assurance Co. The firm prospered until 1849 when the increase in convict transportation and a sharp fall in wool prices led him to write to Jackson: 'You must send very limited Supplies of Goods & no Articles of Luxury as none here can afford more than the common necessaries . . . The exclusively penal character of Van Diemen's Land has drawn the well-directed Capital & Skilful free Labor to the other Colonies'. This letter was sent by Jackson to the Colonial Office without avail, but meanwhile Du Croz opened agencies with merchants at Adelaide and with F. G. Dalgety [q.v.] in Port Phillip. In March 1852 he went with his wife and two children to England where he won confidence as 'an honest and thorough man of business'. With his partner he planned to amalgamate with Dalgety but after he returned to Tasmania early in 1853, Jackson withdrew. Du Croz then bought out his partner and with his family sailed for London in 1854 to establish his own head office. Gervase became manager in Launceston and on 8 August married Jessie Tasmania Massey; he died aged 34 on 19 February 1855, survived by his wife and one son; as a mark of respect all the business houses in the town were closed for his funeral.

Although Du Croz continued to deplore the poverty of Tasmania's economy and never returned to Australia he had a succession of partners in his own firm at Launceston. In London he continued to correspond with Dalgety and by 1857 was his most important partner and chief administrator of the spreading colonial branches. Du Croz represented Tasmania in the General Association for the Australian Colonies in 1860 and at the London International Exhibition in 1862. With Dalgety he attempted in 1871 to improve the preparation of wool in Australia and silenced protests by his assertion that the firm acted simply as brokers and made no transactions on its own account. After his wife died in 1872 he sought to retire but continued his active management until the firm was incorporated in 1884 and then served as a director until 1895. He died aged 76 at his home, Courtlands, Sussex, on 28 May 1897. He left an estate of £200,000 to his two sons, three daughters and a nephew.

P. L. Brown, *Clyde Company papers*, 3-6 (Lond, 1958-68); *Town and Country J*, 7 Oct 1871; *Examiner* (Launceston), 1 June 1897; Dalgety papers (ANU Archives); CSD 1/62/1364 (TA); CO 280/252/464.   ISABELLA J. MEAD

DU FAUR, FREDERICK ECCLESTON (1832-1915), public servant and patron of exploration and arts, was born on 14 September 1832 in London, son of Frederick Du Faur and his wife Mary Elizabeth; his ancestors had migrated from Gascony to England in 1765. He was educated at Brighton and in 1846-50 at Harrow but ill health prevented his entrance to Cambridge. He arrived at Melbourne in February 1853 and went to Bendigo. After a bout of 'colonial fever' he worked his way to Sydney where he joined the Railway Department. In 1856 he returned to London and found his father dead and himself involved in a Chancery suit. After travel on the Continent and advancement of his cultural interests he sailed for Sydney in the *Whitehall* and arrived in July 1863. Next month he joined the Surveyor-General's Office as a draftsman and in 1866 transferred to the Occupation of Crown Lands Office where he initiated a systematic surveying and mapping of runs available for selection. His claim in 1872 that 'I expended not merely an amount of zeal but my private time and energies, not limited by consideration of the mere requirements of my position' was still valid when he resigned as chief draftsman in September 1881, but his map of New South Wales, after ten years of preparation, was destroyed in the Garden Palace fire in September 1882. He ran a pastoralists' agency with J. B. Tonkin in 1881-83, with Francis Gerard in 1885-89, and by himself until 1901. On a visit to Europe in 1887 he talked with friends and Berlin professors, in the interests of his clients, about the possibility of destroying rabbits bacteriologically.

Du Faur was elected a fellow of the Royal Society of New South Wales in 1873 and became chairman of its geographical section. In 1874 he helped to finance the last expedition under Andrew Hume to ascertain the fate of Leichhardt [q.v.]. He shared in equipping a party under Wilfred Powell for exploration in New Britain in 1875 and the expedition under Captain H. C. Everill to the Fly River in 1885. He had been elected a fellow of the Royal Geographical Society of London in 1875. Soon afterwards he suggested that the Australian climate was affected by weather conditions in the Antarctic and hoped that the colonies would share in exploration there. He revived the subject when he helped to found the Geographical Society of Australia and became its first chairman in 1883. In a paper to the society in 1892 he proposed that fifty adventurous young men should charter a steamer and tour in Antarctic waters in the Christmas holidays. Much scientific interest was aroused and in 1907 he renewed his proposal in a paper, 'The effect of Polar Ice on the weather', to the Royal Society of New South Wales. By 1910 Scott, Shackleton and others had joined the 'polar steeplechase', and an Australasian Association, with Du Faur on its committee, was raising funds in support of Mawson's expedition.

In December 1874 Du Faur had been chosen as an observer of the transit of Venus at Woodford. Impressed by the scenery and vegetation in the Blue Mountains, he had already bought land at Mount Wilson where he entertained a wide variety of friends including the artist W. C. Piguenit [q.v.] and the photographer Bischoff, made many excursions in river valleys and was active in developing other beauty spots in the ranges. After living for years in the western suburbs, he built a new home at Turramurra. The reservation of Yellowstone Park and his own ramblings in rugged country inspired him to advocate the preservation of Ku-ring-gai Chase; it was dedicated as a national park in 1894 with Du Faur as managing trustee.

Du Faur published his translations into English verse of Horace's *Odes, Epodes (selected) and Carmen Saeculare* in 1906 and the *Quatrains* of Seigneur de Pibrac in 1907. His most outstanding work, however, was in the art movement in Sydney. An original member of the New South Wales Academy of Art in 1871, he joined its council in 1873 and was honorary secretary and treasurer until 1881. When the National Art Gallery was established in 1876 he was appointed one of the five trustees on its board, acted as secretary and treasurer until 1886 and served as president in 1892-1915. Its progress owed much to his energy, taste and administrative ability.

In 1866 Du Faur married Augusta Louisa, daughter of Major J. H. Crummer [q.v.]; she died on 23 July 1867. At St Mark's Church, Darling Point, on 23 January 1878 he married Blanche Mary Elizabeth, daughter of Professor John Woolley [q.v.]. Du Faur died at Turramurra on 24 April 1915 and was buried in the Anglican churchyard at Gordon. Predeceased by his second wife, he was survived by three of their four children.

His name is commemorated by the Du Faur Rocks at Mount Wilson.

R. A. Swan, *Australia in the Antarctic* (Melb, 1961); C. H. Currey, *Mount Wilson* (Syd, 1968); H. A. MacLeod Morgan, 'Eccleston Frederic Du Faur', *JRAHS*, 42 (1956); Roy Soc NSW, *J*, 49 (1915); Du Faur papers, A1629 (ML).

DUFFIELD, WALTER (1816-1882), miller, pastoralist and politician, was born at Great Baddow, Essex, England, son of William Duffield, farmer. He arrived in South Australia in the *William Barras* in December 1839 and became a tenant on Jacob Hagen's [q.v.] estate at Echunga. In 1847 he moved to Gawler, where with some help from his sister in England he bought the Victoria steam flour-mill; it was burnt down three times, twice by incendiarists, but he rebuilt it each time and added better machinery, larger wheat stores and cottages for his workmen. As his business and exports expanded he acquired other mills at Snowtown, Wallaroo, Port Pirie, and a share in the Union at Gawler. He bought sections in the Gawler special survey in 1851 and began to build up the fine Para Para estate, winning prizes for his hams, wines and orchard produce, and making it a place of attractive entertainment for local functions, picnics and races. In the early 1850s he leased the Princess Royal run and then bought Koonoona station near Burra where by 1863 he was shearing over 40,000 merino sheep. With tireless energy he also acquired over a thousand square miles of pastoral leases, including Outalpa in the north-east of South Australia and Weinteriga on the Darling River, and visited them regularly. He became a local director of the Bank of South Australia in 1859 and joined its Adelaide board in 1873; he was also a director of the Adelaide Marine and Fire Insurance Co., and a member of the Adelaide Club and the Chamber of Commerce. At Gawler he supported all worthy causes, was a pillar of the Congregational Church, opposed state aid to religion and served for many years as president of the local branch of the British and Foreign Bible Society.

Popular for his liberal views and as a practical businessman, Duffield represented Barossa in the House of Assembly in 1857-68 and 1870-71, and was treasurer in John Hart's [q.v.] ministry for five months in 1865-66 and under J. P. Boucaut [q.v.] for twelve months in 1866-67. His most noted legislation was the 1867 Dog Act which remained unamended until 1884. He was elected to the Legislative Council in 1873. Granted a short leave in 1878 he returned to the council but on the urgent advice of his family doctor resigned on 5 March 1880. He disposed of his pastoral leases, made his will and withdrew from all public activities. He died at Para Para on 5 November 1882, aged 66, and was buried in Willaston cemetery. He was survived by his wife Phoebe, née Johnstone, whom he had married in Adelaide on 7 March 1842, and by one son and five daughters. Most of his estate, valued at £117,000, was sold and placed in trust for his children and their descendants.

E. H. Coombe, *History of Gawler 1837 to 1908* (Adel, 1910); Sel cttee on Adelaide-Gawler railway, *Evidence*, V & P (SA), 1854 (122); *Register* (Adel), 20 Feb 1863; *Observer* (Adel), 11 Nov 1882.   MOLLY HUXLEY

DUFFY, SIR CHARLES GAVAN (1816-1903), Irish nationalist and Victorian statesman, was born on 12 April 1816 in Monaghan, Ireland, son of John Duffy, shopkeeper, and his wife Ann, daughter of Patrick Gavan of Latnamard. Reading and dreaming over his few books, he grew up during the struggle for Catholic emancipation and his nationalism was kindled by stories of 1798. He boasted that he was the 'first Catholic emancipated in Ireland' as most of his schooling was at the local Presbyterian academy. He went to Dublin in 1832 to become a journalist, studied the 'panorama of Irish resistance' and 'burned to strike a blow in that hereditary contest'. He was admitted to the King's Inns in 1839 and went to Belfast to edit a Catholic weekly.

In 1842 Duffy married Emily, daughter of Francis McLauglin. He returned to Dublin and, with two young barristers, Thomas Davis and John Dillon, founded his own weekly, the *Nation*; with it he hoped to 'change the mind of his generation and so to change their institutions', to foster a sense of national unity and to educate the Irish people to achieve their national freedom. Daniel O'Connell, hero of Catholic emancipation, revived the movement for repeal of the Union in 1840 and the *Nation* supported him. Duffy was a good business manager; within two years he had a circulation of 11,000 and showed his skill in discerning talent. In 1845 he published the popular *Ballad Poetry of Ireland*, including some of his own poems. In that year he was admitted to the Bar and his wife died. In 1846 he married Susan, daughter of Philip Hughes of Newry.

Davis and other middle-class Protestant intellectuals in Trinity College Historical Society believed that the divisions of Ireland could be transcended only by awareness of a common national heritage; thus their ideas diverged from those of O'Connell. The basis of the repeal movement was the Catholic peasantry, but the *Nation* hoped to bring in the Protestant middle class. The great famine intensified the divisions between the old leader and the young men, and O'Connell forced the issue by demanding a pledge that no resort be made to violence. The Young Irelanders left Conciliation Hall and set up their own confederation. Davis had died in 1845 and without his leadership they were soon divided between the reformers Smith O'Brien [q.v.] and Duffy, and the revolutionaries Lalor and Mitchel [q.v.]. The Paris revolution of February 1848 brought increased activity and a new Treason Felony Act under which Mitchel, O'Brien and other Young Irelanders were transported to Van Diemen's Land; Duffy was imprisoned but, ably defended by Isaac Butt, was freed after his fifth trial. He then revived the *Nation* and helped to organize a League of North and South, of Protestant and Catholic, to send to parliament members pledged to secure the passage of a land reform bill. Duffy represented New Ross in the House of Commons in 1852-55, but his plan for creating an Independent Irish party was wrecked by discreet patronage and by withdrawal of support by Dr Cullen [q.v.], who regarded Duffy as an Irish Mazzini. In despair Duffy sold the *Nation* and in November 1855 sailed for Australia with his wife and children. Lucas, his closest colleague, thought his 'real reason is want of means . . . but he wants to go off in poetry rather than in prose'.

Duffy was welcomed with enthusiasm in Melbourne and Sydney, but settled in Melbourne, 'the capital of Australia; here the popular element is strong and triumphant'. He set up as a barrister but was persuaded to stand for the first parliament under responsible government and £5000 was raised by public subscription, £2000 of it in New South Wales including a donation from Parkes [q.v.], to provide him with a freehold qualification for either House; half this

sum was used to buy a house in Hawthorn and half deposited in a bank. Duffy was elected to the Legislative Assembly for Villiers and Heytesbury. As the only member who had sat in the Commons, he acted as parliamentary schoolmaster to secure close adherence to British procedure, although it was difficult for his opponents to reconcile this new role with the 'Irish rebel to the backbone'. Describing himself as a 'radical reformer', he began his political career by sponsoring a bill to abolish the property qualification for members.

Land reform was at the centre of the radical platform, and Duffy claimed that he suggested to his Young Ireland friend, Wilson Gray [q.v.], the idea of calling a convention modelled on the League of North and South. With his great prominence as a land reformer, Duffy was given charge of the Lands Department in the O'Shanassy [q.v.] ministries in 1858-59 and 1861-63, and his Land Act was passed in 1862. Like the Nicholson [q.v.] Act of 1860 which it modified, the Duffy Act provided for selection after survey within specified agricultural areas and extended annual pastoral licences to 1870. However, loose drafting made it easy for squatters to employ dummies and the Act soon broke down. The agricultural areas were withdrawn, and although some genuine selection took place, the Western District squatters were the chief beneficiaries. Duffy's attempts to amend the Act were defeated; he blamed its failure 'solely on the manner in which it was drafted' by Professor Hearn [q.v.], and the ministry's refusal of support to its amendment.

Tension between O'Shanassy and Duffy had led to Duffy's resignation from the ministry in 1859. O'Shanassy, a self-made early settler, a devout Roman Catholic and an O'Connellite, seemed jealous of the brusque new chum, fresh from the House of Commons, with his literary tastes and his legal knowledge, and his part as a leading Young Irelander in driving O'Connell to his death as O'Connell's son alleged. This early quarrell was patched up in 1861 but revived when O'Shanassy acquired squatting property and moved further away from the 'Popular Party'. When the ministry resigned in 1863, Duffy and three others had been in office long enough to qualify for life pensions of £1000, although the provision was revoked soon after their claims were made. This windfall enabled him to live as a gentleman 'dividing my time between politics and the pruning knife', to buy property at Sorrento and to visit Europe twice before he finally left Victoria.

Duffy made the first of these visits in 1865 to settle his sons at school; in speeches at dinners in his honour and in a public lecture he entered into discussion of the 1866 reform bill, with a spirited defence of colonial self-government in opposition to the criticism of Lowe [q.v.]. On his return to Victoria he took a leading part against the McCulloch [q.v.] government on education and the Darling grant. In the absence of O'Shanassy and Bishop Goold [q.v.], Duffy marshalled Catholic opposition to Higinbotham's [q.v.] education bill in May 1867, and in February 1868 helped to found the *Advocate*, a Catholic lay journal. He wrote its first editorial, 'What shall we do in the pending elections?', to make Catholics aware of the power of their vote. Duffy had also been connected with but made no claim to ownership of the *Victorian*, an Irish Catholic weekly which ran from July 1862 to April 1864.

It was easier for Duffy to attack the government than to form an administration. His religion isolated him from other liberals; he was not popular and his free trade sympathies were out of touch with the mood of the 'Progressive Party'. Early in 1871 he contemplated retiring from active politics to the Speaker's chair but withdrew his candidacy after a riding accident. His influence was still great and he continued to be active in negotiations which accompanied changes of government, without a chance to form an administration himself. However, in June he was called upon by the governor to form a ministry 'because he was the principal agent effecting the organisation of the opposing sections of the Legislative Assembly which defeated the McCulloch administration', free traders under Duffy and protectionists under Berry [q.v.]. The McCulloch government was defeated on its budget proposal for a property tax of 6d. in the £. Some form of direct taxation seemed unavoidable, especially to the opponents of tariff increases, to finance new government responsibilities.

The new alliance was heavily weighted in Berry's favour. An able orator, he announced that this was the first truly radical ministry with no merchants, squatters, bankers or a single Melbourne representative in it. The free trader might organize the alliance but the protectionist treasurer dictated the policy, and the tariff of 1871 was a clear commitment to protection. Duffy was not happy about government control of railways, but his second measure was a bill providing for railway extensions to serve some of the centres represented in this 'provincial' ministry. When the Legislative Council opposed the economy change to a narrower gauge, Duffy averted a crisis by discreet appointments to a joint conference. The ministry avoided commitment on the education question, but Duffy and Berry were both opposed to increased state control. In the recess popular support was stimulated by banquets in country towns and city support by such radical groups as the new Democratic Association. While Duffy was heartened by the 'sympathy and applause of the industrious classes', many members of the assembly resented this appeal to the people over the heads of their elected representatives. Although this popular support was not then well organized, it was vocal enough to alarm business interests and large landowners. Berry's radical programme had aroused conservative opposition which could be easily combined with and channelled into sectarian and national opposition to Duffy's leadership.

Despite David Syme's [q.v.] prayer that Duffy would keep the Pope and the Irish out of his road, his premiership brought to the surface bitter religious and national prejudices. The Irish Catholic minority was large and growing, and Duffy was determined to make Catholic emancipation a reality and to secure for Catholics a fair share of positions of responsibility 'as a policy, proclaimed and defended, not by stealth'. Other factors also militated against Catholic leadership: the Pope's denunciation of liberalism in the Syllabus of 1864, the publication of the doctrine of Infallibility in 1870, the strong line taken by the hierarchy in Australia after the Provincial Council of 1869 particularly on education, and the increased proportion of Catholics shown by the 1871 Victorian census. In this setting the Duffy ministry could be made to appear a serious political danger.

The Opposition under Francis [q.v.] attacked the ministry for its neglect of the education question; after the final defeat the governor refused to grant a dissolution. Catholic clergy then entered the field to fight the new Francis administration in the ministerial elections, in hope of delaying the introduction of an unfavourable education bill. Bishop Goold's pastoral admonition on education was read in churches on the eve of the elections. This clerical interference rebounded on itself and confirmed the opposition of those who disliked Catholics and feared the influence of priests; the 1872 Education Act was carried in the wake of this sectarian bitterness. The education question had awakened the Catholics to the need to organize their vote; it was rarely united but followed personal and political divisions among the Catholic candidates. Duffy thus suffered from the fear of Catholic power, without benefiting greatly from any well-organized Catholic support. The Duffy ministry was short lived, but it was significant in the commitment to protection which reflected Berry's growing power, and in acting as a catalyst in the education question.

The 1871 tariff heightened trade rivalry between the colonies whose leaders now found it necessary to meet more often to discuss common problems. Some federal body would clearly have been valuable but was not possible while rivalry remained intense. Federation had a great academic appeal for Duffy but he found agreement with representatives from the other colonies very difficult. In 1857-62 he had chaired several select committees and urged the need for a conference to discuss federation. His able report for the first committee, 'the political art of Duffy at its highest', came to nothing. In 1870 when the withdrawal of British troops was proposed he chaired a royal commission on federation. Its recommendation that the colonies remain neutral in the event of war involving the mother country aroused more interest than its statements on federation. It involved Duffy in a wide correspondence, brought adverse criticism with the suggestion that he wished to sever the connexion, and was not well received in the colonies or in England. Again as host to the Intercolonial Conference in Melbourne in September 1871 he did nothing to diminish the rivalry between Victoria and New South Wales, but crossed swords with Sir James Martin [q.v.] with skill and relish. Negotiations to renew the border duties agreement of 1867 broke down, and although the colonies accepted the principle of reciprocal trade agreements with each other they could not agree on a joint statement for the Colonial Office. Duffy refused to sign the statement prepared by New South Wales which implied criticism of Gladstone, an 'unexpected gush of loyalty' noted with quiet surprise at the Colonial Office. In the depth of rivalry between Victoria and New South Wales Duffy could not think in federal terms while he was premier of a protectionist colony. Several of his ministers were protectionists vigorously opposed to federation or anything like intercolonial free trade, and in 1877 they were to carry the stock tax which further aggravated relations. The royal commission of 1870 was Duffy's last public move on federation in Australia. In 1890 when interest was reviving, he wrote 'The Road to Australian Federation' for the *Contemporary Review*; soon afterwards he found that Parkes had revived the subject and Duffy wrote to him with some bitterness: 'In the Federal movement, I not merely took the principal part but practically did everything . . . The flowers gathered from so much seed make but a scanty bouquet'.

In 1874 Duffy went to Europe for treatment for a voice ailment. He was asked to stand for parliament but would not accept Butt's Home Rule policy, and he came away from the O'Connell centenary celebra-

tions distressed by the bitterness and divisions he had found in Ireland. On his return to Victoria in 1876 he opposed Berry's stonewall tactics, and was content to take the Speaker's chair in 1877, turning from active politics to writing. He had always thought of himself as a 'poet-statesman', above all enjoying talking about ideas and literature. The Carlyles were his lifelong friends and through them he met many English men of letters. In Victoria he helped Marcus Clarke [q.v.] with employment and literary criticism. He waited in the Speaker's room for a chance to discuss philosophy and history with Charles Pearson [q.v.]. He had been a trustee of the Melbourne Public Library and National Gallery for years, and in Europe was always on the look-out for suitable pieces of sculpture and pictures to send to the gallery.

Duffy was knighted in 1873 and appointed K.C.M.G. in 1877. He was growing weary of colonial politics and 'loathed the task of answering again and again the insensate inventions of religious bigotry' of Orangemen. After his sixtieth birthday he was free to leave Victoria permanently without losing his pension. His wife died on 21 September 1878 and of the few Young Ireland friends left in Australia, O'Grady [q.v.] died in 1876 and Butler [q.v.] in 1879. He complained of 'the exhausting and killing monotony of the Chair'. Like many liberal contemporaries in Europe he had become disillusioned. His private letters were filled with 'the groans of a disappointed reformer'. 'We have lost our way . . . Parliaments have become *such* bear gardens'. He was distressed at the 'naked selfishness of the democracy', at the 'unexpectedly bad class of representatives' returned by manhood suffrage. Compared with the pettiness and meanness 'in the bitter and blockhead cabals of Colonial life', 'Life in London is as little like life in the colony as the tide of the Atlantic is like a waterhole in the Lachlan'. It was not surprising that in 1880 he returned to Europe, 'to work for Ireland but not in Parliament'. He settled at Nice and devoted himself to writing articles for serious journals, letters to *The Times* and solid historical works.

He welcomed Gladstone's land bill in 1881 but would not join the Home Rule League. When the Conservatives came to power with Irish support, he tried to win Carnarvon to his own scheme: a 'Fair Constitution for Ireland'. He continued to stress the need for parliamentary self-government, 'The most perfect system of liberty that exists in the world'. The basis of his claims for Ireland now was the success of self-government in Australia and his own personal success in a free community. He stressed this 'Australian

Example' so strongly that it provoked Dicey in 1886 to write 'Ireland and Victoria', to demonstrate the falsity of the analogy.

The most popular of Duffy's historical works was *Young Ireland* (London, 1880). It was followed by *Four Years of Irish History* (1883), *The League of North and South* (1886), the *Life of Thomas Davis* (1890), *Conversations with Carlyle* (1892) and *My Life in Two Hemispheres* (1898). Duffy contributed a section on the 'Carnarvon Controversy' to R. B. O'Brien, *Life of Charles Stewart Parnell* (1898), and expanded a chapter of *Young Ireland* into a *Bird's Eye View of Irish History* (1892). These histories became classics, but a recent critic has detected a 'subtle bias', for although Duffy makes much of his fairness and keeps close to the documents, these books were written by a patriot for patriotic purposes as yet unachieved, a participant defending himself against O'Connell and Mitchel and complaining that the contributions of Young Ireland had been belittled by later leaders. Duffy appears best as an organizer and scene shifter for the prominence of others. This talent of the old campaigner was not appreciated by the younger generation in the Irish Literary Society. He was its president in the early 1890s and planned to publish Young Ireland writings in a revived Irish Library series, but Yeats ridiculed the romanticism of Young Ireland, was irked by Duffy's prestige and his old-fashioned notions and 'pressed upon an unwilling Gavan Duffy the books of our new movement'.

Duffy's retirement at Nice was enlivened by the four young children of his marriage at Paris on 16 November 1881 to Louise Hall; when she died on 17 February 1889, he brought his daughters from Victoria to look after the household. One of his last political stands was in favour of the Boers to the dismay of the English colony at Nice. He died on 9 February 1903 and was buried at Glasnevin cemetery beside his Young Ireland friends within the circle of the O'Connell monument.

Of the children of Duffy's second wife, Sir Frank Gavan (1852-1936), became chief justice of Australia, Charles Gavan (1855-1932) was clerk of the House of Representatives in 1901-17 and of the Senate in 1917-20, Philip was a surveyor and civil engineer noted for his work in Western Australia on the Coolgardie water supply, and Susan was gifted as a writer. The children of his third marriage were George, president of the Irish High Court, Bryan, a Jesuit educationist in South Africa, Thomas, a missionary in India, and Louise, M.A., who was given an honorary doctorate by the National University of Ireland for her educational work.

Duffy was a man of charm, wit, talent and learning, and a devoted friend. He knew that he was brusque and peremptory in controversy. His enemies complained of his 'morbid vanity' and Deakin wrote of his 'subtlety, finesse and insincerity', but granted him the sincerity of his liberal sentiments. For Duffy was above all a Liberal. Frustrated and disappointed in his work for Ireland, his optimism tempered by his colonial experience, he continued to write to educate and so to free his countrymen. 'Duffy was a liberal by instinct and on reflection, and remained true to his colours to the last'.

W. B. Yeats, *Autobiographies* (Lond, 1926); D. R. Gwynn, *Young Ireland and 1848* (Cork, 1949); A. Deakin, *The crisis in Victorian politics, 1879-1881*, J. A. La Nauze and R. M. Crawford eds (Melb, 1957); J. H. Whyte, *The Independent Irish Party, 1850-59* (Lond, 1958); A. G. Austin, *Australian education, 1788-1900* (Melb, 1961); G. Serle, *The golden age* (Melb, 1963); K. B. Nowlan, *The politics of repeal* (Lond, 1965); L. O'Broin, *Charles Gavan Duffy* (Dublin, 1967); J. M. Ward, 'Charles Gavan Duffy and the Australian Federation movement', *JRAHS*, 47 (1961); J. E. Parnaby, *Sir Charles Gavan Duffy in Victoria* (M.A. thesis, Univ Melb, 1941); J. E. Parnaby, *The economic and political development of Victoria, 1877-1881* (Ph.D. thesis, Univ Melb, 1951); G. R. Bartlett, *Political organization and society in Victoria 1864-1883* (Ph.D. thesis, ANU, 1964); Duffy papers (LaT L); Parkes letters (ML); CO 309/99-104.   JOY E. PARNABY

DUFFY, JOHN GAVAN (1844-1917), solicitor and politician, was born on 15 October 1844 at Dublin, Ireland, the only surviving son of Sir Charles Gavan Duffy [q.v.] and his first wife Emily, née McLauglin. John Gavan Duffy was educated at St Laurence O'Toole's Seminary in Dublin and Stonyhurst College, Lancashire, England. Some time after his arrival at Victoria in the *Morning Light* on 30 August 1859 he took up land north of the Lachlan River and then bought and leased land with his father at Sorrento. In March 1871 he matriculated at the University of Melbourne and next year took the English essay prize. However, he allowed his considerable literary ability to remain dormant, apart from contributions to the *Australasian* under the pen-name of Aulus. Duffy did not complete his university course but was articled to J. G. Duffett, a well-known solicitor, and practised with W. J. Wilkinson from 1876 until the latter's death in 1891.

As a successor to his father, John represented the safe Catholic seat of Dalhousie in the Legislative Assembly in 1874-86 and in 1887-1904. In James Service's [q.v.] first ministry from 5 March to 3 August 1880 he was president of the board of land and works, commissioner of crown lands and survey and minister of agriculture. In 1890 he was postmaster-general in the Munro [q.v.] government until February 1892 when in the newly formed Shiels ministry he was again appointed postmaster-general and also attorney-general. In April 1892 he resigned from these posts to stand for the Speakership but was defeated and returned to the cabinet as a minister without portfolio until the fall of the Shiels government in January 1893. In 1894-99 he was postmaster-general in the George Turner ministry and represented Australia at the Universal Postal Congress at Washington in 1897. He attended the Federal Council of Australasia in 1893 when he was chairman of the Standing Committee and was also a delegate at the Intercolonial Conference of Ministers in Sydney in 1896.

As a member of the Catholic group in parliament Duffy was a frequent spokesman on the education issue; in particular, he opposed non-denominational Christian teaching in schools. His cabinet post recognized the help that he and other Catholics had given Berry in 1877 and Service [qq.v.] in 1880. From then on he remained friendly with the Constitutionalist free-traders and for a time was the only Catholic attending their caucuses. He was prominent also in the Home Rule movement. In 1875 he brought down and carried a bill to enable women to take university degrees; however it was rejected by the Legislative Council. C. H. Pearson [q.v.] described him as 'a popular and genial gentleman, above the average as a speaker and an administrator'.

In the 1880s Duffy helped to promote the idea of Australian exploration in the Antarctic and introduced the proposal to parliament in December 1885. When the first Australian Antarctic Exploration Committee was inaugurated in June 1886, he was a member and became a spokesman for the cause in parliament after his re-election in 1887.

After 1904 he settled down to his law practice and, in partnership with T. E. King, conducted most of the legal business for the Catholic Church. He was a prominent layman of the Church and in 1909 was made a knight of St Gregory. Duffy had married Margaret Mary, daughter of Dr J. B. Callan, on 20 June 1874. He died on 8 March 1917 at his home in East St Kilda survived by his wife, two sons and a daughter.

Australasian, 13 Mar 1886, 6 Oct 1894, 17 Mar 1917; Table Talk, 19 Feb 1892; Speaker (Lond), 23 July 1892; Argus, 9 Mar 1917.

J. R. J. GRIGSBY

DUGDALE, HENRIETTA AUGUSTA (1826?-1918), feminist, was born in London, daughter of John Worrell and his wife, née Austin. Married at 14, she arrived at Melbourne in 1852 with her husband Davies. After his death she married William Dugdale, son of an English clergyman; they had a son Carl, and two daughters. About 1905 she married Frederick Johnson. She made her own clothes, grew vegetables, did carpentry and was an excellent chess player besides taking an active role in public affairs. She died at Point Lonsdale on 17 June 1918, aged 91.

From 1869 Mrs Dugdale had been a pugnacious pioneer of the Woman Movement in Victoria. In 1884 she was president of the first Victorian Women's Suffrage Society, formed on 22 June. With ready words and biting wit she wrote and spoke in the feminist cause. She firmly believed in evolutionary progress and the perfectibility of mankind which to her could only be achieved through the disciplined control of human nature by reason and the co-operation and equality of the sexes. These views were embodied in a booklet, A Few Hours in a Far Off Age (Melbourne, 1883), which she dedicated to George Higinbotham [q.v.] 'in earnest admiration for the brave attacks made by that gentleman upon what has been, during all known ages, the greatest obstacle to human advancement, the most irrational, fiercest and most powerful of our world's monsters—the only devil—MALE IGNORANCE'. The brutality and darkness of her own age she attributed not only to male ignorance and vanity but also to liquor and the illiterate working classes. The emancipation of her sex was to be the primary solution and she exhorted women to throw off their chains, discard their apathy and learn self respect. The weapon of emancipation was the suffrage whereby women could achieve equal social, legal and political privileges with men. Progress also involved elevating the working classes through a more equitable distribution of wealth and the introduction of the eight-hour day. She condemned the monarchy as a reactionary institution constricting human advancement and she bitterly opposed imperial federation; Christianity was another despotism formed by men to humiliate women, and most Christians were intolerant hypocrites. She described herself as a believer in 'true ethics' rather than religious morality.

Mrs Dugdale won adherents among radicals and secularists but met much opposition from conservatives. When she advocated reform of women's dress some accused her of sacrificing her modesty, and when she declared that women should have a place in politics others declared that she was attempting to win notoriety and self glory; yet she established the pattern of demands for female emancipation in Victoria. She stirred many women into positive action to achieve their rights and to gain access to the professions. She was a member of a Victorian group of radical, free-thinking women who believed in temperance, birth control and 'applying the surgeon's knife to rapists'. Although sometimes melodramatic and emotional in her opinions she was forceful and assertive and deserved her place among the founders of Victoria's feminist movement.

A. Henry, 'Marching towards citizenship', F. Fraser and N. Palmer (eds), *Centenary gift book* (Melb, 1934); *Age*, 10 Sept 1883; *Melbourne Review*, Jan 1884; *Herald* (Melb), 12, 28, 30, 31 May, 2, 3 June, 8, 13, 15 Oct 1884; *Punch* (Melb), 5, 12 June 1884; *Liberator* (Melb), 30 Aug, 29 Nov 1885, 4 July, 1 Aug 1886; *Table Talk*, 20 Oct 1899; *Aust Woman's Sphere*, 10 June, 10 July 1902.   JANICE N. BROWNFOOT

DUNCAN, GEORGE SMITH (1852?-1930), engineer, was born at Dunedin, New Zealand, the third son of George Duncan and his wife Elspeth; his parents had migrated from Scotland in 1849. In the mid-1860s George returned to Scotland with his father and elder brothers; he went to school in Scotland and at Clifton College, England. He studied engineering at the University of Edinburgh and on his return to Dunedin, completed his studies at the University of Otago while in the employ of Thompson & Simpson, engineers. He was appointed provincial engineer of the District of Otago and from 1876 engaged in private practice. In 1878 he married Euphemia Kilgour, of Dunedin. In 1879-81 as a partner in the Dunedin firm of Reid & Duncan he built the Roslyn cable tramway, the first cable tramway built outside America. A second line from Dunedin to Mornington was opened in March 1883.

Duncan went to San Francisco about January 1882 and may have met F. B. Clapp [q.v.] who in 1883 engaged Duncan as chief engineer to the Melbourne Tramway & Omnibus Co. When the Melbourne Tramways Trust was set up as the constructing authority for Melbourne's cable tram system, the largest in the world, Duncan was appointed engineer in May 1884. He remained consulting engineer to the company which operated the trams, and with Clapp revisited the United States in late 1883 to investigate the latest developments in the cable system. Duncan made many advances on American practice and was able to construct his lines around curves with greater success than achieved elsewhere. He made

many innovations and among his inventions was the emergency slot-brake. Both he and Clapp insisted on a high standard of maintenance.

In March 1892, five months after the completion of the last line, Duncan resigned as the trust's engineer though he continued as consultant to both the trust and the company. Soon afterwards he left for Europe and America, and in London was elected a member of the Institution of Civil Engineers in recognition of his work. He returned to Melbourne about 1894 and resumed his private practice, specializing in mining engineering. He introduced to Victoria the cyanide process of extracting gold and with his younger brother Alfred, his son and others, established the firm of Duncan, Noyes & Co.

Duncan never lost his eagerness to experiment. He was also a chemical analyst and from about 1912 began to search for a practicable method of extracting gold from sea water. In a laboratory at his home in Black Rock he produced gold but at prohibitive cost. Quiet and modest, and reserved except among his close family circle, Duncan was also an enthusiastic golfer. He died at his home on 4 September 1930, survived by two sons and a daughter.

J. D. Keating, *Mind the curve! A history of the cable trams* (Melb, 1970), and for bibliog; *Argus*, 8 Sept 1930.   JOHN D. KEATING

DUNCAN, SIR JOHN JAMES (1845-1913), pastoralist and member of parliament, was born on 12 February 1845 at Anstruther, Fife, Scotland, second son of John Duncan, sea captain, and his first wife Joan, sister of Walter Watson Hughes [q.v.]. Captain Duncan had first arrived in Adelaide in 1841 and engaged in sheep-farming with his brother-in-law at the Hummocks, but he went back to Scotland and made several voyages o India; in 1854 he returned to South Australia with his family and again joined Hughes on pastoral leases near Wallaroo. There his wife died, he became a justice of the peace and, when copper was found near Wallaroo in 1859, helped to develop the mines. He was a staunch Presbyterian and his obituarist claimed that 'no man ever complied so fully with the Scripture injunction of not letting his left hand know what the right hand did'. He died at Glen Osmond on 24 April 1880, leaving two sons by his first wife and two sons and two daughters by his second.

John James was educated at Watervale Grammar School, Bentley, near Gawler and the Collegiate School of St Peter; in holidays he brought the first four miners from Burra to Moonta and often carted water to his uncle's mines. He worked for three years with Elder [q.v.], Smith & Co. and then took charge of the financial department of the Wallaroo and Moonta Mining and Smelting Co. He went to Britain in 1878, served as South Australian commissioner at the Paris Exhibition and travelled widely on the Continent. On his return he managed his uncle's pastoral properties, took up leases as far north as Lake Eyre and in 1887 inherited the stations of Hughes Park near Watervale and Gum Creek near Burra. On 5 November 1873 he had married Jane Morison, daughter of Arthur Harvey of Durban, South Africa; she died a year later without issue. In London on 27 August 1879 he married Jean Gordon, daughter of James Grant and Mary, née Todd.

In 1871 Duncan was elected to the South Australian House of Assembly for Port Adelaide which then included Wallaroo where the overwhelming mining vote made him one of the first members of parliament to be returned by a labour organization. In 1875-78 he represented Wallaroo after it became a separate electorate. He was elected for Wooroora in 1884 but resigned in 1890 to take a prominent part in the National League, a Conservative association which later became allied with Liberal and Democratic unions against the Labor movement. In 1891 he was returned for the North-Eastern District to the Legislative Council. He held the seat until 1896 and then visited Britain until 1899. He represented the Midland District in the council in 1900-13. In his last years he was leader of the Opposition to Verran's Labor government. Peculiarly loyal to South Australia, he rejected all pleas to nominate him for election to the Federal Senate, although he had forsaken much of the independence that earlier led him to refuse ministerial office three times. At first an impetuous and vehement speaker, he was said to 'wing a sparrow by his gun-shot and disjoint his own shoulder with the recoil'; later he developed 'some oratorical magnetism', and despite 'an irruption of ahs' his speeches were vigorous and authoritative. Right or wrong he was always sincere and a popular choice for the joint committees which hammered out disagreements between the two Houses. Even in his last years when he cheerfully called himself a 'stonewaller', he was never cynical or bitter and prided himself on differing from his opponents 'with honour and without estrangement'.

Duncan was widely respected for his sagacity and immense influence in pastoral affairs, and the administration of big finance and local finance. He held many directorships including the South Australian Savings Bank and was president of the Northern

Agricultural Society and in 1905-07 of the Pastoralists' Association, often representing South Australia on its federal council. He was a captain in the Watervale Volunteers and served for years on the Upper Wakefield District Council. In 1911-13 he was one of the first members elected by parliament to the Council of the University of Adelaide. He was knighted for his public services on 12 June 1913. In addition to his fine homestead at Hughes Park he had a large town house, Strathspey, at Mitcham. After an operation for gall-stones he died at a private hospital in North Adelaide on 8 October 1913. He was buried in the family ground at St Mark's Church of England, Penwortham, the mourners travelling by train to Saddleworth and thence to the cemetery by char-à-bancs. He was survived by his wife, four sons and two daughters. From his estate of £320,000 generous bequests were made to his numerous relations, £1500 to charitable organizations and £5000 to the Presbyterian Church of which he had been a devoted member at Flinders Street. Most of the remaining property was sold and placed in trust for his family and descendants. In memory of W. W. Hughes, he left £100 to maintain his uncle's grave at Chertsey, Surrey, and £50 'to keep clean and repair' his uncle's statue at the entrance of the University of Adelaide; his son John Grant was enjoined to use the surname Duncan-Hughes.

H. T. Burgess (ed), *Cyclopedia of South Australia*, 1 (Adel, 1908); *Observer* (Adel), 24 Apr 1880, 14 Apr 1900; *Mail* (Adel), 16 Aug 1913; *Pastoral Review*, 15 Oct 1913; *Advertiser* (Adel), 9 Oct 1913; *Register* (Adel), 9, 10 Oct 1913.   MOLLY HUXLEY

DUNN, JOHN (1802-1894), miller, was born on 13 February 1802 in the parish of Bondleigh, Devonshire, England, son of Charles Dunn, yeoman farmer. He was educated at a penny-a-week dame school and a boys' school. At 12 he was apprenticed to a miller at North Taunton to escape military service. In 1819 he became an 'improver', wandering from mill to mill in order to learn all aspects of the trade. He was manager of a mill at Bideford in 1830 when the birth of his son John prompted him to keep cows for a supplementary income. Poverty was so close that he was dissuaded from migrating to Canada in 1833 only by a rise in wages. He rented his own mill at Monkleigh, near Bideford, from 1835 until 1840 when he was persuaded by four of his six brothers to join them in South Australia.

With free passages for himself, his wife Anne, their son and three daughters Dunn sailed in the *Lysander* and arrived at Glenelg on 6 September 1840. Determined to make money, he took up an eighty-acre section at Hay Valley (near Nairne), where his second son William Henry was born and where he erected the first windmill in the colony. The returns from dairy and agricultural produce were small so he ordered a steam engine from England and on 1 August 1844 began 'grist' milling for local farmers. Dunn's mill gave impetus to local development and by 1850 Mount Barker had become a wheat producing centre whilst Dunn & Co., doubling its milling capacity, had bought up surplus grain and begun a flour trade with Adelaide. In the 1850s trade was extended to the goldfields of California and Victoria and the sugar plantations of Mauritius. Dunn opened a warehouse and mill in Adelaide in 1856 and built a new mill at Bridgewater in 1860. He acquired two more mills at Nairne in 1864. On the death of his first wife, John Dunn in 1870 married his daughter-in-law's sister, Jane Williams. He retired in 1889 and died at Mount Barker on 13 October 1894. The firm's eleven mills, five with the most modern machinery, then represented an investment of £150,000. They annually had an export trade of some 20,000 tons of flour to Britain, Western Australia, New South Wales and South Africa, some 400 employees, and a payment to farmers of £500,000.

JOHN DUNN junior (1830-1892) was admitted a partner in 1852 but sold out to his father in 1862 to become a missionary in Fiji. On his return next year he built his own mill at Port Adelaide. In 1864 he rejoined the firm and merged his mill with it. In his absence, however, John senior had admitted as partners his son William Henry, son-in-law W. Hill (d. 1885) and brother-in-law G. Shorney (d. 1891). William Henry left the firm in 1878 to farm at Pekina near Orroroo and died in Adelaide on 7 July 1891.

The firm's family composition helped its success and also permitted a conscious mood of innovation. It was the policy of the firm that at least one partner was always travelling. Thus John junior visited Britain in 1866, 1878 and 1890, the second tour including the mills of South Africa, Austria, Hungary and America. After his death at Port Augusta on 6 February 1892 his sons Frederick and Alfred took command and the interest swung from mill modernization to the markets of Asia and the Pacific Islands. The family firm also showed excellent organizational ability. Following the movement of farmers, five mills were established in northern centres, one in the south-east and the mill at Port Adelaide was enlarged

in 1887; all were built on railway lines and thus linked with the firm's private wharves. The whole network was pinpointed with some fifty purchasing agents.

The firm's prosperity enabled the family to pursue political careers. John senior represented Mount Barker in the House of Assembly from 1857 to 1868 when he was unseated by a Court of Disputed Returns for alleged election bribes, and was a member of the Legislative Council in 1869-77. John junior represented Barossa in the assembly in 1875-77 and the council in 1880-88, whilst William Henry represented Onkaparinga in the assembly in 1875-77. Of greater note was the philanthropic bent of the family, all of them Methodists. John senior gave £500 each year to charities, spent £4000 on building the Wesleyan Church at Mount Barker, donated a recreation park to the town, established a university scholarship, built the Salem cottages for aged poor at Mount Barker and, from his estate sworn for probate at £100,000, left some £14,560 to religious, charitable and relief organizations.

H. M. Franklyn, *A glance at Australia in 1880* (Melb, 1881); E. F. L. H(ill), *The staff of life . . . and a sketch of the career of John Dunn* (Adel, 1883); *Mount Barker Courier,* 12 Nov 1886, 4 Feb, 22 Apr, 29 July-19 Aug 1887, 19 Oct 1894; *Observer* (Adel), 11 July 1891, 13 Feb 1892, 20 Oct 1894; *Critic* (Lond), 11 June 1898.
                                M. FRENCH

DUNNE, PATRICK (1818-1900), Catholic priest, was born at Philipstown, King's County (Offaly), Ireland, son of Patrick Dunne, farmer, and his wife Mary, née Rigney. He trained at Carlow Seminary and was ordained on 8 March 1846. After four years of service to his native diocese of Kildare, he volunteered to join the newly formed Melbourne diocese, 'rising above the opposition of dearest relatives and priests'. He arrived in Melbourne in the *Digby* on 7 September 1850 and was appointed to Geelong. After a brief stay, the first of two in that mission, he was transferred to the new mission of Pentridge (Coburg), and acted as chaplain to the 'infamous Stockade'. In October 1851 he journeyed to Ballarat on horseback, celebrated the first Mass on that goldfield and performed many baptisms in the lower Wimmera. In 1853-56 he established at Geelong twelve schools under the Denominational Schools Board, as well as the first Catholic secondary or grammar school.

At Port Fairy in 1856 his independence and turbulence led him into a dispute with Bishop J. A. Goold [q.v.] over trust money for a church building. He also became involved with P. Bermingham, M. McAlroy [qq.v.] and other clerical and lay critics of the Polding [q.v.] and Goold administrations in Sydney and Melbourne. As a result Dunne was virtually banished and spent much time in Rome and Ireland, adding to the rising chorus of complaints levelled at Church management. In December 1858 he returned to Melbourne as a migration chaplain but was forbidden to exercise his priestly functions by Goold's vicar-generals, J. Fitzpatrick and P. B. Geoghegan [qq.v.]. After writing a long document in his own defence, addressed to Polding, Dunne returned to Ireland. Roman authorities were compelled finally to take note of many of his grievances, but Dunne himself, at Goold's instigation, was forbidden to return to Australia. Far from being discouraged he persuaded Irish bishops to allow him to open a minor seminary at Tullamore, County Offaly, which was designed to give an initial training for missionary volunteers to Australia.

In the early 1860s Dunne co-operated with James Quinn [q.v.] in a migration scheme which contributed to the settling of the Darling Downs. The first migrants arrived at Brisbane in the *Erin-go-bragh* in August 1862. Financial difficulties in the new Brisbane diocese, linked with sectarian objections to the migration scheme, brought Dunne to the Goulburn diocese in April 1868 where his zeal was directed by Bishop William Lanigan [q.v.] into constructive work. After a term as first president of St Patrick's College and cathedral administrator at Goulburn he transferred to the Gundagai-Jugiong mission. On the death of his friend Michael McAlroy in 1880 Dunne succeeded as vicar-general, retaining his title and the confidence of his bishop when he was transferred to Wagga Wagga in 1883 and to Albury in 1887. He helped to plan many churches, including St Michael's in Wagga.

Dunne was one of the best-known priests of the last half of the nineteenth century, often injecting a tumultuous note into church affairs and quarrelling with bishops and public officials. He was a pioneer who responded to the demanding challenges to extend his religion in frontier conditions. At times impatient and adopting sledge-hammer methods in newspaper controversy, his total achievement was a tribute to his vision as much as to his methods. Even in retirement in the 1890s he was a respected national figure, still making his determined thrusts into affairs of church and state.

On 21 July 1900 he died at Albury and was buried in the grounds of Newtown Orphanage, now St John's Orphanage, Wirlinga, Albury.

J. F. Hogan, *The Irish in Australia* (Melb, 1888); P. F. Moran, *History of the Catholic Church in Australasia* (Syd, 1895); W. Ebsworth, 'One of the greatest pioneer priests', *Advocate* (Melb), 30 July 1947; T. J. Linane, 'The priest who borrowed a tent', *Light* (Ballarat diocesan J), May 1966-June 1968; Geoghegan letter, 25 May 1850 (Roman Catholic Archives, Melb); J. A. Goold diary and letters (Roman Catholic Archives, Melb).

T. J. LINANE

DUNNE, WILLIAM JOHN (1814-1883), Catholic priest, was born at Ballycallan near Kilkenny, Ireland. After education at Burrell's Hall he entered St Kyran's College and three years later enrolled at the College of the Immaculate Conception at Ratcliffe in Leicestershire. He volunteered for service in Australia, arrived in Sydney in March 1843 and was ordained by Archbishop Polding [q.v.]. He was first attached to St Mary's Cathedral and then given charge of the mission at Windsor. In 1845 he went to Van Diemen's Land to take over the Richmond mission, which then extended from the south coast to the boundary of the Launceston mission. Dunne was reputedly responsible for the building and improvement of seven country churches including those at Richmond, Sorell, Brighton and Jerusalem. When the newly appointed Bishop Daniel Murphy [q.v.] arrived at Hobart Town in July 1866 with a community of Presentation Sisters, Dunne housed the nuns under supervision of the bishop's sister at his Woodburn estate in the Richmond parish.

Later that year Dunne was moved from Richmond and appointed the first Catholic archdeacon of Tasmania. He was stationed at St Joseph's Church in Hobart. When William Hall [q.v.] died in July Dunne became vicar-general; as chief executive of the Catholic Church in Tasmania he was largely responsible for the harmony which existed between Catholic and public educators in the colony. He represented the Church on the Council of Education for sixteen years, sat on royal commissions into education and was active on the boards of several schools. He was closely associated with the building of the orphanage attached to St Joseph's and the formation of the Catholic Ragged School of St Luke's of which he was superintendent. As editor and proprietor of the *Tasmanian Catholic Standard* until 1872, when he visited Rome, he continued to influence Tasmanian educational change. From 1874 his involvement with public education became more difficult after a diocesan synod favoured a policy of separation. Ill health caused him to relinquish his major duties in 1882 and he settled into what he hoped would be gentle retirement as pastor of Coburg and

Brunswick in Victoria, but on 7 March 1883 he died at Coburg. After a ceremonial funeral in Melbourne his body was sent to Hobart and buried beneath the memorial he had prepared for himself in the churchyard at Jerusalem in the Tasmanian Midlands. Both the farewell on his resignation and his funeral were attended by friends and admirers from many denominations.

His will established the Dunne scholarship for local scholars to attend St Ignatius Jesuit College in Sydney, while bequests placed St Joseph's Orphanage in Hobart on a sounder basis and met the initial cost of building at Sandy Bay the Magdalen Home for delinquent girls.

Mercury, 8 Mar 1883; *Argus*, 9 Mar 1883; *Age*, 10 Mar 1883; *Australasian*, 10 Mar 1883, supp; *Catholic Standard*, 2 Apr 1883.

PETER BOLGER

DURACK, PATRICK (1834-1898), pastoral pioneer, was born in March 1834 at Scarriff, County Clare, Ireland, the eldest of eight children of Michael Durack and his wife Bridget, née Dillon. The Duracks were struggling tenant farmers who survived the famine of the 1840s and followed another branch of the family to New South Wales in 1853; they arrived in the *Harriet* in May. Within two months of reaching the Goulburn district Michael Durack was accidentally killed. Patrick settled his mother and family at Goulburn and went to the Ovens River diggings in Victoria. He returned in eighteen months with £1000 and bought a smallholding near Mummel. There he brought his family and soon increased his assets. On 31 July 1862 he married Mary, daughter of Michael and Mary Costello of Tea-tree station near Wheeo.

Life in the settled area of Goulburn provided insufficient outlets for Durack's energy, land hunger and organizing powers. In 1863 with his brother Michael and brother-in-law John Costello [q.v.] he set out with horses and cattle to establish a property in south-west Queensland. All the cattle died in the prevailing drought and the party survived only with the help of desert Aboriginals. Despite this setback the Duracks and Costellos returned to Queensland and in 1868 established Thylungra and Kyabra stations on a tributary of Cooper's Creek. Drought conditions continued but Durack and Costello rode around the country pegging claims to some 17,000 square miles of land between Kyabra Creek and the Diamantina River. As conditions improved, the blocks were stocked and sold to incoming settlers, many of them relations and friends. Durack also bought properties in the towns of Roma where he had a

butchery, Thargomindah, Adavale and Windorah. His hotels, at first built of mud and spinifex with ant-bed floors, flourished in the wake of opal miners and Cobb [q.v.] & Co. services. By 1877 his cattle had increased from the original 100 head to about 30,000 and he began to buy sheep. Eight children, two of whom died in infancy, were born to the Duracks in these years and Patrick maintained a paternal control over the lively pastoral and mainly Irish community of the region. By 1879 he was reputedly 'on his way to his first half million', while Costello had sold up and retired to the Queensland coast.

Still uncertain of his future prosperity in south-west Queensland, Durack was excited by Alexander Forrest's report of more reliable prospects in the Kimberley district of Western Australia. In 1881 he and Solomon Emanuel, a Goulburn banker and pastoralist, financed an expedition to the area. In July 1882 a party led by Durack's brother Michael took ship from Brisbane with horses and provisions to Cambridge Gulf and King Sound. Favourable reports decided the Duracks to take up land on the Ord River and the Emanuels on the Fitzroy. From Thylungra station Durack organized the droving of 7250 head of breeding cattle and 200 horses on a 3000-mile trek, the longest undertaken by Australian drovers up to that time. They reached the Ord River in two years and four months with a loss of half the cattle and several men; the venture cost some £72,000. In 1886 Durack's two elder sons went by sea and set up Argyle station on the Behn River.

In 1885 Durack retired with his wife to Brisbane, first amalgamating his Queensland interests with a group of financial speculators. Inactivity did not suit him and in March 1887 he went to Argyle to help his sons. Later that year he bought goldcrushing machinery from Sydney and began mining on the Kimberley goldfields. Summoned to Brisbane in 1889 he learned that financial disaster had overtaken his Queensland interests. Left with only household possessions Durack took his wife to live at Argyle. He had earlier assigned his north Australian interests to his sons. His wife died of malaria at Argyle on 24 January 1893. In 1896 Durack visited Ireland; he returned to Kimberley and helped to develop his sons' expanding interests but no longer played a major role in his family's affairs. He died at Fremantle on 20 January 1898 and was reinterred on 4 November 1901 beside his wife in the pioneer cemetery at Goulburn.

M. Durack, *Kings in grass castles* (Lond, 1959).

MARY DURACK

DURYEA, TOWNSEND (1823-1888), photographer, was born at Glencoe, Long Island, New York, North America, son of Hewlet Duryea. He was trained as a mining engineer and his experience in the art of photography dated from 1840. He also took an art course. He arrived at Melbourne in 1852 and next year entered a studio partnership with Alexander McDonald in Bourke Street. In 1855 he moved to Adelaide and in February opened daguerreotype rooms over Prince's store at the corner of King William and Grenfell Streets. Later that year Townsend and his brother Sanford formed the partnership of Duryea Bros. They were the first photographers known to have worked outside Adelaide; by 1856 they had visited Auburn, Burra, Clare, Kapunda, Goolwa, Milang, Port Elliot and their near-by villages. In 1857 Duryea used experience gained in America as a shipbuilder to build the thirty-foot cutter Coquette behind the Maid and Magpie Hotel at Magill. Though the cutter was said to be for the River Murray trade, it was used mainly in racing; stakes in private challenges were sometimes £100 a side. Duryea was also interested in copper finds near Wallaroo, and by February 1861 a fine lode of copper had been cut on section 471, the property of 'Mr Duryea and others'. Within a few months the Duryea Mining Association owned fifteen mineral sections in the area.

In 1863 Townsend dissolved the partnership with his brother. His studio was the most popular in Adelaide, patronized by governors, visiting dignitaries and Adelaide's leading citizens. As well as portraits he produced many views, including several notable panoramas of Adelaide. In 1872 he photographed almost all the surviving old colonists and made their portraits into a large mosaic comprising some 675 cartes-de-visite. Duryea was chosen as official photographer in the royal visit of 1867. On 9 November the duke of Edinburgh posed at Duryea's King William Street studio for the first royal portraits made in Australia. Duryea then accompanied the official party throughout the visit, travelling in a specially prepared photographer's van. By the early 1870s Duryea's panoramas, royal portraits and prizes won in Society of Arts photographic competitions had made him famous. He achieved his high standard with the help of skilled operators. Short in build he was extremely energetic, of 'vigorous mind and keen intelligence, his whole character bearing the impress of sterling integrity'. Duryea always made full use of the advertising facilities offered by newspapers and almanacs. His career as a photographer was cut short when his studio and entire collection of 50,000 negatives were destroyed by fire on 18 April 1875. This loss was a serious blow to Duryea and historians alike, as the plates were the best record of early South Australian colonial life ever made. After the fire Duryea moved to the Riverina district of New South Wales and took up a selection near Yanga Lake. In his later years he was crippled by a stroke and became an invalid. He died on 13 December 1888 after a buggy accident and was buried at Parkside near Balranald.

Duryea was married twice in America: first to Madalina and second about 1852 to Elizabeth Mary Smith who accompanied him to Adelaide. In Adelaide on 22 May 1872 he married Catherine Elizabeth Friggins. He was survived by a son and a daughter of the first marriage, four sons and a daughter of the second, and three sons and two daughters of the third. Several of his sons and grandsons became photographers.

J. Cato, The story of the camera in Australia (Melb, 1955); Riverina Recorder, 19 Dec 1888; SMH, 20 Dec 1888; newspaper cuttings, R. J. Noye collection (PLSA).   R. J. NOYE

DUTTON, CHARLES BOYDELL (1834-1904), pastoralist and politician, was born on 16 August 1834 at Patrick Plains, New South Wales, son of Henry Peterin Dutton, a Hunter River squatter, and his wife Sophia Hume, née Bell, whose family also had pastoral interests. By 1857 Charles was aware that the Hunter with its floods and spreading farms was no place for aspiring squatters. His cousins, Robert and William Bell, had already gone as far as Keepit on the Namoi; with them and his brother Archibald, Charles set out to look for suitable land in the north. They settled at Bauhinia Downs on a tributary of the Dawson and from this base the family extended their operations even farther into Queensland. The Bells and the Duttons were among the first applicants for land on the Nive River when the Mitchell district was opened for settlement and their leases included the site of Tambo township. After the initial rush subsided, pressure to stock and work all the runs became more insistent and many leases were allowed to lapse. The Duttons retained Bauhinia Downs which Charles managed, and Goomally where his brother Harry had charge. Later a house in Toowong, Brisbane, and an estate at Cooredulla near Armidale were also acquired.

In 1865 Dutton contested the new pastoral electorate of Mitchell in the Queensland Legislative Assembly but the only two votes cast for him were by his Bell cousins; John Gore Jones also had two votes and was awarded the seat by the returning officer. In

1871 Dutton nominated B. M. Morehead [q.v.] for Tambo but did not stand himself again until 1883 when he was elected for Leichhardt. S. W. Griffith immediately appointed him minister for lands and in 1887 he also acted as minister for works and mines while his friend William Miles [q.v.] was ill. When Miles died in August Dutton relinquished the lands ministry and took control of mines and works. In December when Griffith reformed his government, Dutton became minister for railways but lost his seat in the 1888 election and made no attempt to re-enter politics.

Dutton had a significant share in the idealistic review of legislation initiated by Griffith. He was given responsibility for a comprehensive consolidating land bill which introduced some long-sought reforms and has since been known as the 1884 Dutton Act. It went far towards relieving squatters of their exclusive use of land. The old practice of resuming half of every run, thought to be fairest for all but clearly far from efficient, was again invoked to provide cheap additional areas of agricultural land. The Act also provided for a land administration board with precise legal status, thus clearing away tangles and uncertainties that had bedevilled the operation of earlier land legislation. Although the Act was perhaps the best technical legislation of its kind which Queensland ever had, its weakness was that it miscalculated the relation of the colony's economy with land use and ownership. A land tax was rejected, and the gradual collapse of Queensland's economy over the next decade enforced amendments which eroded the ideals of 1884.

Dutton was mild with no great enthusiasms, a thoughtful spokesman for his department, more interested in facts than in theories. An efficient administrator, he brought with him the practical qualities which had made him a successful squatter. He won repute as a liberal, a humanitarian and one of the earliest squatters to gain the confidence of the Aboriginals whose land had been appropriated. His sense of justice, likeable modesty and freedom from political taint made him ideal for Griffith's assignment. The squatters in the Legislative Council were hostile but Dutton saw the bill through with determination. His legacy to Queensland was a Lands Department protected from undue interference by politicians, and a Department of Agriculture that provided experimental and educational facilities for farmers.

On 1 July 1865 at Brisbane Dutton married Martha Ann Alice, 17-year-old daughter of Captain Richard Coley; Bauhinia Downs was well known for its comfort and hospitality, and his wife's talents as doctor,

nurse and midwife were widely recognized. He died on 5 February 1904 at Cooredulla, and was buried privately by an Anglican clergyman. He left an estate worth over £13,000 and was survived by his wife, two sons and six of their eight daughters.

O. de Satgé, Pages from the journal of a Queensland squatter (Lond, 1901); J. Wright, The generations of men (Melb, 1959); PD (Qld), 1883-88; Weekly Herald (Brisb), 28 Jan 1865; Week, 4, 18, 25 Aug, 15 Sept, 19 Nov 1883, 29 Nov, 6, 27 Dec 1884; Brisbane Courier, 12 Nov 1883, 6 Mar 1884, 18-20 Apr, 7 May 1888; Queenslander, 23 July 1887, 13 Feb 1904.

BEVERLEY KINGSTON

DWIGHT, HENRY TOLMAN (1823?-1871), bookseller and publisher, was born in London, son of Richard William Dwight, mariner, and his wife Anne, née Meade, and grew up at Deptford, Kent. His elder brother, Richard William (1816-1864), migrated to Melbourne in 1853 with his wife Isabella Ann, née Gill, and became a grocer at Emerald Hill. Richard died on 19 August 1864 and was buried in the Melbourne general cemetery.

After experience in the London book trade, Henry migrated about 1855 to Melbourne, bringing with him a large stock of second-hand books. Within months of his arrival, he set up business at 234 Bourke Street East. In 1864 he took over the Glasgow Book Warehouse at 232 Bourke Street which had been opened the year before by Robert Mackay, publisher of Mackay's Australian Illustrated Almanac (1860-1877). Dwight used both premises until 1870 when he retained 232 Bourke Street only.

Although George Robertson, Samuel Mullen [qq.v.] and George Slater had commenced bookselling in Melbourne in 1853, Dwight's knowledge of books and attention to customers' wants attracted A. L. Gordon, Henry Kendall, Richard Henry 'Orion' Horne, Sir Archibald Michie [qq.v.], and others to his shop. There Dwight presided as 'a colonial Quaritch', over a literary coterie of 'lawyers, doctors, divines, journalists—a motley crew, but united in the bonds of bookdom. It was no light privilege to be admitted into the sacred circle'. Dwight was the Melbourne authorized agent for Quaritch of London whose catalogues bore his name.

Dwight issued in November 1859 his Catalogue of a collection of books, old and new, Theological and Miscellaneous . . . Books on Architecture & Building, Brewing and Distilling, Geology, Mineralogy, Mathematics & Natural Philosophy, which he claimed was the first such catalogue issued in the colony. His next catalogue claimed a stock of 10,000 volumes which by August 1862 had grown to 60,000 volumes. The 1865 catalogue contained 508 items of 'a choice selection of Books and Pamphlets, printed in, and relating to, the Colonies of Australia'.

Dwight lived quietly and sought no public prominence. One of the rare references to him in the press was in 1868 when police seized a number of American editions which he had bought at a sale, but the books were soon returned to him 'as one of the most enterprising and respected members of the bookselling trade'.

Dwight was an early and successful publisher, including G. Bourne's *Journal of Landsborough's Expedition from Carpentaria in search of Burke and Wills* (1862) and works by Rev. J. E. Tenison Woods, Thomas McCombie [qq.v.], J. J. Thomas and J. Geary. He also published *Australian Celebrities or Personal Portraits of 100 Theatrical Stars of various magnitudes* (1865), *The Hamlet Controversy. Was Hamlet Mad?* (1867) and *The Cordial and Liqueur Maker's Guide* (1869). Dwight issued verse by R. Horne, G. G. McCrae, E. M. Curr [qq.v.], D. W. Jobson and others. In fiction Dwight published *Lindigo, The White Woman, or The Highland Girl's Captivity among Australian Blacks* (1866) by Angus McLean, and joined with George Robertson and Sampson Low of London in McCombie's *Frank Henly, or Honest Industry Will Conquer* (1867).

Dwight died at his bookshop on 13 June 1871, survived by his wife Elizabeth, née Aldis. He bequeathed his property to the University of Melbourne in reversion upon his wife's death, with annual proceeds to be divided into prizes for the 'encouragement of learning in ancient history, constitutional and legal history, and natural philosophy'. Dwight's bequest was one of the first of substance to the university. When it became effective in 1904 it was valued at £5000.

R. C. Miller, *Books: their history and influence* (Melb, 1883); A. P. Martin, 'Concerning Australian poets', *Australian poets, 1788-1888*, D. W. B. Sladen ed (Lond, 1888); E. Scott, *A history of the University of Melbourne* (Melb, 1936); E. M. Miller, *Australian literature from its beginnings to 1935*, 2 (Melb, 1940); A. Blainey, *The farthing poet . . . Richard Hengist Horne 1802-84* (Lond, 1968); *Leader* (Melb), 24 Mar 1866; *Australasian*, 3 Oct 1868, 17 June 1871; *Herald* (Melb), 13 June 1871.

IAN F. McLAREN

DYMOCK, DAVID LINDSAY (1839-1937), co-operative dairying promoter, was born at Edinburgh, Scotland, son of John Dymock, solicitor, and his wife Margaret, née Waugh. In 1845 he migrated to New South Wales and by the early 1860s had established a dairy farm at Jamberoo, on the Minnamurra River; soon after he set up a highly successful auctioneering business centred in near-by Kiama. In the 1870s he promoted a road over the Jamberoo Mountain to Moss Vale via Robertson, and became captain of the Jamberoo Volunteer Rifle Corps. In 1873 he served on the Church of England school board; he was a leader in the erection of the Jamberoo Presbyterian Church, opened in January 1876, and in 1878 gave the presidential address to the revitalised Jamberoo Young Men's Mutual Improvement Society.

In the late 1870s the south coast dairymen began to consider the 'idea of co-operation' as an alternative to the unsatisfactory system of commission selling of produce through Sydney agents. In the next decade, with Dymock as its leading public advocate, the movement took advantage of the Mort-Nicolle [qq.v.] refrigeration advances and the invention of the mechanical separator to revolutionize dairying. In November 1879 at Kiama he presided over a meeting to consider a central co-operative marketing project. The campaign culminated in 1881 with the formation of the South Coast and West Camden Co-operative Co., the first of its kind in New South Wales. Dymock was chairman of directors until its forced voluntary liquidation in 1899 and takeover next year by (Sir) William McMillan. A breakaway group formed the Farmers Co-operative Society in 1900, parent of the modern Producers' Distributing Society, in whose board room in 1937 was unveiled a tablet stating 'Dymock was the father of co-operation in Australia'.

In the 1880s Dymock promoted the establishment of a 'Herd Book' to tabulate dairy cattle breeding, and introduced a new light tin-lined butter keg. He also helped to introduce overseas developments in milk condensing and separating.

On a holiday trip in 1884, Dymock was commissioned to survey co-operative butter manufacture overseas, particularly in Denmark. He returned with the sole agency for the revolutionary De Laval mechanical separator, which he handed over to a Sydney firm of engineers, Waugh & Josephson. In 1885 he called meetings, explained the Danish factory system, and demonstrated the separator at the Kiama showground. He became a director of the pioneer Albion Park Co-operative Butter Factory, which treated 1700 gallons of milk daily with six De Laval separators. By the end of the 1880s more than a dozen such factories had started in the area, with Dymock a director of at least two,

Waughope and Woodstock, both founded in 1887.

In 1890 Dymock took part in a separatist movement against the Kiama Council and served as an alderman on the new council from 1892 to July 1900. He was also president of the Kiama Agricultural Society for many years, an elder of the Presbyterian Church, a councillor of St Andrew's College within Sydney University and secretary of the Kiama district school board in the 1890s.

In 1864 at Jamberoo Dymock had married Grace Maria Menzies, and before 1914 he retired to Brisbane where he died on 6 August 1937, survived by two sons and two daughters.

F. McCaffrey, *First century of dairying in New South Wales* (Syd, 1909); W. A. Bayley, *Blue haven: centenary history of Kiama municipality* (Kiama, 1960); J. Jervis, 'Illawarra: a century of history, 1788-1888', *JRAHS*, 28 (1942); T. C. Kennedy, A brief history of co-operation as applied to the dairy industry (typescript, ML).   KEN MACNAB

E

EADE, JOEL (1823-1911), builder, architect and educationist, was born on 9 February 1823 at Breage, Cornwall, England, son of James Richard Eade, farmer and miner, and his wife Elizabeth, née Dunnald. At 14 he left school and began work on a farm. In 1840-44 as an apprentice carpenter and joiner he attended classes at the local Mechanics' Institute, 'acquiring a knowledge of drawing and design that lifted him out of the ranks of journeymen'. From 1845 he practised his trade in London, taking charge of a workshop where his employer discovered his drawing skill. In 1851 he went to California and gained a similar position.

In 1857 Eade arrived at Melbourne in the *What Cheer*. After four unsuccessful months on the Ovens goldfields he worked on the Beechworth court-house at £6 a week and was in charge at its completion. In 1859 he sought further contracts in Melbourne and then Daylesford where he had more success and bought land. He returned to Melbourne in 1861 and soon set up as an architect and builder at Collingwood. He was assessor to the borough in 1867-69, a member of the Municipal Council in 1869-75 and mayor in 1870-71. As honorary surveyor he planned new public buildings, including public baths, reformed the council's accounting system in 1873 and served on the parliamentary inquiry into Melbourne and suburban sewerage in 1871. He was a life governor of the Melbourne Hospital, returning officer for the Collingwood School Board and parliamentary elections, and for eighteen years an active magistrate.

Technical education was another improving cause dear to Eade. With support from local protectionist employers he founded the Collingwood School of Design for 'rising operatives' in July 1871 and personally initiated the Auxiliary Artisans' School of Works in March 1872, for which he ran the first juvenile industrial exhibition in Victoria in 1873. He was promptly imitated by John Danks [q.v.] at Emerald Hill and by others at Ballarat. In 1875 at the third exhibition the acting-governor, Sir William Stawell [q.v.], affirmed Eade's view that Schools of Design would be 'incomplete' without Schools of Works 'which practically adopted the instructions given by the others'. In that year Eade also won a certificate of merit at the Intercolonial Exhibition for his pupils' workmanship. He was elected to the committee of the Chamber of Manufactures in 1876 and was later a trustee. In 1879 he served on the executive committee of the Intercolonial Juvenile Industrial Exhibition in Melbourne. Eade's pupils at the School of Design included the inventor, Louis Brennan [q.v.], who showed some of his work at the first exhibition, and the artist, Tom Roberts, who remembered the Samuel Smiles encouragement of 'higher aspirations in lads who might otherwise have dragged on as common plodders'. The closure of the School of Works in 1875 was due partly to Eade's ill health and the lack of a suitable building, but chiefly because of 'apathy of the government and local corporations [and] the jealousy of leading men who had philanthropic fads of their own'. In 1876 he offered land for a technical school of his own design with ground-floor workshops and a drawing school above, but no funds were then avaliable. A Freemason and an Anglican, he died at his Collingwood home on 2 May 1911, predeceased by his wife Maria Sarah, née Heald, whom he had married in 1861, and survived by their only son.

H. M. Humphreys (ed), *Men of the time in Australia: Victorian series*, 1st ed (Melb, 1878); A. Sutherland et al, *Victoria and its metropolis*, 2 (Melb, 1888); *Age*, 4, 5 July 1871, 3 May 1911; *Argus*, 5 July 1871; *Collingwood Mercury*, 31 July, 14 Aug 1875; *Observer* (Collingwood), 23 July 1874, 23 Nov 1876, 7 Feb, 4 Apr 1889, 15, 22 Apr 1897, 12, 19, 26 May 1904.

J. H. RUNDLE

EADES, RICHARD (1809-1867), physician, was born on 15 August 1809 in Dublin, son of William George Eades, wine merchant, and his wife Mary, née Cranwill. He was educated at Trinity College, Dublin (B.A., 1832; M.B., 1836), and London (M.R.C.S., 1834). In the cholera epidemic of 1832-33 he went to Canada as surgeon of a migrant ship and visited hospitals there, in New York and elsewhere in America. He later went to Paris to study botany and chemistry. Back in Dublin, he lectured on materia medica at the Ledwich School of Medicine in 1838 and in 1842 at the Park Street and the Richmond Hospital Medical Schools; he was also physician to the Fever Hospital, Kilmainham, in 1847-48. He was co-opted a fellow of the Royal College of Surgeons in Ireland on 4 October 1844. With his wife and infant he arrived in South Australia in the *Roman Emperor* on 23 October 1848. He registered with the Medical Board on 2 January 1849, built up a successful practice in Adelaide as a physician and took a leading part in democratic politics. The discovery of gold prompted his move to Melbourne in January 1852, but he probably did not work on the goldfields.

Apart from his practice Eades was active in public affairs. He helped to found the Philosophical Institute of Victoria in 1855 and was a member of its council in 1858-59 and of the Royal Society of Victoria in 1860-61 and vice-president in 1860. In 1854 he represented La Trobe ward in the Melbourne City Council and was mayor in 1859-60. On 28 August 1860 when large crowds gathered outside Parliament House to demonstrate against inadequacies of a land bill, Eades courageously read the Riot Act; although the demonstrators clashed seriously with the 'police, no stone was thrown at him. He was physician to the Melbourne Hospital in 1859-66 and official visitor to the Lunatic Asylum in 1856-67. He was appointed city health officer on the death of Dr John Macadam [q.v.] in 1865. An early advocate of the Volunteer Forces, he was assistant surgeon to the Metropolitan Company of Artillery. He was a member of the Burke and Wills [qq.v.] Exploration Committee.

In 1861 he lectured on materia medica in the Government Analytical Laboratory and with Macadam began an extra-mural course for medical students. The enterprise of Eades and Macadam, at a time when the university could not obtain funds, undoubtedly hastened the establishment of the Medical School. When it opened in 1862, Eades was appointed lecturer in materia medica and therapeutics, a position he held until 1867. He was highly regarded as a physician, and as a fluent lecturer held the attention and the affection of his students. His fine baritone voice, his extensive repertoire of Irish songs and his wit made him very popular at special dinners. He died at his home in Windsor on 12 October 1867, and was buried with Anglican rites in the Melbourne general cemetery.

Eades married first, in 1843 at Dublin Sarah Christine Beare by whom he had two sons and three daughters, and second, at Melbourne in 1856 Charlotte Eleanor McKee, née Beare, by whom he had one son and three daughters. He was survived by one son and two daughters of the first marriage and by his widow and her four children. His family was left in poor circumstances and a public meeting was held on 20 March 1868 at the Mechanics' Institute to raise funds for their relief.

C. A. Cameron, *History of the Royal College of Surgeons in Ireland* (Dublin, 1886); *Univ Melb Medical School Jubilee* (Melb, 1914); 'Dr

Eades', *Aust Medical J*, Oct 1867; J. E. Neild, 'The Medical School of the Melbourne University', *Aust Medical J*, May, June 1887; *Illustrated Melb Post*, 16 Aug 1862; *Argus*, 14 Oct 1867; K. F. Russell, History of the Melbourne Medical School (held by author); Medical School letters (Univ Melb Archives).

K. F. RUSSELL

EAGAR, GEOFFREY (1818-1891), accountant, banker, politician and public servant, was born on 17 February 1818 in Sydney, the second son of Edward Eagar [q.v.] and his wife Jemima, née McDuel. He attended the schools of J. D. Lang and W. T. Cape [qq.v.], winning prizes for mathematics and classical studies. He left school at 15 and worked for ten years as a book-keeper for various employers and for another ten years as managing clerk in the large mercantile firm of Thacker & Co. In 1854 he was invited by the board of the Bank of New South Wales to an important new position in the bank's service. As the first branch (later chief) accountant Eagar was responsible for new accounting procedures and the supervision of a rapidly growing number of branches. He was well paid, travelled extensively and established an outstanding reputation as a banker. The directors of the bank were astonished when he submitted his resignation in September 1859 in order to accept appointment to the Legislative Council of New South Wales. His close friends, however, were not surprised, for he had displayed an early and mounting interest in political issues. From 18 he had been an anonymous contributor to many of the colony's newspapers and periodicals, writing with boldness and a reforming zeal on public questions. His former schoolfellows, William Forster, James Martin and John Robertson [qq.v.], had become active politicians and Eagar was anxious to join them.

A liberal, he advocated land reform, compulsory and secular education, and measures to counter political corruption. He believed that the government should play a major role in promoting economic growth, mainly by the judicious construction of public works and a carefully devised fiscal policy. From the beginning of his parliamentary career his brilliant oratory commanded attention but won him few friends, for he had a disconcerting habit of analysing political clichés to show up the inconsistency and shallowness of many of his political associates. This did not prevent him from gaining ministerial office; after only a month in the council he was selected as secretary for public works in Forster's ministry. This ministry survived for only four months and

Eagar surrendered his seat in the council in November 1860. He put his private affairs in order by opening an office in the heart of Sydney, from which he conducted a lucrative business as a consulting accountant and agent. In January 1863 he entered the Legislative Assembly as member for West Sydney and commenced a sustained attack on the Cowper [q.v.] ministry's management of the public finances. When James Martin replaced Cowper as premier in October 1863 he selected Eagar as colonial treasurer in the knowledge that no member of the assembly was better equipped to deal with budgetary difficulties and administrative inefficiency in the Treasury and related departments.

As treasurer from October 1863 to February 1865 and from January 1866 to October 1868, Eagar implemented sweeping financial and administrative reforms. He was primarily responsible for the abandonment of the famous Deas Thomson [q.v.] free trade tariff, the imposition of stamp duty taxation, the establishment of an efficient mechanism for raising overseas loans and the creation of a powerful Treasury organization. He also introduced new accounting procedures and greatly strengthened the staff, thereby making possible for the first time effective Treasury control of expenditure. His measures aroused widespread hostility and he was undoubtedly one of the most controversial figures in the colony's politics. He ruled the Treasury at a particularly difficult time of unavoidable deficit financing associated with a balance of payments crisis. Although a determined reformer and forceful administrator, he was impatient of criticism, almost tyrannical in his treatment of subordinates and inclined to move too swiftly in advance of public opinion on the general question of taxation.

His departure from the political scene followed what appeared to be a fairly straightforward administrative decision affecting the Customs Department. The collector of customs, W. A. Duncan [q.v.], was an influential and highly independent public servant with powerful political supporters, especially Henry Parkes [q.v.]. Duncan resisted Eagar's plans to bring the Customs Department completely under control of the Treasury and was charged by Eagar with insubordination. Duncan apologized on the advice of Parkes but Eagar refused to accept the apology; instead he insisted on Duncan's dismissal, thereby provoking Parkes to resign from the ministry. The 'Duncan affair' quickly became a major topic of interest to parliament and press and Eagar was branded as a tyrant. The ministry resigned partly as a result of the adverse publicity and in 1868 Eagar retired, firmly convinced of the correctness of all his actions as treasurer.

Within months of leaving politics he was financially embarrassed. From this predicament he was rescued in 1871 by the premier, Martin, who found Eagar a senior position in the Treasury and promoted him permanent head in February 1872. Eagar retained this key post until 17 February 1891. The Treasury was very much an institution of his own moulding and, as permanent head, he was in a powerful position to advise the sixteen treasurers who held office between 1872 and 1891. His influence was widely recognized and his ability at times gratefully acknowledged by politicians with some understanding of the complexity of financing a rapidly accelerating flow of government spending on railways and other costly services without resort to heavy taxation. Eagar was the master mind behind the large-scale overseas borrowing programme and skilfully manipulated available funds to keep the government solvent. Like some other public servants whose work outside the public limelight has never been properly investigated Eagar played a role as important for the colony as many of the leading politicians.

Besides his duties in the Treasury, from 1885 Eagar was a member and three times chairman of the Civil Service Board appointed to correct some of the abuses of the patronage system. He was also a member of the History Board which recommended in March 1891 the publication of the *Historical Records of New South Wales*. From 1859 until his death he was auditor for the University of Sydney. He was well known to literary circles as a fine essayist and a fair poet, his main leisure-time activity in his last years being the translation of the Odes of Horace into English verse. His death from a stroke on 12 September 1891 was noted by every Sydney publication in lengthy obituaries and was the cause of a special resolution of the Legislative Assembly on the motion of Henry Parkes, who called him one of the last of the 'most striking figures who watched over the introduction of parliamentary government' in New South Wales.

On 7 March 1843 he had married Mary Ann Arabella Bucknell and made his home at Glebe Point, Sydney. He also acquired a property on the Blue Mountains, with Eagar's Platform (Valley Heights railway station) at his front door. He was buried in the Anglican section of Rookwood cemetery and left an estate of about £3000. He was survived by his wife and three of their four children.

P. N. Lamb, 'Geoffrey Eagar and the Colonial Treasury of New South Wales', *Aust Economic Papers*, Sept 1962; CO 201/508.

P. N. LAMB

EBSWORTH, FREDERICK LOUIS (1816-1884), wool-broker, was born on 22 July 1816 in London, the third son of Thomas Ebsworth and his wife Mary Susannah, née Crook. Thomas Ebsworth was with the London firm of Marsh & Ebsworth which handled John Macarthur's [q.v.] wool; he was the auctioneer in 1821 when a bale of Macarthur's wool brought 124d. per pound.

Frederick came to Australia in the *Caroline* in January 1832 and worked in the Australian Agricultural Co. which his father had helped to promote. In 1834-45 his eldest brother Henry Thomas was secretary of the company in England and another brother, James Edward (d. 1874), accountant and assistant commissioner in Australia; in 1835 Frederick was 'Clerk to the Accountant and Superintendent of Manufactures' at Port Stephens. Later he went back to England and returned in the *Hashemy* on 25 January 1839. In October he set up as a wool-broker in Pitt Street, Sydney, and also acted as agent of the company.

Ebsworth developed wide business interests. In the depressed early 1840s he pioneered the use of steam for making tallow; his method was adopted on a large scale by Henry O'Brien [q.v.] and other graziers. In June 1843 he failed in a bid to float a sheep-boiling company with capital of £10,000. He was a founder and director of the Royal Exchange in 1851, a director of the Commercial Banking Co. of Sydney, a founder and first policy-holder of the Australian Mutual Provident Society and a foundation member and later director and trustee of the Australian Club.

On 18 April 1842 at St James's, Sydney, Ebsworth married Sophia Augusta (d. 1877), second daughter of Captain W. A. Steel of the 34th regiment; they had six sons and four daughters. At the Pitt Street Congregational Church, Sydney, on 11 January 1883 he married Rebecca Ann, daughter of John Gurner [q.v.]. Survived by his second wife and three sons and two daughters of his first marriage, he died at his residence 159 Liverpool Street, Sydney, on 20 September 1884 and was buried in St Stephen's churchyard, Camperdown.

His younger brother, OCTAVIUS BAY-LIFFE, wool-broker and manufacturer, was born in London in 1827. He came to Sydney in the *Catherine Jamieson* on 27 November 1848 with a speculative cargo and letters of introduction from various houses in Leeds. He found the colonial market depressed and about a year later went to San Francisco where he worked as a merchant and commission agent.

Back in Australia after a short time he was partner and probably manager of Thomas Barker's [q.v.] tweed mill in Syd-

ney in 1853-54. In 1855 he became the wool specialist in Mort [q.v.] & Co. In 1858 after a dispute he was dismissed by Mort's partner, E. W. Cameron [q.v.]. He was soon reinstated, but the quarrel recurred and Ebsworth left and in 1860 set up in opposition next door. Though he had been a key man in Mort's firm and popular with the pastoralists, he failed to gain enough clients and was soon forced out of business. Despite his animosity against Cameron, he remained on good terms with Mort.

In 1860-70 he owned Barker's mill in Sussex Street, which manufactured a large variety of cloths and ginned local cotton for export to England during the American civil war. He also had a wool-washing establishment and bought wool, tallow, hide and cotton for numerous overseas and local firms. He was also a director of two investment and building societies, and an auditor of the City Bank and of a local branch of an insurance company. He was a foundation member of the Union Club in 1857 and held office in the Sydney Philharmonic Society.

At Christ Church, Sydney, on 6 July 1852 he had married Frances Mary Barker (1829-1914), second daughter of James Barker. Survived by his wife, four sons and a daughter, he died of diphtheria at Cintra, Burwood, on 23 June 1870 and was buried in St Stephen's churchyard, Camperdown. His estate was sworn at £8000.

A. Barnard, *Visions and profits* (Melb, 1961); *Australian*, 6 Jan 1832, 26 Jan, 31 Oct 1839, 2 Jan 1840; *SMH*, 30 June 1843, 25 Feb 1850; Ebsworth papers (ML).   G. P. WALSH

EDEN, CHARLES HENRY (1839-1900), public servant and writer, was born on 20 March 1839, the younger son of Robert Eden (1800-1879) and his wife Frances, daughter of Rev. Rowland Egerton Warburton; his great-grandfather was Sir Robert Eden, third baronet of West Auckland, and his uncle was Admiral Henry Eden (1797-1888). After sale of his naval commission Eden arrived at Moreton Bay in the *Queen of the Colonies* on 6 April 1863. On 11 May at St John's Cathedral, Brisbane, he married a fellow passenger, Georgina, daughter of Captain F. W. Hill. According to his *My Wife and I in Queensland: an eight years' experience in the above colony with some account of Polynesian labour* (London, 1872), Eden shepherded at Pilton, obtained a post in the Registrar-General's Office through the influence of G. E. Dalrymple [q.v.], spent two years at Mount McConnell under Ernest Henry [q.v.] and searched for gold at Calliope and Gympie in 1867. In Brisbane in 1868 for the duke of Edinburgh's visit he

was appointed on 6 May police magistrate
and subcollector of customs at Cardwell at
a salary of £300. After an inquiry he was
dismissed in March 1870 and left in the
Clarence in May to return to England. In
his book Eden did not mention his appointment at Cardwell; but his claim is evidently
untrue that he left Brisbane in 1868 solely
to join J. E. Davidson in a sugar venture at
Bellenden Plains until carried aboard the
Black Prince unconscious from fever in early
1870. In England Eden turned to writing
and by his death on 16 February 1900 had
published in London some sixteen novels
and many works of exploration and travel,
including *Australia's Heroes* (c. 1875) and
*The Fifth Continent, with the adjacent
islands* (c. 1877).

Most controversial in the colonies for its
disenchanted account of colonial life was
My Wife and I in Queensland. A reviewer
in the *Illustrated London News*, 22 June
1872, found Eden's work to be 'both manly
and gentlemanly' in spirit but thought it
'enough to warn honest men away from
Queensland for some time to come'. In reply
the *Brisbane Courier* accused Eden of 'vilify-
ing the colony that was foolish enough to
provide him with an easy and honourable
position in its service, a man whose sole
recommendation was—that the Duke of
Edinburgh was his friend'. One correspondent, 'A Bohemian', added two days
later: 'Very few men have had a better
opportunity of observing "low life" here
and gauging its utmost depths of depravity,
and nobody could take a greater pleasure in
the task than Eden'.

Eden's elder son Guy Ernest Morton (d.
1954) became a distinguished lawyer and
also wrote for the London stage; he published two novels and a book of Australian
verse, *Bush Ballads* (London, 1907).

D. Jones, *Cardwell Shire story* (Brisb, 1961);
C. T. Wood, 'The Queensland sugar industry
as depicted in the Whish and Davidson diaries', JRQHS, 7 (1964-65), no 3; *Brisbane Courier*,
4, 6 Sept 1872; Justice Department records (QA).

                                    DOROTHY JONES

EDINBURGH, ALFRED ERNEST AL-
BERT, DUKE of (1844-1900), was born on 6
August 1844 at Windsor, England, second
son of Queen Victoria. He entered the navy
in August 1858 and travelled widely as a
midshipman in the frigate *Euryalus*. In the
winter of 1862-63 he was elected King of
Greece but politics dictated his withdrawal
and he was given instead right of succession
to the Duchy of Saxe-Coburg and Gotha. He
was promoted lieutenant in 1863 and in
1866 became both a naval captain and duke

of Edinburgh. He commissioned his first
command, H.M.S. *Galatea*, in January 1867,
left for the Mediterranean in February and
sailed for South America on 12 June for a
state visit to the emperor of Brazil. Then
after two months at the Cape, the *Galatea*
reached Adelaide on 31 October 1867 to
commence the first royal tour of Australia.

After three uneventful weeks in South
Australia, the duke moved on to Melbourne
where a shooting incident between Orange
and Catholic factions and a riot due to inept
handling of a free public banquet marred
the generally enthusiastic atmosphere. He
then visited Tasmania and arrived in Sydney
on 21 January 1868. After a month of festivities he spent a week in Brisbane and
returned to Sydney. Despite rumours of
sectarian strife, he attended a picnic at Clontarf on 12 March where an Irishman, Henry
James O'Farrell [q.v.], succeeded in wounding him seriously. In a frenzy of outraged
patriotism the New South Wales government sought unsuccessfully to uncover a
conspiracy and, overruling the duke's eminently sensible proposal to refer the sentence
on O'Farrell to the Queen, refused to recommend clemency. O'Farrell was hanged on
21 April and the duke who had recovered
completely by 26 March left for England on
26 June. He visited Australia again in-
formally, arriving in Fremantle on 28 January 1869 and leaving Sydney on 3 April. In
both Sydney and Melbourne he dedicated
hospitals commemorating his escape from
death. In 1870 the duke made a final visit to
dock the *Galatea*. He arrived at Sydney on
15 September, visited Melbourne for the Cup
from 22 October to 19 November, and sailed
early in 1871 without any ceremonies.

The duke married Grand Duchess Marie
of Russia on 23 January 1874. He continued
his naval career and on 3 June 1893 became
admiral of the Fleet. On 22 June 1893 he
succeeded to the Duchy of Saxe-Coburg and
Gotha and thereafter lived in Germany
where he died of heart disease on 30 July
1900. He left four daughters, one of whom
became Queen of Rumania; his only son
predeceased him.

Although more reserved than his elder
brother, the duke was reputedly cultured,
intelligent and a fine seaman. His visits
stimulated imperialist sentiment in Australia but the accompanying incidents
aggravated sectarian tensions.

J. G. Knight, *Narrative of the visit of . . . the
Duke of Edinburgh to . . . Victoria* (Melb, 1868);
J. D. Woods, *A narrative of the visit of . . . the
Duke of Edinburgh . . . to South Australia*
(Adel, 1868); J. Milner and O. W. Brierly, *The
cruise of HMS Galatea* (Lond, 1869); B. McKin-
ley, *The first royal tour 1867-68* (Adel, 1970);
P. M. Cowburn, 'The attempted assassination

of the Duke of Edinburgh, 1868', *JRAHS*, 55 (1969); *Australasian*, 27 Feb-13 Mar 1869; *SMH*, 11 Mar-5 Apr 1869.   H. J. GIBBNEY

EDKINS, EDWARD ROWLAND (1840-1905), pastoral manager, was born on 10 January 1840 at Bridgnorth, Shropshire, England, the youngest son of Thomas Oliver Edkins, stationer and sometime mayor, and his wife Louisa, née Winton. When his father died, Edkins migrated to Victoria with his mother and other members of the family; they arrived in 1852. In the late 1850s Edkins began droving and about 1862 was reputed the first to take cattle across the Burdekin River when he drove some 4000 head from New South Wales to stock Bluff Downs, Mary Vale and Wando Vale runs for Robert Stewart [q.v.], Glen Walker and others. In 1864 he learned in Victoria how to inoculate cattle against pleuropneumonia and was employed to inoculate stock on runs near Rockhampton. In 1866 he and his brother Henry ran the boiling-down works at Burketown for the Scottish Australian Co. Ltd, and perfected a technique of curing beef for markets in Batavia and Singapore.

On 26 October 1867 at Emerald Hill, Victoria, Edkins married Edwina Marion, daughter of Dr Walter Huey (1797-1843) of Launceston, Tasmania, and his wife Alethea, née Martin. With his bride he made the long trip from Melbourne to Burketown where he managed Beamesbrook station for the Scottish Australian Co. and where the first two of his eight children died and in 1871 his wife's brother Edward, on leave from India, was fatally speared. In 1872 Beamesbrook was abandoned and Edkins with his family and 12,000 cattle went to manage Mount Cornish station, the western lease of Bowen Downs. Under Edkins's management the station's Shorthorn herd became one of the best known in the colony but drought from 1898 to 1902 reduced the cattle from 36,000 to 1300, despite artesian watering improvements made in 1891-96. Deciding not to restock, the company sold the property to the New Zealand and Australian Land Co. and Edkins went with his wife to Sydney, where he was pastoral inspector for the Scottish Australian Co. Descendants are still in the Longreach district.

In the 1880s and 1890s with Frank Hann [q.v.] Edkins had taken up Lawn Hill in the Northern Territory, and with other partners held Roxborough, Katandra and Dunrobin. He was a justice of the peace from December 1869, and a member until December 1902 and six times chairman of the Aramac Divisional Board. He named several district features and the town of Muttaburra, which he intended to be Mootaburra. He died at Drummoyne, Sydney, on 14 August 1905 and was buried in the churchyard of St Thomas's, Enfield. He was survived by his wife and six children.

D. S. Macmillan (ed), *Bowen Downs, 1863-1963* (Syd, 1963); Reminiscences of Edwina M. Edkins (MS held at Bimbah, Longreach, Qld).
                                ZITA DENHOLM

EDMONDSTONE, GEORGE (1809-1883), butcher and politician, was born on 4 May 1809 in Edinburgh, son of William Edmondstone, naval commissary, and his wife Alexandrina, née Farquharson. At 12 his father died and in 1832 he migrated to Sydney. Later he went to Hobart Town and after some hard times began business in Sydney. He then moved to Maitland and about 1840 he took up Normanby Plains station, but sold out early in 1842 and set up as a butcher in Brisbane, hoping to profit from trade with the newly-settled Darling Downs. He soon achieved prosperity and prominence. Although not a great speaker he was elected to the first Brisbane Municipal Council in 1859 and remained a member until 1866. As mayor in 1863-64 he had much to do with the planning of the first Brisbane bridge and the town hall. He was also involved in the conflict between the council and the government on the new Brisbane waterworks.

In the Queensland Legislative Assembly he represented East Moreton in 1860-67, Brisbane in 1869-73 and Wickham in 1873-77. He seldom spoke in the assembly and made little impression, though in 1870 in company with T. P. Pugh, K. I. O'Doherty and S. Fraser [qq.v.] he tried to organize a Liberal party based largely on Brisbane. In 1877 he was appointed to the Legislative Council in an effort to secure a majority for John Douglas's [q.v.] Liberal government. His appointment was resisted by the administrator, Sir Maurice O'Connell [q.v.], but approved by his successor, Sir Arthur Kennedy.

On 10 July 1837 in Sydney Edmondstone had married Alexis Watson Tilleray. He retired from business because of a heart complaint and died at his home in Breakfast Creek on 23 February 1883, survived by one of his two daughters.

G. Greenwood and J. Laverty, *Brisbane 1859-1959: a history of local government* (Brisb, 1959); *Qld Express*, 17 Feb 1870; *Brisbane Courier*, 24 Feb 1883.   A. A. MORRISON

EDWARDS, SIR JAMES BEVAN (1834-1922), soldier, was born on 5 November 1834 in England, son of Samuel Price Edwards of Donegal. He was educated at the Royal Military Academy, Woolwich, and was commissioned in the Royal Engineers in December 1852. He served with distinction in the Crimea, in the Indian mutiny and with General Gordon's 'Ever-Victorious Army' in China. In 1885 he commanded the Royal Engineers in the Suakin operations and then became commandant of the School of Military Engineering at Chatham. Promoted major-general in 1888, he went next year to Hong Kong as commander of British troops in China.

Following a recommendation of the Colonial Conference of 1887 Edwards was chosen by the British government to inspect the forces of the Australian colonies and to advise on their organization. He arrived at Brisbane in July 1889, inspected fortifications and troops in each colony and reported to the colonial governments in October. In recommendations published in the leading newspapers, he showed that the colonial forces lacked not only cohesion but the organization, training and equipment to fit them for defence of the continent. On questions common to the whole of Australia he proposed an organization which would enable the colonies to combine for mutual defence; he recommended uniform organization and armament, a common Defence Act, a military college to train officers and a uniform gauge for railways. Above all he emphasized the crucial importance of his first and main proposal. 'Looking to the state of affairs in Europe, and to the fact that it is the unforeseen which happens in war, the defence forces should at once be placed on a proper footing; but this is, however, quite impossible without a federation of the forces of the different colonies'.

Radicals accused Edwards of being 'a political tout' obsessed with the invasion of Australia, but the timing of his practical plans enabled Sir Henry Parkes [q.v.] to take the strong initiative which led to the National Australasian Convention of 1891 'empowered to consider and report upon an adequate scheme for a Federal Constitution'. Six months before Edwards arrived Parkes had talked Federation with Deakin in Melbourne and in July 1889 had an abortive exchange of letters with the Victorian premier on the same theme. Edwards later claimed, in an address to the Royal Colonial Institute on 10 March 1891, that Parkes 'saw at once that combined action for purposes of defence was impossible without a Federal Government to direct and control it He therefore became the champion of the great question of Colonial Federation'.

After leaving Australia Edwards carried out a similar mission in New Zealand and returned to Hong Kong. He resigned his command in 1890 and retired in 1893. As a Conservative he represented Hythe in the House of Commons in 1895-99. An ardent advocate of imperial federation he was elected a fellow of the Royal Colonial Institute, joined its council in 1893 and served as chairman in 1909-15. He had been promoted lieut-general in 1891 and became colonel-commandant of the Royal Engineers in 1903. He was described as a far-sighted and progressive officer, fearless in his acceptance of responsibility. Known for his kindly and cheerful nature, he had a great capacity for work and for getting others to work loyally with him. His appointment as C.B. in 1877 was followed by a K.C.M.G. in 1891 and K.C.B. in 1912. He died in London on 8 July 1922.

Edwards was married first in 1868 to Alice (d. 1899), daughter of Ralph Brocklebank; second, in 1901 to Nina (d. 1916), daughter of John Balfour and widow of Sir R. Dalrymple-Horn-Elphinstone; and third, in 1918 to Amy Ann Courtnay, daughter of J. N. Harding.

H. Parkes, *Fifty years in the making of Australian history* (Lond, 1892); B. R. Wise, *The making of the Australian Commonwealth, 1889-1900* (Lond, 1913); J. A. La Nauze, *Alfred Deakin*, 1 (Melb, 1965); E. Salmon, 'Lieutenant-General Sir J. Bevan Edwards', *United Empire*, 13 (1922); F.E.G.S., 'Lieut.-General Sir James Bevan Edwards', *Roy Engineers J*, 37 (1923); *Age*, 15, 23, 24, 26 Oct 1889; *SMH*, 15, 17, 24, 25 Oct 1889; *Advertiser* (Adel), 16 Oct 1889; *Argus*, 24, 29 Oct 1889.   A. J. HILL

EGAN, DANIEL (1803?-1870), public servant, merchant and politician, was born at Windsor, New South Wales, probably the son of Brian Egan. In 1824-35 he was foreman at the government dockyard in Sydney and accepted a gratuity in lieu of a similar post at Trincomalee, Ceylon, when the yard closed. He went into business and acquired several trading vessels. In November 1842 he was elected alderman for Gipps ward in the Sydney Municipal Council, but resigned in September 1843 because of his insolvency. Re-elected in November 1846, he was mayor of Sydney in 1853. From 1848 to 1853 he was a magistrate on the Sydney bench.

As a politician Egan supported the liberals, and favoured an extension of the suffrage and the opening up of the land. He was an elected member of the Legislative Council for the pastoral district of Maneroo (Monaro) in 1854-56 and represented the same seat in the Legislative Assembly in 1856-59 and Eden in 1859-69. In January 1870 he regained Monaro. He was a firm supporter of the Cowper-Robertson [qq.v.] faction for over eleven years; he was postmaster-general under Robertson and Cowper from 27 October 1868 until his death. Though he supported much liberal legislation he vigorously opposed the abolition of state aid to religion and the Public Schools Act (1866).

Egan was twice married. He had two sons and a daughter by his first marriage which took place when he was about 23. His second marriage was to Mary Ann Cahnac on 17 July 1843 at St Mary's, Sydney; there were no children. Egan's second wife and a son and a daughter of her former marriage were lost in the wreck of the Dunbar near Watson's Bay on 20 August 1857. Egan's only surviving son, John Piper (b. 1827), married Marianne, a sister of Richard Brownlow [q.v.], on 14 April 1855.

Egan died after a short illness at the Oxford Hotel, Watson's Bay, on 16 October 1870; his friend Archbishop Polding [q.v.] had administered the last rites, and he was buried in the Catholic cemetery at Petersham.

Egan's grave was soon after the centre of a brief but widespread religious and public scandal. Though he was a staunch Catholic and a benefactor of the Church, certain zealous bigots objected to his burial in consecrated ground because of his alleged association with a woman to whom he was not married. They had his body secretly removed and placed in unconsecrated ground. W. B. Dalley, E. Butler and D. Buchanan [qq.v.] were among the many who condemned their action. The matter was raised in parliament in January 1871, a select committee proposed, and the outrage deplored by most sections of the community and of the Catholic Church. The furore ended when Polding ordered the body to be reinterred in its original grave.

P. Loveday and A. W. Martin, *Parliament factions and parties* (Melb, 1966); *Illustrated Sydney News*, 22 Oct 1853; *SMH*, 11 Mar, 11, 27 Aug 1857, 17, 19 Oct 1870, 28, 31 Jan, 1 Feb 1871; *Town and Country J*, 22 Oct 1870; Perkins papers (NL).   G. P. WALSH

EGGERS, KARL FRIEDRICH WILHELM (1815-1882), printer and journalist, was born in Brunswick, Hanover, Germany, son of a medical practitioner of some repute. He received a good education, including university training. In 1843 he went to London and was employed by the printing firm of Clowes, Gilbert & Rivington. He arrived at Port Adelaide in the *Thomas Lowry* late in 1848. He worked at Dehane's printery

in King William Street and then joined the mechanical staff of the Adelaide *Register* and *Observer*. By February 1850 he was acting as the German reporter for the *Register*. In March 1851 he applied successfully for the position of German interpreter for the Law Courts at a salary of £100.

In September 1851 Eggers became the proprietor of the *Adelaider Deutsche Zeitung*. This paper had been founded in April by Rudolf Reimer, who had then bought the *Süd-Australische Zeitung* and merged the two. Eggers also bought the German printing press and type. He issued the *Adelaider Deutsche Zeitung* twice a week from 1853 to 1862, establishing his printery in the Register Building, Grenfell Street. A few years later he entered into partnership with Georg Eimer, but retired in 1874 after printing the first year's issues of *Der Lutherische Kirchenbote für Australien*. Eggers continued his own printery and resumed the *Kirchenbote* in July 1878. In 1879 he began editing and publishing a book almanac, the Adelaide *Volks Kalender* but because of ill health in October 1880 he had to arrange for the type to be set elsewhere. After several paralytic strokes Eggers died at his home in Angas Street, Adelaide, on 30 January 1882 and was buried in the West Terrace cemetery. He was survived by his widow, Henriette, née Roenfeld, whom he had married on 2 March 1850 at Adelaide, and by a daughter and granddaughter. The *Observer* obituarist praised Eggers's literary tastes, his culture, his many contributions to the English press of the colony and his keen interest in the affairs of German colonists.

His brother, Julius Friedrich Carl (b. 1828), arrived at South Australia in the *Australia* in December 1850, married Henriette Waldemine Friederike Helmke on 8 July 1853, and settled on the land, first at Cockatoo Valley and later on the Kingsford estate, where he died on 25 May 1871. Julius's eldest son, Carl Friedrich Wilhelm, was born at Cockatoo Valley on 10 September 1854. At 15 he managed his father's farm and then branched out on his own at Concordia near Gawler and later at Wasleys. In 1878 he married Anna Marie Konzag. In 1905 he became a justice of the peace. He was president of the National League, a member of the local school board and of the Independent Order of Oddfellows, a trustee of the Lutheran Church and a founder of a new Lutheran church at Wasleys. In 1919 he retired to Adelaide where he died in 1944.

Register (Adel), 5 Jan, 12 Apr 1848, 19 Dec 1850; *Süd-Australische Zeitung*, 30 May 1871; *Observer* (Adel), 4 Feb 1882; German newspaper files, v22 (Adel Inst); CSO letters (SAA); family information.   F. J. H. BLAESS

EGGLESTON, JOHN (1813-1879), Wesleyan minister, was born in January 1813 at Newark, Nottingham, England, son of Frederic Eggleston, confectioner and local preacher, and his wife Ann, née Else. In 1833 he was hired by a Lincolnshire circuit to conduct services. Next year he was accepted by the British Conference as a ministerial probationer and filled appointments at Rotherham, Buxton, Sheffield and Edinburgh before his ordination in 1838 at the Wesleyan Conference in Bristol. There he was persuaded by the newly-appointed general superintendent of Australasian Missions, Rev. John Waterhouse, to accompany him to New Zealand.

After his marriage to Eliza Moulton in 1838, Eggleston embarked with the missionary party and arrived in Hobart Town on 31 January 1839. Because plans were changed Waterhouse and Eggleston stayed in Hobart while the others went to New Zealand. A year later Eggleston left Hobart to take charge of the small Wesleyan society in Adelaide. Primitive living conditions and disagreements with church members over state aid led to his early withdrawal and he returned to Van Diemen's Land where he was stationed at Launceston as a colleague of Rev. William Butters [q.v.] in 1843. Appointments to New Norfolk in 1846, Hobart in 1847, and Sydney in 1850 preceded his transfer to the Collins Street Chapel, Melbourne, where he was active on the Wesleyan Education Committee for the Victoria district. He returned to Sydney in 1856 as general secretary of Australasian Foreign Missions and became responsible for their oversight in New Zealand, Tonga, Fiji and Samoa, which in 1855 had become the charge of the Australasian Conference. Because of the huge correspondence Eggleston was released from circuit duties in 1858. He faced many difficulties: missions in the north of New Zealand were desolated in the Maori wars of 1862 and those in Samoa were the subject of a bitter dispute with the London Missionary Society. Despite Eggleston's efforts to raise money, the amount contributed by the Australasian Church decreased, and the Missionary Committee of the British Conference had to continue substantial grants. After debate the Australasian Conference of 1861 decided to continue the missions despite their financial burden.

Confidence in Eggleston's administration was expressed by his election as president of the Australasian Conference in 1860. He resigned as missionary secretary in 1863 and returned to circuit work at Wesley Church, Melbourne. There he renewed his interest in educational affairs, especially the establishment of the Wesleyan Grammar School

(Wesley College) opened in 1866. He visited England in 1867 and on his return was superintendent of circuits at St Kilda, Brunswick Street, Fitzroy, Clunes and Geelong East. He was appointed treasurer of the supernumerary ministers and ministers' wives fund in 1868 and helped to prepare a plan for the improved government of the Church by annual and general conferences. Failing eyesight forced his retirement in 1878 and he died at Brighton on 23 January 1879. Eggleston was an untiring and earnest minister, evangelical and pietistic in theology. His three sons and one daughter, together with their descendants, became influential in church, law, politics and architecture in Victoria.

J. C. Symons, *Life of the Rev. Daniel James Draper* (Lond, 1870); M. Dyson (ed), *Australasian Methodist ministerial general index*, 1st ed (Melb, 1889); *Spectator* (Melb), 30 Jan 1879.

RENATE HOWE

ELDER, DAVID (1849-1923), businessman and grazier, was born on 19 June 1849 at Dundee, Scotland, son of Douglas Elder and his wife Euphemia, née Adam. In 1854 the family migrated to Melbourne where his father, a shipwright and marine surveyor, later became superintendent of the government dockyard.

Elder was educated at Scotch College. In 1865 he obtained a position with a prominent Melbourne accountant, Andrew Lyell [q.v.], later Lyell & Gowan, and was admitted to the partnership nine years later. In this unusually dynamic firm, which in the 1880s had branches in Sydney and London, he acquired close familiarity with a variety of business attitudes and practices and a wide circle of influential commercial acquaintances. His reputation gained him in 1880 the Melbourne management of the New Zealand Loan and Mercantile Agency Co. Ltd, a rapidly growing pastoral consignment house active in Australia since 1874. As manager and in 1889-1903 as general manager for Australia, Elder led the N.Z.L.&M.A. Co. in an abrasively competitive expansion. 'They desire to absorb everything', lamented one rival manager, 'What other reputable business . . . requires such an adjunct to its sale room as a grog room?' In the 1880s competition between woolbrokers became increasingly concentrated on the liberality of their lending policies. Most lenders ignored the deteriorating prospects of increased pastoral production as easily as the company's directors ignored their chairman's warning that Elder's 'grasping at business is ruinous'. Basic principles of financial management were neglected by many. Unable to meet prospective debenture repayments, its funds locked in overvalued loans, its business riddled with the effects of what *The Times* called the 'gigantic system of continued and complicated dishonesty' devised in New Zealand by some directors, the N.Z.L.&M.A. Co. failed in 1893. Elder's contribution was not negligible: loose control of lending and accounting; interception of a company official's report to the directors specifying very large contingent capital losses on the Australian business. For his role in the Pastoralists' Federal Council in 1891-92 the *Bulletin* described him as the 'Napoleon of the capitalist party'; he was undoubtedly one of the strongest personalities among Australian pastoral financiers and wool-brokers at that time. He secured his way even with his more scrupulous London directors and their successors in the reconstructed company as readily as he created apprehension among his competitors. He retained his position in the Australian management until his retirement at 53 on exceptionally generous terms.

Among other roles outside the industry, Elder was a justice of the peace in Victoria and New South Wales and a commissioner of the Victorian Savings Bank. After his retirement he served as director of a number of Queensland pastoral companies, some of which he helped to promote, of a meat company and of several commercial companies. Elder died at Essendon on 25 August 1923. He was survived by four sons and a daughter and by his wife Emma Ann, daughter of Samuel and Mary Turner of Sandridge, whom he had married on 22 May 1873.

N. Cain, 'Capital structure . . . Pastoral companies in Australia 1880-1893', *Aust Economic Papers*, June 1963; N. Cain, 'Pastoral expansion and crisis in New South Wales 1880-1893: the lending view', *Aust Economic Papers*, Dec 1963; *A'sian Insurance and Banking Record*, 9 Mar 1880, 16 July 1889, 20 Mar 1903; *Pastoral Review*, 15 June 1892; *Argus*, Apr, May 1894; *The Times*, 8 May 1894.   ALAN BARNARD

ELDER, WILLIAM (1804-1882), ALEXANDER LANG (1815-1885), GEORGE (1816-1897), businessmen, and SIR THOMAS (1818-1897), businessman, pastoralist and public benefactor, were born in Kirkcaldy, Scotland, sons of George Elder, merchant and shipowner, and his wife Joanna, née Lang. In 1839 the family decided to extend its business to the new province of South Australia and accordingly Alexander sailed as sole passenger in his father's schooner *Minerva*, 89 tons, with a cargo of rum,

whisky, brandy, tar, fish, biscuits, tinware, gunpowder, agricultural machinery and seed, with which to establish himself. He advertised as a general and commission agent and dispatched the *Minerva* for regular trading between Adelaide and Launceston. He survived the depression in 1841-43 and expanded his activities; he bought pasture lands, established a gasworks and acted as agent for shipping companies and men on the land. When copper was discovered at Kapunda in 1842 he set up as a metal-broker.

William, a sea captain, visited Adelaide in 1840 when he brought out 183 Scottish and Irish migrants. The passengers acclaimed his 'gentlemanly deportment . . . perfect self command and good temper under the most trying circumstances'. He returned to Adelaide in 1844 with his wife, née Malcolm, to join the family business. By 1849, when George joined them in Adelaide after some years in Canada, business was thriving. Alexander was a justice of the peace, director of the Savings Bank and the Adelaide Auction Co., and trustee and treasurer of the Church of Scotland. In July 1851 he was elected for West Adelaide to the Legislative Council where he battled against state aid for religion and against a nominated rather than an elected upper house for parliament. In Adelaide he married the daughter of Rev. John Baptist Austin, a Congregational minister. On 30 March 1853 he resigned from the council and with his wife and children left South Australia. He settled in London in 1855. There he acted as agent for the Adelaide firm until 1884 when with two sons he established A. L. Elder & Co. Much of his trade was with New Zealand where he owned land at Langdale near Masterton and where three sons migrated. Alexander died in London on 5 September 1885 survived by seven sons and five daughters. He left an estate in South Australia worth £317,000 and was well remembered in the colony for his integrity, drive and common sense.

William left South Australia soon after Alexander and retired in Scotland. He died at Cannes in April 1882, survived by his wife. George, 'handsome, with charming manners and the cleverest of the brothers', was chairman of the Chamber of Commerce in 1852 and 1855. A popular speaker, he was urged to enter parliament but refused. He took a great interest in Chalmers Church and laid its foundation stone. He left South Australia in 1855 to live in Scotland, where he was chairman of the North Ayrshire Liberal Association, a deputy-lieutenant of Ayrshire and director of many companies. He died at Knock Castle, Largs, Ayrshire, in July 1897, aged 81.

Thomas migrated to Adelaide in 1854 and worked for a year with George. He then formed a partnership with Edward Stirling, Robert Barr Smith [qq.v.] and John Taylor: Elder, Stirling & Co. In 1856 Barr Smith married Thomas's sister Joanna. She became Adelaide's most renowned hostess but Thomas always lived quietly and never married. Elder, Stirling & Co. financed in 1859 the Wallaroo and Moonta Copper Mines which, after initial risks, brought them great wealth. Stirling and Taylor retired and the two remaining partners formed Elder Smith & Co. which became one of the world's largest wool-selling firms. While still active as agents they built up a huge pastoral territory, spreading further and further from the civilized fringe and moving into the untouched wastes of South Australia, Queensland and Western Australia. They tackled the outback problems by spending many thousands of pounds in fencing and sinking bores though their properties constituted a land mass finally much larger than the whole of their native Scotland. Thomas's holdings included Paratoo (3000 square miles), Umberatana, Mount Lyndhurst and Blanchewater (3000 square miles) and Beltana (900 square miles).

Thomas was an enthusiastic and practical supporter of exploration and saw the camel as the answer to the transport problems of the outback. His first imported batch of breeding camels included three types for speed, stamina and strength; he also brought out Afghans to manage the beasts. From the original 124 camels he bred a sturdy stock at Beltana. A hundred were used in building the overland telegraph line from Adelaide to Darwin in 1872 and they were established as indispensable in P. E. Warburton's [q.v.] 4000-mile journey from the centre of Australia to the western coast in 1872-73. Ernest Giles's [q.v.] exploration in 1875 also succeeded with camels. Thomas financed both these expeditions as well as those of Ross [q.v.] in 1874, Lewis in 1875 and the Royal Geographical Society of South Australia in 1891. He also lent camels and drivers to genuine expeditions of discovery and much land was opened up as a result of his ardent interest in exploration. In 1890 he wrote to Mueller [q.v.] offering to finance a trip to the Antarctic.

Thomas published in Adelaide for private circulation four pamphlets describing early travels of his own. Notes from a pocket journal of a trip up the River Murray in 1856 (1893) reports his two-month journey in Captain Cadell's [q.v.] steamer and attests to his immediate enjoyment of his new home. Narrative of a tour in Palestine in 1857 (1894) describes a spontaneous jaunt from Cairo to Mount Sinai and Jerusalem which Thomas made with a party of Englishmen, his first experience of camel riding. His Travels in Algeria in 1860 (1894) convinced him that the French experiment in colonization was unlikely to succeed, while in Notes from a pocket journal of rambles in Spain in 1860 (1894) he confessed after visiting the art galleries that 'picture seeing is more fatiguing than people think'; but he later gave £25,000 to the art gallery in Adelaide.

Thomas was a member of the Leglislative Council in 1863-69 and 1871-78. He attended regularly and his few speeches suggest him as unemotional, conservative, educated, sensible, and, in discussion, short and to the point. His opinion was listened to with respect. He was particularly interested in the waste lands bill of 1866 for which he voted although as a squatter he stood to lose by it, and after 1871 he continually opposed what he considered extravagant government spending.

Thomas bought Birksgate, Glen Osmond, where he built his own gas plant for lighting, grew bananas in his conservatory, made wine from his own garden grapes, created a zoo and built a tower in the grounds from which he could signal to his yachts as they raced in the gulf. When an overseas ship was sighted he fired a cannon and hoisted the Union Jack as his own shipping advisory service. He began to race horses in 1873 and for ten years competed with varying success. When his head trainer died he sold his racers and concentrated on his stud farm at Morphettville which became one of the best in Australia. In 1878 he was appointed K.C.M.G. and in 1887 G.C.M.G. In 1885 he built a house (later Carminow) on Mount Lofty in Scottish baronial style. He died there on 6 March 1897. His estate was sworn at £615,573 and outside South Australia it probably amounted to some £200,000.

His philanthropy is everywhere evident in South Australia, not least at the University of Adelaide. In 1874 he gave £20,000 to endow chairs in mathematics and general science; in 1883-97 he gave £31,000 to the Medical School, £21,000 to the School of Music and £26,000 for general university purposes. His will also included bequests of £10,000 to Presbyterians, £4000 to Anglicans for their cathedral and £4000 to Methodists for their Prince Alfred College. He left £25,000 for the foundation of Working Men's Homes and £16,000 to hospitals. A statue is in Adelaide.

Elder Smith & Co. Limited: the first hundred years (Adel. 1940); F. Gosse, 'Sir Thomas Elder, G.C.M.G.', PRGSSA, 63 (1962); Observer (Adel), 13 Mar 1897.   FAYETTE GOSSE

ELIOTT, GILBERT (1796-1871), public servant and politician, was born at Stobs, Roxburghshire, Scotland, the third son of Sir William Eliott, sixth baronet, and his wife Mary, née Russell. He entered the army and as a captain in the Royal Artillery served with the occupation forces in France in 1815 and later elsewhere. At Bedrule, Roxburghshire, on 21 April 1830 he married Isabella Lucy, daughter of Robert Elliot, vicar of Askham, Yorkshire.

With his wife and three children he arrived in the *Mary* at Sydney in November 1839. He became a justice of the peace. On the recommendation of the earl of Auckland, a near relation, he was appointed police magistrate at Parramatta by Governor Gipps in June 1842. As visiting justice at the Female Factory he uncovered gross fraud and embezzlement; counter-charges by the superintendent led to an inquiry which found Eliott 'an excellent Public Officer, and a man of unimpeachable integrity'. In 1846 he sought office as comptroller-general of convicts in Van Diemen's Land, but was unsuccessful despite strong support from Gipps and FitzRoy. In January 1854 he became chief of the three commissioners of the city of Sydney. Although this appointment was for six years, a select committee criticized the commissioners' administration and they were replaced in 1857.

Eliott acquired pastoral leases in the Wide Bay area and represented the Burnett district in the New South Wales Legislative Assembly from July to December 1859. His opposition to the separation of Queensland aroused some hostility but in May 1860 he easily won the seat of Wide Bay, a squatter electorate, in the first Queensland Legislative Assembly. Even the Gympie gold rush from 1867 did not shake his hold on the seat. The new assembly had few members with parliamentary experience and so Eliott was speedily chosen as the first Speaker, a post which he retained until his retirement in 1870 without missing a single day's sitting. Always benign and courteous, although firm, he was very popular; one member even started a private subscription for a full-length portrait of Eliott to be presented to him; it is still in Parliament House, though cut down in size. Eliott was approached to accept a knighthood but refused, partly because he was already in line of descent of an old Scottish barony, partly because he felt his means were not adequate to support such a distinction. In 1870 he was given a retirement allowance of £400 a year, and appointed to the Legislative Council. He was appointed C.M.G. in 1871.

Eliott had remained aloof from political controversy except once when, reporting to his constituents after the session of 1862, he spoke very strongly against the way government business was conducted in the assembly. His speech caused a short stir but was soon forgotten. On his property he lived with a quiet dignity and endeared himself to all his neighbours. His retirement was brief. While visiting his son, Gilbert William, a magistrate at Toowoomba, he died suddenly of angina pectoris on 30 June 1871. He was survived by his wife, son and a daughter Frances Willoughby.

HRA (1), 22, 24-25; O. de Satgé, *Pages from the journal of a Queensland squatter* (Lond, 1901); *Qld Guardian*, 18 Oct 1862; *Brisbane Courier*, 16, 19 Jan 1863, 1 July 1871; Governor's dispatches (QA).　　A. A. MORRISON

ELLERY, ROBERT LEWIS JOHN (1827-1908), astronomer and public servant, was born on 14 July 1827 at Cranleigh, Surrey, England, son of John Ellery, surgeon, and his wife Caroline, née Potter. He was trained as a surgeon (M.R.C.S.), but his early interest in astronomy was encouraged by friends at Greenwich Observatory and he was given some access to instruments there. He arrived in the *Moselle* at Melbourne in December 1852 and settled in Williamstown. He wrote to the press in 1853 advocating that an observatory be set up at Williamstown to determine accurate time against which shipmasters in the port could adjust their chronometers. Lieut-Governor La Trobe acted on the suggestion and the observatory was established within the year. Ellery was its first director, a position he retained for forty-two years.

Ellery had a sound appreciation of the directions in which the observatory could be developed, and under his hand it increased in importance in the civil and scientific life of the colony. In addition to his astronomical work he had from the outset made systematic meteorological observations. In 1858 he was appointed to conduct the geodetic survey of the colony, an undertaking which absorbed much of his time until 1874 and which had great influence on the astronomical programmes of the observatory. By 1863 the Williamstown site had become unsuitable and the observatory was moved to the Melbourne Domain where its functions were merged with those of the meteorological and magnetic observatory opened in 1858 on Flagstaff Hill by Professor Neumayer [q.v.]. In 1862, stimulated by the appearance of Donati's comet in 1858, a group of citizens had resumed earlier negotiations to equip the observatory with a major telescope. In 1865, after long discussions, a 48-inch reflector was ordered from Thomas

Grubb in Dublin and arrived in 1868. Until 1908 the Great Melbourne Telescope was the largest in the world, but it ran into trouble from the outset and its failure is said to have retarded the development of large telescopes for thirty years. Its faults lay not so much in the workmanship as in the design. In particular its liability to oscillate in the lightest wind and the susceptibility of the mirrors to tarnish made it almost unmanageable; even Ellery, with his fine instrumental skill, could not do much with it. What he did achieve, sketches of nebulae based on visual observations, was soon made obsolete by the advent of photography for which the telescope could not be used. Ellery had no hand in the design and was one of the few people to emerge with credit from a sorry affair. The telescope was finally acquired by the Mount Stromlo Observatory, where after extensive modification it functions successfully.

Despite the early failure of the telescope, the observatory had won solid repute in the astronomical world by the 1870s. With a staff at one time of twelve and four telescopes the main work developed from providing surveyors with more accurate positions for their reference stars into an extensive programme of mapping the southern skies. Two volumes of star positions, published in 1874 and 1889, constitute Ellery's principal scientific achievement although he published many shorter papers on instrumental problems and such transient phenomena as comets. Similarly the dropping of the Williamstown time-ball became a colony-wide time service, with signals transmitted daily over the telegraph network. The observatory was also the meteorological centre for the colony: it gathered observations and issued forecasts; it collated tidal and magnetic information and finally was responsible for calibrating navigational, surveying and other instruments, functions closely parallel to those of Greenwich Observatory.

Ellery's interests ranged far outside astronomy. A leading member of the colony's scientific community, he was president in 1866-85 of the Royal Society of Victoria which acknowledged that 'his energy long made him the mainspring of our society, and his resourcefulness helped us in many a time of difficulty'. He served on many public bodies, notably as treasurer of the Council of the University of Melbourne, as chairman of the Alfred Hospital, and as a trustee of the Public Library, Gallery and Museum. He was deeply interested and active in the first and later Australian Antarctic Exploration Committees. As early as 1886 he suggested that 'self-registering instruments should be set up on the Antarctic continent

to save a party the trouble and risk of living there during the winter'; seventy years later this plan was put into effect. In 1888 he presided at a Meteorological Conference of directors of Australasian Observatories, held to improve and systematize intercolonial meteorology. In 1873 he helped to establish the Victorian Torpedo Corps (Submarine Mining Engineers) and commanded it until he retired in 1889 as lieut-colonel. In 1885 he was the first president of the Victorian Beekeepers' Club, and edited the *Australian Beekeepers' Journal*.

To his role of scientific pioneer Ellery brought great intelligence, humanity and energy. With invaluable instrumental skill he devised and built an early form of chart recorder for continuous automatic records of quantities such as rainfall and temperature; incidental to this machine he anticipated by several years the invention of the fountain pen. When the Great Telescope became unusable by tarnishing of its mirrors (they were made of a tin-copper alloy known as speculum), Ellery after many trials mastered the technique of repolishing them. By 1890 he could claim that 'the performance of the great telescope is now certainly better than it ever has been'. This would be a noteworthy feat today; for that time it was remarkable. Indeed Ellery was nothing if not versatile. 'He excelled in unexpected and apparently incompatible directions; besides being a good musician, he was a good carpenter . . . a blacksmith, watching him working at an anvil one day, said : "that man has been in the trade; he hammers like a professional"'. To his successor, Baracchi, 'he was one of the originators of every scientific movement in Australia during half a century'. Others emphasized 'the kindly nature and fund of humour' of this 'genial old veteran'. He died in Melbourne on 14 January 1908.

Of his principal honours Ellery was elected a fellow of the Royal Astronomical Society in 1855 and of the Royal Society in 1873, appointed C.M.G. in 1889 and in 1900 was president of the Australasian Association for the Advancement of Science at the Melbourne meeting. In 1853 he had married Amy, daughter of Dr John Shields; she died in 1856. In 1858 he married her sister, Margaret, who died in 1915, survived by one daughter.

Board of Visitors to the Observatory, *Reports* (Melb, 1860-95); H. G. Turner, A *history of the colony of Victoria*, 2 (Lond, 1904); R. A. Swan, *Australia in the Antarctic* (Melb, 1961); Sel cttee on national defences, Evidence, V&P (LA Vic), 1864-65, 2 (D33); C. S. Ross, 'Our observatory: the story of its establishment', VHM, 6 (1917-18); H. Wood, 'Astronomy in Australia', Roy Soc NSW, *Procs*, 84 (1951); Roy

Soc Vic, *Procs*, 21 (1908), p 553; Roy Soc, *Procs*, 82 (1909); *Australasian*, 7, 14 July 1866, 9 Mar 1867, 28 Nov 1868, 22 Oct 1870, 9 Mar 1872, 14 Mar 1885, 27 Feb 1897, 29 June 1901; *Argus*, 12 Jan 1884.　　　　S. C. B. GASCOIGNE

ELLIOTT, SIZAR (1814-1901), merchant and innovator, was born on 13 May 1814 at Burnham, Essex, England, son of John Elliott, flour-miller, and his wife Annie, née Bell. After his father died, he was taken at 4 by his mother to New Brunswick, Canada. There he was educated at the national school and served a seven-year apprenticeship to a merchant-auctioneer. In 1835 he left New Brunswick to join an uncle in Launceston, Van Diemen's Land. Next year he married Sarah Westrip and soon afterwards moved to Sydney, where in 1839 he set up as a grocer. He remained in Sydney until gold was discovered, when he first tried his luck at the Bathurst diggings, then shipped goods to Victoria and finally established a general retail merchant business in Melbourne. Apart from a short stay at Dunedin, New Zealand, in the early 1860s, he lived in Melbourne.

With a strong physique, great energy and passion for scientific experiment, Elliott was above all a tireless advocate of the products of his adopted land. In Sydney his efforts of promotion included colonial wine for the local market, the export of lambskins to China and the import of kauri gum from New Zealand. Particularly notable were his pioneering efforts from 1845 to develop a canned meat export trade in response to the current glut of livestock. He was probably the first in Australia to can meat and was awarded medals at successive Sydney shows. Although he failed commercially he inspired others who were more successful. In Melbourne Elliott's inventive talents won him exhibition medals at various times for tent-making, butter churns, milk pans and wine; in 1859 he had planted a small vineyard at Brighton and for many years devoted much time to fermentation experiments. In 1872 and 1876 he published two editions of *On the introduction of Local Industries into New South Wales*.

Elliott became a public figure of some note in Melbourne. In 1857 he served on the committee to send an expedition to central Australia. Next year he became a Melbourne City councillor and was chiefly responsible for establishing the Public Baths, though he protested bitterly when they were leased to a private contractor known to be 'a molester of ladies'. In 1859 he was appointed a magistrate of the city. In the early 1870s, after his own business had declined, Elliott became a professional fund raiser for the Alfred Hospital. In this role he was among the first to suggest the idea of a 'Hospital Sunday' when church and chapel collections would be donated to hospitals. However, while the Alfred Hospital moved slowly on the idea, the Melbourne Hospital took the initiative, and Elliott lost much of the credit for a device which was to raise large sums for the hospitals.

Elliott's creative efforts faded in the 1870s. His wife died in 1876, survived by two sons and a daughter. He moved to Prahran and lived in retirement though still active physically and as a magistrate. In 1887 he published *Fifty Years of Colonial Life*, and in 1895 the *Prahran Telegraph* ran a series of articles, later published as a pamphlet, on his long and useful life. He died at Prahran on 1 March 1901 and was buried at the Cheltenham cemetery.　　　　E. A. BEEVER

ELLIS, HENRY HAVELOCK (1859-1939), psychologist, critic and editor, was born on 2 February 1859 at Old Croydon, Surrey, England, the eldest child and only son of Edward Peppen Ellis (1827-1914), sea captain, and his wife Susannah (1830-1888), daughter of Captain John Wheatley. In 1866 his father took him in the *Empress* to Sydney. On his return and in the absence of his father Ellis assumed much family responsibility. The influence of his mother's evangelical faith on him was reinforced by the preaching of Rev. John Erck of Merton, but his teacher at The Poplars, Tooting, interested him in wider aspects of religion and introduced him to nineteenth-century literature. On 19 April 1875 Ellis left in his father's *Surry* for Sydney. On the voyage he read widely. He also began a journal which he continued erratically for four years, and consulted it in 1884 for *Kanga Creek* (London, 1922), a much-praised *novelle* based partly on his Australian life; he later used a few incidents in his clinical studies but not, he claimed, in his autobiography begun in 1899 and published as *My Life* in 1940.

Ellis decided to stay in New South Wales. He became a teacher at Fontlands, a private school in Burwood, but lacked qualifications and experience; his salary was reduced and he left at the end of the year. In 1876 he tutored the five children of a retired civil servant at Goonawarrie, near Carcoar. He found the work tolerable enough and revisited Sydney to matriculate at the University of Sydney, but did not proceed to an external course. Despite some material comfort it had been a dark year: he lost much of his faith but not his longing for spiritual assuredness. He retreated again to the country as sole assistant in a Grafton proprietory school. When the owner died, Ellis found himself 'a boy of eighteen—headmaster of a grammar school'. The venture failed and in October he sold out cheaply. He had lodged at Grafton with an auctioneer, with whose daughter he fell in love. He was too reticent to mention the fact but the experience increased his understanding of human affection. On this theme, in his solitude and perplexity, he dwelt more and more.

Back in Sydney, Ellis determined to 'go under the Council [of Education]'. He read hard at the Public Library but disliked his month of training at Fort Street Normal School, where 'the great object is discipline'. He passed his examination and was posted to half-time schools at Sparkes and Junction Creeks, near Scone. He must have been an adequate teacher and, by his own account, was not unhappy. His commonplace books of 1878 reveal intensive reading and a larger interest in natural science. In particular he re-read *Life in Nature* by James Hinton, a physiologist and amateur philosopher, and consulted Ellis Hopkins's edition of Hinton's *Life and Letters*. Hinton's exposition gave the questing Ellis a belief in the inherent righteousness of the search for artistic and scientific truth. The best avenue for his search, Ellis thought, was a medical and not a clerical career. He resolved to return to England and sailed in *La Hogue* in January 1879. On 27 February he confided in his diary: 'These three years I have spent in Australia seem to me like those three during which Paul was in Arabia'. In 1881-89 while studying medicine at St Thomas's Hospital, London, he began editing the 'Mermaid' series of dramatists and then the 'Contemporary Science' series. In 1897-1910 his six-volume *Studies in the Psychology of Sex* appeared; his other publications include *Man and Woman* (1894), *Little Essays of Love and Virtue* (1922) and *Impressions and Comments*, 3 volumes (1914-24). In 1891 he married Edith Oldham Lees, authoress.

Ellis never returned to Australia although he published a paper on 'The Doctrines of the Freud School' in *Transactions of the Ninth Session, Sydney*, 1911, of the Australasian Medical Congress. A photograph of Sparkes Creek, taken by his Australian friend Marjorie Ross, stood by his bedside in his last years. Ellis died without issue on 8 July 1939.

I. Goldberg, *Havelock Ellis, a biographical and critical survey* (Lond, 1926); J. S. Collis, *An artist of life* (Lond, 1959); A. C. Marshall, *Havelock Ellis* (Lond, 1959); H. H. Ellis diaries and commonplace books (ML); records and notes (held by Dr Godfrey Harris, Double Bay, NSW). K. J. CABLE

ELSASSER, CARL GOTTLIEB (1817-1885), musician, was born on 7 June 1817 at Höfingen near Stuttgart, son of Johann Gottlieb Elsässer, teacher, and his wife Johanne, née Belser. Elsässer received his early instruction in music from his father and from the Stuttgart organist Kocher. He completed his studies in Dresden under the minor composer and organist Johann Schneider, returned to Stuttgart, and was active as a conductor and teacher until the political unrest of 1847-48. At this time he replaced the Kapellmeister P. J. von Lindpaintner (1791-1856) who, with his orchestra and the members of the Royal Theatre, was placed under interdict by the King of Württemberg. Late in 1849, after the collapse of the liberal movement in the German States, Elsässer went to England to become music director of a private college run by Dr Heidelmaier at Worksop, Nottinghamshire.

In 1853 Elsässer migrated to Victoria and spent the rest of his life in Melbourne as a music teacher, conductor and composer. The success of some of his pupils, among them Amelia Bailey and Geraldine Warden, speaks for Elsässer's competence as a voice and keyboard teacher.

Retiring in temperament, Elsässer took little part in public life. He conducted the Melbourne Philharmonic Society for one season in 1861 and the opening festival concerts of the German Turnverein next year. He appeared occasionally as guest conductor with various local choral societies but never held a regular position with any of them.

An active composer, he was often represented in contemporary programmes, mostly with part-songs, but also with more ambitious choral and orchestral works. His compositions include the cantata *Praise the Lord* (1860); *Wedding Cantata* (1863), which was performed at Sir Henry Barkly's banquet in honour of the wedding of the prince of Wales; *Peace Festival Cantata*, also known as the *Sieges Cantata* (1871); *Victoria's Dream*, a competition cantata for the Melbourne International Exhibition in 1880; and *Songs of Praise* (1882). Very little of his music was published, however.

A stroke in April 1884 deprived Elsässer of speech but friends supported him until his death on 5 January 1885 at his Hawthorn home. He was buried in the Lutheran section of the Melbourne cemetery. His wife Johanne Louise, née Raff, survived him; they had no children.

Elsässer's impact on music in Australia was probably more generic than personal. With many other emigrant musicians, he brought to Victoria the characteristics of early nineteenth-century German music and helped to form a taste and convention which were perceptibly different from those current in England. This German-oriented movement was never as firmly established in Victoria as it became in South Australia, but its effects persisted well into the twentieth century.

H. M. Humphreys (ed), *Men of the time in Australia: Victorian series*, 2nd ed (Melb, 1882); Musical Soc of Vic, *Catalogue of the musical library* (Melb, 1909), 1st supp (1916), 2nd supp (1920); *Australasian*, 3 June 1871, 3 May 1884, 10 Jan 1885.   KENNETH HINCE

ELSEY, JOSEPH RAVENSCROFT (1834-1857), surgeon, explorer and naturalist, was born on 14 March 1834 in London, the only son of Joseph Ravenscroft Elsey, a Bank of England official. He was educated at Mill Hill School, and trained in medicine at Guy's Hospital (M.B., 1853). In March 1855 he qualified at the Royal College of Surgeons and the College of Chemistry, and soon after was appointed surgeon and naturalist to the North Australian Exploring Expedition, led by A. C. Gregory [q.v.]. Before leaving England in April Elsey sought advice on meteorology from Charles Sturt [q.v.]. In July he reached Melbourne in the *Marco Polo* and went on to join Gregory in Sydney. The expedition, in which Elsey ranked fifth and Ferdinand Mueller [q.v.] sixth, sailed from Port Jackson and reached the mouth of the Victoria River near the end of September. Elsey had made notes on coastal history and natural history, and while quartered at the Victoria was diligent in medical work and the study and collecting of birds and insects; he also bred caterpillars in boxes, gave attention to fish and crocodiles, made geological and meteorological observations, and cultivated vegetables. Some of his most interesting beetles, which frequented treetops, were obtained from the stomachs of high-flying birds. 'You cannot imagine', he wrote to his parents, 'what delight my work as a naturalist affords me. Not a day passes but some wonder or novelty shows itself'.

In June 1856 Elsey, with the two Gregory brothers, Mueller and three stockmen, trekked overland to Brisbane, a journey of more than 2000 miles that took six months. Earlier Elsey had obtained two new species of birds, now known as the lilac-crowned wren and the buff-sided robin, and on the overland journey he discovered a third novelty, the golden-shouldered parrot. These species were named by John Gould [q.v.], who acknowledged the informative nature of numerous field notes furnished by Elsey.

Elsey returned to Sydney and in March 1857 sailed in the *Alnwick Castle* for England. There he was assured that Gregory's tribute to his conduct had been officially noted with 'great satisfaction'. He was then offered appointment as government surgeon at the Seychelles Islands; but his health had become 'seriously and unexpectedly deranged' in London and he went instead to the West Indies, where he hoped to do natural history work in a better climate. He died at St Kitts on 31 December 1857.

The amount and nature of the work done by the youthful Elsey were impressive. He was accorded warm tributes by Gould, by Mueller who named a plant of the genus *Ripogonum* in his honour, and by the zoologist J. E. Gray [q.v.] who gave a new tortoise the generic name *Elseya*. Gregory had given the name Elsey to a tributary of the Roper River, and the pastoral property, Elsey station, established there was the scene of Mrs Aeneas Gunn's *We of the Never-Never*.

J. Gould, *Handbook to the birds of Australia*, 1 (Lond, 1865); A. H. Chisholm, 'J. R. Elsey, surgeon, naturalist, explorer', *Qld Naturalist*, 17 (June 1964) nos 3, 4; J. D. Macdonald and P. R. Colston, 'J. R. Elsey and his bird observations on Gregory's overland expedition, Australia, 1856', *Emu*, 65 (1966) pt 4; A. H. Chisholm, 'J. R. Elsey, explorer of the Never-Never', *JRAHS*, 52 (1966); J. R. Elsey papers (NL); Mueller papers (NL).   A. H. CHISHOLM

ELYARD, WILLIAM (1804-1865), public servant, and SAMUEL (1817-1910), public servant and landscape painter, were the eldest and fourth sons of William Elyard, a half-pay naval surgeon, and his wife Sarah, née Gilbert. Compelled by his health and finances to emigrate to New South Wales, William senior arrived with his family on 18 December 1821, as surgeon-superintendent on the convict ship *John Bull*. William junior was born on 23 May 1804 at Rochester and educated in England. On 6 February 1822 he was appointed temporary clerk in the colonial secretary's office and became second clerk on 1 October. In February 1841 when T. C. Harington [q.v.] resigned, Elyard was already doing much of the executive work of the office. His promotion to chief clerk, when the assistant secretaryship was abolished in the name of economy, was a recognition of the existing state of affairs rather than a fundamental change. Elyard was an important junior link in the Macleay-Darling administrative revolution. On 26 June 1856, as a result of the change to responsible government he was appointed under-secretary. His long service in the colonial secretary's office provided administrative continuity at a critical transitionary time.

Elyard died unmarried and in office on 20 March 1865 and was buried at St Peter's Anglican Church, Cook's River. His funeral cortège, which 'extended the entire length of William-street', was a tribute to 'the importance of his services'. He left most of his estate, consisting of land at Balmain and on the Shoalhaven, to his brother Alfred, but made provision for the children of his late brother Arthur.

Samuel was born on 9 May 1817 on the Isle of Wight. He was educated at Mr Gilchrist's school and the Australian College where he showed talent at portrait painting. He then studied under Conrad Martens [q.v.] and taught drawing. He sought secure employment and on 16 April 1837 was appointed an extra clerk in the colonial secretary's office. On 1 January 1846 he was promoted to second clerk, from which position he was retired on 18 August 1868 with a pension. From his twenties, when he studied under J. S. Prout [q.v.], he specialized in landscape painting in water-colours and oils: he 'always painted his studies directly from nature in colours, and of a large size'. He exhibited in Sydney in 1847 and 1857 and in Paris in 1867. Some of his works are in the Dixson galleries, Sydney. Interested in photography, he himself printed and published facsimiles of his work as *Scenery of Shoalhaven* (Nowra, 1892).

In the 1840s Samuel became mentally disturbed and his brother arranged frequent leave in the country. On 10 April 1849, while delirious from drugs, he went through a form of marriage with Angelina Mary Hughes Hallett, née Scott, an alleged prostitute. He later repudiated the marriage on the ground of his insanity and accused her of blackmail. He published many pamphlets to vindicate himself and, at the same time, to convert the Jews to Protestantism. In mid-1857 he started a journal, the *Salem Standard*, and imported a press with Hebrew type. He suffered from prophetic and royal delusions, but moderated after his retirement and became an Anglican lay preacher and a justice of the peace. He died at Nowra on 23 October 1910.

F. McCaffrey, *History of Illawarra and its pioneers* (Syd, 1922); *Empire* (Syd), 21 Mar 1865; *SMH*, 22 Mar 1865; *Nowra Leader*, 28 Oct 1910; *Bulletin*, 3 Nov 1910; Col Sec in-letters, memorials (NSWA); Elyard papers (ML and Dixson Lib, Syd); MS and printed cats (ML and Dixson Lib, Syd).   M. J. SACLIER

EMBLING, THOMAS (1814-1893), medical practitioner and parliamentarian, was born on 26 August 1814 at Oxford, England, son of John Embling, breechesmaker, and his wife Sarah, née Edwards. Apprenticed at 16 to an apothecary, he studied medicine in London (M.R.C.S., 1837) and became a licentiate of the Society of Apothecaries in 1838. He went into practice at Brompton. On 1 August 1839 he married Jane Webb Chinnock, an upholsterer's daughter; they had three sons and four daughters.

Both Embling and his wife suffered from 'pulmonary affections'; they decided to migrate to Australia and arrived in Melbourne in 1851. Embling had acquired from visits to Hanwell Asylum a pioneering interest in the 'moral treatment' of insanity, and in January 1852 he became the first resident medical officer to Yarra Bend Lunatic Asylum. His first impressions 'were those of great astonishment not unmixed with pain . . . I saw much that was incomprehensible, and much disreputable'. As a matter of principle he removed manacles and other instruments of physical coercion from patients, but the lay superintendent countermanded his orders. His reforms drew the wrath of the colonial surgeon and a select committee of inquiry into the asylum in August found evidence of mismanagement although it reported that Embling's 'whole offence' was 'too much conscientiousness'. Embling resigned and returned to private practice at Gore Street, Fitzroy, where he devoted much attention to the suffering poor.

Embling publicly espoused the popular movement at Eureka in December 1854 and took over the chair at a public meeting which passed resolutions in favour of the diggers' cause. At the Legislative Council elections in 1855 Embling opposed one of Hotham's territorial magistrates and won the North Bourke seat with a triumphant majority. Next year he supported the eight-hours movement and is credited with coining the slogan, 'Eight hours labour, eight hours recreation, eight hours rest'. In the first elections under responsible government he successfully campaigned for the working-class stronghold of Collingwood on a moderately radical programme; as an Independent by faith he won strong support from Dissenters by his vigorous opposition to state aid to religion. In the House Embling twice voted unavailingly to keep the Haines [q.v.] ministry in office. In 1858 his state aid abolition bill lapsed, and as an ardent protectionist he proposed in 1860 a select committee on tariffs which was postponed. At times he displeased some Collingwood radicals by commending too warmly the rights of property. The Nicholson [q.v.] Land Act, he thought, would show people 'the mistake they had made in listening to a class of agitators'. In the 1861 election he opposed the Heales [q.v.] ministry and was defeated. Two years later at a meeting of the second Anti-Transportation League Embling pledged that 600

Collingwood men 'were prepared to go to Western Australia and prevent the landing of the convicts'. Despite the Protection League's doubts about his loyalty his candidature was endorsed in 1866 and he was re-elected. In the following political turmoil Embling was rumoured to have been given the chance to form a cabinet but he was too unreliable as a party man to succeed. Increasingly he dissented from McCulloch's [q.v.] financial policies and at the next elections withdrew from politics.

Embling returned to medicine and his diverse enthusiasms: he advocated penny banks, bathing, medical certification of death, northern exploration, the introduction of camels and llamas, and a transcontinental railway. He died of 'senile debility' at Hawthorn on 17 January 1893, survived by his wife, two daughters and two sons, both doctors. He left instructions that his burial service should be Anglican, the minister an Independent and the formalities those of the Funeral Reform Association. He left an estate of more than £22,000.

Opponents accused Embling of wanting force of character and of 'trimming', but he was an opportunist only in the party political sense, for the cast of his mind was utopian. His eccentricity often derived from superior rationality and independence: for instance, at a time when 'Chinamen' were thought to be inferior undesirables, he welcomed their immigration. As a friend of generous causes he 'wished to make himself useful to the public'.

G. Serle, *The golden age* (Melb, 1963); K. M. Benn, 'The moral versus medical controversy: an early struggle in colonial Victorian psychiatry', *MJA*, 2 Feb 1957; *Argus*, 14 July 1853; *Australasian*, 21 Jan, 25 Feb 1893; G. R. Quaife, The nature of political conflict in Victoria 1856-57 (MA thesis, Univ Melb, 1964).

RICHARD KENNEDY

ERSKINE, JOHN ELPHINSTONE (1805-1887), naval officer, was born on 13 July 1805 at Cardross, Scotland, son of David Erskine and his wife Keith, daughter of the 11th Baron Elphinstone. He entered the navy on 6 May 1819, was commissioned in 1826 and assumed his first command of the gunboat *Arachne* on the Jamaica station in 1829. After service in the Mediterranean, he was promoted captain on 28 June 1839 and served as flag captain to his cousin, Sir Charles Adam, on the West Indies station. From 1845 to 1847 he was on half-pay and in February 1848 was appointed to the *Havannah* as senior officer on the Australian station. Soon after his arrival Erskine made a tour of Samoa, Tonga, Fiji, the New Hebrides, the Loyalty Islands and New

Caledonia between 25 June and 7 October 1849, and next year visited the Solomons and other islands. An account of the first cruise was published in 1853 as *Journal of a Cruise among the Islands of the Western Pacific . . . in Her Majesty's Ship Havannah*. Lively and intelligent, Erskine was popular in Sydney society, became friendly with the Macarthur [q.v.] family and in 1851 published his description of a visit to the goldfields in A *Short Account of the late discoveries of Gold in Australia*. In that year, he contributed an account of his two Pacific voyages to the *Journal* of the Royal Geographical Society.

Erskine returned to England in 1852, entrusted by Sir William Denison with a verbal message to the Colonial Office secretary on Tasmanian affairs; after serving in the Baltic through the Crimean war he was appointed rear-admiral in 1857, A.D.C. to the Queen and second-in-command of the Channel Squadron. He was appointed vice-admiral in 1864 and in 1865 was elected M.P. for Stirlingshire.

With experience of naval anti-slavery operations in the West Indies and the effects of European penetration in the Pacific, he joined the Aborigines Protection Society and became a parliamentary leader of the influential lobby working for the Pacific Islanders Protection Act of 1872. Defeated in the elections of 1874 by Henry Campbell-Bannerman, he retired from the navy and lived in London till his death on 23 June 1887.

JAMES ELPHINSTONE ERSKINE (1838-1911), son of John's brother James, was born on 2 December 1838. He joined the navy in 1852, became a captain in November 1868 and in 1880 served as private secretary to Lord Northbrook, first lord of the Admiralty. In January 1882 he became commodore on the Australian station and in 1884 declared a British protectorate over the south coast of New Guinea. His speech at the ceremony has been considered ever since as a declaration of rights for the indigenous people. On returning to England he became A.D.C. to the Queen, was appointed rear-admiral and served as junior sea lord in 1886. In 1888-91 he was in charge of the Irish coast and in 1895 became commander-in-chief of the North America and West Indies station. Two years later he was knighted and promoted admiral, then after serving as A.D.C. to the King, he became an admiral of the fleet and retired in December 1908. He died at Venlaw, Peeblesshire, on 25 July 1911. In 1885 he had married Margaret Eliza Constable; their son also joined the navy.

C. E. Lyne, *New Guinea. An account of the establishment of the British protectorate*

(Lond, 1885); J. Inglis, *In the New Hebrides* (Lond, 1887); J. W. Lindt, *Picturesque New Guinea* (Lond, 1887); O. W. Parnaby, *Britain and the labor trade in the southwest Pacific* (Durham, North Carolina, 1964); PD (HC), 1872-73; *Colonial Intelligencer*, 1874-78; *The Times*, 4 July 1887, 26 July 1911; W. G. Lawes papers (ML); Vigors journal, G2261 (NL); MS cat under J. E. Erskine (ML); CO 422/3, 4.

H. J. GIBBNEY

ESMOND, JAMES WILLIAM (1822-1890), gold discoverer, was born on 11 April 1822 at Enniscorthy, County Wexford, Ireland, son of Michael Esmond, merchant, and his wife Mary, née Moran. He migrated to Port Phillip in 1840, worked on Westernport stations and then drove a weekly mail coach between Buninyong and the Horsham region. In 1849 he was stirred by news of gold in California and decided to try his luck there. He arrived too late to prospect much on his own as the best claims were occupied, so he worked as an overseer. In 1850 he sailed for Sydney in the same ship as E. H. Hargraves [q.v.].

Esmond returned to Buninyong and was contracting on stations when he met Dr George Hermann Bruhn, a German physician and geologist who was examining the area. He told Esmond of quartz reef he had seen at Burn Bank near Clunes. Esmond hurried there with his workmate, James Pugh; satisfied that the area was auriferous they enlisted the sawyers, Burns and Kelly, to work the claim. On 5 July 1851 Esmond went to Geelong and showed a few ounces of their gold to Alfred Clarke of the *Geelong Advertiser*. To questions about the locality of the find his reply was 'up among the mountains'. He went to Melbourne to buy iron for a cradle and returned through Geelong where on 15 July he told Clarke the locality of the find. Clarke published the news on 22 July and the rush started. On 22 August Esmond sent Clarke fourteen ounces of gold which were later sold in Melbourne, the first marketed in Victoria.

Esmond later moved to Ballarat where he became an influential miner. He fought as section commander under Peter Lalor [q.v.] at the Eureka Stockade. In 1865 he started a venture known as the New North Clunes Goldmining Co.; it was not a success though he persevered and sank some deep shafts. He finally sold it in desperation, only to see the buyers strike it rich in a few months. In his last years Esmond suffered much from Bright's disease and had financial difficulties. Because of his service to the community in first discovering gold, government aid was sought for him, but without success. A public subscription for him at Ballarat had raised over £150 when he died on 3 December 1890. The money was used to build a cottage for his widow Margaret, née McAuliffe; they had three sons and six daughters.

Esmond's repute as the first to discover gold in Victoria is doubtful. William Campbell [q.v.] and others had found gold before him but kept it secret. In 1853-54 the Legislative Council select committee on claims for the discovery of gold in Victoria accepted Esmond's evidence that he had found gold on 28 June 1851 and that his site was revealed on 22 July. However, Louis John Michel had made his find and given full particulars of his site at Anderson Creek (Warrandyte) on 5 July. The committee recommended rewards of £1000 to Michel for discovering and publicizing an available goldfield, to Esmond 'as the first actual producer of alluvial gold for the market'; other rewards were recommended for Campbell, Thomas Hiscock and Bruhn but were not paid for ten years. In defence of Esmond's claim, his find was worth-while and was later sold in Melbourne, while Michel's was very small and given to the mayor of Melbourne as a souvenir. Esmond's find also led to the development of one of the world's greatest gold-producing centres at Ballarat, whereas the goldfields of the Upper Yarra were never important.

A. Sutherland, *Victoria and its metropolis*, 1 (Melb, 1888); V&P (LA Vic), 1859-60, 1, 310; L. Cranfield, 'The first discovery of gold in Victoria', VHM, 31 (1960); *Geelong Advertiser*, 1 Feb 1856; *Argus*, 5 Dec 1890.

LOUIS R. CRANFIELD

EVANS, GEORGE SAMUEL (1802-1868), barrister, editor and politician, was born on 3 June 1802, son of George Evans of London. He was educated at Merchant Taylors' School and the University of Glasgow (M.A., 1827; LL.D., 1830). A scholar of the classics and uncertain of his vocation, he was ordained a Congregational minister, spent six months in 1828 as headmaster of Mill Hill School and then decided on a legal career. He entered Lincoln's Inn in 1832 and in 1837 was called to the Bar, but before he could establish himself he became enthusiastic for New Zealand colonization.

Active in the New Zealand Co. from the first, Evans sailed with his wife Jessie in the *Adelaide* to Port Nicholson (Wellington) in 1839. He was a member of the colonists' self-governing committee and their chief judicial authority as 'umpire'. In 1840 he was made a magistrate and played a leading role in the colonists' efforts to validate their land purchases. Returning to London in 1844, he continued to work for New Zealand and resumed his interrupted legal career until ill health forced him to leave England. He went to New Zealand in 1852 but left in 1853 for Victoria.

Evans quickly became prominent in Victorian public life: the learned doctor of laws and Greek scholar, boasting of his massive work in making notes for a great history in continuation of Gibbon, was a rare figure amongst the colonists. As editor of the *Herald* in 1855-58 he wrote about a thousand leading articles, besprinkled with classical allusions; for his ponderous style and manner, his staff nicknamed him 'Bozzy'. The same style marked his parliamentary oratory. He represented Richmond in the Victorian Legislative Assembly in 1856-59, Avoca in 1859-61 and Maryborough in 1861-64. Always eloquent but apt to bore the assembly with his weighty periods and his constant reference to the virtues of the British Constitution, Evans was a rather comical figure and a source of endless delight to Melbourne *Punch*.

His political career was undistinguished. According to an obituarist, he laid 'more store by the wants of office than was consistent with a high order of political usefulness'. His political views, broadly liberal, were conveniently flexible when salary beckoned. He eagerly accepted office as postmaster-general under O'Shanassy [q.v.] in 1858, and took lands as well when Duffy [q.v.] resigned in 1859, ensuring re-election by his startling adoption of the Land Convention's policy. Evans lost office in 1859, but was again postmaster-general in the third O'Shanassy government in 1861-63. Defeated at the 1864 elections, Evans returned to Wellington in 1865 and successfully prosecuted legal claims which secured his right to much landed property. Evans married twice but had no children; his second wife Harriett, née Strother, died in Wellington on 31 March 1866, and Evans died there on 23 September 1868.

J. L. Forde, *The story of the Bar of Victoria* (Melb, 1913); D. Blair, 'Three Melbourne barristers', *Centennial Mag*, 2 (1889-90); *Argus*, 6 Apr 1859; *Australasian*, 17 Oct 1868; MS cat under G. S. Evans (ML); CO 309/53, letter 25 Oct 1860 and minutes.

JANICE BURNS WOODS

EVANS, MATILDA JANE (1827-1886), teacher and novelist under the pseudonym Maud Jeanne Franc, was born on 7 August 1827 at Peckham Park, Surrey, England, the elder of two daughters of Henry Congreve, schoolmaster. An unfortunate investment robbed her father of a large inheritance and in 1852 he sailed with his family for South Australia where a son had already migrated

in 1849; Matilda Jane's mother died at sea aged 49 and her father died by 'visitation of God' on 26 December 1852 at North Adelaide.

Responsible for the younger children, Matilda Jane was engaged as a governess and later opened a school at Mount Barker. There she wrote her first novel, *Marian, or The Light of Some One's Home*; this tale of Australian bush life was first published in 1861 by the local printer, Arthur Waddy, but ran to several editions in London. On 16 February 1860 at Zion Chapel, Adelaide, she married Ephraim Evans, Baptist minister and widower, of Nuriootpa. He died on 6 April 1863, and her *Beatrice Melton's Discipline* (1880) describes his last years. He had made little provision for his wife and four children, but a public subscription helped Matilda Jane to start a school at Nuriootpa. She then opened a ladies' school at Angaston and in 1868 moved to Angaston House at North Adelaide. Soon afterwards she gave up teaching and devoted her time to the North Adelaide Baptist Church as a deaconess and to writing. She contributed many short stories and articles to local journals, and wrote fourteen novels; some appeared first locally but all were published in London by Sampson Lowe & Co., and ran to at least two editions. In 1888 a collected edition of her Australian tales was produced by her London publishers. Her books were favoured as Sunday school prizes for their strong gospel message, and she found her inspiration and her characters in her own experience and locality. She was also devoted to the cause of temperance. She died of peritonitis at her home in Prospect on 22 October 1886, survived by her two sons, Henry Congreve (1861-1899), who at 24 was chief of staff of the *Advertiser* and in 1889 founded *Quiz*, a social and political weekly, and William James (1863-1904), who became a journalist, collaborated with his mother in the collected short stories, *Christmas Bells* (1882), and wrote *Rhymes without Reason* (1898). They inherited her copyrights, manuscripts and most of her books, but her canary and 'all Miss Warner's books' went to her sister, and other small items to her brothers, her stepson and stepdaughter.

Register (Adel), 25 Apr 1863; *Observer* (Adel), 30 Oct 1886; *Mount Barker Courier*, 27 June 1930.   H. J. FINNIS

EVERARD, JOHN (1825-1886), businessman and politician, was born at Groby, Leicestershire, England, and baptized on 7 April 1825 at near-by Ratby, son of Thomas Everard, farmer, and his wife Mary, née

Breedon. He sailed in the *Adelaide* and arrived at Melbourne on 11 May 1853; a fellow passenger was James McCulloch [q.v.]. Everard first entered business as a merchant and later turned to stock and share broking in partnership with W. L. Horton, becoming a leading member of the Stock Exchange formed in 1861.

As a politician Everard first came to prominence in connexion with the Land Convention and the movement for liberal land settlement laws. In January 1858 he was returned for Rodney as one of the first Conventionist members of the Legislative Assembly. He was re-elected in 1859 but resigned at the end of the year to give Wilson Gray [q.v.] a seat. In 1861 he was returned for North Gippsland, although he did not campaign there. However, he was not sworn in because he had become insolvent when the position of certain Maldon mining companies, with which he was closely connected, deteriorated suddenly in August. His fortunes soon recovered and he began tea broking, at first with J. C. Robertson, and from January 1863 on his own. In April 1864 he was re-elected for North Gippsland at a by-election. He did not stand at the general elections of 1864 and 1866, but in March 1868 was returned for Collingwood. Two hundred of his constituents clamoured for his resignation in October 1869 but he defended himself as an independent liberal reformer in a *Tract for Stirring Times* and in letters to the press. He was defeated for Rodney in 1871 and for Mornington in 1872 but was again successful at Collingwood in 1874. However, in July he again had to resign because of insolvency through losses of over £12,000 in mining speculations and in guarantees on tea ventures. After this setback he concentrated on tea broking and auctioneering. He died at South Yarra on 29 August 1886 and was buried in the Anglican section of the Melbourne general cemetery.

His political principles were always radical and democratic and his devotion to them seems to have affected his business interests. He fought hardest for favourable land laws but was also active in organizations urging protection, the eight-hour system and other liberal causes. He never accepted ministerial office though it was offered to him. His wide influence in politics won him the nickname of 'Warwick'.

At Melbourne in 1856 he had married Mary, daughter of Edward Moss and Jane, née Quinn, of Gortmore, Tyrone, Ireland; they had one daughter and seven sons, one of whom, William Hugh, became Speaker of the Victorian Legislative Assembly. After his wife died, he married at Fitzroy on 19 February 1875 Faith, daughter of William

Cann and Sarah, née Yeandle; they had at least three children.

H. M. Humphreys (ed), *Men of the time in Australia: Victorian series*, 1st ed (Melb, 1878); *Age*, 23 Aug 1861, 31 Aug 1886; *Daily Telegraph* (Melb), 20 Oct 1869, 11 July 1874.

ROBERT A. JOHNSON

EVERETT, GEORGE (1811-1893), JOHN (1816-1902) and EDWIN (1822-1909), pastoralists, were born at Biddesden House near Ludgershall, Wiltshire, England, sons of Joseph Hague Everett (M.P. 1810-12) and his wife Margaret, née Cook. George and John arrived at Sydney in October 1838 in the *Hope*, and later squatted at Ollera (sweet water) fourteen miles from Guyra, in the New England district. When Edwin joined them in 1842 the property was registered in their joint names. George returned to England in 1856 and John in 1858 when he became London agent for the firm. John visited Ollera in 1881 with his son Arthur who took over the managership in 1890. Edwin stayed at Ollera and in 1862 bought the adjoining station of Tenterden.

The Everetts began with 451 sheep; by 1854 Ollera had a registered area of 74,800 acres and carried 8000 sheep and 1200 cattle. The predominant interest was sheep but Hereford cattle became important in the Rocky River gold rush of the 1850s. The station carried 46,000 sheep and 4000 cattle in 1877, but by 1892 free selection had reduced it to 18,000 acres and the sheep to 14,000. The Everetts were excellent pastoralists, keeping abreast of the developing wool industry with marked financial success. The social organization of Ollera was run on paternalistic and almost feudal lines. From the first they brought out migrant families, settled them as shepherds and encouraged them to run a few sheep for themselves and to provide farm produce as well as services for the station. Wages were above average, banking facilities were provided, cottages were built and the station store supplied all needs. By the 1860s Ollera had schools and a fine church; sports and social activities were also encouraged. With work available for all, the families kept together and intermarried, strong in their loyalty to each other and the firm. Free selectors caused no rancour since nine-tenths of them came from the shepherd families and the quixotic Edwin helped his old retainers to choose their land wisely and sometimes gave them part of the deposit. Most of the selectors continued to do seasonal work on Ollera and had the use of station facilities at a reasonable fee. After 1890 the transfer of selectors' land and the rise of trade unions eroded the old social pattern, but respect and affection between descendants of the Everetts and of the old families is still evident.

George died at Bournemouth, England, on 23 September 1893, leaving most of his estate of £23,000 to his wife Arabella Elizabeth, née Hanmer, his daughter and three sons. On 18 September 1858 at Edinburgh John married Helen Wauhope; they had four sons and three daughters. He died in November 1902 at Totton near Southampton. His second son Arthur managed Ollera for many years after 1890 and was followed by his son Thomas Arundel. Edwin died a bachelor at Tenterden station on 12 November 1909, leaving most of his estate worth £31,000 to his nephew Arthur.

Portraits of John and Edwin are at Ollera, together with many other station paintings.

A. V. Cane, Ollera 1838 to 1900: a study of a sheep station (MA thesis, Univ Syd, 1949); Ollera MS (Univ New England Archives).

ALAN V. CANE

EWAN, JAMES (1843-1903), financier, was born on 18 July 1843 near Leith Walk, Edinburgh, son of James Ewan, headmaster and author of geography books, and his wife Mary, née Blair. In March 1849 he arrived at Sydney with his parents in the *Zemindar*. He was educated at his father's school in York Street and at the West Maitland Presbyterian High School. In November 1857 he entered the warehouse of his brother-in-law, John Frazer [q.v.], where he became a partner in 1869 with another brother-in-law, James Watson [q.v.], in John Frazer & Co., wholesale merchants. After Frazer's death in 1884 Ewan and Watson ran the firm until it was liquidated in 1891, 'all the partners retiring on fairly ample fortunes'. They remained trustees of Frazer's vast estate which included five important city buildings. On 25 April 1875 Ewan became a director of the United Insurance Co. and was its chairman in 1877-1903. In January 1878 he became a director of the Australasian Steam Navigation Co. and chairman six months later. He was also a director of the Waratah Coal Co. and sat on the committee of the Chamber of Commerce. By 1879 he had moved to Ranelagh, Darling Point. In March 1882 on medical advice he reluctantly agreed to visit the East and England, after threatening to stay in Sydney if Watson resigned the Treasury to attend to the additional business caused by his absence.

In January 1884 Ewan resumed the unenviable post of chairman of the A.S.N. Co. It had paid no dividends for many years and its shares were far below par. Since the seamen's strike in 1879, which had been directed against the company, and the seamen's agreement of 1884, he foresaw more trouble with labour organizations and decided to realize the company's assets. Its fleet was sold for £200,000, and the appreciation of its landed property and wharves enabled the company to pay its shareholders over 20s. in the £. Ewan himself negotiated with Sir Henry Parkes [q.v.] the sale of their Circular Quay wharf property to the government for £275,000. After the liquidation Ewan retained his interest in shipping and owned with Watson the Grafton wharf property, which was leased to Burns, Philp & Co. for £14,000 a year until resumed by the government in 1900. In 1885 he became a director of the City Bank and as its chairman in 1892-1903 guided it through the crisis of 1893; it was one of four banks in Sydney which did not close their doors, although its dividend was reduced to 4 per cent.

Ewan was public spirited and 'privately an ardent politician' but he never tried to enter parliament. He was a magistrate, a trustee of the Savings Bank of New South Wales, a director and honorary treasurer of Sydney Hospital, a member of the Sydney Benevolent Society and on the committee of the Sydney Bethel Union in 1876. He largely contributed to building the Nepean Cottage Hospital and to Hope House, a convalescent home next to Glenleigh, his country home on the Nepean River. By 1880 he had acquired two stations in Queensland, Gunnawarra, carrying 10,000 cattle, and Waterview; in 1891 he bought Gunningbland near Forbes and later acquired three other stations which were managed by his sons. In 1899 he shore over 60,000 sheep with machines.

Ewan was a member of a tightly-knit family group of Scottish merchants. With 'keen business ability', he was a 'greatly trusted financial man'. He was also a staunch member and a generous supporter of the Presbyterian Church. He died of influenza on 1 August 1903 at Glenleigh and was buried in the Presbyterian section of Rookwood cemetery. He had suffered from chronic bronchitis and nephritis for thirty years. He was survived by his wife Marion Jane, daughter of Rev. John Reid and sister of G. H. Reid, whom he had married in 1872, and by their two sons and six daughters. He left nearly £48,000 to his widow, providing that she did not remarry, and to his children; his eldest son had been disinherited in 1902.

Report of the Royal Commission on strikes (Syd, 1891), p 196; *The City Bank of Sydney 1863-1913* (Syd, 1913); V&P (LA NSW), 1887-88,

3, 981; *Banking and Insurance Review*, Sept 1900, Aug 1903; *SMH*, 3 Aug 1903; Parkes letters (ML).   MARTHA RUTLEDGE

EWART, DAVID (1838-1927), educationist, was born on 31 August 1838 at Alyth, Perthshire, Scotland, son of Thomas Ewart, farmer, and his wife Grace, née McLagan. He was educated at the village Free Church school where he became a monitor and pupil teacher and then won a Queen's scholarship to Moray House, Edinburgh. He completed the course in 1858 and matriculated at the University of Edinburgh but lack of funds forced him to leave the university and take up teaching. He was appointed to the Free Church school in Stuartfield, Aberdeenshire, and in 1861-63 had charge of the Free John Knox School in Aberdeen.

He arrived in Queensland in September 1864 and, while waiting for a vacancy with the Board of General Education, lumped cargo on Raff's [q.v.] wharf. He was appointed assistant master at the Normal School, then went to Eagle Farm and to the head teachership of Rockhampton Central Boys' School. His ability impressed the general inspector, Randal MacDonnell [q.v.], and led to his appointment in 1873 as organizing master and acting inspector. He was promoted district inspector in 1874, senior district inspector in 1876, registrar in 1879 and general inspector in 1882. In 1905-09 he was the first director of education.

His major influence on Queensland education was felt during his years as general inspector when J. G. Anderson [q.v.] was under-secretary of the Department of Public Instruction. Ewart's limited views on pri-mary education, his lack of appreciation of developments in secondary and technical education and his unfavourable reports after visits to the southern colonies retarded educational advance in Queensland. His autocratic manner in dealing with teachers and their problems was criticized in 1888 by the royal commissioners on the civil service who reported that he had so exercised his powers 'as to bring the staff into a frame of mind very little short of rebellion'. While his annual reports had literary merit they also showed that by 1901 there was mounting criticism of Queensland's outdated primary syllabus, method of inspection, over-centralized administration and lack of modern teacher-training facilities. Not until Ewart retired in 1909 and was replaced by R. H. Roe and J. D. Story did Queensland's education system advance towards those operating elsewhere in Australia.

Ewart died in Toowoomba on 4 May 1927 and was buried in the Toowong cemetery, Brisbane. At Aberdeen in 1864 he had married Jane Milne; of their three sons and three daughters, he was survived by William James, a Queensland government architect; David, a senior member of Dalgety's [q.v.]; and Helen who married A. O. Jackson, manager of the Queensland National Bank, Toowoomba.

E. R. Wyeth, *Education in Queensland*, ACER res series no 67 (Melb, c1953); R. Goodman, *Secondary education in Queensland, 1860-1960* (Canberra, 1968); Roy Com on educational institutions, Evidence, V&P (LA Qld), 1875, 2, 192; Roy Com on establishing a university, Evidence, V&P (LA Qld), 1891, 3, 958.

RUPERT GOODMAN

F

FACY, PETER (1822-1890), entrepreneur and temperance worker, was born on 6 October 1822 at Ashburton, Devon, England, son of Peter Facy, woolstapler, and his wife Mary. He arrived with his parents at Hobart Town on 23 January 1825 in the steerage of the *Cumberland*. Peter Facy senior began business as a tanner and fellmonger and profited as one of the colony's first wool exporters; his partners included William Kermode and Henry Hopkins [qq.v.]. He died on 15 June 1832 survived by his widow, two daughters and three sons, Joseph, John and Peter. The sons maintained the business until 1848 when, with the realized capital from its sale, Peter and Joseph went to England.

Peter Facy junior returned to Hobart in the *Jane Frances* in 1849 and entered business with Captain William Fisher as shipowner, sawmill proprietor and timber merchant engaged mostly in intercolonial trade. He was a shareholder in and later senior director of the Tasmanian Steam Navigation Co., the most successful of the shipping companies expanded in the gold rushes. He became president of the Hobart Mutual Building Society and a director of the Bank of Van Diemen's Land in which his family held many shares. Facy retained a lifelong interest in the shipping of Hobart, owning the barques *Kassa, Wild Wave* and *Pet*, the barquentine *Guiding Star*, the steamship *Pinafore*, and the trading ketches *Hero, Priscilla* and *Huon Chief*. He became the local expert on lighthouses, a warden of the Hobart Marine Board and a member of the Consolidated Board which administered Tasmania's lights. Facy personally promoted the building of the system of lights on the Mersey and particularly the lighthouse on the Mersey Bluff at Devonport.

In 1846 Facy helped G. W. Walker and James Bonwick [qq.v.] to found the Van Diemen's Land Total Abstinence Society. He was treasurer of the Tasmanian Temperance Alliance for thirty years and in 1869-90 edited the temperance monthly, *People's Friend*. He was one of the first in Hobart to join the Rechabites and was treasurer for the Southern Cross District in 1858-70. When the Good Templar movement reached Tasmania from America in 1874, Facy and his partner Fisher joined the new Haste to the Rescue Lodge and Facy became its grand treasurer. He was a member of the Congregational Church, a committee member of the Bible Society and a justice of the peace from 1883. He was also an enthusiastic cricketer, a committee member of the Glee Club and an exhibiting member of the Amateurs, Gardeners and Cottagers Horticultural Society. Quiet and unpretentious, he worked to achieve what he conceived to be good ends in many diverse fields and found deep satisfaction in involvement with local affairs. He died on 5 February 1890 at his home in Hampden Road unaware that both the Tasmanian Steam Navigation Co. and the Bank of Van Diemen's Land, the piers of his world, would soon cease to exist. He was interred in the Congregational burial ground at New Town and a memorial in the Melville Street Temperance Hall recalls his role as treasurer to its building fund.

On 5 September 1850 Facy married Elizabeth, the second daughter of James Vautin of the Imperial Audit Department. One of their two sons, also Peter, became secretary of the Tasmanian Steam Navigation Co. and an active licensing law reformer.

Hobart Town Courier, 15 June 1832; *Mercury*, 6 Feb 1890; *People's Friend*, Feb, Mar 1890.   PETER BOLGER

FAIRBAIRN, GEORGE (1816-1895), pastoralist, was born on 28 April 1816 in Berwickshire, Scotland, son of John Fairbairn, sheep farmer, and his wife Jessie, née Johnston. He applied successfully as a shepherd for a free passage to South Australia, where he arrived in January 1839 but soon moved to the Port Phillip District. He managed the Ballan run for eighteen months and after a year in Melbourne became manager of a station on the Glenelg River in September 1842. There he stayed until 1845 when he bought a share in the near-by Fulham run. By August 1846, when George Armytage [q.v.] bought Fulham, Fairbairn had £1000 and 2000 sheep. He had tried to become a partner of Rev. John Lillie [q.v.], but the arrangements broke down and he bought a share in Congbool station. In the gold rush Fairbairn tried his luck at Bendigo and then became a successful gold buyer at Ballarat. In February 1854 he married Virginia Charlotte, daughter of George Armytage; soon afterwards he took his bride to England.

They returned to Victoria in 1861 and Fairbairn bought Eli Elwah station in the Riverina; he continued to buy other unimproved runs in eastern Australia. By 1870 he held several million acres. Tough in constitution—in old age he had a damaged

147

hand amputated without anaesthetic—he travelled thousands of miles by buggy to inspect his properties, always taking with him a Bible, Johnson's *Dictionary* and Boswell's *Life of Johnson*, reading each in turn. In November 1864 he was elected for Dundas and Follett in the Victorian Legislative Assembly; a silent member, he voted faithfully for the McCulloch [q.v.] government. He found politics not to his taste and withdrew in January 1866 although he served long in the Corio Shire Council. Fairbairn was claimed to be one of the four Australians who owned over a million sheep, but he deserved more repute for his pioneering spirit. He developed his runs by wire fencing and watering each paddock, and was an early user of wire netting which he produced expensively by 'puddled galvanizing'. He was also an advocate for exporting frozen meat. His enthusiasm survived the unsuccessful consignment in 1873 and was vindicated in 1879-80 by the *Strathleven* shipment. He became a director of the Australian Frozen Meat Export Co. and supported the canning industry. He also helped to promote the Apollo Stearine Candle Co. and used its products lavishly in his home. Among his many other business interests he was a director of the Union Bank of Australia and the Trust and Agency Co., Melbourne.

In his last years Fairbairn lived in retirement at Lara station near Geelong, and his pastoral empire was divided among his children. He died suddenly at Queenscliff on 18 July 1895, survived by five of his six sons and a daughter.

T. W. H. Leavitt (ed), *Australian representative men*, 2nd ed (Melb, 1887); J. T. Critchell and J. Raymond, *History of the frozen meat trade* (Lond, 1912); S. Fairbairn, *Fairbairn of Jesus* (Lond, 1931); R. V. Billis and A. S. Kenyon, *Pastoral pioneers of Port Phillip* (Melb, 1932); A. Henderson (ed), *Early pioneer families of Victoria and Riverina* (Melb, 1936); P. L. Brown (ed), *Clyde Company papers*, 4 (Lond, 1959); *Argus*, 19 July 1895; *Geelong Advertiser*, 19 July 1895; *Pastoral Review*, Aug 1895.   DONALD S. GARDEN

FAIRFAX, JOHN (1804-1877), newspaper proprietor, was born on 25 October 1804 in Warwick, England, the second son of William Fairfax and his wife Elizabeth, née Jesson, of Birmingham. In 1817 he was apprenticed to William Perry, printer, bookbinder and bookseller of Warwick, and in 1825 joined the London *Morning Chronicle*. He soon returned to Warwickshire and started a printery at Leamington. On 31 July 1827 he married Sarah, daughter of James Reading of Warwick. In 1828 he founded the

Leamington Spa Courier with James Sharp but the partnership broke up in four months. Fairfax carried on as a printer, bookseller and newsagent. In 1835 he became part-owner of the *Leamington Chronicle and Warwickshire Reporter*. Next year he successfully defended a libel suit but, unable to meet costs, had to apply to the Insolvency Court. With his wife, mother and three children, Fairfax arrived at Sydney on 26 September 1838 in the *Lady Fitzherbert* with £5 in his pocket.

Fairfax worked as a journalist and on 1 April 1839 became librarian of the Australian Subscription Library. On 8 February 1841 with Charles Kemp [q.v.] he bought on long-term credit the daily *Sydney Herald* from Frederick Stokes. On 1 August 1842 the title was changed to the *Sydney Morning Herald*. In the first few years the partners had to do almost everything themselves: reporting, editing, leader writing as well as all the mechanical work of producing the paper. In the 1850s the competition of Henry Parkes's [q.v.] *Empire* led to reorganization of the *Herald*. In 1851 Fairfax returned to Leamington and paid his creditors in full, despite an honourable discharge. By request he lectured at the Leamington Music Hall on the Australian colonies and goldfields. In England he also bought the first steam press to be used for printing a newspaper in Australia; it was installed in 1853. On 30 September Fairfax bought Kemp's interest and admitted his eldest son Charles as a partner. Fairfax was in close contact with Parkes, a lifelong friend: information was exchanged and agreement often reached on wages to compositors, the size and price of their papers and no Sunday editions. After Parkes lost the *Empire* he contributed literary and political articles as well as parliamentary summaries to the *Herald*. In 1856 the *Herald* was moved to Hunter Street, the firm became known as John Fairfax & Sons and his second son James became a partner.

While the *Herald* was developing as the major newspaper in New South Wales, Fairfax widened his activities. By 1851 he was a foundation director of the Australian Mutual Provident Society, and in the 1860s a director of the Sydney Insurance Co. (fire only), the New South Wales Marine Insurance Co., the Australian Joint Stock Bank and the Australian Gaslight Co. and a trustee of the Savings Bank of New South Wales. For some years president of the Young Men's Christian Assocation, he was appointed in 1871 to the Council of Education. He helped to establish the Pitt Street Congregational Church where he was senior deacon. Deeply religious and fair-minded, he was well known for his tolerance at a time when sectarian feeling ran high. In August 1856 he was nominated for the South Riding of Cumberland as a Liberal who 'would encourage the formation of Railways' and direct steam communication between Sydney and England. He lost and in 1869 refused Parkes's request to stand for East Sydney but in 1874 accepted nomination to the Legislative Council.

Fairfax built up the *Herald* from a small journal to one of the most influential and respected newspapers in the empire. In 1858 he had built Ginahgulla on Bellevue Hill. He died on 16 June 1877 and was buried in the Congregational section of Rookwood cemetery. He was predeceased by his wife, eldest son and only daughter, and survived by two sons who carried on the *Herald*.

A portrait is in the boardroom of John Fairfax Ltd and miniatures of him and Sarah are held by descendants.

In memorium. Obituary notices and funeral services . . . Hon. John Fairfax, Esq., M.L.C. (Syd, 1877); H. Parkes, *Fifty years in the making of Australian history* (Lond, 1892); *A century of journalism. The Sydney Morning Herald, 1831-1931* (Syd, 1931); J. F. Fairfax, *The story of John Fairfax* (Syd, 1941); Parkes letters (ML); Fairfax uncat MS 459 (ML); MS and printed cats under Fairfax (ML).

J. O. FAIRFAX

FAITHFULL, WILLIAM PITT (1806-1896), pastoralist, was born on 11 October 1806 at Richmond, New South Wales, the eldest son of William Faithful [q.v.] and his wife Susannah, née Pitt. He left school at 15 and entered the office of his uncle, Robert Jenkins [q.v.], a Sydney merchant. After his uncle died he worked for five years as an overseer on the property of his aunt, Mrs Jemima Jenkins. Faithfull did not take up his option for a grant of 320 acres and in 1827 applied for land with acreage more appropriate to his means. The land board assessed his capital at £2232 and in October he was granted 1280 acres on the Goulburn plains. Originally Cooranganennoe, the property became known as Springfield. Faithfull consolidated his assets and in 1835-37 acquired land on the Mulwaree Chain of Ponds. In 1838 with his brother George he overlanded sheep and cattle to Port Phillip. Although attacked by Aboriginals, George founded Wangaratta station on the Ovens River, a district where he bred and grazed sheep with his brother in 1846-48.

Faithfull had founded the Springfield stud in 1838 with ten rams from Sir William Macarthur's [q.v.] Camden Park flock. One of the earliest to recognize the importance of selective breeding, he improved his flock by buying ten rams a year from such noted studs as those of G. H. Cox of Burrundulla,

N. P. Bayley of Havilah and Edward Cox of Rawden [qq.v.]. By 1854 Faithfull held Brewarrina, 32,000 acres in the Murrumbidgee district. In 1871 his son Augustus Lucien took over the management of the stud and concentrated on breeding a pure flock of high class, stronger, heavier-woolled merinos mostly from Tasmanian rams.

W. P. Faithfull became a justice of the peace in 1836 and returning officer for Argyle and warden of the Goulburn District Council in 1843. In 1846-48 he was an elected member of the Legislative Council for Argyle and after responsible government served in the Legislative Council from 13 May 1856 until May 1861 when he joined Sir William Burton [q.v.] in resigning in protest against an attempt by the governor to swamp the council in order to pass the land bill.

On 20 January 1844 in Sydney Faithfull married Mary, daughter of Thomas Deane of Devonshire. Springfield House was built in the early 1840s, and by 1858 its garden was well known for its 'English flowers of every shade in perfection'. His wife got roots and seeds from England every year. The stone woolshed, built in the late 1840s, was one of the earliest in the colony. Faithfull died at Springfield on 24 April 1896 and was buried there by the Anglican bishop of Goulburn. He was survived by five sons and three daughters. He left an estate worth £335,253 with Springfield, grown to over 20,000 acres, Brewarrina, and land in Melbourne, Wangaratta, Mittagong and Sydney. The Springfield stud was left to his youngest son, Lucien, in whose hands it remained until he died in 1942, when it went to Lucien's daughter, Mrs Maple Brown. It is claimed to be the oldest registered merino flock in Australia in the possession of one family.

C. McIvor, *The history and development of sheep farming from antiquity to modern times* (Syd, 1893); R. M. Bedford, *Think of Stephen: a family chronicle* (Syd, 1954); 'The pastoral homes of Australia: Springfield', *Pastoral Review*, Dec 1909; C. H. Bertie, 'Pioneer families of Australia: the Faithfulls', *Home*, Nov 1931; E. W. Cox, 'Famous merino studs: Springfield, the property of A. Lucien Faithfull', *New Nation Mag*, Sept 1935; *SMH*, 21 May 1838; S. Uren, *Massacre of the Faithfull party* (ML); Faithfull family papers (NL); Mowle papers (ML); Col Sec in-letters, 1838 (NSWA); MS cat under Faithfull (ML); newspaper cuttings under Faithfull (ML).   DIANNE PATENALL

FALCONER, WILLIAM ROSE (1818-1869), engineer and civil servant, was the youngest son of William Falconer, member of a respected Presbyterian family of Ayrshire, Scotland. He first migrated to Canada, where he gained engineering experience in the building of gas works in Montreal, Quebec and Toronto. In Canada he negotiated with Bogle, Kerr & Co. of Glasgow and through their agency was appointed engineer-manager of the new Hobart Town Gas Co. for three years from 1 Septemer 1855. Travelling via Liverpool and Melbourne, he arrived in December at Hobart Town where other unrelated Falconers were already active in banking and real estate.

The directors soon accepted his plans for erecting plant and buildings on the site of the present Hobart Gas Works. The project developed smoothly and the first gas-lighting of Hobart streets on 9 March 1857 was a gala occasion. The company had allowed Falconer to accept outside engagements and in 1856 the Launceston Municipal Council retained him to amend and execute the St Patrick's River water scheme. Later when the Launceston Gas Co. was formed he became consulting engineer in charge of building its gas works. He resigned from the Hobart company when his original appointment ended and for a few months devoted his efforts to the Launceston project, which was completed during 1859. Falconer thus brought to Tasmania the benefits of what was then an advanced technology: the gas works he established have remained from that time as the only two operating in the State. He also played a small part in the development of coal mining in the Fingal Valley, and his appointment to the directorship of Public Works, gazetted on 3 January 1859, was widely acclaimed. That post carried with it the offices of· inspector of telegraphs and director of roads and bridges; he was also appointed a member of the Bridgewater (Bridge) Commission and the Committee of Management of St Mary's Hospital in Davey Street, Hobart.

At St John's Church, New Town, on 14 September 1864 Falconer married Harriet, daughter of John James; they had one daughter. Four years later he was paralysed after a fall from his horse and was thereafter confined to his New Town home until he died aged 50 on 26 May 1869. He was buried at St John's Church and the pallbearers included the premier and other leading public figures; the government offices closed at 2 p.m. and many civil servants were among the two hundred mourners. In tribute the *Mercury* noted that he was 'highly respected and esteemed by all who knew him, and throughout his civil service career enjoyed the reputation of an upright official'; the *Examiner* added that he 'had the happy knack of attaching persons to him by the general amiability of his manners'.

By coincidence his mother also died on 26 May 1869 in Glasgow. His widow married William Bone of Richmond; she died on 14 March 1913 aged 74, and was buried in the Falconer family grave: the tombstone was later moved to the Cornelian Bay cemetery.

Tas Mail, 1, 17 June 1869, 23 Mar 1907; Minute books, 1854-58 (Hobart Gas Co.).

R. L. WETTENHALL

FALKINER, FRANC SADLIER (1833-1909), pastoralist, was born on 23 October 1833 at Beechwood, County Tipperary, Ireland, the third son of Daniel Falkiner, a solicitor whose forebears had pioneered the Irish woollen industry, and his wife Rebecca, née Sadlier. He was intended for the Anglican ministry but migrated to Victoria about 1853. He went to the Maryborough goldfields and later opened a store in Ararat where he had some success in assaying and buying gold. On 10 July 1856 at Carisbrook he married Emily Elizabeth Bazley.

Falkiner took up land near Ararat and in 1875 moved to Cliff Cottage, Geelong, where he was appointed government land valuer for the first land tax. The family moved to the drier western plains of New South Wales to benefit his asthmatic son Otway. In 1878 in partnership with J. Ross and Malcolm McKenzie, Falkiner bought from Peppin & Sons [q.v.] the 75,000-acre station of Boonoke and half its total stock. Falkiner bought out his partners in 1882, transformed the property and developed a stud with sheep bred from the original Peppin stock. His rams were characterized by robust constitutions, big frames, high quality fleeces and ability to endure rigorous climatic conditions. Between April 1882 and July 1884 the sale of sheep had brought £74,721. By 1884 Boonoke had 200 miles of fencing. In October 1888 Frederick Parker protested against the award of prizes to Falkiner for stall-fed sheep entered in the grass-fed section at the Deniliquin Pastoral and Agricultural Show. Falkiner was disqualified and accused Parker of similar practices, whereupon Parker sued for libel. Falkiner was acquitted at Deniliquin but Parker appealed as Falkiner had stayed in the same hotel as the jury and allegedly influenced them in his favour. The Supreme Court granted a new trial in Sydney and ordered Falkiner to pay all the costs. Chief Justice Darley [q.v.] severely denounced Falkiner for making a false declaration. He was refused leave to appeal to the Privy Council but the case was apparently settled out of court.

In 1884-1909 Falkiner bought for over £1,000,000 the Riverina stations Moonbria, Tuppal, Moira, Morago and Pericoota. In 1899 all these properties were formed into

F. S. Falkiner & Sons Ltd, with Falkiner, his wife and his sons as directors and each son manager of one station. Later purchases by the company included the Wanganella stud and the Widgiewa estate, later called Boonoke North.

Falkiner died at Boonoke on 8 September 1909 and was buried in the Anglican cemetery, Deniliquin. He was survived by his wife, five sons and four daughters to whom he left an estate of £204,000. In 1912 his widow established a scholarship for boys going from Deniliquin High School to an Australian university. His third son Otway took over the management of the company and his eldest son, Franc, sold out and bought Haddon Rig near Warren.

H. N. Maitland (ed), *New South Wales, 1920-1923* (Syd, 1923); *NSW Law Reports*, 1888; *NSW Weekly Notes*, 5 (1889-90); *Sydney Mail*, 18, 25 Oct 1884; *Australasian*, 8 Dec 1888, 16 Feb 1889; *Pastoral Review*, 15 Oct 1909.

DIANNE PATENALL

FALLON, JAMES THOMAS (1823?-1886), vigneron and wine merchant, was born at Athlone, Ireland, son of James Fallon, farmer, and his wife Margaret, née Norton (Naughton). He was educated at the Athlone Grammar School. On 31 August 1841 he arrived in Sydney as a bounty immigrant in the *John Renwick*. He farmed for some years near Sydney, then opened a store in Braidwood. In 1854 Fallon moved to Albury, opened a general store in Kiewa Street and later became part-owner of the paddle-steamer *Cumberoona*. He was soon one of the town's most important citizens and in 1857 subscribed £100 to a reward for the local discovery of gold. In 1859-62 Fallon was Albury's first mayor.

The Murray Valley Vineyard, 640 acres with 150 under vine, was established about 1858 by a company of which Fallon was a director, but border customs caused a loss of some £7000. About 1861 Fallon acquired the vineyard and soon became a successful vigneron and wine merchant as well as storekeeper. His well-known cellars in Kiewa Street were the scene of many local celebrations. By 1872 he had set up a distillery, a central depot in Sydney and cellars in Melbourne and exported wine to England, America, India, Ceylon and New Zealand. His wines continued to win prizes, notably in 1873 at Vienna and in 1882 at Bordeaux.

Active in community affairs, Fallon became president of the Albury and Murray River Agricultural and Horticultural Society. In 1869-72 he represented the Hume in the Legislative Assembly. In 1872-73 Fallon visited overseas vineyards and in December

1873 addressed the London Society of Arts on Australian vines and wines (printed as *The Murray Valley Vineyard . . . in 1874*). He argued that the British duties discriminated against some colonial wines. He was contradicted by Dr Thudichum, who asserted that Fallon's claims for the strength of colonial wines were opposed to all established scientific facts. On the same visit Fallon engaged L. Frere, a distinguished French vigneron, to manage his vineyard. On his return Fallon had his wines tested for alcoholic strength by the chief inspector of distilleries in Victoria and other impartial officials. The results bore out Fallon's claims as the highest figure obtained was 32.4 per cent without fortification. On 20 June 1876 in London Fallon presented these results, later published as *The Wines of Australia*, before the Royal Colonial Institute to which he was elected a member. Despite criticism by Dr Thudichum and Hubert de Castella [q.v.], Fallon and the Victorian government eventually secured a sliding scale of duties on colonial wines.

In 1871-86 Fallon lived in Sydney between overseas travel. He died unmarried at Manly on 26 May 1886 and was buried in the Roman Catholic section of the Albury cemetery. He left his estate of £20,000 to his brother Patrick who carried on the vineyard; destroyed by phylloxera, it was replanted and wine was made there by the Fallon family until the 1930s. Though his importance as an energetic man in a small town is easy to overestimate, Fallon appears an intelligent and enterprising pioneer, whose initiative and persistence did much for his community and for the colonial wine industry.

H. de Castella, *John Bull's vineyard. Australian sketches* (Melb, 1886); A. Andrews, *The history of Albury, 1824-1895* (Albury, 1912); W. A. Bayley, *Border city* (Albury, 1954); K. M. Ortiz, 'James T. Fallon—one of Albury's founders', Albury and District Hist Soc, *Bulletin*, Dec 1968; *Maitland Mercury*, 14 Jan 1868, 1 July, 20 Nov 1875, 16 Mar 1876; *Town and Country J*, 20 Apr 1872, 15 July 1876, 5 June 1886; *Illustrated Sydney News*, 23 Feb 1878.

W. P. DRISCOLL

FANNING, EDWARD (1848-1917), businessman, was born on 16 March 1848 at Sydney, the second son of William Fanning [q.v.], merchant, and his wife Oriana, née Richardson, who were then visiting New South Wales. Named for his ancestor, the discoverer of Fanning Island, Edward grew up at Bozedown, near Reading, England, and spent some time with the family of Thomas Henry Huxley [q.v.] who had married Oriana's half-sister. Edward was educated at Eton and Trinity College, Oxford (B.A., 1870), and won distinction as an athlete.

In 1871 Edward joined the Melbourne branch of Fanning, Nankivell & Co., a Reading mercantile firm of which his father was senior partner. Tall, handsome, witty, charming and rich, Edward was welcomed by Melbourne society. He played for the Melbourne Cricket Club, followed the Melbourne hounds and bred greyhounds with which he later won the Tasmanian Plate and Great Southern Cup. An accomplished whip, he aroused admiration when he drove his tandem along St Kilda Road and was much in demand to school horses until a bad fall almost killed him.

In the mid-1870s Fanning, Nankivell & Co. invested in the Queensland sugar industry. The firm bought Gairloch, 4600 acres in the Herbert River area, and spent over £120,000 on the plantation. In September 1882 Macknade, 6856 acres with a successful history, was bought from the Neame brothers for £60,000, half paid in cash, the rest remaining on mortgage. Hamleigh plantation was soon added to Fanning, Nankivell & Co.'s holdings. In 1885 the Neames in England had word that 'things were not going at all well at Macknade' and in 1886 Frank Neame sailed to Melbourne. Fanning refused Neame's partnership proposal as the firm had already lost £200,000. Macknade was therefore handed over as it stood in lieu of money owing. Gairloch was put up for auction in Melbourne but no buyers came forward and it was sold in lots for only £20,000. Arthur Neame considered overextension the cause of Fanning, Nankivell & Co.'s failure. Inefficient managers, unsuccessful experiments with Javanese, Sinhalese and Chinese labourers, the low price of sugar and bad seasons contributed to the disaster which was by no means confined to this firm. One bright spot for Fanning in these troubled years was the amendment of the law on marriage with a deceased wife's sister. In 1874 he had married Constance Emily, daughter of David Moore [q.v.], but she died of pneumonia soon after the wedding. His wish to marry her eldest sister Kate was not realized until 4 November 1885.

Fanning, Nankivell & Co. reorganized at the end of the 1880s and as Fanning & Co. continued to ship tea, sugar, ginger and spices to Australia. The depression of the 1890s brought further financial difficulties but Fanning managed to avert ruin, and although he was never wealthy again, 'his own integrity and utter morality in all things led him to positions that gave him financial security'. He was a trustee of Edward Wilson's [q.v.] estate, and chairman of the Equity Trustees Executors and Agency Co. which he helped to found, and of the Australian board of the New Zealand Loan and Mercantile Agency Co. He was a director of the London Bank of Australia, the Carlton, United and Castlemaine Breweries, the East Greta Coal Co., New South Wales, the Colonial Mutual Life Assurance Co. and the North British and Mercantile Insurance Co. He was a member of the Children's Hospital committee and a trustee of the Alexandra and Melbourne Clubs and president of the latter in 1915.

A devout Anglican in his youth, Fanning was impressed by rationalist doctrines but continued to attend church. He remained a crack shot and excellent billiards player, and a great joy in his old age was listening to his large record collection on his trumpet gramophone. He died at his home, Coora-min, Westbury Street, East St Kilda, on 30 November 1917, survived by his wife, two sons, Rupert and William, and one daughter, Beryl.

E. Scott, *Historical memoir of the Melbourne Club* (Melb, 1936); Roy Com into the general condition of the sugar industry, Report, V&P (LA Qld), 1889, 4, 78; *Argus*, 1 Dec 1917; *Pastoral Review*, 15 Dec 1917; Neame diary (Oxley Lib, Brisb, ML); information from Mrs Kingsley Newell, Shoreham, Vic.   J. ANN HONE

FANNING, WILLIAM (1816-1887), merchant, and FREDERICK (1821-1905), army officer and merchant, were sons of William Fanning (1785-1859) and his wife Sophia Cecilia, née Harley. William arrived in Sydney about 1842 and in 1843 entered partnership as a general merchant with George Richard Griffiths [q.v.]. They imported teas from China and wine and spirits. In 1844 William became a member of the Australian Club and in September a justice of the peace. On 6 August he married Oriana, third daughter of G. A. Richardson, M.D. of Jamberoo; her half-sister Henrietta Heathorn married T. H. Huxley [q.v.] in 1855. About 1846 William acquired pastoral interests in the Wellington Valley. In February 1850 he went to England but returned in 1852 and lived at Double Bay. About 1856 he became part-owner of two ships registered in Sydney and was associated with (Sir) Daniel Cooper [q.v.]. In 1854 he had become a local director of the Australian Gold Mining Co., in 1855 a founding director of the Colonial Sugar Co. and a member of the Sydney Chamber of Commerce, and in 1857 a director of the Union Bank of Australia. In 1860 he was living at Hardwicke, near Reading, England, but later at Canterbury House, Canterbury, Sydney, and was the principal partner in Griffiths, Fanning & Co.

In 1838 Frederick enlisted in the Indian army. On 3 October 1840 he became a lieutenant in the 9th Regiment of Native Infantry and on 16 December 1843 was seconded to the revenue survey department, where he became interested in native languages. Promoted captain on 1 January 1852, he retired as a major on 23 July 1858. In May 1850 he had married Sophia (1831-1922), daughter of Rev. Joseph Taylor and his wife Antoinette, née Van Someren. Frederick arrived in 1858 at Sydney where he lived although active in the firm's pastoral ventures. In 1866 the firm owned 195,000 acres with 18,000 cattle in the New England district including Wooroowoolgen near Casino. The brothers owned a further 48,000 acres and Frederick another 28,000 acres. By 1871 he had twenty-two properties in Queensland, mainly in the Maranoa district, as well as three sheep runs near Coonamble with William. Most of these stations were sold by the 1880s. Frederick's eldest son William Joseph managed Wooroowoolgen till his return to England in 1890 when his second brother Francis Grant (1860-1942) took over.

About 1870 William returned permanently to England and lived at Bozedown House near Reading, where he died on 24 June 1887. He was survived by his wife, two daughters and three sons, of whom the second was Edward [q.v.]. Frederick returned to England soon after his brother and lived first at Park Wood, Swanley, Kent, then in Kensington, and assisted at the firm's counting house in Old Bond Street, London. He died at Kensington on 16 February 1905 and was survived by his wife, three sons and a daughter.

L. Huxley, *Life and letters of T. H. Huxley*, 1-2, 1st ed (Lond, 1900); *India Army list*, 1905; J. Huxley (ed), *T. H. Huxley's diary of the voyage of H.M.S. Rattlesnake* (Lond, 1935); MS cat under Griffiths, Fanning & Co. (ML); newspaper indexes under Fanning (ML); information from W. R. Fanning, Toorak, Vic, Mrs B. Kingsley Newell, Shoreham, Vic, and Mrs R. S. Follett, Ashleworth, Gloucester, England.

RUTH TEALE

FARMER, SIR WILLIAM (1832-1908), retailer, was born on 1 July 1832 in England, the third son of Samuel Farmer of Moor Hall, Belbroughton, Worcestershire, and his wife Elizabeth, née White. In 1848 he joined his uncle Joseph in Sydney.

Joseph Farmer was born on 26 June 1814 at Halesowen, Worcestershire, son of William Farmer and his wife Mary, née Walters. Joseph and his wife Caroline, née Harley,

had reached Sydney as bounty immigrants in the *Royal Saxon* on 31 March 1839. In September his wife opened a dressmaking and millinery shop, and a year later Joseph, who had been a farmer, set up as a draper opposite the Victoria Theatre in Pitt Street. He opened a branch at Parramatta and in 1843 acquired new premises. He was interested in racing and in 1845 won three races with his own horses at a drapers' charity meeting. In 1848 the business was temporarily leased to Price & Favenc until William arrived to learn the trade. In the 1870s Joseph returned to England and on 22 November 1890 died at Chapel Hill House, near Margate, Kent, survived by two sons and two daughters. His estate in New South Wales was valued at £33,600.

In March 1854 William took control of the firm in partnership with William Williams and Francis Giles. Two years later they had seventeen employees. In the next forty years the Farmers had many partners: in 1860 Richard Painter succeeded Williams and Giles, and in 1865 John Pope (1827-1912) joined the firm which was styled Farmer, Painter & Pope. By 1866 William Farmer and Painter held two runs, Minore and Geary, in the Bligh and Wellington districts; they still held them in 1871. Painter had retired in 1869 and J. & W. Farmer & Pope became Farmer & Co. Over the years the firm expanded and branched out from drapery. In 1874 G. P. Fitzgerald [q.v.] and W. Seaward (d. 1894) were admitted as junior partners and Farmer returned to England to live at Ascot Place, Berkshire. On 5 January 1897 Farmer & Co. became a public company; Farmer was chairman of directors until his death. His last visits to Australia were in 1894 and 1907.

Farmer became a lieutenant of the City of London and in 1890-91 was sheriff of London, in 1895 high sheriff of Berkshire and in 1898 master of the Worshipful Company of Gardeners. In 1891 he was appointed knight bachelor. He died on 8 July 1908 at Peterley Manor, Great Missenden, Buckinghamshire, predeceased by his wife Martha, née Perkins (d. 1901), whom he had married on 26 January 1864 in England, and survived by one son and three daughters. His estate was valued for probate at over £41,000.

For over a century Farmer & Co. was a leading innovator in Australian retail trading and an important Sydney commercial and social institution: in 1866 it encouraged the Saturday Half Holiday Association and later became the first business house in Australia to close at 1 p.m. on Saturdays. In 1923 the company received Australia's first commercial broadcasting licence and broadcast as 2FC (Farmer & Co.).

153

SMH, 10 Sept 1840, 28 Jan 1843, 15 Jan 1912; *The Times*, 10 July 1908; *Sydney Mail*, 15 July 1908; *Bulletin*, 18 Jan 1912; *Evening News* (Syd), 30 May 1925; business records (Farmer & Co. Archives, Syd).   G. P. WALSH

FARNELL, JAMES SQUIRE (1825-1888), politician, was born on 24 June 1825 at St Leonards, North Sydney, son of Thomas Charles Farnell, brewer, and his wife Mary Ann (1804-1850), daughter of James Squire [q.v.]. He was educated at Parramatta, became adept in bushcraft and as a drover acquired an unusually wide knowledge of the colony. He joined the Californian gold rush in 1848 and returned to live at Kissing Point, Sydney, where he inherited 400 acres from his mother. On 2 May 1860 he won a Legislative Assembly by-election for St Leonards, but as a conservative was defeated for Central Cumberland in December. In 1864-74 he represented Parramatta. An active legislator, he became well versed in parliamentary practices. He supported Sir Alfred Stephen's [q.v.] attempts to extend the grounds of divorce, especially for incurable insanity, and advocated the extension of roads, railways and bridges. In 1870 Farnell bitterly criticized James Martin [q.v.] for 'betraying' his friends and joining Robertson [q.v.].

In 1872-75 Farnell was secretary for lands in Henry Parkes's [q.v.] first government. In 1872-73 he bore the brunt of the rush for mineral leases and dealt with applications for three-quarters of a million acres. In 1874 he carried the Mining Act and from May to July was also secretary for mines without salary to start the new department. In 1874 he was defeated for Parramatta but won St Leonards which he represented until 1882. In 1876-77 he was an able chairman of committees. After the fall of Robertson's government in March 1877, Farnell led 'a third party' of about seven members and created a deadlock in the assembly that was aggravated by the necessity of land reform and by Governor Robinson's reluctance to dissolve parliament without supply. When Parkes's ministry fell in August Farnell refused to serve under Robertson and then under Alexander Stuart [q.v.] though he consented to join S. C. Brown [q.v.] who failed to form a ministry. After the general election Robertson was defeated in December. Farnell declined to join Parkes and on 18 December, as secretary for lands, became the first native-born prime minister of New South Wales. The governor found his ministers 'personally respectable' but observed that his government could exist only while the followers of Parkes and Robertson did not coalesce.

Accepting the governor's opinion that only a new Electoral Act could break the deadlock, Farnell unwisely introduced it before his promised land bill which made many concessions to selectors. On 6 December 1878 the ministry was defeated and resigned after the governor had refused their advice to dissolve. After Robertson failed to form a ministry Farnell agreed to withdraw his resignation in hope of gaining some of Robertson's supporters, but on 20 December the government fell.

In 1882-85 Farnell represented New England and in 1883-85 was secretary for lands in Stuart's ministry. Probably the greatest achievement of his career was the passage of the Crown Lands Act in 1884 after months of debate and obstruction. When G. R. Dibbs [q.v.] reconstructed the ministry after Stuart's resignation, Farnell was appointed to the Legislative Council as minister of justice on 7 October 1885. Two days later he resigned his portfolio because of disparaging remarks on himself and officers of the Lands Department. Thereafter he ceased to be active in politics; in January 1887 he resigned from the council and returned to the assembly for Redfern, still a convinced free trader.

In the 1860s Farnell was a director of the Parramatta River Steam Co. and in the 1870s of the Civil Service Banking and Commercial Provident Society, and a trustee and chairman of the Civil Service Building Society. He was also president of the Sydney Club and a member of the Linnean Society of New South Wales. In 1880 he was a New South Wales commissioner to the Melbourne International Exhibition. Proudly Australian he arranged grants for marking places of historical interest. A prominent Freemason in the Leinster Marine Lodge, Farnell was supposed by critics to draw many electoral votes from his fraternity. In March 1876 he was installed as provincial grand master of the Irish Constitution. He favoured the movement to unite the masonic constitutions in New South Wales and on 3 December 1877 was installed as the first grand master of the Grand Lodge of New South Wales. Though the British Grand Lodges opposed its independence Farnell worked patiently to end discord. Recognition came just before he died on 21 August 1888 at the Boulevard, Petersham. The first function of the United Grand Lodge was to hold a 'Lodge of Sorrow' in his honour. He was buried in the family vault in the churchyard of St Anne's Church of England, Ryde. He was survived by his wife Margaret, née O'Donnell, whom he had married in Sydney on 23 June 1853, and by five sons and six daughters to whom he left an estate of £55,810. His son Frank served in the Legislative Assembly in 1887-98 and 1901-03. A

Herald editorial on his death claimed that Farnell 'was not a violent partisan, but he was a painstaking politician, who generally had a substantial reason to show for his action', and gave him credit for being 'neither a scandal-monger nor a grievance-monger'.

W. Henley, *History of Lodge Australian Social Mother No. 1 . . . 1820 to 1920* (Syd, 1920); K. R. Cramp and G. Mackaness, *A history of the United Grand Lodge of New South Wales* (Syd, 1938); P. Loveday and A. W. Martin, *Parliament factions and parties* (Melb, 1966); V&P (LA NSW), 1861-62, 2, 1347; *SMH*, 15 Dec 1870, 12, 28 Dec 1877, 5 Oct 1885, 22 Aug 1887; *Illustrated Sydney News*, 28 Mar 1874, 26 Jan 1878; *Freeman's J* (Syd), 22 July 1882; *Town and Country J*, 26 Feb 1887; *Syd Q Mag*, 1887; G. C. Morey, The Parkes-Robertson coalition government, 1878-1893 (B.A. Hons thesis, ANU, 1968); Mahon papers (NL); Parkes letters (ML); MS and printed cats under J. S. Farnell (ML); CO 201/583-603.

V. W. E. GOODIN

FARR, GEORGE HENRY (1819-1904), Anglican clergyman and schoolmaster, was born on 2 July 1819 at Tottenham, Middlesex, England, son of George Farr (d. 1826), linen merchant and descendant of a notable legal family, and his wife Eleanora, née Goodall. Sponsored by his guardian and friend, (Sir) John Patteson (1790-1861), he entered Christ's Hospital where he won the gold medal for mathematics and became senior Grecian. At 19 after severe illness he entered Pembroke College, Cambridge (B.A., 1843; M.A., 1854). In 1843 he enrolled at the Middle Temple but left after his mother died. He was made deacon at Ely for Exeter and priest in 1845. He served at St Wenn in 1844-46, Treleigh in 1846-48, St Buryan in 1848-53, Stapleton in 1853-54 and as inspector of schools for Exeter in 1844-54. In 1846 at Woolwich he had married Julia Warren, daughter of Major Robert Hutchinson Ord and his wife Elizabeth, née Blagrave.

Dissatisfied by the state of the Church of England he had written in August 1845 to Julia about 'the principles of the Anglo-Catholic Church . . . We have laws but no one to enforce them. And it is this consideration which has made me hesitate to consider England as my home'. Perhaps for this reason and his wife's health Farr applied for the headmastership of the Collegiate School of St Peter, Adelaide. Chosen from twenty-eight candidates, he sailed for South Australia with his wife, daughter and stepsister in the *Daylesford* and arrived in July 1854.

The first headmaster of St Peter's, Rev. Theodore Percival Wilson (1819-1881), also of Cambridge (M.A., 1847), was addicted to writing pious books for boys and had given the school no definitive character before he returned to England. In contrast Farr's qualifications were athletic as well as academic: at Cambridge he had stroked a college eight and earned pocket money by reporting prize fights for the press. His legal training tempered his religious thinking; he judged character 'not only by the scrapes boys get into but by the way they get out of them', and reputedly overlooked 'almost any fault in a boy except untruthfulness'. He was generally popular with his staff and pupils, blending firmness, sympathy and humour in just proportions and encouraged support for the new Melanesian mission under the son of Sir John Patteson. When in 1864 he talked of resigning over matters of discipline, a deputation of old boys persuaded him to change his mind. With his intellect, convictions and unpretentious manner he was an effective collaborator in Bishop Short's [q.v.] plans for the school and among the colonists. He gave evidence at committees of inquiry into educational issues in 1861, 1868-69 and 1882, and specially opposed state interference in private schools. His wife proved a devoted and tactful helper, first in supervising the school's dairy and poultry and from 1872 the boarding house. In 1860 she helped to found a home for orphan girls, later known as Farr House. When Farr retired in 1879 the school was said to be the pre-eminent educational institution in South Australia and worthy of comparison with any school in England.

Farr served as priest at Semaphore in 1879-83, Mitcham in 1883-84 and St Luke's, Adelaide, in 1884-95. As archdeacon he made many visitations to the vast western and south-eastern regions of the colony. In 1857-96 he was a canon of St Peter's Cathedral. In the University of Adelaide he was warden of the senate in 1880-82 and vice-chancellor in 1887-93. He was also chairman of the Public Library, Museum and Art Gallery in 1869-86. In 1883 he had visited England and his thesis on the development of the law of real property won him a doctorate of laws at Cambridge. He died in Adelaide on 7 February 1904 and was buried in North Road cemetery. His wife died aged 88 on 21 April 1914. Of their three sons and four daughters, Eleonora Elizabeth married E. G. Blackmore [q.v.], Mary married Rev. W. H. Sharp [q.v.] and Clinton Coleridge (1866-1943) was a distinguished physicist.

M. E. P. Sharp et al, *Early days at St. Peter's College, Adelaide, 1854-1878* (Adel, 1936); G. H. Jose, *The Church of England in South Australia, 1-2* (Adel, 1937, 1954); A. G. Price, *The Collegiate School of St. Peter, 1847-1947* (Adel,

1947); Vestry minutes (St Andrew's Church, Walkerville, SA); Farr papers (ML); Watson papers (Soc Aust Gen, Syd).

J. S. DUNKERLEY

FARRELL, JOHN (1851-1904), poet and journalist, was born on 18 December 1851 at Buenos Aires, Argentina, the third son of Andrew Farrell (d. 1897), chemist, and his wife Mary, née Parley (d. 1862). His parents had migrated to South America from Dublin in 1847. Attracted by the goldfields the family arrived in Melbourne in 1852 and settled in the Loddon district, near Baringhup.

Farrell had little schooling and at 11 was on his father's farm, but he found time to read English poetry, to fiddle for the local Christy Minstrels and to share in recitation evenings, activities that were to influence his writing. At 19 he walked to Bendigo and worked in a brewery, then went gold digging at Darwin and cutting timber and droving in Queensland. In 1875 he returned to the family home but soon moved to Camperdown to manage a brewery. Still restless, he tried farming on a selection near Benalla but by 1878 he was again a brewer. For the next nine years he worked for Gulson's breweries at Albury as manager, then at Goulburn and from 1884 at Queanbeyan, where he was a partner in the branch and contributed to the *Queanbeyan Age*.

Later Farrell recalled that 'I never discovered or suspected that I had any literary faculty earlier than 1877', but while at Albury he contributed satirical verses to the local press; they were reissued as *Ephemera: An Iliad of Albury* in 1878. In 1882 *Two Voices: a Fragmentary Poem* appeared, with the first of Farrell's *Bulletin* contributions, including 'Jenny', a long verse narrative that ran for nearly a year. Farrell had only intended the first instalment as a specimen but 'Traill [q.v.] was in America, and in his absence Haynes [q.v.] shoved it in, and I was bound in honour to go on supplying the copy from week to week'. Until 1889 Farrell was a regular *Bulletin* contributor of verse, and he is credited with its first story about Australian life and people: 'One Christmas Day' on 27 December 1884.

In January 1887 *How He Died and Other Poems* was published in Sydney and well reviewed; by November Farrell, now an 'unqualified and ardent believer' in Henry George [q.v.], whose *Progress and Poverty* had converted him in 1884 to a strong belief in single tax, had left brewing and was in Lithgow editing the *Lithgow Enterprise and Australian Land Nationaliser*, one of the movement's earliest journals. By 1889 Farrell was editor of the *Australian Standard* in Sydney and wrote on 'The Philosophy of the Single Tax' for the *Daily Telegraph* between October 1889 and 1 February 1890; in March 1890 he accompanied George on a lecturing tour through three colonies. On his return he became editor of the *Daily Telegraph* but wisely decided that he could not manage a large daily; he resigned, although he continued until 1903 to write its leaders, to review books and as 'Niemand' to run a column. Farrell continued, too, his work as a single tax publicist: his Australian dispatches appeared in the New York *Standard*, while at home he contributed articles and poems to the *Single Tax*.

This grind of journalism prevented Farrell from writing much poetry after 1890, although 'Australia to England', praised by Kipling and recited by elocution students for years, was published in Sydney in 1897, and his 'Hymn of the Commonwealth' was sung by the choir massed in Centennial Park for the Federation inaugural celebrations. In 1903 Farrell began revising his poems for a new edition, but had not finished when he died in Sydney on 8 January 1904. He was buried in the Catholic section of Rookwood cemetery, survived by his wife Elizabeth, née Watts, whom he had married in 1876, four sons and three daughters. His estate was valued at £827.

Later in 1904 a memorial volume of the poems, edited by Bertram Stevens, appeared as *My Sundowner and other Poems*; it was reprinted as *How He Died and Other Poems*, though only three of the poems in the 1887 edition of *How He Died* were included. Despite his contemporary fame, Farrell is not a major Australian poet. Much of his topical satire is now dated, his verse narratives are stilted and his commemorative poems are excessively sentimental; he is more significant as an up-country reader of the *Bulletin* who responded, like the tentative Lawson, to the magazine's encouragement to send in material. But Farrell knew his limitations: when asked once whether he had deserted the Muse, Farrell replied, 'I can't say I ever knew the lady'. To the virtue of humility he added compassion. At his death his friends remembered the rotund Irishman with his drooping moustache and a pipe that was seldom from his mouth but seldom lit, and remembered how his 'rich seducing brogue', his humour and his optimism had brightened dark days in the 1890s. Their tributes are aptly summarized on his gravestone:

Sleep Heart of Gold! 'Twas not in vain
You loved the struggling and the poor,
And taught, in sweet and strenuous strain
To battle and endure.
The lust of wealth, the pride of place,
Were not a light to guide thy feet;
But larger hopes and wider space
For hearts to beat.

D. Thomas (ed), *The early history of Baring-hup* (Bendigo, 1950); B. Stevens, 'John Farrell: poet, journalist, & reformer', *New Zealand Illustrated Mag*, Aug 1904; G. Mackaness, 'Gordon, Kendall and Farrell: some literary curiosities', *Southerly*, 1950, no 1; K. Levis, 'The role of the *Bulletin* in indigenous short story writing during the eighties and nineties', *Southerly*, 1950, no 4; *Bulletin*, 14 Jan 1904; Astley papers (ML); MS cat under Farrell (ML).

B. G. ANDREWS

FARTHING, WILLIAM ARMSTRONG (1818-1886), colliery proprietor, was born in Filey, Yorkshire, England, son of William Farthing, farmer, and his wife Jane, née Armstrong. In 1839 he migrated to New South Wales where he became a bootmaker and leather merchant at Maitland. In 1851 he tried gold mining but in 1853 went into coal mining probably because of his marriage in 1843 to Lillias, sister of James and Alexander Brown [q.v.]. Farthing seems to have managed for the Browns their small mines at Four Mile Creek near East Maitland and was probably still there when he tried to bring Four Mile Creek miners to work in the Browns's Minmi collieries during the strike of 1860.

The extension of the railway towards Singleton made it possible to bring new coal lands into production and Farthing began to mine a seam which he had discovered in the bed of Anvil Creek, near Greta and the new railway. This was an outcrop of the Greta coal measures which were to become the chief source of gas coal for Australia and which were to provide much coal for export to countries in the Pacific region before 1914. Between 1862 and 1871 an average of 10,000 tons a year was produced from the Anvil Creek colliery where from twenty to forty miners were employed and steam power was used to raise the coal and keep the mine clear of water. In 1864 Farthing won a contract for steam coal from the Australasian Steam Navigation Co. and his Anvil Creek coal, when tested in a gas works, yielded twice as much gas as other colonial coals. In 1871 he suffered a financial set-back when the mine caught fire, not spontaneously as Professor Edgeworth David later surmised, but because of the inexperience of a new miner who lit a fire to clear the pit of foul air. Farthing bypassed the fire and reopened the colliery but in 1872 it produced only half as much coal as in 1870. Hampered by low prices and lack of capital, he sold the property in 1873 to the Anvil Creek Colliery Co. Ltd, established with a capital of £30,000.

Farthing retired to his small property near Greta and continued to act as a magistrate and 'acquitted himself on the bench with credit and discretion'. 'Kindly, warmhearted and generous', he was described in 1871 by the *Maitland Mercury* as 'a most energetic and pushing man whose perseverance and industry have merited greater success than he has met with'; he possibly lacked the ruthlessness that would have carried him into the first line of northern colliery proprietors. He did not establish a major mine, his annual outputs were relatively insignificant and he cannot be said to have discovered the Greta coal measures, for others had preceded him in exploiting them. Yet he was the most important of these pioneers and his work at Anvil Creek demonstrated the rich properties of this coal. Aged 67 he died on 6 August 1886 and was survived by his wife, only son and at least two daughters. He was buried with Presbyterian rites in East Maitland.

Newcastle Chronicle, 5 Mar 1864, 1 Feb 1865, 2 Mar 1871, 28 Feb 1874; *Maitland Mercury*, 2 Mar 1871; *Town and Country J*, 1 Oct 1887; Purves papers (ML).   J. W. TURNER

FAUCETT, PETER (1813-1894), judge, was born in Dublin, son of Peter Faucett, blacksmith, and his wife Catherine, née Cook. He was educated at a private church school and at Trinity College, Dublin (B.A., 1840). He then studied law and in 1845 was called to the Irish Bar. After some seven years' practice in Ireland, he migrated to Sydney, arriving in 1852. On 29 December he was called to the colonial Bar of New South Wales. He appeared regularly in criminal proceedings on the Maitland circuit, and his advocacy took him as far as Brisbane, then within the jurisdiction of New South Wales.

On 7 April 1856 Faucett was elected under the new Constitution Act to the first Legislative Assembly of New South Wales for the electorate of King and Georgiana, and again at the general election on 1 February 1858. He surrendered this seat on 11 April 1859 on the dissolution of the second parliament. On 20 January 1860 he won the seat of East Sydney in a by-election, but failed to hold it at the general elections in December. He was returned for Yass Plains in a by-election on 15 August 1861. On 16 November 1863 he accepted the office of solicitor-general in the first Martin [q.v.] ministry, and held it until 2 February 1865. On 2 November 1863 he successfully recontested Yass Plains in another by-election. He represented Yass Plains in the fifth parliament from his election on 10 December 1864 until his appointment on 4 October 1865 as a puisne judge of the Supreme Court of New South Wales.

As solicitor-general Faucett behaved 'with the tranquil earnestness becoming the position of one whose sole concern is to have justice done'. His career as a back-bencher was unspectacular, but it was said of him that 'he had the reputation of being a plain-spoken, sober-sided, solid man'. He interested himself in state support for religious denominations, both for their schools and for their community: in connexion with this question he presented petitions from the United Church of England and Ireland, from the Catholic Church and from the Sydney Jewish Community. He also introduced petitions from Anglican and Catholic churches protesting against the matrimonial causes bill of 1862. Of his two public bills only that on titles to land (1858) became law; three of his four private bills were passed.

As a judge Faucett was sound and careful, and his judgments were rarely overruled. He was not brilliant but was universally lauded for his fairness and courtesy. Slow of judgment, he was greatly influenced by legal precedent. When he resigned on 8 February 1888 because of poor health the chief justice, Sir Frederick Darley [q.v.], paid tribute to his industry and ability. On 9 April he was appointed to the Legislative Council for life. He was active in debate and in 1890 again joined in the protest against the matrimonial causes bill.

Faucett was a member of the faculty of law of the University of Sydney and in 1859-94 a fellow of the senate. He represented the university in June 1888 at the octocentenary celebrations of the University of Bologna and in July 1892 at the tercentenary of his alma mater. He also served on the Women's College Council in 1891-92. He played a leading role in the foundation in 1858 of St John's Roman Catholic College by placing the establishing bill before parliament and serving as a fellow on its first council. He resigned in 1863 but retained his interest in the college. He was also associated with the foundation of St Vincent's Hospital, Sydney. He was 'a most devoted and exemplary Catholic'. On 21 January 1862, aged 49, he was married to Frances Clements, an English immigrant aged 25, in St Mary's Cathedral by Archbishop Polding [q.v.]. His wife died four years later while giving birth to their first and only child, Frances, who survived him. His estate was valued at about £27,314. At his home, Erina, Five Dock, on 21 May 1894 he received the last rites and died next day.

NSW Law Reports, 1888; Express (Syd), 27 Dec 1884; Freeman's J (Syd), 28 Jan 1888, 23 May 1894; SMH, 23 May 1894; Senate minutes 1891-94 (Univ Syd Archives); St John's College, Council minutes, 17 Apr 1893, 7 May 1894 (Univ Syd Archives).   W. B. PERRIGNON

FAUCHERY, ANTOINE JULIEN (1827?-1861), writer and photographer, was born in Paris, son of Julien Fauchery and Sophie Gilberte Soret. After trying his hand at painting and wood-engraving, he turned to literature and contributed in particular to the Corsaire-Satan. In 1848 he left Paris with the photographer Nadar, supposedly to defend Poland but was instead imprisoned for a time in Magdeburg. In 1852 Fauchery sailed from Gravesend in the Emily for Melbourne, where he arrived on 22 October. He went to Ballarat and for two years worked on the goldfields. In 1854-55 he spent several months in Melbourne where, at 76 Little Bourke Street East, he founded the Café-Estaminet Français which was well patronized by non-British residents of the town. He returned to the goldfields and for some months was a store-keeper at the Jim Crow (Daylesford) diggings. This venture failed so he went to Melbourne and on 1 March 1856 sailed in the Roxburg Castle for England. Twelve days later Calino, charge d'atelier, a play he had written with Théodore Barrière, was staged with some success in his absence at the Vaudeville Theatre in Paris. In that year La résurrection de Lazare, a 'drama in letter form' that he had written in collaboration with Henri Murger was published in Paris. Back in France Fauchery published his eight Lettres d'un mineur en Australie in fifteen instalments from 9 January to 8 February 1857 in Le Moniteur Universel. They were supplied with a preface by Banville and brought out as a volume by Auguste Poulet-Malassis, a newly-established publisher who had just won notoriety with his first edition of Baudelaire's Fleurs du mal.

On 15 January 1857 at Montmartre Fauchery married Louise Joséphine Gatineau, who had apparently accompanied him to Australia. In April he applied for an official photographic mission to Australia, India and China, and was granted 500 francs by the French government. On 20 July with a lady who gave her name as Julie Fauchery he sailed from London in the Sydenham and on 2 November reached Melbourne. Throughout 1858 he worked as a photographer with a studio at 132 Collins Street East. His work was outstanding, particularly for his time, but in a letter of 20 February 1859 he complained to the French minister of Public Instruction that 'the people of Melbourne did not understand all that was legitimate in [his] desire' to photograph them. Next day he sailed from Melbourne for Manila. In 1860 the French government gave him 1000 francs to leave Manila and follow the French military expedition to China as photographer and journalist. From July to November 1860 he wrote a series of *Lettres de Chine*, which were published in fifteen instalments in *Le Moniteur*, from 12 October 1860 to 3 February 1861. Taken ill in China, he went to Japan where he died at Yokohama on 27 April 1861 from the combined effects of gastritis and dysentery.

His *Lettres d'un mineur* are his chief claim to interest as a writer, and they paint a vivid picture of life in early Melbourne and on the goldfields. Happily Fauchery, unlike most English commentators of the time, is not given to moralizing; as an ardent Republican of 1848 he is constantly, and at times outspokenly, on the side of liberty, against oppressors of all kinds. Hostile to capitalists and scornful of squatters, he is sympathetic to emancipists, diggers, Jews, and above all Chinese. Though his sympathies do not extend to the Aboriginals, they enable him to write imaginatively on the convict system, and to suggest something of the contribution convict and digger would make to the development of national character. But if he has political sympathies, Fauchery is not a political thinker: he shows virtually no interest in the nature of government in Victoria, and no awareness of its earlier social history. He briefly mentions the insurrection at Eureka, but he was then in Melbourne and glosses over the episode as of little account. Through all his endeavours to come to terms with his new experiences he remains a minor Romantic, one of the lesser writers of *la bohème*; he is at his best in his poetic descriptions of the natural scene, and at his most original when he manages to convey something of the quality of its impact upon a fine French sensibility.

P. Larousse, *Grand dictionnaire universel du XIXᵉ siècle*, 1 supp (Paris, 1877); J. Cato, *The story of the camera in Australia* (Melb, 1955); A. Fauchery, *Letters from a miner in Australia*, tr A. R. Chisholm (Melb, 1965); *Illustrated Melb News*, Jan-Feb 1858; Dossier no F17 2961 (Archives Nationales, Paris); Photograph album under Fauchery (LaT L).

K. M. O'NEILL

FAULDING, FRANCIS HARDEY (1816-1868), manufacturing chemist, was born on 23 August 1816 and baptized at Swinefleet, Yorkshire, England, son of Francis Faulding, surgeon, and his wife Mary Ann, née Hardy; his parents had been married by licence on 7 September 1815. Influenced by his family environment and by the experimental work of Joseph Priestley (1733-1804), chemist and 'discoverer' of oxygen, young

Faulding served an apprenticeship with his father and qualified as a chemist and surgeon. He sailed from Liverpool as a surgeon-superintendent in the emigrant ship *Nabob* and arrived at Sydney in February 1842. Seeking better opportunities he sailed in the *Dorset* for Adelaide, but found the economic slump deeper there than in Sydney. With courage he weathered the storm. At 5 Rundle Street on 19 May 1845 he opened an establishment as 'Chemist and Pharmicien', assuring customers that he would stock only the purest and choicest drugs and personally supervise the dispensing of all prescriptions. He imported supplies from England but necessarily had to rely on his own manufacturing supplies. The pharmacy flourished and the premises were soon too crowded for the manufacturing and wholesale side of his business, so Faulding transferred it to a two-storied warehouse in Clarence Place, off King William Street. By 1850 he had many qualified employees, among them Joseph Bosisto [q.v.], and his salesmen travelled far into the country on horseback with packs of samples. The business suffered in the exodus to Victorian goldfields but quickly revived as Faulding increased his supplies of remedial medicines for livestock, especially after 1861 when he took Luther Scammell [q.v.] into partnership. The firm of F. H. Faulding & Co., wholesale druggists and manufacturing chemists, then founded, survives as one of the oldest in Australia.

Faulding's interests were by no means limited to his business. In 1849 he became a leading shareholder of the South Australian Building and Investment Society, and in 1850 was an active promoter of the abortive City of Adelaide Gas Light and Coke Co. In 1861-62 he was a member of the Adelaide City Council, in 1865 a director of the Bank of Adelaide and in 1867 a trustee of the Savings Bank of South Australia. He visited England in 1857-59, 1861 and again in 1863 when he ordered on behalf of the Adelaide City Council a set of eight bells, the Albert Bells, for the tower of the Town Hall.

On 16 September 1852 Rev. T. Q. Stow [q.v.] married Faulding to Eliza, daughter of R. F. Macgeorge at her father's home, Urrbrae (now in the Waite Agricultural Research Institute); they had no children. Although Faulding was dedicated to the elimination of disease and squalor of afflicted humanity, he was not physically robust. He died on 19 November 1868 at Wooton Lea, the home he had built at Glen Osmond and now part of the Presbyterian Girls' College. He was buried in a vault at the West Terrace cemetery. His estate was valued for probate at £56,000 and his bequests included generous sums to his relations in England and to the missionary work of the Wesleyan

Church. On 1 December 1869 his widow married Anthony Forster [q.v.].

F. H. Faulding & Co. Ltd, *A century of medical progress 1845-1945* (Adel, 1945); *Australian*, 22 Feb, 26 Apr 1842; *Register* (Adel), 20 May 1845, 26 May 1849, 9, 12, 17, 26 Jan 1850.

A. F. SCAMMELL

FAVENC, ERNEST (1845-1908), explorer, journalist and historian, was born on 21 October 1845 at Walworth, Surrey, England, son of Abraham George Favenc, merchant, and his wife Emma, née Jones. Educated at the Werderscher Gymnasium in Berlin and at Temple College, Cowley, Oxfordshire, he arrived in Sydney in 1864. After a year in Sydney he went to a pastoral run near Bowen; for the next fourteen years he worked on stations in North Queensland and occasionally wrote for the *Queenslander*. Late in 1877, when the *Queenslander's* proprietors planned an expedition to prove the practicability of a transcontinental railway to Darwin, Favenc was selected as leader. With O'Malley, Hedley, Briggs and an Aboriginal, he left Blackall in July 1878 and reached Darwin in February 1879; the publication of his reports won him repute and soon afterwards he settled in Sydney where on 15 November 1880 he married Elizabeth Jane Matthews.

Favenc's expert bushcraft and unique knowledge of Queensland were valuable for pastoral investors and he was offered a partnership by De Salis [q.v.] Bros, who aimed at extending their interests into the Northern Territory. Late in 1881 Favenc left Sydney to establish a station for the company on Creswell Creek and in 1882, with Hedley, explored a large area from the overland telegraph line to Creswell Creek. He also made attempts to reach the Gulf of Carpentaria along the rivers east of the station but failed. In February 1883 he successfully offered the South Australian government a report on the country watered by the Macarthur River. He left Powell's Creek on 28 May 1883 with Lindsay Crawford, sometime an overland telegraph officer, and an assistant. They reached the Macarthur's headwaters and by following its course found the only practical road to the gulf. They then returned to the telegraph line by a more northerly track, reaching Daly Waters on 15 July.

On his return to Sydney Favenc's failure to win a magistracy in the Northern Territory and the approaching centenary of New South Wales inspired him to undertake his first major work. His *History of Australian Exploration 1788-1888*, supported by the New South Wales government, was a great success and remains a useful reference. While it was printed he visited Western Australia and wrote *Western Australia. Its past history. Its present trade and resources. Its future position;* this shallow, hasty compilation failed to justify its pretentious title. The government refused any financial assistance but the book helped Favenc to secure a commission from an English syndicate to examine pastoral land in the north-west. He arrived at Geraldton in March 1888 and with two companions spent some months on the upper Gascoyne and Ashburton Rivers. The expedition's report appeared in the *Proceedings* of the Royal Geographical Society in 1889 but his reminiscent articles in the Sydney press were described by West Australians as 'a burlesque and a libel on reality'. In Sydney Favenc worked for the *Evening News* and published five books of fiction and one of verse between 1893 and 1905. They were competent, uninspired and often melodramatic but his faithful portrayals of inland Australia secured him a place in Australian literature.

Favenc was a romantic who could attribute the bad luck on his 1883 expedition to loss of a mending kit made by his wife. In spite of failing health, he talked of more exploration but died in Sydney on 14 November 1908, survived by his wife and daughter.

Evening News (Syd), 16 Nov 1908; *Town and Country J*, 18 Nov 1908; CSO 3554/87 (Battye Lib, Perth); Northern Territory files, 1884, 1886 (SAA); MS cat under Ernest Favenc (ML).

H. J. GIBBNEY

FELLOWS, THOMAS HOWARD (1822-1878), politician and judge, was born in October 1822 at Rickmansworth, Hertfordshire, England, son of Thomas Fellows, solicitor, and his wife Mary, née Howard. He was educated at Eton, then worked in his father's office, studied in Pleaders' chambers and later under the master pleader, Thomas Chitty, serving as his valued assistant for about six years. In 1847 Fellows published in London *The law of Costs as affected by the Small Debts Act and other statutes.* Later he took out a certificate as a special pleader and practised until called to the Bar in November 1852. He sailed to Melbourne in the *Kent*, arriving in April 1853. He was admitted to the Victorian Bar in May, and although inclined first to seek a police magistracy, he persevered at his practice, and after a pro-squatter judgment was appointed standing counsel to the Pastoral Association.

In September 1854 Fellows was returned for the Loddon district to the Legislative Council where he showed an active and lasting interest in legal reform. He followed

Robert Molesworth [q.v.] as solicitor-general in the Haines [q.v.] government in June 1856 and in August contested the Central Province seat in the first Legislative Council under responsible government. At Emerald Hill in his only campaign meeting Fellows repelled electors by his high-handed manner and lost. He campaigned again more amicably in September and was returned for St Kilda to the Legislative Assembly. In February 1857 he succeeded W. F. Stawell [q.v.] as attorney-general but lost office in March when the Haines ministry resigned. He was solicitor-general in the second Haines ministry from April 1857 to March 1858. In May 1858 he was elected for Central Province by a majority of one to the Legislative Council. He represented the Nicholson [q.v.] ministry in the council without portfolio from October 1859 to November 1860; he failed to modify the council's attitude towards the Nicholson land bill and his attempted compromise in August helped to bring down the government. In October 1863 he became postmaster-general in the McCulloch [q.v.] ministry but found its liberal policy uncongenial and withdrew in March 1864.

During the tussle between the two Houses in the 1860s Fellows doggedly defended the constitutional rights of the council. After a tedious tirade in July 1865 he moved that the assembly's appropriation-cum-tariff bill 'be laid aside'. As leader of the Opposition in the council he was sought by Governor Darling in 1866 to form a ministry but his terms were too difficult. In 1867 he angrily moved the council's rejection of the Lady Darling grant tack to the appropriation bill in August and then declined, unless elevated to ministerial status, to advise the governor. To strengthen the constitutional party in the assembly, Fellows contested St Kilda in the general election of February 1868; he was returned and from May to July, as minister of justice in the Sladen [q.v.] cabinet served as leader of the government in the Legislative Assembly.

When conflict between council and assembly abated Fellows accepted other public roles. In 1870 he was appointed a trustee of the Public Library, Museums and National Gallery and a commissioner of the planned intercolonial legislation and federal union inquiries. In 1872 he helped to organize Victorian exhibits for the London International Exhibition of 1873 and served in the commission on the accommodation needs of the Supreme Court branches. Fellows's legal career culminated with his appointment as fifth judge of the Supreme Court of Victoria in December 1872. To attract him from his large and lucrative common law practice at the Bar, the salaries of puisne judges were

raised from £2500 to £3000. Fellows was not an outstanding judge but was valued for his clear expositions, memory for precedent and intimate familiarity with statute law.

Among other activities Fellows was a Prahran councillor in 1861-64 and, because of his attachment to Queenscliff where he spent his summers, was elected one of the first borough councillors in 1863 and mayor in 1865. As a devout Anglican, Fellows gave generously to the Church of England at Queenscliff and to the Anglican school and church near his home in South Yarra, and was privately beneficent. In his youth he was a keen sportsman and in Melbourne often rowed on the Yarra River and played regularly with the South Yarra Football Club. His wife Jane, née Hemmons, and his brother, Rev. Walter Fellows, were present when he died on 8 April 1878 at his home in South Yarra and the Crown Law Offices were closed on the day of his burial at St Kilda cemetery.

H. G. Turner, A history of the colony of Victoria, 2 (Lond, 1904); J. L. Forde, The story of the Bar of Victoria (Melb, 1913); G. Serle, The golden age (Melb, 1963); Argus, 15, 27, 28 Aug, 5 Sept 1856, 25 Jan 1868, 9, 10 Apr 1878; Age, 9 Apr 1878.   CAROLE WOODS

FELTON, ALFRED (1831-1904), businessman and philanthropist, was born on 8 November 1831 at Maldon, Essex, England, the fifth child of six sons and three daughters of Thomas Felton, tanner, and his wife Hannah. He was probably apprenticed to a chemist before migrating to Victoria in 1853. He is said to have made money carting goods to the goldfields before establishing himself as a merchant in Melbourne. In 1857 he was a commission agent and general dealer and in 1861 a wholesale druggist in Swanston Street.

In 1867 Felton bought the wholesale drug house of Youngman & Co. in partnership with its manager, F. S. Grimwade [q.v.]. Renamed Felton, Grimwade & Co. the firm expanded rapidly in the next twenty-five years, and although the depression of the 1890s reduced both its trading and manufacturing activities it remained the largest drug house in the colony and a sound and profitable business, with subsidiary interests in drug houses in New Zealand and Western Australia. The two men also founded other enterprises: in 1872 the Melbourne Glass Bottle Works (ancestor of Australian Glass Manufacturers Ltd) and an acid works which was merged in 1897 with Cuming Smith & Co.; in 1882 the Adelaide Chemical Works Co., in partnership with the principals of Cuming Smith & Co., and the Australian Salt Manufacturing Co., the only failure among their ventures; and in 1885 J. Bosisto & Co., in partnership with Joseph Bosisto [q.v.] founder of the eucalyptus oil industry in Australia. Felton also bought two large estates, Murray Downs and Langi Kal Kal, in partnership with Charles Campbell, senior partner in Cuming Smith & Co. When Felton died on 8 January 1904 his assets were valued at more than £500,000.

Shrewd and upright in business, Felton was mildly eccentric in his private life and opinions. Although probably self-educated, he had a strong interest in literature and the arts, and the bachelor rooms in the St Kilda Hotel in which he spent his last twenty years were crowded with books, pictures and *objets d'art*. He sought no public office, and his many benefactions were usually discreet and anonymous, though he did not shun public controversy in his warm support of the Australian Church, founded by Charles Strong [q.v.]. After his death his will gained him more renown than he had ever sought in life: it established a trust fund, originally of £383,163 but later increased to more than £2,000,000, under the control of a Felton Bequests' Committee of five. Half the income was to be given to charities, especially those for the relief of women and children, and the other half spent on works of art for the Melbourne National Gallery, works judged 'to have an artistic and educative value and be calculated to raise or improve the level of public taste'. In its first sixty years the committee spent £1,237,000 on works of art, to the inestimable benefit of the gallery's collection.

A portrait by Sir John Longstaff from a photograph is in the National Gallery; it shows Felton in old age, in amiable mood on a seat in his partner's garden at Caulfield.

C. Bage (ed), *Historical record of the Felton Bequests*, 1-2 (Melb, 1923, 1927); R. Grimwade, *Flinders Lane: recollections of Alfred Felton* (Melb, 1947); E. D. Lindsay (ed), *The Felton Bequest, an historical record 1904-1959* (Melb, 1963); J. R. Poynter, *Russell Grimwade* (Melb, 1967); *Argus*, 9, 11, 13 Jan 1904; R. Grimwade papers (Univ Melb Archives); Felton papers (held by Trustees and Executors Agency Co. Ltd, Melb).   J. R. POYNTER

FENTON, JAMES (1820-1901), pioneer, was born on 20 November 1820 at Dunlavin, Ireland, son of James Fenton, landowner. He was educated at a Protestant boarding school near the Vale of Avoca. In 1833 his father decided to migrate to Van Diemen's Land, probably because of a favourable report from his cousin, Michael Fenton [q.v.]; the family sailed from Liverpool in the *Othello* but in the Bay of Biscay

the father died and was buried at sea. The ship arrived at Hobart Town in February 1834. James was sent to a boarding school near Hobart, and his mother moved with the rest of the family to Swansea where she had bought land from a son of George Meredith [q.v.]. There she built a home and lived until her death. The property was then taken over by Edward Carr Shaw who had married her daughter Anne. Shaw had come from Ireland in 1830 and was an uncle of George Bernard Shaw.

The Fenton brothers Michael, John and Charles moved to the mainland: Michael and John to Warrnambool in Victoria where Michael became mayor; and Charles to New South Wales. The eldest sister, Elizabeth, had married George Hall who had taken up land on the north coast near Port Sorell. James visited his brother-in-law and became interested in the district. All the lightly timbered country had been taken up between the Mersey River (Devonport) and Emu Bay (Burnie) where the Van Diemen's Land Co. had made a base in 1828, but the heavy forests west of the Mersey were deemed impossible for conversion into farms even with convict labour. In 1840 Fenton went to this area on the Forth River where he had bought a thousand acres from the government. He was the only settler in the district and the nearest post office was at Westbury fifty miles away. He built a hut and made a canoe to cross the river but his greatest problem was the timber. At the Forth estuary, for the first time in Australia, he applied the technique of ringbarking for clearing forest land. The undergrowth was cut down and burned and, when the ringbarked trees died, grass and crops could be grown among them. In 1846 he married Helena Mary, sister of Thomas Monds [q.v.]; they had one son and three daughters.

In 1852 James joined the exodus to the goldfields of Victoria; leaving his family in Launceston he crossed to Port Phillip. On the Yarra he saw a city of canvas from which the male population had gone to the goldfields, and asked himself—'when they come back with gold where will they live?' He concluded that they would want timber for rough-and-ready houses and that it could be readily supplied from Tasmania's north-west forests. He returned home, engaged men to fell and split the trees, and soon sold half a million palings to Melbourne builders. With the profits he acquired more land at the Forth, Leven and Don Rivers; his first object in acquiring this country was to exploit it for timber. Tracks for bullock wagons had been cut by his axemen, some of whom became his tenants on small areas which they gradually cleared.

In 1879 Fenton retired from farming and built a home at Launceston where he wrote *A History of Tasmania from its discovery in 1642 to the present time* (Hobart, 1884). In 1891 he completed *Bush Life in Tasmania fifty years ago*, a first-hand description of a pioneer's life. His wife died in 1892 and he died on 24 June 1901. The beautiful farm lands carved out of the north-coast forests are his best monument.

His son, Charles Benjamin Monds, built a store at the Forth in 1869 and later farmed on the headland at Table Cape where as a guide to mariners he kept a large lantern burning each night and was later instrumental in having a lighthouse erected. He founded the Table Cape Butter Factory, and in 1886-96 represented Wellington in the House of Assembly. In 1869 he had married Rebecca Ditcham; they had eight children, many of whose descendants live in the districts pioneered by their ancestor.

Examiner (Launceston), 25 June 1901.

F. C. GREEN

FERGUSON, CHARLES WILLIAM (1847-1940), vigneron, was born on 11 September 1847 in Perth, Western Australia, son of Dr John Ferguson [q.v.] and his wife Isabella, née Maxwell. He went with his mother to Scotland in 1855 and attended the Dundee Seminary for three years; on his return he became a foundation student at Bishop Hale's [q.v.] School.

Charles left in 1863 to work on his father's properties: Houghton (bought in 1859) and Strelley (first held by R. H. Bland [q.v.]). There he developed the vineyards that pioneered the viticultural industry in Western Australia. Of his father's first vintage, twenty-five gallons of wine in 1859, Ferguson wrote: 'It was my job to drop in more pebbles as evaporation went on, until fermentation ceased. This was tested by a match at the bung hole and when half a dozen burned one's finger before going out, fermentation was deemed to have run its course'. In 1869 he caught the bushranger 'Moondyne Joe' [q.v. J. B. Johns] in the Houghton cellars. Apart from two years in the pearling industry in the early 1870s Ferguson lived at Houghton until he retired in 1911. He experimented with fertilizers for his vines and also the bush system of growing vines, which he considered more economic than the conventional trellis system. He stored his wine in oak casks and in 1903 opened bottling cellars in Prince's Building, St George's Terrace, Perth. At the same time the name Houghton was adopted and used on the registered label. Grapes for a wide variety of red, white and fortified wines were grown at Houghton.

Active in the affairs of the Middle Swan district, Ferguson served on the Swan Roads Board and was a keen member of the Royal Agricultural Society. In 1898 he was made a justice of the peace. For forty years he was churchwarden for St Mary's Anglican Church. He was an enthusiastic cricketer and the pitch he laid down at Houghton became the home of the Swan Cricket Club for many years. In 1876 he had married Dora Charlotte, daughter of Dr Samuel Waterman Viveash and his wife Susan, née Smith; they had nine children. He died at Airlie, Mount Lawley, on 16 January 1940, survived by his wife, four sons and three daughters.

Western Mail (Perth), 17 Apr 1914; *West Australian*, 12 Sept 1935, 17, 18, 19 Jan 1940.

FERGUSON, MEPHAN (1843-1919), manufacturer, was born on 25 July 1843 at Falkirk, Scotland, son of John Ferguson, contractor, and his wife, née Boyd. He arrived in Melbourne with his parents in 1854; after three years at Emerald Hill he moved to Ballarat, where he was indentured to John Price, a prosperous blacksmith. Seventeen years later he returned to Melbourne to establish himself as an ironfounder and railway contractor. The successful completion of one of his first large contracts, a bridge over the Yarra, enabled him to obtain much government work. He built twenty bridges on the north-eastern railway and eight on the Clifton Hill line; he manufactured and erected many footbridges, engine traverses and station verandahs, and he also fabricated the wrought-iron and cast-iron work, some 1300 tons in weight, for the Newport railway workshops. The cast-iron and wrought-iron work for the Maryborough and Seymour engine sheds came from his establishment, and he built up a large trade in bolts, nuts and buffers for the Victorian and other colonial railways.

Ferguson owed his early success to his entrepreneurial and technical skills and to the government's protectionist policy of awarding contracts to colonial firms. By 1885 he was well established. In that year, when Alfred Deakin returned from California and decided that wrought-iron pipes should replace cast-iron in the Melbourne water supply, Ferguson acted promptly. He won government contracts for the supply of wrought-iron piping, and bought the Glasgow Iron Works in West Melbourne where he established a new factory and testing works. He also imported the latest hydraulic machinery and designed a plant said to match any in the world. Ferguson had earlier bought the Carlton foundry, and now employed 300 hands. His outlay was more than covered by an output of £150,000 a year, and he soon had to establish new buildings on a ten-acre site at Footscray.

Ferguson continued his experiments with wrought-iron pipes, and perfected straight-riveted, longitudinal and transverse seams and, more important, pipes with spiral seams. Seventy miles of this lighter piping was used in the Melbourne water supply by 1909, while Ferguson also supplied the pipes for many of the Victorian Water Trusts, the Chaffey brothers' irrigation scheme and similar ventures in New Zealand, Ceylon and Malaya. He also patented a locking bar or rivetless pipe which was first used by the South Australian government. He achieved world-wide attention by defeating overseas competitors for the contract to supply 360 miles of thirty-inch steel main for the Kalgoorlie pipeline in Western Australia. Soon afterwards he won a large contract for the Mona Gas Co. at Tipton, South Staffordshire, despite heavy competition. He designed and manufactured his own plant at Footscray, and shipped it to England where his work was highly praised. One English journal saw it as a 'welcome landmark in the path of Imperial progress', but English contractors were not so pleased. Ferguson continued to expand his bridge and railway work, despite depression in the 1890s, and held many contracts for wrought-iron piping in the Australian colonies. The firm also developed a large general engineering trade, including marine boilers, and won contracts for various sewerage schemes. His continued emphasis on innovation and research, and his policy of reinvesting profits in the firm accounted for much of its success.

Ferguson married first, Agnes Shand, by whom he had five sons and two daughters, and second, Maggie Kennedy, by whom he had one daughter. He died at Falkirk, Royal Parade, Parkville, on 2 November 1919, leaving an estate worth £14,000. He was survived by three sons and three daughters; one son was killed in World War I. The vast industry Ferguson built declined after his death but he had shown what enterprise and research could achieve.

A. Sutherland et al, Victoria and its metropolis, 2 (Melb, 1888); H. Michell (ed), Footscray's first fifty years (Footscray, 1909); 'Men of today. Mephan Ferguson', Scientific Australian, 20 Mar 1886; Argus, 24 Mar 1886, 3 Nov 1919; Vic Engineer, 15 June 1886.

GEORGE PARSONS

FERGUSSON, SIR JAMES (1832-1907), governor, was born on 14 March 1832 in Edinburgh, the eldest son of Sir Charles Dalrymple Fergusson, fifth baronet of Kil-kerran in Ayrshire, and his wife Helen, daughter of David Boyle. Fergusson went to Rugby, succeeded to the baronetcy in 1849 and next year entered University College, Oxford. He left without a degree, entered the Grenadier Guards and served in the Crimean war where he was wounded in November 1854. Elected as a Conservative for Ayrshire he entered the House of Commons in May 1855. He retired from the army on 9 August 1859. In 1857 he lost his seat but held it again in 1859-68. He was under-secretary for India in 1866-67 and for the Home Office in 1867-68. He succeeded Sir Dominick Daly as governor of South Australia and in the Rangatira arrived at Adelaide on 15 February 1869. The duke of Edinburgh was present next day when Fergusson was sworn in.

South Australia was then in severe depression. A run of bad seasons had ruined harvests, copper and wool prices were low, unemployment was high and many people were migrating to Victoria and New South Wales. As a remedy the government tried to implement Strangways's [q.v.] reforms for selling waste lands on easy terms to small settlers but much amendment of the 1868 Act was needed. In the Northern Territory problems of land and settlement were also a costly burden. Disputation in parliament was continuous and sometimes bitter, ministries were short and sometimes stillborn and dissolutions of parliament were too frequent to please the press and some members of parliament. The first crisis was created by dissatisfaction with the budget proposed by Strangways's government. In January 1870 he asked Fergusson to dissolve parliament and despite protests from parliament and press the governor gave his assent. When the new parliament met on 27 May Strangways resigned and John Hart [q.v.] formed a government. On his resignation in November 1871 Ayers and Blyth [qq.v.] failed to form ministries and Fergusson again agreed to dissolve parliament. Blyth resigned when parliament met in January 1872 and Ayers then formed a ministry. The dissolutions granted to Strangways and Blyth were described by the South Australian Register as the 'gravest errors' of Fergusson's administration. The governor was accused of mistaking the passing attitudes of private members as permanent disorganization and of not realizing that in colonial parliaments party formations changed with every issue; Fergusson had 'honestly striven to act for the best' but he suffered gravely from inexperience of colonial institutions. The governor met this adverse criticism calmly and with dignity.

By June 1871 the colony's economy had improved, the 1870-71 wheat harvest was a record and high prices for wool and copper stimulated trade. Fergusson's interest in the colony's economic progress was active, practical but never domineering. On his way to South Australia he had taken steps to initiate colonial trade with India, particularly in remounts for the Indian army. He visited many agricultural shows in country centres and his speeches, which usually advocated the importance of independence, were designed both to encourage the settlers and promote greater production. Church, charitable and educational institutions could rely on his interest and support. His more personal acts included gifts of books to the construction parties on the overland telegraph line and the loan of his yacht to clergymen visiting outlying coastal missions. He took a close interest in the affairs of the Ebenezer Mission School and encouraged moves towards opening an institution for the blind, deaf and dumb, both for children and for adults. In 1872 Fergusson gave his warm support to the formation of a University Association to promote the establishment of a university. The object of the association, which was greatly aided by a most generous act of self-denial by the Presbyterian, Baptist and Congregational Churches, was achieved with the passing in 1874 of the Act which established the University of Adelaide.

Probably Fergusson's greatest achievement as governor was his part in securing the route of the overland telegraph line through the Northern Territory to Port Augusta. He encouraged the South Australian government in its decision to undertake the land route which required landing the submarine cable at Port Darwin rather than Burketown in Queensland, and then risked Colonial Office disapproval by cabling instructions direct to the South Australian agent-general in London in order to secure the British Australian Telegraph Co.'s contract. He watched the progress of the enterprise closely and consistently defended the colony against charges of acting selfishly to obtain the contract. Fergusson was prominent in the celebrations which greeted Charles Todd's [q.v.] return to Adelaide in November 1872 and his deep personal interest in the project was generously acknowledged.

Less generous were criticisms of Fergusson's apparent aloofness from the community. His social functions at Government House were not lavish and were bitterly attacked by men such as Lavington Glyde [q.v.]. In answer to Glyde's charges Fergusson wrote that it was his duty 'to guarantee to those who come on my invitation to Government House that they shall only meet there persons of respectable character'.

His hospitality was also curtailed by his wife's ill health, her confinement in April 1871 and her death in October. Government House levee lists also helped to revive a dispute over precedence, by which the governor gave place to Anglican and Roman Catholic bishops as prescribed in an earlier directive from the duke of Newcastle to Governor MacDonnell. In September 1872 the problem was solved when the Queen assured the colonists that in future no bishop or minister of any religious persuasion should be allowed precedence in the colony.

In November 1872 Fergusson was appointed governor of New Zealand and left Adelaide on 6 December for a short visit to England. In 1875, hoping to return to politics, he resigned his post in New Zealand and was made K.C.M.G. In England he tried in vain to re-enter parliament in 1876 and 1878 and in March 1880 accepted the governorship of Bombay. In February 1885 he was made G.C.S.I., and in March returned to England. In 1885-1906 he represented Manchester, serving as under-secretary in the Foreign Office in 1886-91 and postmaster-general in 1891-92. In 1893 with J. Henniker Heaton, J. F. Hogan [qq.v.] and others he formed an Australian party in the House of Commons. Fergusson was a director of the Royal Mail Steam Packet Co., the National Telephone Co. and similar enterprises. In 1907 he attended the conference of the British Cotton Growing Association at Jamaica, where on 14 January in a violent earthquake Fergusson was killed while walking in the street near his hotel. He was buried in a churchyard near Kingston.

On 9 August 1859 Fergusson married Edith Christian, daughter of James Andrew Ramsay, marquis of Dalhousie; she died aged 32 at Adelaide on 28 October 1871, leaving two sons and two daughters. On 11 March 1873 in New Zealand he married Olive, daughter of John Henry Richman of Warnbunga, South Australia; she died of cholera at Bombay on 8 January 1882, leaving one son. On 5 April 1893 he married Isabella Elisabeth, widow of Charles Hugh Hoare and daughter of Thomas Twysden; she survived him without issue.

E. Hodder, *The History of South Australia*, 2 (Lond, 1893); *Register* (Adel), 16 Feb 1869, 5, 7 Dec 1872; *Australasian*, 12 Sept 1874; CO 124-130.   V. A. EDGELOE

FERRES, JOHN (1818-1898), government printer, was born 1 October 1818 at Bath, England, the second son of Robert Ferres (d. 1820), printer, and his wife Esther, née Chancellor. After elementary education, he was trained in the printing trade and ran a general office in Bath, distributing magazines, newspapers and other publications. He was married on 8 June 1846 to Julia Harriett Langdon of Bath; she died without issue on 17 April 1848. In August Ferres followed his mother, his sisters Hannah Wilton and Eliza Cooper, their husbands and two nephews to Victoria, arriving in Melbourne in December. He spent some time near Alberton, Gippsland, where his family had settled and where his mother died on 23 June 1865, before returning to his trade in Melbourne. There he joined the staff of the *Melbourne Morning Herald* and soon became manager. On his advice a steam-driven printing machine was imported and installed in the *Herald* office.

On 8 November 1851 Ferres was appointed government printer, succeeding Edward Khull [q.v.] and taking over a staff of six and limited plant and machinery. He issued the first *Government Gazette* in January 1852. Work increased with the rapid growth of the colony and by 1887 the staff numbered 278. In 1858, after several moves, the Printing Office was housed in a new building in Gisborne (now Macarthur) Street; as government printer, Ferres resided on the premises. At 60 he was superannuated on a pension of £333 but in 1881 was reinstated; his return, according to the *Australasian*, was 'a distinct gain to the state' for he was 'as competent now . . . as . . . at any time of his life'. Ferres was known for his equable temperament. Garryowen [q.v. Finn] acknowledged his integrity, organizational ability, technical knowledge, capacity to withstand political pressures, cool head, and inexhaustible stock of patience.

Ferres had compiled and published in Melbourne *William Caxton: A Contribution in commemoration of The Festival held in Melbourne, 1871, to celebrate The Fourth Centenary of the First Printing in the English Language*. The French government honoured him with a decoration for specimens of fine printing.

Ferres retired for a second time in 1887 and then lived at Hawthorn where he was a justice of the peace. He died on 21 August 1898 after an illness of two years, and was buried in the Melbourne cemetery. He was survived by his widow Mary, née Davey, whom he had married on 23 January 1851 at the Independent Manse, Collins Street. They had four sons and two daughters.

Garryowen (E. Finn), *The chronicles of early Melbourne*, 1-2 (Melb, 1888); Government Printer, *100 years of service* (Melb, nd); *Australasian*, 17 Sept 1881; *A'sian Typographical J*, Aug 1898; Roberts family papers (held privately).   HARLEY W. FORSTER

FETHERSTONHAUGH, CUTHBERT (1837-1925), pastoralist, was born on 22 June 1837 in Dardistown, County Westmeath, Ireland, son of Cuthbert Fetherstonhaugh and his wife Susan, née Curtis. In 1843 the family moved to Germany and returned to Ireland in 1848. Cuthbert attended school in Frankfurt and Wales and later Belfast Academy. In 1852 his father, two brothers and a cousin left Ireland for Victoria and in May 1853 Cuthbert followed in the *Sussex*.

In Melbourne Cuthbert worked first as a wharf clerk for £2 10s. a week but soon joined a brother as a carrying contractor and cleared £5 a week. He next went surveying on the Upper Goulburn River and then trapped horses with Hunter and Snodgrass [qq.v.] in the ranges. Persuaded by his mother to take more steady employment, he worked on Edward Henty's [q.v.] Muntham run for six years. With Tom Clibborn [q.v.] Fetherstonhaugh laid out the Coleraine steeplechase and won repute as one of the most dare-devil riders of the Western District.

Fetherstonhaugh left Muntham in 1862 and went to Queensland where with two partners he acquired Ban Ban near Gayndah on the Burnett River. Travelling further north Cuthbert was stricken with dysentery. On recovery, he bought the lease of Burton Downs, 300 miles north of Rockhampton, in June 1863 but after a three-year struggle Burton Downs had to be sold. Although penniless and with diminished vitality, he remained adventurous. His reputed encounter with the bushranger Bluecap and his gang was recalled by B. H. T. Boake [q.v.], and he also figured as 'Rev. Herbert Heatherstone' in Rolf Boldrewood's [q.v. T. A. Browne] *The Colonial Reformer*.

Fetherstonhaugh underwent a religious experience in 1865 and in 1872, encouraged by Dean H. B. Macartney [q.v.], he studied for the Anglican ministry. After acting as lay-reader at Templestowe, Doncaster and Anderson's Creek near Melbourne, he was ordained at Wagga Wagga in July 1873 and then took charge of the Brookong-Jerilderie parish. Two of his sermons were published: *Our Father* in 1874 and *Truth and Freedom* in 1876. His stipend of £300 helped him to buy the books he had longed for but his reading led him to question beliefs he had accepted from childhood. Unable to accept major Anglican dogma, he resigned in May 1875 but served at Urana as an unsectarian minister. In 1876 he became manager of Canally station near Balranald and on 16 November in Melbourne he married Flora Agnes Murchison. Next year with partners he bought Goorianawa station in the Castlereagh district and managed it for seventeen years.

In 1886 Fetherstonhaugh helped to form the Commercial and Pastoral Association of New South Wales and in 1890 the Pastoralists' Union. In 1894 he began to advocate inland freezing works and a meat export company. In relevant journals and lectures all over the colony he sought support for his scheme and by August 71,000 shares and £40,100 in debentures had been taken up. In 1895 he visited Chicago to engage experts in canning. In 1898 when the Stockowners' Meat Export Co. was well established he turned to mining in the Gulf Country. Successful, he returned in 1902 to New South Wales, and worked as a government land valuer.

Fetherstonhaugh next bought Mungarie, east of Coonamble. In old age he left its management to his son Cuthbert and lived at Blackheath. His last great interest was the Free Kindergarten Union of New South Wales. In 1918 he published in Sydney his lively autobiography, *After Many Days*, which he continued as 'My religious experiences' (c. 1919), a manuscript now in the Mitchell Library. He died on 10 June 1925 at Wellington, survived by his wife, two sons and one daughter. He left an estate worth £3252.

B. Boake, *Where the dead men lie and other poems*, A. G. Stephens ed, 2nd ed (Lond, 1913); *Australasian*, 6 May 1876; *Pastoral Review*, 16 Apr, 15 Aug 1894, 15 Nov 1895, 16 Aug 1909, 16 July 1925; SMH, 11 June 1925; *Sydney Mail*, 17 June 1925.   J. ANN HONE

FINCHAM, GEORGE (1828-1910), organbuilder, was born on 20 August 1828 at St Pancras, Middlesex, England, the second son of Jonathan George Fincham, organbuilder, and his wife Jane, née Parry. After attending a private school he was apprenticed in 1842-49 to the London organbuilder, Henry Bevington, and then worked as a foreman for James Bishop & Son.

Fincham arrived in Victoria on 9 July 1852 in the *Duke of Cornwall* and set up as an organ-tuner and repairer at 113 Queen Street, Melbourne. Next year he visited the Ballarat diggings but returned in 1854. In 1855 he bought land in Bridge Road, Richmond, where he built his home and a bluestone factory. To finance equipment and stock for his factory, he worked on the new Spencer Street railway station building and later for James Henty [q.v.] & Co. By 1862 he was able to start organbuilding; churches then had funds for pipe organs and interest in organ music was stimulated by the newly-arrived organists C. E. Horsley, David Lee and Rev. G. W. Torrance [qq.v.]. In June 1866 the Victorian government awarded

Fincham £100 for organbuilding with colonial materials and metal pipes of his own manufacture. In 1878 he bought the firm of Lee & Kaye, and in 1881 established an Adelaide branch, managed by Arthur Hobday, his ex-apprentice, until sold in 1894 to J. E. Dodd. In 1904 he opened a branch in Sydney, while he had agents in Perth (1897) and Brisbane (1902).

Fincham's first organ was of ten stops; at the same time he built an organ of seventeen stops. This was the first organ of any considerable size built in the colony; it was opened in the factory on 21 December 1864. His organ for the Melbourne Exhibition in 1866 won an award, the first of many for his work. In 1879 his tender for an organ for the Melbourne Exhibition Building was accepted against overseas competition. The four-manual organ of seventy speaking stops was completed for the 1880-81 Melbourne International Exhibition, and remained in use in the building for nearly fifty years. Altogether he built about 200 organs for cathedrals and churches and supplied pipe work and parts to organbuilders throughout Australasia. His integrity and the quality of the organs he built overcame the prejudice towards colonial work. He was outstanding among Australian organbuilders for his skill, his business ability and his readiness to keep pace with modern trends. He patented many improvements; most of the organs he built had mechanical action and from 1886 some had tubular-pneumatic.

Active in church and community affairs Fincham was a vestryman at St Stephen's Church, Richmond, until 1878 when the family moved to Hawthorn. In 1880 he became a justice of the peace and honorary magistrate. He was a member of the Chamber of Manufactures and was a committee member of the Workingmen's College, the Victorian Society of Organists and the Melbourne Philharmonic Society; he also joined the Metropolitan Liedertafel, the Old Colonists' Association, the Richmond and Hawthorn bowling clubs and the Hawthorn Rowing Club. In 1858 Fincham married Margaret, daughter of Samuel Tilley and his wife Ann, née Warrington. Of their four children, one son died in infancy and Frederick (1861-1878) died in the wreck of the *Loch Ard*; a daughter was born in 1877 while a third son, Leslie V. H. (1879-1955), became a partner of the firm in 1901. Fincham died at Hawthorn on 21 December 1910. His business was continued by his descendants.

E. N. Matthews, *Colonial organs and organbuilders* (Melb, 1969), and for bibliog; Roy Com on the tariff, Evidence, V&P (LA Vic), 1883, 4 (10).   JOHN HENWOOD

FINCH-HATTON, HAROLD HENEAGE (1856-1904), imperial federationist, was born on 23 August 1856 at Eastwell Park, Kent, England, the fourth son of George William Finch-Hatton, tenth earl of Winchilsea and fifth earl of Nottingham, and his wife Fanny Margaretta, daughter of Edward Royd Rice of Dane Court, Kent. His forebears included eminent statesmen and jurists. Educated at Eton and Balliol College, Oxford, Harold went to Queensland at 19 to visit his elder brother, Henry Stormont (1852-1927), who succeeded to the two earldoms in 1898 and held leaseholds in the Nebo district south-west of Mackay. In 1868 the Finch-Hattons' kinsman, Lionel Knight Rice, had begun to acquire the cattle runs later known collectively as Mount Spencer. At separate times in 1881 Henry and Harold became partners with Rice and the station manager, Charles Walter Toussaint. Apparently the partnership was reduced to the two Finch-Hattons by March 1888.

In 1881 Harold had joined the rush to the Mount Britten goldfield, forty-five miles west of Mount Spencer, and invested £16,000 in a pioneer mining undertaking which returned him only some £10,000. In 1883, probably with his brother, he returned permanently to England, although Henry seems to have visited Australia in the mid-1880s. Harold's *Advance Australia! An Account of Eight Years' Work, Wandering, and Amusement, in Queensland, New South Wales, and Victoria* (London, 1885) gave a vivid impression of life on station and diggings and preserved much squatter-lore on many subjects including the Aboriginals. Convinced that the sugar industry could survive only with cheap coloured labour, he advocated government control of the Kanaka trade, not for humanitarian reasons but to free the planters from the politically damaging slur of slave trading. He strongly opposed the Griffith ministry on its Kanaka policy and predicted the rise of a northern separationist movement if the government decided to ban the coolie traffic.

In England Harold failed three times to win a seat in the House of Commons but was returned unopposed for the Newark division of Nottinghamshire in July 1895. His maiden speech on 28 April 1896 demonstrated the limits of ultra-conservatism; he resigned in April 1898, unable to stomach the concessions made to the Liberal Unionists by the Salisbury government. He was the founding treasurer, but otherwise a passive member, of the Imperial Federation League. For a time he was sole member, and then chairman, of the London committee of the North Queensland Separation League. He was also secretary of the Pacific Telegraph Co., formed to link Vancouver and Australia. When not in London he lived at Harlech and was high sheriff of Merionethshire in 1903. Unmarried, he died of heart failure in London on 16 May 1904.

V&P (LA Qld), 1886, 1, 429; The Times, July-Sept 1884, 13-26 May 1898, 18 May 1904; Australasian, 16 Apr 1887; Run registers (QA).

D. P. CROOK
DAVID DENHOLM

FINK, BENJAMIN JOSMAN (1847-1909), businessman, politician and speculator, was born on 21 April 1847 in Guernsey, Channel Islands, the eldest son of Moses Fink and his wife Gertrude, née Ascher. The family arrived at Melbourne on 14 April 1861 in the *Suffolk*. Moses Fink's brother Hirsch had started a small business in Geelong: Moses at first worked for him as an itinerant hawker. Benjamin completed his education at the Flinders School, Geelong, and at 16 went to New Zealand where he worked as a produce dealer.

In 1865 Fink returned to Melbourne and became a clerk for Wallach Bros, an Elizabeth Street emporium. Gifted musically, he demonstrated and sold pianos and furniture to such effect that by 1874 he was joint owner of the store. In 1880 the National Bank lent him £60,000 to buy out his partner, Maurice Aron. In 1883 Fink opened two branches of Wallach's in Sydney, later rebuilding the Melbourne store for £120,000. In the 1880s he also bought large interests in coal-mines, gold-mines and pastoral properties. In 1883-89 Fink was an independent member of the Legislative Assembly for Maryborough, but his political career remained always subservient to his business, which began to expand rapidly. He amalgamated his small Joint Stock Bank of Ballarat with the City of Melbourne Bank, making it the colony's biggest buyer of gold. In the next years the City Bank lent Fink more than £300,000, most of which was lost in speculation. In 1884 he bought W. H. Rocke's furniture business, which gave him control of the most important retail outlets for quality furniture. In 1885 he took over the famous Duke mine at Maryborough, had it pumped dry and won £70,000 worth of gold in three years; he also formed the Mercantile Finance Co. Ltd, which rapidly became one of the biggest land boom companies. In 1888 he erected Fink's Buildings on the corner of Flinders and Elizabeth Streets at a cost of £110,000; he also bought the original Cole's [q.v.] Book Arcade for £40,000, Gresham Buildings for £52,000 and several other sites which were converted into shops and office blocks. He built 'The Block', Melbourne's leading shopping arcade of the day, and took over and rebuilt Georges Ltd. Among the hotels he bought, leased or controlled were the Ballarat Star, Albion, Saracen's Head, Governor Arthur and Rose and Crown. In 1888 he undertook to pay the McCracken [q.v.] family £250,000 for the right to float their brewery into a £2,000,000 public company. He persuaded the Stock Exchange of Melbourne to build on his land at a cost of £220,000; it yielded him a personal profit of £55,000. All these ventures were supported by a complex system of cross-financing which was never fully untangled.

When the land boom collapsed and devalued his speculations, Fink's apparent wealth vanished. The Mercantile Finance Co. alone showed a loss of nearly £1,000,000. He made a so-called 'secret composition' with his creditors, revealing debts of £1,520,000. His estate realized ½d. in the £. Fink left Melbourne hurriedly for London with his family. At least two attempts were made by leading institutions to have Fink's composition set aside on the ground that 'registration was obtained by fraud', but in these cases out-of-court settlements were made and public investigation avoided. Large assets were in the name of his wife Catherine, who was the daughter of his uncle Hirsch and whom he had married on 14 October 1874 at Geelong. After the crash Catherine retained control of the remaining assets and even increased them. In 1892, the year of his insolvency, Benjamin transferred to his wife much land in Melbourne's western suburbs. As late as 1909 Catherine was still subdividing and selling this land in partnership with Sir Thomas Bent [q.v.]. In 1895 the Eighth Union Building Society sold Catherine a fifty-year lease of the Ballarat Star Hotel on which Benjamin Fink had defaulted. In 1899 the Caledonian and Australian Mortgage & Agency Co. Ltd sold her back the freehold of Fink's Buildings, on which Benjamin had also defaulted.

Benjamin Fink died intestate in London on 17 September 1909, after suffering from diabetes for twelve years. He was survived by a son, Harold Nestor, and a daughter, Winifred. In early life Fink undoubtedly had remarkable acumen and energy, but like many others became obsessed by the land boom of the 1880s. His manipulations when the boom collapsed disfigured an otherwise productive career.

T. W. H. Leavitt (ed), *Australian representative men*, 2nd ed (Melb, 1887); G. Meudell, *The pleasant career of a spendthrift and his later reflections* (Melb, 1935); M. Cannon, *The land boomers* (Melb, 1966); *A'sian Sketcher*, July 1888; *Age*, 23 Sept, 30 Nov, 10 Dec 1892, 21 Sept, 16 Nov 1893, 5 Sept 1894; *Table Talk*, 23 Sept, 14 Oct 1892, 10 Mar, 18 Aug 1893, 12

Jan 1894; *Argus*, 22 Sept 1909; Company and insolvency files (VA).   MICHAEL CANNON

FINLAYSON, JOHN HARVEY (1843-1915), newspaper editor, was born on 3 February 1843 at Mitcham, South Australia, the third child of William Finlayson and his wife Helen, née Harvey. He was educated at George Mugg's school, Mitcham, and the Adelaide Educational Institution, where his scholastic record attracted the attention of the proprietors of the *South Australian Register*. He joined its literary staff in December 1861, soon showed ability at parliamentary and law reporting, became chief of the reporting staff in 1866 and contributed leading articles. He also wrote on agricultural subjects for *Farm and Garden* and the *Observer*. In 1876 he travelled in America and Europe, reporting on the Philadelphia Exhibition and appointing foreign correspondents for the *Register*. On his return he was invited to become a proprietor, and in 1878 succeeded John Howard Clark [q.v.] as editor.

Finlayson was appointed a justice of the peace in 1880, and a commissioner for the Adelaide Jubilee International Exhibition of 1887 and for South Australia in the Melbourne International Exhibition of 1888. He was chairman of the Distressed Farmers' Seed Wheat Fund, established by the *Register* in the 1890s, and as a councillor of the South Australian Acclimatization Society attended the fourth International Congress of Zoologists in London in 1898. Failing health induced him to resign the editorship in 1899; he made his fourth journey to England and settled in London as correspondent for the *Register*. He visited South Australia in 1904 and returned finally in 1908 to retire at North Adelaide where he died on 30 March 1915.

As a member of the Congregational Church, one of Finlayson's most consistent interests was free, secular, compulsory education, which he advocated not only as an editor but in the Parliamentary Club of the North Adelaide Young Men's Society and the Education League which he helped to found. He also served on the North Adelaide School Board of Advice. Leading articles in the *Register* show Finlayson's concern with legislation on agricultural and pastoral matters, land and income taxes, votes for women, defence of free trade and constitutional reforms to make the Legislative Council less obstructive. Although indifferent about the Federal Council, his editorials supported the Federation Conventions of the 1890s. On relations between labour and management, the *Register* was fairly liberal, criticizing some of the tactics of both parties in disputes, warily approving the trade union movement and placing high hope in arbitration.

On 20 March 1878 Finlayson had married Alice, daughter of Thomas Shoobridge, a London merchant. A daughter, Katharine, was born on 14 August 1879 and a son, Harvey Pym, on 11 January 1881.

W. J. Sowden, Our pioneer press ... a history (SAA).   J. H. LOVE

FINNEY, THOMAS (1837-1903), merchant and politician, was born on 10 January 1837 at Currakeen House, Tuam, Galway, Ireland, son of Thomas Finney and his wife Eliza, née Cornwall. He was educated privately and in 1856 began work in a drapery business in Dublin. In 1862 with his workmate James Isles (d. 1888), Finney arrived at Brisbane in the *Flying Cloud*. Two years later in partnership Finney Isles & Co. bought a drapery business in Ann Street, Fortitude Valley, and with a staff of five traded as Finney Isles & Co. at the Valley Exchange. By 1869 the business had branches in Rockhampton and Gympie; next year they opened a second Brisbane store, the City Exchange in Edward Street. The firm bought these premises in 1873 and with the acquisition of further property expanded into such lines as tailoring, furniture, furnishing and hardware, an early development of the modern department store. The trading was not consolidated until 1909 when new premises were built extending over a whole frontage between Queen and Adelaide Streets.

Finney was always interested in the welfare of his employees and in 1879 pioneered 6 p.m. closing in Brisbane stores. In 1885, with other firms, he instituted 1 p.m. closing on Saturdays and continued it despite the reversion of other firms to the old Saturday hours of 8 a.m. to 11 p.m. A charity fund of the employees was subsidized £ for £ by the management and was administered by a committee comprising the managing director and two leading employees elected by the staff. The business suffered severely in 1893 from flood waters and from the financial crisis, but soon recovered.

Finney was a licensing justice, a member of the Brisbane Board of Water Works and the Fire Brigade Board. He was also president of the Commercial Rowing Club. He was long a member of the Toowong Shire Council and in 1896 yielded to pressure from his friends and associates and stood successfully for the Toowong seat in the Legislative Assembly; in the 1898 election he retained the seat. In parliament he continued his campaign to improve conditions for shop assistants and similar workers. He visited England in 1898, 1900 and 1901-03, and resigned his seat in 1902.

On 24 May 1864 in the Wesleyan Church, Brisbane, Finney married Kate Pringle Little; when she died less than two years later he married Sidney Ann Jackson whose father was a member of the Irish landed gentry and whose sister married James Isles. In 1881 she bought land at Toowong, and next year built Sidney House, one of the major residences in Brisbane. She died on 13 October 1883 leaving a son and two daughters; under her will Sidney House became the property of her husband. In England in 1901 Thomas Finney married a widow, Janet Edgar Farrow, to whom he left a life interest in Sidney House when he died on 16 December 1903. He was buried at Toowong cemetery. In the 1960s Sidney House was acquired by the Australian Broadcasting Commission, and Finney Isles & Co. was taken over by David Jones Ltd.

E. J. T. Barton, *Jubilee history of Queensland* (Brisb, 1910); L. E. Slaughter, *Finneys 90 years progress 1864-1954* (Brisb, 1954).

A. A. MORRISON

FINSCH, OTTO (1839-1917), ornithologist, ethnologist and pioneer of German colonialism, was born on 8 August 1839 in Warmbrunn, Germany, son of Moritz Finsch and his wife Mathilde, née Leder; his parents were connected with the glass trade. Finsch was trained as a merchant but, with little love for the profession, gladly travelled in the Balkans in 1858-59. He became interested in ornithology and in 1861 was appointed an assistant at the Museum of Natural History in Leiden, Holland, so that he could pursue his studies. He joined the Museum of Natural History and Ethnography in Bremen as a curator in 1864 and became director in 1876. Although his achievements as an ornithologist won him an honorary doctorate from the University of Bonn in 1868, Finsch developed an equally strong interest in ethnology. The offer of the Humboldt Foundation to finance an expedition to the Pacific was made on his repute as an ornithologist, but the expedition in 1879-82 was dominated by his ethnological interests. Finsch also became interested in creating German colonies in the Pacific; after his return he joined the 'South Sea Plotters', a small group of influential men led by the banker, von Hansemann, who pursued similar plans. Finsch supplied them with optimistic information about the local conditions, including the estimated costs of opening a colony on the north-east coast of New Guinea and the

New Britain (Bismarck) Archipelago. This plan had to be postponed, partly because Bismarck was reluctant to acquire colonies and partly because the Queensland government attempted to annex the eastern half of New Guinea in 1883. After the Foreign Office disallowed this annexation and Bismarck granted imperial protection to Luederitz for his plans to establish a German colony in south-west Africa, the way was open for the 'South Sea Plotters'. Finsch was made leader of the expedition sent out to look for harbours, to make friendly contacts with the natives and to acquire land for a colony under German protection. Finsch and his team left Berlin for Sydney on 16 June 1884. They fitted out the small steamer *Samoa* and sailed on 11 September for the Duke of York Islands. Between October 1884 and May 1885 Finsch made five explorations between East Cape and Humboldt Bay on the north coast of New Guinea. He had an exaggerated view of his role and expected a leading post in the administration of the new colony, but failed in negotiations with the Neu Guinea Kompagnie founded by the 'South Sea Plotters'. Despite such honours as the Prussian medal, Finsch became disappointed. In 1886 he married Elisabeth Hoffmann but his disappointment grew as he realized how quickly he was forgotten and how difficult it was to find a suitable post in Germany. At Leipzig in 1888 he published an account of the cruise of the *Samoa*. In 1897-1904 he had charge of a division at the Museum of Natural History in Leiden, Holland, and then at the Municipal Museum in Braunschweig, building up the ethnological collection and working especially on primitive money in the Pacific. Not until he was granted the title 'Professor' by the duke of Braunschweig and honoured at his seventieth birthday by the 'medal for distinguished services for art and science' in silver, did his embitterment lose some of its sharpness. He died at Braunschweig on 31 January 1917.

A. Wichmann, *Nova Guinea*, 2 (Leiden, 1910); *Neue Deutsche Biographie*, 5 (Berlin, 1961); Singelmann, 'Prof. Dr. Finschs Anteil an der Erwerbung des deutschen Suedseeschutzgebietes', *Deutsche Kolonialzeitung*, Oct 1909.

P. G. SACK

FISHER, CHARLES BROWN (1818-1908), grazier, was born on 25 September 1818 in London, the second son of James Hurtle Fisher [q.v.] and his wife Elizabeth, née Johnson. He spent two years on his uncle's farm in Northamptonshire before sailing with his parents in the *Buffalo*. He arrived in South Australia in December 1836, served briefly as a clerk to his father and then joined his elder brother James in Adelaide as merchants and carriers. In 1838 the brothers sought another partner and occupied their first pastoral lease, Little Para, a few miles north of Adelaide. The run was sold in 1840 but the Fisher brothers soon acquired other pastoral leases from which they supplied Adelaide with sheep and cattle. Such leases were then issued on condition that they were stocked within three months with 16 cattle or 100 sheep to the square mile. In 1844 the Fisher brothers were charged by the commissioner of crown lands with understocking their holdings or moving stock from run to run in order to establish occupancy. The charge was not denied but the Fishers do not appear to have lost their leases. In the early 1850s they sent large numbers of sheep and cattle to the Victorian goldfields and used the profits to expand their landholdings. In 1854 they bought Bundaleer for £31,000 and in 1855 Hill River, near Clare, for £160,000; they then claimed 800 square miles under pastoral leases and were again accused of moving stock between their runs to establish occupation. Charles was also buying freehold land including the Levels, near Adelaide, where he started a merino stud. In 1856 he wrote to James in England estimating that they would shear 115,000 sheep that year: 'Such a state of things, I venture to say is unexampled even by golddiggers'.

A noted sportsman, Fisher had ridden at the first race meeting in Adelaide in 1838 and helped to organize the first steeplechase over four miles of stiff country. In the 1850s he imported several thoroughbreds and after he moved to Melbourne in 1865 bought most of his brother Hurtle's Maribyrnong stud in April 1866 and made his début racing under his own colours at the spring meeting of the Victoria Racing Club. He retired from the turf as an owner and sold his stud for a sensational total of £64,376 but continued to import blood sires. Well known at Flemington for his courtly manner and English dress, he was a vice-president of the V.R.C.

Fisher became one of the biggest pastoralists in Australia. In Victoria he bought Cumberland, near Melbourne, and Pirron Yallock, near Colac, for breeding from imported Lincoln sheep and stud Shorthorns: one bull cost him £4000. In South Australia he sold most of his land including Bundaleer and Hill River where he had 50,000 sheep and some 4000 acres under wheat. He bought Yanga near Balranald, Gunbower near Echuca and Thurulgoona on the Warrego River. In 1868 he began to take up leases in Queensland; by 1877 he had sixteen runs but lost them when the Supreme

Court ruled that his claim to qualify as a resident was fraudulent. After his appeal to the Privy Council failed he turned with great enterprise to the Northern Territory. With J. C. Lyon as partner he took Victoria River Downs and other leases, stocking them with some 30,000 cattle overlanded from south Queensland. The partners also attempted to cultivate coffee and rubber near Darwin but without success. By 1887 they held in the territory about 34,000 square miles much of which they stocked and extensively improved. In 1884 Fisher & Lyon sent a trial shipment of cattle to south-east Asia with little profit and in 1890 Goldsbrough Mort [qq.v.] took over some of their leases. Overcapitalization, falling prices and six bad seasons forced Fisher into bankruptcy in 1895. His liabilities were nearly £1,500,000 against assets of £786,000. Destitute, he retired to Melbourne where in November 1896 friends took up a subscription which F. S. Falkiner [q.v.] headed with £500. Later Fisher moved to Adelaide and died at Glenelg on 6 May 1908. Predeceased by his wife Agnes Louisa, whom he had married in 1855, and survived by their only son, he left an estate valued at £1600.

H. H. Peck, *Memoirs of a stockman* (Melb, 1942); G. C. Morphett (ed), *C. B. Fisher* (Adel, 1945); *Australasian*, 16 Mar, 11 May 1895, 6 Nov 1896; *Argus*, 31 Aug 1895; *Register* (Adel), 7 May 1908; CSO letter books, 1844, 1855 (SAA).

J. M. MAIN

FISHER, JAMES COWLEY MORGAN (1832-1913), farmer and missioner, was born in Bristol, England, son of Robert Fisher, magistrate, and his wife Sarah, née Cowley. At 14 he ran away to sea; later he was described as utterly illiterate but not unintelligent. He deserted the *Esperanza* for the goldfields in 1852, soon became a carter and labourer and then settled in Nunawading, near Melbourne, as a charcoal burner. In 1853 at Prahran he married Caroline Chamberlain; they had two sons before she died in August 1855. At Christ Church, Hawthorn, on 8 June 1858 Fisher married Emma Pickis Kefford, aged 18; they had four sons and four daughters.

His mother-in-law, Rhoda Harriet Kefford, had earlier founded the 'New Church of the First-Born' on Swedenborg's principles. By 1863 Fisher had become its leader after ousting a peculating leader; reputedly he also tried to succeed John Wroe [q.v.], evangelist of the Christian Israelites. Fisher taught the imminence of the millennium, the restoration of Israel and the ingathering of the dispersed ten tribes by the spirit of God. His rival testified to his 'strong electro-

biological power' in faith-healing but credited his successes more to luck than ability. On moonlight nights he led his followers through the country-side banging tins to exorcise the devil. He had about one hundred disciples who came from Nunawading, Prahran, Richmond and Ballarat. Lamenting the spread of superstition to Australia, the *Age* declared that they were not 'ignorant clodhoppers' but 'sober, decent, highly respectable' albeit 'of a certain grim countenance'.

The 'Nunawading Messiah' would have remained obscure if one of his closest followers, Andrew Wilson, had not prosecuted him in 1871 for obtaining money by falsely representing himself as the messiah. The law suit failed but was a harvest for the press and the Melbourne waxworks, because Fisher was alleged to practise polygamy. He denied that he had been 'anything more than a preacher of the Gospel according to the law and testimony'. He hired the Haymarket Theatre in Melbourne on 30 July to justify himself but the meeting ended in hubbub. Yet the débâcle did not affect Fisher's standing at Nunawading where he served on school and roads boards.

By 1900 the Fisherites had drifted back to obscurity. Many of them went to the Western Australian goldfields and then settled at Wickepin where they selected over 20,000 acres. Fisher joined them in 1904, built a church and preached regularly. In 1910 he married Ruth Mahala Rentil. After a head injury he became 'a bit queer'. He died aged 81 on 20 January 1913. The Wickepin settlement was an agricultural success and although the sect had died out by the 1930s many Fisherite descendants were still on their holdings.

J. Bonwick, *The Mormons and the silver mines* (Lond, 1872); I. Southall, *A tale of Box Hill* (Box Hill, 1957); D. Duke, 'The Nunawading messiah', *Box Hill City Hist Soc, Papers*, 1 (1964-68); *Age*, 19, 20, 26, 28 June, 6, 10, 12, 26, 28, 31 July, 3 Aug, 27, 28 Sept 1871, 10, 17, 24 June, 1 July 1933; *Argus*, 10, 29, 30 July 1871; *Illustrated Aust News*, 12 Aug 1871.

JAMES GRIFFIN

FISHER, JOSEPH (1834-1907), accountant and parliamentarian, was born on 14 September 1834 at Brighouse, Yorkshire, England, the youngest son of Joshua Fisher, merchant, and his wife Hannah, née Mellor. With his parents, brother and two sisters he sailed in the *Pestonjee Bomanjee* and arrived in South Australia in October 1838. His father opened a grocery in Hindley Street, Adelaide, but died on 3 September 1841, leaving Joseph in Anthony Forster's [q.v.] charge. After five years at the Oddfellows

School he entered his guardian's office. In 1848 Forster was offered a partnership in the *South Australian Register* but soon withdrew; Fisher, who had gone with him, stayed on, graduating from odd jobs to accounts. In 1852 he visited the Victorian goldfields and in May 1853 became a proprietor and commercial manager of the *Register* and *Observer*. Intelligent, tactful and firm, he guided the business through many storms, advancing his own interests and those who worked with him. He retired from the *Register* in October 1865 and sold his share to J. H. Clark [q.v.]. On 10 March 1857 in Melbourne he had married Anne Wood (1834-1917), daughter of Henry Wilkinson Farrar, merchant; they had seven children.

In retirement Fisher travelled widely with his family in the Australian colonies and New Zealand and visited Britain five times. An enthusiastic gardener, his chief delight was to work among his roses and trees in the large grounds of Woodfield, at Fullarton. There he enlarged and renovated his home, built up a fine collection of local art and entertained his friends. In the cricket season he regularly occupied the same front seat in the members' pavilion at the Adelaide Oval and for nearly twenty-five years was vice-president of the Cricketing Association. In 1868-70 he represented Sturt in the House of Assembly and in 1873-81 sat in the Legislative Council. He served on many committees, often as chairman. As an advocate of private enterprise and municipal government he was a sharp critic of parliamentary legislation that he deemed unnecessary and of ministries that ignored the rights of property owners by usurping such irresponsible powers as resuming private land with inadequate compensation. In 1880 when a restrictive Chinese immigration bill reached the council his uncompromising opposition led to its rejection as an unChristian, uneconomic measure that meddled with imperial matters; his firm stand was unpopular and cost him his seat in the 1881 election.

With his integrity, plain speech and geniality Fisher was sought by high and low for advice, and he came to know the ins and outs of every business deal in town. As agent for such colonists as John Ridley [q.v.] who had retired to England he gained further inside information though he rarely used it for personal gain. His own investments, including shares in two large sheep stations and the clipper *Hesperus*, were varied, safe and seldom changed; he claimed that he rarely went to the races and that even when given a sure tip he never placed a bet. His talents were in great demand and his directorships included the Bank of Ade-

laide, the Port Adelaide Dock Co., the South Australian Gas Co. as well as insurance, pastoral and mortgage firms.

In his last twenty years Fisher suffered from gout and diabetes. He died at Woodfield on 26 September 1907, survived by his wife, two sons and a daughter. His estate was valued at £72,400. On 17 April 1903 he had donated £3315 to institutions in order to avoid the 10 per cent succession duty which to him was 'an unjust and unwise exaction . . . tending to check the flow of public spirited benevolence'. The list included hospitals, churches, convalescent homes and parks; the largest gifts were £500 for the National Art Gallery and £1000 to the University of Adelaide to provide for the Joseph Fisher medal and every alternate year a lecture in commerce.

Register (Adel), 26 Oct 1865, 15 Apr 1903, 28 Sept 1907.

FISHER, THOMAS (1820-1884), businessman and benefactor, was born on 23 January 1820 at Brickfield Hill, Sydney, the only son and youngest child of John Fisher and his wife Jemima, née Bolton. His father arrived in New South Wales in the *Perseus* in 1802 as a convict and became the first professional jockey recorded in the colony; his mother, also a convict, arrived in the *Canada* on 8 September 1810 and was promptly appointed government housekeeper at Parramatta; she retired when her husband was granted a free pardon in 1814.

In 1832 when his parents died almost penniless, Thomas was at Sydney Public School and two of his three sisters were in service. He was soon apprenticed to a bootmaker and apparently set himself the goal of financial security. He opened an account with the Bank of New South Wales in 1842 and next year was the owner of a three-storied building near the corner of King and Pitt Streets, Sydney; his bootshop occupied the ground floor, he and his sister Sarah lived in the attic rooms, and the first floor was let as legal chambers. For the next forty years his tenants were the solicitors George Robert Nichols, John Williams and Richard Driver [qq.v.], whose influence extending beyond their active work in local government and parliament, was significant in the establishment of a strong and vociferous 'Native Party'.

Probably advised by his well-informed tenants, Fisher began the second phase of his business career in 1857 by buying small cottages and allotments and lending money on the security of property. Fifteen years later the bootmaker's shop had become a warehouse, and his financial interests ranged from trading ships to suburban hotels. He took no recorded part in public affairs and his only known acts of benevolence were the provision of hot meals for the slum-dwellers in near-by Brougham Place and the maintenance and education of the orphaned children of one of his sisters. When his sister and housekeeper died in 1870 and his own health began to fail, he retired to Darlington. There he walked regularly in the grounds of the University of Sydney and attended Commemoration Day functions, which were open to the public, but remained an unobtrusive, almost anonymous figure.

In the Commemoration Day address in 1879 the chancellor, Sir William Manning [q.v.], stressed the need for a university library and envisioned the day 'when one of our men of great wealth and equal public spirit will . . . earn the gratitude of their country by erecting for the University a library worthy of comparison with like edifices at home'. Next year Fisher made his will in which, after minor bequests, he directed that £1000 be shared among Sydney's major hospitals and asylums and the Sydney School of Arts, and that the residue of his estate, some £33,000, be paid to the University of Sydney 'to found a library'. Fisher died in Sydney Hospital on 27 December 1884 and was buried in Waverley cemetery. His benefaction, the largest till then received by the university, was used entirely for the acquisition of books. The library building, erected from funds provided by the colonial government, was opened in 1909 and in his honour named the Fisher Library.

H. E. Barff, A short historical account of the University of Sydney . . . 1852-1902 (Syd, 1902); H. Bryan, 'Earlier years of the University of Sydney library', JRAHS, 55 (1969); Sydney Gazette, 13, 21 Oct 1810; Fisher papers (Fisher Lib, Univ Syd).   NANCY GRAY

FISKEN, ARCHIBALD (1829-1907), pastoralist, was born on 27 August 1829 near Bothwell, Lanarkshire, Scotland, son of Archibald Fisken (1797-1854) and his wife Eliza, née Inglis. The family with an uncle, Peter Inglis, and his wife, arrived in the Dauntless at Port Phillip in 1840. Inglis bought a station near Ballan and the Fiskens made their home with him. Young Archibald attended the Scots' School in Melbourne and then was tutored at the station. At 17 he was given charge of his uncle's cattle stations, Lal Lal and Warrenheip. He won repute as a stockman for mustering and driving home, with two assistants and small loss, several hundred Lal Lal cattle which had strayed into rugged country beyond the

Goulburn River. He also became known as a fearless whip and daring horseman; he liked to hunt kangaroos and to race horses, once riding the mare Alice Hawthorn at Flemington. He became an honorary life member of the Ballarat Turf Club.

The gold rush to Ballarat brought Fisken labour problems but he made a fortune by slaughtering meat for the diggings. With his profits he bought the two stations from his uncle on terms which he soon paid off. Later land selectors reduced his holdings but he retained 10,000 freehold acres bought at auction. On Lal Lal he built a homestead and became recognized as one of Victoria's best judges of cattle. In 1871 at Ballarat he joined C. W. Gibson's stock and station agency, later named Fisken, Valentine & Co. In 1873 he left his son Archibald to manage Lal Lal, bought Corrabert in Toorak and moved to Melbourne where he could give better attention to his many commitments in Australia and Scotland. At Ballarat he had helped to promote the Agricultural Society, Meat Preserving Co., the Warrenheip distillery and several mining companies, serving in most of them as a director. In Melbourne he supported the Farmers' Club, the National Agricultural Society and Pastoralists' Associations. He became prominent in the wool trade, a director of the Australasian Mortgage and Agency Co. and the Commercial Union Assurance Co. He had shares in several stations and was an active trustee for such large proprietors as Sir Samuel Wilson [q.v.]. He was also a member of the Australian and Melbourne Clubs.

In 1852 Fisken became a justice of the peace and attended the County Court and many Petty Sessions in the Ballarat area. He was also one of the first returning officers for North Grant and Ballarat East, first chairman of the Buninyong Road Board and first president when it became Shire Council; at Buninyong he served as chairman in Victoria's first Local Land Board. A staunch Presbyterian, he was an active member of Scots Church, Collins Street, Melbourne, and a trustee of church property. His colonial experience, courtesy and humour made him an invaluable committeeman. After a serious operation he died in East Melbourne on 13 June 1907, survived by his wife Charlotte Emily, née McNamara (1842-1913), whom he had married in July 1859, and by three of their seven children. His estate was valued at over £53,000.

J. Smith (ed), Cyclopedia of Victoria, 1 (Melb, 1903); A. Henderson (ed), Early pioneer families of Victoria and Riverina (Melb, 1936); Pastoral Review, 17 Sept 1895, 15 Dec 1905, 15 June 1907; Argus, 14 June 1907.
                                    J. ANN HONE

FISON, LORIMER (1832-1907), Wesleyan missionary, anthropologist and journalist, was born on 9 November 1832 at Barningham, Suffolk, England, the thirteenth of twenty children of Thomas Fison, farmer, and his cultivated and idealistic wife Charlotte, daughter of Rev. John Reynolds, who translated seventeenth-century religious writers. After schooling in Sheffield, Lorimer enrolled at Caius College, Cambridge, in June 1855. Tutored by his brother-in-law, Robert Potts (1818-1881), a Trinity don, he showed promise in mathematics. He also performed satisfactorily in classical and theological studies but was rusticated after two terms because of a boyish escapade. The affair left a lifelong wound but he accepted his lot stoically and left England for the Australian goldfields. It was possibly the second visit. In a letter written to Lewis Henry Morgan on 26 March 1880 Fison spoke of a 'return' to Australia after leaving Cambridge, and there is other slender and less dependable evidence to that effect. All that is certain of his Australian experiences until 1861 is that he passed through a severe personal crisis on the diggings: the news of his father's death caused him intense grief and he underwent a paroxysmic religious conversion at an open-air evangelical meeting. He left the goldfields, intending to complete his studies for a degree at the University of Melbourne, but he became a Wesleyan and, learning of the need for missionaries in Fiji, offered himself. He was ordained and in 1863 sailed for Fiji with his Welsh bride Jane, née Thomas.

Fison proved more than a match for the challenge of a still barbarous and turbulent region. According to Rev. Dr George Brown [q.v.], he was 'one of the best missionaries whom God has ever given to our Church'. Large and imposing, kindly and cheery though formidable when aroused, in whom wit, common sense and intelligence combined, Fison became the confidant and adviser of natives, officials and settlers alike in his seven years at the Viwa, Lakemba and Rewa stations. The Fijians were drawn to him by repeated proof of his courage, honesty and devotion, and by the ease with which he learned their languages and customs. He was an eloquent preacher, a splendid conversationalist and a felicitous writer. He worked vigorously against the blackbirders and was of service in the tangle of Fijian, Tongan and international affairs that preceded the cession of the islands to Britain. In 1871 with a large reputation he left for pastoral work in New South Wales and Victoria. His health impaired but with the highest goodwill of the Wesleyan Conference of Australia, he returned to Fiji in 1875 to serve until 1884 as principal of the Navuloa Training Institution, on which he left an enduring mark.

In Fiji in 1869 Fison responded, at the suggestion of Professor Goldwin Smith, to an appeal by the American ethnologist, Lewis Henry Morgan (1818-1881), for information on the kinship systems of primitive peoples. He wrote a well-digested account of the Fijian and Tongan systems in time for inclusion as a supplement to Morgan's illuminating book, Systems of Consanguinity and Affinity of the human family (1871). On his return to Australia in 1871 Fison transferred his new scientific interest to the Aboriginals and through the newspapers sought help in the study. One who responded was A. W. Howitt [q.v.] and in 1872 they entered into a collaboration and loyal friendship that endured until 1900.

They amassed a large body of cohesive data on Aboriginal kinship, family and marriage forms and many empirical features of social organization and culture, by means of direct observation, face-to-face discussions with informants and the circulation of printed lists of questions to Europeans with Aboriginal contacts. This first study of Aboriginal actuality, though among broken tribes, was made by regularized methods under the control of theoretical concepts. Howitt was guided by Fison who understood the classification of kinship terminology and its related categories of thought as few scholars then did. Both were inspired, though not slavishly, by Morgan's evolutionist ideas. In 1880 their compendium, Kamilaroi and Kurnai, was published hurriedly to avert 'secret piracy'. Dedicated to Morgan, it was rightly acclaimed a landmark in anthropology. As none before, it made clear the segmentary character of Aboriginal society, including that most crucial structure, the articulation of territorial groups with social categories, but collapse of the evolutionist perspective and long bickering among contemporary scholars obscured the merit of this pioneer work. Fison wrote his sections in his second period in Fiji, after contributing information to Morgan's Ancient Society (1877).

Although heavily burdened by mission tasks including original works in Fijian, Fison worked indefatigably at anthropology. In 1881 he wrote a brilliant treatise on Fijian land tenure which had effect on three governments and in 1903 earned him tardy commendation from the Colonial Office. He continued to publish gracefully and informatively on a wide range of Fijian customs in 1881-95. Two joint papers of the 1880s remarkably anticipated the essentials of the organismic and structural-functional perspectives of modern social anthropology. The long mortification of never having a degree ended with honorary awards of an A.M. by an American university and a D.D. in Canada.

After four pastoral years in Hawthorn and Flemington Fison retired from the ministry in 1888. Poor and in failing health, he settled in Melbourne to earn a livelihood by journalism. He published *Tales from old Fiji* edited in 1904 and edited the *Spectator and Methodist Chronicle* until 1905, when his lot was eased by the grant of a British government civil list pension of £150. He was a founder and one of the first fellows of Queen's College, Melbourne. In 1892 he was president of the anthropology section at the Hobart meeting of the Australasian Association for the Advancement of Science. In 1894 he was among the representatives of Australian science at the British Association meeting at Oxford, where his work was fully acknowledged. He died at Essendon, Melbourne, on 29 December 1907, survived by his wife, two sons and four daughters.

C. Irving Benson (ed), *A century of Victorian Methodism* (Melb, 1935); C. B. Fletcher, *The black knight of the Pacific* (Syd, 1944); G. Brown, 'Lorimer Fison', *A'sian Methodist Missionary Review*, Feb 1908; J. G. Frazer, 'Howitt and Fison', *Folk-Lore* (Lond), 20 (1909); B. J. Stern (ed), 'Selections from the letters of Lorimer Fison ... to Lewis Henry Morgan', *American Anthropologist*, 32 (1930); *Age*, 31 Dec 1907.   W. E. H. STANNER

FITZGERALD, GEORGE PARKER (1843-1917), was born on 13 February 1843 in Hobart Town, son of James Fitzgerald, a superintendent in the Hobart General Hospital, and his wife Eleanor, née Scott. He was educated at the Hutchins School, and gained experience in Hobart counting houses and shipping offices. At 19 he moved to Sydney and entered Farmer [q.v.] & Co., drapers. His progress was rapid and at 31 he became a junior partner. In Sydney on 28 November 1863 he married Mary Lane; they had ten children. After her death on 3 May 1881 he returned to Hobart where he established an agency for Robert Gray & Co., wholesale merchants. On 5 August 1882 at St John's Anglican Church, New Town, he married Emma Caroline Gwatkin Lovett; they had three children.

Boom conditions in Tasmania favoured enterprise and Fitzgerald was able to buy his principal's business and set up as a wholesaler. He steadily developed his business even after the boom ended and in 1892 entered the retail trade, founding the house which grew into Tasmania's largest emporium. As an innovator he was recognized throughout the Australian retailing trade; he introduced Father Christmas to his shops

and with advancing age was sometimes mistaken for that identity in plain clothes. A fair employer, he never joined in any unworthy victimization of unionists, or shared in the organized boycott of advertisers in the *Daily Post*, Hobart's Labor newspaper. In 1911 his Hobart premises were completely destroyed by fire but he rebuilt his store and in spite of wartime conditions almost succeeded in re-establishing the business before he died.

Fitzgerald was a founding director of the Cascade Brewery Co. Ltd but had few other business associations. However, his involvement in public affairs was unusual for a man so immersed in a demanding business. After returning to Tasmania he became an active supporter of the 'ferocious reformers' who were challenging the insular conservatism which had long dominated Tasmania. In 1886-91 he represented West Hobart in the House of Assembly, serving in the Fysh ministry without portfolio. His radicalism enraged Conservative opponents who saw revolution in his outspoken support of the Trades and Labor Council and Henry George's [q.v.] theories, and near treason in his 'detestation of the Imperial System of Gt. Britain'. He was also an advocate of southern railways but his most constructive work was probably in state technical education; it is recorded that the 'Hobart Technical School was built through his personal exertions'. His least envied public duty was the liquidation of the Bank of Van Diemen's Land, which for years kept him face to face with widespread distress. The rise of the Labor Party disappointed him and by 1904 he was chairman of the National Association dedicated to oppose class legislation. He continued his many public activities until he died after a short illness on 28 March 1917. He left a personal estate of more than £10,000 to his wife, four sons and two daughters, and was buried privately at Cornelian Bay cemetery.

H. Reynolds, 'Regionalism in nineteenth century Tasmania', *PTHRA*, 17 (1969-70); *Daily Post* (Hob), 29 Mar 1917; *Examiner* (Launceston), 29 Mar 1917; *Mercury*, 29 Mar 1917; *Tas Mail*, 29 Mar 1917; family papers.
                                       JOHN REYNOLDS

FITZGERALD, NICHOLAS (1829-1908), politician, brewer and pastoralist, was born on 7 August 1829 in Galway, Ireland, the eighth son of Francis Fitzgerald, brewer, and his wife Eleanor, née Joyes; a brother, Sir Gerald Fitzgerald, K.C.M.G., became accountant-general of the navy in 1885-96. In 1845 Nicholas entered Trinity College, Dublin, studied law in 1848 at the King's

Inns and in 1849 won a scholarship to the new Queen's College in Galway. In 1852 he turned to commerce, partly in Ceylon and India, and arrived in Melbourne in 1859. He joined his brother Edward who had just started the Castlemaine brewery. In 1875 they opened a brewery in South Melbourne. In 1885 they converted to a public company, the Castlemaine Brewery Co. Melbourne Ltd, selling for £75,000; in 1888 it paid a dividend of 25 per cent. They extended business to Newcastle and Brisbane in 1887 and to Adelaide next year. Nicholas was managing director from 1892 till 1906 when, in the great amalgamation of breweries, he became a director of Carlton and United.

In 1863 Fitzgerald was appointed a magistrate and in 1864 was elected for North-Western Province to the Legislative Council after a close contest. As a councillor until 1906 he never accepted office though offered the ministry of defence in the Patterson [q.v.] government. According to J. M. Davies [q.v.], Fitzgerald 'preferred to do his duty as a private member rather than join a Government which did not agree with him on the education issue'. He was a brilliant orator with clear ideas on important political issues. He was a member of the National Australasian Convention in Sydney in 1891 and in 1894 represented Victoria at the Colonial Conference in Ottawa, Canada, where he was staunchly imperialistic. In 1903 he became the Legislative Council's chairman of committees.

With large pastoral interests in the 1880s and 1890s in New South Wales and Queensland, Fitzgerald's main station was Fort Bourke on the Darling but drought forced him to sell many of his holdings. In 1887 he helped to found the National Trustees Executors and Agency Co., planned largely to meet the needs of the Irish Catholics; Fitzgerald was managing director and associated with him were William Cain [q.v.] and Walter Madden. He was chairman of the Dunlop Pneumatic Tyre Co. in the 1890s and a director of the Manchester Fire Assurance Co. and the Bellambi Coal Co.

A prominent Catholic layman, Fitzgerald was awarded the papal knighthood of St Gregory by Pope Leo XIII. He often spoke at public gatherings connected with the Church, and was an enthusiast for completing St Patrick's Cathedral. He presented the laity's address when his friend Archbishop Carr was welcomed to Melbourne and again at his jubilee. His commonest theme was Catholic education. 'Justice', he said, 'has been put aside for power, but no wrong can be sanctified by success . . . The sense of that injustice will never be removed until the law is altered'. He was at his best when speaking to his fellow

countrymen on subjects appealing to their native sympathies.

In 1863 Fitzgerald married Marianne, the eldest daughter of John O'Shanassy [q.v.]; they had seven sons. He died at his home, Moira, Alma Road, St Kilda, on 17 August 1908, survived by his widow. He left an estate valued at £5318.

Argus, 18 Aug 1908; *Advocate* (Melb), 20 Aug 1908; *Austral Light*, Sept 1908; Carlton and United Breweries: a history 1837-1951, MS 500 (NL); National Trustees Executors and Agency Co. Archives (Melb); information from Sir Michael Chamberlin, Kew, Vic.

D. J. DWYER

FITZGERALD, ROBERT (1807-1865), pastoralist and politician, was born on 1 June 1807 at Windsor, New South Wales, the second son of Richard Fitzgerald [q.v.] and his wife Mary, née Ford. He was educated at Fulton's [q.v.] School in Sydney. At 21 his father gave him capital, mostly in livestock, and by 1830 he had been granted 500 acres at Rylstone. In 1832 he acquired more land in partnership with William Lawson [q.v.] on the Liverpool Plains and about 1835 Yarraman by a deal with Bonegarley, 'King of Yarraman Plains', receiving official recognition when Fitzgerald paid cash for the land. In 1840 he inherited his father's lands and the agency for Mrs Macquarie's [q.v.] estate. In his own right he had acquired 19,814 acres in the County of Bligh, 400 square miles in the Gwydir district, farms in the County of Cumberland and extensive leases on the Liverpool Plains. On 24 February 1855 the *Freeman's Journal* could reckon that he was fourth among the colony's 'cormorant squatters'.

In 1840 Fitzgerald became a director of the Bank of New South Wales. With his home in Windsor he was active in local affairs and a judge at the Sydney races. On 11 March 1841 he married Elizabeth Henrietta, daughter of Richard Rouse [q.v.], who brought to him Mamre, St Marys, as her dowry. In November he became a magistrate and in 1842 Master of the Social Lodge, Windsor (Irish Constitution). In 1843 he told electors in the Cumberland Boroughs that he advocated a 'just and liberal system of public education' but refused to recognize 'invidious distinctions' in the selection of immigrants. He stressed his deep interest 'as an *Australian*, in all that concerns the welfare of the land that gave me birth'. He was defeated by one vote and his supporters rioted at Windsor. Meanwhile he had become a member of the Windsor District Council and was active on a committee against squatters' licences.

In 1849 Fitzgerald, despite his equivocal attitude to transportation and the opposition of the *Sydney Morning Herald*, easily defeated Archibald Michie [q.v.] in a by-election for the County of Cumberland, retaining his seat until responsible government in 1856. He was appointed to the new Legislative Council and reappointed in 1861 for life. By 1857 he had rebuilt Springfield, Darlinghurst, and lived there when in Sydney. In addition to his pastoral holdings, Fitzgerald acquired much real estate in Sydney. In 1861 he rebuilt the burnt-out Prince of Wales Theatre (Theatre Royal) in Castlereagh Street. He gave £100 to the organ fund of the University of Sydney.

Fitzgerald died from paralysis on 9 May 1865 at Springfield and was buried in St Matthew's cemetery, Windsor. He was survived by his second wife Charlotte, née Bennett, whom he had married on 8 October 1864, and by one son and five daughters of his first marriage. He left an estate of £90,000 which did not include his pastoral empire.

HRA (1), 22; M. Roe, *Quest for authority in eastern Australia 1835-1851* (Melb, 1965); R. L. Knight, *Illiberal Liberal: Robert Lowe in New South Wales, 1842-1850* (Melb, 1966); *Australian*, 11, 23 July 1840; *SMH*, 18 Jan, 10 Aug 1843, 30 Apr 1844; MS cat and newspaper indexes under Robert Fitzgerald (ML); Col Sec land letters, 2/7852 (NSWA); family papers (held by Richard Evans, MLC, Dabee, Rylstone; E. C. B. MacLaurin of Mamre, St Marys, and others).   E. C. B. MacLAURIN

FITZGERALD, ROBERT DAVID (1830-1892), surveyor and naturalist, was born on 30 November 1830 at Tralee, County Kerry, Ireland, son of Robert David FitzGerald, banker, and his wife Mary Ann, née Bell. He studied civil engineering at Queen's College, Cork, arrived at Sydney in 1856 and was appointed to the Department of Lands as a draftsman in August. In 1868 he was given charge of the roads branch and in 1873 became deputy-surveyor-general. In 1874-82 he was also chief mining surveyor and for some years controller of the Church and School Lands. On the surveyors' licensing board he examined cadet surveyors. After the Crown Lands Act, 1884, he sat on the commission of three to consider the future working of the department; much retrenchment resulted and his own office was abolished on 30 November 1887. In 1888-92 he served on the Public Service Commission.

FitzGerald was an enthusiastic ornithologist and a skilful taxidermist; in addition to some poetry, he contributed twenty articles on the birds of Kerry to the *Kerry*

Magazine in 1855-56. From 1856 his drawings indicate his early interest in Australian natural history. He eagerly accompanied Walter Scott Campbell to Wallis Lake, north of Newcastle, in 1864 and collected ferns and orchids for the greenhouse and gardens of his home, Adraville, Hunter's Hill. In May 1869 with Charles Moore and William Carron [qq.v.] he visited Lord Howe Island; in 1871 he returned to the island and again in November 1876, each time making botanical collections. In 1874 he was elected a fellow of the Linnean Society of London and in 1876 a member of the Royal Society of New South Wales.

With Arthur James Stopps (1833-1931), a lithographer in the Lands Department, FitzGerald published the first seven parts of his *Australian Orchids* between July 1875 and October 1882. These comprised Volume I, dedicated to Charles Darwin [q.v.]. Four parts of Volume II were published before 1892 and the fifth was brought out by his friend Henry Deane. The exquisite lithograph plates, which included enlargements of FitzGerald's painstaking dissections, were hand-coloured by various artists from instructions and sample sheets coloured by FitzGerald. This work brought him fame. J. D. Hooker [q.v.] considered it 'a work which would be an honor to any country and to any Botanist', while George Bentham [q.v.] wrote, 'Thanks to you the Australian Orchideae are now better known than those of any other country out of Europe'. At Balmain on 3 July 1860 FitzGerald married Emily Blackwell, daughter of Edward Hunt, M.L.C., and his wife Hannah Paget, née Mason. Three sons and three daughters survived him when he died at Hunter's Hill on 12 August 1892. He was buried in the Presbyterian section of the old Balmain cemetery.

Described by his friends as sedate and grave but with a fund of Irish humour, FitzGerald was an efficient surveyor, engineer and public servant and a dedicated naturalist whose hobby attained scientific standard and recognition. He saw the need for reserving land in the Blue Mountains and elsewhere. Though he had little inclination to preserve dried specimens, his botanical work bridged the gap between amateur and professional botany in his day. He described many species of orchids for the first time in his *Australian Orchids* and in the *Journal of Botany*, and eyebrows were raised in professional circles when he described the beech orchid, *Dendrobium falcorostrum*, in the *Sydney Morning Herald* on 18 November 1876. He is remembered not only for naming Australian orchids but also by names bestowed in his honour: a spider orchid, *Caladenia fitz-*

geraldii Rupp; the ravine orchid, *Sarcochilus fitzgeraldii* F. Muell., 'the most ornate and beautiful of all Australian species of the genus' (Rupp); and the giant epacrid, *Dracophyllum fitzgeraldii* F. Muell., which he discovered on Lord Howe Island. His grandson Robert David FitzGerald became a poet and surveyor.

W. Woolls,'*In memory of R. D. FitzGerald* . . . (Syd, 1892); J. H. Maiden, 'Records of Australian botanists', Roy Soc NSW, *Procs*, 42 (1908); C. A. Messmer, 'The biography of Robert David Fitzgerald . . .', *Vic Naturalist*, 48 (1931-32); *Sydney Mail*, 3 Sept 1892; records (NSW Department of Lands); FitzGerald papers (ML, NL); information from R. D. Fitzgerald, Hunter's Hill, NSW.   L. A. GILBERT

FITZGERALD, THOMAS HENRY (1824-1888), sugar-grower and politician, was born in October 1824 at Carrickmacross, County Monaghan, Ireland, son of Patrick Fitzgerald, farmer, and his wife Anne, née Dunoyer. He qualified as an engineer, migrated to New Zealand in 1842 and worked as an assistant surveyor. In 1851 he married Jessie Wilson (d. 1901).

Fitzgerald sat in the Provincial Council of Wellington in 1857-58 and of Hawke's Bay in 1859-61, and in the House of Representatives from April to November 1860 as member for Hawke's Bay. A persistent separatist and advocate of provincial rights, he did not remain in any one post long enough to make the mark which his abilities suggested. In 1862 he went to Queensland and was appointed a surveyor based at Rockhampton. In 1864-65 he surveyed the site of Mackay where, impressed with the potential for sugar-growing, he resigned and with John Ewen Davidson started one of the earliest plantations. He erected the Alexandra mill with the first local iron-crushing apparatus in the district. Its success in the 1868 season established the capacity of the district for sugar-growing. Fitzgerald later founded the Meadowlands and Te Kowai mills and the Peri plantation; but his attention was already drawn towards politics.

As in New Zealand, Fitzgerald's political career in Queensland was characterized by forceful spokesmanship of local grievances and lack of persistence in playing the political game. This lack of persistence was partly due to the competing claims of his business interests which as the father of a large family he could not afford to neglect. In September 1866 he was elected to the Legislative Assembly as member for Kennedy; next year with Archibald Archer [q.v.] he championed the northern interests. Together they attempted to establish in Queensland provincial councils like those in New Zealand but failed; they then supported the Mackenzie [q.v.] ministry but, disappointed in their hopes of reduced government expenditure, additional representation for the north and land laws giving the pastoralist greater security, they changed sides in November 1868 and the government resigned. Invited to form a ministry, Fitzgerald failed but consented to join Lilley's [q.v.] Liberal ministry as colonial treasurer. He resigned from the ministry in January 1869 and his seat in June. Lured again by politics in November 1873, he was elected for Bowen. The Mackay sugar industry was then suffering from poor seasons and Fitzgerald's main activity in parliament was to move in 1874 for the introduction of cheap Indian labour for the canefields but the motion was narrowly defeated. He became insolvent in 1875 and resigned his seat; his estate passed out of his hands in 1876.

When the sugar industry boomed in 1879, Fitzgerald hoped to pioneer cane-growing in another district. He sailed north to inspect potential sites. After looking at the Daintree River he settled on the Johnstone River, sixty miles south of Cairns, and in 1880 with help from the Brisbane Convent of Mercy founded Innisfail, the first plantation there. Handicapped by fever, heavy scrub and the fall in sugar prices in 1883 he failed and in 1885 Innisfail passed to a mortgagee. After erecting the Hambledon mill near Cairns in 1886 for Thomas Swallow [q.v.] Fitzgerald retired to Brisbane where he died on 10 November 1888 and was buried in the Catholic section of the Brisbane general cemetery. In the Johnstone district the town of Geraldton commemorated him but was changed in 1909 to Innisfail to avoid confusion with Geraldton in Western Australia. Fitzgerald left eight sons and three daughters. The two eldest sons grew cane in the Innisfail district; the fifth, Charles Borromeo (1865-1907), represented Mitchell as a Labor member in the Legislative Assembly in 1896-1902 and was attorney-general for six days in December 1899.

H. L. Roth, *The discovery and settlement of Port Mackay, Queensland* (Halifax, 1908); S. K. Page and W. J. Doherty (eds), *Jubilee souvenir of Innisfail and district . . . 1873-1923* (Innisfail, 1923); G. C. Bolton, *A thousand miles away* (Brisb, 1963); I. N. Moles, 'The Indian coolie labour issue in Queensland', *JRAHS*, 5 (1953-57); *Brisbane Courier*, 12 Nov 1888; B. Kingston, Land legislation and administration in Queensland, 1859-1876 (Ph.D. thesis, Monash Univ, 1970).   G. C. BOLTON

FITZGERALD, Sir THOMAS NAGHTEN (1838-1908), surgeon, was born on 1 August 1838 at Tullamore, Ireland, son of John FitzGerald and his wife Catherine Naghten, née Higgins. He was educated at St Mary's College, Kingstown, and the Ledwich School of Medicine, Dublin, taking his clinical studies at Mercer's Hospital (L.R.C.S.I., 1857); there he was dresser to Richard Butcher who was surgeon to the Queen and outstanding in pre-Listerian British surgery. In 1857 FitzGerald won a commission in the Army Medical Service but had to resign because of illness. As a ship's surgeon he arrived at Melbourne in July 1858. Almost immediately he was appointed acting house surgeon at the Melbourne Hospital until E. M. James returned from England. FitzGerald then opened a private practice near the hospital in Lonsdale Street West. He had applied for the position of surgeon to the Bendigo Hospital but was beaten on the chairman's casting vote. Elected an honorary surgeon to the Melbourne Hospital in 1860, he held that post until 1901 and in 1902-07 was consulting surgeon. He had similar consulting appointments at St Vincent's, Queen Victoria and Austin Hospitals and in 1884 the first clinical lectureship in surgery created by the University of Melbourne at the Melbourne Hospital. In his long service there he influenced large numbers of medical graduates whose memories of 'Fitz' were among their cherished hospital recollections. When he resigned as senior surgeon his colleagues placed a tablet in the Melbourne Hospital vestibule commemorating his long association with the institution; this tablet is now in the operating suite of the hospital at Parkville.

FitzGerald was extremely rapid, resourceful and successful in the operations possible at that time and he introduced original methods, described in the *Australian Medical Journal* in 1887, in the treatment of inguinal hernia, fractures, cleft palate and talipes. His technical skill was great: his mere tying of a knot in a cleft palate operation was said to be a work of art. Brilliant and dexterous as was his operating, his diagnostic skill was also noteworthy. He seemed to have an extra sense, so that he could describe the position of fragments in a fracture as accurately as if they were demonstrated by x-ray; his deductions from symptoms were equally unerring and his opinion was widely sought by patients.

FitzGerald, under average height with a large handsome head, sideboards, broad shoulders, deep chest and dignified carriage, was a distinguished figure in any assembly. To undaunted surgical courage he added instant resourcefulness; with unexpected developments one operation would change into another as if all had been prearranged and no emergency ever took him aback. He had little facility in the spoken or written word; his occasional lectures were more practical than theoretical, and in the wards students learnt more from what he did than from what he said. Always kind and considerate both with his patients and his colleagues he held high the honour of his calling and became the unquestioned leader of the profession in all the Australasian colonies.

During FitzGerald's life the science and art of surgery and medicine were revolutionized. In a presidential address to the Medical Society of Victoria in January 1900, he reviewed some of the changes from 1860 to 1900 : 'Will such a difference ever re-occur . . . shall we ever again go through such a period of unlearning, such a period of relinquishing beliefs, of learning that most of the remedies in which at one time we had so much faith were in reality delusions, more harmful than beneficial'. In his own branch of surgery he said that it was 'not until 1874, about ten years after Lister had commenced his experiments, that things began to wake up in operative surgery'. Before Lister's researches were published, FitzGerald had been deeply impressed by the differences in the dangers of simple and of compound fractures, and in order to avoid the yet unexplained risks of surgical infection, he devised a whole system of subcutaneous surgery through small incisions. But he had neither the biological knowledge nor the speculative insight that led Lister to his epoch-making discoveries. Perhaps because of his success FitzGerald did not at first fully appreciate Lister's contribution, although his own concern about surgical infection led him to condemn the Melbourne Hospital as a source of wound infection in 1886; he refused to operate for a time and with Richard Youl [q.v.] precipitated an inquiry by a select committee of the Legislative Council. Chaired by J. G. Beaney [q.v.], with whom FitzGerald had been in legal conflict in 1863, the committee's report favoured the hospital. In 1890 FitzGerald gave evidence to the royal commission on charities.

At his death two of his distinguished pupils, Harry Allen, professor of pathology in Melbourne, and George Syme, later president of the Royal Australasian College of Surgeons, wrote appreciations of FitzGerald and his work; both spoke of him as 'a genius'. In 1884 he visited Ireland and became a fellow of the Royal College of Surgeons of Ireland; the examiners were said to have been astounded by the rapidity of his amputations. In May 1897 he was knighted, the first Australian to be so honoured for eminence in the medical profession. In the Boer war he offered his services to the imperial government, and for three months in 1900 was a consulting surgeon in South Africa. For this work he was appointed C.B. in 1900 and thanked by the Victorian government. His South African experiences were published in the *Intercolonial Medical Journal of Australia*, December 1900. He was president of the Medical Society of Victoria in 1884 and 1900, the surgery section at the first Intercolonial Medical Congress in 1887 and the Australasian Medical Congress at Sydney in 1889.

Before his wife died in 1890, beside his private hospital he had built an Italianate mansion, Rostella, a place of gracious hospitality; his tennis court was a miniature club and in his active years he always played before breakfast. With his lucrative practice he maintained a 'handsome brougham complete with two magnificent horses and coachmen and footman in livery' to take him daily to the hospital gates and to the races each week. A skilled four-in-hand driver he loved horses, breeding them at his Doncaster country home and racing under the name of T. Naghten; his most successful horse was Rhesus, winner of the Victorian Grand National Hurdle Race in 1882. A familiar figure at Flemington, he was surgeon to the Victoria Racing Club for many years. Among his collection of fine pictures was Lefebvre's 'Chloe', which has long adorned Young & Jackson's Hotel, Melbourne. Soon after his return from South Africa FitzGerald relinquished his hospital position and most of his private practice because of ailing health. Little benefit was derived from a voyage to England and on a later trip to Cairns he died in the *Wyreena* on 8 July 1908 at sea off Townsville from the after-effects of pneumonia; he was buried with Roman Catholic rites in the Melbourne general cemetery.

On 17 December 1870 FitzGerald married Margaret, daughter of James Robertson, of Struan House, Launceston, Tasmania. Of their three daughters, Ethel married Captain (later Admiral) Lumsden, Eleanor married Edward Cairns Officer, and Kathleen married Colonel Archibald Douglas. On Kathleen's death in 1951, her residuary estate was bequeathed to the University of Melbourne for founding a surgical scholarship in memory of her father.

J. Smith (ed), *Cyclopedia of Victoria*, 1 (Melb, 1903); *Intercolonial Medical J of A'sia*, 5 (1900), pp 1, 549, 13 (1908); *Lancet*, 18 July 1908; *MJA*, 9 July 1966; *Argus*, 10 July 1908; *Age*, 27 Aug 1908.　　COLIN MACDONALD

FITZGIBBON, EDMUND GERALD (1825-1905), civic administrator, was born on 1 November 1825 in Cork, Ireland, son of Gibbon Carew FitzGibbon and his wife Catherine, née Hurley. He claimed descent from the White Knight of Kerry and in Victoria enjoyed the title but outside the colony his claim was disputed. According to a newspaper interview, he professed to have lived in London from the age of 5 and never attended school; 'my education was obtained principally from association with the cultured men who formed my father's circle of friends'. After working as a clerk in London he migrated to Victoria, arriving in September 1852. After a year on the Forest Creek goldfields he read proofs of the papers for the second session of the Legislative Council. In 1854 he became a clerical assistant in the Melbourne City Council office. In 1856 the town clerk, William Kerr [q.v.], resigned and his deputy died after a day in office, throwing heavy responsibilities on FitzGibbon. To cope with a severance crisis in Smith ward (Carlton), FitzGibbon was gazetted town clerk of that ward in June. Soon afterwards he was appointed town clerk of Melbourne.

As town clerk FitzGibbon helped to obtain crown land for public markets, and fiercely opposed attempts to alienate parkland. He prevented the Melbourne Gas Co. from selling its grant of crown land at West Melbourne, and survived an attempt by leading gas shareholders to unseat him as town clerk. He was a pioneer advocate of asphalt paving which replaced broken metal and facilitated the introduction of tram tracks. His prevention of a private tramway company from gaining permanent possession of Melbourne's streets later enabled the tramways to become the property of a trust comprising the interested municipalities. He blocked attempts by electric lighting companies to erect poles in the streets and made possible the public ownership of the city's lighting system. He also campaigned against the pollution of the Yarra by effluent from factories.

From the mid-1860s FitzGibbon negotiated with governments and suburban councils to form the Melbourne and Metropolitan Board of Works to introduce sewerage and to control water supply. Suburban councils resisted until FitzGibbon helped to obtain for them the most favourable terms possible. His appointment in 1891 as full-time chairman of the new board inspired optimism for its future, but he was later criticized by the press for involving the board in more capital expenditure than had been anticipated. He went to London and raised large loans which, according to George Meudell, could have been done more cheaply in Melbourne.

However, in FitzGibbon's fourteen years as chairman Melbourne's sewerage system was completed and its water catchments consolidated.

FitzGibbon's abilities overshadowed those of the part-time amateurs on the City Council and the Board of Works Commission. After part-time study he was admitted to the Bar in 1860. In 1861 he unsuccessfully contested South Bourke electorate as a free trade candidate advocating assisted immigration, the abolition of state aid to religion and a uniform system of secular education with facilities for religious teaching. In the 1860s he was active in the movement to abolish the transportation of convicts to Western Australia. He was a prominent Anglican layman. Through pamphlets, lectures and letters to the press he advocated from the 1870s that the city's administration should serve as a model for the whole colony, and that party conflict should be abolished by involving all parliamentarians in executive government, with departments administered by committees instead of by individual members. To some extent his ideas were realized in the Board of Works. He was appointed C.M.G. in 1892. In Melbourne on 26 July 1873 FitzGibbon married Sarah, née Dawson. He died on 12 December 1905 at his home, White Knights, South Yarra, survived by five sons.

A statue is in St Kilda Road near Prince's Bridge. The Melbourne City Council and the Board of Works have portraits.

G. Meudell, *The pleasant career of a spendthrift and his later reflections* (Melb, 1935); B. Webb, *The Webbs' Australian diary, 1898*, A. G. Austin ed (Melb, 1965); *Observer* (Collingwood), 10 Sept 1874, 20 Sept 1883, 4 Jan 1906; *Australasian*, 4 Oct 1884, 4 Oct 1890; *Table Talk*, 1 May 1891; *Argus*, 6 June 1903; *Punch* (Melb), 28 Jan 1904.   BERNARD BARRETT

FITZHARDINGE, WILLIAM GEORGE AUGUSTUS (1810-1884), solicitor, was born on 8 June 1810 in London, son of William Fitzhardinge (M.P. for County Gloucester 1810-11, created Earl Fitzhardinge 1841), eldest son of the 5th earl of Berkeley and Jane Baldwin, niece of Major-General Thomas Hawkshaw, in the East India Co.'s service. In 1823 he was admitted to Westminster School as a 'Town Boy' (described erroneously as the son of Augustus Fitzhardinge, third son of the earl), became a King's Scholar in 1825 and left in 1826. Next year he was articled for five years to Thomas Clarke who later became solicitor to the Board of Ordnance. About 1833 he married Mary Anne Gahen, and a daughter was born in London on 14 February 1836. Later he moved to Chiswick where a son was born on 20 June 1838.

In August 1838 Fitzhardinge left Plymouth with his family as cabin passengers in the *James Pattison* and reached Sydney on 11 December. A widowed sister of his mother, Mrs Susanna M. Ward, had been in the colony for eighteen years and held several land grants including 1000 acres on the Paterson River, of which she appointed Fitzhardinge superintendent. In March 1839 he and a fellow passenger from England took from her a seven-year lease of Clarendon Park, 500 acres on the eastern side of the river, with three convict servants. The partnership broke up after two months and Fitzhardinge returned to Sydney. On 1 April 1840, after an examination 'as to service, character and on legal matters', he was admitted as an attorney, solicitor and proctor of the Supreme Court. He commenced practice at 4 King Street, where he established the firm of Fitzhardinge & MacKechnie, later successively Fitzhardinge & Son, Fitzhardinge, Son & Houston, and Fitzhardinge, Son & Yeomans, and now incorporated in McCoy, Grove & Atkinson. Fitzhardinge's practice, which became extensive in civil and equity matters, began in a troubled financial period. He acted on occasions for the Bank of Australasia, once in 1843 in a case against John Piper [q.v.]. In that year he acted for Charles Kemp and John Fairfax in an action against J. R. Brenan [qq.v.], and was also reported as appearing with counsel for the defendant in the involved case of Gordon's insolvency in which conspiracy was alleged. Whilst acting for another client, Thomas Broughton [q.v.], he was charged with perjury in an affidavit; the case lasted a week and was then dismissed by the magistrate, Charles Windeyer [q.v.]. He also acted as Sydney agent for Gilbert Wright, a Bathurst solicitor, and it was perhaps this experience which drew his attention to the potentialities of country practice linked with a city firm, which he systematically developed later as his sons grew up.

By 1842 Fitzhardinge had moved from the North Shore to a house in Spring Street. In 1844 he corresponded with Sir William Macarthur [q.v.] and bought olive trees from Camden Park for his new house at Waverley. In the next year 'John Hardy, gardener to Mr. Fitzhardinge' was a successful exhibitor at the Floral and Horticultural Exhibition in Sydney. The family moved to Waterview Bay, Balmain, in 1849 and two sons later established homes in Balmain. Fitzhardinge's first wife died on 5 July 1844, and on 18 November at Christ Church St Lawrence, Sydney, he married Anna Amelia, daughter of William and Eliza

Hyde. She died on 9 June 1865, and on 16 August 1866 he married Harriet Ellen, daughter of Alfred Elyard, solicitor and marshal of the Vice-Admiralty Court. Fitzhardinge's eldest son, William, ran away to sea at 14, and eleven years later was master of a ship trading between Sydney and Manila. Of the remaining nine sons who survived to manhood, five were articled in their father's office and practised as solicitors in Sydney, Wagga Wagga, Dubbo and Glen Innes. One, Grantley Hyde, graduated from the University of Sydney, practised as a barrister and was for twenty-eight years a District Court judge.

Fitzhardinge brought to the colony a family tradition of responsibility to the community and passed it on to his sons, several of whom were active in municipal affairs and in the raising of volunteer regiments. They were no less notable in rowing and sailing. Three sons were members of the crew that defeated Victoria in the first intercolonial boat race on the Parramatta River on 4 February 1863, and two were members of the winning crew in the first 'Intercolonial Gig Race' in Hobart on 30 January 1872. Five of the brothers were foundation members of the Sydney Rowing Club in 1870 and Grantley Hyde in 1874 owned one of the fifteen boats on the register of the Royal Prince Alfred Yacht Club. Fitzhardinge died in Paddington on 12 September 1884 and was buried in the Church of England section of the Randwick cemetery.

Fitzhardinge had a pride in his family traditions and descent and showed his feeling for them in the use of the Berkeley coat-of-arms on his seal and bookplate and by the names he bestowed on his children. Apparently reserved, he was devoted to his family, and his high standard of professional conduct and his industry won him a standing in the community and were passed on to his sons.

Reserved and equity judgments of the Supreme Court . . . 1845 (Syd, 1846); J. Welch, *The list of the Queen's scholars of St Peter's College, Westminster* (Lond, 1852); G. F. R. Barker and A. H. Stenning, *The record of old Westminsters*, 1 (Lond, 1928); *Sydney Herald*, 12 Dec 1838; SMH, 29 Dec 1933, 9 Feb 1934; Macarthur papers (ML).

PETER C. FITZHARDINGE-SETON

FITZPATRICK, COLUMBUS (1810-1877), builder and undertaker, was born in Dublin, son of Bernard Fitzpatrick, convict and later chief bailiff of the Supreme Court of New South Wales, and his wife Catherine, née Milling. On 2 July 1811 he arrived in Sydney with his parents and elder brother in the *Providence*. The family lived at Windsor and Parramatta until 1817 when he was taken to Sydney by his mother, a schoolmistress, who taught him, instructed other children in religion and founded the choir which later became that of St Mary's Cathedral. When the foundation stone of the cathedral was laid by Macquarie on 29 October 1821 Columbus held the trowel for the governor and later recorded his brief speech. Until the end of 1826 he acted as assistant to the two Roman Catholic chaplains, Fathers Philip Conolly and J. J. Therry [qq.v], and was educated by them. In 1824-26 he was in Hobart Town with Father Conolly and on his return to Sydney was apprenticed to a coachbuilder.

In October 1830 Fitzpatrick was granted 100 acres at Narara Creek, near Gosford, but later sold it and bought a smaller block. About 1838 he moved to Goulburn where he became a builder and worked intermittently as an undertaker. An active helper in times of bush fires and floods, he was overseer of local works in 1863-68 while the municipal council was dissolved. An alderman in 1873, he tried several times for election as mayor and finally retired because municipal workmen had to remain unpaid until resolution of the deadlock. He joined the Argyle and Georgiana Roads Association, formed to protect the interests of free selectors. In local politics he was an outspoken advocate of free trade and labour rights and became well known as an electioneering agent, although in 1856 in his only candidature he secured no votes at all.

In 1864 he contributed some personal reminiscences to the *Southern Argus* and became a constant writer for the local press on a variety of subjects from politics to early colonial history. His historical articles attracted much notice but he neglected encouragement to extend and publish them in permanent form. Cardinal Moran used them in 1895, and in 1965 their rediscovery caused much controversy as it was argued that, contrary to Moran's opinion, Fitzpatrick as a first-hand witness contradicted a long-held tradition that a consecrated Host had been left by Father J. F. O'Flynn [q.v.] at the house of William Davis in Sydney.

After conducting a funeral during inclement weather in September 1877 Fitzpatrick became ill and died aged 68 at Goulburn on 8 November. He was survived by his wife Margaret, née Gilligan, whom he had married at Goulburn in 1845, and by three sons and three daughters. One son, Michael, became a clerk of Petty Sessions.

Apart from his significance as an amateur historian, Fitzpatrick's principal interest lies in his willingness to play a leading part in the growing community in which he lived. Although unflinching in religious and political attitudes he was unbiased in carrying out his civic duties. As a writer he used a lucid and vigorous style, highly personal in tone but marked by a quiet good humour which well accounts for his popularity in Goulburn.

P. F. Moran, *History of the Catholic Church in Australasia* (Syd, 1895); C. J. Duffy (ed), *Catholic religious and social life . . . portrayed in the letters of Columbus Fitzpatrick, 1810-1878* (Syd, 1966); E. J. Lea-Scarlett, 'Columbus Fitzpatrick, a neglected historian, and his family', *Descent*, 2 (1965) pt 4; 'The Fitzpatrick family, 1810-1904', Aust Catholic Hist Soc, J, 2 (1966).   E. J. LEA-SCARLETT

FITZPATRICK, JOHN (1810-1890), clergyman, was born in Dublin. He studied for the priesthood at the seminaries of Carlow and Maynooth and was ordained on 30 December 1837 for the Dublin archdiocese. Along with J. A. Goold, Francis Murphy, John Brady, P. B. Geoghegan [qq.v.] and others he was persuaded by Dr W. B. Ullathorne [q.v.] to work in the Australian colonies, and in July 1838 he arrived at Sydney in the *Cecilia*. He was sent first to the Goulburn mission and travelled far into the Riverina, but he was no horseman and after a year moved to the Penrith and Liverpool areas. In 1848 he was invited by Bishop Goold to join him in Port Phillip. Fitzpatrick arrived in Melbourne on 6 November in the *Shamrock* and, apart from a brief pastorate in Geelong in the early 1850s, was Goold's right-hand man for the next thirty-eight years.

As administrator of St Patrick's Cathedral in 1858-79, Fitzpatrick was responsible for adopting W. W. Wardell's [q.v.] plans for the building, and from the first he nurtured the project, begged funds and kept meticulous account of the £150,000 raised and spent in the cause. According to the *Bulletin*, 'in spirit he raised every stone of the walls. He haunted the building like its ghost . . . often the workmen were startled to see his slight, bent figure, with the cassock gathered around it, crossing from aisle to aisle on the foot-wide, windy walls, 70 ft. above the ground'. With his close knowledge and love of architecture Fitzpatrick was often consulted in the building of Catholic churches, colleges and schools in the colony.

In 1851-53 Fitzpatrick was in Rome with Goold. As secretary and vicar-general on his return he handled most of the episcopal correspondence and administrative burdens. His ponderous formality and persistent monetary demands for support of the cathedral irked the priests struggling in the country missions. He seldom ventured beyond Melbourne apart from the occasional deputizing for Goold in opening churches. Clerical and lay discontent reached its peak in the late 1850s with the departure of Fathers Patrick Dunne, Michael McAlroy and Patrick Bermingham [qq.v.].

In 1876 Fitzpatrick was appointed monsignor and papal chamberlain but refused to be addressed by the title. In his last years he lived at the cathedral presbytery while Dean Thomas Donaghy attended to matters of administration. He died there aged 80 on 21 January 1890 and was buried in the cathedral vaults. Obituarists spoke warmly of his 'untiring zeal and self-denial' in building the cathedral without incurring debts. 'Kindly, benevolent, disinterested in gain', Fitzpatrick assigned almost all his property, which was filed for probate at £601, to the cathedral building fund. The sanctuary, chapel and transepts were then unfinished and £27,000 was needed to complete the building. It was proposed that this money be raised and the works completed as a memorial to him.

H. N. Birt, *Benedictine pioneers in Australia*, 1-2 (Lond, 1911); W. A. Ebsworth (ed), *St. Patrick's Cathedral* (Melb, 1939); J. O'Brien, 'The Maneroo', *A'sian Catholic Record*, 22 (1945); *Advocate* (Melb), 25 Jan, 22 Feb 1890; *Australasian*, 25 Jan 1890; *Argus*, 18 Feb, 21 Mar 1890; *Bulletin*, 26 Aug 1899.

T. J. LINANE

FITZPATRICK, MICHAEL (1816-1881), public servant, land agent and politician, was born on 16 December 1816 at Parramatta, son of Bernard Fitzpatrick, convict, and his wife Catherine, née Milling, a schoolteacher, who arrived in Sydney from Dublin in the *Providence* in July 1811. After teaching by his mother, Michael attended St Joseph's denominational school, Beveridge's Mercantile Academy in 1829-31 and J. D. Lang's [q.v.] Australian College in 1832-34 where he formed a lasting friendship with Rev. Henry Carmichael [q.v.]. In 1835-37 Fitzpatrick was an usher at Carmichael's Normal Institution. He became a clerk in the Lands Office in October 1837, a permanent first-class clerk by 1844 and clerk of the Executive Council in 1851. Deas Thomson [q.v.] employed him as his secretary in Legislative Council business.

After the granting of responsible government in 1856, Fitzpatrick was appointed under-secretary to the Department of Lands and Works, and after the department was divided in 1858 became involved in John

Robertson's [q.v.] advanced land laws of 1861. His most significant administrative contribution was the reorganization of the department in 1867, but he lamented that his failure to get a 'Mining Minister' led to inefficiency in the Lands Department after he had retired in 1869. He promptly sought election to the Legislative Assembly; he failed to win the Lachlan seat but held Yass Plains until 1881. His campaign adumbrated positions that he supported throughout his political career: free trade, assisted migration, reorganization and retrenchment in the civil service and more railways. Fitzpatrick was an apt candidate for Yass Plains, an area which held many Catholics and was affected by agrarian radicalism. He favoured the Public Schools Act, 1866, which strengthened the national system of education, and his well-formed, progressive land views, while supporting squatters, did not neglect selectors. He supported the Cowper [q.v.]-Robertson faction until Robertson joined Martin [q.v.] in 1870; in 1872-77 Fitzpatrick followed Henry Parkes [q.v.]. Although a member of some importance, he had also become a land agent. Many of his clients were Riverina squatters for whom his inside knowledge of the Lands Department was useful. David Buchanan and Tom Garrett [qq.v.] often accused him of unethical behaviour for a legislator but Fitzpatrick heatedly denied it.

After the elections of October 1877 Fitzpatrick was second-in-command of a faction of malcontents led by J. S. Farnell [q.v.] and became colonial secretary when Farnell took office in December. Fitzpatrick carried the Lunacy Act, the Sydney Corporation Act and the Water Supply and Sewerage Act. He also attended to some long overdue administrative issues and took a firm stand against any violence towards the Chinese. As Opposition leader in 1879 he supported amendment of the matrimonial causes bill so that it would receive royal assent. His last years in the assembly were enlivened by the controversy over public education. In the angry atmosphere of 1879-80, when Parkes and Archbishop Vaughan [q.v.] were steering close to mutual slander, Fitzpatrick managed to upset both in his principled adherence to the system set up in 1866. As well as state-supported denominational schools he wanted the public schools better organized under a proper department with general religious instruction from visiting clergy. He voted against the third reading of the public instruction bill, and so earned Parkes's biting hostility, which he returned with Irish intensity.

Fitzpatrick died suddenly from apoplexy on 10 December 1881 at his home in Croydon. He was buried in Petersham cemetery without Catholic rites but after a public outcry the Church gave him a requiem mass at St Mary's Cathedral and a graveside service. He was survived by his wife Theresa Anastasia, née Small, whom he had married on 1 August 1846, and by four sons and two daughters.

Administrative ability, liberal views, Catholic faith and capacity for deft negotiation were mixed together in Fitzpatrick. He was never of the first rank, rather an organizer behind the scenes, occasionally betrayed by Irish ebullience and often in difficulties as a politician because of his ability to see several sides to most questions. He was a member of the Linnean Society of New South Wales.

PD (LA NSW), 1881; Sel cttee on the administration of the land law, Evidence, V&P (LA NSW), 1873-74, 3, 905; E. J. Lea-Scarlett, 'Columbus Fitzpatrick, a neglected historian, and his family', Descent, 2 (1965) pt 4; Illustrated Sydney News, 10 Mar 1875, 24 Dec 1881; Echo (Syd), 23, 26 Aug 1878; SMH, 13 Dec 1881; Australasian, 17 Dec 1881; Town and Country J, 17, 24 Dec 1881; Bulletin, 29 Sept 1888; Parkes letters (ML); CO 201/584, 587, 591, 595.

BRIAN DICKEY

FLANAGAN, RODERICK (1828-1862), journalist and historian, was born on 1 April 1828 near Elphin, County Roscommon, Ireland, son of Patrick Flanagan, hatter, farmer and woolsorter, and his wife Martha, née Dufficy. The family went to New South Wales as bounty immigrants in the Crusader and reached Sydney in January 1840. After two years at James Ryder's mercantile and classical school in York Street, Roderick was apprenticed to a printer. He found employment with the People's Advocate and in 1849 he went to Melbourne to work for the Daily News. Returning to Sydney probably in 1851 he founded, in partnership with his brother Edward Francis, the Chronicle, a weekly which expired after six months. In 1852 Henry Parkes [q.v.] employed him on the Empire and he rose to be its editor; he contributed articles and verses to the People's Advocate and Freeman's Journal. He wrote a series of articles, published in the Empire in 1853, on the Aboriginals. These were published posthumously as a book in 1888 under the title The Aborigines of Australia. Flanagan had been greatly moved by the plight of the Aboriginals and his writings discussed their manners, customs and sufferings at the hands of the colonists. He tried to estimate the numbers of Aboriginals in eastern Australia both at the coming of white men and at the time that he wrote. His careful chapter on the Myall Creek massacre was a restrained exercise in the use of evidence to prove guilt.

In 1854 Flanagan joined the staff of the *Sydney Morning Herald* and began work on a history of New South Wales. He left Sydney in November 1860 to take his incomplete manuscript to London and arranged publication with Sampson, Low, Son & Co. When he died intestate on 13 March 1862 only three-quarters of the first volume had been revised. The two volumes were published in 1862 under the title *History of New South Wales with an Account of Van Diemen's Land, New Zealand, Port Phillip, Moreton Bay and other Australasian Settlements*. The preface declared that Australia had acquired enough history to be 'a proper field for the exercise of the historian's labours'. 'The Australian Colonies', he wrote in recommending his own work to English readers, 'are more than any others, an offshoot of Great Britain and the history of New South Wales is, to a very considerable extent, the history of all Australia'. Flanagan used official sources, together with newspapers, earlier histories, periodicals and personal information. The *Empire*, 28 July 1862, noted that his work 'shows his personal sympathy with the progress of liberal opinions . . . Yet we have seen nothing in the book which can be ascribed to political or ecclesiastical partizanship'.

A collection of Flanagan's verse was published posthumously in 1887 under the title *Australian and other Poems*. He was a member of the Australian Literary Institute and the Philosophical Society of New South Wales.

Flanagan papers (ML).   JOHN M. WARD

FLEMING, JOSEPH (1811-1891), pastoralist, businessman and politician, was born on 6 January 1811 near Windsor, New South Wales, son of Henry Fleming, a native-born contractor, and his wife Elizabeth, née Hall. He was educated in Sydney and farmed with his father on the MacDonald River even after his marriage on 29 April 1831 to Phoebe McGinniss of Wilberforce. Although his brother John had been involved in the Myall Creek massacre Joseph was appointed chief constable of Wollombi in 1842 and in 1844 inspector of distilleries, holding both positions until 1846.

About 1836 Fleming with his uncles had taken up Mundowie run on the Liverpool Plains. In 1846 he also acquired Orrabar in New England where he had organized and led the capture of the Gentleman Dick gang of bushrangers in July 1839 and was employed on the collection of the 1841

census. In 1848 he turned to Queensland and by September 1850 at Ipswich had bought town lots on which he established a boiling-down works, sawmill and flour-mill. He was also a partner in the steamer *Bremer* trading to Brisbane, and by February 1851 held eight Maranoa runs covering 128,000 acres. In September 1859 he took advantage of a food shortage at the Tooloom goldrush in northern New South Wales, freighted in supplies and financed a store run by John Drysdale and Gordon Cameron.

Fleming soon became involved in the political life of Ipswich. He joined the faction led by Arthur Macalister [q.v.] and shared in the complicated manoeuvres at the election of the first Queensland parliament, but fell foul of W. B. Tooth [q.v.] with whom he fought a legal action in 1857-61 over the sale of Talavera station. When Fleming won, Tooth planned an appeal to the Privy Council; whether the case ever went to London is doubtful but Tooth somehow secured all Fleming's Maranoa stations. In July 1860 Fleming was appointed a justice of the peace and elected for West Moreton to the Legislative Assembly but never said a word in parliament. The lawsuit, flood damage and falling wheat prices left him in financial difficulties. Desperate to retrieve his position, he took up 400 square miles of new country on the Warrego in August 1861. He could not pay the licence fees and in November 1862 was declared bankrupt for £29,132 on the petition of the Bank of Australasia and had to resign his seat in the assembly and his commission as a justice.

Fleming's wife died in the 1850s survived by five daughters of their nine children. His housekeeper, Mrs Dollmann, soon acquired an active interest in his affairs; his attempts to salvage the Warrego runs by transferring them to her led to a ludicrous incident in which she contrived the arrest of a bailiff employed by the Bank of Australasia. For this and other deviations Fleming failed to acquire a certificate of discharge. When his friend and patron, Macalister, became premier in August 1866, he won West Moreton again in September but was defeated after another session of silence; his parliamentary ventures and some of his business activities were probably designed to serve Macalister's interests. After his political defeat Fleming abandoned public life and confined himself to store-keeping in Ipswich and Roma. An undischarged bankrupt he died at Ipswich on 23 September 1891.

L. E. Slaughter, *Ipswich municipal centenary* (Brisb, 1960); D. G. Bowd, *Macquarie country: a history of the Hawkesbury* (Melb, 1969); V&P (LA NSW), 1858, 1, 919; V&P (LA Qld),

1863, 1, 95; 'Reminiscences of Mrs Susan Bundarra Young', *JRAHS*, 8 (1922); Equity file 6, SCT/U2 (QA); Insolvency file 147/1864 (QA); Registrar's notebook SCT/DJ1 (QA); Col Sec in-letters (NSWA); MS cat and newspaper indexes under Joseph Fleming (ML).   H. J. GIBBNEY

FLEMING, SIR VALENTINE (1809-1884), chief justice, was born on 13 November 1809 at Ashby-de-la-Zouch, Leicestershire, England, the second son of Captain Valentine Fleming of Tuam, County Galway, and his wife Catherine, née Gowan. Educated at Bangor and Trinity College, Dublin (B.A., 1832), he was called to the Bar on 21 January 1838. In 1841 he was appointed commissioner of the Insolvent Debtors' Court in Hobart Town. Though regarded as something of a dandy, he soon won repute for his professional competence.

In 1844 Fleming was appointed solicitor-general. Both he and the attorney-general, Thomas Horne [q.v.], as law officers of the Crown, were often called upon to advise Lieut-Governor Denison and the Legislative Council in 1847. When the judges held that Denison had exceeded his powers in reinstating the Patriotic Six to the Legislative Council, Horne and Fleming expressed the contrary opinion; later the Six were formally appointed under the royal sign manual. When the puisne judge, Algernon Montagu [q.v.], ran into financial difficulties he and the chief justice, Sir John Pedder [q.v.], held that the Supreme Court had no jurisdiction to entertain an action brought against Montagu by one of his creditors. Both Horne and Fleming were asked whether the lieut-governor had power to remove or suspend a judge; they separately replied that he had such power and on 31 December Denison amoved Montagu from office. Denison again sought the advice of his law officers after the Supreme Court had ruled that the Dog Act (so-called) was invalid. Horne and Fleming separately advised that the decision of the Supreme Court was wrong; relying on this advice Denison secured the passage by the Legislative Council of a validating Act.

After Montagu was amoved, Horne was appointed puisne judge; Fleming became attorney-general and in 1851 an official member of the Legislative Council. In 1852 the conflict between the colonists and the official policy of the lieut-governor and the Colonial Office over the continuance of transportation was brought to a head in the Legislative Council. J. W. Gleadow [q.v.] moved for an address to the Queen conveying to her the opinion of the council that the time had arrived for the cessation of transportation. Denison sought in vain to

defeat or delay the motion and in his tactics had the support of the attorney-general. On 19 August 1853 as the colony advanced towards responsible government a select committee was appointed to draft a new constitution. The committee of ten included Fleming and two other members of the legal profession and it reported to the Legislative Council on 28 September. The recommendations were substantially embodied in the new constitution; the bill was passed in October 1854, sent to London and confirmed by an Order in Council in 1855. Fleming, with his drafting experience as attorney-general, probably played a prominent part in drawing up both the committee's recommendations and the bill.

In May 1854 when the health of the chief justice was noticeably declining, Denison foresaw Pedder's early retirement and wrote to the Colonial Office strongly suggesting the appointment of Fleming as chief justice. Sir George Grey replied that if Horne's legal qualifications were at least equal to Fleming's his experience as a judge should weigh in his favour, but if the lieut-governor deemed Fleming the fittest in all respects to be chief justice he would not refuse to sanction the appointment. Pedder had retired before this reply reached Denison who on 7 August appointed Fleming chief justice and wrote to London in glowing terms on Fleming's qualifications and his consistent support of the executive government. In his next dispatch Denison enclosed a letter from Horne protesting against Fleming's appointment and claiming the chief-justiceship in right of seniority. In a covering letter the lieut-governor stated that he considered Fleming better qualified than Horne to act as chief justice and asked for confirmation of the appointment. T. G. Gregson [q.v.] and other determined opponents of Denison and Fleming drafted a petition of protest against Fleming's appointment but it was rejected by the Legislative Council. On 2 January 1855 the secretary of state confirmed Fleming's appointment.

Fleming was knighted in 1856. In his fifteen years as chief justice the most important litigation to come before the Supreme Court was probably the well-known constitutional case of *Hampton v. Fenton* [qq.v.]. In an elaborate judgment, Fleming held for the plaintiff and on an appeal to the Privy Council his judgment was upheld. When Fleming retired in 1872 members of the Bar presented him with an illuminated address testifying to his ability, care, courtesy and constant impartiality. Similar expressions of esteem were made in the Executive Council, a public meeting at Launceston and the press. His pension of

£1000 was two-thirds of his salary as chief justice.

Fleming went to England but returned to Tasmania as acting chief justice in the absence of his successor, Sir Francis Smith [q.v.], in 1872-74. For a few months he acted as deputy-governor and then returned to England where he became a magistrate for Surrey. He died near Reigate on 21 October 1884. In Hobart on 20 March 1852 he had married Elizabeth Oke, daughter of Charles Buckland; they had two sons. After she died he married on 1 August 1872 Fanny Maria, daughter of William Seccombe [q.v.], who survived him.

L. F. S. Hore, *Digest of cases decided in Tasmania, 1856-1896* (Hob, 1897); W. A. Townsley, *The struggle for self-government in Tasmania 1842-1856* (Hob, 1951); *The Times*, 28 Oct 1884; GO 1/95/21, 33/79/404, 33/81/24.

M. GIBSON

FLETCHER, JAMES (1834-1891), coalminer and owner, newspaper proprietor and politician, was born in August 1834 at Dalkeith, East Lothian, Scotland, son of William Fletcher and his wife Ann, née Crawford. As a boy he worked as a coal-miner. He reached Australia in February 1851, went to the goldfields and then settled in Newcastle where he worked in the Burwood and Borehole collieries. He concentrated on helping the miners and was responsible for the Australian Agricultural Co.'s sick and accident fund. In 1860 he was elected chairman of the new Hunter River Miners' Association. Within a year the union was involved in the colony's first serious industrial dispute after the men refused to accept a 20 per cent reduction in hewing rates. Disunity amongst the proprietors gave victory to the union. On 25 November 1861 the union established the New South Wales Co-operative Coal Co. Fletcher was chairman and manager until it failed. He then managed J. & A. Brown's [qq.v.] Minmi collieries but soon returned to manage the revived Co-operative mine until 1880. He represented it on the Masters' Association which he helped to found. He also became managing director of the Wickham and Bullock Island Coal Co. and part-owner of the Ferndale Colliery. In 1874-75 he was mayor of Wallsend and in 1876 of Plattsburg.

In the early 1870s Fletcher upheld the cause of the miners when the coal industry was depressed. He favoured the vend system of controlled marketing which also provided for a sliding scale of wages according to the price of coal. The scheme was adopted to the profit of the mine-owners. In 1876-89

Fletcher was proprietor of the *Newcastle Morning Herald and Miners' Advocate*. At one stage he ran into financial difficulties and was helped by the Browns; in 1884 James Brown sued for recovery of his money but Fletcher was saved from ruin by his friends who raised over £4000.

In 1880-91 as a protectionist he represented Newcastle in the Legislative Assembly. His 'rugged eloquence' and integrity commanded the respect of both sides in the House and he carried six private Acts. He opposed Alexander Stuart's [q.v.] government and the Sudan expedition. In February 1886 because of his mining interests he was strongly criticized for becoming secretary for mines under Patrick Jennings [q.v.] but he had accepted office on the understanding that later he was to be minister of railways. He resigned his portfolio on 23 December. He pleased his constituents with his success in abolishing excessive wharfage dues at Newcastle and advocating the eight-hour system. In March 1888 he won a court case after John Haynes [q.v.] had sued him for assault in parliament. In 1889 he was secretary for public works in G. R. Dibbs's [q.v.] government.

Fletcher had successfully mediated in strikes in the 1880s and in 1890 was appointed to the royal commission on strikes, but after a week poor health induced him to visit Tasmania and Victoria. He died from heart disease and apoplexy in Melbourne on 19 March 1891. He was survived by his wife Isabella, née Birrell, whom he had married at Wallsend in 1854, and by six sons and three daughters. Past master of St James's Lodge, Plattsburg, and a member of Lodge Harmony, Newcastle, he was buried in the Wallsend cemetery with Masonic rites. An editorial in the *Daily Telegraph* claimed that 'he has enriched the Browns and other colliery proprietors; he has advanced the prosperity of Newcastle as no other man has done; he has improved the condition of the miners; and in doing all this he has impoverished himself'. His last years were clouded by financial worries and his estate was valued at only £858. In 1897 a statue was erected by public subscription in Newcastle Lower Reserve 'to commemorate James Fletcher as a friend of the miners'.

E. Digby (ed), *Australian men of mark*, 1 (Syd, 1889); G. H. Kingsmill, *The coal miners of Newcastle, N.S.W.* (Newcastle, 1890); R. Gollan, *The coalminers of New South Wales* (Melb, 1963); *NSW Law Reports*, 1884; *Newcastle Morning Herald*, 1876-1891; *Daily Telegraph* (Syd), 27 Sept 1884; *Town and Country J*, 30 Apr 1887, 26 Jan 1889, 28 Mar 1891.

ROBIN GOLLAN

FLETCHER, JOSEPH HORNER (1823-1890), Wesleyan minister, was born at St Vincent, Windward Islands, the eldest son of Rev. Joseph Fletcher, Wesleyan missionary, and his wife Mary, née Horner. In 1830-37 he attended a Methodist school in Kingswood, England, and then his uncle's school in Bath. He entered business but in July 1842 became a local preacher. He was accepted for the Wesleyan ministry in 1845 and after training at Richmond College, Surrey, he married Kate Green in December 1848. He was sent to Auckland, New Zealand, where he became the founding principal of Wesley College. In 1856 poor health obliged him to take up circuit work in Auckland and New Plymouth, where he witnessed the Maori war. He moved to Queensland and in 1861-64 was on circuit in Brisbane. In 1863 he became the first chairman of the Queensland Wesleyan District.

In 1865 Fletcher was serving at Ipswich when invited to succeed Rev. J. A. Manton [q.v.] as president of Newington College, Sydney. He acknowledged that the main business of the school was secular education in a Christian atmosphere and believed that education could help to overcome sectarianism. He invited distinguished academics to examine Newington students and strongly supported Parkes's [q.v.] education policies. He opposed the formation of a Methodist university college until a strong secondary school was established. He believed that boys should be taught to appreciate orderly conduct rather than to fear punishment and that corporal punishment was degrading and to be used only in extreme circumstances. Under Fletcher Newington developed a high moral tone and a tradition of ,order and respect. After he retired in 1887 the old boys gave him an address of appreciation and a portrait in oils to be hung in the hall. In addition to his normal duties from 1883 he had taught resident theological students. From 1887 he was an effective and progressive full-time theological tutor.

As a preacher Fletcher had exceptional power: he expressed his thoughts in a fresh way with sparkling illustrations and characteristic humour. He combined humility with great spiritual power, prophetic vision and administrative ability. He encouraged the development of institutional church work which grew into the Central Methodist Mission in Sydney. Fletcher was elected as the first president of the New South Wales and Queensland Wesleyan Methodist Conference in 1874 and again in 1884, when he was also president of the General Conference of the Australasian Wesleyan Methodist Church. As conference editor in 1868, 1871 and 1873, Fletcher contributed more than fifty articles, numerous essays and reviews of books to the *Weekly Advocate*. He read widely, deeply and with discrimination. Never robust in health, he suffered months of illness before he died aged 66 at Stanmore, Sydney, on 30 June 1890. He was survived by three sons and two daughters, and buried in the Wesleyan section of Rookwood cemetery. In 1892 his eldest son, Joseph, edited a memorial edition of his *Sermons, Addresses & Essays*.

J. Colwell, *The illustrated history of Methodism* (Syd, 1904); *Jubilee Newingtonian 1863-1913* (Syd, 1914); D. S. Macmillan, *Newington College 1863-1963* (Syd, 1963); *Weekly Advocate*, 5, 12, 19, 26 July, 2 Aug 1890; C. B. Fletcher, 'A footnote to the history of Christian missions', A'sian Methodist Hist Soc, J, 1 (1933); *Town and Country J*, 7 Feb 1874; D. B. Smart, The role of the Methodist Church in New South Wales education to 1880 (M.Ed. thesis, Univ Syd, 1965); J. E. Carruthers, Fathers and founders (typescript, ML).

D. B. SMART

FLETCHER, WILLIAM ROBY (1833-1894), Congregational minister, was the third son of Rev. Richard Fletcher of Grosvenor Street Chapel, Manchester, England. He was educated at the school in Silcoates, Yorkshire, Lancashire Independent College and the University of London (B.A., 1853; M.A., 1856), winning the University gold medal. He had become a member of the Congregational Church in 1847 and in 1856 sailed to join his father in Melbourne. After pastorates in Victoria at Bendigo in 1858-66 and Richmond in 1866-76 he was called to Stow Congregational Church, Adelaide.

Fletcher was a member of the University of Adelaide Council in 1878-87 and vice-chancellor from July 1883 to December 1887. His B.A. degree had been taken in mathematics, classics, and moral and natural philosophy, and his M.A. in philosophy and political economy, but when Professor Davidson [q.v.] was ill in 1879 Fletcher served for a term as acting professor of English language and literature and mental and moral philosophy, and again from August 1881 to July 1883 after Davidson died. He retired from Stow Church in 1890 and went to Egypt and the United Kingdom to collect archaeological antiquities and acquaint himself with the latest developments in theological education. He returned to Adelaide to serve as the principal of the Congregational Training College. In 1892 he was elected chairman of the Australasian Congregational Union then meeting at Wellington, New Zealand. He died aged 61 at Adelaide on 5 June 1894, survived by his wife Eliza, née Duncan, two sons and a daughter.

Fletcher was less an original thinker than a skilful expositor of other men's ideas. He was a popular lecturer and wrote many articles for journals and newspapers including sixty-eight essays on political economy, the 'Dry-as-Dust Club Papers', published in the *South Australian Register* in 1880, and forty-seven lay sermons published in the *Advertiser* in 1884. His other works, published in Adelaide, included his addresses to the Congregational Union, *God in Science and God in Christ: or, the religious teachings of physics and history concerning theism and Christianity*, 1879, and lectures on archaeology, *Egyptian Sketches*, 1892. *A short biographical sketch of the Rev. Wm. Roby Fletcher M.A. together with selections from his lectures, sermons, papers, etc.*, was edited by Rev. J. J. Halley [q.v.] in 1895.

As a preacher Fletcher was persuasive and intellectual rather than emotional. Although he had attended the University of Bonn in 1849 and heard Ritschl lecture, he was by no means an advanced liberal in theology; his acceptance of the 'results' of Higher Criticism was slow and cautious. His intellectual interests were very broad and his library correspondingly large. He was a member of the Australasian Society for the Advancement of Science, president of the Adelaide University Shakespeare Society and of the Young Men's Christian Association. He had a great influence on the intellectual culture of Adelaide and his death was deeply mourned by many outside his own denomination. A public subscription in 1895 raised £160 to found a university scholarship in his memory.

Stow Church Circular, June 1894; *Advertiser* (Adel), 6 June 1894; Univ Adel Archives.

R. B. WALKER

FLOOD, EDWARD (1805-1888), builder, pastoralist and politician, was born on 24 June 1805 in Sydney, illegitimate son of Joseph Flood, an Irish convict. He had little schooling, was apprenticed as a carpenter and became a building contractor. On 22 May 1826 at St James's Church he married Charlotte, daughter of Reuben Hannam, ex-convict. By the early 1840s Flood had acquired real estate in the city and the schooner *Marion Wave*. In 1841 he was a director of the Mutual Fire Insurance Association and bought Narrandera station, 76,000 acres, the start of his pastoral empire. In 1842 he became an alderman in the first city council. Next year he was appointed a magistrate but was fined £50 for striking J. R. Holden [q.v.] who had called the councillors 'idiots'. In 1844-45 Flood joined the Sydney District Council, and in 1849 was mayor of Sydney and a founder of the Sydney Mechanics' School of Arts. A committee member of the Benevolent Society from 1844, he fought in July 1850 for improved conditions for the inmates, asserting that he would not 'herd so many pigs into the same space'. He also advocated the extension of the city franchise to all householders.

Radical in politics, Flood supported Wentworth [q.v.] in the 1843 election for the Legislative Council but later broke with him. An opponent of renewed transportation, he employed two convicts from the *Hashemy* but later denied it. In 1850 he suggested abolishing governorships, perhaps because his refusal to toady to 'autocrats' had brought him into conflict with FitzRoy. In 1851-56 Flood represented the North-Eastern Boroughs in the Legislative Council and belonged to the native-born faction. His political friendship with James Martin and Henry Parkes [qq.v.] began before responsible government. In 1856-57 Flood held the North-Eastern Boroughs in the Legislative Assembly and supported Charles Cowper and John Robertson [qq.v.]. In 1858-59 he represented the South Riding of Cumberland and Canterbury in 1859-60. On 1 October 1859 he became Cowper's secretary for public works but the government fell on the 26th. In a poem, 'Conscience and Flood', in the *Southern Cross* he was savagely accused by William Forster [q.v.] of being 'bought by place and pay' and of treachery to his friends. In return Flood was a fiery critic of Forster's government until he resigned from parliament on 13 January 1860. In 1861 Flood joined the committees of the Society for the Suppression of Cattle-Stealing and the Agricultural Society of New South Wales.

In pastoral affairs Flood was conservative and complained to Parkes that 'we are now quite at the Mercy of the Labouring Classes'. Flood's landholdings are somewhat obscure but by 1851 he seems to have held runs in the Clarence River district, over 650,000 acres on the Lower Darling in addition to Narrandera and runs in the Lachlan district. In the late 1840s, probably with inside knowledge, he offered high tenders for leases on the Lachlan held by James Tyson [q.v.] who had to buy them back for a large sum. By 1866 Flood had sold most of his runs in the Riverina but had acquired twenty-five other runs in New South Wales, one in partnership with Tyson. With S. D. Gordon [q.v.] he held runs of nearly 800 square miles on the Maranoa and Warrego Rivers in Queensland. By 1871 he held thirty-one runs in New South Wales and with partners eighteen in Queensland; he was also sole owner of Gowrie station (Charleville). In 1875-76 he sold a 'large amount of property' but still held Nar-randera, Quambone, Nimben and other runs. In the 1860s Flood built the Blackwall wool stores on Circular Quay and set up a wool-pressing business in Sydney. He also built the first flour-mill on the Murrum-bidgee at Gundagai. He was a director of four insurance companies, chairman of the Queensland Steam Navigation Co., a trustee of the Savings Bank of New South Wales and later a director of two mining companies.

In politics Flood had continued to corres-pond with Parkes and in August 1868 criti-cized the arbitrary power of the chief engineer over contractors for government railways. In October he tried to prevent the dismissal of W. A. Duncan [q.v.] by the colonial treasurer, Geoffrey Eagar [q.v.]. When Eagar returned his letter unopened, Flood published the correspondence in the *Sydney Morning Herald*. In December 1869 he was returned to the Legislative Assembly for Central Cumberland after an election scene when he and Parkes were followed 'by hootings and howlings, which plainly in-dicated the nationality of his assailants'. In the *Herald* Flood complained of the Irish electors; next year the *Freeman's Journal* accused him of 'a total disregard to the interests of all religion' when he suggested the amalgamation of Roman Catholic and Protestant orphanages. He was defeated in 1872 and again in 1874 when he claimed that 'nearly all the Irish vote was against me', but hoped that he would not lose the friendship of Dalley [q.v.]. He refused to contest another seat. He visited England twice in the 1870s and America in 1878.

Tough and self-made, Flood won repute for 'a uniform course of honourable con-duct' but he could be a very hard man in business. He could send Parkes a 'Bottle of the best Irish Whisky', yet leave his wife to die in poverty on 5 May 1879 at Newtown. For years he lived with Jane Oatley, until she died in 1884, and her three children. He died on 9 September 1888 and was buried in the Oatley vault in the Anglican section of Waverley cemetery. He was survived by five sons and four daughters of his legal wife. His will left his youngest son, Joseph Washington, and two Oatley sons residuary legatees to £428,000, and was challenged by his other children on the ground that it 'was obtained by undue influence and fraud' by the Oatleys.

E. Digby (ed), *Australian men of mark*, 2 (Syd, 1889); *SMH*, 4 Nov 1843, 22, 31 July, 19 Aug, 9, 10, 16, 18 Sept 1844, 26, 27 Feb, 23 July, 6, 13 Aug 1850, 14, 17, 19 Oct 1868; *Southern Cross* (Syd), 8 Oct 1859; *Freeman's J* (Syd), 11 Dec 1869, 9 Apr 1870; *Daily Telegraph* (Syd), 11 Sept 1888; *Town and Country J*, 15, 22 Sept 1888; J. Gormly, *Reminiscences*, vol 3 (ML); Parkes letters (ML); MS and printed cat under Edward Flood (ML).   R. W. RATHBONE

FLOWER, HORACE (1818-1899), busi-nessman, was born on 14 December 1818 in London, son of John Flower, merchant, and his wife Martha Deanne, née Wickham. Educated in England, he arrived early in 1838 at Sydney in the *Spartan*, with his brother Philip. He probably joined his brother's firm of Marsden & Flower and then the firm of Flower, Salting [q.v.] & Co. on its formation in 1842. He was later sent to Bradford to study the wool trade, and on his return joined Thomas Must at Portland where, as Flower, Must & Co., they traded as wool-buyers and exporters. Flower was appointed a trustee of the Portland branch of the Port Phillip Savings Bank in 1847 but two years later moved to Port Fairy where Flower, with William Rutledge [q.v.] and Francis Forster, trading as William Rutledge & Co., shipped to the London firm of P. W. Flower & Co. wool, tallow and later gold, and imported necessities and luxuries. The firm had shipping interests, a wine and spirits monopoly and its own wharf.

Flower was the Port Fairy agent for Lloyds of London, a trustee of the Savings Bank, prominent in establishing the hospital and fire brigade and was chairman of the Roads Board in 1860-61. He was a trustee of the Nareeb Nareeb estate and an executor of John McKellar's Knebsworth estate. As a member of the 'Syndicate of Irish Gentry' he took up the 5120-acre Farnham survey and with partners in 1849-68 held several pastoral runs including Argyle, 32,000 acres near Casterton, Burrie Burrie near Dunkeld, The Gums near Penshurst and Kolonga near Bundaberg.

In 1862 William Rutledge & Co. became insolvent, a disaster for which heavy losses in grain transactions and depreciation of landed securities were blamed. The two largest creditors were Flower, Salting & Co. and the Bank of Australasia. Horace Flower accused the bank of relentlessly pursuing him and his partners, and he fought as far as the Privy Council against the local decision which placed them 'in the same category with notoriously dishonest men'; the partners paid 20s. in the £ to their creditors and in 1866 were honourably dis-charged from bankruptcy. Goldsbrough Mort [qq.v.] & Co. offered Flower the management of their new Port Fairy branch, a position he held until it was closed in 1865. He unsuccessfully contested the 1864 Shire Council election but in 1865 was appointed shire secretary.

Early in 1869 Flower sold his home, Leura, and moved with his family to Melbourne. Port Fairy regretted his decision as he was loved for his hospitality, humour and wit and admired for his classical learning and unbending honour. For a time Flower was with the Melbourne office of the auctioneering firm Samuel Macgregor & Co. and he lived first in Carlton and later in Toorak. He died at his home, Englefield, on 19 December 1899, survived by his wife Amelia, née Kirby (Kirk), whom he had married in 1850, and by five sons and four daughters of their twelve children.

English Reports, 16 (1902); A. Henderson (ed), Australian families, 1 (Melb, 1941); M. Rutledge, 'William Rutledge', VHM, 36 (1965); Belfast Gazette, 29 June 1860; Banner of Belfast, 26 Apr, 3 June, 22 July, 12 Aug, 4 Nov 1862; Warrnambool Examiner, 2 Feb 1864; Port Fairy Gazette, 22 Dec 1899.   J. ANN HONE

FOELSCHE, PAUL HEINRICH MATTHIAS (1831-1914), police inspector, was born on 30 March 1831 at Moorburg, near Hamburg, Germany, son of Matthias Foelsche. At 18 he enlisted in a German Hussar Regiment and at 25 migrated to South Australia. In November 1856 he was appointed trooper third class in the Mounted Police. He was transferred to Strathalbyn where on 5 January 1860 he married Charlotte Georgina Smith. He devoted much time to firearms and as an expert in colouring stocks and barrels his services were in great demand by local volunteer corps. While at Strathalbyn he was appointed sub-inspector in charge of the newly-formed Northern Territory Mounted Police. In January 1870 he arrived in the Northern Territory where he spent his remaining years apart from brief visits to Adelaide in 1884 and China in 1897.

After establishing a modest home in Palmerston (Darwin) Foelsche sent for his wife and two daughters. He adapted well to the difficult environment and set an example to the settlers. He remained cheerful and optimistic when others were complaining of hardship and sacrifice. As 'the very best man that could have been selected for the position at that time' he became a great force in the community. He was an excellent conversationalist, speaking and understanding English as well as his German and was very popular. He became 'a perfect encyclopedia on Northern Territory affairs and people'. He also won repute as a dentist and had a large collection of the best dental instruments.

As a policeman Foelsche was a 'veritable sleuthhound of the law', with a natural detective instinct and mental powers that made him dreaded by criminals. His knowledge of the law was such that he was said to be the best lawyer outside the South Australian Bar. He had a keen intellect, studious habits and a retentive memory. When stationed at Strathalbyn he was often selected for special duty where exceptional tact and discretion were required. Police Commissioner George Hamilton (1812-1883) considered him one of the most capable men in the police force, and Lord Kintore, governor of South Australia, described him as intelligent and efficient. In pursuit of his police duties Foelsche was unrelenting and displayed exceptional energy and courage when he led the search for native murderers. His cunning stratagems invariably led to the apprehension of suspects. Soon after he arrived in the Northern Territory he realized the difficulty in administering justice to the natives and made a systematic study of Aboriginal customs and language. On 2 August 1881 his authoritative paper, 'Notes on the Aborigines of North Australia', was read to the Royal Society of South Australia.

About 1873 Foelsche succeeded Captain Samuel White Sweet [q.v.] as leading photographer of the Northern Territory where his work became the main pictorial record of natives, scenery and industries for the next twenty years. At his own expense he distributed thousands of his photographs to prominent persons and societies at home and abroad, spreading his belief in the potential of the northern colony. Anthropological studies sent to Germany earned him the gratitude of the Kaiser, who presented him with a gold hunting watch and signed portrait. As late as 1920 copies of Foelsche's Aboriginal studies were being sent to universities overseas. Many of his original prints survive in Australian archives, and many negatives are in the Noye collection (PLSA) and in the South Australian Museum.

Foelsche was a useful botanical collector and correspondent for F. Mueller [q.v.], who named in his honour Euc. Foelscheana, a well-known Northern Territory tree. In the territory a mountain, river, headland and street in Darwin bear his name. A notable Freemason, he helped to found the Port Darwin Lodge which was named after him. He retired from the police force in January 1904, and was awarded the Imperial Service Order. In his last two years he was confined to his chair and suffered much pain before he died on 31 January 1914.

S. F. Downer, Patrol indefinite: the Northern Territory Police Force (Adel, 1963); Roy Soc SA, Procs, 5 (1881-82); Chronicle (Adel), 5 Feb

1914; *Northern Territory Times and Gazette*, 7 Feb 1914; *Observer* (Adel), 7 Feb 1914; *A'sian Photo Review*, Nov 1955.　　R. J. NOYE

FOLEY, LAURENCE (1849-1917), pugilist and contractor, was born on 12 December 1849 near Bathurst and baptized on 2 May 1852 at Penrith, son of Patrick Foley, schoolmaster, and his wife Mary, née Downs. At 14 he went to Wollongong as servant to Father D. O'Connell. Foley decided not to enter the priesthood and at 18 moved to Sydney and became a building labourer. He joined one of the larrikin gangs which roamed and fought each other in the inner suburbs of Sydney, and became a leader of the 'Green' or Catholic group. He took boxing lessons from Black Perry, a Negro pugilist. On 18 March 1871 Foley fought Sandy Ross, leader of the 'Orange' or Protestant group; the fight lasted seventy-one rounds before police intervened and Foley gained a moral victory. On 17 September 1873 he married Mary Anne Hayes in Ipswich, Queensland.

He abandoned street fighting when taken up by the well-to-do sportsmen of 'the Fancy' including George Hill [q.v.]. Foley became a building contractor but had various prizefights and exhibitions, all of which he won or drew, including in 1877 an exhibition with gloves with Jem Mace, ex-world champion. Foley was challenged by Abe Hicken to a bare-knuckle fight for the Australian championship. After abortive attempts to hold it in Victoria, a special train on 20 March 1879 brought 700 spectators from Melbourne to Echuca and they were then ferried into New South Wales. Foley won in sixteen rounds, and got £600. In Sydney the *Evening News*, 24 March, quoted a Ballarat report that 'Victoria has lost the honourable distinction of being the proud dwelling place of the Australian champion, the glory of Melbourne has departed away, and we in the wilderness are in tears'. Foley was acclaimed at each railway station while returning to Sydney where a benefit concert and subscription fund were organized for him.

About 5 ft. 9 ins. high and weighing 140-149 lbs., Foley combined agility and science with punching power. He fought all comers irrespective of size. He became a publican in Sydney, eventually at the White House Hotel in George Street, where he also gave boxing lessons and for many years ran boxing programmes. He trained many prominent boxers at early stages of their careers. Apart from exhibitions, Foley had one further fight, with 'Professor' William Miller [q.v.] on 28 May 1883 for a £500 purse. Spectators broke up the fight in the fortieth round and it was declared a draw, but Foley conceded the fight. Later he was the official demolition contractor for New South Wales until he resigned in 1903. An associate of E. W. O'Sullivan, he was considered for the position of parliamentary serjeant-at-arms and in 1903 contemplated running for the seat of Yass.

Foley died of heart disease on 12 July 1917, and was buried in the Catholic section of Waverley cemetery. He was survived by a son and two daughters of his first marriage, and by three sons and two daughters of his second wife Mary, née Hoins, whom he had married at Randwick on 12 November 1887. He left an estate of £11,500.

K. Roberts, *Captain of the push* (Melb, 1963); *Evening News* (Syd), Mar-Apr 1879; *Australasian*, 12 Apr, 17 May 1879; *Bulletin*, 10 June 1882; *Argus*, 13 July 1917; *Referee*, 18 July 1917; *Westralian Worker*, 20 July 1917.

W. M. HORTON

FOLINGSBY, GEORGE FREDERICK (1828-1891), artist and art teacher, was born on 23 August 1828 in County Wicklow, Ireland. At 18 he travelled to New York, attended the National Academy of Design and was an illustrator for *Harper's Magazine* and the *Illustrated Magazine of Art*. After wide travel he studied drawing at the Munich Academy in 1852-54, and was briefly a pupil of Thomas Couture in Paris. Returning to Munich he spent five years under Karl von Piloty (1826-1886) who had a major influence on his style and technique. Folingsby stayed in Munich, established himself as a history and portrait painter and exhibited in London, Belfast and elsewhere. In Vienna in 1873 and Philadelphia in 1876 he won first-class medals for history painting. Some reproductions appeared in the *Illustrated London News* and the *Graphic*. Among his major works are 'The First Lesson', exhibited at the Royal Academy, London, in 1869 and in 1871 'Lady Jane Grey's Victory over Bishop Gardiner'.

In 1878 Folingsby decided to leave Europe. The *Report of the Trustees of the . . . National Gallery of Victoria* stated that he would be prepared to settle in the colony if 'sufficient inducement' were offered. He was already known in Victoria for his painting, 'Bunyan in Prison', acquired in 1864, and the trustees commissioned another work for £500. Folingsby's name first appears in the *Melbourne Directory* of 1880. He promptly established himself as a portrait painter and became an examiner of art teachers. He was offered the position of 'Master in the School of Painting' at the gallery, and was appointed on 1 June 1882 at a salary of £600. In September he became director of the National Gallery and master in the School of Art.

Folingsby completely reorganized art teaching methods in Melbourne. Students ceased to copy paintings; following the Munich school they drew and painted directly from life, made academic studies of the antique and still life and progressed to studies in composition. The separate Schools of Design and Painting were co-ordinated. Folingsby did not discourage outdoor sketching but preferred studio finish: 'The man who paints landscape in open air is a fool'. He stressed good drawing and 'broad and simple' work. An exacting and able teacher, he taught the fundamentals of art and a disciplined approach. His interest in history painting may have stimulated awareness of national themes. In November 1883 he initiated annual student exhibitions, and on his advice the travelling scholarship was introduced in 1887. The student exhibitions were commended in the press but he was later criticized for teaching the Munich method of painting with a bituminous base. Among his students were Frederick McCubbin, David Davies, John Longstaff, Rupert Bunny, E. Phillips Fox and Aby Altson. McCubbin later wrote: 'The influence of Folingsby was a great stimulus to us all'. A. Colquhoun found his attitude 'intimate and stimulating'; Bunny felt he had to 'unlearn nothing'. The academic method was, however, considered detrimental to landscape painting.

As director, Folingsby reorganized the gallery and advised the trustees on purchases. He discontinued the frequent cleaning and restoration of paintings, and obtained much needed studios for the Art School. As a painter he was not involved in local art and art organizations, but exhibited with the Victorian Academy of Art in March 1883 and by invitation briefly joined the Australian Artists' Association in 1887.

The National Gallery of Victoria has Folingsby's 'Bunyan in Prison' and 'First Meeting between Henry VIII and Anne Boleyn' as well as various studies, including landscapes. His completed works are realistic, carefully arranged and meticulous in finish; some of his studies are very free and spontaneous. The Historical Collection of the La Trobe Library, Melbourne, has his portraits of William Saurin Lyster, 1883, Sir Charles Sladen, 1884, and James Service [qq.v.], 1886. The Mitchell Library, Sydney, has his portrait of Sir Hercules Robinson. Folingsby's wife Clara, née Wagner, then a recognized landscapist, is represented by broad and high-keyed studies in the National Gallery of Victoria. Folingsby died on 4 January 1891 and was buried in the Church of England section of Kew cemetery, Melbourne. He was survived by his daughter Grace.

His portrait by Sir John Longstaff is in the National Gallery of Victoria.

Report of the trustees of the Public Library, Museums and National Gallery of Victoria (Melb, 1880, 1883-92); Gemmell, Tuckett & Co., Catalogue of oil paintings ... of the late G. F. Folingsby ... to be sold by auction (Melb, 1891); E. La T. Armstrong, The book of the Public Library ... 1856-1906 (Melb, 1906); J. MacDonald, foreword, The art of Frederick McCubbin (Melb, 1916); A. Colquhoun, Frederick McCubbin: a consideration (Melb, c 1919); Argus, 5 Jan 1891; Table Talk, 9 Jan, 20 Mar 1891; Age, 20 Aug 1932; Public Library, Museums and National Gallery of Victoria, Minutes 1882-90 (VA).   RUTH ZUBANS

FOOTT, MARY HANNAY (1846-1918), teacher and poet, was born on 26 September 1846 in Glasgow, Scotland, daughter of James Black and his wife Margaret, née Grant. Her father took his family in 1853 to Melbourne where they lived at Mordialloc. She was educated at Miss Harper's private school and in 1861 attended the Model School as a teacher-trainee. In 1862-68 she was on the staff of the Common School in Fitzroy; in 1867 she had been licensed as a teacher of drawing. In 1869 she was appointed to the Common School in Brighton but soon resigned. In the next five years she spent some time at the National Gallery School, gaining a first certificate in 1874, taught at a Wagga Wagga private school and expressed her literary interests in poems and articles contributed to such papers as Melbourne Punch, the Town and Country Journal and the Australasian.

On 1 October 1874 at Dubbo Mary married Thomas Wade Foott, a stock inspector at Bourke. They lived in Bourke until 1877 when they drove overland to their station, Dundoo, in south-west Queensland. Mary's father was a sleeping partner in the undertaking but the station had its troubles: mortgages were raised in 1880 and 1882. Her husband died on 2 February 1884 after a long illness and in 1885 Mary and her father relinquished all interests in Dundoo. After her husband died she had taken her two young sons to Toowoomba. There she lived until 1885 when she moved to Rocklea, Brisbane. In 1886 she ran a small school and then became editor of the women's page in the Queenslander. By this time she had written most of the poems by which she was to be remembered. They were published in 1885 as *Where the Pelican Builds and Other Poems*. The title poem, much anthologized, uses the legend that the best land outback is where the pelican builds her nest, that is, at the end of the rainbow. It was possibly occasioned by the tragic fate of the Prout brothers. For the *Queenslander* she wrote some poems but mostly contributed notes, articles and reports. In 1890 her *Morna Lee and Other Poems* was published; it included most of the poems in the first volume and added others.

About 1897 Mrs Foott went to Victoria and taught at Trinity High School in Coburg; in 1899 she was teaching in Wagga Wagga. By 1901 she was living with her elder son Cecil who was in the military forces at Townsville. When he married in 1901 she returned to Rocklea and did some tutoring. In 1912 her younger son, Arthur, went with his wife to Bundaberg to join the *News-Mail* and she accompanied them. She became a governess, kept up her literary friendships, especially that with A. G. Stephens, and did some writing and painting. She died in Bundaberg on 12 October 1918 from pneumonia. Arthur was killed in Belgium in 1917 and Cecil died in 1942, a brigadier-general.

From her letters and the memories of her elder son, Mary Hannay Foott emerges as a woman of great courage and initiative. Despite her hardships and difficulties she preserved a bright vitality. Though a minor poet, she was probably the first woman in Queensland to make a mark in Australian literature.

B. Foott, 'Mary Hannay Foott', *Bulletin*, 1 July 1959; Foott family letters (Hayes Lib, Univ Qld and Oxley Lib, Brisb); information from Education Department, Melb.

MARGARET HENRY
CECIL HADGRAFT

FORBES, FREDERICK AUGUSTUS (1818-1878), store-keeper, grazier and politician, was born on 30 September 1818 at Liverpool, New South Wales, son of Francis Ewen Forbes and his wife Mary Anne Taboweur. His father, twenty-one-year-old son of a Scotch merchant family, was sentenced in Calcutta in November 1816 to fourteen years transportation for receiving stolen property; he arrived at Sydney in the *Mary* in March 1817 with his wife, one son and £7000. He became a partner of Edward Eagar [q.v.] in the Indian and South Sea trade. By 1821 he had been granted an absolute pardon but heavy losses with Eagar and in a later partnership with Cooper and Underwood [qq.v.] as well as costly litiga-

tion reduced him to keeping a store at Liverpool.

Frederick was educated at Cape's [q.v.] school and The King's School, spent some time at sea and after his father died on 25 May 1842 took over the store at Liverpool. In 1844 he married Margaret Milner. Late in 1848 he sold out and moved to Ipswich where he opened a new store. He was active in the Queensland Separation movement, secretary of a subscription library and a member of a committee to form a Moreton Bay Steam Navigation Co. He began investing in stations, held at least three runs by 1853 and by 1867 thirty-six runs covering nearly 1000 square miles in the Darling Downs, Maranoa, Warrego and South Kennedy districts.

Although encouraged by Arthur Macalister [q.v.] Forbes failed to win a seat in the New South Wales Legislative Council in April 1856, but in May 1860 he won one of the Ipswich seats in the new Queensland Legislative Assembly. He was defeated at the general election of May 1863 but held the Warrego seat from March 1865 to July 1867 and West Moreton from September 1868 till his retirement in 1875, serving as chairman of committees in 1870-71 and Speaker in 1871-73. Despite his pastoral interests, Forbes never joined the squatting oligarchy but opposed its political domination. He supported the introduction of Kanakas and was described as 'a liberal, with a strong repugnance to radicalism'.

The monetary crisis of 1866-67 affected Forbes's multifarious interests and he became bankrupt on 24 January 1870. His main creditor was the Bank of New South Wales to which he owed £44,621. Unlike some others he recovered rapidly and was discharged by 9 May with sufficient assets to acquire shares in three more stations. After an accident he died at Ipswich on 9 July 1878 survived by eleven of his seventeen children.

V&P (LA Qld), 1867, 811; *North Australian, Ipswich and General Advertiser*, 1858-59; *Town and Country J*, 12 July 1873; Col Sec land letters (NSWA); Bankruptcy files (QA); MS cat and newspaper indexes under F. E. and F. A. Forbes (ML).

A. A. MORRISON

FORBES, HENRY OGG (1851-1932), scientist and explorer, was born on 30 January 1851 at Drumblade, Aberdeenshire, Scotland, son of Rev. Alexander Forbes and his wife Mary, née Ogg. From Aberdeen Grammar School, he went to study medicine at Aberdeen and under Lister at Edinburgh but an eye injury ended his studies and he went to Portugal as a scientific collector from 1875 to 1877. In 1878-84 he was collecting in the East Indies where in 1881 he married a fellow Scot, Anabella Keith.

In 1884 the British Association for the Advancement of Science and the Royal Geographical Society appointed Forbes to lead an expedition to New Guinea. He left London on 1 April 1885 and while engaging carriers in the East Indies lost £800 worth of equipment when a lighter sank. Delayed by this disaster and bureaucratic obstruction, he did not reach Cooktown till August and was immediately invited to travel to New Guinea with Sir Peter Scratchley [q.v.]. He left Port Moresby for the interior with three Europeans and twenty-two Malay carriers on 25 September and since the rainy season was imminent established a base camp at Saminumu, near Sogeri, to acclimatize his carriers and to become acquainted with the natives. On 7 November he joined Scratchley on his fatal visit to the north coast. Forbes then ran short of money but, with no written statement of Scratchley's verbal promise of financial support, could get no immediate funds from the new commissioner, John Douglas [q.v.]. In April he induced Rev. James Chalmers [q.v.] to join him in an attempt to climb Mount Owen Stanley but was forced back by deserting guides and regretfully went to Cooktown in May to pay off his Malay carriers. Promised support from Douglas provided that other colonies contributed, he returned to New Guinea with his wife and while waiting for funds took up duty on 21 June as acting government agent at Dinner Island where he led a punitive expedition against the murderers of Captain J. C. Craig at Joannet Island.

The scant results from Forbes's well-publicized activities had seriously damaged his reputation in Australia and in spite of personal representations he was unable to secure colonial support. However, Douglas appointed him as meteorological observer in Port Moresby. On 1 October 1887 Forbes began his last attempt to reach the main range. With two old New Guinea bushmen and two South Sea Islanders he struggled through difficult country for a month but his carriers deserted, his base camp was plundered and he returned to Port Moresby on 5 November. He failed to win compensation for his private losses and prepared a map which was later declared completely unreliable. Bitter and disgruntled he left for England in February 1888. In 1890-93 Forbes was director of the Canterbury Museum, New Zealand, and then returned to England to enjoy a distinguished scientific career. In 1911 he became consulting director on museums in Liverpool and held that post until he died on 27 October 1932.

Forbes's failure in New Guinea was entirely due to bad luck. Had he been able to do further work his scientific ability and his civilized attitude to natives would undoubtedly have contributed to the opening up of new territory.

British New Guinea, *Annual reports 1886-89*; A. Wichmann, *Nova Guinea*, 2 (Leiden, 1910) pt 2; G. S. Fort, Report on British New Guinea, V&P (LA Qld), 1886, 2, 939; J. M. Hennessy, 'A few months' experience in New Guinea', *JRGSQ*, 1 (1885); W. Macgregor, 'Journey to the summit of the Owen Stanley Range, New Guinea', *JRGS*, 12 (1890); *JRGS* (NSW), 3-4 (1885-86), p 165; *Scottish Geog Mag*, 1885-88; *Australasian*, 23 Apr 1887; newspaper cuttings (ML); Protectorate papers (PNGA).

H. J. GIBBNEY

FORBES, WILLIAM ANDERSON (1839-1879), bush balladist, was born on 13 August 1839 at Boharm, Banffshire, Scotland, son of Lewis William Forbes, Presbyterian minister, and his wife Elizabeth Mary, née Young. He attended a parish school and entered King's College, Aberdeen, in 1854 but on 6 April 1855 the Senatus Academicus minuted: 'Thereafter it was agreed that William A. Forbes, Bursar of the 1st class—having been guilty of repeated contempt of the authority and discipline of the college in spite of repeated warning—should be debarred from attending this college next session—and that his friends should be recommended to remove him altogether'. Forbes is listed as attending Marischal College in 1854-58 but he did not qualify for a degree. His family interpreted his exclusion from King's College as 'a madcap piece of youthful folly; either snowballing or lampooning a professor—the tradition is not exact'.

Forbes is supposed to have run away to sea and to have travelled widely. His poem 'Fragment', includes a subscription: 'Composed on leaving Scotland, June 1862'. About 1884 his brother wrote that 'some twenty-two years ago . . . he stranded somehow on the shore of Queensland'. This would suggest that 1862 was the last time he saw Scotland. This elder brother, Archibald, a noted war correspondent, visited Queensland in 1883 and made inquiries into the life of William, but found nothing more than general reminiscences from old acquaintances: that William had worked on a northern cattle station, shepherded on the Burnett, mined on the Morinish field, farmed in the Mackay district, laboured on the roads near Roma and Mount Abundance and washed sheep for shearing in the Toowoomba area.

Other information may be gleaned from *Voices from the Bush* (Rockhampton, 1869) by Alexander Forbes. He was locally known and refers to himself as 'Alick the Poet'. His poems reveal that he was often homesick but often busy enough to forget that he had his troubles, which he mostly details with wry humour; and that he consoled himself with liquor and tobacco. He held definite views: he believed the miseries of the Queensland drought year of 1867, for example, were intensified by the selfishness of squatters who encouraged immigrants so that cheap labour would be plentiful; and he had the contemporary distaste for the Chinese. Some of the poems deal with life on the Morinish field north-west of Rockhampton, where gold had been discovered by the Smith brothers in 1866 and on which there were about five hundred miners in its heyday. A poem telling of the opening of a quartz crushing machine on 13 August 1868 suggests that Forbes had then been on the field for some time. These poems, rough and ready enough, give some insights into outback life: a miner killed in a caving shaft; a miner lost in the bush; and the evils of bush publicans. More than that, they show Forbes as anticipating, however crudely, the humorous descriptions of J. B. Stephens [q.v.], the mining sketches of Dyson, and the comic anecdotes of Paterson. He wrote no 'galloping rhymes' but he deserves his place as one who, like Gordon [q.v.], wrote bush ballads years before the spate began in the mid-1880s.

At the end, Forbes was in the Warwick district. He fell ill, entered the local hospital and two days later died from obstruction of the bowel on 31 October 1879. He never married.

A. Forbes, *Souvenirs of some continents* (Lond, 1894); H. Scott et al, *Fasti Ecclesiae Scoticanae*, 2 (Edinburgh, 1917).

CECIL HADGRAFT

FORD, RICHARD (1837-1898), administrator and accountant, was born at Liverpool, England, the eldest son of Richard Henry Ford and his wife Sarah, née Swingwood. He was educated at the Collegiate Institute, Liverpool, and then served for three years in the office of Mellor, Cunningham & Powell, Liverpool cotton-brokers. He arrived in Australia in 1852, worked in the office of the Melbourne solicitor George S. Horne and in 1854 went to England and became a clerk with the Liverpool Dock Trust for three years. Ford returned to Victoria in 1858 in the *Ellen Stuart*; he spent three years in the office of the Ballarat solicitors, L. G. & I. Hardy, and then set up as a share-broker in Daylesford. Later he returned to Ballarat to work as a professional accountant, auditor and mining agent and

was elected auditor to the councils of Ballarat and Ballarat East. He won the office of town clerk of the City of Ballarat from fifty-three applicants on 8 May 1871 and was later appointed city treasurer. In 1873 he gave evidence to the royal commission on local government legislation. Three years later when he left Ballarat, councillors, district legal managers and citizens expressed through testimonials and gifts their appreciation of his 'marked ability, and unremitting zeal and energy'.

Ford was chosen from many applicants to serve as first secretary to the new Melbourne Harbor Trust Commission, a post which he held from May 1877 to January 1884. His work was highly esteemed by the trust, and he was sent to London in 1883 with R. Murray Smith [q.v.] to float a loan for £250,000. On 30 January 1884 Ford was appointed third commissioner for a seven-year term under the 1883 Victorian Railways Commissioners Act which transferred general authority over railways from the Board of Land and Works to three commissioners. In 1887 Ford became second commissioner and controlled the department while the chairman, Richard Speight [q.v.], was absent. After the huge construction programme in the 1880s, the railways showed a large deficit in 1890 and the Munro [q.v.] and Shiels governments came into conflict with the commissioners. Ford's appointment was renewed in January 1891 but rudely interrupted on 17 March 1892 when the commissioners were suspended under the 1891 Railway Amendment Act for 'inefficiency and mismanagement'. They were scheduled to appear before the bar of the Legislative Assembly on 7 June 1892 but instead submitted their resignations and rejected the government's charges. The Shiels ministry, unwilling to 'blight or blast' the future of the commissioners, offered them a retirement allowance equal to half their salaries for the unexpired portion of their terms and, for Ford, the option of some other place in the public service. Though greatly distressed, he rallied to accept further responsibility as the legal manager of such major companies as Broken Hill South, North Broken Hill and Rocky River Mining Co.

Ford married Annie Mary, née Maugan; they had two sons and five daughters. His wife died on 5 May 1894, aged 49. Ford became ill in 1898 and was removed from his home, York House, Albert Park, to Auburn. Aged 61 he died there on 23 September and was buried in the St Kilda cemetery, survived by his children.

A. Sutherland et al, *Victoria and its metropolis*, 2 (Melb, 1888); B. Hoare, *Jubilee history* of the Melbourne Harbor Trust (Melb, 1927); L. J. Harrigan, Victorian railways to '62 (Melb, 1962); Ballarat Courier, 29 May 1877; Age, 18 Mar, 8 June 1892; Argus, 26 Sept 1898.

CAROLE WOODS

FORREST, JOHN (1820-1883), Catholic priest and college rector, was born in November 1820, near Buttevant, County Cork, Ireland, the eldest son of Benjamin Forrest and his wife Sarah, née O'Connor. Educated at Bandon High School, at 17 he entered St Patrick's College, Maynooth, and in 1844 was sent to the Irish College in Rome where he was ordained in July 1847 and awarded a doctorate of divinity in theology from the Gregorian University.

Back in County Cork Forrest carried out parish duties. On 14 November 1850 he became a teacher in the new St Laurence O'Toole's University School, Dublin, under the presidency of Dr James Quinn [q.v.]. Late in 1851 Forrest applied in vain for the chair of theology at Maynooth, and after he failed to secure a lectureship at the Catholic University of Ireland in 1853 he resigned his teaching post to resume parochial duties at Bray and later at Kingstown. In 1859 Cardinal Cullen [q.v.] recommended Forrest to Archdeacon John McEncroe [q.v.] as rector for St John's College, University of Sydney, and the Freeman's Journal introduced him to the colony as a 'gentleman of rare learning and a thorough Irishman'.

Forrest visited universities and colleges before leaving Europe and was installed as rector on 7 September 1860. He made his first public appearance on 8 October when he addressed the St Benedict's Young Men's Society on 'The State of Education in the Pope's Dominions'. A temporary building was rented for the college and on 2 February 1861 three students took up residence. The rector and only two students moved into the new building in Michaelmas term, 1863. The council contemplated closure but the rector and fellows accepted liability for the remaining debt. Forrest bore many expenses in carrying out his aims to provide a proper residence for Catholic university students, assist them in their studies and supply lectures on special subjects involving Catholic principles.

As public spokesman for the college Forrest was accepted as a protector of Catholic rights in the colony. Irish Catholics appreciated his attitudes and St John's soon became a meeting place for the Irish bishops of new dioceses. Forrest's sympathies were with them but Archbishop Polding [q.v.], who resisted the Irish national element, seems never to have visited the college while For-

rest was rector. When a new Benedictine coadjutor archbishop, Roger Bede Vaughan [q.v.], arrived in 1873 only one student was resident in St John's. Forrest was prepared to work with Vaughan to raise the status of the college, but Vaughan offered to pay him £400 a year to resign. In 1875 Forrest became parish priest at Balmain. In 1878 he retired from active duties and lived in Belvedere House, Balmain; he died there on 3 August 1883.

The failure of St John's College under Forrest points not to his lack of ability but to the low standard of colonial tertiary education. College finance, too, was straitened. Despite Vaughan's contentions that Forrest had succumbed to drink, the press was loud in his praise when he died. The Herald ascribed to him 'liberal and enlightened views' with 'sympathies . . . as broad as his heart was kind'.

M. Shanahan, Out of time, out of place (Canberra, 1970); Downside Abbey Archives transcripts (Sancta Sophia College, Syd); St John's College Archives (Syd).

MARY SHANAHAN

FORSTER, ANTHONY (1813-1897), politician, financier and newspaperman, was born on 15 May 1813 at Monkwearmouth, Durham, England, son of Anthony Forster, shipwright, and his wife Catherine. He started a business at Newcastle upon Tyne but about 1840 became insolvent. G. F. Angas [q.v.], with whom Forster had been associated in the Northumberland Sunday Schools Society, employed him as his agent and attorney in South Australia to replace Charles Flaxman. Forster arrived at Glenelg in the Siam on 25 April 1841. His main task was to take possession of the Barossa estate for Angas. Forster helped to lay out the town of Angaston and was an efficient manager but was disliked for his pomposity and self-importance. In December 1844 he returned to England in the Symmetry and resigned as Angas's agent.

As agent for the banker Robert Bevan, Forster returned to the colony with his wife Margaret Gibson, née Sims, on 14 May 1846 in the Isabella Watson. He took up sheep farming near Greenock and on Bevan's land laid out the township. A shrewd agent he soon prospered enough to enter business on his own account. In 1850 he became a director of the South Kapunda copper mine. In 1852 Forster went to the Victorian goldfields but returned next year and in May with E. W. Andrews, Joseph Fisher [qq.v.], and others bought the South Australian Register. Forster edited the Register and the Adelaide Observer until November 1864. In

1855 he won the West Adelaide seat in the Legislative Council; a serious riot and voting irregularities brought his victory into dispute and he was not admitted as a member until January 1856. In 1858 he was prominent in guiding through the council R. R. Torrens's [q.v.] Real Property Act. More preacher than debater, Forster held his seat until 1864 when he retired to England for family reasons. At Grasmere, Westmorland, he wrote *South Australia its progress and prosperity* (London, 1866); the *Register* described it as perhaps 'too practical and realistic to rank high in general literature', though particularly able in its chapters on government and the Real Property Act.

Forster, who liked to think of South Australia as a 'land of peace, of plenty, and of good order ... of chapels, bibles, and religious enjoyment', was active in the religious affairs of the colony. In 1843-44 he was a member of the Methodist Newborn Chapel in Hobson Place, Adelaide, and in 1848 presided at the opening of the Independent Chapel at Kensington. He was a successful lay preacher and at 80 published privately a book of hymns. In 1844 he conducted a Sunday school for Aboriginal children at Walkerville. He served on committees of the South Australian Missionary Society, the League for the Maintenance of Religious Freedom and the Auxiliary Bible Society. He was also a committee member of the Literary and Scientific Association and the Mechanics' Institute, first treasurer of the South Australian Institute, a founding member of the Adelaide Club, a fellow of the Royal Colonial Institute and of the Royal Geographical Society and a justice of the peace.

After his wife died in England, Forster visited Adelaide and on 1 December 1869 married Eliza, widow of F. H. Faulding [q.v.]. His last years were spent at St Leonards-on-Sea, Sussex, where he died on 13 January 1897. Predeceased by his wife and all his children, he left most of his property, sworn at £26,550 to his 'reputed niece'. His name is commemorated by a town on the River Murray and a range north of Alice Springs.

A. E. Ridley, *A backward glance* (Lond, 1904); *Register* (Adel), 7 Oct 1848, 15 Aug 1866; *The Times*, 14, 15 Jan 1897; *Observer* (Adel), 23 Jan 1897; W. J. Sowden, Our pioneer press (SAA).   N. S. LYNRAVN

FORSTER, WILLIAM (1818-1882), man of letters and politician, was born on 16 October 1818 at Madras, India, son of Thomas Forster, army surgeon, and his wife Eliza, daughter of Gregory Blaxland [q.v.]. His parents married in Sydney in 1816.

went to India that year, to Wales in 1822 and Ireland in 1825. In 1829 the family returned to Sydney and settled at Brush Farm, Field of Mars, near Ryde. Forster was educated in India at the regimental school of the 14th Light Dragoons, in Ireland at Rev. J. Crawford's school at Donnybrook, and in New South Wales at W. Cape's [q.v.] school and The King's School where in 1836 he won a prize for poetry.

From his parents' families Forster both absorbed the tradition of pioneering harsh but promising lands and acquired the financial resources to reduce the risks of squatting. He went on one of the first overland expeditions to Port Phillip and from 1839 took up depasturing licences and leases and bought land. By 1840 he had a station near Port Macquarie and other property in the Clarence River district. In 1848 he moved into the New England district and in 1849-54 pioneered the Burnett and Wide Bay regions in the Moreton Bay District where he amassed runs of about 64,000 acres. In 1867, when he had retired from active control of his properties, he still leased about 80,000 acres in Queensland. On 8 April 1846 at Parramatta he had married Eliza Jane, daughter of Colonel Charles William Wall and his wife Ann, née Atkinson. When Forster quit his active country life in 1854 and returned to Sydney they had two sons and three daughters; three more daughters were born before his wife died at 35 at Brush Farm in 1862.

Appointed a magistrate in 1842, Forster was removed from the lists in 1849 after a shooting incident in which an Aboriginal was wounded by Gregory Blaxland junior. Forster became one of the most successful squatters of the great pastoral expansion in eastern Australia. With his wife's help and some competent associates he overcame great problems of exploration and settlement in inhospitable and, at times, dangerous regions. He adapted himself to the bush. Never a friendly man, his experience consolidated his independent spirit. To a degree he tamed his environment but it moulded him. He remained a bushman, honourable and unyielding, always an individual, and probably the most erudite and literate of the squatters. His insight enabled him to see himself and his work in a wide social framework. He argued that squatters had rights to security of tenure because of their financial and physical risks and intellectual deprivation; that colonial society gained economically by allowing squatters access to land on reasonable terms. But he also acknowledged that they were using land that did not belong to them and that vast tracts were falling into few hands, with the result that increasing population, which strengthened liberal opinion, would condition radical land reform. He also perceived the political disadvantages of the connexions of squatting with rule from Britain.

Forster somehow found the time to write fine poetry and prose. In the 1840s his country work and the nature of colonial politics both dictated the form of his writing and sharpened his political aspirations. He defended the squatters against Governor Gipps. He found a congenial forum in Robert Lowe's [q.v.] *Atlas*, a sardonic and satirical newspaper which published his best-known early poem 'The Devil and the Governor', of which H. M. Green said 'with the doubtful exception of Deniehy's [q.v.] "How I became Attorney General of New Barataria". . . Australia produced until the twentieth century no satire that could compare with it'. In 1866 G. B. Barton [q.v.] claimed that Forster's writings 'would probably fill several octavo volumes'. He also shone as a critic, especially in exposing the pretensions of F. Fowler [q.v.]. Much of his writing was political and he contributed to Deniehy's *Southern Cross*: notably in 1859 a witty piece on 'The Question of Moreton Bay Separation' in which he described Rev. J. D. Lang [q.v.] as 'The Great Apostle of National Disintegration', and insisted that the Clarence River district should not be taken from New South Wales. Forster discontinued his political essays when he became premier on 27 October 1859 but he kept up his poetry. In 1876 he published the verse play, *The Weirwolf*, in 1877 *The Brothers* and, finally in 1884 his second wife issued *Midas*. To Morris Miller, Forster's verse 'is proficient and convincing', while Barton sums him up as 'a pungent writer . . . [who if he] had devoted himself with more attention to letters than he has done, it can hardly be doubted that he would have gained distinction'. Though his wit is occasionally peevish, there is an inventiveness and technical skill in the whole of Forster's work that places it near the front rank of nineteenth-century Australian literature.

Politics was Forster's chief love. By 1855 his squatting had given him the means and his writing the incentive to enter parliament. In 1856 he won the seat of Murray and St Vincent at the first elections under responsible government. He differed from John Robertson [q.v.] in land reform, especially on the detail of extended period of repayment for land selected before survey, and he was sceptical that any land legislation could do more than reduce the disorder associated with great changes in a new phase of colonial development. Though an Anglican by birth and conviction and one who saw the advantages of denominational schools, he considered that the great

social and economic problems of a vast and sparsely-settled colony with its many kinds of Christians as well as non-believers and Jews made it inevitable that a national system of education should be established. In wanting church and state to be separated he joined the almost unanimous opinion of the colonial intelligentsia. Without a trace of bigotry, he could rebuke and restrain excessive religious or patriotic zeal; in the *Melbourne Review*, 1881 (21), he wrote of the extravagant 'loyalty and attachment to the mother country . . . which was exemplified . . . by a savage burst of indignation against the unfortunate maniac [H. J. O'Farrell, q.v.] who shot the Duke of Edinburgh'. The Catholics admired him, but most were unresponsive to his liberalism. In the 1850s he also sought manhood suffrage and an elective upper house.

Forster served in all ten parliaments until his death in 1882, except the ninth in 1876-80. He held seven different seats at various times. At several elections he lost one seat but won another at a second attempt. In 1859-60 he was premier for five months and in 1863 and 1872 was asked to form ministries; in 1863-65 he was colonial secretary, in 1868-70 secretary for lands and in 1875-76 colonial treasurer. He served under Charles Cowper, James Martin [qq.v.] and John Robertson but was on good terms with none of them; Martin claimed that he was 'disagreeable as an opponent, dangerous as a supporter, but fatal as a colleague'. According to the *Sydney Morning Herald* in 1874, 'Mr. Forster seeks no friends in public life, makes no alliances, asks no one to help him, takes no one into his confidence, and is sometimes evidently repentant that he has ventured to confide in himself'. In 1861 he satirized the Chinese restriction bill and in 1868 he was one of two who voted against the treason felony bill. In 1875 as treasurer he transferred colonial funds from the Bank of New South Wales to the City Bank, of which he was a director, but no impropriety was involved. His durable conflict with Henry Parkes [q.v.] stemmed in part from his criticism of Parkes's poetry, but more significantly from his belief that Parkes had forestalled him with the Public Schools Act, 1866. In 1871-76 and in 1881-82 Forster was a member of the Senate of the University of Sydney. In October 1875 as treasurer he went to London to rectify some financial and other troubles and was agent-general from February 1876. In England he had a resounding quarrel with T. Woolner [q.v.] over Captain Cook's [q.v.] statue, offended polite society with his bushman's clothes and annoyed Parkes and Governor Hercules Robinson with an anti-federation speech to the Royal Colonial Institute and his off-handedness with government business. In December 1879 Parkes peremptorily recalled him.

Despite his political nonconformity Forster was a major parliamentarian. His persistence, independence and honesty helped to check parliament's drift into futility. He insisted that the legislature should mirror society and that no people could prosper if they did not subscribe to the highest ethical standards, he took it on himself to ensure that parliament's actions should be judged on his view of what was right. He was respected and feared as well as hated. He set an example of rectitude so seasoned with waspish efficiency that parliament always listened and often learnt from him. He was also a leading legislator. He introduced over fifty bills, ranging from the regulation of cemeteries to the control of diseases in sheep.

On 8 November 1873 at Armidale he married Maud Julia Edwards; they had three sons and two daughters. He died on 30 October 1882 at Edgecliff and was buried at St Anne's, Ryde. His estate was sworn at £30,000. The *Freeman's Journal's* superlatives caught some of the essential man, 'The boldest, frankest, least selfish and most honourable man who has ever taken part in our public life has been taken away from us'.

G. B. Barton, *The poets and prose writers of New South Wales* (Syd, 1866); D. Dignan, *The story of Kolan* (Brisb, 1964); V&P (LC NSW), 1855, 3, 970, (LA NSW), 1856-57, 1, 1207; *Empire* (Syd), 16 Apr 1856; *Town and Country J*, 27 Mar 1875; *Illustrated Sydney News*, 8 Apr 1875, 25 Nov 1882; *Bulletin*, 13 Nov 1880; *SMH*, 31 Oct 1882; *Australasian*, 4 Nov 1882; Printed cat under William Forster (ML); CO 201/508-09, 523, 526-36, 597.   BEDE NAIRN

FORSTER, WILLIAM MARK (1846-1921), merchant, saddler and philanthropist, was born on 7 October 1846 in Rothbury, England, the third child and elder son of Luke Forster, merchant and saddler of Rothbury, and his wife Anne, née Blackett. On 12 July 1852 the family sailed from Liverpool in the *Ellen* and arrived in Melbourne on 18 October. After attending St Luke's School in South Melbourne, William worked with a softgoods merchant and commission agent, and in 1864 set up as a general merchant at his father's saddlery business in Little Bourke Street. On 1 September 1869 he married Mary Jane McLean; she was born in Balmain, New South Wales, on 27 November 1849 and died in 1908; they had five sons and eight daughters.

From 1871 to 1874 Forster was in Auckland, New Zealand, where he established a saddlery, Forster & Son. He returned to Melbourne and joined his father in Luke Forster & Son, saddlers and harness-makers. In 1903 in partnership with a son and daughter he established Forster & Co., manufacturers of women's clothing in Hosier Lane, Melbourne. On 2 February 1910 he married Mary Alice Gowdie, née Crook. She was born at Fitzroy in 1873 and died in 1930; they had a son.

Concerned for the welfare of children and young people, and conscious of the demoralizing influences in some Melbourne streets and alleys, Forster searched for boys who wandered aimlessly or gathered idly at street corners. Devoting himself unsparingly to their welfare, he established youth services which, in scope and conduct, were far ahead of his time, and he gained a remarkable degree of acceptance and help for his work from influential sections of the community.

In 1883 Forster invited three wandering boys to his home in Toorak to spend the evening with his family. The following week each boy was invited to bring a friend. When the gatherings became too large, the vicar of St John's Church of England, Toorak, lent him the Sunday School Hall. From a spirit of comradeship among these boys and Forster's counsel that they must always try to overcome their obstacles and disappointments, the 'Try Society' emerged, with activities ranging from games and gymnasium to reading, singing and talks from their leader. Late in 1884, when the hall was no longer available, Forster sought co-operation from William Groom, a journeyman hatter, who in 1878 had brought together a similar group of boys in North Fitzroy to form the 'Excelsior Class'. By 1885 the two groups had joined under Groom's leadership to become 'The Try Excelsior Class'. Seeing the urgent need for expansion of the movement, Forster raised funds to provide a salary for Groom, enabling him to devote his full time to the work.

'Try Excelsior' groups were soon formed in St Kilda, Hawthorn, Richmond, South Melbourne and the City of Melbourne. Based on the principles of self help and self government, the groups were notably classless. Provided they could afford it, the boys, aged from 7 to 18, each contributed 1d. a week towards equipment for the class. They elected their own officers and committee. Under the class leader's guidance the committee determined the group's activities, formulated its rules and imposed penalties for breaking them.

In 1886 Forster established the Newsboys' Try Excelsior Class, which met in a shed he was allowed to use in Little Collins Street.

Determined to find permanent accommodation, he approached the government and was granted permissive occupancy of land in the city and £1000 for his building appeal. In 1889 the new building, named the Gordon Institute for Boys, was opened, the General Gordon Memorial Appeal Committee having donated the residue of their funds to Forster's appeal. Forster relinquished the management and leadership of the Gordon Institute Newsboys' Try Excelsior Class in 1890, but retained his seat on the board of management until 1891.

In 1887 the Toorak and South Yarra Try Boys' Society reopened in a new building on land donated by a local resident. In 1888 a farm near Lilydale was lent to the society and funds were given for its upkeep to provide training for boys for whom Forster found work in the country. Through visits and letters of encouragement he kept closely in touch with these boys; their replies show warm appreciation of his understanding and help.

By 1892 Forster had extended the building and the activities of the Try Society to include an employment bureau, penny savings bank and a sickness insurance scheme which for a monthly contribution of 3d. paid a member 5s. a week while unable to work. Classes in carpentry, boot repairing, shorthand, book-keeping, reading and writing, singing and elocution were provided, also a lending library, games rooms, swimming pool and cricket and football clubs. Sunday services and a Children's Church were open to all young people who wished to come. At the wish of its members, the Try Society had now become a club for boys up to 18 who were employed. Schoolboys were admitted only if they were about to seek work. Provided they could afford it, members paid an entrance fee of 1s. 6d. and thereafter 6d. a month. In 1892 classes for girls were held in the society's rooms and by 1893 a Girls' Try Society had been formed in Hawksburn. For lack of premises it disbanded in 1913.

In 1895, as the Gordon Institute proved too far from the city centre for many newsboys, Forster began a second society, the City Newsboys' Try Society, in a store-room in Little Collins Street. Activities followed the pattern usual for Try Societies. To meet the special needs of newsboys, a coffee room also provided hot meals for 1d., following 'Try Society' policy to encourage self help and protect self respect; but no penniless boy went hungry. In 1898-1907 Forster published monthly the *Australian Boys' Paper*, to which he was a regular contributor. Publication ceased for lack of funds, but in 1909 the monthly *Try Boys' Gazette* took its place. In 1901 problems of health and business led Forster to resign the leadership of the City Newsboys' Try Society but he remained on its committee of management. He continued as leader and manager of his Try Society, renamed in 1918 the William Forster Try Boys' Society, until he died in Melbourne on 6 June 1921.

Failing health had finally curtailed Forster's active participation in his societies but his humanity, tolerance and respect for the boys had gained him a special place in their affections. Deeply religious and by creed a Presbyterian, he had great moral courage. With evangelical fervour he continually exhorted the boys to be honest, truthful, kind, courageous and hard working and, above all, to seek guidance from the Scriptures. 'If God be for us, who can be against us?' was the Try Society's motto. Forster's unswerving belief in the literal truth of what he took to be a promise, and his faith in the power of prayer, made all his achievements seem, to him, a natural outcome. Through his magnetism of personality and infectious enthusiasm he carried with him the membership of his societies, and his wife and family shared his enthusiasm in his work. His societies continue and the original Try Society's Committee of Management has never lacked an active member of the Forster family.

H. Wise, *Directory of New Zealand* (Dunedin, 1872-73); *Age, Argus, Herald* (Melb), 1880-1921; Records of Toorak & South Yarra Try Boys' Soc, Newsboys' Try Excelsior Class, Gordon Institute for Boys, and City Newsboys' Try Soc; family papers and information.

RUTH HOBAN

FORSYTH, ARCHIBALD (1826-1908), ropemaker and politician, was born on 10 March 1826 at Garmouth, Morayshire, Scotland, the ninth and youngest son of John Forsyth, carpenter, and his wife Helen, née Young. At 17 he reputedly worked on railway construction and later in the timber trade. In 1848 he migrated to Sydney and became a cedar-getter on the northern rivers where 'his fine stature' impressed his fellow axemen. In 1851 when gold fever struck he tried Ophir, the Turon diggings and then the Victorian fields. On 21 January 1854 he married Sarah Corbett in Melbourne. Later he seems to have been a sawmiller in Apollo Bay, and in 1862 he founded Forsyth & Anthony, general merchants.

Persuaded by the ropemaker James Miller, a boyhood friend, Forsyth sold out in 1864 and the next year founded Sydney's first 'rope and cordage' works on four acres at the corner of Bourke and Lachlan Streets, Waterloo. In 1868 he made his nephew

John (1846-1915) a partner. Starting business at an expansive time in Australia's maritime enterprise, Forsyth had proved his product equal in quality and price to imported rope before free trade was established in New South Wales. By early 1875 the firm had a warehouse and offices in Kent Street and in 1876 A. Forsyth & Co. founded the Kangaroo Rope Works in East Brisbane. In that year his first wife died and on 24 October 1877 at Sandhurst he married Sarah Emmett.

In 1873 Forsyth was a founder of the committee of the Animals Protection Society; he was appointed a magistrate in 1875, joined the committee of the Sydney Mechanics' School of Arts in 1878 and later he became a governor of Sydney Hospital. An 'ardent bowler', he was the founding president of the City Bowling Club in 1880-83, and also a founder of the Randwick Bowling Club.

In July 1885 Forsyth called a meeting to found a Chamber of Manufactures and as its first president drafted a constitution. The plan was premature and it collapsed, but a decade later his nephew John helped to found the permanent chamber. Retired from active business, Forsyth was elected in October 1885 to the Legislative Assembly for South Sydney as an avowed protectionist. He claimed 'he had been a Chartist' and favoured payment of members. He strongly believed that the shareholdings of cabinet ministers in public companies should be limited by statute, and introduced an unsuccessful amendment to the Arbitration Act, but a critic called him a 'bore of the first magnitude'. In September 1886 Forsyth became leader of the new Protection Union. He published many pamphlets and letters on the benefits of Federation and the protection of native industries. His 'conservative, careful policy of management' saved the firm in the 1892-94 depression. In 1894 A. Forsyth & Co. was turned into a private company with 65,000 £1 shares held by his relations. He was chairman of directors until 1897 when he visited Europe. In 1900 electricity and automatic spinners were installed in the Waterloo factory and production rose to over 1500 tons of rope and twine a year.

Well known as a philanthropist, Forsyth presented a new horse-drawn ambulance to the Civil Ambulance Brigade. In 1897 he published *Rapara or the Rights of the Individual in the State*, the history of a utopian settlement in the South Pacific founded on protection and land nationalization. Although the book was criticized in *Liberty*, it was 'admitted that Mr. Forsyth has the welfare of humanity at heart'.

Stern but just, generous and idealistic, he had his children schooled in Germany. In his last years Forsyth felt the heat and built an 'ice-room' in his house, Elgin, Randwick. He died there on 15 March 1908, survived by four sons and five daughters of his first wife, and by his third wife Harriet Grace Walker, whom he had married at 80. He was buried in the Congregational cemetery at Long Bay by a Presbyterian minister. He left £43,500 to his descendants and £625 to ten charitable institutions. A. Forsyth & Co. Pty Ltd was still on its original site in 1972.

Ex-M.L.A., *Our present parliament, what it is worth* (Syd, c1886); D. S. Macmillan, *One hundred years of ropemaking 1865-1965* (Syd, 1965); Sydney Chamber of Commerce, Inc., *We're in business* (Syd, 1968); V&P (LA NSW), 1885-86, 6, 1033; *Liberty* (Syd), Jan 1898; *SMH*, 12, 14, 17 Oct 1885; *Aust Star*, 16 Mar 1908; information from A. Forsyth & Co.

MARTHA RUTLEDGE

FORSYTH, GEORGE (1817-1887), storekeeper and stock and station agent, was born at South Shields, County Durham, England, son of James Forsyth, shoemaker, and his wife Isabella, née Williamson. He arrived in Sydney in the early 1840s and for some years superintended a station on the lower Murrumbidgee River. In 1850 Forsyth with his brother Thomas established a store where the Port Phillip road crossed Tarcutta Creek near its junction with the Murrumbidgee. There on 31 December 1851 he was married by Bishop Broughton [q.v.] to Margaret Anne, sister of John Gordon, a neighbouring pastoralist. In 1855 Forsyth bought a store in Wagga Wagga, then a thriving village of about 300 people. In the next twenty-one years the town's population grew to 3000 and the district prospered, and G. Forsyth & Co. developed a large wholesale and retail business. The firm was a 'universal provider' ever ready to diversify and in 1868 set up a bonded store for wholesale trading. In the gold rush G. Forsyth & Co. established a stock and station agency to capitalize on the thousands of stock passing southward through Wagga Wagga to the markets of Bendigo and Melbourne. In the *Goulburn Herald*, 1856, the firm advertised monthly sales because the travelling stockholders were often willing to sell on the hoof. In the late 1860s the firm of Wilkinson & Lavender emerged from G. Forsyth & Co.

For over twenty years Forsyth was also a civic leader in Wagga Wagga. He was prominent in the establishment and management of the Mechanics' Institute, the hospital, the National school and the Presbyterian Church and was a founding director of the Wagga Wagga Bridge Co. which built the toll bridge across the Murrumbidgee in 1862. He was voted to the chair at many meetings and in 1870-74 he was first mayor of Wagga Wagga. In these faction-ridden years Forsyth was respected for his integrity. In 1876 when he decided to leave the town the *Wagga Wagga Advertiser* suggested that local residents plan 'a right royal parting testimony to the worth of our good King George'. In 1876 Forsyth retired to his property near Yarrangobilly and about 1880 moved to South West Rocks on the Macleay River. He died aged 70 in Kempsey on 26 May 1887 and was buried at Frederickton by a Wesleyan minister. He was survived by his widow and only daughter.

K. Swan, *A history of Wagga Wagga* (Wagga Wagga, 1970); *Goulburn Herald*, 19 July 1856; *Wagga Express*, 27 Aug 1859; *Albury Banner*, 3 Oct 1860, 29 May 1861; *Wagga Wagga Advertiser*, 27 Apr 1870, 23 Feb 1876; Wagga Wagga Bridge Co. report, 31 Dec 1875 (Wagga Wagga Hist Soc Archives).

K. J. SWAN

FORWOOD, WALTER WEECH (1846-1926), engineer and manufacturer, was born on 18 January 1846 in London, son of Frederick Forwood, surgeon. He arrived in South Australia with his parents in 1853, attended the private school of Rev. P. Mercer at Port Adelaide and then, probably because of his mother's family interest in shipping, went to sea. On the Asiatic coast he was impressed by the high wages of mechanics and decided to become an engineer. He worked his way to London and thence to Adelaide where on 1 March 1865 he entered the Colonial Ironworks in Hindley Street as an apprentice. Soon after he became a journeyman in the foundry the proprietor died. A new owner failed to make the business thrive and the staff attempted without success to run it as a co-operative. The trustees then offered the works to Forwood and T. D. Down. They prospered and the firm of Forwood, Down & Co. was founded in 1873.

A boom in gold mining in the Northern Territory turned their attention to mining machinery and with this heavy demand the firm had to expand. It was registered as a limited company in 1897 and when Down died Forwood bought his shares and distributed them among his family. With his five sons he built at Mile End one of the largest engineering works in Australia. He invented and patented new machinery for mining and his products were sold throughout the world. He also made structural ironwork and his bridges spanned the Gawler-Angaston and Brighton-Willunga railways, the Millswood subway and many projects of the Roads Board Department. By 1900 he had a second ironworks at Kalgoorlie.

Active in civic affairs, Forwood represented Gawler ward in the Adelaide City Council for sixteen years, eight of them as a councillor and ten as chairman of the works and highways committee; he represented the council on the Municipal Tramways Trust. In 1908 he represented South Australia at the Franco-British Exhibition in London. He became president of the South Australian and the Associated Chambers of Commerce, a member of the Employers' Federation and a councillor of the Royal Agricultural Society. In 1914 he was appointed to the Coal Board and to the State War Council as an adviser on the manufacture of munitions. He was also a prominent member of the Duke of Leinster Lodge.

On 22 May 1872 at St Margaret's Church, Woodville, Forwood married Harriet Ann Frewin: they made their home at Moorings, Henley Beach. Returning from a visit to America he died at a private hospital in Sydney on 23 November 1926; after a service at Trinity Church, Adelaide, he was buried at North Road cemetery. He left an estate worth £42,000 to his three daughters and two surviving sons.

Register (Adel), 25 Nov 1926.

FOSBERY, EDMUND WALCOTT (1834-1919), inspector-general of police, was born on 6 February 1834 at Wotton, Gloucestershire, England, son of Commander Godfrey Fosbery, R.N., and his wife Catherine Lyons, daughter of John Walcott, naturalist. He was educated at the Royal Naval School, New-Cross, Surrey, and won the Yarborough cadetship for mathematics and navigation but declined to join the navy. He became secretary to Sir Phillip Rose, of Rose & Russell, solicitors to Benjamin Disraeli and some large railway companies. In 1852 he migrated to Victoria and went to the Mount Alexander goldfields. Next year he joined the Victorian police force as a gentleman-cadet and was soon appointed to its executive branch.

In 1861 Fosbery advised Charles Cowper [q.v.] on the reorganization and centralization of the New South Wales police force. On 1 April 1862 he joined the civil service as secretary to the Police Department and acting inspector-general with the rank of superintendent. He was active in reforming a force largely 'composed of men into whose character and antecedents it did not do to inquire too closely'. By 1866 Fosbery could report that despite increased unemployment and distress there was a 'most remarkable decrease of crime'. In 1869 he claimed that seditious meetings had been held before the attack on the duke of Edinburgh [q.v.] and declared it 'improbable that an assassination of that kind should be committed by one man, avowing himself a Fenian, without the connivance and assistance of other Fenians'. In 1874 Fosbery succeeded John McLerie [q.v.] as inspector-general of police. He gave the same attention to minor as to major matters; after complaints by Deas Thomson [q.v.] he even tried hard to 'abate the goat nuisance'. On 13 February 1882 he wrote to Parkes [q.v.] that 'The new Licensing Act though rather difficult to bring into operation is working wonders & will do much to abate the evil of intemperance which was spreading to such an extent here I expect the arrests by the police in Sydney will be reduced this year by *some thousands*'.

Under Fosbery the force increased from 800 men to 2300, despite trouble in recruiting. In 1882 he wrote to Parkes that 'Newly arrived Irish apply, but no others—a good draft of 30 or 40 English from the Met[n]. Police in London would be very useful to me'; pay was bad and constables considered 'dismissal but little punishment'. Fosbery was always left untrammelled to enforce discipline. The duties of the police increased and ranged from chasing truants to collecting statistics in the interior. An able administrator, Fosbery was a member of the Board of Health, chairman of the Public Service Tender Board and from 1900 a member of the board for the administration of the Old Age Pensions Act. As chairman he took a particular and benevolent interest in the charges of the Aborigines Protection Board. He was on the committee of the Discharged Prisoners' Aid Society and chairman of the Charity Organization Society. He was also a trustee of the New South Wales Savings Bank, and a director of the Bank of New South Wales and the United Insurance Co. In 1888 he visited Europe, partly on official business.

In 1901 Fosbery was presented with a silver cigarette box and salver by the duke of York and in 1902 made a C.M.G. At his retirement on 31 December 1903 he was fêted by the mercantile community, the public service and the police force; he followed the latter's advice to use their cheque to visit England and have his portrait painted. On his return in 1904 he was appointed to the Legislative Council; he attended regularly, spoke on many subjects and carried one private Act. He was a member of the Union Club, a member and trustee of the Australian Jockey Club, and a vice-presi-

dent of the Society for the Prevention of Cruelty to Animals.

He died on 1 July 1919 at his home, Eaton, Darlinghurst, and was buried in the Anglican section of Camperdown cemetery. His wife Harriette, née Lightfoot, whom he married at Melbourne in 1854, had died in 1917. He was survived by a son and two daughters of his eight children and his estate was sworn at £23,500.

His portrait by Sir John Longstaff is in the Art Gallery of New South Wales.

V&P (LA NSW), 1866, 5, 629, 1868-69, 1, 805, 1873-74, 6, 67, 1879-80, 2, 950; *Town and Country J*, 14 Nov 1874; *Daily Telegraph* (Syd), 25 Dec 1903, 2 Feb 1904; *SMH*, 2 July 1919; Parkes letters (ML); MS cat under Fosbery (ML).

BRIAN DICKEY
MARTHA RUTLEDGE

FOSTER, JOHN LESLIE FITZGERALD VESEY (1818-1900), civil servant, landowner and author, was born on 19 August 1818 in Dublin, the second son of John Leslie Foster, a Tory member of parliament and baron of the Irish Court of Exchequer, and his wife the Honorable Letitia Vesey, née Fitzgerald. His mother was a sister of Lord Fitzgerald and Vesci and in compliance with his will she and her son John assumed the surname of Foster-Vesey-Fitzgerald in 1860.

'Alphabetical' Foster, as he was known in Victoria, was educated privately and at 17 entered Trinity College, Dublin (B.A., 1839). After studying law for some months he sailed for Sydney and travelled overland to Port Phillip in 1841. He took up a run near Avoca in May 1842 and in 1844 went into partnership with his cousin, W. F. Stawell [q.v.], on a neighbouring property, Rathescar; Foster also acquired land on the Maribyrnong River near Melbourne. His pastoral ventures brought him no great fortune but with his family background they identified him with the colony's conservative squatting element. Although overshadowed by Stawell and often ridiculed in the *Argus*, he carved out a place in colonial society and in 1846-48 and 1849-50 was one of the Port Phillip representatives in the New South Wales Leglislative Council. Forthright in speech but tactful in debate, he was very much aware of his responsibilities and personal honour. In 1843, angered by what he considered a fraudulent land deal, he refused to pay and challenged the seller, Dr F. McCrae, to a pistol duel. When the surgeon declined in provocative terms, Foster publicly horsewhipped him and his mount; the assault cost Foster a £10 fine and £250 in damages. Never courting public approval, he was unpopular with most colonists who saw him as a Tory and opportunist, yet even his enemies admitted his intelligence, capacity for hard work and later his administrative foresight and good sense.

In 1850 Foster sold his land rights and returned to Ireland where he married Emily, daughter of Rev. J. J. Fletcher, D.D., of Dunran, County Wicklow. He published The New Colony of Victoria, formerly Port Phillip (London, 1851), a well-documented account of colonial achievements and prospects, intended as a handbook for prospective colonists and migration agents. Next year he applied for the colonial secretaryship and in 1853 returned to Victoria to take up the post on 20 July. He served under Lieut-Governor La Trobe until May 1854 and then acted as administrator of the colony until Governor Hotham arrived in June. In September 1853 Foster became a member of the committee chosen to draft a new constitution for Victoria. Determined to safeguard established interests, he and Stawell dominated the committee, and the Constitution, accepted with minor amendments, was skilfully framed so that its democratic features were more obvious than its conservatism.

Foster's executive positions in a time of financial difficulty and goldfield unrest made him the target of much criticism. He was blamed for the extravagant public works programme and the growing gap between revenue and expenditure which so alarmed Hotham on his arrival. Certainly the Legislative Council had been rash in voting funds but the public finances were by no means out of control and Foster had foreseen the remedy of appropriating the land and immigration fund. More serious in its consequences for Foster was the goldfields question. While La Trobe had relied heavily on his advice and the Executive Council had met more than once a week early in 1854, Hotham bypassed his officers from the first. Foster bore little responsibility for Hotham's goldfields policy but he remained the focus of public resentment. Far from being oblivious of the miners' problems, he was well aware that economic distress led to social unrest, and proposed that the licence fee be abolished and replaced by an export tax on gold. The proposal was rejected and when Hotham arrived the licence system was more rigorously enforced, with dire results at Ballarat. Under strong pressure from Hotham Foster offered to resign on 4 December 1854; a week later Hotham accepted the offer and promised recompense for the loss of his £2000 salary and £1000 pension. Foster remained in the Legislative Council until elected in 1856 for the Williamstown

seat in the Legislative Assembly; he was treasurer in the short O'Shanassy [q.v.] ministry. He also served on the Council of the University of Melbourne and as a local director of the London Chartered Bank and the Liverpool Assurance Co. In 1857 he returned to England.

Foster was never compensated. Hotham's promise was twice rejected by the Legislative Council and once by the Legislative Assembly. Foster defended himself in spirited letters to J. F. Palmer [q.v.], published in Melbourne in 1855, and in 1867 visited the colony to give evidence to a select committee which in vain recommended his compensation. He admitted that he would not have resigned had he foreseen the lasting resentment against him; clearly he was made a scapegoat for Eureka.

Among his other works Foster published speeches on the Victorian constitution bill in 1853 and on the Eureka crisis in 1854, and Australia (London, 1881). He died at South Kensington on 3 January 1900, survived by a son and two daughters.

G. W. Rusden, History of Australia, 2-3 (Lond, 1883); Garryowen (E. Finn), The chronicles of early Melbourne (Melb, 1888); P. S. Cleary, Australia's debt to Irish nationbuilders (Syd, 1933); A. Henderson (ed), Australian families, 1 (Melb, 1941); G. Serle, The golden age (Melb, 1963); V&P (LC Vic), 1854-55, 1, 425 (LA Vic), 1856-57, 1, 49, 1867, 2 (D18); G. R. Quaife, The nature of political conflict in Victoria 1856-57 (M.A. thesis, Univ Melb, 1964).   BETTY MALONE

FOSTER, WILLIAM JOHN (1831-1909), lawyer and politician, was born on 13 January 1831 at Rathescar, County Louth, Ireland, son of Rev. William Henry Foster of Loughgilly, County Armagh, and his wife Catherine, née Hamilton. The Fosters were a distinguished Anglo-Irish legal family and Catherine was a niece of the duke of Wellington. William John was educated at Cheltenham College, England, and Trinity College, Dublin. Without taking his degree he left in 1852 for the Victorian goldfields. He returned briefly to Britain and in 1854 went back to Victoria, refused a post in the public service and turned to farming at Wollombi, New South Wales. Bored by country life he studied law under A. T. Holroyd [q.v.] at Sydney from February 1858 and on 13 May was admitted to the Bar. He also helped to write a treatise, published in 1870 as Practice of the district courts of New South Wales. In 1859-62 and 1864-70 he was crown prosecutor for the northern districts, and in 1870 for Sydney.

A devout Evangelical, Foster became a member of every diocesan, provincial and general Synod of the Church of England until 1895. In the 1870s he sat on the committees of many church and charitable institutions. A militant temperance advocate, he set the example of total abstinence. He was also active in the Lord's Day Observance Society and the Loyal Orange Institution. In 1877 he told Synod that Orangeism had 'done more for religious liberty in New South Wales than laws, barristers and judges together'. He was also a member of the Aborigines Protection Board.

Appointed to the Legislative Council, Foster was attorney-general in J. S. Farnell's [q.v.] ministry in 1877-78. In November 1880 he resigned from the council and represented Newtown in the assembly. He became an independent member of the opposition to the Parkes-Robertson [qq.v.] government. Although he supported such government measures as the Licensing Act, he made a stir in October 1881 when he became minister of justice in the coalition. As minister of justice Foster found congenial work in implementing the new Licensing Act. To 'Cassius' in the *Freeman's Journal*, 30 September 1882, he was a 'fussy little brusher' and 'the most singularly striking and original specimen of the modern Puritan prig'; the *Bulletin* christened him 'Water Jug Foster'. In January 1883 after a bitter fight he lost his seat to Henry Copeland [q.v.]; but in 1885 he regained it. In 1886 he became a Queen's Counsel and six times acted as a Supreme Court judge on circuit.

On 20 January 1887 Foster became attorney-general under Parkes. In March he refused the Speaker's chair as it would affect his 'already very seriously impaired private means'. Pressed by Chief Justice Darley [q.v.], Foster told cabinet that it was 'of great and pressing importance' to appoint a sixth judge. On 18 May he created an uproar by resigning from the government because he had not been appointed to the judgeship allegedly promised him when he had declined nomination as Speaker. Next day in 'an unseemly, almost disgraceful debate' the Parkes-Foster correspondence was read to the House. The *Sydney Morning Herald*, 20 May, suggested that Foster had 'joined the Ministry, not with the object of serving the country, but for the purpose of advancing his own interests'. Despite a Supreme Court decision that erection of the reredos in St Andrew's Cathedral was not unlawful, he bitterly opposed such 'idolatry'. In September when the cathedral chapter agreed in the 'interests of peace and unity in the Church' to accept a panel of the Transfiguration as a substitute for the Crucifixion panel, he described it as 'identical with one existing in a Roman Catholic Church in Melbourne'. His intransigent and narrow attitude contributed to Bishop Barry's [q.v.] resignation.

On 14 February 1888 Foster was appointed to the Supreme Court bench, Darley reporting to Parkes that he was 'a man of the most upright character, the most unblemished honour'. In May 1890 Foster figured in a famous case when he concurred with his colleagues that under a disused law of George III the colonial secretary could not give permission for Sunday performances, but dissented from them on the need for amendment; 'he did not think the day had come when either public opinion or the legislature would sanction any relaxation of the laws'. In 1891 ill health forced him to seek leave; after a visit to Europe in 1892 he retired in 1894 and moved from his home, Thurnby, at Newtown. He died at Valley Heights on 16 August 1909 from senile decay and was buried in Waverley cemetery. Predeceased by his wife Matilda Sophia, née Williams, whom he had married in Sydney in 1854, he was survived by six sons and two daughters. He left an estate of £10,000.

Ex-M.L.A., *Our present parliament, what it is worth* (Syd, c1886); E. Digby, *Australian men of mark* (Syd, 1889); PD (NSW), 1881, 1887; V&P (LA NSW), 1872-73, 3, 1515, 1887 (2nd S), 2, 1071; SMH, 31 May 1879, 29 Mar, 17 Oct 1881, 27 Nov, 1, 4 Dec 1882, 12 Oct 1885, 19, 20, 21, 25 May, 3, 7 Sept 1887, 23 May 1890, 17 Aug 1909; *Town and Country J*, 5 Nov 1881, 24, 29 Nov 1887, 18 Feb 1888; *Bulletin*, 14 Jan, 21 Oct 1882; *Freeman's J* (Syd), 30 Sept 1882; *Evening News* (Syd), 4 Nov 1893; *Review of Reviews* (Lond), 10 Dec 1894; G. C. Morey, The Parkes-Robertson coalition government, 1878-1893 (B.A. Hons thesis, ANU, 1968); W. W. Phillips, Christianity and its defence in New South Wales circa 1880 to 1890 (Ph.D. thesis, ANU, 1969); Parkes letters (ML).

MARTHA RUTLEDGE

FOWLER, DAVID (1826-1881) and **GEORGE SWAN** (1839-1896), wholesale grocers, were born near Kilrenny, Fife, Scotland, sons of James Fowler, grocer, merchant and Baptist pastor of Anstruther and Cellardyke. David worked in his father's business and in 1854 with his wife Janet, their two children, a servant and goods worth £2300 sailed from London in the *Fop Smit* and in November arrived at Adelaide. There he joined his eldest brother James and sister Margaret who had arrived in the *Anna Maria* in November 1850. David promptly opened a retail grocery with James. They had a hard struggle with competitors but by 1857 expanding business enabled them to acquire new headquarters in King William Street and enter the import trade. After much sickness James died in 1859 and Margaret returned to Scotland. George, who was then working with his father, sailed with Margaret for South Australia in the steamship *Indus* and arrived in July 1860. In a new agreement David and George pooled their joint assets of nearly £20,000. In 1864 George went to Scotland to marry Catherine (Janet) Lamb and returned to Adelaide. Next year their retail trade was dropped and they concentrated on the wholesale business; David visited Britain to set up a buying office in London. He settled there in 1873 to direct the branch, quick to exploit the commercial advantages of the telegraphic link with Australia. In 1877 with David Murray [q.v.] he acquired Pandura station near Port Augusta. With his brother George he gave over £5000 for a new town hall at Cellardyke. Noted for his enterprise, integrity and skill as a commercial statistician, he died aged 55 in London on 11 November 1881.

By then, despite droughts, depressions and financial crises, D. & J. Fowler had reached 'the front rank of the commercial houses established in the South Hemisphere'. The firm had branches at London and Fremantle, agencies in the Northern Territory and on the River Murray, large stores in Port Adelaide and other suburbs, big depots for kerosene and factories for jam, condiments, confectionery and preserved fruit. They also ran a large shipping agency, importing foodstuffs and exporting wool, wheat, flour, meat, butter, copper and tanning bark. By 1896 the firm had spread to Broken Hill and Kalgoorlie, and acquired the bankrupt Adelaide Milling Co. for £82,500 and eleven other flour-mills, and won a leading place as dried fruit packers on the Murray irrigation settlements. While travelling to Britain in 1882 George had met a director of Shell Oil Co. and won from him the agency for Shell products in South Australia; later he built the Shell bulk installations at Port Adelaide. In Britain he also heard of the Macarthur-Forrest cyanide process for recovering gold from mine tailings and helped to introduce the process on his return to Australia in 1884.

Like his brother David, George was an unflinching advocate of free trade. David had contested the East Adelaide seat in the House of Assembly but failed because he rejected protection even of native industry. George was elected for East Adelaide in 1878, represented South Australia at the intercolonial convention on tariffs in 1880 and served as treasurer for two months in Morgan's [q.v.] ministry in 1881. Moderate on most subjects he opposed protective duties and unbalanced electorates. With his 'pretty fair library' and regular copies of

The Times and *Economist* he castigated the raising of government loans without close study of movements in the London money market. In 1884 he failed to win re-election because of his temperance views. With David he had been one of the twenty-five founders of Flinders Street Baptist Church in 1861. George was active in the Sunday school, served as deacon and treasurer and helped to form the Baptist Association and the aged ministers' fund. As president of the Baptist Union he aimed at dissolving church debts and started a building fund and a mission in India. He died at his home in Glen Osmond on 1 October 1896, survived by his wife and leaving an estate valued at £80,000.

In 1891 his daughter Laura Margaret had been the first woman graduate in medicine at the University of Adelaide; later she became a missionary in Bengal. The eldest son, James Richard, was born on 25 May 1865 at Mitcham and educated at Prince Alfred College, Adelaide, Amersham Hall, Buckinghamshire, and St John's College, Cambridge (B.A., 1886; M.A., 1890). In 1892 he married Esther Tinline Murray and became a director in the family firm. In the University of Adelaide he served as a member of the council in 1901-25 and chairman of the board of commercial studies in 1904-22. He was also a governor of the Public Library Board and a director of the Bank of Adelaide. He died in Adelaide on 17 December 1939.

J. Price, *Memoir of George Swan Fowler, Christian merchant* (Adel, 1897); *Years to remember: a record of the first hundred years of D. and J. Fowler Limited* (Adel, 1954); *Observer* (Adel), 26 Nov 1881, 3, 10 Nov 1896; Executors' papers of David Fowler 1871-1925 (SAA).

FOWLER, FRANCIS EDMUND TOWN (1833-1863), journalist and author, was born in London. As Frank Fowler he reported for two sessions in the House of Commons and was a hack journalist for such London newspapers as *The Times*. In 1855-57 he visited New South Wales for his health and intended to write a popular book on his travels. He joined the staff of the Sydney *Empire* and worked mostly in Sydney, with visits to the inland as a correspondent. He wrote articles on colonial *mores* for the *Empire* and *Sydney Morning Herald*.

To get acquainted with the country Fowler involved himself in activities beyond journalism, and 'filled various positions . . . lecturer, government shorthand writer, playwright, magazine projector, editor and . . . candidate for political laurels'. He deplored the lack of merit in colonial literature and soon joined such writers as Richard Rowe ('Peter Possum') [q.v.] who were determined to transcend local apathy and to speak and write with vitality about their responses to Australian society rather than to withdraw into frustration and alcoholism like Kendall and Deniehy [qq.v.]. Fowler identified himself with the colony and had grandiose plans for the establishment of a national literature. In 1856 he tried to form the Literary Association of New South Wales around N. D. Stenhouse [q.v.] but it soon faded. Helped next by Rowe, Fowler founded and edited the literary and critical journal *Month* which focused on the development of a peculiarly Australian idiom. He regularly lectured on an independent Australian culture. As a member he often addressed the Mechanics' School of Arts on poetry, theatre, literature and politics. His lectures were published as *Texts for Talkers* (London, 1860) and he wrote the preface to *Australian Album* (Sydney, 1857). In January 1858 Fowler contested the Sydney seat in the Legislative Assembly but failed; much of his support came from the Stenhouse *camaraderie* and the personal following he had built up by his enlivening contributions to the colonial press.

In 1857 Fowler returned to England with his wife Rachel, née Clarke, whom he had married at a Congregational Church in Sydney on 9 February 1856, and their infant son. He was sent off with a testimonial. He wrote his first major work *Southern Lights and Shadows* (London, 1859) on the voyage. He became editor of the *Weekly Mail*, leader-writer on the *Standard* and contributed occasionally to the *Empire*. He published in London *The Wreck of the 'Royal Charter'*, and *Dottings of a Lounger* (1859) and, as 'Harpur Atherton', *Adrift: or, the Rock in the South Atlantic* (1861). He founded the London Library Co. and was its first secretary. As it began to flourish he died aged 30 from brain fever on 22 August 1863 at Kensington. His widow and children returned to Sydney almost penniless. In 1864 Rowe in Glasgow and Stenhouse in Sydney published *Last Gleanings*, a collection of his works with a brief biography. Fowler's style reveals a poetic, romantic and ebullient personality, although he was severely criticized by W. Forster [q.v.].

G. B. Barton (ed), *The poets and prose writers of New South Wales* (Syd, 1866); J. Normington-Rawling, *Charles Harpur, an Australian* (Syd, 1962); SMH, 1855-56, 27 Feb, 7 May, 12 June, 6, 14 July 1857, 14 Jan 1858, 4 June 1859; A. M. Williams, Nicol Drysdale Stenhouse: a study of a literary patron in a colonial milieu (M.A. thesis, Univ Syd, 1963); Stenhouse letters (ML).   S. B. CLARK

FOWLER, ROBERT (1840-1906), manufacturer and politician, was born on 13 July 1840 in Sydney, the eldest son of Enoch Fowler (1807-1879) and his wife Jane, née Lucas. His father, a native of Tyrone, Ireland, had established in 1837 a pottery on a lease in Parramatta Street West. Robert was educated at the near-by Christ Church School and then entered his father's business.

In June 1844 Fowler's pottery grounds were auctioned and Enoch bought an allotment 208 x 100 ft. at £10 17s. 6d. a foot. In 1848 the pottery was moved to the Glebe, first in Queen Street and then in Bay Street, where a man and four boys were employed making ginger beer bottles and kitchenware. In 1860 he was encouraged by A. T. Holroyd [q.v.] to buy a machine for making four-inch drainpipes which was exhibited at the Parramatta Agricultural Society's show; the manufacture of drainpipes gradually became the mainstay of the works. In 1865 on a five-acre site on Parramatta Road, Camperdown, the firm's twenty-five employees were turning out half a mile of pipes each week. Business expanded rapidly to meet increasing demand; as well as salt-glazed drainpipes and plain bricks, the works made fire bricks, chequered and border tiles, chimney pots and all types of pottery. Robert, who had assisted his father, inherited the firm on his father's death in 1879.

Robert's interests included history, political economy and natural philosophy. He was elected alderman for Cook municipality in 1869 and mayor in 1870; he helped to merge it with Camperdown and became mayor of the new borough in 1870-71. In 1872-84 he was an alderman for Denison ward of the Sydney City Council and was mayor in 1880. In the 1890s he represented Phillip ward. In 1872 he was appointed a justice of the peace and in February 1886 to the royal commission on intoxicating drink. In July 1894 as a free trade and selected local option league candidate he won Sydney-Phillip in the Legislative Assembly. Defeated next year, he was appointed to the Legislative Council. Though inactive as a politician he held enlightened views on many matters including female suffrage.

Fowler was chairman of his district Public School Board and fond of sport, supporting regattas and public school cadet matches. He was a commissioner for New South Wales at the Melbourne Exhibition of 1881 and the Amsterdam Exhibition. Industrious, modest and popular, he was an unostentatious philanthropist and a Freemason as well as a director of Sydney Hospital and the Benevolent Asylum and a governor of the Royal Prince Alfred Hospital for twenty-four years. He also subscribed to the Irish Relief Fund.

He died of cerebral thrombosis after a long illness at his residence, Cranbrook, Australia Street, Camperdown, on 12 June 1906, and was buried in Waverley cemetery. His estate was sworn for probate at almost £42,000. About the time of his death an expansion of the pottery was being planned and soon afterwards another plant was opened at Bankstown and an existing pottery at Longueville taken over. By 1912 business had outgrown the facilities of the Camperdown works and they were transferred to a seventeen-acre site at Marrickville. Robert Fowler's Potteries became a public company in 1922.

At St Barnabas's Church, Sydney, on 2 October 1867 Fowler had married Jane (d. 1923), daughter of Joseph Seale, publican, and his wife Susannah, née Owen; he was survived by three sons and five daughters.

E. Digby (ed), Australian men of mark, 2 (Syd, 1889); Cyclopedia of N.S.W. (Syd, 1907); SMH, 30 May, 26 June 1844, 17 July 1894, 25 July 1895, 14, 15 June 1906; Illustrated Sydney News, 16 Oct 1865, 24 Jan 1880; Bulletin, 21, 28 Aug 1880, 26 Nov 1881; Daily Telegraph (Syd), 5 July 1895; Town and Country J, 14 Sept 1895; Sydney Mail, 20 June 1906; information from R. Fowler, Roseville, NSW.

G. P. WALSH

FOX, HENRY THOMAS (1819-1891), master mariner, marine surveyor and insurance agent, was born on 31 May 1819 at Shaldon, Devonshire, England, son of William Fox, master mariner, and his wife Mary, née Langdon or Thomas. Educated at Rendell's School, Bovey-Tracey, near Exeter, he boarded his first ship, Oporto Packet, in April 1832. On 25 December 1840 he reached Launceston, Van Diemen's Land, as chief mate of the Union. His first command was the Blossom out of Port Phillip in March 1841. On 7 May he reached Sydney in the Shamrock. In 1842-50 he was master of various coastal and Pacific ships based in Sydney, including the Emma and the Phantom owned by Thomas Woolley [q.v.]. On 16 April 1846 at Christ Church, Sydney, Fox married Isobel Pilmor Williamson of Launceston, the sister of Woolley's wife. In 1848 he was alleged to have withheld news of the Californian gold strike from a Sydney Morning Herald reporter.

Intending to go to England, Fox sailed with his wife and daughter in the Mary Catherine to San Francisco in March 1851. He found it an 'accursed place', most of his crew deserted and after news of gold discoveries in New South Wales he returned to Sydney in November. From February to April 1852 he was at the Major's Creek goldfield near Braidwood but found it a 'vile hole'. In June he bought the Emma and sailed her on the Geelong run. On 17 July 1853 he arrived in Sydney as pilot of the American New Orleans, thus concluding his last voyage.

Fox began life ashore as a marine surveyor. From July 1854 he was a member of the Chamber of Commerce and next year was on its committee to have a lighthouse erected on King Island. In 1855 he was praised by the Empire for his lecture on the 'History of the Navigation on the Southern Coasts of Australia'. He wrote letters to the Sydney Morning Herald and in 1856 to the Nautical Magazine and Naval Chronicle on the need to correct discrepancies in charts. In October he was active in moves to establish a nautical school. In March 1859 he was appointed to the Pilot Board, but the government ignored its advice on the Jervis Bay lighthouse and the use of the Sea Witch as a pilot ship. The board declined to fit out the ship and in March 1862 Fox, with Benjamin Darley and Charles Smith [qq.v.], was dismissed. They petitioned the Legislative Assembly for a select committee and were exonerated. On 9 September 1857 Fox had become secretary and surveyor to the Australian General Assurance Co. on condition he ceased his own surveys. From 1865 he was manager of the company; he was also auditor of the City Bank. In 1861 he was appointed to the Steam Navigation Board and in 1875, with Henry Parkes's [q.v.] support, to the Marine Board.

A devout Anglican and a Freemason, Fox had enjoyed taking Bishop Selwyn to New Zealand in 1850. When living in Sydney he regularly attended the 'Garrison' Church. Fond of cricket, concerts and the theatre, he was described in the Empire as 'that attractive combination—the sailor, the man of science and the gentleman'. On 29 April 1891 Fox died at his home, Evandale, Burwood, from chronic bronchitis and was buried in the Newtown cemetery. He was survived by five daughters and his son Harold, who became a notable tennis player and represented New South Wales against Victoria in 1886-1902.

Austral, Lawn tennis in Australasia (Syd, 1912); C. Bateson, Gold fleet for California (Syd, 1963); J. H. Watson, 'Australian mariners of the past', Scottish A'sian, 8 (1917); Empire (Syd), 5, 7 Sept 1855, 28 Feb 1856; H. T. Fox diaries and papers (ML); MS cat and newspaper indexes under Fox (ML).

MARIAN R. HENRY

FOY, MARK (1830-1884), draper, was born at Moystown, King's County, Ireland, son of Marc Foy, French emigré and flour-miller, and his wife Catherine, née Hennessy. He was educated at Banagher and was reputedly intended for the legal profession but because of family problems he was apprenticed to a drapery firm in Dublin. In 1858 he arrived at Melbourne in the *Champion of the Seas*. He probably worked first for Buckley [q.v.] & Nunn and in 1859 went to the goldfields. He had a butcher's shop at Campbell's Creek till 1861 when he moved into a produce store at Castlemaine. In 1863 he went to Bendigo where his brother Francis had a wholesale produce business. Early in 1867 Mark went into partnership with Robert Bentley, a store-keeper. In December 1868 he followed a new rush to Spring Creek, in McIvor Shire, where by January 1869 there was said to be 'a business for every claim at work'. The raw settlement suffered great discomforts and at a public meeting in Foy's premises on 24 February he moved that Spring Creek be constituted a borough. He was elected to a committee for planning separation of the town from near-by Heathcote. Despite the declining mining population and bitter opposition from Heathcote, the new borough of Graytown was proclaimed on 9 August 1869 and named after Wilson Gray [q.v.], a family friend. On 13 September Foy became magistrate for the McIvor General Sessions. He also helped to arrange the first borough election and on 4 November was elected a councillor. However, the town's decline continued and he soon dismantled his shop and went to Melbourne. On 11 February 1870 the partnership with Bentley was dissolved 'by mutual consent'.

Foy set up a new drapery shop in Smith Street, Collingwood, where he prospered, occupying three shops by 1875 and six by 1880. At Carrum Swamp he selected 195 acres in November 1871 and later another 129 acres. In November 1882 he settled the Smith Street business on his eldest son Francis, withdrew his capital, brought in William Gibson as Francis's partner and left with his wife for Europe. In San Francisco his health worsened and he died on 14 January 1884. Soon afterwards Francis sold out to Gibson and moved to Sydney to establish a new business under his father's name.

Energetic and resourceful, Foy was described as a 'Liberal Conservative' and was later said to have donated money to Sir James McCulloch's [q.v.] party. He was also sympathetic to the early closing movement. He was married twice: first in Ireland about 1848 to Mary Macken (d. 21 March 1879) by whom he had six surviving children; and second in Melbourne to Catherine Power (d. 1930) by whom he had one son.

H. M. Humphreys (ed), *Men of the time in Australia: Victorian series*, 2nd ed (Melb, 1882); Mark Foy's Ltd, *The romance of the house of Foy* (Syd, 1935); PD (LA Vic), 27 May 1874; *Bendigo Advertiser*, 2 Sept 1867-18 May 1869; *McIvor Times and Rodney Advertiser*, Jan-Dec 1869; *Collingwood Advertiser and Observer*, Sept-Oct 1870.　　　CECILY CLOSE

FRANC, MAUD JEANNE; see EVANS, MATILDA JANE

FRANCIS, JAMES GOODALL (1819-1884), politician, was born on 9 January 1819 in London, son of Charles Francis and his wife Anne, née Smith. On 14 February 1835 he arrived at Hobart Town as a steerage passenger in the *Sarah*. He became partner in a Campbell Town store in 1840 and later head clerk in the Hobart firm of Boyes & Poynter. About 1850 Duncan McPherson bought the firm and took Francis into partnership; McPherson was consul for the United States and McPherson, Francis & Co. did much business with whaling ships in port. In 1853 Francis moved to Melbourne to open a branch of the firm while McPherson remained in Hobart. The partnership was dissolved in 1860 and next year Francis admitted John McPherson as partner to form Francis & McPherson. Francis was a local director of the Bank of New South Wales until his death; in April 1857 he was elected vice-president and in May president of the Chamber of Commerce. His other interests were legion. He was a director of the Victoria Sugar Co. established in 1857; he had a large part in establishing 'the Australian and Tasmanian Insurance Companies' and in 1857 was a director of the Melbourne Underwriters' Association, known as the Melbourne Marine Insurance Association after 1858. He was interested in gold-mining especially in the late 1850s and in Riverina and Victorian squatting from the late 1870s: in 1884 he held a half-interest in Runnymede, near Casterton, and was buying Monomeith near Cranbourne with P. and J. Bruce. He also invested in coal and Western Australian timber but his favourite hobby was probably the large vineyard he established at Sunbury in 1863.

In 1859-74 Francis represented Richmond in the Victorian Legislative Assembly. On 25 November 1859 he succeeded J. C. King [q.v.] as vice-president of the lands and works board and commissioner of public works in the ministry of William Nicholson [q.v.]. When the cabinet refused to back James Service [q.v.] who threatened to invoke an 1850 Order in Council to make the Legislative Council accept his land bill, Francis resigned with Service on 3 September 1860. This action put him towards the left; so did his mild protectionism. Like other reformist merchants, however, he was separated from radicals by his dislike of agitation and contempt for their administrative capacities. He therefore opposed the part-radical ministry of Richard Heales [q.v.] as incompetent; when it turned wholly radical at the elections of 1861, proposing tariff reform and more administrative action to solve the land question, he despised it the more for its sudden conversion. Like other moneyed reformers he helped to defeat Heales and supported John O'Shanassy's [q.v.] ministry of 1861-63, although except for C. G. Duffy [q.v.] it was thoroughly conservative. Francis then became restless when Duffy's Land Act proved a fiasco and helped to defeat the ministry when Duffy proposed to increase pastoral rents fixed by arbitration under his own Act.

Co-operation in 1862 with James McCulloch [q.v.] earned Francis the commissionership of trade and customs in June 1863 in McCulloch's first administration. It was dominated by men of standing but the presence of Heales and three supporters made it easier for Francis to introduce his 1865 tariff. This first move in Victoria towards protection also began a political crisis. The government's victory at the 1864 elections had forced the Legislative Council to accept a liberal land bill, but it determined to counter-attack on the tariff. The government therefore 'tacked' this to the budget, but the council rejected the combined bill in July. Victoria was in uproar. Francis, while far from joining the radical agitators, supported his tariff against his class and saw it pass in March 1866.

The crisis revived in July 1867. A grant to Lady Darling, whose husband Sir Charles had been recalled for alleged partisanship in supporting the ministry in the earlier crisis, was also tacked with a similar result. Francis disliked the unnecessary disruption but extremism prevailed. He supported his colleagues, especially after Colonial Office intervention had forced their resignation in May 1868, but was soon critical of his party's intransigence. This attitude and his business affairs kept him out of the more radical restoration of the ministry after the crisis but he rejoined McCulloch in April 1870 as treasurer in his more conservative third administration. Faced with falling revenue after the 1871 elections Francis proposed even higher duties but, believing

12½ per cent the limit, suggested Victoria's first property tax for the rest. This proposal brought down the government in July and wrecked its party. Duffy's radical ministry successfully increased duties to 20 per cent but fears of another constitutional crisis united members of all persuasions. McCulloch resigned in the Christmas recess and Francis became leader and in June 1872 chief secretary. His pragmatism and moderation symbolized coalition and 'practical legislation'. His democratic style held together a cabinet of able, self-assertive men, some recently bitter opponents, and his majority soon became overwhelming.

Francis did not shun conflict. The 1872 Education Act, which first provided effectively for free, secular and compulsory primary education, belied claims that as an Anglican he had raised the question merely to undermine his Catholic predecessor. The ancient questions of mining on private property, fencing, impounding and land law liberalization were tackled. Acts were passed to reduce mining accidents and implement a long-delayed railway building programme. Constitutional reform was Francis's personal responsibility. In 1873 his proposals, more radical than politic, would have gone far towards one man one vote and one vote one value, liberalize the council and institute double dissolutions in future constitutional crises. These measures were frustrated by the council but Francis acted with determined moderation. Having given the council several opportunities he fought the 1874 elections on his 'Norwegian scheme' to settle disputes between the Houses by joint sittings. His personal majority was undiminished but reservations on the reform bill made its third reading majority fatally narrow. Simultaneously Francis almost died from pleurisy. A large majority urged him to retain office but he refused; the ministry was reconstructed in July under George Kerferd [q.v.]. The chief secretaryship was kept vacant but Francis left parliament in November and went to Britain.

When he returned in 1876 the assembly was polarized between McCulloch's ruling right and the left under Graham Berry [q.v.]. Disgusted, like many liberals, with Berry's violent agitations and McCulloch's intrigues, Francis refused to stand at the 1877 elections which swept Berry into power. The constitutional crisis of 1877-78 changed his mind. Still favouring constitutional reform he feared radical violence and sided with his class and the constitutionalist party. A vacancy was created in West Melbourne but at the poll in February 1878, and again in the ministerial by-election of April, Francis was defeated by political excitement, Catholic opposition and electoral sharp practice. Not until May was he elected for Warrnambool, his seat thenceforth. The crisis was over but in a close-fought campaign on the nature of council reform his experience greatly helped his party. He was minister without portfolio in Service's constitutionalist cabinet from March to August 1880 but health limited his activities; when Service left for England in March 1881 Francis would not seek the leadership and instead was the recognized adviser of the new leader, Robert Murray-Smith [q.v.]. He took over as leader in April 1882 after Smith became agent-general.

Meanwhile Berry had passed a reform Act but his government had promptly fallen and a scratch ministry was assembled by Sir Bryan O'Loghlen [q.v.] in July 1881. Francis's party, unable to rule alone, gave O'Loghlen a majority but with increasing reluctance, for Francis still mistrusted Berry. Worsening health reduced his influence and he began to doubt the ministry's financial competence; when the disappointing results of a major loan took O'Loghlen to the hustings in February 1883 Francis abandoned him. He stood down in favour of Service but when neither party won a majority accepted a coalition with Berry. His health collapsed and he died on 25 January 1884 at Queenscliff. He was survived by his wife Mary Grant, née Ogilvie, whom he had married at Hobart; they had eight sons and seven daughters. His estate was valued at more than £178,000.

Francis was no political giant. An effective administrator, he lacked the necessary touch of political ferocity and skill in manoeuvre; he also admitted that he was a wretched speaker. With the giants briefly removed in 1872-74, his straightforward, level-headed independence and modesty were what the times required. If he could not inspire awe, fear or passion, he had a rare capacity for winning confidence and affection. He never sought the trappings of power and three times refused a knighthood as inappropriate to colonial society. Had his health allowed, his qualities might have brought him an enviable and continuing political success.

A. S. Kenyon, 'The James Hamilton letters', VHM, 15 (1933-35); Argus, 25 Aug 1859, 1 Aug 1861, 26 Jan 1884; Leader (Melb), 25 July 1863; Illustrated Aust News, 20 Feb 1884; F. K. Crowley, Aspects of the constitutional conflicts . . . Victorian legislature, 1864-1868 (M.A. thesis, Univ Melb, 1947); J. E. Parnaby, The economic and political development of Victoria, 1877-1881 (Ph.D. thesis, Univ Melb, 1951); G. R. Bartlett, Political organization and society in Victoria 1864-1883 (Ph.D. thesis, ANU, 1964). GEOFFREY BARTLETT

FRANKLYN, HENRY MORTIMER (1848?-1900), newspaper proprietor and journalist, was probably the second son of George Jerome Franklyn and his wife Jane, née Mortimer. He went to New York where he worked for an uncle in the liquor trade and contributed gratuitously to periodicals. He later moved to San Francisco where he married the wealthy Helen Hensley on 14 June 1876. Franklyn followed no occupation but managed her affairs. Through unwise speculation, in which his honesty and integrity were questioned, Franklyn lost most of her money and £30,000 of his own; he was declared insolvent in 1878. His wife divorced him and he left the country.

Franklyn arrived in Melbourne in February 1879 and with his remarkable persuasive talents soon promoted the Victorian Review Publishing Co. The Victorian Review, a monthly magazine of high quality and wide recognition, included many important contributors; Franklyn's own articles covered a wide variety of subjects. In 1881 he published A glance at Australia in 1880, a surprisingly comprehensive study of the Australian colonies and their pastoral, agricultural and mercantile development and potential. The aim of his publications was to make Australia known and through them he evolved a blueprint for the country's economic and political development based on free trade and a federated Australia. He was disgusted by Victoria's rejection of the proposed federal council at the 1880-81 Colonial Conference, and in reaction founded in March 1881 the Federal Australian, a weekly devoted to promoting federation. In November he started the World, an evening newspaper. On 25 July 1883 in Melbourne he married the 19-year-old Henrietta Isabel, the youngest daughter of John Seals of Hobart and his wife Emily, née Llandall. They lived in luxury at Virgilius, St Kilda, which Franklyn had bought in 1881 and where a daughter was born on 19 February 1885.

Franklyn's extravagance, including heavy betting on horse-racing, worsened his financial position which declined steadily after 1885 when he borrowed large sums to buy the Victorian Review, Federal Australian and the World. The World was discontinued in June but Franklyn published the others until debts amounting to £70,000 forced him into bankruptcy in February 1886. After the insolvency hearings Franklyn left for England where in 1887 he published The Unit of Imperial Federation, a cause he had adopted in 1885. News of his later prosperity reached Victoria in 1893. He claimed to have inherited £150,000 from an uncle and to have succeeded as an insurance broker, though his estate was valued at only £1255 3s. 10d. when he died on 9 August 1900 in Upper Berkeley Street, London. His will provided for his daughters, Vera Gladys and Helen Ermyntrude, 'in consequence of my wife's extravagance and unsteadiness'.

Franklyn was never specifically charged with dishonesty. By all accounts he was a smooth Yankee type whose sales talk caused many to doubt the sincerity of his ideas and his assumed pose of a patriotic Australian, but he had an immense capacity for work and his knowledge of many subjects made him a skilled commentator on contemporary events.

Argus, 20 Feb, 18, 30 Mar, 10 Apr, 19 May 1886; *Age*, 30 Mar 1886; *Table Talk*, 3 Mar 1893; Insolvency papers (VA).

DONALD S. GARDEN

FRASER, ALEXANDER (1802-1888), businessman and politician, was born on 2 January 1802 at Aldourie, near Inverness, Scotland, first of the ten children of John Fraser, farmer and Free Church elder, and his wife Ann, née Fraser. He left Scotland in 1827 to work in London. In 1831 he married Mary Ann Glannon (1811-1877); next year they sailed for Sydney in the *Rubicon*. Because his wife was ill, Fraser disembarked at Hobart Town where he began business as a coachmaker. Attracted by the preaching of Rev. Nathaniel Turner he joined the Melville Street Wesleyan Church. In 1839, with David Heckscher as partner, he invested in a pastoral run in the Port Phillip District near Sunbury. When the gold rushes disrupted Hobart's economy, Fraser took his family to Bendigo in 1852 and next year started business in Melbourne as an auctioneer and mercantile agent in partnership with Edward Cohen [q.v.]. The partnership was dissolved in 1864 and his two sons, Henry Critchard and Alexander William, became partners in the firm of Fraser & Co. Fraser was also a director of the Australasian Assurance Co.

Fraser lived at St Kilda and in 1857 was elected to its first Municipal Council; in 1859 he became chairman and mayor in 1864-65. In the Legislative Council he represented North-Western Province from 1858 until he retired in 1881. He consistently supported attempts to reform the council by widening the franchise and increasing the number of members. A convinced free trader, he opposed any increase of protective tariffs on imports into Victoria. He was minister of public works and represented the Francis [q.v.] government in the Legislative Council from 1872 until 1874 when he was granted leave to go to Britain, which

he had visited in 1848 and 1862. In 1878 he brought an action against the Melbourne *Age* claiming damages of £10,000 for an article reflecting on his conduct towards a brother who had died in a London workhouse; he was awarded £250.

Fraser's faith in education was evidenced in his long superintendency of the St Kilda Wesleyan Sunday School and his support for the establishment of Wesley College. He was one of the Wesleyan members of the 1866 royal commission on education which recommended the incorporation of denominational schools into a national system. While a member of the Francis ministry he guided through the Upper House the 1872 bill introducing free, compulsory and secular education to Victoria. An active churchman, he held most important offices in the Wesleyan Church and for thirty years was treasurer of the supernumerary fund, which he helped Rev. Daniel Draper [q.v.] to found. Dour and pious, Fraser was conscientious in fulfilling his political duties. He presided at numerous meetings and laid countless foundation stones until illness confined him to bed, two years before he died at his home, Aldourie, St Kilda, on 20 August 1888. He was survived by two sons and several grandchildren.

J. B. Cooper, *The history of St Kilda . . . 1840 to 1930*, 2 (Melb, 1931); G. M. Dow, *George Higinbotham: church and state* (Melb, 1964); *Age*, 22 June 1878; *Argus*, 21 Aug 1888; *Spectator* (Melb), 7 Sept. 1888.

RENATE HOWE

FRASER, ARCHIBALD COLQUHOUN (1832-1896), civil servant, was born at Stirling, Scotland, son of Andrew Fraser (d. 1884), lieut-colonel in the Indian army, and his wife Isabella, née Colquhoun. He was educated at the Royal Military College, Sandhurst, but after an accident abandoned an army career. He attended the University of Edinburgh and in 1851 passed the Scottish law examination. In 1852 he arrived in Melbourne and joined the Victorian civil service. Early in 1854 he went to Sydney where he worked as a clerk and on 11 December joined the New South Wales immigration office at £191 a year. On 14 May 1857 he transferred to the crown law office and by 1 June 1860 had become second clerk to the crown solicitor in charge of criminal business with a salary of £350. On 1 January 1868 he was appointed clerk of the peace for County Cumberland and in 1870 for the whole colony at a salary of £600. In 1881 he was admitted as a solicitor but declined appointment as one of the first stipendiary magistrates in Sydney. From 1

April 1887 to June 1896 he was under-secretary for justice commencing on £960 a year.

Fraser was unusual in allowing his subordinates to be original in their work. At the crown law office his reorganization of Petty Sessions assured gentle treatment for 'certain old and valued officers'. He prepared the Criminal Law and Evidence Amendment Act, 1891, which, *inter alia*, introduced more lenient treatment for attempted suicide. His administration emerged quite favourably from the inquiry into the civil service in 1888-92 and from the royal commission of 1895.

Fraser was a director of the Civil Service Building Society from its formation in 1874 and was credited with the introduction of the 1884 civil service bill which was welcomed by the service before amendment in parliament; from 1 January 1885 to 31 December 1887 he was a member of the Civil Service Board. Reappointed in October 1891, he was chairman in 1895-96. He was active and prescient on the board and clashed with the first chairman, Geoffrey Eagar [q.v.], over defining the limits of the board's authority. Fraser's extensive knowledge of the civil service aided the 1895 royal commission when he analysed the weaknesses of the 1884 Act; his ideas anticipated much of the 1895 Public Service Act which aimed at reform and an end to ministerial patronage. In 1896 although his mental and physical abilities were unimpaired Fraser was a victim of the ruthless retrenchment of the Public Service Board. His enforced retirement caused an important debate in the Legislative Council on the powers of the board and the significance of the 1895 Act. He took up a partnership as a solicitor but died aged 64 on 24 October 1896 after a stroke. He was buried in the Church of England cemetery, Waverley, predeceased by his first wife Helen Maria, née Edson, whom he had married at Sydney in 1866. He was survived by two sons and three daughters, and by his second wife Hope, née McLeod, whom he had married at Melbourne in 1885. His elder son, Archibald Colquhoun (b. 1868), was in 1896 clerk of Petty Sessions at Penrith.

PD (NSW), 1896; *Town and Country J*, 9 Feb 1889; *Evening News* (Syd), 26 Oct 1896; *SMH*, 26, 27 Oct 1896; Civil Service Board, minutes (NSWA); Department of Justice papers, bundle 7722 (NSWA).   BRUCE MITCHELL

FRASER, SIR MALCOLM (1834-1900), civil engineer and administrator, was born in Gloucestershire, England, son of William Fraser of Clifton. He was a surveyor in the province of Auckland in 1857-59, district surveyor in the Native Land Purchase Department in 1859-63, district surveyor on the Canterbury West Gold Fields in 1863-67 and chief surveyor for Westland in 1867-69. He also won repute as a naturalist.

In 1870, recommended by Governor Weld, he was appointed surveyor-general of Western Australia, in succession to J. S. Roe [q.v.]. Fraser soon reorganized his department, reduced its permanent staff to the few officers competent in geodesical and trigonometrical surveying and insisted that the routine field work of pegging and traversing be done by private surveyors at piece-work rates. The permanent staff became inspectors and also conducted a large-scale trigonometrical survey which, when completed in the late 1880s, linked all the coastal regions of Western Australia from the Kimberleys in the north to the Esperance district in the south. This survey led to the making of accurate lithographic maps which were of great value to would-be farmers and itinerant gold seekers as well as giving pastoralists better security of tenure by accurately locating and defining the boundaries of their leases and thereby enabling them to raise loans. Fraser also raised the entrance standards to the surveying profession and, with the help of his deputy, John Forrest, made the Crown Lands Office the most efficient, economical, corruption-free and revenue-producing of the government departments. Fraser encouraged inland exploration and also advised the government on the engineering problems in proposals for building government and private railways.

In 1870 Fraser became a member of the Executive and Legislative Councils and in 1872 was given the additional post of commissioner of crown lands. As colonial secretary in 1883-90 he was the senior member and governor's spokesman in the Legislative Council. He performed this task successfully, though with difficulty because of the irascibility of Governor Broome, the 'Bear Garden' atmosphere at meetings of the Executive Council and the feuding between Broome and Chief Justice Onslow, Attorney-General Hensman [qq.v.] and Surveyor-General Forrest. During his twenty years in the legislature Fraser was associated with several major revisions of the Crown Land Regulations and active in the constitutional discussions which preceded the establishment of parliamentary government in 1890. He represented Western Australia at several intercolonial conferences, and was made C.M.G. in 1881 and K.C.M.G. in 1887. An able administrator, especially during his early years in Western Australia, he merits notice as one of the few who were able to work in harmony with Sir Napier Broome, an achievement which his contemporaries in the colony found difficult to understand and his superiors in the Colonial Office quite amazing. He made few enemies in his long career and his critics merely noticed that he was no exemplar of plain living.

In 1890 Fraser retired to London on a pension. On the recommendation of the first premier, Sir John Forrest, he was appointed Western Australia's first agent-general in England and held the post until 1898. Aged 66, he died at Clifton on 17 August 1900, predeceased on 20 December 1896 by his wife Elizabeth, née Riddiford, whom he had married on 3 October 1861 in New Zealand. Of their three children, the elder son, William (1863-1884), became a station manager and died at Roebourne.

J. S. Battye, *Western Australia* (Oxford, 1924); F. K. Crowley, *Australia's western third* (Lond, 1960); F. K. Crowley, *Forrest: 1847-1918*, 1 (Brisb, 1970); *Western Mail* (Perth), 25 Aug 1900.   F. K. CROWLEY

FRASER, SIR SIMON (1832-1919), contractor, pastoralist and politician, was born on 21 August 1832 at Pictou, Nova Scotia, the youngest son of William Fraser of Inverness and his wife Jane, née Fraser. He was educated at the Pictou Academy and worked on the family farm and flour-mill.

In 1853 Fraser arrived in Australia and after two years at Bendigo had enough capital to move into business. From his shop in Elizabeth Street, Melbourne, he traded in horses and produce from Sydney and soon began tendering for bridge, road and then railway construction. He helped to promote the firm of Collier [q.v.], Barry & Co. which completed the Sandhurst-Echuca railway in September 1864; Fraser's suggestion to use Bendigo gravel as ballast instead of the blue metal specified in the contract enabled the company to clear £100,000, of which Fraser's share was £30,000. With William McCulloch [q.v.], Fraser was later a director of the Deniliquin-Moama railway built in 1876. Next year with Barry and Brookes he contracted to build a section of the line from Port Augusta to Farina in South Australia. In 1865 he went to Queensland where with George Simmie, Thomas Craig and William Forrest he formed the Squatting Investment Co. and bought properties on the Dawson River which were later consolidated under the name of Mount Hutton. The company also held Thurulgoona in the Warrego district where in 1886-87 Fraser engaged the Canadian J. S. Loughead to drill for artesian water. Fraser's *True story of the beginning of artesian*

water supply of Australia was published in Melbourne in 1914. He became a partner in Collins, White [qq.v.] & Co. which also had Queensland properties. Later he bought Nyang near Moulamein in New South Wales. In 1869 he returned to Melbourne and next year with Simmie and Craig bought stations near Echuca.

In 1874 Fraser was elected for Rodney in the Legislative Assembly but did little for Echuca in parliament, confining himself to such metropolitan affairs as the Chamber of Commerce. In 1883 after helping to arrange the Service-Berry [qq.v.] coalition he toured Europe and America. On his return in 1885 he was defeated for the seats of West Melbourne in the assembly and Northern Province in the council, but in August 1886 won South Yarra Province in the council. In 1890-92 he was minister without portfolio in James Munro's [q.v.] cabinet. He was a Victorian representative at the Ottawa Conference in 1894 and at the Australasian Federal Convention in 1897-98. In 1901 he topped the Victorian poll for the Senate where he opposed Labor attacks on private enterprise and stood for re-election in 1906 as an anti-socialist. He supported the Canberra site for the federal capital and advocated private ownership of railways. His term expired in 1913. As grand master of the Grand Lodge of Port Phillip he often defended the Orange cause in parliament.

Fraser was a director of the Australian Widows' Fund Life Assurance Society and of the *Melbourne Evening Standard*. A shrewd judge of men and affairs, his common sense and vigour brought him success in business, not least in the 1890s when Fraser & Co. survived despite the crash of the City of Melbourne Bank, of which he had been a director. After 1885 Fraser lived at Norla, Irving Road, Toorak. In 1862 he had married Margaret Bolger; she died in 1880 survived by two daughters. In 1885 he married Anne Bertha Collins; they had three sons. Fraser was knighted in 1918. On 30 July 1919 he died of bronchitis in Melbourne, survived by his wife, a daughter and two sons.

His portrait, painted by Millais in 1897 for 3000 guineas, is held by descendants at Mundoolun, Tamborine, Queensland.

M. Cannon, *The land boomers* (Melb, 1966); *Table Talk*, 13 Sept 1889; *Punch* (Melb), 17 Dec 1903; *Age*, 31 July 1919; *Pastoral Review*, 16 Aug 1919.   ELIZABETH M. REDMOND

FRASER, SIMON (1824?-1889), auctioneer and parliamentarian, was born at Inverness, Scotland, son of Alexander Fraser, farmer, and his wife Janet. He was educated at local schools and ran an ironmongery at Liverpool before leaving for Queensland in 1862. With J. F. Buckland he founded the auctioneering firm of Fraser & Buckland which later became Fraser & Son, land and commission agents, stock, station and produce brokers of Queen Street, Brisbane.

Fraser entered parliament in November 1868, representing North Brisbane in the Legislative Assembly with Dr K. O'Doherty and T. P. Pugh [qq.v.]. He represented Bundamba in 1873-78 and Brisbane South in 1880-88. A member of the Grey Street Congregational Church, South Brisbane, from its foundation in 1866, and one of the six delegates to the Congregational Intercolonial Conference in May 1883, Fraser was an able representative of liberal Nonconformist opinion. He often reiterated his belief in promoting the interests of the colony as a whole rather than supporting any one interest group. Queensland needed people, he argued, and migration from Europe and Asia should be encouraged; but he objected to coloured labour being introduced for a limited term of years to supply one industry. Referring to the sugar industry in 1874, Fraser declared that 'if any industry could only exist by being bolstered up in that way, the sooner it came to an end the better'. He supported land legislation and railway extension which aimed at settling small farmers, and free, secular, compulsory education to primary level. A member of the Board of Education in 1874, Fraser believed that Queensland should be able to offer a university education but maintained that the government should not subsidize secondary or advanced education since this would not promote self-reliance and independence. He was an originator of the Brisbane Sunday School Union and three times its president.

Under S. W. Griffith and his liberal government Fraser served as chairman of committees in the Legislative Assembly in 1884-88 with 'the strictest impartiality and conscientiousness in the discharge of his duties'. In London on 5 September 1856 as a widower Fraser married Lucy Ann Simpson; they had three sons and five daughters. He died aged about 64 on 8 January 1889 at South Brisbane.

Congregational Union, NSW, *Report of the intercolonial jubilee conference* (Syd, 1883); C. A. Bernays, *The roll of the Queensland parliament 1860-1926* (Brisb, 1926); PD (Qld), 1868-70, 1874-75, 1878, 1880, 1884; *Brisbane Courier*, 9 Jan 1889.

JACQUELINE BELL
M. CARTER

FRAYNE, URSULA (1816-1885), mother superior, was born on 5 October 1816 in Dublin, Ireland, daughter of Robert Frayne, a prosperous businessman, and his wife Bridget. In 1834 she entered the Institute of Mercy, founded in 1832 in Dublin by Mother Catherine McAuley, and took the name Ursula in place of her baptismal name Clara. In 1842 she was appointed Superior of the institute's first foreign mission foundation in Newfoundland and in 1845 went on foundation to Perth, Western Australia, at the request of the newly consecrated Bishop Brady [q.v.] for Sisters to staff his proposed schools. She and her companions arrived in Perth on 8 January 1846.

From the outset the Sisters of Mercy experienced great hardship. So small was the Catholic population that government aid, granted to denominational schools in 1849, was insignificant and the bishop, who was close to bankruptcy, could not be relied on for support. Shocked by the conditions under which the Sisters worked in the first two years, the Dublin mother-house sent money for their return passages. This money Mother Ursula gratefully acknowledged but she refused to abandon the mission. However, she soon realized that Sisters would have to supplement their meagre income. In 1849 she opened the first secondary school in Western Australia, a 'select' fee-paying school catering for an almost exclusively non-Catholic clientele; it brought much-needed security. Its success determined the pattern of future Mercy expansion, which was to establish, almost simultaneously and often within the same building, three separate schools: a 'select' fee-paying school, a primary school and an infants' school. By 1856, despite the impending withdrawal of government aid, the schools of the Sisters of Mercy in Western Australia were flourishing. Probably with some relief, having experienced the bitter Brady-Serra [q.v.] dispute over ecclesiastical jurisdiction and seen her countrymen recalled to Rome, Ursula Frayne responded to a request from Bishop Goold [q.v.] for a Victorian foundation. A similar request came from Bishop Murphy [q.v.] in Adelaide but she was already committed.

She arrived in Melbourne in March 1857 and within six weeks had raised loans to pay off the mortgage on her convent in Nicholson Street, Fitzroy. Rapid expansion followed. Large building programmes were undertaken for educational and social work, culminating in the erection of the first wing of the present 'Academy' in 1870 at a cost of £6000. The Sisters of Mercy were the first teaching nuns in Victoria and under the vigorous leadership of Mother Ursula their establishment included a boarding and day school for girls, together with two primary schools and a domestic training school for orphans. She also founded the St Vincent de Paul's Orphanage at South Melbourne and managed it until the Christian Brothers took over the boys' section, leaving the girls under the care of her Sisters. Although the 1872 Act caused temporary retrenchment in Catholic education, it resulted in expansion for the Nicholson Street community, and Sisters replaced lay teachers when salaries could not be met. Ursula Frayne's first Victorian country foundation was at Kilmore in 1875 and especially dear to her for its rural setting. She died at Nicholson Street on 9 June 1885.

Her letters give evidence of the qualities which distinguished her as a religious: intelligence, blended with shrewd, practical wisdom; tenacity and great powers of endurance; strict and loving observance of the Rule; and a keen Irish wit. A fine Gothic chapel was built by her successor as a memorial within the convent grounds at Nicholson Street. There her remains were interred in a vault flanked by a Celtic cross, reminiscent of her origin.

P. D. Tannock, A history of Catholic education in Western Australia, 1829-1929 (M.Ed. thesis, Univ WA, 1964); M. M. Frayne, Sketches of Conventual life in the bush (typescript, Convent of Mercy Archives, Perth); letters (Benedictine Abbey Archives, New Norcia, WA); notes and letters (Convent of Mercy Archives, Dublin).

IMELDA PALMER

FRAZER, JOHN (1827-1884), merchant, company director and philanthropist, was born in Dromore, County Down, Ireland, son of John Frazer and his wife Sarah, née Waddell. As 'a carpenter and joiner' he arrived at Sydney as a bounty immigrant in the *Margaret* on 23 January 1842, with a brother and two sisters. He first went up country 'to learn something of squatting' on 'a very modest salary indeed', and then worked as a clerk in Sydney. In 1847 he opened his own wholesale grocery business and in 1853 he married Elizabeth, daughter of James Ewan. Her two sisters married William Manson and James Watson [q.v.] who with her brother James [q.v.], became Frazer's closest friends and business partners. In 1858 he moved into larger premises in York Street and next year took Manson as a partner. By hard work, 'integrity, prudence and punctuality' Frazer made John Frazer & Co. into one of the most influential mercantile houses in Sydney. The York Street stores were burnt down in 1865 and rebuilt for £15,000 in massive stone and with modern fire-fighting equipment. From the mid-1860s Frazer speculated in land in Queensland and by 1871 had four runs of his own and eighteen in partnership. In Sydney he had built two large new stores, a bonded warehouse and the impressive Frazer House. He had also sold his home, Ranelagh at Darling Point, and about 1874 bought Quiraing at Edgecliff. His directorships included the Australian Joint Stock Bank, the Mutual Life Association of Australasia and the Sydney Exchange Co. in addition to three other insurance companies, a shipping line, an ironworks and several mining companies. Later he was also a director of the Commercial Banking Co. of Sydney and the Australian Gaslight Co.

Frazer retired from his own business in 1869 and next year visited England. In 1872 he refused for health reasons to contest a seat in the Legislative Assembly but in April 1874, persuaded by Watson, he accepted nomination to the Legislative Council. Though never prominent in the House he contributed much-needed common sense. As a friend and creditor of Henry Parkes [q.v.] he was involved with the governor, Sir Hercules Robinson, in an abortive attempt to exploit coal on land at Jervis Bay. Frazer was appointed a magistrate in 1875 but next year, admitting physical and mental weariness, a feeling of being 'used up' and unable to forget the loss of his three young children, he sailed for England with his family. Apart from a brief return in 1878 to retain his seat in the Legislative Council, he stayed in England until 1880, although homesick for Sydney. He was a representative commissioner at the Melbourne International Exhibition, as he had been at the Paris Universal Exhibition in 1878. Frazer died aged 57 at Quiraing on 25 October 1884, survived by his wife, two sons and two daughters. He was buried in the sumptuous family vault at Rookwood cemetery and left a personal estate worth £405,000.

Frazer's business success was matched by his philanthropy. He had assisted the Sabbath school at the Scots Church for years, wrote 'a hymn to the Creator' and became an elder of the Presbyterian Church, supporting it liberally in his lifetime and in his will. Long active in the Lord's Day Observance Society he left £2000 for an annual prize essay in 'Defence of the Christian Faith'. He served on numerous charitable committees, all of them benefiting under his will. Other gifts included £2500 for drinking fountains, one near Hyde Park and another in the Domain. With an insatiable appetite for culture and mental improvement he denied himself sleep in his youth for literature, history and philosophy. He also collected water colours on his travels and in 1875 he became a member of the Royal Society of New South Wales. In 1876 he joined the Council of St Andrew's College and became vice-president of the Young Men's Christian Association, giving it a library. In that year he also gave £2500 for two bursaries to enable 'poor lads from the bush' to go to the University of Sydney and, at a large farewell banquet in his honour, called for the foundation of a chair of history and conditionally gave £2000 for it. In 1890 his family donated this sum to the university where it was used to found the Frazer scholarship in history.

G. N. Griffiths, *Some houses and people of New South Wales* (Syd, 1949); V&P (LC NSW), 1877-78; *Empire* (Syd), 21 July 1865; *Illustrated Sydney News*, 28 Mar 1874; *SMH*, 23 Feb, 10 Mar 1876, 27 Oct 1884; *Town and Country J*, 26 Feb 1876, 1 Nov 1884; *Bulletin*, 5 Aug 1882; *Sydney Mail*, 1 Nov, 27 Dec 1884; Parkes letters (ML); MS cat under John Frazer (ML); information from Mrs Stuart Bradshaw, and Dr W. W. Phillips, La Trobe Univ.

MARTHA RUTLEDGE

FREEHILL, FRANCIS BEDE (1854-1908), solicitor, was born on 22 November 1854 in Sydney, son of Patrick Freehill (1817-1899), a baker of Ballyconnell, County Cavan, and his wife Margaret, née Cosgrove. His parents arrived in Sydney on 29 April 1844 as bounty immigrants in the *United Kingdom* and by the 1850s Patrick was an organizer of most Irish Catholic movements in Sydney. Francis was educated at St Mary's College, Lyndhurst, and St John's College, University of Sydney (B.A., 1874; M.A., 1876). In 1884 he was elected a fellow of the college; in his will he endowed a scholarship. He was articled to his elder brother and admitted a solicitor on 30 June 1877. He practised in Cowra and Bathurst before inheriting the goodwill of his brother's Sydney firm in January 1880; in 1894 he became a notary public. About 1885 Freehill had become a founding director as well as solicitor of the City Mutual Life Assurance Society Ltd, and remained a director when it was taken over by the Citizens' Life Assurance Co. Ltd. He was a founder of the *Catholic Press* in 1895 and until 1907 a director of the Australian Newspaper Co. Ltd, which also published the *Australian Star* and *Sunday Sun*.

Freehill was first involved in colonial support of home rule for Ireland in 1883, when he promoted the visit of John Redmond [q.v.] and his brother William. Later he organized the visits of John Dillon, Michael Davitt and other Irish delegates. In 1885 he replaced J. G. O'Connor [q.v.] as president of the Irish National League in New South Wales, and showed 'a capacity to govern which few of his friends anticipated'. He ran the St Patrick's Day festivities at Botany

and in 1886 he canvassed funds for Ireland among construction workers on the Prospect dam. When the Papal Rescript was published in 1888, he publicly maintained that papal infallibility did not cover politics. In an article, 'Colonial Know-nothingism', in the *Centennial Magazine* (Sydney, 1889-1890), Freehill defended the colonial Irish against B. R. Wise. Though he never succeeded in entering parliament he was a foundation member of the executive committee of the Australasian Federation League of New South Wales in 1893; in 1897 he was treasurer and a member of its finance committee and in 1899 of the united federal executive formed to co-ordinate the 'yes' campaign for the second referendum on the Commonwealth bill.

In 1896-1908 Freehill was consul for Spain in Sydney. About 1895 he helped to recruit the Irish Volunteer Rifles; commissioned captain in May 1896, he became major in 1900, lieut-colonel in 1904 and retired in 1906. In September 1903 he was created a papal chamberlain. A founder of the Lewisham Hospital, he became secretary and president of its board, giving generously to it and other Catholic charitable institutions.

As a platform speaker, Freehill was fluent and cultivated; his writing was commanding and rich in sarcasm. He spoke French, Italian and Spanish and had an excellent library which he left to the University of Sydney. In 1907 he visited England, Ireland, Spain and the Vatican. He died at Lewisham Hospital on 12 March 1908 and was buried in Rookwood cemetery. He was survived by his wife Eileen Marie, née Molony, whom he had married in Melbourne on 14 April 1888. His assets allowed her to contribute generously to Catholic causes. She was an admirer of Archbishop Kelly and the first Australian woman to become a papal countess in her own right. In 1930 she gave £1000 to found a lectureship in Italian at the University of Sydney. In the 1930s she gave St John's College the gate tower and lady chapel therein and the east oriel window and mosaic floor in the main chapel. She died on 12 June 1942.

A portrait of Freehill is in the dining hall of St John's College.

P. S. Cleary, *Australia's debt to Irish nationbuilders* (Syd, 1933); *SMH*, 1 June 1886, 19 Mar, 16 June 1888, 16 Mar 1908; *Catholic Press*, 17 June 1899; *Daily Telegraph* (Syd), 16 Mar 1908; *Bulletin*, 19 Mar 1908; G. M. Tobin, The seadivided Gael: a study of the Irish home rule movement in Victoria and New South Wales, 1880-1916 (M.A. thesis, ANU, 1969); MS cat under Freehill (ML); A'sian Federation League of NSW papers, MS47 (NL).   RUTH TEALE

FREELING, SIR ARTHUR HENRY (1820-1885), engineer and surveyor-general, was born on 26 July 1820 in London, the eldest son of John Clayton Freeling and his wife Mary, née Coxe. His grandfather, Sir Francis Freeling, baronet, was secretary to the general post office for thirty years. Arthur was educated at Harrow and at 17 joined the Royal Engineers as a second lieutenant. On 18 November 1848 in Hampshire he married Charlotte Augusta, daughter of Sir Henry Rivers. Soon afterwards with the rank of captain he sailed for South Australia to succeed E. C. Frome [q.v.] as surveyor-general and colonial engineer, and arrived in January 1849.

In Canada Freeling had examined roadworks but most of his engineering experience had been in supervising the building of large barracks in England. In addition to his duties in South Australia as surveyor-general and head of the Crown Lands Department he was one of the five commissioners appointed to manage the affairs of the City of Adelaide from September 1849 to June 1852 and was annually elected as chairman of the Central Board of Main Roads in 1850-61. At times he was also an inspector and commissioner of railways and acting colonial architect. In 1855-56 he was a nominated member of the Legislative and Executive Councils. After responsible government he was elected to the new Legislative Council in March 1857 and served as commissioner of public works in the Finniss [q.v.] ministry for four weeks. In August 1859 he resigned from the council because his 'numerous avocations' prevented him from satisfactorily fulfilling his parliamentary duties. He was then a major and honorary lieut-colonel in the Royal Engineers, a captain in the 1st Adelaide rifles and a member and Sunday school teacher in St Andrew's Church of England, Walkerville. His only exploring expedition was to Lake Torrens where in 1857 he examined its navigable possibilities. In 1860 he visited the Kiandra goldfield, reporting that the best access for South Australians was by way of Twofold Bay and the Snowy River. In 1861 he resigned as surveyor-general in favour of G. W. Goyder [q.v.]. Soon afterwards he returned to England. Numerous presentations and addresses testified both to the 'urbanity and impartiality' with which he had maintained the confidence of the public and made many personal friends.

On the death of his cousin in 1871 he succeeded as fifth baronet to the family estates in Sussex. In 1877 he retired from the army as lieut-colonel with the honorary rank of major-general, 'a good practical man and a trustworthy authority on military matters'. He preferred to live quietly and was never 'prominently before the public, either at home or in the colonies', though he maintained interest in Australia as a resident fellow of the Royal Colonial Institute and through his contacts with visiting colonials. He died at his home in Chelsea on 26 March 1885, survived by his wife, a son Harry who succeeded to the baronetcy and a daughter. He left an estate valued at £9000.

PP (SA), 1855-56 (158) evidence, 1857-58 (174); *Observer* (Adel), 24 Mar, 10, 24 Nov, 15, 22 Dec 1860, 4 Apr 1885; *Adelaide Examiner*, 26 May 1860.   GORDON BUXTON

FREEMAN, WILLIAM GLOVER WEBB (1809-1895) and JAMES (1814-1870), photographers, were the sons of an 'unknown gentleman'. William was born in Bristol, England, and about 1836 at Clifton married Margaret Ann, née Dayrell. The brothers had five years' experience in London as professional photographers before William with his wife and family reached Sydney in April 1854 in the *Elizabeth*. In partnership with George Heath he set up as a chemist and druggist. In October 1853 James and his wife arrived in the *Sovereign of the Seas*. The brothers started business in 1854 and soon became the colony's outstanding photographers with the best known portrait studio. Like their competitors they advertised extensively in the press but were more successful in getting long newspaper notices. In that year at the Paris Exhibition the brothers were commended for their daguerreotypes, which were also used industrially as a basis for woodcuts in the *Illustrated Sydney News*. Two of the best photographs were 'Miss Keane' on 11 November and the opening of the Long Cove railway viaduct near Lewisham on 24 March 1855. They also advertised 'Stereo Daguerreotypes' and that 'Invalids and Country Gentlemen could be visited in their homes'. In 1856 the Freemans adopted the collodiotype process and made available portraits of viceroyalty and such prominent figures as the actor, G. V. Brooke [q.v.]; they were also permitted to photograph the first ministry under responsible government, providing that the photographs were not shown in the colony. By 1858, using large-format wet plate photography printed on gold-toned albumen paper, they were able to produce popular harbour and city panoramas; previously such pictures were only available in wood or copper engravings.

The Freemans entered into public affairs and James gave several long and precise addresses: on 8 December he lectured to the Philosophical Society of New South Wales 'On the Progress of Photography and its

Application to the Arts and Sciences' and published the paper in the *Sydney Magazine of Science and Art*, 1859. He forecast the application of photography to the control of engineering, criminal investigation, military and many other purposes. In the late 1860s the brothers visited Britain where James died aged 56 on 22 October 1870 at Haverfordwest, Pembrokeshire. On William's return the firm was advertised as 'photographer to H.R.H. the Prince of Wales'. In the early 1870s he took over the business of Mr and Mrs Oswald Allen, well-known photographers and miniature painters. Freeman took advantage of the carte-de-visite craze and many portrait cartes of the 1870s were imprinted 'Freeman late Oswald Allen'. In 1888 he retired in ill health and left his home in Sydney. He lived for some time at Goulburn and died aged 86 in Newcastle on 9 March 1895, survived by three of his five children. He was buried in the Anglican section of Sandgate cemetery.

S. A. Donaldson letters (ML); pictures and portraits cat (ML); notes and newspaper extracts (held by authors).

KEAST and IRIS BURKE

FRENCHAM, HENRY (1816-1897), goldfields pioneer, was born in Wexford, Ireland. He arrived at Melbourne in 1840 and was first employed in an auctioneering business. Later, as a reporter for the *Port Phillip Gazette*, he set out in June 1851 to search for gold in the Plenty Ranges in an attempt to stop the evacuation of Port Phillip to New South Wales goldfields. On 14 June the Melbourne papers carried the story of Frencham's claim to have discovered gold and his bid for the offered reward. However, assay of his specimens revealed no gold, though on the site where they were found, near Queenstown and not far from Warrandyte, the Caledonian field and mine were later worked.

In November Frencham resigned from the *Gazette* to go prospecting. After working at Ballarat and Forest Creek (Castlemaine) he went with companions to Bendigo which an acquaintance had described as a likely site. In late November the party was successful and Frencham returned to Forest Creek to report the discovery and to apply for protection. Troops arrived on 8 December. On 13 December a letter by Frencham, under the *nom de plume* 'Bendigo', appeared in the *Argus* announcing the discovery; he also claimed to have taken a major role in a demonstration at Bendigo against the new £3 gold licence. Frencham

continued digging at Bendigo till 1854. He then bought an estate at Windsor for subdivision and later a cattle station at Warrandyte where for some time he was manager of the Magnet Gold Mining Co.

In May 1867 Frencham lodged a claim with the minister of mines for a reward for the discovery of the Bendigo field but it was not recognized. He continued to defend these claims in later years, especially as his financial position worsened. In 1890 a select committee was appointed to inquire into his claims. In the course of its proceedings the committee was presented with twelve other claims for the original discovery. The report found 'that Henry Frencham's claim to be the discoverer of gold at Bendigo has not been sustained, but that he was the first to report the discovery of payable gold at Bendigo to the Commissioner at Forest Creek'. No reward was forthcoming.

Frencham returned to Bendigo in March 1895 where he was welcomed by the local council. He died aged 81 in a wooden cottage in Richmond on 3 July 1897, leaving an estate worth £460. He was predeceased by his wife Alicia, née Gainford, whom he had married before 1851, and by whom he had three sons and five daughters.

G. Blainey, *The rush that never ended* (Melb, 1963); *Argus*, 13 Dec 1851, 15 June 1888; *Bendigo Advertiser*, 6 July 1897.

DONALD S. GARDEN

FROUDE, JAMES ANTHONY (1818-1894), historian and man of letters, was born on 23 April 1818 at Dartington, Devonshire, England, son of Rev. Robert Hurrell Froude (1771-1859), and his wife Margaret, née Spedding. In 1830-33 Froude attended Westminster School and after private tuition entered Oriel College, Oxford (B.A., 1842; M.A., 1843). He became a fellow of Exeter College, and in 1849 was appointed headmaster of the High School, Hobart Town, but did not take up the position.

When Froude arrived in Melbourne on 21 January 1885 in the *Australasian*, his twelve volume *History of England from the Fall of Wolsey to the defeat of the Spanish Armada* (1856-70) had established his repute as 'one of the greatest English prose writers of the nineteenth century'. In Victoria Froude was lionized; he stayed with the governor, travelled to Ballarat and other gold towns in a special train and visited sheep stations and vineyards. On 14 February he reached Sydney where again he was fêted although his visit was overshadowed by the dispatch of the Sudan contingent. He found W. B. Dalley [q.v.] 'the most remarkable of all the Australian statesmen' and was influenced by his views on imperial federation. On his return to England he published *Oceana; or England and her Colonies* (1886), hoping to promote imperial federation and a united Oceana.

The book flattered Australians but proved controversial. In a review in *McMillan's Magazine*, August 1886, B. R. Wise declared that 'Mr. Froude saw nothing of the men and women whose sentiments really compose Australian opinion. He came upon us at a time when the popular imagination had been taken captive by military ardour; and he associated only with the wealthy and official class. Were he to return to Sydney now he would form very different impressions'; the Sudan expedition, which had started with such enthusiasm, became the subject of disenchantment. The *Age* claimed that Froude's mind was 'an absolute blank' on the federation of Oceana and that the colonies did not want imperial federation. The *Australian Magazine*, July 1886, referred to Froude as 'our Romantic Historian' and criticized his superficiality, inaccuracies and 'partial and one-sided' observations; *Oceana*, however fascinating as a travel book, was visionary and useless 'as a serious attempt to grasp and understand a complex political problem'. Only the *Sydney Morning Herald* reviewed the book with any favour.

In 1892 Froude was appointed regius professor of history at Oxford. He died on 20 October 1894 at Kingsbridge, Devonshire, survived by one daughter of his first wife Charlotte Maria, née Grenfell, and by a son and a daughter of his second wife Henrietta Elizabeth, née Warre.

W. H. Dunn, *James Anthony Froude*, 1-2 (Oxford 1961, 1963); *Age*, 22 Jan-11 Feb 1885, 6 Mar 1886; *SMH*, 26, 27 Feb 1885, 6 Mar, 15, 25 Sept 1886.   RUTH TEALE

FRY, JAMES (1821-1903), farmer and flour-miller, was born at Cassington, Oxfordshire, England. The ship *Brilliant* brought him and his wife Mary, née Gean, to Victoria in 1854. He settled first at Geelong, and after experience on the goldfields bought a property near Mount Blowhard, about eleven miles from Ballarat, and started grain-growing on an extensive scale. In 1856 he bought a primitive flour-milling plant at Geelong and erected it on his land. The little mill soon prospered and Fry installed in its place the advanced and complete equipment of the Ascot steam flour-mills at a cost of £25,000. The extension of farming around the Ballarat goldfield sup-plied ample grain for the Ascot mill and, with the local mining population as a ready market, Fry's success continued. In 1864 with Gilbert Walker he bought the Ballarat flour-mills from Hassel & Monckton. Walker retired from the partnership in 1867.

Fry soon decided to launch his milling enterprise in other parts of the colony. He leased a mill from John Gillies at Horsham, erected mills at St Arnaud and, to cope with extended business, admitted his former employees, James Johnson, William Fraser and Thomas Roxburgh, into the firm. As farming progressed in the Wimmera and the district was opened by railway, Fry was one of the first millers to take advantage of the new source of supply, setting up branches and sub-agencies in the main townships; by 1880 his firm had additional mills at Ascot, Kingston, Natimuk, Dimboola and Donald. A network of wheat-gathering agencies and buying-stations was also established across Victoria from Kaniva to Numurkah. Headquarters in Melbourne, after 1870 the important centre for flour-milling, were essential and in 1881 Fry's firm leased offices in the A.M.P. buildings and later in Robb's buildings, Collins Street West. The firm was formed into a limited liability company in September 1884 with a subscribed capital of £88,000, increased to £200,000 in 1887. The first issue to the public was made in 1888, raising the authorized capital to £300,000. As well as making Fry's Five Stars Flour a household word in Australia, the company became one of the largest providers of wheat cargoes from Victoria, and undertook multiple services for farmers, from the supply of machinery to land transactions. Through its indenting business large sums were invested on behalf of clients in Australia and England.

Fry retired from the active management of his firm soon after it was floated into a company. He had been overseas several times and decided to devote his time to the agricultural and pastoral pursuits which had always interested and challenged him. He had acquired a property about twenty miles from Glenorchy in 1868 and was one of the first farmers to use dry-farming techniques, demonstrating the potentiality of wheat-growing on the Wimmera plains. He also owned 1800 acres of rich land at Sutton Park, Newlyn, where he died aged 82 on 14 August 1903. He was predeceased in 1901 by his second wife Louisa Ann Coles, née Absolem, a widow whose two sons and two daughters survived him.

A. Sutherland et al, *Victoria and its metropolis*, 2 (Melb, 1888); *Millers' J of A'sia*, 27 Aug 1903, 23 May 1904; *Argus*, 15 Aug 1903.
                                 CAROLE WOODS

FRYAR, WILLIAM (1828-1912), politician, surveyor and mining inspector, was born on 25 January 1828 at Willington, Northumberland, England, son of Thomas Fryar, mining engineer, and his wife Mary Ann, née Scott. He went to Queensland in 1853, and at intervals between 1864 and 1882 worked in the Lands Department as a licensed surveyor in the south-eastern parishes of Maroochy and Mooloolah. On 6 January 1874 he joined the seventh Queensland parliament as an independent member for East Moreton in the Legislative Assembly where he was mainly interested in land policy. In spite of some criticisms he was in general accord with the secretary for public lands, T. B. Stephens [q.v.], and upon the latter's resignation he replaced him in the third Macalister [q.v.] ministry, from 27 May 1875 to its fall on 5 June 1876. He remained member for East Moreton until he resigned in 1877 and then returned to surveying. He had become one of the first directors of the Queensland Evangelical Standard, a Dissenting weekly of strong political character, established on 10 June 1875. In 1882 he became the first Queensland inspector of mines and held the senior post, the Southern Division, until he retired in June 1904. In 1857 at Brisbane he had married Margaret Louisa Lewis; of their ten children only two sons and two daughters survived him when he died in Coorparoo, Brisbane, on 22 December 1912.

Fryar's public life was not entirely smooth. As a surveyor he was involved in some local conflicts; because of his comparative youth and inexperience he was a somewhat unpopular choice as lands minister; his land alienation policy—he was an advocate of throwing open more land to closer settlement—brought scathing criticisms during a particularly stormy and short-lived government; and in his later career as mining inspector he was often attacked by Labor politicians and miners campaigning for elected, rather than appointed, inspectors. Nevertheless it seems clear that his efforts on the miners' behalf were sincere and unremitting, and would have had greater success if the miners themselves had given their inspectors more support. In his twenty-two years as inspector of mines he undoubtedly did much to improve the conditions of the Queensland miner.

PD (Qld), 1874-76; Reports of inspector of mines, Southern division, V&P (LA Qld), 1883-1904; A. A. Morrison, 'Religion and politics in Queensland', JRHSQ, 4 (1951); J. Stoodley, The Queensland gold-miner in the late nineteenth century (M.A. thesis, Univ Qld, 1964); M. Gaylord, Economic development in the Maroochy district until 1915 (B.A. thesis, Univ Qld, 1967).

JUNE STOODLEY

FULLARTON, ROBERT RUSSELL (1829-1895), naval officer and public servant, was born at Irvine, Ayrshire, Scotland, son of James Innes Fullarton, army officer, and his wife Mary, née Kerr. He served his apprenticeship in the Ellen, and first visited Melbourne in 1844. After further voyages he returned in command of the Glenbervie in 1849 and then engaged in coastal trade under Captain G. W. Cole [q.v.] and others.

His temporary appointment as assistant to the harbormaster, Alexander Campbell [q.v.], on 1 January 1853 was made permanent a year later. In 1856 he applied in vain for a position as sea pilot and on 1 July 1865 was appointed master of the lighthouse tender Pharos. In 1868 he was temporary harbormaster of Hobson's Bay and from January 1869 harbormaster at Melbourne under the Harbor Department; he was transferred to the Melbourne Harbor Trust when it was incorporated in 1877. He was elected chairman of the Victoria Steam Navigation Board and president of the Pilot Board of Victoria on 1 October 1880; when the Pilot Board was abolished in 1887 he was permitted by the Melbourne Harbor Trust to accept presidency of the Marine Board of Victoria.

Fullarton's ability in winning promotion was also shown in the Victorian Naval Reserve (later Naval Brigade) in which he was the second to enlist in 1859. He was appointed senior lieutenant in charge of the Port Melbourne Division in 1860 and within a year had command of the whole Naval Reserve. In 1869 he became commander in the Naval Forces and staff officer in charge of the West Coast Military District. In 1871 he resigned his naval command at the government's request in order to frame Naval Reserve Regulations. He enrolled members under the Discipline Act, 1870, and was appointed to command all Naval Reserves. He declined employment as naval commandant in 1878 at the request of the Melbourne Harbor Trust. Involved in several legal cases under the Discipline Act, he appears to have been efficient but officious. In 1885 he was appointed a member of the Council for Defence and honorary aide-de-camp to the governor. He was commandant of the naval forces of Victoria from February 1887 to early 1888 with active command of the fleet. Fullarton devoted his entire leisure to perfecting his knowledge of naval strategy and never missed an encampment, cruise and muster until his retirement from the Naval Brigade in June 1892. He was also an active Freemason.

After fighting a fire on the kerosene-laden ship Habitant on 8 June 1894 Fullarton suffered from over-exertion and influenza. His health deteriorated and he resigned on 16 September. The £1000 voted to him by the Melbourne Harbor Trust went to his widow Christina, née Robertson, after he died at Albert Park on 23 September 1895. He was buried at St Kilda cemetery and left an estate worth £3000 to his widow to maintain their three daughters and a son who was in poor health.

W. P. Evans, *Port of many prows* (Melb, 1969); *Melbourne Harbor Trust jubilee report 1877-1927* (Melb, 1927); *Government Gazette* (Vic), 1855, 1860, 1869, 1885; *Williamstown Chronicle*, 31 Mar 1860, 31 Aug 1867, 28 May 1870, 1871, 14 Aug 1880, 19 Mar 1881, 19 Jan 1884; *Argus*, 24 Sept 1895; *Weekly Times* (Melb), 28 Sept 1895; W. P. Evans, A rocket by night: a history of the Victorian pilot service (Port Phillip Pilot Service); W. P. Evans, Deeds not words: a history of the Victorian Navy (held by author); Victorian Pilot Board records (held by author). WILSON P. EVANS

FULLERTON, JAMES (1807-1886), Presbyterian minister, was born on 11 January 1807 at Aghadowey, County Londonderry, Ireland, the fourth son of Rev. Archibald Fullerton and his wife Elizabeth, née Church. He studied for the ministry at the Royal Academical Institution, Belfast, and the University of Glasgow. Ordained on 2 December 1836 at Benburb, County Tyrone, he was persuaded by J. D. Lang [q.v.] to migrate to Sydney where he arrived on 3 December 1837 in the *Portland*. He ministered at Windsor but Lang's synod, which had separated from the Presbytery of New South Wales, soon appointed him to a third Presbyterian group in Pitt Street. He gathered a strong congregation, especially Ulster families, responsive to his vigorous evangelicalism. His voice failed in 1868 but he remained at Pitt Street until 1886.

In the differences that beset the early Presbyterian Church in New South Wales Fullerton turned against Lang who abused him as 'a mere hibernian driveller with neither ability nor respectability'. In contrast Lang's successor, Dr Archibald Gilchrist, described him as 'the unbending champion of the old theology'. In 1841 Marischal College, Aberdeen, awarded Fullerton an honorary doctorate and he contributed to an anthology, *Lectures on the Sabbath*, by ministers of the Presbyterian Church. In 1844 he published *Ten Lectures*, and edited the *Christian Herald* for some months. In the 1840s he served on the committees of several philanthropic and educational societies as well as campaigning for shorter hours for shop assistants and against transportation. In July 1851 he was tried

in the Supreme Court for 'illegal solemnization of marriage' and discharged on a technicality; later the registrar-general claimed that Fullerton had run a 'marriage shop', conducting over four hundred marriages a year. In 1856 he published *The National Duty of Christian States* and in 1865 as moderator he led the conservative Synod of Australia into the final union which created the Presbyterian Church of New South Wales. In 1877-86 he served on the Council of St Andrew's College after years of opposition to its establishment in the University of Sydney.

Fullerton died in Sydney of pneumonia on 3 July 1886 and was buried in Rookwood cemetery. He was survived by two sons and two daughters of his first wife Mary, née Jenkins, whom he had married on 30 June 1840, and by two sons and two daughters of his second wife Janet, née Young, whom he had married at Melbourne in 1859. His estate, including a farm and shares in a sugar plantation in Queensland, and sixteen houses and sixty-three acres in Sydney, was valued at £13,000.

His brother George (1802-1883), physician, was the second son of Archibald Fullerton. Educated at the Universities of Glasgow (Ch.M., 1831) and Edinburgh (M.D., 1832) he arrived at Sydney in 1841. On 27 March 1845 he became physician to the first medical staff of Sydney Infirmary. About 1849 he returned to Ireland and in 1855 married his cousin Julia Moffatt. Next year they went to Sydney but soon moved to Brisbane. Fullerton became first president of the Medical Board of Queensland, and in 1860 was appointed to the first Legislative Council. In 1863 he resigned the presidency of the Medical Board. He acquired large land holdings at Toolambilla in the Maranoa district. By 1867 he had fourteen runs comprising 584 square miles. In 1870 he published a *Family Medical Guide* which became very popular in the outback. He contributed generously to the Presbyterian Church. About 1878 he returned to Sydney, where he died on 24 September 1883, leaving an estate worth £17,800.

J. D. Lang, *Presbyterian union* (Syd, 1858?); D. S. Myles, *One hundred years. Fullerton Memorial Church* (Syd, 1938); E. H. Stokes, *The jubilee book of the Sydney Hospital Clinical School* (Syd, 1960); Sel cttee on registration of births, deaths, and marriages, Evidence, V&P (LC NSW), 1885-86, 4, 297; *Presbyterian* (NSW), 7 May 1881, 10 July 1886, 20 Aug 1887; *MJA*, 7 July 1962; *SMH*, 5, 10, 17, 19, 22 July 1851, 14 July 1886; *Town and Country J*, 10 July 1886; Pitt St Church registers (Presbyterian Lib, Assembly Hall, Syd); information from A. J. Gray, Scone, NSW.

        ALAN DOUGAN

FULTON, THOMAS (1813-1859), foundry owner, was born on 10 September 1813 at Dundee, Scotland, son of Thomas Fulton (d. 1866), wrought-iron worker, and his wife Isabella, née Wheelwright. He was apprenticed to a machine-maker and did well. Attracted to the Congregational Church by Dr David Russell, he became a dedicated Christian. He decided to migrate to Port Phillip in partnership with Robert Langlands, brother of George and Henry [qq.v.], and arrived at Melbourne with his family in February 1842. With Langlands, Fulton set up an iron foundry on swampy land in Flinders Street. At first they had only a small foot-lathe but built up their business by determination and ingenuity. They erected a steam engine for the first mill in Melbourne and turned rack wool-presses for squatters, Fulton cutting the square-threaded screws by hand as the lathe was too small. When in 1843-44 squatters slaughtered thousands of stock, Fulton developed a technique for boiling them down for tallow. He was in partnership in 1846-55 with George Annand and Robert Smith and then ran the business himself; by 1858 when the gold rush had rapidly increased its output, the firm was employing 150 men. Fulton undertook plumbing and smithy work, made dray wheels, milled flour and was a licensed merchant and insurance agent. That Fulton was well liked by his men as an upright and humane employer is shown by a letter of loyalty and a silver tray they presented him in 1858.

Fulton was the first deacon of the Congregational Church in Victoria. He paid much of the cost of setting up the Lonsdale Street and St Kilda churches and donated £1000 to a £5000 fund to bring ministers from Scotland to cope with the gold rush. In 1858 he attended a church conference in Hobart. As a speaker he was popular for his 'homely and racy eloquence', although he once stood for parliament and was defeated. He was a magistrate and a Melbourne city councillor in 1854-59. A strong advocate of temperance, he also took a prominent part in agitation for separation and abolition of transportation. He formed a land syndicate which invested extensively in Malvern and Gardiner.

On 18 February 1859 Fulton was accidentally thrown to his death down a mine-shaft in Bendigo while checking the installation of machinery. He had intended to open a branch in Bendigo to make quartz-crushing machinery of his own invention. He was survived by his wife Elizabeth, née Black, and seven of their eight children. To Garryowen [q.v. Finn], 'Fulton was the sort of man for an infant settlement; skilful, and industrious, strong of mind, iron in frame,

outspoken, and honest to the backbone'. His headstone was erected by his employees. He died intestate but some of his property later passed to his brothers: William (1825-1879), joiner and patternmaker; James, timber merchant; and Robert, who carried on the foundry.

J. B. Cooper, The history of St Kilda . . . 1840 to 1930, 1 (Melb, 1931); J. B. Cooper, A history of Malvern (Melb, 1935); Age, 16, 18 Nov 1854; Argus, 21 Feb 1859; My Note Book, 23 Feb 1859: Southern Spectator, Apr 1859.
                                    ROSLYN BRERETON

FURPHY, JOHN (1842-1920), engineering blacksmith, was born on 17 June 1842 at Kangaroo Ground, Victoria, the eldest son of Samuel Furphy, farmer, and his wife Judith, née Hare. His parents had arrived from County Armagh, Ireland, in 1841 as bounty immigrants; his father was then described as an agricultural servant and his mother as a dressmaker. He was educated first by his mother and then at government schools at Kangaroo Ground and Kyneton. He was later apprenticed to a Kyneton firm of blacksmiths and implement makers, Hutcheson & Walker, who were pioneers in the local manufacture of farm machinery. In 1864 he set up as a blacksmith in Kyneton and stayed there until 1873 when he moved to the newly surveyed township of Shepparton in the Goulburn valley, where he opened the first blacksmith's and wheelwright's shop. His business expanded into ironfounding and by 1888 his establishment was the most extensive of its kind in northern Victoria. At the foundry he produced a variety of agricultural implements and specialized in modifications to suit local farming conditions. One of his patents was a grain stripper which won first prize at the Grand National Show in 1884 and had a wide sale before the manufacture of the combine harvester. At the International Exhibition in 1888-89 his entry of a grain-stripping machine, a furrow plough and iron swingletrees was among those gaining the highest possible award.

Furphy's most distinctive product was a simple invention which he never patented: a watercart with a 180-gallon cylindrical iron tank, mounted horizontally on a horse-drawn wooden frame with cast-iron wheels. The name Furphy was painted in large capitals on both sides of the tank. These carts, generally known as furphies, were ideal for the transport of water on farms, and an estimated average of 300 were produced annually for about forty years. They were used in large numbers by the Australian army in World War I. Drivers of the carts were noted for spreading gossip, and in time furphy became a synonym for idle rumour. The word was current in this sense by 1916 when C. J. Dennis used it in *The Moods of Ginger Mick*. By coincidence, Furphy's brother Joseph, who wrote *Such is Life* while employed at the foundry, had used the pen-name of 'Tom Collins', which among bushmen at the end of the nineteenth century carried the meaning that furphy now carries.

With his piety and strong sense of duty, John Furphy was prominent in Shepparton affairs. The first religious service in Shepparton was held by the United Free Methodists in his cottage behind the blacksmith's shop in 1873. In his thirty-five years of unbroken association with the Methodist Church in Shepparton he filled every office open to laymen and was well known as an effective preacher. Even his watercarts reflected his moral earnestness. Cast in the metal of one end was a rhymed exhortation to do one's best, and above it an inscription in shorthand warning of strong drink and urging the reader to stick to water.

On 25 May 1866 at Kyneton John Furphy married Sarah Ann Vaughan; they had five sons and four daughters. Furphy lived in Shepparton until 1909 when he moved to Melbourne where he died on 23 September 1920. Descendants still operate the foundry.

T. W. H. Leavitt and W. D. Lilburn (eds), *The jubilee history of Victoria and Melbourne* (Melb, 1888); *Shepparton Advertiser*, 27 Sept 1920; *Shepparton News*, 26 Sept 1932.

JOHN BARNES

G

GAINFORD, THOMAS (1823-1884), Congregational minister and social reformer, was born on 28 February 1823 on Wythmour Head estate near Workington, Cumberland, England, son of William Gainford, farmer, and his wife Jane, née Walker. Educated at the village school, Gainford at 19 was champion wrestler of Cumberland. Discontented with farm work, he became a shipwright at Workington and studied navigation. In 1842 as a ship's carpenter in the *Philomela* on the South American run he had a religious conversion. On his return he evangelized as a 'praying sailor' and worked in Sheerness dockyard. Known as the 'Black Preacher', he became a Wesleyan local preacher, chief ruler in the Rechabites, president of the temperance society and an advocate of the peace movement. At Sheerness in 1850 he married Dinah Briggs.

With little chance of promotion, Gainford decided to migrate and in September 1853 arrived in Sydney with his family in the *Walmer Castle*. He worked for John Cuthbert [q.v.], shipbuilder, and on his own account built wharves for the Peninsular and Oriental Steam Navigation Co.; later he became its superintendent of steamers. Guided by Nathaniel Pidgeon [q.v.] he assisted in the work of the City Mission, especially at the Female Refuge. In 1855 he became coproprietor of a sawmill on the Parramatta River but soon started another on the Richmond River where he also preached to the cedar-getters. In 1857 he went to the Victorian goldfields and preached and did temperance work at Tarrangower (Maldon). He became a magistrate and company manager at Mount Korong (Wedderburn). He was one of the two delegates sent to Melbourne to plead at the bar of the House in protest against the proposed land bill; he was then asked to represent Tarrangower in parliament but refused. In 1859 he left the Wedderburn diggings to become foreman of the patent slip at Stockton, Newcastle, where he preached for the Wesleyans and also served as pastor for the Congregational Church in Brown Street. Next year he was ordained to the Congregational ministry and in 1867 was called to the Ocean Street Church, Woollahra. In 1870 at a much lower salary he became minister of the Mariners' Church. To make it attractive to seamen he renovated the building and grounds and organized a normal congregation. He also ran several benevolent activities particularly in advising the sick poor on hygiene and medical care. The reforms of 'Father Gainford' did much to give the Sydney Bethel Union world-wide repute.

Gainford died at Bethel House, Sydney, on 5 March 1884, survived by his wife and by four of their five sons. An Evangelical, much of his appeal as a preacher lay in his 'transparent goodness'. His repute as a revivalist was enhanced by his influence over such desperate characters as the prizefighter, Tom Sullivan, a notorious New Zealand goldfield murderer, who confessed at his trial that at the Wedderburn diggings he had been nearly persuaded to reform when Gainford told him he was 'a gem in the rough'. Gainford's conversion of the murderers R. F. Nichols and A. Lester at Darlinghurst gaol in 1872 received much publicity. Besides advocating total abstinence Gainford condemned smoking and had a naïve faith in hydropathy and phrenology.

J. and W. R. Gainford (eds), *Memoir of incidents in the life and labours of Thomas Gainford ...* (Orpington, 1886).　NIEL GUNSON

GALE, JOHN (1831-1929), journalist, was born on 17 April 1831 at Bodmin, Cornwall, England, son of Francis Gale, excise officer, and his wife Mary, née Hamlyn. He was educated at Weymouth Grammar School and apprenticed to a newspaper in Newport, Monmouthshire. Converted to Wesleyan Methodism, he entered the ministry, was appointed to colonial duty and arrived at Sydney in the *American Lass* on 24 May 1854. In 1854-57 he travelled widely in New South Wales on a circuit which included Goulburn, Gunning, Queanbeyan and the Canberra district. On 3 January 1857 he married Loana, née Wheatley, and resigned to become a tutor.

Gale declined an invitation to run a sectarian newspaper at West Maitland but moved to Queanbeyan and on 15 September 1860 under primitive conditions started the *Golden Age and General Advertiser*; after 1864 it was named the *Queanbeyan Age and Recorder*. Through his paper he supported free selection and advocated reform in local administration. In 1866 he joined the committee of the new Free Selectors' Protection Association and of the local school board. His newspaper did not prosper and he moved in August 1867 to Braidwood where he founded the *Braidwood Independent* but in November, after a petition from Queanbeyan residents, resumed the *Queanbeyan*

Age. He founded the *Gunning Leader* in 1876, became secretary of the Free Selectors' Association and patriarch of the sons and daughters of temperance. In 1880 he visited Sydney as a delegate from the Queanbeyan Free Selectors' Association and convener of the Land Bill Conference and in 1883 served the first of three terms as president of the New South Wales Land Law Reform Alliance. In 1885 he became a justice of the peace, vice-president of the Land and Industrial Alliance Conference of New South Wales and one of Queanbeyan's first aldermen.

In the 1881 general election Gale had been defeated for Queanbeyan but in 1885 he helped E. W. O'Sullivan to win the seat for the protectionists. In February 1887 Gale was elected for the Murrumbidgee. He was not prominent in parliament and some free selectors complained that he neglected their interests; in 1889 he did not seek re-election. On entering parliament he had sold the *Queanbeyan Age* to four of his children and in April 1887 invested £3000 in the *Manly Spectator* which he founded with Harold Stephen as his partner. Stephen so mismanaged the funds that Gale became bankrupt in March 1890. He returned briefly to Queanbeyan before going to Junee where he established the *Democrat* and remained until 1894 when he became editor of the *Queanbeyan Observer*, owned by his son-in-law, Edward Henry Fallick.

Gale had published short stories and historical articles and after he retired in 1903 continued to write and held several minor official posts including that of coroner. In 1927 he published *Canberra: History of and Legends relating to the Federal Capital Territory of the Commonwealth of Australia*. He often wrote on fishing and had collaborated with Frederick Campbell of Yarralumla in the liberation of the first trout in the Molonglo River in 1889. His earlier writing was forceful and humorous but the dry and pedantic style of his book on Canberra reflected little of his literary ability. His passionate espousal of a flimsy claim for the discovery of Lake George in 1812 reduced his impact as an historian. He died at Queanbeyan on 15 July 1929 and was buried in the Queanbeyan Presbyterian cemetery after a Methodist ceremony. He was survived by four daughters and one son of the eleven children of his first marriage, and by his second wife Elizabeth Ann Forrest whom he had married on 17 January 1921 at Queanbeyan.

E. J. Lea-Scarlett, *Queanbeyan: district and people* (Queanbeyan, 1968); *Town and Country J*, 7 May 1887; *Queanbeyan Age*, 16 Sept 1960, centenary supp. E. J. Lea-Scarlett

GANNON, MICHAEL (1800-1881), builder and innkeeper, was born at Mullingar, Westmeath, Ireland, son of John Gannon, joiner, and his wife Alicia, née Gelshin. In 1820 he and his younger brother James, both carpenters, were sentenced in Meath, Michael for life and James for fourteen years. In December 1820 they arrived at Sydney in the *Almorah*.

In August 1824 Michael, then an assigned servant, married in Sydney Mary Parsonage, who later petitioned Governor Darling for her husband to be assigned to her. They lived in the Rocks area where Gannon worked as a carpenter and joiner. By 1829 he had a ticket-of-leave and in June 1836 his conditional pardon was confirmed. Gannon prospered as a builder and accumulated real estate. By 1843 he was undertaker for Catholic burials and had started as an auctioneer and commission agent in Lower George Street but this business was damaged by his brother's insolvency. Michael then obtained a publican's licence for an inn on Cook's River Road, Newtown, and was settled at Tempe by the end of 1845. Bankrupt within two years he was criticized for fraudulent transactions, contradictory evidence on oath and criminal neglect in failing to keep proper accounts.

From 1848 Gannon 'played an active and largely hidden role in Sydney politics'. In November 1850 he bought for £732 in St George parish a heavily timbered estate of 1905 acres, known as Gannon's Forest and later renamed Hurstville. Buying and selling property he lived at Tempe until he died aged 81 on 9 August 1881, survived by four sons and two daughters. He was buried in the family vault at Cook's River beside his wife who had died on 25 March 1875. His estate, valued at £9581, was bequeathed to members of his family but challenged by some of his relations.

James was granted his ticket-of-leave in 1828 and married Mary Phelps at Sydney in 1829. From carpentry he drifted into innkeeping and sporting activities, notably pigeon shooting. Insolvent in 1843, his personal assets were valued at £62 and included his treasured fowling piece and two dogs. On the fringe of politics in 1865 he was fined £50 for personation and double voting but was pardoned by the governor. As a labourer he died aged 68 at Paddington on 19 February 1871, leaving three children.

E. Digby (ed), *Australian men of mark*, 2 (Syd, 1889); P. Geeves and J. Jervis, *Rockdale: its beginnings and development* (Syd, 1962); M. Roe, *Quest for authority in eastern Australia 1835-1851* (Melb, 1965); Insolvency file (NSW). Philip Geeves

GARDENER, ALFRED HENRY (1831-1881), greyhound owner, was born at Alpheton, near Sudbury, Suffolk, England. He arrived at Sydney in May 1865. He worked until 1871 for Prince, Ogg & Co., warehousemen, and later represented Arthur & Co. Ltd, woollen and softgoods manufacturers of Glasgow, but mostly depended on private means.

Gardener devoted his life to breeding and racing greyhounds. Before his majority he had won several private matches with rejects from Lord Stradbroke's kennel. In 1871 he returned to England and had two successful seasons. Hearing that coursing had been legally recognized in 1873 in Victoria, he thought he might profitably introduce the sport to New South Wales. In 1874 he returned to Sydney with eleven valuable greyhounds and at a meeting at the Royal Hotel inaugurated, with Sir Hercules Robinson as patron, the New South Wales Coursing Club of which he was the first honorary secretary and a lifetime committee member. The first public coursing meeting was held at Bathurst on 8 May 1876 and the first in Sydney in June 1879. By the end of the 1878 season Gardener had given up coursing on his own account and trained for James Weir and George Hill junior of Surry Hills. His most notable season in New South Wales was in 1880 when, after reverses in Melbourne, he beat the Victorian dogs sent to Sydney to challenge his Hopmarket. He imported another three greyhounds from England and by 1881 had profitably put to stud all his imported dogs, whose offspring were already earning valuable stakes throughout the colony.

Gardener gave many prizes and won repute as 'the coursing patriarch of New South Wales'. He was well known on all the important courses: Sunbury near Melbourne, Woodstock, Bathurst, and Rooty Hill near Sydney. Quick tempered, he was often 'boisterous in demeanour . . . in the excitement of the chase'. His hints on racing and the improvements he introduced in breeding were acknowledged by local owners, particularly the sporting brothers William and George Lee [q.v.] of Bathurst and Walter Lamb [q.v.] of Sydney. He died aged 50 at Surry Hills on 28 February 1881 of typhoid fever and was buried in the Anglican section of Rookwood cemetery. Most of his estate of £1500 was left to relations in Suffolk.

SMH, 5 June 1879, 3 Mar 1881; *Town and Country J,* 3 July 1880, 5 Mar 1881; *Daily Telegraph* (Syd), 2 Mar 1881; E. S. Marks, Early coursing in Australia, 1868-1887 (ML).

RUTH TEALE

GARDINER (CHRISTIE), FRANCIS (1830-1903?), bushranger, was born at Boro, near Goulburn, New South Wales, natural son of Christie, a Scottish free settler, and an Irish-Aboriginal servant girl. He went to Victoria and in October 1850 as Francis Christie was sentenced to five years' hard labour at Geelong for horse stealing. Next March he escaped from Pentridge gaol and returned to New South Wales. In March 1854 he was convicted as Francis Clarke at Goulburn on two charges of horse stealing and imprisoned on Cockatoo Island. In December 1859 he was given a ticket-of-leave for the Carcoar district, but broke parole and went south and by the end of 1860 as Frank Gardiner he had a butchery at Lambing Flat but after a brawl was forced to leave. Known as 'The Darkie', he began highway robbery on the Cowra Road. In July 1861 at a sly grog shop near Oberon he shot and wounded Sergeant John Middleton [q.v.]; Trooper Hosie was also wounded although allegedly bribed to let Gardiner escape.

Gardiner joined up with Johnny Piesley; after ranging the old Lachlan Road they moved to the Weddin Mountains and were joined by John Gilbert, Ben Hall [qq.v.] and others. The police under Sir Frederick Pottinger [q.v.] could not catch the gang for it moved too rapidly aided by 'bush telegraphs'.

On 15 June 1862 at the Coonbong Rock near Eugowra Gardiner's gang held up the gold escort and got away with £14,000. Soon afterwards Gardiner, while visiting his mistress Kate, wife of John Brown of Wheogo, narrowly escaped from Pottinger. With her he went to Queensland where as Mr and Mrs Frank Christie they ran a store and shanty at Apis Creek near Rockhampton. In February 1864 he was traced by the New South Wales police and arrested. Tried for wounding Sergeant Middleton with intent to kill, he was acquitted by the jury but found guilty in July on two non-capital charges. Chief Justice Stephen [q.v.] gave him a cumulative sentence of thirty-two years' hard labour. In 1872 W. B. Dalley [q.v.]; who had defended Gardiner, organized petitions to the governor to use his prerogative of mercy. Sir Hercules Robinson decided that Gardiner had been harshly sentenced and in 1874 released him subject to his exile. This decision provoked a public controversy with petitions, counter-petitions and violent debates in the Legislative Assembly, and led to the fall of Parkes's [q.v.] government.

On 27 July Gardiner embarked for Hong Kong and by February 1875 was in San Francisco where he ran the Twilight Saloon. The press continued to note his activities, including his death in Colorado about 1903, but most reports were unsubstantiated.

H. Parkes et al, *Debate on the prerogative of pardon as involved in the release of Gardiner & other prisoners* (Syd, 1876?); H. Parkes, *The case of the prisoner Gardiner the prerogative of pardon* (Syd, 1876); V&P (LA NSW), 1863-64, 1, 1365, 1865, 1, 53, 62, 1865-66, 1, 339, 1873-75; *Sydney Mail*, 26 Mar, 23 Apr 1864; *Australasian*, 20 June 1874, 20 Feb 1875; *Bulletin*, 18 Mar, 11 Nov 1882; CO 201/577-581.

EDGAR F. PENZIG

GARDNER, JOHN (1809-1899), Presbyterian clergyman, was born on 17 April 1809 in Glasgow, Scotland, the third son of Rev. William Gardner and his wife Mary, née Clelland. At 17 he entered the University of Glasgow where for nine years he studied for the ministry of the Church of Scotland. In 1835 he was licensed by the Glasgow Presbytery to preach and after some months in Paisley, became assistant to Rev. R. Smith of Lochwinnoch, father of R. B. Smith [q.v.] of Adelaide. Gardner's first call was from St Andrew's Presbyterian Church, Birkenhead, England, where he was ordained on 26 August 1840, and on 12 February 1844 married Catherine, daughter of John Alexander Forrest, a Liverpool merchant.

In 1843 the disruption of the Church of Scotland raised problems of loyalty for many English Presbyterians but although Gardner had been influenced by Dr Thomas Chalmers and many of his congregation urged him to associate himself with the Free Church movement he decided that the issues did not affect English Presbyterianism. In South Australia many Presbyterians, interested in the Free Church, presented a signed address to its moderator in January 1844. Although the Established Church of Scotland and the United Presbyterians had churches in Adelaide, several influential businessmen decided to establish the Free Church cause and in 1849 applied to the colonial committee of the Free Church in Scotland for a minister. Gardner accepted the challenge and arrived in Adelaide in March 1850. He found no congregation but his amazing zeal and support from such businessmen as Thomas Elder [q.v.] soon built up the Free Church cause. On 6 July 1851 Chalmers Church was opened in Adelaide.

The cause expanded rapidly, often at the expense of the two older Presbyterian churches. In 1854 Gardner formed the Free Church Presbytery; its negotiations in 1860 for reunion of the three churches proved abortive but in May 1865 the Presbyterian Church of South Australia was formed and Gardner was elected moderator of its new presbytery. Prominent in the colony's social and religious affairs, he served on committees of the British and Foreign Bible Society, the Aborigines Friends Association, the Bush Mission, the Benevolent and Strangers Friend Society and the Female Refuge. His lectures in 1853 at the opening of the Young Men's Christian Association, 'The Literary Merits of the Bible' and 'Missions: the Great Enterprise of the Christian Church', were later printed. He visited regularly at the Adelaide Hospital and in politics was active in educational matters and in opposing the bill to legalize marriage with a deceased wife's sister.

In 1868 Gardner accepted a call to St Andrew's Church, Launceston. In 1874 he moved to Queenscliff, Victoria. Elected moderator for 1883, he presided over the general assembly when Charles Strong [q.v.] was tried for heresy. Gardner's staunch defence of traditional Presbyterian doctrines and his skill and tact in handling the case benefited the orthodox party, but he must be held partly responsible if the treatment Strong received at the assembly is considered unconstitutional and unjust. Gardner retired from the active ministry in 1888 and died at Toorak, Victoria, on 10 May 1899. Predeceased by his wife on 30 March 1892 he was survived by three of their five children.

Gardner belonged to the older school of Presbyterian thought and had little sympathy with newer trends in theology. His enthusiasm and organizing ability explain the success of the Free Church cause in South Australia and also characterized his later ministry in Tasmania and Victoria. His Evangelical convictions and sincerity made him outspoken in defence of what he believed to be true and often blinded him to other forms of truth. These qualities, rather than originality, distinguished his life and ministry.

A portrait is in the museum of the English Presbyterian Historical Society and a tablet is in Scots Church, Adelaide.

W. Gray, 'The history of the Presbyterian Church in South Australia' 1839-1938, *Presbyterian Banner*, Feb 1932-Nov 1939; *Observer* (Adel), 26 Sept 1868, 13, 27 May 1899; *Argus*, Nov 1883; *Leader* (Melb), 20 May 1899.

DIRK VAN DISSEL

GARLAND, JAMES (1813-1904), pastoralist and police superintendent, was born on 13 August 1813 at Ellon, Aberdeenshire, Scotland, the youngest son of Thomas Garland, tenant farmer, and his wife Catherine, née Adams. He was educated by Revs J. Milne and W. Lillie, and in 1828 entered King's College, University of Aberdeen (M.A., 1832). In 1835 he bought a commission in the 99th Regiment, transferred to the 28th and arrived at Sydney in June 1836 in the *Strathfieldsaye*. Stationed at Parramatta for a year, he sold out in 1837 and with a fellow officer, William Cadell, took up Darbalara station in wild mountain country on the Tumut River. In June 1839 Garland married Emma Broughton whom he had met when she took refuge from bushrangers with the 'Soldier Officers'. After fifty-three years of marriage Garland wrote that 'never did he cease to bless the bushrangers for sending me such a treasure'. In 1840 he sold Darbalara and lived mostly at Lachlan Vale, Appin, and in 1842 became a magistrate. In the 1840s he took up four other runs on the Upper Murrumbidgee and Hume Rivers in partnership with George Mair. In 1852 Garland held Maragle and Tooma, a total of 80,000 acres. About 1855 he moved to Sydney where he set up a stock and pastoral agency in partnership with Edward Bingham to deal in squatting ventures.

In May 1856 Garland was elected to the Legislative Assembly for the Lachlan and Lower Darling but failed to live up to his maiden speech which the *Empire* thought afforded 'promise of considerable debating ability and decided usefulness in the conduct of public business'. In 1857 he did not seek re-election and next year visited Britain. In 1859 he was defeated for the Tumut seat.

In 1861 Garland & Bingham became insolvent and their estate was sequestrated. Although not involved in the 'reckless conduct' and 'unnecessary expenditure' of his partner, Garland honourably surrendered his private fortune. He was granted his discharge certificate in 1862 but the insolvent estate was not wound up until 1902. On 1 March 1862 he was appointed police superintendent for the north-western district, with headquarters at Tamworth under the reorganization provisions of the new Police Regulation Act, 1862. His district was infested with bushrangers including Captain Thunderbolt [q.v. F. Ward], and raw recruits needed careful training. 'Robberies were of daily occurrence, the mails were being perpetually interrupted, and the commercial world was beginning to lose faith in the postal means of communication'. In May 1868 when a harbourer of 'the very worst of cattle stealers and bushrangers' was appointed to the Commission of the Peace Garland protested and proceeded to make the district 'one of the most peaceful in New South Wales'. A 'just officer' to his men, he

retired on 28 February 1882. He was the first president of the Tamworth Mechanics' Institute and in 1885 was appointed to the local land board. Survived by six sons and four daughters to whom he left £1300, he died on 17 November 1904 and was buried in the Anglican cemetery, West Tamworth.

W. F. Morrison, *The Aldine centennial history of New South Wales*, 2 (Syd, 1888); T. B. Clouston (ed), *Tumut centenary celebrations 1824-1924* (Syd, 1924); *SMH*, 9 May 1844, 24 May 1856, 18 Nov 1904; *Empire* (Syd), 26, 31 May 1856; *Tamworth Observer*, 8, 12 Apr 1882, 19 Nov 1904; *Tamworth News*, 19 Nov 1904; Insolvency file 5328 (NSWA); MS and printed cats under J. Garland (ML); newspaper indexes under J. Garland (ML); WO 17/2320-22.

MARTHA RUTLEDGE

GARLICK, DANIEL (1818-1902), architect, was baptized on 22 January 1818 at Uley, Gloucestershire, England, son of Moses Garlick, plasterer and weaver, and his wife Rachel, née Smith. His father had seen active service at Vittoria, Salamanca and Corunna in the Peninsular wars; after his wife died he decided to migrate to South Australia with his sons Daniel, Thomas and William. They sailed in the *Katherine Stewart Forbes* and arrived in the new colony on 17 October 1837.

Daniel and his father ran a business as builders and timber merchants in Kermode Street, North Adelaide, until the early 1850s when a deterioration in Daniel's health led to a change. His father bought some 450 acres east of Smithfield, about fifteen miles from Adelaide, and with his three sons grew wheat, planted a vineyard and made wine. After their father died about 1860, Thomas and William remained on the farm but Daniel began business as an architect in Gawler. About 1862 he married Lucy King; she died on 26 July 1871 leaving three sons.

Garlick designed many churches and banks in townships north of Adelaide and in 1864 was described as an architect and land and estate agent with offices in Adelaide. Among the buildings which he designed in and around Adelaide in the 1860s and 1870s are the original buildings of Prince Alfred College, St Barnabas College, part of the Collegiate School of St Peter where the original buildings had been designed by others, and the south wing of Adelaide Town Hall. The colleges are in the fashionable neo-Gothic of the time but elsewhere his designs reveal an ability to turn to other styles then current. As the practice expanded, Herbert Louis Jackman, who had served his apprenticeship with Garlick, was his partner until 1899. In 1891 Daniel's son Arthur (b. 1863) joined the firm, 'the business to be carried on at the present offices of H. L. Jackman in Argent Street, Broken Hill'. When the South Australian Institute of Architects was established in 1886, Daniel was prominent among those who founded it. He was its second president, holding office in 1892-1900.

Garlick gave brief service in local government. He was chairman of the district council of Munno Para East in 1855-60 and represented Robe ward in the Adelaide City Council in 1868-70, but he was obliged to discontinue this work to devote all his time to his practice. He was a sidesman of Christchurch, North Adelaide, where he attended for many years. Garlick died aged 84 in North Adelaide on 28 September 1902. He was survived by his second wife Mary Rebecca (1874-1912), a widow whom he had married on 29 September 1877, and by a son and a daughter. He left an estate worth £1150.

A bust sculptured by Jackman is held by Jackman, Gooden, Scott & Swan, architects of Adelaide.

Observer (Adel), 29 Sept 1902; Council minutes (SA Inst of Architects); partnership records (SAA).   GAVIN WALKLEY

GARNSEY, CHARLES FREDERICK (1828-1894), Church of England clergyman, was born on 15 November 1828 at Berry Hill, Gloucestershire, England, son of Thomas Rock Garnsey, incumbent of Christ Church, and his wife Elizabeth, née Hare. His father had been a chaplain in Sierra Leone in 1819-21 and was a firm Evangelical.

Charles was educated at Monmouth Grammar School and articled to a solicitor. Impatient with legal work, he migrated in 1848 to Van Diemen's Land armed with family references. He hoped for outdoor occupation to benefit his health but soon won Bishop Nixon's [q.v.] patronage and tutored his children. He was made deacon in 1853 and became Gell fellow in Christ College and then bursar. He preferred teaching and parochial work to administration and resigned from the college in 1855 to teach at the Hutchins School. Failing appointment as a school inspector, he became Nixon's secretary in 1857 and did good work in a difficult time. Next year he moved to Sydney and taught at Rev. W. H. Savigny's [q.v.] new 'collegiate school' at Cook's River.

In 1860 Garnsey set up his own 'collegiate school' at Windsor. The incumbent, H. T. Stiles [q.v.], who had known his father, had reservations about Garnsey's prospects as a headmaster and as his son-in-law, but the school prospered and he married Mary

Emma Stiles (d. 13 April 1886). Garnsey was ordained priest by Bishop Barker [q.v.] on 18 December 1864 and assumed a large share of the Windsor work. He became incumbent on Stiles's death in 1867. His cricketing prowess and his heroism in a local fire and flood made him popular and enabled him to renovate the church and extend parochial activity. Garnsey had abandoned his early Evangelicalism and, under Nixon's influence, had become a High Churchman, for which he was criticized by local Dissenters and by a group of earnest Low Churchmen led by the astronomer, John Tebbutt [q.v.]. A series of petty incidents made him anxious to serve in a larger sphere and in 1876 he became Canon Allwood's [q.v.] assistant at St James's, Sydney.

Much of the burden of a famous city church with a declining congregation and an ageing incumbent fell on Garnsey, and in April 1878 he became incumbent of Christ Church St Laurence. An energetic pastor, he founded the Guild of St Laurence, opened a mission room for the slum areas, maintained his large school after the withdrawal of state aid and served in many charitable organizations. A Tractarian for many years, he returned in 1884 from a visit to England a proponent of ritualism and his leadership made Christ Church a centre of the liturgical movement in Sydney. He instituted a daily Eucharist with appropriate vestments, furnishings and music. After experience on the *Australian Churchman*, he edited the *Banner and Anglo-Catholic Review* in 1890-92 and helped to found the *Churchman* on 6 July 1894. He was a member of the Church Union and the Churchman's Institute and a patron of religious sisterhoods. In 1877 he had joined the Royal Society of New South Wales. Although a good scholar Garnsey was not an ecclesiastical antiquarian. A vigorous, practical churchman, he sought to link the sacramentalism of his later years to a positive social gospel. He had little local support but his influence extended beyond the diocesan boundaries.

Garnsey died suddenly on 3 December 1894, survived by four sons and six daughters of his first marriage, and by his second wife Marion Laura, nee Walker, whom he had married in 1887. He was buried in Waverley cemetery. A fund was raised for the education of his family and a memorial window placed in Christ Church in July 1895.

W. F. Carter, *The cathedral of the Hawkesbury . . . St. Matthew's, Windsor* (Lithgow, nd); L. M. Allen, *A history of Christ Church St Laurence Sydney* (Syd 1940); R. M. Teale, 'Party or principle?', *JRAHS*, 55 (1969);

Churchman, 7 July, 6 Dec 1895; Garnsey papers (ML); Stiles papers (ML); C. F. Garnsey diaries and memoranda (held by Dr C. D. Garnsey, Turramurra, NSW).   K. J. CABLE

GARRAN (GAMMAN), ANDREW (1825-1901), journalist and politician, was born on 15 November 1825 in London, the third child of Robert Gamman, merchant, and his wife Mary Ann, née Mathews. Intended for the Congregational ministry, he went to Hackney Grammar School and a theological coaching college in Norfolk. In 1842 at Spring Hill College, Birmingham, he was influenced by Henry Rogers, Congregational minister and professor of philosophy. Next year he matriculated at London University (B.A., 1845; M.A., 1848).

In 1848 Garran fell seriously ill with suspected phthisis and was sent to Madeira. On his return to London next year he was advised to migrate to Australia. In 1850 in the *Ascendant* he met G. F. Angas [q.v.] and was appointed 'Christian instructor'. He arrived in Adelaide in January 1851, did some preaching, worked as a journalist and later editor on the *Austral Examiner* and at the elections for the reformed Legislative Council campaigned against state aid to religion. With Adelaide depopulated by the Victorian gold rush Garran spent most of 1852 as a tutor on a Victorian station and later in Melbourne shared in an attempt to start a newspaper. In 1853 he returned to Adelaide as co-editor of the *South Australian Register* with a salary of £200. Next year Garran married Mary Isham Sabine, daughter of a well-to-do chemist and devout Congregationalist.

Invited by John Fairfax [q.v.], Garran joined the *Sydney Morning Herald* as assistant editor in May 1856. He attended the University of Sydney (LL.B., 1868; LL.D., 1870) and in 1873 succeeded John West [q.v.] as editor of the *Herald*. Like many Englishmen of his class and education, Garran had found difficulty in fully adapting to the fluid Australian society. Steeped in the political, social and economic principles of leading liberal British writers he was disturbed by 'the disharmony "produced by conflict" between employer and employee, free selector and squatter, Protestant and Roman Catholic'. The British liberal had become a colonial conservative incongruously upholding *laissez faire* against a slowly rising tide of state control. As a result his editorials often had an unwelcome didactic and righteous tone but they were distinguished by a lucid style, a clear vision of the advantages of an educated democracy and an innate and informed generosity. Failing health forced him to resign at the end of 1885. Under Garran the *Herald* had consolidated its position as a leading Australian newspaper and the most intelligent and knowledgeable journal in New South Wales.

In 1876 Garran had been a commissioner for New South Wales for the Philadelphia International Exhibition, and in 1879 for the Sydney International Exhibition. A director of the Newcastle Wallsend Coal Co. from 1869, he was its chairman in one of its most prosperous periods in 1874-79. He contributed to other Australian newspapers, often under the pseudonym 'Nova Cambria', and was a regular correspondent of the London *Times*. He edited *The Picturesque Atlas of Australasia*, 3 vols (1886). President twice of the Australian Economic Association he was on the Board of Technical Education and a trustee of Sydney Grammar School. He served on the noxious trades commission in 1888, was president of the royal commission on strikes in 1890 and was a member of an inquiry into the Bay View lunatic asylum in 1894. In 1887 Henry Parkes [q.v.] had him appointed to the Legislative Council and he introduced Sir Alfred Stephen's [q.v.] divorce bill when it was finally enacted in 1892. In October he resigned from the council and the chairmanship of the Parliamentary Committee on Public Works to become president of the Council of Arbitration with a salary of £1500. In June 1889 he had been president of the inaugural conference of the Free Trade and Liberal Association, but his views on freedom and individualism had helped to inhibit the attempts of the free traders to form a political party. In 1895 George Reid had him reappointed to the Legislative Council where he represented the government; he was also vice-president of the Executive Council until November 1898.

Described by J. A. Froude [q.v.] in 1886 as 'right-minded even to the point of rigidity', Garran was plagued by ill health for most of his life. He owed much to the tender care of his wife, who with one son and five of their seven daughters survived his death at Darlinghurst on 6 June 1901. He was buried in the Congregational section of the Rookwood cemetery. His son, Robert Randolph (1867-1957), won distinction as a constitutional lawyer and Commonwealth public servant.

R. R. Garran, *Prosper the Commonwealth* (Syd, 1958); P. Loveday and A. W. Martin, *Parliament factions and parties* (Melb, 1966); Mrs C. Bright, 'The Hon. Dr. Garran, M.L.C.', *Cosmos Mag*, 31 May 1895; *Bulletin*, 29 Sept 1883, 15 June 1901; *Argus*, 7 June 1901; *SMH*, 8 June 1901; G. Woolnough, 'Andrew Garran', *Daily Mail* (Brisb), 23 Apr 1927; M. Rutledge, *Sir Alfred Stephen and divorce extension in*

New South Wales 1886-1892 (M.A. thesis, ANU, 1966); P. J. Read, Conservatism and the Sydney Morning Herald: the editorship of Andrew Garran, 1873-1885 (B.A. Hons. thesis, ANU, 1967).   E. K. BRAMSTED

GARRARD, JACOB (1846-1931), trade unionist and politician, was born at Harwich, England, son of Joseph Garrard, revenue officer, and his wife Martha, née Piggott. Educated at Harwich National School and Southwark Borough School, he migrated at 13 with his family to New Zealand and worked on coastal ships. Apprenticed in 1861 to an engineer he moved in 1867 to Sydney where he lived at Balmain and until about 1883 worked in turn at docks owned by T. S. Mort, P. N. Russell [qq.v.], the Australasian Steam Navigation Co. and Davy & Sands. He joined the Amalgamated Society of Engineers and in 1874 became its delegate on the Trades and Labor Council.

Garrard's tenacity and fluency made him one of the most prominent young trade unionists in the 1870s. He was a leader in the 1873-74 strikes that won the eight-hour day for iron-trades workers and he gained valuable experience by seeking support in Victoria for the strikers. Impressed by F. B. Dixon's [q.v.] vision of the social role of trade unions, he contested West Sydney in the 1877 election, claiming that he was 'no railler against capitalism . . . [but] it was class legislation to have a House composed of capitalists and squatters'. Failure sharpened his political ambitions and he widened his electoral appeal by his teetotalism and Orangeism and by serving on the Balmain Borough Council in 1879-86. In 1880 he was mayor and, although the Trades and Labor Council would not officially support him, he was helped by many unionists and won the new seat of Balmain.

In parliament Garrard was one of the best-equipped members to respond to colonial technological, industrial and administrative change in the 1880s. He co-operated with the Trades and Labor Council and F. M. Darley [q.v.] to pass the Trade Union Act, 1881, and sponsored the Employers Liability Act, 1882. He was a member of the Tramway Inquiry Board and acted as an arbiter in coal-industry disputes. In 1887-92 he was a member of the royal commission into the civil service. An unwavering free trader he adjusted to the complex parliamentary situation as protection became more popular. In 1885-86 he was secretary for public works under John Robertson [q.v.] and supported Henry Parkes's [q.v.] ministries in 1887-91. By 1888 he was an accomplished parliamentarian who often acted as temporary chairman of committees and provoked the judgment that 'when he turns his head to the Opposition, and looks at them quizzingly, why, Burke and Fox wouldn't have been able to stand it'. Meanwhile he had left his trade and become a successful estate agent and auctioneer, chairman of the City and Country Investment Land and Building Society and director of the Australian Mutual Prudential and Medical Assurance Society. He retained links with the Labor movement and in 1884, when unveiling the Engineers' Society's new banner, declared that unionists 'desired, while protecting themselves, to lend a helping hand in building up the [country's] great industries'. In 1885 he was responsible for making a public holiday in celebration of the eight-hour objective. In 1886 he became one of the first trustees of the Sydney Trades Hall.

Garrard observed the need for structural political change and in 1889 was on the council of the ephemeral Free Trade and Liberal Association. In 1891 he was on the Parliamentary Executive Committee that organized the elections for the free traders, but could not harmonize his electoral style in Balmain with the novel circumstances posed by the Labor Party. Defeated there he won Central Cumberland at a by-election and refused to join Labor. His radicalism, if somewhat modified, found expression in the revivified Free Trade Party led by George Reid for whom he was an effective organizer. In 1894-98 he was member for Sherbrooke and in 1895-98 minister for education and the colony's first minister for labor and industry under Reid. In the 1890s he continued to reflect his knowledge of industrial affairs and concluded that compulsory arbitration was needed. He proved an energetic education minister with a special interest in technical education. In 1896 Garrard joined the Salvation Army. In 1898 he narrowly lost his seat and in 1899-1912 was a member of the Water and Sewerage Board and its president in 1899-1904. He served on the Kuringai Chase Trust for nearly thirty years and was an active worker for the Methodist Church.

In 1870 at Balmain Garrard had married Rebecca Cavill. Survived by two daughters and two of his five sons he died on 5 November 1931 at Hornsby and was buried in the Methodist section of Gore Hill cemetery. His estate was valued at £3696.

K. D. Buckley, The Amalgamated Engineers in Australia, 1852-1920 (Canberra, 1970); Town and Country J, 2 Apr 1887; Daily Telegraph (Syd), 17 July 1887; SMH, 6 Nov 1931; Trades and Labor Council minutes 1871-86 (ML).
                                             BEDE NAIRN

GARRETT, THOMAS (1830-1891), politician, newspaper proprietor and land agent, was born on 15 July 1830 at Liverpool, England, son of John Garrett and his wife Sarah, née Stafford. On 12 November 1840 he reached Sydney with his parents, bounty immigrants, in the *Argyleshire*. Educated by his father, he was bound at 11 to a printer; he soon ran away to sea in H.M.S. *Fly* but was returned to complete his time. As a journeyman he worked on the *Goulburn Herald*, *Atlas* and *Argus* before trying the goldfields. After three years in the Government Printing Office, Sydney, he and W. F. Cahill founded the *Illawarra Mercury* at Wollongong in 1855. In 1860 with his father he started the *Alpine Pioneer and Kiandra Advertiser* and in 1861 the *Manaro Mercury and Cooma and Bombala Advertiser*. He sold his share in the *Illawarra Mercury* in 1867, formed a partnership with George F. Pickering and for about two years produced the lusty *Bell's Life in Sydney*. He then turned to share-broking and agency work.

Garrett never used the liberal political comment in his newspapers to further his own or his father's political careers. In 1860 he had won the Monaro seat as the acknowledged lieutenant of John Robertson [q.v.] and in 1864 Shoalhaven, his father's old electorate. In 1864-69 he was chairman of committees and parliamentary whip and in 1870 was reputed to have engineered with John Davies [q.v.] the coalition between Robertson and James Martin [q.v.]. In 1867 he joined Orange Lodge No. 2, and in 1869 was suspended for the non-payment of dues but continued to flirt with Orangeism. In July 1871 Garrett resigned to become police magistrate at Berrima but, despite a loan of £200 from Robertson, his estate was sequestrated on 24 February 1872; he owed £2846. Although his certificate of discharge was not issued until September 1887 he represented Camden in the Legislative Assembly in 1872-91. An active legislator and a powerful debater he was 'prominent without having a following of any kind' but many doubted his 'political rectitude'. In the 1870s he became a mining speculator and land agent.

In February 1875 Garrett was rewarded by Robertson with the lands portfolio where his administrative skill firmly established the new Courts created by the Crown Lands Amendment Act which he had tactfully and expertly piloted through the assembly. Overworked and drinking too much, he resigned from the ministry in February 1877 after a censure motion against him was narrowly defeated. He helped to bring down Parkes's [q.v.] government in August, joined Robertson's new ministry but again resigned; rumour held that no cabinet containing Garrett could retain the confidence of the assembly. In 1878 he visited England and America. His growing intemperance may have caused his long spell on the back benches. Early in 1883 he tried to form a 'third party', but by July 1888 when Parkes had to ask him to resign as secretary for lands he was probably an alcoholic.

Garrett's skill as a parliamentary tactician was greatest in adversity. In 1875 he had routed Parkes who charged him with corrupt appointments and he survived a select committee inquiry into an alteration of the 'Report of the Examiner of Coal Fields, on land leased by Messrs Garrett and Greville' [q.v.]. In 1881 he was even more hard pressed when accused of complicity in seeking compensation for E. A. Baker's [q.v.] Milburn Creek Copper Mining Co., for which he had bought shares at call and helped to destroy all written evidence of the deal. Robertson resigned from office in defence of his friend and Parkes's expulsion motion was only narrowly defeated, but in the 1880s John McElhone's [q.v.] repeated questions revealed that Garrett had over 68,000 acres of mineral leases on much of which he paid no rent. He was also a director of the Wickham and Bullock Island Coal Co. Ltd.

Garrett died at Newtown on 25 November 1891 from softening of the brain and was buried in the Anglican section of Waverley cemetery. He was survived by three sons of his first wife Mary Ann, née Craigon, a son by his second wife Marcia, née Grocott, and by his third wife Elizabeth, née McPhillamy, and two infant sons. His estate was valued at £14,816.

Ex-M.L.A., *Our present parliament, what it is worth* (Syd, c 1886); E. Digby (ed), *Australian men of mark*, 1 (Syd, 1889); P. Loveday and A. W. Martin, *Parliament factions and parties* (Melb, 1966); V&P (LA NSW), 1875-76, 4, 735, 1881, 1, 241, 3, 558, 633, 1883-84, 4, 561, 1887-88, 8, 263; *Illustrated Sydney News*, 27 June 1874; *Town and Country J*, 27 Mar 1875, 29 Jan 1887; *Australasian*, 26 Apr 1879; *Bulletin*, 6 Apr 1881; Parkes letters (ML); CO 201/577, 581, 583-84, 587, 591, 595, 597-98.

G. A. PRICE

GARRICK, SIR JAMES FRANCIS (1836-1907), politician and agent-general, was born on 10 January 1836 at Sydney, the second son of James Francis Garrick who migrated in the early 1830s to manage a flour-mill. Like his elder brother, James was articled to a Sydney solicitor. He was admitted to practise in December 1860 and his brother practised in Christchurch, New Zealand. In 1861 Garrick moved to Brisbane, where only four attorneys were then in practice. He went into partnership with Charles Lilley [q.v.], built up a flourishing practice and became solicitor to the City Council.

Garrick represented East Moreton in the Legislative Assembly in 1867-68. In 1869 the Lilley ministry appointed him to the Legislative Council but he soon left for London and after an absence of two sessions his seat was declared vacant. In London he resumed his legal studies and was called to the Bar of the Middle Temple in 1873. Next year he returned to Brisbane and was admitted to the Queensland Bar. He was crown prosecutor of the metropolitan district in 1874-75, the central district in 1875-76 and the southern district in 1877. In 1882 he was appointed Q.C. He re-entered politics in 1877 for East Moreton. In February 1878 he was appointed secretary for public lands and mines in the ministry of John Douglas [q.v.]; in December he became attorney-general and held office for two months before the government fell. From 1879 he was prominent in the Opposition led by S. W. Griffith to the McIlwraith [q.v.] government until November 1883 when Griffith took over the administration and appointed Garrick temporarily as colonial treasurer. In 1883-84 he was postmaster-general, a post that customarily involved leadership of the government in the Legislative Council, to which he was duly appointed. He represented Queensland at the Intercolonial Conference of 1883.

In June 1884 Griffith appointed him agent-general for immigration in London while still holding a seat in the Executive Council as minister without portfolio. Apart from an interruption from June 1888 to December 1890, Garrick held his post in London until October 1895. In his first term he sent to Queensland an average of 10,000 migrants each year, most from Britain but a few from Europe. When hopes of increased German migration were crushed in 1885 by German newspaper stories 'warning against Queensland', Garrick tried to counter them but with little success. In 1886 he unsuccessfully canvassed the possibility of other schemes of state-aided migration from Britain. He took part in settling the New Guinea question after Queensland's abortive annexation in 1883. With other Australasian agents-general he was involved in numerous conferences and private interviews with the secretary of state for the colonies. The latter rejected both Garrick's suggestions for more immediate and effective action in New Guinea and the South Pacific and his protest against the deportation of French criminals to New Caledonia. He arranged with the Admiralty

for the *Paluma* to survey more accurately the Queensland coast and secured other ships for his government. He attended the Postal Union Conference at Lisbon in 1885 and the International Congress at Brussels on customs tariffs in 1888. As an executive commissioner, he prepared Queensland's court for the Colonial and Indian Exhibition in 1886, and was one of Queensland's representatives at the Colonial Conference in 1887. He was appointed C.M.G. in 1885 and K.C.M.G. in 1886.

In his second term as agent-general in 1890-95 Garrick completed the details of a scheme to send Italians to the sugar areas of Bundaberg and the Herbert River as replacements for Kanaka labour. In 1891-92 he publicized a scheme of village settlement but deteriorating financial conditions in Queensland put an end to such plans. When the focus of attention in the agent-general's office switched to commerce and trade, Garrick helped to find and promote new markets for Queensland products and new products for Queensland to develop. The marketing of frozen beef was his main concern. With the War Office he helped to complete arrangements for the defence of Torres Strait, including armaments for Thursday Island. He was active in the Imperial Institute and a Queensland representative on its council. In 1890 he was invited but declined to stand for the House of Commons as a Unionist. In 1895 he was appointed a judge of the Queensland Supreme Court but did not assume office. He was a director of several companies and remained in London until he died at his home on 12 January 1907. He was survived by his wife Catherine, daughter of Dr J. J. Cadell, whom he had married on 3 January 1865, and by three children. His daughter, Katherine, endowed the James Francis Garrick chair of law at the University of Queensland.

Described as a 'brilliant lawyer, a well set up handsome man, cultivated and of great personal charm', Garrick was also a fine speaker, very courtly and diplomatic. Although overshadowed in politics by his friend Griffith, as agent-general he was an active intermediary between his government and imperial officials and an ardent promoter of Queensland's advancement.

R. S. Browne, *A journalist's memories* (Brisb, 1927); C. Lack, 'Colonial representation in the nineteenth century', *JRHSQ*, 8 (1965-66); *Argus*, 12 May 1890; *The Times*, 14 Jan 1907; Col Sec letters to and from agent-general (QA); Griffith papers (Dixson Lib, Syd).

W. ROSS JOHNSTON

GARVAN, JAMES PATRICK (1843-1896), insurance entrepreneur and politician, was born on 2 May 1843 at Cappagh, Limerick, Ireland, son of Denis Bourke Garvan, civil servant, and his wife Anne, née Culhane. In 1847 he migrated to Sydney with his family. Educated at John Armstrong's school in Redfern and Creagh's Elizabeth Street school, he won a scholarship to Sydney Grammar School in 1858 but left when his father died in 1860. Next year he became an assistant clerk in the survey department of the Sydney Municipal Council but was suspended on 29 December 1866 for absence without leave. He resigned on 7 November 1867, remarking, 'it was through taking part in political contests and supporting the losing side'; later he received £21 in damages. He then roved eastern Australia and in 1870-71 at Sydney he was articled to R. R. Bailey and to B. A. Freehill. In 1872 he joined the Hill End gold rush and was a successful legal adviser for several mining companies. In 1875 at Sydney he read for the Bar with W. B. Dalley [q.v.] and Edmund Barton, but gave it up in 1876 and founded the Australian Terminating Building Society. He astutely saw the need for improved water transport and in 1876-79 established and nurtured the North Shore Steam Ferry Co. Ltd; predicting an increase of insurance he also founded the City Mutual Fire Insurance Co. Ltd and the City Mutual Life Assurance Society Ltd.

Garvan had combined gradual success in business with a notable share in sport and public activity through Irish-colonial societies. In the 1860s he had been a competitive sculler and amateur heavy-weight boxer and held the record throw of 121 yards 1 foot with a cricket ball. Next decade he was vice-president of the National Regatta and umpire of championship rowing on the Parramatta River. He was also an outstanding horseman and prize-winning exhibitor of horses at the Royal Agricultural Show. In 1865 he had been corresponding secretary of the Irish National League and in 1876 he was cosecretary of the Daniel O'Connell centenary celebrations. His growing colonial repute and his wealth were augmented in the 1870s by pioneering work in the Lismore and Tweed River district.

Garvan had a natural political instinct and outgrew the constrictions, often sectarian, of municipal affairs. In February 1872 he was defeated for the Hastings seat in the Legislative Assembly but in 1880 won Eden as a free trader. In 1882-83 he claimed that the treasurer, J. Watson [q.v.], and the minister for works, F. A. Wright [q.v.], had breached ministerial standards, but in 1885 supported Henry Parkes's [q.v.] right to criticize members of parliament outside the House. Garvan's political stature increased through his restraining influence in the lively Sydney visit of William and John Redmond [q.v.] in 1883 and by 1885 his tolerance and rationality, revealed as chairman of St Patrick's Day celebrations, helped to allay rising racialism and sectarianism. He became a leading parliamentarian and specialized in informed criticism of governmental accounts; his analysis of railway administration helped Parkes in 1888 to separate it from political influence. As colonial politics ramified in response to financial stresses Garvan, somewhat against his grain, became more actively involved. He concluded that income taxation and extra customs duties were needed and in February 1886 moved the motion that brought down John Robertson's [q.v.] ministry but as minister of justice under Patrick Jennings [q.v.] he could do little to alleviate political confusion. When Parkes made free trade and protection the clear-cut issue at the elections of February 1887 Garvan became a protectionist and toyed with the idea of becoming the party's leader. In January-March 1889 he was treasurer under George Dibbs [q.v.] and in defence of W. P. Crick warned parliament: 'Be careful lest in the exercise of power by a majority you do not stamp out that hope of liberty which must manifest itself more in a minority than anywhere else'. A convinced federationist, chiefly because of his grasp of banking and currency, he was proposed by Parkes as a member of the 1891 convention but was displaced by Dibbs. Pressure of business reduced his zest for politics and he lost his seat in 1894.

Political disorder and Parkes's domination of parliament in 1887-91 had helped Garvan to decide to consolidate his insurance ventures. In December 1886, influenced by the success of the Prudential Assurance Co. of England, he founded the Citizens' Life Assurance Co. Ltd to concentrate on industrial insurance to enable workmen to buy small insurance on low premiums. His integrity and insight helped him, as managing director, to recruit skilful and devoted assistants, and despite envious and ignorant critics the enterprise rapidly prospered. 'As to whether he was the first to introduce Industrial Assurance to any part of Australia is a matter of small importance. There is no doubt whatever that he was the first to prove that [it] could be made to pay in this country'. Under Garvan's eldest son, John, the company amalgamated in 1898 with the Mutual Life Association of Australia to form the Mutual Life and Citizens' Assurance Co.

In 1871 at Sydney Garvan had married Mary Genevieve, daughter of Dr Glissan. Leaving an estate of £21,445 and survived by his wife, six sons and six daughters, he died on 20 November 1896 at North Sydney and was buried in the Catholic section of Rookwood cemetery. His remains were later transferred to South Head cemetery. Edmund Barton aptly pointed to his 'entirety of life, adorned with consistent principle, filled up in the discharge of virtuous duty, with nothing to conceal, no friendship broken, no confidence betrayed, no timid surrender to popular clamour, no eager reaches for popular favour'.

A'sian Insurance and Banking Record, 16 Nov 1889; Aust Financial Gazette and Insurance Chronicle, 7 Mar, 11 Dec 1896; Town and Country J, 21 Apr 1883; Parkes letters (ML); information from Duncan McCorquodale, Wahroonga, NSW.   BEDE NAIRN

GAUNSON, DAVID (1846-1909), solicitor and politician, was born on 19 January 1846 at Sydney, son of Francis Gaunson, grocer and tea dealer and elder in Rev. J. D. Lang's [q.v.] Scots Church, and his wife Elizabeth, née Wakeman. He was educated at schools in Sydney and, after the family moved to Melbourne in the 1850s, at Brighton. In 1862 he was articled to his brother-in-law, J. M. Grant [q.v.] and in 1869 was admitted as an attorney. After three vain attempts in 1871-72 to enter the Legislative Assembly, Gaunson was elected for Ararat at a by-election in May 1875. Under the patronage of Grant and Graham Berry [q.v.], he quickly won repute as the leading young native-born Liberal and was a conspicuous 'stonewaller' against the McCulloch [q.v.] government. He was prominent as a jingoist speaker at the Melbourne demonstration in support of Disraeli in July 1878. During his term as chairman of committees of the assembly in 1880-81, Gaunson was engaged as counsel in defence of Ned Kelly [q.v.] and was prominent in arranging the mass meeting and petition in support of clemency. In July 1881 when he was appointed minister of lands in the stopgap O'Loghlen-Bent [qq.v.] government, his outraged constituents rejected him in the ministerial election.

'Endowed with a musical voice, good presence, fine flow of language, great quickness of mind, readiness of retort and a good deal of industry, ability and humour, he was only disqualified from marked successes by his utter instability, egregious egotism, want of consistency and violence of temper'. Deakin's description appears to be, for him, unusually charitable. As member for Emerald Hill from October 1883 to March 1889, Gaunson made an appalling reputation for himself as the most unruly member and was regarded with pity or contempt by most members. He allied himself with the small opposition group led by Bent in which C. E. Jones [q.v.] was also conspicuous for almost constant obstructionism. In the 1887 session Gaunson spoke 308 times, often for several hours. He was legal adviser to Madame Brussels, keeper of Melbourne's most famous brothel, and to the Licensed Victuallers' Association. As one of the liquor industry's chief parliamentary spokesmen he appeared to overdo his maxim that a man should get drunk once a month for his health's sake. He was accused of accepting money to represent the interests of private individuals in parliament. He also had links with the railwaymen's trade union and often made vicious attacks on R. Speight [q.v.], chairman of the railways commission.

From 1889 Gaunson formed legal partnerships in turn with J. Wallace, F. W. Cumbrae-Stewart and A. McG. Lonie. In the mid-1890s John Wren, financier and gambling entrepreneur, became one of his clients. The association is depicted in Frank Hardy's novel, Power without Glory, in which 'Garside' shows much similarity to Gaunson. He once boasted that he had cheated Pentridge of more deserving tenants than any other practitioner in Victoria. In 1903 he presided over a public meeting in Melbourne addressed by the visiting John Norton. In June 1904 Gaunson returned to politics and was successful as Labor candidate for the public servants who briefly had separate representation. He had not been a member of the Labor Party but signed the platform; almost immediately he left the party in order to support his old friend Bent, who was premier.

In 1875 Gaunson married Margaret McLeod Scott; they had two sons and two daughters. His brother William, who survived him, had been prominent in the 1870s in the Australian Natives' Association and in politics, although he was never elected to parliament. Gaunson had been a church organist in his youth, but he abandoned churchgoing and stated that he worshipped God according to his conscience. He died at Camberwell on 2 January 1909. Bent and Wren were among his pallbearers.

A. Deakin, The crisis in Victorian politics, 1879-1881, J. A. La Nauze and R. M. Crawford eds (Melb, 1957); K. Dunstan, Wowsers (Melb, 1968); PD (Vic), 1884, 523, 1886, 494; Leader (Melb), 26 Sept 1888; Argus, 2 Mar 1889; Bulletin, 7 Jan 1909; Labor Call, 7 Jan 1909.

GEOFFREY SERLE

GAUNT, WILLIAM HENRY (1830-1905), judge, was born on 27 July 1830 at

Leek, Staffordshire, England, son of John Gaunt, banker, and his wife Mary, née Bakewell. Educated at Leek Grammar School and Whitchurch, Salop, he migrated to Melbourne, and entered the Victorian public service and was rapidly promoted. By March 1854 he was chief clerk at Beechworth, the administrative centre of the Ovens goldfield. In July 1855 the resident warden commended Gaunt as 'a highly valuable public servant' with an intimate knowledge of the district and the 'temper and disposition of the miners'. Appointed sub-warden in the Beechworth district in January 1856 and a Chinese protector in August, he was given control of the extensive Woolshed district. When European miners attacked a party of Chinese at the Buckland River diggings in May 1857 Gaunt was sent to restore order. One of his proclamations, issued in Chinese characters, concluded 'W. H. Gaunt, your protector—tremble and obey!' In June he was appointed a police magistrate and next month was sent to take charge at the Buckland where the Chinese had been expelled from the diggings; the police force assisting him was led by R. O'H. Burke [q.v.]. In January 1858 Gaunt was appointed a warden, in November was transferred to Chiltern, north of Beechworth, and in August 1859 was made a commissioner of crown lands.

In February 1860 Gaunt was appointed a coroner of Victoria, acting at Indigo, near Chiltern. In April 1865 he was transferred to Beechworth, became visiting justice of the gaol and later moved to Sandhurst. In January 1869 he was appointed returning officer for the mining district of Ballarat and visiting justice of the gaol. He was associated with this area for the rest of his life and won high repute for his integrity. In 1874 he chaired the inaugural meeting of the first Australian competitive swimming club. For years he studied law and was called to the Bar in December 1873. He was one of the many public servants dismissed by Graham Berry [q.v.] on 9 January 1878 (Black Wednesday). After petitioning the Queen in vain over his dismissal he began practice in Ballarat as a barrister. He soon became a leading authority on mining laws; one of the cases in which he was involved was the lengthy inquest on the bodies of the twenty-two miners drowned in the New Australasian mine disaster at Creswick in 1882. He was appointed a temporary judge of the Insolvency Court in 1889 and a County Court judge in 1891. In 1900 he was chairman of the royal commission which considered Metropolitan Board of Works matters, and in 1902 was president of the inquiry into the unification of municipalities in Victoria.

In 1860 Gaunt married Elizabeth Mary, the youngest daughter of Frederick Palmer; they had nine children. Of the surviving five sons and a daughter, Ernest Frederick Augustus and Guy Reginald Arthur both became admirals and were knighted; Cecil Robert became a lieut-colonel, Clive Herbert a government advocate in Rangoon and Mary (Mrs H. L. Miller) one of the first women students to enrol at the University of Melbourne (1881), although she did not complete her degree; she became a successful novelist.

Gaunt died on 5 October 1905. An anonymous colleague said: 'I don't think he was ever excelled as a police magistrate, and during the many years he was on the County Court bench he earned the highest regard. His capacities were as unquestioned as his integrity, and more could not be said of any judge'.

V&P (LA Vic), 1878, 3, (58); *Government Gazette* (Vic), 22 Feb, 15 Aug 1856, 30 June 1857, 5 Jan 1858, 16 Aug 1859, 3 Feb 1860, 7 Mar, 11 Oct 1862, 28 Mar, 4 Apr 1865, 17 May 1867, 9 June 1868, 22, 29 Jan 1869; *Ovens and Murray Advertiser*, 21 May 1857, 11 Mar 1865; Col Sec in-letters, goldfields, 25 Mar 1854, 21 July, 18 Nov 1855, 22 Aug 1857 (VA); scrapbook and newspaper cuttings (held by M. Desmond Gaunt, Ballarat).

AUSTIN DOWLING

GEIKIE, ARCHIBALD CONSTABLE (1821-1898), Presbyterian minister, was born on 22 July 1821 in Edinburgh, son of Rev. Archibald Geikie and his wife Ellen, née Bayne. From the High School he went to the University of Edinburgh for one session in 1839-40 and then studied in Glasgow for the Congregational ministry at Queen's College and the Theological Academy. In 1843 failing eyesight forced him to quit his studies and he went with his father to Canada. In 1845 he was ordained to the Congregational ministry and wrote for the *Toronto Globe*. In 1852 he returned to Europe and in 1853-54 was minister of the British and American Chapel in St Petersburg. In 1854 he returned to Canada to work in journalism there and the United States. Finding Canadian Congregationalism very different from Presbyterianized Independency, he became a Presbyterian minister in 1855 and settled at St Andrew's Church, Berlin (Kitchener), Ontario. Later he was assistant to Dr John Bayne of Galt, Ontario. In 1843 in Canada he had married Sarah Johnson, daughter of W. H. Wisener of Tennessee. In November 1858 at Orillia, Canada, he married Elizabeth Murdoch (d. 1881).

When Bayne died, Geikie returned to Scotland and was commissioned by the Free

Church of Scotland for service in Australia. He arrived in Sydney in October 1861, joined the Synod of New South Wales and from Bombala ministered in the Monaro. Translated to Bowenfels in 1863, he went in 1866 to St Stephen's, Bathurst, where he had a notable ministry. He worked patiently, drawing on Canadian experience, for Presbyterian union and in 1864 was elected moderator of the General Synod which united the Synods of New South Wales and Eastern Australia preliminary to the final Presbyterian union in 1865. He was elected moderator of the United Church in 1871. Geikie's work was recognized by honorary degrees from Hanover College, Ohio (D.D., 1872), Queen's University, Ontario (LL.D., 1884) and the University of St Andrews (D.D., 1885). He retired from the ministry on 17 December 1895 and in 1893-98 served on the Council of St Andrew's College, University of Sydney. He was a member of the Royal Society of Antiquaries, Scotland. He died at Woollahra on 29 July 1898 and was buried in Rookwood cemetery. He was survived by his third wife Elsbeth Cooper, née McPherson, whom he had married in Sydney in 1886, by a daughter of his first marriage, and by four sons and a daughter of his second. His estate was valued at £3000. Memorial windows are in St Stephen's, Bathurst, and St Andrew's College Chapel.

Geikie had strong convictions and a satirical wit. He shone more as a debater in the Church courts than as a preacher. These skills were always at the service of high ideals of the ministry. His published works included *Christian missions to wrong places, among wrong races, and in wrong hands* (1871), *The Human Sympathies of Christ* (nd), *The Presbyterian Union of 1865 and notices of some who wrought it* (1896) and at least two sermons.

J. Cameron, *Centenary history of the Presbyterian Church in New South Wales* (Syd, 1905); J. Waugh, *St. Stephen's, Bathurst, 1832-1932* (Bathurst, 1932); *Australian Witness*, 1 Jan, 1, 22, 29 Apr 1876, 19, 26 Mar 1881, 27 Jan 1883, 24 May 1885; *Presbyterian Messenger* (Syd), 1 Sept 1898; *Scotsman*, 22 Feb 1896; General Assembly, Minutes 1896, 1899 (NSW Presbyterian Lib, Assembly Hall, Syd); letters and reports, Bowenfels and Bathurst (NSW Presbyterian Lib, Assembly Hall, Syd).

                                        ALAN DOUGAN

GEOGHEGAN, PATRICK BONAVENTURE (1805-1864), Roman Catholic bishop, was born in Dublin and baptized on 17 March 1805. He was orphaned at the age of 8 and relations of his father who were not Catholics arranged for his admission to a Protestant institution. He was rescued by a Franciscan priest and placed in an orphanage. Later the Franciscans sent Geoghegan to school at Edgeworthstown, County Longford, and then to a college in Lisbon. Eager to become a Franciscan priest he was transferred to the Franciscan training school at Coimbra, Portugal. After completing his studies he was ordained priest on Easter Saturday, 1835. He was appointed to St Francis's Church, Dublin, where in 1837 he was interviewed by Dr Ullathorne [q.v.] who was recruiting priests for the Australian Catholic Mission. Geoghegan volunteered to go for seven years. Given £150 for his outfit and passage by the Colonial Office he sailed in the *Francis Spaight* and arrived at Sydney on 31 December. He was appointed to Bathurst but after four months Bishop Polding [q.v.] sent him to establish the first Catholic mission in Melbourne.

Some three thousand Catholics were then in the area out of a population of about ten thousand. Geoghegan lost no time in putting up 'almost in the open air . . . a poor temporary altar' and celebrated the first Mass on Pentecost Sunday, 19 May. A week later he notified his flock that 'a plain commodious church' had to be built and that they were to cultivate 'kind liberable feeling and deportment toward the members of all religious persuasions'. The government gave him a salary of £150 and a land grant at the corner of Elizabeth and Lonsdale Streets where he built a temporary church, a presbytery and a school. On 4 October 1841 he laid the foundation stone of St Francis's Church. In April-September 1842 he was in Sydney and again briefly in 1843. In Melbourne in July he narrowly escaped being hit by a bullet fired in an encounter between members of the Orange Society and Catholics, mostly Irish born, whom he was trying to restrain. He was made vicar-forane by Archbishop Polding. On 23 October 1845 he opened the completed Church of St Francis. On 30 October 1846 he left Melbourne for Hobart Town on his way, it was wrongly thought, for Ireland but was back in April 1847. Rumour then held that he was to be the first Catholic bishop of Melbourne. However, J. A. Goold [q.v.] was appointed to the Melbourne see and on 6 August 1848 chose Geoghegan as his vicar-general. Early that year Geoghegan had visited the new Anglican bishop, Charles Perry [q.v.], but received what even many Protestants regarded as an ungracious rebuff. In March 1849 Geoghegan left for Ireland to recruit priests for the Australian mission. He returned in April 1851. In 1852 to the select committee on education in Victoria 'he gave a most complete exposition of

Catholic views on the respective roles of the Church, the family, and the state in education'.

When Dr Murphy [q.v.] died in 1858 Geoghegan was appointed bishop of Adelaide. He was consecrated in St Francis's, Melbourne, on 8 Septémber 1859 and enthroned in St Francis Xavier's Cathedral, Adelaide, on 1 November. Deeply troubled by the education system in South Australia he 'exhorted pastors and their flocks to an united effort to establish Catholic schools in their respective localities'. With the help of 30,000 francs from the Propagation of the Faith, several schools were opened. He also built twenty new churches and the chancel and side altars of his cathedral. To recruit dedicated priests for the diocese he left for Europe in February 1862 but in Rome on 10 March 1864 was translated at his own request to the new see of Goulburn, New South Wales. In Dublin he was extremely ill when an old throat ailment became a cancer. He died on 9 May 1864 at Kingstown (Dunleary) and was buried in the old Church of St Francis, Merchants Quay, Dublin.

Father Geoghegan, according to one who knew him in the early days in Melbourne, was 'a round, chubby, natty little man, a perfect picture of health and cheerfulness'. At his best when faced with problems, he admitted to being very sensitive and easily hurt, a disposition which led him into errors of judgment as well as much suffering. An inclination to excessive fault-finding alienated some of the priests in Melbourne and Adelaide.

A portrait in oils is in the dining room of the Archbishop's House, West Terrace, Adelaide.

P. F. Moran, *History of the Catholic Church in Australasia* (Syd, 1895); F. Byrne, *History of the Catholic Church in South Australia* (Adel, 1896); F. Mackle, *The footprints of our Catholic pioneers* (Melb, 1924); R. Fogarty, *Catholic education in Australia 1806-1950* (Melb, 1959); Geoghegan papers (Roman Catholic Archives, Syd, Melb and Adel).

OSMUND THORPE

GEORGE, HENRY (1839-1897), social reformer, was born on 2 September 1839 in Philadelphia, United States of America, the first son of Richard Samuel Henry George and his wife Catherine Pratt, née Vallance. Brought up in a puritanical family George was educated at Mrs Graham's school, Mount Vernon Grammar School, the Episcopal Academy and after five months at high school became a messenger boy and then a clerk. In 1855 he sailed for Mel-

bourne in the crew of the *Hindoo*, went on to India and thence to America in April 1856. In December he was in San Francisco where in 1858-59, between bouts of gold-prospecting, he worked as a typesetter. He joined the Methodists and on 3 December 1861 married Annie Corsina, Sydney-born daughter of Major John Fox and his wife Elizabeth, née McCloskey. Irregular employment kept them poor until he became managing editor of the San Francisco *Times* in 1866. By then he had perfected a simple but emotional literary style studded with biblical allusions. A maturing curiosity for social and political problems had emerged in 1865 when he turned from protection to free trade. In 1868 his article 'What the Railroad Will Bring Us' analysed the tendency to concentrate increasing national wealth in fewer hands, a conviction confirmed by a visit to New York. He was an active Democrat but his pamphlet, *Our Land and Land Policy* (1871), argued against private ownership of land, exposed the predatory nature of rent and stressed the need for a tax on land values only. In 1879 his definitive *Progress and Poverty* won him repute as a leading American reformer. In 1880 he settled in New York. In 1880-89 he made several visits to Britain and with the publication of *Social Problems* (1883) became an international figure.

George's theories spread to Australia chiefly through the *Bulletin* in 1883. In 1887 the Land Nationalisation League was founded in Sydney to propagate his and A. R. Wallace's beliefs. Reformed in 1889 as the Single Tax League it was led by F. Cotton, John Farrell [q.v.], E. W. Foxall, C. L. Garland, W. Johnson and P. Meggy. In America in 1889 Garland arranged for George to visit Australia and with Farrell as campaign director he arrived in Sydney on 6 May 1890 in the *Mariposa*. His reforming appeal was still strong but his remedies had been devastatingly criticized even by Australians. His antagonism to socialism and trade unionism alienated much working-class and radical support at a time of political and industrial turbulence and his objections to private property frightened land-owners. Above all, his free-trade views, even in New South Wales, isolated him from the rising tide of protection. This diverse but powerful hostility was increased by the intense fervour of George's supporters: at a banquet on 7 March Garland had introduced him with 'Ecce Homo !' The result of his campaign in Queensland, Victoria, South Australia and New South Wales was negligible. The *Bulletin* especially, the *Sydney Morning Herald* and the *Age* helped to ensure that Georgeism had no future in Australia. He left in June 1890 and died on

28 October 1897 in New York and was buried in Greenwood cemetery, Brooklyn.

George's influence has been overrated by several historians and publicists. None of his doctrines was original and all were theoretically and practically flawed however beguilingly propagated. His views on leasehold and taxation of unimproved land value were held independently by many Australians and their partial legislative adoption owed little to George. His central ideas of the 'unearned increment' and single tax are now historical curiosities.

Henry George jun., *The life of Henry George* (Lond, 1900); L. F. Post, *The prophet of San Francisco* (New York, 1930); S. B. Cord, *Henry George: dreamer or realist* (Philadelphia, 1965); L. G. Churchward, 'The American influence on the Australian Labour Movement', *Hist Studies*, no 19, Nov 1952; F. Picard, 'Henry George and the Labor split of 1891', *Hist Studies*, no 21, Nov 1953; J. M. Powell, 'The land debates in Victoria, 1872-1884', *JRAHS*, 56 (1970).   BEDE NAIRN

GERSTAECKER, FRIEDRICH (1816-1872), writer and traveller, was born on 10 May 1816 in Hamburg, son of Friedrich Gerstaecker (1790-1825), opera singer. At an early age he entered an office but later went on the land. In 1837 he migrated to America where he led 'a wild and adventurous life'. On his return to Germany in 1843 he established himself as a writer of travel books. Factual accounts of his own experiences and guides for intending migrants were followed by novels on American life that made him famous in Germany. In 1849 he went from South America to the goldfields of California and thence to Australia by way of the South Sea islands. He arrived in Sydney in March 1851, took a coach to Albury and attempted to paddle down the Murray River in a self-made canoe. When it was wrecked he tramped 700 miles to Adelaide, 'the wildest and most dangerous march' of his life. He visited the German settlements in South Australia but in August the first news of the gold strike hurried him back to Sydney and the Bathurst diggings. He next went to the Dutch East Indies but in 1852 was back in Germany as an author and journalist, living in turn in Leipzig, Gotha, Coburg, Dresden and Braunschweig. In 1860-61 he was in South America, observing the German colonists there. Next year he visited Egypt and Abyssinia, and a fourth voyage in 1867-68 took him to the United States, Mexico, Ecuador and the West Indies. In 1870 he was war correspondent for a popular journal. He died on 31 May 1872.

Gerstaecker was a prolific writer; the first edition of *Gesammelte Schriften* (Jena, 1872-79) in forty-three volumes is incomplete. His novels and stories, based on experience and an extensive reading of travel books, are unsophisticated narratives of exciting adventures in far-away countries, but contain much ethnographical and geographical detail. The characterization is sketchy and the descriptions of exotic nature lack polish. The great success of his books in Germany was largely due to the sharp contrast they presented between the wide world and its freedom and the narrow parochialism of German life.

The increasing flow of German migrants to Australia probably first aroused Gerstaecker's interest in the continent. In 1849 he compiled a handbook on Australia, *Nord- und Süd-Australien. Ein Handbuch für Auswanderer*, for intending German migrants. His *Narrative of a Journey round the World . . .* (Stuttgart, 1853-54: English translation, London, 1853), vividly describes his adventures in Australia. His most popular Australian novels are *Die beiden Sträflinge* (1856; translated as *The Two Convicts*, 1857), an adventurous story of a noble bushranger which was serialized in the *Examiner and Melbourne Weekly News* from October 1859 to March 1860, and *Im Busch* (1864), set in gold diggings near Sydney. Both deal with problems that he found specially interesting in the Australian scene: the complex relation between convicts, bushrangers, natives and free settlers, the fate of German migrants in Australia and the exciting life of the goldfields. Many of his other works such as *Blau Wasser* (1858), *Inselwelt* (1860) and *Unter Palmen und Buchen* (1865) have an Australian background; in 1853 he translated Charles Rowcroft's [q.v.] *Tales of the Colonies (Bilder aus Australien)*. His books were translated into several languages and, in modernized editions, some of his novels are still favoured reading of young people in German-speaking countries.

E. Seyfarth, *Friedrich Gerstaecker* (Freiburg, 1930), and for bibliog; A. J. Prahl, *Gerstaecker und die probleme seiner zeit* (Mainz, 1938).
                                        LESLIE BODI

GIBBONS, GERALDINE SCHOLASTICA (1817-1901), mother superior, was born in Kinsale, County Cork, Ireland, daughter of Gerald Gibbons, who was connected with Daniel O'Connell and most of the Cork gentry, and his wife Mary, née Sughrue, niece of the bishop of Ferns. Educated in Cork she arrived in Sydney with her family in 1834. Her father's ventures in business were unsuccessful. Geraldine and a sister joined the newly-arrived Sisters of Charity;

on 17 July 1847 Geraldine was professed as Scholastica and began work in the Female Factory at Parramatta. On 9 April 1848 she went to Sydney to establish a home for penitent women in Campbell Street; it was moved to Carter's Barracks in March 1849.

Mother Scholastica succeeded her sister, Mother Ignatius (d. 20 March 1853), as superior of the order in preference to Baptist de Lacy. She launched the appeal to establish St Vincent's Hospital which she entrusted to Sister de Lacy's management while she stayed on alone at the women's home. To relieve the pressure on her, Archbishop Polding [q.v.] decided to found an order following Benedictine rules but suited to Australian conditions. He found a group of volunteers and requested Mother Scholastica to be superior of both orders. On 2 February 1857 she helped to establish the Community of the Good Shepherd which took the name of the Good Samaritan to avoid confusion with a similar congregation in Europe. Both communities prospered under the rule of this efficient, dedicated and retiring nun who always wore the habit of the Charity order while living with the Good Samaritans. In 1859 she was reluctantly involved when St Vincent's Hospital became the centre of an outburst of sectarianism and a cause of Catholic faction fighting. 'The Battle of the Bible', started by a minor misunderstanding, flared up into a major blaze after Sister de Lacy gave a distorted version to J. H. Plunkett [q.v.] and the press.

Mother Scholastica gradually relinquished responsibility in the Charity congregation, although no superior was elected until 1864. On 6 September 1876 she resigned her charge of the Good Samaritans, returned to her original allegiance and served the poor from the Charity Convent in Hobart until 1885. Unable to find the peace she desired, she yielded to the requests of her former novices and returned to Rosebank Convent, Five Dock. Aged 85 she died at Marrickville on 15 October 1901 and was buried in the Catholic section of Rookwood cemetery. In 1945 her body was reinterred at Rosebank College. Two flourishing religious congregations remain as monuments to her zeal and industry.

SMH, 2, 6 June 1859; *Freeman's J* (Syd), 11 June 1859; Roman Catholic Archives (Syd); Sisters of Charity Archives (St Vincent's Convent, Potts Point, NSW); Sisters of the Good Samaritan Archives (St Scholastica's Convent, Glebe, NSW).   C. J. DUFFY

GIBLIN, WILLIAM ROBERT (1840-1887), premier and judge, was born on 4 November 1840 at Hobart Town, son of William Giblin, clerk of the registrar of deeds and deacon in the Congregational Church, and his wife Marion, née Falkiner. He was educated by his uncle and at the Hobart High School but left at 13 to work for the legal firm of Allport [q.v.] & Roberts; he was later articled to John Roberts. Giblin studied not only law but in other fields, reading widely and developing a literary style in his prose and verse. In 1864 he was admitted to the Bar and became a partner of the Hobart barrister, John Dobson, brother of William [q.v.]. His success in the courts was immediate and enabled him on 5 January 1865 to marry Emily Jean, daughter of John Perkins.

Dedicated to the moral and social elevation of the underprivileged, Giblin founded in 1864 the Hobart Working Men's Club, the first of its kind in Australia, and was its president until 1887. He was also a founder and teacher of the Congregational Sunday school and helped in forming football teams to discourage larrikinism. He rowed in early club races and encouraged walking in the mountains. He publicly advocated the building of a railway from Hobart to Launceston for lowering the transport costs of primary producers. All these activities made him popular and in 1869 he was petitioned by hundreds of voters to stand for election to the House of Assembly. He was elected unopposed for Hobart Town and, after electorates were revised, represented Central Hobart in 1871-76 and Wellington in 1877-84. He served as attorney-general under J. M. Wilson [q.v.] for nine months in 1870 and in Kennerley's [q.v.] ministry in 1873-76. He joined the ministry of P. O. Fysh in August 1877 as colonial treasurer and attorney-general, and was premier as well from March to December 1878. From October 1879 to August 1884 he led a coalition government. As premier, treasurer and sometimes attorney-general he reorganized the colony's finances, secured the adoption of an equitable taxation policy and initiated an active programme of public works. In 1883 he represented Tasmania at the Australasian Convention which led to formation of the Federal Council. On 7 February 1885 he was appointed puisne judge of the Supreme Court. As acting chief justice he was administrator of the government in October-November 1886, the first native-born Tasmanian to hold this office. Worn out by heavy responsibilities and heart disease, he died on 17 January 1887.

Alfred Deakin described Giblin as 'remarkably impressive . . . too big for his colony'. By any standards he was a statesman, bringing order out of political chaos and saving the colony from long stagnation.

His integrity, both public and private, was unusually high. He was brilliant and convincing in debate especially on forensic subjects, skills which won him repute throughout Australia. His philanthropy and active Congregationalism were also well known and his lectures on literary topics were in constant demand. He was survived by his wife, four sons and three daughters. His second son, Lyndhurst Falkiner, was a distinguished scholar, soldier and the first Ritchie professor of economics in the University of Melbourne.

Cyclopedia of Tasmania, 1 (Hob, 1900); B. R. Wise, *The making of the Australian Commonwealth, 1889-1900* (Lond, 1913); F. C. Green (ed), *A century of responsible government 1856-1956* (Hob, 1956); *Mercury*, 4 Feb 1885, 18 Jan 1887; correspondence file under W. R. Giblin (TA).
                                                    E. M. DOLLERY

GIBSON, ANGUS (1842-1920), sugar planter and politician, was born on 25 April 1842 at Kilmaurs, Ayrshire, Scotland, eldest son of William Gibson, farmer, and his wife Mary, née Macalister. In June 1863 Angus and his father sailed for Queensland as assisted immigrants in the *Cairngorm* and settled on a market garden at Doughboy Creek, near Brisbane. His mother and five children followed in the *Warren Hastings* on 27 February 1864. The family began growing sugar on a farm called Clydesdale and the mill they established next year became the social and political centre of the district. On 3 February 1880 Gibson was elected to the new Bulimba Divisional Board. The Clydesdale farm proved too small and, after an exploratory trip through northern sugar areas by Angus in 1882-83, the family sold out, formed a partnership with Howes brothers and bought Bingera plantation near Bundaberg. Their new mill had its first crushing in 1885 and by 1889 the partnership under Gibson's management had a capital of £73,000 and held 2658 acres worked by 98 Europeans, 8 Chinese and 200 Kanakas. In 1894 the firm set up a sugar settlement at Watawa and in 1904 the undertaking was floated as a company.

Although dedicated to sugar Gibson was active in many other fields. He was chairman of the Gooburrum Divisional Board in 1888 and a member of the Kolan board in 1895-1900, served on the licensing board, was active in the local Caledonian Society, chairman of the Bundaberg Harbor Board and the Toowoomba Electric Lighting Co. As a prominent Methodist layman, he represented Bundaberg at Queensland's first Wesleyan congress in 1893 and later Queensland at national congresses. In 1899-1920 he was a nominee in the Legislative Council. His rare speeches were mostly on the sugar industry and in 1901 he was prominent in establishing a Sugar Producers and Manufacturers Union. He had married Catherine Martin on 9 November 1866. He died on 28 May 1920, survived by five daughters and three sons, one of whom succeeded him in the firm. A third generation of the family still controls Bingera.

J. Y. Walker, *The history of Bundaberg* (Bundaberg, 1890); D. Dignan, *The story of Kolan* (Brisb, 1964); C. T. Wood, *Sugar country* (Brisb, 1965); *Sugar J and Tropical Cultivator*, 15 July 1901; *Aust Sugar J*, 1909-21; *Bundaberg Daily News and Mail*, 28 May 1920.
                                                    H. J. GIBBNEY

GIFFEN, GEORGE (1859-1927), cricketer, was born on 27 March 1859 at Adelaide, son of Richard Giffen, carpenter, and his wife Elizabeth, née Challand. Coached as a boy by the Goodens, he played for the Norwood Club. In his first game for South Australia against East Melbourne in 1877 he made top score in each innings and for more than a decade virtually carried the South Australian side on his own shoulders. Against Victoria in 1891 he scored 237 and took 12 wickets for 192. In 1892 he made 271 (a score not surpassed for South Australia until Bradman did so in 1935) and took 16 for 166. For ten years against Victoria he averaged 138 with the bat and 11 wickets a match.

In Australia he made twelve centuries, including four over 200, and six times took eleven or more wickets in a match. In England he made another six centuries, coupling one of them with a hat-trick and another with 7 wickets for 11. In first-class cricket Giffen scored 12,501 runs at an average of 29 and took 1109 wickets at 21 runs each. He once took 17 wickets in a match and once 10 wickets in an innings; he also performed three hat-tricks. In his last match against Victoria in 1903 he made 81 and 97 not out and took 15 wickets for 185. He retired from first-class cricket in 1903 but in 1908 was induced to play once more for South Australia against the Fijians.

Giffen toured England in 1882, 1884, 1886, 1893 and 1896, declining the tours of 1888 and 1890. English conditions suited him a little less well than Australian but in 1886 he headed the side's averages both with bat and ball; in two weeks he captured 46 wickets at an average of 6.5 runs, almost certainly a record. In Tests he was the first to make over 1000 runs and to take over 100 wickets. As Australia's captain in 1894-95 he totalled 475 runs and 34 wickets. In

1898 his reminiscences, *With bat and ball*, were published in London. He worked in the Adelaide post office in 1882-1925, and died unmarried on 29 November 1927.

At his best Giffen had remarkable defensive powers. He scored mainly in front of the wicket since the fast Adelaide wicket encouraged driving. He bowled slow-medium off-breaks and his subtle changes of pace obtained many wickets caught-and-bowled through a slower dropping ball. His toll might have been higher if South Australia had played New South Wales a decade earlier and if in Test matches he had not coincided with such formidable bowlers as Spofforth, Turner and Boyle [qq.v.]. With strong faith in his own bowling which sometimes proved expensive, Giffen could be cantankerous as a captain, but he was Australia's first great all-rounder.

A stand in the Adelaide Oval is named after him and a portrait is in the pavilion.

R. H. Lyttleton et al, *Giants of the game* (Lond, 1899); H. S. Altham, *A history of cricket* (Lond, 1926); C. B. O'Reilly, *South Australian cricket 1880-1930* (Adel, 1930); S. Smith, *History of the tests* (Syd, 1946); A. G. Moyes, *A century of cricketers* (Lond, 1950); A. G. Moyes, *Australian bowlers* (Syd, 1953); A. G. Moyes, *Australian batsmen* (Syd, 1954); R. Binns, *Cricket in firelight*, 2nd ed (Lond, 1955).

CHRISTOPHER MORRIS

GILBERT, JOHN (1842?-1865), bushranger, was born in Hamilton, Canada, son of William John Gilbert. In October 1852 he arrived at Melbourne in the *Revenue* with his family. He soon left home and worked as a stable-boy in Kilmore before drifting to the goldfields where he associated with gamesters and petty thieves and attracted suspicion by his flashy dress and 'flush of money'. At 18 after moving into New South Wales he met Frank Gardiner [q.v.] at Kiandra and in 1860-61 joined his raids in the Wheogo district. 'A superb horseman', his 'certain cheerful charm and courage' appealed to Gardiner. On 15 June 1862 Gilbert took part in the Eugowra gold escort robbery and like Gardiner had a £500 reward on his head. Soon afterwards he rescued his brother Charlie and Henry Mann, who had been arrested by Sir Frederick Pottinger [q.v.], and then vanished for about nine months.

In May 1863 Gilbert returned to the Weddin Mountains and became Ben Hall's [q.v.] right-hand man although they did not always work together. In July 1863 with John O'Meally he held up the bank at Carcoar in broad daylight but the alarm was given before they took any loot. He was with Hall in the affair at Bathurst, 'the piratical descent on Canowindra' and the raids on H. Keightley and Goimbla station when Mickey Burke and O'Meally were killed. Early in 1864 Gilbert went to Victoria but soon returned to join Hall and John Dunn. On 17 November the gang robbed the Gundagai-Yass mail after a battle with the police in which Gilbert killed Sergeant Parry. On 27 December the gang rode into Binda, robbed Morris's store and attended a dance at the Flag Hotel. Morris's store was later burnt in revenge for his attempt to capture the bushrangers. In January 1865 they attended the Wowingragang races and mixed with the punters including Pottinger who failed to recognize them. On 27 January at Collector when Constable Nelson was mortally wounded by Dunn, Gilbert took the dead policeman's gun-belt. Between 2 February 1862 and 10 April 1865 Gilbert took part in at least forty-four armed hold-ups and robberies in New South Wales, including the theft of five race-horses and eighteen other mounts.

Gilbert and Dunn were proclaimed outlaws in April under the Felons Apprehension Act with £1000 on each of their heads. Gilbert was shot by Constable John Bright on 13 May and buried in the police paddock at Binalong. Dunn managed to escape but was captured in January 1866 and hanged in March.

Sydney Mail, 20 May 1865; *Illustrated Sydney News*, 16 June 1865; Bertie cuttings, vol 31 (NL).

EDGAR F. PENZIG

GILBERT, JOSEPH (1800-1881), pastoralist and vigneron, was born in May 1800 at Puckshipton, Wiltshire, England, the second of four sons of Joseph Gilbert and his wife Jane, née Pike. He was educated at Marlborough College and on the Continent learnt much of vine-growing and wine-making.

In 1838 his mother died and Gilbert sailed in the *Buckinghamshire* for South Australia. He reached Holdfast Bay on 21 March 1839 and went in search of land while waiting for the sheep he had ordered from Van Diemen's Land. In July he applied for a special survey in Lyndoch Valley where he transferred his Tasmanian sheep and began to build a house. The property was named first Karrawatta and then Pewsey Vale. He soon won repute for his fine wool, careful breeding of imported thoroughbreds and Shorthorn cattle, acclimatization of English deer, his garden and his stables. He planted his first vines in 1847 and was licensed to distil spirits in 1849. The vineyard was destroyed by frosts in 1855 but was soon replanted and before long his wine and cellars won deserved fame. He constructed a reservoir at Pewsey Vale and built a school for resident families and in 1861 a chapel, designed by the architect Edward Hamilton, and named in memory of his brother Thomas of Marden, Wiltshire.

Gilbert soon had to find more land for his increasing flocks. He leased Mount Bryan in 1851, McVittie's Flat in 1853 and several runs on Yorke Peninsula in 1859-70. He bought a large acreage in the hundreds of Hallett and Kingston in 1860-64 and sections in the Upper Wakefield and Hill River special surveys in 1850. He was also a director and trustee of the Mount Remarkable Mining Co. in 1850-54. He leased Owen Springs in the Northern Territory in 1871 and Macumba on the Finke River in 1872. In Adelaide he had also acquired a town acre on which the Bank of Australasïa was built and an original country section where the suburb of Gilberton now stands; it was surveyed and sold in blocks in the 1870s. At Wongalere station on 21 January 1848 Gilbert had married Anna (b. 26 April 1812), sister of Dr W. J. Browne [q.v.]. Anna died of pneumonia on 23 September 1873. Joseph remained active until a week before he died on 23 December 1881. He was buried with his wife at Pewsey Vale and left an estate valued at £37,000. Of their four children the only son, William (1850-1923), was educated at the Collegiate School of St Peter and in England and after pastoral experience managed his father's properties from 1875; on 22 July 1879 he married Mary Young Clindening by whom he had eleven children.

A point on Yorke Peninsula perpetuates Gilbert's name and a memorial tablet is in the church he built. An oil painting of his family by A. Schramm is in the Henry Gilbert private hospital, Le Fevre Terrace, Adelaide.

G. C. Morphett, *The Gilberts of Pewsey Vale* (Adel, 1949); R. Cockburn, Nomenclature of South Australia (revised typescript, SAA, ML); family history and papers (held by Misses Gilbert, Stirling, SA). MARJORIE FINDLAY

GILES, ERNEST (1835-1897), explorer, was born on 20 July 1835 at Bristol, England, son of William Giles, merchant, and his wife Jane Elizabeth, née Powell. Educated at Christ's Hospital he followed his parents to Adelaide in 1850. He moved to Victoria in 1852, tried his luck on the goldfields without success and became a post office clerk in Melbourne. By 1861 he was in western New South Wales where until 1865 he engaged in several expeditions aimed at assessing the pastoral country be-

yond the Darling River. These journeys gave him both the experience and the taste for further exploration.

In 1872 Giles was chosen to lead a small expedition organized by Dr Mueller [q.v.] to investigate parts of central Australia west of the new overland telegraph line. From Charlotte Waters the party followed the Finke valley to the Missionaries' Plain south of the MacDonnell Ranges but found its way blocked to the west by lack of water and to the south by the salt-pans of Lake Amadeus which Giles named. There his second-in-command, Carmichael, insisted on turning back despite Giles's wish to find a route to the coast of Western Australia. This ambition was to inspire his remaining expeditions, the first of which, again backed by Mueller, was assembled next year. Starting further south Giles followed the line of the Musgrave Ranges which, unknown to him, had just been discovered by Gosse [q.v.]. On reaching Mount Olga which he had earlier named from a distance, Giles found from Gosse's draytracks that he had been anticipated but since they soon turned back he was encouraged to persevere. He spent the next summer trying to break through to the west from a base in the Tomkinson Range and in autumn persisted in attacking the desert from a northerly point in the Rawlinson Range. A desperate final effort cost him the life of one of his men, who gave his name to Gibson's Desert, and brought Giles himself close to death; the exhaustion of his supplies compelled him to retreat, defeated, to the overland telegraph line.

Although forestalled by P. E. Egerton [q.v.] and John Forrest, Giles succeeded in his cherished aim of making an overland crossing from South to Western Australia in 1875. Equipped with camels by Thomas Elder [q.v.], he set out from Beltana and went for supplies to Port Augusta whence he proceeded first north-west and then west along a string of waterholes, Wynbring, Ooldea, Ooldabinna and Boundary Dam, until he reached the Western Australian border. He then risked a 312-mile marathon across the Great Victoria Desert before discovering the Queen Victoria Springs; from there he was able to complete his journey to Perth in fairly easy stages. On the return trip in 1876 he went north to the Murchison and Ashburton Rivers, crossed Gibson's Desert and reached the Rawlinson Ranges where he had been held up in 1874. He thus achieved a double crossing of the western half of the Australian continent.

Although Giles found little good country, his expeditions added substantially to the knowledge of central Australia. He published *Geographic Travels in Central Aus-*

tralia from 1872 to 1874 (Melbourne, 1875), *The Journal of a Forgotten Expedition* (Adelaide, 1880) and a full account of his journeys in two volumes, *Australia Twice Traversed* (London, 1889). For his explorations he was made a knight of the crown of Italy, honorary member of several Continental societies and in 1880 fellow and gold medallist of the Royal Geographical Society, London. The South Australian government granted him £250 for each of his expeditions in 1872 and 1874 and a lease of some 2000 square miles in the Northern Territory after 1876 but he was refused official appointment because, as Governor Jervois claimed on 11 October 1881, 'I am informed that he gambles and that his habits are not always strictly sober'. Giles was a land classifier in the Western District of Victoria in 1877-79, briefly revisited the Musgrave Ranges in 1882, represented a prospecting company he had formed in the Kimberleys in the 1890s and joined the rush to Coolgardie. There he became a clerk in the warden's office and on 13 November 1897 died of bronchial pneumonia.

Although Giles made no major discoveries, he is among the more interesting Australian explorers by virtue of his journals which, although overwritten, display a fine descriptive ability and constitute a record of inner experience as well as outward observation. His culture, perception and imagination were no less marked than his skill and determination.

E. B. Dow, *On the Burke and Wills track: the Giles inscription* (Broken Hill, 1937); G. Rawson, *Desert journeys* (Syd, 1948); L. Green, *Ernest Giles* (Melb, 1963); J. Young, 'Recent journey of exploration across the continent of Australia . . .', American Geog Soc, J, 10 (1878); W. H. Tietkens, 'Experiences in the life of an Australian explorer', *JRAHS*, 5 (1919); L. Green, 'A Voss among the explorers . . .', *Quadrant*, 7 (1963); CO 13/139.

LOUIS GREEN

GILFILLAN, ROBERT (1823-1909), merchant and auditor, was born on 5 December 1823 at Borrowstounness, Linlithgowshire, Scotland, son of James Gilfillan, excise officer, and his wife Charlotte, née Anderson. He probably learnt some accounting from his father. In April 1848 he arrived at Auckland, New Zealand, in the *Richard Dart* with merchandise ranging from boots to chloroform. In January 1849 he was licensed as an auctioneer. In April his brother John Anderson arrived in the *Lalla Rookh*. The brothers set up as merchants and commission agents. In June Robert organized a meeting of subscribers to the Presbyterian Church. On 30 July 1852 he

left Auckland in the *Raven* and reached Sydney on 22 August. He described his protracted and uncomfortable crossing in a letter to his parents. He apparently succeeded in disposing of some of his heavy stocks of English goods, returned to Auckland and in February 1853 sailed for London in the *Fancy*. On 28 February 1854 he married Margaret, née Fraser, at Cullen, Banffshire.

He returned to Sydney with his wife in the *Royal Lily* the same year and traded for many years as Gilfillan & Co., importers and merchants. A director of the Australian Mutual Provident Society in 1862-66, he was also its auditor eleven times between 1870 and 1886. Gilfillan lived at Quiberee, Lavender Bay. He died on 17 July 1909 at North Sydney and was buried in the churchyard of St Thomas's Church of England where he had been a regular worshipper. He was survived by his wife, four sons and three daughters. His estate was valued at £1143.

NZ Government Gazette (Province of New Ulster), 25 Jan 1849; *New Zealander*, 29 Apr 1848, 10 Feb, 21 Apr, 30 June 1849, 2 Feb 1853; AMP Soc Archives (Syd); letters and papers (held by Miss H. M. A. Gilfillan, Roseville, NSW).

HAROLD F. BELL

GILL, HENRY HORATIO (1840-1914), explorer, farmer, prospector and newspaper proprietor, was born in October 1840 and baptized on 26 July 1846 at St George's Church, Battery Point, Hobart Town, the eldest son of William Henry Gill and his wife Susannah, née McLowe. Henry's grandfather had been lord mayor of London in 1789 and his father an army lieutenant who had arrived in Van Diemen's Land in the *Regalia* on 30 December 1822 and later became chief clerk in the audit department.

After education at the Hutchins School, Henry found employment as a law clerk, probably intending to enter the legal profession, but he soon found that he preferred an outdoor life and took up farming. He then went to New South Wales where he joined several exploring parties. He returned to Tasmania about 1865, leased Llanavan, a large property near Cape Portland, and took up sheep-farming. He became a justice of the peace for the territory on 13 May 1867. On 3 September 1870 he was married at Llanavan by a representative of the Congregational Church to Sara Inez Jacobs. In 1869-71 he was a member of the George Town Board of Works, and in 1879 a councillor of the Rural Municipality of Spring Bay. Meanwhile he had become associated with Bernard Shaw and Renison Bell in discovering tin; he had himself discovered rich gold deposits near the Whyte River. He never lost his interest in mining. In 1906 with his partner, Thomas Batty, he was credited with the discovery of a diamond at Long Plains near Harvey's Creek.

In 1881 Gill was living at Colville Street, Hobart. He bought the *Southern Star* from its proprietors and on 17 November 1883 from 51 Collins Street launched the *Tasmanian News*, an evening paper bearing the motto *publicum bonum privato est proeferendum*. Over his name as editor and proprietor he wrote: 'We issue our first number with a larger list of subscribers than has ever assisted previous enterprise in the same direction here'. The paper ran for about twenty-eight years but by 1896 Gill had retired from journalism and his wife appeared as proprietor for some years after 1890. In 1887 he was induced to contest the Kingborough seat in the House of Assembly and was elected with a large majority. Sound and thorough in debate he kept himself conspicuous as a liberal and with Dr Crowther [q.v.] was credited with responsibility for half the roads and bridges built in his large district. In 1897 he resigned and sailed for England to float a gold mining company.

In 1886 Gill and some members of parliament had attended the opening of the Fingal railway line; on their return journey on 29 June they were involved in an accident near Campania. At the inquiry he was publicly thanked for walking many miles to Brighton to bring help for the injured. His own injuries were not then apparent but he suffered later effects to the end of his life. He was a founder and first secretary of the Rechab Masonic Lodge and later worshipful master and deputy provincial grand master. He died on 4 March 1914 and was buried in the Cornelian Bay cemetery, survived by his wife and six children. According to an obituarist, 'he was a pure lover of his country, a believer in its possibilities, and an honest and conscientious public man'.

W. H. Twelvetrees, *Diamonds in Tasmania* (Mines Department circular, 4, Hob, 1918); *Critic* (Hob), 6 Mar 1914; papers held by the family.   E. R. PRETYMAN

GILL, JAMES HOWARD (1857-1899), solicitor, was born on 31 August 1857 at Ipswich, Queensland, the second son of Richard Gill and his wife Honora, née Howard. His father, born on 8 March 1819 in London, son of George Gill, trader, and his wife Mary, née Woodcroft, had arrived in Sydney on 24 December 1841 and in January 1843 went to South Brisbane. There he set up as a saddler but in 1849 moved to Ipswich in hope that the squatter capital

would offer better opportunities for his business. On 1 October 1854 he was appointed the Ipswich postmaster at £400 a year. As a public servant he was not permitted to stand for the new Queensland parliament in 1860, but as an original subscriber to the Ipswich Grammar School, Queensland's first secondary school, he was appointed a trustee and in 1890-92 chairman of trustees. On 11 March 1848 he had married Honora Howard; they had two sons and a daughter. After Honora died Gill married Mary Anne Boyd in 1875. He died on 21 December 1913 in Brisbane and was buried in the Ipswich cemetery.

James attended Ipswich Grammar School and was *dux* in 1873-74. He showed promise of a brilliant academic career but in 1875 failed to win a proposed government scholarship in the University of Sydney because the institution of these awards had been temporarily deferred. On 6 March 1876 he was articled to G. V. Hellicar of Thompson & Hellicar, solicitors, and became active in founding and directing the Queensland Law Students' Association. Among his associates was John George Appel, whose sister Annie Louise he married at Brisbane on 31 August 1882. Gill had been admitted as a solicitor in April 1881 and started a practice at Ipswich. In 1884 he entered into partnership with Appel who stayed in Brisbane. When the government decided in 1885 to appoint its own crown solicitor Gill was offered the post and accepted. Although his salary of £1000 was much lower than his receipts from private practice he was persuaded that the new office would lead to further advancement and even to the bench. As crown solicitor Gill won repute, not least in 1892-93 when he was active in the arbitration of John Robb's [q.v.] railway contracts, the shearers' cases after the strikes and the settlements after failure of the Queensland National Bank. His most notable work was his share in drafting the Queensland Criminal Code, a monumental achievement undertaken by the chief justice, S. W. Griffith, in 1894 and passed by parliament in 1899.

Gill's hopes of advancement were never realized. In 1893 he fell foul of the attorney-general, T. J. Byrnes, first over political matters and then over his staff. Family tradition maintains that Byrnes wanted to appoint one of his favourites in Gill's place. In 1893 when the wages of civil servants were reduced by 20 per cent, Gill's salary was cut to £600; its increase to £700 in 1896 was also out of accord with the general rise. His health suffered under the strain of work and conflict with Byrnes and he was twice given leave before he died of tuberculosis on 11 October 1899. He was survived by his wife, who in December 1899 received a government grant of £800, and by a son and two daughters. Some of his descendants still practise law in Queensland.

Brisbane Courier, 12 Oct 1899; Supreme Court and Justice Department records (QA); Gill family papers (held by author).

J. C. H. GILL

GILL, MYRA; *see* KEMBLE

GILL, WILLIAM WYATT (1828-1896), missionary, was born on 27 December 1828 at Bristol, England, son of John Gill of Barton Hill and his wife Jane, daughter of Richard Wyatt, yeoman. Nurtured in Kingsland Congregational Chapel, Bristol, he became a member at 14 and his thoughts turned early to the ministry. After three years at Highbury College, London, and a year at New College, University of London (B.A., 1850), he was discouraged from missionary work, but his eagerness to accompany Rev. Aaron Buzacott to the Cook Islands met with approval and in June 1851 he was accepted by the London Missionary Society. He was ordained at Spa Fields Chapel on 11 July and on 15 November arrived at Hobart Town in the mission ship *John Williams*. With Buzacott and Henry Hopkins [q.v.] he visited Launceston, Melbourne and Geelong on missionary work. On 23 November he reached Sydney where he met Mary Layman Harrison, a pious Anglican. According to Buzacott, he 'had to run the risk of his neck to get her having had to go to the "Turon gold diggings" to get her Father's consent' before they were married by Dr R. Ross [q.v.] on 19 December.

Gill worked at Mangaia, Cook Islands, in 1852-72 except for five months in 1858 at Rarotonga in charge of the institution for training native teachers and a visit to Sydney in 1862-63. In 1872 with Rev. A. W. Murray [q.v.] he visited the principal islands in Torres Strait and on 7 November landed the first teachers, including six Cook Islanders, at Kataw in New Guinea. In 1873 he sailed for England where he read to the Royal Geographical Society his paper 'A Visit to Torres Straits and Mainland of New Guinea'. It was included with other articles in his *Life in the Southern Isles; or, Scenes and Incidents in the South Pacific and New Guinea* (London, 1876), a work that established his repute in mission circles. His more scholarly work, *Myths and Songs from the South Pacific* (London, 1876), published at the instigation of Professor Max Müller, did much to improve the missionary image

among scientific workers. Gill resumed missionary work and was stationed on Rarotonga from April 1877 until he retired in November 1883 after his wife died in July. In December Gill went to Sydney and in January 1884 sailed to New Guinea with another party of Rarotongan teachers. In 1885 he published in London an account of this voyage in *Work and Adventure in New Guinea 1877 to 1885*, a work ascribed to James Chalmers [q.v.] and himself, and *Jottings from the Pacific*. Through the influence of Sir George Grey the New Zealand government had published his *Historical Sketches of Savage Life in Polynesia* (Wellington, 1880), which was revised for missionary readers as *From Darkness to Light in Polynesia* (London, 1894).

In Sydney Gill revised the Rarotongan Bible and in 1887-88 went to London to see it through the press with his second wife Emily, née Corrie (1843-1923), whom he had married on 10 June 1885. In 1889 the University of St Andrews conferred on him an honorary doctorate. He returned to Sydney and lived at Marrickville, dogged by ill health but still active in the scientific pursuits he loved. With Rev. Samuel Ella (1823-1899), a missionary colleague, Gill was prominent in the Australasian Association for the Advancement of Science and contributed to the journal of the Polynesian Society. He also published a pamphlet, *The South Pacific and New Guinea*, in 1892. Evangelical and humanitarian in outlook, Gill had conducted revival meetings in the islands and his reports on the Peruvian 'slave trade' did much to influence the British and French governments to take action. He died on 11 November 1896 and was buried in the Waverley cemetery. He was survived by his second wife and by seven of the ten children of his first marriage. His eldest daughter Honor was married to a missionary in Samoa.

J. King, *Ten decades, the Australian centenary story of the London Missionary Society* (Lond, 1895); R. Lovett, *History of the London Missionary Society, 1795-1895*, 1 (Lond, 1899); J. Sibree (ed), *A register of missionaries . . . 1796 to 1923*, London Missionary Society (Lond, 1923); Polynesian Soc, J, Dec 1896; *New Zealand Herald*, 10 Dec 1881; LMS Archives (Westminster); family papers (held by Mr O. Mcd Gill, Rose Bay, NSW).   NIEL GUNSON

GILLBEE, WILLIAM (1825-1885), surgeon, was born in Hackney, London, son of William Gillbee, probably a captain in the duke of Wellington's regiment, and his wife Sarah, née Ward, a beauty in the court of the duke of Clarence. His father died about

1832 and his mother married Bracee Uppington Barfoot. In 1836 she took her family to Van Diemen's Land as assisted migrants. As Mrs Gillbee she was the first matron of the Lying-in Hospital, Melbourne, in 1856-57. William remained at school in Edinburgh and in 1844 entered the university medical school. He won high praise from his teachers, Sir John Goodsir, Sir Robert Christison, James Miller and Sir James Simpson. In 1847 he left Edinburgh for London where he studied at Guy's Hospital (M.R.C.S., 1848). In November 1849 he sailed as surgeon in the *Windermere* for Hobart Town. His letters show that his family reunion was not happy and in April 1850 as surgeon in the *Raven* he left for California. He fossicked at the goldfields for fifteen months and then returned to Britain for postgraduate training at Edinburgh in 1851-52, again with Sir James Simpson.

Gillbee returned to Victoria in the *Georgiana* in 1852. The crew mutinied at Corio and the captain and Gillbee narrowly escaped death. He opened a practice in Collins Street East and, with his thorough training and obvious ability, he rose rapidly in his profession. He was elected an honorary surgeon to the Melbourne Hospital in January 1854 and was the first in the colony to perform several types of major operations. Prominent in the Medical Society of Victoria, he was its president in 1863. He had helped to found the medical school in the University of Melbourne and became an examiner in surgery in 1862. He was first president of the Victorian branch of the British Medical Association in 1879. A bachelor of genial character and large stature, he was a noted member of the Melbourne, Athenaeum and Yorick Clubs, and as vice-president of the Royal Society of Victoria helped to plan the Burke and Wills [qq.v.] expedition. He was the first assistant surgeon to the Volunteer Force in 1853, became surgeon major in 1867 and later principal medical officer.

Gillbee was senior surgeon at the Melbourne Hospital in 1867 when Joseph Lister announced his principles of antiseptic surgery. Gillbee was the first to apply and advocate these methods in Australasia. In 1868 he published 'On the treatment of abscess and compound fracture by Mr. Lister's new method' in the *Australian Medical Journal* and championed the cause of antisepsis in the 1870s before the principle was accepted generally. In 1875 he was not re-elected by the subscribers to the honorary staff of the Melbourne Hospital. In sympathy, a meeting of 'professional gentlemen' was held to 'protest against injustice and ingratitude on the part of the public'. His colleagues persuaded him to remain on

the committee of management and he was elected its president in 1882, but soon had to resign when a recent graduate, James Barrett (1862-1945), complained of his interference in the management of a patient. A chronic chest complaint undoubtedly contributed to his loss of status and his depression in his last years. In 1883-84 he travelled in New Zealand and England; six weeks after his return he died aged 60 on 4 January 1885. He was buried in the Melbourne general cemetery after an Anglican service, and left an estate of £31,000. His bequest of £1000 to the National Gallery of Victoria for sending an artist to England to paint a picture of Australian historical interest resulted in Philip Fox's 'Landing of Captain Cook', and John Longstaff's 'The Arrival of Burke and Wills at Cooper's Creek'.

Portraits are in the Archives of the Medical Society of Victoria.

D. M. O'Sullivan, 'William Gillbee (1825-1885) and the introduction of antiseptic surgery to Australia', *MJA*, 5 Nov 1966.

DAVID M. O'SULLIVAN

GILLIES, DUNCAN (1834-1903), politician, was born near Glasgow, Scotland, the second son of Duncan Gillies, market gardener, and his wife Margaret. He left school in Glasgow at about 14 and worked in an office until he migrated to Victoria. He arrived in December 1852 and promptly went to the Ballarat goldfields.

Gillies was a successful miner, sharing a productive claim in the Gravel Pits area with several others, including Peter Lalor [q.v.], and later became a working partner in the rich Great Republic mine. Despite his youth and skimpy education he was soon something of a public figure, a frequent speaker for the miners' cause at meetings, a member of the local court and the mining board which succeeded it in 1858 and a delegate to the land convention in 1857. In February 1861 after defeats in August 1859 and November 1860 he was elected for Ballarat West in the Legislative Assembly. His platform was proper representation of local interests and although quiet and cautious in the House he brought forward issues of importance on the goldfields. If as some accounts suggest he was paid by his constituents, he served them truly for some years even though his early radicalism faded and in the constitutional crises of 1865-68 he opposed the government and popular opinion. From the start of his parliamentary career he had studied questions of order, procedure and convention and his growing respect for the Constitution placed him on the conservative side and alienated his constituents. In May 1868 he accepted the post of minister for lands in the Sladen [q.v.] administration but lost his seat at the ministerial by-election.

Gillies was returned for Maryborough to the Legislative Assembly in March 1870. From July 1872 to August 1875 he was commissioner for railways and roads in the Francis and Kerferd [qq.v.] ministries and in 1875 became minister for lands and for agriculture under McCulloch [q.v.]. One of the busiest and most efficient of members and notable for the strength and lucidity of his speeches, he was valuable in office despite a certain coldness and lack of originality. Undoubtedly sincere and hard-working, he was a skilful tactician and a loyal colleague.

As a member of the McCulloch government and an opponent of the land tax Gillies overcame strong opposition from Berry's [q.v.] supporters to win the Rodney seat in 1877, but was promptly challenged on the ground that the lands department had used undue influence on his behalf. Although a qualifications committee found the charge proved, Gillies himself was exonerated but he had to contest a second election. He re-entered the assembly on 7 November, six weeks before the Legislative Council rejected Berry's appropriation bill including provision for payment of members. Gillies was the first to reply to Berry's call for vengeance on 20 December with a terse analysis of the government's motives. In February 1878 he was first again to answer Berry's attempt to justify the Black Wednesday dismissal of scores of civil servants, and was among the strongest opponents of Berry's proposals for reform of the council and his decision to appeal to the imperial parliament to alter the Constitution. Although he conceded that some reform was needed, he argued in defence of the Constitution and traditional parliamentary procedure, refuting Berry's explanations with such clarity that even the most persistent heckler was silenced. Gillies was not learned or given to display, but on this issue his performance was almost scholarly, almost dramatic; it was perhaps the high point of his political career though years of eminence lay ahead.

After Berry's defeat at the polls in February 1880 Gillies was minister for railways under James Service [q.v.] until August. In opposition he continued to take a close, practical interest in railways and was thus the obvious choice for that portfolio when the Service-Berry coalition was formed in March 1883. He knew as well as anyone the difficulty of administering the sprawling and complex department as its impermanent political head. In July he introduced the railways management bill designed to abolish political patronage and increase the efficiency of the department by substituting a board of three commissioners for ministerial control. It was only briefly successful: although Gillies referred all questions to the board for decision and conscientiously refrained from interference, he failed to protect the commissioners from the demands of other parliamentarians. He was similarly amenable to the lobbyists over the 1884 railways construction bill, allowing extensive additions to the already extensive mileage recommended by the commissioners. While minister he assisted the passage of a private bill to allow the Melbourne Tramway and Omnibus Co. monopoly rights to operate in the city and suburbs, a bill he had first introduced in May 1882. In response to critics of this questionable procedure he argued that he would not undertake a new private bill while in office but had been long committed to this one though he had no private interest in it. Gillies also fulfilled the duties of minister for public instruction in the Service-Berry government.

Early in 1886 when Service and Berry retired, Gillies and Alfred Deakin became leaders of the coalition, Gillies at the head of the so-called Conservative wing and Deakin as head of the Liberals. Formerly rather limited in the range of his political activities, Gillies as premier, treasurer, minister for railways and later for mines as well had to cope with the intricacies of international and intercolonial diplomacy, and in a wildly booming economy was responsible for defining the government's financial policy. He was not quite equal to the task. In negotiations with the Colonial Office over French annexation of the New Hebrides he displayed admirable persistence but poor judgment and ignorance of the European situation.

Gillies's government worked consistently to bring about Federation but his determined efforts to initiate closer co-operation between the colonies invariably failed to interest Sir Henry Parkes [q.v.]. His down-to-earth temperament made him suspicious of Parkes and when the old man suddenly proposed in June 1889 that they plan to federate at once Gillies's response was cold. At that stage he saw insuperable difficulties in the way of immediate federation and proposed instead to reform the Federal Council and increase its powers. By October, however, when Parkes suggested a meeting of colonial representatives to plan a federal government Gillies had recovered sufficient optimism to take the lead in inviting Parkes to a less ambitious alternative conference. At that conference in Melbourne in January

1890 Gillies took the chair. Although persuaded that the present was as good as any time to create a federal government, he firmly pointed in his summing-up speech and at the Sydney conference in 1891 to the problems to be overcome. Unmoved by the visionary eloquence of his fellow delegates, Gillies saw only danger in emphasizing the 'bright and noble aspect' of federation.

In his administration of Victoria Gillies was ruled by the same fatal pliancy as he had shown over the Railways Management Act. An inexpert treasurer, for some years he swam with the tide of the boom, building and borrowing freely in response to demands from all sides of the House. In mid-1889 he predicted a surplus of £1,700,000 but by the end of the year the wisdom of his financial management was causing strong doubt among those who discerned the onset of depression. His railways bill providing for eight hundred miles of track increased such doubts but also alienated those members whose demands were not satisfied. The ministry's apparent hostility towards striking unionists further dissipated support for Gillies, and in October the coalition was defeated on a motion of no confidence.

Many blamed Gillies for the depression, while members who had been personally involved in the boom escaped censure; his own conservative reaction increased his unpopularity. In opposition he was a liability and in 1893 he reluctantly accepted the post of agent-general in London. In 1887 while premier he had refused a knighthood. He returned to the Legislative Assembly in 1897 but was never influential again for his health and ability failed. A victim of Bright's disease, he did not retire but lived on his past reputation, and on 14 October 1902 was elected Speaker by a sympathetic and respectful House. Aged 69 he died on 12 September 1903.

Gillies's long career in Victorian politics was not remarkable for originality. His strength lay rather in the mechanics of politics, his skill in debate, his knowledge of tactics and procedure, and above all his ability to hold disparate groups together in a workable parliamentary majority. In the end his habit of placating all interests proved disastrous but for years before his defeat in 1890 it had worked well, contributing largely to the legislative achievement of the coalition.

Gillies was always thought to be a bachelor but at 63 in a London registry office on 15 January 1897 he had married Harriett Turquand Fillan, née Theobald, a widow of 37. She followed him to Melbourne after he returned but was persuaded by his friends to go back to her nursing in Johannesburg without announcing herself to Melbourne society. This episode contrasts strangely with the general pattern of Gillies's personal existence. Cold and reserved to most people, although a few friends knew him to be sincere, warmhearted and a charming conversationalist, he had no family, no lasting business associations. He divided his time between his lodgings, the Athenaeum and Australian Clubs and parliament. Politics was his life.

A portrait by J. M. Munt is in Parliament House, Melbourne.

B. R. Wise, *The making of the Australian Commonwealth, 1889-1900* (Lond, 1913); R. L. Wettenhall, *Railway management and politics in Victoria, 1856-1906* (Canberra, 1961); G. Serle, *The golden age* (Melb, 1963); J. A. La Nauze, *Alfred Deakin*, 1 (Melb, 1965); J. M. Tregenza, *Professor of democracy; the life of Charles Henry Pearson, 1830-1894* (Melb, 1968); G. Serle, 'The Victorian government's campaign for Federation, 1883-1889', *Essays in Australian Federation*, A. W. Martin ed (Melb, 1969); D. Blair, 'The Hon. Duncan Gillies', *Once a Month*, May 1886; *Ballarat Star*, Feb 1861, 13, 14 Sept 1903; *Age*, 14 Sept 1903; *Argus*, 14 Sept 1903.   MARGOT BEEVER

GILMORE, HUGH (1842-1891), Primitive Methodist minister, was born in Glasgow, Scotland. He soon became a homeless orphan and later claimed to have been brought up among the poorest of the poor of that city. These rough beginnings left him with some painful memories but also with a conviction of the goodness of human nature and a broad sympathy with the poor. At 19 while working at Ballast Hills, a suburb of Newcastle upon Tyne, he was converted suddenly and dramatically and became a member and then lay preacher of the Primitive Methodist Church. A probationer in 1865, he was ordained as an itinerant preacher at Stockton-on-Tees in 1870, served in various northern circuits and after six years at Preston migrated to South Australia in June 1889 hoping to improve his health. In 1881 he had refused an invitation to Adelaide.

Gilmore wanted to serve in the city slums but was sent to minister in the pleasant residential area at Wellington Square, North Adelaide. At first he was inclined to think that the colony had no poor but later found much poverty though less widespread than in the United Kingdom. His preaching, marked by a deep sincerity and a forceful simplicity and which rarely employed the usual evangelistic and theological phrases, soon attracted a congregation of very diverse degrees of wealth, education, religious belief and political attachment. The chapel soon had to be enlarged with a gallery.

In 1890 Gilmore was elected president of

the Primitive Methodist conference of South Australia in February, and president of the first intercolonial conference of the Primitive Methodist Connexion at Adelaide in October. In the maritime strike he supported the unions whole-heartedly. In a speech at Port Adelaide on 12 October he condemned capitalism and advocated somewhat vaguely the public ownership of capitalist enterprises. A week later at a large demonstration in Adelaide the unionists cried out two names: Hugh Gilmore and C. C. Kingston. Although he called himself a Christian Socialist his main political object was to promote the Adelaide branch of the Single Tax League. In 1890-91 he was foundation president of the league and of the Society for the Study of Christian Sociology. He also joined a deputation from the Women's Suffrage League which in June 1891 urged the premier, Thomas Playford [q.v.], to adopt a suffrage bill then before parliament.

In many ways an unorthodox Methodist, Gilmore declared that conversion could not be swift and complete, that the real test of a Christian was not attendance at church or class-meeting and that 'experimental' religion was not enough unless justified to the mind. He criticized the Evangelicals who saw the world as a spiritual wilderness but neglected to improve its conditions, thus reducing the gospel to religious individualism. He advocated reform of the physical and material aspects of life as a necessary part of Christian conduct while at the same time he insisted that if need be a man could lead a spiritually good life even in adverse material conditions. The harmony of his religious and political ideals was best seen in the Christian Commonwealth movement which he began in April 1891. Membership was open to all Christians whatever their religious attachments. Its first section was to give relief to the poor; the second to offer friendship, accommodation and employment to strangers; the third to redeem the lapsed and depraved; and the fourth and fifth to deal with political and social questions. To Gilmore the movement was an expression of the true 'spiritual' religion, active and beneficent, in contrast to contemporary 'ecclesiastical' religion, respectable, exclusive and institutional. However, ill health forced him to retire from preaching in July. He died aged 49 on 24 October. His funeral procession included among many others 400 members of labour organizations. He was survived by his wife, four sons and four daughters. His eldest son, Joseph, served in the Primitive Methodist ministry and later was purser in the *Royal Tar* on two journeys to Paraguay.

Gilmore's literary work in England included contributions to the *Quarterly Re-view* and leading articles to the *Primitive Methodist Weekly*. In the colony he was joint-editor of the *South Australian Primitive Methodist* in 1889-91 and his *My Intellectual Quickening* appeared soon after his death. From shorthand notes members of his church compiled *Sermons by the late Hugh Gilmore* in 1892 and one of his many lectures, *The Single Tax*, was published in 1911.

Minutes of the Primitive Methodist Conference, England (1892); *Christian Colonist*, 29 Aug 1890; *Advertiser* (Adel), 24, 26 Oct 1891; information from Mr H. Gilmore, Glenunga, SA.   R. B. WALKER

GLADMAN, FREDERICK JOHN (1839-1884), educationist, was born on 1 February 1839 in London, son of William Gladman, police superintendent, and his wife Rebecca, née Barnes. He attended a Lancasterian school until apprenticed at 14 as a pupil-teacher to Robert Soar, headmaster of the British and Foreign School at Bushey, Hertfordshire. On ending his apprenticeship he was admitted as a Queen's scholar to the Borough Road Training College, London, for one year's teacher-training. In 1859-62 he taught at a small British and Foreign School at Godalming in Surrey. He was appointed headmaster of a larger school at Great Yarmouth in 1863, but only after the school's managers had overcome their reluctance to appoint so young a man. He taught brilliantly, meeting the rigid requirements of the payment by result system then in vogue and at the same time stirring the imagination and capturing, often for life, the affection of his pupils. While at Great Yarmouth he began private studies: in 1869 he matriculated in the University of London (B.A., 1871; B.Sc., 1875). After nine years at Great Yarmouth he was asked to return to the Borough Road Training College as headmaster of the Model and Practising School, a position he filled with distinction. As co-editor with Rev. William Legge he published *The Handy Book of English History* (London, 1874); it was followed by his own *School Method* (London, 1877) and in 1882 by his *School Work* in Jarrold's Pupil Teachers series.

In 1876 the Victorian Education Department had inquired in England for a suitable principal of the Training Institution in Melbourne. Gladman stood out among the applicants because of his experience in teaching and teacher-training, his university record, unusual for one who had begun his professional career as a pupil-teacher, and a glowing testimonial from Matthew Arnold who as a school inspector had examined

Gladman. In March 1877 Gladman arrived in Melbourne and before taking up his appointment in June travelled around Victoria getting to know the system. He published a report foreshadowing many of the criticisms which in the next seven years he made in greater detail and, particularly for so mild a man, with increasing acerbity. He was specially perturbed by the failure to develop procedures to secure qualified teachers, by the low standard required of entrants to the Training Institution and by defects in its professional and academic courses. He recommended changes and campaigned for their implementation but had made little impression on the educational authorities when he died suddenly, probably of diabetes, on 23 November 1884 at St Kilda. He was survived by his wife Sarah Ann, née Howard, whom he had married on 9 August 1860, and by five of their eight children; one son, Philip Howard, became an inspector in the Education Department of Western Australia.

Though many of his recommendations were implemented after his death and through his writing were influential in Australia, Gladman's importance is not primarily that of reformer or theorist. He was a rigorous thinker and well-read by any standards; by colonial standards his opinions were progressive but to British and Continental educationists he would have appeared as intelligently derivative. His great contribution was to bring to a narrow and parochial education system a generous view of the task of schooling, a stern moral and intellectual concern, a pride in the craftsmanship of teaching and a passionate conviction of its importance. His students, many of whom later rose high in their professions, were strikingly influenced by his attitudes. As a memorial to him they instituted the Gladman prize, awarded yearly to the best student at Melbourne Teachers' College.

A'sian Schoolmaster files, 1875-85 (LaT L); Education Department, registered letters 1876-85 (VA).

R. J. W. SELLECK

GLASS, HUGH (1817-1871), speculator, squatter and merchant, was born at Portaferry, County Down, Ireland, son of Thomas Glass, merchant, and his wife Rachael, née Pollock. In 1840 he migrated to Victoria and began farming on the Merri Creek; by 1845 he had established himself as a station agent and merchant. In 1853 he married Lucinda (Lucy), youngest daughter of Captain Nash, Victorian squatter and sometime of the 21st Royal Scots Fusiliers. Within two years Glass had doubled his station holdings and begun stock dealing. At this time he built Flemington House, valued in the 1850s at £60,000; with its artificial lake and white swans, its Corinthian collonaded portico supporting a long balcony, its huge ballroom and its landscaped garden sloping down to the Maribyrnong River, it became the showplace of Melbourne.

As an agent and dealer, Glass speculated in buying and selling stations throughout eastern Australia. He also owned a core of runs from which he sent stock to Newmarket sales, the most notable being the Wimmera and Westernport stations of Moyreisk, Nettyallock, Avoca Forest, Bullock Creek, Weddikar and Glengower. Although Glass invested in mining and suburban real estate, his absorbing interest was the stock and station market and he considered himself primarily a squatter. By the early 1860s he was at his peak; in 1862 he was reputed the richest man in Victoria, worth some £800,000. As a businessman, he was a brilliant organizer with a detailed knowledge of the law which he used to his advantage. He was also alert to the possibilities of manipulating the men who made the law. For instance, in the 1860s he formed and directed an association aimed at influencing parliamentarians to pass land bills sympathetic to the pastoral interest. Although the extent of this control of members is uncertain, James McKean [q.v.] claimed in 1869 that one of Glass's associations had spent £80,000 in influencing members. Without doubt Glass had made himself a force to be feared and reckoned with in Victorian politics. He created around himself an aura of absolute power and self-assurance. At Flemington House he entertained lavishly, while his office was a centre of financial and political influence and Collins Street his court. By his style of life he buoyed up his contemporaries' trust in him, his methods and his empire.

With all his ability Glass was unable to maintain his position. Under selection Glass, unlike other big squatters such as Richard Goldsbrough [q.v.], bought large areas of freehold, mostly by acquiring certificates under the 1865 Land Act and by employing dummies. This latter method of Glass's became notorious and a poem entitled 'The Charge of the Dirty Three Hundred', reputedly written by a clerk in the lands department, was widely circulated:

> 'Pay them all' said H - - - G - - - -
> 'Let them all go to hell
> All that are left of them
> All the three hundred'.

The cost of supporting dummies and buying certificates meant that Glass paid dearly for his land and had to borrrow heavily. Thus his pastoral empire became based on heavily mortgaged assets which after 1865 were shown to be vulnerable.

By the mid-1860s Glass owned 35,000 acres scattered over twenty runs, none of which was particularly productive. In his intrigues to acquire land he often lost sight of its economic potential and bought unwisely. In the late 1850s he had also extended his leasehold interests into parts of Victoria and New South Wales with unreliable water supplies, and droughts in 1865-66 and 1868-69 exposed the weakness of his leases and freehold in these areas. The droughts decimated his assets and reduced the resale value of the remaining stock and of the stations themselves. Glass attempted to extricate himself by selling some of his stations, but did so at a loss. Worse still, three of his purchasers failed in 1869, owing him over £100,000. In that year Glass's business empire collapsed: he assigned his estate to trustees, with debts reckoned at more than £500,000. All that remained was his suburban land which later helped to clear the estate.

Glass's political influence in Melbourne came under attack at the same time. A select committee found him guilty of taking part in corrupt practices and parliament committed him to gaol. The Supreme Court, headed by Sir William Stawell [q.v.], a former partner, promptly reversed parliament's decision, arguing that the legislature had encroached upon the powers of the judiciary. The decision to release Glass was popular and he was widely congratulated. However, the popularity of his release derived as much from the feeling that parliament was corrupt, overbearing and ripe for censure as from any sympathy with Glass himself. None the less his political power had been effectively broken by the scandal.

Glass's personal life was also placed under stress. Lucy, the baby, had died in 1866 and another daughter, Evangelina, died in June 1869 aged eleven months. In addition Glass's own health was deteriorating from cancer of the liver. Survived by his wife and eight children, he died on 15 May 1871 aged 55. The inquest jury found that the immediate cause of death was an overdose of chloral, administered at his own request by his son, with the object of causing sleep to relieve pain. However, the evidence at the inquest by two doctors who attended Glass on his death indicated that the dose was fatal only because of his already diseased condition 'from which he might have died in a few months'.

Glass had enjoyed a career without parallel amongst nineteenth-century Australian financiers and pastoralists. Within ten years he fell from financial heights to bankruptcy and from success as a political manipulator to rebuke by parliament. His strength lay in his vitality and opportunism but he lacked foresight. His political dealings left him open to public criticism while his rash purchases of land strained his financial resources, leaving his pastoral interests exposed to the dangers of drought. In the event his network of power and wealth collapsed.

H. H. Peck, *Memoirs of a stockman* (Melb, 1942); M. L. Kiddle, *Men of yesterday* (Melb, 1961); C. E. Sayers, *David Syme; a life* (Melb, 1965); *Leader* (Melb), 13 Sept 1862; *Argus*, Apr-May 1869, 16 May 1871; *Age*, 16 May 1871; Armytage papers (LaT L).   J. E. SENYARD

GLENNIE, BENJAMIN (1812-1900), Anglican clergyman, was born on 29 January 1812 in Dulwich, Surrey, England, the twelfth son of Dr William Glennie, principal of a private school in Dulwich, and his wife Mary, née Gardiner. He was educated at his father's school and at King's College, London. At 30, after several years on the Continent as a tutor, he entered Christ's College, Cambridge (B.A., 1847). Three of his elder brothers had migrated to New South Wales: Henry, a landowner, James, a doctor, and Alfred, a farmer later ordained. Benjamin arrived at Sydney in January 1848 in the party of Dr W. Tyrrell [q.v.], first bishop of Newcastle.

Glennie was made deacon by Tyrrell at Morpeth on 19 March and appointed to Moreton Bay. There he faced an immense pioneering task, made more difficult by the ineffectiveness of his predecessor, Rev. John Gregor [q.v.], much religious indifference and a nervous condition which threatened the early termination of his ministry. In Brisbane he increased the congregation at the temporary St John's Church and established day and Sunday schools. He also visited Ipswich each month and made an extensive pastoral tour on the Darling Downs. Ordained priest in 1849, he was transferred next year to Drayton on the Darling Downs. In 1850-60 he was responsible for the whole of the Downs but after the diocese of Brisbane was created and his territory divided into parishes, he served at Warwick in 1860-72 and Drayton in 1872-76. He engaged in long and arduous pastoral tours which in the early years averaged 3000 miles a year on foot or horseback. He laid the foundations of a parochial system on the Downs by establishing congregations, buying strategic sites and building churches.

Glennie

A.D.B.

In 1863 Glennie had been appointed the first archdeacon of Brisbane by Bishop E. W. Tufnell [q.v.] but took little part in diocesan administration until Bishop M. B. Hale [q.v.] moved him to the parish of Toowong, Brisbane, in 1876. From 1877 he was full-time archdeacon and, as examining chaplain, was also responsible for training the first local candidates for holy orders. When Bishop W. T. T. Webber [q.v.] arrived in 1886 Glennie retired from active work and was appointed first honorary canon of St John's pro-Cathedral, Brisbane. In 1868 he had married Mary Brougham (1826-1890), daughter of William Crawshaw, master mariner, and his wife Mary; they had no children. He died on 30 April 1900 at Wynnum, near Brisbane.

Though not the first Anglican clergyman at Moreton Bay, Glennie may be rightly ranked as the pioneer of the Anglican ministry in Queensland. He won widespread affection and respect for his devoted pastoral work, his long, patient ministry in the face of many setbacks, his extensive travels and his foresight in laying the foundations of a parochial structure that provided for the future growth of the Church of England. Although often poor through the failure of his people to support him adequately, he was generous with money and by personal exertion raised the nucleus of the fund which made possible the foundation in 1908 of the Glennie School in Toowoomba. He is often referred to as the 'Apostle of the Downs'.

A. P. Elkin, *The diocese of Newcastle* (Syd, 1955); K. Rayner, The history of the Church of England in Queensland (Ph.D. thesis, Univ Qld, 1962); Church of England papers (Oxley Lib, Brisb); Glennie diary 1848-60 (Brisb Diocesan Registry). K. RAYNER

GLENNIE, HENRY (1835-1910), businessman and author often known as 'The Australian Silverpen', was born on 5 August 1835 at Newry, County Down, Ireland, the first son of Joseph Glenny, linen merchant, and his wife Elizabeth, née Grandy, both staunch Irish Protestants. After schooling at Newry he worked for a time with his father until permitted to migrate to Australia. At 18 Glenny arrived in Victoria in the *Phoenix*, eager to try his luck on the Victorian diggings. At White Flat and Eureka he had little success and accepted the offer of the Geelong merchants, J. & T. Bray, to manage a general store in a tent at the Gravel Pits. Although store-keepers as well as diggers had grievances, he came out on the side of officialdom, volunteering for the mounted police patrol on the day after the rising at Eureka. In 1855 he was appointed postmaster and clerk of courts at Beechworth. After a year he resigned and went to Castlemaine to manage a store. He then taught at Blanchard's school for young ladies and gentlemen. There he met 14-year-old Emma Jane Blanchard whom he married on 14 February 1859 at Castlemaine.

In 1857 Glenny had set up a 'Portrait Saloon' in Castlemaine's market square and soon had photographic studios at Ballarat and Kyneton. The chain of studios became the 'Dublin and Melbourne Portrait Rooms of H. Glenny, Artist'. About 1865 he returned to Ballarat where he built a fine house in Victoria Street. He quickly became well known as a successful businessman, investor, speculator, promoter, broker, financier and author. Ballarat's boom years suited his style and character. In August 1875 he became travelling agent in Victoria for the National Mutual Life Association of Australasia and for many years sold insurance in a spectacular manner; in the first year alone he wrote nearly a thousand policies. His work was mainly in northern Victoria and the Riverina but later extended to South Australia and Tasmania. Glenny travelled abroad at least ten times, visiting many countries. He returned to Newry as the local boy who made a fortune in Australia and while visiting England in 1893-94 placed Australian properties worth £1,000,000 on the market. He also sold mining companies and floated the Queen's Birthday Gold Mining Co., Dunolly, on the London Market for £150,000.

Although a prolific author and sometime editor of the *Ovens and Murray Advertiser*, Glenny had no special writing ability. Under the pen-names 'The Australian Silverpen', 'Old Chum', 'Peter Possum', 'A Voice from the East', 'Quince' and 'Rambler' he wrote sketches, essays and comment for many newspapers and religious journals. Many of these items were republished as *Jottings and Sketches at home and abroad* (Belfast, 1888 and 1889); it also included flattering newspaper reports of his own activities. He always signed his name as H. Glenny, J.P., F.G.S., F.R.G.S.

An ardent Wesleyan and temperance advocate, Glenny was the Ballarat representative of the (Royal) Society for the Prevention of Cruelty to Animals and the Prisoners' Aid Society. In 1880 as a justice of the peace he had signed the gaol book to certify that Ned Kelly [q.v.] was hanged by the neck till dead. Admired for his respectability and unblemished character he died in Melbourne on 24 July 1910, survived by his widow and by three sons and two daughters of their thirteen children.

W. B. Kimberly (ed), *Ballarat and vicinity* (Ballarat, 1894); National Mutual Life Assn of A'sia, *A century of life* (Melb, 1969); private papers (held by Misses E. and M. Glenny, Ballarat).   AUSTIN McCALLUM

GLYDE, LAVINGTON (1823-1890), accountant and parliamentarian, was born at Exeter, England, son of Jonathan Lavington Glyde. One of his brothers became a Dissenting minister at Bradford and another a partner of Sir Titus Salt at Saltaire. Educated at Exeter and Denmark Hill School, London, Glyde studied accountancy and the wool trade in Yorkshire and in the *Agincourt* arrived at Port Adelaide in July 1850. He brought a fair sum in cash and a sixty-day draft on the Bank of South Australia, mostly on behalf of relations in Yorkshire. Within a week he lent all his cash at high interest; he tried to borrow on the draft but the manager, Edward Stephens [q.v.], refused so bluntly that Glyde waited till it matured and promptly transferred his account to the Bank of Australasia. To his agencies and money-lending he soon added wool-buying and an export-import business on his own account. Later he included wheat and wine to his speculations and even invested in copper-mines once he modified his extreme caution.

A Congregationalist, Glyde attended Clayton Church and became active in public affairs. In the 1850s as 'A Looker-on' he wrote for the press a series of articles delicately satirical in vein. He supported J. H. Clark [q.v.] in founding the South Australian Institute and served for many years on its governing board. He became a director of insurance companies and chairman of many building societies. Well read and intelligent he never courted public favour but retained his independence. A stalwart Liberal with a strong conservative cast he represented East Torrens in the House of Assembly in 1857-60, Yatala in 1860-75 and Victoria in 1877-84. From the outset he was notable for his grasp of constitutional procedures and specially for his competence in financial issues. In 1858 he served on the select committee on taxation and in a 'protest report' advocated the total abolition of distillation laws. In evidence to a select committee on the Real Property Act in 1861 he complained that the commissioner's powers were too great particularly on mortgaged land. In 1863 he represented South Australia at the intercolonial conference in Melbourne on uniform tariffs and then became treasurer in F. S. Dutton's [q.v.] eleven-day ministry in July. He was then appointed commissioner of crown lands and immigration under Ayers [q.v.] until July 1864. He

held the latter portfolio under John Hart [q.v.] for a week in 1865 and under Ayers from May 1867 to September 1868 and again from October to November. He constantly opposed any interference with wool-growers either by the Pastoralists' Association which, he claimed, 'wanted to turn the colony into one vast sheep run', or by government regulations, although in 1867 as commissioner he had to arrange relief for drought-stricken graziers.

Glyde's greatest work was as treasurer under Arthur Blyth [q.v.] in 1873-75 and Bray [q.v.] in 1881-84. Always a severe critic of government expenditure he closely watched the raising of South Australian loans in London. He fearlessly fought the National Bank in London and forced it to repay with interest a five-year accumulation of unwarranted surcharges for floating loans. The total sum was not large but assured British investors of the colony's budgetary care. In Adelaide he was denounced as pessimist and alarmist and lost his seat in the assembly. For years he fought the muddle and extravagance of departments raising and spending their independent revenues and by 1884 succeeded in consolidating the colony's funds under parliamentary control even though the change gave the colony the first land and income taxes in Australia.

Glyde's wife Mary Ellen, née Hardcastle, died on 16 December 1869. On 20 July 1870 at Clayton Church he married her widowed sister Alice Phoebe Kepert. Although marriage with a deceased wife's sister was legalized next year in South Australia, Governor Fergusson called it 'indecent' and refused to invite the Glydes to a ball at Government House. However, Glyde was gazetted an Honorable in 1875. After resigning from the assembly in March 1884 he visited England with his family. His object was to promote the Talisker mine at Cape Jervis but it suffered heavy losses after he returned to Adelaide. He was accountant to the Insolvency Court in 1885 until he died aged 67 at his home in Kensington, Adelaide, on 31 July 1890. He was survived by his second wife and several children mostly under 21. His estate was valued for probate at £1326.

Frearson's Wkly, 1 Oct 1881; *Bulletin*, 2 Sept 1882; *Observer* (Adel), 4 Aug 1883, 24 May 1884, 2 Aug 1890; CO 13/127.

GODFREY, FREDERICK RACE (1828-1910), squatter and businessman, was born on 11 May 1828 at Bellary, India, son of Colonel John Race Godfrey and his wife Jane Octavia, née Woodhouse. He was educated at Exeter Grammar School and at 19 migrated to Port Phillip to become the partner of his brother Henry who in 1846 had taken up Boort station, 64,000 acres in the Loddon district, where he was the first white settler. In 1850, by converting a swamp into Lake Boort, Frederic became a pioneer of irrigation. He had close contact with the local Aboriginals, one of whom described him as 'the Loddon blacks' best friend'. Later as vice-chairman of the Aborigines Protection Board and as a commissioner reporting on the Aboriginals in 1877 he defended them as intelligent, industrious and honest. While at Boort he sold much stock to the Bendigo goldfields. On 29 April 1854 at St Kilda he married Margaret Lilias, daughter of David Chambers; they had five sons and four daughters.

In 1863 Godfrey sold Boort, moved to Mount Ridley, Craigieburn, and, because he claimed that his tenure in Victoria was threatened by the land laws, bought Pevensey station near Hay in New South Wales. He lived at Mount Ridley for seventeen years, sending stock to the Melbourne markets. He was also active in local government as president of the Merriang Shire Council and member of the Broadmeadows council. In 1874-77 he represented East Bourke in the Legislative Assembly. His rule in politics was to support measures rather than men, thus avoiding party loyalties and attempting to exercise his individual judgment.

Godfrey moved to St. Kilda in 1880 and became a founding director of the Trustees, Executors and Agency Co. Ltd, Melbourne, serving as chairman in 1895-1909. In 1890 he was appointed an honorary commissioner of the Savings Bank. An aspect of his agricultural interest was his original membership of the old Port Phillip Farmers' Association which merged into the Royal Agricultural Society. A prominent Anglican, he was a member of the Church of England Association; he had been appointed the first lay canon of St Paul's Cathedral in 1869 and held other church offices. He showed varied interests as a member of the Melbourne Club for fifty-eight years and its president in 1887, as a justice of the peace, president of the Melbourne Hospital Committee in 1887-1904, commissioner of the State Savings Bank from 1890, member of the committee of the Felton [q.v.] Bequest in 1904-09, founder and vice-president of the Philatelic Society of Victoria in 1892 and a member of the royal commission on charitable institutions in 1890-91. Interested in natural history, he became a member of the Acclimatisation Society of Victoria in 1863 and served as its elected president for several years. With A. A. C. Le Souef

[q.v.] he established the Government Reserve at Gembrook for the Acclimatisation Society and acted also on the committee for the preservation of Wilson's Promontory.

Godfrey's first wife died in 1895 and on 3 October 1898 at St John's Church, Darlinghurst, Sydney, he married Marian, daughter of Richard Walker; they had no children. Godfrey died at St Kilda on 11 September 1910. His enterprise and industry showed that he 'loved Australia and endeavoured to foster a true British spirit of strict honour and industry and patriotism to God, King and Country'.

A. Sutherland et al, *Victoria and its metropolis*, 2 (Melb, 1888); J. Smith (ed), *Cyclopedia of Victoria*, 1 (Melb, 1903); A. S. Kenyon, *Story of Australia: its discoverers and founders* (Geelong, nd); M. L. Drought (ed), *Extracts from old journals written by Frederic Race Godfrey ... 1846-1853* (Melb, 1926); A. Henderson (ed), *Early pioneer families of Victoria and Riverina* (Melb, 1936); M. Cannon, *The land boomers* (Melb, 1966); Godfrey diary (held privately).

MARGARET GRAVELL

GOETHE, MATTHIAS (1827-1876), Lutheran pastor, was born on 29 March 1827 at Neuendorf, near Koblenz, Germany, son of Heinrich Goethe, public servant. He was trained for the Catholic priesthood but at 20 became a Protestant, went to England, met J. D. Lang [q.v.] and married Harriett Alice Wells. They sailed in the *Clifton* to Sydney where on 1 April 1850 Goethe was appointed teacher of mathematics and modern languages at the Australian College and on 9 October he and David Blair [q.v.] were ordained by Lang. In Sydney Goethe conducted religious services in German and French.

In 1852 Goethe went to Melbourne seeking relief from asthma. He held his first German Lutheran service on Christmas Day at the Congregational Church, Collins Street; soon afterwards members of the German Lutheran community asked him to become their pastor. His induction on 25 March 1853 was conducted by seven English ministers of various denominations. Goethe thus became the first Lutheran minister and founder of the Lutheran congregation in Victoria. The government donated land at Eastern Hill and £1500 towards building a church; it was completed and dedicated on 11 June 1854. Goethe founded congregations in Grovedale, Ballarat, Bendigo and Castlemaine, and also held regular services at Hawthorn, Doncaster and other places near Melbourne. In 1856 he went to Moreton Bay and induced three German missionaries to move to Victoria, thus giving Bendigo,

Ballarat and Grovedale their first resident pastors. In that year Goethe formed the first Lutheran Synod of Victoria and became its president, holding office till 1867. He visited Germany in 1857 to recruit Lutheran ministers and teachers for Victoria. By 1860 Lutheran services were held regularly at Melbourne, Grovedale, Ballarat, Bendigo, Tarrington, Thomastown, Berwick and Doncaster, with schools at each centre except Ballarat and Doncaster. Goethe also sought union between the South Australian and Victorian synods but could not overcome the differences on doctrinal questions. In Victoria Goethe worked for co-operation between Protestant denominations, accepted state aid for his church and schools and encouraged Germans to learn English and mix with other settlers. He also made English compulsory in his schools. He edited the first Lutheran monthly paper in Victoria, *Der Pilger in Viktoria* (1853-56). In 1860 he founded *Der Australische Christenbote*, which appeared monthly for fifty years, with Goethe as its editor till 1867. He had published a German calendar in 1854.

In 1867 Goethe left Melbourne for California where he founded the first Lutheran congregation in Sacramento and stayed for eight years. Then he moved to Mexico City where he preached in Spanish and translated the Lutheran catechism into that language. He died on 27 October 1876, survived by his wife and four children.

Although hampered by ill health, Goethe was a good preacher, an accomplished writer, a remarkable linguist and an effective organizer. He taught the virtues of hard work and moral rectitude, the value of education and good citizenship. His own words, 'Nothing is of more moral value, than to foster tolerance even when opinions conflict', sum up the guiding principle of his life.

Die deutsch-evangelische Kirche in Australien (Berlin, 1857); H. Herlitz (ed), *Festschrift . . . evangelische—lutherischen Synode von Victoria* (Melb, 1907); Th. Hebart, *The United Evangelical Lutheran Church in Australia*, J. J. Schultz ed (Adel, 1938); A. Brauer, *Under the Southern Cross: history of Evangelical Lutheran Church of Australia* (Adel, 1956); information from Pastor Seyler, Melb, Rev. F. J. H. Blaess and Rev. M. Lohe, Adel.

S. M. TARNAY

GOLDIE, ANDREW (1840-1891), naturalist and merchant, was born on 24 May 1840 at Kelburne, Ayrshire, Scotland, son of David Goldie and his wife Agness. After a sketchy education and apprenticeship to his father's trade of gardener he migrated in 1862 to Auckland where for

some ten years he was a nurseryman. Back in Britain in 1874 he arranged to collect plants in the South Sea Islands for a London nurseryman but next year in Melbourne he was encouraged by Dr Mueller [q.v.] to go to New Guinea. He arrived at Port Moresby in the mission steamer *Ellengowan* on 28 March 1876 but after some local exploration and two bad attacks of fever left in December for Sydney.

There Goldie published reports of his travels and arranged with E. P. Ramsay [q.v.] of the Australian Museum to take two collectors, Alexander Morton and William Blunden, on his next trip. Accompanied by James H. Shaw, surveyor, the party reached Port Moresby in Goldie's cutter *Explorer* on 17 July 1877. Morton and Blunden went to the Laloki River and set up a camp while Goldie and Shaw sailed to Tupusulei, explored about eight miles inland, climbed the Astrolabe Range and returned westward to Boera and the Laloki River where Shaw was hurt and left for Port Moresby. Goldie joined Morton and Blunden and on 10 November they moved west and found a large river; Goldie gave it his own name and one of his carriers appropriately found traces of gold. In December the party set off to collect on Suau Island but returned to Port Moresby after meeting Charles Dudfield, captain of the schooner *Mavri*, who had been wounded by islanders. Morton left for Sydney and for seven weeks the others explored the south coast: they entered Cloudy Bay, examined the Robinson River, named the Blunden River and Milport and Glasgow Harbours, and in the Louisiade Archipelago named the Redlick group and discovered Teste Island. Early in 1878 Shaw and Blunden went to Sydney where an assay of their gold specimens stimulated a rush. On 28 June 1879 Goldie led four Europeans and twenty carriers to the old camp on the Laloki; they explored as far as the Rouna Falls and returned to Port Moresby in September. Soon afterwards he sailed from Yule Island to Freshwater Bay in his new boat *Alice Meade* and named Alice Meade Lagoon and Goldie Reef.

Weakened by fever and hardship Goldie decided to settle in New Guinea. In May 1878 he had bought land near Hanuabada and set up a trading store. In September 1883 he joined J. B. Cameron, agent of a Sydney syndicate, in buying 17,000 acres at Kabadi. This purchase defied native custom and poisoned his good relations with W. G. Lawes [q.v.]. On establishment of the protectorate Goldie and Cameron sought recognition of the transaction but were refused. In 1886 the government decided to remove European settlement from the Hanuabada area. In exchange for his property Goldie was offered six blocks in the new township at Granville West but after a vigorous paper war with Sir Anthony Musgrave was compensated with £400 for his improvements, and given fifty suburban acres and three town allotments on which he built Port Moresby's first store in January 1887. Despite a report of his death in 1886 Goldie visited Sydney in 1891 but died soon after his return to Port Moresby on 20 November. Although evidence on his estate was destroyed in World War II, he left 3750 shares in Burns Philp & Co. Ltd to three sisters and two brothers.

Goldie was intensely jealous of his repute as an explorer and never allowed subordinates to publish independent reports. He was unpopular in scientific circles because he tended to see his collections as a commercial venture; yet many of the scientific discoveries claimed by him were allegedly made by his associate, Carl von Hunstein, a German naturalist.

T. F. Bevan, *Toil, travel, and discovery in British New Guinea* (Lond, 1890); A. Wichmann, *Nova Guinea*, 2 (Leiden, 1910), pt 1; G. Souter, *New Guinea: the last unknown* (Syd, 1963); G. S. Fort, Report on British New Guinea, V&P (LA Qld), 1886, 2, 939; *Town and Country J*, 19 Jan 1878, 13 Nov 1886; *SMH*, 31 Dec 1879, 19 Jan 1880; W. G. Lawes journals (ML); E. P. Ramsay papers (ML); Protectorate papers (PNGA); MS cat under A. Goldie (ML); CO 243/43.   H. J. GIBBNEY

GOLDSBROUGH, RICHARD (1821-1886), woolbroker, was born on 17 October 1821 at Shipley, Yorkshire, England, the only son of Joshua Goldsbrough, butcher, and his wife Hannah, née Speight. In 1842 he completed a seven-year apprenticeship in near-by Bradford, set up in business in that city and married Emma, daughter of Samuel Hodgson, a Halifax butcher living in Ovenden. His business as woolstapler was small but prospered modestly. His success depended partly on the skill with which he sorted and repacked purchased wools to meet the individual requirements of different manufacturers. With this skill he arrived at Melbourne in the *Warrior* on 29 November 1847 and founded his business in September 1848. His wife remained in England until at least 1850.

At first Goldsbrough's main business was in classing and repacking wool for growers and for merchants who bought it as a way of remitting funds to England, and in classing sheep on properties. The purchase of J. & R. Bakewell's business in 1850 made Goldsbrough the leading broker in Melbourne and provided the occasion to estab-

lish the first regular auction sales of wool in the colony. From 1852 Goldsbrough was assisted by his brother-in-law, Hugh Parker, to whom he gave a share in the profits from 1854 and a formal partnership in 1857. By that time Goldsbrough had entered other branches of the wool trade and industry. With Edward Row and George Kirk he formed the firm of E. Row & Co. in 1853; it became Row, Kirk & Co. in 1860. The partners acted as auctioneers at Goldsbrough's wool sales and developed a large clientele as stock and station salesmen. After the partnership dissolved in 1863 Goldsbrough's own firm began selling stock and stations. As private speculations he and Kirk bought several large pastoral properties on the Murray and Lachlan Rivers, among them Perricoota, Tatallia, Cowl Cowl and Ballingerambill, which they resold advantageously before 1867. Later, in partnership with Parker and perhaps Edward Row's nephew, Goldsbrough developed the Traralgon West cattle station in Gippsland. In the 1870s he was associated with A. W. Robertson [q.v.], John Wagner and Salathiel Booth in such other properties as Midkin, Auburn, Mount Hope, Gunbar, Bael Bael and Murrumbit. Goldsbrough was also a partner in, and probably financed, the hide and skin businesses operated by close relations of Frederick Row and Parker.

The woolbroking partnership was strengthened in 1873 by the addition of J. S. Horsfall [q.v.] and David and Arthur Parker in 1876. By the 1860s woolclassing and packing were minor among Goldsbrough's services; selling wool in Melbourne, consigning it for sale in London on behalf of growers and providing short- and long-term credit for pastoralists were the major elements. Lending to squatters in central Victoria and the Riverina proved very profitable in the decade of squatting boom. At the end of the 1860s a pastoral depression reduced stock and station values, diminished income and a sharp fall in profits placed Goldsbrough at the mercy of banks from which he borrowed the money he lent. Bank forbearance permitted him to extricate himself but heavy capital losses stood as stark reminders of the vulnerability of borrowing short and lending long. To escape dependence on banks Goldsbrough sought to amalgamate with a public company having access to British investment funds. After unsuccessful negotiations with the Australian Mortgage Land & Finance Co. in 1874, a satisfactory merger with the Australasian Agency and Banking Corporation was effected in 1881. Next year, after bidding unsuccessfully to purchase the business of Mort [q.v.] & Co. in Sydney, the new concern opened its own branch there. The amalgamation creating Goldsbrough Mort & Co. Ltd was not carried through until 1888.

Open-minded and generous in many ways, Goldsbrough's charity was an essentially private affair; to public appeals he contributed selectively and rarely with largesse. He had few public interests outside his business and the Victoria Racing Club. Never an owner himself and rarely a large better, he was fascinated by the turf and was a steward of the V.R.C. from its formation until 1886. To horse-racing as to his other private interests he brought a gargantuan zest for living that bore out the promise of his height and girth. His song was loud, his laughter boisterous. While holidaying in England he entertained a champagne-loaded party at the Ascot races in a coach surmounted by a large emu-emblazoned flag, to the immense discomposure of English friends. That his enjoyment of wine and spirits was undiminished nearly forty years after the convivial evenings with cards and claret recalled by Alfred Joyce [q.v.] is apparent from the contents of Goldsbrough's cellar when he died: 150 gallons of whisky, nearly 70 of brandy and 100 of sherry, 36 of sixty-six-year-old port, and much else. Goldsbrough was also exuberant in other ways. His children by his wife Emma Hodgson (1822-1877), possibly as many as three, died young in Yorkshire. More specified natural offspring were credited him by gossip than are consistent with the facts. Liberal use of his surname in the baptism of his friends' and associates' children hardly discouraged invention. His heir was Richard Goldsbrough, son of Frederick Row's wife Elizabeth Selena.

Goldsbrough had begun to withdraw from active management of the firm before the internal tumour, from which he died on 8 April 1886 after a seven-month illness, became apparent. He had devoted thirty years to persuading growers to sell their wool in Melbourne and buyers to travel from England and the Continent to buy it, and to providing services and facilities that would help persuade them. His wool stores, designed with that purpose, formed the basis of a distinctively Australian style of building. He played an important role in the evolution of Australian wool-broking practices, in the creation of a formalized and efficient selling system and in the development of financial techniques that provided the credit basis for Australia's pastoral expansion in 1860-90. In these contributions, arising solely and directly from his business activities, Goldsbrough's significance lies.

A. Joyce, A homestead history, G. F. James ed (Melb, 1942); A. Barnard, The Australian wool market, 1840-1900 (Melb, 1958); Goldsbrough Mort & Co. Ltd, Wool and the nation (Melb, 1960); Goldsbrough Mort & Co. records (ANU Archives); private information from L. Watmough, Sydney.   ALAN BARNARD

GOODCHAP, CHARLES AUGUSTUS (1837-1896), commissioner of railways, was born on 2 April 1837 in Kent, England, son on William Goodchap, architect. Educated at Huntingdon Grammar School, he arrived at Sydney in 1853 and became a clerk in the Colonial Secretary's Office. In 1856 he transferred to the Land and Works Department and in 1859 joined the railway branch of the Department of Public Works. In 1870 he became chief clerk for railways, secretary in 1875 and succeeded John Rae [q.v.] as commissioner on 29 January 1878. He attributed a disastrous collision at Emu Plains next day to the 'dangerous state of disorganization' in the railways and to Rae's unwarranted cancellation of the 'Working Orders' after a near collision at Bathurst in 1877.

Goodchap was commissioner in a railway boom: in 1878-86 over 1300 miles of track were opened, passengers quadrupled, freight doubled and earnings rose from £902,987 to £2,208,294. Despite the increased traffic and inadequacies of the Redfern terminal, management improved. Goodchap claimed that his most important innovations were the introduction of interlocking points and signals and the 'absolute block' system of signalling. He also instigated the training of employees in first aid for the Railway Ambulance Corps and the construction of large maintenance and repair workshops. However, a feud between Goodchap and the engineer-in-chief, John Whitton [q.v.], was damaging and the administration was hampered by political pressures conducive to extravagance in the construction of new lines and patronage in appointments. In debates on Henry Parkes's [q.v.] Government Railways Act, 1888, Goodchap's administration was criticized and he was accused of being more interested in building new lines than in making the railways profitable. The Act set up a corporate body of three railway commissioners to manage the railways and remove them from political influence. On 27 October 1888 Goodchap resigned when, contrary to expectation, he was not appointed to the new commission. Parkes noted that he had 'no practical knowledge' and that the lines were in a dangerous state. Goodchap's employees gave him £500 which he donated for a library for railway employees. Parkes's suggestion that he visit Europe and America as a travelling commissioner was dropped after opposition in parliament.

Goodchap went to England in 1889 and in his absence was elected as a protectionist to the Legislative Asembly for Redfern. Defeated in 1891, he was nominated to the Legislative Council in 1892. In 1871 he had been a founder and honorary secretary of the Civil Service Co-operative Society and in 1885 was appointed to the Civil Service Board on which he supported his friend A. C. Fraser [q.v.]. He was a member of the Union Club and briefly honorary treasurer of the Australian Jockey Club. Unmarried he died from diabetes and pneumonia at his home in Potts Point on 20 October 1896 and was buried with Anglican rites in Waverley cemetery. His estate was valued at £739.

PD (NSW), 1888-89; V&P (LA NSW), 1877-78, 4, 185, 192, 1887 (2nd S), 2, 154, 314, 1888-89, 2, 597; R. L. Wettenhall, 'Early railway management legislation in New South Wales', *Tas Univ Law Review*, July 1960; *Bulletin*, 5 May 1880, 30 June 1883; *Illustrated Sydney News*, 30 Sept 1882; *Australasian*, 28 Apr, 27 Oct 1888; *Town and Country J*, 3 Nov 1888, 2 Mar 1889; Parkes letters (ML).

J. H. FORSYTH

GOODE, SIR CHARLES HENRY (1827-1922), merchant and philanthropist, was born on 29 May 1827 at Hinton, Herefordshire, England, son of Samuel Goode. He left school at 10 to help his father and at 12 was apprenticed to a draper. In 1849 he migrated to South Australia where he opened a shop at North Adelaide and peddled goods first on foot and later by cart. Joined by Thomas Good the business grew rapidly. When Good retired Charles and his brothers Samuel and Matthew opened a warehouse in Adelaide. Charles went to London in 1859 to establish a buying department and returned to Adelaide in 1863. In March 1865 he was elected for East Torrens to the House of Assembly but resigned in November 1866 because of cotton shortages caused by the American civil war. He then directed the business in England for twelve years; after his return the partnership with his brothers was dissolved in 1882 and Goode took W. H. Durrant, his London manager, and W. H. Tite, an Adelaide business associate, as his partners. When Tite retired the firm of Goode, Durrant carried on for many years until it merged with D. & W. Murray [q.v.]. Goode remained a director but had other interests: he had become a justice of the peace in 1866 and was a director of a bank, an insurance society, several manufacturing concerns and the *South Australian Advertiser*.

Best known as a philanthropist Goode had studied social welfare in England and brought knowledge as well as enthusiasm to social work in Adelaide. A staunch Baptist he conducted a men's Bible class at Flinders Street Church for thirty-two years. He also helped to found the Young Men's Christian Association in Adelaide and was secretary of its first committee in 1851; when it was re-established in 1879 he gave long service as its president. He was prominent in founding the Royal Institution for the Blind in 1884, and its only president until 1922. He was a founder of the Adult Deaf and Dumb Mission and of the Adelaide Children's Hospital, serving for years on its board. He was also chairman of the James Brown trust set up to care for sick and crippled children and for sufferers from tuberculosis. In 1898 he published a series of letters to young people as *A visit to Japan and notes by the way*. In January 1912 he was knighted. He not only signed cheques for good causes but gave his services generously and his public philanthropy did not make him unsympathetic to individual claims. According to the *Mail*, 'His name was a synonym for charitable deeds. Despite all the wonderful work done in this respect, his efforts stand right out, and every member of the community is proud to acknowledge the excellence of this prince of philanthropists'.

Goode was twice married: first, on 6 August 1856 at Christchurch, North Adelaide, to Mary Harriet Good, sister of his first partner; and second, on 16 December 1900 to a widow, Helen Augusta Lloyd, née Smith, He had no children but was a good stepfather to the two daughters of his second wife. He died on 5 February 1922, leaving an estate of £32,000.

A portrait in oils is in the Art Gallery of South Australia.

H. P. (Padgham), *32 years: reminiscences of the . . . Baptist Young Men's Bible Class* (Adel, 1911); *Honorary Magistrate*, June 1909; North Adelaide Baptist Church minutes; records held by Goode, Durrant & Murray (Aust) Ltd.

A. C. HILL

GOODENOUGH, JAMES GRAHAM (1830-1875), naval officer, was born on 3 December 1830 at Stoke Hill, near Guildford, Surrey, England, son of Edmund Goodenough, dean of Wells, and his wife Frances, née Cockerell. Educated at Westminster School, he entered the navy at 14. He served first in the Pacific in the *Collingwood*, then in the *Cyclops* off the African coast in 1848-49 and then returned to England to study for his lieutenant's commission. In 1851 he joined the *Centaur* off the east coast of South America and in 1854-55 was in the Baltic during the Crimean war. On the China station in 1856-61 he was present at the capture of Canton in December 1857. For the sake of his health he was allowed to return to England and served in the Channel squadron until 1863 when, as a captain and with an established reputation as a gunnery expert, he was sent to North America as an observer in the American civil war. In 1871, after further service in the Mediterranean, he became a member of the Admiralty's committee on warship design. For about a year he was naval attaché in several European embassies where his professional abilities, grave, reserved manners and linguistic talents all commanded respect.

In May 1873 Goodenough was appointed captain of H.M.S. *Pearl* and commodore of the Australian station. Before leaving England Goodenough, with Edgar L. Layard, the new consul in Fiji, was selected by the government to inquire into the question of annexing or establishing a British protectorate there. He arrived in Fiji on 16 November ahead of Layard and of the papers prepared in the Colonial Office for his information. He soon decided that the local government, which he had been instructed to recognize *de facto*, was maintained only by the presence of the navy and that its relations with the British settlers were hostile. He sided with the settlers and in December reported to the Admiralty, and in February 1874 to the Colonial Office, that Fiji ought to be annexed. With Layard he helped to undermine the existing government and worked for a voluntary cession. By April when the Colonial Office received his report he and Layard had already exceeded their authority by accepting the cession on terms, and in London Gladstone and Kimberley had given way to Disraeli and Carnarvon. Dissatisfied with the *fait accompli* the new ministers sent Sir Hercules Robinson, governor of New South Wales, to negotiate an unconditional cession. Despite Robinson's praise of his work, Goodenough was bitterly disappointed by adverse criticism in Britain and wrote in his journal: 'I share the usual fate of the naval officer, viz., to be broyé on the wheel of difficulty for a civilian to . . . pick my brain afterwards'.

As senior officer on the Australian station Goodenough was well known and well liked. He was a keen race-goer and had strong charitable interests, especially among seamen. His duties included the maintenance of law and order among British subjects in the Pacific and control of their relations with indigenous peoples. On 12 August 1875 while trying to conciliate natives on Carlisle Bay in the Santa Cruz Islands he and others of his party were wounded by poisoned arrows. He refused 'to allow a single life to be taken in retaliation', although some huts were burnt. Tetanus set in and, after gallantly bidding farewell to the ship's company, Goodenough died on 20 August in the *Pearl*, 500 miles from Sydney.

He was buried in the cemetery of St Thomas's Church of England, North Sydney, between two of his men. He was survived by his wife Victoria, daughter of William Hamilton, whom he had married in England on 31 May 1864, and by two sons. One son, William Edmund, became an admiral. His widow published uncontroversial parts of his journal and became a lady-in-waiting to Queen Victoria. In 1876 Goodenough Royal Naval House was established in Sydney by public charity to continue his welfare work for naval men. A bay and island on the Papuan coast were named after him. A stained glass window in his memory is in St Thomas's, North Sydney, a bust by Prince Victor of Hohenloe is in the Painted Hall at Greenwich and another by Achille Simonetti [q.v.] is in the Art Gallery of New South Wales.

V. H. Goodenough (ed), *Journal of Commodore Goodenough . . . 1873-1875* (Lond, 1876); J. D. Legge, *Britain in Fiji, 1858-1880* (Lond, 1958); W. P. Morrell, *Britain in the Pacific Islands* (Oxford, 1960); W. D. McIntyre, 'New light on Commodore Goodenough's mission to Fiji 1873-74', *Hist Studies*, no 39, Nov 1962; D. Scarr, 'John Bates Thurston, Commodore J. G. Goodenough, and rampant Anglo-Saxons in Fiji', *Hist Studies*, no 43, Oct 1964; Goodenough papers (ML); Parkes letters (ML).

JOHN M. WARD

GOODLET, JOHN HAY (1835-1914), timber merchant and philanthropist, was born on 22 March 1835 at Leith, Scotland, son of George Goodlet, merchant, and his wife Mary, née Hay. In June 1852 he arrived in Melbourne where he was employed by C. & J. Smith, builders. In 1855 he went to Sydney with a shipload of American doors, sold them profitably, began importing timber from Jervis Bay and set up a sawmill in Erskine Street with his own wharf. About 1862 James Smith became his partner and by 1881 they were sawing over 100,000 ft. a week and had two other coastal mills, brickworks at Granville producing 200,000 bricks a week and a pottery in Surry Hills making drain and sewage pipes, tiles, terra cotta and chimney pots and stoneware. In 1866-88 Goodlet was a director and twice chairman of the Australian Mutual Provident Society. He was a commissioner for the London Exhibition in 1872 and for the Sydney city railway in 1890-91. He was active in the volunteer corps and became a lieut-colonel of the second infantry regiment.

Goodlet suffered severely in the bank crash of 1893 but soon recovered. As managing director of a limited company he began to make Portland cement at the Granville works, expanded his other branches and prospered greatly. He gave generous help to such charitable institutions as the Thirlmere Home for chronic consumptives at Picton, the Sydney Hospital, Benevolent Society, Royal Hospital for Women at Paddington, the New South Wales Institution for the Deaf and Dumb and the Blind and the Sydney City Mission. Goodlet's major interest was the Presbyterian Church. He was an active convener of the finance committee of the General Assembly of Australia and a member of many other committees. In May 1910 he represented New South Wales at the General Assembly of the Presbyterian Churches and at a World Missionary Conference in Scotland. Chairman of directors of the *Presbyterian*, he guaranteed the loan which founded the new *Messenger* in 1901 and by 1909 had paid off the overdraft. For many years he was Sunday school superintendent at Ashfield where in 1903 he opened the Goodlet institute. In 1870-1914 he served on the Council of St Andrew's College, University of Sydney, and helped to secure its finances, giving 2000 shares in his firm to found the Goodlet scholarships for the students for the Presbyterian ministry. In 1883-92 he was a trustee of Cooerwull Boys' School near Lithgow and in 1888 helped to found the Presbyterian Ladies' College at Croydon. In 1878-80 he had guaranteed half the stipend of three bush missionaries in New South Wales. At Sholinghur, India, he built a hospital after control of the mission there was transferred from Scotland to Sydney.

In 1860 Goodlet had married Ann Alison Panton (1827-1903); she supported all her husband's charities, was president of the first Australian branch of the Young Women's Christian Association in 1880-1903 and won a place on the State Children's Relief Board in 1887. In 1903 he married Elizabeth Mary Forbes (1865-1926), who devoted most of her time to missions. Goodlet died on 13 January 1914. He had no children and left most of his estate of £92,910 to the Presbyterian Church with 30 per cent for foreign missions.

A portrait is in St Andrew's College and memorial windows to him and his wives are in the Ashfield Church.

T. Richards (ed), *New South Wales in 1881* (Syd, 1882); W. F. Morrison, *The Aldine centennial history of New South Wales*, 2 (Syd, 1888); A. D. Gilchrist (ed), *John Dunmore*

Lang (Melb, 1951); *Messenger* (Presbyterian, NSW), 16 Jan 1903, 23 Jan 1914, 6, 13 Aug 1926; *Aurora Australis* (Ashfield), Mar 1914; *Sydney City Mission Herald*, 2 Feb 1914; *A'sian Builder and Contractor's News*, 28 May 1887; *Prices Current* (Goodlet & Smith, Ltd), Oct 1904, Feb 1906, Feb 1907; *SMH*, 14, 15 Jan 1914; The industrial progress of N.S.W. (ML); Walker papers (Presbyterian Lib, Assembly Hall, Syd); General Assembly, Minutes (Presbyterian Lib, Assembly Hall, Syd).

RUTH TEALE

GOODMAN, GEORGE (1821-1908), Anglican clergyman, was born on 17 May 1821 at Peterborough, Northamptonshire, England, the third son of Thomas Goodman, merchant, and his wife Mary, née Dent. He was educated at Kings Cliffe, at Hazelwood School, Edgbaston, and at Camberwell. After two years of commercial experience he entered Christ's College, Cambridge (B.A., 1844; M.A., 1847). He was ordained deacon on 2 March 1845 by the bishop of Chester, J. B. Sumner, on a title to Holy Trinity, Birkenhead, and priest in 1846. Later that year he moved to London as assistant curate at St Bride's, Fleet Street.

In May 1853 Goodman heard the former archdeacon of Melbourne, Thomas Hart Davies, speak on Bishop Charles Perry's [q.v.] desperate need for clergy and later that year he sailed for Melbourne, arriving in December. Perry immediately appointed him his examining chaplain and in January 1855, after a year at Heidelberg, vicar of Christ Church, Geelong. In 1877 Bishop Moorhouse [q.v.] appointed him first rural dean of Geelong and in 1879 he was elected by the Church Assembly a canon of the proposed St Paul's Cathedral. As examining chaplain to Perry and his successors for fifty years and lecturer in homiletics and exegesis in the theological faculty of Trinity College, Melbourne, in 1879-99, Goodman's influence on the clergy of Victoria was lasting and pervasive.

At Geelong Goodman was active in philanthropic and educational activities. He was a member of the hospital committee, president of the Mechanics' Institute and Mrs Austin's adviser in establishing cottage homes for the elderly. Both he and his wife gave evidence to the royal commission on charitable institutions in 1891-93. He had inherited a parochial school which survived until 1879 but his main educational interest centred on Geelong Grammar School which was built opposite Christ Church in 1858. He became secretary of the school council in 1863, the boys worshipped in his church, and successive headmasters, J. Bracebridge Wilson [q.v.] and L. H. Lindon, served as churchwardens throughout his ministry.

Goodman's scholarship was reflected in his preaching and teaching. Both in England and Victoria he contributed articles and reviews on biblical and historical topics to literary and religious journals. In 1865 he published the *Principles and practice of public reading*, a manual which incorporated his own preaching techniques. His *magnum opus* was *The Church in Victoria during the Episcopate of the Right Reverend Charles Perry, First Bishop of Melbourne* (1892). In an introductory note the bishop declared that Goodman was qualified 'by his general ability, by his agreement with me in religious principles and by his experience in the diocese' to accomplish the work satisfactorily. The memoir, published at Perry's expense, displays Goodman's sensitive understanding of Perry as man and bishop.

His evangelical preaching was Biblical rather than popular and his outlook on religion and life was conservative. Although offered preferment he was content to minister faithfully in his familiar sphere and consistently declined to leave Geelong, until he retired in September 1906. On 1 July 1853 he had married Margaret Elizabeth, daughter of Henry Powlett Mortlock, bookseller of Stamford. She had been governess to the marquess of Normanby and a worker at St Bride's, London; she died on 26 September 1901. Goodman died on 25 June 1908, survived by two daughters of their six children.

W. R. Brownhill, *The history of Geelong and Corio Bay* (Melb, 1955); L. L. Nash, *Forward flows the time: the story of Ridley College* (Melb, 1960); *Geelong Advertiser*, 26 June 1908.   JAMES GRANT

GOOLD, JAMES ALIPIUS (1812-1886), Roman Catholic archbishop, was born on 4 November 1812 into a prosperous commercial family in Cork, Ireland. He entered the Augustinian order, made his novitiate at Grantstown, Wexford, and studied divinity at Rome and Perugia. He was ordained in 1835. After meetings in Rome with Dr Ullathorne [q.v.] Goold returned to Ireland and obtained permission from his superiors to volunteer for missionary service in New South Wales. With a testimonial from the Father Provincial of the Augustinians in Ireland attesting his piety, talent and strict observance of rule he arrived in Sydney on 24 February 1838.

Goold began work as assistant to Archdeacon McEncroe [q.v.] and a few months later was appointed to Campbelltown. In his five years there he built schools and several churches, including St John's, and won repute as an outstanding missionary pastor by his piety and diligence. He became a protégé of Archbishop Polding [q.v.], and was appointed by Pope Pius IX as bishop of the new see of Melbourne on 9 July 1847. Polding's inability to secure an assistant bishop delayed Goold's consecration in St Mary's Cathedral until 6 August 1848.

Goold travelled overland to Melbourne, making the six-hundred-mile journey in a coach and four in nineteen days. He was installed in St Francis pro-Cathedral on 8 October. Religious factional strife was then acute and the new bishop became a focus for Catholic loyalties in the Port Phillip District. In November and December he disputed the title 'Bishop of Melbourne' with the Anglican Dr Perry [q.v.]; the Colonial Secretary's Office found their claims equal within the law and contention continued. In 1850 Goold was a central figure in the defence of Irish immigrant orphans who were attacked by officialdom because of their inability to be assimilated into an urban community. Throughout the decade he led Catholic opposition to Anglican claims of precedence at government functions; this dispute culminated when Goold and his clergy boycotted the Queen's birthday levee in 1859. By then his efforts to make the Catholic Church a recognized influence within the colony had been largely successful, but probably more obvious was his direction of the physical growth of the Church.

Goold saw that the most immediate need of the Catholic Church in the Port Phillip District was sufficient clergy not only for the rapidly growing population in Melbourne but also for the scattered rural communities which extended as far west as Portland and north to the ranges. The second need was ecclesiastical and school buildings, including a cathedral. To raise funds for supplementing government grants he launched the Catholic Association in January 1849. In that year with extensive lay and clerical support it raised money for the first mission to Ireland to recruit priests for the diocese. In 1851 Goold visited Ireland for the same purpose, and the first new missions were established and manned by newly-arrived Irish and English priests. A small seminary was attached to St Francis's Church to train clergy until St Patrick's College was opened. The twofold problem of providing sufficient clergy and buildings was accentuated by the gold rushes and permanent pastors could not be appointed to the goldfields until 1853. As well as visiting all the country missions, Goold went to the Ballarat goldfields in November and December 1854 and September 1855. According to some contemporaries, his presence was said to have pacified many diggers and to have contributed to the orderly behaviour of Catholic miners, particularly after the Eureka affair.

In the formative years of his episcopate Goold assumed firm personal direction of the affairs of his diocese. In 1853 he had helped to found the weekly *Catholic Tribune* which soon closed after he withdrew his patronage. He also developed a positive policy for the social and religious improvement of his flock. Throughout the 1850s and particularly after the Legislative Council's select committee recommended government grants to religious denominations in 1852 he was determined to secure the continuity of this aid. He persisted despite pressure from some Catholics who were willing to accept the abolition of government grants and replace them with voluntary donations for support of the clergy and religious education. Before the first communities of nuns arrived in 1857 he had tried hard on overseas visits to obtain such staff for his proposed orphanage, hospital and schools. The introduction of teaching orders for boys after 1865 developed from the same policy.

In Melbourne as at Campbelltown Goold showed great interest in education. One of the first tasks he gave the Catholic Association was to raise funds for building schools in rural areas. He observed that even with grants from the Denominational Schools Board both schools and teachers were lamentably deficient. Central control of Catholic education was established in the 1850s by the bishop and his vicar-general, John Fitzpatrick [q.v.], and was consolidated in 1861 under the Catholic Education Committee. It met regularly under Goold's chairmanship and included representatives of clergy and prominent laity. After the Victorian Board of Education was formed in 1862 he often clashed with government authorities over the role of local Catholic clergymen on school committees. Whenever the board challenged his authority over the membership of such a committee, especially after 1863, Goold withdrew that school from receiving state aid, and a system of voluntary donation took its place. In 1866 Goold refused to appear before the royal commission into education because no episcopally-nominated Catholic had been appointed to it, although the government had invited two Catholic laymen to join it.

Before the 1872 election Goold issued a pastoral admonition, calling on Catholic laity and clergy to withhold their votes from those candidates 'in favour of a scheme of godless compulsory education'. In 1873-84 the Catholic Education Committee acted as a focal point for political action over this grievance. In those years proposals for compromise were often mooted but Goold would

entertain no solution that reduced his authority as exercised through the central committee or his nominees on local school committees. Yet he was concerned about the possible harmful effects of Catholic political rallies even when organized by his committeemen. He also failed to give firm directions to his clerical and lay advisers for strengthening the support of Catholic schools, an increasingly burdensome responsibility for the local clergy and their committees, while he gradually concentrated his attentions on administration of his diocese and the building of its cathedral.

St Patrick's Church on Eastern Hill had been planned early in Goold's episcopate and, after recasting of the plans, the building was almost complete in 1858 when the decision was taken to demolish part of it and rebuild on W. W. Wardell's [q.v.] Gothic design. The decision was strongly opposed by the laity and particularly the clergy many of whom were already finding difficulty in raising funds for local projects, and the new building was started without a public ceremony. In his correspondence and pastorals for two decades Goold appealed for generous donations for the cathedral, and in 1874 from Rome he directed Fitzpatrick to divide the metropolitan area into sections for systematic collection. Although the cathedral project remained for years a focus for opposition, it was praised by the Catholic press and subscriptions were generally filled.

In 1858 Goold had sought support from the Society for the Propagation of the Faith in Rome for a special missionary to the Chinese in Victoria and for the pastoral care of the Aboriginals, but little was done. He visited Rome and Ireland again in 1867, and attended the council session of 1869. In 1873 on his last visit to Rome it was announced that he would become archbishop when Melbourne was made a metropolitan see on 31 March 1874. He had attended the first provincial council of the Catholic Church in Australia at Sydney in 1844 and the second in Melbourne in 1869, advocating in both as in Rome the creation of new Australian sees. He also wanted Irish bishops despite the policy of Polding who favoured Benedictines and other English clergy for Australian appointments.

Archbishop Goold enjoyed good health until the 1880s. At Brighton on 21 August 1882 he was fired at by an old acquaintance, Patrick, brother of H. J. O'Farrell [q.v.] who had wounded the duke of Edinburgh at Sydney in 1868. Goold's health deteriorated steadily after that day, but he continued to display the qualities of devoted pastor by making widespread visitations and confirmations. Throughout his episcopate he had been an unyielding but sincere prelate whose first concern was his church and its interests. He had no broad views or scholastic achievement and ruled his archdiocese with the conservatism and single-mindedness of an Irish bishop in an Irish see. He died after a heart attack at Brighton on 11 June 1886. He was buried within St Patrick's Cathedral, the building of which was perhaps his greatest triumph.

J. F. Hogan, *A biographical sketch of the late Most Rev. James Alipius Goold* (Melb, 1886); P. F. Moran, *History of the Catholic Church in Australasia* (Syd, 1895); *Advocate* (Melb), 1868-86; *Australasian*, 29 June 1872; *Illustrated Aust News*, 1882, 1886; *Argus*, 12, 13, 16 June 1886; *Freeman's J*, 19 June, 3 July 1886; Catholic Education Cttee, Minutes 1861-84 (Roman Catholic Archives, Melb).

J. R. J. GRIGSBY

GOOLD, STEPHEN STYLES (1817-1876), painter, contractor and political organizer, was born in Wiltshire, England, son of Moses Goold and his wife, née Styles. He migrated to Australia in 1841 and settled in Sydney. On 7 March 1843 at St James's Church of England he married Margery Balfour, an Irish housemaid. He helped to found the Loyal Orange Institution in 1845 and as an active Primitive Methodist became a prominent lay preacher and a trustee of the Kent Street Chapel. He achieved modest success in his trade as a painter and glazier and probably did some building and contracting as well.

After the attempted assassination of the duke of Edinburgh, Goold joined the Protestant Political Association formed in March 1868. It sought the 'self defence and maintenance of Protestant principles' by securing the return of Protestants to parliament and the city council. Goold was active in the association especially when his own branch at Waterloo emerged as the centre of opposition to John Davies's [q.v.] attempts to force it to take sides in politics. Goold unsuccessfully opposed Davies for the presidency in November but they remained closely linked in politics. Goold began to campaign actively for municipal and parliamentary candidates who had the association's support and late in 1869 he became its paid itinerant organizer. In January 1870 he was elected grand master of the Loyal Orange Institution and established it in country districts where he also established agencies for its weekly *Protestant Standard*. With publicity by its editior, Rev. John McGibbon [q.v.], and his own organizing abilities Goold built up the institution from 30 lodges and fewer than 3000 members in early 1870 to 120 lodges and over 16,000

members by the end of 1875 when ill health forced him to resign. In 1870-76 he represented Phillip ward in the Sydney Municipal Council. In 1871 he had been appointed a magistrate and in 1874 became mayor of Sydney. In December he won the seat of Mudgee in the Legislative Assembly. He retained a strong Evangelical antipathy for Roman Catholicism as an organized religion but was genuine in his charitable concern for Catholics as individuals. Rather than use his positions to advance the Protestant cause, he seems to have regarded them as signs of the increased respectability that his activities had brought him.

Aged 59 Goold died of hypostatic disease and debility on 28 August 1876, survived by his wife, a son and three daughters. He was buried in Camperdown cemetery by his old Orange friend, Rev. Zachary Barry [q.v.]. For a social aspirant with religious commitments, Goold's funeral was a fitting reward. Over 1000 people attended the graveside and the pall-bearers included the premier, the Speaker and the mayor of Sydney.

Aust Protestant Banner, 10 Nov, 4 Dec 1868; *Freeman's J* (Syd), 1 Dec 1870; *Protestant Standard*, 25 Feb 1871, 2 Sept 1876; *SMH*, 1 Sept 1876.

MARK LYONS

GORDON, ADAM LINDSAY (1833-1870), poet and horseman, was born on 19 October 1833 at Fayal, Azores, the only son of Adam Durnford Gordon, a retired captain of the Bengal cavalry and teacher of Hindustani, and his wife Harriet Gordon, who were cousins. His parents were in comfortable circumstances, his mother having inherited £20,000. He was educated at Cheltenham College, the Royal Military Academy at Woolwich in 1848-51 and the Royal Worcester Grammar School in 1852. Even in his early years he established a pattern of interests which he sustained throughout his life. As an adolescent he was taught riding and by 1852 was beginning his racing career. His fecklessness was apparent early. He himself said that his 'strength and health were broken by dissipation and humbug'.

His father secured Gordon an offer of a position in South Australia. He sailed in the *Julia* and arrived in Adelaide on 11 November. On the 24th he joined the South Australian Mounted Police. He had hoped for a captaincy, and according to his own account was very near getting one 'but the rules compelled a man properly speaking to serve as a trooper'. He seems to have been content with his lot, since he wrote to his friend Charley Walker, 'I have done well, my boy, which you will be glad to hear and have got an easy billet in a station that suits me well, with the hope of a speedy promotion'. For two years he was stationed at Penola in the Mount Gambier region where he led a routine life with no remarkable incidents or exploits to interrupt his daily duties. He resigned on 4 November 1855 ostensibly to become a drover. His superior officer wrote that he had conducted himself 'remarkably well' and that he was sorry to lose him. Instead of droving Gordon took up horse-breaking in the south-east. He was in touch either directly or indirectly with his family in England, and his father gave him financial assistance until his death on 17 June 1857. In that year Gordon met J. E. Tenison-Woods [q.v.] who was able to supply him with books and whose friendship stimulated Gordon's interest in literature.

On 29 April 1859 Gordon's mother died and on 26 October 1861 he received from her estate a legacy of £7000. Meantime he had continued as horse-breaker and steeple-chase rider in country areas. The main records of him in this period concern his successes and failures at race meetings in the Penola and Mount Gambier districts. The legacy brought him relative prosperity. On 20 October 1862 he married Margaret Park, who was born in Glasgow. She had little education but was an excellent horse-woman. Even her hard work and practical good sense could not save Gordon from his financial imprudence and increasing melancholia. In March 1864 Gordon bought Dingley Dell, a cottage near Port MacDonnell. He also speculated in land and was mortgagee for several landholders. His first publication, 'The Feud', appeared in the Border Watch, 30 August. A new phase in Gordon's life began on 11 January 1865 when he received a deputation asking him to stand for the South Australian parliament. In the next two months he managed to combine steeplechasing and political campaigning. The sitting members were defeated and with John Riddoch, a loyal friend and lifelong supporter, Gordon was returned to the House of Assembly for the Victoria district, topping the poll. He combined his parliamentary duties with steeplechasing, travelling to races in Adelaide, Ballarat and Melbourne and publishing poems. He resigned on 10 November 1866, probably because he had invested in land in Western Australia. On 11 December with Lambton Mount he landed at Bunbury with some 5000 sheep; in a few months his flock had been reduced by about one-third. In March 1867 he returned to Adelaide, gave up his temporary home in Glenelg and went back to Mount Gambier. His only child, Annie Lindsay, was born at Robe on 3 May. In June his first two volumes of poetry were

published: Ashtaroth on 10 June and Sea Spray and Smoke Drift on the 19th. Their financial failure together with his losses in Western Australia and racing must have dissipated much of the legacy from his mother's estate.

On 22 November he rented Craig's livery stables in Ballarat, and in January 1868 he joined the Ballarat Troop of Light Horse. In March he was promoted senior sergeant but suffered a serious horse-riding accident, one of many that undermined his physical condition. On 14 April his daughter died. These private misfortunes, together with the failure of the livery stables, led to his wife's departure from Ballarat on 25 September. A small legacy enabled Gordon to settle his debts and on 1 October he left to stay for two months in Melbourne with Robert Power. His reputation was then growing. The Australasian printed articles on his feats of horsemanship, and he was praised for his poetic talents by the Colonial Monthly. In spite of private difficulties he continued his racing career, adding to his renown for recklessness and daring. In the early months of 1869 he was riding in various parts of Victoria, and in May he took lodgings in Brighton where his wife rejoined him. He was also continuing to publish poetry and prose. On 12 March 1870 he had another bad riding accident and wrote to Riddoch, 'I am hurt inside somewhere'.

In 1868 Gordon heard that he was heir to the family estate, Esselmont, in Scotland. He was convinced of his right to the estate but determined not to return to England. His letters show his increasing melancholia and preoccupation with financial difficulties. He hoped, by acquiring Esselmont, to guarantee his wife's financial security. In June he received news that the entail of Esselmont had been abolished and therefore he would not receive the inheritance. On 23 June 1870 his Bush Ballads and Galloping Rhymes was published and Henry Kendall [q.v.] showed him a proof copy of the enthusiastic review he had written. At dawn the next morning Gordon went to the beach at Brighton and shot himself.

The pattern of Gordon's life was strange. If the purpose of his migration to Australia was to escape the debilitating attractions of the company into which he had fallen as a young man in England, the life that he led merely served to exacerbate his own temperamental weaknesses. His real love was steeplechasing yet he had sufficient poetic talent to develop into a more substantial writer than he ever became. Long after he died, enthusiastic admirers made pilgrimages to his grave, to Dingley Dell and to other places associated with him. A bust unveiled on 11 May 1934 in West-minster Abbey by the duke of York attests his extraordinary popularity. His literary reputation has now declined. His popular ballads with their narrative drive and vital-ity are in marked contrast to his more am-bitious poems which, heavily imitative of Romantic and Victorian poetry, are marred by carelessness and inattention to detail. But his successes and failures in his poetry, as in his own life, are a reflection of the tastes and interests of his time.

A statue by Paul Montfort is near Parlia-ment House, Melbourne.

E. Humphris and D. Sladen, *Adam Lindsay Gordon* (Lond, 1912); J. K. Moir, Adam Lindsay Gordon (LaT L); Gordon letters (ML, copies RHSV); Gordon material, D3532 (SAA).

LEONIE KRAMER

GORDON, ALEXANDER (1815-1903), barrister, was born in London, the eldest son of Alexander Gordon, solicitor. Educated in London he served in an attorney's office, entered the Inner Temple in November 1837 and in November 1841 was called to the Bar. He worked mostly in equity until 1857 when his health and his desire for profes-sional advancement prompted his migration to Sydney. He soon became prominent at the Bar and won repute for his advocacy in *Purves* v. *Attorney-General and Lang*, which included a Privy Council decision in his favour. In 1858-74 he appeared in about three-quarters of the reported equity cases. This specialization was unusual in colonial practice and may have impeded his further progress. Although appointed Q.C. his chief interest lay outside the law courts.

Gordon was an Evangelical Anglican de-vout in promoting religion and philan-thropy. He served on such charitable com-mittees as the Home Visiting and Relief Society and the Prince Alfred Hospital and on many ecclesiastical and educational bod-ies. He was a director of the Sydney Dio-cesan Committee and Educational and Book Society, represented his church on the Denominational School Board in 1859-66 and was a fellow of St Paul's College in 1867-74. At St Paul's, Redfern, he was a churchwarden and taught a Sunday school and men's Bible class. However, his main work for the Church of England was legal and constitutional. In the 1840s the colonial church had contemplated schemes for synodical government. Gordon first believed that a constitution should be based on a voluntary compact but soon decided that full legislative sanction was required. He helped to draft a bill discussed by the dio-cesan conference in 1858. Despite serious differences with other Anglican lawyers he

emerged as the foremost advocate of parlia-mentary action and the legal tie with the Church of England. In 1866 he was largely responsible for the Church of England Pro-perty Management Act, the preamble of which referred to the constitutions accepted by conferences within the dioceses of New South Wales; though more indirect than he hoped, the constitutions were to be recorded in the Supreme Court. In 1872 he helped to create a constitution for the Church in Aus-tralia and Tasmania. In 1862-74 he was chancellor of the Sydney diocese and in 1867-68 registrar. In all this activity his close co-operation with Bishop Barker [q.v.] led to charges of undue influence over his bishop but they were untrue. Both men were Erastian Low Churchmen and were as one in defending Anglican denominational schools and in securing concessions in the public schools bill, 1866.

In 1874 Gordon returned to England but after a few years came back to Sydney and resumed his work in the courts and the church. He helped to resolve the problems which arose over the election of Barker's successor in 1882-83, devised a legislative settlement for church property and became chancellor in 1884. Predictably, he opposed Parkes's educational reforms in 1879-80 and began to acquire political interests. In 1883 he was appointed to the Legislative Council by his friend Alexander Stuart [q.v.]. He supported Stuart's land legislation but on constitutional grounds opposed the Sudan policy of W. B. Dalley's [q.v.] ministry. Al-ways more lawyer than politician, Gordon spoke most often on legal subjects. Late in 1885 he retired to England but retained colonial interests: he supported the church's stand on divorce reform, spoke on the problems of Australian Anglicanism to meetings of English churchmen and in 1889 published *The Future of the Empire; or, a brief statement of the case against Imperial Federation*. Between 1867 and 1884 he had published ten pamphlets chiefly on church law and polity. Gordon died at Puckle-church, Gloucestershire, on 12 December 1903. By his wife Anne, née Chambers, he had a son, Alexander (1858-1942), who was a judge of the New South Wales Supreme Court in 1910-28 and was knighted in 1930.

W. M. Cowper (ed), *Episcopate of the Right Reverend Frederic Barker . . . A memoir* (Lond, 1888); J. G. Legge, *A selection of Supreme Court cases in New South Wales from 1825 to 1862*, 2 (Syd, 1896); R. Border, *Church and state in Australia 1788-1872* (Lond, 1962); *Supreme Court reports* (NSW), 1861-74; *Church Sentinel*, Dec 1858; *SMH*, 15 July 1871; *Aust Churchman* (Syd), 26 Dec 1903; V&P Synod, 1866, 1874, 1886, 1904 (Syd Diocesan Registry).

K. J. CABLE

GORDON, GEORGE (1829-1907), engineer, was born at Arbroath, Forfarshire, Scotland, son of Robert Gordon and his wife Margaret, née Auton; the family home was Cargield House, near Dumfries. After apprenticeship in England with a consulting engineer he spent six years in Holland, four of them as chief engineer of the Amsterdam Water Co., and then served for ten years as chief district engineer of the Madras Irrigation and Canal Co. As an hydraulic engineer he offered his services to the Victorian government and in 1871 was asked to report on the public waterworks but the appointment was cancelled. In October the Duffy [q.v.] government opened fresh negotiations and on 5 May 1872 Gordon arrived in Melbourne to become chief engineer of the lands and works board. On 2 February 1875 he became chief engineer of the water supply department and held the post till Black Wednesday, 9 January 1878. His dismissal was raised in parliament and he petitioned the governor and the Queen for reinstatement and compensation but to no avail.

In 1880 Gordon was appointed to a water conservancy board to report on supplying water to the northern plains of Victoria for stock and domestic purposes. The twelve reports in 1880-81 and two on irrigation in 1882 and 1884 were cautious. The board concluded that the best means of supplying water was by using the natural channels and building cheap works for diversion and storage under the control of local trusts. These principles met with spirited opposition from advocates of large-scale irrigation such as Hugh McColl [q.v.] but became the basis of the Victorian Water Conservation Act of 1881 and later legislation in 1883-84. The board was then dissolved and Gordon was virtually dismissed. Again his case was raised in parliament where his work, particularly the Stony Creek weir, was criticized. In the controversy opinions of his ability ranged from adulation to condemnation. The political overtones of the quarrel confuse any assessment of his talent and even later writers disagree as to whether his reports and works have been vindicated by time.

In the next two decades Gordon managed his own engineering firm, consolidated the wealth he was amassing in private ventures, worked occasionally for the lands and works board and was consulted by the governments of Tasmania and New South Wales. He continued his interest in water schemes and in 1889 was a founding partner of the Lake Boga Irrigation Co. He also held land in the Chaffey Bros' scheme at Mildura.

Gordon published several articles and pamphlets on irrigation and water conserva-tion, including a report on water supply for Invercargill, New Zealand, after a visit in April-May 1878. He was a fellow of the Victorian branch of the Royal Geographical Society. He died aged 78 at his home, Ellerslie, Toorak, on 25 February 1907, survived by two children of his first marriage, and by his second wife Violette Elizabeth, née Eddington, and their three sons and one daughter. He left assets of over £8000.

F. W. Eggleston, *State socialism in Victoria* (Lond, 1932); C. S. Martin, *Irrigation and closer settlement in the Shepparton district, 1836-1906*, J. L. F. Woodburn ed (Melb, 1955); PD (Vic), 20 Nov 1884, 24 June 1886; J. H. McColl, 'Hugh McColl and the water question in northern Victoria', VHM, 5 (1916-17); *Argus*, 14 Sept 1878; Gordon papers (LaT L).

DONALD S. GARDEN

GORDON, PATRICK ROBERTSON (1834?-1915), inspector of stock and brands, was born probably near Aberdeen, Scotland, son of an engineer and his wife Mary, née Lamb. Educated at a country academy and Marischal College he migrated to Victoria in 1853 to manage Peechelba station on the River Ovens for an English syndicate in which he held a share. He soon won high repute for his management, racing stud and knowledge of animal diseases. In 1864 he became metropolitan inspector of stock in Sydney where his work on the bovine pleuro-pneumonia outbreak attracted further notice and won him an invitation from the Queensland government to draft a diseases in sheep bill. In February 1868 he became chief inspector of stock for Queensland, establishing the first stock branch (later the Departments of Agriculture and Stock, and of Primary Industries).

As Queensland then had no parliamentary draftsman, Gordon had to draft his own bills. His greatest achievement was the Brands Act in 1872, which established a new system of stock brands, won him world fame and the additional post of registrar and chief inspector of brands. Other notable measures for which he was responsible were the first Marsupial Act, 1877, the Meat and Dairy Act, 1893, and the Diseases in Stock Act, 1896, after a tick infestation which Gordon was prominent in defeating. In 1875 he had induced the government to inquire into the decay of native grasses. In 1889 on his advice the government secured the services of Drs Germont and Loir of the Pasteur Institute in Paris, and an effective vaccine against bovine pleuro-pneumonia was discovered. Gordon also advocated innoculation of cattle and tubercular tests as well as closer liaison between officers seeking to improve animal health. He was prominent in the campaign against scab and endeavoured to encourage the production of mohair. He appeared to his contemporaries as the driving force behind his whole department.

In addition to his departmental reports Gordon published several pamphlets. After he retired from the public service on 31 December 1903 he wrote many articles for the *Queenslander* and *Courier* under the pseudonym of 'Jumbuck'. He also had a large share in the discussions leading to the formation of the National Agricultural Association (Royal National Association) and with Gresley Lukin [q.v.] and John Fenwick organized its formal launching at a public meeting in June 1875, presided over by the governor, William Cairns. A capable violinist, Gordon also helped to found the Brisbane Musical Union and was its secretary for many years. At Sydney on 13 May 1868 he had married Emily Florence Roberts. He died at Sandgate, Brisbane, on 28 August 1915, survived by three sons and four daughters of their thirteen children. His death certificate gave his age as 85 and at marriage as 34; when he retired in 1903 his age was officially given as 69.

A. L. Clay, 'Patrick Robertson Gordon', *Aust Veterinary J*, July 1959; *Brisbane Courier*, 30 Aug 1915; *Queenslander*, 4 Sept 1915; *Qld Country Life*, 28 May 1959.

A. A. MORRISON

GORDON, SAMUEL DEANE (1811-1882), merchant, pastoralist and politician, was born on 12 October 1811 at Ballynahinch, County Down, Ireland, son of David Gordon, farmer, and his wife Mary, née Deane. Educated at private schools in Ireland he arrived in Sydney about 1830. He worked in several Sydney mercantile houses before becoming a merchant. At Liverpool he had a large store by 1840 and later the agency for the Albion brewery. In the 1840s he turned to pastoral speculation and leased Banandra run, 50,000 acres on the Murrumbidgee. In 1848 he sold his Liverpool store and moved to Sydney where he set up as a wine and spirits merchant. In 1854 he was appointed a magistrate and next year became a director of the Sydney Exchange Co., the Hunter River Railway Co., the English, Scottish and Australian Bank and the Sydney Insurance Co. He was on the committee of the Sydney Bethel Union. On 22 October 1839 at East Maitland he had married Eliza, daughter of Peter Dickson of Kirkcudbrightshire; she died in 1856, leaving a son and four daughters.

Gordon first took an interest in politics as a supporter of Rev. J. D. Lang [q.v.]. He won Durham in the first parliament under

responsible government and was re-elected in 1858. In 1859-60 he represented Illawarra. A conscientious member with liberal and progressive views especially on constitutional reform, education, land and railways, he supported the Cowper-Robertson [qq.v.] faction and was a convinced free trader. In the 1860 general election Gordon was defeated but appointed on 2 September 1861 to the Legislative Council, pledged to its reform.

In the 1860s Gordon became a director of the New South Wales Marine Assurance Co. and the Australian Gaslight Co., and chairman of Mitchell's Creek Quartz Mining Co. and the Mutual Life Association of Australasia. He bought real estate in Sydney and in 1867 had a total of 460 square miles in four runs on the Darling Downs, two in the Leichhardt district and six in Gregory. With Edward Flood [q.v.] as partner he had another 726 square miles in seven runs in Maranoa and nineteen in Warrego. By 1871 he had disposed of his own Queensland stations, acquired six in the Bligh district of New South Wales, and with Flood still held five Maranoa runs and thirteen in Warrego.

A prominent Presbyterian, Gordon was a founder of St Andrew's College, Sydney, and member of its council. He was also a vice-president of the Highland Society and a member of the Victoria Club and the Linnean Society of New South Wales. He joined the committee of the Chamber of Commerce in 1867 and in the 1870s served briefly on the committees of the Benevolent Asylum, the Sydney Infirmary and Dispensary and the Hospital for Sick Children, and was a vice-president of the Young Men's Christian Association and the Horticultural Society of New South Wales and a councillor of the Agricultural Society of New South Wales. He died on 24 July 1882 of brain disease at his home, Glenyarrah, Double Bay, and was buried in Rookwood cemetery. He was predeceased by his second wife Emily, née Fielding, and by five sons and two daughters. His three surviving daughters each inherited a house and, with their children, a fortune valued at £215,862.

V&P (LA NSW), 1870-71, 1, 732; SMH, 21 May 1842, 19, 21 Dec 1843, 15 Oct 1851, 31 Mar 1856, 1 Jan, 30 Apr 1868, 25 July 1882; *Empire* (Syd), 23 June 1856; *Bulletin*, 9 May 1881, 29 July 1882; *Town and Country J*, 29 July 1882; *Illustrated Sydney News*, 5 Aug 1882; MS and newspaper indexes under S. D. Gordon (ML).

G. J. ABBOTT
MARTHA RUTLEDGE

GORE, JOHN (1846-1931), Salvation Army officer, was born at Sutton, Lincoln-

shire, England, son of William Gore, shoemaker, and his wife Martha, née Marsh. On
3 September 1867 he was converted at a
Christian mission conducted by 'General'
William Booth. For two years he helped
Booth in the mission which in 1879 became
known as the Salvation Army. In 1870 Gore
married Sarah Simpson and in April 1878
they arrived with three children at Adelaide
in the *Clyde*. He found work as a plate-layer
and had charge of laying the second track
from Adelaide to the port. Deeply religious,
he became active in the Bible Christian
Church.

In 1880 Gore met Edward Saunders, who
had been a member of Booth's mission and
had arrived in Adelaide in 1879. They decided to hold meetings on Booth's lines and
next evening preached in the notorious
Light Square. They were abused by the mob
but continued to preach. Convinced that the
effort was worthwhile, they wrote to Booth
asking him to send officers '*as fast as fire and
steam can bring them*'. Encouraged by
Booth, Gore and Saunders decided to hold
their first official Salvationist meeting on
Sunday, 5 September, at the open forum in
Botanic Park. The meeting was successful
and barracks were soon built at the corner
of Hindley and Morphett Streets. In February 1881 when two Salvation Army
officers arrived, sixty-eight converts and
supporters marched to the port to greet
them. Their numbers increased and by 1882
the Salvationists had started in Sydney.

Gore decided to become a full-time officer
and in October 1883 was appointed to
Kapunda. There his family suffered much
hardship: the eldest son was attacked for
'being an Army boy' and his mother's
wrists sprained when she went to his rescue;
and after meetings he and his helpers often
had to leave the hall by the back door to
avoid angry mobs. Known in army circles
as 'John and Sarah', they were stationed in
turn with rapidly-growing corps at Bowden,
Moonta, Port Pirie, Port Augusta and Norwood. Transferred to New South Wales in
1889 they served at Wallsend, Leichhardt,
Penrith, Parramatta, Wagga Wagga and
Wollongong. Everywhere his unorthodox
methods and fiery preaching attracted audiences but his forthright testimony won
many lasting converts. Widely known as
'Salvation Gore' he retired from active service in 1902 with the rank of adjutant and
later became staff-orderly at colony headquarters. In 1924 he was the first Australian
officer to receive the 'Order of the Founder'.
On 12 March 1927 he unveiled a commemorative tablet in Adelaide's Botanic Park
where the army had begun its official Australian operations. His wife died on 14
August 1915 and on 25 May 1916 Gore

married an elderly widow, Esther Willings,
who cared for him until he died aged 85 at
Mortdale on 28 December 1931. He was survived by six children of his first marriage.
Three of them were Salvationist officers; the
eldest son, William, became a major and
composed band music of international renown.

P. Dale, *Salvation Chariot . . . 1880-1951*
(Melb, 1952); S. James, 'Salvation Army in
South Australia', *Victorian Review*, 7 (1882);
War Cry (Eastern Australia), 20 Dec 1924, 2
Apr 1927, 16 Jan 1932, 29 June 1940.

P. Dale

GORE, ST GEORGE RICHARD (1812-
1871), pastoralist and politician, was born
on 26 March 1812 at Dublin, the eldest of
five sons of Thomas Gore and his wife Elizabeth, née Corbet; his father was rector of
Mulrankin, County Wexford, and brother
of the seventh baronet of Manor Gore. Educated by his father he entered Trinity College, Dublin (B.A., 1831; M.A., 1834). He
was called to the Bar and practised in London until 1839 when he decided to migrate.
With his brother Ralph Thomas, naval
officer, he arrived in the *Bengal* at Sydney
in February 1840. On 17 August he married
Frances, daughter of Edward Caldwell of
Lyndhurst.

In November 1841 Gore's widowed mother
arrived at Sydney in the *Fairlie* with three
sons: Robert, barrister; St John Thomas,
army officer; and William Francis, student.
In May Gore and a partner had been licensed to settle on the Darling Downs on a
run they named Yandilla. In 1844 William
was ordained an Anglican priest and next
year Ralph and Thomas joined their
brother on the Downs where Thomas soon
acquired the Tummaville run. Robert was
drowned when the *Sovereign* was wrecked
in March 1847. After a dispute in 1848 Gore
took up a new run called Bodumba, leaving
Yandilla to a family combine: William,
Ralph and Robert's mother-in-law, Margaret
Baldock. After Ralph died in England in
1860, his widow married Osmond Priaulx
who joined the partnership.

Gore took an aristocratic pride in the
proper management of his estate and the
welfare of his employees but his indiscreet
comments and membership of the squatter
clique made him unpopular outside Warwick where he was elected to the Legislative
Assembly without opposition on 20 May
1860. On 14 January 1862 he became secretary for public lands and works in the
Herbert [q.v.] ministry but was defeated by
an organized sectarian vote in the by-
election resulting from his acceptance of

public office. On 3 July 1863 he was nominated to the Legislative Council where he represented the government; from 13 September 1866 to 15 August 1867 he was postmaster-general under Arthur Macalister [q.v.] and from 28 January to 3 May 1870 under Charles Lilley [q.v.]. Gore surrendered his Bodumba and Canning Creek leases in 1869 and acquired a stud property called Lyndhurst, near Warwick, where he died on 16 August 1871, leaving four sons and three daughters. He is commemorated by a statue in Warwick, a street in Toowoomba, a highway and a railway station.

His eldest son ST GEORGE RALPH was born on 21 September 1841 in Sydney and spent his early years on his father's property. In 1866 he joined a family friend, C. J. Graham [q.v.], on a station in the Peak Downs district but after three disastrous years abandoned the venture and became clerk of Petty Sessions at Nanango. On 3 February 1873 he was transferred to Brisbane as clerk in the Registrar-General's Office, became a deposition clerk in the Brisbane Police Court in 1874, clerk assistant of the Legislative Council in 1876 and chief clerk of the Colonial Secretary's Office in 1877. On 6 April 1876 he married Eugenia Marion, daughter of E. I. C. Browne [q.v.]. When his cousin, the 8th baronet, died unmarried on 31 December 1878 Gore succeeded to the title. He used it in spite of some derision from local democrats, stayed in Queensland and on 1 January 1880 was appointed immigration agent and chief inspector of Pacific Islanders and of Distilleries. In 1884 when two officers of the recruiting ship *Stanley* were tried for violence in New Britain Gore was alleged to have approved their actions. Sir St George died at his home in Brisbane on 17 October 1887, leaving four children.

H. S. Russell, *The genesis of Queensland* (Syd, 1888); M. J. Fox (ed), *The history of Queensland*, 1 (Brisb, 1919); T. Hall, *The early history of Warwick district* (Toowoomba, 1923); D. Gunn, *Links with the past* (Brisb, 1937); J. Trude, Notes on Yandilla station (Oxley Lib, Brisb); Glennie diary (Oxley Lib, Brisb); run registers and mortgage records (QA); MS cat and newspaper indexes under Gore (ML); I. Elliot, Family history (held by St G. Ralph Gore, Wycanna, Talwood, Qld).

A. A. MORRISON

GORE, THOMAS JEFFERSON (1839-1923), Churches of Christ minister, was born on 23 March 1839 in a log house at Bloomfield, Nelson County, Kentucky, America, son of Volney Gore and his wife Elizabeth, née Stone, both of whom descended from early English settlers in Vir-

ginia. Educated in Lexington at Transylvania University (A.M., L.Th., 1863), he first ministered to the Hustonville Christian Church, Kentucky. In 1866 he accepted an invitation to the Grote Street Church of Christ, Adelaide, where he served from 3 March 1867 to 1885 and in 1893-98. His other pastorates were at Norwood, York (Kilkenny), Glenelg, Unley and Henley Beach; but all the congregations in South Australia came under his influence because of his readiness to leave his own pulpit to visit them on special occasions. When he arrived in the colony the membership of Churches of Christ was 500; by 1923 it had reached 7000. He probably did more to mould the thought and direct the energies of the communion than any other member. Thorough knowledge of the scriptures gave his pulpit work an expository nature, and the eloquent presentation of his subjects always drew large congregations. He was also a diligent pastor. To prepare young men for the ministry he organized a Bible Students' Training Class in 1867 and continued to lead it for fifty years. Later he was invited to be principal of the College of the Bible, Glen Iris, Victoria, but reluctantly declined because of his age. His scholarship and facile pen found scope as the editor of the Australia-wide periodical, *Christian Pioneer*, and he contributed to other religious publications. Wide sympathies and sound judgment made him tolerant towards all who did not share his deep convictions, and a highly respected citizen and counsellor in every community where he served. He visited his homeland twice and maintained strong connexions with the Disciples there.

On 17 November 1868 at Mitcham Gore married Jane, daughter of the Hon. Philip Santo, member of the Legislative Council and founding member of the Grote Street Church; they had four children before she died. On 5 October 1876 he married her sister Sarah; they had seven children. He died at his home in Unley on 4 July 1923, survived by his wife, three sons and four daughters.

A. S. Gore, *Thomas Jefferson Gore* (Melb, 1926); H. R. Taylor, *The history of Churches of Christ in South Australia* (Adel, 1959).

HERBERT R. TAYLOR

GORMLY, JAMES (1836-1922), bushman and politician, was born at Foxborough Hall, Elphin, County Roscommon, Ireland, son of Patrick Gormly, grazier, and his wife Mary, née Docray. In January 1840 his parents and five children arrived at Sydney as bounty immigrants in the *Crusader*. They settled in the Illawarra district where James was lost in the mountains for forty-eight hours. In 1844 the family moved to Nangus on the Murrumbidgee and in 1849 settled at Gundagai. James had little education but helped to tend his father's stock and became expert in bushcraft. At 15 he briefly visited the Turon diggings. In the 1852 flood at Gundagai all the Gormlys were drowned except James and his brother Thomas. Next year they took stock to the Victorian markets and then had some success on the Victorian goldfields. In 1858 James married Mary Jane Cox at Ten Mile Creek, Holbrook.

About 1854 Gormly had settled at Wagga Wagga where he won government mail contracts and soon had 300 horses and a large staff on 500 miles of mail routes in western New South Wales; one of his coachmen was the Tichborne claimant, Tom Castro [q.v. Orton]. In 1872 he sold out to Cobb [q.v.] & Co. and next year selected land for himself and six children near The Rock. In 1876 he moved to new selections and bought some freehold land. In 1875 he had leased Coronga Peak, 182,000 acres in the Bourke district; after adding fences and tanks he sold it at a profit and took up Wilga Downs, 256,000 acres on the West Bogan, which he also sold well. In 1882 he returned to Wagga Wagga, bought urban real estate and advanced his farming interests.

In 1875 he was foundation president of the Wagga Wagga Free Selectors' Association and in 1877 attended the conference of free selectors in Sydney. In 1883-86 he served on the Wagga Wagga City Council and was twice mayor in 1884-85. He also became president of the Mechanics' School of Arts and the Murrumbidgee Pastoral and Agricultural Association. In the Legislative Assembly he represented the Murrumbidgee in 1885-94 and Wagga Wagga in 1894-1904 and was a member of the Legislative Council in 1904-22. A protectionist and Irish Catholic, he advocated the cause of selectors and farmers' unions in parliament and carried his vigorous political campaigns to every small settlement by rail, coach or buggy. His speeches reflected his detailed and practical knowledge of matters affecting smallholders. An effective 'roads and bridges' member he carried three private Acts.

Gormly was an expert amateur rider and at 9 was reputed to have ridden in his first race at Gundagai. With Camel he won 22 races and came fourth in Wagga's marathon 'Ten Mile Race'. For over fifty years he was a member of the Murrumbidgee Turf Club, often acting as steward and handicapper, and in 1885 gave the club a gold cup; he was also president of the St Patrick's Day Race Club. He continued to ride in races long after he was in parliament. In 1913 he was foundation president of the Wagga Wagga and District Horse-breeders' Association and often judged thoroughbreds at Riverina shows. In the early 1900s Gormly wrote many articles about his experiences for the local papers and in 1921 published his *Exploration and settlement in Australia.* Small, wiry and energetic, he had great powers of endurance. He carefully nurtured his Irish brogue all his life. Gormly died aged 86 in Wagga Wagga on 19 May 1922 and was buried in the Catholic cemetery. Predeceased by his wife in 1917, he was survived by five sons and three daughters. His estate was valued at £14,000.

Ex-M.L.A., *Our present parliament, what it is worth* (Syd, c 1886); R. J. E. Gormly, *Hon. James Gormly . . . a Murrumbidgee pioneer* (Pymble, 1959); G. L. Buxton, *The Riverina 1861-1891* (Melb, 1967); K. Swan, A *history of Wagga Wagga* (Wagga Wagga, 1970); J. Gormly reminiscences (newspaper cuttings, ML); printed cat under Gormly (ML).

GORDON BUXTON

GOSMAN, ALEXANDER (1829-1913), Congregational theologian and social reformer, was born on 21 February 1829 at Crail, Fife, Scotland, son of John Gosman, builder, and his wife Catherine, née Auchterlonie. He attended the parish school, spent about three years in business in Leith and Dumbarton and then taught in schools in Dundee and Greenock. He moved to Glasgow as assistant English master at the High School and also taught and acted as chaplain in the Glasgow Asylum for the Blind. He decided to study for the ministry in 1850 and entered the University of Glasgow and the Congregational Theological Hall. He was ordained on 27 June 1855 at Haddington, East Lothian. In September 1857 he married Jane, daughter of William Buchanan of Alexandria, Dumbartonshire.

In response to appeals by the Colonial Missionary Society Gosman sailed with his wife and daughter in the *Great Britain* and arrived at Melbourne on 21 September 1860. In his first pastorate at Ballarat Gosman won repute as a scholar and preacher and was called in 1863 to the Independent Church, Alma Road, St Kilda. He was appointed lecturer in 1864 and later professor of English and metaphysics at the Congregational College of Victoria; in 1876-1913 he was its principal. In 1878-83 he was an examiner in logic and mental and moral philosophy at the University of Melbourne and in 1878-1905 ministered to the Congregational Church at Hawthorn. Elected chairman of the Congregational Union of Victoria in 1869, 1883, 1895 and 1904 he was also the first chairman of the Congregational Union of Australasia in 1904-07. He visited Britain in 1884 and was a delegate to the first International Congregational Council in 1891 and the second at Boston in 1899. In 1904 he was awarded a doctorate of divinity by the University of St Andrews.

Gosman always considered himself a 'public servant', basing his sermons on the 'needs' of the people as suggested by public opinion and interpreting the new doctrines of evolution and 'Higher Criticism' of the Bible to a questioning generation. He published articles and reviews in such periodicals as the *Victorian Review* and anonymously wrote weekly leading articles on social, philosophical, scientific and political subjects for the *Daily Telegraph* in the early 1880s. He was often in open controversy with more orthodox churchmen such as Bishop Moorhouse [q.v.], and his pamphlet, *Mr Justice Higinbotham* [q.v.] *on The Orthdox Faith. A Review and a Vindication* (Melbourne, 1887), earned the judge's admiration. Gosman also defended his colleagues who tackled evolutionary subjects, and reserved his judgment when Rev. John Campbell's 'new theology' earned widespread censure.

From the 1860s Gosman had campaigned for the use of the Bible as an historic and literary text in State schools. As a founder of the Bible in State Schools League and a vice-president of the National Scripture Education League he advocated adoption of the New South Wales system for Victoria. In the scripture election campaign led by Bishop Clarke in 1894 Gosman withdrew from its council, disapproving the lessons recommended by the royal commission on education and describing the proposed referendum as a 'hopeless muddle'. He was similarly insistent in pressing for a chair of mental and moral science at the university in 1882 and in advocating divinity degrees in 1909 on purely secular grounds.

Gosman's humanity was early aroused by the poverty of many migrants. From Ballarat he informed the *Haddington Courier* that clerks and middle-class men should not emigrate if they were making a living. Eager to champion the 'toiler' against the excesses of individualism he crusaded for social justice. He was the first president of the Anti-Sweating League in 1895-1902, and active in the Charity Organization Society and the Leongatha Labour Colony; his name was said to be a 'household word' in the 1890s. His involvement with labour and socialism was not on party lines but accorded with his belief that natural law ought to be the ultimate appeal in all personal, social, industrial and political matters. Gosman argued for free trade as an antidote to unemployment and was committed to the concept of progress, visualizing the eventual removal of poverty and inequality of opportunity. When the Victorian Factories Act was amended in 1896 he became chairman of the shirt (wages) board and his handling of its four hundred or more determinations to the satisfaction of employers and employed was deemed a 'triumph of conciliation, conscientiousness and common sense'. His lecture series in the eastern colonies were published as *Socialism in the light of Right Conduct and Religion* (Melbourne, 1891). Gosman was a delegate to the Bathurst Federal Convention in 1896. He penned much verse in the cause and one of his federal anthems was printed by order of the Victorian government. At Brisbane in 1895 he deplored the possibility of Japanese raids and, with his faith in a 'Greater Britain', hoped that Australian federation would help to hasten imperial federation.

Outside his denomination, Gosman's closest friends were Charles Strong, H. G. Turner [qq.v.], the philosopher Henry Laurie and Alfred Deakin. Despite his liberal theology Gosman insisted on certain shared orthodoxies and his humanitarian emphasis prevented friction with his Evangelical colleagues, though he was often 'confused and perplexed' by their actions. A keen believer in church union, he refused to be bound by historic creeds. While he and his influence survived, Congregationalism could make a contribution to Australian life out of proportion to its numbers. He died from bronchial pneumonia on 15 January 1913, survived by his widow and six of their seven children. Of his sons, John had a produce business in Melbourne and Sydney, and William, sometime principal of Camberwell Grammar School, was assayer and ore expert to the Mount Lyell Mining Co. The second daughter, Janie Buchanan, married William Warren Kerr, a noted Congregational layman.

A portrait by McCubbin is in the Congregational College of Victoria, Kew.

A. Sutherland et al, *Victoria and its metropolis*, 2 (Melb, 1888); Congregational Union, *Jubilee volume of Victorian Congregationalism 1888* (Melb, 1889); R. E. W. Kennedy, 'The Leongatha Labour Colony', *Labor Hist*, May 1968; *Congregational Year Book, 1860-1913*; *Congregationalist* (Melb), 10 Feb 1913; *Congregationalist* (Syd), 10 Feb 1913; *Table Talk*, Nov 1895; *Australasian*, 24 June 1905; *Age*, 20 Jan 1913; F. H. Cutler, A history of the anti-sweating movement in Victoria, 1873-96 (M.A. thesis, Univ Melb, 1956); Gosman papers (LaT L).
NIEL GUNSON

GOSSE, WILLIAM CHRISTIE (1842-1881), explorer and surveyor, was born on 11 December 1842 in Hoddesdon, England, the second son of William Gosse and his wife Agnes, née Grant. His father, a medical practitioner, was a cousin of the naturalist, Philip Henry Gosse (1810-1888). In 1850 Dr and Mrs Gosse with four sons and two daughters migrated to Adelaide hoping to cure the father's bronchitis. Dr Gosse became an active citizen of Adelaide, among other achievements originating the Home for Incurables, forming the second branch of the British Medical Association outside England and becoming the first warden of the Senate of the University of Adelaide. He sent his eldest and youngest sons to the Collegiate School of St Peter and the two middle ones to J. L. Young's [q.v.] Educational Institution which produced the better results: William won distinction as an explorer and the third son, Charles, achieved it as a doctor of medicine specializing in eye diseases. When Charles was killed on 1 July 1885 by an accident with a bolting horse, a lectureship in ophthalmic surgery was founded at the University of Adelaide in his memory.

William, described by his sister Agnes as 'of an exceedingly gentle and thoughtful temperament', joined the surveyor-general's department in 1859 and was sent on a trigonometrical survey of the far north. By 1868 he was working in the south-eastern district when he married Gertrude Ritchie of Melbourne; she died the next year.

In 1872 the South Australian government invited William to lead a party to explore a way from central Australia to Perth. Major Egerton Warburton [q.v.] hoped to get this leadership but the government thought he was too old at 58. His champion, Thomas Elder [q.v.], promptly fitted out another expedition with Warburton as leader. The rival parties, scrupulously avoiding each other, both set off from Alice Springs station in April 1873. Gosse, instructed 'to avoid mention of Mr Warburton's party', was harassed by trying to avoid the other's tracks and find a separate, manageable way of his own. Gosse's party consisted of Edwin Berry, second-in-command, William's youngest brother Henry as collector, two other white men, Winnall and Nilen, three Afghans and an Aboriginal boy. Elder lent them camels; they also had horses and provisions for eight months. The party proceeded westwards for four months, one of their camps being at Ayers Rock which on 19 July Gosse discovered, named and with astonishment described in his diary. On 17 September Gosse decided it was futile to proceed further west with so little water discoverable and that little drying out; the party turned back, returning by a different route and reaching, exhausted, Charlotte Waters telegraph station on 19 December. Although the expedition did not achieve its stated object it provided details of over 60,000 square miles of country and Gosse's maps prepared the way for John Forrest's successful crossing from east to west of that same territory in 1874.

In 1874 William married Agnes, daughter of Alexander Hay [q.v.]; they had three children, William, (Sir) James and Agnes. In 1875 he was made deputy surveyor-general and, in July 1881, not being well, was granted a year's sick leave. William planned to revisit England but on 12 August had a heart attack and died within hours, aged 38, at his home in Adelaide.

Anglo-Australian (A. G. Hay), *After-glow memories* (Lond, 1905); Report and diary of Mr W. C. Gosse's central and western exploring expedition, 1873, V&P (SA), 1874, 2 (48).

FAYETTE GOSSE

GOTCH, JOHN SPEECHLY (1829-1901), businessman, was born on 4 December 1829 at Kettering, Northamptonshire, England, son of John Gotch (1791-1869), farmer, and his second wife, née Lefevre (according to one report, Mary Ann Fever). For some months in 1843 he attended school at Tollington Park, London. By February 1844 he was apprenticed to John Meadows, chemist and druggist, of Market Harborough near Leicester. After a five-year apprenticeship and six months as an assistant, Gotch migrated to America. In September 1849 he left Liverpool in the *Shenandoah* for Philadelphia where he was employed by a dentist without pay for six months; later he became assistant to a dentist in New York.

In February 1853 Gotch sailed for Australia in the Baltimore clipper *Peytona* but was wrecked off Mauritius. There he practised dentistry until he left Port Louis in the *Emma Colvin* and reached Melbourne on 24 December. When his gold digging in the Castlemaine district proved fruitless he returned to Melbourne in 1854 and sold newspapers for an elderly Scotsman, Alexander Gordon, who in December 1853 had leased a stall in the western market and become advertising agent for the *Argus*. They soon became partners as Gordon & Gotch. They recognized the opportunities in the colony's rapid growth and by 1859, when Gordon sold his interest to Gotch and returned to Scotland, the firm was pre-eminent in Melbourne as news and advertising agents and as distributors of newspapers and periodicals from Britain. Gotch introduced his brother William into the business in 1860 and his brother-in-law Alfred Jones in 1861. A branch was opened in Sydney that year, another in London in 1867 and a Brisbane house in 1875, each with a partnership in which Gotch held at least a half share and was directly involved in their management: he even went to London in 1874 to tackle a financial crisis created by a defaulting clerk. The branches were not uniform in their activities which extended from the export and distribution of newspapers and magazines through printing and publishing such works as the *Australian Handbook* in 1870-1906 to advertising, a press telegraph service and the import of stationery and printing supplies including machinery. Later the London branch engaged in general exports and the Australian offices took over agencies for importing such goods as pianos and sewing machines.

The success of these operations led to fragmentation of the original firm and to the end of Gotch's exclusive ownership of the Melbourne house. In 1885 Gordon & Gotch Ltd came into being, with Gotch holding 165 of the 300 shares of £100 each as well as being chairman of directors and president. In 1897 when the company became a proprietary he held 205 shares; the firm did not expand its share capital till 1907. He disposed of his interests in the London and Sydney branches in 1890-91 and steered the company through the depression of the early 1890s, taking on himself all the losses resulting from the failure of the New Oriental Bank in 1892. After branches were opened in Perth in 1894 and Wellington in 1899 he became less active in business.

Gotch had acquired pastoral interests, mainly in the Western District, but his name remains almost exclusively associated with his firm. For years he was president of the Authorised News Agents' Association of Victoria but, apart from this and his links with the East Melbourne Congregational Church and such charities as the Austin Hospital, the Collingwood Crêche and the Society for the Prevention of Cruelty to Children, he does not appear to have been active in public affairs.

On 17 September 1856 Gotch married Elizabeth Miller Jones of Bedford; of their nine children four died in infancy and a fifth predeceased her father. He died on 23 September 1901 at his home in East Melbourne and was buried in the Anglican section of the Melbourne general cemetery. He was survived by his wife who died in 1914 and by two sons and two daughters. The sons, John Gordon and Edward Speechly, and a son-in-law, H. Courtney Dix, were long associated with the firm.

Gordon & Gotch ... *fifty years' progress* ... *1853-1903* (Brisb, 1903); R. F. Bell, *Gordon &*

Gotch, London ... *1853-1953* (Lond, 1953); *Gordon & Gotch (A'sia) Ltd, Centenary 1853-1953* (Melb, 1953); *Age*, 25 Sept 1901, 18 Feb 1914; *Argus*, 25, 26 Sept 1901; *Weekly Times* (Melb), 28 Sept, 5 Oct 1901; Defunct Trading companies, Gordon & Gotch Ltd papers (VA); family and business reminiscences (Gordon & Gotch (A'sia) Ltd Archives, Melb).

WALLACE KIRSOP

GOULD, CHARLES (1834-1893), geological surveyor, was born on 4 June 1834 in England, son of John and Elizabeth Gould [qq.v.]. After graduating from the University of London (B.A., 1853), he won the duke of Cornwall's exhibition at the Royal School of Mines in 1854 and a Board of Trade certificate with many first-class passes in 1856. He then travelled with his father in eastern North America early in 1857, worked with the Geological Survey of Great Britain and left for Hobart Town on 12 April 1859. His initial contract at £600 a year with travelling expenses was to make a geological survey and prepare a book on the geology of Tasmania. The contract, first offered on the recommendation of Sir Roderick Murchison, was renewed several times. His surveys covered much of the colony and added greatly to geographical knowledge of western Tasmania. He named peaks along the West Coast Range after contemporary English scientists. He also served as a coal commissioner from March 1862 to June 1867, as a gold commissioner of the western district in 1862 and a magistrate of the territory.

Gould's wide experience, careful observation and well-developed stratigraphic and structural senses led to the first establishment of the order and correlation of Ordovician to Lower Devonian rocks over much of Tasmania, to the correct deduction of the succession of Permian and Triassic coals and Jurassic dolerite and to the suggestion of mining for coal under dolerite sills as along the Mount Nicholas Range, the development of which he strongly urged. The first recognition of glacial deposits in Tasmania was his. His strategy in looking for gold was sound and economical and his results, though negative, still stand. He tried to make the public aware of the dangers of relying too much on analyses of single samples.

An impression of incompleteness is conveyed by his reports and papers; something more or better soon was a common promise and the colonial secretary did not always get the reports when he wanted them. Another area of continuing tension was that of the function of the Survey: Gould wanted a regional geological survey and the secretary a mineral prospecting unit, preferably one for gold; but the final compromise was rather closer to Gould's stand. Combined with these difficulties, the depressed finances of the colony in 1868-74 probably led to the lapse of Gould's contract in August 1869. Gould then seems to have acted as a geological consultant and land surveyor in Tasmania, the Bass Strait islands and New South Wales where he was licensed as a surveyor on 29 January 1873. While in Tasmania he was actively interested in its Royal Society and the fauna and flora. He left Tasmania late in 1873 and seems to have returned to London where he stayed until at least June 1874. From 1880 he travelled in Burma, Singapore, Siam, Hong Kong, China, Korea and Japan, apparently advising on mining properties. He also collected ornithological specimens and material for his *Mythical Monsters* (London, 1886), a rather credulous book, the culmination of an interest extending at least as far back as his Tasmanian days. He returned to Europe early in 1889 but soon sailed to Buenos Aires. He travelled in South America until he died, probably unmarried, in Montevideo, Uruguay, on 15 April 1893.

G. Blainey, *The peaks of Lyell*, 1st ed (Melb, 1954); *Government Gazette* (NSW), 29 Jan 1873; C. P. Whitley, 'John Gould's associates', *Emu*, Oct 1938; 'Charles Gould to John Gould', *Vic Naturalist*, 56 (1939-40); A. H. Chisholm, 'Mrs John Gould and her relations', *Emu*, Apr 1941; *Mercury*, 14 May 1862; Col Sec letters (TA); information from G. Edelsten, Winchester, England.   MAXWELL R. BANKS
                                 M. L. YAXLEY

GOWLLAND, JOHN THOMAS EWING (1838-1874), naval officer, was born on 10 July 1838 at Leysdown, Kent, England, the eldest son of Captain Thomas Sankey Gowlland and his wife Mary, née Ewing. He entered the Royal Naval School, Greenwich, became captain of its 800 boys and in 1853 joined the navy as a master's assistant. He saw active service with the Baltic squadron in the Crimean war and at 16 won a medal for taking a prize back to England. He then served in the survey of the Chincha Islands off Peru, of Vancouver Island and Straits and in determining the northern boundary of the United States of America. As a commander he won the goodwill of the Indian chiefs and was specially thanked by the Admiralty for his excellent charts; his name is perpetuated in several places on the Pacific coast. He returned to Europe by way of Sydney and as first assistant surveyor worked in the Mediterranean.

Gowlland was appointed to the Australian survey as chief assistant in 1865.

When Captain Sydney retired Gowlland took command of the survey of the New South Wales coast and compiled Admiralty charts of the coast and the tidal waters of the Richmond, Clarence, Hunter and Hawkesbury Rivers. He also surveyed the waters of Port Jackson and made the first plans of Garden Island. From 1871 his services were retained at the expense of the New South Wales government. In that year he commanded the *Governor Blackall* on a voyage to Cape York to observe a total eclipse of the sun. In 1872 he volunteered to command a relief expedition to search for the brig *Maria* wrecked off Bramble Reef. For rescuing thirty-four pitiful survivors he was given handsome pieces of plate and the thanks of the premier, Sir James Martin [q.v.]. In 1873 Gowlland returned to England and was promoted staff commander. He was a fellow of the Royal Geographical Society and a member of the Institution of Civil Engineers, London, and the Royal Society of Victoria. He wrote several pamphlets on the winds and currents of the eastern coast of Australia and many press articles on marine subjects. He returned to Sydney and while surveying Middle Harbour was drowned in an accident off Dobroyd Point on 14 August 1874. He was buried with full naval honours at the cemetery of St Thomas's Anglican Church, North Sydney, and survived by his wife Genevieve, née Lord, whom he had married in Sydney on 12 October 1865, and by two sons and a daughter.

Gowlland's journals and papers were clearly written and skilfully illustrated with sketches of ships, coastlines and nautical scenes, some in colour. His Australian charts, much in use until recent years, are highly regarded, and a copper engraving of the Hawkesbury, Broken Bay and Port Jackson, probably his finest work, was found about 1940 in possession of the government printer. A memorial window is in St Thomas's Church, North Sydney, and a compass designed by him is in the Admiralty at Slough, England.

L. S. Dawson, *Memoirs of hydrography 1856-1864* (Eastbourne, nd); G. C. Ingleton, *Charting a continent* (Syd, 1944); V&P (LA NSW), 1872, 2, 1383; G. C. Ingleton, 'A brief history of marine surveying in Australia', *JRAHS*, 30 (1944); *Naval and Military Gazette*, 42 (1874); *SMH*, 17, 18 Aug 1874; *Town and Country J*, 22 Aug 1874.

                              ELEANOR E. BARRON

GOYDER, GEORGE WOODROOFE (1826-1898), surveyor-general, was born on 24 June 1826 in London, eldest son of David George Goyder, physician and Swedenborgian minister, and his wife Sarah, née Etherington. The family later moved to Glasgow where George studied surveying and was articled to a railway engineer. He migrated to Sydney in 1848. After three years with an auctioneering firm he visited Melbourne and went to Adelaide where he decided to settle. In June 1851 he entered the South Australian civil service as a draftsman and on 10 December at Christchurch, North Adelaide, married Frances Mary Smith.

Goyder joined the Department of Lands as chief clerk in January 1853. In quick stages he rose from second assistant to assistant surveyor-general in January 1857. In April he took charge of an exploration to report on country north of pastoral settlement. He was amazed to find Lake Torrens full of fresh water and its flourishing eastern surroundings very different from the desert described by E. J. Eyre [q.v.] in 1839. His exuberant report persuaded the surveyor-general, Captain Freeling [q.v.], to examine the area in September. No more rain had fallen but hot winds had killed the vegetation and turned the lake into a bed of mud. Freeling returned to criticize Goyder for mistaking flood for permanent water, being misled by mirage and misconceiving the value of the northern country. Although Goyder had proved that Eyre's horseshoe of salt lakes was penetrable and thereby opened the way to further exploration, he was too conscientious to ignore his blunder and in 1859 at his own request led survey parties to triangulate the country between Lakes Torrens and Eyre and to sink wells. When Freeling resigned Goyder was recalled from the north to become surveyor-general on 19 January 1861 at a salary of £700.

Goyder's northern surveys had attracted many large pastoralists who soon demanded modified conditions for their leases. With extra duties as inspector of mines and valuator of runs Goyder went north to classify grazing leases, rents and rights of renewal. In less than twenty months he rode over 20,000 miles, visiting 83 stations and handling his departmental correspondence each night. When his valuations were published the outback lessees complained bitterly and inside pastoralists demanded reassessment while smallholders and urban anti-squatters condemned any concession to hungry graziers. In this three-sided struggle four ministries rose and fell but Goyder stood firm. In 1865 three commissioners were sent north to reassess rents but found the country in severe drought. In November Goyder was directed to go north and from his own observations to lay down on the map 'the line of demarcation between that

portion of the country where the rainfall has extended, and that where the drought prevailed'. With a small mounted party he went to Swan Reach on the River Murray and thence north-west to Pekina, east to Melrose and returned through Crystal Brook to Adelaide. A map published in 1866 showed his line of travel with a wing sweeping east from the Murray to the Victorian border and another from Spencer Gulf far to the west.

Goyder's rainfall line was first used for the reassessment of leases and the relief of stricken pastoralists. After the drought broke in 1867 he cautiously admitted that his line separated 'to a certain extent' lands suitable for agriculture and those fit only for grazing. This statement strengthened the urban land reformers in the general election in April 1868. Led by H. B. T. Strangways [q.v.] they introduced 'Agricultural Areas' where sections up to 320 acres were to be sold at auction on credit, thus enabling small farmers to compete against wealthy speculators. When the new Act was passed in January 1869 Goyder had chosen six areas, each with easy access to the coast. While the new sections were marked out he took 150 men to the Northern Territory where incompetence and delay in the surveys were causing much discontent. His prompt and firm action soon restored confidence. He recommended Palmerston (Darwin) as the capital site, completed the survey of 665,860 acres in six months, reported on traces of minerals and located a million acres of average quality suitable for the growth of tropical products. He sailed for Adelaide in November and next February visited Victoria to see the working of land regulations there. He disliked random selection before survey but his mission led to amendments of Strangways' Act. Liberal extensions of credit to new farmers and good seasons in the 1870s brought land sales of nine million acres for the decade. With larger sections and better opportunities to buy land in well-watered areas he discouraged attempts at farming beyond his line. He pursued this policy as chairman of the railways commission in 1874-75 but northern newspapers claimed that the southern districts were full and ridiculed the accuracy of the line. Scorning Goyder's warnings the government yielded in 1874 and made land available beyond the line. Farmers pushed north and had fair harvests but the onset of bad seasons in 1880 left them in dire distress. At great expense they had to be relocated south of the line, their sections reverting to sheep runs spoiled by wind erosion and destruction of native vegetation.

One of Goyder's many enterprises sprang

from the colony's severe shortage of timber. He did his utmost to preserve trees and encourage planting. In 1873 he recommended the use of forest reserves and in 1875-83 was chairman of the Forest Board with J. E. Brown [q.v.] as chief conservator. Another constant project of Goyder's was water conservation. Starting with wells and dams on northern stockroutes he persuaded the government to spend £300,000 on drainage in the south-east in 1867. In 1871 he inspected pumping machinery and irrigation works in Britain and America and returned to Adelaide with much knowledge of boring for artesian water. He advised many pastoralists on water problems and rejected such impracticable schemes as irrigating the Adelaide plain by a canal from the River Murray. His paper on the development of water conservation in 1883 indicated the immense scope of his inquiries.

Nicknamed 'Little Energy', Goyder was reputed the ablest administrator and most efficient public servant in the colony. A martinet in office hours he won the respect and affection of his subordinates. As 'king of the lands department' he served under 24 different commissioners of crown lands through 34 changes of ministry and helped to amend over 60 Lands Acts. Costs of his department rose from £15,000 in 1861 to £165,000 in 1883 when his power began to wane but in the same time he quadrupled the colony's revenue from land sales and leases. Disgruntled graziers, farmers and miners all charged him with partiality but it was never proved. In fixing rents, boundaries and valuations he was scrupulous and firm, and his rulings were tolerated because of his integrity and honour. In fieldwork his powers of observation were almost uncanny; he brought fortunes to many settlers but remained comparatively poor. He tendered his resignation in 1862, 1873 and 1878 but each time was persuaded to withdraw it by increments to his salary. He was earning £1250 a year when he retired on 30 June 1894 and was then given £4375 in lieu of a pension. In October leading citizens gave him a purse of a thousand sovereigns. He was appointed C.M.G. in 1889.

Goyder consistently overworked himself and his health suffered. For years after 1861 he had scurvy and in 1869 returned from Darwin with 'nervous and muscular debility' and was ordered complete rest. His wife was then recuperating in England where she died on 8 April 1870 at Bristol from an overdose of sleeping pills. In 1871 Goyder took nine months leave and visited Britain and America leaving his nine children with Ellen Priscilla Smith, his deceased wife's sister. On 20 November he married her: they had one son and twin daughters.

Goyder died on 2 November 1898 at his home Warrakilla, near Aldgate, leaving an estate of £4000.

D. W. Meinig, *On the margins of the good earth* (Chicago, 1962); PP (SA), 1857-58 (72, 153), 1865-66 (62, 78, 154), 1869-70 (31), 1870-71 (78), 1873 (105), 1890 (60); *Argus*, 7 June 1870, 1 June 1883; *Observer* (Adel), 22 Mar 1887; *Australasian*, 27 Oct 1894; F. J. R. O'Brien, Goyder's line (B.A. Hons thesis, Univ Adel, 1952); K. R. Bowes, Land settlement in South Australia, 1857-90 (Ph.D. thesis, ANU, 1963).

GRAHAM, CHARLES JAMES (1839-1886), grazier, newspaper proprietor, parliamentarian, public servant and businessman, was born on 7 October 1839, son of John Graham (1790-1862), vicar of Hinxton, Cambridgeshire, England, and his wife Frances Maria. He was educated at Uppingham, Bury and Peterhouse, Cambridge (B.A., 1862). He then went to Sydney in the *Montmorencey* and in 1865 moved to Queensland because of delicate health and hope of greater opportunities. He gained experience on the Darling Downs with the Gore [q.v.] brothers and joined St George junior in taking up properties on the Peak Downs. After difficult years in 1866-68 Gore turned to other vocations while Graham struggled to establish himself in the central district. He became editor of the *Peak Downs Telegram* with a share in the profits; in partnership with Mackay, a printer from Rockhampton, he took over the newspaper and soon became sole owner.

In 1872 as an independent Graham won the Clermont seat in the Legislative Assembly; not a single vote was registered against him in the town and his electors paid him a salary of £300. He was secretary for public lands from 15 July 1873 to 8 January 1874 when the Palmer [q.v.] ministry was defeated. When the 1875 session ended he resigned because of financial difficulties. Griffith, leader of the new government and a political opponent of Graham, offered to appoint him under-secretary for public instruction to supervise the establishment of Queensland's new educational system under the 1875 Act which set up a system of state education but also provided for 'non-vested' schools. After consultation with Palmer, Graham accepted the office and held it from 17 January 1876 to 31 October 1878. His administration was so successful that on his resignation he received not only a testimonial from all the government teachers in the colony but also high praise from the nuns of All Hallows, the leading Catholic girls' school.

Graham moved to New South Wales in search of a cooler climate and greater financial stability. In partnership with George Walker Waddell, formerly manager of the Australian Joint Stock Bank in Clermont, he took over a brewery at Orange and ran it profitably. Active in public causes in the town, he became captain in the local Volunteer Force. In 1884 he applied without success for appointment as under-secretary for public instruction in New South Wales. He sold the brewery and in January 1885 sailed for England partly to renew old links, partly for a difficult operation on the foot of his young son. In January 1886 he left for Australia in the *Parramatta*, aware that he had heart trouble. It afflicted him severely near Colombo but the stay there revived him. Rough seas again aggravated his complaint and he had to go ashore at Albany where he died on 18 March 1886 of valvular disease of the aorta. He was survived by his wife Mary Joseph, née Enright, and three children.

V&P (LA NSW), 1884, 1, 436; Centenary report of the Queensland Public Service, V&P (LA Qld), 1959-60, 1, 58; *Brisbane Courier*, 22 Mar, 6 Apr 1886; *Western Advocate* (Orange), 24 Mar 1886.
           A. A. MORRISON

GRAHAM, SIR JAMES (1856-1913), physician and politician, was born on 29 July 1856 at Edinburgh, son of Thomas Graham, marble polisher, and his wife Jane, née Square. He was educated at the University of Edinburgh (M.A., 1879; M.B., C.M., 1882). In 1884 he migrated to Sydney and in January 1885 became resident medical officer at the Royal Prince Alfred Hospital. A year later he resigned to lecture in anatomy at the University of Sydney (M.B. *ad eund.*, 1886). In July he returned to the hospital as medical superintendent. He left for Europe in August 1888, was awarded honorary degrees at Berlin, Paris and Vienna, and for his thesis on 'Hydatid disease in its clinical aspects' won a gold medal at the University of Edinburgh (M.D., 1888). He returned to Sydney in 1889 and was appointed honorary assistant physician at the Royal Prince Alfred Hospital; in 1896 he became a director on its board. He also lectured to nurses in clinical medicine and later in midwifery at the University of Sydney in 1897-1912. At his private practice in Liverpool Street he had many Chinese patients and at the hospital was reputed 'to see sixty out-patients in twenty minutes', but despite his speed he was very popular.

In July 1894 as a free trader and Liberal Graham was elected for Sydney-Belmore to the Legislative Assembly after a brilliant campaign. He advocated graduated income tax and higher probate duties and in the assembly helped to pass medical and dentistry bills. He was defeated at the election in July 1901 and in 1906 opposed J. C. Watson for South Sydney in the Federal parliament without success. In September 1907 as a vice-president of the Liberal Association he won the Labor stronghold of Surry Hills in the New South Wales Legislative Assembly but was defeated in September 1910. A prominent leader in municipal reform he had been elected to the Sydney City Council in 1898. He was president of the Citizens' Vigilance Committee during the 1900 plague scare and in 1901 was elected mayor and knighted by the duke of York in Sydney. At the end of his term he was given a presentation at the Town Hall and a testimonial from the registered dentists. He then visited England with his wife Fanny, née Millard, whom he had married at Newcastle in 1890; she had been on the nursing staff of the Royal Prince Alfred Hospital.

Among his many public offices Graham had helped to found the Women's Hospital in 1895 and was associated with it until 1907. With Professor Anderson Stuart he organized the University of Sydney Medical Society and was its first president in 1886. He was also the first chairman of the Dental Board, a founder and president of the Surgical Appliance Aid Society and the Australian Trained Nurses' Association, a director of Sydney Hospital, a member of the Board of Health, a medical officer of the Benevolent Society, a councillor of the local Royal Society, a trustee of Sydney Grammar School, a director of the City Bank of Sydney and the English, Scottish and Australian Bank and a member of the Australian Club. Under his guidance and influence, the Royal Prince Alfred Hospital became an excellent training ground for the medical profession. In parliament and local government he sought to alleviate the needs of the sick and poor, contributed to the establishment of old-age pensions and helped to give Sydney better sanitation. With his firm principles and demands for better medical services he was often in conflict with fellow directors and parliamentarians. He died on 8 March 1913 at Darlinghurst and was buried in the Anglican section of Waverley cemetery. He was survived by his wife and one son. His estate was valued at £20,000.

Prince Alfred Hospital Gazette, 1902-13; G. H. Abbott, Inaugural address . . . sixth annual reunion, RPAH Officers Assn, *Year Book*, 1935; letter-books, annual reports 1883-1900 and newspaper cuttings (RPAH, ML).
           MARGARET CALDWELL

GRAHAM, JAMES (1819-1898), merchant, agent and politician, was born on 5 February 1819 at Ennis, County Clare, Ireland, son of James Moore Graham, Irish-born surgeon in the Scottish Fife Militia, and his first wife Anna Maria, née Ievers. He was educated at Ennis College and, after the family moved to Fife in 1832, at Madras Academy, Cupar. There in 1836 he was employed by Pagan & Christie, bankers and solicitors, and on 10 May 1838 was appointed clerk in charge of the National Security Savings Bank of Fife, of which Christie was actuary. Graham immediately deposited 10s. in the bank but resigned in August, sailed in the Alfred in September and arrived in Sydney on 7 January 1839. To his parents he wrote, 'I left my happy home, a home that was endeared to me by the warmest ties of affection, and which contained all that was near and dear to me on this earth'. However, he had a testimonial from Pagan & Christie with 'most cordial wishes for his prosperity and success'.

With three companions and a young servant Graham started overland in April for Melbourne to establish an agency for the Sydney· merchant, S. A. Donaldson [q.v.]. They travelled through drought-burnt country, crossed the Murray River, saw a promised land which 'gladdened both man and beast' and reached Melbourne on 10 May. Graham's instructions from Donaldson were 'to get settlers to give us wool, and give them in exchange either money at a reasonable rate of advance or sugar, tea, tobacco etc. at the market price'. Young and talented, he soon established a successful business which included investments in land and buildings for Donaldson's clients. In the 1840s he was a director of the Port Phillip Steam Navigation Co., the Melbourne Fire and Marine Insurance Co. and the Melbourne Auction Co., treasurer of the Commercial Exchange, member of the management committee of the Port Phillip Theological Education Society, secretary of the Australia Felix Immigration Society, a trustee of the Government Savings Bank and a commissioner for insolvent estates. By the mid-1840s, though still conducting Donaldson's Victorian affairs, Graham was in business on his own account. He admitted Frederick Lamb as a partner in 1853. Graham was nominated that year to the Legislative Council but resigned in 1854 to visit Britain.

In Cupar the freedom of the burgh was conferred on him after he gave £100 for distribution to the poor to enable them 'to lay in a few necessaries or comforts for the coming winter'. Alarmed by reports of increasing depression in Melbourne he hurried back and in January 1857 was busy at 91 Little Collins Street East penning admonitions to his debtors. He returned to Cupar in 1858 to collect his family and reached Melbourne in October 1860. His association with Lamb had been dissolved in 1857 and next year he formed Graham Bros & Co. His brothers, Edward and Charlie, were admitted as partners. That partnership was dissolved about 1870 but Graham retained the firm's title. His son, Francis, became a partner on 1 January 1876 and on 31 December 1897 another son, Harry, was admitted.

Goods ranging from silk to ore crushers, from brandy to corrosive sublimate were sold by Graham Bros & Co. and bales of Victorian wool were shipped to England. Much of the business was on commission: the firm managed the affairs of such retired investors as the ex-lieut-governor C. J. La Trobe, selling his colonial land in Jolimont and investing the proceeds. Among his other clients were the overlander, Joseph Hawdon [q.v.], and the squatter and financier, William Campbell [q.v.]. In addition Graham acted as executor of many deceased Victorian estates. Despite the increasing commitments of his firm Graham was also a director of the Melbourne and Mount Alexander Railway Co. and the St Kilda and Brighton Railway Co., chairman of the Melbourne Exchange Co., a director of the English, Scottish and Australian Bank, the London Guarantee and Accident Co., the Australasian Insurance Co. and chairman of the North British Mercantile Insurance Co., the South British Marine Insurance Co. and the Standard Insurance Co. of Scotland. His interests in station properties included Yering, View Hill, Tragowell, Dunock Forest and Koolomurt in Victoria. He also became consul for Sardinia in 1859 and later for United Italy. He was a founding member of the Melbourne Club and its president in 1865, a founding member of the Old Colonists' Association, a Freemason and an Anglican. In 1866-86 he represented Central Province in the Legislative Council but was not prominent in politics and usually voted as a Conservative. He retired from politics 'to concentrate on business and personal affairs'. Though still active in the firm particularly in managing the affairs of friends and absentee colonists, Graham's letters in his last years were written in a shaky hand.

On 24 September 1845 Graham had married Mary Alleyne, née Cobham; of their eighteen children, eight died young. He died at South Yarra on 31 July 1898, leaving an estate worth more than £189,000. Strong in talent and business associations, industrious and honest, close in his attention to detail, he was one of Victoria's most prominent men of commerce. A good provider rather than a high liver, his life and the outstanding collection of records he left for historians form a fascinating reflection of colonial Victoria's commercial history.

A portrait of Graham is held by a great-grandson, F. J. O. Graham of Sydney, and another is in the Melbourne Club.

Fife Herald, 16, 23 Nov 1854; Graham Bros & Co. records (Univ Melb Archives); Minutes of directors' meetings (National Security Savings Bank, Cupar, Fife).   FRANK STRAHAN

GRAMP, JOHANN (1819-1903), vigneron, was born on 28 August 1819 at Eichigt near Kulmbach, Bavaria. He migrated from Hamburg in the Solway and arrived at Kingscote on 16 October 1837. He worked on Kangaroo Island for the South Australian Co., and in 1839-40 helped to build the company's wharf at Port Adelaide. After working in an Adelaide bakery he turned to farming at Yatala. In 1847 he moved to Jacob's Creek in the Barossa valley and planted a vineyard. In 1850 he made his first octave of wine, a type of hock later known as Carte Blanche. The pioneer vigneron in the district, he did most of the work by hand but was soon able to expand his vineyard, build a cellar and improve his equipment. He was active in the Lutheran Church and in the 1860s served on the Barossa East District Council, took his turn as chairman and among other achievements helped to provide Rowland Flat with a public school; he had been naturalized by 1872. Years of exposure and hard work affected his skin and he gradually withdrew from the business. In old age he successfully cultivated citrus fruit. On 9 August 1903 he died at his home, leaving an estate of £10,600. He was survived by his wife Eleonora, née Nitzschke, and by 3 sons, 3 married daughters, 48 grandchildren and 19 great-grand-children.

His eldest son GUSTAV was born on 18 June 1850 in Adelaide and after attending the public school in Rowland Flat helped his father until 1874. On 17 April he married Louisa Koch and at Rowland Flat his father gave him forty-four acres which he called Orlando. There he planted vines and in 1877 transferred his father's wine business. He built large cellars at Orlando in 1886, steadily increased his acreage and added to the fermenting and storage capacity. He served in the Barossa District Council for fifteen years and was an active member of the local school board and of the Lutheran Church, acting as treasurer of its Aboriginal mission at Koonibba, Denial Bay. He died at Angaston on 11 July 1927, leaving an estate of £11,420. He was sur-

vived by his wife and by two sons and four daughters of their ten children.

In 1912 the business of Orlando wines was converted into a limited company, G. Gramp & Sons. The youngest son of the third generation, LOUIS HUGO (b. 1895), later became managing director and won wide repute as an expert judge of wines. He increased the capacity of the winery to 3,500,000 gallons. With other South Australian vignerons he was flying to Canberra for a conference on the wine industry but was killed when the air liner Kyeema crashed into Mount Dandenong on 25 October 1938. He was survived by his wife Hulda, née Braunack, and by two sons and two daughters. His brother Fred took over the management of the company.

H. T. Burgess (ed), Cyclopedia of South Australia, 2 (Adel, 1909); G. Gramp & Sons Ltd, 100 years of wine making, 1847-1947 (Adel, 1948); Observer (Adel), 15 Aug 1903; Advertiser (Adel), 26 Oct 1938.

GRANT, JAMES MACPHERSON (1822-1885), politician, was born at Alvie, Inverness-shire, Scotland, son of Louis Grant and his wife Isabella, née McBean. The family migrated to Sydney in 1836. James was articled to the solicitors, Chambers & Thurlow. He qualified in 1847 and soon became Thurlow's partner but was restless. In 1844 he had visited New Zealand, and fought in the Hone Heke war; in 1850 he made a speculative voyage to California and next year went with his brothers to the Bendigo diggings. He was a legal adviser to co-operative companies and one of the seven guarantors for Ebenezer Syme [q.v.] who bought the Age, and was one of its early contributors. By 1854 he was a prospering Melbourne solicitor. In Sydney he had shown radical sympathies and in Bendigo was an active political speaker. Now he threw himself, without charge, into the successful defence of the Eureka Stockade rebels.

In November 1855 Grant was elected for Sandhurst to the Legislative Council and in October 1856 for Sandhurst Boroughs to the new Legislative Assembly. He decided not to stand in 1859 but was persuaded to contest Avoca, his constituency thenceforward. He soon established himself as a legal reformer and republican radical. These views, his fondness for drink and the tendency for outbursts of sudden ferocity to sweep away his normal urbanity damaged his practice, but his political position rapidly improved. In Heales's [q.v.] ministry on 20 February 1861 Grant became vice-president of the board of land and works and commissioner of public works. The ministry fell in November 1861 but in James McCulloch's [q.v.] coalition of June 1863 Grant became vice-president of the land and works board and commissioner of railways and roads; in September 1864 he became president of the board and commissioner of crown lands and survey.

His land bill, on which the government had fought the 1864 election, was passed in March 1865 but the exigencies of finance and coalition and the power of the council made compromises necessary; despite Grant's vigorous administration his stronger safeguards against evasion only made it more expensive. However, Clause 42 authorized smallholding licences near goldfields at ministerial discretion; Grant's regulations developed these licences until from November 1868 they were widely available for up to 160 acres. Administrative powers were used to ensure genuine settlement. Generally it worked, despite scandals. Grant had some responsibility for these because of the disorganization of his office and his reluctance to delegate authority, yet few thought him corrupt.

A constitutional crisis and these scandals delayed amending legislation until December 1869. Grant's second Act extended free selection before survey to 320-acre lots at 20s. an acre paid over ten years and retained the safeguards of improvement conditions, a revocable licence for the first three years and extensive ministerial discretion. Imperfections remained but scandalous evasion ended.

Grant's career seemed to be finished. He had held office for nearly six years when McCulloch's government fell in September 1869, and the Land Act was passed under its successor. Yet when McCulloch regained power in April 1870 Grant was dropped. Despite the ministry's more conservative tone the parting was amicable; ill health was probably the explanation. Grant was certainly poor and characteristically had waived his inchoate rights when ministerial pensions had been abolished. The government therefore put £7000 on the estimates for his family; he resigned in July but immediately had the vote deleted because it threatened to provoke another constitutional crisis. At the 1871 election he re-entered the assembly. His health had improved; he had temporarily abandoned alcohol and his financial anxieties were allayed by a public subscription of £3000 and the introduction of payment of members. Moreover, the current lands minister was allegedly pro-squatter.

When McCulloch fell in June 1871, Grant readily accepted his old post in the radical ministry of C. G. Duffy [q.v.] but little was

achieved before the government fell in June 1872. Duffy soon nominated Grant leader of the Opposition but it was disintegrating and Grant lacked authority to hold it together. That was the achievement of Graham Berry [q.v.] in 1875-76. Grant served in his first cabinets as minister of justice from August to October 1875 and May 1877 to March 1880. In the constitutional crisis of 1877-78 he was a keen supporter of tough measures against the council. He broke with Berry in 1880 for seeking a compromise reform bill and was omitted from Berry's ministry in 1880-81. After Berry's Reform Act was passed Grant helped Sir Bryan O'Loghlen [q.v.] to defeat the ministry in July 1881 and became his chief secretary and minister of public instruction. Grant's prestige was invaluable to a weak ministry; his education post also diminished fears that O'Loghlen might tamper with the secular education system. The ministry fell in March 1883 after a snap election but Grant declined to lead the Opposition because he supported the policies of the liberal and conservative coalition although he deemed such alliances unparliamentary. Soon afterwards his health gave way. He died aged 63 on 1 April 1885 and, after a service at Elsternwick Presbyterian Church which he had helped to found, was buried in Melbourne general cemetery. He was survived by his wife Mary, née Gaunson, a son and three daughters.

Compact and sturdy, Grant always looked impressive with a fine forehead and bold eyes but he had never sought first place. He was not obtrusive in debate, organization or agitation and, although a convinced protectionist, generally ignored finance. Probably he suffered from self-doubt, yet he was quick, ingenious and strong on detail and could speak clearly and effectively. When parliament voted £4000 to his widow it settled a debt of honour.

E. C. Booth, *Another England* (Lond, 1869); R. Carboni, *The Eureka stockade* (Melb, 1947); M. L. Kiddle, *Men of yesterday* (Melb, 1961); PD (Vic), 1856-85; *Argus*, 22 July 1856, 2, 4, 6 Apr 1885; *Leader* (Melb), 21 June 1862, 4 Apr 1885; *Ovens and Murray Advertiser*, 18 Apr 1874; G. R. Bartlett, Political organization and society in Victoria 1864-1883 (Ph.D. thesis, ANU, 1964); Black papers (La T L); Governor's dispatch, 11 Sept 1869, CO 309/91.

GEOFFREY BARTLETT

GRAVES, JAMES ABRAHAM HOWLIN (1827-1910), politician, was born on 14 December 1827 at Maryborough, Queen's County, Ireland, the elder son of Captain

John Baker Graves and his second wife Anne, née Howlin. He was educated at the Ecôle Normale, Boulogne, and in Dublin at Feinaigle's School and in 1845 at Trinity College. On 5 October 1852 he married Julia Maria, daughter of William James Harvey of Kyle, County Wexford. There they lived on estates inherited through James's mother although early financial difficulties made them sell some land on 6 May 1858 in the Incumbered Estates Court to meet family charges. This sale eased their troubles but in November 1863 the Wexford Masonic Lodge noted with regret that 'for furtherance of your temporal prospects' he intended to migrate.

He landed at Melbourne in 1864 and became a pastoralist in the Riverina where, according to tradition, his family joined him three years later. In 1872 he went to Melbourne as sub-manager and inspector for the London and Australian Agency Corporation. He also dealt in Victorian properties and leased stations in the north-east and Gippsland where he pioneered the breeding of Red Poll cattle. A restless vigour also led him into such enterprises as development of the Port Welshpool fisheries, a directorship in Thomas Bent's [q.v.] Heights of Maribyrnong Estate Co. and ownership in 1888-89 of the *Trades Hall Gazette*.

Graves represented Delatite in the Legislative Assembly in 1877-1904 except for the 1900-1902 session. He was chairman of the police appeal board in 1877, an anti-squatter member of the royal commission on closed roads in 1878, commissioner to the Melbourne International Exhibition and a chairman of the visiting committee to the industrial and reformatory schools in 1879. He resigned from the royal commission on the police force in 1881 on becoming commissioner of trade and customs in the O'Loghlen [q.v.] ministry of 1881-83. Thereafter his services were little used for he had become notorious for his inconstancy of principle. Berry and Service [qq.v.] could not discover his final position on their reform bills of 1879 and 1880 until his crucial vote was cast against each. When a reform measure was adopted in 1881 Graves resurrected loyalty to the liberal platform which, he argued, Berry had betrayed, and his seconding of O'Loghlen's successful no-confidence motion won him the portfolio. Delatite electors were also familiar with his enthusiasm for Orange principles in Protestant areas and ecumenical spirit at meetings predominantly Catholic. He was especially skilled in subverting the electoral committees of opposing candidates. He was assiduous in serving Delatite's grazing, selector and mining interests but in Melbourne his 'lightning changes' suggested

place-hunting, hard bargaining and unreliability. Deakin dismissed him as 'the most sinuous and uncertain of fence-sitters'. Others concluded that if Graves spoke in favour of a measure his vote would go against it. His many conservative beliefs and his representation of a farming district added to his reputation as an uncertain liberal supporter in a crisis. He opposed high tariffs but was ready to hold the trade and customs portfolio. Apart from the removal of duties on tea and wine, protection was scarcely altered while he was commissioner: the slipperiness of the ministerial benches and the creation of the royal commission into the tariff meant that the government asked little of Graves beyond staying power.

Later Graves continued to vote as an independent Liberal, opposing coalition from 1883 and later supporting Sir George Turner. His parliamentary experience was recognized by his election as deputy-chairman of committees in 1887 and chairman in 1903. He was always a strong critic of 'class legislation', whether emanating from the Legislative Council, landholders, radicals or Labor, and claimed that progress demanded 'practical, non-political measures', with government encouragement of the small, independent man of capital. He died at South Yarra on 23 November 1910, predeceased by his wife in 1901 and a son, James Warden, in 1906, and survived by his elder son, John Crosbie, and three daughters.

H. M. Humphreys (ed), *Men of the time in Australia: Victorian series*, 2nd ed (Melb, 1882); J. Sadleir, *Recollections of a Victorian police officer* (Melb, 1913); L. Monod (ed), *The Red Poll herd book of Australasia*, 1 (Melb, 1921); A. Deakin, *The crisis in Victorian politics, 1879-1881*, J. A. La Nauze and R. M. Crawford eds (Melb, 1957); PD (Vic), 1877-1900, 1903; *Age*, 4, 9, 12, 16 July 1881, 8, 16 Feb 1883, 24 Nov 1910; *Table Talk*, 15 Feb 1895; *Argus*, 24 Nov 1910; *Toora and Welshpool Ensign*, 2 Dec 1910; J. H. Graves estate papers (Equity Trustees Co., Melb); Heights of Maribyrnong Estate Co. Ltd, package 1215 (VA); information from L. J. Graves, Mansfield, Vic.

C. F. DOXFORD

GRAVES, JOHN WOODCOCK (1795-1886), composer, was born on 9 February 1795 at Wigton, Cumberland, England, son of Joseph Graves, plumber, glazier and ironmonger, and his wife Ann, née Matthews. His father died in 1803 leaving nothing but debts, and John had little schooling. At 14 in Cockermouth he was apprenticed to his uncle George, painter of coach signs. John learned to use brush and pen but attributed his best education to an old bachelor, Joseph

Falder: 'He fixed in me a love of truth and bent my purpose to pursue it'. Fond of drawing and painting, Graves at one time hoped to study art; later he painted several portraits in oils. About 1815 he completed his apprenticeship, left Cockermouth and acquired interests in a carding mill at Caldbeck. Later he became interested in coal-mining in West Scotland and neglected the woollen mill. His connexion with it ended in blows and a lawsuit which he lost. At Caldbeck he had met the farmer, horse-dealer and huntsman, John Peel (1776-1854), with whom he spent much time. One evening in 1824 Graves wrote impromptu the five verses 'D'ye ken John Peel?' and sang them to the old Cumberland rant of 'Bonnie Annie'. The song quickly became famous and as its author Graves is best remembered. After Peel's death he wrote 'Monody on John Peel' and 'At the Grave of John Peel'.

In 1834 Graves left for Van Diemen's Land in the *Strathfieldsay* with his wife and six children as assisted immigrants and some £10 in cash. He tried various occupations, was granted 640 acres on Bruny Island and in September 1835 applied for the post of keeper of the proposed lighthouse on South Bruny. In May 1836 he advertised himself as willing to repair, paint and varnish carriages, paint portraits and heraldic devices and undertake japanning, plumbing and glazing. In 1837 he sought an official appointment to report on coal-mines at Port Arthur; in May he asked the lieut-governor for help in opening a slate quarry at Davey River and in June for employment as a lithographer. In 1842, after detention at the government asylum in New Norfolk for apparent insanity, he went to New Zealand where he studied flax-growing, invented a machine to improve the preparation of flax and attempted to evolve a better weaving loom. He returned to Hobart Town about 1845. Erratic and eccentric, he lived on Satellite Island with his son Joseph, with whom he carried on 'a very fierce war'. In 1856 he was described as 'a most violent and dangerous person and certainly unfitted to be at large'.

Graves married twice. His first wife, Jane Atkinson of Rosley, Cumberland, died within a year of marriage. Four years later he married Abigail Porthouse. Of their eight children, the eldest, John Woodcock, became a successful lawyer in Tasmania, and Joseph owned large timber mills at Southport. For some years Graves lived with John at Caldew in Cavell Street, West Hobart, but Joseph was his mainstay in later life. Graves died at Hobart on 17 August 1886 and was buried in the Queenborough cemetery. In 1958 a memorial was erected in St David's Park.

H. Machell, *John Peel* (Lond, 1926); *Hobart Town Courier*, 30 Jan 1835, 20, 27 May 1836; correspondence file under Graves (TA).

A. W. CAMPBELL

GRAY, JAMES (1820-1889), civil servant and parliamentarian, was born at Ballybay, County Monaghan, Ireland, son of Orange parents. He dabbled in Irish politics and, by his own account, became a voluntary exile and migrated to Hobart Town.

On 17 January 1848 Gray became a clerk in the registry of deeds at a salary of £78. From December 1851 he was ill for eight months and when he recovered became bench clerk to visiting justices at the Hobart penitentiary at a salary of £100. In July 1854, with a reference from Lieut-Governor Denison as 'a very useful man and one in whom you can confide', he was appointed a clerk in the department of roads and public works. After six months he was promoted a second-class clerk at £150 a year. Flattering testimonials from past and present directors of his department and from several members of parliament won him promotion in January 1860 to chief clerk and doubled his salary. When reorganization of the department was mooted in 1868 Gray collected more testimonials praising his fidelity, attention and untiring exertion 'as one of the most efficient officers in the service'. In July 1870 he offered to accept a lower salary 'if the exigencies of the public service required'. He was then earning, in addition to his salary, emoluments of £60 for extra work under the Loans Act and £50 from the Bridgewater commissioners. In November 1871 he was notified of the abolition of his office and applied for his pension, claiming that it should be computed not only on £300 but on the £410 he had received for 'a much greater number of years than required by the Superannuation Act'. His claim was approved by the Executive Council but parliament demurred; on 1 January 1872 Gray was given a pension of £144 for his salary but only a lump sum of £50 for the loss of his extra earnings.

An ardent Irishman, Gray named his home Ulster Lodge and devoted much time and eloquence to the cause of 'the little property-holder'. Elected to the House of Assembly for West Hobart in August he soon won repute for the variety and force of the petitions he introduced and of his questions in the House. Although described as 'a fellow of infinite jest and of a most excellent fancy', his light banter often demolished departmental extravagances and strengthened his appeals for the underprivileged. After his wife died, he resigned in April 1877 and took his only daughter to Ireland. He returned to Hobart in 1880 but she stayed with relations and reputedly became a nun. In 1881 he contested the Pembroke seat in the Legislative Council without success but in 1882-89 in the assembly represented Sorell, a rural electorate which owed him much for its roads and bridges. In November 1883 he represented Tasmania at the Irish National Convention in Melbourne and renewed acquaintance with the president, K. O'Doherty [q.v.], whom he had known 'in the days of his exile'.

Habitually anti-government, Gray was often twitted for his political convictions but none doubted his geniality and benevolence to even casual acquaintances. Late in 1888 ill health kept him away from parliament but,‘hearing of designs to dislodge the ministry of P. O. Fysh, he struggled to his place and successfully defended the Conservative premier. The effort hastened Gray's death at 69 in Hobart on 21 January 1889. He was buried in Cornelian Bay cemetery.

Advocate (Melb), 10 Nov 1883, 26 Jan 1889; *Mercury*, 17, 22, 23 Jan 1889; CSD 7/49/D1009 (TA).

GRAY, MOSES WILSON (1813-1875), politician and judge, was born in Claremorris, County Mayo, Ireland, son of John Gray and his wife Elizabeth, née Wilson. He was educated at Cork, at Hazelwood School, Edgbaston, and at Trinity College, Dublin (B.A., 1835). He entered the King's Inns in 1834 and was called to the Irish Bar in 1845 but seldom practised. In 1835 he was appointed an assistant commissioner to the poor law inquiry in Ireland. He then went to America where he studied at the University of Michigan, was admitted to the Bar and travelled in the mid-west and Canada to examine a plan for the colonization of impoverished Irish tenantry. He returned to Dublin in 1848 and published a pamphlet, *Self-paying Colonization in North America.* Believing that Ireland's main problems were constitutional he strongly sympathized with opponents of the 1800 Act of Union. He joined his brother in managing and editing the *Freeman's Journal,* and in 1852 with C. G. Duffy [q.v.] went to France to see John Dillon. In 1855 after hopes for settlement of the Irish land question collapsed Gray and Duffy sailed in the *Ocean Chief* and arrived in Melbourne in 1856.

Gray was admitted to the Victorian Bar, worked as a law reporter for the *Age* and later the *Argus* and became the dedicated leader of the popular 'unlock the lands' campaign. He was a committee member of the new Victoria Land League and in July 1857 was elected president of the Land Convention, his skill and inspiration winning the esteem of delegates. He denounced the 'barefaced iniquity' of the Haines [q.v.] government's land bill and advocated an alternative measure based on free selection, abolition of sale by auction and open pasturage over crown lands. He joined a deputation to request the government to withdraw its land bill and his experience of the American land system greatly helped the convention's subcommittee on land. He was president of the council formed after the convention dissolved in August. Though inclined to trust the O'Shanassy [q.v.] government, he was shocked when it compromised with the Legislative Council on electoral reform in October 1858. Gray declared that the convention would have to fight its own battle on the hustings and led a deputation to the government to warn of 'national calamity' if land reform were delayed. At a ministerial by-election for Richmond in April 1859 he supported G. S. Evans [q.v.], misled by his specious advocacy of a semi-convention land policy. Because of this mistake Gray felt obliged to resign as president of the convention but remained a council member; he was also active in the United Australian Society and the Eight Hours Labor League.

The convention distrusted the new Nicholson [q.v.] ministry's land policy and decided to support Gray against the treasurer, J. McCulloch [q.v.], in a by-election at East Melbourne on 8 November 1859. Gray lost by 350 votes but on 11 January 1860 was returned for Rodney. Sitting with the 'Corner' group in the assembly he plunged into the debate on the Service [q.v.] land bill but was soon 'half bewildered' when the government deferred the squatting question and failed to defy the Legislative Council. He renewed his hopes in July when Service threatened to invoke an 1850 Order in Council to open the lands on easy terms but was disgusted by the Nicholson government's resignation and weak resumption of office. On 28 August Gray urged the assembly to listen to the agitators outside parliament and fervently wished that every man had 'a vote, a rifle and a farm'.

Gray's passion for land reform did not exclude other pressing issues. As one of the poorest in the assembly he appreciated the need for payment of members. He also sought legislation for secular education, mining on private property, light duties on imports for revenue purposes and repeal of the Masters and Servants Act and the gold export duty. He introduced a barristers' admission bill and when returned for Rodney on 3 August 1861 advocated reform of the Legislative Council. He declined office in the tentative Duffy ministry of 1860 and in the Heales [q.v.] ministry of 1860-61. Though uncommitted to the Heales ministry, Gray defended the legality of J. H. Brooke's [q.v.] occupation licences as a prelude to a real 'people's land bill'. He was bitterly disappointed in December 1861 when Duffy introduced a land bill which fell far short of convention aims and the 1861 Robertson [q.v.] Acts in New South Wales. Gray's efforts to secure easier purchase terms, stricter residence conditions and more liberal commonage were rebuffed and after parliament was prorogued in June 1862 he left for New Zealand, declining a banquet and pecuniary testimonial but attending a simple social at the Trades Hall.

Gray joined the Dunedin Bar and in 1864 became district judge of the Otago goldfields. He was competent and conscientious and many of his decisions were published in the *New Zealand Jurist and Reports* but his diffidence, constant self-doubt, and indifference to material advancement led him to reject more lucrative positions.

Gray maintained an avid, critical interest in the countries he had known and during the American civil war identified with the North as the upholder of human freedom. He had married in the United States and taken his wife to Ireland but she returned to America with their son Wilson who later fought in the Union army. After strenuous circuit travelling, overwork, failing health and distress at the prospect of retirement, Gray died aged 62 on 4 April 1875 at Lawrence, and was buried in Dunedin. Though he died with a sense of futility in his Victorian work, many of his opinions on land selection prevailed in later legislation. The Victorian Legislative Assembly paid him high tribute in 1877 and G. Higinbotham [q.v.], whom he had always admired, eulogized him at the opening of the Trades Hall Council Chamber in 1884 for his services to the democratic land movement and for his perfect example, his absolute self-abnegation and unyielding adherence to principle.

Busts were placed in the Trades Hall Council Chamber and Parliamentary Building, Melbourne, and a portrait by J. Irvine is in the Hocken Library, Dunedin.

C. G. Duffy, *The League of north and south* (Lond, 1886); C. G. Duffy, *My life in two hemispheres*, 2 (Lond, 1898); G. Serle, *The golden age* (Melb, 1963); R. Stout, 'Moses Wilson Gray', *Melbourne Review*, 7 (1882); *Leader* (Melb), 12 July 1862; *Age*, 17 Apr 1875, 8 Mar 1884; L. C. Duly, The land selection acts in Victoria 1859-69 (M.A. thesis, Univ Melb, 1959).
                                      CAROLE WOODS

GREEN, RICHARD (1808-1878), merchant, was born on 24 November 1808 at Essendon, near Hertford, England, son of Isaac Green (1770-1837) and his wife Frances (1775-1857). He arrived in the *Eliza* at Hobart Town on 2 May 1831 accompanied by Mathias Gaunt, M.D., R.N., his wife Frances, sister of Richard Green, and their four children and niece, Hannah Jackson (1810-1904). After crossing the island with a bullock team over rough bush tracks, Gaunt and Green jointly took up land at Windermere on the River Tamar. Green at first lived in a cottage belonging to the father of 'Philosopher' Smith [q.v.]; built on a hill overlooking Swan Bay, it was surrounded by a palisade to keep out the Aboriginals. Later a farm house was built at Windermere. At St John's Church, Launceston, in May 1835 Green married Hannah Jackson.

About 1883 Green was accountant and general manager of the firm of James Henty [q.v.] & Co., Launceston. When the partners retired in 1843 he carried on the business as merchant in his own name. Described in 1851 as a shipping agent he bought the barque *Tiberias* and left Launceston for the Victorian goldfields. He was successful there and later returned to Launceston. A liberal donor to ecclesiastical and public institutions, he was a member of the standing council for Church schools at Launceston and elected an alderman in 1847, a member of the Marine Board and master warden, managing director of the Launceston Gas Works, and chairman of the Launceston and Western Railway Co. and the Cornwall Fire and Marine Insurance Co. He was the first chairman and managing director of the Mount Bischoff Tin Mining Co. and Smelting Works from its formation, and chairman of the Tasmanian Copper Co. He was a member and repeatedly president of the Chamber of Commerce, and took an active interest in all public affairs. He was an energetic member of the Church of England and served on the synod from its formation. In a long association with the Church Grammar School, Launceston, he was a trustee from 1850 and secretary and treasurer from 1864. He died at his home in Cimitiere Street, Launceston, on 23 September 1878, survived by his wife and by four sons and one daughter of their seven children. At his funeral 'the flags of the vessels in harbour were hoisted half-mast, and many business establishments in Launceston partially closed their doors, as a token of respect for the memory of the deceased gentleman'.

His second son, Alfred, became a solicitor in 1859 after serving his articles under William Henty [q.v.] of the firm of Gleadow [q.v.] & Henty, founded in 1826; his son, Alfred Lawrence, was admitted to the Bar in 1900 and in 1912 the firm became known as Ritchie & Parker Alfred Green & Co. In 1972 A. L. Green's two sons, Richard Martin and Alfred John, great-grandsons of J. W. Gleadow, were members of the firm which held the record of having the same continuous family interest for the second longest term in Tasmania and probably the third in Australia.

Church News (Hob), Oct 1878; Examiner (Launceston), 24, 26 Sept 1878; correspondence file under R. Green (TA).   R. M. GREEN

GREEN, SAMUEL (1841-1904), clergyman, was born on 2 February 1841 at Uppingham, Rutland, England, son of Rev. John Green, a Dissenting clergyman, and his wife Martha Margaret, née Holmes. His early ambition was to join the East India Civil Service. In 1863 he won a high place among applicants but changed his mind; he went instead to South Australia and offered himself for the Anglican ministry. Trained by Bishop Short [q.v.], he was ordained in 1865. As parish priest he worked mainly at Port Adelaide in 1865-66 and 1868-93 and Glenelg in 1893-1904.

One of the first High Churchmen in a strongly Evangelical colony, Green asserted the catholicity of the Church of England and introduced such innovations as weekly celebrations of Holy Communion and choral Eucharists, with the so-called 'ritualistic devices' of processional cross, altar candlesticks and incense. In 1869 a petition against ritualism was circulated through the diocese by militant Evangelical laymen who urged synod to remove Green and three other clergy from the diocese. Synod refused almost unanimously to debate the motion. Short investigated complaints about Green's services and concluded that 'not a hint had been breathed of false doctrine' by the priest. Green claimed to be 'as firm a Protestant (according to the Prayer Book) as could be found'. His sincerity and tact won over his congregation and most laymen in the diocese. He was appointed clerical secretary of synod in 1870 and served on the standing committee for thirty-five years. A forcible debater and an efficient administrator, he was a recognized authority on Church polity and was mentioned at least once as a probable bishop.

Green also promoted the revival of spiritual discipline, conducting Lenten observance and retreats. He was closely connected with the Confraternity of the Blessed Sacrament and with early work of the Kilburn Sisterhood. As canon missioner of the diocese in 1896-1904 he conducted parish missions designed to strengthen the life of the Church. He was also keenly aware of social problems. Although scarcely a Christian Socialist, he was an energetic supporter of local institutes and was closely connected with the Port Adelaide Workingmen's Association, founded in 1872 and the Homestead League, formed by G. W. Cotton [q.v.] in 1885.

Green decided to stand for Port Adelaide in 1878 in protest against the constitutional exclusion of ministers from parliament. Backed by local clergy, he had an enthusiastic response when 800 port electors attended a meeting to hear him and declare him a fit candidate. Proclaiming his principle vindicated, he stepped down before polling day.

Sharing the views of Bishop Kennion [q.v.], Green actively supported co-operation between capital and labour. In the 1887 shipping stoppage at Port Adelaide he addressed 3000 strikers, urging them to return to work, and warning them that not the employers but cunning men in their own ranks might be using the strike for selfish gains. The dispute ended after he arranged a conference between unionists and shipowners. He then seemed uncertain of labour principles but in the maritime strike of 1890 he told a large meeting that 'men were striking for their corporate existence—for unionism, by which they had managed to raise their lives. The owners had not a stake like that to fight for'. He also urged employers to initiate a permanent board of conciliation. Respected by both sides, he claimed 'many friends among the employers, but tenfold more among the men'.

A popular speaker, Green gave many public lectures, often using lantern slides. Some addresses were more scholarly than others: his 'Courtship' was acclaimed a masterpiece. He also ran a Spiritualist circle, with his wife as 'an effective Planchette medium', at the Port Adelaide Institute in 1880-81.

In 1865 Green had married Ellen Elizabeth, daughter of Rev. Edward Bayfield; they had no children. He died of heart disease at Glenelg on 23 July 1904.

F. R. Meleng, Fifty years of the Port Adelaide Institute (Adel, 1902); Observer (Adel), 17 Apr, 29 May 1869, 13 Apr 1878, 20 Sept 1890, 30 July, 13 Aug 1904; Advertiser (Adel), 16 Dec 1884, 13 Oct 1887, 25 July 1904; Review (Adel), 1890-94; Diocesan synod, Reports 1864-1905 (Diocesan Registry, Adel).

JANET SCARFE

GREENE, MOLESWORTH RICHARD (1827-1916), pastoralist was born on 14

January 1827 at Dublin, the eldest son of Lieutenant William Pomeroy Greene, R.N. and his wife Anne, née Griffith. Molesworth was educated in Paris. In 1842 he went with his parents to Port Phillip in the *Sarah* which his father had chartered for his household, hunters, two race-horses, two bulls and a cow, a library and a prefabricated house; they arrived in December. Woodlands, some miles from Melbourne, was chosen as the site for the family's new home.

In the next years Greene gained useful experience in bush life. A 'fine young fellow' with much character, he assumed responsibility for the family when his father died in 1846. With his brother, Rawdon, he took up a run west of the Whipstick scrub near Tandara and stocked it with 300 cattle. In 1848 he bought J. Moore's [q.v.] half of Glenmore station, near Bacchus Marsh; his uncle, C. J. Griffith [q.v.], held the other half. In that year the firm of Griffith & Greene bought Mount Pyramid near Echuca and William Campbell's [q.v.] Mount Hope station and famous Camden flock. Greene then visited England and on his return in 1851 became engaged to Emma, sister of Rolf Boldrewood [q.v. T. A. Browne]; they were married on 27 July 1854 at Woodlands.

With Frederick Darley [q.v.] and Robert Massie, Greene acquired Merungle station on the Lachlan. He then ventured into Queensland where with Lloyd Jones and A. T. Sullivan he took up Bulloo Downs and extended his holdings to include Tickalaro, Onepah, Dynevor Downs and others. He established an excellent Shorthorn herd and in 1899 his enthusiastic letter to the British Australasian Society on prospects in Queensland was published in London. Crippled by the long drought ending in 1902 he confined his rural activities to six dairy farms in Gippsland and Greystones near Bacchus Marsh. On this 10,000-acre property he built an imposing house with a magnificent view and, supplemented by the smaller Beremboke property five miles away, ran horses, cattle and 11,000 sheep. His flock was merino with a long-wool cross to maintain a good standard for wool, carcass and lamb production. He won renown for his husbandry, for his improvements in the conservation of water, firebreaks, cultivation of artificial grasses, especially lucerne, and tree plantations and for his use of share-farming both at Greystones and on his Gippsland farms.

For years Greene was a justice of the peace, a trustee of the Melbourne Public Library, National Gallery and Museum, a member of the Melbourne Club and its president in 1883, and vice-president of the Pastoralists' Association of Victoria and Southern Riverina. He was chairman of directors of the South Broken Hill Mining Co. in 1916 and respected as an authority on financial matters. On the Bacchus Marsh Shire Council he was described as its 'watchdog', always reminding his colleagues of their financial responsibilities. A liberal donor he rarely refused a deserving cause and supported Trinity College and the Trinity Women's Hostel. In his youth he was a noted amateur rider with great physical strength and his nephew thought him a 'perfect marvel' at 84: 'a man who rode on the run every day; read without glasses, and was up in all the topics of the day'. He died at East Melbourne on 10 October 1916 and was buried at the Melbourne general cemetery; he was survived by a son and two daughters, one of whom married Sir William Allardyce, later governor of the Bahama Islands and in 1920-22 of Tasmania.

M. F. E. Stawell, *My recollections* (Lond, 1911); *Pastoral Review*, 18 May 1903, 15 Nov 1905; *Argus*, 11 Oct 1916; *Werribee Express*, 14 Oct 1916.

J. ANN HONE

GREENUP, RICHARD (1803-1866), medical practitioner, was born on 15 March 1803 at Darcy Hay, near Halifax, England, third son of George Greenup, clothier, and his wife Elizabeth, née Marsh. On 19 May 1826 he entered Queens' College, Cambridge (M.B., 1831; M.D., 1836) and then practised at Salisbury, where in 1837 he married Jane, daughter of William Bird Brodie, banker, and his wife Louisa, née Hussey. Greenup moved to Calne where he practised and was visiting physician for ten years to asylums in North Wiltshire. As surgeon in the *John Knox* he arrived in Sydney on 29 April with his wife and children. He opened a private practice but was soon involved in helping to organize the new University of Sydney, became its secretary on 17 March 1851 and later was also treasurer and registrar. He was an examiner for medicine in 1856 and for chemistry and experimental physics in 1858.

Greenup was appointed medical superintendent at the Lunatic and Invalid Establishment at Parramatta on 20 March 1852 at a salary of £600. He joined the asylum in July and his duties included those of medical officer of the Protestant Orphan School, visiting surgeon to the gaol and the Destitute Roman Catholic Children's Institute, and official visitor to the Tarban Creek Asylum where Dr F. R. H. Campbell [q.v.] was superintendent.

Although the Parramatta asylum was for incurable lunatics, Greenup decided that his patients would benefit from humane treatment. He soon stopped the detention of refractory patients in cells and permitted them to exercise, albeit in 'leathern belts with handcuffs'; later even this restraint was relaxed. Orderly systematic visiting was introduced, male inmates were encouraged to work in maintenance, gardening and supplying wood to the orphan schools while female patients made clothing for the institution. In 1853 he could report that out of 253 patients two were cured and three improved and in 1863 that twenty were cured and six improved out of 476 inmates. He gave evidence at select committees on the management of asylums and alleged wrongful detention of lunatics. Critical of 'inquisitorial duties of a single medical man acting as Official Visitor', he supported the recommendation for a mixed board, and suggested a limited number of visits and duties similar to those prescribed in England. The increasing congestion at Tarban Creek was a constant problem. His plan to increase the intake at Parramatta by transferring invalid male patients to an auxiliary establishment was fulfilled in 1858. He pleaded in vain for a new and bigger asylum at Parramatta but his proposal to buy a near-by farm for asylum inmates was accepted in 1864. On 17 July 1866 during routine inspections he was stabbed in the abdomen by James Cameron, a lunatic with a homicidal record. He died two days later and his large funeral was conducted by Bishop Barker [q.v.]. He left an estate of £1610.

Among his honorary appointments Greenup was a trustee of the Protestant Orphan School in May 1852 and medical adviser to the government in December 1854. In a smallpox scare in 1858 he supported compulsory vaccination and in a pamphlet next year abridged for colonial use a letter by Dr John Simon on the subject. He was a visiting justice to the Parramatta gaol in 1859 and joined the board of management of the Government Asylum for the Infirm and Destitute in 1862. A fine, authoritative figure, Greenup was active in community affairs and often lectured on literary, philosophical and historical subjects. He was a member of the Anglican Church and Bible societies, a financial supporter of St John's Church, a lay reader at St Paul's, Castle Hill, and conducted services at the asylum for inmates who attended voluntarily. With strong views about the colony's defences he chaired a large public meeting which led to the formation of the Parramatta Rifle Corps; he became its honorary surgeon in May 1861.

His widow petitioned parliament in October 1866 for financial assistance but received only her husband's superannuation of £700.

Mrs Greenup later went to Queensland, bought Rotherwood on the Darling Downs and died there on 31 July 1894, leaving an estate of £9200. Her two sons and two of her four daughters married into pastoral families.

K. M. Brown, *Medical practice in old Parramatta* (Syd, 1937); V&P (LC NSW), 1854, 2, 9, 1855, 3, 763; (LA NSW), 1858, 3, 375, 1862, 2, 595, 1863-64, 2, 938, 4, 902, 960, 985, 1021; D. I. McDonald, 'Dr Francis Campbell and the Tarban Creek Asylum, 1848-1867', *JRAHS*, 53 (1967); SMH, 20, 21, 23 July 1866, 14 Aug, 4, 12 Sept 1867; *Church Chronicle*, 8 Aug 1866; Univ Syd Archives; information from N. B. Greenup, Canberra.   NAN PHILLIPS

GREENWAY, CHARLES CAPEL (1818-1905), archdeacon, was born on 13 March 1818 in Sydney, son of Francis Howard Greenway [q.v.] and his wife Mary, née Woore. He was educated at Cape's [q.v.] School in Sydney and in 1848 leased Collymangool, 33,000 acres on the Barwon River in the Gwydir district, where he developed an abiding interest in the Aboriginals and gained a knowledge of the Kamilaroi tongue.

At 32 Greenway decided to enter the church and began his clerical training in the diocese of Newcastle under Bishop Tyrrell [q.v.], and in 1854 was stationed at Newcastle. He was not made deacon until 1866 when he moved to Bundarra where for twelve years his flock responded warmly to his pastoral care. In 1867 he was ordained priest. A thorough bushman, he travelled regularly throughout his huge parish which included Warialda, Inverell, Bingara and Barraba from which new parishes were set up in 1871-77. He was active in the affairs of the diocese of Grafton and Armidale and in 1874-79 a member of the Diocesan Council. In 1878 his appointment to Grafton reflected Bishop Turner's [q.v.] high opinion of his work. Much of the credit for building Christ Church Cathedral at Grafton was due to Greenway's persistent efforts. In May 1882 he was appointed the first archdeacon of Grafton. He recognized the need for decentralized administration in the dual-titled diocese and was instrumental in gaining the approval of the diocesan synod in 1884 for two archidiaconal councils, a step towards the establishment of a separate coastal diocese thirty years later. He was appointed commissary when Bishop Turner retired to England in 1892; after Turner died in April 1893 he became administrator of the diocese and presided over the special synod which in 1894 elected Bishop Green. Early in his colonial career Bishop Tyrrell had spoken of Greenway's energy and perseverance and later Bishop Turner had written: 'Mr. Greenway commands my affection. With all his oddity there is a genuineness worth a great deal. I do not care about his brusque manner. I never tire of him. A bad preacher (on dit) but a good priest all agree'.

Greenway retired at the end of 1894 and lived on the family property at Tarro on the Lower Hunter. He died on 18 October 1905 in the Hillside private hospital for the insane, Gladesville, and was buried in the Anglican section of the Field of Mars cemetery. He was survived by his wife Emma, née Brown, a son and two daughters. A memorial window is in Christ Church Cathedral, Grafton.

K. H. Aubrey, The Church of England in northern New South Wales . . . (M.A. thesis, Univ New England, 1964); Greenway papers 1817-1903 (ML).   KEITH H. AUBREY

GREENWOOD, JAMES (1839-1882), Baptist pastor and politician, was born at Todmorden, Lancashire, England, son of Richard Greenwood, factory worker, and his wife Betty. He studied theology under Edward Bean Underhill (1813-1901) and philosophy and economics at the University of London (M.A., 1866). At St Pancras Church of England on 26 June he married Mary Ann Wallis Ward.

Greenwood became pastor of the Baptist Church in Nottingham where he absorbed the politics of the Midlands Dissenters. In July 1870 he arrived in Sydney, called by the Baptist Church in Bathurst Street. In June 1874 he convened a meeting of the clergy and prominent laymen of the Protestant churches to consider 'the propriety of establishing a more efficient and unsectarian system of public instruction'. In August the first public meeting of the Public School League was held and in September Greenwood published its manifesto: New South Wales Public School League, for making Primary Education national, secular, compulsory and free. In the Sydney Morning Herald, 27 September, its four principles were summarized: the league aimed at making education universal by adopting a uniform system embracing all children of school age and was opposed to the support of denominational education from public funds. He also published a Speech . . . in reply to the Hon. Henry Parkes [q.v.] on Education and Sermons for the People. Greenwood was also invited by the Public School League to stand for parliament but he insisted that he could serve the league and the country better out of parliament.

His parishioners were becoming restive over his secular and political commitments, and in 1876 he resigned from the Bathurst Street Church and abandoned all his pastoral duties. According to his daughter's 'Recollections', Greenwood had found Baptist theology restrictive. In January 1882 he lectured on 'Free Thought' and told his large audience why he no longer believed in Christian dogmas: he referred to the imperfections of the Bible which 'contained passages which he never dared to read to wife or daughter . . . If it was to be commonly used it should be made decent by expurgation as Shakespeare had been'.

In 1877-80 Greenwood represented East Sydney in the Legislative Assembly. In 1878 he gave notice of a motion on the league platform but it was never put. However, the first three of the league's objectives were embodied in Parkes's Public Instruction Act, 1880. The editors of A Century of Journalism (Sydney, 1931) claimed that Greenwood was largely responsible for the Act. An active and conscientious member, he was an able public speaker but lacking in tact. He had written in the Sydney Morning Herald on the education question even before 1876 when his resignation from pastoral duties freed him to work for that paper and for the Echo. He was widely read and the breadth and variety of his knowledge made him a competent statistician and he was credited with improving many government statistical returns. He died aged 44 at Paddington on 6 November 1882 and was buried in Rookwood cemetery; no minister of religion officiated. He was survived by his wife, one son and three daughters.

A. G. Austin, Australian education, 1788-1900 (Melb, 1961); A. C. Prior, Some fell on good ground . . . the Baptist Church in New South Wales, 1831-1965 (Syd, 1966); A. R. Crane, 'The New South Wales Public School League 1874-1879', Melbourne studies in education 1964, E. L. French ed (Melb, 1965); D. Morris, 'Henry Parkes—publicist and legislator', Pioneers of Australian education, C. Turney ed (Syd, 1969); Baptist Mag (Lond), 1850-70; Banner of Truth, 1880-82; A. L. Green, Recollections of a pioneer's daughter, Mary Gilmore papers (ML); letters (Central Baptist Church, Syd); minutes 1867-78 (Baptist Assn of NSW); minutes 1869-80 (Bathurst St Baptist Church, Syd).   DAVID MORRIS

GREEVES, AUGUSTUS FREDERICK ADOLPHUS (1805-1874), physician, politician and newspaper editor, was born at Knaresborough, Yorkshire, England, son of John Greeves, merchant, and his wife, née

Wilkinson. He studied medicine at Edinburgh (L.R.C.S., 1827) and in England (M.R.C.S., 1828) and practised at Knaresborough and Harrowgate. In 1840 he migrated to Port Phillip in the *Lord Goderich*.

Greeves was one of the surgeons who performed the first local operation with chloroform in 1848 but he had other interests besides his medical practice. In 1841 he had become proprietor of the British Hotel and later the Yarra Steam Packet Hotel on Queen's Wharf. He was vice-president of the Debating Society and a founding member of the Australia Felix Lodge of the Independent Order of Oddfellows. In May-June 1842 he edited the *Port Phillip Gazette* in the absence of George Arden [q.v.] but next year retired from the staff. In November 1843 he was elected to the Melbourne corporation and became an alderman in 1846 and mayor in 1849. Prominent in local politics, he was active in the Port Phillip separation movement, in drafting petitions to the Colonial Office and in 1848 supporting the movement for the recall of Superintendent La Trobe and the election of Earl Grey as a Port Phillip representative in the New South Wales Legislative Council. He was also influential in having a bridge built over the Yarra River and instigating the reservation of sites for the future town hall and parliament.

Greeves was a member of the Victorian Legislative Council in 1853-56 and served on the select committee which drafted the constitution. He was elected for East Bourke to the new Legislative Assembly in November and next March in the O'Shanassy [q.v.] government became commissioner of trade and customs. In April he was defeated in the ministerial elections but was appointed to the Melbourne sewerage and water commission; after his re-election for East Bourke in June he successfully proposed the Yan Yean amendment bill and held his seat until August 1859. From February 1860 to July 1861 he represented Geelong East and in September-October 1860 was president of the board of land and works and commissioner of crown lands and survey in the Nicholson [q.v.] ministry; many squatters were grateful for his administration of the new Land Act. In 1864-65 he represented Belfast in the assembly. As a Conservative he had opposed the secret ballot and supported high property qualifications, and was often accused of political opportunism. He won some repute for oratory but his style of speech was also described as 'pedantic fluency'. According to William Kelly [q.v.], he was 'a painstaking man, who, with . . . a fair share of small ability, and a great ambition for public fame or notoriety, has given all his time . . . to the study of public questions'.

In 1869-70 the Oddfellows presented Greeves with a testimonial and £500 which he offered to the University of Melbourne for an exhibition in his name for the sons of Victorian Oddfellows; in September 1871 the offer was rejected because of its exclusive conditions. He died aged 69 at his home in Swanston Street on 23 May 1874, survived by his wife Elizabeth, née Milner. He was buried in the Melbourne general cemetery after an Anglican service and a litany read by the Oddfellows who also erected his headstone.

L. Becker, *Men of Victoria* (Melb, 1856); W. Kelly, *Life in Victoria*, 1 (Lond, 1859); Garryowen (E. Finn), *The chronicles of early Melbourne*, 1-2 (Melb, 1888); *Aust Medical J*, 19 (1874), p 160; D. M. O'Sullivan, 'David John Thomas . . . a founder of Victorian medicine', *MJA*, 30 June 1956; *Argus*, 8 Apr, 1 May 1856, 25 May 1874, 8 July 1933; G. R. Quaife, The nature of political conflict in Victoria 1856-57 (M.A. thesis, Univ Melb, 1964).

R. W. G. WILLIS

GREGORY, SIR AUGUSTUS CHARLES (1819-1905), explorer and surveyor-general, was born on 1 August 1819 at Farnsfield, Nottinghamshire, England, the second of five sons of Joshua Gregory (1790-1838), lieutenant in the 78th Regiment, and his wife Frances, née Churchman. His father had been wounded and in lieu of a pension accepted a land grant in the new Swan River settlement where in 1829 the family arrived in the *Lotus*. Aided by a neighbour, Surveyor-General Roe [q.v.], Augustus became a cadet in his department in 1841 and was soon promoted an assistant surveyor. He worked mainly in the country, marking out roads and town sites and issuing pastoral licences, often with his brothers as his chainmen. He also designed an apparatus to operate the first revolving light installed on Rottnest Island.

Gregory's resource, bushcraft, facility for invention and technical expertise won him the confidence of his superiors and in 1846 he was given command of his first expedition. In seven weeks with his brothers Francis and Henry Churchman (1823-1869) he travelled north of Perth, and returned in December to report good grazing land and a promising coal seam on the Irwin River. Impressed by his enterprise a group of colonists invited him in 1848 to lead a settlers' expedition to map the Gascoigne River and seek more pastoral land. Although repelled by dense scrub the party charted part of the Murchison River and found traces of lead which led to the opening of the Champion Bay district centred on Geraldton.

Gregory continued to mark out roads and stockroutes and look for grazing land and minerals until 1854 when Governor Fitzgerald reported to the Colonial Office in glowing terms of his skill and ability to abide by instructions. The imperial government had already decided to sponsor a scientific exploration across the north of Australia and Gregory was chosen to lead it. With eighteen men, including his brother Charles, Ferdinand Mueller [q.v.] and other scientists he sailed from Moreton Bay in August 1855 and in September reached the estuary of the Victoria River. After initial set-backs Gregory led several forays up the Victoria River and traced Sturt's Creek for 300 miles until it disappeared in desert. Turning east the party explored the Elsey, Roper and Macarthur Rivers, crossed and named the Leichhardt and then travelled to Brisbane by way of the Flinders, Burdekin, Fitzroy and Burnett Rivers. In sixteen months the expedition had journeyed over 2000 miles by sea and 5000 by land. The natural resources discovered did not measure up to expectations, but Gregory was awarded the gold medal of the Royal Geographical Society and his report later stimulated much pastoral settlement.

Although Gregory attributed his success to 'the protection of that Providence without which we are powerless', the smooth passage and thorough scientific investigations of the expedition owed much to his leadership. Paradoxically it was too successful to be recognized as one of the most significant journeys led by one of the few unquestionably great Australian explorers. Modest, unromantic and resolute in following instructions, he did not dramatize his report, boasted no triumphs and sought no honours despite his admirable Aboriginal policy and meticulous organization. He excelled as a surveyor and manager of men, horses and equipment, and invented improvements for pack-saddles and pocket compasses. His seasonal knowledge and bushcraft were unparalleled and he was the first to note the sequence of weather patterns in Australia from west to east.

Gregory's qualities were again displayed in 1858 when he led an expedition for the New South Wales government in search of Leichhardt [q.v.]. From Juandah station he went west, crossed the Warrego and Barcoo Rivers but after finding traces of the lost explorer was forced by drought to abandon the search and travel south to Adelaide. This was his last major expedition. He marked the southern boundary of the new colony of Queensland and in 1859 became its first commissioner for crown lands and surveyor-general. He relinquished lands in 1863 but remained in charge of surveys until September 1879.

Gregory had the most onerous duties in the new government for land was the colony's greatest resource. He was responsible for classifying and controlling an area of 670,000 square miles inhabited by only 12,000 people with differing concepts of land alienation and use. Widely divergent physical and climatic conditions, haphazard records and a staff lacking in both quality and quantity, made his task unenviable and later unpopular. Although he worked with speed and efficiency, his 'qualities as an explorer were not matched by his ability to institute and oversee a large, complicated and important Government department'. He had little patience for administrative process but relied on a combination of practical experience, technical skill and a network of intimates which included squatters, bushmen, explorers and surveyors. His social and political ties with the 'Pure Merinos' coloured his judgment and influenced his administration of land law. The most powerful civil servant in Queensland, he rarely hesitated to translate his own inflexible views into administrative action. His memorandum of 17 August 1867, which gave much of the best land on the Darling Downs to the pastoralists, was Queensland's greatest concession to the squatters since the 1847 Order in Council. Although personally incorruptible, Gregory had little interest in smallholding and in 1868 his statement to the Legislative Council openly revealed that he had no confidence in the main principles of agricultural selection and in the ideological and social assumptions that lay behind it. He must be held culpable for condoning abuses of which he had ample proof, and much legal trouble ensued later from his deliberate laxity, secrecy and determination to remain dictator of his department. Yet justification can be pleaded. Not only did he have to translate the complex and often contradictory proposals of raw, factious politicians into reality but he also had to cope with continuous pastoral expansion. That he neglected the interests of the smallholder is true but equally valid is the record of his great services to a new colony struggling with immense problems.

Gregory was appointed to the Legislative Council on 10 November 1882. Always a critic of the government, he opposed all radical legislation and social reform and allied himself with the most reactionary squatting group in the House. He spoke more often than most members and his advice was freely sought and given, particularly on land and technical matters. He joined the Freemasons in 1855 and was grand superintendent of the Royal Arch Lodge in 1891. In 1863-1905 he was district grand master of Queensland lodges operating under the English Constitution. He was also a staunch Anglican and won repute for his private charity. He maintained his scientific interests and associations. A trustee of the Queensland Museum in 1876-99 and member of the Aborigines commission in 1876-83, he was elected president of the Australasian Association for the Advancement of Science in 1895. In local government at Toowong he served as president of the divisional board and in 1902 became first mayor. For his public services he was made C.M.G. in 1874 and K.C.M.G. in 1903 for his contribution to Australian exploration. He died unmarried at Rainsworth, his Brisbane home, on 25 June 1905 and was buried in Toowong cemetery.

In Brisbane Gregory published five geological reports on southern Queensland and such significant pamphlets in 1878 as *The Real Property Act of 1877, Meridian Line and laying out lines of latitude on the ground* and the *Supply of Water to the City of Brisbane*. His report to the British government, 'Papers relating to an expedition undertaken for the purpose of exploring the Northern portion of Australia' was printed by the House of Commons in 1857, and his collected papers and records and those of his brother Francis were published in 1884 by the Queensland government as *Journals of Australian Explorations*; this laconic chronicle seldom does justice to his many qualities and achievements.

A portrait by Ugo Cantini in 1891 is in the Masonic Museum, Ann Street, Brisbane.

His brother FRANCIS THOMAS, born on 19 October 1821, became a cadet in Western Australia, assistant in 1847 and a staff surveyor in 1849. His field-work ranged wide and included the streets of Fremantle and the harbour at King George Sound. Under Augustus in 1852 he supervised the road-building by convicts with tickets-of-leave but resented the time wasted on accounts, correspondence and inquiries, and claimed that hired labour was much less expensive. On a routine survey of the Murchison River in 1857 he explored its upper reaches and for his initiative was given command of an expedition to the Gascoigne River in 1858. After covering 2000 miles in 107 days he reported guardedly against settlement before a port was opened in Exmouth Gulf. In 1859 he declined a lucrative post in Victoria because he had to visit England. There he joined others in urging the government and the Royal Geographical Society to found a colony on the north-west coast of Australia with all the necessary equipment and 'a

large body of Asiatic labourers'. A grant of £2000 was offered subject to an equal subsidy from the colonial chest. Although Surveyor-General Roe modified the proposal and settlement was postponed, Gregory went to Nicol Bay in 1861 and traced many northern rivers. For these explorations he was awarded the founder's medal of the Royal Geographical Society in 1863. His report became a handbook for northern settlement by pastoralists and pearlers. He also collected many botanical and geological specimens which were later housed in C. G. Nicolay's [q.v.] museum at Fremantle. He moved to Queensland in 1862 where in 1864 he married Marion Scott, daughter of Alexander Hume; they had four sons and one daughter. Gregory was appointed commissioner of crown lands in the Toowoomba district and to the Legislative Council in 1874. He was postmaster-general in 1883 and led the opponents to payment of council members in 1886. He died at Brisbane on 21 August 1888.

Known as Frank, he was ambitious and less imperturbable than Augustus and was once described as 'a smooth, not altogether trustworthy fellow'. He and his brother were called 'the squatting proconsuls of the Darling Downs', but their contribution to Australian exploration remains unchallengeable. The family name is commemorated at widely scattered points on the continent, and not least by the *Andansonia gregorii*, a baobab found and named by Mueller on the Victoria River.

J. P. Thomson, 'Sir Augustus Gregory', *Qld GJ*, 18 (1903-04); *West Australian*, 26, 27 Oct 1888; *Brisbane Courier*, 21, 28 Nov, 5 Dec 1903; *Queenslander*, 1, 15 July, 1 Aug, 2 Sept 1905; B. R. Kingston, Land legislation and administration in Queensland, 1859-1876 (Ph.D. thesis, Monash Univ, 1970). D. B. WATERSON

GREGORY, DAVID WILLIAM (1845-1919), cricketer, was born on 15 April 1845 at Wollongong, son of Edward William Gregory (1805-1879), bootmaker, and his wife Mary Anne, née Smith (1817-1901), who were married on 25 May 1835 at Sydney. Edward William arrived in Sydney on 28 July 1814 in the *Broxbornebury* with his parents and two brothers. A capable cricketer himself, he founded probably the most famous family in Australian cricket. In 1861-84 five of his eight sons played for New South Wales in international or intercolonial matches: twenty of his descendants represented New South Wales in cricket and other sports.

David was educated at the St James Model School and in 1861 joined the Auditor-

General's Department. In 1883 he became inspector of public accounts and later paymaster of the Treasury until he retired in 1908. Meanwhile he had joined the National Cricket Club in Sydney and in 1866 played his first intercolonial match against Victoria. In 1867-75 he was a member of the Warwick Club and for two seasons had the best averages both as a batsman and a bowler. With his brothers Edward James and Charles Smith (1847-1935) he played a celebrated series of single wicket matches against Victorian players. He captained New South Wales and in March 1877 the combined New South Wales and Victorian side that defeated J. Lillywhite's English team in what is known as the first Australia-England Test match.

In 1878 with John Conway of Victoria Gregory organized the first Australian team to visit England. Gregory captained the side which was financed by £50 from each player. It played thirty-seven matches and won thirteen of 'seventeen eleven-a-side games, including a renowned victory at Lords on 27 May against the Marylebone Cricket Club that established the repute of Australian cricketers in England and inspired *Punch* into verse:

The Australians came down like a wolf on the fold,
The Marylebone cracks for a trifle were bowled;
Our Grace before dinner was very soon done,
And Grace after dinner did not get a run.

The team also toured America. Gregory introduced a new conception of big cricket leadership with masterly control of bowling changes, placement of fields and team rungetting. The team's success proved not only a stimulus to Australian cricket but also an impetus, often overlooked, to Australian nationhood.

In 1883-89 Gregory was secretary of the New South Wales Cricket Association. He died from heart disease on 4 August 1919 at Paddington and was buried by an Anglican clergyman in the Congregational section of the Gore Hill cemetery. He was survived by four sons and three daughters of his first wife Mary Ann, née Hitchings, by two sons of his second wife Lilies Leslie, née McMillian, and by his third wife Ellen, née Hillier. He was predeceased by four sons and two daughters of his first marriage and one daughter of his second.

EDWARD JAMES GREGORY, brother of David, was born on 29 May 1839 at Sydney. He played with the National, East Sydney and Bathurst Cricket Clubs. He represented New South Wales against English teams led by H. H. Stephenson in 1862, G. Parr in 1864, W. G. Grace in 1874 and J. Lillywhite

in 1876. Next year in Melbourne he played in the first England-Australia Test match. An aggressive batsman he was known as 'Lion-hearted Ned'. In 1878 he retired from big cricket and became curator of the Sydney Cricket Ground which was laid out under his supervision. In 1861 at Sydney he had married Ellen, née Mainwaring; they had three sons and five daughters. He died on 22 April 1899 and was buried in the Anglican section of the Waverley cemetery.

His son SYDNEY EDWARD, born on 14 April 1870 at Sydney, played for New South Wales against Queensland in 1889. Next year he visited England with W. L. Murdoch's [q.v.] Australian team and was in every touring side until 1912 when he was also captain; he played in 52 Tests against England and batted 92 times to score four centuries and 2193 runs, averaging 25.8. Known as 'Little Tich', Gregory was a superb fielder especially at cover-point; a strong driver with excellent leg-side shots, he improved the art of footwork and in 1894 he scored 201 against England, a record for the Sydney Cricket Ground until Bradman scored 234 in 1946. Gregory died at Randwick on 31 July 1929 from a gastric ulcer and was buried in the Anglican section of the Randwick cemetery. In 1892 at Sydney he had married Mary, née Sullivan; they had one son and one daughter.

'Argus', *Australian cricketers' tour through Australia, New Zealand and Great Britain* (Bathurst, 1878); F. J. Ironside, *Australasian cricketing handbook* (Syd, 1880); H. W. Hedley, *At the wickets* (Melb, 1888); A. G. Moyes, *Australian cricket: a history* (Syd, 1959); *Wisden Cricketers' Almanack*, 1879-80, 1900, 1911, 1920, 1930; *Aust Cricket Annual*, 1895-98; *Sydney Mail*, 29 Apr 1899, 13 Aug 1919, 14 Mar 1928, 7, 21 Aug 1929, 23, 30 Dec 1931.

R. ELSE-MITCHELL

GREGSON, JESSE (1837-1919), company superintendent, was born in Kent, England, son of William Gregson, solicitor, and his wife Caroline Augusta, née Hilder. Educated privately and in schools at Rochford, Hadleigh, London and Salisbury, he was articled at 15 to his father. Uninterested in the law and unsettled by his mother's death in 1852 and his father's remarriage in 1855 he left for Sydney in January 1856 and arrived with £50 in gold and letters of introduction to R., E. and F. Tooth [q.v.] and others. He was coolly received by the Tooths but assisted warmly by Alexander Busby, a fellow passenger.

Unable to find suitable work in Sydney, Gregson accepted Busby's invitation to visit him at Llangollen station near Cassilis. He then worked for Dr Traill at Collaroy, a near-by station, where he learnt stock management, helped with the lambing for 15s. a week and in 1858 became head overseer at £80 a year. In May 1860, as Busby's partner, he overlanded 5000 ewes to a new station, Rainsworth, near the future town of Springsure in Queensland. In his memoirs Gregson recalled the hard first years: by 1867 plant and buildings had been established but 'we had made no progress in reducing the station debt or in bettering our position'. In that year he entered a new term of partnership of seven years and celebrated it by investigating the use of wire fencing in Victoria. With the decision and resolution which characterized his whole career, he soon fenced 20,000 acres on Rainsworth: 'I was very proud of this exploit, the more so because I was the first to start wire fencing in that district'.

In 1870 Gregson accompanied Busby, who had been elected to the board of the Australian Agricultural Co., on a visit to Warrah, the company's station on the Liverpool Plains. Four years later Busby recommended him as superintendent of the company to replace E. C. Merewether [q.v.]. Invited to England, he was appointed to the position and held it from 1875 to 1905. Under the London court of directors, he had charge of one of the most important enterprises in Australia. He applied himself with vigour to the care of the company's extensive pastoral and mining properties and his detailed reports to London reveal his energy and precise knowledge. In 1877-78 at Warrah 25,000 sheep died in a severe drought, a disaster which made Gregson doubt the value of pastoral investment, but by 1880 Warrah had 113,000 sheep and complete rabbit-proof fencing. He was responsive to increases in the value of company land that followed railway extensions and began the sale of property that in May 1893 culminated in the disposal of the Port Stephens estate. With Nelson Brothers he built a chilling and freezing works at Aberdeen.

Gregson soon mastered the coal-mining industry and became the outstanding spokesman of the colliery proprietors. In his dealings with the miners' union Gregson was both just and hard. He believed that it was wrong for miners employed by different companies to make common cause in a single union, and notably in 1882 he attempted several times to split the union by cutting the hewing rate and precipitating a strike. His aim was a union restricted to employees of his company: 'my objection was not therefore to trade unionism as a principle but to the Borehole Miners [A.A. Co.] continuing to join lots with those whom they have really very little in common'. His policy was opposed to the essential principle of unionism and Gregson was seen by unionists as their most determined opponent. On the other hand he was respected as a man of his word.

In the late 1880s Gregson began to take a leading part in the preparation of employers for the conflict between capital and labour which broke out in 1890. From 1888 he corresponded with shipowners and other employers, advocating the importance of united action. In the maritime strike he joined the intercolonial conference of employers which directed the strike on the employers' side and in 1890-91 he served on the royal commission on strikes. His knowledge of mining and industrial relations was also called on when he was appointed to the royal commission which prepared the case for the Coal Mines Regulation Act, 1896. This Act laid down much more rigorous regulations for health and safety of miners than any provided by previous Acts.

In 1870 Gregson had married Catherine, née Woore, widow of A. G. Maclean [q.v.], surveyor-general of New South Wales. He died aged 82 on 3 August 1919 at Katoomba and was buried in the Anglican section of Sandgate cemetery. Most of his estate of £17,500 was left to his surviving children. Much of his family life had been centred on a home built in 1880 at Mount Wilson in the Blue Mountains where they summered each year from December to April and Gregson pursued his amateur but informed interest in botany. The director of the Botanic Gardens wrote to the Sydney Morning Herald soon after Gregson died: 'Not only did he send large collections of dried plants and seeds on his own initiative, but nothing gave him greater pleasure than to hunt the neighbourhood for plants unrecorded from the area. He was a splendid correspondent, and followed up the life histories of a number of plants concerning which we had but little information, and in a few cases they turned out to be new to science'. His specimens are preserved by the National Herbarium of New South Wales.

R. Gollan, The coalminers of New South Wales (Melb, 1963); Gregson papers (ML); A.A. Co. papers (ANU Archives).

ROBIN GOLLAN

GRESHAM, WILLIAM HUTCHISON (1824-1875), land reformer and idealist, was born at Hull, Yorkshire, England. He was later fond of recounting his varied youthful experiences at sea and in the backwoods of North America. In the early 1850s he migrated to Melbourne where, aged 29, on 15 March 1853 he married Jane Ingles who was born at Greenock, Scotland, in 1830. In

1855 Gresham joined Charles Ingles and John Adams as merchants in Footscray. Next year the partnership set up as ship-chandlers in Melbourne and in 1859 at Sandridge (Port Melbourne). Gresham also had a patent fuse factory at Footscray in 1867, managed the Evelyn Tunnel Gold Mining Co. in 1872 and his own commission agency and ship-chandlery at Sandridge in 1873-75.

Gresham had been a friend of J. S. Mill and continued to correspond with him after migrating. He was thus steeped in the latest British political and social philosophy which he tried to introduce into Australia. Mill remarked 'that Victoria deserved to be congratulated that she had such an enlightened politician as Mr. Gresham'. In the late 1860s Gresham began to pepper Melbourne and country papers with his ideas of reform on many political, social and economic questions. He also held office in several intellectual and political societies including the Working Man's Political Association and the Eclectic Association. He was best known for his work in the Land Tenure Reform League which in October 1870-November 1873 was a counterpart of the English association backed by Mill. The league was associated with the radical Democratic Association of Victoria and advocated state ownership of all lands with a single tax. In letters to newspapers and seven published tracts Gresham and his supporters carried out a wide campaign and won many important subscribers. The league may have had some influence on Berry's [q.v.] land tax bill, 1877. To implement his ideas Gresham contested the Sandridge seat in the Legislative Assembly in 1866, 1868 and 1874 but despite his organization of well-attended public meetings he failed each time because he handicapped himself by 'repudiating canvassing as an infringement of the sanctity of the ballot box'. Although he had many friends and admirers, his reforms were too bound in philosophical thought and jargon, and his style of speaking and writing was too nervous.

In August 1873 Gresham was elected to the Sandridge Borough Council where he was very active and became involved in many projects. His business suffered and he bought the small Felix Holt to compete for trade by sailing down Port Phillip Bay to meet incoming ships. At 3 a.m. on 13 May 1875 with two boatmen he left Sandridge but ran into a storm. His battered boat was washed ashore near Mornington but despite thorough search the bodies of the three men were never found. Gresham's wife and eight children were left destitute but his fellow councillors raised a relief fund of over £500 to buy a house for his family. A daughter, Ada, taught mathematics at the Presbyterian Ladies' College in 1876.

H. Mayer, Marx, Engels and Australia (Syd, 1964); Argus, 29 Jan 1866, 19 Feb 1868, 11 Mar 1871, 22 Apr 1874; Age, 4 Jan 1872, 18 May, 11 June, 6 July 1875; Daily Telegraph (Melb), 13 Feb 1872, 10 Feb 1874; Sandridge Reporter, May 1873-May 1875; F. B. Smith, Religion and freethought in Melbourne, 1870 to 1890 (M.A. thesis, Univ Melb, 1960).

DONALD S. GARDEN

GREVILLE, EDWARD (1822-1903), politician, was born in Bristol, England, son of Charles Greville and his wife Agnes, née Cole. About 1852 he migrated to Victoria and next year moved to New South Wales where he established a newsagency in Sydney. In 1861 with Charles Octavius Bird as partner he started a telegraphic and advertising agency in Bridge Street mainly to supply news to country papers, and for a time was Reuter's agent. The partnership dissolved in 1866 when Greville successfully sued Bird for debts. Greville continued the business on his own, acquired extensive agencies for wholesale stationers' and printers' supplies and published the Illawarra Express. In the 1880s it was known as the Greville Telegram Co. and was competing with Reuter.

Defeated in December 1869 allegedly by Catholic intimidation, Greville was narrowly elected to the Legislative Assembly for Braidwood in October 1870 after a bitter campaign involving the Protestant Political Association which supported him even though he professed to be an independent. He was not a local resident but represented Braidwood competently until 1880. In 1877 he was one of seven members who in turn voted both the Parkes and Robertson [qq.v.] ministries out of office. He favoured the working class and the development of natural resources but his monotonous speeches were few and uninspired. With the secretary for lands, Thomas Garrett [q.v.], Greville owned a 2000-acre coalfield at Teralba near Newcastle and the unauthorized alteration of an official report on their land led Greville in 1876 to move for a select committee which cleared the proprietors of blame.

In 1872 as Greville & Co. he had begun publication of the Official Post Office Directory of New South Wales, which in 1875 was expanded to include a gazetteer and essays on the geography, history and natural resources of the colony. The New South Wales government bought about a thousand copies of the 1875 edition for official use. In 1883 his first Official Directory and the Almanac of Australia (later

The *Year Book of Australia*) favoured Federation and included descriptive and analytical sections by experts. In later issues he introduced such novel features as a prize for the discovery of the most errors in the previous edition and persuaded leading political figures to adjudicate on prize essays. His appointment in 1879 to the Sydney committee for Fiji at the International Exhibition probably originated the later belief that he had been officially appointed Fijian consul in Sydney by King Thakombau. In 1882 Greville became a trustee of the Free Public Library and sat on the royal commission of inquiry into the friendly societies; in 1883 he was a commissioner for the Amsterdam Exhibition and in 1884-92 for land titles in New South Wales. In 1892 he was appointed to the Legislative Council. Lacking any outstanding personal qualities, Greville remained a well-known but shadowy figure who apparently made no attempt to correct imprecise rumours about his career. At St Kilda, Victoria, on 10 January 1863 he had married Eliza Maria Tuckwell, née Sinclair. He died aged 81 at Centennial Park, Sydney, on 9 July 1903 and was buried in the Church of England cemetery, Waverley, leaving an estate of £2400.

V&P (LA NSW), 1875-76, 4, 725; *Illustrated Sydney News*, 27 June 1874; dossier file on Edward Greville (Soc Aust Gen, Syd); printed cat under Greville (ML).   E. J. LEA-SCARLETT

GRIBBLE, JOHN BROWN (1847-1893), missionary, was born on 1 September 1847 at Redruth, Cornwall, England, son of Benjamin Gribble, miner, and his wife Mary, née Brown. He arrived at Port Phillip in 1848 with his parents. They settled at Geelong where John was educated and at 20 married Mary Ann Elizabeth Bulmer.

In October 1876 Gribble was admitted to the ministry of the United Free Methodist Church, but soon joined the Congregational Union of Victoria and became a home missionary at Rutherglen and Wahgunyah near the Murray River. His travels took him into the Riverina where he preached at Jerilderie, became its first resident missionary, had an encounter with the Kelly [q.v.] gang and made contact with the remnants of Aboriginal tribes. In 1879 he visited Maloga mission on the Murray, toured the Murrumbidgee with Daniel Matthews [q.v.], at Jerilderie published A *Plea for the Aborigines of New South Wales*, and with £6 15s. and the help of his wife opened the Warangesdah Aboriginal Mission at Darlington Point. They built huts, dormitories

and a church and made several converts. In 1880 the mission received a government grant and was visited by Bishop Thomas [q.v.], of Goulburn, who baptized nineteen Aboriginals and decided to sponsor the mission. Gribble was made a stipendiary reader that year, deacon in 1881 and priest in 1883. With help from the government, diocese and Aborigines Protection Association the mission prospered but the costs rose to £1200. In 1883 a report on Warangesdah by the protector of Aborigines provoked a government inquiry which led to the reform of the Aborigines Protection Board.

In 1884 Gribble was invited by Bishop Parry [q.v.] of Perth to work in Western Australia and went to England where he raised funds and published *Black but Comely*, a description of Aboriginal life in Australia. In 1885 he opened a mission on the Gascoyne River but was strongly opposed by settlers who exploited native labour. In 1886 he published *Dark Deeds in a Sunny Land*: this fierce castigation of his opponents created a furore and the welfare of the Aboriginals was obscured by much blackening of reputations until 1905. In 1887 the mission was abandoned and Gribble returned to New South Wales where he opened a mission on the Darling River for the Aborigines Protection Association. In 1889-90 he was rector of Temora where he built the first church; after losing all his belongings when the rectory was burnt down he became rector at Batlow. In both parishes he continued to devote much time to the Aboriginals. In 1892 he went to Queensland to open Yarrabah mission near Cairns. Suffering from malaria he retired to Sydney where he died on 3 June 1893. His tombstone in the Waverley cemetery described him as the 'Blackfellows' Friend'.

Gribble was survived by his wife, four sons and five daughters. His eldest son, Ernest Richard Bulmer (1869-1957), helped his father to found the Yarrabah mission and was in charge of it in 1894-1910. He was rector of Gosford in 1911-14, head of the Forrest River Mission, Western Australia, in 1914-28, chaplain of the Palm Island Aboriginal Settlement in 1931-41 and canon of North Queensland diocese in 1941-57. In 1932 he published *The Problem of the Australian Aboriginal* and in 1933 *A Despised Race: the Vanishing Aboriginals of Australia*. He was appointed O.B.E. in 1956.

R. T. Wyatt, *The history of the diocese of Goulburn* (Syd, 1937); P. Hasluck, *Black Australians* (Melb, 1942); B. Thorn (ed), *Letters from Goulburn* (Canberra, 1964); V&P (LA, NSW), 1883, 3, 919, 937.

GRICE, RICHARD (1813-1882), pastoralist, businessman, philanthropist and churchman, was born on 30 October 1813 at Bootle, Cumberland, England, son of William Grice and his wife Sarah, née Parke. For many generations his family had been farmers and businessmen in Cumberland and conducted a private family bank. He was educated at Walker's School, Whitehaven, and gained early farming experience on a family property. At 25 he decided that England held little future for him and he was encouraged to try his fortune in the Port Phillip District. Amply supplied with funds by his family, he sailed with his equal partner Benjamin Heape and two shepherds from Liverpool in the *Alice Brooks* and arrived at Adelaide in September 1839. A few weeks later the party went on to Melbourne where the partners immediately set up in business, Grice investigating pastoral opportunities and Heape managing the import and export of a wide variety of goods; they also financed other business ventures.

Grice explored the Western District by bullock dray and then went to Van Diemen's Land where he bought 2168 ewes and 8 Leicester rams. Within a few years, both singly and in partnership, he had become one of the principal pastoralists in the colony. He also held pastoral properties in Queensland. One of his early holdings was the Mount Alexander run near Castlemaine. Despite being speared in the back by a marauding party of Aboriginals, Grice admired the local tribesmen and described those on the Goulburn River as the tallest and finest looking men he had seen in the country. His first homestead at Mount Alexander was a hut made of slabs between which the fingers could be pushed; he commented that it would not be good enough for a cow-house in England. In 1842 he wrote to his father that it was wrong to believe that Australian beef and mutton would be poor and light: 'We can challenge the world almost in either'. On 21 August 1844 he married Anne Lavinia, daughter of James Hibberson, proprietor of a Derbyshire posting establishment. In 1847 they visited Europe and then settled in Melbourne. When Heape died in 1855, Grice admitted into partnership T. J. Sumner, who had been a clerk with the firm. Sumner's eldest daughter, Annie Ruth, married Grice's eldest son, James, and the firm became known as Grice, Sumner & Co. It was by then one of the oldest and foremost mercantile houses in the Australian colonies. By 1874 the firm also held large stations in Victoria, New South Wales, South Australia and Queensland and shipped guano from Malden Island until 1914.

Grice was a director of the Union Bank.

In 1859 he was chairman of a royal commission into the public service which condemned the 'degrading system of patronage and the absence of any rules for appointment, dismissal, leave or superannuation'. He died at his home in Fitzroy on 4 November 1882, survived by his wife and by three sons and four daughters of their twelve children. He left an estate valued at £320,000.

In 1850-63 Grice had anonymously given £1000 a year to cover almost the total cost of building St Mark's Church, Fitzroy. For many years he provided £1000 for the maintenance of home missionaries and £1000 for the general needs of the church. The Church of England *Messenger* estimated his gifts to the church at nearly £40,000. After Grice died the dean of Melbourne recalled that he arranged his benefactions with such modesty that practically nobody who enjoyed the fruits of his generosity ever knew their source. Archbishop Lowther Clarke said that 'no one else had assisted the Church of England in such a princely way'. The sacred communion vessels at St Paul's Cathedral were given in his memory. His name is also commemorated in several buildings at the Old Colonists' Homes. He had been a vice-president of the Melbourne Hospital and one of the principal supporters of the Melbourne Benevolent Home.

G. Goodman, *The church in Victoria during the episcopate of the Rt Rev. Charles Perry* (Melb, 1892); I. Selby, *History of Melbourne* (Melb, 1924); R. V. Billis and A. S. Kenyon, *Pastoral pioneers of Port Phillip* (Melb, 1932); A. Henderson (ed), *Early pioneer families of Victoria and Riverina* (Melb, 1936); G. Serle, *The golden age* (Melb, 1963); *Age*, 6 Nov 1882; *Argus*, 6 Nov 1882; family papers (held by author).   J. S. LEGGE

GRIFFIN, THOMAS JOHN AUGUSTUS (1832-1868), policeman, gold commissioner and murderer, was born on 27 July 1832 in County Antrim, Ireland, son of John Loftus Griffin and Anne, née Thompson. He entered the Royal Irish Constabulary and then volunteered for service in the Crimean war where he won two decorations and a commission in the Turkish contingent. He arrived in Victoria early in 1857 and on 29 April at Essendon married Harriett Klister, supposed to be a wealthy widow. He deserted her and in May 1858 joined the New South Wales police. Next February he was appointed chief constable at Rockhampton. At Brisbane he became by exchange chief constable in November 1860 and was soon promoted clerk of petty sessions, reputedly because of his friendship with the sister of a leading politician. On 18 October 1863 he was appointed police magistrate and gold commissioner on the Clermont field where his overbearing manner made him unpopular. He came close to penury by heavy losses in Chinese gambling dens and heavy demands from his wife whose discovery of his whereabouts also lost him the support of the politician's sister.

In June 1866 Oscar de Satgé [q.v.], chief magistrate of Clermont, discovered that Griffin had stolen a letter addressed to him in criticism of the commissioner's work and asked for a civil service inquiry into this flagrant abuse of duty. The inquiry was held in Brisbane where few witnesses could attend and Griffin was exonerated. Rumours that he had embezzled money entrusted to him by miners led to a public meeting in Clermont and a petition for his removal, but before it could be presented he was transferred to Toowoomba as police magistrate; later he moved to Rockhampton as gold commissioner. In 1867 he was given custody of £252 by some Chinese miners but when the moment for settling came in October he was unable to pay. Soon afterwards he drew £8151 from the bank to pay for gold delivered from Clermont by the escort, extracted £252 with which he paid the Chinese and dispatched the remainder with the two troopers of the Peak Downs gold escort. Griffin accompanied the escort and at the Mackenzie River shot both troopers and stole the money. Although he himself took part in the investigation, so many of the missing notes were traced to him that he was arrested. Sentenced to death on 18 March 1868, he confessed his guilt and was hanged in the Rockhampton gaol on 1 June. A week later his body was exhumed and reburied after removal of the head. Despite the offer of a reward for apprehension of the offenders, the head is reputed to have remained for years as a souvenir in an upper-class Rockhampton home.

Queensland Supreme Court reports, 1 (1860-68); O. de Satgé, *Pages from the journal of a Queensland squatter* (Lond, 1901); J. T. S. Bird, *The early history of Rockhampton* (Rockhampton, 1904); *Morning Bulletin,* 1867-68; *Australasian,* 11 Apr 1868; Col Sec letters 1868 (QA); Supreme Court records (QA).

A. A. MORRISON

GRIFFITH, CHARLES JAMES (1808-1863), pastoralist and politician, was born in August 1808 at Kildare, Ireland, the fifth son of Richard Griffith (1752-1820) and his second wife Mary Henrietta, daughter of Walter Hussey Burgh, barrister. Charles studied at Trinity College, Dublin (B.A., 1829; M.A., 1832), and was admitted to the Irish Bar. In 1840 he migrated to the Port Phillip District and with James Moore [q.v.] took up Glenmore run near Melton. In 1848 Moore sold his share to Griffith who, with his nephew, M. R. Greene [q.v.], bought Mount Hope and Mount Pyramid near Echuca. Hours of solitude in the Australian bush prompted Griffith to write *The present state and prospects of the Port Phillip District of New South Wales* (Dublin, 1845), a guide for intending migrants and a denunciation of insecure squatting tenures. He finished this book in 1844 while visiting Dublin and in 1846 he married Jane Catherine Magee.

Griffith was nominated to the new Victorian Legislative Council on 31 October 1851 but became the elected representative of Normanby, Dundas and Follett in June 1853. His steely attitude towards the gold diggers' agitations and his advocacy of an imported aristocracy and the representation of interests rather than population in debates on the constitution in 1854 branded him a Tory but he showed foresight in warning against too many parchment checks on constitutional amendments. As a commissioner of sewerage and water supply from April 1853 and president from January 1854, Griffith proved competent and in his pamphlet *Observations on the Water Supply of Melbourne* (Melbourne, 1855) refuted criticisms of the Yan Yean reservoir project. He was appointed a magistrate for Bacchus Marsh in 1852, acted as a commissioner to organize the transfer of Victorian exhibits to the Paris Exhibition in 1855 and became a director of the Bank of Victoria. In 1856 as a candidate for Dundas and Follett in the new Legislative Assembly he outlined his political creed : state aid for religion specially in country districts, land sales by auction and the protection of squatting licences, a combined education system and increased government aid to country schools. He won narrowly from his sole opponent on 21 October but in November was defeated by Francis Murphy [q.v.] for Speaker in the assembly. He supported the Haines [q.v.] ministries but resigned from the assembly in February 1858 to visit Britain. He returned in 1862 and became chairman of the common schools board and commissioner of lands titles.

Griffith was a devout Anglican, even alienating some electors by insisting on Sunday observance. He helped to persuade his relation, Rev. H. B. Macartney [q.v.], to migrate to Victoria in 1848 and in January 1849 was honoured when Bishop Perry [q.v.] visited his station near Bacchus Marsh. Perry respected Griffith's principles and religious zeal and in 1854 made him chancellor, the highest lay office in the Melbourne diocese. Griffith was a prominent founder of the bishopric endowment fund and helped to establish the Melbourne Church of England Grammar School. He died without issue on 31 July 1863 at his home in Dandenong Road, South Yarra, leaving a legacy of £1000 to the Anglican Church.

G. Goodman, The church in Victoria during the episcopate of the Rt Rev. Charles Perry (Melb, 1892); R. V. Billis and A. S. Kenyon, Pastoral pioneers of Port Phillip (Melb, 1932); Argus, 22 Nov 1853, 19 Jan, 18 Mar 1854; Portland Guardian, 15, 17 Oct, 5 Nov 1856; G. R. Quaife, The nature of political conflict in Victoria 1856-57 (M.A. thesis, Univ Melb, 1964).

CAROLE WOODS

GRIMM, GEORGE (1833-1897), Presbyterian minister, was born on 9 June 1833 at Brechin, Forfarshire, Scotland, the eldest son of Robert Grimm and his wife Mary, née Arnott. After a meagre education he was apprenticed to a stonemason. He attended night school, encouraged by the parish minister, Dr James McCosh, later president of the College of New Jersey (Princeton). Dr Thomas Guthrie of Edinburgh described Grimm in his autobiography as 'a youth of superior talents and early piety . . . he commenced latin grammar, and placing the books before him while at his daily work, he studied and finally mastered it'. He saved enough to pay fees at Aberdeen Grammar School in 1855-56 and then, maintaining himself by manual work and private teaching, won a second-class prize in Greek and the senior-class Straton gold medal in Humanities at the University of Edinburgh (M.A., 1861). After three years at the Free Church New College he offered his services to the colonial committee of the Free Church. On 8 June 1865 he married Mary Hetherington at Sowerby Bridge, Yorkshire.

Sent to Queensland that year Grimm arrived in Brisbane and was inducted to Dalby. In 1870 he was transferred to Young and Grenfell in New South Wales. When Young and Grenfell became separate parishes he moved to Young where St Paul's Church and manse were built. In 1879 he was moderator of the New South Wales General Assembly and in 1880-97 served at Balmain West (Rozelle). There another St Paul's Church and manse were built and another congregation was established at Drummoyne where a church was built and named in his memory. Grimm was a faithful pastor; his preaching is said to have been 'evangelical, lucid, scholarly and improving,

impaired by a somewhat awkward delivery'. But his greatest gifts were academic. In 1873-97 he was tutor in apologetics and systematic theology in the Theological Hall, St Andrew's College, and from 1886 a college councillor. He also studied botany and astronomy. Using original sources and journals he wrote widely on Australian history and contributed many articles to the Sydney Evening News and the Town and Country Journal. His many books and pamphlets included The Australian Explorers (1888), The Unveiling of Africa (1890), A concise history of Australia (1891), The Sabbath: Patriarchal, Jewish & Christian (1892), Twelve Lectures on the Immortality of the Soul and the Life Everlasting (1892) and The Bulwarks of our Faith (1893).

Grimm died at Balmain on 2 June 1897, and was buried in the Presbyterian section of Rookwood cemetery. Of his surviving three sons and six daughters, his eldest son, Arthur Hetherington, was a member of the New South Wales Legislative Assembly for Ashburnham in 1913-20 and Murrumbidgee in 1920-25, and briefly a minister without portfolio.

Testimonials & certificates in favour of George Grimm, M.A. (Brechin, 1861); J. Cameron, Centenary history of the Presbyterian Church in New South Wales (Syd, 1905); C. A. White, The challenge of the years: a history of the Presbyterian Church . . . New South Wales (Syd, 1951); Aust Witness, 9 Dec 1876, 8 May, 10 July 1880; Presbyterian (NSW), 11 July 1897; Town and Country J, 15 Nov 1879; SMH, 3 June 1897; General Assembly, Minutes 1894, 1898 and Grimm papers (Presbyterian Lib, Assembly Hall, Syd).

ALAN DOUGAN

GRIMWADE, FREDERICK SHEPPARD (1840-1910), businessman and parliamentarian, was born on 10 November 1840 at Harleston, Norfolk, England, second son of the seventeen children of Edward Grimwade and his wife Anne, née Johnson. After attending Queen Elizabeth's Grammar School, Ipswich, he was apprenticed to his father's firm of wholesale druggists at Ipswich and London. In 1862 he was invited to manage a wholesale drug-house established in Melbourne by Edward Youngman, another of his father's former apprentices. Grimwade arrived in Victoria in 1863; three years later Youngman was drowned in the wreck of the London, and in 1867 Grimwade borrowed £8000 from his father and with Alfred Felton [q.v.] bought Youngman's business, renaming it Felton, Grimwade & Co.

The partners prospered. Within three years they had recouped the whole purchase price of £24,000, and the firm was soon the largest drug-house in the colony, with subsidiary interests in Western Australia and New Zealand. Grimwade and Felton also founded a number of other enterprises: in 1872 the Melbourne Glass Bottle Works, ancestor of Australian Glass Manufacturers Ltd., and an acid works which was merged in 1897 with Cuming Smith & Co.; in 1882 the Adelaide Chemical Works Co. in partnership with the principals of Cuming Smith's, and the short-lived Australian Salt Manufacturing Co.; and in 1885 a partnership with J. Bosisto [q.v.] & Co. Grimwade was also chairman of the Royal Bank in 1888-1910. The depression of the 1890s interrupted the progress of these enterprises but all except the salt venture survived to resume profitable growth in the twentieth century. When Felton died in 1904 Felton, Grimwade & Co. became solely a Grimwade concern.

Grimwade was a shrewd businessman of great probity and his strong character and forthright opinions on current issues made him a prominent figure. His views were conservative but moderate: as chairman of the Melbourne Chamber of Commerce in 1883 he pleaded for less bitterness in political conflict, for pragmatic legislation and administration and for co-operation between merchants and manufacturers despite their disagreements over protection. Although a free trader by conviction, he signed the mildly protectionist report of the royal commission on the tariff in 1881-83. Persuaded to stand for the Legislative Council in 1891 he was elected unopposed and represented North Yarra Province for thirteen years; he kept aloof from political faction and did not seek office but often spoke in debate on a wide range of issues. He was suspicious of welfare legislation, opposed bills on sweating, workers' compensation and old-age pensions, and as a member of the royal commission on state banking in 1894-95 stoutly resisted proposals for radical government interference in the banking system. On constitutional questions, however, he showed an increasing liberalism, gradually abandoning his opposition to one man one vote and even to female suffrage; he once rebuked his fellow-councillors for their 'rank Toryism'. The two subjects on which he spoke most often were gambling, which he vainly hoped would be prohibited, and the legalization of cremation, a cause he pleaded with great vigour and eventual success.

Grimwade abandoned the Nonconformity of his upbringing to become a prominent layman in the Church of England. He deplored increasing secularism, especially in education, and served for many years on synod and the councils of the Boys' and the Girls' Grammar Schools. He played some part in the Charity Organization Society and, if less notable a philanthropist than Felton, he had, unlike his partner, a family to maintain. In 1865 he had married Jessie Taylor Sprunt (1842-1916); they had nine children, of whom four sons and three daughters lived to maturity. His substantial mansion, Harleston, built at Caulfield in 1875, was presented to Melbourne Grammar School in 1917 by his sons and renamed Grimwade House. In 1895 he bought Coolart, a property on Westernport Bay where he bred bloodstock despite his aversion to gambling. In his last years a diabetic condition undermined his health but he remained active in business affairs until a few days before he died at Caulfield on 4 August 1910.

Grimwade's third son, Alfred Sheppard (1874-1941), became a surgeon. The other three all carried on their father's business; Edward Norton (1866-1945) succeeded him as senior partner, Harold William (1869-1949) combined business with a distinguished military career and Sir Wilfrid Russell (1879-1955) worked with his brothers in developing the enterprises founded by Grimwade and Felton into some of Australia's largest public companies.

R. Grimwade, *Flinders Lane: recollections of Alfred Felton* (Melb, 1947); J. R. Poynter, *Russell Grimwade* (Melb, 1967), and for bibliog.
                        J. R. POYNTER

GRIVER, MARTIN (1814-1886), Roman Catholic bishop, was born on 11 November 1814 in Barcelona, Spain, son of James Griver and his wife Teresa Coni. He studied humanities and theology in Barcelona, won an honours degree in philosophy and entered the School of Medicine (M.B., B.S., 1845). On 17 December 1847 he became a priest and ministered in his native town.

In 1849 Griver was recommended to Bishop Salvado [q.v.] and joined the missionaries gathered in Barcelona for service in Western Australia. In December he landed at Fremantle with Dr Serra [q.v.] and his band of monks, but opposition to Serra by one of the party on the voyage became on shore a public struggle to prevent the monks from joining the mission at New Norcia, and to have Serra ousted from the leadership. Griver had hoped to work with Salvado in the new northern diocese of Port Victoria but after some difficulty led the monks instead to New Norcia. Though appointed superior by Serra, Griver was soon sent with seventeen brothers to Guildford where they arrived after an arduous and difficult journey on foot. From Guildford he went to Serra's new foundation, New Subiaco, and then to Perth. In 1851 he had to handle a delicate situation which had arisen from the unexpected return of Bishop Brady [q.v.], and his marked differences of opinion with Serra. Griver then had only a scanty knowledge of English but displayed great competence, courage and an edifying humility in difficult circumstances. He had wanted to join the Benedictines but, because of Serra's mismanagement, did not become a professed monk. He discharged his priestly office with zeal and prudence in Perth and Fremantle, travelled all over the country and in 1858 visited the colony's furthest outposts, from Albany in the south and Geraldton in the north. Many benefited from his knowledge of medicine on these tours.

When Serra went to Europe in 1859 Griver was left in charge of the administration of the diocese and was confirmed in this appointment in 1862. His first duty was to separate the New Norcia Mission from Perth. Indefatigable in the discharge of his apostolate, he devoted special attention to the welfare of convicts and poor and orphan children. Under his prudent management and with the aid of Bishop Salvado's intervention with the governor, the long-debated question of education and independent schools at last found a satisfactory solution in 1871 when assistance was provided to all schools in the colony. His greatest joy and glory was to complete in January 1865 the Cathedral of the Immaculate Conception in Perth. Serra had collected abundant funds and valuable gifts for it in Europe and Benedictine friends provided its design and promised adequate labour for its construction; Griver had invited Bishop Salvado of New Norcia to solemnize the laying of its foundation stone in 1863.

In 1869 Griver went to Rome where in 1870 he attended the Vatican Council and was consecrated bishop of Tloa in partibus; his title was changed to Perth after Brady died in 1871. Since the Benedictine monks had retired to their New Norcia mission, Griver had to recruit priests for the growing colony. To this task and the welfare of his diocese he applied himself whole-heartedly, visiting Rome in 1882 and the Plenary Council of Australasia at Sydney in 1885. His death in Perth on 1 November 1886 was widely lamented. Kind and considerate in all his dealings with others, he himself followed the ascetic and austere life of the anchorite. When his body was being prepared for burial at St Mary's Cathedral, it was found that he had been wearing two small wooden crosses, the nails of which were deeply embedded in his flesh.

P. F. Moran, History of the Catholic Church in Australasia (Syd, 1895); J. T. Reilly, Reminiscences of fifty years' residence in Western Australia (Perth, 1903); Centenary of the Catholic Church in Western Australia (Perth, 1946); J. T. McMahon, One hundred years: five great church leaders (Perth, 1946); B. C. Cohen, A history of medicine in Western Australia (Perth, 1965); Perth Gazette, 4, 18 Jan 1850; Inquirer, 2 Mar 1870; D. A. Mossenson, A history of state education in Western Australia (Ph.D. thesis, Univ WA, 1962); M. Griver, papers and letters (Roman Catholic Archives, Perth, and New Norcia).   E. PEREZ

GROOM, WILLIAM HENRY (1833-1901), politician, publicist and newspaper-owner, was baptized on 7 March 1833 at Plymouth, England, son of Thomas Groom, cordwainer, and his wife Maria, née Harkcom. After primary schooling he was apprenticed to a baker. On 26 October 1846 he was convicted of stealing and sentenced at the Plymouth Quarter Sessions to seven years' transportation. From Pentonville he was sent to Sydney in the Hashemy and arrived in Sydney on 8 June 1849. He was conditionally pardoned in October and worked near Bathurst. Later on the Turon diggings he became a shop assistant. By 1853 he was assistant manager of Byrnes & Co., Sofala, and correspondent of the Bathurst Free Press and Mining Journal. In March Groom was a delegate of the Turon Miners' Committee to a meeting at Bathurst in protest against licence fees. Although credited with 'good moral conduct, strict honesty and sobriety, and good character' Groom was accused of stealing gold on 12 December 1854. The charge was dismissed but he initiated libel proceedings. He appeared at the Bathurst Circuit Court on 28 February 1855 and was sentenced to road labour for three years. On his release he migrated to Queensland where in August 1856 he set up as a store-keeper and auctioneer at Drayton. He was financed by a Cornishman, John Thomas Littleton, whose daughter Grace (b. 8 June 1838) he married in 1859. The business prospered and in 1862 Groom acquired the Royal Hotel, Toowoomba; despite insolvency in 1866 he bought another hotel. In 1872 he built a store and hotel at Stanthorpe but returned to Toowoomba in 1874 and bought a share in the Toowoomba Chronicle. As sole proprietor in 1876-1901 he made it the most powerful newspaper on the Darling Downs. In 1861 he became Toowoomba's first mayor, an office he later held five times, and had long association with many other local authorities and societies.

On 11 August 1862 Groom won a by-election for Drayton and Toowoomba in the Legislative Assembly. Apart from an interlude in 1866 he held his seat until elected first Federal member for Darling Downs in 1901. This record was unequalled in Queensland politics, but he was never a key Brisbane figure and seldom influential. Although able and acceptable as Speaker in 1883-88 he held no executive office and his main contributions to the colony's affairs were his consistent agrarian radicalism and membership of the royal commissions on the sugar industry in 1889 and crown lands in 1897. He succeeded in satisfying the material needs and advancing the causes of his electorate while maintaining a balance between its differing sections. Selectors, artisans, Germans and Irish all constantly supported him despite his leadership of the Darling Downs 'bunch'. However, the importance of this group had been overestimated; it had little effect on colonial policy and was never a cohesive body. Groom could not retain the loyalty of his protégés and the Downs as a whole, and the rise of Labor, coupled with the Griffith-McIlwraith [q.v.] coalition which he never accepted, alienated him from major political influence.

Groom's main legislative interest was land policy and his radicalism was always of the country rather than the town. An advocate of self-improvement through education, hard work and self-denial, he reiterated that moral virtue was rewarded with material blessings. Believing that progress was an immutable law of nature, he claimed that advance on the Downs meant replacement of large pastoral estates by the settlement of a contented yeomanry. He advocated free selection on the American pattern and in 1868 successfully sponsored the inclusion of homestead clauses in the Land Act. In 1877 he campaigned for larger homesteads and in 1883 adopted the principle of a minimum economic acreage for the family farm. Despite his optimism most selectors were soon in difficulties from lack of capital, credit, markets, transport facilities and uncertain world prices. Groom's panacea was agricultural protection, a policy he finally succeeded in persuading the Queensland parliament to accept.

Groom died in Melbourne on 8 August 1901 and was buried in the Anglican section of the Toowoomba cemetery. He was survived by his wife who died on 22 January 1932 and by four sons and three daughters. One son, Sir Ernest Littleton (1867-1936), succeeded him as member of the House of Representatives for Darling Downs, and another, Henry Littleton (1859-1926), served in the Queensland Legislative Council for sixteen years.

A life's work: 34 years in parliament: What Mr. Groom has done for Toowoomba (Toowoomba, 1896?); C. A. Bernays, Queensland politics during sixty years (Brisb, 1919); D. B. Waterson, 'The remarkable career of Wm. H. Groom', JRAHS, 49 (1963-64); Plymouth, Devonport and Stonehouse Herald, 25 July, 31 Oct 1846; SMH, 14 Dec 1854; Toowoomba Chronicle, 9 Aug 1901; Brisbane Courier, 9 Aug 1901; M. Cameron, W. H. Groom: agrarian liberal (B.A. thesis, Univ. Qld, 1965).

D. B. WATERSON

GRUBB, WILLIAM DAWSON (1817-1879), attorney, politician and entrepreneur, was born in London. In March 1832 he arrived in Van Diemen's Land in the Sovereign with his sister Maria Susanna and her husband Henry Reed [q.v.]. He worked briefly in the business of his brother-in-law and then returned to England to complete his studies and read law. While there he married Marianne, daughter of Joseph Beaumont of Molgreen House, Huddersfield, Yorkshire. He returned to Launceston in 1842 and was admitted a barrister and solicitor of the Supreme Court, and with Henry Jennings set up a partnership which continued until the latter moved to Melbourne. Apart from his successful practice, Grubb's main business ventures were in timber and mining. He built a sawmill at Pipers River in partnership with William Tyson; a private Act was passed in 1855 to permit the building of a tramway to the junction of the Launceston-George Town Road at Mowbray but before the line was completed the timber market had failed and the project did not succeed. Similarly his investments in mining were often unfortunate and he was reputed to have lost over £50,000 in timber, gold, coal and railway investments. However, the New Native Youth and Tasmania gold mines were profitable and appear to have compensated largely for his losses in other directions: the Tasmania mine was said to have paid dividends of over £700,000 by 1900. Grubb represented Tamar in the Legislative Council from 1869 until he died aged 62 on 8 February 1879. He was survived by three sons and two daughters.

His eldest son, FREDERICK WILLIAM, was born in 1844 at Launceston. Educated at Horton College, Ross, he was articled to his father and to the Hobart firm of Allport [q.v.], Roberts & Allport. In 1867 he went into partnership with his father and carried on the practice alone from 1874 when his father retired; in 1884 he disposed of it to W. Martin and F. C. Hobkirk. In the Legislative Council he succeeded his father as member for Tamar in 1879 and in 1881-1911 represented Meander. He also carried on his father's interest in investment: in mining as a director of the Western Silver Mine, Zeehan, and in the pastoral industry managing Bengeo merino stud at Lemana until replaced by his son Percival Beaumont. In 1871 Frederick married Alice, daughter of Edward Archer, Northbridge, Longford; they had a son and a daughter. Alice died on 14 October 1877, and on 3 December 1879 he married her cousin Isabel Madeline, daughter of Joseph Archer; they had one daughter. He died at Launceston on 28 April 1923.

Cyclopedia of Tasmania, 2 (Hob, 1900); *Cornwall Chronicle*, 10 Feb 1879; *Examiner* (Launceston), 30 Apr 1923; correspondence files under Grubb and Reed (TA).   M. J. SACLIER

GUERARD, JOHANN JOSEPH EUGEN VON (1812-1901), artist, was born in Vienna, son of Bernhard von Guerard and his wife Josepha Schulz von Leichtenthall. His father was a court painter to Francis I of Austria and his mother the daughter of a field marshal in Vienna. Guerard early showed artistic talent and his father took him in 1826 to Italy where he studied old masters before settling at Naples in 1832. For six years he painted landscapes in southern Italy and Sicily. He then moved to Dusseldorf where he studied under Johann Wilhelm Schirmer at the academy and exhibited regularly at Leipzig and Berlin. He left Dusseldorf in 1848 possibly for the Californian goldfields. In 1852 he sailed from England in the *Windermere*, lured by the gold rush. He arrived at Geelong on 24 December and two weeks later left for Ballarat. His diary describes his luckless year on the goldfields, but he made many pencil sketches, now in the State Library of Victoria. At St Francis's Church, Melbourne, on 15 July 1854 he married Louise Arnz of Dusseldorf.

For sixteen years Guerard travelled and sketched in the wilds of Victoria, Tasmania, New South Wales, South Australia and New Zealand, sometimes in company with such scientific expeditions as those led by A. W. Howitt [q.v.] in 1860 and G. B. von Neumayer [q.v.] in 1862. Later he transferred many of his pen and pencil sketches to canvases commissioned by wealthy patrons. Influenced by the Austrian Biedermeier school, he painted grandiose mountain landscapes reminiscent of Europe's alpine artists. Archibald Michie [q.v.] presented 'The Valley of the Mitta Mitta' to the Melbourne Art Gallery in 1866 and in 1870 the trustees bought for £157 10s. his 'Mount Kosciusko, seen from the Mount Hope Ranges, Victoria'. Guerard occupied studios in Collins and Bourke Streets in the 1850s, and then lived for nearly twenty years in Gipps Street, East Melbourne. In Melbourne his first years had been difficult and in 1855 he tried to sell many paintings by lottery. The *Argus*, 1 February, reported his failure: 'While Tom Barry [q.v. J. Atkins] can leer and sneeze on our public stage at £100 per week a first rate painter like M. Guerard has been driven from the shores of Victoria from inability to procure bread by the exercise of his genius'. In October 1856 he was an active founder of the Victorian Society of Fine Arts, and in January 1857 its only exhibition included his views of Mount Abrupt and Hobart Town. The *News Letter of Australasia*, January 1858, criticized his 'very peculiar' style and in February sourly opposed the purchase of 'M. Guerard's fine picture of Fern Tree Gully . . . for . . . the Queen'. Although few locals would subscribe for the painting, Queen Isabella of Naples later bought two of his early works and many others went to Dusseldorf, America, Natal, England and exhibitions in Paris, London and Vienna.

Guerard's elaborate album of tinted lithographs, *Australian Landscapes* (Melbourne, 1867), was based on the Western District views which he exhibited in 1858 and which Governor Barkly so admired that he commissioned a similar series of pen and ink drawings. Much of his work was engraved for periodicals and he illustrated S. D. Bird's [q.v.] *On Australasian Climates* (Melbourne, 1863).

At its exhibition of 1865 the Royal Academy accepted Guerard's 'Fall of the Wetterboro Creek, with the romantic view of the Jamison's Valley, in the Blue Mountains between Sydney and Bathurst'. In 1870 he became a charter member of the Victorian Academy of Artists; he had six pictures in its first exhibition and many others later. In 1873 paintings were sent to London for the International Exhibition and in 1876 he was one of the first Australian artists represented in the Centennial Exhibition at Philadelphia. In 1870 he was appointed first master of painting at the National School of Art, Melbourne, and curator of the National Gallery of Victoria. Among his earliest students were Frederick McCubbin, Tom Roberts, Rupert Bunny, E. Wake Cook and Bertram Mackennal, but he was a better painter than teacher and left little mark on them; he resigned because of ill health in 1881.

Described by William Strutt [q.v.] as 'delightful', Guerard must have had great physical endurance to undertake his long and arduous journeys. He was a member of the 'charmed circle' of writers and artists and bon viveurs who gathered around

James Smith, Nicholas Chevalier, R. H. Horne [qq.v.] and others, and was active in the Royal Society of Victoria, serving on its council in 1866-67. He was fluent in English, French, Italian and German, but signed his name in the German form. In 1870 the emperor of Austria had awarded him the cross of the order of Franz Joseph.

In 1882 Guerard returned to Europe where his wife died in London on 12 January 1891. When the Australian banks crashed in 1893 he lost all his investments and apparently lived in poverty until he died aged 89 in Chelsea on 17 April 1901. He was survived by his only child, Victoria, who was born on 4 September 1857 in Melbourne and married Reginald Blunt at Dusseldorf on 20 December 1885.

A. Graves, *The Royal Academy of Arts*, 2 (Lond, 1905); E. LaT. Armstrong, *The book of the National Gallery of Victoria . . . 1856-1906* (Melb, 1906); U. Thieme and F. Becker, *Allgemeines Lexikon der bildenden Künstler* (Leipzig, 1912); Bernard Smith, *Australian painting 1788-1960* (Melb, 1962); B. Finemore, 'Selected recent accessions in Australian painting', *Art Bulletin of Vic*, 1967-68; *Argus*, 4 Oct 1855, 29 Dec 1857, 5 Aug 1858; *Illustrated Aust News*, 27 July 1867; Guerard diary (ML); W. Strutt papers (ML); H. G. Turner papers LaT L); family papers (held by Edward Comstock, Sydney).   MARJORIE J. TIPPING

GUILFOYLE, WILLIAM ROBERT (1840-1912), landscape gardener and botanist, was born on 8 December 1840 at Chelsea, England, son of Michael Guilfoyle (d. 1884), nurseryman, and his wife Charlotte, née Delafosse, of Huguenot origin. His father migrated to Sydney with his family in 1853 and set up a nursery at Redfern; another at Double Bay was more successful. After private teaching by his uncle, Louis Delafosse, William attended Lyndhurst College, Glebe, and was encouraged in botanical study by W. S. Macleay and John MacGillivray [qq.v.]. He made several tours in northern New South Wales and Queensland collecting specimens, some of which he sent to Ferdinand Mueller [q.v.] in Melbourne to be identified. In 1868 he joined the scientific staff of H.M.S. *Challenger* in its scientific expedition through the South Sea islands, and then grew sugar and tobacco on his father's land near the Tweed River.

On 21 July 1873 Guilfoyle was appointed curator of the Royal Botanic Gardens, Melbourne, at a salary of £500. His predecessors, Dallachy [q.v.] and Mueller, had been more interested in developing the gardens for scientific than aesthetic and recreational purposes. Guilfoyle, inspired by the tropical landscapes he had seen, extended and remodelled the gardens. When he designed an extension he made a coloured sketch of his conception and then by a process of improvement brought it to the planting stage. Sweeping lawns, cunningly planned foliage and informal vistas filled the area which was expanded to over one hundred acres. When the south bank of the Yarra was straightened to prevent floods Guilfoyle secured the adjoining section and transformed a billabong into a series of lakes. He created a fern gully in a hollow and on a hill overlooking the Yarra built a Temple of the Winds as a memorial to La Trobe, founder of the gardens. The temple was designed in the classical tradition but instead of the usual acanthus motif Guilfoyle used the native staghorn fern. He also designed several summer houses or kiosks. Paderewski, who planted an American red chestnut to mark his visit on 26 October 1904, remarked that Guilfoyle did with his trees what a pianist tried to do with his music. Conan Doyle claimed that the gardens were 'absolutely the most beautiful place' that he had ever seen. Guilfoyle also managed the 62 cultivated acres of the Government House land and 156 acres in the outer Domain. He also designed private gardens; probably the best known is at Coombe Cottage, Dame Nellie Melba's home at Coldstream, near Lilydale. Melbourne's Botanic Gardens had gained world-wide repute before Guilfoyle retired in September 1909. He then lived at Jolimont and is credited with the attractive treatment of the creek which runs through Fitzroy Gardens. In 1890-91 and 1896 he visited England and Europe.

Guilfoyle did not neglect botanical studies in order to indulge his genius for landscape gardening. He started the medicinal ground in the gardens and also grew plants of economic value. His publications included *First Book of Australian Botany* (1874), revised and reissued as *Australian Botany especially designed for the Use of Schools* (1878); *The A.B.C. of Botany* (1880); *Australian Plants* (1911?) and many pamphlets.

Guilfoyle died on 25 June 1912 at East Melbourne, survived by his wife Alice, née Darling, whom he had married at Melbourne in 1888 and by their only son William James. His brother John was curator of the reserves under the Melbourne Metropolitan Parks and Gardens Committee in 1891-1909.

F. Clarke, *In the Botanic Gardens* (Melb, 1938); P. C. Morrison (ed), *Melbourne's garden* (Melb, 1946); J. H. Maiden, 'Records of Australian botanists', *Roy Soc NSW, Procs*, 55 (1921); *Australasian*, 17 Jan 1891; *Age*, 26 June

1912; *Argus*, 26 June 1912; information from Roy Botanic Gardens & National Herbarium, Melb.   ALAN GROSS

GUNSON, JOHN MICHAEL (1825-1884), medical practitioner, was born in Limerick, Ireland, son of Robert Gunson, a Protestant merchant, and his Catholic wife Jane, née Shepherd. He was reared as an Anglican but became a Catholic. At 14 he was sent to school in France for about five years and in 1845 was entered as a student at the Dublin Lying-In Hospital. After six months he was given a certificate by the hospital authorities and went to Paris where by 1848 he had a dozen certificates for attending lectures but no formal degree. In June he was admitted a member of the Royal College of Surgeons in England and then practised in Oxford. In May 1852 he sailed from Liverpool as surgeon in the *Grasmere* and arrived in South Australia on 28 August. Next April he was registered as a medical practitioner and opened a practice in Adelaide. He visited Europe and creditably passed 'a rigorous examination' at the University of Heidelberg (M.D., 1865), and in 1866 at Limerick married Mary Sarah Lucas. He returned to Adelaide with his wife and practised at his home in Angas Street. In 1867 he was appointed an honorary medical officer at the Adelaide Hospital but soon resigned. He retired in 1876 and at Marryatville built a large house which was bought by Sir Edwin Smith [q.v.] and later became Loreto Convent. In 1879 he took his family to Europe intending to stay, but returned after two years and built another house at Kensington Gardens.

Gunson joined the Adelaide Philosophical Society in February 1877 and read a paper 'On the Philosophy of Food, according to recent Scientists'. An influential layman in the Catholic Church he was active for years as president of the Young Men's Society, surgeon to the Hibernian Benefit Society and director of the Catholic Building Society. On 22 August 1881 at Adelaide he was installed a knight of St Gregory the Great. When John Redmond [q.v.] visited Adelaide in 1883 Gunson chaired the meeting although as a firm believer in 'Home Rule' he was no advocate for an 'Irish Republic'. In the University of Adelaide (M.D. *ad eund.*, 1877) he served on its first council in 1874-79 and senate in 1877-84. He died on 3 May 1884 and was buried in the Catholic section of West Terrace cemetery. Of his three sons, William and George were lawyers and John Bernard a medical practitioner who married Annie Elizabeth, granddaughter of Sir John Morphett [q.v.].

Dr Gunson's brother, WILLIAM HENRY, was born in Limerick and educated at Rev. John Hogg's College. He migrated to Adelaide with his brother in 1852 and was briefly associated with the *South Australian Register*. He then joined the customs department at Port Adelaide but moved to Melbourne where he worked for the *Age*. He was converted to Catholicism independently of his brother. About 1858 he joined the staff of the *Ballarat Times* and from 1860 ran the *Daylesford Express*. In February 1868 he became the first editor of the *Advocate*, a Catholic weekly in Melbourne. Cultured and gifted, he maintained a scholarly literary style in his leading articles for nearly thirty-four years. He died aged 73 at his home in Windsor on 28 December 1901. He was survived by his wife Mary Elizabeth, née Lynch, and by their three sons and two daughters.

Register (Adel), 31 Jan 1877, 22 Aug 1881, 3 May 1884; *Argus*, 3 Jan 1902; *Advocate* (Melb), 4 Jan 1902; A. A. Lendon, Dr J. M. Gunson (SAA); information from F. D. Minogue, Melb Diocesan Hist Com.

SALLY O'NEILL

GUNTHER, WILLIAM JAMES (1839-1918), Anglican clergyman, was born on 28 May 1839 at Wellington, New South Wales, son of Rev. James William Gunther and his wife Lydia, née Paris. His father, a German-born missionary, had a long and distinguished career in the Mudgee district and was an archdeacon of the diocese of Bathurst when he died in 1880. In 1852-57 William was educated at The King's School, Parramatta, where he won three scholarships, and at Queen's College, Oxford (B.A., 1862; M.A., 1865). He was made deacon in 1863 by the bishop of Chester, ordained priest by the bishop of Lichfield in 1864 and Bishop Barker [q.v.] secured him a curacy at Stapenhill, Derbyshire. In 1865 Gunther returned to Sydney and on 1 January 1866 was licensed as curate of St Phillip's Church, where he won Barker's commendation. In 1867-1909 he was incumbent of the old and important parish of St John, Parramatta. In 1868 he joined the committee of management which aided G. F. Macarthur [q.v.] in reviving The King's School. Later he helped to associate the school with the diocesan synod, and remained on its council and other school committees for many years. When the local denominational school closed, he converted it into St John's Grammar School and prepared pupils for entry to The King's School. From 1883 he was a fellow of St Paul's College, University of Sydney.

Gunther's activity in education was a part of his involvement in the affairs of the diocese. He had become an episcopal examining chaplain in 1868 and rural dean of Parramatta in 1870. In 1875 he was secretary of the provincial synod and in 1877 was made a canon of St Andrew's Cathedral; meanwhile he became an active member of many diocesan organizations. In the episcopate of Bishop Saumarez Smith, his responsibilities grew heavier. He delivered the presidential address to the 1897 synod and when Rev. W. M. Cowper [q.v.] died in 1902 declined the offer of the deanery, as he had of two country bishoprics. He became vicar-general and commissary, the principal clergyman of the diocese and an important figure in provincial and general synods. A firm Evangelical, he did his best to moderate the bitter party feelings in Archbishop Smith's last years. When he presided over the synod which in 1909 chose J. C. Wright as Smith's successor, Gunther was able to avoid the confusion and disorder which had marked earlier elections. He left Parramatta in 1910 but retained his extraparochial appointments until 1916 when, having administered the diocese five times in twenty years, he resigned. Aged 79 he died on 16 June 1918 and was buried in the Anglican cemetery, Parramatta. He was survived by his wife Mary Jane, née Willis, whom he had married on 7 July 1868, and by three sons and two daughters.

In addition to his administrative duties and membership of a wide variety of religious bodies, Gunther was a prominent ecclesiastical historian. He wrote pamphlets and articles on St John's Church, The King's School, Samuel Marsden [q.v.] and early Australian church history. His results were sometimes uncritical but he did invaluable work in preserving old books and records. He was president of the (Royal) Australian Historical Society in 1906 and began the systematic study of Sydney's Anglican history.

S. M. Johnstone, *The history of The King's School, Parramatta* (Syd, 1932); V&P Synod 1897, 1909, 1917, 1918 (Syd Diocesan Registry); *Church Standard*, 21 June 1918.

K. J. CABLE

GURNER, HENRY FIELD (1819-1883), solicitor, was born on 31 March 1819 in Sydney, the second son of John Gurner [q.v.] and his wife Rebecca Ann, née Gallefant. He was educated at W. T. Cape's [q.v.] School, became a clerk under his father in the Supreme Court in 1834, then worked for the crown solicitor, Francis Fisher, and in 1841 was admitted as an attorney, solicitor and proctor in New South Wales. On 10 February he was appointed deputy-registrar and clerk of the Supreme Court of New South Wales for the Port Phillip District and in May became the first attorney, solicitor and proctor admitted in Melbourne. He entered private practice in November but on 6 January 1842 became clerk of the peace and crown solicitor at Port Phillip and in September agreed to act until December as the first town clerk of Melbourne. Gurner was crown solicitor of Victoria from July 1851 until he retired in November 1880.

Gurner's attachment to his native land and legal work was reflected in his valuable collection of Australiana (list published in 1878) and his own publications: *The Rules and Orders of the Supreme Court of New South Wales for the District of Port Phillip* (1841), *Practice of the Criminal Law of the Colony of Victoria* (1871), and *Chronicle of Port Phillip now the Colony of Victoria from 1770 to 1840* (1876). He was well known and respected in Melbourne and was a member of the Melbourne Club from 1844 and president in 1870. He lived with his family in William Street, Melbourne, until 1854 and then moved to a house in Princes Street, St Kilda, with a view overlooking Hobson's Bay. Gurner Street, St Kilda, was named in his honour. During a brief recall as crown solicitor he died at the Melbourne Club on 17 April 1883 and was buried in the St Kilda cemetery; he left an estate worth £61,000. His wife Augusta Mary, daughter of Edward Curr [q.v.], was a skilled horsewoman and travelled widely before she died aged 88 in 1917. Of their eight surviving children, Henry Edward and John Augustus were barristers and the latter became crown prosecutor in Victoria.

J. A. Gurner, *Life's panorama* (Melb, 1930); E. Scott, *Historical memoir of the Melbourne Club* (Melb, 1936); *Argus*, 18 Apr 1883; *Australasian*, 21 Apr, 12 May 1883.

CAROLE WOODS

GURNEY, THEODORE THOMAS (1849-1918), mathematician, was born on 10 October 1849 at Aldersgate, London, son of Thomas William Henry Gurney and his second wife Theophila, née Hope. His grandfather, William Gurney, was rector of St Clement Danes, and his father was a scholar at St John's College, Cambridge (B.A., 1837; M.A., 1851), a master at Christ's Hospital in 1837-62 and vicar of Clavering with Langley, Essex, in 1862-74. Theodore was educated at home by his father and private tutors, and in 1869 entered St John's College, Cambridge (B.A., 1873; M.A., 1876). Successful in mathematics, he won a college scholarship and a university Bell scholarship in 1871, graduated 3rd wrangler in mathematics in 1873 and was elected a fellow at St John's in November 1874. In 1877 on the recommendation of (Sir) G. G. Stokes, Lucasian professor of mathematics, Cambridge, and Sir Charles Nicholson [q.v.] he was chosen from a large number of applicants to succeed M. B. Pell [q.v.] as professor of mathematics and natural philosophy in the University of Sydney.

At the University of Sydney Gurney developed new courses, organized the laboratories and won repute as a fine teacher. In 1884 he visited Europe and bought additional apparatus for the department of natural philosophy. In the University Senate he was an elected member in 1894-96 and ex officio as dean of the faculty of arts in 1894-96. In 1877 he had become a member of the Royal Society of New South Wales. At St James's Church, Sydney, on 10 March 1879 he married Johanna Cornelia (b. 1846), widow of Captain F. W. Wragg of Chesterton Hall, Cambridge, and daughter of J. C. Pelgrim of Leerdam, Holland.

Together the Gurneys contributed greatly to the general activities of the developing university, notably in helping to promote the Musical Society and the establishment of the Women's College of which Mrs Gurney was a member of the council in 1892-93. However, Gurney failed to fulfil the undoubted promise of his achievements at Cambridge and in 1902 a committee, appointed to seek his successor, wrote to the eminent Cambridge mathematician, (Sir) Joseph Larmor: 'There is very considerable activity in all other branches of science here, but research in mathematical matters is absolutely non-existent. The present professor, Gurney of your College, has held the chair for 25 years. Mentally equipped with every gift except ambition he has as you know never published a line'. Gurney retired from the University of Sydney and returned with his wife to England. They identified themselves closely with the Parish Church of St Andrew, Chesterton, where they are both commemorated by a marble tablet. Gurney died on 4 September 1918, and his wife on 7 September 1922, both at Chesterton Hall. Gurney Crescent in Seaforth, Sydney, and Gurney Way, Cambridge, were named after him.

University of Sydney, Reports, V&P (LA NSW), 1877-78, 2, 418, 1885-86, 4, 351; Archives section (Westminster Public Lib, Lond); St John's College Archives (Cambridge).

I. S. TURNER

GUTHRIE, THOMAS (1833-1928), pastoralist, was born on 25 April 1833 in Duns, Berwickshire, Scotland, the youngest son of David Guthrie, merchant, and his wife Agnes, née Gray. His father had business connexions in Hobart Town and Thomas joined his elder brother there in December 1847. He worked for some months on William Downie's sheep station near New Norfolk. In 1849 the brothers left for California with a cargo of wooden-frame houses. In Honolulu they learned that others had preceded them to San Francisco with similar cargoes so they sold their houses and returned to Port Phillip. In 1851 the brothers took livestock to Lyttelton, New Zealand, and survived shipwreck on the way back. Thomas became a gold buyer at the Forest Creek and Ballarat diggings. He bought gold for £2 7s. 6d. an ounce and then made the hazardous journey to Melbourne alone, selling the gold to Dalgety [q.v.], Cruickshank & Co.

In 1854 Thomas went to Scotland and returned in 1855. In 1857 he joined George Synnot's stock, station and wool broking firm in Geelong. Guthrie was a brilliant auctioneer and in 1861 became a full partner. Synnot & Guthrie built stock saleyards on thirty-six acres of Drumcondra, Geelong, owned by Guthrie. They held weekly sales and with C. J. Dennys [q.v.] were founders of the Geelong wool market. In 1860 Synnot & Guthrie acquired for £16,000 Quambatook run in the lower Avoca district. When the partnership dissolved in 1866 Guthrie kept Quambatook and retired from wool broking. His brother-in-law, Gideon Rutherford, became his partner and they improved Quambatook to carry 64,000 sheep. Mary Oliver, née Rutherford, whom Guthrie married on 15 September 1864, was a remarkable woman. When her first husband died in 1857 she bought Morambo and the adjoining Fairview. Her understanding of pastoral affairs was a great help to her husband in his adventurous enterprises. She died on 4 September 1918.

When Quambatook was opened for selection Guthrie secured only 1640 acres. Rutherford withdrew from the partnership when the best of the run was taken by selectors. By buying out those who failed Guthrie gradually increased his freehold to 14,700 acres. At Rich Avon East, the leasehold of which he acquired in 1864, Guthrie bought 23,000 of the original 40,000 acres. His other properties were Rich Avon West, Avon Plains, Brim and Davis Plains in the Wimmera and Mount Muirhead, South Avenue, Mount Graham, Avenue Range and Woakwine in the south-east of South Australia. At Rich Avon Guthrie built up a merino stud with selected ewes from the

Ercildoune stud and rams from T. F. Cumming's [q.v.] stud at Stony Point. Guthrie never stayed long at Rich Avon and in 1873 he installed a manager and moved his family to Geelong where the children could attend school. He bought the Hermitage which remained the Guthrie home for thirty years.

In 1882 Guthrie embarked on his most spectacular venture. At public auction he bought 1200 square miles on the Barkly Tablelands, called the run Avon Downs, soon expanded it to 2300 square miles, and in the next three decades spent £100,000 on improvements and increased its carrying capacity from 14,500 to 70,000 merinos. Some of the sheep were overlanded from Rich Avon, a grave error which Guthrie soon realized because of the distance to travel. He managed the station mostly from Victoria and was probably the first to run large numbers of sheep in the Northern Territory. His wool was carted 200 miles to Burketown and shipped to England; he once topped the London market with scoured merino wool from Avon Downs. The station also carried 400 horses and 9000 Shorthorn cattle, which later replaced the sheep entirely. He erected the first forty-seven miles of telephone line in the territory and claimed to be the first to bore for subterranean water there. By his drive and interest the Camooweal Hospital was established.

Guthrie was a sturdy Scot with a magnificent physique and constitution. Although primarily a businessman he loved the hardship and excitement of pioneering and left the management of his Victorian and South Australian properties, much reduced by closer settlement, to his sons while he opened up new areas. He died on 18 October 1928 at South Yarra, survived by five of his six children. His sons were Thomas Oliver, of Rich Avon; Arthur Donaldson, station manager; and James Francis, senator.

J. Smith (ed), *Cyclopedia of Victoria*, 2 (Melb, 1904); A. Henderson (ed), *Australian families*, 1 (Melb, 1941); C. E. Sayers, *Shanty at the bridge; the story of Donald* (Donald, 1963); *Pastoral Review*, 15 Feb 1910, 16 Nov 1928; *Mount Wycheproof Ensign*, 2 Nov 1928.

J. ANN HONE

GWYNNE, EDWARD CASTRES (1811-1888), lawyer, legislator and judge, was born on 13 February 1811 at Lewes, Sussex, England, son of William Gwynne (1774-1825), rector of St Michael's, Lewes, and of Denton. Educated at St Ann's Grammar School and an establishment near Sheffield, he was articled first with Charles Willis, attorney, of Cranbrook, Kent, and then with Few & Co., London. He practised as an attorney until 1837 when he was appointed clerk of court by Sir John Jeffcott [q.v.], the first judge of the Supreme Court of South Australia. Jeffcott had no power to make the appointment but Gwynne had already quitted legal practice and decided to sail for Adelaide in the *Lord Goderich* as superintendent of emigrants. He was relieved of this office by the British consul in Brazil where the ship put in because the cabin-passengers were close to mutiny. Partly for this reason he did not impress Governor Hindmarsh and his appointment as clerk of court was not confirmed when he arrived on 15 April 1838. He was admitted to the Supreme Court, served as partner in turn with Charles Mann [q.v.], William Bartley, E. Klingender and W. J. Lawrence and quickly became prominent at the Bar, particularly in equity. He was legal adviser to the South Australian Mining Association which opened the Burra Burra mine in 1845.

Gwynne was a nominee in the Legislative Council in 1851-54. He was defeated for East Torrens in the Legislative Council election of 1855, but after responsible government in 1857 was elected to the Legislative Council and in August was attorney-general in John Baker's [q.v.] ten-day ministry. He resigned from the council on 30 August 1859 because of his appointment as third judge of the South Australian Supreme Court on 26 February. In 1867 he became second judge and primary judge in equity. He was acting chief justice from December 1872 to June 1873. In February 1877 he was given leave to visit England and retired from the bench on 28 February 1881 on a pension of £1300. Apart from service in the Supreme Court he had acted three times as commissioner of insolvency, and in October 1885 was granted the title of Honorable.

Gwynne was the first member of the South Australian Bar to be elevated permanently to the bench. He was popular and respected although his political views were conservative. He was a staunch, if unsuccessful, supporter of state aid to religion, an upper chamber of members nominated for life by the Crown and representation related to property-holding, and was one of the most fervent opponents of Torrens's Real Property Act, 1857-58. The highlights of his judicial career centred on Judge Boothby [q.v.]. While still at the Bar, Gwynne had clashed with Boothby and was contemplating departure to Melbourne rather than suffer more humiliation when in 1859 he was appointed third judge, partly in order to facilitate majority decisions and to provide for circuit courts, but also as a means of resolving difficulties between Boothby and the chief justice, Cooper [q.v.]. Despite

Boothby's disrespect to his brother judges, particularly after R. D. Hanson [q.v.] succeeded Cooper, Gwynne managed for a time to remain aloof from the discord between Boothby and Hanson and between Boothby and the Bar.

The parting of the ways began when Cooper retired and Boothby was not made chief justice. Gwynne and Hanson overruled Boothby when he claimed that Hanson was improperly appointed because he had not been admitted a barrister in England, Ireland or Scotland. This argument was equally applicable to Gwynne as Boothby reiterated at every opportunity, although Gwynne joined Boothby in doubting the validity of the Real Property Act, 1857-58, the Registration of Deeds Act, 1862, the various Local Court Acts and the existence of the Court of Appeals. The imperial parliament tried to rectify matters by legislation which culminated in the Colonial Laws Validity Act, 1865, the full implications of which were accepted by Gwynne but not by Boothby who continued privately and publicly to attack the validity of the appointments of Hanson and Gwynne. They were finally compelled to refuse to sit with Boothby and in 1867 supported his amoval. Throughout these difficulties Gwynne stood out as a staunch upholder of the law as he saw it. His will and ability to do so speaks highly of his character, pertinacity and high repute in the colony. In May 1870 he resigned his primary judgeship after a dispute with the government. The governor refused to accept his resignation until convinced that Gwynne, despite settlement of other grievances, would not act both as primary judge in equity and as a member of the Full Court. In 1871 a new Equity Act was passed to empower the Executive Council to require any judge of the Supreme Court to act as primary judge in equity. This Act was strongly opposed by the judges who deemed it 'an attack on the Bench' and requested that it be reserved for consideration by the Crown, but the royal assent was given on 16 May and Gwynne was soon reappointed.

Independent and outspoken Gwynne was never appointed chief justice despite his seniority. Like his colleague, R. I. Stow [q.v.], he was chagrined in 1876 when S. J. Way, Q.C., was appointed to succeed Hanson as chief justice. Gwynne showed his displeasure by refusing private converse with Way. Further difficulties arising from his reluctance at an advanced age to adjust himself to the new system of procedure introduced by the Supreme Court Procedure Act, 1878, led to his retirement.

In private life Gwynne was a keen farmer, orchardist and viticulturist. In 1840 he bought a large property in the area now known as Glynde after his home Glynde Place. He also had a substantial farm in the Inman Valley where he bred horses for show and for racing. He was a keen horseman and in 1854 was appointed captain of a volunteer troop of cavalry. On 24 July he had married Marian, daughter of Richard Eales Borrow of Adelaide. He died at Glynde on 10 June 1888 survived by his wife (d. 19 December 1896) and eight of his thirteen children.

Mount Gwynne in the Northern Territory was named after him by J. M. Stuart [q.v.] in 1860.

A. J. Hannan, *The life of Chief Justice Way* (Syd, 1960); PP (SA), 1867 (22), 1870 (68, 68a, 68b, 163), 1871 (54); *Register* (Adel), 11 June 1888; *Homes and Garden* (SA), Apr 1950; R. M. Hague, History of the law in South Australia (SAA).   DAVID ST LEGER KELLY

H

HACK, WILTON (1843-1923), utopist, was born on 21 May 1843 at Echunga, South Australia, the second child of Stephen Hack and his wife Elizabeth Marsh, née Wilton (1815-1915). Stephen had migrated from Gloucester to South Australia in 1837 with his brother J. B. Hack [q.v.] and went on to Sydney for cattle which he took by sea to Portland and then overland to Adelaide in two batches. While his brother acquired land and a whaling station, Stephen stayed in Adelaide, busy with a large kitchen garden, dairy, livery stable and contracts for his working bullocks. He went to Gloucester in 1841 to see his parents and to marry, returning to Adelaide with his wife in 1842. Like his brother, Stephen became insolvent but was discharged in 1844. He recovered slowly by dint of hard work and careful management of stock and land. In 1857 he led an exploration into country north of Streaky Bay and found enough pasturage and water to justify government payment for the expedition. In 1873 he retired to Gloucester where he died aged 78 on 14 May 1894.

Wilton was sent to his Quaker grandparents in Gloucester and educated at Sandbach Grammar School, Cheshire, and the University of Heidelberg. He joined his father at Long Desert station east of the River Murray bend and soon took up Pinnaroo station but had to abandon it in the 1865-67 drought. He became a drawing master in Adelaide schools and on 10 May 1870 married Anna Maria, daughter of George Stonehouse, Baptist minister. Determined on a life of service 'in fields not tended by others', he began visiting prisoners at Yatala gaol. In 1873 he went to Japan as a missionary. Language problems and military unrest cramped his activities so he hired a translator, bought a printing press and distributed thousands of religious tracts even to priests and officials. He gathered a few followers but ran out of funds. He became a teacher of English in a government school but was soon dismissed. In 1876 he visited Adelaide where he negotiated with the government for the admission of a few hundred Japanese families in the Northern Territory. Back in Japan he told the government that South Australia would provide free passages for the migrants but this was promptly denied in Adelaide and the whole project was rejected by the Japanese authorities.

Hack returned to Australia in 1878. He floated several gold mines in New South Wales with some success. In South Australia at Mount Remarkable he attempted a socialistic village settlement for the unemployed. Attracted to theosophy he visited India and Ceylon several times studying eastern religions, on which he wrote and lectured. In 1890 he went to England to promote gold mines in Western Australia but had to borrow from his father for his return fare to Adelaide. He settled at Glenelg and devoted himself to painting in oils and water-colours until his only daughter married and his wife died. Two of his sons moved to Western Australia and in 1915 he visited them. A serious accident prevented his return and 'in consequence of the kindness bestowed on him by his nurse', Minnie Alice Wierk, he married her on 26 April 1916. Hack died at Beverley, Western Australia, on 27 February 1923, leaving small legacies to his four surviving children and some £1500 to his wife.

J. Cross, 'Wilton Hack and Japanese immigration into north Australia', PRGSSA, 61 (1959-60); V&P (SA), 1857-58 (156); Advertiser (Adel), 2 Mar 1923; Hack family letters, 1488 (SAA).

HADDON, FREDERICK WILLIAM (1839-1906), journalist, was born on 8 February 1839 in Croydon, Surrey, England, son of Richard Haddon, schoolmaster and landscape artist, and his wife Mary Caroline, née Wykes. Adopted by an uncle he was educated at private schools, but prevented from studying law by his uncle's death and in 1855 entered the service of the Statistical Society of London. In 1859 he became assistant secretary for the society and for the Institute of Actuaries of Great Britain and Ireland. He helped to edit the Journal of the Statistical Society and contributed statistical articles to other London journals. Edward Wilson and Lauchlan Mackinnon [qq.v.], proprietors of the Melbourne Argus, engaged Haddon in 1863 and in December he arrived in Melbourne with them in the Great Britain. Haddon worked first as a contributor to the Argus and then as sub-editor. He became co-editor of the new weekly Australasian in 1864 and sole editor in 1865. He was promoted editor of the Argus on 1 January 1867. Under his guidance it became, according to R. E. N. Twopeny [q.v.], 'the best daily paper published out of England'. Meanwhile Saturday night gatherings at his lodgings in 1867-

68 and quarters which he briefly shared with Marcus Clarke [q.v.] attracted talented literary friends who in 1868 formed the Yorick Club. Haddon, one of the first trustees, withdrew as the club lost its Bohemianism but retained ties with Marcus Clarke and in 1870 went with him to Tasmania.

In 1873 Haddon left for Europe and early next year, after a survey of leading English newspapers, he recommended that the *Argus* adopt the 'telescopic system' of varying the newspaper's size according to the availability of news. Wilson, fired with Haddon's enthusiasm, sought reform of the *Argus* administration and a reduction in the paper's price. The editorial council, resentful of his alleged 'backstairs influence' over Wilson, cursorily dismissed Haddon's system. Mortified, he refused to attend daily policy meetings and so jeopardized his editorial position. Wilson attributed his conduct to 'habits of self-indulgence' and subsequent poor health. Ignoring desperate warnings from Wilson and Mackinnon against making the *Argus* subservient to free-trade dogma and the constitutionalist party, Haddon continued to pontificate on these subjects and in January 1879 he went to England to stop Berry's [q.v.] 'embassy' from gaining imperial reform of the Victorian Legislative Council. He lobbied British statesmen, interviewed editors, wrote 'nervous and forcible' letters to *The Times* and other journals and compiled a pamphlet sympathetic to the council, *The constitutional difficulty in Victoria. Statement of facts for the information of English readers* (London, 1879). In June he left London and returned by way of America. Despite a price reduction from 3d. to 2d. in 1884 and to 1d. in 1893, the *Argus* failed to rival the *Age* in circulation, but Haddon continued as editor in more stable circumstances than before.

Wilson described Haddon as a 'safe and good Editor' who lacked brilliance but kept the *Argus* free from libel actions. Later critics also noted Haddon's ability to encourage new writers, his disciplined yet frank relations with the staff and his insistence on efficiency. He was Melbourne correspondent for *The Times* in 1895-1903, but retired from the *Argus* in 1898 to represent the trustees of Wilson's estate on the management board of the *Argus* and *Australasian*. He served on the inquiry into the finances of the Royal Melbourne Hospital and undertook other work relevant to charitable bequests from the Wilson estate. He went to London for the coronation in 1902, and for some years was president of the Victorian Poultry and Kennel Club.

Haddon married Annie Jane King in June 1875. She died in 1877 aged 37. Haddon died on 7 March 1906 at his home, Heronwood, South Yarra, survived by his second wife, Alice Annie Good of Sandhurst, whom he had married on 31 January 1883, and a daughter by his first marriage. His estate was valued for probate at £2558.

G. Meudell, *The pleasant career of a spendthrift and his later reflections* (Melb, 1935); B. Elliott, *Marcus Clarke* (Oxford, 1958); *Bulletin*, 21 Feb 1880, 26 May 1883; F. W. Haddon letters (LaT L); J. S. Johnston letters (Univ Melb Archives).   CAROLE WOODS

HAGENAUER, FRIEDRICH AUGUST (1829-1909), Moravian missionary, was born on 10 March 1829 at Hohenleuben, Saxony, of Lutheran parents. He left school at 14, worked for two years with his father and then on railway construction. Influenced by Pastor Lohe and Dr Schmid at Greiz, he applied in 1850 to study at Herrnhut, Ebersdorf, where the Brotherhood of Moravian priests accepted him as a missionary trainee in 1851. On 27 November 1856 he was instructed to go to Victoria with F. W. Spieseke who had returned to Europe after the Lake Boga Mission, established with La Trobe's help in 1851, was abandoned.

Hagenauer and Spieseke arrived at Melbourne in May 1858. By December, following Governor Barkly's suggestion, they had selected a Wimmera River site on Antwerp station, where the squatter, Horatio Spencer Ellerman, gave material assistance and the Ebenezer mission school was opened next January. In 1858 several missionaries including Spieseke and Hagenauer had given evidence to a select committee on the alleviation of Aboriginals' 'absolute wants'. The Central Board appointed to watch over the interests of the Aborigines, which first met on 7 June 1860, set up two stations and planned more government depots and missions financed by various churches. In February 1862 after negotiations between the Moravians and the Presbyterian Church of Victoria Hagenauer and his wife arrived in Gippsland where the Presbyterians hoped to secure two large reserves on Green Hills station with support from the central board. Objections by squatters led the board of land and works to change the site and in August 1863 some 2356 acres were secured at Lake Wellington on the River Avon. The Hagenauers moved to this reserve calling it Ramahyuck. Hagenauer believed in 'kind, firm, just and business-like treatment' and used the 'patriarchal principle' to control the Aboriginals. Thanks to generous subsidies and continuous assistance by a trained teacher, Ramahyuck was described in 1877 as the most successful of all missions. The Aboriginals had well-constructed homes, learned rural tasks, cultivated crops, vegetables and fruit and tended sheep and cattle. In 1872 the school, taught in 1864-66 and 1870-76 by Rev. Carl Kramer, was the first in the colony to secure 100 per cent in marks under the results system introduced in 1862-63. After the 1877 royal commission on Aboriginals, Hagenauer and Kramer were asked to tour the Murray area and persuade nomads to move into the reserves and mission stations. Hagenauer was also successful in training half-castes for rural work; and the number at Ramahyuck rose to 85 but dropped to 63 in 1888 as the half-castes became independent of the mission. For the Moravian Board in Saxony Hagenauer travelled in 1885 to North Queensland investigating Aboriginal needs and his report led to new government reserves and the Mapoon mission.

Tireless in his devotion to Aboriginals Hagenauer became religious superintendent for Anglican missions at Lake Tyers and Lake Condah and for two Presbyterian missions. As director of four of the colony's six stations he had much influence but often quarrelled with the board over supervision of the secular side of the missions and complained of the 'iron rule' of the secretary, Robert Brough Smyth [q.v.]. On 1 July 1889 Hagenauer became acting secretary and general inspector for the board at a salary of £450. Hagenauer resigned as secretary in 1906 and died aged 80 at Lake Tyers on 28 November 1909. On 15 June 1861 at St Paul's Church, Melbourne, he had married Christiana Louisa Knobloch, a missionary from Saxony; she died on 23 October 1917. Of their nine children, seven were born at Ramahyuck. A son was acting secular manager at Ramahyuck until it closed in 1908.

A conscientious and effective administrator, Hagenauer was 'wise in counsel, patient in effort and resolute in action'. In addition to material on Aboriginal language included in Brough Smyth's *Aborigines of Victoria* (Melbourne, 1878) he published papers on *Mission Work among the Aborigines of Victoria* (1880), *Report of the Aboriginal Mission at Ramahyuck, Victoria* (1885), and *Notes of a Missionary Journey to North Queensland* (1886).

S. L. Chase (ed), *The Moravian mission at Lake Boga* (Melb, 1856); A. Massola, *Aboriginal mission stations in Victoria* (Melb, 1970), and for bibliog; M. Manning, 'Life of Ernest Albert Le Souef', *JRWAHS*, 6 (1962-68) pt 4; L. J. Blake, 'Education at Ebenezer', *Educational Mag* (Vic), Feb 1967; *The Gap*, 7 (1969); information from Miss R. L. Hagenauer, Box Hill, Vic.   L. J. BLAKE

HAINES, WILLIAM CLARK (1810-1866), politician, was born at Hampstead, England, son of John Haines, physician, and his wife Jane, née Bliss. He was educated at Charterhouse and in 1829-32 at Caius College, Cambridge (B.A., 1833), where by family tradition he was a friend of Thackeray.

After practising surgery in England for some years, Haines migrated to Victoria about 1841 and bought property near Geelong with John Highett [q.v.] in 1842; the partnership was dissolved in 1846. Haines had given up farming by 1850 when he divided 2849 acres into forty-nine farms stretching from Pollocksford on the Barwon River across the Geelong-Colac road at Moriac. By 1851 he had sold five farms to C. J. Dennys [q.v.] and others were sold in the 1850s. Haines became well known in the Geelong district as territorial magistrate, district trustee of the Port Phillip Savings Bank and member of the Grant District Council in 1843. In 1851 he was a government nominee in the first Legislative Council; his resignation in August 1852 in protest against the intended issue of leases to the squatters won him the support of smallholders and radicals, although Haines was always a conservative. He was elected member for Grant in the council in August 1853 and became an official nominee from December 1854 to March 1855. He served on many council committees, including one for licensing in September 1854 when he took a firm anti-temperance stand. With J. L. V. F. Foster, W. F. Stawell [qq.v.] and others he helped to draft the new Victorian Constitution.

In December 1854, after Foster resigned, Haines became colonial secretary. His loyal and conscientious service was acknowledged by Governor Hotham, who wrote to the Colonial Office: 'Single handed I never could have coped with the difficulties with which I found this Colony surrounded, but I have had an able assistant and above all, a gentleman by my side, who has the invaluable habit of looking at his object and marching straight to it'. As the chief civil servant in Victoria Haines implemented the moves to resolve the financial crisis of 1854-55, reform goldfields administration and institute local government in suburbs, shires and country towns. He also shared with Hotham the many criticisms levelled at the administration.

In the council Haines was a reluctant, almost inarticulate speaker except when forced to clarify a government plan or defend a constitutional issue. He could be roused to speak on a few subjects on which he felt strongly, such as the unfair advantages of pastoral licensees over landowners.

Another subject was education, which he claimed should be 'the work of the people themselves', financed by local rates and government grants, supervised by local authorities who understood local needs and property values, and preferably dominated by the churches.

In October 1855 news reached Victoria that the imperial parliament had passed the new Victorian Constitution Act. The Executive Council persuaded Hotham to forgo his powers at the earliest possible moment and to transfer sovereignty to it until elections could be held to choose the new parliament. Haines, Stawell, Andrew Clarke and H. C. E. Childers [qq.v.] were released from their duties in November 'on political grounds' and immediately reinstated as members of the first ministerial cabinet. The action was condemned by the majority of the Legislative Council who also accused these officials of acting to ensure their right to retiring pensions. Haines later offered to share his £1000 pension with Foster, who declined.

As chief official Haines was accepted as the nominal leader of the government in the Legislative Council. In the debates on electoral procedures for the forthcoming elections, William Nicholson [q.v.] gained support in the council when he advocated the use of secret ballot. Haines argued that secret ballot would mask rather than prevent bribery and when Nicholson's proposal was approved by a slight majority Haines resigned. Nicholson was unable to form a government and when the council resumed early in January 1856 Haines was recalled by the acting-governor, Major-General Edward Macarthur [q.v.]. Reluctantly Haines accepted the principle that the ballot question was to be decided by the legislature rather than by the ministers and an amended electoral bill became law in March.

In the first parliament under the new Constitution in November 1856 Haines was member for South Grant in the Legislative Assembly and led the first ministry. From the beginning his government was insecure despite the stability and confidence of the previous months. Uncertain of a majority in the assembly, he relied heavily on the advice of Stawell while his opponents were comparatively united under J. O'Shanassy [q.v.]. In March 1857 after several narrow victories Haines's ministry was defeated. O'Shanassy took office but was soon defeated and on 29 April Haines was reinstated, leading a cabinet mainly chosen by McCulloch [q.v.]. His government lasted until February 1858 when it was defeated by a mixed group of democrats, anti-Catholics and squatters during debates on the redistribution of electorates. Haines re-

signed and later that year left for North America and Europe.

While holding office in 1857-58 Haines swam with the current of Victorian affairs, yielding to pressure from strong colleagues and influential groups. Although he always opposed the hold of the squatters on crown lands, his land bill of 1857 had acknowledged the contention of the powerful squatting group that security of tenure for pastoralists was necessary for Victoria's prosperity. Again in 1857 when he needed A. Michie's [q.v.] support, he gave government backing to Michie's private bill which would have cut down the church influence in education that Haines himself favoured. Despite his dislike of what he called 'a naked democracy' his government had to accept the principle of manhood suffrage for assembly elections, although the bill introduced included provisions for plural voting and complicated residential qualifications. The onset of an economic crisis and unemployment from 1857 also circumscribed reforms by Haines's administration. He encouraged assisted immigration but it was not popular and had to be reduced. Finance to implement plans to extend the railway system could not be arranged before Haines lost office. Business interests scotched suggestions for a national bank and little was done to extend and reform the civil service.

Haines's reputation was high when he returned to Victoria in October 1860. Representing Portland he took his place in the Legislative Assembly in November. He was treasurer in O'Shanassy's ministry till the government fell in June 1863 and represented Victoria at the intercolonial tariff conference that year. Under O'Shanassy he shared in improvements to electoral procedures, transport, local government and legislation on real estate. In the main issue of state aid to education Haines continued to work with O'Shanassy to reduce the power, prestige and financial status of the secular state schools, although in 1862 Richard Heales [q.v.] managed to carry a bill to establish a single board of education.

In the 1864 election Haines lost at Portland but was elected for Eastern Province to the Legislative Council. In the controversy over protection late in 1865 he was deeply involved in debates on the constitutional aspects of the tariff appropriation bills. His friends blamed his distress over this issue for the carbuncle which caused his death at 55 in his city home at South Yarra on 3 February 1866. He was buried in St Kilda cemetery. He was survived by his wife Mary Ann, née Dugard, whom he had married in London in 1835, and by five sons and two daughters.

Haines had been a member of the Council

of the University of Melbourne in 1853-65 and vice-chancellor in 1857-58. He sponsored horse-racing at Geelong as well as international and intercolonial cricket matches; in 1861 he was made a trustee of the Melbourne Cricket Ground. He was a grand master of the Scottish Freemasons, a member of the Melbourne Club and a prominent Anglican. A contemporary journal described him as 'a man of no brilliant talents but of immense weight of character—honest, jovial, undisguised old English Tory'. His hard work, patient affability and undoubted integrity were acknowledged by all but he lacked decisiveness and originality. 'Honest Farmer' Haines, as he was sometimes dubbed, was an admirable senior official but less successful as a minister of the Crown.

W. Kelly, *Life in Victoria*, 1 (Lond, 1859); H. G. Turner, *A history of the colony of Victoria*, 2 (Lond, 1904); W. R. Brownhill, *The history of Geelong and Corio Bay* (Melb, 1955); G. Serle, *The golden age* (Melb, 1963); PD (LA Vic), 1861-62, (LC Vic), 1865; E. Scott, 'The history of the Victorian ballot', *VHM*, 8 (1920); *Age*, 5 Feb 1866; *Argus*, 5 Feb 1866; *Illustrated Aust News*, 23 Feb 1866; W. Hammond, 'Early history of the Barrabool Hills', *Geelong Advertiser*, Dec 1898-Jan 1899.

BETTY MALONE

HALE, MATHEW BLAGDEN (1811-1895), Anglican bishop, was born on 18 June 1811 at the manor of Alderley, Gloucester, England, son of Robert Hale Blagden Hale and his wife Lady Theodosia Eleanor, youngest daughter of Joseph Bourke, third earl of Mayo and archbishop of Tuam. His father was a direct descendant of Sir Mathew Hale, lord chief justice of the King's Bench in 1671-76.

Hale was educated at Wotton-under-Edge, Gloucester School and Trinity College, Cambridge (B.A., 1835; M.A., 1838; D.D., 1857). After six months in Lausanne he read theology for a term at Cambridge and was made deacon by the bishop of Gloucester on 5 June 1836 and ordained priest in June 1837. His family dissuaded him from going to the West Indies on missionary service, and in Gloucester he was curate at Tresham with Kilcott in 1836, Wotton-under-Edge in 1838 and permanent curate of Stroud in 1839. In 1840 he married Sophia Clode by whom he had two surviving daughters, Amy and Mary. His wife's and his mother's deaths in 1845 severely affected his health. He resigned from Stroud, was rector of Alderley for a year and then curate of Atworth, living with his father in Wiltshire.

Soon after Augustus Short [q.v.] was

consecrated bishop of Adelaide in 1847 he invited Hale to become archdeacon and examining chaplain in South Australia. Eager for missionary work among the Aboriginals, Hale accepted and sailed in the *Derwent* with his daughters and Short's party. On arrival in December he was given charge of St Matthew's, Kensington, and soon afterwards of St John's, Adelaide. When Short visited the Western Australian section of his diocese in October 1848, Hale went with him and on the Vasse at John Molloy's [q.v.] home found five daughters 'who although being in the most complete seclusion, possess a grace and dignity and ease of manner which would do honour to the most refined society'. At St Mary's, Busselton, on 30 December 1848 Hale married the eldest daughter, Sabina Dunlop.

Hale's observation of work among Aboriginals and half-castes in Western Australia spurred his intention to help the natives in South Australia. In 1850 he persuaded Lieut-Governor Young to grant him £200 and a year's rations to found an institution where Aboriginals from Adelaide could receive practical training in isolation from corrupting influences. Boston Island was chosen as the site, but it lacked fresh water, so Hale bought the lease of Poonindie run, twelve miles from Port Lincoln, and had it declared a native reserve. There natives were brought after schooling in Adelaide to be taught farming and to receive further instruction in Christianity. So successful was the venture that in 1853 Hale took over Pastor C. W. Schurmann's Aboriginal school in Port Lincoln and in exchange for a government grant of £1000 a year he agreed to receive any natives or half-castes sent to Poonindie by the protector of Aborigines. Sharply rising costs in the gold rushes and the failure of the crops in 1854 proved formidable challenges, but once through the first decade the institution managed to become self-supporting. By 1856 the residents at Poonindie had risen from 19 to 62, a total of 110 natives had been received and the buildings and stock were worth £4700. Many material difficulties had been solved by Hale's personal generosity and by 1860, despite criticism of the high incidence of deaths from lung complaints, the institution had demonstrated the capacities of the Aboriginals in useful employment. After his father died in December 1855 Hale returned to England on family business. He visited Western Australia en route and from observations in that colony published *The Transportation Question* (Cambridge, 1857), advocating 'a Reformatory Colony' instead of 'a Penal Settlement'.

Recommended by Short, Hale was appointed the first bishop of Western Australia and on 25 July 1857 was consecrated at Lambeth by the archbishop of Canterbury and by the bishops of London and Ripon. His episcopate was most notable for his attempts to introduce secondary education. In Perth on 28 June 1858 he opened a boys' college founded on the model of the Collegiate School of St Peter, Adelaide, but seven years elapsed before he could vest the property in trustees and obtain a grant from the Society for Promoting Christian Knowledge to reimburse his initial private outlay. Known as 'the Bishop's School', it trained many community leaders but the indifference of the colonists to education and the trustees to management as well as the scarcity of suitable permanent staff combined to defeat his efforts. In 1872 he wrote, 'There is no such thing as convincing the people that education pays. Making their sons messengers on a sheep station pays, and that settles the question . . . Parents won't use the school so it's no use to keep it struggling on'. The school passed out of church control when the trustees arranged for it to be taken over by governors appointed by the government. Hale's attempt to found a girls' boarding school in 1860 suffered similar lack of response and cost him the return fares of the schoolmistress whom he had brought from England.

As a member of the Board of Education Hale believed that Governor Kennedy's introduction of the Irish National system in government schools was in the interests of the colony. In 1871 he vigorously opposed an attempt to give Roman Catholic schools a separate grant, but later saved sectarian division by proposing state aid for all private schools. Hale wanted the government to treat every denomination alike but would tolerate no state interference in church affairs. When Governor Hampton interfered with the duties of convict chaplains and attacked Hale for alleged lack of efficient supervision of his clergy, the bishop's representation to the Colonial Office was a major factor in Hampton's recall.

Hale had consulted with his clergy since 1860 and because of the size and isolation of his diocese he appeared to sense no urgency in settling the mode of church government. Just before the meeting in Sydney to found a general synod for the Australian Church in 1872, he introduced synodical government to his diocese, following the constitutional model of consensual compact devised in Adelaide by Bishop Short in 1855. The population of Western Australia rose in 1857-75 from 13,368 to 26,709, while the Anglican clergy increased from 8 to 17 and the number of churches from 14 to 28 with 9 new rectories. Although 59 per cent of the population claimed Anglican allegiance

in 1875, more than three-quarters of clerical stipends was paid by the government. Hale's liberality in building the Bishop's House at his own expense was a fine gesture to the diocese struggling in poverty. Constant travelling in his huge diocese had brought on repeated attacks of lumbago and in 1875 when it was suggested that he should succeed Bishop Tufnell [q.v.] in Brisbane Hale protested against 'putting a man of sixty-four in such a position'. Somewhat typically he added, 'Nevertheless as I have always professed to go by duty and not by choice [and] if the bishops should unanimously say that . . . I should go, I should consider that a sufficient indication of my duty'.

The Australian bishops were unanimous and Hale was installed in Brisbane on 15 December. His concern for the more remote parishes was a feature of his work in Queensland and by 1878 he had arranged the division of his huge diocese, with G. H. Stanton [q.v.] taking charge of North Queensland. Another sign of progress was the increase of clergy; in 1875 he found 25 clergy ministering in the whole colony and in 1885 had 35 in the subdivided diocese of Brisbane. His introduction of a Clergy Widow and Orphan's Fund to the diocese in 1877 showed his concern for the welfare of his priests but his attempts to improve the lot of the Aboriginals and the Chinese had little effect. Hale always struggled against the congregational spirit of a diocese in which established parishes prospered whilst isolated centres were neglected. He tried to create a strong central fund to assist these centres but the response was so meagre that he registered his protest by resigning in 1876. Only after Bishop Barker [q.v.] intervened and the Diocesan Council promised greater efforts did Hale withdraw the resignation; yet by 1878 only £2200 had been collected, most of it by the bishop's personal efforts and his own private gift of £300. When Barker resigned in 1881, Hale as senior bishop presided over the General Synod of the Church of England in Australia until Alfred Barry [q.v.] was appointed bishop of Sydney and metropolitan bishop of Australia in 1884.

Hale retired in March 1885 and returned to England where he continued to promote the Church's mission to the Australian Aboriginals by his writings. He died at Bristol on 3 April 1895, survived by his second wife and by five sons and three daughters.

Hale was more a missionary than an administrator. He could win the confidence of people in all classes and his generous and paternal disposition earned him the title of 'the good bishop'. Although never profound, he remained a disciplined and serious scholar and his conservative theological views were respected more for their wisdom than for their originality. Compared with contemporaries like Short, Perry and Tyrrell [qq.v.] he lacked nothing in unselfish devotion to duty. His letters after retirement show his continued interest in the development of the Church in Australia while his wide experience in three Australian colonies made him a valued adviser.

A. Burton, Hale School, Perth . . . 1858-1900 (Perth, 1939); F. Alexander (ed), Four bishops and their see (Perth, 1957); A. de Q. Robin, 'Mathew Blagden Hale and the Poonindie experiment', Univ Studies in History, 5 (1968); Western Mail, 6 Nov 1919, 23 Sept 1925; West Australian, 25 July 1936, 8 Jan 1938; K. Rayner, The history of the Church of England in Queensland (Ph.D. thesis, Univ Qld, 1962); A. de Q. Robin, The life of Mathew Blagden Hale (Ph.D. thesis, Univ. WA, 1971); P. U. Henn, The Perth episcopate of Bishop M. B. Hale 1857-75 (Battye Lib, Perth); A. Burton (ed), M. B. Hale diary 1856-75 (Battye Lib, Perth); Hale letters, 1848-75 (ML, Perth Diocesan Registry); Hale papers, 1835-91 (Univ Bristol, ML, NL, Battye Lib, Perth).

A. DE Q. ROBIN

HALES, FRANCIS (1822-1900), Anglican clergyman, was born in County Limerick, Ireland, son of Francis Hales, quartermaster in the 40th Regiment, and his wife Catherine. He went with his parents to Sydney in 1826, Hobart Town in 1827 and Bombay in 1829. His father died in January 1832, leaving an estate in Hobart valued at £144. Francis returned to Britain with his mother; they lived with his guardian, Henry Rocke, on the Isle of Man. In 1842 Hales entered Trinity College, Dublin (B.A., 1846), became curate at Castlebar, and was made deacon and in 1847 priested by the bishop of Tuam.

Hales and his young wife Ann Augusta, née Stoney, sailed in the Stag with Bishop Perry's [q.v.] party and arrived at Melbourne in January 1848. Sent on a missionary tour of scattered settlements in Gippsland, Hales returned after four months to take over the large parish of Heidelberg. 'Earnest, sensitive and spiritual', he was almost over-zealous in his duties. At first he preached on alternate Sundays in the Presbyterian Chapel, but soon raised funds for building St John's Church which was opened on 26 October 1851. At other centres in the parish he was less successful and became temperamental and tactless. After a row with his trustees over the site for a vicarage he moved his family into part of the church, but under pressure from the

bishop resigned in 1853. His parishioners gave him 350 sovereigns and bought his 'few sticks of furniture for fabulous prices'. With his wife and four children he sailed in the Clarence and arrived at Launceston in November as chaplain of Trinity parish. The incumbent, Rev. John Yorker, who was also chaplain of the gaol with a government salary of £200, left in December on sick leave, privately agreeing to pay £150 of his salary to Hales as his locum. Despite many protests, the colonial secretary insisted that Hales was entitled to only half the salary. In February 1856 Yorker resigned and Hales was appointed rector of Trinity and gaol chaplain with the full salary. Later the colonial secretary found that Yorker had drawn only £50 each year and Hales was given the balance. He had more arguments with the government in 1867 when the gaol appointment terminated and as a public servant he was superannuated at £18 a year.

In his long years at Trinity Hales served under four bishops: Nixon in 1854-62, Bromby in 1864-82, Sandford [qq.v.] in 1883-89 and Montgomery in 1889-1900. He became one of the first canons of St David's Cathedral, Hobart, in 1872, and archdeacon of Northern Tasmania in 1877; he represented Tasmania at General Synod in 1876, 1881 and 1888 and administered the diocese in 1882-83 and 1888-89. His grasp of financial matters and acquaintance with every church property in his archdeaconry were immensely valued by synod. He was also a successful organizer of fund appeals for missions and church building, not least for replacing his old church by the new Holy Trinity in 1898. His preaching was expository and clear, though he preferred 'a feast of reason and flow of soul' with friends in his study. He was an initiator of many public movements and opposed lotteries, capital punishment and government interference with church affairs. Although he had supported a 'university scheme' for Tasmania in 1857, he advocated 'a Hobart College affiliated with the Universities of Melbourne and Sydney' in 1889; after the University of Tasmania was created in 1890 he became a member of senate and was its warden in 1896-1900. At least six of his sermons were published, including a dissertation against marriage with a deceased wife's sister. For years he had suffered from asthma but found 'the trip across Bass Strait a perfect cure'; for this reason he often sought leave to visit Victoria and in 1889 took three months' leave in New Zealand. Perhaps the highlight of his career was on 14 July 1896 when as a patriarchal figure he presided over a large audience of Protestants and Catholics at the jubilee of his ordination. Aged 78 he died at his home in

Launceston on 9 July 1900, predeceased by his wife and survived by at least six of their nine children.

Cyclopedia of Tasmania, 2 (Hob, 1900); *V&P* (Tas), 1889 (145); *Church News* (Hob), 1 Aug 1896, 1 Aug 1900; *Examiner* (Launceston), 11 July 1900; CSO 5/175/4154, 24/241/9537 (TA); GO 33/26/953 (TA); CSD 1/53/1031, 4/99/1121, 13/48/710 (TA).

HALES, THOMAS (1847-1901), jockey, was born in Portland, Victoria, one of the ten children of Matthew Hales, blacksmith, and his wife Margaret, née Ward. The family moved to Penola and then Robe, South Australia. Although forbidden by his father to become involved with racing, Tom at 12 found school drab, ran away from home and found refuge at Edward Stockdale's station, Lake Hawden. There he first met Adam Lindsay Gordon [q.v.] whom he described as 'the most competent horse-breaker I ever saw'. Later at Penola Gordon as a police trooper arrested Hales for throwing stones at bullocks in the Penola stockyard, but released him when reminded of their meeting at Stockdale's station.

At 13 Hales rode his first winner, Euclid, in a match race for £50 against another horse ridden by a well-known professional rider. However, the name of Hales had little significance in racing until 1872 when he went to Melbourne with the Adelaide trainer, H. Tothill, and was asked by the owner, T. J. Ryan, to ride The Ace in the Melbourne Cup. His mount ran second to The Quack but his handling of it was appreciated by knowledgeable observers.

At a time when the horse was every man's mode of transport and the skill of a professional jockey had to be outstanding to set him apart from his fellows, Hales was sought by the richest owners in Australia. For James Wilson, master of the powerful St Alban's (Geelong) stable and stud, Hales won the Victorian Derby and Oaks on the filly Briseis, and for W. A. Long [q.v.] won the 1880 Australian Jockey Club Derby, the Victorian Derby and the Melbourne Cup on the unbeaten Grand Flaneur. He also rode for E. De Mestre [q.v.], but it was association with James White [q.v.] of Kirkham stud, New South Wales, that won him repute as 'the [Fred] Archer of Australia'. Chiefly on White's horses, notably Abercorn, he won three Sydney Cups, six Australian Jockey Club Derbys and seven St Legers, seven Victoria Derbys and ten St Legers, and six Australasian Champion Cups. In 1872-94 from 1678 mounts he won 496 races, had 332 seconds and 195 thirds, the prize money totalling £336,680. Al-

though corruption was then rife in Australian racing he preferred to rely on his skill. Perhaps his best tribute came from the bookmaker, Joe Thompson [q.v.], who often suffered from this skill: 'I never saw Hales lose a race once he had it won, and that is more than I can say of any other jockey I have ever seen'.

Hales held an interest in Milby station on the Lachlan River in 1883-88 and bred horses at Haleswood, his 600-acre property near Tallangatta, Victoria. He died aged 54 at Moonee Ponds on 26 October 1901, predeceased by his first wife Harriet Amelia Blackler, and survived by his second, Frances Selina Coles; they had no children.

A. Sutherland et al, *Victoria and its metropolis,* 2 (Melb, 1888); N. Gould, *The magic of sport* (Lond, 1909); D. M. Barrie, *The Australian bloodhorse* (Syd, 1956); M. Cavanough and M. Davies, *Cup Day* (Melb, 1960).

MAURICE CAVANOUGH

HALFEY, JOHN (1825-1889), businessman and politician, was born on 16 September 1825 at Southport, Lancashire, England, son of John Halfey, boarding-house keeper, and his wife Sarah, née Nixson. On 21 February 1849 at Gretna Green he married Elizabeth Veach, servant at a Southport inn. They lived in northern England for some months and a daughter was born at Penrith early in 1850. About August Halfey left his wife and some time after February 1851 migrated to Victoria, apparently under the name of his brother-in-law, Richard Johnson. On the goldfields near Bendigo he was eminently successful. By 1855 Halfey had resumed his own name and settled in Melbourne with a substantial capital to follow commercial pursuits. Early in 1860 his wife filed a petition for divorce in England and after an undefended suit obtained the dissolution of their marriage in 1862. On 14 February 1863 at Geelong, three months after the decree was made absolute in England, Halfey married Annie, daughter of John Lane, master mariner, and his wife Lucy, née Ward.

For some years after 1861 Halfey served on the Kew Municipal Council and was second mayor in 1862-63. In 1864 he was elected for Sandhurst to the Legislative Assembly but was soundly defeated in 1868. In that year and 1870 he failed to win a seat for Southern Province in the Legislative Council and in 1871 for Richmond in the assembly. He was active in parliament only on mining questions and in advocating a strong protective tariff. He was appointed official assignee of insolvent estates in January 1872 and while in office also became official liquidator in May and commissioner of the Supreme Court in November. He resigned these posts in September 1884 to stand for the Legislative Council, but was unsuccessful then and in September 1888.

Halfey had many mining interests especially around Bendigo, valuable holdings in such firms as the Australian Alliance Assurance Co. and the Colonial Bank and was a prominent director of many important companies. In 1871 he had joined a syndicate which acquired the Melbourne Newspaper Co. Ltd, and for many years was chief partner of S. V. Winter [q.v.] in managing the *Herald* newspaper. By 1886 its circulation was over 25,000 copies daily. On 4 January 1889 Halfey died while working at the *Herald* office in Little Collins Street. His estate was valued for probate at over £190,000 with assets evenly divided between city property and company shares. His wife, by whom he had three sons and two daughters, left their home, Ordsall, Kew, went to England and died in 1909. She was buried beside Halfey in the Anglican section of the Boroondara cemetery where their grave was reputed to have the tallest monument.

H. M. Humphreys (ed), *Men of the time in Australia: Victorian series*, 1st ed (Melb, 1878); *Bendigo Advertiser*, 1 Nov 1864; *Herald* (Melb), 4 Jan 1889; *Argus*, 5 Jan 1889; family information.   ROBERT A. JOHNSON

HALFORD, GEORGE BRITTON (1824-1910), professor, was born on 26 November 1824 at Petworth, Sussex, England, the second son of James Halford, merchant of Haverstock Hill near London, and his wife Nancy, née Gadd. Privately educated, he studied medicine at St George's Hospital, London (M.R.C.S., 1852; L.S.A., 1854), and obtained the M.D. at St Andrews in 1854. He became a member of the Royal College of Physicians in 1859 and a fellow in July 1870 but was never formally admitted. In 1850 he had been house surgeon at the Westminster Hospital and in 1856 senior house surgeon to the Liverpool Royal Infirmary and Lunatic Asylum. He was also honorary surgeon to the Bridgnorth Infirmary and in 1857 physician to the Royal Hospital for Diseases of the Chest, London; he also had a private practice. In October he was appointed lecturer in anatomy at the Grosvenor Place School of Medicine adjoining St George's Hospital. There he investigated the physiology of the action and sounds of the heart in animals, birds and man, a work of first-rate importance.

In 1862 planning for the medical school at the University of Melbourne was well advanced and lectures to first-year students had begun under John Macadam [q.v.]. Professors James Paget and Richard Owen were invited to select a suitable candidate for the first chair of anatomy, physiology and pathology. Assisted by Sir Redmond Barry [q.v.] then in London, they chose Halford who had worked with Owen on the heart and whom Paget described as 'one of the most distinguished experimental physiologists of the day. His name would give distinction to any University'. Halford's appointment was endorsed and he gave up his practice to collect specimens for a museum and books for a library, for which the Council of the University of Melbourne had sent him £500. With his wife and family he left England on 6 September in the *Agincourt* and arrived at Melbourne on 23 December.

Halford lived at first in a rented house in Madeline Street, Carlton, and until the building for the medical school was completed in May 1864 held his lectures and practical classes in anatomy and physiology in the converted coach-house of his private residence in May 1863. In that year he was admitted M.D. (*ad eund.*) in the University of Melbourne. The curriculum for the medical course had been prepared by A. C. Brownless [q.v.] and the Medical School Committee before Halford arrived. At the professorial board he protested against the poor scientific content of the first year, notably the absence of natural philosophy. For seven years he was the only full-time lecturer in the medical school and the sole lecturer in anatomy for which he was given a demonstrator in 1869. As well as teaching in three rapidly expanding disciplines Halford was examiner in French for matriculation and arts students. In 1871, as president of the professorial board, he fired an early shot in the long battle over the admission of women students by informing the council that he proposed to allow women who passed the relevant examinations to sign the matriculation book. This plan was quickly stopped by the council and women were not admitted to the university until 1880. Halford served on the council of the Royal Society of Victoria in 1864-67 and 1871 and was vice-president in 1868 and 1870.

In 1876 the faculty of medicine was established and took over administration of courses from the Medical School Committee. Halford was elected dean and held office until 1886 and again in 1890-96. In 1880 he went on leave to England for a year to inspect and work in departments of physiology. On his return he presented plans to the council for expansion of the physiology laboratories and division of his chair so that he would be responsible only for physiology; the proposals were accepted and in 1882 Halford became professor of physiology and Harry Brookes Allen professor of anatomy. From 3 students in 1862 the school had 180 by 1882 and 240 by 1896.

At 72 Halford applied for extended leave but although appointed for life he had no provision for a pension and was placed on half-pay and given leave. He retired to Inverloch, Gippsland, and his health improved after a visit to England. His place in the university was taken by Charles James Martin, who was appointed lecturer and later acting-professor. When Martin resigned in 1903 the council offered to pay Halford his half-salary for life if he resigned the chair. He agreed and W. A. Osborne was appointed professor of physiology. Deductions from both Martin's and Osborne's salaries were made to pay Halford's pension.

Halford arrived in Melbourne with an enviable record as a research worker. Had he remained in England he would have become an international figure. Instead he made a name for himself as a teacher in Melbourne and founded a tradition which was followed by his successors. Certainly he hoped to continue the work on the heart but his teaching burden was too great and the university had no money for research. The high repute of the Melbourne Medical School was made at the expense of his own. His later researches damaged rather than added to his record. In trifling arguments on comparative anatomy he favoured Richard Owen against T. H. Huxley [q.v.] and like many contemporaries disagreed with Charles Darwin [q.v.]. In experiments with snake venom he pursued with fervour the ammonia treatment of snakebite but, although it did not become the universal antidote that he hoped, he was honest enough to declare that his ideas were wrong. Of some thirty papers and pamphlets, his most important were published in London before he came to Melbourne. The best, *The action and sounds of the Heart; a physiological essay* (London, 1860), deserves reprinting.

At Hanover Square, London, in 1857 Halford had married Louisa Henrietta, eldest daughter of the late Thomas Millar; they had twelve children. He died at Inverloch on 27 May 1910, survived by his widow, six sons and three daughters. He was buried in the Inverloch cemetery. By then he had been forgotten, and no substantial obituary appeared in the journals. His family established the Halford Oration in his memory in 1928. In 1928-47 the lectures were delivered at the Institute of Anatomy, Canberra, but in 1948 by agreement with the family the fund was transferred to the Uni-

versity of Melbourne and the orations have since been delivered in Melbourne.

Univ Melb Medical School Jubilee (Melb, 1914); W. A. Osborne, 'George Britton Halford, his life and work', MJA, Jan 1929; R. R. Stawell, 'The foundation of a medical school and the progress of medical education', MJA, 3 Jan 1931; A. L. Kenny, 'Halford the man', MJA, 1 Feb 1941; *Truth* (Melb), 11 June 1910; K. F. Russell, History of the Melbourne Medical School (held by author); Council minutes, medical school letters and faculty of medicine minutes (Univ Melb Archives).

K. F. RUSSELL

HALL, BENJAMIN (1837-1865), bushranger, was born in February 1837 at Breeza, Liverpool Plains, son of Benjamin Hall and his wife Elizabeth; both parents were ex-convicts. He became a stockman and with John Macguire leased a run, Sandy Creek, near Wheogo. On 29 February 1856 at Bathurst he married according to Roman Catholic rites Bridget Walsh of Wheogo. Her sister became Frank Gardiner's [q.v.] mistress. About 1860 his wife left him taking their infant son. In April 1862 he was arrested for armed robbery at a race meeting on the orders of Sir Frederick Pottinger [q.v.]. He was acquitted but soon afterwards detained for his share in the Eugowra gold escort robbery. He was not committed for trial but on his return to Sandy Creek found most of his stock dead and his home burnt down. Embittered, Hall joined John Gilbert [q.v.] and became leader of a gang of bushrangers.

Hall was probably the most efficient of the bushranger leaders. His men were well armed and superbly mounted, often on stolen race-horses which easily outpaced the police nags. Some of their holdups seem designed only to defy the police: on their daredevil raid on Bathurst in October 1863 they took little loot and at Canowindra they offered food, drink and festivity to all for three days, but drank little themselves and left the town empty-handed. On 24 October in a raid on Henry Keightley's homestead at Dunn's Plains Burke was shot. Hall prevented Vane from shooting Keightley in revenge and accepted the £500 ransom procured by Mrs Keightley. Vane surrendered and in November O'Meally was shot. While Gilbert visited Victoria, Hall was joined by 'The Old Man' (James Mount) and Dunleavy, neither of whom lasted long. Gilbert returned and John Dunn joined the gang. In 1864 they concentrated on the Sydney-Melbourne Road south of Goulburn. On 15 November they held the road near Jugiong and robbed some sixty travellers; while holding up the Gundagai-Yass mail Gilbert shot Sergeant Parry. On 27 January 1865 Constable Nelson was shot at Collector by Dunn. In April the Felons Apprehension Act outlawed bushrangers and made it a felony to harbour them. Their only safety was to keep on the move. Hall with £1000 on his head decided to quit but was betrayed. On 5 May he was ambushed and shot by the police near Goobang Creek on the Lachlan plain. His body, riddled with gunshot wounds, was buried in the cemetery at Forbes. His funeral was 'rather numerously attended' for his reckless courage, courtesy to women, humour and hatred of informers had won him a sympathy not shared by his more bloodthirsty colleagues.

Sydney Mail, 30 July, 20 Aug 1864, 20 May 1865; *Empire* (Syd), 8 May 1865; *Illustrated Sydney News*, 16 May 1865; G. C. Richardson (ed), History of the Richardsons of Rossford and Rich Hill (extract from Professor J. J. Auchmuty, Univ Newcastle).

EDGAR F. PENZIG

HALL, GEORGE WILSON (1836-1916), trade unionist, journalist and politician, was born at Brighton, England, where his father was an agent for the British and Foreign Bible Society. He arrived in Melbourne in 1853 and later became a compositor. In 1873 he was secretary of the Melbourne Typographical Society and editor of its *Australasian Typographical Journal*. Unable to win worthwhile support and continually involved in petty disputes with employers, the society tried to improve its bargaining power through collective action with other workers. In July 1874 Hall called an inaugural meeting of the Trades and Labor Council. Though it failed to win major objectives and by 1875 was almost defunct, Hall as its secretary gained some prominence in October by organizing a public meeting to protest against the gaoling of two tanners at Castlemaine. He also seconded a motion by Thomas Bent [q.v.] which called for a system of arbitration. The government seemed prepared to discuss proposals for courts of conciliation but nothing was achieved.

In 1878 Hall left his union post to become editor-proprietor of the *Mansfield Guardian*. A few months later when the Kelly [q.v.] gang shot three police from Mansfield, Hall published a pamphlet, *The Kelly Gang or The Outlaws of the Wombat Ranges* (Mansfield, 1879). Next year he moved to Benalla and covered the capture of the Kellys at Glenrowan for the Melbourne *Argus* and his own *Benalla Standard*. Police handling of the Kellys led Hall to agitate for an inquiry into the police force which in 1881 was set up with Hall as a commissioner.

Hall was elected for the Moira seat in the Legislative Assembly in July 1880. He had long been concerned at the prevalence of sweating in the printing industry and gave influential support to the printers' public campaign for factory reform. In May 1883, at the request of W. C. Smith [q.v.], Hall joined the enlarged royal commission on shop employees and with officials of the Typographical Society lobbied for new legislation. Although active in parliament Hall held no portfolio but was a whip for the Service-Berry, Munro [qq.v.] and Shiels ministries. He was also a staunch advocate for temperance.

From about 1886 Hall was a leader of the country section of the Liberal-protectionists in the Deakin-Gillies [q.v.] coalition. In 1887-88 Hall held that more was to be gained by staying with the government than by opposition but at the 1889 election he announced his breakaway and, backed by the Victorian Farmers' Protection Association, won the new seat of Shepparton and Euroa. Although he did not always maintain an independent position he was prominent in exacting budgetary concessions from the government in 1889 on behalf of farmers. He lost his seat in 1891 and went on an official lecture tour of England to attract migrants to Victoria. After attempting in vain to re-enter parliament in 1894 and 1897 he retired from public life. He was married first to Marian Burton, second to Mary Juliet Worthington and third to Mary Hughes. He died in Melbourne on 21 September 1916 aged 80, survived by his widow and by three sons of the first marriage; two children of the second marriage predeceased him.

R. T. Fitzgerald, *The printers of Melbourne; the history of a union* (Melb, 1967); *Benalla Standard*, 29 Sept 1916; *Mansfield Courier*, 30 Sept 1916; M. G. Finlayson, Groups in Victorian politics, 1889-1894 (M.A. thesis, Univ Melb, 1964).

R. T. FITZGERALD

HALL, HAYDEN HEZEKIAH (b. 1825), merchant and mail contractor, was born on 27 August 1825 in Hartford, Connecticut, United States of America, son of Elisha Hall. At 15 he entered Canandaigua College and was later apprenticed to an uncle who had steam-engine works in New York. About 1846 he began building steamers on Lake Ontario, in 1848-50 promoted shipping in China and in 1852 ran steamers among the Philippine Islands. On 23 March 1854 he arrived at Sydney in his *General Urbistonolo*; when no buyer offered, he renamed her *Ben Bolt* for the Hunter River trade. In 1855 as 'the handsome American' he rented James Paterson's wharf and store at Morpeth. Declared bankrupt in December, he was discharged on 8 March 1856 and left for New York where on 27 January 1857 at a Baptist Church he married Rachel, née Cole. In September 1857 he opened the 'American Stores' in West Maitland, but on 11 December 1862 was again declared bankrupt; released next March he returned to America.

In 1864 Hall settled in Sydney as a partner of Samuel Hebblewhite & Co. He floated the Mineral Oil Co. to manufacture kerosene from Hartley shale and persuaded Ebenezer Vickery [q.v.] that his Illawarra land would yield oil. Hall left Sydney in July 1866 to have Vickery's shale samples tested at Yale University but the results were negative. On 1 November Hebblewhite & Co. went bankrupt: Hall severed the partnership and returned to Sydney in February 1867; after litigation the estate was released in May.

In December 1866 Hall was appointed United States commercial agent in Sydney. He reported to the secretary of state that earlier consuls had stood in bad repute with the New South Wales government 'owing to their ungentlemanly conduct'. In 1867 he encouraged the migration to California of some 300 labourers and their families by issuing under his official seal worthless certificates of employment on the Central Pacific Railroad. The migrants' destitute condition on arrival brought inquiries in Washington and London, and Henry Parkes [q.v.] published a caution in the *Government Gazette*, 21 July 1868. In reply to Governor Belmore, Hall fulsomely explained the 'stigma that now rests on me'.

In 1868-69 Hall failed to interest three American companies in his 'favourite idea' of a steamship line from Sydney to San Francisco. On 6 January 1870 he signed a mail contract with the New Zealand government and chartered three ships. Competition and lack of a New South Wales subsidy forced him in September 1871 to abandon the project and on 30 November he was again declared bankrupt. Next January he sought in vain a United States subsidy, mentioning his 'past services in opening up the Pacific by a mail line . . . and holding it at great loss'. For some months after February 1872 he assumed the title of 'United States Consul' but was repudiated by Washington. In May his estate was released and on 19 November Hall tendered privately to the New South Wales and New Zealand governments for a permanent monthly mail service with passengers between Sydney and San Francisco. In 1873 the contract was signed in London,

with Hall as managing director of the Australasian and American Mail Steam Ship Co., although some members of the Legislative Assembly claimed that Parkes had been bribed into a dubious contract. The first chartered steamer left Sydney on 13 January 1874 but in June the company's San Francisco agents arrested three of its ships for debt. In haste Hall left Sydney on 1 August but six weeks later the company and his own estate were sequestrated. He failed to raise funds in London and advised the colonial governments on 24 February 1875 that his company could not pay the penalties for non-fulfilment. In April he was employed by the Pacific Mail Steamship Co. of New York, which took over the mail contract. In September he returned to Sydney and next May his private estate was released. The company's affairs were never settled. Hall left Sydney in March 1876. For some years he promoted the building of a railway and canal in Mexico. In the 1880s his name was in New York directories as 'manager' and later 'president' of unspecified companies, and living in Brooklyn and New Hamburg. His last known address was a New York office in 1888.

V&P (LA NSW), 1868-69, 2, 111, 1870-71, 67, 1873-74, 2, 963, 1875, 3, 1; SMH, 16, 17, 27 Oct 1873; *Town and Country J*, 6 June 1874; *New York Times*, 30 Dec 1879; Dispatches from U.S. consuls in Sydney, 1836-1906, vols 6-7 (ML, NL); Parkes letters (ML); Bankruptcy papers (ML); information from New York Gen and Biog Soc.   RUTH TEALE

HALL, THOMAS SIMPSON (1808-1870), pastoralist, was born on 19 August 1808 at Bungool on the Hawkesbury River, son of George Hall and his wife Mary, née Smith. His parents arrived in the *Coromandel* in 1802 with four children, as members of a small group of Presbyterian immigrants who settled on the Hawkesbury and founded at Ebenezer the chapel which in 1972 is the oldest church on the mainland of Australia. George Hall, whose family had been tenant farmers of the dukes of Northumberland, built Percy Place in Windsor, became a substantial farmer and encouraged his sons to search for new grazing land. They were among the first settlers in the Upper Hunter district and selected land in biblical fashion with Archibald Bell [q.v.] of Richmond. By 1828 the Hall family held 4700 acres at Dartbrook and at Gungal and employed nine convicts, eight of them Protestant.

Thomas managed the Dartbrook property for the family partnership and later inherited it. He bred station horses, Durham cattle and merino sheep. He responded to the urgent need for good cattle-dogs and imported a pair of wall-eyed blue 'merles', a cross between the Scottish collie and Italian greyhound. In 1840 he produced a merle-dingo cross that combined the speed and silence of the dingo with the collie's intelligent obedience. 'Hall's Heelers' became famous among Hunter Valley cattle-men and were in much demand for station work. After 1870 a pair were taken to Sydney where the breed was improved, chiefly by the Bagust brothers, who 'bred a lot and drowned a lot' until by 1890 the blue cattle-dog bred true.

By 1850 the Hall brothers had over 200,000 acres in the Maranoa district of Queensland and over 270,000 acres in New England and the Liverpool Plains and by 1870 their estates included Gundibri, Nandowra and St Heliers in the Upper Hunter, and leaseholds of 100,000 acres in the Gwydir district, 525,000 acres in New England and 437 square miles in Queensland. Despite his far-ranging pastoral interests, T. S. Hall was an efficient magistrate, a member of the first Scone District Council and on the committee of the Scone Benevolent Association. His support for the Presbyterian Church was generous and sustained. He retained strong links with his birthplace, contributed to the building of the Windsor School of Arts and in 1856 presided at the first meeting of the Windsor Literary Society. He died at Dartbrook House on 28 May 1870 and was buried in Dartbrook private cemetery. He was survived by his wife Anne, née McGinnis, whom he married on 1 July 1835, and by eight daughters.

J. Steele, *Early days of Windsor* (Syd, 1916); *Sydney Mail*, 13 Apr 1938; biographies of Hawkesbury pioneers (held by R. M. Arndell, Pitt Town, NSW).   NANCY GRAY

HALL, WILLIAM SHAKESPEARE (1825-1895), J.P., explorer, pastoralist and pearler, was born on 25 December 1825 in London and baptized at St Mary's Church of England, Lambeth, on 6 May 1827, the second son of Henry Edward Hall (1790-1859), squire of Shakerstone Manor, Leicestershire, and his wife Sarah Theodosia (1793-1858), née Branson. His parents' families both claimed connexions with the poet. He sailed for Western Australia with his parents, two brothers and three sisters in the *Protector*, chartered by his father and another settler, and reached Fremantle in February 1830. They safely landed many livestock, farming equipment, a 25-ton sloop and a jolly-boat, necessities and luxuries, and ten servants and apprentices. The value of this cargo en-

titled his father to a land grant of some 16,594 acres which was taken up at Mandurah. Unfortunately the land proved unsuitable. After several years of hardship in which their first house and all its contents were destroyed by fire and their sloop was wrecked on Hall's Bank, the family moved to Perth and later bought a partly-improved property at Wongong near Armadale.

Educated chiefly by Rev. J. B. Wittenoom [q.v.], Shakespeare Hall farmed at Wongong until 1852 when he went to the Victorian goldfields. After eight unsuccessful years he returned to Western Australia and joined the expedition under Francis Gregory [q.v.] which in 1861 explored the north-west. In 1863 for John Wellard, Hall took up the first sheep station, Andover, in the Roebourne district. His early diary gives much insight into the toil and difficulty of pioneering. At that time the only communication with the south was by occasional sailing boats and the second settlers in the district were the Withnell family who arrived in April 1864. Like his father Hall was short in stature but had prodigious strength. By the end of his second year much of the station's development had been achieved and he turned to pearling with Malay and Aboriginal divers and later to business pursuits in Roebourne and Cossack where for some years he was chairman of the municipality. On a hot summer night on 11 February 1895 he had a heart attack while swimming in Cossack Creek and was drowned. An obituarist described him as 'one of the most brilliant, upright, honest and valued lives that has ever lived amongst us'. A wrought iron screen in the Roebourne Anglican Church and a tombstone at his grave in Cossack were erected 'as a mark of appreciation and respect by the North West Pioneers'.

On 2 November 1868 he had married Hannah Boyd (1849-1911), daughter of George Lazenby, architect, and his wife Mary Ann, née Wells. Three of their children survived infancy: Henry Ernest (1869-1941), Hannah Joy (1876-1960) and Harold Aubrey (1871-1963) who like his father and grandfather was highly knowledgeable of the Aboriginals, their customs and language, and was singularly successful in his relations with them.

A. R. Richardson, *Early memories of the great nor'-west* (Perth, 1909); W. S. Smart, *Mandurah and Pinjarrah* (Perth, 1956); A. Hasluck, *Thomas Peel of Swan River* (Melb, 1965); P. Hasluck, 'The first year in the north-west', *JRWAHS*, 1 (1929); H. A. Hall, A partial vocabulary of the Ngäloomä Aboriginal tribe (Univ NSW, Univ WA); W. S. Hall papers (Battye Lib, Perth, and held by author).

H. MARGARET WILSON

HALLEY, JACOB JOHN (1834-1910), Congregational minister, was born in London, son of Dr Robert Halley, classical tutor at Highbury College, and his wife Rebecca, née Sloman. His father, author of works on Nonconformity and sometime principal of New College, London, was of Perthshire farming origins and his mother a descendant of Rev. Henry Jacob, one of the first Independents. After schooling at Manchester, where his father was pastor of Mosley Street Chapel, Halley entered a warehouse. He was active in chapel affairs, especially the Juvenile Missionary Society, and at 17 was preaching at cottage services. 'He knows nothing', said his father, 'but his manner pleases people'. About 1855 on medical advice he migrated to Sydney where he joined a business firm, became a lay preacher and helped to form the Young Men's Christian Association. He later represented the firm in Yass and preached for the Methodists but was persuaded by Rev. J. L. Poore [q.v.] to enter the Congregational ministry. In 1857-59 Halley attended lectures at the University of Sydney but did not complete his degree, probably because of disagreement with his lecturers. He also worked as an evangelist at Newtown and helped to gather a congregation at Petersham.

At the request of a Lower Darling squatter Halley volunteered for bush missions and on 21 March 1860 was ordained and appointed to the district. In 'cabbage-tree hat, fly-veil, riding breeches, and high boots' he reached the station and was joined by his friend, Price Fletcher, a field naturalist who took him on expeditions. He covered his large parish by buggy, but exposure during flood conditions brought back his old complaints and he sought more settled work. He went to Melbourne but soon moved to Maryborough and opened preaching stations at the goldfields of Rodborough, Norwood, Amphitheatre and McCallum's Creek. In 1864 he succeeded Rev. A. Gosman [q.v.] at Ballarat and in 1872 moved to Williamstown. As secretary of the Congregational Union and Home Mission of Victoria in 1872-1909, Halley concentrated on conserving the principles of Independency and evangelism. He strengthened the denomination by his financial acumen and by building up home mission work. His own experience had impressed him with the importance of the 'jackaroo parson' and his recruits, many from itinerant Methodist backgrounds, included J. B. Gribble [q.v.], M. M. Whitton, James Dare and Daniel Gunson. Halley himself tirelessly visited the scattered stations by train and buggy, and lectured in the towns on such subjects as 'Naples, Vesuvius and Pompeii'. He was

chairman of the union in 1871-72 and 1908-09, attended the meetings of the Congregational Union of England and Wales at Manchester in 1881 and was a delegate to the International Congregational Council at Boston in 1899. He died suddenly on a tram in Melbourne on 19 January 1910 aged 75, survived by his wife Margaret, daughter of Rev. Richard Fletcher and sister of Rev. W. R. Fletcher [q.v.] whose biography he had edited in 1895. Of his three daughters, Gertrude became a medical inspector of schools in Tasmania and Ethel a missionary in Shanghai.

Of liberal Evangelical outlook and strong temperance views, Halley worked well with men of other religious backgrounds. His friend Dr L. D. Bevan described him as 'made on large lines . . . intelligent, large sympathied, well read, a man not thrusting himself into visibility and notice, but seen and recognized'.

A portrait by McCubbin is in the Congregational College of Victoria, Kew.

Mrs Halley et al, *Memorials of Rev. J. J. Halley* (Melb, nd); L. J. Bevan (ed), *The life and reminiscences of Llewelyn David Bevan* (Melb, 1920); E. M. MacQueen, *The story of a church* (Melb, 1966); *Argus*, 20 Jan 1910; *Vic Independent*, Feb 1910.   NIEL GUNSON

HALLIDAY, WILLIAM (1828-1892), pastoralist, was born at Dumfries, Scotland, son of William Halliday and his wife Margaret, née Harvey. He learnt sheep farming from his father. In 1852 at Dumfries he married Marion, née Irving, and migrated to Victoria where he worked for the Wilson brothers in the Wimmera. With James Richmond [q.v.] he acquired a run near St Arnaud where he became a shire councillor. He suffered little encroachment by selectors but disliked the Victorian land laws and in 1873 bought Brookong station in New South Wales, reputedly for £100,000. At great expense he ringbarked large areas and in 1876 opened a private telegraph line to Urana. Some weeks later when rain fell he bought by telegram 150,000 sheep in the depressed Victorian market and emerged from the drought with a profit. By 1889 he had 48,650 acres of leasehold and shore over 200,000 sheep. He also ran cattle and after 1887 grew wheat as a sideline.

Halliday allowed selectors water and stock forage in dry times and in 1888, after a trip to Britain, was paid the 'unique compliment' of a public dinner by the selectors. He was a liberal donor to the Presbyterian manse at Urana, the hospital, public school and School of Arts; he was also an active magistrate, president of the Urana turf club and vice-president of the cricket club. He subscribed £1000 to the Sudan expedition in 1885 and gave the refund to the Goodenough [q.v.] Royal Naval House in Sydney. On 31 August 1885 he was appointed to the Legislative Council; he attended regularly and took a house in Woollahra but was never an enthusiastic politician.

Halliday was an early and vigorous member of the Pastoralists' Union of New South Wales and took a firm stand against the Amalgamated Shearers' Union. In August 1888 he refused its demands to employ only union labour and when strikers picketed his woolshed, wired Sydney for forty Colt revolvers and called the police. After the Riot Act was read, nine shearers were arrested and on 19 October were tried at Wagga Wagga and sentenced to imprisonment. On 19 September 1890 in the maritime strike Halliday, complete with waistcoat, gloves and black topper, drove one of the wool drays under police escort from Darling Harbour through the unionists' ranks to Circular Quay where the Riot Act was read. He died at Quiraing, Woollahra, on 25 August 1892, predeceased by his wife and survived by a son and four daughters to whom he left £274,919.

W. G. Spence, *History of the A.W.U.* (Syd, 1911); W. A. Bayley (ed), *Billabidgee* (Urana, 1959); *Town and Country J*, 25 Aug 1888; SMH, 20 Sept 1890, 26 Aug 1892; *Bulletin*, 27 Sept 1890; *Pastoral Review*, 15 Sept 1892; *Wagga Express*, 27 Aug 1892; Labor Council of NSW records (ML).　　　　RUTH TEALE

HALLORAN, HENRY (1811-1893), civil servant and poet, was born on 6 April 1811 at Cape Town, son of Laurence Halloran [q.v.] and his wife Lydia (Laura) Anne, née Hall. After some years in England he went to Sydney with his mother in 1822. Educated at his father's school, in 1827 he became a clerk in the Survey Department. In 1841 he married Elizabeth Henrietta, daughter of Joseph Underwood [q.v.]. He became chief clerk and in 1859 supervised the merger of the Crown Lands Office with the Survey Department.

A close friend and correspondent of Henry Parkes [q.v.] Halloran in 1841 promised to subscribe to a volume of poetry that Parkes hoped to publish. From the 1840s Halloran's own verses were published in newspapers and magazines. Accepted in Sydney's literary circles, he encouraged young writers and was reputed to have found Henry Kendall [q.v.] a job in the Colonial Secretary's Department. 'A scholar as well as a poet', his work was admired by Daniel Deniehy [q.v.] who considered some of his verses 'remarkable for their classic grace' and 'manly gentleness', but believed that those 'connected with home affections . . . [gave] him the truest title to the rank of poet'. Halloran also made 'charming' translations from the Greek poems of Anacreon.

In February 1866 Parkes appointed him under-secretary in the Colonial Secretary's Department and in 1867 a justice of the peace. In 1870 he served on the board for opening tenders for pastoral runs. He undertook extra administrative duties and in 1867 and 1873 was a member of the commissions to make arrangements for welcoming the duke of Edinburgh and the public funeral of W. C. Wentworth [q.v.]. His contemporaries credited Halloran with a remarkable organizing ability. He retired on a pension in 1878 and was made a C.M.G. Between 1875 and 1880 he was a New South Wales commissioner for exhibitions in Philadelphia, Melbourne, Paris and Sydney. Parkes would not find Halloran any additional work after 1878. He set up as a land agent but was unhappy and soon retired to write poetry at his home, Mowbray, Ashfield. Inclined to be querulous, he disputed for years with the government over compensation for land resumed at Ashfield.

In 1887 he published *Poems, Odes and Songs*, dedicated to Lady Carrington. Much of his later poetry was written for special occasions and revealed his loyalty to the throne. These poems were unimaginative and he was 'quite unable to break free of conventions'. He published *A Few Love Rhymes of a Married Life* (1890) but also enjoyed boxing and was a lieutenant in the volunteer cavalry. He died on 19 May 1893 at Ashfield and was buried in St John's Church of England cemetery. He was survived by four sons and four daughters of his first wife (d. 1889) and by his second wife Julia Margaret (Bella), née Guerin, and their eight-month-old son. Bella was the first woman graduate of the University of Melbourne (M.A., 1885) and contributed to magazines and journals. Halloran's estate was valued at £2700.

G. B. Barton (ed), *The poets and prose writers of New South Wales* (Syd, 1866); V&P (LA NSW), 1872, 1, 666; SMH, 4 July 1887; *Town and Country J*, 20 May, 3 June 1893; Parkes letters (ML); MS and printed cats under H. Halloran (ML).　　　　BRIAN DICKEY

HALY, CHARLES ROBERT (1816-1892), pastoralist, parliamentarian and public servant, was born on 11 April 1816 at Amboise, France, son of Colonel Charles William Haly and his wife Ann, née Hutchings. His father's Irish lineage was documented over 800 years. The family moved to Newfoundland. In 1838 Charles and his brother William sailed from Plymouth in the *James Pattison* and arrived at Sydney in December. They settled first on the Hunter River but soon moved to the Gwydir River where they assembled a large party of men and sheep and went north to the Logan district. By 1842 they were seeking land in the Burnett district and were listed in 1846 as the holders of Taabinga, a sheep run of 305 square miles. William returned to England in 1859 and died in 1861.

Unlike many other squatters Charles soon became aware of the dangers in over-exploiting land and as one of the first to detect intestinal worms in sheep he advocated remedial measures. In 1853 at Tamrookum in the Logan district he married Rosa Harpur. His homestead at Taabinga reflected spacious ideas, with some walls of two-foot-thick sandstone blocks and the interior woodwork in cedar, both produced on his property. A keen lover of good horseflesh, he imported Arab and English sires and became widely known for the quality of his horses.

In 1860 Haly was elected for the Burnett to the first Queensland Legislative Assembly. With a new forum for advocating protection of the land, he continually recommended the preservation of indigenous grasses and the use of steam-ploughs and irrigation. He supported measures to deal with stock diseases and for supplying the capital with water from the Upper Brisbane River basin, and secured the abolition of the salt duty. Though never outstanding as a parliamentarian he won wide respect for his honesty and consistency; according to the *Brisbane Courier*, he would vote even against his own interests if the proposal were for the general good. Always cheerful and hearty, he was welcome everywhere. He held his Burnett seat until 1863 and again in 1865-67 and 1869-71, and in 1876-78 he represented Leichhardt.

Despite his efforts he experienced much trouble through diseases in his sheep and the rapid spread of speargrass. Forced to sell Taabinga, he became police magistrate at Dalby on 26 April 1882 and on 1 January 1891 also clerk of Petty Sessions. On 26 August 1892 he died in office, survived by eleven of his fourteen children.

J. E. Murphy and E. W. Easton, *Wilderness to wealth* (Nanango, 1950); A. A. Morrison, 'Some lesser members of parliament in Queensland', JRQHS, 6 (1959-61); *Queenslander*, 3 Sept 1892; Register of officers 1870-1910, COL 429 (QA).   A. A. MORRISON
                                        M. CARTER

HAM, THOMAS (1821-1870), engraver, lithographer and publisher, THEOPHILUS JOB (1828-1892) and CORNELIUS JOB (1837-1909), were sons of Rev. John Ham and his wife Ann Job, née Tonkin. Thomas was born on 17 February 1821 at Teignmouth, Devon, England, Theophilus on 9 July 1828 at Bilston, Staffordshire, and Cornelius on 13 January 1837 at Birmingham. The family arrived at Melbourne in the *Dublin* on 13 December 1842, intending to go to Sydney but Melbourne Baptists persuaded John Ham to stay and in July 1843 he became the first minister of the Collins Street Baptist Church. In August 1847 he resigned to go to the Bathurst Street Church in Sydney.

Thomas had trained as an engraver and in 1843 was commissioned to engrave the corporation seal for the Town of Melbourne. With his business in Collins Street, East Melbourne, he was sole contractor for engravings and lithography for the government and designed and engraved currency notes for various banks. He also took up land with another brother, Jabez, on the River Plenty in 1845 and in 1846-47 at Lalbert in the Wimmera district. In 1847 he published a map showing the squatting districts of 'Australia Felix'; it ran to six editions in 1851-61. Other maps published in 1849-54 included *Melbourne and Geelong Districts* (1849), *Map of the Suburban Lands of the City of Melbourne* (1852) and *Plan of the City of Melbourne* (1854). Ham lithographed the first Victorian stamps issued in January 1850: 1,800,000 'Half-length' stamps for 1d., 2d. and 3d. values, and also lithographed fifty brass cancelling-seals. In 1852 he engraved the plate for the 2d. 'Queen-on-Throne' stamps and printed 500,000 direct from the plate.

From July 1850 to August 1852 Thomas, Theophilus and Jabez jointly published the *Illustrated Australian Magazine*, the first of its kind in Australia. Thomas engraved and lithographed the maps and plates, many of them drawn by W. Strutt [q.v.]. *Ham's five views of the gold fields of Mount Alexander and Ballarat*, drawn by D. Tulloch, was engraved and published by Thomas in 1852, followed in 1854 by *The Diggers Portfolio* and *The Gold Diggers Portfolio*, each with plates. In 1853 as a land and commission agent Thomas had opened the Central Land Office at 35 Swanston Street, and in 1855 was joined by Cornelius in what became the long-standing firm of C. J. & T. Ham. Thomas also opened a quartz works at Taradale in 1855 but in December 1857 joined the Victorian Geological Survey Office where he had charge of the lithography of sale plans. Four lithographs were printed from stone at lectures given by him in December 1859 and April 1860. Later that year he transferred the agency business to Cornelius and moved to Brisbane, where he was lithographer in the Survey Office from 1860 and chief engraver in 1866-70. With his brother-in-law, William Knight, he formed Thomas Ham & Co., general engravers, lithographic artists, printers and photographers, but the firm was dissolved in November 1868. With Knight, John Collings and W. S. Warren, Thomas then developed sugar plantations on the Albert River and later bought a farm at Redcliffe. He lithographed and published several maps in Queensland, including *Atlas of the Colony of Queensland* (c. 1868), and engraved maps for the government. He died at Brisbane on 10 March 1870. On 18 September 1851 in Melbourne he had married Mary Jull, daughter of John Collings. Of their five sons and four daughters, Alice contributed poems to many journals and her collected verse, *Coward or Hero*, was published in Brisbane in 1928.

Theophilus worked with Thomas on the River Plenty and at Lalbert and then on the *Illustrated Australian Magazine*. After 1852 he started his own commission agency and later became a timber merchant. In 1867 as a partner he joined the firm of C. J. & T. Ham. On 6 October 1868 he married Elizabeth, daughter of William Perry of Paddington, Sydney. She died in 1874 aged 28, leaving a son and a daughter. Theophilus died on 29 August 1892 at Richmond and was buried in the Anglican section of the Melbourne general cemetery. His estate was valued at £56,959.

Cornelius was educated at private schools in Melbourne and Sydney. In 1852 he became a clerk with Henry and John Cooke, Melbourne merchants who were first proprietors of the Melbourne *Age*. Henry Cooke married Amelia Ham, one of their three sisters. Cornelius joined Thomas in the firm of C. J. & T. Ham where he became famous as an auctioneer. In 1870 he was elected to the Melbourne City Council and in 1879-1909 was alderman for La Trobe ward. As mayor in 1881-82 he helped to establish the Working Men's College and for many years was on its council. He served in the royal commissions on the International Exhibition in 1880-81 and on public instruction in 1881, represented Melbourne Province in the Legislative Council in 1882-1904 and was minister without office in the Munro [q.v.] ministry from November 1890 to February 1892. He was a director of the Metropolitan Gas Co., chairman of the London and Lancashire Fire Insurance Co. and of the Citizens' Life Assurance Co. and a cofounder of the Australian Deposit and Mortgage Bank which suspended payment

in 1892. He was an active temperance worker and president of the Young Men's Christian Association. In the Baptist Church he served on the Home Mission Committee in 1871, was president of the Union in 1884-85 and one of the first trustees of its fund. Predeceased by his wife Hattie White, sister of G. R. Latham, United States consul, whom he had married at Carlton in 1868, he died on 10 December 1909. He left an estate worth £64,179 to three sons and six daughters.

J. Smith (ed), *Cyclopedia of Victoria*, 1 (Melb, 1903); C. L. Pack, *Victoria, the half-length portraits* (New York, 1923); F. J. Wilkin, *Baptists in Victoria . . . 1838-1938* (Melb, 1939); J. W. Collings, *Thomas Ham* (Melb, 1943); J. R. W. Purves, *Half lengths of Victoria* (Lond, 1953); F. G. A. Barnard, 'Some early Victorian maps', *VHM*, 6 (1917); *Melb Bulletin*, 18 Nov 1881, 1 Dec 1882; *Table Talk*, 26 Dec 1889, 27 Jan 1893; *Australasian*, 3, 17 Sept 1892, 25 Jan 1896, 3 Nov 1900, 18 Dec 1909; *Argus*, 11 Dec 1902, 11 Dec 1909.

IAN F. McLAREN

HAMILTON, EDWARD WILLIAM TERRICK (1809-1898), pastoralist and company director, was born on 26 November 1809 at Loughton, Essex, England, son of Rev. Anthony Hamilton (1778-1851) and his wife Charity, née Farquhar. His elder brother, Walter Kerr, was bishop of Salisbury in 1854-69. Edward was educated at Eton and Trinity College, Cambridge (B.A., 1832; M.A., 1835), and a fellow in 1834-42. He was admitted to the Inner Temple on 2 November 1832, but later decided to abandon law to follow 'a pastoral life' in New South Wales, hoping thereby to make enough money to enable him to return to England and live as a leisured gentleman.

In August 1839 he joined his brother, Captain H. G. Hamilton, R.N., and a friend, George Clive, in buying the pastoral property, Collaroy, near Cassilis, from W. S. Davidson [q.v.]. Edward, who was junior to Clive in the venture, went out to New South Wales to manage the property, arriving with his brother in February 1840. For almost fifteen years Hamilton managed Collaroy, along with other properties that he acquired. The partnership, although stormy, was financially successful after many vicissitudes. In January 1855 he returned to England, and the partnership was angrily dissolved.

From the beginning Hamilton had moved in the same colonial circles as the Macarthurs, Deas Thomson [qq.v.] and their fellows. In July 1843 he was appointed one of the six unofficial nominees in the Legislative Council. He resigned in 1846, was reappointed in December 1848 and retired in 1850. He took little part in colonial politics and his most controversial public act was to castigate his fellow squatters because they opposed Gipps's proposed squatting regulations of 1844. In 1851-54 he was the first provost (chancellor) of the University of Sydney.

Hamilton was governor of the Australian Agricultural Co. from August 1857 to September 1898. He must be credited for most of the company's increased profits after 1857, not least because he chose capable subordinates. Hamilton retained other connexions with New South Wales: he became its representative agent in London in January 1863 and kept in touch with colonial acquaintances.

Hamilton had large intellectual powers and a high opinion of his abilities. Although not vindictive he was very argumentative. He was quick to portray himself as the victim of 'the treachery of false friends' and at times he wrote acid comments on colonial leaders with whom he associated. He was an Anglican whose views were often intolerant, and he never doubted his superiority over members of the middle class and the lower orders although his ideas were slightly 'liberalized' by his years in the colony. On 14 August 1844 he had married Ann, daughter of John Thacker, of Berkshire and New South Wales. In 1865-69 Hamilton represented Salisbury in the House of Commons and was sheriff of Berkshire in 1879. He died on 28 September 1898 at his home, Charters, Sunningdale, Berkshire, predeceased by his wife and survived by two sons and six daughters.

SMH, 15 Apr, 2 May 1844; Collaroy papers (ML); Macarthur papers (ML).

J. R. ROBERTSON

HAMILTON, JOHN (1834-1924), parliamentarian, company director and merchant, was born on 11 July 1834, at Hobart Town, the second son of William Hamilton and his wife Mary Anne Wilson, née Beaugarde. His parents had arrived in Van Diemen's Land in the Lindsays from Ireland on 23 June 1832. At 9 John was sent to the boarding school of Rev. John Burrowes [q.v.] at Brighton, and then to the Hobart Town Grammar School where he distinguished himself by winning the blue ribbon and medal for general attainments. This school became associated with the new Hutchins School, where he was enrolled in 1849. After leaving school he was apprenticed to Askin Morrison [q.v.], a successful merchant and shipowner. Hamilton worked first in the counting house on the New (Prince's)

Wharf and later was promoted to an administrative post. When Morrison retired in 1871 and transferred his business to James Macfarlane [q.v.] Hamilton continued with the new owner.

In Elizabeth Street, Hobart, his father had established William Hamilton & Sons, general importers, cabinet and chair manufacturers and undertakers, but when he retired in 1878 the business was discontinued. On the same site Hamilton set up the firm of John Hamilton & Co., merchants, shipping, commission and insurance agents. He was also interested in the timber industry and in 1887 owned sawmills at Surges Bay on the Huon River. He represented Glenorchy in the House of Assembly from 20 June 1887 until 3 March 1903. He became a justice of the peace on 17 February 1885 and was reappointed on 4 May 1895. He was vice-president of the Chamber of Commerce in 1889 and president in 1892. In that year he was a local commissioner for the Chicago Exhibition and World Fair. From March 1888 to March 1892 he was manager of the Cascade Brewery Co. in Hobart, and acted as an adviser in 1893. He was a director of the Hobart Gas Co. and of the Tasmanian Steam Navigation Co. which later merged with the Union Steamship Co. of New Zealand. He was an honoured member of the Church of England synod for many years, first representing the parish of Glenorchy and later of Battery Point. In January 1887 he proposed the building of a deanery on land adjoining St David's Cathedral; by September it was ready for occupation. At St Luke's Church, Richmond, on 22 June 1861 he had married Ellen Morgan.

In 1924 Hamilton was believed to be the oldest living member of the Masonic fraternity in Australia. He had been grand secretary for many years, held the rank of deputy past master of the order and was chairman of directors of the Masonic Hall Co. while their hall was built in Murray Street. He died at his home in 95 Montpelier Road on 17 August. After a service in St George's Church conducted by Bishop Hay, he was buried in Queenborough cemetery and later reinterred at Cornelian Bay cemetery. His descendants included many prominent medical practitioners.

W. R. Barrett, History of the Church of England in Tasmania (Hob, 1942); Mercury, 18, 20 Aug 1924; family papers.

E. R. PRETYMAN

HAMILTON, JOHN (1841-1916), politician, was born on 19 August 1841 in Melbourne, son of John Dinwoodie, saddler, and his wife Janet, née McFarlane. According to his own account, he was educated in Melbourne and by a private tutor in England, and then went to Rockhampton planning to enter the pastoral industry. Instead he was attracted in 1862 to the Calliope gold rush and in 1867 to Gympie where next year, as John Hamilton, he became a magistrate. He later claimed to have offered the New Zealand government one hundred picked men who had seen active service to fight in the Maori wars but was rejected because they ended in 1872. He also claimed to have been offered the commissionership of the Palmer diggings opened in 1873. Although not formally qualified, he practised as a doctor and in 1877 at the Hodgkinson gold rush in North Queensland was surgeon to the hospital. There he quarrelled interminably with the local warden and won damages of £150 from an editor who accused him of seducing a friend's daughter, but became popular enough to go into politics.

Elected for Gympie to the Legislative Assembly in 1878, Hamilton supported McIlwraith's [q.v.] Conservative party next year, and after leaving the Gympie district became a member for Cook in 1883. He and his running-mate, F. A. Cooper, were returned after a hectic election in which ballots were alleged to have been rigged in their favour at one or two mining camps. On appeal Cooper was unseated but Hamilton held his seat until 1904. He spoke consistently and often in favour of northern interests and supported the North Queensland separation movement, the use of Pacific Islanders in the canefields and a succession of Conservative leaders from McIlwraith to Philp. Appointed whip to the Griffith-McIlwraith coalition of 1890, he was an influential back-bencher but at times rebelled, leading a successful revolt in 1893 against the reduction of parliamentary salaries and supporting in 1899 the successful move to oust A. S. Cowley [q.v.], the ministerialist nominee, as Speaker. In 1902 Hamilton denounced the protector of Aborigines, Walter Edmund Roth, whom he accused of undue interference in the exploitation of a half-caste girl. He lost his post as government whip in 1903 when the Philp ministry was overthrown by a 'Lib-Lab' coalition.

Defeated by a Labor candidate for Cook in 1904, Hamilton lived quietly in retirement. After several weeks' illness he died unmarried on 7 December 1916 at the Brisbane hospital. Renowned in his earlier years as an all-round athlete, especially as boxer, swimmer and crack shot, he was respected by his contemporaries as 'a man's man'. As a goldfield doctor he was reputed to treat any down-and-out miner without fee but to thrash any malingerer who took advant-

age of his generosity. In the Legislative Assembly, busy with the minutiae of parliamentary work and increasingly dependent on its camaraderie, he seemed almost pathetic but was saved by his obvious delight in the cut and thrust of debate at its keenest and most aggressive.

V&P (LA Qld), 1879 (2nd S), 2, 1179, 1883-84, 449; PD (Qld), 1902; *Bulletin*, 8 May 1880; *Brisbane Courier*, 8 Dec 1916.

G. C. BOLTON

HAMILTON, SIR ROBERT GEORGE CROOKSHANK (1836-1895), civil servant and governor, was born on 30 August 1836 at Bressay, Shetland, Scotland, son of Rev. Zachary Macaulay Hamilton and his first wife Anne Irvine, née Crookshank. Educated at the Grammar School and at the University and King's College, Aberdeen (M.A., 1857; LL.D., 1885), he entered the War Office and was sent to the Crimea as a commissariat clerk. He returned in 1857 and worked in the Office of Works, and in 1861 became accountant to the Board of Education, then a rapidly expanding complex. In 1868 he published his *Book-keeping*, which ran to at least seven editions by 1899. In 1869 Hamilton was appointed to the yet more difficult post of accountant to the Board of Trade, where he reorganized the Board's financial department. In 1872 he became assistant secretary to Playfair's civil service inquiry commission, and in 1874 its secretary. In 1878 as accountant-general of the navy he simplified the naval estimates making them intelligible to the public. In 1879 he served on Carnarvon's commission on colonial defences, and in May 1882 he became permanent secretary to the Admiralty. After the Phoenix Park murders he was lent to the Irish administration and was permanently appointed under-secretary with a C.B. in April 1883. On 12 January 1884 he was made K.C.B. While in Ireland he became convinced of the advisability of Home Rule, and had some share in influencing both Earl Spencer and W. E. Gladstone. These sympathies probably caused his removal from the under-secretaryship in November 1886.

Hamilton was compensated by appointment as governor of Tasmania and took up his duties early in 1887. Unlike other governors he had no constitutional crises to face, though the Van Diemen's Land Bank failed in August 1891 and had to be wound up. The only ministries in his governorship were led by P. O. Fysh from March 1887 to August 1892 and Henry Dobson [q.v.] from August 1892 to 1894; he insisted on calling them prime ministers instead of premiers. He promoted public works, especially railways, and encouraged the investment of British capital in the colony. He also encouraged Federation : he presided over the meeting of the Federal Council of Australia at Hobart in 1887 and opened its second and third sessions in 1888 and 1889. He also opened the sixth Trades Union Congress in Hobart in 1889. The greatest contribution he and his second wife made was to the colony's cultural life. Soon after arrival he organized extensive celebrations for the Queen's jubilee, which included three balls, an address with 22,500 signatures and masses of jubilee cake handed to all and sundry. He was president of the Royal Society of Tasmania and actively supported the Australasian Association for the Advancement of Science. He helped to found the University of Tasmania and several technical schools, and opened many museums and art galleries. His wife formed a Literary Society at Government House.

In 1893 Hamilton returned to England and the civil service. He was appointed to the royal commission inquiring into the working of the Constitution of Dominica and in 1894, on Morley's nomination, served on the commission on the financial relations between England and Ireland. In November he became chairman of the Board of Customs. He died at South Kensington on 22 April 1895 and was buried at Richmond, Surrey.

On 18 August 1863 he had married Caroline Jane Ball, daughter of Frederick Augustus Geary, of Putney, Surrey; she died in 1875, leaving three sons and one daughter. On 4 July 1877 he married Teresa Felicia, second daughter of Major Henry Reynolds (d. 19 July 1859) and his wife Ann, née Cox; they had two sons and one daughter.

Cyclopedia of Tasmania, 1 (Hob, 1900); A. M. Morris, *Lady Hamilton's Tasmania* (Hob, 1966); V&P (HA Tas), 1892, 1, 237; *Australasian*, 8 Jan 1887, 5 Nov 1892, 1 Jan 1895; *Mercury*, 29 Nov 1892; *The Times*, 23, 27 Apr 1895; GO 23/24/62, 25/23/259 (TA).

RICHARD REFSHAUGE

HAMILTON, THOMAS FERRIER (1820-1905), pastoralist, was born at Cathlaw, the third son of Colonel John Ferrier Hamilton of Cairnhill and Westport, Scotland, and his wife Georgina, daughter of the second Viscount Gort. Following family tradition, Thomas went to the Edinburgh Military Academy. In 1839 he arrived at Sydney in the *Abberton*, with his cousin J. C. Riddell [q.v.]. Together they rode to Port Phillip where they took up Cairnhill in the Gis-

borne district. In 1845 Hamilton visited Scotland. In 1861 the partnership was dissolved with Riddell keeping Cairnhill and Hamilton acquiring Elderslie, New Gisborne, where he built his homestead and eventually owned 1536 freehold acres.

Hamilton was a member of the Gisborne Road Board and president of the Shire Council for many years. He was made a justice of the peace and with F. A. Powlett [q.v.] and George Airey opened the Kilmore bench. His duties as magistrate took him on several expeditions after Aboriginals who had raided stations in the Loddon and Campaspe district and on one expedition he led a detachment of ten soldiers sent from Melbourne. At the request of the police commissioner, Captain F. C. Standish [q.v.], he mediated on labour difficulties with the men employed on the Bendigo-Melbourne railway. In 1872 Hamilton was elected for Southern Province to the Legislative Council. He was particularly interested in mining legislation, extension of railways to Gippsland and free education. In 1883 he visited France as a commissioner for Victoria at the Bordeaux Exhibition and while overseas had a serious accident. On his return to Victoria he retired from the Legislative Council in August 1884.

Hamilton was an early member of the Melbourne Cricket Club and president for nine years. In a match against Richmond in 1861 he was described as 'impenetrable to the bowling though he could not hit at all'. He played against the visiting English side in 1862 and always took a great interest in the organization of local matches in the Gisborne district. He was president of the West Bourke Agricultural Society for many years. An athlete and racquet champion of Great Britain he was an early member of the Melbourne Club, serving on its committee in 1849-52 and as president in 1872. His last years were very quiet and he was practically unknown to the younger generation in Gisborne. He died on 7 August 1905 aged 85, survived by two of his five sons and six daughters. He was predeceased by his wife Elizabeth, whom he had married in 1851; she was the daughter of Sidney Stephen, a judge in New Zealand.

J. Smith (ed), *Cyclopedia of Victoria*, 3 (Melb, 1905); *Argus*, 8 Aug 1905; *Woodend Star*, 12 Aug 1905; *Werribee Express*, 19 Aug 1905.

J. ANN HONE

HAMMOND, MARK JOHN (1844-1908), gold-miner and politician, was born on 15 November 1844 in Sydney, the elder son of John Hammond, who had arrived in May 1841 in the *Moffatt*. He attended school in Newtown but at Christmas 1852 went with his father to the Braidwood goldfields. Late in 1853 the family moved to Sofala where Mark became a blacksmith and a successful jockey. In January 1861 at Lambing Flat he lost his money in a hotel venture; in September he joined the rush to Forbes but contracted typhoid and went home. In December 1862 he struck payable gold at Lambing Flat but next year was almost crippled by a scorpion bite and returned to Sofala. In 1868 he joined a mining company at Hill End and in 1872, as a partner of Beyers & Holtermann [q.v.], his dispirited change in direction of a tunnel led to the discovery of the world's greatest specimen of reef gold. In June 1873 he retired to Sydney with independent means. On 14 July 1869 at the Roman Catholic Cathedral, Bathurst, he had married Mary Anne Fitzpatrick.

After being tricked into a fraudulent mining adventure, Hammond lived in Sydney and Bathurst. In 1880 he joined the rush to Temora and as a 'counterpoise' speculated in urban real estate. He narrowly survived the 1893 depression and later censured socialist legislation which depressed the property market. On 24 September 1876 he had been elected an alderman of Ashfield municipality and mayor in 1882. In January 1883 he helped W. A. Hutchinson [q.v.] to found the Municipal Association and became one of its vice-presidents. After failing to win the Canterbury seat in the Legislative Assembly in 1882, he was elected in April 1884. Defiantly independent of party and enraged by any suggestion of a monopoly, he was labelled a 'glaring example of municipal madness'. His parliamentary speeches were larded with figures and quotations from John Stuart Mill. In 1886 he described the income tax bill as 'infamous and immoral', and published a pamphlet, *Land Taxation on Capital Value*. In 1881 he had campaigned in the *Daily Telegraph* to give financial independence to municipal corporations. In 1883 his pamphlet, *Proposed Establishment of Corporation Gas Works at Ashfield*, showed his wide research into costs and in 1884 his bill, fixing a maximum rate for domestic gas, was enacted as a government measure. Amendments to allow municipalities to mortgage their rates to build gas works were vigorously resisted in the Legislative Council but, with pressure from the Municipal Association, were passed in August 1886.

Hammond retired in January 1887 and went to England in 1889. On his return he became vice-president of the Ashfield Bowling Club and a member of the Ashfield Horticultural Society. In 1891 he was made a justice of the peace and in 1900-03 had

a city office as a mining agent. After Federation he supported Edmund Barton in the Australian Democratic and Liberal Reform League. After surfing at Manly he died of heart failure on 4 February 1908 and was buried in the Roman Catholic cemetery at Bathurst. His estate was valued at £30,712. He was survived by his wife, two sons and a daughter.

Ex-M.L.A., *Our present parliament, what it is worth* (Syd, c 1886); Municipal Assn of NSW, *Procs*, 1883-88; *Daily Telegraph* (Syd), 29 June 1894; *Advertiser* (Ashfield), 8 Feb 1908; *Bathurst Daily Argus*, 8 Feb 1908; *National Advocate*, 8 Feb 1908; M. J. Hammond papers (ML); MS cat under M. J. Hammond (ML).

RUTH TEALE

HANCOCK, HENRY RICHARD (1836-1919), mine superintendent, was born on 1 April 1836 at Horrabridge, Devon, England, son of George Hancock. He had a good education and much experience of assaying and surveying in local mines. At 23 he went to South Australia to manage a silver-lead mine near Strathalbyn. In 1862 he moved to Yelta in the area where copper had been found at Wallaroo in 1860 and Moonta in 1861 by shepherds of W. W. Hughes [q.v.]. After exploratory work by the Tipara Mining Association revealed great wealth the Moonta mine was opened in 1862 with James Warmington as captain (superintendent). Later that year he was replaced by his brother William, whose resignation was soon demanded by the miners. They won after a three months' strike, and in 1864 Hancock was appointed superintendent of the Moonta Mining Co.

Hancock's comprehensive report on the mine's various ores and his plans for expanding output soon won him repute, but his first need was more hands. The first miners at Moonta had come from Burra and Kapunda, and on his recommendation many more were brought from Cornwall and the Victorian goldfields. He also encouraged the tribute system by which independent miners could bid for their pitches and employ their own men; tributers numbered eighteen in 1862 and by 1874 represented nearly half the mine's workforce of 900. An enthusiast for machinery he introduced a steam-engine to replace hand-worked pumps, winches and ore-crushers; by 1865 tramways had reduced barrow work and by 1866 a railway replaced wagon teams for carrying ore to the smelters at Wallaroo. The mine's engineering shops were the best in the colony and enabled Hancock to experiment in replacing the slow and arduous labour of drilling holes by sledge hammer in the hard Moonta rock. He designed and patented a percussion drill driven by compressed air and capable of boring forty feet of shot-holes in an eight-hour shift. For separating sulphides from the ores he made and patented a jigger which was also used later at Broken Hill.

In 1864-73 the output of the mine trebled and gave shareholders some £840,000 in forty-four dividends, but variations in the price of copper were reflected in the miners' wages and employment. In 1873, Moonta's best year, Hancock persuaded the directors to maintain constant production and employment by assuring a minimum weekly wage of £2 for bad years. The miners were duly notified but in 1874 copper fell from £110 a ton to £87 and Hancock was ordered to reduce all wages to £1 16s. His protest to the chairman, then in Britain, was successful but meanwhile the miners downed tools and elected a strike committee. Their wives soon used brooms to 'sweep the insurgents out of the mine' and work was resumed.

In building 'Australia's little Cornwall' Hancock had personal assets. A commanding figure with a flowing beard, he wore a grey bell-topper and long black coat and spoke in cultured accents. A devout Wesleyan, he went to chapel twice each Sunday and early superintended the Sunday school. His large two-storied mansion, surrounded by native trees, was adequately staffed and connected by telephone to the stables where he had a special carriage. The mine office was equipped with speaking tubes and from a look-out on its roof he could survey the surface workings. In his own room he had a 'pulpit' desk, his papers far above the range of prying eyes. Most of his workmen lived in humpies scattered among the mallee scrub on the mining leases. When the town of Moonta was surveyed in 1865 the miners were expected to move into it but they preferred their rent-free homes, thus making themselves semi-tenants while employed on the mine. At one stage some 6000 people lived on the Moonta leases and the company found that it had assumed the functions of government with Hancock as a kind of chief justice.

However deep his concern for the welfare of his people, Hancock was a strict ruler. He compelled all employees to join the medical club at a small weekly rate, but medicines and consultations were free and sick pay was provided. He encouraged cricket, football, chess and glee clubs and many mutual improvement societies. He established a brass band, library and reading room and a compulsory night school for boys from the mine's sorting tables. He also helped to round the Point Pearce Mission for Aborig-

inals from the Moonta area, the local school of mines, the gas company and the Agricultural, Horticultural and Floricultural Society, serving on their boards for many years. For his varied powers Captain Hancock was held in awe. Any summons to his office was dreaded as an employee was liable to be questioned about things that had nothing to do with his work, and men who were sacked usually found no other job in the district.

After amalgamation of the Wallaroo and Moonta Mining and Smelting Co. in 1889, Hancock became its general manager and his benevolent bureaucracy brought many advantages to Wallaroo. He retired in 1898 and was succeeded by his eldest son, Henry Lipson, who managed the Moonta mine until it closed in 1923. In 1880 Captain Hancock had taken up Nalyappa, 30,000 acres of grazing land extending from the coast to the Maitland Road. He managed it from the mine office until it was subdivided and sold in the late 1890s. His first wife Sarah Annie had died of typhoid at Moonta on 27 June 1870, leaving two sons and a daughter. In Adelaide on 28 August 1872 he married Loveday Maria Jolly of Moonta. Hancock died at his home, Iveymeade, Burnside, on 14 January 1919. He left an estate valued at £21,000 to his wife, seven sons and three daughters.

SA Dept of Mines, *Centenary of the discovery of copper at Wallaroo-Moonta* (Adel, nd); O. Pryor, *Australia's little Cornwall* (Adel, 1962); *Register* (Adel), 15 Jan 1919.

OSWALD PRYOR

HANDFIELD, HENRY HEWETT PAULET (1828-1900), Anglican clergyman, was born on 12 December 1828, the fifth son of Edward Handfield, naval commander, of Hermitage House, near Dublin, and his wife Louisa, née Cokely. He was educated at Uppingham School and the Collegiate Institution, Liverpool. After his parents died he became the ward of Bishop Perry [q.v.] and in 1848 arrived at Melbourne with him in the *Stag*. He became an assistant at the Melbourne Diocesan Grammar School under R. H. Budd [q.v.] and was made deacon by Perry on 21 December 1851. He was licensed as assistant curate to Archdeacon Thomas Hart Davies at St Peter's, Eastern Hill, ordained priest in 1852 and succeeded to the charge of the parish in December 1854.

While locum tenens of the parish before appointment as its incumbent, Handfield reorganized the school associated with it and added a bluestone chancel, two transepts and a gallery to the original church. In 1855-56 he was in England with Perry. In 1857 the bishop published a general circular to his clergy forbidding the practice of intoning and chanting portions of divine service. Privately, at the prompting of indignant clergy and laity, he rebuked Handfield for liturgical extravagances at St Peter's and expressed concern at some of Handfield's theological opinions. However, by September 1865 Handfield had moved the organ from the gallery and sported in full view a robed and chanting choir. His peculiar relationship to Perry seemed to shield him from disciplinary consequences of their various disagreements over this and other matters.

With equal perseverance for community welfare, he played a leading role in the opening and direction of a day school and centre for worship in the Richmond area in 1857, and founded St Peter's Evening School in 1858. His zeal for education included the new university. His notorious choir sang at the laying of the foundation stone of Trinity College in 1870 and he served on its council in 1871-1900. He was also a founding member of the theological faculty and a lecturer in 1879-1900. He had helped to form the Melbourne and Collingwood City Mission in 1856 and managed his parochial finances so well that by 1868 half the church collections were given away to good causes. In 1876 he was appointed chaplain of the Victorian Volunteer Force.

Handfield stood high in the opinion of the Church assembly which elected him both to the board responsible for the appointment of Bishop Moorhouse [q.v.] in 1876 and to the chapter of the new cathedral in 1879. Moorhouse made him rural dean of the city of Melbourne. As the leading promoter of Moorhouse's vision of a 'Mission to the Streets and Lanes', Handfield circulated the public appeal in 1885 and encouraged Sister Esther to move into the Little Lonsdale Street Mission House in 1888, thus playing a part in founding the Community of the Holy Name. He was the first chaplain of the mission and the first warden of the Sisters. On 10 November 1853 Handfield had married Mary Leigh, eldest daughter of William Upton Tripp of Collingwood; they had no children. He died on 8 August 1900 at St Peter's vicarage.

Esther, Mother foundress of the Community of the Holy Name (Melb, nd); *Holy Trinity Church, East Melbourne, 'The story of the century', 1864-1964* (Melb, 1964); *Argus*, 9 Aug 1900; *Leader* (Melb), 18 Aug 1900; *Weekly Times* (Melb), 18 Aug 1900; MS records (St Peter's, Eastern Hill, Melb, Community of the Holy Name, Cheltenham, Vic).

B. R. MARSHALL

HANN, WILLIAM (1837-1889), and FRANK HUGH (1846-1921), explorers and pastoralists, were the sons of Joseph Hann and his wife Elizabeth, née Sharpe. The family migrated from Wiltshire in 1851 to the Westernport district in Victoria. In 1862 Joseph Hann was attracted to the newly-opened upper Burdekin district in Queensland where in partnership with Richard Daintree [q.v.] and some Melbourne investors he took up Bluff Downs, Maryvale and Lolworth stations. After Joseph was drowned in the great Burdekin flood of January 1864, his sons struggled with hostile Aboriginals, speargrass, dingoes and falling wool prices and in 1870 William had to overland their last 19,000 sheep to Victoria; Lolworth and Bluff Downs were surrendered and he ran cattle at Maryvale.

In 1872 William was given charge of a well-organized official party to explore the interior of the Cape York Peninsula. The country was difficult and Hann was often irked by assistants whose bushcraft was less competent than his. Dense scrub prevented him from reaching his goal on the Endeavour River but the party located some fair pastoral country and discovered and named the Tate, Daintree and Palmer Rivers. On the latter he reported traces of gold which led to J. V. Mulligan's [q.v.] prospecting party and a dramatic gold rush. The new fields soon provided Hann with a market for his cattle and he prospered. In 1886 after a trip overseas he introduced axis deer from Ceylon to the Maryvale district. He was also a benefactor of St James's Cathedral, Townsville, and a member of the Dalrymple Divisional Board. He died suddenly while swimming near Townsville on 5 April 1889, survived by his wife and two daughters; a son had died in infancy. A daring horseman and whip and a first-class bushman, Hann was notable among the first generation of North Queenslanders.

Frank Hann, born on 19 October 1846, managed Lolworth station in 1865-70 and in 1875, when the cattle industry revived, took up Lawn Hill station in the Gulf country. Refusing to sell in good times, he was overtaken by low prices, poor seasons and the outbreak of redwater fever in the 1890s, and walked off the station in 1894. Penniless and very miserable he overlanded to Western Australia with 6 Aboriginals and 67 horses in 1896. He searched in vain for suitable country in the Nullagine district and in 1897 decided to return to Queensland but was diverted to a short-lived gold rush at Mount Broome in the West Kimberley district. In the winter of 1898 he penetrated the Leopold Ranges, till then a barrier to expansion, discovered and named the Charnley and Isdell Rivers and located some fine areas of pastoral country. This feat of bushmanship and endurance was remarkable for Hann was over 50 and suffering from the after-effects of a broken thigh and the area he traversed was one of the most difficult in Australia and peopled by unwelcoming Aboriginals. He took up over 1000 square miles of the new country but had no funds to buy stock and it was pioneered by established Kimberley families. Hann lived in Perth for four years and then turned to prospecting. Authorized by the Western Australian government to explore the inland desert, he opened a track from Laverton to the Warburton Ranges on the South Australian border in 1903 and investigated a rumour of gold at Queen Victoria Springs in 1907. An accident put him on crutches in 1918 and he retired to Cottesloe, Perth, where he died unmarried on 23 August 1921. In his last years he had corresponded with Daisy Bates on appealing for more government attention to Aboriginal welfare. Each of his diaries in the Battye Library, Perth, is prefaced by the motto, 'Do not yield to despair'.

R. L. Jack, *Northmost Australia*, 2 (Lond, 1921); J. Black, *North Queensland pioneers* (Charters Towers, 1931); G. C. Bolton, *Richard Daintree* (Brisb, 1965); V&P (LA Qld), 1873, 1031; Hann papers (Battye Lib, Perth, and held by E. Clarke, Maryvale, Charters Towers).

G. C. BOLTON

HANNELL, JAMES (1813-1876), publican and politician, was born on 1 December 1813 at Parramatta, the eldest son of two convicts, James Walton and Elizabeth Hannell. Educated at Christ Church School, Newcastle, he served with the Newcastle police in 1833-36. On 12 March 1836 he married Mary Anne Sophia, second daughter of Edward Priest, lighthousekeeper at Port Stephens.

In 1839 Hannell became Newcastle's first auctioneer and later bought the Ship Inn. This venture flourished and he soon achieved influence by his successful support of Major D'Arcy Wentworth in the first Legislative Council elections in 1843. In 1845 at the District Council elections he proposed Henry Usher who was later the chief benefactor of the new Newcastle Hospital, with which Hannell was closely associated. In 1855 he declined Henry Parkes's [q.v.] invitation to join 'the chosen men in the new parliament', but in 1859, standing as a Liberal, he was narrowly defeated for Newcastle by Arthur Hodgson [q.v.]. In December 1860 Hannell unseated Hodgson. An ardent free trader he supported Robertson's [q.v.] land proposals and opposed state

aid to religion. In 1866 he voted unreservedly for Parkes's education bill. He resigned his seat in 1869 in favour of his friend, Sir James Martin [q.v.]. In 1872-74 Hannell represented Northumberland. A 'roads and bridges' member, he seldom permitted faction ties to hamper him.

Hannell was active in agitating for the incorporation of Newcastle and became its first mayor in 1859-62, serving again in 1868-69 and 1871. In 1859-64, 1866-71 and 1873-76 he represented city ward in the Newcastle Council. When Wickham was proclaimed a municipality in 1871, largely by his efforts, he became its first mayor. Familiar with the control of meetings, he successfully led both Newcastle and Wickham Councils through their formative years. He had been gazetted a justice of the peace in 1857 and regularly attended the Newcastle bench. Prominent as a churchwarden and trustee of Christ Church Anglican Cathedral, he became embroiled in an altercation between Canon John Fletcher and Bishop Tyrrell [q.v.]. In 1862 in parliament Hannell raised the parishioners' objections to the bishop and later initiated a fruitless Supreme Court action against him. Martin told Hannell that the parishioners' case had been 'blundered all through', but later even Tyrrell lauded 'the energy and ability with which he performed his duties as chairman of committees'.

For the Newcastle Hospital, Hannell organized concerts in which he took part as a comic singer. He was a key figure in establishing the Newcastle Mechanics' School of Arts and in 1858 was appointed one of the first trustees of the Newcastle National School. In 1867 he became a member of the Board of the Newcastle Public School. He was president and judge of the Newcastle Jockey Club, organizer of the first regatta and president of the Regatta Committee for over thirty years. He died at Mary Ville, Newcastle, on 31 December 1876 and was buried in Christ Church cemetery. He was survived by his wife, three sons and six daughters. His estate was valued at under £1000.

D. O'Donnell, *The Christ Church Cathedral controversy, 1861-1866* (Newcastle, 1967); V&P (LA NSW), 1860-74; Registers, 1826-56, and vestry minutes, 1859-90 (Christ Church Cathedral, Newcastle).

DAN O'DONNELL

HANSON, SIR RICHARD DAVIES (1805-1876), judge and author, was born on 6 December 1805 in London, the second son of Benjamin Hanson, fruit merchant. Educated at a Nonconformist school in Melbourn, Cambridgeshire, he was articled at 17 to the Methodist John Wilks, admitted an attorney in 1828 and practised briefly in London. With his family he attended the King's Weigh-House Chapel under Rev. Thomas Binney [q.v.], whose intellect challenged his own and confirmed his aggression as a Nonconformist. Hanson talked of migrating to Canada but joined the legal firm of Bartlett & Beddome. His conservative employers, dismayed by his utopian ideals, soon dismissed him without a testimonial.

Through Robert Gouger and John Brown [qq.v.] Hanson was influenced by E. G. Wakefield [q.v.] and drawn into promoting the province of South Australia. He drafted an early proposal in 1831 and supplied the South Australian Land Co. with charters and precepts of the seventeenth-century colonies in America and persuaded his relations to sign its petition in 1832. At the South Australian Association's public meeting in Exeter Hall on 30 June 1834 he was entrusted with an important resolution and announced his intention of migrating. In the Morning Chronicle, 3 July, he replied to criticism of the meeting by The Times. In August with Gouger and others he persuaded the duke of Wellington to support the South Australian bill and, when it was passed, contributed colonial articles to the Morning Chronicle. In February 1835 he reviewed the anonymous New British Province in the Eclectic, joined a legal firm in Southampton, tried to float a land company and helped to organize the South Australian Literary Association. His inaugural address claimed that many minds in England were restricted by privilege; even if men could not be made perfect, a reasonable community could be formed with instructed people. In 1836 he was persuaded to give evidence to the select committee on the disposal of land in British colonies and to apply for appointment as judge in South Australia. Despite strong support he failed, and withdrew from the South Australian venture.

Early in 1837 Hanson joined the Globe as a political critic. In 1838 he was appointed assistant commissioner of inquiry into Canadian crown lands and migration at a salary of £660 and arrived at Quebec with Lord Durham. He went to work with a will on his special report, later printed over his name in the appendix of the Durham report, and showed clearly that under the 1790 Constitutional Act land reserves had been administered erroneously. In Canada he worked with Dominick Daly, later governor of South Australia. Hanson returned with Durham to England and continued as his private secretary until the report was printed. According to Henry Reeve, editor

of the Greville papers, he gave a copy to The Times before it was submitted to the government.

Hanson was then appointed by the New Zealand Co. to draft legal documents and seek investors to buy land orders. After the principal agent, Colonel Wakefield, sailed hurriedly in May 1839 in the Tory, the directors sent Hanson, as second agent, in the Cuba in August to speed the surveys. He arrived at Port Nicholson (Wellington) on 3 January 1840 but his hopes of making a quick fortune and returning to England were foiled when the consul, William Hobson [q.v.], negotiated the Treaty of Waitangi. In May Hanson went to the Chatham Islands, beyond Hobson's jurisdiction, and with stores and guns bought some 200,000 acres. The Colonial Office later disallowed the deal, but soon after his return to Wellington Hanson was charged by the colonel with buying land without authority and withholding the deeds as security against the uncertainty of the company honouring his bills. As the private agent of several absentee land buyers and the elected vice-president of the Council of Government Hanson was well placed to defy Colonel Wakefield and the company. He helped restive colonists to organize protests against the company's delay in making rural sections available and in September was deputed with G. S. Evans [q.v.] and Henry Moreing to interview Governor Gipps in Sydney. The result was a ruling that the company's land agreements with Maori chiefs should be confined to blocks of 100,000 acres in which individual settlers were to select their sections. In December the deputies returned to Wellington by way of Auckland where Hanson made his peace with Hobson.

In 1841 Hanson's breach with the company deepened but in October he was also ostracized by the settlers as a 'government man' when Hobson made him crown prosecutor for the southern districts at £200 a year. Supported by a few independents he founded the New Zealand Colonist and Port Nicholson Advertiser in August 1842. Its premises caught fire and the last number, 1 August 1843, appeared in black borders with the motto, 'Not dead but speaketh'. The Wairau massacre on 17 June had alarmed many settlers who clamoured for vengeance, but Hanson refused to prosecute until Rauparaha and Rangihaeta were committed by a police magistrate and advised Governor Robert FitzRoy, who arrived at Wellington early in 1844, not to retaliate. FitzRoy followed this advice and became intensely unpopular, but Hanson assured him that any other course would have brought every Maori into revolt. Hanson was attacked for accepting appointment as a magistrate and commissioner of the Court of Requests with the right of private practice, and vilified by Jerningham Wakefield in *Adventure in New Zealand* (1845). Disgusted by the relentless native policy of Governor Grey in 1846, he decided to leave New Zealand but did not resign his legal posts for a year.

In July Hanson arrived in Adelaide where his friend, John Brown, had kept him in touch with local affairs, especially on proposals to grant state aid to religion and education. Hanson promptly helped to revive the League for the Preservation of Religious Freedom and as one of its most active secretaries wrote tracts, spoke at meetings and contributed to the *South Australian Register* in 1846-49. On 7 October 1846 he was admitted 'a barrister, solicitor, attorney and proctor' in the Supreme Court. With an office in King William Street he started a practice. He had been in the Legislative Council Chamber in September when the non-official members walked out in protest against Lieut-Governor Robe's reservation of royalties on copper, and in June 1848 won popularity as junior counsel to J. H. Fisher and E. C. Gwynne when Judge Cooper [qq.v.] decided against seignorage. In 1849 he appeared in over a hundred cases, but in December was thrown from his gig, damaging his hip permanently. He appeared in court on a crutch after three months, and made Richard Hicks his partner. In 1848 he had bought a house in Sturt Street where on 29 March 1851 he married Ann, née Hopgood, aged 24, the widow of Captain Scanlon of New Zealand. In 1855 he moved to a larger house on East Terrace when his brothers and sisters began to join him. He gradually acquired seven sections of Mount Lofty where he later built his family home, Woodhouse.

In 1851 Hanson stood as a voluntaryist for Yatala in the first part-elective Legislative Council but his victory was disputed. In June he was appointed acting advocate-general in place of the ailing William Smillie (d. 1853) at a salary of £500, with the right of private practice and 'without the obligation hitherto required of voting with the government'. Although the ordinance for state aid to religion had expired in February, some grants were given to churches, but Hanson stopped them and in August helped to throw out the state aid bill at its first reading in the Legislative Council. He then drafted and introduced the Education Act with aid for school buildings and teachers' stipends and became a member of the first Board of Education. In 1852 he had a leading role in the passage of the Bullion Act, the Grand Jury Abolition Act and the District Councils Act, the first of its kind in Australia designed to encourage local democracy.

On the select committee for drafting the colony's constitution in 1853 Hanson proposed a lower house with a low franchise and a nominee upper house on trial for nine years. He was criticized for abandoning 'pure democracy' but argued that his plan was as much as the Colonial Office would accept. This constitution was rejected in London and in 1855 Governor MacDonnell arrived with a decided preference for a unicameral legislature. He was persuaded by a newly-elected council to endorse a bicameral constitution: an assembly to be elected by manhood suffrage under secret ballot and the 'cross in the square' system, and a council guarded by householding voters. This constitution was sent to London in January 1856 and received the royal assent in June. When the news reached Adelaide in October, B. T. Finniss [q.v.] formed a ministry with Hanson as his attorney-general.

On 9 March 1857 at the first elections under responsible government Hanson won the second of six seats for the City of Adelaide. The Finniss ministry fell on 21 August and after two short governments Hanson formed a ministry on 30 September; with some reconstruction it lasted until 9 May 1860. As advocate-general he had introduced forty-six bills and twenty-one as attorney-general. He employed only one clerk but was seldom absent from the legislature, served on many select committees, helped to form the parliamentary and law libraries and made his home a meeting place for politicians in need of advice. Hicks attended to much of his court work, but prominent cases like his defeat of the Anglican claim to a cathedral site in Victoria Square made Hanson the acknowledged leader of the South Australian Bar.

Sir Charles Cooper resigned as chief justice and was replaced by Hanson who was graciously farewelled from the House of Assembly on 21 November 1861. The appointment was challenged by Judge Boothby [q.v.] who had told MacDonnell in June 1860 that he would automatically succeed Cooper and that neither the governor nor Executive Council could appoint anyone else. In chambers Boothby reiterated this claim, denying the right of Hanson and the third judge, Gwynne, as mere attorneys, to sit in the court or to pass opinion on the dicta of the 'Senior Judge'. Overruled, he announced that he would appeal to higher authority. The threat was carried out but the Colonial Office advised him to submit his case to the Judicial Committee of the Privy Council. Unwilling to pay the costs, Boothby desisted but the incident and his rebuke for not sending his protest through the governor added to his annoyance. In January 1861 MacDonnell, himself a barrister and former chief justice of Gambia, had confessed to his superiors that 'no measures are possible which would prevent Mr. Boothby's peculiar idiosyncrasies breaking out from time to time in prejudice to the interests of justice', but Hanson was more tactful. When both Houses sent addresses to the Queen for Boothby's removal, Hanson had opposed them declaring that 'we have a Judge against whose character and integrity not one syllable is brought . . . It would be wrong to punish [him] for expressing his conscientious opinion on the validity of laws, which it is his sworn duty to do'.

One of Hanson's first duties in the Supreme Court was to inquire into the validity of local legislation, much of which he had drafted. He recommended various amendments to several Acts, 'not because he considered them necessary but merely to set the minds of people at rest'. Gwynne sometimes deprived him of a majority in the court especially in cases connected with the Real Property Act. Hanson had been sceptical about its validity in 1857 and redrafted 'Torrens's [q.v.] clumsy and unprofessional attempt to improve the law'; when it was passed he advised the governor to assent to it on the Queen's behalf, and worked hard to simplify its operation.

In parliament Hanson's ablest speech had been against the amendment of money bills by the Legislative Council whose members looked only at the letter of the law and ignored its obvious intention. This distinction was all-important to Hanson and he expounded it clearly in his minority judgment in *Dawes* v. *Quarrel*, when it was decided that the South Australian legislature had no 'power to establish courts' as these words were omitted from the Constitution Act. Hanson argued that as the Act specifically established representative institutions and the making of laws for peace, order and good government, it was 'somewhat singular that the Imperial Parliament should have deliberately deprived South Australia, under the pretence of providing for its better government . . . of creating Courts of Justice . . . I must confess this seems to me to raise a very strong presumption against the construction now contended for'. In contrast Boothby stuck to punctilio and, because he deemed the Constitution Act invalid, found fault with a large and indefinite number of Acts passed by the colony's legislature. The imperial parliament came to the rescue with validating Acts but they had little effect on Boothby. To him the colony's entire legal system was

different from that of Britain and therefore repugnant to the laws of England.

By 1866 the administration of justice was in confusion and uncertainty. Boothby was accused in the press of bullying counsel, dictating to juries, quashing informations, discharging prisoners in criminal trials and bringing equity cases to a standstill. Petitions for his removal poured into parliament and both Houses sent addresses to the Queen, but were advised that the only remedies were by appeal to the Privy Council or 'to remove him at your own responsibility'. Hanson remained outwardly imperturbable but had been deeply hurt in 1863 when Boothby and his eldest son with fourteen other colonists persuaded Bishop Short [q.v.] to carry a protest to Governor Daly against Mrs Hanson attending a ball at Government House. Daly angrily rebuked the bishop for spreading slander and named the protesters in his report to London after Hanson 'spoke to me very earnestly of their unfairness'; inquiry revealed that she had been Hanson's housekeeper before she married him and that all their six children had been born in wedlock in 1853-63.

In the Full Court on 12 April 1867 the chief justice declared that 'the remarks of my learned colleague have ceased to annoy or affect me in any way because I feel . . . that by dwelling upon his fancied rights and fancied wrongs, he has incapacitated himself judicially from any reliable conclusions . . . and therefore I look upon them as should any other utterance founded upon mental or moral illusion'. Four days late Hanson and Gwynne conferred and adjourned the sittings until next term Boothby dissented and tried in vain to conduct the Court by himself. On 24 Apri Hanson and Gwynne wrote to the governor seeking remedial measures but disclaiming any personal motives or inability to overcome obstructive difficulties. Boothby was given time to prepare his defence before trial by the governor and his Executive Council. He was found guilty of misbehaviour and 'amoved' from office on 29 July.

Despite his 'steady flow of carefully measured words, weighted with calm and logical reasoning', Hanson often claimed that he turned to law to please his father but wished he was rid of it, especially its 'archaic procedures' such as public executions. A voracious reader in his leisure, he turned readily to science and theology and was moved to share his knowledge. He believed in inevitable human progress and abhorred the mental barriers that hindered it. He saw the Bible as 'God's main instrument in the education of the world' only if read with a spirit of inquiry instead of infallible authority. His first public lecture on this theme was to the South Australian Library and Mechanics' Institute in March 1849 and shocked his audience. He emerged again to lecture in 1856 to the East Torrens Institute and in 1857 to the South Australian Institute on the power derived from adult self-instruction. By 1860 he was propounding law in nature in relation to scripture to the Adelaide Philosophical Society. Members of the Bible Society were present and asked him to resign; when he refused, they elected a new president. Hanson moved on to law in creation, rejecting Lamarck as 'absurd' but confessing attraction by Darwin's [q.v.] theories, however incomplete. In 1865 his *Law in Nature and other Papers* was published in Adelaide and London; its argument that the Bible should not be exempt from inquiry was highly praised by Bishop Colenso, whose sermons on the Pentateuch had greatly influenced Hanson.

Hanson applied for leave to visit Britain and sailed in February 1869. In March he published *The Jesus of History* which he had started to write in 1866 and finished on the voyage. The book was well documented although he lamented his inability to read German sources except in translation. Working from the first three gospels, especially Matthew, he succeeded in 'fusing the evangelical narratives into a clear and consistent whole', rejecting the romance of Renan and the miracles but judicially interpreting the record 'as an inquirer before the fall of Jerusalem'. The 'trained sifter of evidence and weigher of probabilities' was neither orthodox nor rationalist and reached his conclusions only after years of struggle. 'It is no slight matter', he wrote, 'to part with convictions that have been cherished for years ... But perhaps the belief in a God, who is both just and merciful, may rest with equal confidence upon the instincts of our nature and our experience ... as upon ... a slavish submission to the dogmas of a self-styled infallible Church'. Nor could he resist an analogy between 'the letter of Scripture' and 'the broad principles upon which it is based' and the strictness, rigidly technical and practically unjust in English law which, although reformed, was too often administered by men trained under the old system. William Sanday in *The Authorship and Historical Character of the Fourth Gospel* (1872) disagreed with the unnamed author of *The Jesus of History* but commended his 'admirable ability' while Samuel Butler in *The Fair Haven* (1873) admitted 'very great obligations ... to the ablest of all the writers who have treated the subject'.

On 9 July Hanson was knighted by the Queen at Windsor Castle after at least four recommendations from the governors, Daly and Fergusson. Prompted by Renan's *Saint Paul* (1869) Hanson sketched out his *The Apostle Paul and the Preaching of Christianity in the Primitive Church* on the voyage to Adelaide in 1870. Before it appeared in 1875 over his name, his slight *Letters To and From Rome, A.D. 61-63* was published in 1873 over the pseudonym C.V.S. His *Paul* was more original, penetrating and rationalistic than his life of Jesus yet he was still careful of expressing opinions that would wound his friends. He also confessed that 'with a few mental supressions, I could join in the prayers ... and sermons in the churches of the denomination with which from my childhood I have been connected, the old words bringing back something of the old feelings'.

From 18 November 1872 Hanson acted as governor until April 1873 when Governor Musgrave arrived. With the latter he had very cordial relations, each helping the other with friendly comment on their publications. Hanson gave enthusiastic support to the founding of the University of Adelaide and, when the Act was passed in 1874, its councillors elected him chancellor and invited him to give the inaugural address on 25 March 1876. It was prepared but not given. He died suddenly of heart disease in his garden at Woodhouse on the 4th, and was buried with a state funeral. Survived by his wife, a son and four daughters, he left an estate of about £5000.

HRA (1), 21; D. Pike, *Paradise of Dissent*, 2nd ed (Melb, 1967); PP (SA), 1851-60, 1861 (141), 1863 (53), 1866-67 (33), 1867 (22, 23), 1868 (184); *Register* (Adel), 16 May 1849, 22 Aug 1850, 29 June 1855, 21 July 1856, 3 Feb 1857, 6 May 1876; C. H. Spence, 'Sir Richard Hanson', *Melb Review*, July 1876; H. Brown, Sir Richard Davies Hanson (Fred Johns thesis, Univ Adel, 1938); H. S. Chapman and S. Revans letters (Alexander Turnbull Lib, Wellington, NZ); A. Musgrave letters (copies ML, NL); Governor's confidential dispatches, 1863-66 (SAA).

HARCUS, WILLIAM (1823-1876), Congregational minister, editor and author, was born at Newcastle upon Tyne, England, son of William Harcus, Congregational minister and author of tracts. Educated by his father, he worked as a journalist until he decided to enter for the ministry. For three years he studied under Rev. John Frost in the Congregational Theological Institution at Cotton End, near Bradford, and shared in student preaching. His first ministry was at Loughborough, near Leicester, and at Newport on 26 December 1848 he married Eliza

Oliver. He then moved to Doncaster where he was active in the Association of Congregational Ministers of Yorkshire and won repute for his 'sincerity, genial spirit and sociable disposition'. His next ministry was at Toxteth Park, Liverpool, where he helped to found an evangelical alliance and became its secretary. He also resumed his literary pursuits and contributed to many religious journals, notably the *Christian Witness*, for which he wrote a 'thoughtful and illuminating' series on the lives of the Apostles. Indifferent health, a low stipend and the needs of a young family induced him to resign. With glowing testimonials from Congregationalists and other denominations he sailed in the *Lord Raglan* with his wife, three sons and three daughters; they arrived at Melbourne on 25 November 1860 and soon went to Adelaide.

Harcus ministered at Clayton Congregational Church, Kensington, until 1865 and thereafter remained an active member, preaching often and helping to raise funds. After some differences with his parishioners in 1862 he had joined the *South Australian Register*. In 1867 he moved to the *South Australian Advertiser*, was literary editor until J. H. Barrow [q.v.] died in 1874 and full editor until 1876. Prolific and versatile, his work was always frank, clever and very readable. He won repute for his fair editorials and sound judgment even when controversial. In July-December 1874 his 'Laconic Leaders', a series on public men, aroused criticism in some quarters but, as 'Onkaparinga', he answered firmly in a series entitled 'Post and Rail' in the *Garden and Field*, 1875.

Harcus was appointed a justice of the peace in May 1871 and often acted as coroner. Commissioned by the government in 1873 he published *Handbook for emigrants proceeding to South Australia*, for which he was paid £143 15s. The Adelaide edition included an appendix in German by K. F. W. Eggers [q.v.], and the London edition, 'for gratis distribution', ran to at least seven reprints each of 10,000. For the Philadelphia Centenary Exhibition he was commissioned by the government to write *South Australia: its history, resources and productions*; dedicated to Governor Musgrave, it was published in London and Adelaide in 1876. Pressed by many duties he died aged 53 on 10 August at his home in Hackney, and in compliance with his own request was buried at Clayton Church. He was survived by his wife, six children and some grandchildren and left an estate worth £900.

Register (Adel), 11 Aug 1876; *Illustrated Adel News*, Sept 1876.

HARDING, GEORGE ROGERS (1838-1895), judge and author, was born on 3 December 1838 at Taunton, Somerset, England, the only son of George Rogers Harding, LL.B., vicar of Gittisham, Devon, and his wife Elizabeth, née Winter. Enrolled in 1856 at Magdalene College, Cambridge, he did not take a degree but entered Lincoln's Inn in 1858 and was called to the Bar in 1861. In 1860 he had published in London *A Handy Book of Ecclesiastical Law* which ran to several editions; later he concentrated on equity. On 7 May 1861 he married Emily Morris of Stone House, Worcester, sister of the wife of E. I. C. Browne [q.v.].

In October 1866 Harding and his wife arrived at Brisbane where he was immediately admitted to the Bar, the first equity counsel in the colony. He soon won repute for his skill, integrity and kind treatment of juniors. In April 1876 he was appointed a commissioner under the 1872 Civil Procedure Reform Act and in July 1879 became senior puisne judge of the Supreme Court of Queensland. Scrupulously fair, he was highly respected for his judgments, even those taken to the Privy Council; the only case to make him unpopular was the conspiracy trial after the 1891 strike when his harsh sentences clearly revealed his prejudice. With great energy he published at least five legal treatises ranging from *A Time Table of Proceedings under the Judicature Act* to *The Acts and Orders relating to Insolvency*. He built up a fine library, some of which was later acquired for the Oxley Memorial Library, and while on the bench converted the very small collection at the Supreme Court into a large and important library. In 1883-84 he was acting chief justice in the absence of Sir Charles Lilley [q.v.], and in 1890 visited England on leave.

In 1868 Harding had bought a house in St John's Wood, Brisbane, and extended it as his twelve children were born. He always kept an open house and became famous for his hospitality. Among his guests in 1881 were Prince Albert and Prince George on their Australian tour. After his wife died Harding married Isabella Grahame, sister of E. R. Drury's [q.v.] wife, on 23 December 1889. After hearing a case in the Supreme Court in August 1895 Harding became so ill that he could not be taken home. In great pain for three days he was treated in his chambers where, unable to return to court, he delivered his judgment and died on the 31st. His funeral was one of the largest up to that time in Brisbane.

Town and Country J, 16 Aug 1879; *Bulletin*, 7 July 1883; *Brisbane Courier*, 2, 3, 4 Sept

1895; Jack cutting book no 10 (Oxley Lib, Brisb).

A. A. MORRISON
M. CARTER

HARDMAN, EDWARD TOWNLEY (1845-1887), geologist, was born on 6 April 1845 at Drogheda, Ireland. He was educated at Drogheda and graduated in mining with many prizes as an associate of the Royal College of Science, Dublin. In 1870 he was appointed a geologist in the Geological Survey of Ireland. He was elected a fellow of the Royal Geological Society of Ireland in 1871 and of the Chemical Society of London in 1874.

Hardman was chosen by the Colonial Office for the temporary post of government geologist in Western Australia. He arrived at Perth in March 1883, when colonists were greatly interested in the possibility of finding an economic goldfield. In 1872 the government had offered a reward of £5000 for the discovery of the colony's first workable goldfield, and in November 1882 a prospecting party led by Philip Saunders had reported showings of gold from the headwaters of the Ord River in the East Kimberleys. Saunders had expressed the opinion that payable gold would occur in the vicinity, and as a result he had been approached to lead a government expedition to prospect the area thoroughly. However, on Hardman's arrival in Perth it was decided that he would be better qualified than Saunders to investigate the gold prospects. Hardman was therefore sent to the Kimberleys as a member of survey parties in 1883 and 1884. His published reports and maps of these expeditions are the first geological accounts of the district.

In the 1884 expedition Hardman found good showings of alluvial gold in several watercourses and concluded that there was a 'great probability of payable gold being obtained in this part of the Kimberley'. His report stimulated great interest, and several prospecting parties set out in 1885. Payable gold was found at Hall's Creek on 14 July 1885 by Charles Hall, John Slattery and their party, in the same general area where Saunders and Hardman had reported finding gold showings.

While in Western Australia Hardman also described the geology of the Bunbury-Nannup area and investigated the prospects of supplying Perth with artesian water. He made a brief visit to the Victorian goldfields in 1885 to compare the rocks there with those of the Kimberleys. He had hoped that his appointment would be made permanent, but the Legislative Council demurred at the cost, and in October 1885 he returned to his duties with the Geological Survey of Ireland. The permanent appointment of a government geologist in Western Australia was finally approved in 1887, and it was believed that Hardman would accept the post, but he contracted typhoid fever and died in a Dublin hospital on 30 April 1887 aged 42. He was survived by his wife and two children.

Before leaving Western Australia Hardman had applied for the reward for discovering the Kimberley goldfield, but several others, including Hall's party and Saunders, claimed the find and much bitterness was generated by the conflicting applications. Hardman was a strong personality and most outspoken in pressing his claim. However, doubt was expressed on the propriety of rewarding a government officer for a discovery made in the course of his official duties. In May 1888 the Executive Council finally decided not to pay the reward to any claimant, as the required conditions on the quantity of gold shipped within two years of the discovery had not been fully met. However, £500 was paid as a gratuity to Hardman's widow in recognition of his services to the colony, and Hall's party also received £500. Saunders, the first to find gold in the Kimberleys, received nothing.

Hardman was the author of many important publications dealing with the geology of Ireland, but is principally remembered for his pioneering work in Western Australia which led to discovery of the colony's first goldfield. It gave the impetus to prospecting which resulted in the much larger finds of the 1890s, but Hardman's early death denied him the opportunity to take part in the great mining developments of those exciting years.

A.B.W., 'Obituary. Edward Townley Hardman', Geological Mag, July 1887; West Australian, 17, 18 June 1887; Inquirer, 22 June 1887; file 10560/96 (WA Mines Dept).

PHILLIP E. PLAYFORD

HARDY, ARTHUR (1817-1909), pastoralist, barrister and quarry-owner, was born on 3 May 1817, the sixth son of eight children of Thomas Hardy (1775-1849), surgeon of Walworth, Surrey, and his wife Harriet, née Hurst. Until 1836, when Thomas inherited the Yorkshire manors of Birksgate and Shepley, the Hardys attended the South Place Unitarian Chapel in London where they were influenced by the minister, William Johnson Fox, a friend of John Stuart Mill and other Philosophical Radicals. In 1830 Fox introduced Arthur's elder sister Harriet (Mrs John Taylor) to Mill, thus beginning the romance which culminated in their marriage in 1851, two years after Taylor's death.

Arthur attended Camberwell Grammar School and in 1838 was reading for the Bar. Threatened by tuberculosis he decided to follow his elder brother Alfred (1813-1870), who also had tuberculosis and in 1836 had joined Colonel Light's [q.v.] survey party, hoping that an open-air life would cure him. Suffering at times from 'very violent' pain in his chest, Arthur sailed for South Australia and arrived in the *Platina* on 9 February 1839 equipped with books on farming and sheep husbandry, a Sussex shepherd, land orders bought by his father for four town acres and four 134-acre country sections and a box of specie worth £1000 entrusted to him by a London capitalist, Marmaduke Hart, under articles of copartnership for seven years.

Hardy began mixed farming in what is now the suburb of Paradise. Prolific crops from rich soil, high prices and Hart's capital soon enabled him to stock a sheep run on the River Light. In 1845, after inspecting the coast of Spencer Gulf he took another run in the Port Lincoln district, leaving his sheep in the care of Henry Price. In Adelaide he was also establishing a law practice, prompted by Governor Gawler who sought his help in drawing up proper indictments. In 1848-50 he visited England where he married Martha, sister of Henry Price. On his return Hardy bought a bluestone quarry at Glen Osmond and in 1851 built the mansion, Birksgate, supplementing it in 1857 with Mount Lofty House, the first summer retreat on the highest ridge of the Adelaide Hills. In 1854, to enable his quarry workers and their families to 'avoid the inducement to pass their evenings at the only public house', he built the colony's first country Mechanics' Institute, later enriching it with books selected by the Mills from their personal library. In August he tried in vain to persuade the Legislative Council to help him build a railway from the city to Glen Osmond. In 1851-57 he was president of the Court of Disputed Returns, in 1857-74 served on the Central Board of Education and in 1875-87 represented Albert in the House of Assembly. On 14 October 1857 he became an original trustee of Adelaide's first Unitarian Church and in 1863 was honorary secretary of the committee which founded and built the Adelaide Club. In 1867-84 he was the first district grand master of the English Freemasons in South Australia. In the 1860s he sent his eldest son to Marlborough. 'Mere school education can be got here', he explained to a relation in England, 'but most of the boys turn out either very badly or the minority puffed up with conceit'.

Reputed one of Adelaide's richest men, Hardy was living beyond his means when depression hit the colony's banks in February 1886; his debts amounted to more than £40,000 and he had to assign his estate to a trustee for his creditors. Unable to regain financial independence he kept up appearances as doyen of the legal profession, even in his nineties tricycling to Glenelg station to catch the train to his Adelaide office. Predeceased by his wife, he died at Glenelg on 13 July 1909, survived by two sons and two daughters.

Although well-read, conscientious in public duties and generous, Hardy usually emptied the House when he rose to speak. He is best remembered as a planter of trees, some of them enclosed in the Arthur Hardy flora and fauna reserve at Mount Lofty.

E. J. R. Morgan, *The Adelaide Club 1863-1963* (Adel, 1963); *Honorary Magistrate*, July 1906; *Register* (Adel), 14 July 1909; M. Hardy, A history of the Hardy family in South Australia (SAA); Hardy papers (SAA); Arrangements by deed, 3390 (SAA).   JOHN TREGENZA

HARDY, JOHN RICHARD (1807-1858), gold commissioner and pastoralist, was born on 18 May 1807, the third son of Robert Hardy, vicar of Walberton, Sussex, England, and his wife Sophia-Adair, née Hale. He was educated at Charterhouse and at Trinity Hall and Peterhouse, Cambridge (B.A., 1831). A cricketer he played for Cambridge in 1829. In 1832 he migrated to Sydney where he edited the *Australian* for two years and reputedly introduced round-arm bowling into Australian cricket. On 18 May 1837 he married Clara, fourth daughter of John Stephen [q.v.] and sister of Alfred Stephen [q.v.].

In 1837-43 Hardy was an able police magistrate at Yass where he acquired property and reduced the bushranging threat. In bitter quarrels with local settlers he was supported by Cornelius O'Brien [q.v.] but in 1843 after accusations of irregular magisterial procedures Hardy was suspended. In 1849-51 he was police magistrate at Parramatta. On 15 June 1850 his estate was sequestrated and the order was finally discharged in 1888. Soon after the discovery of gold was announced in 1851, Hardy was appointed chief gold commissioner of crown lands for the New South Wales goldfields at a salary of £600. His instructions were to implement the government's newly-devised goldfields regulations, preserve the peace and 'put down outrage'. Much of his time was spent in riding over the goldfields issuing licences, settling disputes, allotting claims and buying and dispatching gold.

Colonel G. C. Mundy and Captain J. E. Erskine [qq.v.] praised his administrative qualities and testified to his fairness, rectitude, adaptability and humanity.

In September 1852 in evidence to a Legislative Council select committee inquiring into goldfield management, Hardy opposed any alteration of the charge for licence fees and advocated that gold found on private land be accessible to licensed applicants. He hotly defended himself against imputations of improper preference to his brother William. Erroneous information implied that Hardy had not satisfactorily accounted for some moneys collected, and he considered himself the victim of 'an atrocious slander'. In December 1852 the committee reported that Hardy's professed views and opinions were 'of a character wholly incompatible' with his office, and recommended the abolition of his commissionership with compensation and the offer of a suitable vacancy in the public service. However, Hardy retired to his property, Hardwicke, at Yass. In 1855 he published a pamphlet, Squatters and Gold-diggers, their claims and rights. As a founder of the Yass Mechanics' Institute in 1857, he gave its opening address. He died without issue on 21 April 1858 and was buried according to Anglican rites in the garden at Hardwicke. He left a large estate to his wife and brother Charles, who were charged to make adequate provision for his brother William.

J. E. Erskine, A short account of the late discoveries of gold in Australia (Lond, 1851); Australian Journalist, The emigrant in Australia or gleanings from the gold-fields (Lond, c 1852); G. C. Mundy, Our antipodes, 1-3 (Lond, 1852); A. G. Moyes, Australian cricket: a history (Syd, 1959); N. Keesing, Gold fever (Syd, 1967); Further papers relative to the discovery of gold in Australia, PP (GB), 1854 (1719); Illustrated London News, 3 July, 23 Aug 1852; Yass Evening Tribune, 19 Aug 1920; Deas Thomson papers (ML); Insolvency file 2072 (NSWA); newspaper cuttings, v.41A (ML).

NANCY KEESING

HARDY, THOMAS (1830-1912), vigneron, was born on 14 January 1830 at Gittisham, near Honiton, Devon, England. He arrived at South Australia on 14 August 1850 in the British Empire and worked for a year with John Reynell [q.v.]. He then went to a cattle property at Normanville where he joined a butchery business after gold was discovered and drove cattle to the Victorian diggings. In 1853 he returned to South Australia and bought Bankside on the River Torrens three miles from Adelaide, where he planted ¾ acre of Shiraz and Grenache vines, two acres of fruit trees and built a wine cellar. In 1857 his first vintage

was sent in hogsheads to England and in 1859 he visited England with wine samples. He bought more land in 1863, enlarged the vineyard to 35 acres and planted olives (Hardy's Mammoth), oranges, lemons, almonds and vines for raisin and currant production. By 1865 he was producing 14,000 gallons of wine and by the mid-1870s 53,000 gallons from his own vines and from about forty other growers.

In 1874 Hardy bought a disused flour-mill at McLaren Vale. About 1876 he bought the adjoining Tintara vineyard from Alexander Charles Kelly (M.D., Edinburgh, 1832) who had arrived from Scotland on 11 March 1840, was assistant surgeon at Adelaide Hospital and after visiting Scotland in 1846 settled at Morphett Vale where he took up vine-growing. In 1861 he bought what became the Tintara vineyard, cleared the land, planted vines and in 1864 built his home. In 1876 he retired to Norwood and died on 9 October 1877 aged 66, survived by his wife, two sons and three daughters. He published The Vine in Australia (Melbourne, 1861), Wine-growing in Australia, and the teachings of modern writers on vine-culture and wine-making (Adelaide, 1867) and his 'Wine-growing in South Australia' was included in the Chamber of Manufactures' South Australian Industries (1875). One of his sons worked for Hardy.

In 1884 Hardy bought 480 acres next to Tintara and by 1885 had 40,000 gallons of wine maturing, most of it bought by P. B. Burgoyne & Co., London. By 1901 Hardy held 540 acres of vines, had made his sons partners and as Thomas Hardy & Sons Ltd owned stores at Mile End and cellars in Currie Street. His wines won many awards in Australia and overseas, the first a trophy worth £100 at Sydney in 1880.

Hardy was chairman of the wine committee of the Adelaide display in 1886 which led to the Colonial and Indian Exhibition in London. He often lectured on wine-growing, joined the Phylloxera Board in 1889 and was president of the Wine Growers' Association in 1891. His many tours abroad included the Continent, America and South Africa; he visited laboratories in Britain and Montpellier Viticulture College to look at research on wine diseases, and examined the working of the Covent Garden fruit market. He was vice-president of the South Australian Horticultural Society and the Chamber of Manufactures, chairman of the West Torrens Board of Advice and a justice of the peace. He published articles first in the local press and then as Notes on Vineyards in America and Europe (1885) and A Vigneron Abroad. Trip to South Africa (1899). Hardy had married Joanna Holbrook in 1853. He died at Bankside on 10 January 1912, survived by two sons and two daughters. His estate was valued at £46,000.

J. J. Pascoe, *History of Adelaide and vicinity* (Adel, 1901); E. Whitington, *The South Australian vintage 1903* (*Register* reprint, Adel, 1903); Hardy & Sons Ltd, *The Hardy tradition* (Adel, 1953); *Register* (Adel), 3 Nov 1877, 11 Jan 1912.   SALLY O'NEILL

HARE, CHARLES SIMEON (1808-1882), merchant and parliamentarian, was born in London, son of a carpenter. After schooling in London he joined a bank. While young he visited America and later claimed experience in the working of agricultural colleges in various States and knowledge of the education system of Boston. On 5 October 1836 he arrived with his wife Anna Maria in the *Emma* at Kangaroo Island. There he became book-keeper and accountant for the South Australian Co. but was no longer required when the company moved to Adelaide. He settled at Port Adelaide and did contract work, including pile-driving for the government wharf. He later bought land at Plympton but maintained a strong interest in the port area.

In 1851 Hare was elected to the Legislative Council for West Torrens, winning the seat by two votes on a platform of state aid to education, universal suffrage, vote by ballot, two-year parliaments, no nominees and no taxation; he also supported property qualifications and unpaid members. He resigned in 1854 over disagreements on the framing of the new Constitution and became comptroller of convicts. With A. H. Freeling and C. Bonney [qq.v.] Hare was a commissioner of the Adelaide-Gawler railway. He represented Yatala in the House of Assembly from March to May 1857 but resigned to superintend the Yatala stockade, a post he held for less than two years. He had been commissioner of the city and Port Adelaide railway and in July 1860 became manager of railways. In May 1865 he was dismissed, with compensation, for upsetting the governor's express train on a visit to Port Adelaide. He left to work a plantation in Fiji but after many losses returned to Adelaide 'more like a shirt hung on a handspike' than an able-bodied man.

In 1874 Hare became manager of a small mine near Moonta and took part against the miners in the Moonta strike in April. In 1878-80 he represented Wallaroo in the House of Assembly, speaking most often on the subject of education, particularly in support of free schools. Another interest was the use of the Murray River for irrigation on which he published a pamphlet. He

was an advocate of total abstinence and the originator of such charities as the Indian Relief Fund. He visited England in 1880-81 but suffered from a kidney disease and on 22 July 1882 he died aged 74 at his home in Adelaide. Survived by his wife, he was buried in the West Terrace cemetery. His estate was valued at less than £1200.

Former colleagues in the House of Assembly acknowledged his 'racy intelligence and independent character'. Eccentric, much travelled and almost patriarchal, he was always 'an antagonist in conflict of opinion and a champion of weak causes'.

D. Pike, *Paradise of Dissent*, 2nd ed (Melb, 1967); PD (SA), 25 July 1882; *Observer* (Adel), 29 July 1882; *Pearsons Mthly Illustrated News*, Aug 1882.

HARGRAVE, JOHN FLETCHER (1815-1885), judge, was born on 28 December 1815 at Greenwich, England, son of Joshua Hargrave, hardware merchant, and his wife Sarah, née Lee. Privately schooled, he went in 1830 to King's College, London, where he won a certificate of honour for rhetoric, and to Trinity College, Cambridge (B.A., 1837; M.A., 1840). He had enrolled at Lincoln's Inn in 1836, was called to the Bar in 1841 and practised in chancery for ten years. In 1841 he published an edition of part of Blackstone's Commentaries and in 1842 *Treatise on the Thelluson Act; with practical observations upon Trusts for Accumulation*. On 20 September 1843 he married his cousin, Ann Hargrave of Leeds. In 1849, despite strong testimonials, he failed to gain office as a police magistrate. Unremitting study 'unhinged his mind' and in 1851 with a legacy from his father he retired from the Bar. He dabbled in 'railway and other public matters' until his wife committed him to the new asylum at Colney Hatch, Middlesex. Gradually recovering, he was advised to leave England and in February 1857 arrived at Sydney with his family. He was admitted to the local Bar and became a foundation judge of the District Court. He never forgave his wife and could not endure her presence so she returned to England. According to Sir Alfred Stephen [q.v.], Hargrave's judgeship was 'disastrous for women suitors' because he habitually decided against them, but otherwise he mastered his disability.

Hargrave resigned from the bench in February 1859 to become Charles Cowper's [q.v.] solicitor-general and from March to October represented in turn East Camden and Illawarra in the Legislative Assembly. From November until June 1865 he was a member of the Legislative Council. He was solicitor-general under William Forster [q.v.] and attorney-general and government representative in the council under John Robertson [q.v.] and twice again under Cowper. Using politics for his own advancement Hargrave secured silk in 1863, though he had practised little in the colony, and a place on the Supreme Court bench on 22 June 1865. His swearing-in was boycotted by the Bar. As primary judge in equity he was reliable but temperamental and talkative, making a show of his learning. His appointment as first divorce judge in 1873 was strikingly inappropriate. As a member of the Full Court he so aggravated Chief Justice Stephen as to provoke his resignation. Hargrave was also immune to criticism. Accused in 1869 of exceeding permitted expenditure when on circuit, he retorted that the dignity of his position demanded more than the prescribed allowance. He admitted that he did not sit in court before 11.00 a.m. and ignored complaints that he rarely sat after 1.00 p.m. His health was affected by constant quarrelling with the new chief justice, Sir James Martin [q.v.], and his mind, seemingly in decline before his pensioned retirement in 1881, was said to be 'entirely gone' a year later.

Hargrave's greatest contribution was in promoting legal education. He became reader in general jurisprudence at the University of Sydney where Professor Woolley [q.v.] heard with 'the most intense gratification' his first lecture on 3 August 1858, though others found his methods overpoweringly didactic and homiletic. His course of twenty lectures was published in 1878. He also delivered many occasional addresses on law outside the university. In 1864 he was licensed by the university to conduct a boarding house for law students in his leased residence at Upper William Street, Rushcutters Bay. Before insanity overwhelmed him, Hargrave saw his colonial career as 'one long journey of successful toil and victorious conflict'. He died on 23 February 1885 from an 'effusion on the brain' and was buried in the Anglican section of Waverley cemetery. He was survived by his wife, a daughter and three sons, of whom the second, Lawrence, became a noted aeronautical experimenter.

V&P (LA NSW), 1861, 1, 623, 1870-71, 1, 793, 1876-77, 3, 719, 1881, 1, 108, 246, 2, 699; H. W. H. Huntington, Australian judges (ML); A. Stephen, A trio of judges, uncat MS 211 (ML); J. F. Hargrave papers (ML); Lawrence Hargrave papers (NL). J. M. BENNETT

HARGRAVES, EDWARD HAMMOND (1816-1891), gold rush publicist, was born on 7 October 1816 at Gosport, Hampshire, England, son of Lieutenant John Edward Hargraves and his wife Elizabeth, née Whitcombe. Educated at Brighton Grammar School and Lewes, he went to sea at 14 and arrived at Sydney in 1832. He worked on a property at Bathurst, gathered bêche-de-mer and tortoise shell in Torres Strait and in 1834 took up 100 acres near Wollongong. In 1836 at Sydney he married Elizabeth, née Mackay. In 1839 they moved to East Gosford where he became an agent for the General Steam Navigation Co. and with her dowry bought land and built the Fox under the Hill Hotel. In 1843 he forfeited his property, left his wife to look after a store and took up land on the Manning River.

Hargraves sold out and sailed for California on 17 July 1849. He returned to Sydney in January 1851, planning to win a fortune not so much by finding gold but by claiming the government reward for discovery of a payable goldfield. On his way to the Wellington district he saw promising specimens at Guyong and on 12 February, with John Lister, found five specks of gold in Lewis Ponds Creek. In the next weeks he traversed much of the area with slight success, but his campaign depended on finding rich deposits so he enlisted Lister and William, James and Henry, sons of William Tom [q.v.], to continue the search. Hargraves had taught them Californian panning techniques and how to make and use a wooden cradle.

Hargraves returned to Sydney in March and interviewed the colonial secretary Deas Thomson [q.v.]. Encouraged by news from the Tom brothers, Hargraves wrote to the *Sydney Morning Herald* describing in general terms the rich fields. When sure of the government reward some weeks later he announced in the press the specific areas where gold existed and left for Bathurst early in May. He ignored pleas by the Toms and Lister for secrecy, named the area Ophir and whipped up enthusiasm in the Bathurst district. By 15 May over 300 diggers were at Ophir and the first gold rush had begun.

Although Hargraves exaggerated and falsified his finds he never denied his main purpose. The government gave him £10,000 and from 1877 an annual pension of £250. He was also showered with testimonials, valuable cups and other trophies. In 1851 he became a commissioner of crown lands for the gold districts and a justice of the peace. In 1853-54 Hargraves visited England, lived in style, met the Queen and in 1855 published *Australia and its Gold Fields*, which was probably ghosted. Some £3000 poorer he returned with a builder to erect, entirely of cedar, a fine house at Norah Head. He entertained lavishly and by the early 1860s was virtually penniless. Invited by governments he prospected in Western Australia in 1862 and South Australia in 1863. In 1861 he had begun to appeal to the Victorian government for the balance of its £5000 reward, of which he had received only £2381 6s. 1d. in 1854. When petitions failed, he sought help in 1867 from J. S. Butters [q.v.] who persuaded a member of the Legislative Assembly to move for payment. The motion was lost and Hargraves went to Melbourne and in the *Age* charged politicians with corruption. Inquiry by a select committee found none of his charges proven. Deserted by the manipulators he had tried to use, he claimed to be specially shocked by Butters who had paid his hotel bills as a fellow Freemason but cast doubts on his honesty.

In New South Wales Lister and the Tom brothers realized too late that they too had been used by Hargraves. In 1853 a Legislative Council select committee heard long arguments about the 1851 events and, while upholding Hargraves's key role, recommended that £1000 be granted to the men taught by Hargraves and a similar amount to Rev. W. B. Clarke [q.v.]. Hargraves's polemical account of the matter in his book did not silence the increasingly bitter Toms and Lister. From 1870 they bombarded parliament with petitions and campaigned in pamphlets and press. Their persistence was rewarded in 1890 when a Legislative Assembly select committee found that although Hargraves had taught the others how to use the dish and cradle, 'Messrs Tom and Lister were undoubtedly the first discoverers of gold obtained in Australia in payable quantity', but the legend of Hargraves, 'the discoverer of gold' persists. He died in Sydney on 29 October 1891 and was buried in the Anglican section of Waverley cemetery. He was survived by two sons and three daughters and left an estate worth less than £375.

C. Swancott, *The Brisbane Water story*, 4 (Woy Woy, 1955); G. Blainey, *The rush that never ended*, 2nd ed (Melb, 1969); V&P (LC NSW), 1853, 2, 747; V&P (LA Vic), 1864-65, 2 (E6), 1867, 2 (D23); (LA NSW), 1890, 4, 1053, 1087; PD (Vic) 1867; G. Blainey, 'The gold rushes: the year of decision', *Hist Studies*, no 10, May 1962; *Town and Country J*, 12 Feb 1876; J. Clifford, Edward Hammond Hargraves, the gold discovery and crisis of 1851 (B.A. Hons thesis, Univ New England, 1963).

BRUCE MITCHELL

HARKER, GEORGE (1816-1879), businessman, philanthropist and politician, was born at Pateley Bridge, Yorkshire, England,

son of Robert Harker and his wife Nancy, née Richardson. One of nine children, he was educated at local schools and at 13 was apprenticed to a Harrogate chemist. After working in Leeds, Harker had a chemist's business in Prescot where he was treasurer of the Anti-Corn Law League. In 1845 he married Sarah Rigby, by whom he had four sons and three daughters.

Harker migrated to Melbourne, arriving in February 1846. For four years he had a farm on the Heidelberg Road and then moved to Melbourne to become a grain merchant in association first with W. L. Lees and then with his brother, Thomas. Harker's business enterprises prospered and by 1856 he was financially secure enough to devote most of his time to public work. He retired from active business and was elected for Collingwood to the first Victorian Legislative Assembly. Although a democrat and connected with the Central Province Reform Association, he associated with a group of liberal, Nonconformist merchants rather than the radicals; in March 1858 he accepted H. S. Chapman's [q.v.] invitation to become treasurer in the second O'Shanassy [q.v.] ministry. He lost Collingwood in August 1859 but in October won Maldon, which he held till March 1860 when he resigned to visit England with his wife and children. Representing Collingwood in 1864-65 and 1871-74 he maintained an independent course, usually liberal, sometimes staunchly conservative. He introduced bills for payment of members and the abolition of state aid to religion in 1864-65 without success and had radical views on the land question and property tax but was vehemently opposed to protection and strictly constitutional on the clash with the Legislative Council. A very active and conscientious member, if at times out of touch with the political realities, he retired from politics and went to live at Lilydale.

Perhaps more effective than his parliamentary work were Harker's years of charitable service, particularly to the Victorian Asylum and School for the Blind; he was chairman of the provisional committee which founded this institution in 1866 and chairman of its board till 1879. He served on the committee of management of the Melbourne Hospital and as treasurer of the Benevolent Asylum in 1864-70, and was connected with many other charities whose interests he carefully watched in parliament. In 1871 he was chairman of a royal commission which recommended reduction of the number of charitable institutions receiving government aid. He also contributed generously to the funds of the Congregational Church, where he regularly attended but for reasons of conscience was never a member. He represented the Independents on the 1867 royal commission on public education and was a member of the Board of Education from September 1867 till December 1871, when he resigned in the course of a dispute between the board and the Catholic bishop, J. A. Goold [q.v.]. Although sincere and benevolent with a strong sense of public duty and a deep concern for the poor and afflicted, he was often involved in sectarian squabbles.

When Harker retired as a merchant in 1856 he probably retained some commercial connexions, particularly with the importing firm run by his brother in Flinders Street, and became very actively involved in the development of local companies. He also had interests in mining, railways and banking, and was a founder and director of the Collingwood Gas Co. and the Victoria Life and General Insurance Co., with which he remained linked until at 63 he died suddenly in Melbourne on 25 April 1879.

Report of the provisional committee of the Victorian Asylum and School for the Blind, 1866 (Melb, 1866); *Congregational Year Book, 1880*; G. Serle, *The golden age* (Melb, 1963); PD (Vic), 1864-65, 1871-74; *Examiner* (Melb), 6 Aug 1859; *Argus*, 3 Mar 1860, 26 Apr 1879; *Age*, 26 Apr 1879; G. R. Quaife, The nature of political conflict in Victoria 1856-57 (M.A. thesis, Univ Melb, 1964).

MARGOT BEEVER

HARPER, CHARLES (1842-1912), agriculturist, legislator and newspaper proprietor, was born on 15 July 1842 near Toodyay, Western Australia, only son of Charles Harper and his wife Julia Gretchen, née Lukin. He was educated by his father, a barrister of Gray's Inn who became a colonial farmer and later an Anglican clergyman. According to family legend, his mother gave him at 16 a horse and cart, a gun, a barrel of salt pork and £50, and sent him to find himself a farm. He travelled south-east and leased land between York and Beverley, where he farmed for several years and developed the 'Harper fence', using local timber instead of imported wire. In 1861 and 1864 he joined the search for pastoral land in the Yilgarn district and made botanical and geological observations. In 1866 he sailed for Roebourne with sheep and, after a year of exploration with S. Viveash, was fluent in the local Aboriginal language and took up pearling. He and Viveash spent a year building the boat *Amateur*, and with the proceeds of pearling Harper was able to buy a one-third interest in the 883,000-acre de Grey station in 1871. In 1878 Harper sold his share in de Grey and joined Alex McRae

in a smaller station, Yanrey, in the best Ashburton country; he held this interest until 1904.

In 1879 he bought the *Western Australian Times* with Sir Thomas Cockburn-Campbell [q.v.] as his nominal partner and managing editor. On 23 March Harper married Fanny, daughter of Robert de Burgh of Caversham, and settled at Woodbridge, near Guildford, on the 470 acres selected by Governor Stirling in 1829. There he developed a productive sheep, dairying and orchard property of major significance in local agricultural research. He was the first to irrigate with artesian water in Western Australia, and designed successful earthworks to conserve for his orchard the rich silt washed down the Swan River. He co-operated with George Compere, government entomologist, in a search for parasites to combat indigenous pests, sent to Japan for orchard stock, consulted Swan Valley vignerons about improved methods and vines, invented a shearing machine and patented a food product from the core of the blackboy tree and a process for treating septic tank effluent.

An early advocate of mixed wheat and wool farming, Harper wrote extensively on agricultural and pastoral topics, passing on the results of his experiments and reading through his daily *West Australian* and the rural weekly *Western Mail*, both founded in 1885. He advocated experimental farms, giving a lead on his own properties and in partnership with W. Catton Grasby, whom he brought from South Australia in 1905 to be agricultural editor of the *Western Mail*. Harper and his son Walter, working with Grasby, discovered the soluble-phosphate deficiency of local soils long before superphosphate was generally used in the colony. They are also credited with developing the first local wheat varieties, Gresley and Wilfred, named after two Harper sons killed at Gallipoli on 7 August 1915. These wheats were used in Western Australia and New South Wales for many years. Harper supported the co-operative movement and early guaranteed an overdraft of £10,000; his son, Walter, was chairman of the Westralian Farmers Co-operative Ltd for thirty years.

Believing that public life demanded the highest integrity, Harper was persuaded to enter politics only after thorough personal stocktaking, but he soon won respect and distinction. He represented the North District in the Legislative Council in 1878-80, York in 1884-90 and Beverley in the new Legislative Assembly in 1890-1905. In parliament he showed the breadth of his knowledge in quiet, clear speeches. A strong supporter of land ownership, he contended that the state, in parting with land, did not part with the power to tax it, but opposed a project for a land tax in 1887 because the colony had so few wealthy landowners. He served on several select committees, was chairman of royal commissions on customs in 1893, the Coolgardie water scheme in 1902, forestry in 1903 and immigration in 1905, and was chairman of committees in 1897. In many ways an 'independent English country gentleman', he disliked urban concentration, heavy government spending and disciplined party politics. In 1886-88 he and his newspapers took the conservative side in the quarrels surrounding Governor Broome and in the controversy over Rev. J. B. Gribble's [q.v.] allegations of maltreatment of the Aboriginals. In 1899-1900 he broke with Sir John Forrest over Federation and lavish public spending. In December 1903 he was nominated Speaker by the Liberal premier, Walter James. After the 1904 elections he declined reappointment and went into opposition to James, thus becoming one of the few independents responsible for the accession to power of Western Australia's first Labor government, although he believed that the party needed experience in office to temper its radical tendencies. In August 1905 he voted against the Labor ministry and retired before the next general election. However, the findings of his royal commission on immigration provided a framework for expansive rural policies in 1906-14.

Harper died at Woodbridge on 20 April 1912, survived by three sons and four daughters of his ten children. Among his memorials is the Guildford Grammar School, which originated in 1896 in the billiard-room at Woodbridge with fourteen pupils, three of them Harper girls, and after moving to its present site in 1901 was bought by the Anglican Church in 1911.

W. B. Kimberly, *History of West Australia* (Melb, 1897); F. R. Mercer, *The life of Charles Harper* (Perth, 1958); F. K. Crowley, *Australia's western third* (Lond, 1960).

O. K. BATTYE

HARRAP, ALFRED (1820-1893), merchant, shipowner and leader of volunteers, was born in England. He first saw Van Diemen's Land as a junior officer of the *Children* in September 1837 and was so impressed by the colony that he later migrated. With Charles Groom of Carrick as partner he bought a farm in the foothills of the Western Tiers. Though menaced at first by bushrangers and escaped convicts, the venture prospered. He became honorary secretary of the local ploughing association in 1848. In 1853 he took charge of a produce

store in Westbury and on 26 November at Windermere married Amelia, the daughter of Edward Tobin, R.N. By 1857 Harrap had accumulated some capital and experience and set up as a grain merchant in Launceston. With his integrity and resource the business prospered. He added fine wool to his other produce and won repute for shipping his consignments in good order and condition. Later he became an importer of farm machinery and supplies, bought his own ships for coastal trade and held regular auctions. His premises became an exchange, described as 'a friendly, informal meeting place for producers and buyers'.

Active in public affairs, Harrap served for years on the Launceston Municipal Council and was mayor for six terms; a member of the Marine Board he was master warden for six years. He was also a church-warden of St John's Anglican Church, a director of the Commercial Bank of Tasmania for twenty years and in 1877-91 vice-consul for Sweden and Norway. Most notable was his record in the Launceston Volunteer Artillery. He first joined it on 29 June 1860 and became a captain within six months. By 1870 the artillery had a force of 22 with 100 rifles and accoutrements, estimated to be adequate 'for the proper defence of Launceston'. In March 1877 the volunteer artillery in Hobart was disbanded and the guns and gear were returned to the military stores, but Harrap protested. Praising his zeal, the government permitted the Launceston corps to continue but with no 'pecuniary assistance' except for ball ammunition used in practice. When the town clock stopped in 1878 Harrap organized the firing of a noon gun with a daily parade. With government approval, he enrolled fifty new volunteers and twenty bandsmen. He was allowed no cash for uniforms but was promoted major in January 1879 and, by calling a public meeting at the Town Hall, raised the money and also persuaded the cabinet to provide a new parade ground. He served as aide-de-camp to several governors on their visits to Launceston and retired in 1886 as a lieut-colonel. He died aged 73 at his home in St John Street on 26 January 1893, predeceased by his wife in 1890 and survived by four daughters and one son, George Edward (1856-1937), who continued the business and held high office in the volunteers.

A. Harrap & Son Pty Ltd, *A century of service* (Launceston, 1957); J. Reynolds, *Launceston; history of an Australian city* (Melb, 1969); *Daily Telegraph* (Launceston), 27 Jan 1893; *Examiner* (Launceston), 27 Jan 1893; CSD 10/33/544, 60/1430, 63/145, 13/36/476 (TA).

JOHN REYNOLDS

HARRIMAN, BENJAMIN COSWAY (1830-1904), civil servant, was born on 17 November 1830 at Tiverton, Devon, England, son of John Harriman, manager of a lace factory, and his wife Phillipa, née Cosway. His father had followed the lace machinist, John Heathcote, from the Nottingham district to Tiverton after the Luddite riots. Benjamin was educated at schools in Tiverton. He arrived at Melbourne in 1854, became a clerk in the police department and as an expert shorthand writer was often deputed to report on Yarra bank political meetings. He also assisted Professor Hearn [q.v.] and others to organize Mechanics' Institute lectures. Although he never completed a degree in the University of Melbourne he took first- and second-year classes in 1861-62, gaining second-class honours in both years. In 1858 he had married Isobel Ellen, daughter of a government shorthand writer, J. H. Webb, and niece of G. H. F. Webb [q.v.].

After entering the Victorian Law Department in 1860, Harriman became chief clerk in 1870 and secretary in 1872. He supervised his department conscientiously, dispensed with much red tape through efficient and courteous service, tried to offer the best advice to the Berry [q.v.] government in the constitutional conflict of the late 1870s, and maintained the smooth functioning of the courts and the transaction of the colony's legal business despite the public service disruption of 1878. When his health began to deteriorate under the strain of work he was given a year's leave in 1884 to visit England. On his return to Melbourne he undertook the additional responsibilities of reorganizing the Titles Office, investigating frauds in the Registrar-General's Department and extirpating fraudulent practices from his own department. A severe illness forced him to take eight months' leave in 1890 and next year he retired on a substantial allowance.

One of the few criticisms made of Harriman's generally exemplary public service career was that as secretary of the Law Department his affability sometimes resulted in the injudicious disclosure of information to the press. An example of his indiscretion occurred after his retirement when he exacerbated an uneasy situation in the Chaffeys' Mildura irrigation colony in September 1892 by informing disgruntled settlers that they were entitled to free water. A Freemason, Harriman held office in many Victorian societies. After his retirement he lived at Ellendale, Frankston, but died at Darlinghurst, Sydney, on 26 May 1904 at his daughter's home and was buried in Cheltenham cemetery, Victoria. He left a widow, three sons and three married daughters.

Table Talk, 11 Feb 1887, 24 Jan 1890; *Leader* (Melb), 15 Feb 1890; *Mildura Cultivator*, 10 Sept 1892; *Argus*, 30 May 1904.

CAROLE WOODS

HARRIS, JOHN (1819-1895) and GEORGE (1831-1891), businessmen, were born in London, sons of John Harris and his wife Sarah, née Walton; their grandfather was probably the emancipist, John Harris [q.v.]. As a carpenter their father was given free passages for himself, his wife and six children in the *Indiana* and arrived on 15 October 1833 at Sydney; he became a publican and died aged 56 on 29 May 1844 and was buried in the La Perouse cemetery.

His elder son John joined the business of his uncle Joseph Underwood [q.v.] in April 1842 and on 3 May married his cousin, Catherine Lucy Underwood. In June with George Thornton as his partner he set up a mercantile and shipping agency at Brisbane. In November the partnership was dissolved but John continued the agency. In the squatting rush of 1848 the business expanded rapidly and in August George arrived in Brisbane to work for John. The brothers quarrelled often and in 1852 George went to the goldfields at Bendigo. At John's invitation he returned to Brisbane and became a partner in the agency. Soon afterwards John went to London to set up an office as resident partner. Under John the business had been confined to wool export, wharf management, shipping agencies and wholesale imports from London. George was more venturesome; he added a fleet of coasting ships, opened a fellmongery, tannery and boot and harness factory, and when cotton boomed in the American civil war bought suitable land and set up a processing plant near Ipswich. On 13 October 1860 at St Paul's Anglican Church, Ipswich, he had married Jane, daughter of George Thorn; they had three sons and three daughters. One daughter married R. G. Casey and another C. L. Hill [qq.v.].

In the 1870s George speculated in mining properties at Gympie and Stanthorpe but lost heavily. His brother, increasingly alarmed at the firm's seeming instability, visited Brisbane several times and sent agents to report on its progress. George resented this interference and, attributing it to parsimony and over-caution, decided that the partnership had broken down. On 29 August 1876 he petitioned to have the firm declared insolvent. The proceedings for winding up the firm ended in October 1878 and he soon opened his own business as George Harris & Co.

With his wide interests George was prominent in Brisbane affairs. In May 1860 he was appointed to the Queensland Legislative Council and served until August 1878. At various times he was consul for the United States of America, for Italy and for Belgium. In 1862 he had leased Newstead House, the old government residency, and later bought it. There he entertained lavishly until the property was lost during the bankruptcy proceedings. He died on 28 March 1891 at North Quay, Brisbane, and John on 27 May 1895 probably in England.

N. Bartley, *Australian pioneers and reminiscences*, J. J. Knight ed (Brisb, 1896); L. E. Slaughter, *Newstead House* (Brisb, 1955); *Illustrated Sydney News*, 9 May 1891; C. Lack, 'A merchant prince of the sixties', *Brisbane Courier*, 24 July 1937; Col Sec land letters 2/7874 (QA); Insolvency file 188/1876 (QA); RHSQ records; CO 385/5.   CLEM LACK

HARRIS, JOHN (1838-1911), alderman, was born on 10 August 1838 at Maghera, County Londonderry, Ireland, son of John Harris, banker, and his wife Nancy Ann, née McKee. In 1842 he arrived in Sydney with his parents who were kinsmen of Surgeon John Harris [q.v.]. He was educated at Dr Fullerton's [q.v.] school, the Normal Institution and the University of Sydney, but left without a degree to manage the large metropolitan real estate inherited from his father. He lived at Bulwarra House, Ultimo, where much of his property was situated. Harris Park was named after the family. In 1869 he married Lizzie Henrietta Dingle Page.

In 1874-83 and 1886-1911 Harris represented Denison ward in the Sydney City Council. In 1875 he became a magistrate and in 1877-80 represented West Sydney in the Legislative Assembly. In his first term as mayor in 1881, under power granted by the 1879 City Improvement Act and accompanied by civic authorities and the press, he made three dramatic inspections of the slums, a potential fever threat to the city. His visits, vividly described by 'The Vagabond' [q.v. J. S. James] in the *Daily Telegraph*, shocked the public. Harris was ruthless in condemning buildings, including his own Central Police Court. Tall and robust, his private wealth gave him independence. As mayor he entertained in princely style and the mayoress instituted popular monthly receptions. Harris began the reclamation of Blackwattle Bay and resumption of the Rocks and Darling Harbour but the council lacked power to carry out these schemes. In December 1882 he was re-elected to the assembly for South Sydney, defeating John Davies [q.v.] whom Harris accused of fraudulently acquiring a cheque. In June 1883 Davies sued him for £20,000 damages for libel and won after a long and sensational trial, although Harris had to pay damages of only one farthing. In December he retired from the city council and after his wife died in 1885 did not seek re-election to the assembly.

In December 1886 Harris was re-elected to the council and in a policy of reform in December 1887 defeated Sydney Burdekin [q.v.] by three votes to be mayor in the centennial year. To the reformers, 'only a very rich man could afford to reduce the mayoral expenditure'. Harris himself paid for his entertainment and donated his £1000 honorarium to the University of Sydney for a scholarship in anatomy and physiology. At the same time he embarked on strict retrenchment and sacked 250 council employees without impairing efficiency, boldly attacked graft and unearthed 'corporation frauds'. On 3 May 1888 he chaired a large public meeting at the Town Hall to demand the prevention of Chinese landing from the *Afghan* and the total prohibition of such immigration. Heading a procession from the Town Hall to Parliament House he was 'swept into the corridor as if borne upon a tidal wave' and forced through the lobby doors while the crowds outside were in 'wild disorder'.

Harris was mayor for the fifth time in 1889 and on 27 November officially opened the new Town Hall. He left the finances of the corporation sounder than he found them and fought for a modern building construction bill to regulate the height and fireproofing of buildings. In 1896 he urged the corporation to acquire the Australian Gaslight Co. but the government was not interested. He was five times mayor and Richard Meagher twice nominated him in vain as lord mayor as a fitting climax to his public service. Generous and benevolent, 'Honest John' was honorary treasurer of the Benevolent Asylum and a director of the Randwick Orphan Asylum and Sydney Hospital. He died on 7 November 1911 at Bulwarra from chronic nephritis and was survived by five sons and three daughters. He was buried in the Presbyterian section of Rookwood cemetery with Masonic rites. He left £97,000.

E. Digby (ed), *Australian men of mark*, 2 (Syd, 1889); *Bulletin*, 28 Aug 1880; *SMH*, 22, 23, 26-30 June, 13 Sept 1883, 4, 5 May 1888, 8 Nov 1911; *Town and Country J*, 24 Dec 1887, 23 Nov 1889; *Daily Telegraph* (Syd), 29, 30, 31

Oct 1969; newspaper cuttings, vols 135, 156 (ML); MS and printed cats under John Harris (ML); CO 201/608.   MARTHA RUTLEDGE

HARRIS, RICHARD DEODATUS POULETT (1817-1899), schoolmaster and Church of England clergyman, was born on 26 October 1817 at Sydney, Nova Scotia, Canada, eldest son of Charles Poulett Harris, bookseller and private schoolmaster of Manchester, and his wife Anna Maria, daughter of Richard Stout, judge and member of the governor's council on Cape Breton Island. His mother came from a family of American Loyalists and his father, the illegitimate son of John, fourth Earl Poulett, was commissioned in the 60th Regiment; when it was reduced in 1817 he returned to England. Richard was enrolled in 1837 at Manchester Grammar School and in 1839 entered Trinity College, Cambridge (B.A., 1843; M.A., 1852). Interested in the physical sciences and modern languages, and evangelical in outlook, he chose to become a schoolmaster. He was second master at Sheffield Collegiate School in 1843, vice-principal of Huddersfield College in 1844-47 and second master in 1847-49, and classical master at Blackheath Proprietary School, Middlesex, in 1849-57. He was ordained deacon by Bishop Sumner of Chester in 1847 and priest by Bishop Prince of Manchester in 1849. On 25 June 1844 he had married Catherine Prior, eldest daughter of William Hall, a brewer of Cambridge; they had two sons and four daughters.

Through the agency mainly of Rev. Robert Whiston, M.A., headmaster of the Cathedral Grammar School, Rochester, Harris was induced to accept the rectorship of Hobart Town High School, a proprietary school founded in 1848 by leading Presbyterians and Free Churchmen. Keen to get his services and those of his brother-in-law, Rev. F. W. Quilter, M.A., who was to be second master, the shareholders increased their indebtedness from £300 to £715 and appointed him for three years at a salary of £800 with half the school fees above that amount. His wife died on 27 June 1856 and five months later he sailed from Gravesend in the *Mercia* with his daughter Charlotte and two sons, arriving at Hobart on 17 March 1857. On 13 July 1858 he married Elizabeth Eleanor (b. 24 October 1833), eldest daughter of John Wilward, merchant, of Tessierville, Hobart; they had four daughters.

Harris soon won confidence and respect. By 1860 more than 100 parents, Christians of all denominations and Jews, had enrolled their sons. Despite the high enrolment the shareholders felt obliged in 1861 to lease the school to Harris who was to pay an annual rent of £100 and maintain two (Newcastle) scholarships valued at £12 a year. In 1862 the school's finances were still insecure and the building was offered to the government for £1800 as a university college, on the assumption that Harris would become the first principal. When the government refused, the shareholders made a new agreement with Harris. He was charged with assaulting boys with a cane in March 1860 and June 1868, the first case being dismissed and the second settled out of court, but he maintained the school's pre-eminent position in the colony until 1878 when he lost his midlands boarders to Horton College and Launceston Church Grammar School. Thereafter his health declined and in 1885, suffering acute physical pain and mental depression, he surrendered to Christ College, with the shareholders' agreement, all leasehold rights in return for an annuity of £300. The school was closed on 15 August 1885 and he retired to his home, Cliff House, Peppermint Bay, Woodbridge. In his rectorship High School pupils had won five exhibitions, ten gold medals and twenty-two scholarships at the Council of Education's annual examinations and nine times headed the degree list, a record approached only by his friendly competitor, the Hutchins School. Though keen for success in public examinations he also insisted on broadening his pupils' experience. Instruction was given in singing, mechanical drawing and carpentry while participation in sport was encouraged and regular dances were organized for boarders.

In retirement Harris regained health sufficiently to continue his long-standing connexion with the movement for a university. At the royal commission on superior and general education in 1859 he had argued the importance of secondary schools for a university or surrogate institution, and in 1860-90 he was an appointed member of the Council of Education. For the royal commission of 1883 he prepared a plan to transform the council into a university senate and sought a public system of education from primary school to university under the unified control of a government department. His part in the negotiations preceding the University Act in 1889 is obscure. On 16 May Rev. James Scott recommended a teaching university with a salaried chancellor and proposed Harris for the position 'as one who has done the state pre-eminent service'. The proposal was rejected but in 1890-96 he was the first warden of senate.

He divided his leisure mainly between his books, Church, Masonic Lodge and sport; he was a trustee of the Cricket Association and a member of the Hobart Club. He read widely in the sciences and cultivated an inherited facility with modern languages. He established in 1872 a prize for French at the High School and became proficient enough in German to conduct divine service for German migrants on 22 November 1870 and take charge of the German consulate in 1872 in the consul's absence. A member of the Tasmanian auxiliary of the British and Foreign Bible Society and a thoughtful expositor of scripture, he was in demand as a preacher, especially at Trinity Church where he was a communicant. Melancholy in outlook and prone to depression, he had much sadness in his family life. He mourned the separation from the three daughters left in England and the early death of his son Richard from severe burns. His second daughter Charlotte Maria became of unsound mind, was committed to an institution in February 1872 and died a few years later. He died at Woodbridge on 23 December 1899.

R. Brown, *A history of the island of Cape Breton* (Lond, 1869); J. M. Browne, *Family notes* (Hob, 1887); *Rector and grand master: a memoir of . . . R. D. P. Harris* (Launceston, 1903); PP (HA Tas), 1889 (145); *Hobart Town Courier*, 12 Jan 1854, 18, 20, 28 Mar 1857; *Colonial Times*, 25 Jan 1855, 18, 21 Mar 1857; *Mercury*, 17, 22, 23 July, Aug 1855, 28, 30 Aug 1860, 29, 31 May 1862, 19 Apr 1864, 7 Aug 1866, 2, 3 June 1868, 25 Dec 1872, 1 Oct 1875, 4 Oct 1876, 8 Mar, 10 Oct 1877, 22 Aug 1881, 12, 22 Dec 1882, 27 July 1885, 25 Dec 1899; *Tas Mail*, 28 June 1890; Letters testimonial, 5 Feb 1847 (Cheshire Record Office); Davenport diaries 1861-88 (TA); M. Allport letters, 4 Jan 1875 (TA); Shoobridge papers (TA); Walker papers (Univ Tas Archives); Hobart Town High School ledger (TA); CSD 8/2/725, 16/25/290 (TA); WO 31/379.

E. L. FRENCH

HARRISON, HENRY COLDEN ANTILL (1836-1929), 'father' of Australian Rules football, was born on 16 October 1836 at Jarvisfield, the property of his uncle, Major Henry Colden Antill [q.v.], near Picton, New South Wales, son of John Harrison [q.v.] and his wife Jane, née Howe, a relation of William Redfern, Thomas Reiby, George Howe and H. S. Wills [qq.v.]. In 1850 the family settled in Melbourne where Harrison attended the new Diocesan Grammar School. His education was interrupted in 1852 by a visit to the goldfields, where he sympathized with the diggers' grievances. In 1853 he became an officer in the Customs Department and in 1888 transferred to the Titles Office where he became registrar.

Harrison's career as a public servant was worthy, but he was most distinguished as a sportsman. For nine years he was the champion 'pedestrian' of Victoria, defeating all comers in sprints and over hurdles and steeples. His contests with the Ballarat champion, L. L. Mount, aroused great interest. A Ballarat publican and race-horse-owner, Walter Craig, was said to have once held £10,000 to wager on Mount; after Harrison won, Craig offered to finance him in a foot-racing tour of England, but Harrison preferred his amateur status.

Melbourne's first football club was founded in 1858 by Harrison's cousin, T. W. Wills [q.v.], a talented cricketer who was seeking a winter pastime. Harrison played in the first games, and was in succession captain of three football clubs. Wills had learned his football while at school at Rugby but considered that game 'unsuitable for grown men, engaged in making a livelihood'. The Victorian clubs evolved new rules which were consolidated in a code drafted by Harrison and adopted in 1866. It incorporated the distinctive features of the Australian game: no tripping or 'hacking', no 'off-side' rule, the 'mark' and carrying the ball. Harrison thus earned his honorific title as 'father of Australian Rules football'. He retired from playing in 1872 but maintained his interest in football. He became a vice-president of the Football Association formed in 1877; he was chairman in 1905 of the conference which formed the Australian National Football Council and was elected its first life member; he was an honoured guest at the jubilee dinner in 1908 at which Alfred Deakin proposed the toast to Australian football. He also maintained his physical fitness; in 1898 he rode a bicycle from Melbourne to Sydney in ten days to see the final Test match against Stoddart's English 11. In 1923 in Melbourne he published in his autobiography, *The Story of an Athlete*.

Harrison was handsome, lean and well groomed, somewhat unbending and puritanical, upright and honourable. He died in Melbourne on 2 September 1929, predeceased by his wife Emily, a sister of Tom Wills, and survived by four daughters. His coffin carried a wreath of violets in the shape of a football. His name is commemorated by Harrison House, the headquarters of the Victorian Football League.

IAN TURNER

HARRISON, JOHN (1802-1869), sea captain, squatter, agitator and stationmaster, was born in Cumberland, England, son of George Harrison and his wife Anne. He joined the navy as a midshipman and was a lieutenant in H.M.S. *Ganges* when he retired about 18 to command his father's ships. Later he went to Sydney to join a relation, H. C. Antill [q.v.], near Picton. On 12 February 1831 at St Philip's Church, Sydney, he married Jane, née Howe, a relation of H. S. Wills [q.v.].

Harrison visited England with his wife about 1833 and on the return voyage his father was drowned. He planned to grow sugar in Tahiti but in May 1835 his *Friendship*, carrying government stores, was wrecked on Norfolk Island. He sought compensation in land without success and in 1837 with his family overlanded to Port Phillip. They settled in 1838 on the River Plenty and built a homestead, but by 1844 were squeezed out by other squatters. Harrison searched for land in Gippsland but lost most of his cattle and in 1845 took up Swanwater, 70,000 acres near St Arnaud, where he ran sheep. After losing the use of his right arm in a shooting accident in 1850, he divided the run, sold it on terms and moved with his family to Fitzroy.

Active in democratic movements, Harrison had campaigned against increased taxation in March 1844 and in April attended the first meeting of the Separation Society. In June on Batman's Hill under a flag designed by Harrison with a white star centred on a crimson ground, militant squatters met to demand a clear policy on land tenure, while Harrison urged stockholders to form a pastoralists' society to fight against taxation and for separation. Always ready to air grievances in the press, his letter to the governor in Sydney in July 1845 declared that the proposed sale of crown lands by auction would enrich the wealthy but ruin poor squatters. In August he advocated more zeal for separation and in October sought better police protection and rural roads. At the first Legislative Council elections in 1851 the Victorian branch of the Australasian Anti-Transportation League campaigned in support of anti-transportation candidates and appointed Harrison as organizer on 29 July. A provocative and lucid speaker, he worked hard and travelled widely but his job ended in September when the elections began. Harrison took his two eldest sons to the goldfields but he could not dig and was soon agitating for better conditions. In December at Bendigo he presided over a large meeting in front of his tent to protest against increased licence fees. At Mount Alexander he was a delegate at a meeting of some 30,000 diggers and urged them to unite in the Victoria Gold Mining Association. With Dr W. Richmond he carried the diggers' protest to Melbourne and had some success. In October 1852 at Forest Creek he was a delegate from Bendigo at a big meeting which petitioned the governor on such

subjects as police protection and a proposed export duty on gold. He joined the deputation to Melbourne, but the petition failed: extra police were sent to the area and the export duty was rejected.

Although Harrison's role as an agitator was often exaggerated by his enemies, he was undoubtedly outspoken. At a public breakfast for E. H. Hargraves [q.v.] in December, he shocked all present by attacking the army and navy as inadequate safeguards for the colony and by hinting at republican measures. In the *Argus*, 25 May 1853, he appealed to the diggers to send the money they had collected for his wages. At a meeting in the Temperance Hall, Melbourne, a subscription list was organized because he had 'shown himself at all times a firm and faithful advocate of civil liberty and good order'. In September Harrison toured the country calling for the lands to be unlocked and the franchise extended to diggers. He had no direct part in the Eureka uprising, but on 7 December 1854 in Swanston Street spoke to the great gathering which repudiated the armed resistance of the miners at Eureka but supported a peaceful settlement and withdrawal of troops. In 1857 Harrison was again involved in the land question. At a meeting on 23 June he vehemently opposed the land bill which permitted the occupation rights of squatters, claiming that 'when the gold broke out the lands ought to have been thrown open to the people'. He represented Collingwood at the Land Convention which demanded free selection anywhere and abolition of auction and open pasturage.

At times Harrison had been an auctioneer and gold-buyer. In 1859 he joined the Victorian railways and became stationmaster at North Williamstown but asthma forced him to resign in 1864. Aged 67 he died on 21 July 1869 and was buried in the Williamstown cemetery. He was survived by his wife who died in 1879 and by seven children. Of his four sons, Henry Colden Antill, with his cousin T. W. Wills [qq.v.], was a founder of Australian Rules football.

HRA (1), 18; Y. S. Palmer, *Track of the years: the story of St. Arnaud* (Melb. 1955); G. Serle, *The golden age* (Melb, 1963); B. Kent, 'Agitations on the Victorian gold fields, 1851-1854', *Hist Studies*, no 23, Nov 1954; *Port Phillip Gazette*, 20, 23 Mar, 27 Apr, 29 May, 5 June 1844, 16 July, 2 Aug 1845; *Argus*, 30 July, 18 Dec 1851, 31 Mar, 16 July, 19 Aug, 23 Oct 1852, 28 June, 12 Sept, 31 Oct 1853, 23 June 1857, 28 July 1869; *Herald* (Melb), 9 Aug, 12 Sept, 22 Dec 1851, 31 Mar, 23, 26 Oct, 29 Nov 1852, 22 July 1869; *Geelong Advertiser*, 12 Aug, 18 Sept 1851; *Age*, 7 Dec 1854, 23 July 1869; *Williamstown Chronicle*, 24 July 1869, CO 201/254/153.   DOROTHY KIERS

HART, JOHN (1809-1873), mariner, merchant and parliamentarian, was born on 25 February 1809 in England. He went to sea at 12 and visited Hobart Town in September 1828 as a seaman in the *Magnet*. In November 1829 as second mate in the *Britannia* he went to Western Australia and then became well acquainted with the southern coast from Perth to Sydney. In 1832 he was master of the *Elizabeth*, owned and built by John Griffiths [q.v.] at Launceston, and often visited Kangaroo Island to land and pick up sealers and collect seal and wallaby skins and salt. In 1833 he took Edward Henty [q.v.] from Launceston to Portland and returned with whale oil. He then went to New Zealand for pine and potatoes, visited Kangaroo Island, sailed up Gulf St Vincent and stood on the future site of Adelaide. In 1835 he went to England to buy a ship for Griffiths and supplied the South Australian Colonization Commission with information and Colonel Light [q.v.] with sailing directions. Hart sailed in the *Isabella* with J. B. Hack [q.v.] and family as passengers and arrived at Launceston on 1 January 1837. He soon left for Adelaide with livestock for Hack but on a second voyage the *Isabella* was wrecked off Cape Nelson. When Hack heard of the disaster he gave Hart two acres in Adelaide and invested £1500 in a schooner which Hart used as a coastal trader. In 1839 he joined Hack and other partners in a whaling venture at Encounter Bay and managed it for £500 a year; Hack was bankrupted in 1841 and Hart later engaged him as an accountant. With Hagen and John Baker [qq.v.] Hart ran the whaling station in 1842-46 and as his fortunes recovered he bought larger ships. He twice visited Britain and in 1845 married Margaret Gillmor Todd of Dublin.

Hart retired from the sea in 1846 and settled in Adelaide. He bought and leased land in various parts of the colony, ran cattle and acted as agent for absentees. He also invested in copper mines at the Burra, Paringa and Montacute in 1845, Princess Royal and Mount Remarkable in 1846 and Yorke's Peninsula in 1848. He was also a director of the Forest Iron Smelting and Steam Sawing Co. at Cox's Creek and a copper-smelting venture at Port Adelaide, but lost heavily on mineral land at North Kapunda. In 1860 he was deeply involved in the Great Northern Copper Mining scandal but was exonerated after inquiry. In 1849 he had helped to form the short-lived Adelaide Marine Association Co. and the company intending to build a railway from Adelaide to the port; later he bought shares in the National and the Union Banks. Perhaps his best-known achievement was at Port Adelaide where in 1855 he built a flour-mill with twice the grinding capacity of any other in the province, believing that South Australia was to be the granary of the continent.

Hart was elected in 1851 to the Legislative Council for the district of Victoria, resigned in 1853 to visit England and was re-elected in 1854. In the House of Assembly he represented Port Adelaide in 1857-59 and 1862-66, Light in 1868-70 and the Burra in 1870-73. He was treasurer under Baker in 1857, Hanson in 1857-58, Ayers in 1863 and in 1864, and Blyth [qq.v.] in 1864-65. He was chief secretary under Dutton [q.v.] in July 1863 and led his own ministries in 1865-66, 1868 and 1870-71 when he introduced the title of premier. As a councillor he had been a moderate conservative but in the assembly he developed into a tough politician, pleasant enough but something of a schemer. His greatest interests were port and shipping charges. He violently opposed government railways and later advocated their sale, declaring that the only duties of parliament were to protect the country from foreign aggression or internal disorders and provide for the administration of justice and the protection of property. He opposed government borrowing and provision of water and drainage. By 1862 he was in favour of direct taxation of property on condition that free trade displaced customs duties. He maintained that education should not be free as knowledge was not appreciated unless paid for, and advocated a direct tax for secular education. He claimed that public service was a privilege and an honour, and that members should be paid for time lost in private pursuits rather than the value of services rendered. He had brought in a shipload of coolies in 1853 and continued to advocate migration from India and China as well as from Britain, especially after 1863 when South Australia took over the Northern Territory where as president of a company he had applied for 25,000 acres.

While Hart was in office he planned Goyder's [q.v.] survey expedition and carried the bill for the overland telegraph to Darwin although he criticized its route through Port Augusta. He was appointed C.M.G. in 1870 and died suddenly on 28 January 1873 at his home, Glanville, near Port Adelaide. He was survived by his wife and a large family, to whom he left an estate valued at more than £50,000. A son, John, represented Port Adelaide in the House of Assembly in 1880-81.

G. D. Combe, *Responsible government in South Australia* (Adel, 1957); D. Pike, *Paradise of Dissent*, 2nd ed (Melb, 1967); *Observer* (Adel), 24 Mar 1853; W. H. Baynes, John

Hart: the public record, 1831 to 1872 (B.A. Hons thesis, Univ Adel, 1961).

SALLY O'NEILL

HART, WILLIAM (1825-1904), businessman and parliamentarian, was born on 2 April 1825 in London, son of William Doubleday Hart (1801-1847). At 8 he went with his parents in the *Helen Mather* to Launceston where his father started a hardware business, the first of its kind in northern Tasmania. Educated at Launceston, William was apprenticed to his father and in 1846 established his own wholesale ironmongery and machinery business. Despite years of depression his firm prospered and he began investing his profits in land and the Commercial Bank of Tasmania. In 1856 he was elected to the Launceston City Council and served as alderman until 1875 and as mayor and chief magistrate of the city in 1863 and 1869. He was also warden of the Marine Board, chairman of the Hospital Board and the Chamber of Commerce and on the committee of the Benevolent Society. In 1873 he became an original shareholder of the Launceston company which bought the Mount Bischoff Tin Mining Co. and in October 1877 with William Grubb [q.v.] he bought the Tasmania gold mine at Beaconsfield; as a director of both mines and later many others he amassed a large fortune. His powerful influence as a financier, director and property owner induced local wits to call Launceston 'Hartsville'. Those who knew him best attributed his success to godliness and hard work in obedience to the scriptural injunction, 'Whatever thy hand findeth to do, do it with all thy might'. An enthusiastic and generous supporter of the Wesleyan Church and its Sunday school superintendent, Hart gave freely to all denominations and their charities.

Large, impressive and genial Hart showed no trace of condescension or self-importance. He represented Central Launceston in the House of Assembly in 1877-85 and Launceston in the Legislative Council from 1885 to 1902. A staunch Liberal, he opposed government interference in commerce and industry. He held no ministerial office but served in many select committees on mining regulations, customs duties on imported machinery, gas and electricity supplies and increased immigration. He was always ready to introduce petitions from churches, Ladies' Prayer Unions, the Association for the aid of Destitute and Fallen Women and for such purposes as temperance, raising the age of consent, neglected children and the enfranchisement of women. His most notable contribution in parliament was a part-successful effort to save the depositors and shareholders from ruin after the Bank of Van Diemen's Land failed in 1891. In 1901 he was granted sick leave but exceeded his time and forfeited his seat. Diligent friends promptly renominated him and he was elected unopposed in November, though unable to travel to parliament in Hobart. He died at his home, Bifrons, in Launceston on 17 February 1904, leaving much real estate and £69,000. He had transferred his hardware business to his sons in 1886 and among other bequests he left £5000 to the Methodist Church in Tasmania.

At Launceston on 2 November 1847 Hart married Mary Huysey; they had twelve children. She died on 7 January 1883 and Hart married Emma Noble (d. 1931) on 25 November 1884.

J. Reynolds, *Launceston; history of an Australian city* (Melb, 1969); *Examiner* (Launceston), 1891-93, 8 Feb 1904; *Daily Telegraph* (Launceston), 8 Feb 1904; *Bulletin*, 25 Feb 1904.

JOHN REYNOLDS

HARTLEY, JOHN ANDERSON (1844-1896), educationist, was born on 27 August 1844 at Old Brentford, Middlesex, England, the eldest son of Rev. John Hartley, Wesleyan minister, and his wife Sarah, née Anderson. He was educated in 1853-60 at Woodhouse Grove School near Bradford, Yorkshire, and taught there in 1860-67 before graduating from the University of London (B.A., 1868; B.Sc., 1870). He became second master at the Methodist College, Belfast, and in 1870 married Elizabeth Annie Green, sister-in-law of his headmaster, Rev. Robert Crooke, LL.D. In that year he was appointed headmaster of Prince Alfred College, Adelaide, where he arrived on 20 January 1871. The college had opened in 1869 and he was its second headmaster. Under him it became firmly established, its first students matriculating at the University of Melbourne in 1872. He achieved a major change in the college's management when the position of resident governor was abolished in 1875 and full authority over the school was vested in the headmaster.

In May 1871 Hartley was appointed to the Central Board of Education which administered the public schools of the colony. His interest and initiative were soon recognized; his repute survived his resignation from the board after dispute with the government and on 16 March 1874, after reappointment, he was elected chairman. Many of his recommendations were incorporated in the 1875 Education Act. Appointed president of the Council of Education on 1 December 1875, Hartley resigned his headmastership. The abolition of the council in 1878 centralized the administration of the Education Department further with Hartley as inspector-general of schools. Aided by the optimism generated by prosperity, he acted vigorously to create an efficient and centralized school system under his close direction. His autocratic methods aroused opposition and in 1881-83 a royal commission inquired into his administration. Exonerated and unrepentant, Hartley denied effective powers to the boards of advice set up to provide local participation in the administration of the department.

After studying European systems of elementary education, Hartley revised the curriculum in 1885 to broaden its scope but depression and retrenchment undermined his achievement. Desperately justifying expenditure to a parsimonious legislature, and knowing that higher education was impractical, he strove to improve the standard of education in the elementary schools. In 1885 he founded the *Education Gazette* to carry his ideas to teachers and edited it until 1896. He travelled the country speaking to teachers' associations on the new methods, prepared arithmetic books and teachers' manuals, produced primers and reading charts, designed copy books and in 1889 founded *The Children's Hour* and in 1891 the *Adelaide Poetry Book* as supplementary reading for children.

Hartley was a founder of the University of Adelaide. Appointed to the executive council of the Adelaide University Committee in October 1872 and to the first council of the university in November, he worked on the committee preparing a scheme for professorships and lectureships. In June 1877 he was appointed to the first senate. He was active on the council and defended its prerogatives against senate attempts to acquire greater powers. On the finance, education and library committees and on the faculties of arts and science his influence was important in framing regulations and statutes. The public examination system introduced in 1886 was largely his inspiration, ending the domination of classical studies and binding the secondary schools more closely to the university. He served as vice-chancellor in 1893-96.

Over the years he held many other positions. Societies associated with the schools enjoyed his patronage. In 1895 he was appointed to the first council of Roseworthy Agricultural College. He was president of the board of management of the Public Teachers' Provident Fund, on the board of management of the Public Service Provident Fund and a founder of the Public Service Association, initiating and editing its journal. A member of the board which founded

the Adelaide Children's Hospital, he and his wife worked on its committees. He remained true to his Wesleyan upbringing and served on committees of the Wesleyan Conference. He regarded no position as a sinecure. This remarkable activity ended sadly. On 8 September 1896, while riding home from his office on his newly-acquired bicycle, he collided with a horse ridden by a butcher's boy. He died from head injuries on the 15th, survived by his wife and an adopted daughter, Muriel. He left an estate valued at £3400.

Stern and austere, Hartley's idea of relaxation was to walk to his office figuring out complicated mathematical problems. He won respect from all but affection from only a few. His acts of kindness did not overcome the awe with which he was regarded. By nature he was autocratic and his Wesleyan faith and sense of mission inculcated in him a rigorous sense of duty which tolerated no failing in his subordinates. The education system he had founded was admired in other colonies, and men he had inspired, like W. L. Neale in Tasmania and Alfred Williams in South Australia, were to attain prominence. The Hartley studentship at the University of Adelaide is his only memorial, other than the department which he founded and which still bears traces of the imprint he gave it.

G. E. Saunders, John Anderson Hartley and education in South Australia (B.A. Hons thesis, Univ Adel, 1958); G. E. Saunders, Public education in South Australia in the nineteenth century (M.A. thesis, Univ Adel, 1968).

G. E. SAUNDERS

HARVEY, WILLIAM HENRY (1811-1866), botanist, was born on 5 February 1811 at Summerville, County Limerick, Ireland, the youngest son of Joseph Massey Harvey, a prosperous Quaker merchant, and his wife Rebecca, née Mark. From childhood he had a passion for natural history and was encouraged at Ballitore School, County Kildare. On leaving school he was apprenticed to his father but took no interest in the business although it provided the finance for his studies, particularly botany. At 20 he began a long association with William Jackson Hooker who commissioned him to describe certain groups in the new edition of the *British Flora* and introduced him to many botanists including James Bicheno and Robert Brown [qq.v.]. Through J. D. Hooker [q.v.], Harvey received algal collections from expeditions to the Pacific and southern hemisphere. These he described in his *Nereis Australis* (London, 1847-49) and as a contributor in J. D. Hooker, *Flora Tasmaniae* (London, 1860).

Attracted by 'Robert Brown's Country' and by a family friend, Governor Bourke, Harvey wanted to visit New South Wales, but in 1834 his brother Joseph was appointed colonial treasurer at Cape Town. William was made his deputy and after Joseph died in 1835 became treasurer. In office he continued his botanical work, publishing A *Manual of the British Marine Algae* (London, 1841), and preparing three volumes of *Flora Capensis* (Cape Town and Dublin, 1859-1865) in collaboration with O. W. Sonder from Hamburg. Ill health led to his resignation in 1842 and he went to Dublin, hoping for a salaried botanical post at Trinity College. Although he was awarded an honorary doctorate in 1844 and entered the United Church of England and Ireland, he was not appointed to the vacant chair of botany but only as curator of the herbarium. However, in 1848 he became professor of botany of the Royal Dublin Society and in 1856 he was appointed to the chair of botany at Trinity College; he held all three posts until 1866.

In 1849 Harvey's tour of the United States as guest of the Smithsonian Institute and Harvard University led to many publications on American algae. Granted leave by Trinity College he sailed for Western Australia, arriving at Albany on 7 January 1854; after a month at Cape Riche he went overland to Perth where he visited Fremantle and Rottnest and Garden Islands. Harvey had already studied the algal collections of Brown and J. A. L. Preiss [q.v.] and as an authority on European, American and South African algae he was well equipped to evaluate the Australian marine flora. He found it exciting and collected 10,000 specimens, and some were described in 'Some Account of the Marine Botany of the Colony of Western Australia' (*Transactions* of the Royal Irish Academy of Science, 1855). Many new algae were named after botanists in the colony. He reached Victoria in September 1854 and collected extensively in Port Phillip and Westernport Bays and at Port Fairy. On advice of Ferdinand Mueller [q.v.] and Dr Daniel Curdie he discovered at Queenscliff many new algae, naming them after Victorian associates and publishing the collection in *Phycologia Australica* (London, 1858-63). In January 1855 he went to Tasmania. At George Town he shared Rev. John Fereday's enthusiasm for seaweeds and at Deloraine collected seeds and land plants with W. Archer [q.v.]. At Hobart Town he associated with G. W. Walker and R. C. Gunn [qq.v.]. He collected seaweeds at Eaglehawk Neck and Dead Island, and also gave much

attention to the Port Arthur penal establishment. In Sydney he accepted George Bennett's [q.v.] hospitality and with the botanist, Charles Moore [q.v.], went by steamer to Newcastle. In the *John Wesley* he visited New Zealand, Tonga and the Fiji Islands and returned after six months to Sydney. After recuperation at Kiama he sailed by way of Valparaiso for Dublin, arriving in October 1856.

Despite failing health Harvey published his monumental works which are still used as working manuals, particularly in Australia. Shy and taciturn in company, he was verbose and flowery in his writings. His herbarium is at Trinity College, Dublin, but some duplicates from his travelling sets are in the National Herbarium of Victoria. Two sets of his 'Algae Australiae Exsiccatae' in book form are in the Mitchell Library, Sydney. Harvey was also interested in theology and revealed his views in a letter to his friend Josiah Gough, published as *Charles and Josiah: or friendly conversations between a Churchman and a Quaker* (1862). To Darwin [q.v.] and the Hookers he was a 'first-rate botanist' despite his published criticism of the *Origin of Species*. In 1861 he had married Miss Phelps of Limerick but died of tuberculosis on 15 May 1866 at Torquay in the home of W. J. Hooker's widow.

L. J. Fisher (ed), *Memoir of W. H. Harvey, with selections from his journal and correspondence* (Lond, 1869); L. Huxley, *Life and letters of Sir Joseph Dalton Hooker* (Lond, 1918); J. H. Maiden, 'Records of Australian botanists', Roy Soc NSW, Procs, 42 (1908); Letters to W. J. Hooker, Hooker's J of Botany, 6 (1854), 7 (1855); D. A. Webb, 'William Henry Harvey . . . and the tradition of systematic botany', Hermathena, 103 (1966); MS cat under W. H. Harvey (ML).   SOPHIE C. DUCKER

HASSELL, JOHN FREDERICK TASMAN (1839-1919) and ALBERT YOUNG (1841-1918), pastoralists and parliamentarians, were the first two of five sons of John Hassell and his wife Ellen, daughter of Charles Boucher [q.v.]. Their father was born in 1788, son of Francis Carolus Tennant Hassell, shipbroker and merchant, and Sarah, née Govey, of London. According to family tradition, he early joined the navy, transferred to the mercantile marine and then to the Chilean navy where he was taken prisoner by the Peruvians for about a year. He arrived in Van Diemen's Land in 1822 as first mate in the *Belinda* and in 1825-35 commanded ships trading out of Hobart Town, Launceston and Sydney. On the Tamar River in 1828 he was granted 500 acres where he ran cattle. About 1837 he returned to England where in partnership with Frederick Boucher [q.v.] he bought the *Dawson* and stocked it with merchandise. On 19 September 1838 Hassell married and a week later sailed for King George Sound. There he sold some goods and took up 20,000 acres (Kendenup station). He sailed to Tasmania, sold the *Dawson*, the remaining cargo and his Tamar grant. In Sydney he bought sheep, cattle and farming equipment and chartered the *China* to carry the stock to Albany where he arrived on 6 March 1840. He drove his 850 sheep and cattle to Kendenup station and took up more land. By 1850 he had 25,000 acres freehold and 38,000 leasehold, mostly on Kendenup and Jerramungup stations. His partner Boucher had borrowed heavily from the British and Australasian Bank in London but when it failed in 1841 he assigned his assets to the bank. Hassell thus had the bank as partner in his enterprises and had a long struggle until accounts were settled. From 1840, apart from three years in England in the 1860s, he lived mostly at Albany where he had a business importing merchandise and station supplies, keeping the accounts of his properties and arranging wool shipments to England. He died on 15 August 1883, survived by his wife, five sons and a daughter.

His eldest son, John Frederick, was born in Tasmania on 24 June 1839 and his second son, Albert, at Albany on 15 November 1841. Both grew up in Albany and worked on Kendenup where J. F. became manager in 1856. In 1861-63 Albert managed Jerramungup and was the first white settler to travel overland for 200 miles to Esperance. In 1864-78 the brothers were in partnership: J.F. ran the business in Albany and Albert managed Kendenup and, apart from two years, the other stations. From 1882 J.F. was agent in Albany for the Peninsular and Oriental Steam Navigation Co. until Fremantle became its port of call in 1900. In 1893-94 he was a nominee in the first Legislative Council under responsible government. In 1900-01 he represented Albany in the Legislative Assembly. In 1894 when the family properties had been divided, he received Kendenup and remained sole proprietor until it was sold and cut up for closer settlement after he died at Albany on 15 February 1919. He was survived by his wife Isabel, née Morison, whom he had married in 1868, and by their five daughters.

Albert Hassell won a by-election and in 1871-74 represented Albany in the colony's first part-elective Legislative Council. Under responsible government he represented Plantagenet in the Legislative Assembly in 1890-1904 and in 1897-98 was an elected Western Australian representative at the Australasian Federal Convention. He was an active member of the Plantagenet and Albany Road Boards in 1871-1910 and a justice of the peace in 1872-1918. In 1878 with his youngest brother, Arthur Wollaston (1851-1906), as partner he had leased most of the family properties. With Saxon rams imported by J.F. and careful breeding, Albert improved their flocks and in 1889 at the Paris Universal Exposition was awarded a *grand prix* for twenty-five fleeces and in later exhibitions in France and Western Australia won gold medals for his wool displays. Interested in horse-racing and breeding, he won the Plantagenet Cup in 1877 and 1879 and the Metropolitan (Perth) Cup with Corisande in 1879. He bred Satyr which won two Onkaparinga Cups in South Australia, and Bas Blanc which won many races in Western Australia. In 1894 he received Jerramungup in the division of the family properties. It was held by his family until 1950 when it was sold to the government for a land settlement scheme. He died in Melbourne on 20 September 1918, survived by his wife Ethyl, née Clifton, whom he had married in 1878, and by three sons and three daughters of their ten children.

The success of the Hassell family depended on the co-operation of John and his sons, the whole enterprise operating as one entity. A resolute pioneer who despite depression and isolation never lost confidence in the colony, John Hassell contributed greatly to southern settlement and his name is commemorated by a highway from Albany to Jerramungup.

Inquirer, 22 Aug 1883; *West Australian*, 30 Apr 1886, 21 Sept 1918, 17 Feb 1919; *Albany Advertiser*, 25 May 1956; LSD 1/5/293 (TA); correspondence file (Battye Lib, Perth); family records held by Dr C. W. Hassell, Perth, and W. A. Hassell, Cordinup, Albany.

C. W. HASSELL

HAVERFIELD, ROBERT ROSS (1819-1889), grazier, newspaper proprietor and editor, was born on 26 February 1819 at Bideford, Devon, England, son of Captain R. T. Haverfield, R.N. and his wife, née Ross. His mother, daughter of a Scotsman and his Creole wife, had inherited valuable estates in Jamaica. Robert went to a private school in Great Torrington and to the Bideford Free Grammar School where he read privately in the classics. He intended to study at Cambridge but his mother's income was cut by slave emancipation and he decided to migrate. He arrived at Sydney in the *Perfect* on 1 February 1838, stayed for a few months near Goulburn with a fellow passenger, Captain Kennedy, and then joined a friend in Melbourne.

Attracted by livestock, Haverfield drove cattle for Joseph Holloway and sheep for Lauchlan Mackinnon [q.v.]. He then worked as a clerk for George Cavenagh [q.v.] of the *Port Phillip Herald*, but soon left to manage a sheep station at Honeysuckle Creek. He moved west with cattle for Holloway, took up stations in the Wimmera with Joseph Jardine in 1846-48 and on his own account leased Sand Hills and Gerahmin in 1850-51 and Nurmurnemal in 1850-52. On these stations he won the trust of local Aboriginals and learnt their language.

By late 1853 Haverfield had parted with his leases and was working an alluvial claim near Bendigo. In a misunderstanding over licence regulations he was arrested and imprisoned for an hour before his mates released him. Angrily he renounced the diggings and invested his capital in a printing plant and on 9 December with A. M. Lloyd he produced an issue of the *Bendigo Advertiser and Sandhurst Commercial Circular*, the first newspaper published on the Victorian goldfields. Though fearless in denouncing goldfields administration, he insisted that political rights should be secured by constitutional means. Short of capital he sold out to Angus Mackay [q.v.] & Co. in May 1855 and worked a quartz claim in White Horse Gully. He agreed to edit a second Sandhurst paper, the *Courier of the Mines and Bendigo Daily Mail*, for a co-operative company in 1856 but this venture failed in March 1857 and he found employment with Mackay & Co. On their behalf he went to Heathcote to start the *McIvor News and Goulburn Advertiser* in 1858 and then wrote for the *Bendigo Advertiser*. In 1859 he became manager of F. Cadell's [q.v.] business on the Murrumbidgee and Darling. North of Menindee he met Burke's [q.v.] party and reported its progress for the *Bendigo Advertiser*. In November 1861 he was appointed secretary to the royal commission on Burke and Wills [q.v.] and next year government arbitrator in the reassessment of runs for the Ovens district under the new Land Act.

At Echuca Haverfield, as editor and part-owner with Mackay and J. J. Casey [q.v.], published the first edition of the weekly *Riverine Herald* in July 1863. He also invested in the vineyard company and was elected to the borough council but had to resign because his firm had contracted to print council advertisements. He became sub-editor of the *Age* in 1869 but soon returned to Echuca and in August 1870 became chief editor of the *Bendigo Advertiser*. On 29 January 1888 he was presented with a testimonial to his outstanding journalistic ability and service to the community.

In the 1850s Haverfield had contributed stories, verses and yarns to the *Illustrated Australian Magazine* usually under the signature of 'O.W.N.Y.' He sent tales and rhymes to the *Leader* in 1869 and contributed to the *Melbourne Monthly Magazine* and *Once a Month*; in 1884 he lectured on his early colonial experiences. In 1863 he had married Mariana Rubina Collier; they had four sons and a daughter. A Freemason, he was popular and respected, especially by his younger colleagues. He wrote for the *Bendigo Advertiser* almost until he died on 20 April 1889. He was buried at the Back Creek cemetery where Archdeacon Mac-Cullagh [q.v.] read the service.

G. Mackay, *The history of Bendigo* (Melb, 1891); R. V. Billis and A. S. Kenyon, *Pastoral pioneers of Port Phillip* (Melb, 1932); S. Priestley, *Echuca: a centenary history* (Brisb, 1965); *Bendigo Advertiser*, 22 Apr 1889; J. A. Panton memoirs (LaT L).

CAROLE WOODS

HAWKER, GEORGE CHARLES (1818-1895), politician and grazier, was born on 21 September 1818 in London, the second son of Edward Hawker (1782-1860), and his first wife Joanna Naomi, née Poore. His father retired from the navy on half-pay in 1830 and attained flag rank in 1837. Through John Macarthur [q.v.] he was granted land near Braidwood in New South Wales; he bought sections in New Zealand and in South Australia, a colony for which he was later active in securing a colonial bishop.

George was educated at schools on the Continent and in England and at Trinity College, Cambridge (B.A., 1841; M.A., 1854). With his brother Charles he arrived at Adelaide in September 1840 in the *Lysander*. Their brother James Collins (1811-1901) had arrived with Governor Gawler in 1838 and worked on surveys before returning to England where, finding his brothers had just left, he sailed to join them. George had gone north with E. J. Eyre [q.v.] and impressed by the country asked his father for help. The admiral replied generously and the brothers bought 2000 Macarthur merino ewes from Thomas Icely [q.v.] near Bathurst and overlanded them to the Barossa Valley. Aboriginals stole their sheep but Hawker retaliated forcefully and made peace on his own terms. When their Barossa run was bought he moved north and found good water in December 1841 at Bungaree. By 1848 the brothers had leased 500,000 acres; James sold his share to George and took up Moorundi on the Murray River,

Charles settled on the Anama section and George later bought 130,000 acres of Bungaree when the run was auctioned by government. In 1854 he brought John Noble from England as his overseer. As shepherds were replaced by wire fences Noble took charge of the merino stud. Hawker had already bought Rambouillet rams from France but on Noble's advice turned to rams from Wanganella and with them Bungaree became famous for its hardy and large-framed sheep, capable of walking long distances to water. Noble served the family well for nearly sixty years.

In 1851 Hawker failed to win Stanley in the Legislative Council but in 1858-65 represented the Victoria district in the House of Assembly. He was Speaker and chairman of committees from April 1860 to December 1864 despite a temperance pledge which was imperfectly observed. With his family he went to Germany for a cure. Apart from a brief visit to the colony in 1868 he lived at Heidelberg until 1874. He represented the Victoria district in 1875-84 and North Adelaide in 1884-95. He was treasurer under Arthur Blyth [q.v.] for eleven days in 1875, chief secretary under Boucaut [q.v.] in March-June 1876 and commissioner of public works under Boucaut in 1877-78 and under Morgan [q.v.] in 1878-81. His special interests were pastoral affairs and railways. When Morgan retired Hawker was asked to form a ministry but refused; for this and similar actions he was accused of 'pusillanimity' and later shocked his colleagues by voting with the 'labour party'.

At Bungaree Hawker planted a fine garden and orchard. He was prominent in the Royal Agricultural and Horticultural Society and in the 1850s and 1860s won prizes for his exhibits. In 1889 he visited India to look at irrigation methods and on them published several articles in the *South Australian Register*. He was a councillor of the Zoological Gardens. A keen supporter of horse-racing, coursing and cricket he was a founding member of the Hamley Racing Club and later a steward of the South Australian Jockey Club. He also liberally supported St Andrew's Anglican Church, Walkerville.

On 16 December 1845 Hawker had married Bessie Seymour; of their fifteen children, six sons and six daughters survived. Hawker died at his home The Briars, Medindie, on 21 May 1895 and was buried at North Road cemetery. Before his death he had been informed that he would receive a knighthood in the birthday honours; his widow's appeal for a posthumous award was approved by the Queen in September 1895. Hawker left an estate worth £305,800; his collection of paintings and statues was left first to his wife and then to the Art Gallery of South Australia.

J. C. Hawker, *Early experiences in South Australia* (Adel, 1889); W. Hawker, *Reminiscences of George Charles Hawker* (Adel, nd); *Register* (Adel), 2 Feb 1863, 22, 23 May 1895; *Observer* (Adel), 3 Nov 1903; CO 13/111, 149.

HAY, SIR JOHN (1816-1892), pastoralist and politician, was born on 22 June 1816 at Little Ythsie, Aberdeenshire, Scotland, son of John Hay, farmer, and his wife Jean, née Mair. Educated at King's College, University of Aberdeen (M.A., 1834), he studied law in Edinburgh but abandoned it. In 1838 he married Mary, née Chalmers. They arrived in Sydney on 1 July in the *Amelia Thompson*, and soon settled at Welaregang on the Upper Murray. In partnership with his brother-in-law, James Chalmers, he was a very successful squatter. In 1840 P. G. King [q.v.] arranged for Strzelecki [q.v.] to visit Welaregang and wrote to Hay: 'I fancy your zeal for such excursions will induce you to accompany him'.

Active in local affairs, Hay strongly opposed border duties on goods crossing the Murray River. In 1856 he was elected as 'a conservative and squatting representative' for the Murrumbidgee to the first Legislative Assembly. He carried a motion of no confidence against Charles Cowper's [q.v.] first ministry and attacked the legality of appointing James Martin [q.v.] attorney-general. Hay declined to form a ministry himself and recommended H. W. Parker [q.v.], whom he joined as secretary of lands and works in 1856-57. His squatter-oriented land bill was stillborn but in 1857-59 he retained his seat and in 1859 won the Murray. In 1860 he strongly opposed John Robertson's [q.v.] land bills and carried his amendment to ensure survey before selection. At the ensuing general election he was one of Robertson's few opponents to be re-elected.

David Buchanan [q.v.] deplored Hay's 'artificial and affected' manner, but admitted that 'as an Opposition leader, Mr. Hay conducts his opposition in a manly, dignified, and honourable way . . . If he attacks the Government, it is on some great and constitutional question—not on the appointment of two or three policemen'. When Hay was elected Speaker on 14 October 1862 Governor Young reported that he was of the 'very first standing in the Colony in point of fortune, manners, education and character'. Hay won the respect of all parties for impartial discharge of his duties. In 1864 his opposition to Riverina separation led him to give up his Murray seat and he won Central Cumberland. He resigned as Speaker in 1865 and from the assembly in 1867 when appointed to the Legislative Council.

Although Hay had lived in Sydney since 1856 he maintained his Murrumbidgee runs and as partner of Thomas Holt [q.v.] had fourteen more in the Leichhardt district. He was chairman of the Mercantile Bank of Sydney and a director of the Australian Mutual Provident Society and the European Assurance Society. In 1872 he refused to join Henry Parkes's [q.v.] ministry but next year became president of the Legislative Council on Parkes's recommendation. Worried by the frequent lack of a quorum, in 1874 he had the size of the council increased. In 1879 he told Deas Thomson [q.v.] of 'unpleasant relations with the Assembly, partly from a little injudicious management of details by those who have taken the lead amongst us, but chiefly I fear from a spirit of hostility to the Council on the part of leading men in the House'. Believing that the duty of the council was to assist the government unless some important principle was involved, Hay was unremitting in his efforts to get 'laws passed in the best form possible'. Ever jealous of the council's dignity, he complained to the governor of 'sacrilege' after Alexander Stuart's [q.v.] government had put seventy-five beds in the council chamber during an all-night debate on the land bill in 1884.

Hay had many honorary duties: besides speaking at innumerable banquets he was vice-president of the New South Wales commissions for exhibitions at Philadelphia, Paris, Sydney and Amsterdam. He was president of the Highland Society of New South Wales and vice-president of the Agricultural Society of New South Wales and the Australian Club and a founder of the Union Club. He was appointed K.C.M.G. in 1878 and in 1879 members of the Legislative Council commissioned Achille Simonetti [q.v.] to sculpture his bust. Parkes wrote of Hay that 'Among Conservatives he would be held to be a Liberal; among extreme Democrats he would be regarded as a Conservative'. In the Freeman's Journal, 16 September 1882, 'Cassius' discerned his 'pragmatical shrewdness apt at a moment's notice to degenerate into meanness, a vision very narrow, but very sharp, a reverence for No. 1 exceedingly profound'. Hay died without issue at Rose Bay on 20 January 1892 and was buried by an Anglican clergyman in the Presbyterian section of Waverley cemetery. His wife died ten days later. Most of his estate of almost £59,000 was left to the children of his brother James. A Riverina town is named after him.

The Australian portrait gallery (Syd, 1885); H. Parkes, Fifty years in the making of Aus-

tralian history (Lond, 1892); Town and Country J, 26 July 1873, 5 Oct 1889; Bulletin, 18 Jan 1881; S. A. Donaldson, ministry letters (ML); Parkes letters (ML); CO 201/523, 526, 557, 570, 577, 591, 595, 598, 600, 602.

A. W. MARTIN

HAYDON, GEORGE HENRY (1822-1891), writer and artist, was born on 26 August 1822 at Heavitree, Devon, England, the second son of Samuel Haydon, retired naval paymaster, and his wife Elizabeth, née Roberts. His elder brother, Samuel James Bouverie (1815-1891), was a well-known sculptor. A younger brother, Edward, migrated to South Australia in 1849 and died at Adelaide in 1858. Educated mainly by his father who had liberal sympathies, Haydon showed artistic talent and was apprenticed to an architect in Exeter in 1837. Looking for adventure, he arrived in the Theresa at Melbourne in July 1840 with £40 and hopes of a fortune. He worked as a clerk in William Kerr's [q.v.] bookshop, as an architect designing terraced cottages and then for the newspapers. J. B. Were [q.v.] was 'very attentive' to him, engaged him to design his warehouse and employed him as a storeman. Haydon was one of Melbourne's first drawing masters and also sold sketches to the papers. In November the Sydney Monitor copied a paragraph from the Port Phillip Gazette on his drawing of 'the sea monster which was killed on the coast'. His sketch of Melbourne brought him belated fame when reproduced in the Australasian Sketcher, 10 July 1875. Most of his drawings were sold for 10s. 6d. or given to friends so that only those in his journals survive. He also collected natural history specimens for friends in England.

Haydon was concerned about Aboriginals, 'these children of the wilderness'; he stoutly defended them against the prejudices of the colonists, studied their language and customs, and earned their respect. His particular friend and shooting companion was Benbo, of the Werribee 'tribe', who once saved his life and was the subject of many sketches. To Haydon the protectorate system was 'a pack of humbug' and harmful to the welfare of the Aboriginals. He disliked G. A. Robinson [q.v.] but was a firm friend of William Thomas [q.v.], the 'only worthy man' amongst the protectors. Haydon spent much time with friends at Western Port. On French Island he burnt mangroves for barilla, with Robinson blazed a stock route through the bush from Corinella to the Albert River, worked as architect for a shipbuilder, sold sketches and hunted rabbits, mutton-birds and swans.

With Were's help Haydon sailed in the *Abberton* for England in January 1845, 'without £5,000 but with a clear conscience', a bottle of Yarra water for christening purposes and a kangaroo rat which died on the ship. Before leaving he wrote: 'I can do all kinds of bush work in the carpentering way. I can drive bullocks, paint a house, wash, mend and tailor, cobble shoes, reap, grub trees, fence ... a very pretty stock of knowledge to enter an English drawing room, with'. At Exeter he set up as an authority on emigration and gave many lectures. Using George Arden's [q.v.] *Latest Information with regard to Australia Felix* as a basis for a descriptive prospectus, Haydon published *Five Years' Experience in Australia Felix* (Exeter and London, 1846) which was widely reviewed. Very few of his own adventures were narrated and the illustrations, based on Haydon's sketches, were drawn by the painter, Henry Hainsselin, and another friend, Charles Risdon, made the engravings. Haydon married Risdon's sister, Clarissa, at Langtree, Devon, on 20 December 1851; they had four sons and one daughter. In 1849 Haydon was appointed steward of the Devon County Lunatic Asylum at Exminster and in 1853-89 was steward of Bridewell and Bethlem hospitals, London. In 1865 he was called to the Bar at the Middle Temple.

In Australia Haydon had cultivated the image of the colonial frontiersman in his dress and writings. His insistence on the bush virtues of hospitality, mateship and self-reliance found some expression in his novel, *The Australian Emigrant, A Rambling Story, containing as much fact as fiction* (London, 1854). The illustrations, again based on his sketches, were drawn by Watts Phillips. Besides contributing sketches and ideas to *Punch*, Haydon illustrated several privately printed books in the 1860s. He continued to correspond with friends in the colonies and even lectured to his mental patients on his French Island adventures. Haydon died at his home, Ettrick, Putney Lower Common, on 9 November 1891.

A blue-eyed giant, Haydon was an advocate of temperance from his Melbourne days and, although an inveterate pipe smoker, believed in the cult of the healthy body. He found companionship in the volunteer movement, in angling and in Freemasonry. His most intimate friends were the *Punch* cartoonists, John Leech, Charles Keene and George Cruickshank, and the actor Samuel Phelps. He was the subject of Keene's sketch 'the gigantic angler' in *Punch* almanac 1885, said to be an excellent portrait, and drawings of Haydon as a young man are in his personal sketchbook.

R. Howitt, *Impressions of Australia felix* (Lond, 1845); G. S. Layard, *The life and letters of Charles Samuel Keene* (Lond, 1892); M. H. Spielmann, *The history of 'Punch'* (Lond, 1895); E. M. Heddle, *How Australian literature grew* (Melb, 1962); N. Gunson, *The good country: Cranbourne shire* (Melb, 1968); A. W. Greig, 'Letters from Australian pioneers', *VHM*, 12 (1927); *Herald* (Melb), 27 May 1884; *Illustrated London News*, 14 Nov 1891; J. Whitlock, Gentleman felix: the biography of George Henry Haydon (held by Mrs H. R. Haydon, Kingsgate Castle, Kent); G. H. Haydon, Australian diaries and sketches, 1840-45 (microfilm, NL).   NIEL GUNSON

HAYES, CATHERINE (1825-1861), soprano, was born on 29 October 1825 in Limerick, Ireland, daughter of Arthur Williamson Hayes, musician. At 14, after an impecunious childhood with her mother and sister, she won the patronage of Edmond Knox, bishop of Limerick, and sang at private concerts before the city's Protestant aristocracy. A subscription enabled her to study singing in Dublin and her first public appearance was at the Rotundo on 3 May 1839. She saw a performance of *Norma* in September 1841 and decided on a career in opera rather than concerts. She left for Paris in October 1842 and studied with Emmanuel Garcia and in Milan with Felice Ronconi. She made her continental début with the Italian Opera at Marseilles in Bellini's *I Puritani* on 10 May 1845 and was soon engaged as *prima donna* with La Scala, Milan. On 10 April 1849 she made her London début with the Royal Italian Opera of Covent Garden. *The Times* was reasonably enthusiastic, Queen Victoria invited her to Buckingham Palace, the public adored her. In 1851, following the dazzling example of Jenny Lind, she decided to tour America. At New York on 23 September Lind's ex-agent, William Avery Bushnell, became her manager. Her progress through the United States and Canada was triumphant: at San Francisco from November 1852 to May 1853 her fees averaged £650 a month, the 'semi-civilised' gold miners bidding up to £1150 to hear her sing.

Under Bushnell's direction Catherine went to Sydney where her arrival in September 1854 aroused 'an excitement wholly unparalleled in the theatrical annals of this colony'. The *Sydney Morning Herald* exhausted its vocabulary of praise in detailing every nuance of her appearance at the Victoria Theatre on 3 October. Audiences respected her *bravura* passages from opera but were more affected by her singing of such simple ballads as 'Home Sweet Home' and 'Oh Steer My Bark to Erin's Isle'. On 18 October Judge Therry [q.v.] farewelled her before a huge crowd at Circular Quay with assurances that she would be remembered with 'admiration, respect and esteem', and Catherine gave the proceeds of her farewell concert to the Destitute Children's Asylum. Her Melbourne season was almost as spectacular. Her first concert in the redecorated Queen's Theatre was, according to the *Age*, 'a great event in our local history'. She visited Geelong, gave a concert in Adelaide and then left for Calcutta where she arrived unannounced in January 1855. The audiences were not affluent and she returned to Sydney.

At the Prince of Wales Theatre she initiated a daring season of grand opera complete with elaborate sets, supporting soloists and large choruses. The season was launched on 14 August with Bellini's *La Somnambula*. Through the efforts of the *prima donna* the experiment was a huge success although the sets lacked stage machinery, the supporting artists were uncertain and the choruses were ragged. The season continued with the *Bohemian Girl* and *Norma* until on 17 September she left for Melbourne. The performances suffered some initial setbacks but on 22 October at the new Theatre Royal *La Somnambula* was presented to 'a house gorged almost to suffocation'. Early in November the public rejected *Lucia di Lammermoor* and she decided to end her engagement, but her farewell appearance in *Norma* convinced the management that audiences were still interested. The season was revived by the *Bohemian Girl*, *Elisir d'Amore*, *La Somnambula* and *Lucrezia Borgia* with performances of *Norma* when attendances lagged. Her last Melbourne appearance was in *Linda di Chamounix* on 21 December. In 1856 she returned to London where on 8 October 1857 she married Bushnell. She occasionally appeared in London theatres and toured the country districts but restricted her performances after her husband died in France on 2 July 1858, aged 35. Her health had suffered from her tours and from a riding accident in America. She died on 11 August 1861 in London and was buried at Kensal Green cemetery, leaving an estate of £16,000.

E. Blom (ed), *Groves' dictionary of music and musicians*, 5th ed (Lond, 1954); P. L. Brown (ed), *Clyde Company papers*, 6 (Lond, 1968); *Dublin Univ Mag*, Nov 1850; *SMH*, 12 Sept, 4, 18, 19 Oct 1854, 16 Aug 1855; *Freeman's J* (Syd), 14, 21 Oct 1854, 18 Aug 1855, 14 Aug 1861; *Age*, 30 Oct, 7-9, 23 Nov 1854, 23 Oct, 2, 9, 20 Nov, 22 Dec 1855; *Bengal Hurkaru*, 8, 12, 19 Feb 1855; *The Times*, 14 Aug 1861.

DENNIS SHOESMITH

HAYES, WILLIAM HENRY (1829?-1877), adventurer, swindler and black-

birder, best known as 'BULLY', is said to have been born in Cleveland, Ohio, United States of America, son of Henry Hayes, innkeeper, to have gained some knowledge of seafaring on the Great Lakes and to have roamed the Pacific engaging in the many trades that ocean offered in ways often not short of piracy. Although he is stated to have made a voyage to Melbourne and Sydney in the American barque *Canton* in 1853 his first recorded arrival in Australia was at Fremantle in January 1857 as master of the *C. W. Bradley* which he had acquired at Singapore by devious means. For three years he engaged in several audacious maritime frauds ranging from Fremantle to San Francisco. On 25 August 1857 at Penwortham, South Australia, he married, probably bigamously, Amelia Littleton.

In January 1860 Hayes reappeared in Sydney after his stolen *Ellentia* foundered, and was charged with indecent assault on a young girl in that ship. The case was dismissed but the *Empire* printed a scathing account of his character and past activities which was rebutted by forged letters to the *Sydney Morning Herald*. For debt he was imprisoned in Darlinghurst gaol but released when declared insolvent. After some time in the Hunter Valley with the Glogski and Buckingham minstrel troupe he sailed for New Zealand as a passenger in the *Cincinatti* with his theatrical companions. There he reputedly 'married' Rosa Buckingham who, with her child, brother and a young nursemaid, were drowned near Nelson in August 1864; Hayes alone escaped. For some years he sailed New Zealand waters in various craft which he obtained by fraud and deception until in May 1866 he bought the *Rona* and with a wife and children on board became a South Sea trader and blackbirder. The *Rona* was lost off Manihiki, Cook Islands, and in Samoa he joined the American blackbirder, Ben Pease, in the *Pioneer* which later returned to Samoa as the *Leonora* with Hayes in command. In January 1874 Louis Becke, later famous for his South Sea tales, joined the *Leonora* at Milli in the Marshall Islands and for several months cruised with Hayes.

On 15 March 1874, while lying at Kusaie in the Caroline Islands, the *Leonora* was totally lost on a reef but her company escaped. Supported by a few of his scallawag crew and comforted by five native wives, Hayes set up a trading station and terrorized the natives. When H.M.S. *Rosario* arrived in September complaints against Hayes's violent behaviour were made by missionaries, some of his crew and the native king. To avoid arrest Hayes made off in a small boat with one companion, was picked up at sea by the American whaler *Arctic* and landed at Guam in February 1875. After various episodes in the Philippines he re-appeared at San Francisco, where he sailed on his last voyage in the yacht *Lotus* in October 1876 accompanied by a woman, said to be the wife of the owner, and a crew of two. The many versions of Hayes's death all agree on the main facts. In April 1877 the *Lotus* was cruising near Jaluit in the Marshall Islands. After repeated quarrels between Hayes and a sailor, Hayes was killed by a blow from an iron fitting and his body cast overboard. The death was reported when the yacht reached Jaluit but his mur-derer was never brought to justice.

Notorious in every Pacific port, Hayes became a legendary figure, first in Rolf Boldrewood's [q.v. T. A. Browne] *A Mod-ern Buccaneer* (1894), based on a Louis Becke manuscript, and later as a principal char-acter in many of Becke's own tales of the South Seas. Although uneducated Hayes had infinite resource, great plausibility and was undoubtedly a rogue in the grand manner. He was survived by a wife and twin daughters in Samoa.

R. Lovett, *James Chalmers: his autobiog-raphy and letters* (Lond, 1902); T. Trood, *Island reminiscences* (Syd, 1912); B. Lubbock, *Bully Hayes, South Sea pirate* (Lond, 1931); A. T. Saunders, *Bully Hayes*, 2nd ed (Perth, 1932); A. G. Day, *Louis Becke* (New York, 1966); F. Clune, *Captain Bully Hayes* (Syd, 1970); *Government Gazette* (Qld), 28 Aug 1875; *SMH*, 7, 12 Jan 1860; *Empire* (Syd), 9 Jan 1860; 'Cleveland born pirate', *Cleveland Mid-week Review Pictorial*, 30 Nov 1932; Bank-ruptcy papers (NSWA).   JOHN EARNSHAW

HAYNES, JOHN (1850-1917), journalist and politician, was born on 26 April 1850 at Singleton, New South Wales, son of John Haynes, schoolteacher, and his wife Mar-garet, née Daly. Haynes began his career in journalism with the Morpeth *Leader* as an apprentice compositor. He worked for several country newspapers, moved to Syd-ney in 1873, joined Samuel Bennett's [q.v.] *Empire* and later his *Town and Country Journal* and *Evening News* which he sub-edited. In 1880 with J. F. Archibald [q.v.] he started the *Bulletin*, building circulation in 18 months to 15,000. They first lost fin-ancial control to J. Woods and then to W. T. Traill [q.v.] who retained it when the part-nership was formally reconstituted in 1883. Haynes held a minority interest in the *Bulletin* until 1885. His contribution to its early success was large but declined under Traill's proprietorship.

Haynes was resourceful in dealing with continuing financial problems and was fer-tile of ideas, taking as models the new

journalism overseas and Bennett whom he greatly admired. He wanted to combine seriousness of purpose with bright, provoca-tive journalism, saw the exposure article as a way of doing this and wrote a damaging reply to the proprietor of the Clontarf pleasure gardens. For failure to pay costs of the libel action that followed, he and Archi-bald were imprisoned for six weeks in 1882. Haynes hoped to make the *Bulletin* politi-cally important, eschewing sectarianism and supporting free trade, but Traill was pro-tectionist. Haynes published the free-trade *Haynes Weekly* in 1885-87 and *Weekly News* in 1890-91. In 1895 he started the weekly *Elector* which, enlarged and renamed *Newsletter*, ran until 1917. On his own he was not particularly successful and was involved several times in bankruptcy proceedings.

In 1887 Haynes was elected to the Legis-lative Assembly for Mudgee as a supporter of Parkes [q.v.]. He held the seat until 1894 and Wellington in 1894-1904. He remained a consistent supporter of free trade and decentralization, and professed concern for public integrity and the dignity of parlia-ment but was a vituperative and unruly member. His sharp wit, argumentative nature and readiness to allege corruption and impropriety involved him in many dis-putes, including an unsuccessful action against James Fletcher [q.v.] for assault in 1888 and later a bodily attack on W. P. Crick. He made bitter enemies amongst pro-tectionists by publicly repudiating his Catholic faith in the 1887 election, and afterwards often attributed sectarian inter-est to political opponents. He opposed the federal constitution bill as undemocratic and inimical to development of local govern-ment and decentralization. On the federal issue he voted against G. H. Reid in Sep-tember 1899. Haynes remained a free trader but distrust of party left him isolated as party allegiance firmed. He was narrowly defeated in 1904 and failed to secure re-election until 1915 when he won Wil-loughby as an independent democrat. He lost to a Nationalist in 1917. He was vehe-mently loyal, conspicuous for doubting the loyalty of resident Germans and demanding measures against them.

After his defeat in 1904 Haynes continued through his *Newsletter* the long feud with W. N. Willis, E. W. O'Sullivan, Crick and others. His repeated allegations of corrup-tion were partly vindicated by the 1906 royal commission on lands administration. He had sworn out the warrant for the arrest of Willis who took out a writ against the *Newsletter* to silence it; Haynes repeated his charge in contempt of court, for which his son, the nominal proprietor, was gaoled.

Haynes died on 15 August 1917 in North Sydney and was buried with Anglican rites in the Presbyterian section of Rookwood cemetery. He was married three times : in 1871 to Sarah Bedford by whom he had one daughter and five sons; in 1892 to Mary Duff without issue; and in 1899 to Esther Campbell by whom he had a son and a daughter.

C. Pearl, *Wild Men of Sydney* (Lond, 1958); A. G. Thomson, 'The early history of the *Bulletin*', *Hist Studies*, no 22, May 1954; 'Early *Bulletin* memoirs', *Newsletter*, 1905; *Town and Country J*, 28 May 1887; *Australasian*, 28 Apr 1888; *Daily Telegraph* (Syd), 16 July 1894; *Bulletin*, 29 Jan 1930.   HEATHER RADI

HAYTER, HENRY HEYLYN (1821-1895), statistician, was born on 28 October 1821 at Eden Vale, Wiltshire, England, son of Henry Hayter and his wife Eliza Jane, née Heylyn. He was educated privately in Paris and at Charterhouse, where he was a contemporary of Charles Du Cane and George Bowen, and lived in the headmaster's house. He migrated to Melbourne in 1852 and in June 1857 at St Peter's Church, Eastern Hill, married Susan, daughter of William Dodd and his wife Sarah.

In May Hayter began to take temporary assignments on behalf of the assistant registrar-general, William Archer [q.v.]. As one of the five collectors of statistics for Victoria, he was responsible for the western provinces of Ripon, Dundas, Follett and Normanby, and the pastoral district of the Wimmera. After this work ended, he submitted early in 1859 his report which displayed excellent ability and a wide knowledge of the economy, social condition and geography of these districts. The quality of his work led to his appointment as assistant registrar-general of Victoria on 1 September at a salary of £300. In May 1874 the statistical section of the Registrar-General's Office became a separate department with Hayter in charge as first government statist. He started on a salary of £610 with a staff of six and served until 1895.

Until the mid-1880's Hayter was without a peer amongst Australian statisticians and he, rather than Timothy Coghlan or R. M. Johnston, made Australian statistical reporting unequalled in the world. His renown began when he replaced the *Statistics of Victoria* with the *Statistical Register* in 1859. By the early 1860s he had embarked on a large-scale amplification of the *Register*, aiming at a detailed, accurate and penetrating description that would convey in simple but meaningful quantities as many of Vic-

toria's characteristics as he could measure. The *Register* soon surpassed the standardized form of statistical reporting demanded by the Colonial Office. Hayter's *Progress of Victoria* (1873) was the immediate precursor of the *Victorian Year Book* for 1873, published in 1874. This slim volume quickly became a popular source book and annual editions in the series grew by 1895 to more than 1000 pages. The notes and descriptive material became so comprehensive that volumes could be used without reference to the *Statistical Register*, and were praised in England and America for their general utility.

In 1870-72 Hayter had served as secretary to the royal commission inquiring into the working of the Victorian public service; he had also attended to his normal duties but his health suffered and he took leave to recuperate. He went to New Zealand where his advice to the government led to extensive improvement in statistical reporting. He also compiled *Notes on a Tour of New Zealand* (Melbourne, 1874). In 1875 he represented Victoria at a conference in Tasmania where statisticians of other colonies accepted his system as the pattern to be adopted. In 1879 he went to England as secretary to Graham Berry's [q.v.] 'embassy'. The House of Commons committee inquiry into the reorganization of British statistical collection twice sought Hayter's evidence on his aims and procedures, and highly commended him for his valuable advice and services. In 1881 he was a member of the Social Science Congress in Melbourne.

In the third issue of the *Victorian Year Book* (1875) Hayter had introduced a summary tabulation of Australian statistics. His leadership in moves towards uniformity emerged even more strongly in the field of census-taking. He had been responsible under the registrar-general for the Victorian censuses of 1861 and 1871. His ambition for statistical uniformity in Australia was realized in 1881 when the Colonial Office recommended each colony in the empire to hold its census on the day chosen by the United Kingdom. In an elaborate report he rejoiced that 'for the first time the populations of the Australasian colonies and of Great Britain and Ireland have been enumerated simultaneously'.

For his distinguished work Hayter was created C.M.G. and named by the French government as an officer of the Order of Public Instruction in 1882, and appointed chevalier of the Order of the Italian Crown in 1884. He was an honorary member of the Royal Statistical Society of London, the Statistical and Social Enquiry Society of Ireland, the Statistical Association of Tokyo and the Royal Societies of South Australia and Tasmania. Among his published professional works, three papers were read to the section for economic and social science and statistics at the first congress of the Australasian Association for the Advancement of Science in 1888 at Sydney. In his leisure Hayter wrote *Carboona, A Chapter from the Early History of Victoria* (1885) and *My Christmas Adventures; Carboona, and Other Poems* (1887).

Despite his skill in measuring social trends, Hayter had shared in the Victorian land and building boom of the late 1880s. In 1887 he became a director of the Metropolitan Bank and Metropolitan Building Society. These institutions were forced to close their doors on 3 December 1891 and later went into liquidation. Hayter had borrowed £32,000 from the bank to invest in the society and was in debt for £36,000. Composition with his creditors was put through the Insolvency Court in secret and allowed for payment of 3d. in the £1. When he realized that the failure of the bank and society was inevitable Hayter asked the government to release him from his official post, but the cabinet persuaded him to remain and to conduct the 1891 census. Due to retire with a pension on 31 March 1895, he died on the 23rd at his home in Armadale. He was survived by his wife (d. 1911) and one son.

M. Cannon, *The land boomers* (Melb, 1966); V&P (LA Vic), 1875-76, 2 (11), 1883, 3 (49); *Town and Country J*, 24, 30 Mar 1895; *Argus*, 25 Mar 1895; *Australasian*, 30 Mar 1895.

I. J. NEESON

HAYWARD, THOMAS (1832-1915), farmer, merchant and legislator, was born on 1 September 1832 at Honington, Suffolk, England, the eldest son of Thomas Hayward, of Ringshall Hall near Stowmarket, and his wife Maria, née Canler, of Cotton Hall. Educated at Needham Market and Ipswich Grammar Schools he lived as a farmer-landowner's son until attracted to Western Australia by his cousin, Robert Henry Rose [q.v.], who had invited his mother Elizabeth, née Canler, sister and brother Charles to join him. They arrived at Fremantle in the *Devonshire* in September 1853.

Hayward soon went to York and Northam to buy sheep for butchering in Perth, but after several other unsatisfactory ventures he and Rose took up land near the road between Mandurah and Bunbury, where they ran cattle. Later they leased the Wedderburn estate founded by Dr John Ferguson [q.v.]. They suffered heavy losses of cattle and the Rose brothers departed to

their own farms. Hayward stayed for some years and then moved to Bundidup, twenty miles from Bunbury, where he established an estate of 4136 acres. In 1861 he married Catharine, daughter of Joseph Keys Logue and his wife Elizabeth, née Goodwin, settlers in the Swan district. Their wedding present to Catharine was a herd of dairy cattle. This gift and her resolute character persuaded Hayward, who was seriously inclined to return to England, to stay in Western Australia. Of their seven children, four daughters and two sons survived childhood.

In 1862 Hayward began to import farm implements from the manufacturers, Ransomes, Sims & Jefferies, whom he had known at Ipswich. He left the farm in his wife's capable hands until their son Thomas was given control. Increasing custom and a growing grocery business induced Hayward in 1874 to live next door to his store near the Bunbury wharf. After surviving the depression of the 1870s and enjoying the prosperity of the gold boom, Hayward retired in 1898 from direct control of his business in favour of his younger son George and son-in-law Arthur Foreman.

Always active in local affairs, Tom Hayward, justice of the peace, held at various times every senior position in the local government of the Wellington district, the Wellington Agricultural Society and the Bunbury Hunt Club. He was an original director of the Bunbury Building Society in 1882 and chairman in 1885-1913. When Sir John Forrest transferred to the Federal parliament, Hayward in 1901 contested the vacant seat of Bunbury as 'the old dog for a hard road', defeating the young mayor, James Newton Moore, probably by drawing votes from the wharfsiders whose political activities were supported by George Hayward. Always opposed to G. W. Leake [q.v.], Hayward gave early support to George Throssell and A. E. Morgans of the Opposition, but in 1902 publicly announced that he would vote as an independent. He moved to the new country electorate of Wellington in 1904 and in 1911 retired when the electorates were again redistributed. His benevolence and public spirit had won him the respect of many friends and customers throughout the southern districts. He died at Bunbury on 24 September 1915, in the same year as his wife.

Thos Hayward & Son Ltd was then managed by Foreman and F. W. Roberts who became a partner in 1910 after the untimely death of George Hayward. In 1919 an up-to-date department store was built away from the wharf to anticipate the southward extension of Bunbury's business area. Allied to a large Perth retail firm, Thos Hayward

Pty Ltd was still a thriving business in 1971, the third oldest commercial establishment and the oldest retail store in Western Australia.

Bunbury Herald, 2, 25, 28 Sept 1915; *South Western Times*, 9 June 1959, 25 Jan 1962; Hayward family notes (Battye Lib, Perth); papers held by Mrs V. Lowe and Mrs T. Sanders, Bunbury.   A. C. STAPLES

HEADLAM, CHARLES (1816-1898), pastoralist, was born on 22 November 1816 at Eggleston, County Durham, England, youngest of the six children of John Headlam and his wife Ann, née Slade. The family arrived at Hobart Town in the *Skelton* (Captain Dixon) on 22 November 1820. They lived at first in Hobart where John Headlam ran a school; he was granted 775 acres on the Macquarie River in 1823 but appointed a manager to look after his land which he called Egleston. He continued teaching in Hobart and later in Launceston till 1830 when he took his family to Egleston; aged 67 he died on 11 March 1843.

Charles took over the management of Egleston. His skill with stock and his business ability enabled him to expand the original holding of 775 acres until he became the largest landholder in Tasmania, his properties covering 80,000 acres. In addition to Egleston which had grown to 8600 acres, he occupied the well-known estates of Charlton, Lemont, Woodbury and Nant, and several large properties in the lake district. His sheep numbered up to 60,000, and to cope with them he was the first in Tasmania to introduce shearing machines which were installed in the Egleston woolshed in the early 1890s. He was appointed a territorial magistrate on 11 May 1847 and later district coroner. In September 1852 he wrote to the Colonial Secretary advocating the continuation of transportation of convicts for he was then finding difficulty in obtaining sufficient men to work his properties. He served for many years on the Campbell Town Municipal Council and on the Water and Road Trusts. On 14 June 1842 he had married Eleanor, only daughter of John Bayles of Rokeby on the Macquarie River. Headlam died at Egleston on 14 October 1898 and was buried in the Presbyterian cemetery at Kirklands. He was survived by six sons, who inherited his properties, by four daughters and by some fifty grandchildren.

Examiner (Launceston), 17 Oct 1898; GO 33/77/696 (TA); Headlam family records.
                                      A. W. TAYLOR

HEALES, RICHARD (1821-1864), politician and temperance reformer, was born in London, son of Richard Heales (1801-1882), an ironmonger who migrated to Victoria, and his wife Elizabeth. He served an apprenticeship as a coachbuilder in London and at 19 married Rhoda, née Parker; in February 1842 they arrived at Melbourne as bounty emigrants in the *Himalaya*. At first unable to find work except as a day labourer, Heales was by 1847 listed in the almanacs as 'coachbuilder, Collins Lane'; later he had a business in Lonsdale Street.

A fervent believer in temperance, Heales had probably been active in the cause in London, and soon became its most energetic leader in Victoria. In February 1843 he was made secretary and his father president of the newly-formed Total Abstinence Society. Heales was mainly responsible for the building of the Temperance Hall in 1847 and by 1850 was widely known as a temperance speaker. In November he entered the Melbourne City Council, defeating John O'Shanassy [q.v.] in Gipps ward. He had told his constituents that he hoped the time was near when 'the nomination and the poll would no longer be the arena of vice and intemperance, but when the election of the candidate would be the pure result of the people's choice', and proposed, successfully, that the practice of holding council elections in public houses be discontinued. This success, his support for secret ballot, anti-transportation and early closing, together with his temperance work, won him repute as a democrat and reformer dedicated to the social and moral improvement of the working classes.

About 1852 Heales went into partnership with Edmund Ashley, a fellow passenger in the *Himalaya* and an abstainer, and in December sailed for England where for three years he worked for temperance and probably the affairs of his business partnership. By 1857 Ashley & Heales were established in Therry Street, Melbourne, as importers and suppliers of coachmaking materials, and active in the blackwood timber industry in the Dandenong Ranges. Back in Melbourne Heales found that the corrosive forces of the gold rushes had almost destroyed the temperance movement. He set about resuscitating the Total Abstinence Society and organized aid for the Temperance Hall which was in severe financial difficulty. In April 1857 the movement was reviving and he established the Temperance League to co-ordinate the work of existing societies. He was president of the league and of the Total Abstinence Society until 1864.

Heales resumed his political career in August 1856 when he agreed to stand for the Melbourne seat in the Legislative

Assembly. His policy was popular and included the establishment of a general system of education and a system which would provide land for bona fide agriculturists but leave no opportunities for speculators. A working man himself, he told a meeting at North Melbourne that if elected he would be 'the exponent of the wishes and opinions of the working classes'. Despite support from two meetings of working men, Heales was not elected, but in 1857 won a by-election at East Bourke and in 1859-64 represented East Bourke Boroughs. Although a working-men's representative, Heales asserted often in 1857-60 that he sought justice for all and would not legislate for any particular class. In 1857 he supported Haines's [q.v.] land bill, believing that although large tracts of land should always be available for agriculturists, squatters should be allowed to keep their runs at a fair rent until required for closer settlement. He opposed the introduction of the Chinese tax, supported the recognition of homeopathic doctors and in 1859 brought in a bill to abolish ministerial pensions. As was to be expected, he often advocated better regulation of liquor trading and in 1859 moved for a select committee to investigate the subject.

Heales came suddenly into political prominence in August 1860 when, with C. G. Duffy [q.v.], he moved that the assembly support only a government pledged to go ahead with the land bill over which the Nicholson [q.v.] ministry had resigned. Though the motion was lost, Governor Barkly asked Heales to form a government. After approaching Nicholson without success, he negotiated with Duffy but they withdrew when it became clear that the late government and its opposition would unite against them, and Barkly refused to guarantee a dissolution in the event of their defeat. Nicholson resumed office but was defeated in November and, after much confusion and factional manoeuvring, Heales became chief secretary in a ministry brought together by J. H. Brooke [q.v.]. Its members were radical in outlook but depended on the conservative support of C. H. Ebden [q.v.] and O'Shanassy who, unwilling to take office themselves, allowed Heales to assume the burden. They gave him little co-operation. He was defeated on a no-confidence motion in June 1861 after achieving important reforms in the civil service but little else. He then persuaded Barkly to grant a dissolution and announced a very radical policy of Legislative Council reform as a preliminary to land reform, protection to industry and a general system of education. Also included was payment of members

which Heales had earlier opposed. With the support of the Protectionist League and the goldfields electorates, the ministry was narrowly returned but lasted only until November.

Heales's term of office had been humiliating, but he emerged from it a stronger, bolder and more skilful politician with a flair for compromise as he showed next year when he forced past the antagonistic O'Shanassy government a bill to establish a single board of education. The common schools system established by this Act was far from Heales's voluntaryist ideal, but it was a substantial advance towards a secular system and probably as much as parliament could then be persuaded to accept. When James McCulloch [q.v.] took office in June 1863 Heales joined him as minister for lands, hoping at last to achieve a liberal land bill which could not be evaded. He had opposed the 1862 Land Act as likely to favour the squatters and brought in two bills to amend it; his provisions included the reservation of ten million acres for agricultural selection and very strict conditions of payment. Both bills were returned by the council and allowed to lapse. In April 1864 Heales was granted leave from parliament for the sake of his health. Aged 42 he died on 19 June at his Elsternwick home from tuberculosis, aggravated by overwork. He was survived by his wife, six sons and two daughters. Parliament voted £3000 for his family's support and Healesville was later named after him.

Heales was one of the first of Victoria's public men to die in office, but the crowds who lined Swanston Street to watch his funeral procession from the Alma Road Congregational Church to the Melbourne general cemetery were not merely seeking a spectacle. He was a popular figure, honoured for long devotion to the temperance cause, respected for his unselfishness, humility and honesty, and admired for his business success and his increasingly important political work. Even the conservative *Argus* regretted the loss of a serviceable politician; to the *Age* his death was a public calamity.

Garryowen (E. Finn), *The chronicles of early Melbourne*, 1 (Melb, 1888); International Temperance Convention, *Temperance in Australia* (Melb, 1889); C. G. Duffy, *My life in two hemispheres*, 2 (Lond, 1898); J. B. Cooper, *The history of St. Kilda . . . 1840 to 1930*, 2 (Melb, 1931); G. Serle, *The golden age* (Melb, 1963); *Argus*, 2 Nov 1850, Aug, Sept 1856, 20 June 1864; *Leader* (Melb), 15 Mar 1864; H. Bolitho, The Heales ministry, 1860-61 (B.A. Hons thesis, Univ Melb, 1960); J. S. Gregory, Church and state in Victoria, 1851-72 (M.A. thesis, Univ Melb, 1951). MARGOT BEEVER

HEARN, WILLIAM EDWARD (1826-1888), political economist, jurist, politician and university teacher, was born on 21 April 1826 at Belturbet, County Cavan, Ireland, second of the seven sons of Rev. William Edward Hearn (d. 1855) and his wife Henrietta Alicia, née Reynolds, of Kinsale, Ireland. His father, then curate and later vicar of Killargue, County Leitrim, and of Kildrumferton, County Cavan, was a grandson of Archdeacon Daniel Hearn (d. 1766), an Englishman who had settled in Ireland early in the eighteenth century. Hearn married first in Dublin in 1847 Rose (d. 1877), daughter of Rev. W. J. H. Le Fanu, rector of St Paul's, Dublin, a member of a celebrated Irish literary family of Huguenot descent, and second at Melbourne in 1878 Isabel, daughter of Major W. G. St Clair, 9th Regiment, Dublin.

After early education at Portora Royal School, Enniskillen, Hearn in 1842 entered Trinity College, Dublin (B.A., 1847; M.A., LL.D., 1863). He had a brilliant career, graduating as first senior moderator in classics and distinguishing himself in logic and ethics. He also studied law at Trinity College under the eminent jurist, Mountifort Longfield, and at the King's Inn, Dublin, and Lincoln's Inn, London. He was admitted to the Irish Bar in 1853.

When the Queen's Colleges, established for Ireland by Peel's Act of 1845, were opened in 1849, Hearn was nominated professor of Greek at the College of Galway. In 1854 he was chosen by a committee, acting in London for the newly-established University of Melbourne, as the first professor of modern history and literature, political economy and logic. By 1857 his formal responsibilities had been reduced to the subjects of history and political economy, but his versatility was shown by his ready assumption in 1855-56 and again in 1871 of the duties of the professor of classics. One of four original professors, Hearn had probably been attracted to Melbourne by the high salary of £1000 with accommodation in the university building. The choice was amply justified by his academic and public career in a small but lively and growing society, to the intellectual and public life of which he contributed much in the generation after the discovery of gold.

Classes in the university were small but Hearn, who arrived early in 1855, taught a wide range of courses almost single-handed. He was a popular lecturer in a discursive style, much respected personally and as a teacher by students who included such men, later distinguished in literature, law and politics, as Alexander Sutherland [q.v.], Samuel Alexander, H. B. Higgins, Isaac Isaacs and Alfred Deakin. In 1873 Hearn

was appointed dean of the new faculty of law, surrendering his title of professor but retaining the emoluments and privileges of that position, and lecturing in legal subjects including constitutional law and jurisprudence. He played an active and sometimes stormy part in university politics and administration. In May 1886 he was elected chancellor, but his term as a university council member expiring in October, he was defeated in a strenuously fought contest and so was automatically ineligible for re-election to the chancellorship.

Before his arrival in Melbourne Hearn had published in 1851 *The Cassell Prize Essay on the Condition of Ireland*, and had written, probably in 1853-54, an 'Essay on Natural Religion', a manuscript of some 250 pages defending the argument from design for the existence of a beneficent creator against evolutionary doctrine as it was known in pre-Darwinian form (copy in the Baillieu Library, University of Melbourne). In Melbourne he wrote four books, all characterized by a graceful clarity of style and wide learning, if also by cautious and sometimes superficial judgments. The first three were in their time well known outside Australia and still have modest places in the history of their disciplines; they were indeed remarkable books to have emerged from a colonial society. *Plutology or the theory of the efforts to satisfy human wants* (Melbourne, 1863; London, 1864), a textbook of political economy, was highly praised by Jevons [q.v.], Marshall, Edgeworth and other eminent economists. Close examination shows it to be less original than they supposed; Hearn drew heavily on a number of writers not well known in England for his reassessment of 'classical' political economy. But his book emphasized a new approach to the question of economic progress, stressing the stimulus of demand rather than the difficulties of supply, and was remarkable for its early, though rather shallow, attempt to apply Darwinian doctrines to the evolution and organization of economic society. Of *The Government of England* (1867), concerned with the growth of constitutional law and conventions, the jurist, A. V. Dicey, wrote in 1885 that it 'has taught me more than any other single work of the way in which the labours of lawyers established in early times the elementary principles which form the basis of the constitution'. *The Aryan Household* (1878) was concerned with the early social institutions, such as the family and the household, of the supposed progenitors of Western European peoples. Hearn's last book, *The Theory of Legal Duties and Rights* (1883), gave the theoretical reasoning behind his practical attempts to codify the laws of Victoria.

These books brought the young University of Melbourne to the notice of scholars in Europe and America. He also published various pamphlets and lectures and was an active, though anonymous, journalist, writing extensively until 1888 for the leading 'conservative' Victorian newspaper, the *Argus*, and its weekly counterpart the *Australasian* founded in 1864.

From his first years in Victoria Hearn took a prominent part in public affairs. He was an early advocate of adult educational classes and founded the People's College at the Melbourne Mechanics' Institute in an attempt to give, by lectures and examinations, some kind of formal educational qualification other than a university degree. In 1856 he was appointed a member of a board to make suggestions to the Victorian government for the organization of the civil service. Its report, avowedly based on the recent Northcote-Trevelyan report on the British civil service, recommended the establishment of an independent board to control both admission by examination, and promotion. In 1859-60 a royal commission, of which Hearn was a member, presented a weakened version of these recommendations, dropping the board but retaining entrance by examination. An Act of 1862 was based on this report; Hearn argued in 1883, when it was superseded by the more effective Act introduced by James Service [q.v.], that it had never been fairly tried.

Hearn was a prominent layman of the Church of England, being chancellor of the diocese of Melbourne in 1877-88 and active in the affairs of Trinity College, founded in 1872 as an Anglican residential college of the university. He practised little at the Victorian Bar, to which he was admitted in 1860; his appointment as Q.C. in 1886 was a recognition of his scholarly work in the field of law. His main practical venture in law, his drafting of the Land Act of 1862, had unfortunate consequences. According to the author of the Act, C. G. Duffy [q.v.], Hearn was selected by the attorney-general, R. D. Ireland [q.v.], as draftsman because much care and long consideration would be needed. But there were faults in drafting, which Ireland later admitted were well known to him at the time. These allowed the ostensible purpose of the Act, the dispersal of large pastoral estates, to be evaded within the law by pastoralists acting through their agents or 'dummies', though the fault seems to have been Ireland's rather than Hearn's.

In January 1859, to the indignation of the chancellor of the university, Sir Redmond Barry [q.v.], Hearn offered himself unsuccessfully as a candidate at a by-election for the Legislative Assembly, an action which induced the university council to pass a statute, not repealed for a century, forbidding professors to sit in parliament or to become members of any political association. In 1874 and 1877 he was again defeated in elections to the assembly; he met the university council's protest on the first occasion by pointing out that his standing for parliament was not inconsistent with the tenure of his office, which was now that of a dean, not a professor. In September 1878 he was at last elected to parliament to represent the Central Province in the Legislative Council, at a time when fierce political strife between the 'Liberal' followers of the premier, Graham Berry [q.v.], and the conservative element in the colony had culminated in a prolonged deadlock between the two Houses and a rejection of the annual appropriation bill by the council.

By English standards Hearn was a mild conservative, cautious about state intervention in economic affairs but not implacably opposed to it, and a free trader in a colony where 'liberals' or 'radicals' were almost unanimously protectionists. On such questions his opinions were unchanged during his parliamentary career, and he was easily represented by the *Age* to be an illiberal reactionary. In fact he soon gained the respect of both sides of the House as being, on most matters, a more or less neutral and well-informed technical critic of legislation, concerned to improve its form and to suggest practical amendments. From 1882 he was regarded as the 'unofficial leader' of the House. In his last years he was engaged in drafting an immense code of Victorian law, based on a Benthamite-Austinian view of jurisprudence. It was introduced as a draft bill, provoked formal admiration and recommended for adoption by a committee to which it was referred. Regarded as too abstract by practising lawyers, it was quietly abandoned in favour of simple consolidation.

When Hearn died in Melbourne on 23 April 1888 Victoria lost a scholar who had tempered the rawness of colonial life with learning and intellectual distinction and brought lustre to the name of its young university. Black-bearded and bespectacled, he was witty and courteous, though ambitious and sometimes devious in controversy. If the width of his reading and the lucidity of his style helped to conceal a certain superficiality in his scholarship, and the extent of his debts to others, it was nevertheless a considerable achievement in his circumstances to have written several books which gained high praise from the leading authorities in their fields, and were still occasionally referred to a century after their publication. He founded no 'school' in the university; post-graduate studies, affected by the example and ideas of an influential teacher, lay far in the future. But he set an example of humane learning, especially in history and law, to many leaders of Victorian and Australian life in the generation after his death.

Hearn was survived by four of the six children of his first marriage. His only son, William Edward Le Fanu, who had been a medical practitioner at Hamilton, Victoria, died in Western Australia in 1893. His second surviving daughter, Rosalie Juliet Josephine (d. 1934) married in 1884 James Young, a Victorian grazier. Of their three sons, James was chaplain to the New Zealand artillery in World War I and Charles Le Fanu (d. 1921) after serving as captain in that war, was headmaster of the Cathedral Grammar School, Christchurch. Hearn's eldest surviving daughter, Charlotte Catherine Frances (d. 1943), and the youngest, Henrietta Alice (d. 1927), also moved to New Zealand. By his second marriage Hearn had no children.

D. B. Copland, W. E. Hearn: first Australian economist (Melb, 1935); J. A. La Nauze, Political economy in Australia: historical studies (Melb, 1949); G. Blainey, A centenary history of the University of Melbourne (Melb, 1957); J. A. La Nauze, 'Hearn on natural religion: an unpublished manuscript', Hist Studies, no 45, Oct 1965; Argus, 24 Apr 1888; A. Sutherland, 'William Edward Hearn', Argus, 28 Apr 1888; Univ Melb Archives; information from Archdeacon Young, Motueka, New Zealand.

J. A. LA NAUZE

HEATH, GEORGE POYNTER (1830-1921), naval officer and public servant, was born on 19 June 1830 at Hanworth, Norfolk, England, the second son of Rev. Charles Heath and his wife Mary Anne, née Poynter. Educated at Cheltenham College he joined the navy as a cadet in 1845. In 1846-53 he served in H.M.S. Rattlesnake (under Owen Stanley [q.v.] till 1850) and in the Fantome and the Calliope on the Australian station. He then returned to England where he worked at the Admiralty drawing charts of areas surveyed by the Rattlesnake. Late in 1859 as a lieutenant he applied for the government post of marine surveyor in the new colony of Queensland and was appointed. On 23 February 1860, before sailing, he married Elizabeth Jane, sister of Joseph George Long Innes [q.v.]; they had three sons and six daughters.

In his thirty-year tenure of office in what became the subdepartment of harbours, lighthouses and pilots, Heath was responsible for supervising the opening of 13 new ports,

establishing 33 lighthouses, 6 lightships and 150 small lights and marking 450 miles of the inner route through the Barrier Reef. In 1862 he was appointed portmaster of Brisbane and was also a member of the Immigration Board and the Marine Board of which he became chairman in 1869 when he retired as a naval commander. A prominent Anglican he served in 1876-89 as chairman of committees in synod. His large home at Norman Creek was the venue for many gay social activities. In November 1887 he retired from the public service because of ill health and later returned to England. He lived quietly on his pension at South Kensington, London, and died on 26 March 1921, predeceased by his wife in 1893.

R. S. Browne, A journalist's memories (Brisb, 1927); J. H. Thorburn, 'Major lighthouses of Queensland', Qld Heritage, 1 (1967), no 7; Col Sec letters COL 1 (QA); Treasury registers (QA); CO 234/1/123, 2/586, 55/420, 237/2.
H. J. GIBBNEY

HEATON, SIR JOHN HENNIKER (1848-1914), journalist and postal reformer, was born on 18 May 1848 at Rochester, England, the only son of Lieut-Colonel John Heaton and his wife Ann Elizabeth, née Henniker. Educated at Kent House School, Rochester, and King's College School, London, he went in 1864 to New South Wales where he spent several years as a jackeroo before turning to journalism. He worked on the Cumberland Mercury, the Goulburn Evening Penny Post and while on the Cumberland Times served for three months as acting town clerk of Parramatta in 1869-70. He joined the Sydney weekly Australian Town and Country Journal and travelled widely in country districts on its behalf. In 1880 the Bulletin, which later lampooned him unmercifully, credited the paper's early success to his 'unceasing labours'.

On 16 July 1873 at the Holy Trinity Church Heaton had married Rose, daughter of Samuel Bennett [q.v.]. Though he had independent means and in 1878 his wife inherited a one-fifth share in her father's newspapers, Heaton continued to work as a journalist as well as interesting himself in public affairs. In 1879 he published a pioneer reference work, Australian Dictionary of Dates and Men of the Time. As no local press was equipped for such a job, the government printer was authorized to print it at the author's expense. To Heaton's indignation he insisted on censoring the text, lost part of the manuscript and among other cuts deleted a paragraph under the head of 'Pure Merinos' which did not relate to sheep. Heaton's later court action against the government printer failed and the book was published in London; though crammed with useful information, it was marred by many inaccuracies.

In 1883 Heaton left New South Wales and by 1884 was settled in London. In 1886-1910 he represented Canterbury as a Conservative in the House of Commons. However, business and sentimental ties often drew him back to Sydney; he also acted for the colony as a commissioner at the 1883 Amsterdam Exhibition and the 1886 Indian and Colonial Exhibition in London. He was a member of the Colonial Party led by Sir Charles Dilke and J. F. Hogan [qq.v.] in the House of Commons and was dubbed 'the Member for Australia' by the English press; this sobriquet was resented and ridiculed by Australian radicals and nationalists.

Heaton hoped that Australian nationalism would not sever ties with Britain but his imperial federationism was practical; planning 'to stick the Empire together with a penny stamp', he campaigned long for cheaper postal and telegraphic charges. His original scheme for imperial penny postage was derided in 1886 but in 1898 became the rule from Britain to all parts of the empire except Australia. Heaton argued that the shipping contracts which kept Anglo-Australian postal charges high bore no relation to the cost of transporting mail but were a form of subsidy to the merchant marine. In 1905 the first penny letter from Britain to Australia was posted and in 1911 Australia at last reciprocated. By then Heaton had espoused a new cause, penny-a-word telegrams throughout the empire. Long critical of the monopolistic practices of the major telegraph companies, he had represented Tasmania with some success at the 1885 International Telegraphic Conference in Berlin and had given evidence on the subject to the 1887 Colonial Conference in London. He won many deductions in cable rates, brought international telegrams within the reach of the ordinary man and enabled Australian newspapers to give a fuller coverage of world news.

In London Heaton was a fellow of the Royal Colonial Institute and the Royal Society of Literature, and lectured to the latter on Australian Aboriginals. Chess was his favourite recreation; he also collected Australiana and at one stage owned the *Endeavour* journals of Sir Joseph Banks [q.v.]. Heaton had four times declined a knighthood and in 1912 was made a baronet. but his health was deteriorating. Taken ill while travelling on the Continent, he died at Geneva on 8 September 1914. He was survived by his wife, four sons and two daughters.

Heaton had an attractive personality and was a devoted husband and father as well as an urbane clubman and celebrated raconteur. Abuse and ridicule never disturbed him and despite stubborn pursuit of his enthusiasms he made no enemies. Happily self-aware, he recognized that he owed his remarkable success as a postal reformer to being 'a sort of Paganini' who played 'perfectly on one string'.

E. Salmon, *Twelve men of today* (Lond, 1892); R. Porter, *The life and letters of Sir John Henniker Heaton* (Lond, 1916); H. Robinson, *Britain's post office* (Lond, 1953); PD (NSW), 1878-79; V&P (HA Tas), 1885 (127, 128); *Bulletin*, 6 Mar 1880; *Australasian*, 6 Jan 1906; *Daily Telegraph* (Lond), 21 Feb 1912, 10 Sept 1914; *Argus*, 10 Mar 1914, 10 Apr 1915; Parkes letters and document 654b (ML).   B. K. DE GARIS

HEIDENREICH, GEORG ADAM (1828-1910), Lutheran minister, was born on 25 September 1828 at Tiefenort in the duchy of Saxe-Weimar-Eisenach, the eldest son of Johann Georg Heidenreich and his wife Veronika, née Blaufuss. Influenced by the preaching of Dr L. A. Petri in Hanover, he resigned his post in the mint and in 1862 entered the Mission Seminary in Hermannsburg, Hanover, an institution which trained Lutheran missionaries and pastors for service overseas and sent a total of forty-five ordained men to Australia and New Zealand.

Heidenreich was in the first group of four clergy sent to Australia. With twenty-four others he was ordained on 19 March 1866 at Hanover in the presence of George V of Hanover and the royal family. With his wife Anna, née Meyer, whom he married on 19 April at Scheessel, he arrived at Port Adelaide on 24 August in the *Sophia*. He was sent to the parish of Bethany, near Tanunda in the Barossa valley, where he served for forty-four years. His most notable contribution was in Aboriginal mission work for which he had a consuming zeal. Enjoying the highest respect of Theodor Harms, director of the Hermannsburg Mission Society, he was superintendent of its mission work in Australia in 1875-94 and in New Zealand in 1875-77 and 1889-92. In conjunction with the Evangelical Lutheran Synod of Australia, he guided the establishment of the Hermannsburg Mission in Central Australia. The long trek with some 3000 sheep from October 1875 to June 1877 was mostly under drought conditions but he tirelessly travelled between the various sections of the caravan, arranged all stages of the journey and selected the site for the station. He continued to support the mission after the church body to which he belonged had withdrawn. This created intra-church tensions which led to the establishment in 1902 of the Evangelical Lutheran Church of Australia on the Old Basis. Heidenreich served as its president until he died on 8 August 1910, survived by six sons and three daughters.

His second son, JOHANNES HEINRICH SIEGFRIED, was born on 28 July 1868, trained in the Hermannsburg Mission Seminary and the University of Erlangen in 1888-94 and ordained at Bethany on 14 October 1894. As assistant to his father and then pastor in Freeling, he covered great distances in South Australia in pastoral service. His forthright leadership exerted a deep influence. He succeeded his father as president of the Evangelical Lutheran Church of Australia on the Old Basis from 1910 to 1926 when it amalgamated with the United Evangelical Lutheran Church in Australia. In 1928-45 he was vice-president of the united body and president of its South Australian district in 1933-43. His active ministry continued until 1953 and he died on 5 June 1959.

The fifth son, FRANZ THEODOR PAUL, was born on 1 March 1874 and became a flour-miller at Salisbury, South Australia. He was well known in football circles as president of the Norwood Football Club from 1940 until his death on 6 December 1962.

P. A. Scherer, *Venture of faith* (Hermannsburg, NT, 1963); Evangelical Lutheran Synod of Aust reports, 1904-26, and Heidenreich files (Lutheran Church Archives, Adel).

H. F. W. PROEVE

HEIR, FANNY; *see* CATHCART

HELMS, RICHARD (1842-1914), zoologist and botanist, was born on 12 December 1842 at Altona, Hanover, Germany, son of Frederick Helms, Lutheran minister, and his wife Caroline. He migrated in 1858 to Melbourne where he worked for a tobacconist. In 1862 he moved to Dunedin where he turned to dentistry and later to watchmaking. Fluctuating between Australia and New Zealand, he extended his extraordinary versatility to zoology. Although self-taught, he became so zealous as a collector that many new species of New Zealand insects and a number of shells were named after him.

In 1888 Helms became a collector for the Australian Museum in Sydney. He worked first in the Snowy Mountains. From Jindabyne in February 1889 he wrote to E. P. Ramsay [q.v.], curator of the museum, that riding, walking and collecting material occupied him virtually from dawn to midnight each day. Later he made excursions to the regions of the Darling and Richmond Rivers. He was reputed to have had 'the wisdom of a savage as to where a bird would nest or a beetle would burrow', but despite his main interest in zoology he discovered new species of plants, some of which were named in his honour by Mueller [q.v.].

In 1891 Helms was appointed naturalist to an east-west expedition sponsored by Sir Thomas Elder [q.v.] and led by David Lindsay [q.v.]; the party of 8 white men and 5 Afghans with 44 camels started from Warrina, South Australia, in May and, after great difficulty in arid country, crossed into Western Australia in July and dispersed in the Murchison region early in 1892. Results of the expedition were disappointing, but Helms made important collections of fauna and flora. The discussion of these collections by scientists of the Royal Society of South Australia was published in its *Proceedings*, 16 (1892-96), together with a paper by Helms on anthropology. In 1896-99 he was biologist to the Department of Agriculture, Western Australia. He wrote papers on his studies of the honey-bee, ticks and other parasites, noxious weeds, plant diseases and exotic birds. He also published informative material on his finds in excursions to the East Kimberleys and the Abrolhos Islands.

Helms returned to New South Wales in 1900 and as a bacteriologist in the Department of Mines and Agriculture published many papers in the *Agricultural Gazette* and other journals. He retired in 1908 and worked on his extensive collections and made further excursions. On a visit to the Solomon Islands he caught a chill and died in Sydney on 17 July 1914, leaving a reputation as one of the most versatile and diligent natural scientists in Australia. He was buried in the non-sectarian section of the Gore Hill cemetery. Survived by two daughters, he was predeceased by his wife Sarah Ann, née Reay, whom he had married at 36 in Greymouth, New Zealand.

A. Musgrave, *Bibliography of Australian entomology 1775-1930* (Syd, 1932); H. M. Whittell, *The literature of Australian birds* (Perth, 1954), W.B.A[lexander], 'Obituary: Mr. Richard Helms', Roy Soc WA, *Procs*, 1 (1914-15); 'Presidential address', Roy Soc NSW, *Procs*, 49 (1915).

A. H. CHISHOLM

HELY, HOVENDEN (1823-1872), explorer, landowner and politician, was born at Tullamore, King's County, Ireland, son of Frederick Augustus Hely [q.v.] and his wife Georgina Susannah Lindsay, née Bucknell. As an infant he went with his family to Sydney. Educated under W. T. Cape [q.v.] and at The King's School, Parramatta, he worked for two years as a clerk in the Colonial Secretary's Office. In 1841 under the trustees he managed his father's estates near Brisbane Water and Wyong, in which he inherited at 21 a fifth share. In 1857 his sister's marriage settlement necessitated a private Act, Mrs Mann's Trust Act, to enable the trustees to sell part of the estate. Although described by Ludwig Leichhardt [q.v.] as a 'likeable idler', Hely joined his unsuccessful expedition of 1846-47. Leichhardt later accused him of disloyalty and dereliction of duty, after Hely and his relation, J. F. Mann [q.v.], had also disgusted Leichhardt 'with their bawdy filthy conversations or with their constant harping on fine eating and drinking'. Mann's published account of the expedition in 1888 accused Leichhardt of incompetence but did not dispel the charges against Hely. In December 1851 Hely was appointed head of the official search for Leichhardt after the original appointee had drowned, but revealed little imaginative leadership. According to the *Empire* in 1864, the expedition 'established nothing whatever'.

In 1856-57 Hely represented Northumberland and Hunter in the first Legislative Assembly. He was an ineffective politician with a record of assisting relations by patronage. In 1858 before a trip to England Hely borrowed heavily on his property. At Clapton, Somerset, he married Mary Gertrude Church in 1859. His financial problems did not abate after they returned and in 1860 he again borrowed heavily. In July 1862, after fourteen years on the Gosford bench, Hely and three other local magistrates were dismissed after an inquiry into a public display of ill feeling between them that had influenced their legal decisions. In 1865 Hely was declared bankrupt, but he received his certificate of discharge in 1868 after claiming that iron ore and coal were discovered on his property. He died aged 49 on 8 October 1872 at Branthwaite, the home of Rev. W. B. Clarke [q.v.]. He was buried in St Thomas's Church of England cemetery, North Sydney. He was survived by his wife to whom he had left £700 in goods, and by six sons and a daughter.

J. F. Mann, *Eight months with Dr. Leichhardt, in the years 1846-47* (Syd, 1888); *Empire* (Syd), 17 May 1856, 20 June 1864; *Queenslander*, 15 Dec 1900; *Truth* (Syd), 30 Apr 1911; P. P. King papers (ML); Insolvency file 7038 (NSWA).   KEN ELFORD

HEMMANT, WILLIAM (1838-1916), draper and politician, was born on 10 October 1838 at Whittlesey, Cambridgeshire, England, son of William Hemmant, farmer, and his wife Elizabeth, née Burdock. At 21 he migrated to Victoria, worked as a miner at Ballarat and in 1860 moved to Brisbane where he established a drapery shop in partnership with Alexander Stewart. The premises were destroyed in December 1864 by a fire which engulfed a whole city block. After completing the arduous task of rebuilding, Hemmant left for England in November 1865.

At Coates, Cambridgeshire, on 20 September 1866 he married Lucy Elizabeth Ground. He sailed for Queensland on 2 January 1867, leaving his wife to follow. Turning to politics, he led an attack on the Brisbane City Council for financial mismanagement and was elected an alderman in 1868, but in August 1870 lost South Brisbane to T. B. Stephens [q.v.]. In September he joined the committee of a political reform association pledged to defeat the squatting oligarchy and with its backing defeated John Douglas [q.v.] in a by-election for East Moreton in November 1871. As treasurer under Macalister [q.v.] from January 1874 to June 1876 Hemmant was described as the most influential minister after McIlwraith [q.v.] retired. His tariff policies introduced moderate protection in Queensland.

Hemmant resigned on 5 June 1876 and went to England as resident partner for his firm but corresponded with S. W. Griffith and served as commissioner for Queensland at several exhibitions in Europe. Early in 1880 he wrote to Griffith alleging scandals in the purchase of railway lines and in contracts for the conveyance of immigrants. Inquiry by a select committee and a royal commission found little substance in the allegations but, when Griffith became premier, Hemmant acted as agent-general in 1885 and represented Queensland at the International Postal Union Congress.

As an investor and client of the Australian Joint Stock Bank, Hemmant was appointed to its London board in 1876. In August 1893 he sold out of Stewart & Hemmant but continued to serve the firm as a commission agent until 1900 while devoting himself mainly to the bank. In 1897 he chaired the London meeting which accepted a new reconstruction scheme and in 1911 was commended for his service in transforming the Australian Joint Stock Bank into the Australian Bank of Commerce. He was a director of the new bank until he died on 20 September 1916. Of his ten children, a daughter married Sir James, son of R. T. Atkin [q.v.], an old parliamentary colleague; his son George was chief secretary in Nigeria and retired in 1934.

C. A. Bernays, *Queensland politics during sixty years* (Brisb, 1919); G. Greenwood and J. Laverty, *Brisbane 1859-1959* (Brisb, 1959); *Brisbane Courier*, 6 Dec 1864, 10 Aug, 7 Sept 1870, 30 Oct 1871, 12, 13 Jan 1893; *A'sian Insurance and Banking Record*, 19 June 1897; *Draper of A'sia*, 27 May 1902; P. D. Wilson, Political career of Hon. A. Macalister (B.A. Hons thesis, Univ Qld, 1969); Griffith papers (Dixson Lib, Syd); Bank of NSW Archives (Syd).   H. J. GIBBNEY

HENDERSON, SIR EDMUND YEA-MANS WALCOTT (1821-1896), soldier, administrator and police commissioner, was born on 19 April 1821 at Muddiford, Hampshire, England, son of Vice-Admiral George Henderson and his wife Frances Elizabeth, née Walcott-Sympson. Educated at Bruton, Somerset, and the Royal Military Academy, Woolwich, he was commissioned in the Royal Engineers and in 1839-45 served in Canada. In 1848 at Halifax, Nova Scotia, he married Mary Murphy.

In 1849 Earl Grey appointed Henderson comptroller of convicts in Western Australia and he sailed in the *Scindian* with seventy-five convicts, seventy pensioners and some free migrants; they arrived at Fremantle on 1 June 1850. He was instructed to 'examine and report upon the public works which can be undertaken with the most advantage . . . and to exercise a general control of convict labour', but no accommodation had been arranged and he had to lease premises, commenting that a 'woolshed makes excellent barracks'. His work was hampered by an anti-transportation party and by the arrival of more convicts. The first transportees had been chosen for their physical fitness and were soon sent to private employment to relieve the labour shortage without contaminating the morals of the community. Henderson thought highly of these convicts, urged that their terms of servitude be shortened and was pleased when they married. He informed Governor Fitzgerald of improvements in the English penal code but was snubbed when the Executive Council reduced wages and rations for ticket-of-leave men. In retort Henderson appointed prisoner-constables and refused most of the normal duties of the commissariat and the Ordnance Office.

Despite the arrival of sickly, turbulent Irish convicts in 1853, Henderson had the complicated system in working order by 1855. A permanent gaol of limestone had been built at Fremantle with officers' quarters and cottages for the guard, and he had planned a harbour. Fitzgerald was replaced in June 1855 by Kennedy who respected Henderson but differed on 'matters of principle'. His wife had died and he

returned to England with his son in February 1856. He gave evidence on the abolition of transportation to a select committee of the House of Lords and advocated a system of marks, a scheme proposed by his energetic superintendent, Thomas Dixon. The system, based on industry and education, enabled prisoners to earn recommendation for tickets-of-leave by accumulating marks, but Henderson was distressed when he learned that Dixon had been summarily dismissed for fraudulent insolvency. In 1857 he married Maria, daughter of Rev. J. Hindle of Higham, Kent, and returned to Western Australia in 1858.

As a supernumerary of the Royal Engineers, Henderson agreed to take over the colony's public works but when the corps withdrew after three years he had much difficulty in carrying out any but the most ordinary work. By 1862 he told Governor Hampton that the department should be less costly under charge of a civilian. The convict system was then established with limited transportation and Henderson wanted to resign. Nearly 6500 convicts had arrived, fifteen hiring stations were established, road-gangs were working all over the colony and 'remarkable order and quiet' prevailed. Humane and liberal, he had reduced corporal punishment to a minimum and established in the gaol a library, classes and lectures. He was also patron of the Fremantle Workingmen's Association. With complimentary addresses from both colonists and convicts, he left the colony in the *York* on 7 February 1863.

In England Henderson gave evidence on penal systems and transportation to a royal commission, sold his commission as lieut-colonel and accepted appointment as director of convict prisons. When Sir Joshua Jebb died in 1863, Henderson became surveyor-general of prisons and inspector-general of military prisons. In 1869 he became chief commissioner of the metropolitan police which he expanded from 9000 to 13,000. He also instituted a criminal investigation department and a police orphanage. He was made C.B. in 1868 and K.C.B. in 1878. On 8 February 1886 a demonstration of unemployed in Trafalgar Square led to serious riot and much damage to public property. The failure of police to control the crowds was blamed on Henderson and he resigned. Through the Home Secretary, H. C. E. Childers [q.v.], he was given the highest rate of pension, £1000. He was also presented with a purse of £1000 and a portrait by Edwin Long, and London cabmen gave him a silver model of a hansom cab. Henderson had a good sense of humour, wide repute as a raconteur and competence in water-colour sketching. He died on 8 December

1896 in London, survived by several daughters.

E. H. Yates, *Celebrities at home*, 3 (Lond, 1879); PP (GB), 1856, 1863; *Inquirer*, 28 Jan 1863, 10 Sept 1873, 11 May 1887; *Vanity Fair*, 6 Mar 1875; *Illustrated London News*, 4 Dec 1886, 6 Dec 1896; *The Times*, 10 Dec 1896; *Testimonials* 228, 229A, Feb 1863 (Battye Lib, Perth); CO 18/97, 102; CSO 1850-1863 (Battye Lib, Perth).   WENDY BIRMAN

HENDERSON, JOHN BAILLIE (1836-1921), hydraulic engineer, was born in London, son of Hector Charles Henderson and his wife Mary Ann, née Norriss. Educated in Scotland as an engineer, he arrived in Victoria in 1861 and in September was appointed a temporary road overseer under the Board of Lands and Works. In 1863 he resigned and went to Gippsland where he married Elizabeth Child. He rejoined the public service in 1866 as an engineer and surveyor in the Water Supply Department. He served as executive engineer under Lieut-Colonel Sankey on the Coliban water scheme near Bendigo and was responsible for completing the Geelong water supply but in January 1878 he was suddenly discharged on Black Wednesday.

Henderson went to Queensland where on 10 April he became resident engineer of northern waterworks. Five years later he was appointed to the new office ot government hydraulic engineer. Soon afterwards he became interested in Robert Logan Jack's [q.v.] theory of artesian water in Queensland. In 1885 he and Jack collaborated in an investigation and on their recommendation an American drilling plant started work at Blackall in December 1885. Meanwhile an improved plant operated by the Canadian, J. S. Loughead, on Thurulgoona station under contract to Simon Fraser [q.v.] had commenced work in February 1887 and it struck the first water in February 1887. Henderson then secured Loughead's services and the first government bore was completed at Barcaldine on 16 November.

Henderson's activities were not confined to drilling. He kept records of bore output and, when some diminution of supply was observed in 1891, he and Jack recommended government control of artesian waters. A bill to impose such control was rejected by the Legislative Council and was not finally passed until 1910. Henderson travelled thousands of miles all over Queensland and often visited other colonies to study new developments. He introduced the gauging of rivers, provided the first flood-warning sys-tem in Queensland and in 1904 was briefly responsible for Clement Wragge's [q.v.]

weather bureau. Henderson produced no technical literature but was elected to numerous professional societies in Australia, Britain and America. He retired from office in December 1916 and died aged 85 in Brisbane on 15 February 1921, survived by his wife, two sons and a daughter.

S. Fraser, *True story . . . of artesian water supply of Australia* (Melb, 1914); Report on artesian water supplies . . . in the Great Artesian Basin, PP (Qld), 1954-55, 2 (56); American Soc of Civil Engineers, *Trans*, 85 (1922); *Queenslander*, 26 Feb 1921.   H. J. GIBBNEY

HENDERSON, WILLIAM (1826-1884), clergyman, was born on 5 December 1826 at Dalserf, Lanarkshire, Scotland, the eldest son of William Henderson, farmer, and his wife Margaret, née Hamilton. He studied divinity at the University of Glasgow and for two years at Hanover where he also learnt to speak German fluently. In 1853 he accepted a call to Victoria and on 19 April he married Isabella, daughter of Rev. Charles Thomson. In the Free Church mission led by Dr Adam Cairns [q.v.] they left Edinburgh in the *Hurricane* and arrived in Melbourne on 10 September.

Henderson was immediately inducted to the charge at Williamstown and in 1857 was called to Ballarat. Very popular amongst his congregation, the Roman Catholic poor and the Lutheran miners to whom he preached in German, he was sharply criticized by more orthodox Presbyterian clergy and laymen who objected to his activities in the sporting and social life of the youth of Ballarat. He held a commission in the volunteer militia and never hesitated to speak out on political issues. In 1864 he was a founder of Ballarat College where he convened the committee for five years and was a visiting lecturer.

Henderson was respected for his superior powers of debate, transparent humility and evangelical fervour. He was also known for 'advanced' views and hostility to theological rigidity. He denounced what he considered ecclesiastical hypocrisy, especially Sabbatarianism, and with the backing of the Ballarat presbytery agitated for greater doctrinal freedom in the Presbyterian Church. When Charles Strong [q.v.] was expelled in 1883 Henderson was one of his few clerical supporters though they differed on some theological questions. Rev. R. Hamilton's comment that Henderson's views 'at times ran too much in the German groove to be much relished by the Church in general', reflected a contemporary prejudice against theologians who criticized the narrowness of Anglo-Saxon dogma. However, he was moderator in Victoria in 1872-73 and represented Victoria at the Pan-Presbyterian Council in Edinburgh in 1877. Many of his sermons and addresses were published and as one of Ballarat's best-known public lecturers he tackled such diverse matters as European politics and Darwinian evolution which he never feared as a threat to Christian faith. His most notable works were *Christianity and Modern Thought* (1861), a series of lectures on Christian apologetics, and *If, and What? Twelve Lectures on the Foundations of Christian Theism* (1882). In 1878-80 he edited the *Presbyterian Review*, though his reforming spirit aroused some opposition from members of the General Assembly.

Henderson suffered from diabetes and was granted leave for eighteen months by his congregation. A visit to New Zealand brought little relief and he died at Ballarat on 22 July 1884. His funeral was attended by many prominent dignitaries; even the anti-clerical Sydney *Bulletin* waxed sentimental on his death. The mayor of Ballarat and other leading Victorians initiated a financial appeal to relieve his widow's poverty, and the tower of St Andrew's Kirk was completed as a memorial to him. Of his two sons and six surviving daughters, Charles James became superintendent of the Bank of Australasia and Isabella Thomson founded Clyde Girls' School.

R. Hamilton, *A jubilee history of the Presbyterian Church in Victoria* (Melb, 1888); *Monthly Messenger*, Aug 1884; *Ballarat Courier*, 25, 28, 30 July 1884; *Ballarat Star*, 28 July, 8, 9 Aug 1884; *Bulletin*, 2 Aug 1884; notes from Miss L. M. Henderson, South Yarra, Vic.   DON CHAMBERS

HENNING, RACHEL BIDDULPH (1826-1914), letter-writer, was born on 29 April 1826 at Bristol, England, the eldest child of Rev. Charles Wansbrough Henning (1795-1840) and his wife Rachel Lydia, née Biddulph. Her mother's death in 1845 left Rachel responsible for her three sisters and only brother, Biddulph. His health had been early impaired by scarlet fever and in August 1853 he left for Sydney in the *Great Britain* with his sister Annie. Rachel soon decided to join him and a year later sailed in the *Calcutta* with her sister Amy. They lived with Biddulph on a leased farm at Appin, then on his own farm on the Bulli Mountain.

Rachel's letters, never intended for publication, dated from the time Biddulph left England, and were mostly addressed to her sister Etta who married Rev. Thomas Boyce in England, and to Amy who in 1855 married Thomas Sloman [q.v.] of Bathurst. Her 'slightly mordant sense of humour' first showed in her shrewd comments on her fellow passengers: 'Mr and Mrs Donaldson [q.v.] are in their own eyes the great people on board, he being actually a member of the Australian Parliament (I did not know they had one)'. After a placid existence in English country houses, Rachel disliked the heat and the bush life 'extremely' and 'did not care enough about Australian flowers' to make a botanical collection or to use two letters of introduction from Sir William Hooker of Kew. Miserably homesick she went to England in the *Star of Peace* and lived mainly with the Boyces. In 1861 she returned to Australia in the *Great Britain*.

Biddulph had moved to Queensland and in 1862 Rachel and Annie joined him on his run, Exmoor, in the South Kennedy district. From the moment of reaching Queensland Rachel revelled in station life. She had 'never liked parties' or meeting strangers, and found 'a complete emotional, social and intellectual felicity within the family circle'. She loved the wild flowers and 'beautiful' scenery and discovered that 'hardly anything [was] pleasanter than a gallop over a plain with the wind rushing by you and the ground flying under your horse's feet'. A lover of animals, she soon had a 'train' of nine poddy lambs which she took for walks with the dogs.

Rachel left Exmoor in October 1865 and on 3 March 1866 married Deighton Taylor, Biddulph's overseer who was ten years her junior. They lived on the Myall River where Taylor managed a timber-logging business, and then bought a farm, Peach Trees, near Stroud. In 1872 they sold it and moved to another farm, Springfield, near Wollongong. Rachel created gardens wherever she lived. She also loved music and poetry, which she sometimes wrote. In 1896 she sadly left her beautiful flowers at Springfield and moved to Ryde, where Taylor died in 1900. After Biddulph's wife died, Rachel and Annie lived with him at Passy, Hunter's Hill. She died there without issue on 23 August 1914 and was buried in the Anglican section of the Field of Mars cemetery. From her estate of £3433 she left legacies to the Animals Protection Society and the King Edward Home for Dogs.

The Letters of Rachel Henning, edited by David Adams and illustrated by Norman Lindsay, were first published in the *Bulletin* in 1951-52 and later in at least three paperback editions. Her letters read like a novel with 'darling' Biddulph the hero, and give an invaluable picture of colonial life; with vivid descriptions and shrewd, if not always charitable, observations on people, they have both charm and humour.

MS cat under Henning (ML); family papers (privately held).   MARGARET CALDWELL

HENRY, ERNEST (1837-1919), pastoralist and founder of copperfields and towns, was born on 1 May 1837 at Harrington, Cumberland, England, the second of four sons of Captain James Henry and his wife Mary Francis, fourth daughter of John Norris of Hughenden Manor, Buckinghamshire. The family had migrated to North America from Ayrshire, Scotland, in the early seventeenth century and settled on land near Boston. In the war of independence (1775-1783) they espoused the Loyalist cause and the sons fought against the American rebels. The lands of the Henrys were confiscated and the grandfather, James, settled in Jamaica as a sugar planter : when he died his sons, James and Charles Edward, were taken to England by their mother.

At 16 Ernest made his first voyage to Australia as a junior officer in the *Victoria* of the Australian Royal Mail Steamship Co. He returned to England after the Crimean war broke out and was commissioned an ensign but was invalided before the war ended. With his brothers, Arthur and Alfred, he arrived at Melbourne in February 1858. In 1859 when Queensland was separated from New South Wales he travelled overland to Brisbane and with G. E. Dalrymple and P. H. Selheim [qq.v.] explored the region of the Bowen and Burdekin Rivers, following the latter to the Valley of the Lagoons. All three explorers took up pastoral runs : Henry formed Baroondah, a sheep and cattle station on the Dawson River in 1860 and in 1861 leased Mount McConnell on the Burdekin River; Selheim took up Strathmore on the Bowen and Dalrymple the Valley of the Lagoons. From Rockhampton to Mount McConnell Ernest and Arthur took the first herd of cattle to arrive on the Upper Burdekin. Henry sold Baroondah in 1863 and accompanied Hugh Devlin to the Flinders country, an exploration which resulted in his occupation of Hughenden station and the later development of the town named after his mother's home of Hughenden Manor.

In 1865 Henry sold Mount McConnell and Hughenden and abandoned pastoral pursuits. In 1866 he went exploring and prospecting for minerals and in May 1867 on the Cloncurry River discovered the rich outcrop of copper ore which was later known as the Great Australian Copper Mine. Henry and his partners worked it until 1879 when it was sold. In 1882 he discovered copper mines at Argylla, fifty miles west of Cloncurry, and at Mount Oxide,

ninety miles from Argylla, and held these interests until 1913. Henry was a superb horseman with an iron constitution and survived many adventures and encounters with the Aboriginals. Once he abandoned his exhausted horse, walked across rough country for twelve hours, swam the flooded Suttor River and walked barefoot over burnt grass for ten miles to Mount McConnell station. In January 1884 at Argylla he was saddling his horse when a disgruntled Aboriginal drove a spear into his back. Unarmed and bleeding, Henry grappled with his attacker who escaped. Prostrate for seventy-two hours he induced some natives to swathe him with flannels soaked in hot water; every night he heard the Aboriginals disputing if they should kill him. On the fifth day he struggled to his horse and rode to Cloncurry. His reminiscences are in the Oxley Memorial Library.

On 18 August 1870 Henry married Marion Elizabeth, daughter of William Thompson and Mary Ann, née Northcote; she was born at Manchester, Lancashire, in 1845, became a fearless horsewoman and died at Warwick on 26 December 1888. Henry died at Epping, New South Wales, on 26 March 1919. He was survived by a daughter, Ernestine Marion, and by a son, Arthur Douglas, who followed mining and grazing pursuits and at 80 died in Queensland in June 1954. Ernest left an estate of £37,000. His younger brother, Alfred, was for many years police magistrate at Clermont and Townsville, and later a journalist and sugar-planter at Ingham; he then followed journalism in Sydney where he died on 22 February 1917.

G. C. Bolton, *A thousand miles away* (Brisb, 1963); J. Farnfield, *Frontiersman* (Melb, 1968); *Bulletin*, 3 Oct 1907.   CLEM LACK

HENRY, LUCIEN FELIX (1850-1896), artist, was born at Sisteron, France, son of French parents. He studied under Viollet-le-Duc and at the Ecole des Beaux Arts under Gerome. A communard, he was sentenced to death for political offences in the 1871 Paris commune but was exiled to New Caledonia. In June 1879 after a political amnesty he went to Sydney where on 6 January 1880 he married a widow Juliette Lopes, née Lebeau, according to Presbyterian rites. 'After a struggle' he was appointed instructor at the first modelling school in the Sydney Mechanics' School of Arts. In 1883 his appointment as art instructor at the Sydney Technical College was probably due to Edward Combes [q.v.]. In 1884 Henry was paid £250 a year for teaching 'Geometry, Perspective, Freehand, Drawing and modelling' and was also given the fees of all students entering his classes. In 1886 he asked for a salary increase for his additional work in teaching and preparing diagrams for the design class; he also taught privately. In 1888 he arranged the New South Wales court at the Melbourne Intercolonial Exhibition. A founder of the Art Society of New South Wales, he was a committee member by 1884 and often exhibited for the society.

Active as both an artist and a teacher, Henry worked in many fields including sculpture, modelling, terracotta work, architecture and design. He discovered the artistic possibilities of the waratah and advocated the use of Australian colours, fauna and flora for decorative art. He executed many portraits and busts and designed the stained-glass windows in Sydney Town Hall. His series of Australian designs, now in the Museum of Applied Arts and Sciences, show his technical skill. He also drafted a 'majestic' design for a stillborn parliament house. Although not a member of the Heidelberg school he sympathized with its efforts to develop a distinctively Australian art, but failed in his own similar ambitions. Handsome, 'with a Victor-Hugo head and the Victor-Hugo enthusiasm', a magnetic personality and tireless energy, Henry exercised a powerful influence for good on Australian sculpture and on his students who included the well-known B. E. Minns, Sydney Cathels, G. H. Aurousseau and Lucien Dechaineux.

On 25 May 1891 Henry returned to France after a farewell banquet. In that year he published in Paris the Legend of the Waratah and dedicated it to Fred Broomfield, prominent in Labor circles in New South Wales. In Sydney, 'with intent to vex and harass', bankruptcy proceedings were taken against him by his stepson at the instance of his wife who also started divorce proceedings. Henry died on 10 March 1896 at Le Pavé, St Léonard, Haute-Vienne, where he was buried. He left his estate of £23 to Harry André Henry, who was living with him at Le Pavé and whom he left to the guardianship of Elizabeth Kenny of New South Wales. Aged 58 Juliette Henry died on 25 January 1898 at Sydney and was buried in the Catholic section of Waverley cemetery. Before her death she had lectured on French literature in Tasmania and wrote French plays that were translated by Lady Hamilton, wife of the governor.

R. T. Baker, The Australian flora in applied art (Syd, 1915); Bernard Smith, Australian painting 1788-1960 (Melb, 1962); A. McCulloch, Encyclopedia of Australian art (Lond, 1968); G. H. Aurousseau, 'Lucien Henry, first lecturer in art at the Sydney Technical College', Technical Gazette of NSW, Aug 1912; Illustrated Sydney News, 4 Apr 1889; SMH, 18 May 1891; Board of Technical Education, Minute books 1883-89 (NSWA); Bankruptcy file, 8815 (NSWA).

ARTHUR McMARTIN

HENSMAN, ALFRED PEACH (1834-1902), attorney-general and judge, was born on 12 May 1834, the second son of John Hensman, solicitor, and his wife Mary, née Wilkinson, of Springhill, Northampton, England. He went to India and was commissioned in the 1st Madras Fusiliers, but soon resigned because of ill health. He entered the Middle Temple in 1852 and the University of London (B.A., 1853). Called to the Bar in 1858, he became counsel for the Treasury at the Leicestershire Assizes and later a revising barrister. In December 1882 he was appointed attorney-general for Western Australia.

With his wife Emily, née Rowden, and two children Hensman arrived at Perth in the Ballarat on 11 May 1884. He soon won repute as a dignified and reliable lawyer but socially was reserved and somewhat haughty; only intimate friends appreciated his dry humour and genuine benevolence. He was diametrically opposed in temperament and political philosophy to Governor Broome, whose inability to distinguish between administrative and legal matters increasingly irritated him. The governor questioned Hensman's right to give legal advice officially to stipendiary magistrates sitting in civil jurisdiction on cases between private litigants. Hensman tried to indicate the different functions of the attorney-general as judicial officer, and the governor as executive officer, but to little avail. He also maintained that Broome should confine his opinions to points of law and not extend them to questions involving the application of law to facts, especially as he seemed to have privately advised one of the litigants. In the Executive Council on 24 March 1886 the governor presented a minute accusing Hensman of 'disloyalty and improper official conduct', of anti-government conspiracies and actions designed to cripple the administration. Hensman was not permitted to answer the charges and immediately resigned, finding it 'impossible for a man of honour, or for one who has any respect for himself to do otherwise'. He expected his resignation to be transmitted to London and was appalled when Broome not only accepted it but also interdicted him, suspended his salary and demanded his resignation from the Legislative Council. Hensman declared his interdiction illegal and refused to resign from the Legislative Council pending advice from the Colonial Office. Lengthy dispatches passed between Broome and the

Colonial Office, and the affair was aired in the House of Commons. In January 1887 Edward Stanhope, the secretary of state for colonies, vindicated Hensman and ordered Broome to pay his salary in full. At the same time Hensman was offered the attorney-generalship of the Barbados, which he refused. Not satisfied he side-stepped protocol and solicited the aid of his brother, Arthur, to act as his 'representative' in London. These efforts were thwarted by a statement from the new secretary for state for colonies: 'With regard to your brother's complaints . . . that in a quarrel reaching the length attained by that between Sir F. N. Broome and Mr. A. P. Hensman, both parties are so carried away by their antagonism as to put themselves more or less in the wrong, whatever may have been the merits of the original dispute'.

Many colonists sympathized with Hensman, and on 6 November 1886 a public meeting in the Town Hall, well attended by his supporters, indicated that he was moving into the political arena. With his liberal background, he was concerned with social and political reforms. He had always been a staunch advocate for responsible government and since his student days supported the move for the emancipation of women: in convocation of the University of London in 1874 he had urged that they be admitted to degree courses and in Western Australia he pressed for female suffrage and opportunities for higher education. He represented Greenough in the Legislative Council in 1887-89 and practised as a barrister until his elevation to the Supreme Court as puisne judge in 1892. He strengthened it with his command of legal principle and his practicality, always treating the rules of court as servants, not masters. In keeping with his liberalism he was a champion of local autonomy, never yielding to English practice or precedent unless bound to do so. He published a handbook on English constitutional law and an address on Western Australia, which he delivered to the Royal Colonial Institute in London in 1889. Aggravated by continuous disparagement in the *West Australian*, Hensman sued the proprietors, C. Harper [q.v.] and J. W. Hackett, for libel in 1888. The case was decided in favour of the plaintiff who received £800 damages, but it had sordid overtones when the defendants formally objected to its being heard by the chief justice, A. C. Onslow [q.v.], an old friend and supporter of Hensman.

A competent violinist Hensman was active in encouraging musical appreciation in Perth and in recognition for his contribution he was presented with a baton by the Perth Musical Union in October 1889. On a visit to England he died on 5 October 1902,

survived by his wife and son, Harold William, a barrister in his father's firm in Perth.

PD (WA) 1886; Executive Council minutes, PP (WA) 1886, 1888; P. J. Boyce, 'The governors of Western Australia under representative government, 1870-1890', *Univ Studies in History*, 4 (1961-62) no 1; *West Australian*, 16 Jan, 17 Apr 1883, 31 Mar, 1, 14 Apr, 13 Sept 1886, 16 May-21 Aug 1888, 20, 29 Mar, 30 Oct 1889, 8 Oct 1902; *Daily News* (Perth), 23 Nov 1886; *Inquirer*, 29 Dec 1886; *Twentieth century impressions*, 134 (Battye Lib, Perth); Hensman papers (Battye Lib, Perth); Supreme Court records, 270, 1888 (Battye Lib, Perth); CSO, 1883-87 (Battye Lib, Perth); CSR, 1886-87 (Government House, Perth).

WENDY BIRMAN

HENTY, HENRY (1833-1912), **HERBERT JAMES** (1834-1902), merchants, and **THOMAS** (1836-1887), grazier, were the sons of James Henty [q.v.] and his wife Charlotte, née Carter. Henry was born on 9 May 1833 at Launceston, Van Diemen's Land, Herbert in October 1834 at Worthing, Sussex, and Thomas on 24 August 1836 at Launceston. They were educated at Launceston and the junior department of King's College, London. The family visited England in 1833-34 and 1848-51. The father then set up the firm of James Henty & Co. in Melbourne. Henry worked as a clerk in the firm and Herbert in the Bank of Australasia until 1856 when they became partners with their father.

Thomas briefly represented the firm at Launceston, and then managed in turn the family stations of Round Hill near Albury and Muntham near Coleraine. Herbert made his home at Roxeth, Kew, and was elected a member of Kew Municipal Council in 1864 and mayor in 1868-69. He also served on the Melbourne City Council, in one session of the royal commission on education in 1881-82 and as president of the Melbourne Hospital in 1882-84.

Henry was elected for Grenville in the Legislative Assembly in 1866 but resigned next year when the bill for payment of members was passed in the Lower House. He gradually took over the management of the family business from his father who died in 1882. Henry was then chairman of the Colonial Mutual Life Assurance Society, commissioner of the Savings Bank and president of the Chamber of Commerce, while Henty & Co. had more than £90,000 in land and investments. He went to England and returned in 1884 to find that Herbert had managed the family business with such imprudence that the firm was in difficulties. Although in 1885 it was liquidated and reformed with Henry in partnership with Thomas and his uncle Francis [q.v.], they soon discovered that Herbert had signed unrecorded guaranties in the old firm's name for some £81,000, including £33,000 to the notorious H. M. Franklyn [q.v.]. In November Henry filed his schedule in the Insolvent Court, the firm's deficit amounting to £149,518. In May 1886 he was granted an unconditional discharge. In 1889 Francis died leaving Henry as executor of his estate of £300,000. Two daughters disputed Henry's administration and, although some agreement was reached, a writ was issued against Henry. When heard in 1901 the case went against him but the judgment was reversed when he appealed in 1904.

Thomas had moved to Melbourne about 1878. For some years he served on the committee of the Victoria Racing Club and owned several well-known race-horses. In 1884-87 he represented Southern Province in the Legislative Council but seldom spoke in debates. In 1869 he had married Lucy Mary, daughter of J. D. Pinnock [q.v.]; they had eight sons and two daughters. He died at Middle Brighton on 22 September 1887. In 1861 Herbert had married Frances Emma, daughter of Sir Francis Murphy [q.v.]. In 1896 he moved to Deniliquin where he died on 12 August 1902, survived by a son and a daughter of his four children. Henry was described by a friend as 'simple and trusting' and 'the soul of honour'. A lay canon in the Anglican Church, he became a trustee of Bishop Perry's [q.v.] Victorian estate in 1892. He died at his home, Tarring, Kew, on 20 October 1912, survived by his wife Marion Anne McKellar, whom he had married at Geelong on 26 May 1859, and by four sons and three daughters of their nine children.

F. G. A. Barnard, *A jubilee history of Kew 1860-1910* (Melb, 1910); M. Bassett, *The Hentys, an Australian colonial tapestry* (Lond, 1954); *Australasian*, 28 Nov 1885, 1 May 1886, 24 Sept 1887, 5 Mar 1892, 21 Oct 1912; *Illustrated London News*, 22 Sept 1888, Aust supp; *Age*, 24 Dec 1901, 30 July 1904; *Argus*, 24 Aug 1902, 30 July 1904; Henty papers (LaT L).

SALLY O'NEILL

HERBERT, SIR ROBERT GEORGE WYNDHAM (1831-1905), politician and public servant, was born on 12 June 1831 in Brighton, Sussex, England, only son of Algernon Herbert and his wife Marianne, née Lempriere. His father was a barrister, author, antiquarian, sometime fellow of Merton College, Oxford, and fifth son of the first earl of Carnarvon. Robert was thus second cousin to H. H. M. Herbert, fourth earl of Carnarvon and his exact contem-

porary, a connexion of the first importance in his life. Privately tutored he went in 1844 to Rev. Edward Coleridge's house at Eton where he and Carnarvon were constant companions. Despite reputed laziness at Eton he won the Newcastle scholarship in 1849 and entered Balliol College, Oxford (B.A., 1854; B.C.L., 1856; D.C.L., 1862), taking in 1852 a first in classical moderations and in 1853 a second in *literae humaniores*; in 1854, having won literary and legal prizes, he was elected a fellow of All Souls. In December W. E. Gladstone, chancellor of the exchequer, asked Coleridge to recommend a suitable private secretary. Herbert was approached, accepted the post and held it from 1 January 1855 until either the fall of Lord Aberdeen's coalition in February or earlier after an alleged 'divergence of opinions' with his chief.. Herbert turned to legal studies. After his father died in June 1855, he inherited the family house and some copyhold property in Ickleton, Cambridgeshire, but the legacy yielded little income for all his father's capital was left to his mother and two younger sisters. He lingered over his legal studies and was not called to the Bar of the Inner Temple until 30 April 1858.

Herbert's political and public prospects had been diminished by the fall of the Aberdeen ministry, but hopes revived when the Conservatives were returned in February 1858. Prompted by Carnarvon, undersecretary at the Colonial Office, Gladstone offered Herbert a private secretaryship but it carried no salary and was refused. Herbert's career then took a decisive and unusual twist. Sir George Bowen was appointed governor of the new colony of Queensland in June 1859. In July the duke of Newcastle authorized him to select a private secretary who could also become colonial secretary of Queensland, 'independent of local influences'. Advised by 'friends in the Colonial Office', he eventually chose Herbert who accepted because he wanted a public appointment, was not anxious to practise law and no longer had high-placed political friends. Perhaps some of his cousin's new-found interests rubbed off on him.

Herbert had been appointed to no sinecure. He was part of a Colonial Office experiment, for Queensland began as a strict Crown colony with the prospect of immediate responsible government. Commissioned as colonial secretary on 12 December 1859, Herbert was told that he would hold the post only if he secured election to the Legislative Assembly and sufficient votes in the House. He had disadvantages: he was young and book-learned, a 'new-chum' and interloper, an aristocrat and careful dresser, who had yet to prove that he could run a government. In his favour he had intellectual strength, great administrative ability and a personality which enabled him to win 'the goodwill of all persons, especially of the *ladies*'. In the brief Crown colony government he drew on Bowen's experience and personally negotiated the financial settlement with New South Wales. When parliament met on 22 May 1860 his potential rivals, such as Arthur Macalister [q.v.], could find no complaint against him. Since he was already in office, warmly approved by the press and known to have the governor's favour, only a candidate with outstanding claims could have challenged him. None existed in Queensland. Herbert's own political strength was shown in his unopposed return for three constituencies. He chose to sit for Leichhardt in the north. Thus Bowen's original Executive Council became the colony's first responsible ministry.

As premier, Herbert cannot be understood without reference to his political ancestry. He was a product of nineteenth-century English conservatism, and a touch of the eighteenth century was manifested in his political methods. The factions and individualism of Queensland politics and parliament and its lack of a party system help to account for Herbert's success. He made no attempt to create a party, although he sedulously fostered conservatism. He relied first on Bowen's wish to have him as premier, with the necessary corollary that he always emphasized the governor's power of decision. This tactic was eventually noticed and not altogether approved, yet it helped him to command votes in the Legislative Assembly. Just as pertinently, Herbert cultivated a range of groups and individuals. He was also helped by his detachment and 'appearance of polite candour and friendly frankness'. Though long unable to overcome the jealousy of W. H. Walsh [q.v.], he persuaded the Brisbane lawyer, Macalister, to join his ministry in July 1861, a favour which led the original treasurer, R. R. Mackenzie [q.v.], to resign in September 1862. Anxious to retain the support of squatters, Herbert filled the post first with T. de Lacy Moffat and then J. P. Bell [qq.v.]. In contrast, when the first attorney-general, Ratcliffe Pring [q.v.], had to resign for drunkenness in the House, Herbert replaced him with Charles Lilley [q.v.], an urban radical. Political calculation seems to have been absent from Herbert's appointments of such key civil servants as surveyor-general, police magistrates and commissioners of crown lands, but he made rather more justices of the peace than necessary and critics detected political purpose in some of his expenditure on public works. These exercises in political management matched Herbert's performance in parliament. Aware of his reserved, dry manner, he never attempted oratory and never gave anything away. He used mannerisms to disconcert opposing speakers while his own speeches carried into the legislature the administrative ability which was his main strength. Clear, concise and fluent, they persuaded by their content rather than by his slightly halting delivery.

With a secure majority Herbert favoured strong executive government, promoting measures carefully planned and drawing on the warnings and examples of other places; one illustration was his comprehensive land policy of 1860. Despite his conservatism in constitutional matters, he adjusted carefully to progressive public opinion; though a staunch Anglican, he ended state aid to religion and introduced National education against the strong opposition of Bishop Tufnell [q.v.]. He was much concerned, like Peel, for national credit and for economy and efficiency in the civil service. In the absence of income tax, his main source of revenue was the tariff while loan funds were devoted to such developmental works as railways, telegraphs and harbours. His leading objects were to extend settlement especially on the north coast, encourage immigration, diversify the economy and establish a firm basis for stable government. He sought to extend Queensland's trade to Asian markets and to introduce 'Malays and other black labour' for plantation work. In all these aims he had some personal as well as public interest for he invested heavily, though not profitably, in cotton-planting and in the Valley of Lagoons, a large sheep station on the Burdekin.

Before Herbert visited England in July 1862 some of his qualities were beginning to lose effect. In June he had even withdrawn an electoral reform measure for fear of defeat. His conservatism had drawn fire from the *Courier*, Brisbane's most influential newspaper, and he was deemed too anxious to accommodate opinions in the legislature merely to stay in power. His low view of ordinary colonists caused critics to remind him that he had been appointed to office in a very special way and now had to cultivate popular opinion. His ability and integrity were respected, and in London his Australian reputation was enhanced by such things as his public remonstrance against a proposal to renew convict transportation. In his absence Macalister had acted as premier and, though the *Courier* had found Herbert's colleagues even less acceptable, it suggested to the traveller that he was no longer indispensable. On his return in April 1863 the assembly reproached him for going to England without leave and only his cool tact saved the motion from becoming a censure. Soon afterwards a popular railway bill was passed only by the Speaker's casting vote. The colony's first parliament was dissolved and at the general election in May a determined attempt was made to defeat him. He sought local credit by standing for North Brisbane and lost, but won the rural electorate of West Moreton after a bitter contest.

The new parliament confirmed Herbert's power. He anticipated and received better majorities than ever in the assembly, and the leadership of the Legislative Council went to his friend, John Bramston [q.v.]. To Herbert the official Opposition, led by Mackenzie and later joined by Walsh, was 'feeble'. He passed the measures he wanted and indulged his preference for the office work of government over that of parliament, but by 1865 he was 'weary and sick and disgusted with colonial politics'. For two years he had withdrawn increasingly from colonial society, except for such pastimes as horse-racing, yachting and seabathing. His circle of friends was restricted and when not at his office or Government House, where Bowen required him more often than he liked, his greatest pleasure was Herston, his and Bramston's stone house in a well-stocked seventy acres about three miles from town. He decided that he must have another 'taste of civilization' and in November told his ministers of his decision. In February 1866 he turned the premiership over to Macalister and when parliament met in April he sat as a private member.

The pleasure of many members at his 'political decease' and Macalister's first term in office were short. In July a crisis was precipitated by the failure of Agra & Masterman's Bank in London. To replace funds borrowed from this source, the ministry proposed to issue inconvertible government notes, 'greenbacks', but Bowen insisted that his Instructions required him to reserve any such measure for consideration by the British government. Macalister resigned as premier and Bowen instantly recalled Herbert, commissioning him on 20 July a member of the Executive Council without portfolio to avoid any ministerial re-election. In the assembly Herbert steered the legislation for securing loans from local and southern banks to tide the government over its troubles. Both Bowen's Instructions and Herbert's Peelite mind prescribed no more than these 'ordinary remedies'. Macalister had panicked and the mobs were loud in Brisbane, but the governor and his minister imposed orthodoxy with a margin of 18 votes in a House of 32. Herbert's electors in West Moreton sent him a glowing memorial but he resigned on 7 August.

He sailed on the 20th with some unfriendly press but also with power of attorney from Macalister's new ministry to supervise the sale of colonial debentures in London.

A career in England was always thought in Queensland to be available to Herbert. He was now fairly done with politics and little else remained for him in the colony, even though he told Carnarvon of his probable intention to return 'to look after . . . sheep and cattle'. Carnarvon, then secretary of state, tried but failed to arrange his cousin's employment in the Colonial Office. Instead, Herbert accepted an assistant secretaryship at the Board of Trade. In 1870 he became an assistant under-secretary in the Colonial Office and in May 1871 permanent under-secretary. His experience and aristocratic connexions had served him well. He brought to the Colonial Office some of the empire-mindedness which Carnarvon was issuing from the opposition side of the House of Lords. With Carnarvon's return to the Colonial Office in February 1874, there began a remarkable partnership in policy making for the colonies. By seeking to strengthen the upper echelons of the Colonial Office, by promoting co-operation between Britain and the larger colonies, by attempting to reorganize military relations with those colonies and by asserting British claims to the south-west Pacific, the cousins were responsible in the colonial sphere for earning the label of 'imperialist' for Disraeli's second ministry. Carnarvon's enthusiasms were partially discredited when he fell out with his colleagues in January 1878 and Herbert's reputation suffered also. However, he was a fixture in the office and carried through into the era when the 'scramble for Africa' transformed the nature of European imperial activity. Although this process was chiefly the concern of the Foreign Office, Herbert constantly advised his chiefs, emphasizing the need for Britain to maintain her or her colonies' supremacy especially in Africa and the Pacific. He retired in 1892.

After Carnarvon died in 1890 Herbert undertook the general editorship of his cousin's speeches and writings, including several volumes on colonial and imperial affairs. Among other duties he served in 1893-96 as agent-general for Tasmania, advised the sultan of Johore, chaired meetings of the Royal Colonial Institute and helped to found the British Empire League. He approved Joseph Chamberlain's strong policies and in 1900 he consented to return briefly to the Colonial Office as permanent under-secretary. In 1903 he accepted the chairmanship of Chamberlain's tariff 'Commission' where he exhibited the qualities which had won him the name of 'the perfect civil servant', imperturbable and efficient, with an outwardly gracious manner which, as in Queensland, was tempered by occasional acidity and intolerance of fools. He was made K.C.B. in 1882 and G.C.B. in 1892. He was also chancellor of the order of St Michael and St George. Unmarried he died on 6 May 1905 at Ickleton, his death attended by the comparative obscurity which he had chosen since 1867. Perhaps it was his dedication to the civil service which led the *Saturday Review* to proclaim him 'a solid rather than a brilliant member of a singularly interesting family'.

Cambridge history of the British empire, 3 (Cambridge, 1959); J. Farnfield, *Frontiersman* (Melb, 1968); *Qld Heritage*, 1 (1967) no 6, and for bibliog; B. R. Kingston, Land legislation and administration in Queensland, 1859-1876 (Ph.D. thesis, Monash Univ, 1970); Sir Everard im Thurn papers (Roy Anthropological Soc Lib, Lond).   B. A. KNOX

HERLITZ, HERMANN (1834-1920), Lutheran pastor, was born on 10 June 1834 at Niese, Saxony, Germany, of Jewish parents. In London about 1859 he became a Christian and soon afterwards entered the Missionary Seminary at Basel, Switzerland. On 17 August 1862 he was ordained a Lutheran pastor at Durlach, Baden, and received a call from Matthias Goethe [q.v.] to serve as pastor at Germantown (Grovedale) near Geelong. When Herlitz arrived there later that year he found a temporary Lutheran preacher in possession of the church and rectory. The community split and Herlitz had to conduct his services in a schoolhouse. With administrative skill he kept records of the community, managed its financial affairs and marshalled its few educated members to help with its schooling needs, even recruiting his wife Wilhelmine, née Feldmann, whom he married in 1864. He also ministered to near-by districts and visited Melbourne and Ballarat. In 1868 he was called to succeed Goethe as pastor of Melbourne, which till 1876 included care of the Doncaster, Thomastown and Berwick communities.

As president of the Victorian Synod in 1868-1914 Herlitz worked for Australia-wide unity of the Lutheran Church, but was only successful in part for he insisted on calling ministers from the Basel Seminary which had unionistic tendencies and emphasized the nonconfessional, Protestant nature of the Church; he also exercised his right to give communion to non-Lutherans. Although these issues prevented union with most of the South Australian congregations, the General Synod was formed, including

the communities of New South Wales in 1876 and Queensland in 1890. Herlitz was also president of this synod and in 1884, at his insistence, it joined the Melbourne Council of Churches. Almost as well known in South Australia and New South Wales as in Melbourne, he dedicated the Sydney Church in 1883, inducted new pastors and visited Germany to recruit ministers for Australia. Yet he was still active as a pastor and took pride in the many religious services he had personally conducted, and in his own church which was rebuilt in bluestone in 1874. Herlitz formed a church choir which also gave performances under his direction as synodal meetings, and his daughter Marie was church organist for twenty years. In 1867-1910 Herlitz edited *Der Australische Christenbote*, an official monthly which he twice enlarged. In 1907 he also edited *Festschrift* which commemorated the jubilee of the Evangelical Lutheran Synod of Victoria.

Keenly interested in social welfare, Herlitz was cofounder in 1873 of the Hospital Sunday Fund, in 1887 formed the Immigration and City Mission to help newcomers and to minister to the sick and aged in hospitals and in 1900 served on the royal commission on religious instruction in state schools. As a prominent member of the Charity Organisation Society of Melbourne, founded in 1887 by Edward Morris [q.v.], he read a paper on 'Workmen's Colonies for the Unemployed' in 1890 and helped to organize a labour colony. He retired in 1914 and lived with his son Hermann who was medical superintendent of the Cheltenham Hospital for the Aged in 1908-35. For many services Herlitz received a German decoration in 1903. He died at Melbourne on 9 June 1920 and was buried at the Melbourne general cemetery.

Th. Hebart, *The United Evangelical Lutheran Church in Australia*, J. J. Schultz ed (Adel, 1938); R. E. W. Kennedy, 'The Leongatha Labour Colony: founding an anti-utopia', *Labour Hist*, May 1968; Hundert jahre, Drei faltigskeit kirche, 1853-1953 (held by Holy Trinity Church, Melb); Minutes of the Church, 1863-1960 (held by Grovedale Lutheran Church); information from Pastor Seyler, Melb, Pastor Simpfen-dorfer, Grovedale, Mr F. D. O'Brian, Burwood, and Dr H. Carlile, Malvern, Vic.   S. M. TARNAY

HERNSHEIM, EDUARD (1847-1917), master mariner and entrepreneur, was born on 22 May 1847 at Mainz, Germany. He was educated at the local gymnasium and after studying chemistry briefly in Darmstadt began preparation to follow his father in a legal career. When his father died in

1863 the plan was abandoned. He worked on a large estate near Aschaffenburg where he read widely in travel books and, at the suggestion of his uncle, secured a berth in 1865 as volunteer seaman in the *Ceres* on a world trip. Returning to Hamburg in 1866 he took a course in the marine school at Kiel in 1867 and later became captain of a ship trading between China and Australia. The experience thus gained induced him to start his own business as a trader in the Pacific Islands. In 1872 he established a base in the Palau Islands at Malakal and bought the sailing ship *Coran*. In March 1875 he was joined by his brother Franz who had been in business in Mexico; together they made a reconnaissance through the Palau Islands, Yap, Duke of York Islands and New Britain, and set up another trading station at Port Hunter. Franz then returned to Europe to raise capital. Despite such setbacks as the destruction of one station by earthquake and another by native attack, the business slowly prospered and in February 1878 the brothers acquired the steamer *Pacific*. The firm then bought land at Matupi, Raluana, Kabakaul and Kurakaul and began to concentrate on the copra trade.

In 1883 Eduard went to Hamburg for funds and as the business then extended over the whole of the north-west Pacific his lobbying in Germany was an important factor in the decision to adopt an active colonial policy. In recognition of this activity Eduard was appointed German consul in the north-west Pacific Islands and was also able to arrange a merger of interests with the *Deutsche Handels-und Plantagen-Gesellschaft* from which the *Jaluit Gesellschaft* emerged. In 1892 Eduard retired to Germany, donating his ethnographic collections to museums in Berlin, Hamburg and Mainz. The firm was reputed to be particularly sound and in 1909 became a limited company of which he was managing director. The expropriation of most of his Pacific assets in 1914 was a staggering blow from which Hernsheim never recovered. He died in Germany on 13 April 1917.

H. Weyhmann, 'Eduard Hernsheim', *Südsee Bote. Organ des Südsee-Vereins* (Leipzig), 1 Apr 1918; Hernsheim papers, FM4/2218 (ML).

H. J. GIBBNEY

HERZ, JULIUS (1841-1898), musician, was born on 13 March 1841 in Mecklenberg-Schwerin, Germany. He was educated at a preparatory school in Berlin and then at the Berlin *Konservatorium* under Professor Julius Stern. He was a *Konservatorium* master until he migrated to Victoria in 1865. In Melbourne Herz became a member of the first committee of the Victorian Musical Association founded by C. E. Horsley [q.v.], and helped to found the Prahran and South Yarra Musical Union. In 1870 he was one of the twenty-five members whose meetings at the Adam and Eve Hotel led to the founding of the South Yarra Liedertafel; it soon became the Metropolitan Liedertafel and by 1891 had 1090 subscribers. In 1873 Herz organized the Brighton Harmonic Society. He was organist in several Melbourne churches, notably Christ Church, Hawthorn, and choirmaster at St James's Cathedral. He also gave private lessons in vocal and instrumental music, composed songs and *morceaux* and served on the board of examiners of the Musical Association of Victoria.

As conductor of the Metropolitan Liedertafel in 1870-92 Herz organized visits of Melbourne music societies to other capitals. In 1881 he took eighty members to Sydney, a visit which led to the founding of a Liedertafel there. In December 1882 he organized a musical festival, the first of its kind in Melbourne. In the Town Hall with a choir of about 1000 and an orchestra of over 100 musicians, he directed performances of Handel's *Messiah* and Beethoven's *Ninth Symphony*, attracting audiences of nearly 3000 people; on other nights at the Athenaeum he ran 'smoke concerts' which were equally popular. In 1888 he took groups of members to Adelaide where they earned £700 in three days of concerts, and 154 members to Sydney, giving several concerts in the University Hall for the centenary celebrations. In 1889 he helped to found the Society of Musicians of Australia patterned on the Royal Society of Musicians in England. In 1890 Herz was entrusted with the business management of the Victorian Orchestra and worked hard but in vain to continue it after the government guarantee ceased in July 1891. He is credited with persuading Francis Ormond [q.v.] to give £20,000 for establishing the chair of music within the University of Melbourne. He organized the great operatic carnival in the Exhibition Building in Melbourne; the profits of £4000 were devoted to the founding of music scholarships in the university.

Herz had found a friend and patron in Sir William Robinson and in 1892 went to Western Australia after Robinson became governor there. They collaborated in the composition of an opera which Herz produced when he returned to Melbourne in 1894. In 1867 he had married Anna Margarita Freyberger; they had eight sons and one daughter. Herz died at Mordialloc on 23 August 1898 and was buried in the Cheltenham cemetery.

H. M. Humphreys (ed), *Men of the time in Australia: Victorian series*, 2nd ed (Melb, 1882); *Australasian*, 7 Jan, 30 Dec 1882, 27 Aug 1898; *Melb Bulletin*, 19 Jan 1883; *Illustrated Sydney News*, 28 Mar 1891; *Age*, 24 Aug 1898; *Argus*, 24 Aug 1898; *Table Talk*, 26 Aug 1898; Annual reports and guard books (Metropolitan and Melb Liedertafel).

MAUREEN THERESE RADIC

HETHERINGTON, IRVING (1809-1875), Presbyterian minister, was born on 23 June 1809 at Whaite, Dumfriesshire, Scotland, son of Richard Hetherton, farmer, and his wife Louise, née Carruthers. He adopted the name of Hetherington, entered the University of Edinburgh in 1825 and was licensed by the Church of Scotland Presbytery of Lochmaben on 3 August 1835. Eskdalemuir desired him as minister but the duke of Buccleuch presented the living to another. After a time Hetherington accepted appointment as missionary at Portobello, Joppa and Easter-Duddingston. As a result of Dr Lang's [q.v.] visit to Scotland in 1836 Hetherington offered for service in New South Wales and was accepted. He was ordained by the Presbytery of Lochmaben on 25 February 1837, sailed in the *John Barry* from Dundee and arrived in Sydney on 13 July.

The Presbytery of New South Wales appointed Hetherington to the parish of Singleton, an area of 1500 square miles where he began work in September. While there he was engaged in bitter controversy with an Anglican minister over apostolic succession, which resulted in Hetherington becoming a stronger contender for the Presbyterian system than hitherto. In the disruption of 1843 his sympathies lay with the Free Church of Scotland which was opposed to the patronage system. His evangelical views also made him more akin to the Free Church but, when its main supporters withdrew in 1846, he remained with the Synod of Australia which included in its official title 'in connection with the Church of Scotland', for he believed that Australian Presbyterianism should not be embroiled in Scottish controversies.

When the Scots Church, Melbourne, became vacant through the resignation of James Forbes [q.v.], Hetherington accepted a call to the church and was inducted on 13 June 1847. His acceptance was a matter of surprise and criticism, for it was one thing to remain in the Synod of Australia in the interests of unity, but quite another for an alleged upholder of the Free Church to take over the church and manse that Forbes had vacated on that very principle. Further, at that stage of Melbourne's growth Forbes

was able to provide ordinances of religion according to Presbyterian usage for all who desired them. The Scots Church congregation was greatly depleted by the withdrawal of Free Church supporters. The resignation of the three remaining elders in 1851 from differences with Hetherington led to acrimonious discussion in the Melbourne presbytery, the other ministers of which were strong supporters of those that remained in the Church of Scotland in 1843. Gradually the congregation built up again, assisted greatly by the influx of population after gold discovery. A new manse was built in 1852, the stipend increased at least twice and in 1859 a spire was added to the church.

Hetherington was active in the negotiations for union of the various branches of Presbyterianism in Victoria. On the whole his influence was conciliatory, but his annotations to a memorandum of Rev. Dr Macintosh Mackay of the Free Presbyterian Church led to controversy and disruption of that church. Both before and after union Hetherington discharged many administrative tasks on behalf of his denomination and in May 1860 was appointed clerk of the General Assembly of the Presbyterian Church of Victoria.

Hetherington possessed clarity of thought and expression. He was devoted to the work of the ministry and at his best in the pastoral office. In his public prayers, according to F. R. M. Wilson, he 'attained to a variety and fervency of truly devotional utterance which the writer has seldom seen equalled and never surpassed'. At the same time he lacked much as a preacher and, however suitable a choice for the Melbourne of 1847, he was really quite unsuited for a city charge of the type that Scots Church became. His sermons, while most assiduously prepared, were heavy in style, and increasing difficulty in reading his manuscript impaired their delivery. He was later embroiled in several controversies which he pursued relentlessly : for example, his intervention on behalf of Scotch College in its claim against Chalmers Church of portion of the manse garden. This quarrel led *Melbourne Punch* to publish its famous cartoon of Dr Adam Cairns [q.v.] and Hetherington passing each other in the street, each with chin in the air and umbrella under arm, over the caption 'How these Christians hate one another'.

In 1868-74 Hetherington had P. S. Menzies as colleague. He accepted graciously the fact of a crowded church for Menzies and an empty one for himself. They differed theologically but remained friendly until Menzies died early in 1874. Hetherington died on 5 July 1875 after a short illness. He was twice married: first on 24 February 1837 to Jessie Dalton Carr of Workington, Cumberland, who died without issue at sea on 12 May; and second in 1842 to Margaret McAllister Shannon of Mount Keira, New South Wales, who died on 20 December 1870, survived by seven of her nine children.

F. R. M. Wilson, *Memoir of the Rev. Irving Hetherington* (Melb, 1876); *SMH*, 15 Oct 1846; *Punch* (Melb), 17 Nov 1870; Church of Scotland presbytery minutes, 1847-54 and Vic synod minutes, 1854-59 (Presbyterian Assembly Hall, Melb).

F. MAXWELL BRADSHAW

HEYNE, ERNST BERNHARD (1825-1881), botanist and horticulturist, was born on 15 September 1825 at Meissen, Saxony, son of Carl August Heyne, M.D., and his wife Marianne, née Tierof. He graduated at the University of Leipzig with a diploma in botany. An accomplished linguist and mathematician, he obtained a post in the Royal Botanic Gardens, Dresden. In 1848 he was chosen to lead a botanical expedition in Spain, but it was cancelled because of political troubles. Heyne's brother Carl, who had become involved in politics, killed an officer in a duel and fled to America. Although not implicated, Ernst also decided to migrate. He left Hamburg for Melbourne in the *Godefroi*. His journey and arrival on 13 February 1849 are described in his letters. Published in German as *Australia Felix* (Dresden, 1850), they contain shrewd observations of the climate, soil, vegetation, water supplies and economy and habits of the colonists as well as advice to prospective migrants. After his father died, his mother had founded a school in Dresden. In 1851 she migrated with her daughter Agnes to join her son in Melbourne where she continued her educational work.

In 1854 Heyne was employed at the Melbourne Botanic Gardens as chief plantsman. When Mueller [q.v.] became director Heyne was appointed his secretary and went with him on several Victorian expeditions. He helped to classify much of the botanical material collected by Mueller in the 1850s, and is commemorated by *Aster heynei* F. Muell. = *Olearia xerophila*, and *Cyperus heynei* Boeckel. = *Cyperus ornatus* R. Br. His own large herbarium was destroyed after his death.

Heyne moved to Adelaide in January 1869 and made an extensive collection, since lost, of local seaweeds. He is credited with finding *Dicksonia antarctica* on the eastern slopes of the Mount Lofty Ranges. The identification of these tree-ferns, now extinct in South Australia, is authenticated by a specimen in the Melbourne Botanic Gardens: the label written by Mueller reads: Mount Lofty, S. Austr. 1870—E. B. Heyne.

Heyne established a nursery at Hackney, near Adelaide, and opened a shop for seeds and plants in Rundle Street. He contributed regularly to the *South Australian Register* and the *Observer* in the 1870s, chiefly on the cultivation of forest trees, forage plants and pasture grasses. The colonists were then interested in finding the crops best suited to their soil and climate, and those plants and trees likely to prove of economic and industrial importance. Heyne translated many articles and pamphlets on viticulture from German, French and Spanish, and wrote on the best methods of treating plant diseases, especially dodder in lucerne and oidium in vines. At a meeting sponsored by the Chamber of Manufactures in 1870 after a lecture by Dr Schomburgk [q.v.] Heyne spoke on the importance of growing trees, hedges, hickory, yellow willow, sultana vines, tobacco, sunflowers and mulberries. He had published *Vines and their Synonyms* in 1869 and became secretary to the Vignerons' Club, which in 1876 presented him with a gold watch as a tribute to his work. In 1871 he published *The Fruit, Flower and Vegetable Garden*, which was enlarged as *The Amateur Gardener* in 1881 and ran to four editions. His *Rueckblick* in German had appeared in the 1850s.

Heyne was a sincere adherent of the Evangelical Lutheran Church, but on 3 December 1870 at the Unitarian Christian Church, Adelaide, he married Wilhelmina Laura, daughter of Henrich Edouard Hanckel, bookseller of Norwood, and his wife Johanne, née Von Bruno; they had two sons and three daughters. Heyne continued to work until he became ill with asthma and nearly blind. He died on 16 October 1881 at his home in Norwood. His son Carl was still at Roseworthy Agricultural College and, when he qualified, managed his father's shop and nursery with a partner.

Though serious, Heyne was cheerful and sociable with many friends. He delighted in conversation and was a prodigious writer. Though overshadowed by Mueller, his botanical and horticultural work greatly contributed to the early development of two colonies.

J. H. Maiden, 'Records of Victorian botanists', *Vic Naturalist*, 25 (1908-09); J. B. Cleland, 'Dicksonia in the Mount Lofty Ranges', *South Aust Naturalist*, 43 (1968).

F. M. McGUIRE

HICKSON, ROBERT ROWAN PURDON (1842-1923), civil engineer, was born on 15 September 1842 in County Kerry, Ireland, son of Rev. George Hickson and his wife Rebekah Charlotte, née Purdon (Hewson). He was educated at St Columba's College, Dublin. In 1860 he was articled to James Barton, engineer-in-chief for public works in Northern Ireland, and in 1864 became his chief assistant. In 1866-72 he was resident engineer and harbourmaster at Carlingford, County Louth, and in 1873-78 managing engineer of the harbour-dredging department at Barrow-in-Furness, Lancashire. In 1874 he was elected an associate member of the Institution of Civil Engineers and in 1876 a full member. On 1 August 1866 at Dundalk he had married Sophia Haire.

On 9 March 1876 he sailed with his family in the *Bangalore* for Adelaide as engineer-in-chief for South Australian harbors and jetties. In 1876-80 he was responsible for reorganizing the dredging appliances and services, constructing the breakwater at Victor Harbor and many other improvements. After his department was abolished he moved to New South Wales where on 30 August 1881 he joined the Department of Public Works as assistant engineer at Newcastle, with charge of the water supply of the Hunter district and all river and harbour works to the Queensland border. In 1888 he moved to Sydney as acting engineer-in-chief. In 1889 he was nominated to the Board of Water Supply and Sewerage, became commissioner for roads, reorganized his department and insisted on first-class workmanship and sound administration. He significantly improved bridge design and road construction, and extended metropolitan water supply and sewerage. When various branches of the Public Works Department were amalgamated in 1895 he became engineer-in-chief and in 1896-1901 was under-secretary for public works.

After bubonic plague broke out on the Sydney waterfront Hickson was appointed chairman of an advisory board on harbour-foreshore resumption in 1900. In 1901 he became first president of the Sydney Harbour Trust and began a programme of improvements which among other things provided a vast wharfage, diverted sewers discharging into the harbour bays and instituted measures for preventing pollution of port waters. In 1907 he studied the principal ports and harbours of Europe. He sat on royal commissions on improvements to Sydney and suburbs in 1908-09 and on railway decentralization in 1910-11. When he retired on 31 December 1912 he had been responsible for the expenditure of £6,250,000 in capital works on the Sydney waterfront. The Imperial Service Order had been conferred on him on 24 June 1910.

In retirement he was consulted by the British government on harbour improvements in Fiji. He died at Lindfield on 28 June 1923 and was buried in the Anglican section of the Northern Suburbs cemetery. He was survived by his wife, five sons and two daughters to whom he left £8000. A road from Circular Quay to Sussex Street was named in his honour.

J. M. Antill, 'Robert Rowan Purdon Hickson: civil engineer', *JRAHS*, 55 (1969), and for bibliog.
                         J. M. ANTILL

HIGGINS, PATRICK (1825-1882), contractor and pastoralist, was born in Sligo, Connaught, Ireland, son of John Higgins, farmer and tenant of Lord Palmerston, and his wife Margaret, née Lunuy. Educated at the Sligo Academy, he became a successful contractor and, attracted by the gold discoveries, in 1852 migrated to Victorian with his brother John. He followed Palmerston's advice to continue his career and with his brother in 1853 won a contract to make part of the Mount Alexander Road which led to the goldfields at Castlemaine, Chewton and Bendigo. He obtained many other road-making contracts from the Public Works Department but in 1857 changed to railway construction and carried out the extensive earthwork of the Melbourne and Suburban Railway Co. He also made part of the Melbourne-Echuca line and engaged in some profitable squatting ventures with Hugh Glass [q.v.]. In 1858 he became a magistrate. By 1866 Higgins was probably the leading public-works entrepreneur in Victoria. In that year he won the contract to construct the Lithgow section of the zigzag railway in the Blue Mountains west of Sydney. He completed it in 1869 and, assessing the great economic potential of the area, promoted the Lithgow Valley Coal Co. and the Lithgow Pottery. In 1867 he had become a magistrate of New South Wales. He consolidated his wealth with profitable squatting investments on the Lachlan and Murray rivers.

Higgins was not so fortunate in his personal life. In 1855 in Melbourne he married Rose, daughter of John Lynch, of Sligo. Next year she died giving birth to a son. In 1872 Higgins was taking the boy to Europe to finish his education when he was lost overboard between Sydney and Melbourne. Distraught and stricken with heart trouble, Higgins went to Europe and America and proved a discerning and observant traveller.

On his return to Sydney in 1876 he determined to enter public life. By then he was recognized as an entrepreneur whose pioneering had benefited both Victoria and New South Wales as well as himself. An associate of other leading industrialists and pastoralists, including the relatively small Irish-Catholic group headed by P. A. Jennings [q.v.], he was a director of the Sydney Tramway and Omnibus Co., the Intercolonial Life Assurance and General Association, the Intercolonial Board of Executors Trustees and Agency Co. and other companies.

His popularity did not enable him to enter the Legislative Assembly. In 1877, despite a progressive and liberal programme, which included enlightened nonsectarian views on education and immigration, he was defeated at Hartley by J. Hurley [q.v.]. In 1879, a year of crisis for denominational education, Henry Parkes [q.v.] appointed him a commissioner for the International Exhibition in Sydney, and in 1881 a Sydney representative for Melbourne's Exhibition. In accepting Parkes's nomination to the Legislative Council in December 1880 Higgins said he was 'impressed with a full sense of the responsibility which loyalty, duty and independence impose'. The only Catholic member, Higgins was making a worthy mark in the council when he died suddenly from heart disease on 28 January 1882. With Jennings in charge, his body was taken to Melbourne and buried in the general cemetery. £10,000 of his estate of £44,000 was left to his brother, John, and substantial charitable bequests complemented similar gifts he had made when alive.

L. J. Harrigan, *Victorian railways to '62* (Melb, 1962); *Bulletin*, 1 Jan 1881; *SMH*, 30 Jan 1882; *Australasian*, 4 Feb 1882; Parkes letters (ML); CO 201/591.   BEDE NAIRN

HIGHETT, WILLIAM (1807-1880), businessman and politician, and JOHN (1810-1867), pastoralist, were born at Weymouth, Dorset, England, sons of Joseph Highett and his wife Elizabeth, née Harding. In February 1830 the brothers arrived at Hobart Town in the *Elizabeth*. Though bound for Sydney, they stayed in Van Diemen's Land and applied for land. With highly respectable testimonials and a combined capital of £507, they were granted 500 acres which they located at George Town. Later they acquired much land at Launceston and Campbell Town. John managed these properties while William became accountant of the new branch of the Van Diemen's Land Bank at Launceston in May 1832. When

it closed he joined the Tamar Banking Co. as cashier in January 1835. By 1859 the brothers had sold all their Tasmanian land.

In partnership with his cousin, Thomas Austin [q.v.], John took up Mount Hesse station in the Port Phillip District in 1837. In 1842-46 his partner was W. C. Haines [q.v.]. John later bought much suburban land at Geelong. On a commanding site above the River Barwon he built a large residence, Highton House. He was a successful farmer and flour-miller and well known as a horseman and breeder. He died at Queenscliff on 16 January 1867, survived by his wife Sarah, née Moore, whom he had married in Tasmania on 1 September 1846, and by four sons and two daughters.

In 1838 William became first Melbourne manager of the Union Bank of Australia and in 1840 a local director with the title of managing director. He resigned in 1842 to visit Europe but on his return in 1845 was reinstated as a local director. He was a founder and director of the Bank of Victoria, the Melbourne Banking Corporation Ltd and the Victoria Fire and Marine Insurance Co. and had many shares in the Hobson's Bay Railway Co. He also helped to found the Melbourne Mechanics' Institute. An early member and trustee of the Melbourne Club, he shared in negotiations for its new site although his role was difficult because the Bank of Victoria wanted to buy the old property.

Highett was active in the separation movement and in 1853 was a government nominee in the Legislative Council. In 1856 he failed to win a seat in the new council but was elected for the Eastern Province in May 1857. He supported state aid, National schools, railway extension and the opening of crown land with moderate compensation for the squatters. A conservative and industrious councillor, he retired in 1880. In 1847-66 he held a squatting lease near Benalla. He was also an early landowner in Moorabbin Shire, part of which was named for him, and by the late 1870s had 6117 acres, valued at £15,292, in addition to land in Richmond and other suburban areas. For years he was a trustee of St Stephen's Anglican Church, Richmond. In his last years he suffered from gout but continued to play whist on Saturday evenings at his club. He died on 29 November 1880, unmarried and intestate.

Garryowen (E. Finn), *The chronicles of early Melbourne*, 1 (Melb, 1888); A. Sutherland et al, *Victoria and its metropolis*, 2 (Melb, 1888); E. Scott, *Historical memoir of the Melbourne Club* (Melb, 1936); W. McIlroy, 'Melbourne's land sales', *VHM*, 17 (1939); *Argus*, 22 Apr 1857, 30 Nov 1880; CSO 1/453/10074 (TA); GO 33/18/866 (TA); LSD 1/76/19 (TA).

J. ANN HONE

HIGINBOTHAM, GEORGE (1826-1892), politician and chief justice, was born on 19 April 1826 in Dublin, the sixth son of Henry Higinbotham, merchant, and his wife Sarah, née Wilson. He attended the Royal School, Dungannon, and at 18 entered Trinity College, Dublin (B.A., 1849; M.A., 1853). In 1847 he joined the London *Morning Chronicle* as a parliamentary reporter and in 1848 enrolled at Lincoln's Inn. In June 1853 he was called to the Bar and in December sailed for Melbourne in the *Briseis*. In March 1854 he was admitted to the Victorian Bar and in September married Margaret Foreman.

Higinbotham combined journalism and law in the colony. He wrote for the *Melbourne Morning Herald* and at 30 became editor of the *Argus*. His editorials suggest his struggle to reconcile his high-principled liberalism with colonial exigencies. One of his reporters, Charles Bright [q.v.], recalls his dislike of making snap decisions on political issues and says that his scrupulous attention to every detail 'from leading article to minutest paragraph' led to slowness in publication that might be compared with his later repute for pedantry on the bench, despite the conciseness of many of his judgments. On a matter of principle Higinbotham clashed with the proprietor, Edward Wilson [q.v.], and resigned in July 1859.

In 1861 he was elected for Brighton to the Legislative Assembly. As attorney-general in the McCulloch [q.v.] ministry in 1863-68 he was unquestionably the leading radical in Victoria. He established a local precedent by declining private briefs while attorney-general but after resigning from the ministry he returned to the Bar. He was defeated at Brighton in 1871 but represented East Bourke Boroughs in 1873-76. In 1880 he was appointed to the Supreme Court bench and became chief justice in 1886.

Higinbotham had started his political career with all the perplexities of an inexperienced politician testing the practicability of his theories. The uncertainties and adjustments in his thought were illustrated in 1862 by his support of C. G. Duffy's [q.v.] land bill and Richard Heales's [q.v.] common schools bill though he soon saw the weaknesses in both. By 1864 he publicly confessed a mistake in his judgment over the Duffy Act which gave temporary security of tenure to squatters, whom he called 'the wealthy lower orders', but achieved little for smallholders. He tried to redress the balance by supporting Grant's [q.v.] 1865 Land Act but later became even stronger in his views. By 1873 he was affirming that 'property was robbery', that crown lands should be available only on thirty-three-year leases and a progressive property tax levied to make great estates unprofitable.

Higinbotham's dogged struggle for educational reform was perhaps of more immediate importance, but that too revealed his hardening in the face of obstruction. Under him the *Argus* had encouraged educational development but he presented no clear solution for the religious difficulty. During 1861 he advocated a private-enterprise approach. Relying on the authority of J. S. Mill, he proposed that parents should initiate new schools and the government confine itself to financial help. He recognized the need for a state school system but faced the dilemma that, although the state could not engage in spiritual education, education without religion was 'mere instruction'. Yet in 1862 he supported Heales's Act, which created a Common Schools Board with power to establish schools, because he had found that public indifference led to neglect of education. The Act satisfied no one. State aid to church schools was continued but bitter competition emerged between the national and denominational schools and between the denominations themselves. The compromise was costly, and ineffective in bringing education to outlying districts.

By 1867 Higinbotham was convinced that 'in justice to the equal rights of the children of all classes' the state must take full responsibility for national education and withdraw aid to denominational schools. This conclusion had been unanimously reached by the royal commission set up in 1866 with Higinbotham as chairman to prepare a public instruction bill. In five months the commissioners met fifty-two times often for long hours. Higinbotham never missed a meeting. The secretary, David Blair [q.v.], claimed that the amount of work was two or three times greater than usual for commissions and that 'the unremitting zeal of their Chairman acted like a charm on the Commissioners'.

Wanting education rather than mere instruction, the commissioners allowed a place in the national system for 'common Christianity' but not for sectarian doctrine. When Catholics rejected this as state-sponsored Protestantism and appealed for a special grant, Higinbotham could see no way out. In the assembly he suggested that, if Protestants united in providing religious instruction, the case for Catholic aid might later be reopened.

The commission achieved little more than to expose the nature of the dilemma. McCulloch gave no support to its draft bill and Higinbotham was attacked on the one hand for not introducing a fully secular measure and on the other for withdrawing aid from the churches. The Anglican and Catholic clergy battled to retain state aid and those denominations most in sympathy with the bill withheld support in fear of strengthening the Catholic case for a separate grant. Isolated, Higinbotham withdrew his bill convinced that henceforth only a fully secular measure would do. This last important attempt to find a place for religion in the national system may well have hastened the secular solution, for Higinbotham's failure enlightened public and political opinion by revealing the difficulties of compromise—a lesson that he repeatedly pointed out in the House. Although out of parliament when the 1872 Act was passed, Higinbotham had pre-eminently cleared the way for it. He had battled hardest for a religious sentiment in education, yet in 1876 on his last day in parliament he argued that all Christian references be expunged from school textbooks since they offended Jewish parents and children, a recommendation that was later adopted.

In Higinbotham's fifteen-year pilgrimage to extreme state secularism, his personal piety remained unshaken. He was born and buried an Anglican, however unorthodox. In an 1887 address, *The Opening of the Unitarian Church*, he expressed sympathy with that church which 'alone . . . preserves the idea of the unity of God', 'the simplicity of . . . the Semitic ideal', and welcomes the 'distinctive views . . . of independent thinkers'. He liked to belong to a congregation, but no Christian church, he once said, could set up the 'shadow of a rational claim' to be 'the sole Church of Christ'. The clergy of all denominations were 'the greatest enemies to religious education', their sects mere 'competing companies or corporations' displaying a 'pestilent energy in collecting property' as 'proof of vitality'. He believed that the churches and the clergy came between man and his Maker, whereas men, united in their rationality, could find 'God, revealed to the intellect in every minute movement of matter' if they merely tried 'to catch the sound of that one voice which alone above the din of nineteen centuries still makes itself heard'. In attacking clerical orthodoxy in his 1883 lecture, *Science and Religion*, in the Scots Church, he provoked a spate of pamphlets, lectures and sermons and precipitated the virtual expulsion of his chairman, Charles Strong [q.v.], from the Presbyterian ministry.

Higinbotham's deeply religious sense explains many of his political beliefs: his dislike of greed or even private gain; and his belief in the laity and individual judgment unfettered by religious or political authority. Passionately religious and demo-

cratic, he believed in the common man as the source of political authority.

In the *Argus* between December 1856 and April 1858 he enunciated democratic principles in a battle with his proprietor who advocated multiple electorates to prevent manual workers from gaining a majority vote, and special representation of property interests. Higinbotham retorted that 'the most complete equalisation of political rights' came from recognizing that rich and poor had an equal stake in good government, whereas the representation of minorities would favour the rich. He also opposed John O'Shanassy's [q.v.] conservative scheme for the 'excessive multiplication of small constituencies', warning that it would make elected members mere delegates of 'local prejudices and local rapacity' thus encouraging 'bawling demagogues' to win votes by 'extravagant flattery'.

In the *Argus* and later in the assembly Higinbotham held that parliamentarians should vote on every issue by conviction, not in deference to their party or constituents but in support of competent and honest government. Party bonds were 'factious' and impeded the exercise of private conscience. In practice his fidelity to this principle became paralysing and led him to retire from politics. Disapproving Berry's [q.v.] stonewalling tactics, yet convinced that McCulloch was actuated by 'shameful' place-seeking which led him to enact 'a naked farce', Higinbotham could support the actions of neither: nor could he overlook his differences with the party he preferred, for this would be taking a party line. His principles forced him into inaction and resignation, despite requests that he become leader of the Liberal Party.

As attorney-general he had side-stepped this dilemma. Although theoretically opposed to party government, he had kept in office a heterogeneous ministry, the longest since responsible government, and united his followers against the common enemy, the Legislative Council. He was satisfied that the issue, not party loyalty, won him support. His personal wars against the council and the Colonial Office's ill-informed interference with domestic affairs were part of his strategy to make the Legislative Assembly supreme in Victoria. He seized on any challenge to responsible government and any ambiguities in the 1855 Constitution Act to establish precedents in the development of colonial democracy; whether or not he was always legally sound is still not settled by constitutional historians.

In 1864 he reprimanded Sir Redmond Barry [q.v.] for informing the governor of his intention to take a holiday. 'No officer in his department', said Higinbotham, should communicate directly with the governor on official business. In that year he also clashed with Chief Justice Stawell [q.v.] who disagreed with his ruling that the Executive Council was entitled to suspend judges. The imperial law officers upheld Higinbotham but, less concerned with personal victory than with interference from the British ministry, he advised the judges that the decision was 'in no way binding'. He was jealous of the independence of the judiciary except when it conflicted with the independence of the colonial government.

His militant resistance to imperial incursions into domestic affairs was matched by an equal determination that the colonies respect their obligations to the imperial government and to the governor as its sole agent in imperial affairs. In such cases the governor ceased to be responsible to his colonial ministers and, wearing his other hat, was solely responsible to the imperial government.

An opportunity to show the distinction arose in January 1865 when the *Shenandoah*, calling itself a Confederate ship, sought permission to berth at Hobson's Bay for coal and repairs. In an unaccustomed alliance with Melbourne's upper crust, who entertained the ship's officers at the Melbourne Club, Higinbotham advised against the United States consul's request that the ship be seized as a pirate. The United States held Britain responsible for the damage later done by the ship and a tribunal at Geneva in 1872 awarded $15,500,000 for damages done by the vessel. Higinbotham explained that the governor had been answerable to Britain in this dispute and that the ministers, acting merely as advisers, were not responsible for the governor's decision and were therefore not bound to resign if he had rejected their advice.

Higinbotham's principles were again tested in the dispute between the assembly and the council over the so-called protective tariff of 1865. Higinbotham, professedly a free trader, denied that the measure was based on protectionist principles. It merely altered the list of goods dutiable for revenue and was not designed to protect home industries. Protectionists wanted a stronger measure while free traders claimed that the bill contravened their principles. For Higinbotham their argument was a mere 'intellectual puzzle'—a quibble. He predicted that the council would reject the measure, not on principle but out of self-interest, and so advised the ministry to attach it to the appropriation bill.

In the ensuing deadlock between the Houses, Governor Darling used a legal trick to pay public expenses. He borrowed from the London Chartered Bank which sued for repayment and the Crown offered no defence. After elections in which the ministry was supported, and after conferences between the assembly and council (from which Higinbotham was excluded), the appropriation bill was passed on 17 April 1866. On that day Darling received his recall for having expressed disapproval of the Opposition and for raising money by methods of doubtful legality, in both of which Higinbotham had been his mentor.

The removal of Darling rekindled the constitutional struggle. In May 1866 the Legislative Assembly voted £20,000 to Lady Darling and prepared an address of sympathy and gratitude to her husband. The first deadlock ended just in time to make way for the second. After the council rejected the appropriation bill including the Darling grant, parliament was dissolved in August 1867 and the ministry was again returned. Months of confusion followed. The new governor, Manners-Sutton, was tactlessly advised by the Colonial Office not to recommend the grant to the legislature; the government resigned and was followed in May 1868 by the Sladen [q.v.] ministry. Without a majority it resigned in July. The McCulloch ministry then resumed office, but Higinbotham refused to be attorney-general, explaining in December 1869 that he could not hold office in a ministry that prevented him from submitting his case on colonial independence.

Until his final retirement from the assembly Higinbotham remained uncertain about how to reduce the council's powers. He criticized proposals for reducing the property qualifications of electors and members of the council, maintaining that such reductions would not curb the powers of the council but only strengthen it, since it could claim to be more representative while still not being truly responsible. J. G. Francis's [q.v.] 'Norwegian Scheme' of April 1874, to force the two Houses to sit jointly after the council had rejected a bill in two consecutive sessions, exposed Higinbotham's uncertainty. He criticized the measure and suggested that Victoria would be ideally suited to a one-House system because it lacked an hereditary nobility and antagonistic social classes, but he recognized that the time was not ripe.

Meanwhile in 1869 Higinbotham had defined colonial responsible government with clarity and force. His five resolutions, all passed by the assembly, were provoked by conservative Victorian colonists in London who had called a conference on colonial affairs. Incensed at this interference of an 'irresponsible' body of expatriates, he was impelled to clarify the position after a debate on 8 May 1868 in the House of Lords where six of the seven speakers had implicitly denied the existence of responsible government. Only Lord Chancellor Cairns affirmed the principle that Higinbotham held sacred: 'If it was to be laid down . . . that the Secretary of State at home was to hold in leadingstrings the Ministry of the Colony, then the pretence of free colonial institutions was simply a delusion and a mockery'.

Sensing a direct challenge to colonial independence, Higinbotham declared in his resolutions that the London conference should not be sanctioned, that Victoria wished to remain within the empire, that imperial legislation should not interfere with the colony's internal affairs, that the Colonial Office had no right to advise or instruct the governor on domestic issues but could merely advise on the royal assent to colonial bills, and that the assembly should support the ministry in designing measures to establish the independence of the colonial legislature. He asserted that Victoria had never had responsible government because of the anomaly that a 'foreign minister' advised the Crown to accept or reject colonial legislation.

The secretary of state for colonies, he said, was less to blame than 'the chief clerk of the Colonial Office'. The Colonial Office, like the Athenian democracy, 'was governed by the poodle dog of a courtesan'. The dog engrossed the courtesan, who engrossed her lover, 'and the lover ruled the fierce democracy'. Similarly 'the million and a half of Englishmen who inhabit these colonies . . . have really been governed . . . by a person named Rogers'. As a member of the empire Victoria had to control its own defences but had no right to negotiate with foreign nations. In domestic affairs, however, the colony should have complete autonomy as a responsible government. Ministers should deal directly with the appropriate imperial ministers, not through the Colonial Office which was 'a mere straw image of official intrigue, and unlawful arbitrary interference'. 'If you reason with it, you degrade yourselves. If you go to it, and strike it in the face with the back of your gloved hand, you will see it tumble in a heap at your feet'.

Higinbotham also attacked what he called illegitimate instructions to governors empowering them to use, regardless of ministerial advice, the prerogative of mercy in capital punishments. In 1874 Carnarvon ruled that the governor had the right to a final decision only after seeking written ministerial advice but Higinbotham still denounced the instruction as 'a glaring instance of . . . flagrant illegality' which in practice 'could not be obeyed'.

Invited in 1880 to become a Supreme Court judge, he wrote to the premier, James Service [q.v.], about the governor's instruction to call on the judge to report in writing on any case of capital punishment and to appear before the Executive Council. Higinbotham claimed that the Queen had no power to issue this instruction, and that he would 'officially and openly refuse to comply . . . and would pray that the commands of the Crown for my assistance . . . should be conveyed to me through and in accordance with the advice of Her Majesty's Advisers for Victoria'. His stand on this question was a sequel to his earlier battle with the judges. The conditions he laid down were tested four years later. In May 1884, after sentencing Henry Morgan to death for murder, he refused to report to the Executive Council unless requested by the attorney-general. As attorney-general Higinbotham had insisted on the answerability of judges to him: twenty years later as a judge the position was reversed and he insisted on his answerability to the attorney-general. In both cases his principle was upheld.

On a similar principle he insisted that the governor should refuse to inform the Colonial Office on domestic policy. When he became chief justice he should have become administrator in the governor's absences, but he made it clear that as acting governor he would act on this principle. He was therefore by-passed. The insult was never remedied but gave rise to much correspondence with the secretary of state for the colonies whom he successfully convinced in 1892 that the governor's instructions should be redrafted to meet his objections.

As chief justice, Higinbotham still saw himself as a liberal politician who should exploit any legal case that furthered responsible government. The opportunity arose most clearly in *Toy* v. *Musgrove*, a case involving Chinese immigration and Victoria's power to exclude aliens. The collector of customs, Musgrove, refused entry to Chinese passengers in the British ship *Afghan* when it arrived at Melbourne in 1888. Toy brought an action against Musgrove to the full Supreme Court. The defence argued that, under a law restricting Chinese immigration, the governor and the ministry had acted properly. Higinbotham maintained that, since no international law conflicted with Victoria's legislation, the governor had to act as the 'local sovereign'. A lengthy argument then raged around what constitutional rights the governor and his ministry did have. Mr Justice Hartley Williams [q.v.], with some regret and sense of shock, concluded that Victoria had neither the legal right to restrict immigration nor the constitutional justification for claiming responsible government. 'I awake to find', he concluded, 'that we have merely an instalment of responsible government'.

Zelman Cowen says that the case 'must be almost unique in the law reports' in providing 'an elaborate examination of the scope and nature of responsible government', and it gave Higinbotham 'a unique opportunity to expound his political philosophy'. Higinbotham, however, often outvoted on the bench, carried only one of the five judges with him. When Musgrove appealed to the Privy Council it ruled that common law supported Victorian law and aliens had no enforceable right to enter British territory. The constitutional question was thus avoided.

Higinbotham's persistent battle for colonial independence in domestic affairs was equalled by his insistence on Victoria's imperial dependence in foreign affairs. To many his position was paradoxical and ran counter to the nationalistic spirit that soon culminated in Federation. When in 1883 Queensland took possession of south-eastern New Guinea in the name of the Queen, Higinbotham justified the annexation, not as a ministerial decision, but as an act of the governor for the imperial government with no legal effect until ratified in Britain. In the event Queensland's possession was disallowed in London but colonial pressure led to the proclamation of a protectorate in 1884.

In July 1883 at a public meeting Higinbotham had moved that the Crown should annex New Guinea and the New Hebrides to protect them from receiving criminals from other European nations and from recruiting native labour for Queensland, a traffic which savoured of slavery and which that colony's government could not control. All civilized nations, he said, had a right to annex unoccupied territory, though he admitted that he did not fully understand how the right originated or could be defended. However, by 1885 Higinbotham was describing all annexation as the act of 'robbers' justified solely by 'priority of possession'. The Colonial Office could have settled the problem by acceding to colonial requests or by rejecting them, thus forcing the colonies to decide whether to leave the empire. Instead it 'vacillated' and compromised while Germany annexed northern New Guinea. The colonies continued to press their claims without being forced to face the international responsibilities of independence from Britain. This temporizing Higinbotham described as 'the imbecility of the Colonial Office' which pro-

duced in Germany 'a just sense of distrust'.

Deakin saw the protests at England's inaction as a possible prelude to Federation, but to Higinbotham that movement was a 'dangerous mode of thought or rather no thought'. Although not necessarily opposed in principle to Federation, he saw in the negotiations the danger of a compromise in which rights, wrested from the imperial government over thirty years in interpreting the Constitution, could be reversed. Rather than risk the loss of democratic achievements, he would have postponed Federation 'to the date of the Greek Kalends'. He also feared its connexion with republican sentiment, which he thought people of understanding would reject 'for better reasons than the feeble sentimentalism which now seems to be the sole tie between Great Britain and its self-governing dependencies'. He wanted the colonies to continue the existing union with Britain and avoid 'the heavy burdens and the tremendous risk entailed by separation'.

As politician and judge, Higinbotham's dedication to democracy sprang from concern not only with constitutional forms but also with giving an equal voice to the underprivileged. Early he had seen individualism as the means to this end, but experience led him to recognize the need for collective action. While editor of the *Argus* he had scouted the idea of labour representatives in parliament, believing that all men were one and could be relied on to care disinterestedly for the rights of the worker. By 1890, however, he felt impelled to subscribe to the maritime strike funds, less out of concern about the rightness of the strike than about the employers' refusal to negotiate. He saw the unionists fighting with unequal odds against entrenched interests. Diehards demanded that the artillery should drag him from the Supreme Court and shoot him, and critics accused him of impropriety in using his official title in his letter to the Trades Hall, but to this day the Seamen's Union lays a wreath on his statue on each anniversary of his death. In the *Argus* Higinbotham had supported the Eight Hour Movement and later endeared himself to the labour movement. In 1884 he was guest speaker at the opening of the Trades Hall Council Chamber, where his portrait was hung above the president's chair.

Higinbotham's support of the working man sprang from respect and affection evinced in his lack of snobbery that mixed strangely with his courtly and elegant manners. Women were among the underprivileged whom he defended: in 1873 he excited ridicule from the press by advocating the female franchise. The *Australasian* scoffed, 'Mr. Higinbotham can surely not desire to see the denizens of Little Bourke Street or Romeo-land brought in cabs full to the polls', and begged him to leave alone 'our monopoly of our wives and daughters'. At the royal jubilee in 1887 he used the occasion to express his regard for the Queen and thus to expound his views on women's rights. He did not regret that the 'age of chivalry with all its foolery is past', but 'the age of true honour for women' had not yet fully come. Higinbotham was ever chivalrous to women and personally content that they should have it both ways.

Undoubtedly Higinbotham had more than a touch of the ascetic and the Puritan. He became president of the Permissive Bill Association which campaigned for legislation to restrict the sale of liquor by local option. This issue diverted the energy of many churchmen, and even of Higinbotham, when popular opinions on education were being tested in the 1871 election. In 1873 he argued in parliament for a permissive bill, already twice rejected by the council, as one which would empower the majority to compel the minority to prohibition. The *Australasian* accused him of being the 'infallible Pope' establishing a 'moral dictatorship'. In 1881 when the association was superseded by the Victorian Alliance, he was invited to become its president. He declined because he believed that the president should be in parliament, able to organize public opinion in every recess and to bring forward a bill 'session after session'. He was not a fanatical teetotaller but, like many nineteenth-century radicals, he argued that those who tried to remove the 'thraldom' of liquor were 'the truest friends of the working millions' and 'at the foundation of all social and political reform'.

Convinced that men should be protected from the temptation to gamble, Higinbotham attacked raffles at a ladies' bazaar in 1866: Melbourne *Punch* retorted with a cartoon, 'The Puritanical Prig'. He disliked, even more than gambling, public displays of charity. His grandson, the late Charles Reade, believed that one reason why he left instructions with his wife to destroy all his private papers at his death was to conceal the extent of his private gifts. His ready response to public charities and his private generosity were well known. His son-in-law recalled Higinbotham's belief in the rule, 'Give to him that asketh'—a rule that led his fellow barristers to protest against the procession of undesirable persons to his chambers.

While many legal colleagues made large fortunes, Higinbotham never acquired great wealth. His charges were modest, according to Theodore Fink, 'probably less than half of that of others of his time'. He disapproved

the extra salary of £500 more for chief justices than puisne judges, and so he set it aside to provide festive dinners for his colleagues every year. As a barrister he would not defend a case unless he believed in it, but he could be stern and his cross-examinations were said to be 'deadly enough to make villains tremble'.

Always the scholar, he was painstaking and even laborious in his hearing of cases, while his judgments exhibited lucidity, elegance and usually economy. As attorney-general, royal commissioner and judge he was an indefatigable worker, often working into the early hours and then sleeping in his rooms. Possibly the greatest monument to the demands he made on himself was his consolidation of the statutes as attorney-general in 1865 and again as chief justice in 1890. For his efforts he gained the rare honour of thanks of both Houses. After being slighted over the acting governorship, Higinbotham must have enjoyed wry pleasure in this public compliment and in refusing a knighthood, which he described as a 'base, contemptible distinction' that merely gave a man 'a handle to his name'.

Ironically Higinbotham tended to blame himself for exhibiting too little of what his critics described as an excess of fixity of purpose. In his 1884 address to the Trades Hall he remarked that 'stubborn adherence to principle was the most honest expression of a politician's view' and 'experience has led me to the conclusion that almost all compromises, almost all concessions . . . are so many abandonments of principle'. No doubt he had in mind his own political shifts over such policies as land reform. His doggedness in fighting the Legislative Council after the deadlocks wearied some politicians, and as judge his persistent battle with the imperial government for an irreversible definition of responsible government irked some legal colleagues.

Yet opponents and admirers alike respected his probity, and most succumbed to his kindliness, charm and personal magnetism. William Shiels wrote: 'I really loved him. I never knew a more knightly nature than his: and yet it was a unique one, too, from its almost weird blend of contraries'. Shy yet firm, gentle yet ferocious, personally courteous yet impersonally acrimonious, he was indeed a puzzling mixture. His oratory only Deakin, his disciple, could rival. Speaking with a softly modulated Anglo-Irish voice, Higinbotham began his speeches shyly and hesitatingly until under the compulsion of his logic and rhetoric he was carried often to impassioned heights. Deakin described his speeches as 'slow', 'grand', 'stately and impressive with . . . dignity in style and grace of phrase, yet terribly intense and effective' in his 'admirable climaxes'.

Deakin also recalled his 'cherubic' manner, his 'mildness and sweetness', and his profile 'cameo-like in its delicacy, and clear blue eyes, still, calm and far-seeing when not ablaze with passion'. His granddaughter Hilda Morris never · forgot his chiding her for looking into a private garden. 'Ever since then', she writes, 'I have looked straight ahead and respected privacy', and here perhaps is the true explanation for the destruction of his private papers.

This most loved and most hated politician was 'the red radical' or, as Shiels assessed him, Australia's 'noblest if not its greatest man', according to the point of view. For Price Warung [q.v. Astley] he was 'the greatest of Australia's dead' who 'won from privilege and class ground they have never since been able to recover'.

Warned against over-exertion in his last years, Higinbotham characteristically ignored the advice, asking his doctor only to tell him frankly if his mental powers were at all impaired. He died on 31 December 1892, survived by his wife, two sons and three daughters. At his request he had a private funeral.

E. E. Morris, A *memoir of George Higinbotham* (Lond, 1895); G. M. Dow, *George Higinbotham: church and state* (Melb, 1964), and for bibliog; Z. Cowen, *Sir John Latham and other papers* (Melb, 1965); information from Miss H. Morris, Sussex, England, late Mr C. Reade, Corowa, NSW, and M. Cullity, Toronto, Canada.   GWYNETH M. DOW

HIGINBOTHAM, THOMAS (1819-1880), engineer and civil servant, was born in Dublin, the third son of Henry Higinbotham, merchant, and his wife Sarah, née Wilson. Educated in Dublin at Castle Dawson School and the Royal Dublin Society House, Higinbotham moved to London about 1839. At first he worked for a firm that promoted railway companies, and often appeared before parliamentary committees on railways. He then worked for several years as an engineer on British railroads and won high repute in his profession. He was elected a member of the Institution of Civil Engineers on 7 February 1854.

In 1857 Higinbotham followed his younger brother George [q.v.] to Melbourne. He joined his brother's household first at Emerald Hill and after 1860 near the beach at Brighton in a villa which Thomas was chiefly responsible for designing. He never married and lived with his brother, sister-in-law, nephews and nieces till 1880 in a relationship characterized by remark-

able tolerance, friendship and respect despite strong differences in political opinion.

After a short time in private practice in Melbourne Higinbotham was appointed inspector-general of roads and bridges. In 1860 he became engineer-in-chief of the Victorian railways. He supervised the surveying and construction of all new Victorian lines and also guided the settlement of such railway questions as city stations and facilities and the lighting of trains. He fearlessly contested proposals that he considered unsound, such as cheap narrow-gauge lines, and showed great vision in advocating a railway renewals fund, construction of Melbourne's outer-circle railway and adaptations to permit unbroken rail traffic between Sydney and Melbourne. At the government's request in 1874-75 he investigated and reported on the latest developments in railway construction and management in Europe, America and India. With other senior public officials he was removed from office in January 1878 by the Berry [q.v.] government. In the next two years he was invited by the South Australian, Tasmanian and New Zealand governments to report on their railway systems. In March 1880 the Service [q.v.] government reappointed him engineer-in-chief of the Victorian railways, but the ministry soon fell and he was unhappy under its successor. He had decided to resign but died in his sleep on 5 September.

Higinbotham was one of that select band of English railway engineers who exercised a profound influence on the development of Australian communications in the second half of the nineteenth century. They provided practically the only mark of distinction in the Australian colonies' railway departments of the day. But their efforts were not enough to provide firm foundations for sound management as political pressures developed. Though Higinbotham did not live to see the change, his own Victorian service became the first candidate for management by public corporation when the system of political control was formally discredited in 1883.

Higinbotham was an Anglican and for many years a member of the Royal Society of Victoria. His loss was greatly lamented by a society in which public officials of such widely-acknowledged integrity were all too rare. His property, valued at £21,000, was left to his brother George and his family with the request that the family name be changed to Verner, the maiden name of his paternal grandmother. This odd request was not a condition and was therefore ignored.

E. E. Morris, A *memoir of George Higinbotham* (Lond, 1895); R. L. Wettenhall, *Rail-*

way management and politics in Victoria,
1856-1906 (Canberra, 1961); L. J. Harrigan, Victorian railways to '62 (Melb, 1962); N. G.
Butlin, Investment in Australian economic
development, 1861-1900 (Cambridge, 1964);
Roy Soc Vic, Procs, 17 (1880-81); Age, 6 Sept
1880; Argus, 6 Sept 1880.

R. L. WETTENHALL

HILL, CHARLES LUMLEY (1840-1909),
grazier, parliamentarian and cattle-breeder,
was born at Tickhill Castle, Yorkshire,
England, son of Charles John Hill, colonel
of Hussars, and his wife Lady Frances Charlotte Arabella, daughter of Frederick Lumley and granddaughter of the fourth earl of
Scarbrough. Educated at Rossall School, he
entered Pembroke College, Oxford, in
October 1860 but did not take a degree. He
migrated to South Australia in 1863 and
had some experience on a station near Port
Augusta. In 1864 he moved to Queensland
where he soon became manager of Northampton Downs. In 1865 with his Oxford
friends, William Holberton and William
Thomas Allen, he bought sheep, drove them
to the Barcoo River, took up part of Isis
Downs and later acquired the runs of West-
lands, Avington and Thornleigh. They had
much trouble with the Aboriginals and Hill
was prominent in measures to suppress
them. The stations were sold when his partners returned to England.

In 1878 Hill was returned unopposed to
the Legislative Assembly for the Gregory
district where he had bought a share in
Rosebrook station. At first he supported
Palmer and McIlwraith [qq.v.] but, disappointed at not receiving a portfolio, he
joined Morehead and de Satgé [qq.v.] in
forming a cave within the government
ranks. He was further alienated in 1880
when Morehead joined the ministry.
McIlwraith's proposal for a transcontinental
land-grant railway made Hill and other
western graziers fearful of their properties
and he strongly opposed the project in the
press and public meetings. In 1882 he sold
his properties, resigned his seat and sailed
for England.

In 1883 Hill returned to Queensland and
failed in his first attempt to win the Cook
seat. He won it at a by-election in 1885 and
was an independent supporter of S. W.
Griffith. In 1886 he was a representative of
the assembly on the joint committee to discuss the deadlock arising from the Legislative Council's opposition to a money bill.
Contemporary press comment suggests that
he was rather too aristocratic to be popular.
In 1888 he returned to pastoral pursuits and
became a cattle-breeder. At Bellevue, near
Esk, he built up a fine Hereford stud. On 24

July 1904 he had married Edith Maud Taylor, a widowed daughter of George Harris
[q.v.] and sister-in-law of R. G. Casey [q.v.].
Aged 69 Hill died of malaria at Bellevue on
28 October 1909. His widow managed his
estates and won repute for her business
ability and as a grazier and cattle-breeder;
she died on 6 July 1925 at Southport and
was buried in Toowong cemetery.

Boomerang (Brisb), 16 Feb 1889; Pastoral
Review, 15 Aug 1906; Telegraph (Brisb), 7 July
1925.
A. A. MORRISON

HILL, GEORGE (1802-1883), butcher,
alderman and sporting patron, was born on
25 March 1802 at Parramatta, the eldest son
of William Hill and Mary Johnson. His
father, transported for life for felony,
reached Sydney in the Ganges in 1797. Next
year his mother arrived in the Britannia on
a seven-year sentence. William became
superintendent of the government slaughter-
house, had an absolute pardon in 1813 and
was a butcher in Pitt Street in 1828.

George had little education and at 10 ran
cattle on the coast. In 1828 he was helping
his father and by 1832 had three inns in
Pitt Street. On 18 June 1832 at St James's
Church of England he married a widow,
Mary Ann Hunter. He accumulated real
estate and in 1838-50 held Yanko, 56,000
acres on the Murrumbidgee, but his main
occupation was a butcher with his own
slaughter-house.

In 1842 Hill was elected for Macquarie
ward to the first Sydney Municipal Council
and in 1844 became a magistrate. In July
1848 he was elected to the Legislative Council for the Counties of St Vincent and Auckland but soon vacated his seat. In municipal
politics he belonged to the Australian-born
faction and in 1850 was mayor. He brought
'dignity and respect' to the office and was
praised by Bell's Life in Sydney for reforming abuses in the police courts. He also dispensed liberal hospitality and was elected
for a second term, but the Supreme Court
declared his election invalid to the displeasure of Governor FitzRoy. In 1856 Hill
was nominated to the first Legislative Council after responsible government and in May
1861 resigned in support of Sir William
Burton [q.v.]. In 1856-57 he again represented Macquarie ward in the Municipal
Council. He was a trustee of the New South
Wales Savings Bank in 1850-83 and sat on
the committees of the Benevolent Asylum
and the Cumberland Agricultural Society.

In the 1830s Hill was treasurer of the
Sydney races and a subscriber to the Parramatta races. In 1842 his horse Toby won a
trotting match at Homebush. In the early

1850s he was several times on the Anniversary Regatta Committee. Known as a 'gentleman of the fancy' he backed Laurence Foley's [q.v.] fight at Echuca and later leased him a hotel in York Street. Hill's 'jovial face and bluff, kindly ways' were well known. He built a mansion, Durham Hall, Surry Hills, and died there on 19 July 1883 after his buggy had collided with a tram. He was buried in Randwick cemetery, survived by his second wife Jane, née Binnie, and by five sons and five daughters. His estate was valued at £59,200.

Hill was recognized as head of a large family closely connected with the Wentworths and the Coopers [qq.v.]. One of his daughters married Fitzwilliam, W. C. Wentworth's eldest son; another married Sir William, second son of Sir Daniel Cooper. Hill's brother Richard was Wentworth's brother-in-law and his sister Elizabeth was Cooper's wife. Another daughter married her cousin J. R. Hill [q.v.]. His brother Edward Smith Hill (1819-1880) was a naturalist and a trustee of the Australian Museum; in 1874 he was largely responsible for the dismissal of the curator, Gerard Krefft [q.v.], and served as a New South Wales commissioner for exhibitions in Philadelphia, Paris and Sydney. George Hill is not to be confused with his nephew, George (1834-1897), who was prominent in coursing and owned Malta which won the Sires Produce Stakes in 1875 and the Epsom in 1876; in 1891-92 he won the Epsom and Doncaster with Marvel.

C. H. Bertie, *The early history of the Sydney Municipal Council* (Syd, 1911); M. Roe, *Quest for authority in eastern Australia 1835-1851* (Melb, 1965); V&P (LC NSW), 1853, 2, 617, (LA NSW), 1862, 2, 493, 1866, 2, 69, 1869, 2, 463; *Bell's Life in Sydney*, 9, 16, 30 Nov, 7, 14 Dec 1850, 4 Jan 1851, 24 Jan 1852; *Empire*, 4, 11 Jan 1851; *Bulletin*, 10 June 1882; MS cat and newspaper indexes under George Hill (ML); information from J. H. Luscombe, Town Clerk, Sydney.   MARTHA RUTLEDGE

HILL, HENRY JOHN (1847-1926), mail contractor and coach proprietor, was born on 26 March 1847 at Walkerville, South Australia, son of Henry John Hill and his wife Susanna, née Rofe. Known as John he was educated at a Presbyterian school at Alberton and then joined his father's carrying business, Henry Hill & Co. After training in office work John went into outside management. In 1866 Cobb [q.v.] & Co., of which his father was a member, bought out the coaching business of W. Rounsevell [q.v.]. Hill became local manager of Cobb & Co., bought their branch in 1871 and formed the new firm, John Hill & Co., which included H. R. Fuller and George Mills with Hill as the active manager. The business boomed and by 1882 it was sold to John Hill & Co. Ltd. Hill's coaches served most of South Australia and despite competition from the railways, especially in the south and south-east, the firm opened many new routes to offset the loss in trade. Hill often had a thousand horses at work and he opened large service stables at Broken Hill. Before World War 1 the firm amalgamated with H. Graves to form Graves, Hill & Co. Ltd. In 1877 Hill was a partner of C. B. Fisher [q.v.] in at least three Queensland runs. In 1888-95 he served as a railway commissioner at a salary of £1000 and then resumed his work with Hill & Co.

Hill was president of the Royal Agricultural Society in 1905-06, became a life member and chaired its finance and horse committees for thirty years. He was prominent in the Pirie Street Methodist Church and Sunday school for over sixty years and was elected a member of the General Wesleyan Conference in 1884, 1890 and 1894. He was also trustee of the Savings Bank. A keen cricketer for North Adelaide, he scored one of the first centuries on the Adelaide oval in a match against Kent Club in January 1875. He was also active in the Adelaide Bowls Club. On 9 October 1867 he had married Rebecca Eliza Saunders. She died in February 1921 aged 73. Hill died at his home in North Adelaide on 18 September 1926. He left an estate of £16,300 to his surviving seven daughters and six sons, one of whom was the Test cricketer, Clem (1877-1945).

Observer (Adel), 8 June 1895, 25 Sept 1926; *Register* (Adel), 20 Sept 1926.

HILL, JAMES RICHARD (1836-1898), banker and financier, was born on 22 February 1836 in Sydney, the third son of Richard Hill [q.v.] and his wife Henrietta, née Cox. He joined the Bank of New South Wales as a junior clerk on 23 May 1851 and worked at head office as clerk, ledger-keeper and teller until October 1856 when he took charge of the bank's agency at the Rocky River diggings near Armidale. In November 1857 he became manager in Tamworth and next August was transferred to the branch at Tarrangower (Maldon), Victoria.

In February 1862 he went to Dunedin, New Zealand, as superintendent of the bank's gold-buying agencies in Otago and in September became manager at Christchurch. In 1868 he was appointed inspector for New South Wales and in 1870 investigated irregularities in New Zealand where in 1871 he became inspector. Finding the bank's affairs in a sorry state, Hill energetically worked to restore the position. His letters revealed him as touchy, cautious, hard-working and likeable, but his temper was fierce as recalcitrant branch managers discovered. A hypochondriac prone to accident, he was thrown on his head from a Cobb [q.v.] & Co. coach, bitten by the only venomous creature in New Zealand and worked himself almost to a breakdown in the 1870s. In the 1879 financial crisis he wrote to the general manager, Shepherd Smith [q.v.], that 'downright hard work and the worry and anxiety which have accompanied it, have had a most telling effect on me . . . it has aged me before my time', and sought permission to retire. However, he stayed on until 1882 when he took eighteen months' leave. He resigned in 1884 and went to Sydney to assume charge of the Wentworth and Cooper [qq.v.] estates, to whose owners he was connected by marriage.

In 1886 Hill became a director of the bank and in 1894 was elected its first president to have risen from junior clerk. Widely recognized as a shrewd financier, he was deputy-chairman of the Australian Mutual Provident Society, a director of Tooth's brewery, manager of the Australian interests of R. L. Tooth [q.v.], a member of the Union Club and in 1884 a commissioner of fisheries. Active in public charity, he was a director of Sydney Hospital and of the Aborigines Protection Association. He died after a lingering illness at Vaucluse on 23 August 1898 and was buried in the family vault in the Anglican section of Waverley cemetery. His will was sworn at under £11,000. At St Michael's Church, Sydney, he had married on 9 February 1867 his cousin Sophia Helena, eldest daughter of George Hill [q.v.]. His wife and daughter survived him.

K. Sinclair and W. F. Mandle, *Open account: a history of the Bank of New South Wales in New Zealand, 1861-1961* (Wellington, 1961); *A'sian Insurance and Banking Record*, 19 Sept 1898; *SMH*, 19 Feb 1867, 24, 26 Aug 1898; Bank of NSW Archives (Syd).   G. P. WALSH

HILL, RICHARD (1810-1895), pastoralist and politician, was born on 22 September 1810 at Sydney, the third son of William Hill, emancipist butcher, and Mary Johnson. Educated at Wood's school and by W. T. Cape [q.v.], he was apprenticed as a carpenter. In the late 1820s he managed W. C. Wentworth's [q.v.] Vaucluse estate and later was agent for his city property. At St Philip's Church on 27 January 1832 he married Henrietta, daughter of Francis Cox, emancipist, and sister of Wentworth's wife. In 1842 he took over the Carpenter's Arms from his brother George [q.v.], and like him was a butcher with his own slaughterhouse. About 1848 he took up Mungyer, 76,000 acres on the Liverpool Plains, and in 1849 he and his brothers visited the Californian goldfields. In about 1839-60 he owned a large orchard, The Orangery, on the Lane Cove River and was often rowed to it by ten Aboriginals; it was described by George Bennett [q.v.] in *Gatherings of a Naturalist in Australasia* (London, 1860). Hill set up a boiling-down works to provide manure, exported oranges to the Victorian goldfields and at its peak the orchard's profits were £50 a day.

A magistrate from 1855, Hill sat on the committees of several agricultural and horticultural societies and was a councillor of the Agricultural Society of New South Wales. In the early 1860s he went to New Zealand and took up a large run near Invercargill. On his return he acquired three runs on the Lower Macquarie, including Butterbone; they were largely managed by his sons. From 1866 he was a director of the United Insurance Co.

Hill was 'nurtured in politics' by Wentworth. In 1868-77 he represented Canterbury in the Legislative Assembly. Active and vigilant, Hill's imagery was 'most amusing, being purely Australian'. Fond of ornithological jokes, he described James Martin's [q.v.] 1871 coalition as 'five kookaburras mixed up with one rosella—the Robertson [q.v.] rosella making the rest acceptable'. He mostly associated with other native-born politicians like Richard Driver and Edward Flood [qq.v.]. In 1867 he tried to prevent the dismissal of W. A. Duncan [q.v.] and in 1874 with W. B. Dalley [q.v.] and Driver urged the governor to release the bushranger, Frank Gardiner [q.v.]. In 1872 he helped to organize Wentworth's public funeral and in 1880 was appointed to the Legislative Council and a commissioner for the Sydney International Exhibition. In 1882 he was a commissioner for fisheries. Hill was a close friend and correspondent of Henry Parkes [q.v.] and in 1887 told him 'knowing that you are a *Good Catholic*; & with a loving desire to eat fish on Friday's I have much pleasure in sending you a very fine Schnapper'.

From boyhood Hill spent much time hunting and fishing with Aboriginals whom he regarded as his 'sable countrymen'. He found the Aboriginal 'the life and soul of the party, full of humour, an excellent mimic' and a hunter with no superior in the bush. In 1881 he was a councillor of the Aborigines Protection Society and in

June 1883 as a founding member of the Aborigines Protection Board helped to get a parliamentary grant for them. In 1892 with George Thornton [q.v.] he published *Notes on the Aborigines of New South Wales*. An Aboriginal boy lived with him all his life.

Survived by ten sons and one daughter, Hill died at his Bent Street home on 19 August 1895. He was buried in the Anglican section of Waverley cemetery beside his wife who had died on 27 September 1892. His estate was valued at £132,000.

V&P (LA NSW), 1866, 5, 788, 1878-79, 7, 593; *Australian*, 26, 28 Dec 1842; *SMH*, 15 Oct 1857, 13, 30 Jan 1871, 18, 27 Oct 1877, 21 Aug 1895; *Illustrated Sydney News*, 17 Oct 1874; *Bulletin*, 15 Jan 1881; Parkes letters (ML); MS and printed cats and newspaper indexes under Richard Hill (ML).

MARTHA RUTLEDGE

HITCHCOCK, GEORGE MICHELMORE (1831-1912) and WALTER MICHELMORE (1832-1923), businessmen, were sons of William Hitchcock, South Molton, Devon, England, and his first wife Mary Elizabeth, née Tope. George was born at Barnstaple on 7 October 1831 and Walter on 11 August 1832. After attending Denmark Hill School they were apprenticed to their uncle George, a London draper who also employed George Williams, founder of the Young Men's Christian Association.

In 1849 the Hitchcock family migrated in the *Amity Hall* to Geelong where in June 1850 they established Hitchcock Bros & Co., general dealers, wool-brokers and merchants. Walter and his father went to the Ballarat goldfields in September 1851 but were more successful at Forest Creek near Castlemaine. His father became a peoples' commissioner at Castlemaine to protest against police tyranny in May 1853. Devout Congregationalists, father and son organized regular religious services, first in a marquee and later in the Castlemaine hall which William built as well as his own home. Known as the 'Duke of Muckleford' he was auctioneer, merchant, proprietor of livery stables and founder of the first local newspaper. In May 1854 he represented landowners and merchants before the directors of the Mount Alexander Railway Co. In November he was host to Mrs Chisholm [q.v.] and offered to establish a home for girls in Castlemaine. He was vice-president of the local Friendly Aid Society, chairman of the hospital committee, promoter of schools and chairman of the municipality but he lost heavily in mining speculations and was declared insolvent in October 1859. In May 1860 he moved to Brisbane and in 1861 to Sydney where he had relations who had served in the London

Missionary Society. Aged 55 he died in Melbourne on 29 April 1867, survived by his second wife and several children.

In 1852 Walter had returned to Geelong; in September 1853 he and his brother George joined William Bright & Co., drapers and clothiers, and in January 1877 became sole partners. As buyer for the firm Walter had moved in 1863 to London where in 1865-66 his efforts to secure machinery and finance for a woollen mill at Geelong were strongly opposed in England but helped to create an independent colonial industry. In July 1881 he withdrew from the firm but under the management of George and later his son Howard (1869-1932), Bright & Hitchcocks became the largest department store in Victoria outside Melbourne.

In Geelong George became a town councillor in 1875 and a justice of the peace in 1891. He was also active in the Chamber of Commerce and in 1890-1912 chairman of the council of the Gordon Institute of Technology. In 1859 he had married Annie, daughter of John Lowe, a prominent Wesleyan; they had two sons and a daughter. George died at Geelong on 8 May 1912 and the G. M. Hitchcock Art Gallery was named in his honour.

Active in civic affairs, Walter was elected secretary of the Citizens' Committee formed in 1858 to secure a navigable harbour, and chairman of the Geelong and Western District Exploration Committee which was discredited by claiming a gold discovery that failed in 1861. In London he acted as agent for civic and church groups in Geelong and was prominent in obtaining its celebrated post office clock. Among other religious and philanthropic work he led a committee to aid dependents of people drowned in the *London* in 1866, served on the finance committee of the Young Men's Christian Association, was active in the Free Churches Federation, and in the Colonial Missionary Society founded by T. Binney [q.v.] was treasurer in 1882 and chairman in 1884-1904. He was also addicted to collecting Australiana but perhaps his greatest passion was the volunteer fire-brigade movement. In Geelong he rarely missed a fire or lost an opportunity to promote the movement and in 1883 on one of his visits to Australia was honoured with life membership as an honorary captain. In London he donned his uniform to ride in the annual mayoral procession, waited on royalty and published his *Reminiscences of a Volunteer Fireman in Australia and England, 1854-1912*.

In 1857 at Geelong Walter married Mary, daughter of William Burrow, mayor; she died in 1858, leaving one daughter. On 13 December 1860 he married Amelia Woollard; they had three children. She became a

Roman Catholic and died estranged from him in August 1908. Walter died in Somerset on 12 July 1923.

J. Smith (ed), *Cyclopedia of Victoria*, 2 (Melb, 1904); J. E. H. Williams, *The life of Sir George Williams* (Lond, 1906); C. Irving Benson (ed), *A century of Victorian Methodism* (Melb, 1935); Bright & Hitchcocks Pty Ltd, *100 years of progressive service 1850-1950* (Geelong, 1950); J. T. Massey, *The Y.M.C.A. in Australia: a history* (Melb, 1950); I. Southall, *The weaver from Meltham* (Melb, 1950); W. R. Brownhill, *The history of Geelong and Corio Bay* (Melb, 1955); *Mount Alexander Mail*, 26 Jan 1909; information from Mr D. Grant (Castlemaine Hist Soc); Hitchcock family papers.   NIEL GUNSON

HIXSON, FRANCIS (1833-1909), naval officer and public servant, was born on 8 January 1833 at Swanage, Dorset, England, son of William Hixson, master mariner, and his wife Annie, née Manwell. He joined the navy and in February 1848 as master's assistant in the *Havannah*, helped to survey parts of the Australian east coast, New Zealand and the South Seas and returned to England in December 1851. He then served in the *Impregnable* and in February 1852 joined the *Herald* in the expedition to survey and take possession of New Caledonia. They arrived to find the French already in occupation so they surveyed among the Fijian islands and along the Australian coast and went to Sydney. In 1855 Hixson became acting second master. In 1858 he won the silver medal of the Royal Humane Society for the rescue of a drowning seaman. Three months after the *Herald*'s cruise ended at Sydney in May 1860 Hixson was awarded his master's certificate. Next year the *Herald* reached England in July. He served in the *Pelorus* in 1861 and in the *Orpheus* in 1862 on surveys of the New South Wales coast. Hixson's log books reveal him as an able master with scientific attainments and curiosity, and as a keen observer of society in the South Pacific.

On 1 January 1863 Hixson resigned and was appointed superintendent of pilots, lighthouses and harbours in New South Wales. These duties were incorporated in April 1872 as the Marine Board of New South Wales with Hixson as its president; when it was abolished in March 1900 none of his decisions had been reversed by the Board of Trade. He was co-opted for other posts : member of the Fisheries Commission, the Defence from Foreign Aggression Commission and the board for maintaining colonial warlike stores in 1870 and chairman of the Pilot Board; he was chosen to establish an observatory at Goulburn to observe the transit of Venus in 1874. He advocated the building of more lighthouses, claiming that he wanted the coast 'illuminated like a street with lamps'. In 1893 and 1898 he represented the colony at marine conferences in Hobart and New Zealand.

Hixson was best known for his work with the Volunteer Naval Brigade. Its numbers steadily increased after he took command. In the 1880s an artillery unit was added and after a visit to England he reorganized the colony's naval forces. In the Boxer war of 1900 he took a contingent to Hong Kong where the Royal Navy took over. For forty years he had been chairman of the Sailors' Home in Sydney; he also served on the committee of the Royal Naval House, helped to found the Royal Shipwreck Relief, was president of the Humane Society of New South Wales and took great interest in the *Vernon*, a training ship for the rehabilitation of orphan boys.

On 2 November 1861 at St Thomas's Church, North Sydney, Hixson married Sarah, second daughter of Francis Lord. He died of heart failure at his home in Double Bay on 2 March 1909 and was buried with naval honours. He was survived by his wife, three sons who had also been active in the naval brigade, and three daughters, two of whom married grandsons of John Fairfax [q.v.].

Town & Country J, 24 Feb 1877, 13 Feb 1886; *Daily Telegraph* (Syd), 3, 6 Mar 1909; SMH, 3 Mar 1909; MS cat under Hixson (ML).
                                        RUTH TEALE

HOBBS, WILLIAM (1822-1890), medical practitioner, was born in London, son of James Hobbs and his wife Anne, née Phillips. He was admitted a member of the Royal College of Surgeons in London on 15 May 1843. Accompanied by his aged mother, he arrived at Moreton Bay on 1 May 1849 as surgeon of the *Chasely*, the second of J. D. Lang's [q.v.] migrant ships. After a brief period at Drayton on the Darling Downs, he commenced practice in Brisbane in September. Apart from a few months in 1850 when he relieved as resident surgeon of the Brisbane Hospital on the death of David Ballow [q.v.], he remained in private practice in Brisbane throughout his professional life. At various times he held appointments on the honorary staffs of the Brisbane Hospital, the Lying-in Hospital and the Hospital for Sick Children. He was for many years medical officer to the immigration depot and the gaol. He was health officer for Brisbane in 1854-88 and a member of the Medical Board of Queensland in 1860-88. Professionally he was well regarded and is credited with having administered in 1854 the first chloroform anaesthetic in Brisbane.

Hobbs had many nonprofessional interests and appears to have been active in various local cultural organizations and in the Aborigines' Friends Society. He was prominent in local agitation against Earl Grey's proposed resumption of transportation in the 1850s. Like some other colonial medicos he had an inquiring mind and an interest in experiment. He became a protagonist of the medicinal use of dugong oil, a form of therapy for which he coined the name 'Elaiopathy'; samples of his oil were sent to the Paris Exhibition in 1855 but he failed in an attempt to produce and market it commercially. At his property at Humpybong (Redcliffe) he discovered a spring with alleged anti-anaemic virtues. He grew cotton and is said to have sent samples to the editor of the *Economist* but again lost money through backing the Caboolture Cotton Co.

In 1861 Hobbs was nominated to the Legislative Council and, in fact if not in name, as minister without portfolio and leader of the government in that chamber was appointed to the Executive Council. Early in 1862 he resigned from the executive but remained a member of the Legislative Council until October 1880. Politically his most fertile period was in the early years; he played a major part in the passage of the Contagious Diseases Prevention Act, 1868, and the first Health Act, 1872. Apart from the medical area, he was especially active in questions of land tenure. He was a member of the Immigration Board, the Board of Education and the Central Board of Health. His later years were clouded by the findings of the 1876 royal commission on lunatic asylums which reported evidence of neglect in the reception house at Petrie Terrace where he was visiting surgeon. This led to an acrimonious debate in the House with his fellow member, Dr K. O'Doherty [q.v.].

In 1853 Hobbs married Anna Louisa, sister of Edmund Barton. Aged 67 he died on 8 December 1890 at Wickham Terrace, Brisbane. Of their eight children, two sons predeceased him in accidents. The home which was built for him by Andrew Petrie [q.v.] in 1853 became the temporary residence of Governor Bowen and still stands as the deanery of St John's Cathedral.

V&P (LA Qld), 1863 (2nd S), 485, 1864, 1107, 1311, 1875, 2, 1316, 1877, 1, 1109, 1885, 1, 91; *Government Gazette* (Qld), 25 Feb 1860, 13 Oct 1862; F. McCallum, 'Physician and health officer, a Brisbane pioneer', *Health*, 5 (1927); C. G. Austin, 'Newstead House and Capt. Wickham, R.N.', *JRHSQ*, 3 (1937-47); family information.   OWEN POWELL

HODGKINSON, CLEMENT (1818-1893), public servant, was born at Southampton, England, son of Enoch Hodgkinson and his wife Mary, née Millais. He studied civil engineering in France and then worked at topographical fieldwork and mechanical drawing in England. At 21 he inherited money and went to New South Wales where in 1840-42 he was a contract surveyor for the government on the northern rivers. He returned to England in 1843 and published *Australia, from Port Macquarie to Moreton Bay* (London, 1845). As an engineer he worked on railways in France, Belgium and Holland, and lectured at the College of Geodetic Engineers, Putney.

Hodgkinson arrived at Melbourne in the *Tory* on 15 December 1851 intending to take up grazing but instead joined the Surveyor-General's Office in January 1852. For the select committee on Melbourne's water supply and sewerage he contoured the city area, including Richmond and Collingwood, and worked with James Blackburn [q.v.] on plans for the Yan Yean water supply. In 1854 he was promoted district surveyor for the Counties of Evelyn and part of Bourke. He became honorary consulting engineer for the municipal councils of Emerald Hill, Prahran, East Collingwood and Richmond in 1856 and for the Mornington district in 1857. As vice-president of the Philosophical Institute of Victoria in 1856 and 1858 he read papers on the geology of the Upper Murray and railway problems, and was elected to the first council of the Royal Society of Victoria in 1860.

Although Hodgkinson suffered from rheumatism and intended to retire, he was appointed acting surveyor-general in October 1857, and deputy to the surveyor-general, C. W. Ligar [q.v.], in March 1858. After reorganization in 1860 he became assistant commissioner and secretary of the new Board of Crown Lands and Survey. New land legislation in the 1860s greatly expanded the board's work. Deluged daily by a large variety of administrative detail, Hodgkinson also helped to draft amendments to the Lands Act, attended local hearings and served on many committees of inquiry, not least the 1871 royal commission on forests, a subject of major interest to him. He applied for the post of surveyor-general when Ligar retired in 1869 but A. J. Skene [q.v.] was appointed. Hodgkinson continued as secretary but new duties increased faster than he could delegate them. His health gave way in June 1873 but against medical advice he returned to work in July. In 1874 his management was criticized at a public inquiry and he retired on a pension in May. In 1879 Hodgkinson joined the Central Board of Health and the Melbourne

Harbor Trust where he helped Sir John Coode [q.v.] by his knowledge of Australian timbers for docks and piers. He became a commissioner for the westward extension of Melbourne in 1887 and for the International Exhibition and for sanitation in 1888. In 1891 he chaired an inquiry into the River Yarra floods.

Hodgkinson was married first, to Matilda Chapman without issue; second, to Amelia Hunt by whom he had five sons and a daughter; and third, to Annie Davis Smart by whom he had three sons and a daughter. He died aged 75 at his home in Hawthorn on 5 September 1893 and was buried in the Melbourne general cemetery.

K. A. Patterson, 'Clement Hodgkinson', VHM, 39 (1968), and for bibliog; *Illustrated Aust News*, 2 Oct 1893.   H. W. NUNN

HODGKINSON, WILLIAM OSWALD (1835-1900), sailor, explorer, journalist, miner, goldfields warden and politician, was born on 31 March 1835 at Handsworth, Warwick, England, son of William Oswald Hodgkinson, civil engineer, and his wife Harriet, née Brown. Educated at Birmingham Grammar School he early began his varied and energetic career. In 1851 he first viewed Australia as a midshipman in the mercantile marine. By 1853 he was in government service on the Tarnagulla and Forest Creek goldfields in Victoria, and may have shared in the Eureka affair in 1854. He then returned to England and was a clerk in the War Office until 1859, when he sailed for Melbourne to join the literary staff of the *Age*. His reporting brought him into contact with R. O'H. Burke [q.v.], whose expedition he joined in 1860. At one stage he rode to Melbourne and back, over 800 miles in twenty days. He fortunately missed the fatal later half of the expedition, became one of A. Howitt's [q.v.] search party and then, requested by the South Australian government, became second-in-command of the 1861 McKinlay [q.v.] relief party. He claimed that Goyder [q.v.] taught him surveying to enable him to qualify for the post. This expedition, after finding Gray's grave, discovered the Diamantina, crossed the McKinlay Range to the Leichhardt River, and went through the Burdekin country to Bowen.

Hodgkinson became editor of the Rockhampton *Morning Bulletin*, then founded a short-lived weekly and in 1866 gave Mackay its first newspaper, the *Mercury*. He soon sold out, returned to Rockhampton and in 1868 appeared with a crushing battery on the young Ravenswood goldfield. There and at the Cape field he became well

known, floating several companies and joining other mining ventures. In 1870 he moved to the Etheridge goldfield for his first post as mining warden and police magistrate, his impact winning him election to the Legislative Assembly for the Burke district in 1874. Still restless, he resigned his seat in 1875 to lead a government expedition to examine the area between the Etheridge and Cloncurry fields and new country in the south-west and to report on it for mining, pastoral and agricultural purposes. This last officially-sponsored expedition in Queensland opened up the last major unexplored area, taking him to the Diamantina, Mulligan and Herbert Rivers, north to Normanton and up the Cloncurry and Flinders Rivers to Brisbane. In January 1876 his friend J. V. Mulligan [q.v.] discovered the river and goldfield which he named after Hodgkinson.

In 1878-83 Hodgkinson was mining warden, on the Etheridge to 1881 and then on the Palmer where in 1884 he was temporarily suspended pending investigation of one of his reports. To the select committee of inquiry it more closely resembled a prospectus boosting a mine in which Thomas McIlwraith [q.v.], premier and minister for mines, was interested, and aimed at investment in the field while glossing over its languishing condition. However, the committee admitted that McIlwraith had asked for a report, and that Hodgkinson had strong faith that untapped reefs would revive this old alluvial field. But more than scandal was needed to halt Hodgkinson. By 1886 he was warden for Gympie, the premier goldfield, and chosen by the new premier, Griffith, as special commissioner to examine sites for prospective government-subsidized central sugar-mills and alternative claims for continued coloured labour. On his recommendation two central mills were tried at Mackay but in vain.

Hodgkinson had supported McIlwraith, but in 1887 Griffith offered him the new portfolio of mines and works. Opposition papers in 1888 claimed that this was Griffith's best election card for the north where he was disliked but Hodgkinson was 'deservedly popular with most mining communities'. Requested to stand for six electorates he chose Burke and was successful, but the Griffith government was not. In 1890 he was given the curious portfolio of mines and public instruction under the Griffith-McIlwraith coalition. He initiated several important mining Acts before his defeat by J. P. Hoolan in 1893 when Labor first began to sweep the mining electorates.

Like many other miners Hodgkinson went to Western Australia where he represented an English syndicate and won wide respect as an expert on mining. In 1896 he was in Sydney until appointed in 1899 first editor of the *Queensland Government Mining Journal*. He died of influenza on 23 July 1900, predeceased by his wife Kate, née Robertson, whom he had married in Rockhampton, and survived by three of their four children.

Hodgkinson had 'a ready pen and a ready tongue' but his literary style was described as 'chiefly distinguished by its great diffuseness', and to C. A. Bernays [q.v.] he was 'voluble' in parliament. Such a failing was perhaps a safety-valve for his explosive energy. In the politics of the pre-Labor era he called himself a working man's representative. Reputed an admirer of Peter Lalor [q.v.] he supported the miners' stand against Chinese encroachment on the goldfields and later against the employers' attempts to cut wages and employment. In 1890 he linked himself with Thomas Glassey as 'a new power in the House' which was alarming to the more conservative, though he was too far to the right to satisfy the demands of Labor in the 1890s. Exploration was probably his most notable achievement.

H. M. Humphreys (ed), *Men of the time in Australia: Victorian series*, 2nd ed (Melb, 1882); R. L. Jack, *Northmost Australia*, 2 (Lond, 1921); G. C. Bolton, *A thousand miles away* (Brisb, 1963); PD (Qld), 1874-75, 1888-92; V&P (LA Qld), 1883-84, 1607, 1884, 3, 241, 1885, 1, 1157, 1886, 2, 1; Goldfields reports, 1878-84, 1886; M. Walmsley, 'William Oswald Hodgkinson, 1838-1900', Hist Soc Cairns J, Dec 1963, Jan 1964; *Brisbane Courier*, 24 July 1900.

JUNE STOODLEY

HODGSON, SIR ARTHUR (1818-1902), squatter, politician and squire, was born on 29 June 1818 at Rickmansworth, Hertfordshire, England, the second son of Rev. Edward Hodgson (1776-1854) and his third wife Charlotte, daughter of Francis William Pemberton of Bombay, India, and sister of Colonel F. C. Pemberton of Trumpington Hall, Cambridge. C. P. Hodgson [q.v.] was his younger brother.

Educated at Eton in 1828-33 Hodgson entered the navy and in 1833-37 was a midshipman in H.M.S. *Canopus* on the China station. In 1837-38 he was at Corpus Christi College, Cambridge, and in 1839 went to Sydney. After experience on a station, he leased Cashiobury run in the New England district. Persuaded by Patrick Leslie [q.v.] to seek new land, Hodgson and his partner, Gilbert Eliott [q.v.], moved north in July 1840 and in September took up Eton Vale, the second run on the Darling Downs. Although he occupied the choicest pastoral country in Queensland, Aborigi-

nals, scab, low prices, transport difficulties and mercantile depression so beset him that in the first ten years 'he could not realize the small capital he brought out with him'. He even hawked legs of mutton around Brisbane, probably more as a symbolic gesture than an attempt to help his finances. On 30 March 1842 Hodgson married Eliza (1822-1902), the second daughter of Sir James Dowling [q.v.]; they had seven children. A daughter, Annie Frances, married Viscount Lifford, and two others the sons of baronets. Eton Vale became the centre of Darling Downs society, and the Hodgsons unofficial leaders of the Pure Merinos. By the 1850s his economic position was secure and he served as general superintendent of the Australian Agricultural Co. in 1856-61.

Hodgson entered political life as the prime mover of the Moreton Bay and Northern Districts Separation Association, but his trenchant advocacy of convict labour, colonial peerages, National education and a restricted franchise drew the fire of the lower orders. Despite defeat by J. D. Lang [q.v.] in a twice-disputed election for Stanley County in 1854, Hodgson won the Clarence and Darling Downs seat in the New South Wales parliament in 1858 and Newcastle in 1859. In 1868-69 he represented Warrego in the Queensland Legislative Assembly and served in R. R. Mackenzie's [q.v.] ministry as secretary for public works and goldfields in September-November 1868 and as colonial secretary in the Lilley [q.v.] ministry from January to November 1869 when Hodgson left the colony. As a politician he was not a success. Though an excellent lecturer his attitudes were too obsolete and inflexible for a developing colony, and despite his straightforward character he was intolerant in debate. While travelling in England and Europe in 1862-67 he had represented Queensland at exhibitions in London and Paris; he played the same role at Vienna in 1874, Paris in 1878 and London in 1886. For these services he was appointed C.M.G. in 1878 and K.C.M.G. in 1886.

In 1870 Hodgson settled in England. He visited Queensland several times and helped to promote the frozen meat trade. His profits from Eton Vale steadily rose to a peak of nearly £20,000 in 1874, covering the capital invested in the 90,000 freehold acres and 83,000 sheep. He was singularly fortunate in his two Scotch managing partners, John Watts and Robert Ramsay [qq.v.], in Queensland, together with his own business sense and rare capacity to refrain from speculation. In 1873 Hodgson had bought the Clopton estate near Stratford-on-Avon and as a squire devoted himself to charitable, sporting and social activities. He was mayor in 1883-88, high steward of the borough in 1884-89, deputy-lieutenant and high sheriff of Warwickshire in 1881 and was also honorary colonel of the 2nd battalion, Royal Warwickshire Regiment. He was upright and inflexible but made few enemies as his ambitions carried him to high place. A staunch Anglican, he died at Clopton House on 24 December 1902. His privately printed pamphlets on Shakespeare and *In Memoriam* were issued in memory of his wife in 1903. In Queensland a hamlet near Roma and a farming district on the Darling Downs were named after him.

His portrait by H. J. Thaddeus is in the Stratford-on-Avon Town Hall and an engraving from an original drawing by C. W. Walton is in the Mitchell Library.

H. S. Russell, *The genesis of Queensland* (Syd, 1888); F. H. Hodgson, *In memory of Sir Arthur Hodgson* (np, 1904); R. Gollan, *The coalminers of New South Wales* (Melb, 1963); PD (Qld), 1869; *Warwick Examiner and Times*, 5 June 1869; *Brisbane Courier*, 3 July 1869, 27 Dec 1902; *The Times*, 25 Dec 1902; *Pastoral Review*, 15 Jan 1903.   D. B. WATERSON

HODGSON, CHRISTOPHER PEMBERTON (1821-1865), explorer, writer and diplomat, was the fourth son of Edward Hodgson, vicar of Rickmansworth, Hertfordshire, England, and his wife Charlotte, née Pemberton. Educated at Eton and Cambridge, he followed his eldest brother Arthur [q.v.] to Sydney in 1839 and in 1840 joined him on the Darling Downs where they took up Eton Vale station, using it as a headquarters for wider squatting and pastoral activities. In 1844 Hodgson was managing Condamine station when Ludwig Leichhardt [q.v.] arrived to prepare for his journey to Port Essington. He was persuaded to make Hodgson a member of his party 'in consideration of former obligations' and 'as he was fond of Botanical pursuits'. The expedition set out on 1 October but on 5 November Hodgson returned to Jimbour with the American Negro cook, Caleb, for their provisions were already running short and Hodgson was suffering from the 'additional fatigues'. On hearing a rumour that the expedition had been massacred Hodgson organized a search party which followed Leichhardt's tracks to the Bigge Range before provisions ran out and dissension put an end to the excursion.

Hodgson returned to England where he published his *Reminiscences of Australia, with Hints on the Squatter's Life* (London, 1846). In 1849 he published *The Wanderer*, 'all my wanderings in poetry—commencing at Holland and skimming over all the places

I had visited' with some reference to Australia, and *El Ydaiour*, jottings of travel impressions. In his memoirs he confessed to a predilection for regular bush life and to fondness for studying botany and geology. From October 1851 to March 1855 he acted as unpaid vice-consul at Pau in Bayonne, France, and then at Caen. In February 1859 he was appointed consul at Hakodate, Japan, where he was also French consul. He left the diplomatic service in 1861 and died, unmarried, at Hakodate on 11 October 1865.

L. Leichhardt, *Journal of an overland expedition . . . Moreton Bay to Port Essington . . . 1844-1845* (Lond, 1847); H. S. Russell, *The genesis of Queensland* (Syd, 1888).
                                      BEVERLEY KINGSTON

HODGSON, RICHARD (1855-1905), psychical researcher, was born on 24 September 1855 at Melbourne, son of Richard Hodgson, importer and later unsuccessful mining speculator, and his wife Margaret, née Hyde. He attended the Central Common School and in 1871 matriculated to the University of Melbourne (B.A., 1874; M.A., 1876; LL.D., 1878). He was intended for the law but his interest fixed on philosophy. While an undergraduate Hodgson became interested in the contemporary debate about immortality and supernatural phenomena : his student crony, Alfred Deakin, introduced him to spiritualist literature and took him to his first seance. Hodgson abandoned the Wesleyan Methodism of his upbringing. His backsliding distressed his parents and, he believed, helped in 1875 to break his romance with his cousin Jessie D—, who was to die four years later. Hodgson never married.

In 1878 he entered St John's College, Cambridge (B.A., 1882; M.A., 1893). Preoccupied with the relations between physical manifestations and impalpable forces, he sought a physical foundation for psychical beliefs in Herbert Spencer's doctrine that beyond all everyday experience there lay an unknowable of which man has an indefinite consciousness. When T. H. Green exposed the holes in this argument Hodgson published a wild defence and was in turn drubbed by Green (*Contemporary Review*, December 1880, January 1881).

Hodgson's rash onslaught was characteristic of him. He was privately tenacious of his search for unseen powers and publicly boisterous and independent. He nearly failed to graduate from Cambridge in 1882 because the ceremony involved kneeling to the vice-chancellor and Hodgson avowed that he would kneel to no man; but his friends persuaded him. He also asserted himself by wearing brown evening dress. Hodgson was a genial hearty, excelling in boxing and swimming. He was muscular, 5 ft. 8 ins. tall and moved with distinctive grace. None the less his Cambridge mentors in philosophy thought their loud-voiced Australian student 'inconveniently' forthright. After graduating he spent six months at the University of Jena and in 1883-84 was Cambridge University Extension lecturer in philosophy and English literature in the north of England. In 1884 he was appointed to lecture on Herbert Spencer at Cambridge.

Meanwhile the supernatural had become his trade. Since 1879 he had participated in the seances arranged by the Sidgwicks, F. W. H. Myers and other Cambridge investigators and in 1882 he had become an early member of the Society for Psychical Research. His supernatural experiences began in September 1884 with the touch of disembodied hands in the dark in his room at St John's. About this time too he was experimenting with hallucinatory drugs. He afterwards became convinced that he had received premonitions of the deaths of three friends and of his mother.

The S.P.R. in 1884 was intensely curious about the occult transactions associated with Madame Blavatsky in India. In November Hodgson was sent to investigate. After fours months at Adyar, the Theosophists' headquarters, he made three chief findings. He determined that the Coulombs, two disreputable apostates from Adyar who claimed to have helped fake the phenomena, were telling the truth. He demonstrated how the Mahatma letters, missives purported to have arrived from gurus in Tibet, were composed in Madame Blavatsky's inimitable slapdash English and that several were in her handwriting; and he concluded that the letters, rather than having travelled the astral plane, had been conveyed in the mails and were 'precipitated' from the ceiling at Adyar through a trapdoor manipulated by string from Madame's bedroom. Finally Hodgson established that the altar cavity at the Adyar shrine, in which Mahatma letters and a china pin-tray had materialized, had backed on to a wall with an opening through to Madame Blavatsky's boudoir. His report is a monumental examination of credulity and the ease of crude deception (*Procs*, S.P.R., vol. 3).

His Indian experience deepened Hodgson's passionate interest in legerdemain and puzzles. His yearning to believe and his own psychic experiences made him the hammer of cheats. Among the luminaries of the S.P.R. he was almost alone in devising worthwhile experiments: he had a genius for detecting the mechanics of fraud. In 1886-87 Hodgson and S. J. Davey exposed

mediumistic slate-writing as bogus, virtually ending it as a spiritualist technique. Also with Davey he produced classic papers on malobservation and lapse of memory among participants in psychical research (*Procs*, S.P.R., vols 2, 4, 6, 8). In 1894 he began the unmasking of Eusapia Palladino, the physical medium who for years had convinced the leading investigators of Europe.

In 1887 Hodgson became secretary of the newly-founded American Society for Psychical Research. Henceforth in Boston, on a meagre salary, he lived in a single room to which no one was admitted, working obsessively at the supernatural. He was introduced by William James to the trance medium, Mrs Leonore Piper, and became absorbed in studying her. Hodgson was sceptical of her earlier communications but at last in 1896-97 he found solace by accepting her 'control's' utterances as empirical evidence of the survival of personalities after death and of their power to communicate with the living (*Procs*, S.P.R., vols 8, 13). He was now convinced of the goodness and unity of the cosmos. He had 'not a mere consciousness of something there; [but] fused in the central happiness of it . . . a startling awareness of some ineffable Love and Wisdom' amounting to 'the one perception of Reality'. Mrs Piper's 'controls' gave him news of his mother and Jessie D—, and of Madame Blavatsky, whose 'spirit was in the deepest part of Hell'. Hodgson's conversion is celebrated by spiritualists as a milestone in the science. However, his memoranda of his later transactions with Mrs Piper remain undecipherable and unpublished. After his conversion Hodgson himself developed mediumistic powers and, alone in his room, received communications which again are unpublished. But he retained his scepticism about other mediums and, as joint editor of F. W. H. Myers's posthumous *Human Personality and its Survival of Bodily Death* (1903), he probably caused the deletion of references to Myers's sittings with Mrs Thompson.

Socially Hodgson remained ebullient and clubbable. Yet he was restless to explore the other side, remarking in mid-1905, 'I can hardly wait to die'. On 20 December he suffered heart failure while playing handball. In accord with a longstanding promise messages from Hodgson arrived through Mrs Piper, but after William James pronounced them inconclusive, communication ceased.

A. L. Piper, *The life and work of Mrs. Piper* (Lond, 1929); A. T. Baird, *Richard Hodgson* (Lond, 1949); Hodgson letters, William James papers (Harvard Univ); Soc for Psychical Research Archives (Lond).   F. B. SMITH

HODGSON, WILLIAM (1809-1869), Church of England clergyman, was born on 15 December 1809 in London, the youngest son of Haygarth Hodgson, bookseller. He was educated at Richmond, Surrey, at Richmond Grammar School, Yorkshire, and at Sidney Sussex College, Cambridge (B.A., 1832; M.A., 1835). He was made deacon on 25 January 1835 and ordained priest on 31 January 1836 by Bishop John Bird Sumner in the Cathedral at Chester. Appointed curate in the large Lancashire parish of Whalley, he became perpetual curate at Brathay, Westmorland, in 1842 with a stipend not more than £100.

The small stipend and the remote situation had compensations for a man of Hodgson's tastes and character. The circle of scholars who lived in the district included John Harden, whose daughter Jane married Rev. Frederic Barker [q.v.]. In 1846 Harden wrote to the Barkers that he was charmed 'with Mr. Hodgson's sermon'. Soon after his enthronement as bishop of Sydney in May 1855 Barker invited Hodgson to become principal of Moore College. It opened on 1 March 1856 with three students under the Rev. W. M. Cowper [q.v.] as acting principal and Hodgson arrived in Sydney with his wife Mary Ann and three daughters in September. Plans for the erection of a chapel, library and accommodation for twelve students were approved on 27 November, the buildings around three sides of a triangle to cost about £11,000. The chapel was dedicated on 17 December 1857 and student quarters were completed, but the other buildings were delayed through shortage of funds.

Hodgson soon won repute as one of the best classical scholars in New South Wales and Victoria. He was a most acceptable preacher, a faithful teacher and pastor, a publicist on his Church's behalf and a quiet and self-effacing gentleman. He was a devoted Evangelical and strove to establish a high academic standard for the students under his care. The lack of connexion between the college at Liverpool and the University of Sydney was a handicap beyond his control. He served the college with marked ability and success until he resigned in December 1867. In that time forty-six of his students had been ordained. On 29 January 1868 he was farewelled at a public meeting in Sydney. Bishop Barker spoke of him in terms of high praise: 'I have never been in any degree disappointed in the expectations which I had formed concerning you ... I can not but feel deeply your departure'. He recalled that he had known Hodgson in his 'quiet and beautiful parish in the Lake District. I knew you as the faithful pastor and as the efficient tutor of young men. I knew you as the able preacher, and ever listened to your Scriptural and interesting addresses with much edification and profit'.

Hodgson sailed for England on 2 February 1868. His health had been worn out and in October the bishop of Carlisle presented him with the living of Clifton near Penrith in Westmorland at a stipend of £150. In September 1869 Jessie Clay, née Harden, and her daughter visited the Hodgsons: 'Mr. H. took us over his church and shewed me a great deal in his study'. On 2 December he died at Clifton rectory and was buried at Brathay. His wife died in 1892. The great work of Hodgson's quiet unassuming life had been the successful foundation of what is now both the oldest and the largest Anglican Theological College in Australia.

A century of Brathay Church, 1836-1936 (Kendal, 1936); M. L. Loane, A centenary history of Moore Theological College (Syd, 1955); Aust Churchman (Syd), 25 Jan, 3 Oct 1868, 19 Feb 1870; Mrs J. S. Barker diaries (ML); Jessie Clay diary (held privately); SPG letters D17, D29 (microfilm, ML).   M. L. LOANE

HOFFNUNG, SIGMOND (1830-1904), merchant, was born in Kalisz, Poland, the elder son of Rev. Samuel Hoffnung and his wife Caroline. In 1836 his father migrated to England with his family, became minister and cantor of the small Jewish community in Newcastle upon Tyne and in 1840 moved to the Exeter Synagogue. Sigmond was educated in Liverpool but lack of money forced him to leave home and become a junior salesman with a West Country firm. He became friendly with a customer, Henry Nathan, who lent him £500 to buy assorted goods and take them to Sydney. Hoffnung arrived early in 1852 and opened a wholesale business in Wynyard Square. He soon sold his stock, repaid the loan, then made arrangements with Nathan to act as his buyer. Hoffnung prospered and in 1855 moved to larger premises in George Street. Knowledgeable about the needs of settlers, he visited England in 1857 to replenish his stock and to swell his capital and made a formal partnership with Nathan. In Sydney on 26 May 1858 he married Elizabeth Marks of Raymond Terrace.

Hoffnung was prominent in Jewish activities. He was auditor of the York Street Synagogue in 1857 and remained one of its leaders. He served on committees to raise money for distressed Jews in Palestine, the Sydney Jewish Sabbath School, the Sydney Hebrew Certified Denominational School and the Jewish Philanthropic and Orphan Society. In 1866 he was treasurer and a benefactor of the Great Synagogue's building committee, president of the York Street Synagogue and in 1870-76 a member of its board of management. In 1875 he organized the Hebrew Ladies' Bazaar at which his wife alone raised £1285 towards the Great Synagogue building fund.

In 1870 S. Hoffnung & Co. moved into new premises designed by Thomas Rowe [q.v.] in Pitt Street and in 1871 opened a Brisbane branch. The firm also established other branches in Australia, New Zealand and Fiji and had its head office in London. They also had a large factory in Sydney making saddlery and harness. Their range of wholesale goods included American canned fruits and jams, watches, glass and china, ironmongery, rocking-horses, firearms, iron safes and patent medicines. Hoffnung set up the first opal-cutting business in Australia and exported uncut diamonds and sapphires for industrial use. In 1875 he was on the committee of the Trade Protection Society of New South Wales.

In 1877 Hoffnung returned to England and took charge of the London office. His brother Abraham, who had been a successful merchant in America, Canada and Liverpool, joined S. Hoffnung & Co. in 1886. Abraham spent some years in Australia and in London was chargé d'affaires for Hawaii before its annexation. In 1889 Sigmond retired from the firm, which in 1899 became a private company and in 1902 a public company which later had its headquarters at 153 Clarence Street, Sydney. With his brother he restored the Exeter Synagogue. Aged 74 he died on 27 August 1904 in Queen's Gate, Kensington, London, and was buried in the Golders Green cemetery. He was survived by his wife; their only child Sidney, who married Violet, daughter of Sir Julian Goldsmid, took the name Hoffnung-Goldsmid by royal licence, became a director of the company and died in 1930.

W. F. Morrison, *The Aldine history of Queensland*, 2 (Brisb, 1888); S. Hoffnung & Co. Ltd, *The house of Hoffnung 1852-1952* (Syd, 1952); 'Some treasures of the Great Synagogue', Aust Jewish Hist Soc, J, 3 (1949-53); *Bulletin*, 4 Dec 1880; records (Synagogue, York St, Syd).   GEORGE F. J. BERGMAN

HOGAN, JAMES FRANCIS (1855-1924), teacher, journalist, author and politician, was born on 29 December 1855 near Nenagh, County Tipperary, Ireland, the only son and younger child of Rody Hogan and Mary, farm workers. The family migrated to Melbourne in the *Atalanta* in 1856 and settled in Geelong. James was educated at St Mary's Catholic School, Geelong, and for a year at St Patrick's College, Mel-

bourne. He contemplated taking religious orders but in 1872 turned to teaching after passing his examination through the Victorian Education Department. Near Geelong he taught first at Anakie, then at Flinders school and in 1877-81 was headmaster of St Mary's.

While teaching Hogan contributed to newspapers and journals and the success of his work inspired him to become a professional writer. His first article, 'The Tests of Efficiency in Public Schools', appeared in 1873. In 1878 *The Catholic Case Stated . . .* attracted wide attention. This pamphlet was essentially an emotional statement defending the claim of the Catholic denomination in Victoria to state aid for the secular instruction given in Catholic schools. Hogan contributed regularly to the *Geelong Advertiser*, to Mortimer Franklyn's [q.v.] *Victorian Review* and to the *Advocate*, a Catholic weekly.

In 1881 Hogan abandoned teaching, went to Melbourne, became sub-editor of the *Victorian Review* and soon joined the *Argus*. He continued to contribute to a variety of papers and maintained an active association with Irish-Catholic movements. In 1884-87 he presided over the Victorian Catholic Young Men's Society and was secretary to the committee which organized the erection of the O'Connell statue in the grounds of St Patrick's Cathedral, Melbourne. In 1886 he published a biographical sketch of Archbishop Goold [q.v.] and an anthology of his own work under the title *An Australian Christmas Collection*. Next year he went to England seeking a wider field for his writing. In London he published his best-known work, *The Irish in Australia* (1887), which ran to three editions. Although praised by Sir Charles Gavan Duffy [q.v.] in the *Contemporary Review*, it offers an uncritical assessment of the Irish contribution to Australian development and fails as an objective study. Hogan contributed to many journals and became recognized as an authority on Australian affairs. His larger works published in London included *The Australian in London and America* (1889), *The Lost Explorer* (1890), *The Convict King . . . Jorgen Jorgenson* [q.v.] (1891), *Robert Lowe* [q.v.], *Viscount Sherbrooke* (1893), *The Sister Dominions* (1896) and *The Gladstone Colony* (1898). These works were of variable quality, the best being the Lowe biography and *The Sister Dominions*. The others were somewhat superficial, while the fictional works were marred by melodrama.

In 1893 Hogan gained pre-selection for the middle division of Tipperary and on 26 February was elected unopposed to the House of Commons. As a member of parliament till 1900 he took a stand as an Irish Nationalist, supporting the government of Ireland bill. Colonial affairs were the subject of his other parliamentary interests and he acted as secretary of the Colonial Party, an unofficial grouping of British parliamentarians who had had first-hand experience in some part of the colonial empire. The group was led by Sir Charles Dilke [q.v.]. Hogan returned to Australia only once, for the inauguration of the Commonwealth in 1901. He then returned to England where he lived quietly until his death in London on 9 November 1924. He never married and was survived by his sister Margaret.

While Hogan's career was marked by dedication, his achievements were small and marginal in their effect. Single-minded and steadfast, he had a rigid personal morality and a strong conception of the responsibilities of citizenship. As a writer Hogan was a conscientious and competent journalist but his creative work was not outstanding.

Table Talk, 3 Mar 1893, 17 Nov 1894; *Advocate* (Melb), 13 Nov 1924.

JOHN R. THOMPSON

HOLDEN, GEORGE KENYON (1808-1874), solicitor and politician, was born in Worcester, England, son of Adam Holden, sugar-refiner, and his wife Maria, née Gillam. Educated probably at Worcester Grammar School, he studied law. He met leading writers and statesmen and travelled widely while helping Sir James Mackintosh with his *History of England* (1830). Holden was admitted as a solicitor in England and in December 1831 arrived in Sydney. While private secretary to Governor Bourke until 1837 he also engaged in modest importing. He was also a stipendiary magistrate at Campbelltown in 1833-37 and then became crown prosecutor in the Quarter Sessions but resigned in December 1838 after the judges insisted that a barrister should hold the position. Within five years his practice as a solicitor had more than compensated for that blow to his prestige; his clients included leading business and landed families. After 1843 he was a partner of H. Chambers and W. G. McCarthy.

Holden's 'energy, intense conscientiousness and unswerving tenacity of purpose' allowed him to pursue many interests. In 1849-50 he was secretary to the Law Commission and in 1849 served on the Board of National Education. In politics he never belonged to any faction or contested a parliamentary election. From the 1840s he was closely associated with Henry Parkes [q.v.] and other rising men. In 1851-54 he was active in the Australasian League for the Abolition of Transportation. He worked for more representative government in the colony but as a member of the New South Wales Constitution Committee he led a moderate group which in fear of 'democratic' excesses sought to postpone responsible government. He assisted anti-squatter candidates at the elections in 1849 and 1856. He wrote pamphlets and letters to the press and to the Mechanics' School of Arts gave addresses on such subjects as 'without education it was impossible for any democracy to exist'.

In 1856 Holden was appointed to the Legislative Council and in May 1861 resigned in support of Sir William Burton [q.v.] over the swamping of the council. He was reappointed in June. An admirer and correspondent of John Stuart Mill, Holden had always believed that the council should be elective, and while serving in the select committee on the Legislative Council bill he drafted a measure which embodied the Hare system of proportional representation. The attorney-general disagreed with the new bill so Holden piloted it through the council. Though it was lost in the assembly, he received international recognition for his advocacy of proportional representation. A free trader, he urged law reform and supported the abolition of state aid to religion. He promoted the introduction of the Torrens [q.v.] title system. After the 1862 Real Property Act set up the Land Titles Office, he resigned from the council and gave up his lucrative practice to become chief examiner of titles on 1 January 1863; when his salary of £1200 a year was reduced in December he threatened to resign.

At the height of his influence in the 1860s, Holden was president of the Sydney Mechanics' School of Arts, a trustee of the New South Wales Savings Bank, a director of the Liverpool and London Fire and Life Insurance Co. and in 1864-65 chairman of the National Schools Board. In 1866 he was attacked by David Buchanan [q.v.] for writing to the press on the education bill while holding public office, but the government declined to interfere. Only one of Holden's three pamphlets, *The Moral and Intellectual Culture of the People* (Sydney, 1853), was widely read but all were significant expressions of colonial liberalism. Modest in business, cautious in politics and pragmatic in argument and public service he refused to lead popular movements and on principle avoided the clash of classes and of parties. Aged 67 he died at Darlinghurst on 16 April 1874 and was buried in the Canterbury cemetery. He was survived by his wife Eliza Punette Clunes, née Mackenzie, and by five sons and three daughters. His goods were valued at £10,000.

A. Halloran, 'Some early legal celebrities', *JRAHS*, 12 (1926-27); *SMH*, 6, 12, 13 Dec 1861, 4, 18 Sept, 1 Oct 1862, 18 Apr 1874; *Empire*, 17 Apr 1874; *Town and Country J*, 16 May 1874; Parkes letters (ML); Deas Thomson papers (ML).   T. H. IRVING

HOLDSWORTH, PHILIP JOSEPH (1851-1902), public servant and writer, was born on 12 January 1851 at Sydney, the only son of Philip Risby Holdsworth, a respected boatbuilder, and his wife Kate, née Bevan. His father was prominent in temperance and early protectionist movements in Sydney. Philip Joseph was educated at Fort Street High School. In 1870 he told N. D. Stenhouse [q.v.] that he was temporarily unemployed. On 8 March 1871 he became a clerk in the revenue branch of the Treasury and in May 1878 assistant receiver. He was reputed to be a 'good financial man'. On 10 August 1890 he became secretary under J. Ednie Brown [q.v.] in the Forestry Department, until its abolition in 1893 when, despite a personal appeal to Sir Henry Parkes [q.v.], he was retrenched on a small pension.

As early as 1869 Holdsworth was probably a sub-editor of the *Illustrated Sydney News* and became its editor in the 1880s. In 1888 he supervised the publication of a special centenary issue. When the paper changed hands he left and in the 1890s contributed to a number of Sydney journals such as the *Bulletin*, *Freeman's Journal* and *Athenaeum*. He was a founding member of the Athenaeum Club in the early 1880s. Slightly dandified in dress, he was generous to individuals and causes of which he approved. He was associated with the memorial committee for Kendall (d. 1882) [q.v.] with whom he had become friendly in the early 1870s.

Holdsworth's writing is of little permanent interest. He published only one book, *Station Hunting on the Warrego . . . and Other Poems* (Sydney, 1885). Most of the verse had been written when he was young and is conventional in both subject and style. One or two later pieces enjoyed some favour with his contemporaries: 'Quis Separabit' and 'My Queen of Dreams' were singled out for praise. In prose he attempted a brief history of Australia, a pamphlet on the Lost Ten Tribes of Israel and a number of pen-portraits of notable contemporaries. His most important work was probably his prefatory note to the 1886 edition of Kendall's poems. He was accepted as an amiable member of the literary community rather than a significant writer. He died suddenly on 19 January 1902 at his home in Ocean Street, Woollahra, and was buried in the Anglican section of the Rookwood cemetery.

He was survived by his wife, Charlotte Emily, née Atkins, whom he had married in Sydney in 1869, and by his only son.

SMH, 21 Jan 1902; Parkes letters (ML); newspaper cuttings and notes under P. J. Holdsworth (ML).   H. P. HESELTINE

HOLROYD, ARTHUR TODD (1806-1887), physician, explorer and jurist, was born on 1 December 1806 in London, the youngest child of Stephen Todd Holroyd, merchant, and his wife Elizabeth, née Lofthouse. Educated at private schools and Ripon Grammar School, Holroyd studied medicine in Winchester at 18, the Webb Street School of Anatomy, Southwark, the University of Edinburgh (M.D., 1830) and Christ's College, Cambridge (M.B., 1832). Prominent in medical associations, he had become a fellow of the Zoological Society of London in 1826 and of the Linnean Society in 1829. In 1830 he married Sophia Rachel Abbs of Durham. He practised as a physician in London but, dissatisfied with his prospects, entered Lincoln's Inn in 1835. He studied Italian in Rome and in Egypt explored above the second cataract, and became the first European to cross the Bayuda desert to Khartoum and the first Englishman to visit Kordofan. His disclosures of horrifying slave hunts led to their abolition by Mahommed Ali Pasha. Familiar with Arabic he travelled through Sinai, Palestine and Syria. In 1839 in London he read a paper on his Kordofan expedition and was elected a fellow of the Royal Geographical Society. In May 1841 he was called to the Bar at Lincoln's Inn and practised on the northern circuit. A director of the Commercial Bank of London, he was interested in the New Zealand banking system and in 1843 migrated there. In Wellington he practised as a barrister and solicitor, and moved to Sydney in 1844 after the Kororareka affair.

Holroyd was admitted to the New South Wales Bar on 31 October 1845 and built up a lucrative practice, sometimes acting as crown prosecutor. He represented Western Boroughs in the Legislative Council in 1851-56 and in the first Legislative Assembly in 1856-57 when he was chairman of committees. In 1861-64 he sat for Parramatta and in 1863 became secretary for public works under James Martin [q.v.]. Cleared by a select committee in April 1864 from the charge that he had abused his trust by selecting mineral lands at Illawarra, he resigned his portfolio in October after W. M. Arnold [q.v.] charged him with having obtained the appointment of Dr Hamilton to the commission of the peace 'for a pecuniary consideration', a charge which failed after investigation at the bar of the House.

In 1860 as acting chairman of the Quarter Sessions Holroyd roused public indignation by his leniency to a prisoner convicted for horse-whipping J. D. Lang [q.v.]. Holroyd maintained that if persons published offensive matter they must expect personal attacks or civil actions. In May 1866 he was appointed master in equity of the Supreme Court. In 1879 he acted as a Supreme Court judge for a month and became the first master in lunacy. In 1881 solicitors complained about his 'extraordinary conduct' but the minister of justice found his offence was 'more to be attributed to infirmity of temper than to any more serious misconduct'. He resigned both masterships and in 1885 published *Suakim and the Country of Soudan* for the information of the New South Wales contingent.

Holroyd had many interests. He was a director of the Australian Mutual Provident Society and the Ophir Gold Mining Co. and a member of the Chamber of Commerce. At his Merrylands estate, Sherwood Scrubs, he experimented with English fodder plants, cultivated an orangery, and manufactured agricultural drain-pipes and tiles at his Sherwood Drain and Tile Works (later Walker Benson Pty Ltd). In 1872 he was largely responsible for establishing the municipality of Prospect and Sherwood (Holroyd) and was its first mayor. With a bowling green of his own, he published a pamphlet on bowling and its rules in 1874 and was patron of the New South Wales Bowling Association. He was also a trustee of the Agricultural Society of New South Wales and the Sydney Grammar School, an original fellow of St Paul's College, University of Sydney, and a committee member of the Union Club. He had a notable collection of African and Aboriginal arms and curiosities. Holroyd was a prominent Freemason and in 1867-77 was district grand master of the English constitution.

Holroyd died at Sherwood Scrubs on 15 June 1887 and was buried in Rookwood cemetery. He was survived by his only child Emily Sophia, daughter of his first wife, and by his second wife Elizabeth, née Armstrong, whom he had married on 5 August 1868 in the Parramatta Registry Office. Emily wrote books on the Far East. His estate, valued at £13,000, was sequestrated in 1889. He left his library and £500 to St Paul's College and £200 to the Zoological Society of New South Wales.

H. S. Chapman, *The New-Zealand portfolio* (Lond, 1842); V&P (LC NSW), 1855, 1, 423, 1856-57, 2, 172, (LA NSW), 1863-64, 1, 1315, 1398, 4, 257, 1864, 1, 135, 1881, 2, 705; J. Jervis,

'The beginnings of settlement in the parish of St. John', *JRAHS*, 19 (1933-34); *Empire* (Syd), 22 Apr, 3 July 1856; Macarthur papers (ML); Insolvency file 1191 (NSWA).

H. T. E. HOLT

HOLROYD, SIR EDWARD DUNDAS (1828-1916), judge, was born on 25 January 1828 in Surrey, England, the second son of Edward Holroyd, a commissioner of the London Bankruptcy Court, and his wife Caroline, née Pugsley. In 1841 he entered Winchester College, where he twice won the Queen's medal for Latin and English essays, and in 1846 he went to Trinity College, Cambridge (B.A., 1851; M.A., 1854). He entered Gray's Inn in November 1851, was called to the Bar on 6 June 1855 and practised in London.

Encouraged by his friend, A. B. Malleson, a former London attorney who had practised in Victoria since 1857, Holroyd migrated and was admitted to the Victorian Bar on 27 July 1859 and to the Tasmanian Bar in 1867. As in London he supplemented his income by free-lance journalism but soon abandoned it as his law practice rapidly expanded. A sound equity lawyer, he also became expert in mining and commercial law. His ability was marked by offers of a seat on the Supreme Court bench in 1872 and 1873. He then declined but accepted elevation on 22 August 1881, two years after he had taken silk. He had been appointed to the royal commission inquiring into the constitution of the Supreme Court in 1880, and later joined in recommending adoption of the English Judicature Acts under which the systems of common law and equity were amalgamated. He helped to prepare Victoria's Judicature Act, passed in 1883 despite the strenuous opposition of the judges, Robert Molesworth and Hartley Williams [qq.v.].

Holroyd's austere manner, dry humour, learned appearance and zeal for detail seemed in sympathy with an equity judgeship. After the Judicature Act he sat chiefly at common law adapting himself to it most competently, particularly in criminal cases. Ever industrious, he was respected also for his fairness and, by the Bar, for his courtesy, though he could strike out warmly and was impatient of loose legal argument. He was no precisian in matters of form but, it was said, often savoured a legal nicety as an artist might delight in a fine picture. These habits delayed proceedings and some counsel claimed that his meticulous noting of evidence cramped their cross-examination style. Otherwise he was practical and authoritative and his judgments, models of prose, had a good record for withstanding appeals.

He became senior puisne judge and sometimes acting chief justice, and was knighted in 1903. Thereafter his growing deafness and slowness in court aroused public comment. He resigned on 9 May 1906 and was uniquely complimented on his eightieth birthday by the presentation of a bound address signed by the Victorian Bar.

He was an enthusiastic member of the Imperial Federation League and its president for many years. His speech at its inaugural meeting in the Melbourne Town Hall on 5 June 1885 attracted much notice, especially for its concept of federal inter-responsibility in politics and defence, and for his contention that colonial taxation or subsidy for imperial purposes deserved representation of those who paid. He was a member and sometime president of the Athenaeum and Savage Clubs.

In Melbourne on 19 April 1862 Holroyd had married Anna Maria Hoyles, daughter of Henry Compton, of Totnes, Devon; they had two sons and three daughters. Their household was run somewhat strictly, due partly to Holroyd's dislike of frivolity, though he was otherwise sociable and permitted himself to be 'unconventional in manner and appearance' at home. He was fond of sport and enjoyed good health almost until he died on 5 January 1916 at his home, Fernacres, Alma Road, St Kilda.

J. L. Forde, *The story of the Bar of Victoria* (Melb, 1913); P. A. Jacobs, *Judges of yesterday* (Melb, 1924); P. A. Jacobs, *A lawyer tells* (Melb, 1949); *Leader* (Melb), 13 June 1885; *Argus*, 6 Apr 1906, 6 Jan 1916.

R. G. DeB. Griffith

HOLT, JOSEPH THOMAS (1851-1942), producer, theatre entrepreneur and actor best known as BLAND, was born on 24 March 1851 at Norwich, England, son of Joseph Frederick Holt and his first wife Marie, née Brown. His father, actor-manager in the Norwich Theatre, went to Melbourne with his wife in September 1854 at the suggestion of George Coppin [q.v.]. From Geelong he went to Hobart Town and Launceston and in September 1855 opened at the Prince of Wales Theatre in Sydney. Before leaving Australia in April 1857 he had played in most of the goldfields centres of Victoria. In 1858 he returned to Melbourne with his family, including Bland, in the *Josephine*. A successful tragedian, Holt played Othello to G. V. Brooke's [q.v.] Iago; in 1862 as joint lessee of the Theatre Royal, Melbourne, he engaged such players as Brooke, Anna Bishop, Joseph Jefferson [q.v.] and others. When the lease ran out he went to Dunedin for about two years before returning to England. In September 1878 he became joint lessee of the Duke's Theatre, Holborn. He died in London in October 1903.

Bland Holt was educated at the Church of England Grammar School, Brighton, Victoria, and at the Otago Boys' High School, Dunedin. At 6 he had made his first stage appearance at the Royal Theatre, Sunderland. At 14 he became a professional actor and for the next nine years toured the United States and England. He returned to Sydney in 1876 with the rights, bought from his father, for Paul Merritt's play 'The New Babylon'. It opened at the Victoria Theatre, Sydney, with Myra Kemble [q.v.] as leading lady, and began Bland's career as one of Australia's foremost actor-managers. His first repertoire of 'twenty-four new and original dramas' borrowed from Drury Lane included *The Bells of Haslemere*, *A Million of Money*, *The White Heather*, *The Fatal Card*, *The Prodigal's Daughter* and *The Great Millionaire*. Dubbed the 'King of Melodrama', he became famous for his spectacular effects: in one play he used horses, hounds and a stag; in another, horses galloped along Little Bourke Street to make their last run on the stage of the Theatre Royal; and in others he introduced balloon ascents, trained pigeons, a human bridge, diving scenes and the first motor car used on stage. Holt played in many of his own productions as a fine comedian, a capable dramatic actor and a superb pantomime clown. Many of the plays he produced he revised substantially and despite highly-qualified assistants he managed almost every detail of his productions himself. He leased the Lyceum Theatre in Sydney and the Theatre Royal in Melbourne and his plays had record runs. His first wife, known on the stage as Lena Edwin, died in June 1883. In 1887 he married Florence, daughter of William Curling Anderson. She appeared with him in many of his plays.

Holt later introduced an Australian flavour into some productions: *The Breaking of the Drought* in 1907 was described as 'true in every detail to Australian scenes, types and characters'; he even induced Henry Lawson to write a play for him but it was unplayable. He retired in 1909 after touring the Continent, North America and New Zealand with his wife and his private secretary Lucy, daughter of George Coppin. Until his death on 28 June 1942 he lived at Mere House in East Melbourne, Sunning Hill in Kew and The Anchorage, Sorrento. Quiet and hard-working, Holt maintained a harmonious theatrical company; among the actors he encouraged were John Cosgrove, Dorothy Brunton, Madge Titheradge, Vera Pearce and Marie Lohr. He also introduced a high standard of stagecraft into Australian theatre. His wife survived him; they had no children.

A. Bagot, *Coppin the great* (Melb, 1965); H. Porter, *Stars of Australian stage and screen* (Adel, 1965); *Australasian*, 2 June 1883, 11 Dec 1909; *Bulletin*, 18 May 1901; *Age*, 30 June 1942; *Argus*, 30 June 1942; Clarence Holt diary (ML).   DENNIS SHOESMITH

HOLT, THOMAS (1811-1888), wool merchant, financier and politician, was born on 14 November 1811 at Horbury, Yorkshire, England, son of Thomas Holt, wool merchant, and his wife Elizabeth, née Ellis. Educated at schools in Pontefract and Wakefield, he entered his father's business in Leeds at 14, and in 1822-32 represented the firm in Europe. In 1835 he became a partner when a branch was opened in Berlin. There on 20 March 1841 Holt married Sophie, daughter of Frederich Eulert.

After reading J. D. Lang's [q.v.] *Historical and Statistical Account of New South Wales* he decided to migrate and with his wife arrived on 16 November 1842 at Sydney in the *Helvellyn*. He succeeded as a wool-buyer, was made a magistrate and as one of Sydney's most prominent financiers was a foundation director and member of several gold-mining, insurance and railway companies. In 1850 he became a director of the Sydney Tramway and Railway Co. after he had successfully proposed that Charles Cowper [q.v.] resign as chairman and remain manager. In 1855 Holt retired from active business though he retained most of his directorships into the 1860s and in the 1870s was a director of the City Bank. In 1851-80, either alone or with partners, he acquired interests in numerous New South Wales and Queensland pastoral properties totalling about three million acres.

Holt twice failed to enter the Legislative Council, but after responsible government in 1856 won Stanley Boroughs in the first Legislative Assembly, becoming colonial treasurer under S. A. Donaldson [q.v.]. A free trader and opposed to a nominated Upper House, he paid much attention to financial subjects although some of his ideas were 'considered somewhat unsound'. Interested in education, he published two speeches on the subject in December. Addicted to writing to newspapers, Holt inexorably sought improvement in many public issues including immigration, swamp drainage and refrigeration of food. In 1861-64 he represented Newtown in the assembly. In 1865 D. C. Dalgleish [q.v.] accused him of personation at the Glebe. Holt was committed by the magistrate, D. C. F. Scott, but

a bill was not filed and a later summons against him was dismissed. Holt failed in a court action against Scott and in an attempt to have him removed. He won £500 damages from Dalgleish, but declined to collect it.

Holt had sold some of his runs after the gold rush and in August 1861 bought an estate extending from Botany Bay to Port Hacking and including Cook's [q.v.] landing place where he erected an obelisk in the centenary year. He also tried to raise sheep on pastures sown with imported grass and then cattle, scientific oyster-farming, timbergetting and coal-mining, each without success. He campaigned for the damming of George's River to supply Sydney with water but the government rejected his scheme.

Holt built a stone 'Victorian Gothic' mansion, The Warren, overlooking Cook's River and stocked its grounds with rabbits for sport, alpacas and other exotics. He lavishly entertained his friends and visitors including royalty at picnics and shoots. In 1866-68 he visited Europe and collected works for his large art gallery. Generous to charities, Holt lost 'a small fortune' trying to keep the *Empire* afloat and liberally assisted Frank Fowler's [q.v.] *Month* and other improving magazines.

As a member of the Legislative Council in 1868-83 Holt introduced three bills and in 1878 condemned 'the cruelty and degradation of compelling accused persons to stand in the dock during their trial'; the speech was published as *Judicial Treatment of the Accused*. In 1873-76 he served on the Council of Education, and was a commissioner for exhibitions at Philadelphia in 1876, Paris in 1878 and Amsterdam in 1883. He was a founder of the Royal Prince Alfred Hospital and a director in 1873-83. He joined the Commission of Fisheries in 1880, was a vice-president of the Agricultural Society of New South Wales and a member of the Royal Society of New South Wales. A memorial village at Sutherland for elderly citizens was named in his honour. An active and charitable Congregationalist, he gave at half its value in 1864 his residence, Camden Villa, for the establishment of Camden College, of which he became a council member and trustee.

In 1881 Holt went to Europe and devoted himself to the poor of London and the Salvation Army, and helped the work of Rev. A. Mearns and Dr Barnardo. In 1888 he published *Christianity, or the Poor Man's Friend*. He died at his home, Halcot, Bexley, Kent, on 5 September, survived by his wife, three sons and three daughters. His estate was valued at nearly £330,000.

F. Cridland, *Story of Port Hacking, Cronulla and Sutherland shire* (Syd, 1924); P. Geeves and

J. Jervis, *Rockdale: its beginning and development* (Syd, 1962); V&P (LC NSW), 1854, 2, 32, 1855, 2, 576, (LA NSW), 1869, 2, 502, 1878-79, 7, 53; SMH, 9, 11 Jan 1850, 29 Apr 1864, 2 Mar 1865, 21 Apr 1866, 9 Apr 1871, 19 Dec 1877, 15 Sept 1888; *Empire* (Syd), 21 Apr 1856; *Illustrated Sydney News*, 16 May 1865; *Town and Country J*, 17 Oct 1874, 15 Sept 1888; *Bulletin*, 12 Feb 1881; Parkes letters (ML); CO 201/542, 545.   PHILIP GEEVES

HOLTERMANN, BERNHARDT OTTO (1838-1885), gold miner, merchant, sponsor of photography for the encouragement of immigration and member of parliament, was born on 29 April 1838 in Hamburg, son of John Henry Holtermann and his wife Anna, née Nachtigall. Not wishing to spend three years in military service, he left Germany in 1858, sailed from Liverpool in the *Salem*, reached Melbourne on 7 August and went on to Sydney in the *City of Sydney*, arriving on 12 August. There he hoped to meet his brother Herman but found that he had gone to the goldfields. Unsuccessful in gaining any job on land through his lack of English, Holtermann sailed on 13 September as a steward in the schooner *Rebecca* for the Pacific Islands and returned to Sydney on 20 January 1859. He became a waiter at the Hamburg Hotel where a successful miner almost induced him to go to Adelong. After a few months he met the Polish miner, Ludwig Hugo Louis Beyers, and went with him to the Tambaroora (Hill End) area. In 1861 they began prospecting on Hawkins Hill but for five years had little success; in order to hold the claim, Holtermann was forced to undertake a variety of occupations. Once he nearly lost his life through a premature explosion of blasting powder. By 1868 he was licensee of the All Nations Hotel and on 22 February at Bathurst he married Harriett Emmett; Beyers married her sister Mary on the same day.

In 1871 some rich veins were found but they petered out, but next year one of the eight owners sold his share to M. J. Hammond [q.v.] who without authority sealed off the shaft and began a new drive to the west. Rich new veins were immediately encountered, but Hammond had sold out at a substantial profit before 19-20 October when the night shift uncovered the world's largest specimen of reef gold, 630 lbs. Later it was brought to the surface almost intact. Holtermann had warned against rash investment in a letter to the *Sydney Morning Herald*, 20 November 1871. When copies of the paper reached Hill End, he was burnt in effigy but later returned to public favour and became a founding member of the first Hill End Borough Council. In 1874 on the

heights of St Leonards he completed a palatial house with a tower embodying a stained-glass window depicting him standing beside the 'nugget'.

At Hill End Holtermann had met the travelling photographer, Beaufoy Merlin, and his young assistant, Charles Bayliss, and watched them at work. He welcomed Merlin's idea that a great series of 10 ins. by 12 ins. photographs should be made of the settled areas of New South Wales and Victoria and sent abroad to advertise the colonies and encourage migrants. The major part of New South Wales was completed when Merlin died in September 1873, but Bayliss continued with even more grandiose plans. After great difficulties he succeeded in taking the view of Sydney from the tower of Holtermann's house on two single negatives, each over 5 ft. by 3 ft.; these were the largest photographs ever taken by the wet-plate or collodion process at a time when the techniques of enlarging had not been developed. Some of these photographs were made available to the government for international exhibitions at Philadelphia in 1876 and Paris in 1878 where they won medal awards. Another set was mounted on a roll of cloth and taken by Holtermann to America and the Continent where they were exhibited in pleasure gardens and at special gatherings. He returned from abroad with a number of agencies which he vigorously promoted. He had always been interested in medicine and his 'Life Preserving Drops', compounded from the formula of a German doctor, were very popular.

After two earlier defeats, Holtermann was in 1882 elected as a member for St Leonards, proclaiming himself 'a man of indomitable energy and perseverance', 'the staunch friend of the working man' and 'an earnest supporter of every public movement having for its object the advancement of your electorate'. He attended parliament regularly until 1885, being specially interested in immigration and in the progress of North Sydney, including the building of a 'North Shore Bridge' to which he was willing to contribute £5000. He died on his forty-seventh birthday and was buried in St Thomas's cemetery, survived by his wife and by three sons and two daughters. He left an estate of £54,000 mostly in local land investments. He is chiefly remembered today by the vast collection of photographic plates that he sponsored and his family preserved, and those taken by Merlin and Bayliss at Hill End and Gulgong, which made possible the reconstruction of these settlements in their hey-days.

E. Digby (ed), *Australian men of mark*, 1 (Syd, 1889); K. Burke, *Gold and Silver* (Melb,

1971); *Town and Country J*, 2 Nov 1872, 22 Apr 1876; *Bulletin*, 13 Mar, 22 May 1880; *A'sian Photo Review*, May 1953; Holtermann photographic collection (ML).

KEAST BURKE

HOLYMAN, WILLIAM (1833-1919), master mariner and shipowner, was born on 17 December 1833 at Barton upon Humber, Lincolnshire, England. His parents took him to Hull where his training for maritime service commenced at Trinity House School. His father was lost at sea in 1839. In 1847 Holyman began his apprenticeship on a coastal ship trading out of Hull. He completed his articles in 1854 and then joined the barque *Elizabeth Ratcliffe*, sailing to Launceston where she berthed on 12 June. Holyman left his ship to join the schooner *Victory*, sailing between Tasmanian and Victorian ports. In 1855 he transferred to the coastal trader *Amelia Francis* (Captain William Chapman). On 15 December Holyman and Chapman married daughters of James Sayer at Devonport, Holyman to Mary Ann; they had three sons and a daughter.

Holyman settled at Devonport and worked on barges owned by his father-in-law. In 1861 he returned to active command in the ketch *Cousins*. Ten years of profitable trading in her on the north coast of Tasmania encouraged him to buy the paddle-steamer *Annie* in 1871. This venture was not a success and she was sold in 1873, discouraging Holyman from further use of steamships for many years. All his sons qualified as master mariners and in turn commanded ships which were added to the fleet of the family company, William Holyman & Sons. In 1882 the company registered their ships as the White Star Line. In 1883 Holyman's only daughter Susannah married Harry Wood, a shipbuilder at Devonport. This added an important service to the Holyman company, which later bought several ships for enlargement and renovation at Wood's shipyard.

Holyman retired from the sea in 1886 and visited England with his wife. He then gave his full attention to management of the company, to his interest in music, reading biblical history and community affairs. He was an active founder of the district library and Chamber of Commerce and was elected to the town board, later becoming its chairman. He was a prominent Freemason and Oddfellow and a member of the Protestant Alliance Federation. After his wife died in 1900, the management of the company was again revised with William, the second son, assuming the management of the company from his father and transferring its head office to Launceston. The company continued to expand its fleet and its operations. In 1911 they bought automobiles to carry mail from Launceston to Beauty Point, the first regular mail service by motor car in Tasmania; pastoral estates of 27,000 acres were also developed on the islands of Bass Strait. Later the company inaugurated a commercial airline.

Holyman senior died at his home in East Devonport on 18 August 1919, survived by three sons, a daughter, thirty-one grandchildren and eighteen great-grandchildren. His son William died aged 63 at Launceston on 29 September 1921, leaving an estate of £57,155 to his wife Honora, four sons and five daughters.

Cyclopedia of Tasmania, 2 (Hob, 1900); C. Ramsay, *With the pioneers* (Hob, 1957); *Tasmanian year book* (Hob, 1968), p. 570; *Examiner* (Launceston), 19 Aug 1919, 30 Sept 1921.
W. F. ELLIS

HOOKER, SIR JOSEPH DALTON (1817-1911), botanist and explorer, was born on 30 June 1817 at Halesworth, Suffolk, England, second son of the distinguished botanist, Sir William Jackson Hooker (1785-1865), and his wife Maria Sarah, eldest daughter of Dawson Turner, banker and naturalist of Norwich. His father, later director of the Royal Botanic Gardens, Kew, was, from 1820 to 1841 Regius professor of botany in the University of Glasgow and Joseph was educated at Glasgow Grammar School. At 15 he began to attend classes at the University of Glasgow, at first in classics and mathematics and later in medicine (M.D., 1839). He already had a wide knowledge of botany based on work in his father's herbarium and on extensive plant-collecting in the British Isles. His degree enabled him to join the Naval Medical Service and to accompany a scientific expedition to the Antarctic. The expedition, commanded by James Clark Ross, sailed in 1839 in two ships, *Erebus* and *Terror*: Hooker was assistant surgeon and naturalist in the former. They visited Ascension, St Helena, the Cape, Kerguelen, Van Diemen's Land, New Zealand, Tierra del Fuego and the Falkland Islands, and sailed along a vast extent of the coast of Antarctica. Van Diemen's Land was visited twice, during August-October 1840 and March-May 1841, and there was a brief stay at Port Jackson. The expedition returned to England in 1843.

The results of Hooker's botanical explorations of these lands were published under the general title *The Botany of the Antarctic Voyage*, in three large and important volumes: *Flora Antarctica* (1844-47), *Flora*

Novae-Zelandiae (1853-55) and *Flora Tasmaniae* (1855-60). Local naturalists helped by sending large collections of plants to Kew and the valuable aid of R. C. Gunn and William Archer [qq.v.] from Tasmania was acknowledged in the dedication of the third volume. These works, splendidly illustrated by the botanical artist, Walter Hood Fitch, are distinguished by Hooker's insight into morphological problems and by the importance of his theories developed in the introductions. The books, reprinted in 1963, remain indispensable for the study of plants of these southern lands; they are also especially significant because they belong to a critical period in the history of biology. In 1858 the assumption that species of plants and animals were unchanging was challenged by Alfred Russel Wallace and Charles Darwin [q.v.]; their historic paper was presented to the Linnean Society of London jointly by Hooker and the geologist Charles Lyell. It was followed on 24 November 1859 by the publication of Darwin's *Origin of Species by Means of Natural Selection*. Darwin's views on evolution had long been known to Hooker: their friendship dated from 1839. But while Hooker in *Flora Novae-Zelandiae* notes the problems raised by the variability of plants and by the facts of plant geography, for practical reasons he accepts the permanency of species. In the introductory essay to *Flora Tasmaniae* he supports the theory of evolution as brought about by variation and natural selection. This essay, the first published statement in support of Darwin's theory, is based on Hooker's independent studies of plants and particularly on their geographical distribution.

Hooker was a pioneer plant geographer. After returning from the Antarctic and working on fossil plants as a member of the Geological Survey of Great Britain, he sought an opportunity to study the vegetation of mountains in the tropics. In 1847, helped by a small grant from the Treasury, he sailed for India. In 1848-49, from headquarters at Darjeeling in the north-eastern Himalayas, he explored Sikkim and eastern Nepal, reaching the Tibetan passes. Hooker's versatility and keen observation in many fields is shown in his *Himalayan Journals*, first published in 1854: this is an outstanding travel book appealing to scientists in many fields. Of his extensive collections of plants the rhododendrons were especially notable and many species were for the first time introduced into cultivation in England. He also carried out a detailed topographical survey of the area and this formed the basis for subsequent official maps.

Hooker returned to England in 1851. In 1855 he was appointed assistant director of the Royal Botanic Gardens, Kew, and in 1865 succeeded his father as director. He combined administration with research, wrote and edited many scientific papers, prepared important colonial floras, and collaborated with George Bentham [q.v.] in producing the classic *Genera Plantarum* (1862-83). A further aspect of the work at Kew was the distribution of plants grown in its nurseries; one result was that seeds of the rubber tree, *Hevea brasiliensis*, were obtained from Brazil, young plants raised, and sent to Ceylon and Malaya, thus founding the rubber industry in Asia. Hooker also engaged in botanical exploration in Lebanon in 1860, Morocco and the Atlas Mountains in 1871 and North America in 1877.

Hooker's outstanding achievements were recognized by many awards including C.B., 1869; K.C.S.I., 1878; K.G.S.I., 1897; and O.M., 1907. He was elected a fellow of the Linnean Society in 1842 and of the Royal Society in 1847 and had the high distinction of being president of the Royal Society from 1873 to 1878. He also received degrees and honours from many British universities and from learned societies in Britain and the Continent. In 1885 he retired and made his home at Windlesham, near Sunningdale, Berkshire, where he continued to work on the Indian flora and on the genus *Impatiens* (Balsam). He died at his home on 10 December 1911 and was buried in the churchyard of St Anne's Anglican Church at Kew Green.

In 1851 Hooker married Frances Harriet, daughter of Rev. John Stevens Henslow, rector of Hitcham and professor of botany in the University of Cambridge; they had four sons and three daughters. After the death of his wife in 1874 Hooker married, in 1876, Hyacinth, daughter of Rev. William Samuel Symonds and widow of Sir William Jardine: they had two sons.

L. Huxley, *Life and letters of Sir Joseph Dalton Hooker* (Lond, 1918); W. B. Turrill, *Pioneer plant geography. The phytogeographical researches of Sir Joseph Dalton Hooker* (The Hague, 1953); W. B. Turrill, *Joseph Dalton Hooker. Botanist, explorer and administrator* (Lond, 1963); M. Allan, *The Hookers of Kew, 1785-1911* (Lond, 1967).

WINIFRED M. CURTIS

HOOLEY, EDWARD TIMOTHY (1842-1903), explorer, pastoralist and writer, was born on 3 October 1842 at sea in the *Bolivar*, son of Daniel Hooley and his wife Ellen, née Barry. The family went to Van Diemen's Land where the father was overseer on a pastoral property for three years before moving to a farm near Coleraine,

Victoria. Educated at a school in Portland, Hooley gained much practical knowledge of agriculture and bushcraft working with his father. He became a sheep and cattle dealer but in 1864 joined the Camden Harbour Pastoral Association, formed in Melbourne for acquiring leases in north-west Australia. With sheep, cattle and horses Hooley sailed in the chartered schooner *Stag*. The arrival at Camden Harbour was disastrous: the country was parched and the sheep died from poisonous plants. Hooley turned to exploration and made a short trip to the head of the Harding and Sherlock Rivers. He then joined T. C. Murray, crossed the Fortescue River and with difficulty forced a passage through the rugged Hamersley Range, naming both Mount Murray and Mount Anderson. Impressed by the pastoral quality of the country, the two men went to Perth to acquire more sheep. Hooley reported his findings to the surveyor-general, J. S. Roe [q.v.], and for his services was granted a lease of 100,000 acres by the government. He soon bought 2000 sheep and shipped them to Champion Bay, hoping to open a stock route to the north. Leaving the Geraldine mine in May 1866, he followed F. T. Gregory's [q.v.] track of 1858 with seven men, including two Aboriginal prisoners and two teams of horses, and for the first week, Dr Bompas, who accompanied them as naturalist. The party proceeded along the Murchison to the Gascoyne, then struck north past the Lyons and Henry Rivers. Hooley named Gregory's Spring and Mount Roe and arrived at Nickol Bay after a journey of three months and a loss of only eight sheep. Appreciative settlers presented him with a fine gold watch.

Interested in new developments, Hooley was attracted to the pearling industry. In 1868 he rode 1300 miles from Point Walcott to Albany on horseback to join a ship for Melbourne. In May 1869 in his schooner *Liberty*, 54 tons, he arrived at Fremantle accompanied by his wife Jane, née Maze, whom he had married on 4 December 1861 at the Catholic Church in Portland, and by their daughter. He intended to use the schooner for coastal trading and pearl fishing but was faced with labour problems, drought, low wool prices and hostile Aboriginals on his isolated property. He soon accepted an offer to manage a stock company at Guildford and then, with William New as partner, established a sheep station at Williams, south of Perth. Although it was reasonably successful Hooley yearned for the north and in 1882 overlanded to the Ashburton. On the way he lost almost half of his 6500 sheep and cattle but settled at Mount Hubert and took up

an additional 400,000 acres at Mount Mortimer and a cattle run near the Henry River.

Five years later in Perth Hooley became manager of J. H. Monger's [q.v.] mercantile company; when it was absorbed by Dalgety's [q.v.] he became joint manager and later managing director until ill health forced his retirement in 1900. Appointed to the Legislative Council in December 1891, he ceased to be a member when it became wholly representative, but represented Murchison in 1894-97 and De Grey in 1897-1900 in the Legislative Assembly. In 1880 he had served on a commission to investigate the pearl-shell fishing grounds, and was appointed to the board of advice for administrating the Scab Act of 1879. Hooley was a justice of the peace, director of several companies and member of the committee advising the government on Western Australian representation at the Melbourne Exhibition in January 1888. A keen sportsman, he was often handicapper at race-meetings and served for a term as chairman of the Turf Club. His publications include the novel *Tarragal, or Bush Life in Australia* (London, 1897) and numerous articles in local papers, under the pseudonym 'Bucolic'. After retirement he and his wife went to Switzerland where he died at Vevey on 3 August 1903. He was survived by his wife, twin sons and five daughters. In December 1964 a plaque was erected at The Elms in William Street, Perth, to commemorate his contribution to Western Australia.

F. W. Gunning, *Lure of the north* (Perth, 1952); R.E.C., 'Some early Dalgety personalities', *Pastoralist and Grazier*, Apr 1960; *Inquirer*, 1 Mar, 29 Apr, 6 May 1868; *Perth Gazette*, 17 Apr, 1 May 1868; *Herald* (Fremantle), 13 Mar 1869; *West Australian*, 31 Oct 1882, 12 Aug 1884, 7 Mar 1885, 22 Mar, 22 May 1886, 19 Aug 1887, 1 July 1890, 5 Aug 1903, 18 June 1949, 14 June 1968; *WA Bulletin*, 28 July 1888; *Dalgety's Review*, WA, 25 Aug 1949; *Northern Times* (Carnarvon), 21 Jan 1965; J. B. Downes, The Western Australian pearling industries (thesis, Teachers College, 1941, Battye Lib, Perth); J. Crawford, The story of the Williams district (Battye Lib, Perth); Journal of expedition with stock, Perth-Point Walcott (Battye Lib, Perth).

WENDY BIRMAN

HOPE, LOUIS (1817-1894), grazier, sugar planter and miller, was born on 29 October 1817, the seventh son of John Hope, fourth earl of Hopetoun, and his second wife Louisa Dorothea, née Wedderburn. He became a captain in the Coldstream Guards and in 1843 went to New South Wales, moving north to Moreton Bay in 1848. In

1853 at Ormiston he took up land surveyed by J. C. Burnett [q.v.] and with Robert Ramsay [q.v.] as partner bought Kilcoy station which became entirely his in 1863. He served in the Queensland Legislative Council in 1862-82.

At Ormiston and Kilcoy Hope lived as a landed aristocrat, building on each station a comfortable colonial house, though with every precaution against marauding Aboriginals. Reputedly he was once invited to attend Governor Bowen, then visiting Cleveland, but refused, declaring that a mere knight should attend on him as the son of an earl. However, at Ormiston he became a major figure in establishing the colony's sugar industry. Some twenty acres were put under sugar cultivation with Kanaka labour from 1865 onwards. He had a mill built and in 1864 produced three tons of sugar and fifteen cwt of molasses. He supplied plants for the several experiments of John Buhôt [q.v.] and cuttings for plantations in the Oxley district. He also advised another sugar pioneer C. B. Whish [q.v.]. In August 1865 the Queensland parliament refused his petition for a grant of at least 2000 acres, but in 1867 he was given the right to take up 2560 acres. Of these 1800 were taken up near the mouth of the Coomera River (Hope Island) and 760 acres at Kilcoy.

As early as 1862 suggestions had been made that Whish should buy the Ormiston property but the price was too high. In 1870 Hope negotiated with Pruche Aubry, a French sugar planter from the island of Bourbon, but the price of £20,000 was still too high. However, Aubry was installed as manager and sublet thirty acres to his son-in-law, Victor Noaques. Hope retained the mill and, after a dispute over the milling of Noaques's cane, a court awarded £1207 damages against Hope in May 1874. Swearing he would never again crush a stick of cane, Hope dismantled the mill and sold it in 1875, some of the machinery going to J. P. Bell [q.v.] at Jimbour. Hope retained his Kilcoy lands. In 1882 he sold the Coomera property and returned to England where he lived at the Knowle, Hazlewood, Derbyshire. He died on 15 August 1894 at Geneva, Switzerland.

On 12 October 1859 he had married Susan Frances Sophia, daughter of W. J. Dumaresq [q.v.]. He was survived by his wife (d. 4 December 1901), three sons and five daughters. When St John's Anglican Cathedral in Brisbane was opened in 1910 the family donated a grey granite pulpit as a memorial to their parents. Ormiston House is now owned by Carmelite Sisters and on the front lawn is a memorial to Hope, erected by the sugar interests in Queensland.

C. T. Wood, *Sugar country* (Brisb, 1965); F. W. S. Cumbrae-Stewart, 'Notes on registers etc. in St. John's Cathedral', *JRHSQ*, 1 (1914-19); Whish diaries (Oxley Lib, Brisb).

A. A. MORRISON

HOPE, ROBERT CULBERTSON (1812-1878), medical practitioner and pastoralist, was born on 12 May 1812 at Morebattle, near Kelso, Roxburghshire, Scotland, son of Robert Hope, landowner, and his wife Joan, née Culbertson. He studied medicine, surgery and midwifery and won a prize in surgery at the University of Edinburgh (M.D., 1834). He then worked as an assistant to John Douglas at Hawick in Roxburghshire. On 18 April 1838 he sailed from Leith as surgeon in the *Lady Kennaway* and arrived in Sydney on 12 August. He practised medicine in Campbelltown for eight years. On 12 August 1846 he married Catherine Elizabeth, eldest daughter of Rev. Thomas Hassall and granddaughter of Rev. Samuel Marsden [qq.v.].

In 1847 Hope overlanded to the Port Phillip District where his brothers George and James held grazing leases. He practised medicine at Geelong until he and George took up land at Batesford, near Geelong, where Robert built Lynnburn and George built Darriwill. They built a flour-mill at Batesford on the Moorabool River and another on the Barwon River near Inverleigh. When gold was discovered at Ballarat and Bendigo the two brothers increased their fortunes by supplying meat, bread and vegetables to the diggers using the route from Geelong to the goldfields. They were early viticulturists in the Geelong district and their vineyard on the Moorabool River thrived until phylloxera ruined the vines in 1877. They had a joint interest in Darriwill, Barwonleigh and Lake Wallace station near Edenhope.

In 1856 Robert was elected to the Legislative Council as a member for South Western Province. To assist him in his political work he bought Summerlea in St Kilda. In the council he quickly won repute for his conservatism and his severe judgments on the behaviour of his fellow members. He took a stand against every attempt to reduce the privileged position of men of property in elections to both the assembly and the council. He also defended the pastoral tenants of crown lands against free selectors. In 1860 he was chairman of the Board of Agriculture. He retained his council seat until 1864 and represented South-Western Province from 1867 until failing health forced him to resign in 1874. He had been chairman of committees in 1864 and 1870-74. He was a joint founder of the Mechanics'

Institute at Batesford, a justice of the peace, president of the Geelong and Western District Agricultural and Horticultural Society and a leading Presbyterian.

Hope died at Hawthorn on 24 June 1878. Of his nine sons and two daughters, Robert managed a cattle station in Queensland for his father before buying Birrark station near Condobolin; Thomas Culbertson practised medicine in Geelong; Charles became assistant manager of Goldsbrough Mort [qq.v.] & Co. and John was a government surveyor in East Gippsland.

A. Henderson (ed), *Australian families*, 1 (Melb, 1941); Hassall papers (ML); Hope papers (held by author); MS cat under Hope (ML).

MANNING CLARK

HOPKINS, FRANCIS RAWDON CHESNEY (1849-1916), grazier and writer, was born at Colaba, Bombay, India, the eldest son of Francis William Hopkins, naval officer, and his wife Margaret, née McNeil. He was educated in England and studied for the Indian Civil Service but at 16 migrated to Victoria. He worked for his uncle, John Wilson, at Woodlands on the Wimmera River in 1866-71, managed Toorangabby station on the Murray in 1871-75 and then assisted Sir Samuel Wilson [q.v.] on his scattered pastoral leases. In New South Wales Hopkins managed Perricoota from about 1878 and in 1885 with Alexander Wilson bought Errowanbang near Carcoar. He managed it until 1889 when, with Wilson and Charles Hebden (1851-1915), he acquired Coubil and Welbondongah in the Gwydir district. Hopkins soon became active on the Pastures Protection Board and in 1890 helped to found the Pastoralists' Union of New South Wales, serving on its executive for some years.

While managing stations Hopkins took to writing plays, although his success in this hobby was largely due to the encouragement of his friend, the actor-manager Alfred Dampier [q.v.]. In 1876-82 Dampier produced five plays by Hopkins: *Good For Evil* (1876), *All For Gold* (1877), *Only a Fool* (1880), *£ S D* (1882) and *Russia As It Is* (1882). None of these plays had an Australian setting, and all were derived or adapted from European works; although his writing had some literary pretensions, his plays were unashamedly melodramatic. The most popular, *Good For Evil*, was published as *Clay and Porcelain: A Drama of the Present Day* (Melbourne, 1875); it was produced by Dampier in London in 1881 though with no apparent success.

Hopkins's publications other than drama included the *Australian Ladies' Annual* (Melbourne, 1878), with contributions from J. C. Couvreur (Tasma), Ada Cambridge [qq.v.] and others, and *Confessions of a Cynic: Social, Moral and Philosophical* (Echuca, 1882). Later he published collections of his short stories as *Birds of Passage and Other Stories of our Old Country* (1908) and *The Opium Runners* (1909). They reveal no great talent for this medium and although the settings are often Australian rural, titles such as 'Love Is Blind' and 'His Great Mistake' indicate some of the themes. Others are of interest in so far as they reflect political and social attitudes, for example 'Heathens of The Bush' in *Birds of Passage* for its relevance to White Australia. In 1909 Hopkins returned to the dramatic form when he published anonymously *Reaping the Whirlwind*. He described this play, which was set in the future, as aiming to arouse Australians on the subject of defence: it portrayed the capitulation of Australia to an Asiatic invader. For some years Hopkins reviewed books for the *Australasian Pastoralists' Review*. At a time when the *Bulletin* school dominated the local literary scene, Hopkins's spasmodic writings represent a comment from that usually less articulate group, the squatters. He also dabbled in water colours and pen and ink drawings but his approach to the arts was that of the competent amateur.

On 8 January 1884 at Hawthorn, Victoria, Hopkins had married Sarah Jane Kennedy, daughter of a lands department official. Aged 68 he died on 20 July 1916 at Errowanbang after an accident in a mining shaft. He was buried at Carcoar with Anglican rites and was survived by his wife and their only son.

H. M. Humphreys (ed), *Men of the time in Australia: Victorian series*, 2nd ed (Melb, 1882); Websdale Shoosmith Ltd, *Souvenir of the dramatic works of F. R. C. Hopkins* (Syd, 1910); *SMH*, 22 Aug 1916; *Pastoral Review*, 16 Aug 1916.

JOHN RICKARD

HOPKINS, JOHN ROUT (1828-1897), pastoralist, was born on 18 August 1828 at Hobart Town, the second son of Henry Hopkins [q.v.] and his wife Sarah, née Rout. The family lived in England in 1840-42 and after their return to Van Diemen's Land John received a thorough grounding in sheepbreeding, spending some time at David Gibson's [q.v.] famous stud. In 1845 he was sent to manage Murdeduke, one of his father's Western District runs, and then became owner of Wormbete, also near Winchelsea. In 1850-55 Hopkins acquired freehold of 20,000 acres and bought the adjoining St Stephen's and River stations.

In 1854 and 1855 he occupied the Mount Hesse run. Hopkins greatly improved his land and developed a special Wormbete merino which he inbred successfully from then onwards, shearing up to 26,000 sheep a year.

Hopkins was on the Barrabool Shire Council for thirteen years and its first president, and on the Winchelsea Shire Council for thirty-two years and president in 1870-71, 1878-82 and 1884-88. He was a justice of the peace and took a great interest in Geelong's growth, fostering both religious and sporting activities. In 1850 with John Gray and Rev. Ben Cuzens he secured land at the corner of Ryrie and Gheringhap Streets for the use of the Independent Church. In later years Hopkins was a prominent Anglican layman and synod member. A keen oarsman who thought nothing of riding twenty-five miles to Geelong for training, Hopkins was president of the Corio Rowing Club. He was an enthusiastic sailor and for a time was commodore of the Royal Victorian Yacht Club. He was also president in 1884 of the Geelong Cricket and Football Clubs. In 1871 he became a provisional director of the newly-formed Geelong Meat Preserving Co. which collapsed in 1874.

Hopkins had a long and uneventful political career. In the Legislative Assembly he represented South Grant in 1864-67 and 1871-77 and Geelong in 1892-94. In parliament he was concerned mainly with the issues of local government. In 1880 he was vice-chairman of the Geelong Group of the Municipal Association and was elected mayor of Geelong in 1892.

Hopkins was married first, on 1 August 1850 to Eliza Ann (d. 1885), daughter of George Armytage [q.v.], by whom he had six sons and seven daughters; and second, to Mrs Susan Emily Rucker (d. 1890). Hopkins died on 20 December 1897 survived by his third wife Alice Roberta Purkiss, whom he had married in 1892. His estate was valued at £74,700.

A. Sutherland et al, *Victoria and its metropolis*, 2 (Melb, 1888); Pastoral Review Pty Ltd, *The pastoral homes of Australia*, 1 (Melb, 1910); A. Henderson (ed), *Early pioneer families of Victoria and Riverina* (Melb, 1936); W. R. Brownhill, *The history of Geelong and Corio Bay* (Melb, 1955); *Hobart Town Courier*, 13 Dec 1839, 1 Aug 1850; *Geelong Times*, 21 Dec 1897; *Pastoral Review*, 15 July 1909.

J. ANN HONE

HOPKINS, LIVINGSTON (YOURTEE) YORK (1846-1927), cartoonist best known as 'HOP', was born on 7 July 1846 at Bellefontaine, Ohio, United States of America, son of Daniel Hopkins (1800-1849), surveyor, and his wife Sarah, née Carter. He attended school in Bellefontaine, where he caricatured the teacher, and in Kalida and Toledo, Ohio. At 17 he left a clerkship to join the 130th Ohio Volunteer Regiment, which was reviewed in Washington by President Lincoln before it saw service near Petersburg, Virginia, in the summer of 1864. Hopkins, however, spent most of his time picketing the lines and relieving his boredom by drawing. Mustered out in September 1864, he took a job as a railroad messenger, worked on newspapers in Ohio and Illinois and in 1870 moved to New York. By then a freelance 'Designer on Wood', he contributed to newspapers and comic magazines, and illustrated books. In 1880 *A Comic History of the United States*, which he wrote and copiously illustrated, was published but a patriotic reading public was not amused. On 9 June 1875 at Toledo he had married Harriet Augusta Commager.

In 1882 Hopkins met W. H. Traill [q.v.] who so inspired him that by February 1883 Hopkins had arrived in Sydney with his wife, three children and a two-year contract with the *Bulletin*. Soon he was joined by 'Phil' May [q.v.], lured by Traill from England, and together they contributed much to the *Bulletin's* popularity and prosperity. Their skill, enhanced by improved methods of reproduction, attracted other artists to the magazine. Best known of 'Hop's' cartoons were the Sudan war and Federation series, and those that caricatured Parkes, Dibbs [qq.v.], Reid, Lyne, Wise and other public figures. In 1904 he published a selection of his work, *On the Hop*, but his output steadily declined until his virtual retirement in 1913, by which time he was a director of the *Bulletin*.

'Hop's' draftsmanship was inferior to May's and though his political satire was racy and irreverent, it lacked toughness; as the *Bulletin* put it, 'he used his gift for gaiety and mirth, searing or scathing none'. Yet Hopkins remained the most popular of the *Bulletin* cartoonists and, for its proprietors, perhaps the most useful. He diligently kept notebooks of ideas and captions, and constantly referred to the scrapbooks of his past work. His 19,000 drawings included social satire, jokes, *Bulletin* calendars and postcards, and illustrations for such publications as F. J. Donohue's *The History of Botany Bay* (1888). His interpretation of the politicians and the regular appearance of his symbolic figures and menagerie of allegorical animals did much to explain the gospel of economic and racial isolationism, Republican nationalism and cultural chauvinism that the *Bulletin* preached before Federation.

Tall, angular, urbane, a keen player of bowls and maker of violins, Hopkins was not always the puckish imp of his cartoons. Although he moved easily in the Athenaeum Club and Bohemian circles and ran an artists' camp with Julian Ashton at Balmoral, he was observant of propriety and in private sometimes authoritarian and moody; publicly he could be awesome, though not all agree with Norman Lindsay that he was an 'inflexible autocrat' and 'quite humourless'. Hopkins died at Mosman on 21 August 1927 and was cremated at Rookwood. Predeceased by his wife, he was survived by a son and four daughters. His estate was valued at over £44,000.

Portraits of 'Hop' by William Macleod, Ashton and W. T. Smedley are in the Art Gallery of New South Wales. He was an etcher and a painter as well as a cartoonist, and samples of his work are in the Mitchell Library, Australian National Library, and art galleries at Geelong and Castlemaine and in most States.

Official roster of the soldiers of ... Ohio in the war of ... 1861-1866, 8 (Cincinatti, 1888); D. J. Hopkins, *Hop of the Bulletin* (Syd, 1929); O. F. Bond (ed), *Under the flag of the nation* (Columbus, 1961); N. Lindsay, *Bohemians of the Bulletin* (Syd, 1965); *Bulletin*, 1883-1913, 28 Aug, 4 Sept 1927, 29 Jan 1930; ' "Hop": his confessions', *Lone Hand*, Dec 1913-June 1914; *Daily Telegraph* (Syd), 10 July 1927; *SMH*, 22, 23 Aug 1927; M. Mahood, The political cartoon in N.S.W. and Victoria, 1855-1901 (M.A. thesis, Univ Melb, 1965); L. Hopkins, Scrapbooks 1874-1925 (ML); MS cat under Hopkins (ML, Dixson Lib); information from Miss A. Hopkins, Mosman, NSW.

B. G. ANDREWS

HOPWOOD, HENRY (1813-1869), founder of Echuca, was born in Bolton, Lancashire, England, son of Henry Hopwood, manufacturer, and his wife Mary, née Kelly. His bookshelves in later years suggest that he acquired at least a passing acquaintance with some Latin authors. On 11 December 1832 as a gilder in Liverpool he married a widow Fanny Wagdin (Walkden), née Roberts(?). On 8 March 1834 as a labourer he was convicted at the Lancaster Assizes for receiving stolen silk and sentenced to fourteen years' transportation.

Hopwood arrived at Hobart Town in the *William Metcalfe* on 4 September. For 'orderly conduct' he was made a police constable in February 1835. For breaching regulations by living with a woman not his wife in 1838 he was sentenced to a roadgang for a year. In May 1839 he 'aided and assisted' the abduction of his master's daughter and was sent to Port Arthur for two years. He received a ticket-of-leave on 22 December 1842 and rejoined the police. He was conditionally pardoned on 15 January 1846. In February 1844 he had submitted plans for supplying water to Launceston from the South Esk River. In 1845 he was 'an active, intelligent and well-disposed' clerk to a district constable's office but was denied a post in the public service when he applied in April 1846.

When his sentence expired Hopwood moved to Port Phillip and became overseer of boiling-down works on the Murray River near the future site of Echuca. When the works closed, he knocked together the huts, licensed them as the New Road Inn and had a punt for crossing the river. In 1853 when F. Cadell and W. R. Randell [qq.v.] demonstrated the navigability of the river, Hopwood sent his plans for a town to Lieut-Governor La Trobe and, perhaps with prior knowledge, leased a section of the Wharparilla run, newly gazetted as the site for a future town. Early in 1854 the town of Echuca was surveyed and named, and the first land sales held in April. Hopwood was a keen bidder. He built his Criterion Hotel 'of iron and bits and pieces' where the Echuca Club now stands, and claimed that his new punt cost £1500. In January 1855 he became postmaster at Hopwood's Ferry; by March he had opened a butchery, bakery and boiling-down works and by November a large iron store. In 1856 his remarkable pontoon bridge spanned the Murray, and in 1857 he bridged the Campaspe River, his rights secured by a special Act. Later he built a brick store, organized a school, planted a vineyard, published a newsletter and in March 1859 opened the Bridge Hotel.

Hopwood's first wife died early in 1857, and in 1859 he married Charlotte Walters of Bendigo. After a brief retirement to St Kilda he returned to Echuca in August 1860 to run the Bridge Hotel. As patron of the town he was largely responsible for attracting A. Mackay and J. J. Casey [qq.v.] to publish the *Riverine Herald* at Echuca in 1863. In 1864 he leased the Bridge Hotel to a manager and retired from public life, save for a blustering six months from August when he served on the Echuca Road Board. Aged 55 he died of typhoid on 1 January 1869. His daughter Alice, born in Tasmania about 1845, married James McCulloch [q.v.] in 1867 and died without issue in 1895.

Energetic and resilient, Hopwood's undisclosed conviction undoubtedly corroded his public self-confidence. He was noted for arrogant outbursts, stormy quarrels and petty disputes, but also for intense loyalty to friends and kindness to those he deemed needy.

S. Priestley, *Echuca: a centenary history* (Brisb, 1965); *Argus*, 1853-68; *Riverine Herald*, 1863-68; Col Sec files 1851-56 and Chief Sec files 1856-60 (VA); Hopwood letters (Echuca Hist Soc).   SUSAN McCARTHY

HORDERN, ANTHONY (1819-1876), merchant, was born on 16 July 1819 in London, the eldest son of Anthony Hordern and his wife Ann, née Woodhead, of Retford, Nottingham. The Horderns were a banking family from Uttoxeter, Staffordshire. They disapproved the father's marriage and he migrated in the *Phoenix*, arriving at Sydney in March 1825. He set up as a 'coachmaker, wheelwright and smith' and later as a grocer and publican. His wife opened a shop as a haberdasher and bonnet and corsetmaker and her success provoked a rumour that Hordern was her assigned convict. In 1839 he bought three lots in Melbourne and later settled there. He died on 9 June 1869, survived by four sons and two daughters and by his wife who died at Darling Point, Sydney, on 18 January 1871.

Anthony was educated by J. D. Lang [q.v.]. He went to Melbourne in 1839 and in 1842 became a town councillor. About 1844 he returned to Sydney and with his brother Lebbeus (1826-1881) opened a drapery on Brickfield Hill; in 1855 Anthony started on his own in the Haymarket. He also speculated in city real estate and in 1869 won Phillip ward in the city council. About 1860 he built Retford Hall on Darling Point. In 1864 his son-in-law Henry Bull and next year his eldest son Anthony (1842-1886) became partners in the firm. In 1869 his second son Samuel replaced Bull and the firm became Anthony Hordern & Sons. Survived by two sons and two daughters, Hordern died at Sydney on 21 August 1876 and was buried at Rookwood cemetery. On 17 July 1841 at Windsor he had married Harriett, daughter of Samuel Marsden, tanner.

His eldest son, ANTHONY, was born on 24 July 1842 at Melbourne. Educated in Sydney and at Rugby, England, he toured Europe and at 18 entered his father's firm. In 1878 Hordern and his brother Samuel signed a formal deed of partnership for thirty years. According to the *Bulletin*, 22 May 1880, they 'fairly rule[d] the retail trade of the metropolis and the colony in general'. They adopted the trade-mark of the spreading oak over the motto, 'While I live I'll grow'. In 1878 Anthony had visited America and London, and in 1879 opened the 'Palace Warehouse' and the 'Palace Emporium' in the Haymarket. In 1881-82 he opened offices in Britain, the Continent, America and China. Interested in Western Australia, he put to the Colonial Office in 1873 a scheme for 10,000 settlers and in 1883 proposed to the Legislative Council a land-grant railway; later he formed a syndicate in England to construct the line and encourage migration. Leaving an estate of £190,800, Hordern died at sea from brain fever on 16 September 1886 and was buried at Albany where in 1889 an obelisk was erected to his memory. He was survived by four children and his wife Elizabeth, née Bull, whom he had married in 1864.

SAMUEL was born on 14 July 1849 at Sydney. Educated at Fort Street School and Camden College, he joined his father's firm at 17 and in 1886 paid £158,252 for Anthony's share, becoming sole proprietor of 'Anthony Hordern and Sons, Universal Providers, Palace Emporium, Haymarket [ONLY]', to distinguish it from five other competing Hordern shops in Sydney. On 10 July 1901 fire destroyed all the Haymarket complex but Samuel leased the Exhibition building and opened there next day. In 1905 he had new premises on Brickfield Hill. He was generous to his staff of over 4000 and provided a cafeteria and other amenities. City and suburban land speculation added to his wealth and his success brought comments on his 'glorified sockselling' and 'insolent monopoly'.

Samuel gave privately to many charities. A federalist and imperialist, he gave £10,000 to the Dreadnought Fund. In 1892 he was commodore of the Prince Alfred Yacht Club and an active member of the Royal Sydney Yacht Squadron. His love of the country led him in the 1880s to buy Milton Park and Retford Park, near Bowral, where he bred Jersey and Ayrshire cattle. After winning the Sydney Cup in 1893 with Realm and the Metropolitan in 1896 with The Skipper, he concentrated on breeding horses. He kept homing pigeons and was vice-president of the Royal Agricultural Society. He died at Darling Point on 13 August 1909 and was buried in the Anglican section of Rookwood cemetery. He was survived by four of his five sons, by four daughters and by his wife Jane Maria, née Booth, whom he had married on 11 November 1875 at Sydney. In 1910 his estate of £2,925,925 was upheld by the Privy Council after two sons of Anthony had tried to upset the 1878 deed of partnership. His eldest son, Sir Samuel (1876-1956), became governing director of Anthony Hordern & Sons when it was made a private company in 1912.

W. B. Kimberly, *History of West Australia* (Melb, 1897); J. S. Battye (ed), *Cyclopedia of Western Australia*, 1 (Adel, 1912); T. J. Redmond, *History of Anthony Hordern and Sons . . . 1823 to 1932* (Syd, 1938); *Bulletin*, 21 Jan

1882; *SMH*, 2, 6 Oct 1884, 14, 16 Aug 1909, 2 May 1910; *West Australian*, 22 Sept 1886; *Drapers' Record* (Lond), 21 Aug 1909; Anthony Hordern & Sons, Fire insurance papers, 1901 (ANU Archives).   RUTH TEALE

HORNE, RICHARD HENRY (1802-1884), poet, was born on 31 December 1802 at Edmonton, near London, the eldest of three sons of James Horne (d. 1810), quartermaster in the 61st Regiment; his grandfather was Richard Horne, secretary to Earl St Vincent. Richard was brought up at the home of his rich paternal grandmother and attended John Clarke's School where John Keats was also a pupil. In April 1819 Horne entered Sandhurst Military College but left in December 1820. In 1823 after reading Shelley's *Queen Mab*, he decided to become a poet.

In 1825 Horne sailed as midshipman in the *Libertad* to fight for Mexican independence. After two years in America he returned to London, where in 1833 he published his first book *Exposition of the false medium and barriers excluding men of genius from the public*. In the next decade he published three poetic dramas, contributed prolifically to literary magazines, edited the *Monthly Repository* in 1836-37 and served on the royal commission on child employment in factories in 1841. His most famous year was 1843 when he published his epic *Orion* at a farthing a copy to show his contempt for public taste. It ran to six editions in a year and made him a celebrity. During the Irish famine he was correspondent for the *Daily News*. In 1847 he married Catherine, daughter of David Foggo.

In 1852 Horne faced a crisis : his marriage was failing; he was impoverished; he was discontented in his work on Dickens's [q.v.] *Household Words*; and he was torn between the practical and poetic sides of his nature. Tempted by dreams of fortune on the Australian goldfields and a chance to escape, Horne arrived at Melbourne in September. He soon became commander of the private gold escort and in 1853 assistant gold commissioner at Heathcote and Waranga. He was erratic in both posts and was dismissed in November 1854. By 1855 his English ties were severed, his wife having requested a formal separation. In Melbourne he became clerk to Archibald Michie [q.v.], and lived with a Scottish girl; their son, born in 1857, died after seven months. In September 1856 as a radical Horne contested Rodney in the Legislative Assembly but lost. As a commissioner of sewerage and water supply in 1857 when Melbourne's new reservoir was under public attack, he did little to appease

the critics. By 1860 he was again unemployed and living at St Kilda with a female companion. He was well known at Captain Kenney's swimming baths, lectured at Mechanics' Institutes on 'The Causes of Success in Life' and failed to win the Belfast (Port Fairy) seat. He helped to found the Tahbilk vineyard on the Goulburn River. In 1862-63 the Royal Literary Fund assisted him.

In June 1863 Horne was made warden of the Victorian Blue Mountain goldfield near Trentham : 'my Siberia'. Again he began to write seriously and found tranquillity. On visits to Melbourne he held court at H. T. Dwight's [q.v.] bookshop, and became friendly with G. G. McCrae and Marcus Clarke [qq.v.]. In 1864 he published a lyrical drama, *Prometheus the Fire-Bringer*, and in 1866 for the Melbourne Intercolonial Exhibition a masque, *The South Sea Sisters*; it contained a rhythmic representation of an Aboriginal corroboree which brought acclaim. In 1867 he celebrated the arrival of the duke of Edinburgh with a cantata, *Galatea Secunda*, signing himself Richard Hengist Horne, the name by which he was henceforth known. In Australia he produced no significant poetry but some good prose: *Australian Facts and Prospects* (London, 1859), and an essay, 'An Election Contest in Australia' in *Cornhill*, 5 (1862). Disillusioned, he sailed in June 1869 for England where he became a literary doyen, producing many new works all artistically worthless. His poverty was relieved in 1874 by a government pension, and he died at Margate on 13 March 1884.

E. J. Shumaker, *A concise bibliography of the complete works of Richard Henry-Hengist-Horne* (Ohio, 1943); C. Pearl, *Always morning: the life of Richard Henry 'Orion' Horne* (Melb, 1960); A. Blainey, *The farthing poet . . . Richard Hengist Horne* (Lond, 1968), and for bibliog; R. H. Horne papers (ML).

ANN BLAINEY

HORNE, THOMAS (1800-1870), judge, was born in London, the eldest son of Thomas Horne; his grandfather was keeper of the Manor House School, Chiswick. Educated at Westminster School and Christ Church, Oxford (B.A., 1822; M.A., 1825), he entered Lincoln's Inn and was called to the Bar in February 1827. Recommended by the Colonial Office through his uncle Sir William, attorney-general, he arrived at Hobart Town in the *William* on 31 January 1830 with his wife Maria and two daughters. He was admitted to practise in the Supreme Court and set up chambers in Murray Street. Within a year he was engaged in lively politics. At first he supported Lieut-Governor Arthur's campaign against the Aboriginals but soon joined the anti-Arthurites after a slight at Government House. He was a leader of every movement against the government and was editor of the malcontents' *Colonist* until March 1833. At a meeting on 28 February 1835 'he proposed to bring here and set at liberty every man who was convicted of crime in England', a statement that shocked even his radical friends.

This recklessness also pervaded Horne's business affairs. His speculations led him into debt and to pay one creditor he had to borrow from another. He was forced to sell his grant at Cape Portland and purchased lots at Battery Point and Glenorchy, and later admitted to losses of £20,000 in trading with New Zealand and £2000 in other investments. His brother Alfred, who arrived at Hobart in November 1831, was also involved and when his capital was lost he too sold his grant at Cape Portland.

Increasing debts and the needs of his large family forced Horne to accept the post of solicitor-general in January 1841; he also acted as attorney-general when Edward McDowell [q.v.] was dismissed in July until Thomas Welsh was appointed in November. Erstwhile friends of the *True Colonist* claimed that his financial troubles had placed him in the power of the ruling clique, but he was even more deeply in debt when in December 1843 he offered his resignation to Lieut-Governor Sir Eardley Wilmot in order to claim the benefit of the Insolvent Act. The lieut-governor refused to accept his resignation and offered him every possible assistance, including the post of attorney-general next March when Welsh was dismissed for duelling.

With a salary of £900 and the right to private practice, Horne's prospects seemed more settled but, when he replaced A. S. Montague [q.v.] as puisne judge in January 1848, much criticism was levelled at his financial embarrassment. The appointment was challenged in the press and the Supreme Court, but upheld by the chief justice, Sir John Pedder [q.v.]. Lieut-Governor Denison ignored the criticism of his puisne judge but in 1854 when Pedder retired Denison recommended the solicitor-general, Valentine Fleming [q.v.], as chief justice, arguing that Horne's independence of judgment was threatened by his precarious finances. Despite Horne's protests and a petition with more than 2500 signatures, Fleming's appointment was confirmed by the Colonial Office.

With the advent of responsible government, Horne was elected to the Legislative Council as member for Hobart, and a special Act was passed in January 1857 to enable him as a judge to be also president of the council without salary. In September 1860 he was attacked in the council by William Archer [q.v.] over the judgment of the acting chief justice, Robert Molesworth [q.v.] in the case of *Horne* v. *Gilles* in the Supreme Court of Victoria. The judge found that Horne and his cousin Francis Sharpe Horne had exerted undue influence on the latter's father in the execution of his will. At the same time Joseph Solomon alleged that, while a plaintiff in a suit to be heard before Horne, he had been approached by Horne for a loan of £500 which he had refused. To prevent his amoval, Horne resigned and an Act was hurriedly passed to grant him a full pension of £800 though he had been a judge for only thirteen of the fifteen statutory years.

This unusual action caused some indignation but did not prevent Horne from topping the poll for Hobart in the House of Assembly elections in May 1861. In July an appeal by F. S. Horne against the judgment in *Horne* v. *Gilles* was upheld and with his cousin he was cleared of any fault but imprudence. Horne served in the assembly until 1866. Aged 70 he died at his home in Collins Street on 23 September 1870 and was buried at St David's burial ground. He left no real property; his large house in Fitzroy Place had been sold in 1857 and other investments had gone to pay creditors. Even his detractors acknowledged his 'benevolence and kindness of character' and although not brilliant as lawyer or judge he was competent and painstaking in his profession.

W. Murray (ed), *Horne* v. *Gilles* (Melb, 1860); E. M. Miller, *Pressmen and governors* (Syd, 1952); R. W. Baker, 'The early judges in Tasmania', PTHRA, 8 (1960); *Hobart Town Courier*, 2 Sept, 11 Dec 1830; *Colonial Times*, 13 July 1831, 24 Jan 1857; *Colonist* (Hob), 15 Mar 1833; *True Colonist*, 8 Sept 1835, 1 May 1840; *Examiner* (Launceston), Oct 1860; *Mercury*, 15 July, 9 Nov 1861, 26 Sept 1870; G. T. W. B. Boyes diary (Roy Soc Tas); CSO 1/612/13968, 657/14745, 5/281/7385 (TA); GO 33/10/318, 33/12/69, 33/81, 45/1 (TA).

MARY NICHOLLS

HORROCKS, JOSEPH LUCAS (d. 1865), medical attendant, merchant and mining superintendent, was found guilty of forgery at the Central Criminal Court, London, on 10 April 1851 and sentenced to transportation for fourteen years. He arrived at Fremantle in the *Marion* on 31 January 1852, was granted a ticket-of-leave in June 1853 and a conditional pardon on 19 April

1856. Although he was married, his wife
does not appear to have joined him in
Western Australia.

In 1852 Horrocks worked in the medical
section of the convict establishment at Fremantle. This experience and the scarcity of
medical officers led him to apply for the
post of medical attendant at Port Gregory,
which he accepted at a reduced salary of
£20 a year because of his limited qualifications. In September 1853 he left Fremantle
in the brig *Hero*. At Port Gregory his duties
were to attend the medical needs of all
officers of the civil establishment, ticket-of-
leave men and sick natives in the area, purposes for which he had acquired a large
supply of surgical instruments and medicines from Fremantle. His requisition for
more in October was considered excessive
and much reduced. He won repute for
generosity to the poor in supplying prescribed drugs at low costs and was soon
widely known as 'Doc'.

Late in 1854 Horrocks returned to Fremantle in the *Daphne* but soon went to
Wanerenooka where he opened a store, took
an interest in agriculture and was knowledgeable enough to experiment with such
crops as tobacco, hops, fruit and wheat,
believing that the lack of fresh fruit and
vegetables was a prime factor in the high
incidence of scurvy. Unimpressed by the
rough humpies of miners, Horrocks built a
stone cottage for himself and several more
which he leased at low rentals. On 26
December 1859 he was appointed postmaster
at Wanerenooka and in 1864 succeeded in
giving the district improved postal services.
He began agitating for a railway from
Gwalla to Champion Bay, and organized the
construction of the Wanerenooka road,
employing men and supplying tools at his
own cost. Through George Shenton [q.v.]
he became interested in copper and lead and
was connected with the Wanerenooka mine
which produced ore worth £40,000 in its
first ten years. He was also instrumental in
starting mines at White Peak and Yanga-
nooka, and at Gwalla, worked by skilled
miners from Cornwall, his surrounding freehold of 100 acres was later increased.

Deeply conscious of social and economic
problems, Horrocks argued that many convicts were more 'sinned against than sin-
ning'. He was concerned for the progress of
the sandalwood industry and the need for
improved knowledge as agricultural and
pastoral lands became available; he urged
the government to foster the mining industry in the Victoria district by good roads,
to provide steam-driven machinery and to
discourage public zest for quick profits. As
an employer he was sympathetic; once he
started a sustenance scheme for the unemployed to collect stones and build walls.
In October 1864 he petitioned for closure
of the Miner's Arms, a public house opened
by John Hoskins. Of those who signed it
ninety were employed by Horrocks and
many names were forged; the resident
magistrate found that Horrocks had been
selling illicit liquor since 1858.

With a dogmatic belief in individual
rights Horrocks was responsible for building an undenominational church at Gwalla,
its foundation stone engraved with 'My
house shall be called a house for all people'.
Pulpits were installed, one for Anglicans
and one for Nonconformists while anti-
ritualists had a reading desk; the bell was
later removed to Wesley Church in Perth.
Horrocks died from general debility on 7
October 1865 and was buried in the grave-
yard near his church. His property reverted
to the Shenton family.

J. T. Reilly, *Reminiscences of fifty years
residence in Western Australia* (Perth, 1903);
PP (GB), 1852 (1517); J. M. Drew, 'Early
Northampton: an undenominational church',
JRWAHS, 2 (1932); A. Carson, 'The Champion
Bay country', *JRWAHS*, 3 (1939); *The Times*,
10 Apr 1851; *Perth Gazette*, 20, 27 Oct 1863;
Countryman (Perth), 1 Jan 1959; CSO 1853-64
(Battye Lib, Perth); Convict records (Battye
Lib, Perth).   WENDY BIRMAN

HORSFALL, JOHN SUTCLIFFE (1837-
1916), wool-broker and pastoralist, was born
on 12 September 1837 at Haworth, Yorkshire, England, son of Jones Horsfall and his
wife Martha, née Sutcliffe. As a boy he was
impressed by his father's friend, Branwell
Bronte. Horsfall was educated in Bradford
and then worked in the family woollen
mills. Discontented he migrated to Victoria
in June 1856. In 1857 he joined the firm of
Richard Goldsbrough [q.v.] as a travelling
representative and in 1864 was given a share
of the profits as well as his £1000 salary.
In 1873 he became a partner. Horsfall extended the business and built up a large
personal following. In 1877 he became a
director of the Australian Agency and
Banking Corporation Ltd which in 1881
merged with R. Goldsbrough & Co. In 1888
the firm amalgamated with Mort [q.v.] &
Co. of Sydney to form Goldsbrough, Mort &
Co. Ltd. Horsfall remained a director and
was on the local committee of management.
His policy of lower dividends, increasing
reserves and squaring advances with securities was popular with the London board but
not among his fellow committeemen.

Horsfall's first pastoral investment was
Ensay in Gippsland. In the drought of the
late 1880s he acquired Widgiewa, Moma-

long and Kerarbury in the Riverina, financed by Goldsbrough, Mort & Co. When he resigned in 1889 a committee of shareholders exonerated him from a charge of embezzling £25 but could not stop a pamphlet war between him and Andrew Rowan [q.v.], each accusing the other of improperly taking large advances from the company. In 1890 Rowan sued Horsfall for £25,000 damages for libel. Next year the case went to arbitration and Rowan was awarded £50 but costs were shared. In 1892 Horsfall became pastoral adviser to the New Zealand Loan and Mercantile Agency. About 1894 he returned to Goldsbrough, Mort & Co. as pastoral adviser; his secret price was a £10,000 advance to his son-in-law, Rupert Carrington, and in 1904 his agreement with the firm was not renewed. Influenced by his neighbour, Samuel McCaughey [q.v.], in 1892 Horsfall introduced Vermont blood into his stud merinos and by 1905 had won eight championships at the Sydney Sheep Show and in 1906-07 bred the grand champion rams. He was a vice-president of the New South Wales Sheepbreeders' Association. In 1909-12 he sold all his stations except Kerarbury and became curmudgeonly with fears of 'certain poverty impending, thanks to labour legislation which is very hard on large land-holders like myself, simply confiscation in many cases'.

In 1912-16 Horsfall reluctantly gave £10,000 for a chapel in memory of his daughter Edith at Trinity College in the University of Melbourne after Dr Leeper had accepted his unmatriculated nephew. A friend of Maurice Brodzky, he had probably supplied information for the exposures in Table Talk of fraudulent Victorian companies in the early 1890s. Horsfall visited England at least once and New Zealand many times. He equipped and sent 300 bushmen to the Boer war. His great pleasure was boating and he kept a small fleet at Widgiewa. He died on 11 June 1916 at Toorak, survived by a son and several daughters of his first wife Mary, née Maiden, and by his second wife Agnes, née Mahoney. He had already provided for his daughters and his son Richard inherited nearly £115,000.

A. Rowan, Letter . . . to the shareholders, Goldsbrough, Mort & Co. Ltd (Melb, 1889); A. Bird, The Horsfall chapel, Trinity College (Church of England Hist Soc, Melb, nd); M. Cannon, The land boomers (Melb, 1966); A'sian Insurance and Banking Record, 16 Nov 1889; Australasian, 12 Apr, 17 May 1890, 28 Mar, 15, 25 Apr 1891, 5 Sept 1896, 30 Oct 1897; Pastoral Review, 15 June, 15 Sept 1892, 15 Jan 1894, 15 July 1905, 15 July 1916; Goldsbrough Mort & Co. records (ANU Archives); information from Dr A. Barnard, ANU.   K. J. SWAN

HORSLEY, CHARLES EDWARD (1822-1876), musician, was born on 16 December 1822 in London, son of William Horsley, composer and musician, and his wife Elizabeth Hutchins, daughter of the composer, Dr J. W. Callcott. Horsley was a piano pupil of Ignaz Moscheles and a friend of Mendelssohn on whose advice he went to Germany to study under Moritz Hauptmann and Louis Spohr. Horsley was the prototype for the hero of Charles Auchester, a novel by Elizabeth Sheppard. He taught music and became well known as a pianist and organist. For the Liverpool Philharmonic Society he composed at 24 the oratorio David and three years later Joseph. He was organist of St John's, Notting Hill, London, in 1853-57.

Horsley arrived at Melbourne in the British Trident on 10 December 1861. He was appointed organist at Christ Church, South Yarra, but resigned after six months. In 1865 he was organist at St Stephen's Church, Richmond. In 1862-65 Horsley was conductor of the Melbourne Philharmonic Society; he won praise for his ability to conduct expressively but was said to be incapable of keeping the beat at all clearly. His cantata Comus, composed in 1854, was performed for the first time in Australia on 7 December 1862. His David was first produced in Melbourne on 30 June 1863 and he was hailed as a 'genius and an accomplished exponent of his art'. In 1866 he organized the musical festival during the Melbourne Exhibition and at the opening ceremony on 24 October conducted The South Sea Sisters, a masque written by R. H. Horne [q.v.] and set to music by Horsley. Always careless with money he lost heavily over the music festival and in May 1867 was declared insolvent. In June, intending to return to England, he sailed in the Wonga Wonga for Sydney where he took part in the opening recitals on the new organ of St Andrew's Cathedral and later taught organ pupils.

Horsley returned to Victoria in 1870 and was appointed organist to St Francis's Church. In April the mayor of Melbourne commissioned him to compose a cantata to a poem by Henry Kendall [q.v.]; titled Euterpe it was performed at the opening of the new Melbourne Town Hall on 9 August and in 1876 at the Crystal Palace, London. Though highly regarded as a musician, Horsley was eccentric and impulsive. His erratic behaviour bred scandal and he lived in one boarding house after another. In 1871 he decided to leave the colony and at a farewell concert in May an appreciative audience gave him a warm ovation. He returned to England where at Liverpool he was well received and formed the Ballad and Madrigal Troupe. In January 1873 he was appointed organist to St John's Chapel of the Trinity Corporation, New York, and conductor of the Church Music Association. He died in New York on 28 February 1876.

Among Horsley's other works was the oratorio *Gideon*; he also wrote chamber music, piano works, songs, anthems and a church hymnal. In Melbourne he wrote long comments for the press on musical events of note. He edited a collection of glees by his father in 1873 and his own *Text Book of Harmony* was published in London in 1876.

H. M. Humphreys (ed), *Men of the time in Australia: Victorian series*, 2nd ed (Melb, 1882); F. C. Brewer, *The drama and music in New South Wales* (Syd, 1892); G. Peake, *Melbourne Philharmonic Society . . . historical souvenir* (Melb, 1913); W. A. Carne, *A century of harmony* (Melb, 1954); E. N. Matthews, *Colonial organs and organbuilders* (Melb, 1969); *Age*, 6 Oct 1862, 10 Aug 1870; *Argus*, 8 Oct 1862, 1 July 1863, 18 Aug 1865; *Herald* (Melb), 8 Oct 1862; *Australasian*, 20 May 1871, 25 Jan 1873, 6 May 1876; Annual report, 1894-95 (Metropolitan Liedertafel); Guard book, 1853-87 (Melb Philharmonic Soc).

MAUREEN THERESE RADIC

HOSE, HENRY JUDGE (1826-1883), Church of England clergyman, was born in London, son of Rev. John Christian Hose. In 1837-45 he attended the City of London School, a new institution with a liberal educational policy, and became first president of its Old Boys' Club in 1851. With the school's Beaufoy mathematical scholarship he entered Trinity College, Cambridge (B.A., 1849; M.A., 1854). He became mathematical master at Westminster School and in 1853 published parts of *The Elements of Euclid*, claiming that it was clearer and simpler than Simson's edition on which it was based. In that year Hose was made deacon and in 1854 ordained priest. In 1850 he had married Ann Hornby in London.

In 1856 Hose was chosen warden of St Paul's College within the University of Sydney. He arrived with his family in Sydney on 11 December and began with non-resident students until the college buildings were ready late in 1857. The college was restricted by statute to providing tutorial and religious facilities for resident undergraduates, but did not train ordination candidates and could not command the full support of the Church of England. In an underpopulated university and under these conditions, students were not easy to attract. The warden's policy was to infuse as much as possible of the corporate life of the Oxford and Cambridge colleges into St Paul's. He was a vigorous tutor and

preacher and his regular choral services were of high standard. He also taught mathematics at the university and examined in Church schools. In the college chapel he delivered sermons on the life and ministry of Elijah, which were printed in 1861 at the request of the congregation of local residents that he had built up.

By 1860 St Paul's was declining. The warden had lost the right to examine the religious attainments of Anglican candidates for degrees, and a parliamentary select committee had condemned the college as superfluous. Student numbers dwindled and financial difficulties increased. The college council, especially its leading member, Chief Justice Stephen [q.v.], laid much of the responsibility on Hose. In May 1861 they investigated charges that Hose's public conduct had brought discredit upon the college. He contested the legality of the inquiry but the main charge was upheld. Probably he was partly to blame. His mercurial temperament reacted to setback or success; an admirer later recalled 'a certain geniality and freeness of manner which, judged by the severe standard of the world's conventionality, sometimes amounted to a fault'. The tact of Bishop Barker [q.v.] prevented a public breach.

In May 1862 Hose left for England where he taught at Dulwich College and his brother's private school at Hampstead. In 1867 he was mathematical master at the Derby School and assistant curate at St Peter's Church. He became principal of the new Anglican Training College of St Mary, Conway, in 1874. The position proved uncongenial, and after a curacy at Ellingham, Norfolk (1876-79), Hose ended his teaching career at Bishop's Stortford Grammar School. He corresponded with friends in New South Wales and ministered privately to Australians in England. He died at Bishop's Stortford on 16 June 1883, survived by several children.

B. Tacchella (ed), *The Derby School register, 1570-1901* (Lond, 1902); A. E. Douglas-Smith, *The City of London School*, 2nd ed (Oxford, 1965); V&P (LA NSW), 1859-60, 4, 165; *Aust Churchman* (Syd), 23 Aug 1883; K. J. Cable, 'The University of Sydney and its affiliated colleges, 1850-1880', *Aust Univ*, 2 (1964); St Paul's College Council, Minute books 1856-62 (Univ Syd Archives). K. J. CABLE

HOSKINS, JAMES (1823-1900), miner and politician, was born in London, son of James Hoskins, wine merchant. He was early sent to boarding school and from 1840 'discharged clerical duties' in the Anglican Church. He later worked as a policeman and a 'booking porter'. On 5 December 1847 in the Baptist Chapel at Stroud Hoskins married Caroline Day; they had one son Thomas. In 1849 Hoskins left England without his family. About 1853 he arrived in Sydney and went to the goldfields where he had some success and made many friends. He soon became the literary exponent of the miners' grievances. Elected in 1859 to the Legislative Assembly for Goldfields North he was the first to represent a par-ticular class. Hoskins was supported by miners' voluntary contributions, intended to supply him with £600 and complete freedom of action. In February 1863 he resigned for pecuniary reasons and became overseer of northern roads; he had risen to super-intendent before he resigned in June 1867. In July 1868 he regained his old electorate and represented Patrick's Plains in 1869-72 and Tumut in 1872-82. He became a land and commission agent and in 1876 was senior partner of the firm of Hoskins & Blomfield.

A moderate liberal who idolized J. S. Mill, Hoskins maintained an independence that was often censured as treachery. In turn he supported and opposed each ministry until 1877. In 1875 he refused office under John Robertson [q.v.]. As secretary for public works under Henry Parkes [q.v.] in 1877 Hoskins's behaviour became somewhat more stable. In 1878-81 he was secretary for lands in the Parkes-Robertson coalition. Hoskins had severely criticized the management of the Departments of Public Works and Lands. 'Fearless in reforming the abuses of his Lands department', in August 1880 he was instrumental in the suspension of the under-secretary for lands, W. W. Stephen [q.v.], and the accountant after an inquiry into the embezzlement of £800.

In 1880 Hoskins carried an amending Land Act, obviously influenced by Robertson. After Robertson resigned from the ministry in November 1881, Hoskins's land policy was challenged by the colonial treasurer, James Watson [q.v.]; cabinet solidarity was undermined and on 28 December Hoskins resigned his office. He had long suffered from rheumatic gout but Robertson's facile return to the ministry as acting premier and secretary for lands cast doubts on the ostensible reasons for Hoskins's resignation. In 1882 he visited England and America to recuperate and on 26 September resigned from parliament. In 1889 he was appointed to the Legislative Council. Aged 77 he died on 1 April 1900 at Strathfield and was·buried in the Anglican section of Waverley cemetery. Most of his estate of £17,235 was left to his son Thomas. who was located by his executor, Henry Clarke [q.v.], before 1907.

D. Buchanan, *Political portraits of some of the members of the parliament of New South Wales* (Syd, 1863); *V&P* (LA NSW), 1870-82; *Tamworth Examiner*, 2, 20 July 1859; *SMH*, 1 July 1868, 22 Dec 1869, Mar 1877, Nov-Dec 1881, 2 Apr 1900; *Town and Country J*, 7 Apr 1877; *Bulletin*, 5 June, 31 July 1880; G. C. Morey, The Parkes-Robertson coalition government, 1878-1893 (B.A. Hons thesis, ANU, 1968); Parkes letters (ML).

G. C. MOREY

HOTHAM, SIR CHARLES (1806-1855), naval officer and governor, was born on 14 January 1806 in Dennington, Suffolk, England, the eldest son of Frederick Hotham, prebendary of Rochester, and his wife Anne Elizabeth, née Hodges. He entered the navy on 6 November 1818 and on the Mediterranean station was promoted, rapidly for peacetime, lieutenant in 1825 and postcaptain in 1833. In 1842 on the South American station he was in command of the steam sloop *Gorgon*; she ran aground in Montevideo Bay in 1844 and he displayed stubbornness and skill in refloating her. In November 1845 he commanded the squadron on the Parana River and, with help from a French force, defeated the Argentine insurgents under General Rosas. In 1846 he was made K.C.B. and appointed commodore on the west coast of Africa in May. His talent for languages prompted Lord Malmesbury in April 1852 to appoint him head of a mission to Paraguay to negotiate a commercial treaty. Lord Clarendon, Malmesbury's successor, thought the attempt futile and sent his recall, but the dispatch crossed one bearing home the completed treaty. However, Hotham was not appreciated by the Aberdeen ministry, and this as well as his quality is why the duke of Newcastle appointed him lieut-governor of Victoria on 6 December 1853.

The extraordinary changes occasioned by the discovery of gold gave Victoria the reputation of being a most difficult colonial post. Hotham had diplomatic and naval successes to recommend him and, compared with his predecessor La Trobe, was an impressive appointment. The colonial press and public as well as Newcastle were enthusiastic. But Hotham's own preferences emerged in 1854 when the Crimean war broke out and he applied unsuccessfully for a ship rather than take up his governorship. He arrived in Melbourne on 22 June. He soon appreciated the need to increase revenue, strengthen administration and allay goldfields discontent by extending political privileges and improving the licence system, but he totally misunderstood his position as governor of a sizeable Crown colony, particularly Victoria, for which a new constitution providing 'responsible' government was then under consideration in London. He courted the working population, especially miners, while remaining clearly authoritarian. Yet he upset the firmest supporters of authority, the propertied and official classes, by his declarations of 'democratic' principles and his refusal to call regular meetings of the Executive Council. He was obstinate and secretive with his councillors and, unwilling to delegate matters to his officials, he soon exhausted himself with work. When introducing reform of government finance he unnecessarily disparaged his predecessor and the existing officials. Despite the weight of public opinion against the mining licence fee, he proved unwilling to abandon it. Thus in the Eureka crisis he could depend on little help from the officials, and his popularity, though still existing, was a fragile thing.

To Hotham the crisis was a rebellion. Reasonably enough he regarded it as analogous to the Chartist assemblies, speeches and marches in England in 1848, and his policy resembled that of Sir Charles Napier demonstrating to would-be insurgents the futility of challenging a strong military force. It might have worked, but unlike Napier Hotham was neither cool nor well informed. His communications with officials in Ballarat were poor and on 3 December they precipitated armed action which Hotham in Melbourne wrongly interpreted as proof of the continuing danger of insurrection. His diplomatic talents therefore had little room for exercise. He had already set up a royal commission to inquire into discontent on the fields, and now urged on its work; he also arranged the resignation of the chief secretary, J. L. F. V. Foster [q.v.], who was unpopular among the miners. But his fear of 'revolutionaries' remained; he kept troops ready and refused an amnesty for the Eureka prisoners. By mid-January 1855 his popularity had collapsed. In March when the royal commission recommended reform of the licence system he foolishly maintained that the fee was right in principle, but the remedial measures passed in the Legislative Council show clearly that Hotham had lost such weak political grasp as he possessed. Among other ineptitudes he alienated the capable auditor-general, H. C. E. Childers [q.v.].

Fortunately for Hotham six months of political quiet followed Eureka. His post had been raised to a full governorship on 3 February 1855 and the imperial government commended him for suppressing the 'outbreak', though not for his policy towards the ringleaders. His competence was already questioned in the Colonial Office and more so when the colonial reformer, Sir William Molesworth, became secretary of state in July. He rebuked Hotham for high-handed treatment of the Legislative Council over his taxation proposals in June. He also supplied hints on the governor's place in responsible government but Hotham handled awkwardly the inauguration of the new Constitution and ministerial government in November. In that month he sent his resignation to London and foreshadowed a justification of himself. His health was failing and on 17 December he caught a chill while opening the Melbourne gasworks. He died on the 31st, survived by his wife Jane Sarah, daughter of Lord Bridport, whom he had married on 10 December 1853.

W. Hadfield, Brazil . . . and the Falkland Island, with the Cape Horn route to Australia . . . from the sketches by W. G. Ouseley and C. Hotham (Lond, 1854); G. Serle, The Golden Age (Melb, 1963); Gentleman's Mag, May 1856.   B. A. KNOX

HOULDING, JOHN RICHARD (1822-1918), store-keeper and novelist, was born on 22 April 1822 in Essex, England, son of Joseph Houlding, contractor, and his wife Sarah, née Olly. He worked in a London lawyer's office and claimed to have met Charles Dickens [q.v.] whose literary style he later tried to imitate. In January 1839 he arrived at Sydney in the Hashemy. He became a solicitor's clerk and then entered T. W. Smart's [q.v.] auctioneering office. In February 1840 he went to New Zealand where he bought land, but in February 1841 returned to Sydney. At Raymond Terrace he became postmaster, store-keeper and ship-owner, and in 1852 sold his store and retired, enfeebled. In 1854 he visited England and on his return in 1855 lost his 'moderate fortune . . . unused to the peculiar dealings of some of the cute citizens' of Sydney. He had a nervous collapse and while on his back began writing.

In May 1861 Houlding told his patron, N. D. Stenhouse [q.v.], 'Though I can scarcely hope you will be favourably impressed with it, as a literary production, I do trust you will recognize its useful design'. His first novel, Australian Capers (London, 1867), was reprinted as Christopher Cockle's Australian Experiences (Sydney, 1913). It records the downfall of an inexperienced migrant and his conversion to Christianity. Houlding's style was vigorous, humorous and loaded with such similes as the passenger whose 'tongue was as active as a duck's tail'.

Invited by John Fairfax [q.v.], Houlding wrote for the Sydney Mail as 'Old Boomerang'; his early contributions were published as *Australian Tales and Sketches from Real Life* (London, 1868). He also wrote short stories for religious and secular journals under seventeen pen-names, including 'J. R. H. Hawthorn'. His second novel, *Rural and City Life: or, The Fortunes of the Stubble Family* (London, 1870), was also partly autobiographical. His later novels, popular as Sunday school prizes, were shorter and more didactic examples of 'a sanctified literary imagination': they appeared as *Investing Uncle Ben's Legacy, a Tale of Mining and Matrimonial Speculations* (1876), *The Pioneer of a Family; or, Adventures of a Young Governess* (1881), *Launching Away; or, Roger Larksway's Strange Mission* (1882), *In the Depths of the Sea* (1885) and *A Flood That Led to Fortune* (1886).

In Sydney in 1843 Houlding had married Elizabeth, née Hannaford. He lived quietly at his home, Hawthorn, Woolwich, and supported such charitable institutions as the *Vernon* training ship for destitute boys. He was also a Methodist lay preacher, a founder of the New South Wales Temperance Alliance and twice declined to stand for parliament. In the 1890s failing eyesight forced him to abandon writing. He died on 25 April 1918 and was buried in the Methodist section of Rookwood cemetery. He was survived by two daughters, of whom the elder, Lucy Hannah, married Rev. William Kelynack [q.v.]

Maitland Mercury, 2 Sept 1848; W. H. G. Freame, 'Old Boomerang', *Hawkesbury Herald*, 20 May 1906; *SMH*, 27 Apr 1918; J. E. Carruthers, Australian scenes and sketches, 1-2 (ML); MS cat under J. R. Houlding (ML).

RUTH TEALE

HOUSTON, WILLIAM (1846-1932), public servant, was born on 14 June 1846 in Sydney, son of William Houston, surgeon, and his wife Mary Anne, née Harris. Educated at Dr W. S. Creeny's Lyceum School and privately by Dr Stanley, Houston joined the Department of Lands in 1863 as a cadet surveyor. Next year he became a supernumerary draftsman and by 1877 had risen to first-class draftsman. In 1878 he reorganized the numerous branches of the Lands Department, his work providing the basis for later decentralization of administration after the 1884 Crown Lands Act. Appointed inspector of Local Land Boards and Crown Land Offices in 1885, Houston implemented the new Act's provisions on pastoral runs so skilfully that he was promoted chief inspector in 1886. In that year he also served on a commission of inquiry into the department's operations, which led

to estimated savings of over £73,000 and a further annual saving of £30,000 resulted from his reorganization of country land offices in 1887.

In October 1888 Houston became assistant under-secretary of lands and on 7 January 1890 was appointed under-secretary. On 1 March 1900 he became a commissioner of the Land Appeal Court and held office until it was dissolved on 10 December 1921. He had also served as deputy administrator of Norfolk Island affairs and in 1903 as the State's royal commissioner had carried out the division of New South Wales into electorates under the Commonwealth Electoral Act, 1902. In 1906 he was awarded a C.M.G.

In 1864-80 Houston was active in the Volunteer Artillery and in April 1872 was made a second lieutenant. In 1875 he was adjutant at the Campbelltown encampment. A sportsman and a good shot, he loved sailing and 'was almost continually on the water' until prevented by official duties. He was also an 'omnivorous reader'. He died on 3 January 1932 at his home in Bondi and was buried in the Anglican section of Waverley cemetery. He was predeceased by his wife Rose Anna Williams, whom he had married in the Sydney Unitarian Church on 15 September 1869, and was survived by three sons and three daughters.

Houston was not a spectacular or controversial public figure but he contributed significantly to land administration and departmental organization in New South Wales. He is a good example of the sort of official who could achieve senior rank even before the reform of personnel practice which followed the creation of the Public Service Board in 1895.

PP (Cwlth), 1903, 2, 165; *PD* (NSW), 1921; *Government Gazette* (NSW), 6 Mar 1900; *Illustrated Sydney News*, 27 Jan 1894; *The Times*, 9 Nov 1906; *SMH*, 4 Jan 1932; K. W. Knight, The development of the Public Service of New South Wales 1856-1895 (M.Ec. thesis, Univ Syd, 1955).   KENNETH W. KNIGHT

HOWARD, STANLEY (1850-1883), Church of England clergyman, was born on 11 February 1850 at Wadsley, Yorkshire, England, the fourth son of Rev. Thomas Henry Howard, perpetual curate of Wadsley, and his wife Maria, née Wilson, whose family had built the church and held its patronage. His father was related to the ducal family of Norfolk but had been a Quaker businessman before conforming to the Church of England. Howard was educated at Milton Abbas School, Dorset, and in 1869 became a pensioner at St John's College, Cambridge, but his health failed before he could take his degree. Early in 1872 he accepted an invitation from Bishop Barker [q.v.] to move to New South Wales.

Howard studied for the ministry at Moore College, Liverpool, under Canon R. L. King [q.v.]. On 8 June 1873 he was made deacon; he was ordained priest by Barker on 23 May 1875. He served curacies at St Peter's, Cook's River, and at the important parish of St John's, Darlinghurst. He also acted as domestic chaplain to the bishop who continued to take a personal interest in him. In 1876 with Barker he toured North Queensland to renew the campaign to secure a bishop for that region. In 1878 he returned to England where at St Peter's, Clifton, Bristol, he married Mary Anna Nash. He also re-entered St John's College, Cambridge (B.A., 1879; M.A., 1883).

Howard returned to Sydney in November 1878 and was appointed to the new parish of Bowral-Nattai in the southern tablelands of New South Wales. In 1880 he built a parsonage at Bowral on the model of the vicarage erected by his father at his Somerset parish of Warmley, planned other church buildings and promoted a school of arts. When Howard was inducted at Bowral he was described as 'a young gentleman of delicate health but possessed of indomitable perseverance; well educated, possessing a grand substitute for affectation—good common sense, an able preacher, and withal a gentleman'. In his brief colonial career he tactfully served as intermediary between an ageing bishop and his changing diocese, and did much to link the predominant school of churchmanship in the diocese of Sydney to comparable developments in the Church in England. He died at Bowral on 19 September 1883 where he was buried. He was survived by his wife (d. 1943), two daughters and a son, Rev. Charles Stanley Allan Howard (b. 1879), who served at Opa in the New Hebrides.

W. M. Cowper (ed), *Episcopate of the Right Reverend Frederic Barker*, D.D. (Lond, 1888); *Aust Churchman* (Syd), 23 Jan 1879; *Guardian* (Syd), 26 Sept 1883; M. A. Howard, Tales of a grandmother, S. Howard ed (ML); S. Howard diaries and family papers (held by Rev. C. S. A. Howard, Melb).   K. J. CABLE

HOWITT, ALFRED WILLIAM (1830-1908), explorer, natural scientist and pioneer authority on Aboriginal culture and social organization, was born on 17 April 1830 at Nottingham, England, the oldest surviving son of William Howitt [q.v.] and his wife Mary, née Botham. He was educated in England, Heidelberg and Univer-

sity College School, London. In 1852, under the press of family needs, he went with his father and brother Charlton to Melbourne where they had been preceded in 1840 by William's youngest brother Godfrey [q.v.]. A reunion was one purpose of the visit but William and his sons also intended to try their fortunes on the new goldfields. They did so with modest success at intervals in the next two years. The experience turned the course of Alfred's life. He learned to live with confidence in the bush, and its natural phenomena, so strange and as yet so little studied, stimulated his mind to their scientific study. In 1854 his father and brother returned to England but Howitt elected to remain, thoroughly at home in the Australian scene.

Young and handsome, of short and wiry build and notably calm and self-possessed, he fulfilled his mother's prophecy that 'someday Alfred will be a backwoodsman'. For a time he farmed his uncle's land at Caulfield but, unattracted by the life, turned again to the bush and as a drover on the route from the Murray to Melbourne made the passing acquaintance of Lorimer Fison [q.v.]. An experienced bushman and ardent naturalist, Howitt was sent in 1859 by a Melbourne syndicate to examine the pastoral potential of the Lake Eyre region on which P. E. Warburton [q.v.] had reported rosily. He led a party with skill and speed from Adelaide through the Flinders Ranges into the Davenport Range country but found it desolated by drought and returned to warn his sponsors. His ability as a bushman and resourceful leader came to public notice when, after briefly managing a sheep station at Hamilton and prospecting in Gippsland, he took a government party through unexplored alpine country to gold strikes on the Crooked, Dargo and Wentworth Rivers. He was an obvious choice as leader when in 1861 the exploration committee of the Royal Society of Victoria decided to send an expedition to relieve or, as the worst fears sensed, to rescue Burke, Wills, King [qq.v.] and Gray. Howitt's discharge of this assignment was exemplary. Without blunder or loss he twice led large parties on the long journey to Cooper's Creek. He soon found King, the only survivor, and took him to a public welcome in Melbourne but avoided the limelight for himself. Then, at request, he returned to bring the remains of Burke and Wills to the capital for interment. On the second expedition he had explored a large tract of the Barcoo country.

For his services Howitt was appointed police magistrate and warden of the Omeo goldfields, and in 1863 began a distinguished career of thirty-eight years as a public official, twenty-six of them as magistrate. In 1889 he became acting secretary of mines and water supply and in 1895 commissioner of audit and a member of the Public Service Board. He retired in January 1902 on a pension but served on the royal commission which in 1903 examined sites for the seat of government of the Commonwealth, and was chairman of the royal commission on the Victorian coal industry in 1905-06.

Such a career would have sufficed an ordinary man but Howitt attained greater things within it. Physical and intellectual fatigue seemed unknown to him. 'What are they?' he asked drily at 75 when Fison inquired if he never felt the infirmities of old age. In his long magistracy he travelled enormous distances annually (in one year, it was said, 7000 miles) on horseback throughout Victoria. He read while in the saddle and studied the natural scene with such assiduous care that from 1873 onward he began to contribute to official reports, scientific journals and learned societies papers of primary value on the Gippsland rocks. He pioneered the use in Australia of thin-section petrology and chemical analysis of rocks. His fundamental contribution was his discovery and exploration of the Upper Devonian series north of Bairnsdale. He also made important studies of the Lower Devonian volcanics in East Gippsland and compiled magnificent geological maps of the area. In botany his *Eucalypts of Gippsland* (1889) became a standard authority and he collected hundreds of varieties of ferns, grasses, acacias and flowering plants. But his greatest eminence came from his work in anthropology, which was his main interest and relaxation after 1872.

On his expedition to the Barcoo Howitt had met members of the Yantruwanta, Dieri and other tribes while they were uninfluenced by Europeans. He learned, though inexpertly, something of their ecology, languages, beliefs and customs. The experience confirmed in him a dissociation between the Aboriginals as an object of scientific interest and as a challenge to social policy. Family letters show that he went to central Australia sharing the racial and social prejudices of the day. His attitudes softened later but nothing in his writings suggests that he ever agreed with the condemnation of Europeans for their treatment of native peoples expressed in his father's polemical *Colonization and Christianity* (1838). Even in official roles—he was for a time a local guardian of Aboriginals in Gippsland and in 1877 sat on the royal commission which inquired into their whole situation—his attitude appears always to have been that of the dispassionate scientist. His view of their problems did not extend beyond charitable paternalism and segregated training in institutions. His dealings with Aboriginals were cordial and appreciative if somewhat calculated, and he had no difficulty in finding long-serving helpers among them in all his inquiries. But he saw them as a people doomed to extinction by an extraordinary primitivity, and this quality aroused his scientific interest.

In the 1860s Howitt read widely and deeply on the evolution of man and society in the literature of Darwin [q.v.], Lubbock, Galton and Tylor, and probably knew something of Maine, McLennan and Bachofen. He turned this new-found thought towards the Aboriginals and about 1864 began, without definite aim, to record all he could learn of the Kurnai and other south-eastern tribes. He needed only occasion and motive to synthesize his knowledge with the brilliant vision which 'ethnology' was beginning to hold out—a new, universal, comparative science of custom. Both were provided when Fison returned to Australia in 1871 from Fiji. Howitt responded to Fison's public request for information and help in a study of the kinship, affinity and marriage systems of the Aboriginals, and in 1872 the two entered into an enthusiastic collaboration.

Howitt as anthropologist developed through four phases. The first in 1861-71 was one of unwitting preparation. In the second in 1872-80, after induction by Fison into the viewpoint and methods of Morgan's *Systems of Consanguinity and Affinity of the Human Family*, he immersed himself in systematic study. He gave all his leisure to direct inquiries in the field, the development of elaborate questionnaires, their circulation to possible informants, to voluminous correspondence and to writing. In 1873-78 he published twelve brief but informative memoirs, some of which drew on the data collected in the 1860s. In 1879 he completed his part of *Kamilaroi and Kurnai*, which appeared under his and Fison's names in 1880 and was recognized throughout the world as a landmark in the new 'anthropology' replacing 'ethnology'. Howitt's clear account of social organization was, when based on fact, rightly praised, but its reliability was later questioned.

In 1881-90, his third and probably best phase, Howitt continued active and productive. He wrote eighteen substantial papers, some of them of permanent value if their substance is rid of adherence to Morgan's evolutionist hypotheses, by which Howitt was progressively captivated. He shared the contemporary presumption that social phenomena could be understood through their development, which comprehends what is most significant in their nature. But the substance of his work disproves that he supposed development to exhaust the significances. His scientific mentality was excellent, cautious towards the possibility of 'false facts' and ready to see his own theories toppled. He was sharply aware that co-existent facts also required explanation. Such contemporaries as Lubbock, McLennan and Lang, with rival theories about the development of particular institutions, and successors like Mathews, Thomas, Malinowski and Radcliffe-Brown, some of whom revolted against 'conjectural history', did not readily see that his work had importance independently of the overriding obsession that the stratified evidences of pristine family, sexual and marriage forms were visible like fossils in a living society. More appreciative eyes, disregarding such outmoded views, now recognize that Howitt greatly widened the base, improved the methods and deepened the insights of a nascent science. He wrote in a careful, informed way on a wealth of empirical topics —boomerangs, canoes, name-giving, cannibalism, migrations, wizardry, songs, message-sticks, sign-language—but most valuably on the kinship structures and intergroup relations of social life.

In two productive years, 1883 and 1884, Howitt showed his growing span and competence in seven papers, two of them with Fison. One, on initiation, was praised for its lucidity and detail by Tylor, who read it for Howitt to the Royal Anthropological Institute, London, on 11 December 1883. It set a new standard of ethnographic description and analysis and, with a second paper on the same subject, made possible the first comprehension of the form, management and significance of initiations as ceremonious disciplines shaping personality under social, moral and religious sanctions. Other papers made serviceable if now superseded distinctions between 'local' (geographical or territorial groups) and 'social' (marriage, descent and kinship categories) organization which in cross-relationship give Aboriginal society its characteristic structure. For this achievement Howitt most deserves remembrance.

As early as 1878, in his schematic presentation of Brabrolong kinship and his first sketch of Kurnai initiation, he showed some grasp of the anatomy of Aboriginal society. Its emergence in the papers of the third phase is a fascinating anticipation of insights that did not mature fully for another half century. By 1890 he wrote so explicitly, in comparative contexts, of the 'social structure' or the 'organic structure' of Aboriginal society that he must be credited with Fison as the first to adumbrate the essence of the 'structural-functional' per-

spective in modern social anthropology. No one before him could have written from empirical knowledge that 'aboriginal society as it exists in Australia is organized in a comparatively complete manner', and that 'the whole of the customs which form the foundation and the superstructure of aboriginal society ramify so much that in order to understand any part it becomes necessary to study the whole'. These insights were far removed from the imaginary stratigraphy of fossil customs.

In his last phase, 1891-1907, Howitt was a high official with little opportunity for fieldwork yet wrote with unflagging zeal two dozen papers and The Native Tribes of South-East Australia (1904); although a summation of his work it is probably not his best memorial. In his last years he still had formative ideas to offer on many topics, including the ritual significance of the newly-discovered bullroarer and the ethnological puzzle of the Tasmanian and Australian Aboriginals. His output was the more remarkable in view of protracted, and on his part courteous, controversy with anthropological critics, the counter-attraction of botanical and petrological research and the cares of high office. After the only illness of his life he died on 7 March 1908 and was buried at Bairnsdale. He was predeceased in 1903 by his wife Maria Robinson, daughter of Judge Boothby [q.v.], whom he had married in 1864, and was survived by two sons and three daughters.

Howitt was a fellow of the Geological Society of London and the Royal Anthropological Institute of Great Britain, and a councillor of the Royal Society of Victoria. He was much honoured towards the end of his life. The Royal Society of New South Wales awarded him the Clarke memorial medal in 1903 and the Australasian Association for the Advancement of Science the first Mueller [q.v.] medal in 1904. When he visited England that year the University of Cambridge awarded him an honorary doctorate in science and he was made C.M.G. for services to the State and to science. In 1907 he was president of the Adelaide meeting of the Australasian Association for the Advancement of Science, but he is best remembered as one of 'the band of brothers', Fison, Spencer and Gillen, who laid the foundations of Australian anthropology.

P. Corris, Aborigines and Europeans in Western Victoria (Canberra, 1968); D. J. Mulvaney, 'The ascent of Aboriginal man', M. H. Walker, Come wind, come weather (Melb, 1971); W. B. Spencer, 'Alfred William Howitt', Vic Naturalist, 24 (1908); J. G. Frazer, 'Howitt and Fison', Folk-Lore (Lond), 20 (1909); M. E. B. Howitt, 'The Howitts in Australia', VHM, 3

(1913-14); D. J. Mulvaney, 'The Australian Aborigines 1606-1929 : opinion and fieldwork', *Hist Studies*, no 30, May 1958; A. P. Elkin, 'A Darwin centenary and highlights of field-work in Australia', *Mankind*, 5 (1959) no 8; D. J. Mulvaney, 'The anthropologist as tribal elder', *Mankind*, 7 (1970) no 3; Howitt papers (LaT L and held by Mrs M. H. Walker); information from D. J. Mulvaney and D. E. Barwick (ANU).

W. E. H. STANNER

HOWITT, WILLIAM (1792-1879), author and traveller, RICHARD (1799-1870), poet, and GODFREY (1800-1873), physician and natural scientist, were born at Heanor, Derbyshire, England, sons of Thomas Howitt and his wife Phoebe, née Tantum, daughter of a Staffordshire Quaker.

William was born on 18 December 1792 and educated at Quaker schools in Ackworth and Tamworth. He wanted to continue his studies but his father, imbued with Rousseau's teachings, apprenticed him to a cabinet maker. William tore up his articles and worked on his father's farm, roamed the countryside, studied nature and taught himself languages, botany, chemistry and dispensing of medicines. At the Friends' Meeting House, Uttoxeter, on 16 April 1821 he married Mary Botham. They lived at Hanley, Staffordshire, where William set up as a druggist. In 1822 they went to Nottingham and in 1823 began their long literary partnership by publishing *The Forest Minstrel, and other Poems*. William became a borough alderman, a leader in the church disestablishment movement and a supporter of Daniel O'Connell. The family moved to Esher in 1836 and to Germany in 1840. They returned to England in 1843 and made their home a forum for writers, artists and philanthropists.

In 1852 William and two sons sailed for Victoria where they spent two years on the diggings. They gained little gold but much colonial experience; although William revelled in the free bush life and strange flora and fauna, and was stimulated by repulsing bushrangers, he found scope for reform in the land laws, in the gold commissioners and 'the comic-opera police force'. His experiences are reflected in *A Boy's Adventures in the Wilds of Australia* (1854), *Land, Labour, and Gold; or, Two Years in Victoria* (1855), *Tallangetta, the Squatter's Home* (1857) and *The History of Discovery in Australia, Tasmania, and New Zealand* (1865). He returned to England in 1854. The family continued their writing and philanthropy until 1870 when they settled in Rome. At Tra Fontane he persuaded the Trappist Monks to plant malarial swamps with eucalyptus seeds from East

Gippsland. With his wife, Howitt is credited with 180 published works. He also remained active as a self-styled radical crusading for truth, his actions motivated by love of freedom and hatred of injustice. He died in Rome on 3 March 1879, survived by his wife who died on 30 January 1888 and by three children.

An oil painting by C. Hoffmann is held by Mrs R. W. Jowsey, East Bairnsdale, Victoria.

Richard began as a druggist in partnership with William in Nottingham and then opened his own shop. With his brother Godfrey he arrived at Port Phillip in 1840. He farmed on the Heidelberg Road until his return to England in 1844. His lively *Impressions of Australia Felix during four years residence in that colony* (London, 1845) was regarded as the 'most reliable description of Australian life at that date'. He also published volumes of poetry in 1830, 1840 and 1868. He died in 1870.

Godfrey, born on 8 October 1800, was educated at Mansfield, tutored by William and entered the University of Edinburgh (M.D., 1830). He practised in Leicester and in Nottingham was honorary physician to the General Hospital and to the City Infirmary. On 6 April 1831 at the Friends' Meeting House, Castle Donington, he married Phoebe Bakewell. In 1839 he decided to migrate and with his family, a nephew and his wife's brothers arrived at Port Phillip in the *Lord Goderich* in April 1840. Howitt erected the prefabricated wooden cottage he had brought from England, and by 1845 his land extended from Collins Street to Flinders Lane with a frontage to Spring Street where he made a large garden. He also had pastoral interests near Yea and Cape Schanck and a farm at Caulfield.

Howitt was early associated with the Melbourne Hospital; in 1847 he became president and honorary physician of the Melbourne Benevolent Asylum and joined the new Port Phillip Medical Association; in 1853-71 he served on the Council of the University of Melbourne and on the Medical School Committee. In 1854-55 he was first vice-president of the Philosophical Society of Victoria and a member of its successor, the Royal Society of Victoria, in 1859-68.

Howitt won wide repute as a botanist and entomologist. He helped to found the Entomological Society of London, was a member of the Botanical Society of Edinburgh and in 1839 published *The Nottinghamshire Flora*. In Victoria Mueller [q.v.] named the monotypic genus Howittia, a native blue-flowered mallow, 'in acknowledgement of his devotion to botany'. He died at Caulfield on 4 December 1873, survived by three sons and a daughter. To the University of Melbourne he left his books on botany and entomology, his entomological collection and £1000 for scholarships in botany, geology and zoology.

Bronze medallions by Thomas Woolner [q.v.] of Howitt and his family are held by descendants.

M. Howitt (ed), *Mary Howitt. An autobiography* (Lond, 1889); C. Woodring, *Victorian samplers: William and Mary Howitt* (Lawrence, 1952); A. Lee, *Laurels & rosemary* (Lond, 1955); A. Lee, *In their generations* (Plainfield, 1956?); M. H. Walker, *Come wind, come weather* (Melb, 1971); W. Howitt, Autobiography (held by author); Howitt family letters (held by author).

MARY HOWITT WALKER

HUBBE, ULRICH (1805-1892), journalist, farmer, teacher, interpreter, land agent and legal scholar, was born on 1 June 1805 in Hamburg, the third son of Heinrich Hübbe (1771-1847), notary and registrar of the Hamburg Admiralty. He was educated at Johanneum Gymnasium and read law at Jena and Berlin in 1826-30 and at the University of Kiel (D.U.L., 1837). He had held a junior post in the Prussian Civil Service but became a barrister in Hamburg where he helped religious groups, including one led by Pastor Fritzsche [q.v.], to migrate to South Australia. After the great fire in Hamburg in 1842 he went to England and with aid from G. F. Angas [q.v.] sailed in the *Taglione*, arriving at Port Adelaide on 15 October. He leased 560 acres in the Barossa Valley and tried to sublet it. He did not succeed and on 29 June 1843 was gaoled for insolvency. After discharge he was naturalized and opened schools at Kensington in 1847 and Buchfelde in 1851. In 1855 he returned to Adelaide and taught languages, of which he was reputedly fluent in eleven.

In 1856 the press became interested in methods of transferring and encumbering real property. Hübbe advocated the system of registration and indefeasibility of title used in Hamburg and other Hanse towns. He was brought to the notice of R. R. Torrens [q.v.] who in 1857-58 piloted through the parliament the original Real Property Act, which simplified the registration of land titles now used throughout Australia and many other countries. Hübbe assisted Torrens in several ways. At Angas's expense he published in 1857 *The Voice of History and Reason brought to bear against the Absurd and Expensive Method of Encumbering Immoveable Property*, which encouraged the movement for reform, criticized the first draft of Torrens's measure and translated the Hanseatic system of land

registration and transfer. He advised Torrens and his supporters in the passage of the bill and was responsible for important changes in its second and final readings. Although spurned by Torrens, he helped to defend the Act from attacks by the legal profession and by Boothby and Gwynne [qq.v.] in the Supreme Court. He was secretary of a committee formed for that purpose of the Land Titles Association in 1874. He also wrote pamphlets defending the Real Property Act from its opponents, particularly Gwynne.

In 1857-66 Hübbe was government German interpreter at £100 a year and was compensated with £75 when he lost office. He applied for many other government posts without success but retained his interest in law reform. He ardently supported the abolition of primogeniture which was effected in 1867 and gave evidence to the royal commission on Real Property, Intestacy and Testamentary Causes Acts in 1873. He proposed a consolidation of statutes passed in, or applicable to, South Australia with tables of amendments and repeals, drafted a bill to make succession on intestacy uniform and suggested an index and epitome of the colony's laws; all these failed to attract official interest. He abandoned teaching and, after acting as a land agent, interpreter and translator, became editor of the *Neue Deutsche Zeitung* in October 1875, but resigned in April 1876. His eyesight failed and he lived with his daughter, Isabel, in Spalding and later moved to White Hut where both his wife and daughter were teachers. In 1884 friends petitioned the House of Assembly for a grant because of his indigent circumstances and his unpaid contributions to the Real Property Act. He was later given £250. Always of a literary bent he wrote a few minor poems and an unpublished epic on the progress of German civilization towards free trade. When he finally went blind, he learned to read by Dr Moon's raised-type method and presented copies of the gospels to the Blind School for the use of fellow Germans.

Though deeply religious, Hübbe disagreed with Kavel [q.v.] on such matters as mixed marriages, but he joined the Adelaide Lutheran congregation in 1855, became a lector in 1857 and by 1867 was a leading member of Bethlehem Church. He opposed the abolition of the Bible in schools; though tolerant towards other denominations he was anti-authoritarian in both church and state. He gave much advice and help, both secretarial and legal, to his fellow Germans in the colony and was active on committees for protecting German interests. His main importance, often underestimated, lies in his contributions to the Real Property Act.

Anthony Forster [q.v.] was one of several who later claimed that without Hübbe's help the Act might never have been passed.

In 1847 Hübbe had married Martha, daughter of John Gray of Glasgow and widow of Colonel Fuessli, a Swiss officer and early migrant to South Australia. Of their four children, a son was a captain in the 3rd South Australian Bushmen's contingent in the Boer war in 1899 and was killed in action. Hübbe was reputedly learning to speak Gaelic when he died at Mount Barker on 9 February 1892. He was buried in Hahndorf cemetery, predeceased in 1885 by his wife.

A. Brauer, *Under the Southern Cross* (Adel, 1956); PD (SA), 1884; PP (SA), 1884 (112); 'The Real Property Act', *PRGSSA*, 32 (1930-31); E. Tilbrook, 'The Hübbe memorial at Clare', *PRGSSA*, 41 (1939-40); *Lutheran Almanac*, 1934, 1968; *Register* (Adel), 29 Aug 1884; *Observer* (Adel), 11 Oct 1884.

DAVID ST. LEGER KELLY

HUDDART, JAMES (1847-1901), shipowner, was born on 22 February 1847 at Whitehaven, Cumberland, England, son of William Huddart, shipbuilder, and his wife Frances, née Lindow. After schooling at St Bees in 1856-60 he joined his uncle, Captain Peter Huddart, who had a coal and shipping business at Geelong. About two years later James was sent to open a branch at Ballarat and in the mid-1860s he became sole proprietor when his uncle retired. On 1 September 1869 he married Lois, daughter of James Ingham, a consulting engineer in Ballarat.

The business expanded and in 1876 Huddart joined a rival, T. J. Parker, and they formed Huddart, Parker & Co. with J. H. Traill and Captain Thomas Webb as equal partners. By 1878 they had bought William Morley's coal business in Melbourne where they made their headquarters. They used sailing ships until 1880 when three modern steamers were bought. The expansion of the coastal trade in coal, cargo and passengers meant continual additions to the fleet and new branches at Newcastle in 1880 and Sydney in 1881. Regular trade with Queensland began in the mid-1880s, with Tasmania in 1889 and with South and Western Australia in 1890. In 1889 the firm became a limited liability company with a capital of £300,000, the four partners taking up equal shares and the dynamic Huddart becoming managing director.

Huddart was chairman of the Victorian Shipowners' Association in the 1870s, a commissioner of the Melbourne Harbor Trust in 1882-85 and 1889-92 and a committee member of the Melbourne Sailors'

Home and the Victorian Shipwreck Relief Society in 1883-84. At conferences he vigorously advocated shipowners' rights, especially in the maritime strike of 1890, but he claimed that his full business life prevented him from entering politics.

Huddart's ambitions reached beyond the Australian coastal service. On his own account he had two steamships built in England in 1887, formed the New Zealand and Australian Steam Navigation Co. and entered the New Zealand trade in 1892. After March 1893 the financial crisis in Australia and the monopolistic position of the Union Steam Ship Co. of New Zealand made this venture impractical. Huddart, Parker & Co. inaugurated its own trans-Tasman service later the same year.

Thereafter, Huddart concentrated on a project which he believed God had entrusted to him, that of linking Canada and Australasia with England by a fast mail service, the 'All-Red Route'. By securing a transhipment agreement with the Canadian Pacific Railway, he was voted a subsidy of £25,000 for ten years by the Canadian government. This enabled the Canada-Australia leg to begin. Subsidies were also sought from Australasia and Fiji but only New South Wales responded with an offer of £10,000 for three years.

In 1895 Huddart moved to England where he tried to establish a twenty-knot Atlantic service, the other sea leg of the 'All-Red Route'. It required much larger steamers and an annual subsidy of £225,000 of which Canada was expected to pay two-thirds and England one-third. Huddart's plan won full support from the Canadian government and the postmaster-general in London, but was opposed by vested interests and critics within the British government. After a change of ministry Huddart's plans were shelved and later rejected. The implied lack of confidence in his ability led a new government in Canada to reject the Atlantic scheme. Meanwhile he continued to promote the Canadian-Australasian service in hope of financial support from New Zealand. His contract demanded a fourteen-knot, four-weekly mail service and after four years a third steamer was needed, but his private fortune was exhausted and he had to seek finance elsewhere. A new Canadian-Australian Royal Mail Steamship Co. was floated with shares held equally by Huddart and the New Zealand Shipping Co. The *Aorangi*, 4268 tons, was bought and made her first run to Canada in May 1897, the year Huddart formally severed his connexion with Huddart, Parker & Co. However, the new firm had no working capital and the earlier profit expectations did not equal the heavy losses. In February 1898 the winding-up order was issued, a month after the New Zealand government subsidies were authorized.

In recognition of his efforts to establish the England-Canada-Australia route, Huddart was elected a fellow of the Royal Geographical Society on 25 November 1895. His health had been deteriorating since 1893 and the mental strain of later events weakened his constitution. He died on 27 February 1901 at Eastbourne, England, and was survived by his wife, two of his three sons and a daughter. The oldest son joined the shipping firm of Birt & Co. Ltd in Brisbane; the second read engineering at Oxford; and the youngest, Cymbeline, midshipman in H.M.S. *Doris*, was killed on 25 November 1899 in the South African war.

J. F. Hogan, *The Sister Dominions* (Lond, 1896); Huddart Parker Ltd, *Huddart Parker Limited 1876-1926* (Syd, 1926); J. H. Hamilton, 'The "All-Red Route", 1893-1953', *British Columbia Hist Q*, 20 (1956); *Age*, 1 Mar 1890, 14 Dec 1935; *Argus*, 1 Mar 1890, 9 Feb 1920; *The Times*, 1, 4 Mar 1901, 8 Jan 1910; *Whitehaven News*, 7 Mar 1901; Huddart, Parker & Co. Ltd records (Univ Melb Archives).

G. R. HENNING

HUDSON, HENRY (1836-1907), engineering contractor and manufacturer, was born in London, the eldest son of William Henry Hudson (1814-1882), builder and contractor of Plymouth, and his wife Elizabeth Ann, née Dugdale. His father migrated to New Zealand with his wife and family in 1839 and about 1843 moved to Sydney.

Henry was educated at Christ Church School, Sydney, and apprenticed to a joiner; he was first employed by his father who was contractor for the woodwork of the University of Sydney and St Andrew's Cathedral. He visited the Victorian diggings and in 1860 with his father established a small joinery works at Redfern; by July 1870 they employed eighty-seven men and boys. His brothers Robert (1841-1915), William (1843-1891) and George (1848-1907) joined the firm and in 1876-77 Hudson Bros completed a government contract for two hundred railway wagons at £70 each. They also built passenger carriages and in 1881, after Henry visited the United States in connexion with bogie cars, began to produce them too. In 1881-86 Hudsons built the Coast (Prince Henry) Hospital and carried out many large contracts for timber and joinery. In July 1883 the rolling-stock plant was moved to Granville (Clyde). In the 1880s Hudson became chairman and managing director of a new company, Hudson Bros, which embraced the Redfern and Clyde workshops and sawmills at Pyrmont, Bathurst and the

Myall Lakes. The company's report for 31 December 1883 revealed a net profit of £30,000. In 1884 they employed about 1000 hands, and incorporated the firm of R. A. Ritchie [q.v.] of Parramatta and Wickham.

In 1885 the government accepted 'Hudson's Temporary Scheme' to ameliorate Sydney's grave water shortage. It required about 1100 men and was completed in January 1886 for about £78,000. The government was often criticized for accepting the contracts of Hudson Bros without calling for tenders, but the quality of their engineering was never questioned. Hudson Bros also manufactured mining, refrigerating and all types of agricultural machinery. In 1887 Hudson and other engineers were unsuccessful in securing government contracts for the manufacture of locomotives to alleviate a slump. Railway contracts fell away in the depressed 1890s but Hudson Bros kept going until 1898 when it was liquidated and a new firm, Clyde Engineering Co. Ltd, was formed on 30 September to take over the Granville works. Hudson later became general manager.

In 1874 Hudson was a founding trustee of the Equitable Permanent Benefit, Building, Land, and Savings Institution; he was a president of the Employers' Association and in 1889 a vice-president of the Free Trade Association. He became an alderman for Redfern in 1868 and mayor in 1873 and 1880. The government sought his opinion on municipal, engineering and labour questions, and in November 1890 he served on the royal commission on strikes.

Aged 70 Hudson died from heart disease at his residence, Glenhurst, Darling Point, on 9 May 1907 and was buried in Waverley cemetery. He was survived by his wife Mary Ann, née Turner, whom he had married on 17 July 1858 at St Paul's Church, Redfern, and by three of his five sons and three of his six daughters. He left an estate of £12,000 with debts amounting to £19,000.

The Hudsons were important pioneers in the engineering and construction industries and their relations with labour were generally good, though they did not introduce the eight-hour day for fitters and turners until November 1882. Henry Lawson, who worked for them at Clyde in the 1880s for 30s. a week and at their Newcastle branch, praised them in his *Fragment of Autobiography*: 'Hudson Brothers were not Grinders. If they had been they mightn't have failed . . . They imported the best mechanics they could get, treated and paid them well . . . Their work for Australia deserves to be . . . credited to them'.

B. Hardy, *Their work was Australian* (Syd, 1970); V&P (LA NSW), 1873-74, 5, 132, 1877-78,

4, 83, 1883-84, 5, 505, 1887-88, 6, 891; PD (NSW), 1887, 245, 981; 'Early rolling stock builders'. Hudson Brothers', A'sian Railway & Locomotive Hist Soc, *Bulletin*, no 153, July 1950; *Town and Country J*, 9 July 1870, 28 July 1883, 20 Sept 1884, 28 Mar 1885, 23 Mar 1889, 17 Oct 1891, 15 Oct 1898; *SMH*, 7 Sept 1870, 15 Apr 1881, 8 Nov 1882, 1 Oct 1887, 5 Oct 1892, 10, 18 May 1907, 16 Jan 1915; *Illustrated Syd News*, 2 Sept 1882; *Sydney Mail*, 13 Dec 1884.   G. P. WALSH

HUFFER, JOHN (1833-1898), schoolmaster and inspector, was born in Condover, Shropshire, England, son of James Huffer, farmer, and his wife Sarah, née Jones. He spent eighteen months at Highbury Training College, London. In 1857 with his wife Harriett, née Sedgwick, whom he had married in 1854, he arrived in Sydney to become Isaac Coburn's [q.v.] assistant master at the St James's Model School. In 1858 he succeeded Coburn as headmaster and in 1862 was headmaster and training master. Huffer worked with 'zeal and good judgment' to support and extend the reforms initiated by Coburn and did much to raise the quality of instruction in about a hundred Sydney diocesan schools. In 1867 after application he was appointed an inspector under the Council of Education. In 1867-72 he worked in the Camden district and in 1873-76 in the Bathurst area. Like Coburn he found the pressure of work and inflexible requirements of the new position almost insuperable. Friction soon developed with his administrative superior, William Wilkins [q.v.], because of his laxity with correspondence and reports, and his failure to maintain his inspection programmes. However, Huffer greatly improved and extended elementary education in his districts. His ideas on school organization and teaching methods were modern, and he was always positive and encouraging when commenting on the teachers' work. He repeatedly condemned the ineffectiveness of local boards and strongly advocated compulsory school attendance.

At Bathurst Huffer found the work of the inspectorate so rigorous that by 1875 he was suffering from severe 'nervous exhaustion'. His work fell hopelessly behind. Wilkins's solicitude soon turned to disapproval when it was falsely rumoured that Huffer's neglect arose from his desire to become an Anglican clergyman. His work continued to deteriorate and Wilkins advised him to resign. Huffer refused and was dismissed. In 1877 he was reappointed and transferred in 1880 to the new Department of Public Instruction but was again dismissed for inefficiency in December. Superannuated, he retired to

Upper Bankstown where on 18 May 1898 he died of heart failure after chronic bronchitis and was buried in the Anglican section of Rookwood cemetery. He was survived by his wife and a daughter, Mary Jane.

Denominational School Board, *Annual reports* (Syd, 1854-65); Council of Education, *Annual reports* (Syd, 1868-79); K. J. Cable, 'Saint James' Church, King Street, Sydney, 1819-1894', *JRAHS*, 50 (1964); Council of Education, Miscellaneous in-letters 1867-70, Minute book 1868, Secretary's private letters 1874-75 (NSWA).   CLIFF TURNEY

HUGHES, JOHN BRISTOW (1817-1881), landowner, was the eldest son of John Hughes of Edge Hill, Lancashire, England, and his wife Maria, née Bristow. Hughes went to South Australia from India in 1839 and in 1841-42 leased land at Bundaleer, north of Burra. Impressed by the mid-north, he advised his younger brothers Herbert Bristow (1820-1892) and Bristow Herbert to join him. They took up land next to Bundaleer at Booyoolee and then moved to the site of Laura, a town named after Herbert's wife Laura, née White, whom he married in 1854. Later they had headquarters at Booyoolee and Herbert bought out his brother's interest in 1858. In 1870 he journeyed up the River Darling to inspect suitable properties and bought Kinchega from George Urquhart and the English, Scottish and Australian Chartered Bank. Within a few years he had taken up runs totalling two million acres in an area extending from the River Darling to the Pinnacles near the South Australian border, in one place crossing what became the Broken Hill mining leases. In 1879 he had his own paddlesteamer and barge on the Darling. Herbert died at Adelaide in May 1892; his wife died in January 1909 aged 80.

At Bundaleer John Bristow made substantial improvements to the property and showed an interest in the welfare of the families of his men. By 1850 he had a house at Walkerville, Adelaide, and was writing often to the press on affairs of public interest. He was an active promoter of St Peter's Collegiate School. In 1853 he failed to win the seat of Light in the Legislative Council but in 1855 succeeded at East Torrens. He was a member for Port Adelaide in the first House of Assembly in 1857 and a warm supporter of R. R. Torrens [q.v.], serving in his ministry as treasurer from 1-30 September. He resigned from parliament on 24 September 1858, soon sold Bundaleer to C. B. Fisher [q.v.] for £32,000 and went to England. In London he wrote to *The*

Times denouncing the prospectus of the Great Northern Copper Mining Co. and in June 1860 gave evidence in South Australia before the government's inquiry into the scandal. Daunted by the land regulations of the 1858 Land Act Hughes moved to Victoria where he took up Ganawarra and Pine Hills near Echuca and later bought Brung Brungie on the Wannon River near Coleraine. His cattle were badly hit by pleuropneumonia and about 1873 he returned to South Australia. In Victoria in 1869 he gave evidence before an inquiry into railway extensions.

In Adelaide Hughes busied himself with public matters. He twice failed to win a seat in the House of Assembly but continued to air his views in the press on subjects including St Peter's, railways, finance and anti-ritualism. At Adelaide in 1876 he published *South Australia: its Position and Prospects—Letters by J. B. Hughes, Esq., on Railway Extension, Mr. Boucaut's proposed addition of £3,000,000 to its Public Debt, and on Payment of Members*. He was prominent in the Church Association. In 1881 he visited the Western District of Victoria. At Point Lonsdale on 26 March he was drowned. His wife Margaret died three months later at Kent Town, Adelaide; they were survived by several children.

D. Pike, *Paradise of Dissent* (Melb, 1967); PP (SA), 1860, 2 (83), 1864, 2 (213); R. H. B. Kearns, 'A pioneer pastoralist of the West Darling district', Broken Hill Hist Soc, *Papers*, 1970; *Observer* (Adel), 2 Apr 1881; R. Cockburn, Nomenclature of South Australia (rev typescript, SAA, ML).   SALLY O'NEILL

HUGHES, SIR WALTER WATSON (1803-1887), pastoralist, mine-owner and public benefactor, was born on 22 August 1803 at Pittenweem, Fife, Scotland, son of Thomas Hughes and his wife Eliza, née Anderson. He attended school in Crail and was apprenticed to a cooper, but soon went to sea and for some years was whaling in the Arctic regions. Hearing of good openings for enterprise in the East he voyaged in 1829 to Calcutta where he bought the brig *Hero* and traded in opium in the pirate-infested Indian and China seas.

In 1840 Hughes arrived in Adelaide where he settled to mercantile pursuits with Bunce & Thomson. On 21 September 1841 he married Sophia, daughter of the pastoralist and solicitor, James Henry Richman. In the financial crisis of 1840-43 Hughes turned to sheepfarming near Macclesfield in the Adelaide Hills and by careful management salvaged enough to buy another flock which he took north. In 1851 he took up The Peak at Hoyleton in the mid-north and in 1854 with his brother-in-law, John Duncan [q.v.], and family leased the vast Wallaroo station.

From observations in northern Yorke Peninsula, Hughes expected that mineral deposits existed there and instructed his shepherds to look out for any traces. In 1860 a shepherd, James Boor, made the first discovery of copper on the Wallaroo property. Hughes became the largest shareholder in the Wallaroo Mine Co. when it was founded. Soon afterwards another shepherd, Patrick Ryan, found copper on Hughes's Moonta property. After an amazing race to Adelaide, his horsemen managed to forestall rival claimants. The dubious acquisition of the mineral lease led to inquiry by a select committee which reported against Hughes but the Supreme Court and the appeal of rivals to the Privy Council failed to dislodge him. The matter was finally settled out of court by Hughes paying other claimants several thousand pounds and in 1868-69 an Act validated his lease. Several companies had been formed to work the discoveries. The Moonta mine had phenomenal success and was the first in Australia to pay over £1,000,000 in dividends. The Wallaroo mine was also profitable but salt water made it costly. Hughes always maintained that there was rich copper in the hills facing Hoyleton and Blyth and sank many trial holes but without success.

Hughes also owned large properties northeast and north-west of Watervale and planted the first Riesling vines at Springvale where in the early 1860s he established Hughes Park station. He also bought Gum Creek near the Burra, its 896 square miles carrying 60,500 sheep. In 1872 he bought the Lake Albert and Peninsula estate, a property later increased to more than 33,000 acres. He also owned Torrens Park near Mitcham, which was later sold to Robert Barr Smith [q.v.] and then became Scotch College. He had served on the last Adelaide Municipal Council in 1842-43 but apparently took no part in the controversies with Governor Grey. In 1871 he stood for the Legislative Council without success. In 1873 he joined with Thomas Elder [q.v.] in paying for Colonel Warburton's [q.v.] exploration to the north-west.

In 1872 the council of the new Union College, which included Hughes's friend, Rev. James Lyall [q.v.] of the Flinders Street Presbyterian Church, approached him for a donation. His gift of £20,000 so exceeded the council's expectations that it decided to use the money to found a university instead. Hughes wanted two professorships to be endowed and reserved the right to nominate the lecturers already teaching at the Union College. The council of the University Association foresaw difficulties in these proposals and their desire to have them modified nearly caused Hughes to withdraw his gift; the problem was solved when one Hughes professor died and the other resigned within five years of the opening of the University of Adelaide. Because Hughes's gift inspired others to make similar ones, he is often called the 'Father of the University'.

In 1864-70 Hughes was in England and returned there permanently in February 1873, living at Fan Court, Chertsey, Surrey. In 1880 he was knighted for his services to South Australia. After a long illness he died on 1 January 1887, predeceased by his wife in June 1885 without issue. Both were buried in the village churchyard of Lyne, near Chertsey. His vast property was left to relations, including the children of Sir James Fergusson whose second wife was Lady Hughes's sister.

Hughes, like Thomas Elder, William Milne [q.v.] and Robert Barr Smith, was one of the many Scotsmen whose public spirit and rise in influence were outstanding in the colony. Shrewd, gentle and kind, he had little formal education but shared the Scottish respect for learning. A window in his memory in the Flinders Street Presbyterian Church is now in Scots Church, Adelaide. In front of the university which his generosity brought into being is his statue, carved by F. J. Williamson and presented by the Duncan family in 1906.

R. Cockburn, *Pastoral pioneers of South Australia*, 1 (Adel, 1925); A. J. Hannan, *The life of Chief Justice Way* (Syd, 1960); O. Pryor, *Australia's little Cornwall* (Adel, 1962); G. Blainey, *The rush that never ended*, 2nd ed (Melb, 1969); *Register* (Adel), 5 Jan 1887, 29 Nov 1906; *Adelaide News*, 20 Feb 1933.

DIRK VAN DISSEL

HULL, HUGH MUNRO (1818-1882), civil servant, was born in London, the eldest son of George Hull [q.v.] and his wife Anna, daughter of Captain Hugh Munro of the Coldstream Guards. He sailed for Sydney with his parents and sister in the convict transport *Tyne*, and in September 1819 arrived at the Derwent where his father became assistant commissary-general. The family home was soon established on a 2560-acre land grant at Tolosa, Glenorchy; his father was transferred to Launceston in 1823 and after a few months Hugh became a boarder at Dr Thompson's Academy in Hobart. In 1829 he returned to Launceston

to assist his father as a 'volunteer clerk'. On a visit to his office Lieut-Governor Arthur promised him a formal civil service appointment when he reached a suitable age. When his father retired in 1831 the family returned to Tolosa where Hugh joined them.

Hull was presented by his father at Government House in 1834 and became a clerk in the governor's office. Arthur took a personal interest in him, giving him books to read, and encouraging him to broaden his knowledge. He soon tired of the long daily rides between Tolosa and town, and after August 1835 lived in Hobart. He became senior clerk and keeper of the records in the colonial secretary's office in 1841 and in 1848 chief clerk in the governor's office. He got on very well with Lieut-Governor Denison, for whom he had great respect, and who when he left the colony glowingly acknowledged Hull's services and gave him a gold watch. Vigorous in community affairs Hull was also secretary of the new Tasmanian Public Library and of the committee for the review of convict expenditure, acted as unofficial government statist and as meteorologist at Government House and was a fellow of the local Royal Society.

The second phase of Hull's career began in June 1856 when he became police magistrate for the Bothwell, Hamilton and later, Green Ponds districts, living at Bothwell and also holding office as justice of the peace, coroner, chairman of Quarter Sessions, commissioner of the Court of Requests, returning officer for Cumberland electorate, chairman of Bothwell Road Trust and manager of Bothwell and Hamilton Savings Banks. Pluralities were then common and like many contemporaries he was pleased to recite his long list of offices. Nearly 40, he considered himself hale and hearty, weighed exactly nine stone and could ride fifty miles without much fatigue, but the harsh inland climate and strenuous duties affected his health; in October 1857 his doctor advised him to give up riding and that meant the end of his country magistracy. Soon after responsible government was granted, he became assistant clerk-librarian of the House of Assembly, acting clerk in 1862 and clerk in 1864-82. He also served as secretary to royal commissions, organizer of Tasmania's exhibits at intercolonial and international exhibitions and secretary to the reception committee for Prince Alfred's visit in 1867 as well as putting his spare time to good use by developing his talents as scholar, lecturer and writer. He produced and published many statistical summaries, abstracts of legislation, newspaper articles, catalogues, calendars and guides to Tasmania. The government bought thousands of his *Hints to*

Emigrants, and his *Guide* of 1858 and *Royal Kalendar and Guide* of 1859, published by C. E. Walch [q.v.], were forerunners of *Walch's Tasmanian Almanac.* Elected a member of the Royal Colonial Institute in 1873, he became a corresponding member of other intercolonial and overseas societies. He was elected manager of St John's Presbyterian Church of which he was a member, and other societies and associations availed themselves of his services as secretary. One of his greatest satisfactions was his organizing, at first through the Oddfellows' lodge, of a volunteer rifle company. In 1861 he was commissioned a captain and by persistent practice became a champion rifle shot.

Quiet, genial and obliging, Hull was a good family man. He took a close interest in his brothers and sisters, the twelfth of whom was born in 1841. On 31 October 1844 he married Antoinette Martha, daughter of James Aitkin, sheepfarmer and magistrate of Epping; they had two children before she died in July 1852. In raising his young family Hull was helped by his late wife's aunt, whose daughter, Margaret Basset Tremlett, he married on 3 January 1854. Hull died in Hobart from a heart attack on 3 April 1882, survived by his second wife and eleven of their twelve children. His second son, Hugh, had joined him on the parliamentary staff in 1868 and rose in the civil service to head the Stores Department.

Hull's obituarist in the *Mercury* declared that 'seldom in the longest lifetime has any man filled so many honorary positions'. Two of Hull's own writings furnish the main accounts of his career: *The Experience of Forty Years in Tasmania* (London, 1859); and a memoir written on extended leave in 1875.   R. L. WETTENHALL

HUMBLE, GEORGE BLAND (1839-1930), teacher and town clerk, was born on 22 December 1839 at Leyburn Moor House, near Richmond, Yorkshire, England, son of Thomas Humble, farmer, and his wife Jane, née Bland. He was educated at the Wesleyan School at Richmond and the Wesleyan Normal Institute, London, where he taught until appointed headmaster of the Wesleyan School, Marylebone. Invited by the government of Western Australia to teach at Greenough Flats, he sailed in the *Robert Morrison* on 25 August 1861 and after a stormy voyage arrived at Fremantle on 13 July 1862. He taught for a year in a primitive schoolhouse at Greenough, was nearly drowned in the floods of 1863 and survived another fierce storm as he sailed south to become headmaster of the Fremantle Boys' School. Conscientious in his work, he was

respected by his pupils who presented him with an illuminated address and silver tea service when he resigned in 1889.

Humble had been commissioned second lieutenant in the Volunteer Rifle Corps in 1864, and in 1870 sponsored a memorial to the military commandant to change it into the Fremantle Rifle Volunteers. He was promoted first lieutenant and became captain in command. An unpleasant letter in the *West Australian,* 9 May 1888, caused him to tender his resignation, but he recalled it at the request of his officers and men. His popularity and enthusiasm were duly acknowledged by the gifts of a gold locket and a major's presentation sword when he retired in 1889.

Elected councillor for Fremantle North ward in January 1874, Humble could not take his seat as his simultaneous application for the post of part-time clerk of works was successful. When Fremantle was made a corporation in 1883 he became town clerk. In 1892 his position was amalgamated with that of the secretary of the local board of health so that he could become a full-time officer to the council. With manifold duties he undoubtedly worked very hard and probably devoted much private time to council work, despite his concurrent employment as part-time secretary of the Fremantle Benefit Building and Investment Society. In November 1893 the auditor reported to the Fremantle Town Council that far too much clerical work was expected of Humble and that his responsibilities extended beyond the duties defined in the by-laws. Urged by the auditor to respect the secretarial status of the town clerk, the council accepted the report and unanimously moved that 'the worthy town clerk . . . should be placed in his proper position as their chief official and responsible adviser'. However, Humble was shocked in March 1904 when the new mayor, F. Cadd, demanded his resignation, declaring that he was not satisfied with the administration of council affairs. Although divided on the issue, the councillors agreed to accept Humble's resignation and granted him twelve months leave on the maximum gratuity provided by the Act. In 1905 Humble was narrowly defeated as a candidate in the mayoral election.

With an abiding interest in the Wesleyan Church, Humble also was deacon at the Congregational Chapel with Rev. J. Johnston [q.v.] and later instrumental in building the Johnston Memorial Church at Fremantle. A prominent Freemason, justice of the peace and active sportsman, Humble was a founding member of the Fremantle Cemetery Board and planned his own funeral six weeks before he died on 23 October 1930. He was predeceased in January

1908 by his wife Ellen, daughter of Stephen Allpike, master blacksmith, whom he had married in 1864 at the Congregational Chapel, Fremantle. Of their two sons and five daughters, John Alfred Ernest (1867-1912) founded a business in Fremantle and maintained his father's association with the volunteer movement, which merged with the 11th Infantry Regiment and from which he retired as major and second-in-command in 1909.

J. K. Ewers, *The western gateway* (Fremantle, 1948); G. F. Wieck, *The volunteer movement in Western Australia, 1861-1903* (Perth, 1962); *West Australian*, 9, 21, 24 May 1888, 21 Apr, 10 June 1889, 6 Sept 1890, 27 Oct 1930; *Western Mail* (Perth), 25 Jan 1908; Fremantle Town Council minute books (Battye Lib, Perth, Council Chambers, Fremantle).   WENDY BIRMAN

HUMBLE, WILLIAM (1835-1917), manufacturer, was born on 9 April 1835 in Whitby, Yorkshire, England, son of Thomas Humble, farmer, and his wife Jane, née Bland. He was apprenticed in his native town and then worked for Hornsby & Sons, agricultural implement makers at Grantham and also for Bates & Vaughan, Middlesbrough. He arrived at Melbourne in the *Electric* in 1858 and joined Thomas Fulton's [q.v.] foundry as a journeyman. In 1860 he moved to Geelong where he was employed at the Corio Foundry, chiefly in casting postal pillar boxes. In 1861 with John Simmons and Ward Nicholson he bought the Western Foundry in Geelong. Business was good. Simmons died in 1863 and next year Humble and Nicholson decided to control the business themselves. Their partnership lasted until Nicholson retired in 1900.

By 1866 Humble & Nicholson were able to buy the Vulcan Foundry in Geelong. Their success continued through the 1870s and 1880s as Victorian manufacturers benefited from the large government contracts that resulted from the policy of protection. By 1888 Humble & Nicholson had won £60,000 in government contracts, their main source of profits; they built the £5000 bridge at Cressy, the hydraulic crane at Echuca and boilers, tanks and pumps for several public authorities. They also had an extensive private market linked to the agricultural economy around Geelong. The firm made the Ferrier woolpress, began building reaping and binding machines in 1872 and was one of the first Australian companies to manufacture refrigerating machines on the absorption principle. From 1900 Humble was in partnership with three of his four sons: Thomas Strong and William Henry were practical engineers and George Bland

was an accountant who had worked for the Commercial Bank for fourteen years.

Humble was active in community affairs. A councillor from 1869, he ended his municipal career as mayor of Geelong in 1888-89. He was the first treasurer of the Gordon Technological Institute and one of its original three trustees. He was also a trustee of the Geelong Free Library and a member of the board of the Geelong Hospital. As a zealous Methodist he staunchly supported temperance and was a director of the short-lived Geelong Coffee Palace Co. Ltd in 1888-89. He was closely associated with James Munro and M. H. Davies [qq.v.] but never extreme in his views. He helped to form the short-lived Chilwell Gold Mining Co. and was a director in 1878-79. In politics he was a protectionist but his evidence to the royal commission on the tariff in 1883 suggests that this allegiance was more a matter of profit than principle. His great sustaining interest was his business and he was always a keen inventor. In 1869 he began to manufacture velocipedes and later built the first car made in Geelong. The chassis and body were made in the foundry and a De Dion engine was added to the car which his family used for many years. Humble died at Geelong on 27 February 1917, survived by his wife Mary, née Strong, whom he had married in 1861, and by three sons and one daughter.

A. Sutherland et al, *Victoria and its metropolis*, 2 (Melb, 1888); J. Smith (ed), *Cyclopedia of Victoria*, 2 (Melb, 1904); W. R. Brownhill, *The history of Geelong and Corio Bay* (Melb, 1955); *Geelong Advertiser*, 28 Feb 1917.
                                          GEORGE PARSONS

HUME, FERGUSSON (FERGUS) WRIGHT (1859-1932), novelist, was born on 8 July 1859 in England, the second son of Dr James Hume. The family migrated to New Zealand where the father helped to found Ashburn Hall in Dunedin. Fergus was educated at Otago Boys' High School, continued his literary and legal studies at the University of Otago and was articled to the attorney-general, Robert Stout. Soon after his admission to the Bar in 1885 Hume left for Melbourne where he became managing clerk for the solicitor, E. S. Raphael.

With ambitions as a playwright, Hume decided to write a novel to attract the attention of theatre managers. On the advice of a leading Melbourne bookseller he chose the style of Emile Gaboriau, then popular in translations, and produced *The Mystery of a Hansom Cab*, a 'crude but ingenious' tale in which he based his descriptions of low life on his knowledge of Little Bourke Street.

Melbourne publishers 'refused even to look at the manuscript on the ground that no Colonial could write anything worth reading', so he determined to publish it himself and had 5000 copies printed by Kemp & Boyce in 1886. According to Hume this edition was sold out in three weeks and another was demanded. Some months later he sold his rights to a group of Australian speculators for £50. In London the great success of the Hansom Cab Publishing Co.'s edition in 1887 led to many more printings for which Hume received no further payment. Even his claim to authorship and original publication was publicly disputed, although he wrote a preface to a revised edition in 1896.

With the success of this first novel and the publication of another, *Professor Brankel's Secret* (c. 1886), Hume chose a literary career and in 1888 settled in England. There he published some 140 novels, most of them mystery stories set in England, America, Africa or on the Continent which he often visited. Only *Madam Midas* (1888) and its sequel *Miss Mephistopheles* (1890) were set in Australia, although fifteen others had colonial associations. His novels had clever plots but no great literary worth and none enjoyed the popularity of *The Hansom Cab* which played an important part in the growth of escapist literature.

Hume was reputed to be deeply religious and to avoid publicity but in his later years he lectured at young people's clubs and debating societies. He died at Thundersley, Essex, on 12 July 1932.

N. K. Harvey, 'Towards a bibliography of "The Mystery of a Hansom Cab" ', *Biblionews*, Sept 1958; *Table Talk*, 6 Jan, 13 Apr, 27 July 1888; *Australasian*, 21 Jan 1893, 23 July 1932; *Bulletin*, 4 Oct, 15 Nov 1902; *Otago Daily Times*, 13 July 1932; *The Times*, 14 July 1932; J. K. Moir, 'Australian thriller: Fergus Hume's "Hansom Cab" ', *Argus*, 2 Dec 1944, supp; G. James, 'A literary mystery', *Age*, 30 Oct 1965.

PAULINE M. KIRK

HUMFFRAY, JOHN BASSON (1824-1891), politician, was born in Newtown, Montgomeryshire, Wales, son of John Humffray, master weaver, and his wife Jane, née Basson. After a liberal education he was articled to a solicitor but abandoned his studies and went to the Victorian goldfields. He arrived at Melbourne in the *Star of the East* on 19 September 1853.

Humffray soon settled at Ballarat and made his first public speech in November 1854. He saw the diggers' grievances as symptomatic of an essentially unrepresentative political system for which he demanded reform by moral suasion. As secretary of the Ballarat Reform League he worked tirelessly to bring the diggers' needs before the governor, the public and an official inquiry. When the league was influenced by advocates of physical force he withdrew after pleading before a sullen and armed crowd to revert to constitutional agitation. Humffray dissociated himself from the Eureka rebellion but soon resumed his 'moral force' campaign. His popularity was little impaired; elected the first of three miners' representatives, he appeared before the commission of inquiry into discontent on the goldfields, citing maladministration, lack of political representation and difficulty in obtaining land as the diggers' grievances.

In 1855 Humffray initiated the Victorian Reform League with little success but with Peter Lalor [q.v.] he was elected unopposed to represent Ballarat in the Legislative Council. In 1856 he was elected with a large majority for North Grant to the new Legislative Assembly. As an independent democrat he joined the opposition to the Haines [q.v.] ministry. He was minister for mines under Heales [q.v.] from November 1860 to November 1861 and chairman of the royal commission on mining in 1863. Defeated at the polls in 1864 he remained outside parliament until 1868 when he was returned for Ballarat East. Defeated again in 1871 and 1874 he retired from politics. He had supported himself before 1859 by running a book-store in Ballarat and he also owned the Buck's Head Hotel until it was sold by creditors in 1868. In 1872 parliament voted him £300 in payment of his claim to a pension for having held office as a minister.

In parliament Humffray had zealously represented Ballarat's mining and commercial interests, introducing legislation on civic development, goldfields administration, land surveying and mining on private property. At first he lent his magnificent voice and powerful rhetoric to the Chartist cause but in later controversies remained silent or evasive. In support of schools he swung from the National system to the dual system and remained undecided about compulsory education. After supporting the Land Convention in 1857 he angered his constituents by voting in 1862 for a ten-year extension of squatting leases. His inconsistencies, together with his withdrawal from Eureka, led to bitter accusations of self-interested opportunism, though to some contemporaries he was a shrewd but sincere politician.

Humffray lost money in mining speculations and in his last years was dependent on charity. After a long illness he died aged 66 on 18 March 1891, survived by his wife Elizabeth, née Phillips, daughter of a Shropshire lawyer, and by one son. His funeral address was given by a Congregationalist minister and at his own request he was buried near the diggers who fell at Eureka. His only publication was a small booklet, *Ballaratiana* (1881).

A crayon portrait by T. Flintoft is in the La Trobe Library, Melbourne.

W. B. Withers, *The history of Ballarat*, 1st ed (Ballarat, 1870); G. Serle, *The golden age* (Melb, 1963); V&P (LC Vic), 1854-55, 2 (A76); *Argus*, 16 Dec 1887; *Ballarat Courier*, 21 Mar 1891; G. R. Quaife, The nature of political conflict in Victoria 1856-57 (M.A. thesis, Univ Melb, 1964).   DIANE L. LANGMORE

HUMPHERY, FREDERICK THOMAS (1841-1908), merchant, financier and politician, was born on 16 September 1841 at Oldbury, near Berrima, New South Wales, son of Thomas Bott Humphery and his wife Mary Ann, née Thorn. Educated in private schools, he entered commerce at 13. Recommended by Sydney merchants and bankers, he was appointed on 30 May 1864 an official assignee of insolvent estates while retaining his private business as a commission agent. He was receiver and manager of large pastoral and mining estates, a liquidator under the Companies Act and often arbitrated in commercial and financial issues. About 1871 he acquired a cattle station at Mount Debatable and three others near Gayndah in the Burnett district of Queensland, holding them until 1908.

In September 1880 Humphery failed to win Shoalhaven in the Legislative Assembly after the Sydney *Echo* falsely claimed he was 'a disguised denominationalist', but held the seat in 1882-87. As a supporter of Alexander Stuart [q.v.] he spoke mainly on financial questions. He preferred an income tax to a land tax on improved valuations which, he claimed, would oppress free selectors as well as moderately wealthy metropolitan landowners. In December 1887 he was appointed to the Legislative Council where he used his 'large experience in the administrative details of the laws of property and commerce'. He never accepted ministerial office but served on the parliamentary standing committee, on royal commissions into the civil service and city and suburban railways and in 1900-03 as acting chairman of committees. As a member and vice-chairman of the Public Works Committee he initiated enabling legislation for various companies in 1894-97.

Humphery had resigned as official assignee when he entered politics but retained his business interests. He was a director and in 1905 chairman of the Mutual Life Association of Australasia, a founding director and later chairman of the Perman-

ent Trustee Co. of New South Wales Ltd, a director of the Commercial Banking Co. of Sydney, chairman of the Federal Bank of Australia and many other public companies. In 1896-1901 he was also a vice-president of the Hospital for Sick Children. He died on 10 April 1908 at the Hotel Australia from diabetes and heart failure and was buried in the Anglican section of Waverley cemetery. He was survived by a son of his first wife Helena Annie, daughter of Rev. George King [q.v.], whom he had married on 20 January 1875, and by his second wife Lucy Alice Matilda, daughter of W. J. King, and two daughters. His estate was valued at £16,774.

Cyclopedia of N.S.W. (Syd, 1907); *Shoalhaven Telegraph*, 30 Sept, 28 Oct, 4, 11, 20, 25 Nov, 2 Dec 1880, 2, 6, 14 Dec 1882, 14, 17 Oct 1885, 15 Feb 1888, 15 Apr 1908; *SMH*, 11 Apr 1908.   RUTH TEALE

HUNGERFORD, THOMAS (1823-1904), pastoralist and politician, was born in September 1823 at Cork, Ireland, son of Emanuel Hungerford, captain in the South Cork Militia, and his wife Catherine, née Loan(e). In May 1828 Captain Hungerford and his family arrived at Sydney in the *Alexander Henry*. In November he bought 1920 acres at Wallis Plains on the Hunter River and in December was granted 2560 acres which he exchanged in 1833 for a similar grant on Baerami Creek. Thomas was educated in Maitland and in 1843 with his brothers took up Thungalier run on the west bank of the Barwon. In 1847 he became manager and in 1849 introduced the swinging gate for drafting cattle. In 1852 his father gave the Baerami grant to Thomas who married Emma Hollingsworth Wood on 19 June at St Mary's Church of England, West Maitland.

In 1857 Hungerford took up thirteen blocks on the Culgoa and about 1858 occupied Gnomery and Wyambah, 250,000 acres on the Warrego in Queensland, where he ran cattle. Hungerford on the New South Wales border was named after him. In 1860 at Baerami he successfully introduced ringbarking on a systematic scale into Australia. His example was followed by the neighbouring Whites [q.v.] and by 1870 the practice was general in the Hunter Valley. By 1877 Hungerford had 20,000 freehold acres at Baerami and had greatly improved its carrying capacity. Over eighty tons of oranges were harvested annually and a flour-mill was built by the creek. In April 1872 his wife died, leaving him with ten children, and in August he married

Catherine Mary Mallon. About 1875 he built a sandstone homestead for £5000.

Hungerford's election in June 1875 to the Upper Hunter seat in the Legislative Assembly was declared void in July and in August he tried in vain to defeat John McElhone [q.v.]. In 1877 he won Northumberland, one of the colony's most radical constituencies. He retired in 1880 to attend to his private business. In 1881 as Hungerford & Sons he took up three million acres in the Gulf country of Queensland and Cudelgo, 1500 square miles in South Australia near the Queensland border. In 1882 he again represented Northumberland and in 1885-87 the Upper Hunter. He supported the Parkes-Robertson [qq.v.] ministry but later voted for ad valorem duties. The Bulletin claimed that he was 'too high-minded to be manipulated' and that his 'breadth of ideas' and 'large experience' added to his legislative debating power.

Hungerford took a great interest in Aboriginals, learned their language and compiled a dictionary for his own use. He was known for his strong character and 'buoyancy of spirit in the face of difficulties'. By 1889 the Hungerfords owned or rented 3000 square miles and ran over 50,000 cattle, but the depression of the early 1890s and the long drought sent their overdraft up to £250,000; by 1896 the Bank of New South Wales had taken over Baerami and the other stations. Hungerford died at Ashfield on 4 April 1904 and was buried in the Anglican cemetery, Enfield. He was survived by five sons and four daughters of his first wife and by his second wife, three sons and three daughters. Baerami was sold in 1905 and the estate wound up in 1915.

Ex-M.L.A., Our present parliament, what it is worth (Syd, c1886); E. Digby (ed), Australian men of mark, 1 (Syd, 1889); I. Ellis, A history of the Baerami Creek valley (Muswellbrook, 1970); V&P (LA NSW), 1875, 2, 275, 1875-76, 1, 769, 1883-84, 1, 260; Maitland Mercury, 1880-94; Bulletin, 11 Feb 1882; SMH, 5 Apr 1904; Town and Country J, 13 Apr 1904; Court of Claims case 428, 1835 (NSWA); Surveyor-general records (NSWA); MS cat under Emanuel Hungerford (ML).   IAN ELLIS

HUNT, CHARLES COOKE (1833-1868), surveyor and explorer, was born probably in England, son of John George Hunt, auctioneer, and his wife, née Cooke. He seems to have acquired a master's certificate at Liverpool in 1859 and as a navigator arrived in Western Australia about 1863 and lived with an uncle at Newleyine. On 21 October he was appointed junior assistant surveyor to go with W. Padbury [q.v.] to the country around Nickol Bay. There he explored the coast, entered Port Hedland and discovered the pass, later named after him, between the De Grey and Nickol Bay districts. In 1864 with Governor Hampton and the York Agricultural Society as patrons he was sent to explore the country 300 miles east of York on which H. M. Lefroy had reported hopefully. Hunt discovered Hampton Plains and much grazing land. In 1865 he set out again, intending to clear a track for sheep and cattle and to sink wells along the route, but severe drought forced him back with some wild dogs he had captured to the dismay of local settlers. However, he blazed a tree at a place later named White Hope where gold was discovered in 1919. In 1965 the eastern goldfields branch of the Royal Western Australian Historical Society planted a kurrajong and raised an obelisk with a plaque near the site of Hunt's marked tree. Sir John Kirwan later claimed that rumours in 1865 had Hunt discovering gold but that the government suppressed the news.

In 1866 Hunt was a road surveyor in the Northam district and then returned to the country east of York intent on deepening the wells he had sunk. He was accompanied by four white men and by Tommy Windich [q.v.], an Aboriginal who later served John Forrest. Hunt pressed on clearing and sinking wells until he was driven back by ophthalmia and sickness. In 1867 he moved to the Geraldton district as surveyor of roads. He became ill in December, entered hospital in January 1868 and died from heart disease on 1 March aged 35. He was survived by his wife Mary Ann, née Seabrook, whom he had married on 27 December 1864 at Beverley, and by a son Walter (d. 1918) and a daughter Emily. His widow married Charles Frederick Edwards on 20 March 1884.

Hunt's diaries and letters are in the Battye Library, Perth. He was a thorough surveyor and excellent draftsman, who never named discoveries after himself. Forrest was reputed to say, 'Will I ever find a place where this man has not been before me'. While the names of Ford and Bayley were heralded as discoverers of the Coolgardie bonanza, they were probably able to penetrate east of York only with the aid of Hunt's tracks and wells.

E. Millett, An Australian parsonage (Lond, 1872); F. A. Law, The history of the Merredin district (Merredin, 1961); C. M. Harris, 'The eastern goldfields early explorers, 1863-1866. H. M. Lefroy-C. C. Hunt', JRWAHS, 3 (1938-48); Perth Gazette, 13 Mar 1868; Governor's dispatches, v. 8-9 (Battye Lib, Perth); Survey Department, Official letterbook v. 3 (Battye Lib, Perth).   KIM ROBERTS

HUNT, JOHN HORBURY (1838-1904), architect, was born in October 1838 at St John, New Brunswick, the eldest son of William Hunt and his wife Frances, née Horbury. His father, a sixth-generation North American, was a carpenter and builder in Waltham, near Boston, before moving to Canada in 1853. In 1856 Hunt began training as an architect under Charles F. Sleeper of Roxbury, near Boston. He soon transferred to Edward Clarke Cabot who closed his office when the American civil war broke out. Hunt decided to migrate to India. He sailed in the *Tropic* and arrived on 5 January 1863 at Sydney. He met the acting colonial architect, James Barnet [q.v.], who persuaded him to settle. Hunt joined the staff of E. T. Blacket [q.v.], the colony's leading architect. His sound training and knowledge of construction were important acquisitions to the office and by 1865 he was Blacket's chief assistant, supervising and designing many country commissions. His unusual ideas and forceful personality so influenced the character of work emerging from Blacket's office that his seven years there became known as Blacket's 'queer period'.

In May 1869 Hunt left Blacket and went into partnership with John Frederick Hilly. Ten weeks later it was dissolved and Hunt set up his own practice. The buildings that began to flow from his office had freshness, vitality and originality. For thirty years he produced highly-individual buildings, mostly ahead of their time. His architecture was marked by power, character and the use of revealed 'natural' materials. His skill with timber and brickwork was particularly outstanding and he was a master of complexity of form and asymmetrical balance. He also found wealthy clients who were interested in quality regardless of cost. Among the best ecclesiastical buildings Hunt designed were St Matthias's Church, Denman (1871), St John's, Branxton (1873), St Luke's Osborne Memorial Church, Dapto (1882), the Anglican Cathedrals at Armidale (1871) and Grafton (1880) and the Chapel of the Sacred Heart Convent at Rose Bay (1896). His best domestic work included Cloncorrick at Darling Point (1884), Booloominbah at Armidale (1888), Camelot at Narellan (1888), Pibrac at Warrawee (1888) and Highlands at Wahroonga and Tudor House at Moss Vale (1891).

On 21 February 1871 Hunt became a founding member of the local Society for the Promotion of Architecture and Fine Art, forerunner of the Institute of Architects of New South Wales. He resigned in 1873 and rejoined in 1887. As president in 1889-95 he determined to put it on a sound basis but his tactless efforts led to schism and he was left with only fourteen members. However, he reconstituted the institute and in 1891 saw it incorporated and in 1893 granted alliance with the Royal Institute of British Architects, to which he had been elected a fellow in 1891. In 1893 he became an honorary member of the American Institute of Architects.

Quick-tempered, energetic and constantly embroiled in public and private arguments, Hunt was a renowned eccentric. His lack of love for his fellows was balanced by an inordinate love of animals and he was an active member and vice-president of the Animals Protection Society. From 1895 his fortunes deteriorated: his practice collapsed in the depression and never revived. His wife Elizabeth, née Kidd, whom he had married on 4 September 1867 at St James's Church, Sydney, died on 10 March 1895. His enthusiasm was replaced by lethargy from the onset of Bright's disease and he became a recluse. Insolvent in 1897 he sold his home, Cranbrook Cottage, Rose Bay, in 1902 to pay his debts. He died in St Vincent's Hospital on 27 December 1904. He was saved from a pauper's funeral by two old friends and with Presbyterian rites was buried beside his wife in the Anglican section of South Head cemetery.

J. M. Freeland, *Architect extraordinary* (Melb, 1971), and for bibliog.

J. M. FREELAND

HUNT, THOMAS (1841-1934), journalist, was born on 15 September 1841 at Cappawhite, County Tipperary, Ireland, the third son of John Hunt and his wife Anne, née O'Brien. He was educated in parish schools. With his parents and four others of the family he arrived in Victoria in 1858 and settled at Kilmore, the home of two older sisters who had reached there four years earlier.

Hunt rejected an opening in the Colonial Bank and joined the staff of the *Examiner and Kilmore and McIvor Weekly Journal*, at the same time studying law. In 1865 he founded the *Kilmore Free Press* with which he incorporated the *Examiner* in 1868. He remained editor and proprietor of the journal until 1933. He acquired or established other country papers, the *Seymour Express* in 1872, the *Lancefield Mercury* in 1874, the *Nagambie Times* in 1878 and the *Moira Independent* in 1883, but they had passed from his possession by the 1890s. So also had much of his real estate on the collapse in 1891 of the Imperial Banking Co. Ltd, of which he was a director with Sir Benjamin Benjamin [q.v.]. In 1868 Hunt had married Catherine Mary, daughter of

Martin Flynn of Melbourne; she died without issue in January 1914.

In 1874 Hunt stood for the Legislative Assembly seat of Kilmore in a three-cornered contest, one of his opponents being Sir John O'Shanassy [q.v.]. Hunt won the seat by forty-four votes, a victory which he later cited to explain some of the differences that developed between O'Shanassy and himself. He retained his seat through changes of distribution which made him member for Kilmore, first member for Kilmore and Anglesey in 1877-88 and member for Anglesey in 1889-92. He served on two royal commissions: one on closed roads in 1878-79 and the other on gold-mining which included in its report of 1891 a recommendation for the redevelopment of the Reedy Creek fields, one of Hunt's particular interests. After defeat in 1892 he returned to journalism, except for a short trip to Ireland in 1896 as Victorian representative at the Irish Nationalist Party Convention in Dublin.

In March 1903 Hunt was re-elected to the Legislative Assembly for Anglesey which became Upper Goulburn after 1904. In November 1908 he became president of the board of land and works, and commissioner of crown lands and survey in Bent's [q.v.] ministry. His tenure in office was brief for Bent's fall in January 1909 also terminated Hunt's parliamentary career. He then remained in Kilmore where he died on 8 December 1934.

Quiet in parliament, Hunt was voluble over a wide field in his editorials and private conversation. He was an early supporter of Sir Graham Berry [q.v.] and the ideal of a 'yeomanry' of smallholders. His association with Irish and Catholic affairs and public figures was close and continuous and he attained the status of a leading voice in the Irish community before the end of the 1860s.

A. Sutherland et al, *Victoria and its metropolis*, 2 (Melb, 1888); J. Smith (ed), *Cyclopedia of Victoria*, 3 (Melb, 1905); P. S. Cleary, *Australia's debt to Irish nation-builders* (Syd, 1933); J. A. Maher, *The tale of a century: Kilmore, 1837-1937* (Melb, 1938); M. Cannon, *The land boomers* (Melb, 1966); *Table Talk*, 16 Oct 1896; *Age*, 10 Dec 1934; *Argus*, 10 Dec 1934; *Aust Worker*, 19 Dec 1934; G. M. Tobin, *The sea-divided Gael: a study of the Irish home rule movement in Victoria and New South Wales, 1880-1916* (M.A. thesis, ANU, 1969); information from Mrs M. Figgin, Kilmore, Vic.   K. SIMPSON

HUNTER, GEORGE (1853?-1890) and **ROBERT** (1853?-1936), traders and government officials in New Guinea, were twins born probably to an English county family.

In July 1883 Robert arrived in New Guinea with W. E. Armit's [q.v.] expedition. He was described then as 'a good fellow, when sober'. In November George joined his brother and for some time they earned a precarious living by trading and bêche-de-mer fishing. When Sir Peter Scratchley [q.v.] arrived as special commissioner, the Hunters were taken on his staff. George was nominally superintendent of bêche-de-mer fisheries while Robert was supposedly forester and superintendent of natives, but both acted as patrol officers with duties all over the occupied territory, negotiating with native tribes, investigating murders, conducting punitive expeditions and representing the administration in many private exploration parties. In the disruption after Scratchley died they were the senior representatives of British authority in New Guinea for a hundred days.

In 1887 George, the more reliable of the two, was appointed government agent at Rigo and settled there with a native woman while his brother retained a roving commission. Dr William Macgregor described them as 'active, seasoned, dashing men, but they are not truthful, are intemperate, quite uneducated, destitute of patience, harsh and domineering with natives and revengeful'. He therefore refused to confirm Robert's appointment when selecting officers for his government but kept George at Rigo where he could be closely supervised. In May 1890 news of George's death, allegedly from fever, reached Port Moresby; months later it was learned that his native woman, kept against her will, had conspired with a lover and some relations to suffocate him as he lay ill. Two natives were executed for the murder and seven were imprisoned. Robert remained around Port Moresby as a contractor and sandalwoodcutter. He married Namodia of Tatana village. Later he received a government pension and died on 28 August 1936.

Although the Hunter brothers were not particularly moral, they were undoubtedly capable bushmen. Their work in opening up new areas and pacifying tribes laid the foundation for most of the later policy of government exploration and pacification.

British New Guinea, *Annual reports* 1886-90; S. F. Denton, *Incidents of a collector's rambles in Australia, New Zealand, and New Guinea* (Boston, 1889); A. Wichmann, *Nova Guinea*, 2, pt 2 (Léiden, 1910); L. Lett, *The Papuan achievement*, 2nd ed (Melb, 1944); *Australasian*, 7 July, 29 Dec 1883; Administrator's letter books, Protectorate papers (PNGA).   H. J. GIBBNEY

HUNTER, HENRY (1832-1892), architect, was born on 10 October 1832 at

Nottingham, England, younger son of Walter Hunter, architect, and his wife Tomasina, née Dick. Educated at Sedgely Parish School, Wolverhampton, he studied architecture under his father and then at the Nottingham School of Design under T. S. Hammersley. Henry and his three sisters migrated to South Australia in 1848 with Walter and Tomasina and, after their parents died, to Hobart Town where they joined the eldest brother, George, who died on 31 October 1868.

Henry went to the Bendigo goldfields but failed to raise funds to pay his family's debts in Adelaide. Back in Tasmania he worked at Port Esperance in the timber trade on his own account and as manager for J. D. Balfe [q.v.]. He moved to Hobart probably to a stationer's business but in 1856, encouraged by Bishop R. W. Willson [q.v.], he began to practise as an architect. Among his earliest commissions was St Peter's Hall, Lower Collins Street, and in the next thirty years he designed such ecclesiastical buildings as All Saints Church, Macquarie Street; the Church of the Apostles, Launceston; the Mariners' Church, Franklin Wharf; Church of the Sacred Heart, New Town; the Presentation Convent, Hobart; the Deanery, Macquarie Street, and St David's Sunday school. He was supervising architect for St David's Cathedral, planned by Bodley & Garner, London.

On 12 September 1860 Willson laid the foundation stone of St Mary's Cathedral, Hobart, adapted from William W. Wardell's [q.v.] design; as supervising architect Hunter carried out the work with 'integrity, honesty and zeal'. Bishop Daniel Murphy [q.v.] opened the cathedral on 4 July 1866, but the construction was faulty and the pillars of the central tower began to move as the foundations settled, and stone fell from the arches. Hunter and Major Goodfellow examined the work and recommended that the cathedral be rebuilt. A public meeting in February 1876 decided that the central tower, aisles and walls be demolished and rebuilt according to the original plan. Hunter, now Hobart's most successful architect, supervised the demolition but deemed it unwise to attempt the suggested repairs. In 1878 the foundation stone was laid for a new cathedral designed by him.

At an inquiry by Bishop Murphy into the failure of the earlier building, Hunter claimed he had not supervised the work because of other commitments and blamed the contractor, John Young [q.v.]. Certainly Hunter's services had been in heavy demand but he had issued payment certificates to Young and neglected to employ a clerk of works to guard his principal's interests. Young had been badly served by his foreman

but no blame was attached to Wardell who in preparing the designs had noted that he could not advise on suitable foundations.

Hunter prepared plans and was awarded first premium in a competition conducted by the Hobart Municipal Council for a town hall. His design was acclaimed a fine composition of unusual breadth and unity of line but was not accepted. His design for the Hobart Museum won a competition in 1860 and construction began next year. Two years later he was commissioned to build municipal offices. He designed and built the Derwent and Tamar Assurance Offices, the Masonic Hall, Hobart, and the Australian Mutual Provident Society's Building. He planned wards and other offices for the General Hospital and designed many schools for the Board of Education; warehouses, the Marine Office and a 'picturesque grandstand' at Elwick race-course were among other buildings entrusted to his care. In 1876 he revised costs for capital works at two Hobart gaols.

Hunter was choirmaster at St Joseph's Church, Macquarie Street, for over thirty years, a commissioner for the New Norfolk Hospital for the Insane in 1866 and property valuation commissioner for Glenorchy, Hobart and Launceston in 1874 and a territorial magistrate in 1881. He served on the Central Board of Health in 1866-88, the Tasmanian Board of Education in 1875-84 and, after it dissolved in 1884, the Council of Education for which he was examiner in drawing from 1875. On the Board of Education he had been active in developing non-denominational schools. Before the 1883 royal commission on public education, he criticized the board whose meetings were mainly for ratifying decisions already taken by the chairman and secretary. He advocated an education department under ministerial control with a director advised by a board for checking political patronage. He agreed that a neutral secular system was desirable but insisted that 'every possible encouragement and inducement' be given to clergymen for religious instruction which he thought was the basis of all learning.

On a visit to Queensland Hunter formed a partnership with his son, Walter, and former pupil, Leslie G. Corrie, and settled at Brisbane in 1888. This partnership was replaced in 1891 by Hunter & Son. Although specializing in domestic architecture his firm designed the Queensland Deposit Bank and All Hallows' Convent. Prominent in the Queensland Institute of Architects, he served on its council and was president in 1890 and vice-president in 1891. In 1856 at Melbourne Hunter had married Celia Georgina, daughter of Lieutenant John Robertson of the 70th Regiment, Bengal;

she survived him with one son and three daughters of their seven children when he died in Brisbane on 17 October 1892.

Hunter was one of the few notable Roman Catholic professional men in Hobart and had long given the congregation of St Joseph's Church 'the beautiful example of a devout Christian life'. He had also dominated the architectural scene in Tasmania where his admiration for Augustus Pugin, leader of the English Gothic revival movement, influenced his work especially in the churches he designed. His treatment of this style gave a pleasing effect to even the smallest church while his use of local materials enabled him to blend a wide range of building stone in a delicate manner. He brought wide experience and mature judgment to his profession and was generous in sharing his knowledge with those who studied under his direction.

S. M. Robinson, Historical brevities of Tasmania (Hob, 1937); Roy Aust Inst of Architects (Qld), Buildings of Queensland (Brisb, 1959); J. M. Freeland, Architecture in Australia; a history (Melb, 1968); W. T. Southerwood, Planting a faith in Hobart (Hob, 1970); V&P (HA Tas), 1876 (31), 1882 (43), 1883 (45); Building and Engineering J, 19 Mar, 29 Oct 1892, 13 May, 8 July 1893; A. C. Walker, 'Henry Hunter and his work', A'sian Assn Advancement of Science, 19 (1928); Hobart Town Gazette, 2 Jan 1855, 10 Feb, 1 Dec 1874, 6 Jan 1885, 19 Jan, 29 June 1886, 10 Apr, 24 July 1888; Freeman's J (Syd), 30 Oct 1860, 5 Dec 1868; Tas Catholic Standard, 1 Feb 1877; Brisbane Courier, 2 Apr 1888, 18 Oct 1892.

D. I. McDONALD

HURLEY, JOHN (1796-1882), innkeeper, pastoralist and politician, was born in Limerick, Ireland, son of John Hurley and his wife Mary, née Hassett. In October 1823 he was sentenced in Limerick to seven years' transportation for insurrection and in 1824 reached Sydney in the Prince Regent. By 1828 he had been assigned to Captain Terence Murray [q.v.] on whose Lake George grants he worked and became superintendent. He was freed from servitude in 1830 and by 1832 had become an innkeeper at Campbelltown. He operated coaches from the King's Arms and was also agent for others in 1839. In 1841 he moved to the Royal Hotel and by 1844 had other hotels in the area.

Hurley bought land near Campbelltown where he bred horses and had a stud of Clydesdales at Mount Gilead. 'So favourably was his name known for the quality of his stock, that his horses were eagerly sought for the Indian market'. A keen sportsman, he sent his horses to local race meetings and from 1836 was judge at the Campbelltown races.

Under the 1836 Act Hurley took out his first pastoral lease in 1837 and later others between the Lachlan and Murrumbidgee Rivers. By 1849 he had 40,000 acres at Houlahan's Creek and 50,000 acres known as the Cootamundra run on which the town was founded in 1861. Hurley also provided its coach service. Apart from visits to his runs he lived in Campbelltown where he was a member of the first District Council and Roads Trust. In 1859 he was elected to the Legislative Assembly for Narellan but defeated in 1860; he held the seat in 1864-69 and in 1874-80. In the assembly he was a 'roads and bridges' member. He never introduced a bill and although he claimed to have voted in most major divisions in the 1860s he rarely did so in the 1870s. He called himself a liberal and free trader and advocated 'pensions to the old and infirm', triennial parliaments and amendments to the Land Acts.

After defeat in the 1880 election Hurley retired to his home, Alpha House. He was known as 'a friend of the poor' and was reputed to have assisted Caroline Chisholm [q.v.]. Aged 86 he died at Campbelltown on 27 November 1882 from senile decay. Predeceased by his wife Mary, née Byrne, whom he had married at Campbelltown on 10 January 1837, he was survived by three sons and three daughters, to whom he left £25,303.

W. F. Morrison, The Aldine centennial history of New South Wales, 2 (Syd, 1888); V&P (LA NSW), 1866, 1, 737; SMH, 16 Dec 1869; MS and printed cats and newspaper indexes under John Hurley (ML); information from K. J. W. Willott, Campbelltown and Airds Hist Soc.

MARTHA RUTLEDGE

HURLEY, JOHN (1844-1911), mining speculator and politician, was born on 2 June 1844 at Sydney, son of Farrell (Fergus) Hurley and his wife Catherine, née Critchley. His family moved to Maitland where he was educated. He became a digger and soon acquired an interest in various mines, including the Hill End mine. On 23 March 1867 he married Elizabeth Ann, née Letcher.

In 1871 Hurley became a justice of the peace and in 1872-74 represented Central Cumberland in the Legislative Assembly. He became a supporter, friend and creditor of Henry Parkes [q.v.]. In the early 1870s Hurley was active in Protestant politics and was a founder and director of the Protestant Hall. He was a proprietor of a paper company at Liverpool but competition from Melbourne defeated it and on 1 July 1875 his estate was sequestrated. Granted his certificate of discharge in March 1876, he won Hartley in April and held the seat until 1880. An active legislator, he repeatedly attempted to carry a bill to limit usury and to ameliorate the disabilities of Dr Beer, an abortionist. A Freemason of the Irish Constitution and an active Orangeman, he carried in 1878 a resolution to open the Museum and Free Public Library on Sundays. For this and his involvement in a dubious licensing case he was attacked by the *Protestant Standard* and Rev. John McGibbon [q.v.], whom he successfully sued for libel. Virulently anti-Catholic he tried in November 1879 to initiate a bill for inspecting 'all Convents, Nunneries or Monasteries'. His enemies often charged him with being a lapsed Catholic which he strenuously denied. He asked repeated questions in the House and 'never cared how much he endangered his own popularity, or whom he offended'.

In 1878 Hurley bought the Burrum coal-mines and in vain petitioned the Queensland government for concessions to build a railway from the mines to Maryborough. He visited England in January 1881 and in November 1883 was elected to the Queensland Legislative Assembly for Maryborough but in March 1884 was forced to resign through insolvency. He returned to New South Wales and failed as a sawmiller and mining speculator. In February 1886 his estate was again sequestrated. In the 1885 general election he had been defeated in both Hartley and Mudgee, but in February 1887 he won Hartley as a free trader although he did not get his certificate of discharge until October. In December 1888 as a share-broker he was again insolvent but the order was soon discharged. On 3 July 1890 he had to resign his seat because of bankruptcy but was re-elected on the 26th. About 1890 his wife died; on 22 April 1891 at Redfern he married Emma Wilson.

In 1892 Hurley was charged with Francis Abigail [q.v.] and other directors of the Australian Banking Co. with conspiracy to defraud the shareholders. Despite inability to fee a defence counsel he was acquitted but the episode was 'the most painful of his life'. In 1891 and 1894 he attempted to return to parliament and struggled to restore his finances. In 1893 he advertised himself as a 'mining agent' and manager of four companies. In December 1900 he failed to get his certificate of discharge but in 1901 won Hartley and in 1904-07 was chairman of the Public Works Committee. A justice of the peace he was a councillor of the Liberal and Reform Association and a director of the Randwick Orphan Asylum.

Generous and over-confident in the value of his mining interests, Hurley was admired for his 'rugged honesty, and independence, and fearlesss outspokenness'. He finally obtained his certificate of discharge in April 1911. He died on 10 December and was buried in the Anglican section of Waverley cemetery. He was survived by the ten children of his first wife, by one daughter of his second wife, and by his third wife Annie Elizabeth, née Garling, and their only son.

V&P (LA NSW), 1873-74, 6, 54, 1879-80, 4, 910, (LA Qld), 1878, 1, 269, 2, 493, 1879 (2nd S), 2, 1151, 1880, 2, 973; SMH, 29 Oct 1877, 27 Mar 1878, 13 Jan, 13 Oct 1881, 19 May 1887, 20, 22-27 Aug, 2 Sept 1892, 11 Dec 1911; Echo (Syd), 31 Jan, 3, 4 Feb 1879; Protestant Standard, 19 June, 27 Nov 1880; Bulletin, 22 Mar 1884, 23 Feb 1889, 12 July 1890; Town and Country J, 7 May 1887; Evening News (Syd), 11 Dec 1911; Parkes letters (ML); Insolvency files (NSWA).

MARTHA RUTLEDGE

HURST, GEORGE (1816-1885), Methodist minister, was born on 26 September 1816 at Burbage, Leicestershire, England, son of Benjamin Hurst, nurseryman, and his wife Elizabeth, née Dudley. In July 1839 he was accepted as a preacher on trial by the Liverpool Conference and spent nineteen years on English circuits.

In 1858 Hurst volunteered to work in New South Wales and in 1859 was appointed to the Sydney north circuit (York Street). In 1862-64 he was at Bourke Street, Surry Hills. An able speaker, he soon proved to be a forceful debater in the Church courts. In 1859-64 he was a member of the Missionary and Connexional Committees. Interested in languages and literature, he helped to re-establish the *Christian Advocate and Wesleyan Record* in April 1864. He was transferred to Wollongong in 1865 and in 1867 returned to Sydney to superintend the Newtown circuit, where he was re-elected to the Missionary and Connexional Committees. In 1869-70 he was at Maitland. As president of the Australasian Wesleyan Conference at Adelaide he declared that he preferred 'solid instruction' at weekly class meetings and 'wholesale literature' in the libraries to the theatrical exhibitions and scenes for the display of youthful vanity fostered by the Young Men's Christian Associations and mutual improvement societies. In 1871 he was the first clerical general secretary of the Church Sustentation and Extension Society for New South Wales and gave his services gratuitously. In 1878 he was elected president of the New South Wales and Queensland Annual Conference. In his retiring address in February 1879 he referred to the friction arising from the difficulty most churches found in 'raising suitable men for their work'.

In 1881 Hurst became a supernumerary minister at Burwood but remained a member of the Connexional Committee and most other administrative and theological committees. In 1883-85 he was a general treasurer of the Australasian Wesleyan Methodist Missionary Society which he was under 'a financial obligation to serve'. He had long been a councillor of Newington College. In 1884 Rev. William Taylor, founder of the Central Methodist Mission in Sydney, described Hurst as 'that Nestor of the Conference . . . a rugged old conservative . . . with his rough white head, his deep-set eyes all but covered by shaggy eyebrows'. He was thanked by the 1884 Conference 'for his great zeal and labour in raising the funds necessary' to secure young ministers from England.

Hurst died at Burwood on 1 July 1885 and was buried in the Randwick cemetery. He was survived by his wife Susannah Wean, née Ross, whom he had married at Burbage in 1842, and by two sons and two daughters of his ten children. His estate was valued at £37,550. At his memorial service Rev. W. Kelynack [q.v.] paid tribute to Hurst's clear judgment 'that went so thoroughly to the heart of questions, the resolute will that . . . laboured to translate conviction into action'.

M. Dyson (ed), *Australasian Methodist ministerial general index*, 1st ed (Melb, 1889); W. Hunt (ed), *Methodist ministerial index for Australasia* (Melb, 1914); W. B. Taylor, *Life story of an Australian evangelist* (Lond, 1920); *Minutes of the London Wesleyan Methodist Conference*, 14 (1858-60); *Minutes of the A'sian Wesleyan Methodist Church* (1869-71); A'sian Wesleyan Methodist Church, *Minutes of the 12th NSW and Qld conferences* (1884-86); *Christian Advocate and Wesleyan Record*, Apr 1865; *Weekly Advocate*, 1879, July 1885.   S. G. CLAUGHTON

HUSSEY, HENRY (1825-1903), evangelist, millenarian, printer and historian, was born on 27 August 1825 at Kennington, England, the second son of George Edward Hussey (d. 1842), who claimed Norman descent, and his wife Catherine, née Burt (d. 1874). After many small businesses failed in England, his father took the family to South Australia in 1839 and his mother became their mainstay through modest shopkeeping ventures. Henry tried the sea before entering the printing trade in which, despite some early schooling in England, he believed his education began. By 1850 he had a business and in the gold rushes printed the *South Australian Register* and the *Adelaide Observer*. From printing Hussey progressed to publishing Evangelical and millenarian journals, and to bookselling at his Bible Hall and Tract Depot in Adelaide.

Seriously minded, Hussey had taught in Trinity Sunday school at 19, an event he saw as the start of his Christian life. Though baptized and confirmed in the Church of England and later a lay reader, he was concerned about the doctrine of baptism, finally rejecting the sprinkling of infants in favour of the immersion of true adult believers. In the United States in 1854 he met Alexander Campbell (1788-1866), founder of the Disciples of Christ and advocate of adult baptism, whose views Hussey accepted; he was baptized by Campbell at Bethany, Virginia. On his return to Adelaide Hussey left the Church of England and associated with a Church of Christ but differences over administration led him to resign and work independently. He attracted followers, notably in the McLaren Vale district and elsewhere south of Adelaide, and baptized them in local streams.

In 1867 Hussey became copastor at the Christian Church, an undenominational assembly at Bentham Street, with its founder, Thomas Playford [q.v.]. Playford died in 1873 and Hussey was pastor at Bentham Street until 1891. Millenial advocacy was important in the Christian Church and he claimed to have preached on it once a month; he also gave long service on an advent committee and lectured in other colonies. Some tensions in the assembly after Hussey retired led to his return in 1894 but discord continued.

Hussey's printing and publishing encouraged him to literary endeavours and in 1862 his entry in the Gawler Institute competition for a history of South Australia won the prize. To compile this work he had access to government archives and to the private papers of G. F. Angas [q.v.]. Through this introduction and possibly some mutual religious sympathies, Hussey became Angas's secretary in 1865. Angas later acquired Hussey's manuscript and with help from the Angas family it was edited in England by Edwin Hodder and published in 1893. Hussey supported Angas's opposition to Roman Catholicism and their propaganda included the distribution of 2000 copies of Foxe's *Book of Martyrs* and the organizing of a successful petition against precedence for prelates. This experience of public debate led Hussey to stand for Encounter Bay in the House of Assembly in 1874, but he incurred the displeasure of some of his religious followers and withdrew before the poll. After Angas died in 1879 Hussey was authorized to gather material for his biography which was also edited by Hodder and published in England in 1891. Hussey's autobiography refers to many diaries and private papers of Angas which do not seem to have survived.

Hussey's achievements in history and biography, though somewhat filtered, were more enduring than his adventism, though his evangelical career was long and enthusiastic. His youthful experiences at sea and his overseas travels indicate his physical courage. Gertainly he had principle, declaring his theological position frankly and declining any pastoral stipend. Angas's employment of him testifies to his organizing ability and his great industry is evidenced by his books, publishing, preaching and philanthropic committee work. His strong puritanism and intolerance must have robbed him of some humanity, impelling him to sell his Shakespeare on becoming a Christian and his horse-tram shares because the company provided Sunday transport. Though said to be genial and obviously emotional in the Victorian manner of words, his laconic references to his family in his autobiography suggest preoccupation with theological debate. The respect of his followers testifies to his sincerity and, no less significantly, to the remarkable religious climate in South Australia in the nineteenth century. He died at Adelaide on 6 May 1903, predeceased on 25 June 1860 by his wife Mary Ann, née Reid, whom he had married on 19 December 1858, and by one son (d. 1888). He was survived by his second wife Agnes, née Neill, whom he had married on 11 November 1861 and who died on 5 August 1920; she bore him a son and two daughters.

Hussey's publications include *The Australian colonies together with notes of a voyage from Australia to Panama* (London, 1855?), *Nebuchadnezzar's image: being the substance of a lecture on prophecy* (Adelaide, 1878), *More than half a century of colonial life and Christian experience* (Adelaide, 1897) and *The scripture history of The Christ and of the Antichrist* (Adelaide, 1900). He also edited or contributed to the *Christian Advocate and Southern Observer*, the *Church Intelligencer and Christian Gleaner*, and the *Australian Quarterly Journal of Prophecy*.

Observer (Adel), 16 May 1903; notes, 165 (SAA). 　　　　　　　　G. L. FISCHER

HUTCHINSON, WILLIAM ALSTON (1839-1897), manufacturer, merchant, colliery director and politician, was born on 26 March 1839 at Garrigill, near Alston, Cumberland, England, son of Thomas Hutchinson, store-keeper, and his wife Jane, née

Phillipson. He was educated at Alston Grammar School and in 1857 arrived at Melbourne in the *Commodore Perry*, apparently lured by the goldfields. He went to Castlemaine and Ballarat but turned to trading. In 1860 he visited an uncle in Newcastle, New South Wales, where he set up as a store-keeper. In 1861 he married Barbara Telena, daughter of James Steel, a colliery engineer.

In 1872 Hutchinson moved to Sydney where in 1876 he founded a successful soap and candle factory in Abattoir Road, Balmain. In 1878 he was elected an alderman. Described by a local newspaper as a 'dark horse', he became mayor in February 1881 and began a vigorous term of office in which the Town Hall buildings were completed as well as other improvements. In 1883 Hutchinson, aided by the mayor of Sydney, John Harris [q.v.], formed the Municipal Association which he hoped would 'weld together the scattered municipalities of the colony as a whole, with a common interest to strengthen and help each other for their mutual good'. He was the association's acting secretary and in 1897 its vice-president.

On 2 December 1882 Hutchinson was elected for Balmain to the Legislative Assembly. As a politician he was earnest if not particularly distinguished; he supported Alexander Stuart's [q.v.] 1883 crown lands bill and carried two private Acts. As the company's chairman he had successfully promoted the Redhead Coal-Mine Railway Act of 1883. In 1885 he did not seek re-election, reputedly 'disgusted by the great waste of time and the heated feelings that so distinguished the Assembly'. In 1884 he set up as a merchant in Bond Street, Sydney, and returned to municipal affairs, serving as alderman of the Glebe for nine years and its mayor in 1896; he was also a justice of the peace. He was a commissioner for New South Wales at the 1886 Colonial and Indian Exhibition in London and at the 1893 World's Columbian Exposition in Chicago. He later developed a wide range of business interests and became a director of several companies and managing director of the Hetton Colliery. He was keenly interested in the building society movement and a director of the New South Wales Institution for the Deaf and Dumb and the Blind. He died at his home, Alston, Glebe Road, on 20 June 1897 and was buried in the Anglican section of Waverley cemetery. He was survived by his wife and by three sons and five daughters of their eleven children. His probate was sworn at £36,000.

Hutchinson had the drive and acumen to prosper in the expanding commercial life of the colony. He also had much feeling for public welfare and the well-being of ordinary citizens without neglecting his own material advancement. The *Sydney Morning Herald* justly commented that he was held in general respect.

E. Digby (ed), *Australian men of mark*, 1 (Syd, 1889); V&P (LA NSW), 1883, 2, 547-55; *Balmain Independent*, 12 Feb 1881; SMH, 23 June 1897; S. N. Hogg, Balmain past and present (ML).   HARRY HARPER

HYAM, SOLOMON HERBERT (1837-1901), produce merchant and politician, was born on 16 May 1837 at Sarah's Valley, Jamberoo, New South Wales, the second son of Michael Hyam, a London bootmaker, and his wife Charlotte Rebecca (Catherine Mary), née Broughton. Michael had arrived at Sydney in the *George Canning* in December 1827 and became a shoemaker but had the 'ingenuity' to acquire a 'landed estate'. Although Governor Darling called him a 'perfect Jew' and was reluctant to give him a promised grant, Hyam received 1280 acres near Kiama in 1829. He founded Jamberoo where he built an inn and store and cut cedar. In 1847 he sold the property, moved to the Shoalhaven district and died at Nowra on 3 September 1879.

Solomon was educated at home and went to Melbourne for commercial training at 19. In Sydney he became a commission agent but in 1860 was declared insolvent, attributing it to 'great losses' from the Shoalhaven floods. His discharge was certified in October 1861, the year he married Sarah, daughter of Samuel Priestley, produce merchant. Hyam joined his father-in-law's business and reopened as a commission agent in 1866.

Hyam established himself as a wholesale produce merchant with great success. He was elected an alderman of Balmain in 1874 and mayor in 1876-79. In 1875 he had become a magistrate and regularly attended the Water and Central Police Courts where he was known for his unofficious decisions.

In 1879 he retired from the Balmain Council for business reasons but in 1885-87 he represented Balmain in the Legislative Assembly as a protectionist. However, he supported John Robertson's [q.v.] free-trade ministry, allegedly because opposition to Balmain's senior member, Jacob Garrard [q.v.], would have destroyed his popularity. He rarely spoke in the assembly but carried a private Act. In 1886-1901 he served on the Commission of Fisheries and became expert in pisciculture and oyster-farming. In 1886-87 he sat on the royal commission on the excessive use of intoxicating drink. On 30 April 1892 he was appointed to the Legislative Council and from July 1900 was a member of the Public Works Committee.

Hyam's business expanded and in 1886-97 he was a director of the Citizens' Life Assurance Co. In the 1880s he bred pure Jersey cattle in partnership with his brothers near Shoalhaven and won many prizes in agricultural shows. Well known as a yachtsman Hyam's four boats won many races and he was active in arranging intercolonial contests. He built a house at Katoomba where he made a famous garden. He was president of the Balmain Rowing Club and the Katoomba Cricket Club and was a trustee of the Australian Museum and the Katoomba reserve. Uninterested in Jewish community affairs, Hyam was not a member of the Great Synagogue when he died on 7 November 1901 at Katoomba. He was buried in Rookwood cemetery with prayers read by his nephew Hyam Moss. He was survived by his wife, three sons and three daughters. In the 1880s his daughter Lottie was Sydney's 'most famous amateur pianist'.

HRA (1), 14; Ex-M.L.A., *Our present parliament, what it is worth* (Syd, c1886); E. Digby (ed), *Australian men of mark*, 1 (Syd, 1889); *Book of Shoalhaven* (Nowra, 1926); SMH, 9 Nov 1901; *Hebrew Standard of A'sia*, 15 Nov 1901; *Town and Country J*, 16 Nov 1901; Col Sec land letters 2/7887 (NSWA); Insolvency file 5219 (NSWA).   GEORGE F. J. BERGMAN

I

IEVERS, WILLIAM (1818-1901), estate agent, was born on 22 December 1818 at Limerick, Ireland, son of George Hawkins Ievers of Mount Ievers, County Clare, and his wife Margaret, née O'Shaughnessy. The Ievers were a prominent Anglican county family and claimed descent from a sixteenth-century English peer. Ievers early became a Roman Catholic, following his mother's religion; he may also have been influenced by the Oxford movement. Although his family wanted him to be a doctor he joined the navy at 15. He saw action in Constantinople, the Greek archipelago and in 1836-37 the wars of the Spanish succession. He married Mary Harrison of Limerick on 26 July 1838. In that year he transferred to the mercantile marine and as a master sailed to the Spanish Main, Chile, Peru, Canada and the South Seas. Sometime before 1848 he retired from the sea and settled in Dublin as a merchant.

Ievers decided to migrate and with his wife and six children sailed in the *Rienzi* as purser, arriving in Melbourne on 22 April 1855. The family lived first at Madeline (Swanston) Street. Ievers first worked as a storeman and packer for a softgoods firm, and in 1859 started his own real estate business. His agency was in Cardigan Street, Carlton, and from there moved to its present site in Lygon Street in 1886. A second office, opened in Collins Street in 1885, became a focal point for auctions in Melbourne. The Ievers firm was one of the largest in Melbourne and flourished in the 1870s and 1880s. In 1862 Ievers began his association with the Melbourne Corporation and was rate collector and valuer for twenty-five years. In 1875 he had joined the executive of the Victorian Protection League. He was vice-president of the National Reform and Protection League which was the basis of Liberal organization for the 1877 election. He contested North Melbourne and Carlton in the Legislative Assembly without success and in 1880 was again vice-president of the Reform League.

In 1890 the Ievers family moved to their newly-built home, Mount Ievers, in Royal Parade. The firm came unscathed through the depression of the early 1890s as Ievers had relied on commissions rather than speculations during the land boom. However, his investments did include interests in the Colonial Permanent Building Society, of which he was a founder and director. He supported many charities and as early as 1861 had helped to form the benefit system

of the St Patrick's Society. His children were educated at St George's School, Carlton, and he contributed to building the Church of the Sacred Heart (St George's). He was a justice of the peace from the late 1880s and in 1895 was elected city councillor for Smith ward in place of his eldest son who died that year. Irish affairs still interested him; he had visited Ireland in 1890 with William junior and the Freedom of the City of Limerick was bestowed on them. His impressions of the trip were recorded in *Fifty Years After; or, Old Scenes Revisited A.D. 1890* (Melbourne, 1894). He subscribed to Devlin and Dillon's fund for the Home Rule cause.

His wife Mary died in 1898 and Ievers on 14 January 1901. Archbishop Carr, who had often visited Mount Ievers, presided at the funeral. Ievers's liberal and tolerant views had enabled him to exercise a moderating influence in Church affairs and the young men who attended his seminars on economics and politics were also impressed by his liberalism. He left an estate of about £100,000. His son George erected a memorial statue to him over a drinking fountain in Argyle Place, Carlton. Terrace houses built by Ievers still survive and near-by streets bear his name.

The eldest son, WILLIAM, was born on 17 November 1839. After experience in a grocery business and a warehouse, he joined his father's firm as a partner in 1880. The first in the family to win an election, he entered the City Council for Carlton South in 1881 and held the seat until 1895. He shared his father's political views, and after two defeats was elected in 1892 to the Legislative Assembly for Carlton, on a protectionist platform. He supported the Shiels ministry, female franchise and, through National League of Victoria, the Irish Home Rule movement. When the Melbourne and Metropolitan Board of Works was formed in 1890 he became a commissioner. His interests included amateur acting; he was an original member of the Melbourne Shakespeare Society and also joined the Garrick Club. In 1878 he was a committee member of the Melbourne Athenaeum and its president in 1880. With his brothers and friends he founded the Beefsteak Club in 1886; its objects were to promote good fellowship and conversation upon things 'philosophic, literary, musical, artistic and social' and was patterned on the old club in London. William supported many charities and was a justice of the peace. He presided over the

455

royal commission on banking for only a few sessions before he had a rowing accident and died suddenly on 19 February 1895. After a Mass at St George's, Carlton, he was buried at Melbourne general cemetery, his funeral procession including members of the Carlton Football Club of which he had been a vice-president. He was unmarried.

The second son, GEORGE HAWKINS, was born on 24 August 1845. He too joined the family firm and on his father's death in 1901 filled the vacant seat on the Melbourne City Council. A justice of the peace, he was on the committee for the Talbot Epileptic Colony, contributed to the Homoeopathic Hospital and served on the boards of the Immigrants' Homes and the Women's Hospital. He set up the William and Mary Ievers Trust which still contributes to charity. He died on 15 July 1921, survived by his wife Marianne, née Webb. They had no children. His statue is at the corner of Gatehouse Street and the Avenue, Parkville.

The third son, ROBERT LANCELOT, was born in 1854 at Dublin. He shared the family interest in charities and was a member of the board of the Homoeopathic Hospital for nineteen years from 1891, and on the committee of management of the Austin Hospital in 1892-1903. Unmarried, he died on 29 October 1910.

J. F. Deegan, *Chronicles of the Melbourne Beefsteak Club* (Melb, 1890); A. Henry, *Memoirs of Alice Henry* (Melb, 1944); *Table Talk*, 14 Feb 1890, 5 May 1893; *Advocate* (Melb), 23 Feb 1895, 19 Jan 1901; *Carlton Gazette*, 23 Feb 1895; *Weekly Times* (Melb), 23 Feb 1895; *Illustrated Aust News*, 1 Mar 1895; *Argus*, 15 Jan 1901; *Herald* (Melb), 15 Jan 1901; J. E. Parnaby, The economic and political development of Victoria, 1877-1881 (Ph.D. thesis, Univ Melb, 1951); G. R. Bartlett, Political organization and society in Victoria 1864-1883 (Ph.D. thesis, ANU, 1964); R. E. Kennedy, The charity organization movement in Melbourne, 1887-97 (M.A. thesis, Univ Melb, 1967).

SYLVIA MORRISSEY

INGHAM, WILLIAM BAIRSTOW (1850-1878), trader and government agent, was born on 4 June 1850 at Blake Hall, Mirfield, Yorkshire, England, son of Joshua Ingham and his wife Mary, née Cunliffe. He was educated at Malvern College and matriculated in University College, Oxford, but in 1873 left without a degree to join his brother Thomas on Malahide station in Tasmania. In 1874 Ingham began searching for a property of his own and selected a 700-acre sugar plantation called Ings on the Herbert River in north Queensland. He soon became popular, was appointed a justice of the peace and the first township, surveyed

late in 1875, was named after him on the petition of the residents. When his first crop failed from disease, he bought the 7-ton stern-wheel steamer *Louise*, which he used as a general carrier on the Herbert River, and soon afterwards abandoned the plantation. Late in 1876 he moved to Cooktown with a friend, A. T. Clarke, and set up a general water-transport service. He carried diggers to the Hodgkinson goldfield, did some exploring and won repute for seamanship and honesty.

The reported discovery of gold in New Guinea in 1877 inspired Ingham to start trading there. In January 1878 he chartered the 13-ton stern-wheel steamer *Voura*, armed her with three small cannon and sailed for Port Moresby. Before leaving, he had written to the colonial secretary in Brisbane offering to act as unpaid government agent at Port Moresby. The *Government Gazette*, noting his appointment to the post, arrived in the schooner *Colonist* on 22 April with the first wave of a small gold rush but without any official instructions. Ingham therefore did what seemed necessary: he carried out minor police actions, offered to receive and forward mails, confiscated a schooner suspected of illegal activities, deported two prostitutes, recorded land transactions and reported to Brisbane what was going on in New Guinea. On 25 April he persuaded a meeting of native chiefs to petition for British protection and on 13 May recommended annexation. On 3 June the colonial secretary wrote his only letter to Ingham, cautiously approving his activities, emphasizing that he had no legal authority and instructing him to discourage ideas of annexation. At the same time he instructed H. M. Chester [q.v.], a deputy-commissioner for the western Pacific, to visit Port Moresby and report. Copies of the correspondence were then sent to London and to Levuka.

After a visit to Cooktown, Ingham returned to Port Moresby early in October and heard that the natives of Brooker Island (Utian) in the Calvados Chain had massacred the bêche-de-mer party under Captain Edwin Redlich and captured some weapons. Ingham promptly left for the island and arrived there on 24 November. Believing that he understood natives, he soon made them surrender the arms but three days later he and most of his crew were killed in a surprise attack. Hearing of the massacre on 5 December at Dinner Island, Rev. Samuel Macfarlane of the London Missionary Society sailed at once to Brooker where he saw the *Voura* broken up and was convinced that no one had survived. In March 1879 H.M.S. *Cormorant* ineffectually bombarded Brooker. H.M.S.

Wolverene later carried out a more determined punitive operation and retrieved a
few of Ingham's effects. One survivor of the
massacre testified early in 1879 that the
party was roasted and eaten the same night.

PD (Qld), 1878; Further correspondence on
New Guinea, PP (GB), 1883 (Cmd 3617); *Gov-
erment Gazette* (Qld), 30 Mar 1878; *Australasian*, 25 Jan 1879, supp; Qld Supreme
Court papers, 1880/2012 (QA); biog notes held
by E. R. Ingham, Orange; CO 234/38, 39; Col
Sec letters, 1878-79 (QA).   H. J. GIBBNEY

INGLIS, JAMES (1845-1908), author,
merchant and politician, was born on 24
November 1845 at Edzell, Forfarshire, Scotland, the fourth son of Rev. Robert Inglis,
Free Church minister, and his wife Helen,
née Brand. Educated in Edinburgh at the
Normal School, Watt Institution and the
University, he went to New Zealand at 19,
worked at Timaru and joined the west coast
gold rushes. In 1866 he went to India at the
instigation of his brother Alexander, a Calcutta tea merchant, and became an indigo
planter in Bihar and the North-West Provinces. He revelled in tiger shooting and
pigsticking, and published sporting verses,
Tirhoot Rhymes (Calcutta, 1873), under the
pseudonym 'Maori', and *Sport and Work on
the Nepaul Frontier* (London, 1878). In 1875
he became famine commissioner for Bhagal-
pur. After visiting Scotland Inglis returned
to manage extensive government territory.

A rheumatic cripple, in 1877 he left Calcutta commissioned by the Alahabad
Pioneer Mail to write on the Australian
colonies as 'a field for Anglo-Indian capital'.
As 'Maori' he also wrote for the *Echo* and
Sydney Mail. His letters to the *Pioneer* were
published as *Our Australian Cousins* (London, 1880). His health regained, Inglis edited
the *Newcastle Morning Herald* for a year
and became secretary of the Australasian
Accident Assurance Association. In 1879 he
married Mary (d. 1903), née Nichol, and
joined Cowan & Co.

The agent of the 'Calcutta Tea Syndi-
cate', Inglis sold tea at the 1880 Sydney
International Exhibition. As India's execu-
tive commissioner at the 1881 Melbourne
Exhibition he was paid £1000 for his report
to the Indian government on Indian-
Australian trade, and then won the exclu-
sive Sydney agency of the Indian Tea
Association of Calcutta. In 1883, with W. P.
Brown, he traded as Inglis, Brown & Co.
He travelled widely and won renown for
his lectures on India and Scottish poets, and
was a founder, president and trustee of the
Commercial Travellers' Association of New
South Wales. About 1887 he dissolved his

partnership, sold the agency and set up as
James Inglis & Co. By 1889 he had taken his
buyer, John Parker, into partnership. In
1884 Inglis had bought Craigo in Strathfield
where he showed that Indian crops and rare
plants could be grown with success. In
March 1885 he visited New Zealand and
published his letters to the Sydney press in
Our New Zealand Cousins (London, 1887).

In 1885-94 Inglis represented New England in the Legislative Assembly. In 1886 he
was vice-president of the Freetrade Association. Known as 'Tiger' or 'Rajah', he was
described by Sir Charles Dilke [q.v.] as 'an
out-and-out free trader, a fluent witty
speaker, a popular lecturer, and . . . author
of some . . . of the stiffest Indian "tiger
stories".' Despite hopes of becoming the first
minister of agriculture, he accepted the
ministry of public instruction in 1887 under
Henry Parkes [q.v.], whom he admired.
After a rebuke he wrote: 'I hope under your
wise leadership to become myself a wiser,
more thoughtful & more useful man'.

Inglis tried to fulfil the government's
promise of retrenchment but was attacked
for his economies. He was often baited in
the House by those 'birds of evil omen',
Melville the undertaker and Walker [qq.v.]
the ex-spiritualist. Inglis's suggestion that
technical education should be under 'direct
ministerial control' brought him into conflict with the Board of Technical Education,
but he was defended by the *Sydney Morning Herald*. He improved the 'economy and
efficiency' of his department despite 4000
new enrolments and 128 new schools. His
duties involved country tours and opening
'pestilential bazaars', and while serving his
electorate he also found time in 1888 to
publish *Tent Life in Tigerland*, which was
travestied by 'Hop' [q.v. L. Hopkins] in the
Bulletin. In December the government's
decision to lease the tramways involved
Inglis in rumours of fraud and corruption.
He cleared himself in parliament and before
a royal commission, but the government fell
next January.

By 1893 James Inglis & Co. were selling
over 600,000 lbs. of 'Billy Tea' and over
1,000,000 lbs. of packaged teas a year. The
firm had a branch in Brisbane and agencies
in New Zealand, Tasmania and Western
Australia. In 1892-94 Inglis was twice president of the Sydney Chamber of Commerce
but was hard hit by the depression. He
invested in several unprofitable mines and
sought backing on the London Stock Exchange through his brother Robert, a leading broker, who found his brother Jim 'a
bit trying when you try to tackle business
as it is understood here'. Ill and worried
Inglis went to England in 1894. In April
he addressed the Royal Colonial Institute on

'Recent Economic Developments of Australian Enterprise' (*Journal*, vol. 25, 1893-94) and was elected a fellow. In Edinburgh he published *Oor Ain Folk* and, after 'a glorious fortnight among the grouse', completed *The Humour of the Scot* (1894).

Inglis returned to Sydney in February 1896 and as president of the New South Wales Chamber of Mines advocated reform of the 'antiquated' mining laws. Aware of the value of advertising, Inglis sent quart-pots filled with 'Khaki blend' tea to New South Wales soldiers in the Boer war. He bought a bundle of lyrics from Angus & Robertson [q.v.] and chose 'Waltzing Matilda' to wrap round 'Billy Tea' as a free gift. The song was set to music by Marie Cowan, his accountant's wife. Later Inglis allowed F. A. Todd to use it in his *Australasian Students Song Book*. According to the *Review*, October 1900, he was 'instrumental in getting nearly three-quarters of a million of foreign capital introduced into various ventures in New South Wales.

In 1901 Inglis withdrew his nomination for the Senate because of his heart condition and his wife's illness. He was a trustee of the Savings Bank of New South Wales, a director of the Royal Prince Alfred Hospital, the Manchester Fire Insurance Co. and several mining companies, a councillor of the Zoological Society of New South Wales, patron of the Retail Grocers' Association, fellow of the London Society of Arts, a member of the Edinburgh University and Athenaeum Clubs and a prominent supporter of Scottish societies. By invitation he wrote odes to celebrate the 'Commonwealth' and 'Coronation Day' and often wrote to the press. In March 1904 James Inglis & Co. was sued for libel by A. C. Godhard of the Co-operative Coupon Co. whose 'coupon system' Inglis had attacked as 'a pernicious incubus'. After direction by Chief Justice Darley [q.v.] the jury found for Inglis, but after the High Court had granted a new trial the case was settled out of court.

Inglis never 'got over the need for arduous work & plenty of it' to maintain his position. He took up golf and bowls, and his letters showed tenderness to his delicate wife, and humour and warmth to his relations. He died childless at Craigo on 15 December 1908 from kidney disease. Buried in the Presbyterian section of Rookwood cemetery, he was survived by his second wife Ethel Kate Mason, née Macpherson, whom he had married on 13 December 1905. His estate was valued at £9181 but his debts exceeded his assets by £1443.

Ex-M.L.A., *Our present parliament, what it is worth* (Syd, c1886); O. A. Mendelsohn, *A waltz with Matilda* (Melb, 1966); V&P (LA NSW), 1887-88, 4, 24, 1889, 1, 645; *NSW State Reports*, 4 (1904); *NSW Weekly Notes*, 21 (1904); *Cwlth Law Reports*, 2 (1904-05); *Bulletin*, 22 Oct 1881, 2 Mar 1889, 5 Aug 1893; *SMH*, 29 July 1886, 2 June 1887, 3, 16 July, 17 Aug 1888, 17 Mar-1 Apr 1904, 16 Oct 1908; *Centennial Mag*, 1 (1888-89); *Cosmos Mag*, 2 (1896); *Banking and Insurance Review*, 15 Oct 1900, 31 Oct 1908; Parkes letters (ML); letters and scrap-books (held by Mr K. Lee, Inglis & Co., Syd).   MARTHA RUTLEDGE

INNES, FREDERICK MAITLAND (1816-1882), journalist, lay preacher, farmer and politician, was born on 11 August 1816 at Edinburgh, son of Francis Innes and his wife Prudence, née Edgerley. Educated at Heriot's, Edinburgh, and Kelso Grammar School, he worked for his uncle, manager of estates for his relation, the duke of Roxburgh. In 1836 Innes sailed in the *Derwent* and arrived in Hobart Town in 1837. He joined the *Hobart Town Courier* and was prominent in reviving the Mechanics' Institute. In 1838 he married Sarah Elizabeth, youngest child of Humphrey Grey, a prosperous free settler who had migrated from Ireland in 1826.

Innes transferred to the *Tasmanian* but resigned in 1839 and went to England. There he published *Secondary Punishments* (1841), a pamphlet on prison discipline, and became secretary to the British and Foreign Aborigines' Protection Society. With his wife and family he returned in the *Mandarin* to Hobart in 1843, acting as superintendent of Parkhurst boys on the voyage. He rejoined the *Courier* but left in 1845 to edit the *Observer*; he resigned next year, moved to Launceston, became a lay preacher in the Presbyterian Church and worked for the *Cornwall Chronicle*. After a short but stormy term as co-editor with D'Arcy Wentworth Murray, Innes retired to his wife's property, Mona Vale, at Evandale. He lived there for six years in comparative obscurity. In 1856 he was appointed justice of the peace and coroner and elected unopposed for Morven in the new House of Assembly. After five months in the Opposition he became colonial treasurer and held office until November 1862.

In 1859 the colony was reputedly run by a triumvirate, F. Smith [q.v.], W. Henty and Innes, respectively called Seedy, Greedy and Needy. In that year he also tried to create a ministry of lands and works, but the attempt was not successful until 1869. Increasingly Innes undertook such public responsibilities as postmaster-general, minister for immigration, acting colonial secretary and chairman of the Board of Education. Although re-elected for Morven in 1861, he represented Campbell Town in the

Legislative Council in 1862-72. He was appointed to the Library Committee, became chairman of committees in 1864 and president of the Legislative Council in 1868. He was elected for Selby to the House of Assembly in November 1872 and formed a ministry, acting as premier and colonial treasurer. This alliance with old political enemies failed and in August 1873 Innes became leader of the Opposition. In 1875 he crossed the floor to replace P. O. Fysh as treasurer, and was elected for North Launceston but by July 1876 was again in the Opposition. In 1877 he lost North Launceston but won South Esk in the Legislative Council and in 1878 became president. Despite chronic illness he attended every session he could until he died at Launceston on 11 May 1882. He was survived by his wife, seven sons and five daughters to whom he left an estate of £10,700.

Innes as a journalist was particularly concerned with education and prison reform. His 1837 Mechanics' Institute lecture was published as On the Advantages of the General Dissemination of Knowledge. In 1838 he advocated a colonial university and was later instrumental in founding the Tasmanian associate of arts. He bitterly attacked sectarian teaching in government schools. He generally supported Alexander Maconochie's [q.v.] prison reform theories, agreeing that the fundamental problem was 'how to punish so as to do good; to punish with a just measure of severity so as to reform the criminal and prevent the repetition of the crime'. Maconochie had given a large sum to the Tasmanian in 1837 and this may have influenced Innes in his attitude. He was never an ardent anti-transportationist but advocated a gradual cessation of transportation and maintained that the assignment system was economically sound. Although he could see no improvement for colonist or convict under the probation scheme, he praised Lord Stanley's proposals for female convicts. Regretfully he saw that self-government would not be granted while transportation continued, and signed the anti-transportation petition to Lieut-Governor Denison.

Concerned by the colony's economic condition, Innes urged the government to put more money and energy into agriculture and printed a long article, with estimates on roads, both main and branch, to provide access for produce. He was also interested in Major Cotton's [q.v.] irrigation proposals. In the economic slump of the 1840s Innes urged farmers to avoid speculation and to calculate their returns over several years rather than annually. A free trader always looking for markets, he advocated capitalizing on European crop failures and the re-

mount trade with India. He represented Tasmania at an intercolonial congress on free trade in 1873.

Conservative on colonial constitutional issues, Innes feared that self-government would be too democratic. To him public opinion and good government could never be compatible. As a politician he continued his interest in education, served on the Council of Education and was a commissioner of an education inquiry, a guardian of the Queen's Asylum for Destitute Children, a supporter of the Ragged Schools Association and instrumental in encouraging teachers from England to migrate to Tasmania. He was also a commissioner for the New Norfolk Asylum, railways, charitable organizations and penal discipline.

A portrait is in Parliament House, Hobart.

K. H. Dougharty, A story of a pioneer family in Van Diemen's Land (Launceston, 1953); Tasmanian, 6 Aug 1848; Cornwall Chronicle, 4 May 1850; Mercury, 4 July 1873; C. M. Elliott, Frederick Maitland Innes; a study in liberal conservatism (B.A. Hons thesis, Univ Tas, 1964); Leake papers (TA).   C. M. SULLIVAN

INNES, SIR JOSEPH GEORGE LONG (1834-1896), politician and judge, was born on 16 October 1834 in Sydney, the eldest son of Major Joseph Long Innes, superintendent of police, and his wife Elizabeth Anne, daughter of Thomas Reibey and his wife Mary [q.v.]. Educated at W. T. Cape's [q.v.] school and The King's School, Parramatta, he became a clerk in the Survey Department at 17 and in December 1851 clerk of Petty Sessions and of Gold Commissioner Zouch [q.v.] at Sofala. He won repute as an amateur cross-country rider and once used a belt filled with gold dust to adjust his weight. In 1854 he became associate to Chief Justice Stephen [q.v.] and in 1856 entered Lincoln's Inn, London. He was called to the Bar in 1859 where he practised until he returned to Sydney in 1862. He was admitted to the New South Wales Bar on 28 February 1863. On 5 July 1865 he married Emily Janet, daughter of John Smith [q.v.], pastoralist.

Innes became a Queensland District Court judge. Despite promises of promotion he returned to the New South Wales Bar in 1869 and sometimes acted as crown prosecutor. In 1870 he presided at the royal commission on the working of the Gold Fields Act; many of its recommendations, such as the establishment of a Department of Mines, were embodied in the 1874 Mining Act.

In March 1872 Innes was elected to the Legislative Assembly for Mudgee and in

May joined Henry Parkes's [q.v.] first ministry as solicitor-general. Stephen described Innes as 'a man of undoubted integrity and talent . . . a staunch Churchman and, if the term be permissible in Australia, a conservative'. In September 1873 he was appointed to the Legislative Council to represent the government and in November replaced Edward Butler [q.v.] as attorney-general. Attached to Parkes, Innes was impressed by 'the cordial character of the relations—official and private—existing' in the ministry. In 1874 he went with Governor Robinson to Fiji for the cession of the islands to Britain. He was responsible for vesting in the Crown the absolute ownership of all lands not the bona fide property of Europeans or other foreigners or needed for the maintenance of chiefs and tribes. A member of the temporary Fijian Executive Council he drafted the provisional code for the administration of justice and was knighted in January 1875.

In 1875-80 Innes was chairman of committees in the Legislative Council and in 1878 president of the royal commission on Berrima gaol. In 1880-81 he was minister of justice in the Parkes-Robertson [q.v.] coalition. Openly ambitious for promotion to the bench, he became a puisne judge of the Supreme Court on 14 October 1881. His appointment was criticized by the Bulletin which asserted that he had 'never attained eminence at the Bar'. In 1883 the Sydney Morning Herald and Echo 'indulged in a string of invective' against Innes after he had convicted the Herald of contempt of court. Known as a judge with deep sympathy and strong emotion, he was once so agitated after pronouncing the death sentence that he told the defence counsel to discover for the prisoner something of benefit which he could report to the Executive Council. Chief Justice Darley [q.v.] claimed that he had a singularly acute mind, was a well-read and able lawyer, a learned and fearless judge, and at all times a genial and cultured gentleman.

Innes negotiated with the government the acquisition of Chisholm House, settled on his mother by Mary Reibey, as the site for the present Sydney General Post Office. In 1889-90 he visited England and restored his health in 'the quiet and homely life' of an Inverness-shire cottage with grouse shooting. He told Parkes that he had 'not the ability or the inclination for the society of very distinguished men. If I could shine like you, my dear old Chief, and teach them all a thing or two I might like it better'. Devoted to sport, Innes hunted in the 1870s and played cricket until the 1880s. Interested in drama and art, he was a trustee of the Free Public Library from 1879 and of the National Art Gallery of New South Wales.

He was also on the committee of the Goodenough [q.v.] Royal Naval House. Innes died in England on 28 October 1896. He left his estate of £34,414 to the 'unfettered discretion' of his wife, who survived him with five sons and one daughter. His son, Reginald Heath, became chief judge in equity of the New South Wales Supreme Court.

Cyclopedia of N.S.W. (Syd, 1907); W. Blacket, May it please your Honour (Syd, 1927); Correspondence on the cession of Fiji, PP (GB), 1875 (Cmd 1114); C. H. Bertie, 'Pioneer families . . . Long Innes', Home, June 1932; Bulletin, 6 Nov 1880, 22 Oct 1881, 21 July 1883; Norton Smith & Co. papers, Reibey estate, A5327 (ML); Parkes letters (ML); CO 201/569, 599.   K. G. ALLARS

IRELAND, RICHARD DAVIES (1816-1877), barrister and politician, was born in County Galway, Ireland, son of James Stanley Ireland, army captain, and his wife Matilda, née Davies. He was educated at Trinity College, Dublin (B.A., 1837), and called to the Bar in 1838. Attracted by politics, he supported Irish confederation in 1848. Like many talented Irish lawyers, restricted by the overcrowded state of their profession, he decided to migrate to Victoria. He arrived with his family in 1852 and served on a committee for welcoming Smith O'Brien [q.v.] in 1854.

Ireland was admitted to the Victorian Bar in 1853 and to the New South Wales Bar in 1867. He won repute for his brilliant defence of the Eureka defendants in 1855, and for twenty years was Victoria's leading criminal lawyer. His cleverness and audacity in court earned him appointment in 1863 as Queen's Counsel, some £140,000 in fees, the idolization of juries and the grudging respect of judges. Ireland was neither industrious nor learned and resorted to alcohol for his best performances, but few juries could resist his shrewd mixture of eloquence, wit and vituperation. Sir John Madden described him as knowing sufficient law to steer his way through its difficulties without allowing his stronger parts to be embarrassed by its limitations.

Ireland very early established himself in Victorian politics, entering the Legislative Assembly in 1857 at his third attempt. No electorate tolerated him for long but, in a period when members were not paid and urban lawyers were often the only candidates available for a rural or mining constituency, he represented Castlemaine in 1857-59, Maryborough in 1859-61, Villiers and Heytesbury in 1861-64 and Kilmore in 1866-68. Consistent only in his anxiety for office, Ireland's politics were unduly opportunist. He was solicitor-general in the second O'Shanassy [q.v.] ministry in 1858-59, a government chiefly representative of urban capital, and attorney-general in the radical Heales [q.v.] government formed in 1860. He resigned in 1861, ostensibly because he had free-trade views and anticipated an O'Shanassy coalition, but probably because his colleagues refused him a pension for serving two years as a minister, though it was granted in 1863. In O'Shanassy's third ministry in 1861-63 C. G. Duffy [q.v.] sponsored the Land Act of 1862, while the sympathies of O'Shanassy and attorney-general Ireland lay with the squatting and capitalist classes. Ireland clearly foresaw the consequences of Professor Hearn's [q.v.] errors in drafting the bill but said nothing to his colleagues; indeed, he was almost certainly one of the ministers, consulted by Niel Black [q.v.], who advised that the Act should be evaded by the squatters. In 1867 Ireland admitted in debate that he had thought the 1862 Act unworkable and that he believed it undesirable to clog alienation of the land with conditions of settlement. He did not hold office after 1863, and following the revelations of 1867 his election committee warned him not to return to Kilmore. Although he tried another constituency, he was never re-elected, 'a signal instance of public justice', according to the outraged Duffy.

Although Ireland's abilities were outstanding, his career did not fulfil the expectations held for him by many of his contemporaries. Charming, convivial, a clever mimic and dramatic raconteur, he was reputed to have spent four fortunes before his health failed. He died on 11 January 1877 in South Yarra, predeceased by his wife Sophia Mary, née Carr; they had six sons and four daughters.

C. G. Duffy, *My life in two hemispheres*, 1 (Lond, 1898); J. L. Forde, *The story of the Bar of Victoria* (Melb, 1913); J. B. Cooper, *The history of St. Kilda . . . 1840 to 1930*, 1 (Melb, 1931); M. L. Kiddle, *Men of yesterday* (Melb, 1961); R. Carboni, *The Eureka stockade* (Melb, 1963); G. Serle, *The golden age* (Melb, 1963); A. Dean, *A multitude of counsellors* (Melb, 1968); D. Blair, 'Three Melbourne barristers', *Centennial Mag*, 2 (1889-90); *Illustrated Sydney News*, 3 Mar 1887.

JANICE BURNS WOODS

IRONSIDE, ADELAIDE ELIZA (1831-1867), painter, was born on 17 November 1831 in Sydney, the only surviving child of James Ironside, commission agent, and his wife Martha Rebecca, née Redman. Educated by her mother, she wrote patriotic prose and verse for the Sydney press, in-

fluenced by Rev. J. D. Lang [q.v.]. In 1855 she designed a banner and presented it to the First Volunteer Artillery Company of New South Wales. She studied languages with Rev. Matthias Goethe [q.v.] and was esteemed by D. H. Deniehy [q.v.]. At Lang's suggestion in April 1855 she and her mother sailed for London. In January 1856 on reaching Italy Adelaide found that among 'these seers of the Beautiful, the spirit of the Pure and mystical School of Umbria became almost Divine'.

In Rome Adelaide began 'a *siege* and a *battle*' to become an artist and worked up to eighteen hours a day. She was visited by the Prince of Wales and W. C. Wentworth [q.v.], each paying £500 for a painting. In 1859 she won renown with 'The Pilgrim of Art, crowned by the Genius of Art'. In 1861 Pope Pius IX received her in private audience and allowed her to study fresco painting in Perugia and to copy works in the Papal collections. In 'The Marriage in Cana' she revealed her republicanism by modelling the heads of Christ and the bridegroom on Garibaldi. In 1862 she visited London where both pictures were hung at the Great Exhibition but, forced 'from over-study' to rest for six months, she toured Scotland.

A proposal to buy 'The Marriage' for £1000 for the new Town Hall in Sydney failed to win subscriptions. Her ambition was to return and fresco the walls of Sydney's public buildings. In 1865, on a second visit to London, she formed a deep friendship with her teacher John Ruskin who told her 'I cannot separate the nonsense from the sense in you—there is a great deal of both'. Prevented from painting by two years of illness, she died of tuberculosis in Rome on 15 April 1867. An obituarist in the *Athenaeum* commended 'her rich, Titian-like colouring, united to a purity of feeling, that recalled the visions of Beato Angelico'.

Lang's proposal in 1868 to publish her Australian wild-flower paintings failed. In 1871 her 'Manifestation of Christ to the Gentiles' was exhibited in Sydney and in 1880, with 'The Pilgrim' and 'The Marriage', was hung at the opening of the National Art Gallery of New South Wales. The first Australian-born artist to study abroad, Adelaide's works were long forgotten in a shed at the gallery. 'The Marriage in Cana' is now in the dining hall of St Paul's College, University of Sydney.

H. E. Badham, *A study of Australian art* (Syd, 1949); W. Dixson, 'Notes on Australian artists', *JRAHS*, 7 (1921); *Town and Country J*, 14 Jan 1871; J. D. Lang papers (ML); Macarthur papers (ML); MS cat under Ironside and uncat MS set 272 (ML); information from Canon A. P. B. Bennie, St Paul's College, Syd.

RUTH TEALE

IRVING, CLARK (1808-1865), merchant, pastoralist and politician, was born in Bromfield, near Wigton, Cumberland, England, son of Thomas Irving, farmer. He probably gained business experience in London and Carlisle. In 1833 he married Adelaide Thanet, daughter of a London banker. About 1836 he arrived in Sydney as an emissary of British capitalists. In 1839 he set up in Sydney with Richard Lamb as watchmakers and jewellers; they were also merchants, agents and wool-buyers, but the firm was dissolved in 1842. Irving continued his cautious investments and in 1843 bought Casino station on the Richmond River. Manager and later director of the Australasian Sugar Co., he made substantial loans to the company. In 1845 he became official assignee and trustee of insolvent estates. Well known in Sydney, he was secretary of the committee to farewell Caroline Chisholm [q.v.] and steward at a public dinner for W. C. Wentworth [q.v.]. By 1856 Irving had stations in the Darling Downs, Gwydir and Maranoa districts, and grazing leases of 279,040 acres in the Clarence district where he installed boiling-down works and was the first to salt beef for export. He established a Shorthorn herd at Tomki (Casino) and in 1863 paid £200 for a pedigree cow.

In 1856-57 Irving represented the Clarence and Darling Downs in the first Legislative Assembly after responsible government but local dislike of leadership from Sydney and doubts about his attitude to the separation of Queensland cost him his seat. In 1859-64 he sat for the Clarence as an anti-separationist. Although he favoured farmer-settlement on agricultural reserves, he opposed free selection before survey. In 1859 his preemptive purchases were questioned in parliament and strongly criticized. Convinced that the Clarence River provided the best seaport for Armidale and New England, he obtained a government grant of £20,000 to improve navigation on the river, and secured additional grants for roads, a gold escort, a telegraph line and other benefits. He invested heavily in the Grafton Steam Navigation Co. and in 1860 became managing director when it was renamed the Clarence and Richmond Rivers Steam Navigation Co. In 1859 he had founded the first newspaper at Grafton, the *Clarence & Richmond Examiner*. A justice of the peace, he was active in most local organizations.

In 1858 Irving was a foundation director of the Newcastle Wallsend Coal Co. and a director of the Australian Joint Stock Bank, the Australasian Steam Navigation Co. and two copper-mining companies. In 1861 he was importing sugar through David Jones [q.v.] & Co., but was accused by R. M.

Robey [q.v.] of causing losses to the Australian Joint Stock Bank and forcing him to sell his sugar refining business at a loss. Their personal antipathy led to a pamphlet war and threats of law suits.

In 1862 Irving arranged a meeting of bishops and laymen, and donated £2000 to promote the foundation of an Anglican diocese of Grafton and Armidale. He guaranteed another £2000 from his electorate. Entrusted with the formal application for the new see by Bishop Tyrrell [q.v.], he visited England to seek another £3000 and to supervise the launching of the paddle-steamer *Agnes Irving*. In his absence his seat was declared vacant, but he was re-elected. He lost his fortune by speculating in Spanish railways and died aged 57 from pneumonia at Brighton, England, on 13 January 1865. He was survived by his widow, four sons and two daughters, who returned to Australia.

R. M. Robey, *To the shareholders of the Australian Joint Stock Bank* (Syd, 1861); *Report of the proceedings of the shareholders of the Joint Stock Bank* (Syd, 1861); A. P. Elkin, *The diocese of Newcastle* (Syd, 1955); L. T. Daley, *Men and a river* (Melb, 1966); *SMH*, 22 Apr 1847, 22 Sept 1859; *Clarence & Richmond Examiner*, 15 Nov, 6 Dec 1859, 29 May, 11 Dec 1860, 16 Apr, 5 Aug 1861, 11 Feb, 20 May 1862, 8 Aug 1865, 30 Jan 1866; *Armidale Express*, 25 June 1859; J. McFarlane, 'Our early days', pt 45, *Daily Examiner*, 1959; W. H. Fox dossier, 4/800 (Soc Aust Gen, Syd); Adelaide Irving letters and Clark Irving file (Richmond River Hist Soc); Newspaper indexes under Irving (ML).   LOUISE T. DALEY

IRVING, MARTIN HOWY (1831-1912), professor, headmaster and civil servant, was born on 21 February 1831 at St Pancras, London, son of Edward Irving (1792-1834) and his wife Isabella, née Martin. His father was the famous Scots preacher who was declared a heretic by the Church of Scotland and founded the Irvingite or Catholic Apostolic Church; Thomas Carlyle called him 'the freest, brotherliest, bravest human soul mine ever came in contact with'. From King's College School, London, Martin won a Balliol College scholarship and matriculated in November 1848. He was the university junior mathematics scholar for 1850 and obtained first-class honours in classics and second-class in mathematics (B.A., 1853; M.A., 1856). He had signed the Thirty-nine Articles of the Church of England at matriculation, holding that subscription did not preclude his special witness as a member of the Catholic Apostolic Church, but he would not take holy orders as required for most Oxford fellowships. In 1854 he became classics master of the non-denominational City of London School.

In November 1855 Irving was chosen to succeed the first professor of 'Greek and Latin Classics with Ancient History' at the University of Melbourne. He arrived at Melbourne in 1856 and began teaching in July. Early next year his title was changed to professor of classical and comparative philology and logic. Although students were few, he delivered eighteen lectures a week in Greek, Latin, logic and English. In the final honours school he introduced rhetoric and aesthetics applied to English literature. In 1858 he successfully urged the examination for degrees of students who were unable to attend lectures, but the council rejected his schemes for an associate in arts diploma for non-members of the university in 1857 and for the abolition of compulsory Greek for arts degrees in 1858. As an examiner of matriculation English, Greek, Latin, French and German he became an ally of schoolmasters advocating curriculum change.

In January 1871, with the offer of a higher salary and better accommodation for his large family, Irving became non-resident headmaster in charge of secular studies at Wesley College, Melbourne. A resident clerical president was responsible for religious education and the care of boarders. Under Irving the school achieved great success at public examinations. Numbers grew rapidly to a peak in 1873, not surpassed at Wesley until 1900. He deplored the low level of matriculation requirements and built a sixth form of boys staying at school after matriculation. He placed an Arnoldian stress on character formation and trust in the sixth form as 'a democracy of gentlemen'. In December 1875 he bought the Hawthorn Grammar School. Numbers doubled in his first year, new buildings followed and the school became one of the biggest in the colony. He continued to insist on English, arithmetic and Latin as studies most apt to develop 'the faculties of imagination and correct reasoning', but the school also offered Greek, mathematics, history, geography, chemistry and book-keeping. Games were stressed as 'an indication of a school's vigour'.

As a councillor in 1875-1900 and vice-chancellor from May 1887 to May 1889 Irving was an ardent university reformer. In the senate and council of the university he led a 'caucus', composed mainly of schoolmasters, who constantly challenged the administration of the chancellor, Sir Redmond Barry [q.v.]. In Barry's absence overseas, Irving attempted in vain to unseat the chancellor and not until Barry died

in 1880 were new chairs instituted in natural philosophy, engineering, pathology, chemistry and English, French and German languages, while the addition at matriculation of natural science subjects and an honours standard marked the culmination of ten years' agitation. The 'caucus' caused Chancellor W. F. Stawell's [q.v.] resignation in 1882, but growing opposition to the influence of outside educational interests in the university delayed the appointment of a successor. Irving, a reluctant nominee, failed by one vote for the chancellorship in May 1887 when Dr Brownless [q.v.] was appointed in conservative reaction to the unstable years of factional strife.

Irving's equable temperament, administrative capacity, vitality and manifest probity inspired confidence. In 1872 he was offered the post of permanent head of the Victorian Department of Education. He was chairman of the Victorian board of the Australian Mutual Provident Society in 1878-84. Intended for the post of full-time, salaried vice-chancellor he was proposed by the University of Melbourne Council in 1888 but rejected by the professoriate. In February 1884 he was appointed one of the three foundation commissioners of the Public Service Board of Victoria, and left Hawthorn College in charge of his son, Edward. When the board was disbanded in 1893 Irving was granted a pension. He left Australia in 1900 and apart from a brief visit to Melbourne in 1906 lived in England. A devoted adherent of the Catholic Apostolic Church he died on 23 January 1912 among his fellow believers at Albury, Surrey.

Large and athletic, Irving had a commanding presence. James Froude [q.v.], who had known his father, described 'the same finely-cut features, the same eager, noble and generous expressions' in the son but found him 'calmer and quieter'. Irving had won his college and the university sculls in 1852, and founded the University of Melbourne Boat Club in 1859, stroking the fours. He was a founder of Victorian amateur rowing. An expert rifle shot, he encouraged the sport in schools. He joined the Volunteer Rifles in 1862 and was lieutenant-colonel in command of the First Battalion Victorian Militia in 1884-90. He had married Caroline Mary Brueres in 1855; they had four sons and five daughters. She died in 1881 and on 6 July 1882 Irving married Mary Mowat; they had one son and three daughters. Two daughters of the first marriage, Margaret and Lilian, were principals of Lauriston Girls' School, Armadale, while a son, Godfrey George Howy (1867-1937), became deputy-quartermaster-general in the Australian army.

J. Lang, *Victorian Oarsman* (Melb, 1919); E. Nye (ed), *The history of Wesley College 1865-1919* (Melb, 1921); G. Blainey et al, *Wesley College. The first hundred years* (Melb, 1967); *Age*, 20 Dec 1871, 15 Dec 1875, 23 Dec 1876; *Argus*, 20 Dec 1871, 20 Dec 1876, 25 Jan 1912; Professorial Board, Senate and Council minutes (Univ Melb Archives).

G. C. FENDLEY

ISAACS, ROBERT MACINTOSH (1814-1876), barrister and politican, was born at Tortola, Virgin Islands, West Indies, the youngest son of Robert Glover Isaacs. Educated in England, he entered the Middle Temple, was called to the Bar on 12 January 1839 and practised in London. On 27 July 1841 at St Pancras he married Barberina Rogers-Harrison. In 1843 Isaacs migrated to Sydney and was admitted to the Bar of New South Wales on 24 November. By the end of 1854 he was sufficiently prosperous to afford a visit to England. He returned to Sydney in December 1855, after surviving shipwreck at Cape Otway.

In 1856 Isaacs refused appointment as attorney-general in the first ministry in the new parliament as he preferred to concentrate on his developing practice. In *Reminiscences of thirty years' residence in New South Wales and Victoria* (1863) Roger Therry [q.v.] classed him among the leading Sydney counsel. In February 1857 he was appointed to the Legislative Council, but resigned in May 1861 in support of Sir William Burton [q.v.]. A Conservative, Isaacs had served on the general committee of the New South Wales Constitutional Association in 1860. In November 1865 he won the Yass Plains seat in the Legislative Assembly and in January 1866 became solicitor-general under James Martin [q.v.]. A verbose and plodding orator, Isaacs probably fulfilled his potential and his ambitions in the honourable but unspectacular position as second legal officer of the Crown. In 1868 he attacked the governor's refusal to grant Martin a dissolution after the ministry had been defeated. His distant electors were caustic about his brief appearances amongst them and he lost his seat in November 1869.

Harassed by ill health Isaacs moved in 1871 to Hobart where he practised as a barrister and acted as chancellor of the Anglican archdiocese. He returned to Sydney in 1872 and became crown prosecutor in the western districts, with a modest financial security but much exhausting travel. He was a member of the Philosophical Society of New South Wales. Weakened by typhoid fever he died aged 61 at his home in Darlinghurst Road, Sydney, on 26 March 1876. He was buried in the Anglican section of Balmain cemetery. He was survived by his wife, two sons and four daughters, leaving an estate valued at £6250.

Church News (Hob), 1 Apr 1876; *SMH*, 20, 31 Jan 1866, 27 Mar 1876; *Illustrated Sydney News*, 31 Mar 1876; CO 201/548.

JOHN R. FORBES

IVORY, JAMES (1820-1887), pastoralist and diarist, was born on 10 June 1820 probably at Edinburgh, one of the four sons of James Ivory, Scottish judge, and his wife Anne, née Laurie. In October 1840 he arrived in Sydney with a friend, David Graham, and in January 1843 they took out a squatting licence for Eskdale run near Ipswich in Queensland. They slowly acquired more land until about 1848 when the partners separated, Graham taking up the Tabragalba run leaving Ivory with Eskdale. In 1853 Ivory was joined by his brother, Francis Jeffrey, and in September 1854 left for Scotland where in 1855 he married a cousin Harriette Jane Oakley Laurie at Burntisland, Fife.

Ivory returned to Queensland in July 1856 without his wife and infant son. His affairs prospered and he took up land at Bundambah where by 1879 he held over 18,000 acres. He experimented with pastures, began to grow sugar cane and other tropical crops and invested heavily in the cotton boom of the early 1860s. He sailed again for Scotland in August 1862 and returned in August 1864. In February 1868 he bought the valuable Bremer Mills property and soon went to Scotland for his wife and family. While waiting in Sydney for a ship he saw the shooting of the duke of Edinburgh at Clontarf. Ivory left for Queensland in October 1868 with his wife and two young children, leaving his eldest son, James, at school in England, but ten years' separation had alienated his wife and almost from the time he reached Brisbane he was beset by family friction. James arrived in 1875 and sided with his mother but was later forbidden the house while a nephew who joined him in the late 1870s was imprisoned for fraud. Despite the discovery of coal on his property, Ivory's affairs steadily became more confused and, when he died at Ipswich on 11 March 1887, his trustees had to seek a private Act to enable them to wind up his estate.

Ivory was cultured and intelligent, interested in music, literature and foreign affairs. Despite a strong puritanical streak he drank moderately and raced his own horses. From the early 1850s he wrote long letters in diary form to his family in Scotland and the surviving 1275 pages in the Mitchell Library are an invaluable record of a Queensland squatter from 1862 to 1883.

His brother, FRANCIS JEFFREY, was born in 1831 probably in Edinburgh and worked on Eskdale till 1856 when he and another brother, Alexander Laurie, bought Eidsvold station from the Archer brothers [q.v.]. From December 1873 to November 1878 Francis represented the Burnett in the Legislative Assembly; in 1879 he was called to the Legislative Council. In 1881 he was appointed clerk assistant in the assembly and in 1893 became serjeant-at-arms as well.

When gold was discovered at Eidsvold, the property was heavily mortgaged and in 1887 was taken over by the Australian and New Zealand Mortgage Co. Ivory died in Brisbane on 21 January 1896, leaving a block of land, a life insurance policy and some uncollected debts to his wife Hester Mary, née Edwards, whom he had married in 1881.

V&P (LA Qld), 1890, 1, 454; Piper papers, vol 2 (ML); depasturing licences (NSWA); yearly returns of licences for occupation (NSWA); cattle mortgage books (QA); pastoral rent registers (QA).   H. J. GIBBNEY

J

JACK, ROBERT LOGAN (1845-1921), geologist and explorer, was born on 16 September 1845 at Irvine, Ayrshire, Scotland, son of Robert Jack, cabinet-maker, and his wife Margaret, née Logan. Educated at the Irvine Academy and at the University of Edinburgh, he joined the Geological Survey of Scotland in 1867 and by 1876 had contributed greatly to Scottish geology by mapping the coalfields.

In 1876 Jack was appointed geological surveyor for northern Queensland and arrived at Townsville in 1877. In 1879 Jack became government geologist for the whole colony. He was president of the geological section for the first meeting of the Australasian Association for the Advancement of Science in 1888, and president of the Royal Society of Queensland in 1894. He resigned his government post in 1899 to explore for an English company the metalliferous deposits of Szechuan in China. When the Boxer rising broke out he and his son Robert Lockhart made their way to Burma through 450 miles of uncharted mountain country known in World War II as 'The Hump'. In 1901-04 he practised as a consultant mining geologist in London. He then returned to Australia and for five years was a consulting engineer in Western Australia. He served on the royal commission on the Collie coalfield and presided at another on the ventilation and sanitation of mines and the prevalence of lung disease among miners. By 1910 he was a consulting geologist in Sydney.

Jack's geological work for Queensland is outstanding in both quality and quantity and remarkable for its accurate and detailed observation. His recognition of the basinal structure of western Queensland and its potential for artesian water led to the first government bore in the Great Artesian Basin being sunk at Barcaldine in 1887. He personally mapped and appraised the Bowen River coalfield and coal prospects near Cooktown, Townsville and the Flinders River, and reported on twelve goldfields including Mount Morgan, Charters Towers and the Palmer as well as the Stanthorpe and four northern tinfields, the Argentine and other silver mines, the Chillagoe and Koorboora mining districts and the sapphire deposits of Withersfield. Many of his deductions have stood the tests of additional evidence, but his theory that the richly auriferous ores of Mount Morgan were deposited on a pre-desert sandstone landscape by a thermal spring has proved unacceptable.

In collaboration with Robert Etheridge, who described the fossils, Jack brought all his previous work together and analysed it in *The Geology and Palaeontology of Queensland and New Guinea*, 3 vols (Brisbane, 1892). The two men had already collaborated in *Catalogue of Works, Papers, Reports, and Maps, on the Geology, Palaeontology, Mineralogy, Mining and Metallurgy, etc. of the Australian Continent and Tasmania* (London, 1881). Jack published several other shorter compilations on the geology of Queensland, and in 1899 issued the final edition of his geological map of Queensland. In his last major publication, *Northmost Australia*, 2 vols (London, 1921), he gave detailed accounts of all the explorations of north Queensland, including his own. Many of his geological journeys were through unexplored country, especially Cape York Peninsula. On a journey in 1880 he was speared in a surprise night attack by Aboriginals.

Jack died at Sydney on 6 November 1921, survived by his wife Janet Simpson, née Love, whom he had married at Glasgow in 1877, by his son Robert Lockhart who became hydrologist for South Australia and later chief geologist of the Broken Hill Pty, by his stepson James Simpson Love, a well-known grazier in north Queensland, and by two stepdaughters. He was buried in the Presbyterian section of Waverley cemetery.

Spare, quiet and active he was correct in dress and had an ingrained democratic outlook. Some of his letters are in the Geological Survey Office, Brisbane.

D. Hill, 'Robert Logan Jack: a memorial address', Roy Soc Qld, *Procs*, 58 (1946); printed cat under Robert Logan Jack (ML).

DOROTHY HILL

JACOB, ARCHIBALD HAMILTON (1829-1900), politician, was born on 31 July 1829 at Jessore, India, the second surviving son of Captain Vickers Jacob (1789-1836), Indian army and later merchant and landholder in New South Wales, and his wife Anne (1796-1836), née Watson. He was educated at La Martinière College, Calcutta, and from 1840 at Lincoln College, England. Ill health forced him to abandon his studies at Chester for the Anglican Church and employment with the Liverpool and Manchester Bank. With his brother Robert he arrived at Sydney in 1851, acquired five acres at Raymond Terrace where he built a house and later bought a few hundred acres of his father's property. He became clerk of Petty Sessions for Raymond Terrace in 1852 and agent for the sale of crown lands in 1857 but resigned both posts in 1864 and turned to agriculture.

In 1872-80 Jacob represented the Lower Hunter in the Legislative Assembly. He spoke often on various subjects and served on many select and standing committees, but his independence was pronounced. In November 1877 he surprised many members by becoming secretary of mines in John Robertson's [q.v.] tottering ministry which he had opposed in a censure motion. At first an assiduous local representative, he increasingly ignored the needs of his electors and condemned Parkes's [q.v.] 1880 Education Act as costly and unnecessary. In that year he moved permanently to Sydney and held his seat by only three votes. In 1882, as a supporter of Alexander Stuart [q.v.], he lost Morpeth to Robert Wisdom [q.v.], partly because of rumours that Catholic priests were canvassing for him. In October 1883 he was appointed to the Legislative Council.

The council's relative calm and sobriety suited Jacob's temperament. He won repute as deputy-chairman of committees when the Land Act was passed in 1884 and was chairman in 1887-1900. A staunch Conservative, Jacob opposed payment of members, superannuation for civil servants and income tax proposals. He wanted a fixed membership for the council and defended its right to amend money bills. He was quick to detect infringements of privileges and skilfully used his knowledge of standing orders to delay assembly measures, especially during Reid's fiscal manoeuvres in 1894-95. He had the best attendance record of his contemporary councillors but for years feuded with the Daily Telegraph and the Sydney Morning Herald, alleging that they misreported his speeches.

Jacob kept his political and private roles separate. A devout Anglican and a founder of St John's Church at Raymond Terrace, he opposed the opening of parliament with prayer, claiming that it was a private matter. He died at Ashfield on 28 May 1900 and was buried in the Anglican section of Rookwood cemetery. He was survived by five sons of his wife Mary (1830-1897), née Snodgrass, whom he had married in 1853. His estate was valued at £17,500.

An historical and genealogical narrative of the families of Jacob (priv print, Syd, nd); Bulletin, 29 May 1880; SMH, 29 May 1900; Daily Telegraph (Syd), 29 May 1900; Town and Country J, 2 June 1900; Norton Smith & Co. papers (ML).   G. N. HAWKER

JAMES, CHARLES HENRY (1848-1898), businessman and land speculator, was born on 7 December 1848 at Enniscorthy, County Wexford, Ireland, son of James James, farmer, and his wife Catherine, née Shiels. He arrived in Victoria probably in 1867. He reputedly began business as a grocer in North Melbourne and at some stage lived in South Australia. About the end of the 1870s, in partnership with his brother-in-law Percy Dobson, James began to buy, subdivide and sell Melbourne suburban real estate. He was widely acknowledged to have been Melbourne's first 'land boomer', and while the boom lasted was one of the most successful. Many of James's real estate techniques were adopted by his solicitor, M. H. Davies [q.v.]. By 1887 he could claim to have already sold £3,000,000 worth of land, chiefly in the northern and north-eastern suburbs, and at the height of his fortunes in the late 1880s was believed to be a millionaire. He then operated a string of companies, including the Dominion Banking and Investment Corporation floated in 1888, owned extensive tracts of agricultural land in Victoria and held pastoral properties in New South Wales. By that time also he lived in a flamboyant world of his own creation: Illawarra, his 'French Renaissance' mansion in Toorak and the Empire Buildings, his 'Domestic Tudor' office block in Collins Street.

In 1887 James entered the Legislative Council for Southern Province, in which his farm holdings and most of his subdivisional activities were located, but even his staunch supporter, the Argus, admitted that he could 'scarcely aspire to the character today of a well-informed politician of mature opinion', though he was 'in sympathy with the settled interests of the community'. In his three years in the council he spoke seldom and then mostly on issues of personal interest such as the development of northern suburbs.

James's fortunes plummeted in the depression of the 1890s. Already by 1890 he had earned much notoriety from the bankruptcy proceedings of his ex-clerk Harold Sparks and the financial convolutions of the Dominion Bank. In July he was replaced as president of the Whittlesea Agricultural Society by an overwhelming vote of its members. He did not seek re-election to the Legislative Council when his term expired in September. He managed to stave off his financial collapse longer than most of his fellow-speculators: his Dominion Bank did not liquidate until the end of 1895; he himself survived until declared bankrupt in May 1897. Weakened on all sides by deflated land, shares and building values, repeated bank failures, bad debts and drought, he could repay only .6¾d. in the £ on his debts of £851,842. During the bankruptcy proceedings James retired to Sydney and after a severe illness died at Burwood on 2 October 1898. He was survived by his wife Harriette Hardy, née Dobson, whom he had married about 1873 in Melbourne, and by five daughters and a son. He was buried with Presbyterian rites at Boroondara cemetery, Melbourne.

Age, 1887, 3 Oct 1898; Argus, 1887, 3 Oct 1898; Table Talk, 1889-90; insolvency papers (VA).   E. A. BEEVER

JAMES, HENRY KERRISON (1814-1883), Anglican official, was born in England, son of John James and his wife Harriet Eliza, née de Yough. His father migrated to Sydney in 1823 and soon became deputy-sheriff. Henry arrived at Sydney in the Ferguson on 26 March 1829. He was appointed clerk to the archdeacon in 1834 and then became secretary to Bishop Broughton [q.v.]. In 1836 the diocesan registrar refused to keep the records of births, marriages and deaths, and James offered to do it. In the next twenty years he compiled meticulous indexes to all existing registers, from which he was able to satisfy inquirers. On 24 January 1838 he had married Leonora Margaret Bannatyne. In 1857 they suffered a crushing blow when their eldest son was drowned in the wreck of the Dunbar.

In December 1856 the diocesan registrar proposed that the new Registrar-General's Department take over all Church of England registers and indexes and that the government pay James £3000 compensation for his services. The money was put on the estimates but the bill lapsed in October 1858. For searches James had imposed an arbitrary scale of fees based on what the traffic would bear and in December 1859, when he began to refuse searches, his right to compensation was questioned. Three years later a bill for arbitration failed and the problem remained unsolved.

In 1862 James became registrar of the Sydney diocese and ex officio secretary of the Moore College Trust. In July 1866 it was discovered that all trust moneys had been lodged in his private account without any record of disbursements. Though pressed by the trustees he refused for a year to provide adequate accounts and in October 1867 was permitted to resign. In 1864 he had secured a personal loan of £2000 from Bishop Tyrrell [q.v.] of Newcastle by a lien over his rights to compensation, and in 1867 executed a second deed assigning the registers and his compensation to George Hart, a New Zealander, as security for the

payment of several debts including that to Tyrrell. The assignee had power to dispose of the collateral.

When James asked a fee of twenty guineas for the baptismal certificate of the earl of Limerick, the Colonial Office was aroused. In response to a dispatch of October 1877 a bill was prepared early in 1879, proposing compulsory transfer with arbitrators to determine compensation. Threats of legal action by the Church authorities and Hart's representatives caused delay, and the Clergy Returns Transfer Act was not passed until late in that year. James received £5000 compensation and the records were taken over by the registrar-general in 1881. Aged 69 James died on 1 February 1883 and was buried in Haslem's Creek (Rookwood) cemetery. He was survived by six daughters and predeceased by six sons.

Bradshaw's Railway Guide, A narrative of the melancholy wreck of the 'Dunbar' (Syd, 1857); M. L. Loane. A centenary history of Moore Theological College (Syd, 1955); V&P (LA NSW), 1858, 2, 1220, 1859-60, 2, 49, 1860, 465, 1878-79, 7, 879, 1879-80, 1, 453, 1881, 5, 621; Aust Churchman, 19 Oct 1867; Australian, 26 Jan 1838; Town and Country J, 23 Nov 1878; Bishop Barker diary, 1867 (ML).

H. J. GIBBNEY

JAMES, JOHN CHARLES HORSEY (1841-1899), public servant, was born on 30 January 1841 at Rome, son of John James, rector of Avington, Berkshire, England, and his second wife Theodosia Mary, née Tennant, of Staffordshire. At 13 he went to Rugby, where he excelled in Greek and Latin, matriculated on 29 May 1860 and entered Exeter Hall, Oxford (B.A., 1864). He enrolled at the Inner Temple, was called to the Bar in 1866 and practised on the Oxford circuit.

Since the last convicts had arrived from England in 1868, the colony of Western Australia had continued to make steady economic progress. The increase in land transactions had led the government to introduce the Torrens [q.v.] system of land transfer in 1875 and, through the influence of his friend, the earl of Carnarvon, secretary of state for the colonies, James was appointed first commissioner of land titles on 9 July. He arrived at Perth in September. James was anxious to maintain close contact with the authorities in order to succeed in his chosen career. Between 1876 and 1880 he was twice appointed acting registrar, master and keeper of records of the Supreme Court and for a time acted as a puisne judge. In 1887 he served as an official member of the Legislative Council while the surveyor-general was in London. On 29 September he became a police magistrate in Perth and resident magistrate in Guildford. Three years later he was appointed a special magistrate but refused admission to the Bar on legal grounds. In June 1897 he became a police magistrate for the whole colony.

Witty, genial and nicknamed 'Jimmy the Title', he was chosen to present enamelled cups to school children in 1897 during the diamond jubilee celebrations. He took an active interest in the affairs of the Victoria Public Library (State Library of Western Australia) and other educational institutions. He was an acknowledged amateur actor, well known for his knowledge of Shakespeare's plays. He was also interested in music, painting and sculpture, was prominent at race-meetings and enjoyed yachting and cricket. After a short illness he died on 3 February 1899 at Goderich Street, Perth.

James had published *Historical table of the statutes and alphabetical index of their contents* (Perth, 1891); *Historical table of the statutes and an alphabetical index of their contents, together with proclamations, orders in council etc. . . .* (London, 1896); *Statutes of the realm adopted by ordinances and acts of council* (London, 1896); *The Statutes of Western Australia, 1832-1895,* 3 vols (London, 1896). In Perth on 16 September 1885 he had married Rebecca Catherine, eldest daughter of C. H. Clifton, justice of the peace, and his wife Maria Elizabeth, née Glyn. Of their seven children, the youngest son, Meyrick Edward Clifton, had great acting ability and likeness to Field-Marshal Montgomery, and acted as his 'double' in 1944 during the campaigns in North Africa.

W. B. Kimberly, *History of West Australia* (Melb, 1897); M. E. C. James, *I was Monty's double* (Lond, 1954); F. M. Johnston, *Knights and theodolites* (Syd, 1962); *West Australian,* 10 Sept 1875, 31 Jan 1887, 15 Oct 1890, 4 Feb 1899, 16 Feb, 10 May 1963; *WA Bulletin,* 22 Dec 1888; *Inquirer,* 10 Feb 1899; *Western Mail,* 10 Feb 1899, 30 Sept 1954; H. G. Clifton, *Yesterday and today, 1829-1929-1949* (Battye Lib, Perth).   E. ZALUMS

JAMES, JOHN STANLEY (1843-1896), author, best known as 'The Vagabond', was born on 15 November 1843 in Walsall, Staffordshire, England, the only son of Joseph Green James, an attorney whose family had an ironfoundry, and his wife Elizabeth. Educated locally, he was articled to his father but after a disagreement went to London where he struggled to make a living, first by engrossing legal documents, then by casual journalism. After an interlude as a railway clerk and station-master in Wales,

he returned to journalism in London about 1868. By his own account, he was imprisoned as a spy for some weeks in Paris in 1870 and then in London wrote on the Franco-Prussian war. When it ended he reported the formation of the Agricultural Labourers' Union under Joseph Arch in Warwickshire. However, his uncorroborated account of success as a London journalist must be treated with reserve. About 1872, after renewed dispute with his father, he went to America where he changed his name to Julian Thomas and, so he later claimed, made an unhappy and short-lived marriage with the widow of a Virginian planter. Having failed as a journalist, in 1875 he went to Sydney 'sick in body and mind, and broken in fortune'.

In April 1876 the Melbourne *Argus* published 'A Night in the Model Lodging-House' written anonymously by James and signed by 'A Vagabond', the first of a series on 'the social life and public institutions of Melbourne from a point of view unattainable to the majority'. The most substantial of the series were based on his first-hand reports of what it was like to be 'inside' certain institutions: to gather material, he spent a day in the Immigrants' Home, was admitted to the Benevolent Asylum and worked as the porter at the Alfred Hospital, an attendant at lunatic asylums and dispenser-cum-dentist at Pentridge gaol. His accounts of these institutions combined intimate knowledge of their day-to-day working with a breadth of perspective gained from his knowledge of other societies. His shrewd observation, practical judgments and suggestions for reform reveal a compassionate spirit behind his cultivated flamboyancy. His articles were successful partly because of the mystery of their authorship. James wrote with an experienced and authoritative air, casually mentioning associations with prominent men and implying his involvement in public affairs in England and America. He could not measure up to the image that he had so successfully fixed in the minds of his readers, and the revelation that Julian Thomas was the Vagabond produced an inevitable sense of anticlimax from which he never really recovered.

In December James was at the high-water mark of his career: his articles were being published as *The Vagabond Papers*; he was a public figure, sufficiently well known to be portrayed in the Christmas pantomime. Farewelled by fellow journalists and presented with an illuminated address and 308 sovereigns, he sailed in August 1877 to write for the *Sydney Morning Herald*. His 'Impressions of Sydney' appeared in September but next month he was in Cooktown reporting for the *Argus* on the influx of

Chinese gold diggers. By Christmas he was back in Sydney writing without much effect on its low life. In 1878, sent to New Caledonia to report on a native uprising, he shocked readers with details of the brutality of the French colonial administration which he condemned strongly. These reports, together with later articles on his experiences in the New Hebrides and New Guinea, were collected in *Cannibals and Convicts* (1886).

Apart from this book James's later journalism is of little interest. In 1881 a nine-month trip on a collier to China, Japan, British Columbia and California resulted in a series of travel articles in the *Argus*. Some of these articles were collected in *Occident and Orient* (1882). Helped by Alfred Dampier [q.v.] who took the leading role he wrote a 'colonial' melodrama, *No Mercy*, which toured the colonies in 1882. In 1884 he began the 'Picturesque Victoria' series for the *Argus*, and descriptive articles of this kind became, with intervals, his main occupation. In 1886 he was the *Argus* correspondent at the Colonial and Indian Exhibition at South Kensington. In 1887 he transferred to the *Age* and visited New Caledonia and the New Hebrides, and in 1889 Tonga and Samoa. In 1890-92 he was secretary to the Victorian royal commission on charities. He continued to write occasional articles, mostly for the Melbourne *Leader*, until he died on 4 September 1896 in squalor at Fitzroy.

The *Age* obituarist reported that James had been born in Wales, the *Argus* Virginia; his true identity was not publicly known until 1912. The role of 'Vagabond', mysterious, cosmopolitan, sophisticated observer of the antipodes, satisfied both his sense of self-importance and his desire to hide. *The Vagabond Papers* were his main achievement. Although he had literary ambitions, notably in drama, his talent was for journalism. Outwardly egotistical and reckless, he had a generous and sympathetic nature. Probably his early life had helped to develop in him a keen feeling for those in need, a feeling expressed in his best work and commemorated after his death in a memorial erected by public subscription.

Julian Thomas (J. S. James), *The Vagabond papers*, M. Cannon ed (Melb, 1969); 'The Vagabond', *Bulletin*, 17 Oct 1896; J. B. Cooper, 'Who was "The Vagabond"?', *Life* (Melb), 1 Jan 1912.   JOHN BARNES

JAQUES, THEODORE JAMES (1823-1893), registrar-general and solicitor, was born on 6 October 1823 at Rochester, England, son of William Jaques, surveyor, and his wife Jane, née Hill. The Jaques family

reached Sydney in July 1830 in the *Roslyn Castle*. Theodore was educated at the Sydney College under his brother-in-law, W. Cape [q.v.]. In 1839 he became a junior clerk in the Supreme Court Registry Office. He applied for admission as a solicitor by virtue of his service to the Registry Office. Despite strong opposition from the legal profession the judges ordered that if he passed examination he could apply again. On 24 December 1856 he was finally admitted a solicitor but did not practise for many years. In 1852 he became a commissioner for affidavits. In 1857 he was made deputy registrar-general, and took charge of the deeds branch. In the early 1860s he opposed the introduction of the Torrens [q.v.] titles system because it did not record marriage settlements and trusts. In 1864 Jaques was appointed registrar-general, a magistrate in 1865 and as chairman of the Land Titles Commission by 1867 advocated the handing to his department of all records of births, marriages and deaths, particularly those held by the Anglican registrar, H. K. James [q.v.].

Jaques retired on 15 December 1870 because of ill health. He practised as a solicitor and in 1873 was appointed commissioner for affidavits for Victoria in New South Wales. In 1874 he went into partnership with his nephew, Alfred E. Jaques, who in 1878 joined Stephen & Stephen [qq.v.] to establish the legal firm, Stephen, Jaques & Stephen, while Theodore continued to practise on his own. In September 1860 he had joined the Volunteer Infantry; he was commissioned captain in the Balmain company in December, promoted major in 1868 and retired as lieut-colonel in 1885. For years he was a vice-president of the Rifle Association of New South Wales. Jaques lived in Balmain and was active in local affairs and secretary of the Balmain Mechanics' School of Arts. He represented St Mary's Anglican Church, Balmain, on six synods. In 1876-79 he was registrar of the diocese of Sydney.

Jaques died from pernicious anaemia on 23 July 1893 and was buried in the Balmain cemetery. Predeceased by his wife Mary Ann (d. 4 December 1858), née Cook, he was survived by a son and a daughter. He left no will but his estate was sworn for probate at £13,826.

V&P (LA NSW), 1858, 2, 1278, 1879-80, 5, 1165; SMH, 10 Mar 1876, 25, 26 July 1893; *Town and Country J*, 29 July 1893; information from Gordon Jaques and Stephen, Jaques & Stephen.   MARTHA RUTLEDGE

JARDINE, JOHN (1807-1874), pastoralist and magistrate, was born on 5 March 1807 at Spedlins Tower, Dumfriesshire, Scotland, the fourth son of Sir Alexander Jardine and his wife Jane, née Maule. He joined the 1st Regiment of Dragoons in 1835, married Elizabeth, daughter of Captain W. H. Craig, R.N., sold his commission as captain on 10 May 1839 and sailed with his wife for Sydney. They arrived in the *Dryade* on 3 January 1840 and settled on the Coralgie run near Wellington. In financial difficulties by 1848 he was appointed commissioner for crown lands in the Bligh district. Ten years later government retrenchment left him with ten dependants and no occupation. He moved to Queensland and in 1861 was appointed police magistrate and gold commissioner at Rockhampton. When the new settlement of Somerset was established at Cape York in 1863, he became government resident and with his third son, John, erected the first buildings. He served as resident until December 1865 when he returned to his old office at Rockhampton. He died there on 27 February 1874, survived by his wife, five sons and two daughters.

His eldest son, FRANCIS LASCELLES, was born on 28 August 1841 at Orange and educated at Sydney Grammar School. When his father was posted to Somerset, Frank and his brother Alexander overlanded the stock. Accompanied by four Europeans and four Aboriginals they left Rockhampton on 14 May 1864 with 42 horses and 250 cattle. On the ten months' trek of 1200 miles they were constantly harassed by Aboriginals, forced their way through jungles, scrub and swamps and crossed at least six large rivers. At the Mitchell River on 13 December they withstood a major Aboriginal attack. Clad in tatters, wearing hats of emu skin and living on turkey eggs, they reached Somerset on 2 March 1865 with 12 horses and 50 cattle. Both brothers were elected fellows of the Royal Geographical Society and received the Murchison grant. In 1866 Frank settled on a station near Somerset and acted as a sort of deputy government resident in 1868-69, 1871-73 and briefly in 1878, filling the office when no one else was available. Confusion between his government and personal activities led to frequent complaints and in 1875 he was superseded by H. M. Chester [q.v.].

On 10 October 1873 at Somerset Jardine married the seventeen-year-old Sana Solia, niece of the King of Samoa; they had two sons and two daughters. In 1884-86 he was in charge of transport for the construction of the Cape York telegraph line and in 1890 was prominent in searching for survivors from the wreck of the steamer *Quetta*. After the government station was moved to Thursday Island in 1877, Jardine's home at Somerset was the centre of civilization on Cape York. Elaborate dinners for visiting

dignitaries were served on silver plate made from Spanish dollars found by Jardine on a reef in 1890. He died of leprosy at Somerset on 18 March 1919 and was buried near the beach at Somerset. He was survived by his wife, two sons and two daughters.

A brother, Alexander William, was born on 9 November 1843 near Sydney, shared in the Cape York expedition, served on many government works in Queensland, became chief engineer for harbours and rivers and died in London on 20 March 1920.

F. J. Byerley (ed), *Narrative of the overland expedition of the Messrs. Jardine* (Brisb, 1867); A. J. Richardson, *Private journals of the surveyor . . . Jardine's overland expedition to Cape York* (Brisb, 1867); R. L. Jack, *Northmost Australia*, 1-2 (Lond, 1921); J. Farnfield, *Frontiersman* (Melb, 1968); V&P (LA Qld), 1867 (2nd S), 2, 1187, 1868, 519, 1868-69, 673; Palmer papers (Oxley Lib, Brisb); Col Sec land letters (NSWA); Col Sec letters (QA); MS cat under Jardine (ML).   CLEM LACK

JASPRIZZA, NICHOLAS (1835-1901), orchardist, was born in Dalmatia. He arrived in New South Wales about 1864, went to the Lambing Flat diggings where he ended up at the Three Mile diggings. Realizing that victualling the miners was probably more profitable than digging for gold, he planted vegetables on a quarter-acre plot. Drought and floods reduced his capital from £25 to one shilling, but he hawked his first crop of vegetables around the diggings and made £50 profit. He then acquired a four-acre block on which he planted vines and fruit trees. By 1884 he had accumulated 900 acres and also ran 20 head of cattle and 600 sheep. In 1876 he had introduced cherry-growing to the Young district. He first planted Kentish cherries and conducted grafting experiments to produce a suitable variety. By 1893 he had 100 acres under cherries with 7000 full-grown and 300 young trees and 60 acres under vines.

At about 8 p.m. on 8 May 1901 Jasprizza was shot dead through the window of his house at McHenry's Creek, Three Mile. A young man was acquitted of his murder at Young Circuit Court on 30 September. The government then offered a reward of £100, which the family increased to £300, for information leading to a conviction, but the crime remains unsolved. He was buried in the Catholic cemetery at Young.

Jasprizza's life, apart from its unfortunate ending, was typical of many early pioneers: obscure beginnings, disappointed gold digger, small selector and success through shrewd judgment and hard work. He was survived by four sons and two daughters of his first wife Bridget Mary Bowles (d. 1884), née Tunney, whom he had married on 18 February 1867 at Sixteen Mile Rush, near Young, and by his second wife Rosetta, née Johnstone, whom he had married at Young on 7 February 1886. His estate was valued at £9500; his sons took over the cherry orchard which in 1907 was said to be the largest in Australia. Many descendants live in the Young district.

W. A. Bayley, *Rich earth* (Young, 1956); *Burrangong Chronicle*, 5 Aug 1893; *Burrangong Argus*, 11 May 1901; *SMH*, 10, 16 May 1901; Newspaper cuttings, vol 44 (ML).

G. P. WALSH

JEANNERET, CHARLES EDWARD (1834-1898), steamboat-owner and politician, was born on 9 February 1834 in Sydney, the eldest son of Henry Jeanneret. His father, born on 31 December 1802 in London, was apprenticed to an Oxford surgeon in 1817-22 and went to the University of Paris (B.L., 1823), the City Dispensary, London (L.S.A., 1824), and the University of Edinburgh (L.R.C.S.; M.D., 1825), where he was president of the Plinian Natural History Society. He practised in London until 1828 when he applied for a post in Australia but was recommended for a land grant in proportion to his capital. Reluctant to sell out before certain that the colonial climate would suit him, he was assured at the Colonial Office that he could visit Sydney and reserve land while he returned to England to sell his property. He arrived at Sydney in December 1829 and soon applied for a reserve grant but was told that he must take out a bond for £500 to remain in the colony for three years. Protesting against this condition he opened a practice as a surgeon and dentist. His *Hints for the Preservation of the Teeth* (1830) was the first dental publication in Sydney. In 1831 he gave public lectures on chemistry and was active in a dysentery epidemic. At St James's Church on 11 December 1832 he married Harriett Merrett. Each year he announced his projected departure for England, and in 1835 through the governor petitioned the Colonial Office for justice in obtaining a land grant, but the regulations had been changed. In 1839 he petitioned again in vain from Hobart Town. Appointed superintendent of Aboriginals at Flinders Island in 1842, he was dismissed in 1844. After many complaints he was reinstated with arrears of pay but in April 1847 lost his post. He petitioned again in 1849 but the Colonial Office rejected his claims. By 1851 he was in London where in 1853 his final petition ran to sixty-two pages. After publishing his vindication Dr Jeanneret gave up the battle and turned to medical practice. In 1854 he was active in the cholera epidemic in London and later published pamphlets on his methods of treatment. He died of senile decay on 17 June 1886 at Cheltenham, survived by his second wife Frances Ann Barnett, whom he had married on 13 November 1874 at Great Malvern, Worcestershire.

Charles spent his early years at Flinders Island where he learnt seamanship and navigation. At 18 he visited Europe and then spent three years on the Bendigo goldfields. He moved to Sydney where he married Julia Anne Bellingham on 12 June 1857. He joined the Bank of New South Wales and bought land at Hunter's Hill where he lived. He became a partner in Henry Porter's general agency and actively engaged in farming, mining and preserving meat. He financed the building of many large houses in the river suburbs. By 1869 he was a shareholder in and manager of the Parramatta River Steam Co. and in 1873 was manager of the Parramatta and Hunter's Hill Steam Ferry Co. After the two companies had become heavily indebted and amalgamated Jeanneret bought the goodwill and the five steamers in 1875. He added fifteen steamers, renamed the firm Parramatta and River Steamers and extended the steamboat service to Gosford and the Hawkesbury. By 1884 he was also owner of the Mosman's and Neutral Bay Ferry Co. In 1888 he sold out of shipping. In 1881 he had built the Parramatta Tramway connecting the wharves and the western end of the town after parliament passed his private Tramway Act.

Jeanneret was an alderman of Hunter's Hill and mayor in 1870-71, 1877-78 and 1890. From 1886 he represented Bourke ward in the Sydney City Council and was interested in water and sewerage management. As a magistrate he administered 'strict justice and sound common sense' in the Water Police Court. Defeated for Central Cumberland in 1875, he represented Carcoar in the Legislative Assembly in 1887-94 as a free trader. He supported Henry Parkes [q.v.] and federation. He visited England in 1888 and North America in 1893. By 1891 his financial position was precarious. After three withdrawn bankruptcy petitions, his estate was sequestrated in 1897. He owed about £30,000 and his wife's money was inextricably entangled with his estate. A prominent Freemason, he was one of the oldest members of Lodge Harmony. He died from cancer on 23 August 1898 at his son's home, Wyrallah, Richmond River. He was buried in St Anne's Church of England cemetery, Ryde. He was survived by his wife, eight sons and two daughters.

HRA (1), 17, 18; V&P (LA NSW), 1880-81, 2, 1045; Aust Dental J, 24 (1952); Bulletin, 29 Dec 1883; Australasian, 10 July 1886, 18 May 1889; SMH, 25, 30 Aug 1898; MS and newspaper indexes under Jeanneret (ML); Insolvency files (NSWA); CO 201/245, 280/252, 315, 324/86.   MARTHA RUTLEDGE

JEFFERIS, JAMES (1833-1917), Congregational minister, lecturer and journalist, was born on 4 April 1833 at St Paul's, Bristol, England, the elder son of James Jefferis, carpenter and undertaker, and his wife Sarah, née Townsend. Educated at Bristol Grammar School he entered his father's building business and ran a Sunday school in Brunswick Square. A wealthy uncle, W. H. Townsend, civil engineer and surveyor, wanted James to join him but, finding him resolved to enter the ministry, offered to put him through Oxford or Cambridge with prospects of a benefice if he then entered the Anglican Church. Jefferis was strongly attracted to Dissent and declined. In 1852 he entered New College, a Congregational institution affiliated with the University of London (B.A., 1855; LL.B., 1856), where he learned to reconcile scientific discovery with religious belief and encountered liberal theological tendencies.

The London Missionary Society invited Jefferis to serve in India but he declined. In April 1858 he accepted a call to the Congregational Church at Saltaire, a model settlement of the alpaca king, Sir Titus Salt. Jefferis, though not formally ordained, settled happily there but physicians soon found him tubercular and advised him to go to Madeira. Instead Jefferis decided to accept T. Q. Stow's [q.v.] invitation to help to form a Congregational Church in North Adelaide. Ordained on 16 December 1858 at Westminster Chapel he sailed from Liverpool in the Beechworth a week later with his young wife Mary Louisa (d. 1864), née Elbury, whom he had married on 21 October at the Brunswick Chapel, Bristol.

Jefferis reached Adelaide on 24 April 1859 and on 15 May Stow opened services for the new church. Jefferis's preaching attracted worshippers and the North Adelaide Congregational Church was soon constituted with him as its pastor. The new church in Brougham Place was opened in February 1861. Adherents of other denominations, attracted by his eloquence and manly and liberal approach to religion, helped to swell the congregations. Jefferis's morning sermons were expositions for the faithful company, but he was convinced that a preacher should relate religion to life and in the evening services applied Christianity to topi-

cal questions. In 1860 he started the North Adelaide Young Men's Society, one of the first in the colony. The future leading citizens who passed through it were remembered as 'the Jefferis boys'. Repudiating the notion that Congregationalism's mission was to the thoughtful urban middle classes, Jefferis assisted in home missions for the country and the predominantly Catholic poor of Lower North Adelaide. He also served on the committees of benevolent institutions and as local secretary for the London Missionary Society in 1863 led agitation against blackbirding in the South Pacific. On 11 April 1866 at St Kilda Congregational Church, Melbourne, he married Marian (d. 1930), née Turner.

An earnest promoter of education, Jefferis failed in the 1860s to lead Congregationalists into establishing a first-class unsectarian school in Adelaide. This experience and a visit to England in 1868 persuaded him to support compulsory, comprehensive and secular education under the state. He inspired Congregationalists in 1871 to seek Presbyterian and Baptist co-operation in opening an academy for nonsectarian higher education and theological training. Union College was formed in March 1872; classes began in May with Jefferis as tutor in mathematics and natural science. W. W. Hughes [q.v.] soon offered an endowment of £20,000. Jefferis helped to persuade the college council and Hughes that so large a sum should be used to establish a university in Adelaide. Jefferis was a member of the University Association formed in September and of the university council in 1874-77 and 1894-1917.

Jefferis often wrote leading articles on social and political subjects for the South Australian Register and the Advertiser which in 1876 unavailingly offered him the editorship and a partnership. His renown had spread beyond South Australia and in 1863 and 1875 John Fairfax [q.v.] tried in vain to entice him to Pitt Street Congregational Church, Sydney. In the 1870s Jefferis declined calls to churches in England, Melbourne and Adelaide but in 1877 he accepted a call to Sydney with a stipend of £1000.

Jefferis began at Pitt Street on Easter Sunday and soon repeated his Adelaide successes. The press amply reported his lectures, many of which were published as pamphlets. He also fostered the activities of the Young Men's Literary Society and extended Pitt Street's 'evangelical efforts among the neglected poor' in the slums; his abolition of pew rents removed an imagined barrier to artisans and set an example. He joined the successful campaign to divert the revenues of the Church and Schools Estates from the Anglican, Roman Catholic, Presbyterian and Wesleyan Churches to public education, supported the Public Schools League and delivered a weighty reply to Archbishop Vaughan's [q.v.] attack on the public schools. He modified his views on secular education and considered that Parkes's [q.v.] Public Instruction Act of 1880 with its provisions for nonsectarian religious teaching, was sufficient safeguard for both liberty and religion. In 1884 he joined Bishop Barry's [q.v.] abortive movement to strengthen the religious provisions of the Public Instruction Act by introducing daily worship in public schools. Determined to restore the sanctions of Christianity 'with more than their old authority', Jefferis now claimed 'a vital union between religion and the State' which the withdrawal of state aid to the denominations left unchanged. But he broke with Barry's committee over denominational teaching in the schools, and would have nothing but unsectarian 'common Christianity'. For years he advocated the New South Wales Act as the solution to the religious problem in Australia.

By 1889 Jefferis was showing signs of weariness. His public ministry had crowded out visits to his congregation and he confessed that he could not manage alone the pastoral responsibility. His wife's health was also broken and she needed a change. In September he asked for fifteen months' leave and for an assistant pastor who would share his stipend. Convinced that the Pitt Street church had little future he also suggested the sale of the property, using the proceeds for a new suburban church, a memorial hall for mission work and denominational city headquarters. Although the deacons were disposed to accept his proposals, some church members opposed the plan and criticized him personally. Jefferis promptly resigned, refused any presentation and in December sailed with his family for England.

In September 1890 Jefferis began a ministry at New College Chapel, but London's air aggravated his chest and he moved to Belgrave Congregational Church, Torquay, Devon. There he ministered to an increasing congregation and addressed Congregationalist regional and national meetings, but years in Australia had not inured him to the inferiority of a Nonconformist minister in England. His desire to return to Australia was obvious from the English letters he contributed to the *Australian Independent*, except for the dark months after he lost some £10.000 in the 1893 bank crash. He declined calls to two churches in Sydney but in 1894 returned to Brougham Place where he had been happiest.

Under Jefferis the building was renovated and a large debt almost extinguished, but he had reached his zenith at Sydney and utterances once greeted as progressive sounded conservative in the 1890s. He was still influential in denominational and public affairs and continued to write for the *Advertiser*, but pastoral demands weighed heavily upon him. In 1900 he was assisted by W. H. Lewis, a Welshman, to whom he gave half his stipend of £500. He retired from the active ministry on 21 April 1901. In 1909 he edited *Historical Records of the North Adelaide Congregational Church* to which he contributed an 'Historical Sketch'.

Convinced that Australia was destined to be a new and nobler nation spreading Christianity, civilization and liberty throughout the southern seas, he had begun to advocate federation in the 1870s in leading articles in the *Advertiser*. Although an idealist, his study of constitutional law—he obtained his LL.D. by examination from the University of Sydney in 1885—and his knowledge of federal history in America and Canada equipped him for the practical issues. In a lecture at the Adelaide Town Hall in June 1880, published as *Australia Confederated*, he rejected Parkes's 1879 proposal for a legislative union and advocated the Canadian Constitution as the 'safest' example. He repeated the lecture in Sydney in August 1883 relating it to the current annexation question and in 1889 gave two more lectures on the subject. After his return to Adelaide Jefferis supported the federal movement with more lectures and sermons and enlisted the support of the South Australian Council of Churches, which he had helped to form in 1896, in the 1898 campaign for a 'yes' vote. Though his influence cannot be measured he deserves a place in the history of Australian federation as one of its most persistent advocates.

While critics marvelled at his versatility and his dogmatism, Jefferis satisfied many that Christianity was relevant to contemporary issues. He gave trade unionism his blessing but advocated compulsory industrial arbitration. Faced with secular schemes for social salvation he maintained that Christianity was the true socialism. The only prominent churchman to denounce the New South Wales contingent to the Sudan in 1885, he recognized the need for controlled immigration from Asia but denounced the 'White Australia Policy' as 'high treason against the laws of God and man'. He remained Puritanical and condemned the theatre, dancing, gambling, prostitution and other 'moral dangers', but would not advocate teetotalism as the panacea for all social ills.

A consistent contender for a more organized Congregationalism, Jefferis was three times chairman of the Congregational Union of South Australia and twice in New South Wales. In 1883 he persuaded reluctant Congregationalists in New South Wales to mark their jubilee by a conference of Australasian Congregational Churches and presided at it. The conference anticipated the formation of the Congregational Union of Australia and New Zealand in 1888 but he later declined to act as its chairman. He also supported Protestant union and often co-operated with other denominations in common causes. In Adelaide he had helped to form the Evangelical Alliance in 1869 and served as its president; in Sydney he was the moving force behind the impressive United Thanksgiving Service for Protestants at the centenary of New South Wales in 1888. A persistent critic of Roman Catholicism, especially its exclusiveness and authoritarianism, he sometimes linked the Salvation Army with it.

Genial but always dignified and sometimes chilling, Jefferis was much caricatured by cartoonists; hoary age made his leonine appearance even more awesome. In retirement he continued to preach, particularly on special occasions. His oratory no longer appealed to the young but he remained a revered figure in the Union Assembly of which he became a life member in 1901. He built Elbury House, Gilberton, and at Encounter Bay in 1894 bought the Fountain Inn, renaming it Yelki; in summer he held services in the old bar. To the last he walked long distances daily, especially at the bay where he became well known to fishermen as he gathered seaweed and rocks for his natural history collection. He died peacefully at Encounter Bay on Christmas Day 1917 and was buried privately at Brighton cemetery. He left an estate worth £14,500, and was survived by a daughter of his first wife and by his second wife, two sons and five daughters.

His second wife Marian was zealous in philanthropic causes. In Adelaide she campaigned for cottage homes for destitute children and in Sydney in 1878 formed a committee that induced the Parkes government in 1881 to introduce the boarding-out system for orphaned or neglected children. An original member of the State Children's Relief Board, she also advocated cottage homes with foster parents and founded one for twelve children in Newtown. She donated land at Encounter Bay for the Congregational Church in memory of Jefferis.

The Jefferis medal in philosophy commemorates his service to the University of Adelaide. Portraits are in the North Adelaide Congregational Church and Stow Memorial Church.

J. B. Austin (ed), Farewell sermon by Rev. James Jefferis (Adel, 1877); L. Robjohns, Three-quarters of a century (Adel, 1912); E. S. Kiek, Our first hundred years (Adel, 1950); H. G. Pope, Our first century (Adel, 1959); Aust Christian World (Syd), 11 Jan 1918; SA Congregationalist, Jan, Feb 1918; SMH, 18 Dec 1889; Advertiser (Adel), 17, 18 Apr 1901, 27 Dec 1917, 29 Sept 1930; Register (Adel), 18 Apr 1901; Mail (Adel), 22 Mar 1913; Observer (Adel), 29 Dec 1917; B. Dickey, Charity in New South Wales, 1850-1914 (Ph.D. thesis, ANU, 1966); W. W. Phillips, Christianity and its defence in New South Wales circa 1880 to 1890 (Ph.D. thesis, ANU, 1969); Jefferis papers and newspaper cuttings (North Adelaide Congregational Church); North Adelaide Congregational Church records (SAA); records (Pitt Street Congregational Church, Syd).

WALTER PHILLIPS

JEFFERSON, JOSEPH (1829-1905), actor, was born on 20 February 1829 at Philadelphia, United States of America, son of Joseph Jefferson, actor, and his wife Cornelia Frances Burke, née Thomas. He grew up among theatre people, began his stage career at 4 and, after his father died in 1842, relied on acting for a living. At 21 he married Margaret Clements Lockyer. In 1856 he visited Europe and in September joined Laura Keene's company in New York. In 1861 his wife died, leaving four children.

With his eldest son, Jefferson went to San Francisco for a season and then sailed for Sydney, hoping to recover his health. He arrived in the Nimrod on 13 November and opened with Rip Van Winkle, Our American Cousin and The Octoroon. In March 1862 at Melbourne he played a season at the Princess Theatre for about six months. He was immediately popular. Within a week or so in Melbourne, 'not to have seen Jefferson was equivalent to exclusion from conversation in society of all classes'. Critics praised his 'fresh and genial' acting and his refined taste; in retrospect an admirer claimed that his acting combined 'the delicacy, the exquisite finish, the grace and airiness of French comedy with the naturalness and the blended humour and pathos of the best school of English comedians'. He was described as a slender but wiry, compact figure with the intellectual face of a Hamlet: 'a singularly charming companion for a conversational hour'.

In September Jefferson was engaged for the opening of George Coppin's [q.v.] Royal Haymarket Theatre, playing in Our American Cousin. He also played in the country districts of Victoria, including Ballarat and Bendigo. Between theatre seasons Jefferson spent some weeks at a station in the Western District and explored the Murray River. With Melbourne as his base he went first to

Tasmania where he played, among other things, *The Ticket of Leave Man* to an appreciative audience including many ex-convicts. Then in April 1864 he played a season at Dunedin, New Zealand, returning via Sydney. In April 1865 he left Melbourne for London where he arranged with D. G. Boucicault's [q.v.] father a revised version of *Rip Van Winkle*. The play was a great success and he went to America where his role as Rip Van Winkle became legendary. He retired from the stage in 1904 and died on 23 April 1905 at Palm Beach, Florida; he was buried at Buzzard Bay, Massachusetts. His second wife Sarah Isabel, née Warren, whom he had married on 20 December 1867, survived him. Jefferson was also a talented amateur artist and a keen fisherman. His attractive *Autobiography* (London, 1890) included an account of his Australian years and was reported with interest in the colonial press.

W. Winter, *Life and art of Joseph Jefferson* (New York, 1894); A. Bagot, *Coppin the great* (Melb, 1965); *Examiner* (Melb), 5 Apr 1862; *Australasian*, 21, 28 Dec 1878, 28 June 1890, 29 Apr 1905.   DENNIS SHOESMITH

JENNER, CALEB JOSHUA (1830-1890), businessman and politician, was born on 9 December 1830 at Alfriston, Sussex, England, son of Thomas Jenner and his wife Sarah, née Ralf. At 19 he migrated and arrived at Melbourne in February 1850. He may have spent some time in the Ballarat area during the early gold rushes but from the mid-1850s lived in Geelong where he and his brother Thomas had an iron and coal importing business. In March 1863, already well known as a supporter of protection for local industries and apparently successful in business, he was elected for South-Western Province to the Legislative Council and moved to Melbourne.

Jenner was soon established in Melbourne as an ironfounder and importer with premises in Flinders Street and as first chairman of the Land Mortgage Bank. These were his main interests until about 1870 when he gave up ironmongering for the gentler pursuits of importer, investor and company director. In the 1870s he was on the boards of the National Insurance Co., the Commercial Bank of Australia and the Land Mortgage Bank; he was also from 1875 a commissioner for the savings banks of Victoria. He was briefly chairman of William McCulloch [q.v.] & Co., and chairman of the McCulloch Insurance Co. and the Indemnity Fire and Marine Insurance Co. which succeeded it. Later he became chairman of Langlands [q.v.] Foundry Co.

Jenner's political career was distinguished for his behaviour in the parliamentary crises of the 1860s and 1870s. After the rejection of the McCulloch tariff in 1865 he urged the Legislative Council to act with discretion, and sought ways and means of compromise among members of both Houses; he did the same in 1868 and 1878. Business-like, he wanted the country governed efficiently and he was also sympathetic with the Legislative Assembly. He believed that the future prosperity of Victoria depended on the combination of a liberal land law, encouragement to native industry and immigration, and therefore favoured such measures as the 1865 tariff which almost all his fellow councillors opposed. His belief that the council franchise should be widened and his support for the abolition of state aid to religion—he was active in the Baptist Church and represented it on the 1867 royal commission on education—further separated him from them. Twice he became government representative in the council, for McPherson's [q.v.] government in 1869-70 and Duffy's [q.v.] in 1871-72. Yet at heart Jenner was conservative, with firm views on the virtues and duties of privilege and wealth which are evident in his speeches on council reform, immigration and payment of members. Although often against the council on important questions he had its confidence and respect, and from September 1874 to July 1883 was chairman of committees. He retired from parliament in July 1886.

Many of the companies with which Jenner was connected failed in the 1890s but he did not live to see the collapse of the boom he had helped to create. He died at his Mornington home, Beleura, on 27 June 1890, leaving an estate valued at more than £120,000 to his wife Eliza Ann, daughter of Rev. Isaac New of the Albert Street Baptist Church, and to the surviving four sons and six daughters of his thirteen children.

F. J. Wilkin, *Baptists in Victoria . . . 1838-1938* (Melb, 1939); PD (Vic), 1863-86; *Argus*, 28 June 1890; *Table Talk*, 25 July 1890.
                MARGOT BEEVER

JENNINGS, ELIZABETH ESTHER ELLEN (1864-1920), actress, best known as 'ESSIE JENYNS', was born on 5 October 1864 at Brisbane, the only child of Charles Jennings, chemist, and his wife Emily, née Moss. Her father died about 1877 and her mother went on the stage as 'Kate Arden' and soon married William James Holloway, actor-manager. As Essie Jenyns, Elizabeth had her first speaking role in 1879 at the Theatre Royal, Hobart, under the tragedian,

William Creswick, and next played in George Rignold's [q.v.] production of *Henry V* in Adelaide. By 17 she had played such roles as Ophelia, Desdemona and Lady Teazle. Holloway worked Essie very hard; Nellie Stewart [q.v.] attributed her unhappy adolescence to 'stepdaughter's luck', though she was often ill.

In 1884 Essie visited Europe with her mother and Holloway. She saw Sarah Bernhardt act, watched the foremost French directors instruct students at the Paris *Conservatoire*, and in London saw the actress, Mary Anderson, in whose roles she was to excel, although unfavourable Australian critics later called her 'Mary Anderson and water'. With his own 'Shakespeare Company' Holloway opened in Sydney in September 1886, claiming that Essie, who had not acted overseas, had been 'pronounced by eminent critics to be the foremost actress in Australia'. The *Evening News*, 13 September, praised her 'pleasing' performance and voice in the melodrama, *A Ring of Iron*. Overnight she became the star Holloway had advertised. After fourteen weeks at the Opera House and sixteen at the Criterion in Sydney she played for twenty weeks at the major theatres in Melbourne, Adelaide, Hobart and Brisbane. Excelling in such roles as Rosalind and Portia, she gave a much-needed boost to the ailing production of Shakespeare. She became the first star in George Darrell's [q.v.] *Sunny South*. One reviewer observed that audiences were so mesmerized by her great beauty and fascination that they were unable to judge her acting. Although she showed little original interpretation, smitten admirers claimed that she had 'infinitely more soul' than any contemporary comic actress, and she was a native-born Australian.

At the height of her success on 5 December 1888 Essie married John Robert Wood, a prominent cricketer and son of a wealthy Newcastle brewer. Holloway had plans for her to try her luck in London but she saw her marriage as an excuse to retire from the stage. Later she claimed that although she missed the hard work in the theatre she had only acted for a living. In the 1890s the Woods toured Europe for five years in their yacht *Imogen*. Essie described their Mediterranean cruise in *Yachting Ways and Yachting Days* (London, 1892). Her early retirement into respectable and wealthy domesticity made her the heroine of women's magazines and apart from charity, patriotic and benefit performances she emerged only once from retirement to play in a special Sydney presentation of *The Merchant of Venice* under Ellen Terry in 1914. The Woods later lived at Putney Hill, London. Essie died at Killara, Sydney,

on 6 August 1920 and was buried by an Anglican minister in the Presbyterian section of the Sandgate (Newcastle) cemetery. She was survived by her husband, a son and a daughter. Her estate was valued at £1697. She left her 'presentation copy of Shakespeare (1623)' to the National Art Gallery of New South Wales as a gesture to the people of Sydney 'for their loyalty to me'.

N. Stewart, *My life's story* (Syd, 1923); *Centennial Mag*, 1888; *Australasian*, 15 Dec 1888, 25 Jan 1902; *Imperial Review*, Jan 1889; *Cosmos Mag*, 30 Apr 1895; *Bulletin*, 1 Feb 1902; *Shakespearean Q*, Apr 1922.

HELEN M. VAN DER POORTEN

JENNINGS, SIR PATRICK ALFRED (1831-1897), pastoralist and politician, was born on 20 March 1831 in Newry, County Down, Ireland, son of Francis Jennings, linen merchant, and his wife Mary, née O'Neill. He was a direct descendant of John Jennings of Ballymurphy who in 1633 forfeited his Irish estates rather than change his Roman Catholic religion. Educated in Newry and in Exeter, England, he lacked the money to study for the Bar and trained for a business career with a firm in Exeter. In 1852 he went to Victoria. He joined the 1855 rush to New Bendigo (St Arnaud), but his keen commercial sense led him into store-keeping. When his ventures extended into quartz-crushing and grazing land, the prosperous store was run by members of his family who had migrated with his mother in 1857, the year he became a magistrate.

In 1858 Jennings declined to run for the Wimmera seat in the Legislative Assembly and in 1859 failed to win Crowlands, but he polled well in St Arnaud where he concentrated on organizing a town community with roads, drainage, water and a court. An original member, he was chairman of the local council. In 1862 with Martin Shanahan, a fellow Irish Catholic, he acquired Warbreccan station near Deniliquin in New South Wales. In 1863 he moved to the station after marrying Shanahan's eldest daughter Mary Anne, whose sister married a brother of Archbishop Vaughan [q.v.] and brother, John, married a daughter of John O'Shanassy [q.v.]. When Shanahan died in 1882 his son carried on the partnership with Jennings. By then they also held Garawilla near Gunnedah and Denobillie and Ulimambri near Coonabarabran. In 1874 they acquired Westbrook, 80,000 acres on the Darling Downs, Jennings's final home after Warbreccan was sold in 1885.

In defending his pastoral leases under the 1861 Robertson [q.v.] Land Acts, Jennings had no scruples in using his own dummies against speculating selectors but was consistent in his support for closer settlement. He joined the Riverine Association founded in 1863 but did not support separation, although he would have benefited from close Victorian markets. In 1865 he refused to take the district's grievances to the imperial government in London as he believed they should be settled locally. When James Martin [q.v.] visited the Riverina in 1867 and offered Legislative Council nominations to increase the Riverina's meagre representation, Jennings was the only member of the association to accept; in 1867-70 he served in the council and in 1870-72 represented the Murray in the Legislative Assembly. Defeated at Mudgee in 1874, he represented the Bogan in 1880-87.

In January 1883 Jennings was vice-president of the Executive Council in Alexander Stuart's [q.v.] ministry but in July resigned, explaining that 'his own people' were discontented with his position in cabinet. In 1885 he was briefly colonial secretary in G. R. Dibbs's [q.v.] government and then led the Opposition. When Robertson fell, Jennings failed to coalesce with him and reluctantly formed his own ministry in 1886. He was the first practising Catholic premier of New South Wales and the only non-Labor one. His comment that he was not 'a prominent politician' undervalued his importance as he had been offered ministerial office early in 1870 and twice later.

As premier and colonial treasurer Jennings was unfortunate in inheriting a serious financial crisis that helped to precipitate a major political dislocation. Always a free trader, he had promised his Bogan constituents that 'We will be no party to sneaking in protection'. However, his policy to meet the crisis included not only retrenchment, increased stamp duties, and land and income taxes but also a proposal to impose a 5 per cent *ad valorem* tariff and new specific duties. He rightly regarded this as a trivial breach of free-trade principles, and the best available fiscal compromise. His customs bill provoked intense debate in the colony. Its passage through the assembly was finally secured by parliamentary tactics which made its opponents label the government 'a brutal ministry'. But the rest of Jennings's programme was blocked and the deficit rose to about £2,000,000. Within the harassed ministry, relations between Jennings and Dibbs deteriorated; prorogation in October gave temporary respite from external but not internal tensions, and in January 1887 Jennings resigned his uncongenial task.

According to a friend, Jennings's political career had been 'an accidental diversion' from more rewarding pursuits. By the 1880s he had already shown his capacity as an organizer, administrator and benefactor in less controversial fields. In 1875 he was a New South Wales commissioner for the colonial exhibition in Melbourne, and next year representative commissioner for New South Wales, Queensland and Tasmania at the Philadelphia Exhibition. He was the executive commissioner for the 1879 Sydney International Exhibition and its success owed much to his administrative capacity, his equable temperament and his range of informed interest in agricultural and commercial matters. A vice-president of the Agricultural Society of New South Wales in 1876-87, he helped to procure it a permanent site in Moore Park. He was a fellow of the University of Sydney Senate in 1883-91 and a trustee of the National Art Gallery of New South Wales in 1885-97. His lifelong interest in music was combined with his interest in higher education when he gave £1000 towards an organ for the University of Sydney in 1879. Music was his major cultural interest. In St Arnaud he had led local amateur concerts and sometimes joined visiting professional singers in public performances of Rossini and Verdi. His enthusiasm for Wagner was one of the few radical traits in a consistently conservative character. He was president of the Sydney Liedertafel, and his patronage rescued it from an embarrassing situation in 1882. He was a member of the Union Club and in the 1880s was a local director of the London Chartered Bank of Australia, the Intercolonial Life Assurance Annuity and General Association and the Colonial Mutual Life Assurance Society.

In 1878-97 Jennings made the largest individual contributions to Catholic building appeals, especially for St Mary's Cathedral to which he presented a window in memory of his wife who died in 1887. He was a fellow of St John's College within the University of Sydney in 1868-72 and 1874-91; his 'princely liberality' enabled his friend, Archbishop Vaughan [q.v.], to open a library there and Jennings's generous gifts are commemorated by a stained-glass window with his family crest. At his unsuccessful Victorian election in 1859 he had opposed government aid to religion and favoured National education, but by 1879, though his daughter was at a non-Catholic school, he took a prominent part in meetings against Parkes's [q.v.] public instruction bill. Thereafter he supported the Catholic bishops' policy of organizing a separate education system.

Though Irish, Jennings was neither Parkes's 'damned Fenian' nor the 'proud and unflinching home ruler' of Catholic obituary tributes. His concept of Home Rule was conservative, and his support for John Redmond [q.v.] in a hostile Sydney in 1883 was more an indication of his generous nature than of his political beliefs. His emotional involvement in British policy led him to write a long letter to the *Sydney Morning Herald* praising Disraeli's handling of the 'Eastern Question', later published as *The Berlin Congress from an Australian Standpoint* (Sydney, 1878). One of the two New South Wales representatives at the 1887 Colonial Conference in London, he was hesitant about taking the initiative on behalf of New South Wales, though he did support the creation of an imperial fleet for Australian waters. He was a delegate to the 1891 National Australasian Convention in Sydney, but again had difficulty in working with Dibbs. In 1890-97 he was a nominee in the Legislative Council where his brief speeches were all on federation.

If Jennings's ideas of gentlemanly behaviour had been disturbed by his experience of parliamentary disorder in 1886 he retained an obvious enjoyment of public recognition. He was created C.M.G. in 1879 and K.C.M.G. in 1880 for his work for the International Exhibition. He was awarded an honorary LL.D. by the University of Dublin in 1887. He received several papal honours: in 1874 he was made a knight of St Gregory the Great, in 1876 a knight commander of the order of Pius IX, and in 1885 he received the Grand Cross of this order which conferred on him the title of marquis. He had no hesitation in seeking honours, and wrote to Cardinal Moran explaining his suitability. His fascination with titles was shown in an anonymous article he contributed to the *Freeman's Journal*, and later republished over his name as *An Essay on Knighthood, being an historical sketch of the Equestrian Orders* (Sydney, 1878), in which he defended the institution against the criticisms of 'our most conscientious democrats'.

In the 1890s a combination of drought, financial crises and failing personal health greatly reduced his pastoral wealth and his capacity to respond to new circumstances. One by one he lost control of his New South Wales properties. By 1893 he held only Westbrook and succeeded in selling part of it for closer settlement. Survived by a daughter and two sons he died in Brisbane on 11 July 1897 and was buried in Sydney in the family vault in Waverley cemetery. His estate in New South Wales was sworn for probate at £4400.

Y. S. Palmer, *Track of the years* (Melb, 1955); R. B. Ronald, *The Riverina* (Melb, 1960); P. Loveday and A. W. Martin, *Parliament factions and parties* (Melb, 1966); G. L. Buxton, *The Riverina 1861-1891* (Melb, 1967); D. B. Waterson, *Squatter, selector, and storekeeper* (Syd, 1968); A. W. Martin, 'Pastoralists in the

Legislative Assembly . . . 1870-1890', *The simple fleece*, A. Barnard ed (Melb, 1962); *Town and Country J*, 17 May 1890; P. N. Lamb, The financing of government expenditure in New South Wales, 1856-1900 (Ph.D. thesis, ANU, 1963); Parkes letters (ML); MS cat under P. A. Jennings (ML); Roman Catholic Archives (Syd); Univ Syd Archives; CO 201/598.   A. E. CAHILL

JERVOIS, SIR WILLIAM FRANCIS DRUMMOND (1821-1897), governor, was born on 10 September 1821 at Cowes, Isle of Wight, the eldest son of General William Jervois and his wife Elizabeth, née Maitland. Educated at Dr Burney's Academy near Gosport, he entered the Royal Military Academy at Woolwich and was commissioned second lieutenant in the Royal Engineers in 1839. He studied for two years in the School of Military Engineering at Chatham where his work at the drafting board was renowned for its excellence.

Jervois was posted to the Cape of Good Hope in 1841. He began the first survey of British Kaffraria and was twice cited for the quality of his work. He commanded a company of sappers and miners at Woolwich and Chatham in 1849-52 and then went to Alderney. He became the commanding royal engineer for the London military district in 1855, assistant inspector-general of fortifications at the War Office in 1856 and lieut-general and director of works for fortifications in 1862.

Especially interested in the American civil war, Jervois twice visited the United States to examine its defences and travelled three times to Canada. He sketched the harbour defences of Portland and Boston from rowing-boats while disguised as an artist. In 1865-74 he lectured on iron fortifications and inspected British defences from Gibraltar to the Andaman Islands. In 1863 he was made C.B. and in 1874 K.C.M.G.

In April 1875 Jervois was appointed governor of the Straits Settlements, succeeding Sir Andrew Clarke [q.v.], and his decisions irrevocably committed Britain to a place on the Malay archipelago. He distrusted Malays and had little respect for them; for the Chinese in Singapore he showed much sympathy and later strongly defended oriental migration to both Australia and New Zealand; in South Australia he was credited with having 'done much to modify unreasonable prejudice against Chinese labour'.

Early in 1877 Jervois was asked to survey the defences of Australia and New Zealand. Accompanied by Colonel P. H. Scratchley [q.v.] he completed his investigation of

New South Wales defences by the end of May and planned to go to the other colonies. At Melbourne in June he was notified of 'promotion' as governor of South Australia, though in truth he was transferred because Lord Carnarvon at the Colonial Office was unhappy with his active interference on the Malay mainland. On 2 October Jervois arrived at South Australia from Melbourne in H.M.S. *Sapphire* and was sworn in. The colony was in political crisis; when the Colton [q.v.] ministry resigned Jervois won general approval by resisting pressures to dissolve parliament and J. P. Boucaut [q.v.] became premier. For the rest of his term Jervois was 'singularly free of political complications' although he clashed once with the House of Assembly over representation. His term also coincided with good rainfall and unprecedented extension of agricultural land. He laid the foundation stone of the University of Adelaide and of the new institute and art gallery in 1879. He turned the sod of the colony's first tramway, opened new railways and visited the far northern and southern limits of settlement, even buying land for himself.

He was a popular chairman of meetings of the Bible Society, the City Mission and other philanthropic institutions and lectured in aid of funds for the Young Men's Christian Association. He reported on South Australia's defences in December 1877, oversaw the construction of the new Houses of Parliament and a vice-regal summer house at Marble Hill, and promoted both horse-racing and Turkish bathing in Adelaide. Some critics complained that he did not entertain democratically enough, but he met them with characteristic forthrightness by making public his invitation lists. His wife Lucy, née Norsworthy, whom he had married in March 1850, founded a Young Women's Institute and was active in charity work.

In 1882 Jervois was made governor of New Zealand and left Adelaide in January 1883, the *Register* claiming that he was 'not only one of the ablest and most judicious but also one of the most deservedly popular of our Governors'. One of his three sons was appointed adjutant of the local military forces. His younger daughter was married in the colony. He left New Zealand in March 1889. In 1892 he revisited South Australia and New Zealand and became colonel-commandant of the Royal Engineers in 1893. He died on 17 August 1897 after a carriage accident and was buried near Virginia Water, Surrey. His many published papers and lectures include *Defences of Great Britain and her dependencies* (1880) and *Colonisation* (1882). His name is remembered by a bridge in Adelaide and by mountains and a mine in Central Australia.

Roy Engineers J, 2 May 1898; *Australasian*, 23 June 1877; *Advertiser* (Adel), 6 Jan 1883; *Register* (Adel), 6, 8, 9, 10 Jan 1883; CO 13/135-141; family papers (copies held by author).   ROBIN W. WINKS

JEVONS, WILLIAM STANLEY (1835-1882), economist and logician, was ninth of the eleven children of Thomas Jevons, iron merchant of Liverpool, England, and his wife Mary Anne, daughter of William Roscoe, historian. After schooling in Liverpool, he attended University College School, London, in 1850-51 and in October entered University College where he studied mainly scientific subjects, though he was already interested in social conditions and the occupations of the people of London. He had decided to leave University College before taking a degree and to go into business in Liverpool. Early in 1854 he was recommended for a position of assayer at the new Sydney Mint. He accepted, mainly for his family's sake since his expected income would be relatively high, and his father's firm had been bankrupted in 1848 after the railway boom collapsed. After learning the techniques of assaying he sailed for Sydney, arriving on 6 October.

The original arrangements had envisaged his private practice as an assayer, with a retainer and payment by the Mint for work done on its behalf, but Jevons was soon employed by the Mint at a fixed salary. With regular hours and security of income he was able to devote much time to his scientific and intellectual interests. He made good use of his opportunities. His professional work was highly competent and he made some improvements in the standard processes; but the interest of his years in Sydney, both for his own career and for his modest but distinct contribution to Australian history, lies in his private occupations.

A systematic, careful and imaginative observer and speculator on causes, Jevons was a pioneer of scientific meteorology in Australia. From 1855 he made and recorded elaborate daily observations which were published at regular intervals in Henry Parkes's [q.v.] *Empire*. He concluded this work with several detailed articles, published in 1859, on Australian climate. According to H. C. Russell [q.v.], government astronomer, writing in 1888, his 'was the most valuable contribution to the meteorology of Australia that had been made up to the time of its publication'. In 1857 Jevons became interested in the new art of wet-plate photography. His photographs—portraits, interiors, urban and landscape scenes—were not known outside his Sydney contemporaries and family until 1953. Though not the earliest Australian amateur collection, they are considered to be possibly the most interesting of the period both for their technical and pictorial quality.

Known in Sydney as an able, if diffident, scientific observer and writer, Jevons was also quietly extending his interests in social and economic phenomena, and recording his speculations and plans in his journals and home-letters. In solitary journeys on foot to various parts of New South Wales, including the diggings at Braidwood, he was interested not only in geological and botanical observations but in the lives and habits of the people and the growth of new towns. As he read and reflected on books on political economy and statistics he began to see his lifework as the scientific study of social phenomena. He published several articles in the *Empire* on theoretical aspects of land and railway policy in New South Wales and single-handed attempted a 'social survey' of Sydney in 1858, the data for types of houses, location of trades, etc., coming from his own notes and observations.

Though Jevons, as he recalled in later years, was happy and healthy in Sydney, even the prospect held out to him of a large income in private business could not alter his firm resolve to return to England to pursue the work to which he had now decided to devote his life. His years in Australia were decisive in his intellectual development, turning youthful interests into creative activity. In April 1859 he sailed for England by way of America. In 1860 he returned to University College (M.A., 1862), concentrating on logic, mathematics and political economy. He soon began to publish the studies in logic, economics and scientific method which give him a high and enduring place in intellectual history. He was tutor and professor at Owens College, Manchester, in 1863-76 and professor of political economy at University College, London, in 1876-80. In August 1882 he was drowned while swimming.

In 1867 Jevons had married Harriet, daughter of John Edward Taylor, founder of the *Manchester Guardian*. Of their three children the oldest, Herbert Stanley (1875-1955), geologist and economist, published his *Essays in Economics* (1905) while a lecturer at the University of Sydney. A daughter, Harriet Winefrid (1877-1961), a pioneer in professional social work, presented some of his Australian manuscripts to the Mitchell Library.

H. A. Jevons (ed), *Letters and journals of W. S. Jevons* (Lond, 1886); J. A. La Nauze, *Political economy in Australia* (Melb, 1949), and for bibliog of Jevons's Australian writings; J. M. Keynes, *Essays in biography* (Lond, 1951); I. Burke, 'Australia's first pictorialist', *A'sian Photo-Review*, 62 (1955); R. Könekamp, 'William Stanley Jevons (1835-1882). Some biographical notes', *Manchester School*, 30 (1962); 'Sydney in 1858', *SMH*, Nov-Dec 1929; MS cat under W. S. Jevons (ML).

J. A. LA NAUZE

JEWELL, RICHARD ROACH (1810-1891), architect and superintendent of public works, was born in Barnstaple, Devon, England, son of John Jewell, joiner, and his wife Margaret, née Roach. He was articled to an architect and builder in his native town and later worked on the construction of many buildings, including churches, a college, fortifications and a military prison. Jewell married Eliza Jane Arthur. She was very frail and, after their first child was born, he decided to take her to a more temperate climate. They migrated to Western Australia and arrived at Fremantle in the *Will Watch* on 24 February 1852. Two sons and four daughters were born in the colony.

Jewell was first employed in the building section of the Convict Establishment, but soon transferred to the Department of Public Works and was appointed foreman in January 1853 at a salary of £150. Although he suffered a small financial loss by changing his position, prospects were good and he was glad to move from Fremantle to Perth. Governor Fitzgerald then appointed him to act as superintendent of public works and supervisor of the towns of Fremantle and Perth. The *Perth Gazette*, 8 July 1853, commented that 'a foreman of works is not all that is required where expenditure of a very considerable amount of public money requires the most careful supervision'. Jewell's talent in controlling finance was well exercised in the next few years, when the government's financial stringency compelled a policy of 'make do and mend' in public works. His activities were at first confined to repairing buildings, roads and bridges, and supervising the construction of the boys' schools in Perth and Fremantle. The impact of transportation of convicts brought greater prosperity, and Jewell began to take part in designing such major buildings as the court-house and gaol in Perth, using limestone quarried at Fremantle and transported up river by barge, a costly process which he soon replaced by bricks made by James Brittain in East Perth.

Conscientious and diligent, Jewell worked hard. His duties included supervision of works under construction and routine office chores and he often worked on plans and specifications long into the night. For most of his thirty-two years in office he was the only qualified architect in the colony, and wrote that 'only a professional colleague' could appreciate the magnitude of his task. In lasting evidence of his prodigious industry are such major and minor buildings as the Perth Town Hall, Wesley Church, Public Trust Office, the Treasury, pensioners' barracks and the cloisters in Perth; among his many works in the country were Toodyay gaol, Roebourne residency and police station, Greenough police station and Geraldton residency (later hospital). At times Jewell was acting director of public works and commissioner for railways. He retired with a liberal pension as superintendent of public works in 1884. Predeceased by his wife on 19 July 1884, Jewell died on 1 June 1891 at his home, Belvedere, Perth.

J. and R. Oldham, *Western heritage* (Perth, 1961); *Church of England Mag*, Sept 1871; J. and R. Oldham, 'Documents on Australian architects—Richard Roach Jewell', *Architecture in Aust*, 55 (1966); *Inquirer*, 25 Oct 1882, 30 July 1884; *West Australian*, 26 July 1884; *Possum*, 14 Jan 1888; M. B. Hale diary (Battye Lib, Perth); R. R. Jewell, Letter-book 1855-61, A523 (Battye Lib, Perth); CSO, 1852-84 (Battye Lib, Perth).   RAY OLDHAM

JOHNS, JOSEPH BOLITHO (1827?-1900), bushranger known as 'MOONDYNE JOE', was born in Wales, son of Thomas Johns, blacksmith. He became an ironworker in Glamorganshire and on 23 March 1849 was sentenced to ten years' imprisonment for larceny. He was transported to Western Australia and arrived at Fremantle on 1 May 1853.

Granted an immediate ticket-of-leave and in 1855 a conditional pardon, Johns by 1860 was living in the Toodyay district. Suspected of rounding up and branding cleanskin horses, working from an isolated gorge on the Avon River known as Moondyne Springs, he was arrested on a charge of horse stealing in 1861. While awaiting trial he escaped from Toodyay gaol but was recaptured to serve three years' imprisonment. Released, he was again sentenced in 1865 to ten years for killing an ox with the intent of stealing the carcass. Determined not to serve this long sentence and protesting his innocence, Johns from November 1865 to March 1867 made four attempts to escape, three of them successful. With two companions, he was once at large for two months in the unsettled Darling Range. Recaptured he was placed in irons in solitary confinement in a specially reinforced cell with triple-barred windows at Fremantle gaol. Allowed out for exercise on medical advice, he escaped again in 1867 through a clever trick and for two years roamed the hill country east of Perth. He was recaptured while raiding a wine cellar and sentenced to a further term in Fremantle prison. He was released in 1871 and gained his conditional pardon in 1873.

After his release Johns became respectable and worked in the Vasse district as stockman and timber-feller and at Fremantle as carpenter and shipwright. He is reputed to be the discoverer of one of the Margaret River caves named after him. In 1879 he married a widow Louisa Frances Hearn, née Braddick, who died in 1893. In 1900 Johns was finally ordered to the Mount Eliza depot for the destitute and because of increasing senility was transferred to the Fremantle asylum where he died on 13 August.

Moondyne Joe is popularly described as Western Australia's only bushranger of note. No Ned Kelly [q.v.], he neither held up mail coaches nor attacked banks; he raided poultry runs, visited half-way houses and perhaps stole horses. Yet through his determined bids for freedom against the harsh prison discipline of the convict period he became a romantic figure in the eyes of the public. His small triumphs over authority inspired John Boyle O'Reilly [q.v.], a Fenian convict who escaped from Western Australia to the United States, to write in 1887 a novel on convict life in Western Australia featuring a fictitious and highly romantic Moondyne as central character. The twentieth century has seen further romantic legends grow around his name.

Welshman, 30 Mar 1849; *Herald* (Fremantle), 27 Feb 1869; M. C. Carroll, Behind the lighthouse, a study of J. B. O'Reilly's sojourn in Australia (Ph.D. thesis, Univ Iowa, 1954); Fremantle register, 1900 (Fremantle Gaol); Fremantle prison records, convict register 1853 (Battye Lib, Perth); Police Court records, Mar 1900 (Perth Police Court); Police Department records, 12, 19 Aug, 2 Sept 1861, 20 Nov 1865, 14 Mar 1868 (Battye Lib, Perth).   M. TAMBLYN

JOHNS, PETER (1830-1899), engineer and businessman, was born on 19 April 1830 at Pembroke, Wales, son of Thomas Johns, builder, and his wife Elizabeth, née Tudor. The only record of his first twenty-five years is a testimonial that he worked in 1854-56 as a foreman in rebuilding the Crystal Palace at the London suburb of Sydenham.

Johns migrated from Liverpool as a steerage passenger in the *Champion of the Seas* and reached Melbourne in June 1856. In his first years in the city he assembled prefabricated-iron houses imported from England. When the demand for these houses waned, he built iron roofs, stores and

verandahs. By 1862 he was more a manufacturer than a builder, and his small workshops in Flinders Lane made iron gates and
verandahs, and shaped the structural iron
for bridges and buildings. For at least a
decade he was a working artisan as well as
owner of the business.

About 1870 he engaged an excellent
engineer, Thomas Pearce, who had served
his time in the famous Birmingham workshops of Boulton & Watt. With Pearce as
foreman, the new engineering shop made
machines which bent, guillotined and cor-
rugated sheet iron. It also manufactured
hydraulic lifts which were increasingly used
in wool stores and tall city buildings in the
1880s. By the height of the building boom
in 1888 the blacksmith's and engineering
shops rambled over two acres of valuable
city land and employed an average of 120
men.

Johns wisely floated his business into a
public company, Johns' Hydraulic & General Engineering Co., in 1888. He received
more than half of the issued shares, the first
instalment of £25,000 cash and the post of
managing director which he held until failing health made him resign. In 1892 his
company became known as Johns & Waygood, after taking over the Australian business of the English elevator manufacturer,
Richard Waygood & Co.

His was a quiet success story in the
tradition of Samuel Smiles. In the kind of
business which had a high risk of failure,
he succeeded through a rare blend of
caution and enterprise; in the booming
1880s he was outstripped by some competitors but in the depressed 1890s he outstripped them. He took pride and pains in
his work and was generous to his employees,
giving them nearly half of his own shares
in the new public company. He was universally said to have been honourable in
his dealings and meticulous in his workmanship. He superintended the Wesleyan
Sunday school in Carlton for many years,
and a high proportion of his employees and
shareholders—and perhaps even clients—
were Wesleyan. Nevertheless his association in later years with Thomas Bent [q.v.]
must have pursed some Wesleyan lips; Bent
was the first chairman of Johns's public company and was allowed to keep the chair
after he had lost his power, money and
reputation. The likely explanation for the
liaison was simply Johns's loyalty to any
man who had treated him well.

Johns had married Charlotte Eliza Barrett
three months after reaching Melbourne.
When he died at Hawthorn on 24 September 1899 he left eight children, of whom
the best known was Alfred, a dashing play-
boy who toured England with the Australian cricketers in 1899. Descendants of
Johns are still prominent in the firm he
founded.

G. Blainey (ed), *One hundred years: Johns &
Waygood Limited, 1856-1956* (Melb, 1956);
Johns & Waygood Ltd papers (ANU Archives);
family papers (held by Mr P. Johns, Johns &
Waygood Ltd, Melb).   GEOFFREY BLAINEY

JOHNSON, EDWIN (1835-1894), school-
teacher and civil servant, was born on 2
January 1835 at Liverpool, England, son of
Samuel Johnson and his wife Elizabeth, née
Crabtree. Educated at the Liverpool Quakers
School, he was apprenticed at 14 as a pupil-
teacher. About 1853 he won a Queen's
scholarship to Kneller Hall, Twickenham
Training College, under Rev. Dr Frederick
Temple, later archbishop of Canterbury,
who recommended him for employment by
the New South Wales Board of National
Education in 1854. Johnson reached Sydney
in 1855 and was appointed assistant master
at the William Street National School. In
1857 he married Rebecca, née Hanly. In
that year he also brilliantly passed the
teacher-classification examination and as a
result was invited by William Wilkins
[q.v.] to lecture on elementary mechanics
at the Fort Street Model School. Johnson
became headmaster of a new model school
at Deniliquin in 1861 and inspector of
schools in the Hunter River district in 1863.

His advice was often sought by Wilkins.
Both were influenced by the Swiss educator,
Pestalozzi, and believed that teaching
should be adapted to the natural stages of
the child's development and that all teachers
should study psychology. Johnson was
quick to criticize bookish, dull and stereo-
typed teaching, and emphasized 'cultivation
of the intelligence' and teaching the child
'to discover for himself'. He also advocated
infant schools and encouraged the local
Teachers' Mutual Improvement Society. In
1867-77 he was inspector of schools in the
Sydney district and supervised the training
department at the Fort Street Model School
and on-the-job training of assistant inspectors. He advocated in vain a residential
teachers-training college but introduced
half-time schools in sparsely populated districts. He also promoted amendments in the
instruction of pupil-teachers, extended infant schools and introduced military drill
to improve school management and discipline. In 1870 his wife died in childbirth
leaving him with an infant daughter and
six other children.

Johnson sought promotion to senior inspector in 1877 but was transferred to the
Cumberland district. His administrative

talent was recognized in 1880 when Wilkins nominated him for chief inspector with the new Department of Public Instruction. In that post he played an important part in working out educational details of the new administration. In 1884 he succeeded Wilkins as under-secretary and combined loyalty to the previous régime with some readiness to introduce change. Known for his 'affable and genial' disposition and flexible views, Johnson did much to extend a formal English approach to kindergarten work and to establish school savings' banks, the Public Schools Athletic Association and a scheme whereby some students could work for arts degrees at the University of Sydney while at training college.

In 1887 Johnson took 'extended leave' to visit Britain and North America. He gained 'a thorough insight into all that was being done in those countries in the advancement of primary and technical education'. On his return he added cookery, agriculture and manual training to the primary school curriculum and technical and scientific studies to high school courses. On 8 April 1894 he died of cancer at his home in Summer Hill. He was buried in the Anglican section of Waverley cemetery and survived by a son and six unmarried daughters.

Board of National Education, *Annual reports* (Syd, 1855-65); Council of Education, *Annual reports* (Syd, 1866-69); *Reports of the minister of public instruction* (Syd, 1881-95); *NSW Educational Gazette*, 1 May, 1 June 1894; Board of National Education, Fair minute books 1855-66 (NSWA); Council of Education, Sec's private out-letter book 1867, 1874-75, Minute books 1871-80, Miscellaneous in-letters 1867-75 (NSWA).   CLIFF TURNEY

JOHNSON, ROBERT EBENEZER (1812-1866), solicitor and politician, was born in London, son of Richard Johnson, gentleman, and his wife Elizabeth, née Phillips. He arrived in Sydney about 1833 and on 30 October 1834 at St James's Church married Elizabeth Byrne. He was articled to J. W. Thurlow, then to G. R. Nichols [q.v.] and was admitted a solicitor on 12 February 1842. In March 1843 he sued Thomas Revel Johnson for libel after the *Satirist and Sporting Chronicle* had attributed his pocked face to 'the commission of sin in early life, and the effects of mercury'. The case was dropped when T. R. Johnson was gaoled for editing an obscene publication. Johnson lived in style but on 8 December 1847 became insolvent 'through misfortune'. Next year he was discharged and his insolvency did not affect his standing as a solicitor. From about 1851 to 1864 he was in partnership with his brother Richard. In the early 1850s

he moved to Brooksby, Double Bay, with its famous convict-built garden. In 1853 he was joint secretary and treasurer with A. H. Stephen [q.v.] of the St Paul's College Building Committee and contributed £200. He was a fellow of the college until 1866 and a member of the Benevolent Society Committee.

In 1856 Johnson was appointed to the first Legislative Council after responsible government. An active law reformer he carried the Insolvents Act Amendment Act and an Act anent stamps on conveyances. In 1857 he went to England and on his return in November 1858 resumed his seat. He carried the Registration of Deeds and the Supreme Court Verdicts and Judgments Acts but was unable to effect other legal reforms. He served on many committees, devoted himself 'to the details of measures' and was ready 'at all times to give assistance to other members'. In 1860 he joined the New South Wales Constitutional Association which aimed at securing for parliament 'the services of gentlemen whose standing and education are a guarantee that they will support sound constitutional principles', but it failed in the 1860 elections during ferment over the land question. On 10 May 1861 he resigned from the council in support of Sir William Burton [q.v.]. In 1863 Johnson was reappointed and continued his attempts at such legal reforms as arbitration. He introduced thirty bills on nineteen different subjects. Johnson was 'most insistent on the power of the council to amend money bills' and had led the councillors who had threatened to refuse the 1860 Appropriation Act. In 1864 he urged that James Martin's [q.v.] customs bill should be amended. Johnson was 'an effectual speaker and influential leader'. His friend, Sir Alfred Stephen [q.v.], thought that he was 'probably the most useful man in either House'; he worked with Stephen in many congenial 'pursuits and plans'.

An active clubman, Johnson served on the committees of the Union Club in 1863-66 and the Australian Club in 1866. He was a loyal supporter of the Church of England. Aged 54 he died suddenly at Brooksby from apoplexy on 6 November 1866 and was buried in the Anglican section of Randwick cemetery. Alexander Campbell [q.v.] said in the Legislative Council that 'No one could be in his company long . . . without being both edified and amused'. Survived by his wife, three sons and two daughters, he left goods valued at £5000, but his finances were again 'considerably involved'.

In memorium. The Honourable Robert Johnson, M.L.C. (Syd, 1866); G. N. Griffiths, *Some houses and people of New South Wales*

(Syd, 1949); *Satirist and Sporting Chronicle*, 25 Feb 1843; *SMH*, 22 Nov 1858, 11, 24 Feb 1864, 8, 9 Nov 1866; *Empire* (Syd), 26 May 1860, 8, 9 Nov 1866; P. Loveday, Parliamentary government in New South Wales, 1856-1870 (Ph.D. thesis, Univ Syd, 1962); Macarthur papers (ML); Minter, Simpson & Co uncat MS 424, item 64 (ML); MS and printed cats and newspaper indexes under Robert Johnson (ML); Insolvency file 1709 (NSWA).

MARTHA RUTLEDGE

JOHNSTON, JAMES STEWART (1811-1896), politician, newspaper manager and vigneron, was born on 7 February 1811 in West Lothian, Scotland, the only son of James Johnston, part-proprietor of the Adambrae papermill at Mid Calder, and his wife Mary, née Stewart. Orphaned early, Johnston was brought up by his mother's family. He studied medicine at the University of Edinburgh but in September 1834 went to Demerara, British Guiana. He returned to Edinburgh in September 1836 and was briefly a book-keeper. In May 1838 he arrived in the *Jane* at Hobart Town where he joined the office of the superintendent of convicts. In April 1840 he moved to Melbourne where he became a book-keeper to the merchants J. F. Strachan [q.v.] & Co., opened the Southern Cross Hotel in West Bourke Street which he ran until about 1846, and bought land at St Kilda. In 1841-46 he held the Eumemmering cattle station near Dandenong with Edward Wilson [q.v.]. Late in 1848 Johnston and Wilson bought the *Argus*; in 1852 Johnston sold out to James Gill who was soon replaced by Lauchlan Mackinnon [q.v.].

In 1844 Johnston was returned unopposed to the Melbourne City Council for Bourke ward and became an alderman in 1848. A fluent, pungent speaker, he joined the anti-La Trobe party in the council. He advocated the separation of the Port Phillip District from New South Wales, addressed public meetings on anti-transportation in 1849-50 and in 1851 was elected to the Victorian executive of the Australasian League. A familiar figure in the celebrations of the St Andrews and Burns Societies, Johnston was invariably welcome for his rousing after-dinner speeches and rallying songs.

In November 1851 Johnston was elected with W. Westgarth and J. O'Shanassy [qq.v.] to represent the City of Melbourne in the Legislative Council where with other urban liberals he opposed government nominees and squatters' representatives. In the council he denounced transportation and in December 1851 and November 1852 advocated the substitution of an export duty for the gold licence tax. He also proposed the opening of agricultural lands near the goldfields and the limitation of pastoral leases to intermediate districts. He argued for a National education system and initiated an abortive voluntaryist bill. Scornful of the colony's administration, he moved a want of confidence in the 'weak, vacillating and spiritless executive' in November. When it was defeated he resigned and left for Scotland.

Back in Victoria in July 1858 Johnston stood for Southern Province in the Legislative Council but lost. Next year he was returned with A. Michie [q.v.] for St Kilda to the Legislative Assembly. He supported the Nicholson [q.v.] ministry while it lasted, but was only a shadow of the former 'fiery, knock-down Johnston'. His inability to identify with the 'popular party' became apparent in debates on the 1860 land bill when he opposed Land Convention demands for selection before survey and deferred payments, though he genuinely sought enactment of the bill. After the Nicholson ministry was defeated in November, he declined the post of chief secretary but accepted the portfolios of vice-president of the board of land and works and commissioner of public works in the Heales [q.v.] ministry. In February 1861 he resigned from the ministry with his colleague R. S. Anderson [q.v.] when Heales compromised with assembly demands to reduce expenditure. In May Johnston became a commissioner of National education. He was commissioner of public works in the O'Shanassy government from November 1861 to June 1863 and held his assembly seat until 1864. A street in Collingwood commemorates his parliamentary career.

Johnston attracted public notice again in 1865 as one of the executive councillors who petitioned the Queen against the McCulloch [q.v.] government's controversial handling of financial matters. Johnston contested the 1868 general election as a constitutionalist who believed that the assembly was attempting to coerce the council in the Darling grant controversy. He was defeated at West Bourke in January and Warrnambool in February but because of his involvement with the *Argus* did not again try to re-enter parliament.

In 1867 Johnston represented Mackinnon's interests in the *Argus* and was admitted to editorial council meetings in 1870. He was temporarily general manager of the *Argus* in 1871 and from June 1879 to May 1881. One of his other business interests was the Australian Alliance Assurance Co. of which he was an original director. He leased his Marli Terrace flats on the Esplanade, St Kilda, and the Saracen's Head Hotel in Bourke Street, and became increasingly absorbed by his vineyard at

Sunbury. In 1863 he had applied for twenty-six acres at Sunbury but later increased his acreage, ordered a variety of vine cuttings and built a concrete house, Craiglee, where he lived with his family from January 1866. His wines later won awards at overseas exhibitions. He was a Shire of Bulla councillor in 1869-70 but his Melbourne interests demanded supervision and in 1872 he moved his family back to Marli, St Kilda. He often visited Craiglee but entrusted much of the work to his younger sons. An original member of Scots Church, Melbourne, he defended Charles Strong [q.v.] in the 1880s but did not defect to the Australian Church.

In 1887 Johnston went to Scotland with his wife and youngest son and on 12 August 1892 made his last public appearance in Melbourne. Confined for months to his room after a fall, he died at Marli on 10 August 1896 and was buried in the St Kilda cemetery. About 1830 he had married Louise Busten who soon died in Ireland; their daughter Louise married J. L. Currie [q.v.] in 1852. On 22 September 1837 he married Henrietta Swanston in Edinburgh but she died after a mental illness in Melbourne, leaving two sons and one daughter. On 17 January 1854 at Edinburgh he married Mary Inglis; the eldest of their four sons, William Edward, became a judge.

Garryowen (E. Finn), The chronicles of early Melbourne, 1-2 (Melb, 1888); G. Serle, The golden age (Melb, 1963); Argus, 24 May 1881, 11 Aug 1896; Johnston letters (Univ Melb Archives); Johnston diaries (held by Lady Johnston, Camberwell, Vic).

CAROLE WOODS

JOHNSTON, JOSEPH (1814-1892), Congregational minister, was born on 9 March 1814 at Stamford, Lincolnshire, England, son of John Johnston, businessman. Educated privately and at Stamford Grammar School, he taught for two years at Wisbech and then at Stamford, and became a member of the Congregational Church at Grosvenor Street, Manchester. In 1838 he was accepted by the London Missionary Society and as a 'Normal Schoolmaster' sailed in the Camden by way of Sydney for Tahiti with John Williams [q.v.]. On arrival Johnston began a boarding school at Papara for the sons of chiefs and other youths likely to become useful as schoolmasters or assistants to the missionaries. On 28 December 1840 he married Harriett, daughter of Rev. George Platt, a senior missionary on the Society Islands.

Johnston visited Australia for his health in January 1842 and then sailed for six months among the islands of Western Poly-

nesia intent on starting new missions. Tahiti became a French protectorate that year and trouble began between the natives and the French. The refusal of English missionaries to accept state aid led to much conflict and they left the island in 1850. Weakened in health Johnston returned to England where for three years he travelled and preached for the London Missionary Society.

In 1853 Johnston was sent to Fremantle by the Colonial Missionary Society and arrived in the Sabrina on 13 June. He rented a cottage in Fremantle and held meetings in one of its rooms and then in the court-house until the Congregational Chapel was opened in June 1854. In his pastoral duties he made journeys on horseback between Fremantle and Bunbury and was a conscientious and hard-working cleric. At a time when the Congregational Church in Perth had frequent changes of ministers Johnston was a stabilizing influence to Congregationalism in the colony. He was a mover towards Congregational Union in Western Australia and became its first chairman.

Concerned with the intellectual as well as the spiritual needs of the colonists, Johnston often lectured to the Fremantle Mechanics' Institute and when it showed signs of becoming a 'gentlemen's club' he and Rev. George Bostock were instrumental in founding the Fremantle Workingmen's Association. They won the governor's approval and gained a grant for their purpose. Johnston held various offices on the committee; he effectively worked to achieve the amalgamation of the two institutions and was vice-president when they became the Fremantle Literary Institute in 1868. He retired from active work in 1886 and died on 16 February 1892. He was survived by his wife (d. 1896), and by a daughter, Eliza Mary, who had married Samuel J. F. Moore in 1870. His son, Joseph Taylor, had been drowned in 1876 aged 27.

The Congregational Church at Fremantle, completed in 1877, was later named the Johnston Memorial Church in his honour.

S. H. Cox, Seventy years history of the Trinity Congregational Church (Perth, 1916); WA Bulletin, 12 May 1888; Candidates papers, diaries and letters (LMS Archives, Livingstone House, Westminster, microfilm NL); J. Johnston diaries and CSR, 1863, 1867, 1869 (Battye Lib, Perth).

M. MEDCALF

JOHNSTONE, ROBERT ARTHUR (1843-1905), explorer and police officer, was born at Richmond, Van Diemen's Land, youngest of the six sons of John Johnstone, grazier, and his wife Annie Elizabeth, née Meed.

His grandfather was George Johnston [q.v.]. The family moved to Victoria in 1851. Like his five brothers and a sister, Robert was sent to Scotland for education. He returned to work with stock in Queensland in 1865 and for a time managed Apis Downs. In April 1867 at Landsdowne, Mackay, he married Maria Ann Gibson, who was born on 30 November 1847 at Watson's Bay. A Presbyterian, Johnstone attended the Church of England after his marriage.

In 1868 Johnstone became manager of the first sugar plantation at Bellenden Plains, about twenty miles north of Cardwell, for Trevillian & Co. It changed ownership in 1871 and Johnstone, who trained as a cadet at Fort Cooper, was appointed sub-inspector of native police to the Cardwell district. Cardwell was then Queensland's most northerly port. In the 1870s northern frontiers were rapidly expanded by gold discoveries and exploration, and the increased European activity on land and sea was accompanied by significant increases in Aboriginal hostilities.

Settlers, bushmen and shipping, disabled or not, were attacked while massacres, cannibalism and surreptitious murders were reported often. Johnstone's patrols, punitive or otherwise, took him beyond Trinity Bay and west of the ranges, and were interwoven with the accounts and reports of such hostile activities as the wreck of the brig *Maria* (1872), the Goold Island murders (1872), the Green Island massacres (1873), the attack on the *Albert and Edward* 1874), the Conn murders (1875), the Dunk Island murders (1877) and the *Riser* wreck and massacres (1878). Rather anonymous complaints of the extremity of measures taken by Johnstone against the Aboriginals who killed and ate the captain and crew of the *Maria* reached the Queensland parliament. Politicians were satisfied by Johnstone's denial and Cardwell people, more aware than suburban dwellers of the risks Johnstone faced for their protection, presented him with a testimonial of appreciation with particular reference to the wreck of the *Maria*: the original is now held by the Johnstone Shire Council.

In charge of native police Johnstone in 1873 accompanied G. E. Dalrymple [q.v.] on the north-east coast expedition to explore the coastal lands as far as Cooktown. Mounts Annie and Arthur in the Seymour range were named after members of Johnstone's family and Dalrymple named the Johnstone River after him; he had first found it when investigating the Green Island massacres. On this expedition he climbed Mount Bellenden Ker, not Bartle Frere, a supposition which has led to controversy and counter claims. In 1876 he discovered and

named the Barron River when searching for a route over the ranges behind Trinity Bay to serve the new goldfields. With this route found, Cairns was begun with his assistance. In 1879 he escorted James Tyson [q.v.] over the Tully River lands which led to their selection, and T. H. Fitzgerald [q.v.] to the Johnstone River lands which led to the beginnings of Innisfail. He briefly tried grazing on the Herbert at his property Molonga but soon rejoined the public service. In 1881 he took his family in a dray to Winton where he became the first police magistrate and conducted its first land sale. He was transferred to Bundaberg in 1882 and to Howard and Tiaro in 1887. He lived at Maryborough in 1890-1900 and then moved to Beenleigh. He was living at Toowong when he died on 16 January 1905. He was survived by three sons and four daughters of his nine children.

Sometimes known as 'Black' because of his tan, or 'Snake' because he often teased children by producing snakes from his shirt, Johnstone was a keen naturalist and observer of the flora and fauna in northern scrubs. His reminiscences of North Queensland appeared as 'Spinifex and Wattle' in the *Queenslander*, 1903-05. These articles emphasize the things of nature which delighted him on his patrols. A freshwater crocodile and species of freshwater turtle are named after him.

G. E. Dalrymple, *Narrative and reports of the Queensland north-east coast expedition, 1873* (Brisb, 1874); D. Jones, *Cardwell Shire story* (Brisb, 1961); information from Mrs H. M. Hassall, Mundubbera, Qld and Dr J. W. Johnstone, Melbourne.   DOROTHY JONES

JOHNSTONE, THOMAS (1829-1909), Presbyterian minister, was born on 11 January 1829 near Lochmaben, Dumfriesshire, Scotland, son of William Sibbald Johnstone, grazier, and his wife Elizabeth, née Renwick. He was educated at the parish school, matriculated at the University of St Andrews in 1847 and studied for the ministry. In 1856 he was licensed as a probationer by the Presbytery of Chanonry, Ross, and applied for service in New South Wales.

Johnstone arrived at Sydney in 1857 and was appointed by the Synod of Australia to East Maitland, but was soon called to Armidale, then within the Presbytery of Maitland. He began his ministry on 17 April 1857 and vigorously covered a wide area of New England, including Walcha, Hillgrove, Kilcoy, Wandsworth and Guyra as well as the town and district of Armidale. He described himself as an 'evangelical boundary rider'. He was often absent from home for long periods and annually travelled over 6000 miles on horseback. He baptized more than 3000 infants and joined over 800 couples in marriage. In 1865-76 he was clerk of the Presbytery of New England after the union of the Presbyterian Church in Australia. In 1882 St Paul's Church was built in Armidale.

A conventional Scottish Established Church minister, Johnstone devoted his life to the parish. He declined all calls elsewhere and the moderatorship several times. That severe critic, J. D. Lang [q.v.], described him as 'an able, zealous and successful minister of our Church'. He was an earnest preacher with a rugged eloquence and forceful diction, an affectionate pastor, a fond parent and a loyal friend. Physically large and strong, he was sociable, impulsive, warm hearted and sometimes impatient. He continued to live in the old manse after he had gained a colleague, Rev. Peter McQueen, because of his failing health. In 1894 he was awarded an honorary doctorate by the University of St Andrews. In 1903 he became minister emeritus. He died at Armidale on 3 February 1909 and was buried in the Presbyterian cemetery. He was survived by his wife Eliza Jane, née Glass, whom he had married at Armidale on 5 July 1866, and by five sons and three daughters. His estate was valued at £5272.

The Johnstone Memorial Hall was built and dedicated in 1912.

J. D. Lang, Free Church morality (Syd, 1876); J. Cameron, Centenary history of the Presbyterian Church in New South Wales (Syd, 1905); C. A. White, The challenge of the years (Syd, 1951); Presbyterian Messenger (Syd), 12 Feb 1909; Presbyterian Church (NSW), General Assembly minutes, May 1909; Armidale Chronicle, Feb 1909; information from Miss Jennifer and Mr I. McL. Johnstone, Armidale.

ALAN DOUGAN

JONES, AUBER GEORGE (1832-1887), pastoralist and newspaper owner, was born in Van Diemen's Land, the third son of Robert Jones of Pleasant Place, Jericho, and his wife Harriet. He spent his early years in Tasmania and at Richmond on 6 May 1854 married Hannah Maria (d. 1874), daughter of John Joseph Moore, owner of the Guardian. In 1855 he took out an auctioneer's licence for his 'Midland Sale Yards' and seems to have been connected with the Mercury in the 1850s. He moved to Melbourne and studied for the Anglican priesthood under Bishop Perry [q.v.], but 'discovered . . . that other pursuits were more congenial to his tastes and suited to his natural abilities'.

About 1860 he went to New South Wales

to manage Gobbagombalin station near Wagga Wagga and by 1866 had acquired Marrar. He soon established himself as a successful pastoral speculator, buying and selling stations and stock. In the 1860s and 1870s he held Barmedman, Buddigower, Kockibitoo, Woolongough, Glenariff and Wangagong and other runs in the Lachlan district and on the Bogan. He lived in Wagga Wagga and regularly visited his stations. In 1868 with Thomas Darlow he established the town's second newspaper, the Wagga Wagga Advertiser (later Daily Advertiser). Jones also owned valuable business premises in the main street, served on the Hospital and Pastoral Association Committees, donated a cup for intertown cricket competition and generously supported the public school, heading the subscription list with £100 for a new building.

In the 1870s Jones refused to stand for the Legislative Assembly because of his business commitments. Defeated in 1880, he represented the Murrumbidgee in 1882-85. He considered the Land Act 'the greatest abortion ever cast forth', and opposed any amendment of the 1880 Public Instruction Act and further Chinese immigration. Robustly independent, he claimed that 'in my representative capacity I would be neither Protestant nor Catholic, neither squatter nor selector, neither am I a ministerialist nor an oppositionist. I am perfectly unfettered and shall take my seat as your true representative'.

In 1883 Jones moved to Grenfell. Aged 55 he died at Young from apoplexy on 30 December 1887 and was buried in the Anglican section of the Wagga Wagga cemetery. To his obituarist in the Wagga Wagga Advertiser he had long 'occupied the foremost position among men of note in the district'. He was survived by two sons and four daughters of his first wife. His will expressly excluded his second wife Mary Milford, daughter of Judge Callaghan [q.v.], whom he had married on 21 January 1878, from 'any direct or indirect benefit' from his estate of £162,418 and from 'the slightest control or authority' over any of his children.

K. Swan, A history of Wagga Wagga (Wagga Wagga, 1970); Hobart Town Courier, 8 May 1854; Cornwall Chronicle, 14 July 1855; Wagga Wagga Advertiser, 12 Oct 1868, 6 Mar, 21 Apr, 15 May, 2 June 1869, 27 May 1874, 27 Feb 1878, 20 July 1880, 31 Dec 1887; Daily Advertiser (Wagga Wagga), 10 Oct 1928.

K. J. SWAN

JONES, CHARLES EDWIN (1828-1903), politician, was born at Devonport, England, son of John Jones, a Welshman, and his wife Elizabeth, née Tucker. He followed his father's trade and became a tailor, active in radical and temperance causes and vehement against Roman Catholics. In 1850 at Devonport he married Anne Letitia Angear; next year they sailed for Melbourne where he worked as a tailor until 1862 when he made a composition with his creditors. In 1861 he had a sensational but successful battle to enter the City Council and shake the dominant Irish faction. He remained a councillor until October 1865. Sporadic campaigns against 'the Irish ministry' of John O'Shanassy [q.v.] brought associations with the protectionist left which made him forget earlier free-trade activities.

In 1864 the Orange order persuaded him to stand for Ballarat East as a supporter of the moderate coalition of James McCulloch [q.v.] who had overthrown O'Shanassy. After a rowdy campaign, long remembered for his description of the local Irish as 'savages of Bungaree', he was elected in November. He immediately became government whip, so relieving his chronic poverty. Otherwise he lived by writing for the Collingwood Observer until 1867 when he became literary editor of the Ballarat Evening Post. His parliamentary services and creation of the successful ministerial organization for the 1865-66 elections raised hopes of office. Disappointed, he defected to the protectionist Opposition in October. Despite his return to McCulloch in the Darling grant crisis the defection cost him his seat at the general election in February 1868. At the climax of the crisis in May, during the minority Sladen [q.v.] ministry, he dramatically defeated the lands minister at the Ballarat West ministerial by-election, and excelled in the Opposition's anti-Catholic agitation. His reward came in July when he was made commissioner of roads and railways and vice-president of the board of lands and works in McCulloch's second ministry, but previous intrigues with the conservative Opposition and involvements in corrupt land operations emerged in a series of accusations, court cases and parliamentary inquiries. He gambled by resigning office and seat in March 1869 and won the ensuing by-election. Expelled from the Legislative Assembly in April, he was commonly regarded by his constituents as innocent, or no worse than others, and was re-elected. He was narrowly defeated in 1871 only because the large number of candidates split the voters and he had accidentally annoyed the temperance interest.

Jones turned itinerant lecturer, but after a marital upheaval he left in 1872 for America. He lectured and worked as a journalist, spending much time with the Mormons in

Utah and in Wisconsin, and returned to Victoria late in 1881. He lost a by-election at Geelong in April 1882; at the 1883 general election he missed Ballarat West by only the returning officer's casting vote, and won it easily in 1886. Meanwhile he had established in Melbourne the lively People's Tribune, which ran from November 1883 to November 1886; in the speculative boom of the 1880s he became a land agent.

His membership of a group of Opposition freelances, noted for abuse and obstruction, led to a crushing defeat at Windermere in 1889. After a senseless attempt for East Bourke Boroughs in April 1892 he left for Western Australia where he was first a librarian and then a 'teacher of memory culture'. His attempts to enter parliament failed and in April 1901 he almost lost his deposit standing for Fremantle as a protectionist in the first federal elections. Returning to Ballarat he sought Reform League preselection in 1902 but failed and did not poll. He died poor at Korumburra on 18 March 1903. His wife had died on 3 June 1863, leaving three sons and three daughters, and on 17 February 1865 he married Charlotte Ryan who bore him two sons and three daughters. He also appeared from a court case in 1873 to have become the husband of Rebecca Einley.

Jones was brisk and energetic; he delighted in notoriety and intrigue, eventually to his own destruction. Although no grand orator, his command of audiences and especially of hecklers was outstanding. Although no model citizen, his impudence gives him a curious attraction.

M. L. Kiddle, Men of yesterday (Melb, 1961); PD (Vic), 1886, 270; Argus, 6, 13, 17 Sept 1861, 9 Nov 1866, 5-8 Mar 1869, 30 Sept 1870, 5-8 Oct 1870, 9, 10 Apr 1873, 24 Feb, 6 Oct 1887, 4 Feb 1889; Ballarat Star, 3 Nov 1864, 19 Mar 1903.
                                    GEOFFREY BARTLETT

JONES, JOSEPH (1823-1887), politician, was born at Ruthin, Denbighshire, Wales, son of John Jones, shopkeeper, and his wife Ann, née Hughes. On 26 July 1853 he arrived in Victoria with his wife in the United. After a short time on the goldfields, he settled first in a tent at Ballarat East and then in Bridge Street as a spice and coffee merchant in a partnership with G. C. Clemesha, which lasted until April 1862. His own business as a merchant failed in 1876.

A founder of the Ballarat Mechanics' Institute in 1859, Jones was president three times and served on the committee of management for many years. He was vice-president of the Ballarat Chamber of Commerce when it revived in 1870. He was an active supporter of the Brown Hill Literary Institute which organized serious lectures and debates on scientific and social questions. Brought up a Quaker, he became a free-thinker and lectured to the Sunday Free Discussion Society in the 1870s. He was a foundation member of the Australian Secular Association in 1880.

Jones was a teetotaller and in the 1840s had been a Chartist. He retained his popular sympathies but his belief in free trade and orderly politics placed him, like many other liberals, on the side of the Legislative Council in the constitutional crises of the late 1860s. He was then very active in political organization and public speaking in and around Ballarat. When the excitement died down he was persuaded to stand for Ballarat West at the elections of 1871. In the campaign he reiterated that, although an ardent free trader, he was prepared to put aside his private views for the sake of the mining community and the need for mining reform. Helped by a split among the local radicals he and W. C. Smith [q.v.] were elected.

Jones supported the McCulloch [q.v.] ministry's proposals in 1871 to meet a deficit by imposing a moderate increase in duties and a new property tax as preferable to a more protectionist budget. After the government was defeated in June, Jones supported the radical and protectionist Duffy [q.v.] ministry of 1871-72 on all but its tariff, and was one of the few free traders and constitutionalists to oppose the moderate coalition which defeated it and ruled until July 1874. In August 1875 when Berry's [q.v.] radical ministry took office pledged to maintain the 1871 tariff and meet a deficit wholly by a progressive land tax, Jones supported McCulloch's amendment calling for lower duties and a more equitable distribution of direct taxation, and when the McCulloch ministry was formed in October became vice-president of the board of lands and works. Although defeated at the ministerial elections he won the Villiers and Heytesbury by-election in February 1876. In May 1877 Jones lost his seat but, after Berry's attack on the Legislative Council reached its climax in January 1878, became secretary of the National Registration Society. It was formed by Berry's leading opponents to counteract radicalism and to protect their interests in the composition of the electoral rolls; later it helped to create local constitutionalist organizations. Jones was returned for Villiers and Heytesbury to the assembly in December 1879, held his seat at the general election of February 1880 which dismissed the Berry ministry, but lost it when the defeat of Service's [q.v.] constitutionalist government led to another

election in July. Jones was defeated again in 1883.

Jones died in Ballarat on 22 September 1887, survived by his wife Priscilla, née Greaves, two sons and one of their four daughters. He enjoyed the esteem of many friends and was solidly supported by the Welsh community in Ballarat. Sections of the city honoured his memory by flying flags at half-mast when he died. He was buried in the Society of Friends' section of Ballarat new cemetery.

W. B. Withers, *The history of Ballarat*, 2nd ed (Ballarat, 1887); *Ballarat Star*, 8, 10 Feb 1871; *Argus*, 23 Sept 1887; *Ballarat Courier*, 23 Sept 1887; *Hamilton Spectator*, 1 Oct 1887; *Liberator* (Melb), 9 Oct 1887; F. B. Smith, Religion and freethought in Melbourne 1870 to 1890 (M.A. thesis, Univ Melb, 1960).

G. J. HOUGH

JONES, SIR PHILIP SYDNEY (1836-1918), physician and surgeon, was born on 15 April 1836 at Sydney, the second son of David Jones [q.v.] and his second wife Jane Hall, née Mander. Educated in Sydney at the schools of W. T. Cape [q.v.], T. S. Dodds at Surry Hills and Henry Cary [q.v.] at Darling Point, he went in 1853 to University College, University of London (M.B., 1859; M.D., 1860). In 1861 he became a fellow of the Royal College of Surgeons by examination, was house surgeon, house physician and resident medical officer in University College Hospital, studied in Paris and returned to Sydney.

Jones opened a practice in College Street. In 1862-72 he was honorary surgeon at the Sydney Infirmary where he performed the first successful reported ovariotomy in 1870. In 1873 he became honorary consulting surgeon. A member of the building committee of Prince Alfred Hospital, he was a director in 1878-83 and in 1904-18 and an honorary consulting physician from 1887. In 1873 he was appointed to the New South Wales Board of Health. He visited Europe in 1875 and on his return in 1876 gave up general practice and became one of the first consulting physicians. In that year he moved his home to Strathfield while keeping his rooms in the city. In 1881 he sat on the royal commission on quarantine. In 1883-86 he visited Europe and in 1883 represented the New South Wales government at the Medical Congress in Amsterdam. Interested in science and education, he was an examiner in clinical medicine at the University of Sydney, a fellow of its senate in 1887-1918 and vice-chancellor in 1904-06. He was a founding member of the Linnean Society in

1875, a member of the Royal Society of New South Wales from 1867 and honorary secretary of its medical section and a trustee of the Australian Museum until 1918. In 1892 he was president of the third session of the Intercolonial Medical Congress of Australasia. In 1895 he served on the royal commission on the notorious poisoner, George Dean; against J. E. Rogers but with Dr F. N. Manning [q.v.] he found the evidence compatible with attempted suicide and secured Dean's release. In 1896-97 he was president of the New South Wales branch of the British Medical Association, and in 1909 of the New South Wales Medical Board.

Jones strongly believed in the open-air treatment of tuberculosis and was a founder of the Queen Victoria Homes for Consumptives which in 1897 took over J. H. Goodlet's [q.v.] sanatorium at Thirlmere. He was president of the King's Tableland Sanatorium for Consumptives at Wentworth Falls and in 1912 was appointed to the Tuberculosis Advisory Board. In 1914 he was a leader in founding the National Association for the Prevention and Cure of Consumption and was its first president. He published several papers on the dissemination and treatment of the disease. In 1905 he was knighted for his work in combating tuberculosis.

Charitable and philanthropic, Jones was honorary medical officer of the City Night Refuge, vice-president of the New South Wales Institution for the Deaf and Dumb and the Blind and a strong supporter of the Kindergarten Union. A devout Congregationalist, he was deacon first at Pitt Street, then at Burwood and in 1889 at Trinity Church, Strathfield, which seceded with its minister from Burwood. He worked for the Congregational Union of New South Wales and the auxiliary to the London Missionary Society and was a member of council of Camden College, the Congregational theological college. Grave and shy in manner, he put service before ambition. Never physically strong he conserved his energies and was active in old age. He died on 18 September 1918 and was buried in the Congregational section of Rookwood cemetery. He was predeceased by his wife Hannah Howard (d. 1892), daughter of Rev. George Charter, whom he married at Wollongong on 8 April 1863. They were survived by three sons and four daughters to whom he left £61,000.

A portrait by Percy Spence is in the Great Hall, University of Sydney.

E. Digby (ed), *Australian men of mark*, 1 (Syd, 1889); C. Pearl, *Wild men of Sydney* (Lond, 1958); J. A. Garrett and L. W. Farr, *Camden College, a centenary history* (Syd, 1964); V&P (LA NSW), 1894-95, 3, 679, 707; MJA, Sept 1913, Mar 1926; A. Jackson, The

days of David Jones (David Jones Ltd Archives, Syd); printed and periodical cats under P. S. Jones (ML).
JOHN GARRETT

JORDAN, HENRY (1818-1890), dentist, parliamentarian and public servant, was born on 22 November 1818 at Lincoln, England, son of John Jordan, a Wesleyan minister descended from an old Devonshire family, and his wife Elizabeth, née Jefferies. Tutored by his father, he entered Kingsford College, Bristol, and then studied medicine in London. His health failed and he visited America. On his return he studied dentistry in London and built up a lucrative practice in Derby. His *Practical observations on the Teeth* (London, 1851) ran to two editions, was highly praised in England and America and later won him election to the Odontological Society of Great Britain. Though attracted by holy orders, he was persuaded by the Wesleyan Missionary Society to go to South Australia. He was sent to the mission for Aboriginals at Mount Barker but his health soon deteriorated and he returned to dentistry, bought a practice in Sydney and in February 1856 moved to Brisbane. On 9 June 1857 he married Sarah Elizabeth Hopkins, daughter of Nathaniel Turner, an early missionary in New Zealand.

Jordan joined Queensland's first board of education and served as a visiting chaplain at Brisbane gaol. In 1859 he lectured on self-reliance to the Albert Street Wesleyan Church. From May to November 1860 he represented Brisbane in the colony's first Legislative Assembly. In 1861 he was sent to London as commissioner and immigration agent. He wrote a pamphlet on emigration to Queensland, 'the future cotton-field of England', lectured widely and dedicated himself to attracting migrants to the colony. His superior, R. G. W. Herbert [q.v.], visited England in 1862-63 and found fault with Jordan's lack of discipline. In turn Jordan complained of his miserable allowance which caused him to spend part of his own income on lecture tours and to bargain with Mackay Baines & Co. of the Black Ball line for sending a migrant ship each month to Queensland in exchange for land orders. The bargain started well with one-class ships for free migrants but Black Ball soon began to carry paying cabin passengers and then to demand cash for its land orders. The Queensland Treasury objected to this demand and Jordan became the scapegoat. He tendered his resignation and returned to Brisbane in 1864 but the public sympathized with him. Exonerated by a select committee, he went back to London and held office until December 1866.

In 1868-71 Jordan represented East Moreton in the Legislative Assembly. He then turned to journalism and promoted a sugar plantation. In 1873 he failed to win election for Logan, but in 1875 became registrar-general and acted both as statist and commissioner of the Real Property Act; for his work on the 1876 census he was elected an honorary member of the Statistical Society of London. In 1883 and 1888 he won the assembly seat of South Brisbane. As minister for lands and works in 1887-88, he wrote a pamphlet on the amendments of C. B. Dutton [q.v.] to the Land Act, and succeeded in appointing Professor Edward Mason Shelton of Kansas State Agricultural College as instructor in agriculture.

Jordan maintained his interest in religious affairs, describing himself as an 'old' Wesleyan and still part of the Church of England. Partly because of his faith, he strongly opposed Kanaka labour. He died at his home, Sherwood, on 30 June 1890, survived by his wife and by four sons and three daughters of their eleven children.

V&P (LA Qld), 1864, 2, 917, 957, 975, 1865, 651, 671, 1866, 1061, 1867, 2, 63; PD (Qld), 1864, 108, 196; *Brisbane Courier*, 17 June 1865, 26 July 1873, 1 July 1890; B. R. Kingston, Land legislation and administration in Queensland, 1859-1876 (Ph.D. thesis, Monash Univ, 1970); Griffith papers, MS 448-49 (Dixson Lib, Syd).

A. A. MORRISON

JOSEPH, SAMUEL AARON (1824-1898), merchant, was born on 14 October 1824 in London, son of Aaron Joseph of Streatham and his second wife Frances, née Cohen. In January 1843 he arrived in the *Prince of Wales* at Wellington, New Zealand, and began in business. He became skilled in native languages and interpreted for Governor Grey when he pacified the Maoris. Joseph moved to Sydney in 1856 and with J. L. Montefiore [q.v.] founded the well-known firm of Montefiore, Joseph & Co. Influential in commercial circles, he became chairman of the City Bank of Sydney and director of various companies, including the Australian Mutual Provident Society in 1862-66· and 1880-84 and chairman of the Sydney Exchange Co. in 1888. In 1886 he was foundation president of the Commercial, Pastoral and Agricultural Society of New South Wales. Prominent in the Sydney Chamber of Commerce, he was president in 1887-89 and in 1888 attended the first Congress of Australasian Chambers of Commerce held in Melbourne.

A convinced free trader, Joseph had won West Sydney in the Legislative Assembly in 1864. He resigned in 1868 and visited England. In 1881 he was appointed to the Legislative Council but his seat lapsed in 1885 because he was again absent in England. Reappointed in 1887, he resigned in August 1893. He was a New South Wales commissioner for the Sydney, Melbourne, Calcutta and Adelaide Exhibitions. An eloquent speaker, Joseph was active in Jewish affairs, a member of the board of management of the York Street Synagogue and a joint treasurer of the Great Synagogue Building Fund. He was also interested in the Hebrew School and with others negotiated for the York Street Synagogue in a dispute with the Macquarie Street Synagogue. Later he was a trustee of the Hebrew section of the new Haslem's Creek (Rookwood) cemetery.

With his wide banking and commercial links, Joseph was hit by the financial crisis in 1893. He died on 25 September 1898 at his home in Nelson Street, Woollahra, and was buried in the Jewish section of Rookwood cemetery. He was survived by his wife Matilda Philippa, née Levien, whom he had married in 1856, and by a son and two daughters. His estate was valued at £12,000.

Sydney Mail, 13 Feb 1864; SMH, 26 Sept 1898; Aust Jewish Hist Soc Archives; AMP Society Archives.

HAROLD F. BELL

JOSEPHSON, JOSHUA FREY (1815-1892), businessman and judge, was born at Hamburg, son of Jacob Josephson and his wife Emma Wilson, a widow née Moss. His father, a jeweller and a Jewish Christian, had reached Sydney in May 1818 in the *Neptune*, sentenced to fourteen years for having forged £1 bank notes in his possession; in 1820 Joshua arrived with his mother in the *Morley*. He became an accomplished pianist, flautist and vocalist and by 1834 was teaching music. He was the first honorary organist at St Peter's Church, Cook's River. On 1 December 1838 he married Louisa (d. 1862), née Davies, a sixteen-year-old pupil whose sister married John Robertson [q.v.]. They lived at Enmore House, inherited from his father in 1845. Articled to James Norton [q.v.] Josephson was admitted as a solicitor on 17 February 1844.

Elected to the Sydney City Council in 1844 for Cook ward, he became mayor in 1848 and a justice of the peace. He was a member of the founding committee of St Paul's College, University of Sydney. A friend and business associate of T. S. Mort [q.v.], he helped to establish the Sydney Dry Dock Co., the Hunter River Railway Co. and the Sydney Insurance Co. On 9 June 1855 he was admitted to the New South Wales Bar. Next year he went to England, entered Lincoln's Inn in November and was called to the Bar on 30 April 1859. Roger Therry [q.v.] wrote that Josephson bought £2000 to £3000 worth of pictures and sculptures in Italy for his house. He returned to Sydney, practised as a barrister and in 1862 became a land titles commissioner under the new Real Property Act. In the 1860s he was a director of the Australian Joint Stock Bank, the Sydney Insurance Co. and the Australian Mutual Provident Society. He was a commissioner for the 1867 Paris Exhibition. After an early association with Mort in pastoral properties he acquired extensive interests, some, in partnership with George Oakes [q.v.] in pastoral runs in the 1860s, chiefly in the Bligh, Wellington and Warrego districts. He also invested in city real estate.

In 1864 Josephson survived a petition against his return to the Legislative Assembly for Braidwood. In November 1865 he was defeated for the Speakership. In 1868 he became Robertson's solicitor-general, but resigned from parliament and his directorates in September 1869 when appointed a District Court judge and chairman of Quarter Sessions for the western district. Judge Cary [q.v.] disturbed the government by complaints that Josephson had wrongfully induced him to retire by promises and a monetary payment. The question of whether a judge could be removed for misconduct before appointment was unresolved because Josephson was cleared of any intentional moral wrong but was reprimanded for great imprudence and indiscretion in negotiating with Cary while solicitor-general. In 1873 the barrister, Simon Belinfante, alleged misdemeanours by Josephson in his judicial functions at Mudgee. He again escaped dismissal although the Court found that some of his decisions had been 'exceedingly wrong'.

Josephson resigned in 1884 to devote more time to his private affairs and later became a partner in F. L. Barker & Co., wool-brokers. Enmore House was sold and demolished in 1883 when he built St Killians, Bellevue Hill, which later became Aspinall House, Scots College. He died there aged 76 on 26 January 1892 and was buried in the Anglican section of Rookwood cemetery. He was survived by four sons and eight daughters of his first wife, a daughter of his second wife Katerina Frederica (d. 1884), née Schiller, whom he had married in April 1868, and by his third wife Elizabeth Geraldine, née Brenan. His estate was valued at almost £170,000 and he left many of his statues to the National Art Gallery of New South Wales.

V&P (LA NSW), 1865, 1, 105, 501, 1865-66, 1, 33, 1869, 1, 36, 1870, 1, 273, 609, 1873-74, 1,

187, 193; G. H. Abbott, 'Reminiscences of Newtown and neighbourhood', JRAHS, 24 (1938); Bulletin, 11 Nov 1882; Appeal book, W. C. Wentworth v. J. C. Lloyd & others, 2, 1 (ML); A. B. Spark diary (ML); Attorney-General papers (NSWA); MS cat and newspaper indexes under J. Josephson (ML).　　　H. T. E. HOLT

JOUBERT, JULES FRANCOIS DE SALES (1824-1907), adventurer and entrepreneur, was born on 31 July 1824 at Angoulême, Charente, France, the third son of Auguste Alexis Joubert, naval officer, and his wife Rose Elizabeth, née Civadier. From a school in Bordeaux he went to the College Bourbon, Paris. In May 1839 he sailed as a passenger in the frigate Heroine. After visiting New Zealand, he went to Sydney in the Martha in 1839. In May 1837 his brother Didier Numa (1816-1881), agent of Barton Fils, wine and spirits merchants in Bordeaux, had reached Sydney in the Cova Nelly and moved to New Zealand; in December 1839 he returned to Sydney with his wife Louise (Lise), née Bonnefin, whom he had married at Kororareka on 23 November. After 1843 he settled at Hunter's Hill and became a successful merchant.

Jules left Sydney as interpreter in the corvette Aube. He returned in 1841 and became chancellor at the French consulate. A strong Orleanist he resigned in 1848 and on 27 April at St Mary's Church he married Florence Sarah Imlac, daughter of Robert Owen [q.v.]. Lured by copper, they went to Adelaide in 1849 where Joubert invested in land and buildings. In February 1850 his infant daughter died and on 16 April Florence died of typhoid fever with their three-week-old son. Next year Joubert was imprisoned for debt. In 1852 he went to the Mount Alexander goldfield in Victoria, soon contracted to build government quarters and then ran a store at Sawpit Gully (Elphinstone). Late in 1853 from Sydney he victualled the French forces annexing New Caledonia and in mid-1854 sailed with a cargo for Madagascar.

At Christ Church, North Adelaide, on 27 February 1855 he married Adelaide, née Levi. They settled at Hunter's Hill where Joubert had been buying land since 1847. He started contracting and with some seventy artisans from Lombardy built many stone houses in the area. In the early 1860s both Jouberts were active in moves to sell the Field of Mars common and use the proceeds to build bridges over the Lane Cove River at Fig Tree and the Parramatta River at Gladesville. They also petitioned for the incorporation of Hunter's Hill. Jules was first chairman of the council in 1861-62 and Didier first mayor in 1867-69. Jules started a ferry service and in 1865 was chairman of directors of the Parramatta River Navigation Co. but in December 1866 he was declared insolvent. His nephew Numa was later proprietor of the Hunter's Hill and Lane Cove River ferries.

A member of the Agricultural Society of New South Wales, Joubert was honorary secretary in 1867 and later paid secretary. Artistic and volatile, he revitalized the society, moved the annual show from Parramatta to Sydney and enlarged it to include non-agricultural exhibits. The 1870 show was held in the society's new building in Prince Alfred Park. He also edited the society's *Journal*. In 1874 he sought united colonial representation at the 1876 Philadelphia Exhibition. In 1878, as secretary to the New South Wales commission, he organized the exhibits for the Paris Exhibition where he arranged French participation at the 1879 Sydney Exhibition. He was made a chevalier of the Legion of Honour for having sent £12,000 to French flood victims in 1875 but on his return found himself excluded from the commission for the exhibition which he had conceived and organized. In July Henry Parkes [q.v.] confirmed John McElhone's [q.v.] questions in the Legislative Assembly that Joubert and Edward Combes [q.v.] had 'shipped out private property as returned exhibits'. In August after prolonged infighting Joubert was dismissed as secretary by the Agricultural Society for misleading the council.

Joubert left Sydney in disgust. With R. E. N. Twopeny [q.v.] he ran exhibitions in Perth in 1881 and Christchurch, New Zealand, in 1882. In India for most of 1882-83 he organized the Calcutta Exhibition. In Melbourne as a theatrical agent he built the Alexandra Theatre but went bankrupt in 1887. He represented New South Wales at the 1888 Melbourne Exhibition and managed the exhibition in 1889-90 at Dunedin where in 1890 he published his reminiscences, *Shavings and Scrapes in Many Parts*. About 1890 he went to Tasmania where he organized exhibitions at Launceston in 1891-92 and Hobart in 1894-95. He died in Carlton, Melbourne, on 24 August 1907 and was buried in the Boroondara cemetery. He was survived by his second wife, eight sons and two daughters.

I. Brodsky, *Hunter's Hill, New South Wales 1861-1961* (Syd, 1961); V&P (SA), 1855 (21); V&P (LA NSW), 1861, 2, 1336, 1865-66, 3, 429, 1878-79, 1, 607, 1879-80, 1, 208; *Australasian*, 18 July, 12 Sept 1874, 5 Jan 1878, 1 Feb, 23 Aug 1879, 2 Apr, 16, 23 July 1887; *Town and Country J*, 17 Apr 1875; SMH, 12 June, 21 Aug 1879, 17 Mar 1956; *Bulletin*, 20 Nov 1880, 29 Apr 1882, 26 May 1904; *Pastoral Review*, 16 Sept 1907; L. E. Lesser, Show business: a history of theatre in Victoria, 1825-1948 (M.A. thesis, Univ Melb, 1949); MS cat under Joubert (ML); Insolvency file 8059 (NSWA); CO 201/558, 44.

MARTHA RUTLEDGE